D1403830

## MyEconLab *Picks Up Where*

### **Instructors** choose MyEconLab:

"MyEconLab's e-text is great. Particularly in that it helps offset the skyrocketing cost of textbooks. Naturally, students love that."

**—Doug Gehrke, Moraine Valley Community College**

"MyEconLab offers them a way to practice every week. They receive immediate feedback and a feeling of personal attention. As a result, my teaching has become more targeted and efficient."

**—Kelly Blanchard, Purdue University**

"Students tell me that offering them MyEconLab is almost like offering them individual tutors."

**—Jefferson Edwards, Cypress Fairbanks College**

"Chapter quizzes offset student procrastination by ensuring they keep on task. If a student is having a problem, MyEconLab indicates exactly what they need to study."

"MyEconLab helps both students and instructors. There's something there for everyone."

"Someone has already pulled out articles that relate to economics and to the chapter at hand. As much as MyEconLab helps the student, that helps the instructor."

**—Diana Fortier, Waubonsee Community College**

# Lectures and Office Hours Leave Off

## Students choose MyEconLab:

*In a recent study, 87 percent of students who used MyEconLab regularly felt it improved their grade.*

"It was very useful because it had EVERYTHING, from practice exams to exercises to reading. Very helpful."

**—student, Northern Illinois University**

"I like how every chapter is outlined by vocabulary and flash cards. It helped me memorize equations and definitions. It was like having a study partner."

**—student, Temple University**

**Chart 2. Helpfulness of Study Plan Practice Questions and Feedback**
From a recent nationwide survey of students using MyEconLab (conducted by Contemporary Solutions)

90% of students surveyed who used the Study Plan practice questions and feedback felt it helped them to prepare for tests.

*n = 227*

"It made me look through the book to find answers so I did more reading."

**—student, Northern Illinois University**

"It was very helpful to get instant feedback. Sometimes I would get lost reading the book, and these individual problems would help me focus and see if I understood the concepts."

**—student, Temple University**

**Chart 3. Recommendation to a Friend**
From a recent survey of Texas A&M students using MyEconLab (conducted by Contemporary Solutions)

83.9% of students surveyed would recommend MyEconLab to a friend.

*n = 33*

"I would recommend MyEconLab to a friend. It was really easy to use and helped in studying the material for class."

**—student, Northern Illinois University**

"I would recommend taking the quizzes on MyEconLab because it gives you a true account of whether or not you understand the material."

**—student, Montana Tech**

# Microeconomics

Global Edition

# Microeconomics

**Third Edition**

**Global Edition**

## R. Glenn Hubbard
Columbia University

## Anthony Patrick O'Brien
Lehigh University

Boston   Columbus   Indianapolis   New York   San Francisco   Upper Saddle River
Amsterdam   Cape Town   Dubai   London   Madrid   Milan   Munich   Paris   Montreal   Toronto
Delhi   Mexico City   Sao Paulo   Sydney   Hong Kong   Seoul   Singapore   Taipei   Tokyo

Editor in Chief: Donna Battista
AVP/Executive Editor: David Alexander
International Acquisitions Editor:
  Laura Dent
Executive Development Editor:
  Lena Buonanno
Editorial Assistant: Gavin Broady
AVP/Executive Marketing Manager:
  Lori DeShazo
Marketing Assistant: Justin Jacob
Managing Editor: Nancy H. Fenton
Senior Project Manager: Kathryn Dinovo
Senior Manufacturing Buyer: Carol Melville
Senior Media Buyer: Ginny Michaud
Art Director, Cover and Interior:
  Anthony Gemmellaro
Designer, Interior: Wee Design Group and
  Anthony Gemmellaro
Designer, Cover: Jodi Notowitz
Manager, Visual Research: Beth Brenzel
Photo Researcher: Rachel Lucas
Manager, Rights and Permissions:
  Zina Arabia

Image Permission Coordinator:
  Kathy Gavilanes
Manager, Cover Visual Research &
  Permissions: Karen Sanatar
Text Permissions Project Supervisor:
  Michael Joyce
Director of Media: Susan Schoenberg
Content Leads, MyEconLab: Douglas A.
  Ruby and Noel Lotz
Senior Media Producer:
  Melissa Honig
Supplements Production Coordinator:
  Alison Eusden
Full-Service Project
Management/Composition: GGS Higher
  Education Resources, a Division of
  PreMedia Global, Inc.
Printer/Binder: Courier, Kendallville
Cover Printer: Lehigh Phoenix
Text Font: 10.5/12 Minion

Credits and acknowledgments borrowed from other sources and reproduced, with permission, in this textbook appear on appropriate page within text (or on page C-1).

Microsoft® and Windows® are registered trademarks of the Microsoft Corporation in the U.S.A. and other countries. Screen shots and icons reprinted with permission from the Microsoft Corporation. This book is not sponsored or endorsed by or affiliated with the Microsoft Corporation.

If you purchased this book within the United States or Canada you should be aware that it has been imported without the approval of the Publisher or the Author.

Many of the designations by manufacturers and sellers to distinguish their products are claimed as trademarks. Where those designations appear in this book, and the publisher was aware of a trademark claim, the designations have been printed in initial caps or all caps.

10 9 8 7 6 5 4 3 2 1

ISBN 13: 978-0-13-512552-6
ISBN 10:    0-13-512552-9

**For Constance, Raph, and Will**
*—R. Glenn Hubbard*

**For Cindy, Matthew, Andrew, and Daniel**
*—Anthony Patrick O'Brien*

# About the Authors

**Glenn Hubbard, policymaker, professor, and researcher.** R. Glenn Hubbard is the dean and Russell L. Carson Professor of Finance and Economics in the Graduate School of Business at Columbia University and professor of economics in Columbia's Faculty of Arts and Sciences. He is also a research associate of the National Bureau of Economic Research and a director of Automatic Data Processing, Black Rock Closed-End Funds, KKR Financial Corporation, and MetLife. He was formerly a director of Capmark Financial, Duke Realty, Information Services Group, and Ripplewood Holdings. He received his Ph.D. in economics from Harvard University in 1983. From 2001 to 2003, he served as chairman of the White House Council of Economic Advisers and chairman of the OECD Economy Policy Committee, and from 1991 to 1993, he was deputy assistant secretary of the U.S. Treasury Department. He currently serves as co-chair of the nonpartisan Committee on Capital Markets Regulation. Hubbard's fields of specialization are public economics, financial markets and institutions, corporate finance, macroeconomics, industrial organization, and public policy. He is the author of more than 100 articles in leading journals, including *American Economic Review, Brookings Papers on Economic Activity, Journal of Finance, Journal of Financial Economics, Journal of Money, Credit, and Banking, Journal of Political Economy, Journal of Public Economics, Quarterly Journal of Economics, RAND Journal of Economics,* and *Review of Economics and Statistics.* His research has been supported by grants from the National Science Foundation, the National Bureau of Economic Research, and numerous private foundations.

**Tony O'Brien, award-winning professor and researcher.** Anthony Patrick O'Brien is a professor of economics at Lehigh University. He received his Ph.D. from the University of California, Berkeley, in 1987. He has taught principles of economics for more than 15 years, in both large sections and small honors classes. He received the Lehigh University Award for Distinguished Teaching. He was formerly the director of the Diamond Center for Economic Education and was named a Dana Foundation Faculty Fellow and Lehigh Class of 1961 Professor of Economics. He has been a visiting professor at the University of California, Santa Barbara, and the Graduate School of Industrial Administration at Carnegie Mellon University. O'Brien's research has dealt with such issues as the evolution of the U.S. automobile industry, sources of U.S. economic competitiveness, the development of U.S. trade policy, the causes of the Great Depression, and the causes of black-white income differences. His research has been published in leading journals, including *American Economic Review, Quarterly Journal of Economics, Journal of Money, Credit, and Banking, Industrial Relations, Journal of Economic History,* and *Explorations in Economic History.* His research has been supported by grants from government agencies and private foundations. In addition to teaching and writing, O'Brien also serves on the editorial board of the *Journal of Socio-Economics.*

# Brief Contents

# Contents

# PART 7: Information, Taxes, and the Distribution of Income

# FLEXIBILITY CHART

The following chart helps you organize your syllabus based on your teaching preferences and objectives:

| Core | Optional | Policy |
|---|---|---|
| **CHAPTER 1:** Economics: Foundations and Models | **CHAPTER 1 Appendix:** Using Graphs and Formulas | |
| **CHAPTER 2:** Trade-offs, Comparative Advantage, and the Market System | | |
| **CHAPTER 3:** Where Prices Come From: The Interaction of Demand and Supply | | |
| | **CHAPTER 4 Appendix:** Quantitative Demand and Supply Analysis | **CHAPTER 4:** Economic Efficiency, Government Price Setting, and Taxes |
| | | **CHAPTER 5:** Externalities, Environmental Policy, and Public Goods |
| **CHAPTER 6:** Elasticity: The Responsiveness of Demand and Supply | | |
| | **CHAPTER 7:** Firms, the Stock Market, and Corporate Governance | |
| | **CHAPTER 7 Appendix:** Tools to Analyze Firms' Financial Information | |
| **CHAPTER 8:** Comparative Advantage and the Gains from International Trade | **CHAPTER 8 Appendix:** Multinational Firms | |
| | **CHAPTER 9:** Consumer Choice and Behavioral Economics | |
| | **CHAPTER 9 Appendix:** Using Indifference Curves and Budget Lines to Understand Consumer Behavior | |
| **CHAPTER 10:** Technology, Production, and Costs | **CHAPTER 10 Appendix:** Using Isoquants and Isocosts to Understand Production and Costs | |
| **CHAPTER 11:** Firms in Perfectly Competitive Markets | | |
| **CHAPTER 12:** Monopolistic Competition: The Competitive Model in a More Realistic Setting | | |

| Core | Optional | Policy |
|---|---|---|
| **CHAPTER 13:** Oligopoly: Firms in Less Competitive Markets | | |
| **CHAPTER 14:** Monopoly and Antitrust Policy | | |
| | **CHAPTER 15:** Pricing Strategy | |
| **CHAPTER 16:** The Markets for Labor and Other Factors of Production | | |
| **CHAPTER 17:** The Economics of Information | | |
| | | **CHAPTER 18:** Public Choice, Taxes, and the Distribution of Income |

# Preface

When George Lucas was asked why he made *Star Wars*, he replied, "It's the kind of movie I like to see, but no one seemed to be making them. So, I decided to make one." We realized that no one seemed to be writing the kind of textbook we wanted to use in our classes. So, after years of supplementing texts with fresh, lively, real-world examples from newspapers, magazines, Web sites, and professional journals, we decided to write an economics text that delivers complete economics coverage with many real-world business examples. Our goal was to keep our classes "widget free."

## NEW TO THE THIRD EDITION

The effects of the severe economic downturn that began in 2007 with the bursting of the housing bubble continued through 2009. Unemployment rose to levels that had not been seen in decades, and the crisis in the financial system was the worst since the Great Depression of the 1930s. Policy debates intensified during 2009, as Congress passed and President Barack Obama enacted the Recovery and Reinvestment Act, the largest package of spending increases and tax cuts in history. The Federal Reserve sailed into uncharted waters as it developed new policy tools to deal with the unprecedented financial turmoil.

Other long-running policy debates continued as well, as reform of the health care system, the looming cost increases of Social Security and Medicare, environmental policy, and changes to the tax system all received attention from economists, policymakers, and the public. In this new edition, we help students understand these recent economic events and the policy responses to them. As in the first and second editions, we place application at the forefront of the discussion. We believe that students find the study of economics more interesting and easier to master when they see economic analysis applied to the real-world issues that concern them.

Here is a summary of the changes in this third edition. See the next section for details on each of these changes:

- The book provides new coverage of recent debates and policies related to immigration, health care, and pollution.
- The book includes new coverage of the recession and financial crisis of 2007–2009.
- All companies in the chapter openers have been either replaced with new companies or updated with current information.
- All chapters include new *An Inside Look* newspaper articles and analyses to help students apply economic thinking to current events and policy debates.
- There are new *Making the Connection* features to help students tie economic concepts to current events and policy issues.
- Figures and tables have been updated, using the latest data available.
- Approximately 30 percent of the end-of-chapter problems have been either replaced or updated.

In this new edition, we have taken the opportunity to make many changes throughout the text, concentrating on three key areas:

***Policy debates, including immigration, health care, and pollution.*** The number of jobs requiring technical education and training continues to increase. In Chapter 1, "Economics: Foundations and Models," we use the debate about restricting H-1B worker visas to introduce students to positive and normative economic analysis. In Chapter 8, "Comparative

Advantage and the Gains from International Trade," we explore the "Buy American" provision in the 2009 stimulus package.

As this book goes to press, Congress is debating a bill to overhaul the health care system. In Chapter 2, "Trade-offs, Comparative Advantage, and the Market System," we discuss the trade-offs involved in health care spending and the Medicare and Medicaid programs. We revisit the topic of health care in Chapter 5, "Externalities, Environmental Policy, and Public Goods," where we discuss projections of health care spending and the role of the U.S. government in the health care system. In Chapter 16, "The Markets for Labor and Other Factors of Production," we discuss whether U.S. firms are handicapped in competing with foreign firms by paying for their employees' health insurance. We return to the health care topic in Chapter 18, "Public Choice, Taxes, and the Distribution of Income," with a news article and analysis on a proposed soda tax to pay for health care.

The United States has made progress in reducing air pollution since Congress passed the Clean Air Act in 1970. In Chapter 5, "Externalities, Environmental Policy, and Public Goods," we use the economic concepts of marginal cost, marginal benefit, and efficiency to discuss environmental policy, including President Barack Obama's proposed cap-and-trade policy to reduce emissions of carbon dioxide.

*The recession and financial crisis of 2007–2009.* Today's students feel the effects of the worst economic crisis since the Great Depression of the 1930s. The problems in the financial system have proven that it is important for students in both microeconomics and macroeconomics courses to understand the basics of how financial markets work and the role of government in financial regulation. In Chapter 7, "Firms, the Stock Market, and Corporate Governance," we cover the basics of the stock and bond markets, discuss why stock prices fluctuate, and examine the role of the principal-agent problem in the financial meltdown of 2007–2009. We return to the financial crisis in Chapter 17, "The Economics of Information," where we use Bernie Madoff's "Ponzi" scheme to illustrate moral hazard.

*Real-world company examples and newspaper articles.* As in previous editions, we open each chapter by highlighting a company to establish a real-world context for learning and to spark students' interest in economics. We have chosen new companies for some chapters and updated the information in the other chapters. As in previous editions, each chapter closes with the *An Inside Look* feature, which shows students how to apply the concepts from the chapter to the analysis of a news article. We have replaced all the *An Inside Look* features in this edition. Here is a snapshot of some of these changes:

Chapter 1, "Economics: Foundations and Models," opens with a discussion of Microsoft and Bill Gates's view of worker visas. The *An Inside Look* feature presents an article and analysis on whether immigrants displace or complement domestic workers.

Chapter 3, "Where Prices Come From: The Interaction of Demand and Supply," opens with a discussion of Red Bull and the market for energy drinks. The *An Inside Look* feature presents an article and analysis of how advertising helps Red Bull increase the demand for its energy drink.

Chapter 7, "Firms, the Stock Market, and Corporate Governance," opens with a discussion of the runaway success of the private company Facebook. The *An Inside Look* feature presents an article and analysis about Facebook and profits.

Chapter 9, "Consumer Choice and Behavioral Economics," opens with a discussion of how Oprah Winfrey's endorsement of the Kindle e-reader caused a dramatic increase in demand for the product. The *An Inside Look* feature presents an article and analysis on the power of Oprah Winfrey's endorsements.

Chapter 16, "The Markets for Labor and Other Factors of Production," opens with a discussion of the salary of New York Yankees pitcher CC Sabathia. The *An Inside Look* feature presents an article and analysis of the salaries of college basketball coaches.

The following are further changes to this third edition:

- There are new *Making the Connection* features, which help students tie economic concepts to current events and policy issues, as well as new sections, figures, and tables:

    Chapter 1 includes a new *Making the Connection*, "Should the Host Government Protect the Migrant Workers?"

    Chapter 2 includes a new *Making the Connection*, "Facing the Trade-offs in Health Care Spending."

    Chapter 3 includes three new *Making the Connection* features: "Is the Big Mac an Inferior Good?" "The Aging of the Baby Boom Generation," and "Red Bull and the Future Demand for Energy Drinks."

    Chapter 4 includes a new *Making the Connection*, "The Consumer Surplus from Broadband Internet Service."

    Chapter 5 includes revised graphs of the economic effects of government taxes and subsidies to improve student understanding of this sometimes difficult subject, and a new *Making the Connection*, "Should the Government Run the Health Care System?"

    Chapter 6, "Elasticity: The Responsiveness of Demand and Supply," includes a new section and table on "Some Estimated Price Elasticities of Demand."

    Chapter 7, "Firms, the Stock Market, and Corporate Governance," includes a new section and figure on "Why Do Stock Prices Fluctuate So Much?" and a new *Making the Connection*, "How Important Are Small Businesses to the U.S. Economy?"

    Chapter 8 includes two new *Making the Connection* features, "How Caterpillar Depends on International Trade" and "The Obama Administration Develops a Trade Policy."

    Chapter 9 includes two new *Making the Connection* features, "Are There Any Upward-Sloping Demand Curves in the Real World?" and "A Blogger Who Understands the Importance of Sunk Costs."

    Chapter 11 includes several cost and revenue graphs that have been redrawn for increased clarity, as well as a new *Making the Connection*, "Easy Entry Makes the Long Run Pretty Short in the Apple iPhone Apps Store."

    Chapter 12 includes a new *Making the Connection*, "The Rise and Decline of Starbucks."

    Chapter 13 includes two new *Making the Connection* features, "Singaporean Car Owners Experience Petrol Price Rollercoaster," as well as "Can We Predict Which Firms Will Continue to Be Successful?"

    Chapter 14 includes two new *Making the Connection* features, "Monopoly on Connection," and "Have Google and Microsoft Violated Antitrust Laws?"

    Chapter 16 contains a new *Making the Connection*, "Are U.S. Firms Handicapped by Paying Their Employees' Health Insurance?"

    Chapter 17 includes a new *Making the Connection*, "Moral Hazard, Big Time: Bernie Madoff's 'Ponzi' Scheme."

- Figures and tables have been updated using the latest data available.

- Approximately 30 percent of the end-of-chapter problems have been either replaced or updated.

- Finally, we have gone over the text literally line-by-line, tightening the discussion, rewriting unclear points, and making many other small changes. We are grateful to the many instructors and students who made suggestions for improvements in the previous edition. We have done our best to incorporate as many of those suggestions as possible.

# The Foundation:
## Contextual Learning and Modern Organization

We believe a course is a success if students can apply what they have learned in both personal and business settings and if they have developed the analytical skills to understand what they read in the media. That's why we explain economic concepts by using many real-world business examples and applications in the chapter openers, graphs, *Making the Connection* features, *An Inside Look* features, and end-of-chapter problems. This approach helps both business majors and liberal arts majors become educated consumers, voters, and citizens. In addition to our widget-free approach, we also have a modern organization and place interesting policy topics early in the book to pique student interest.

We are convinced that students learn to apply economic principles best if they are taught in a familiar context. Whether they open an art studio, do social work, trade on Wall Street, work for the government, or tend bar, students benefit from understanding the economic forces behind their work. And though business students will have many opportunities to see economic principles in action in various courses, liberal arts students may not. We therefore use many diverse real-world business and policy examples to illustrate economic concepts and to develop educated consumers, voters, and citizens.

Several chapters illustrate our approach:

- **A STRONG SET OF INTRODUCTORY CHAPTERS.** The introductory chapters provide students with a solid foundation in the basics. We emphasize the key ideas of marginal analysis and economic efficiency. In Chapter 4, "Economic Efficiency, Government Price Setting, and Taxes," we use the concepts of consumer surplus and producer surplus to measure the economic effects of price ceilings and price floors as they relate to the familiar examples of rental properties and the minimum wage. (We revisit consumer surplus and producer surplus in Chapter 8, "Comparative Advantage and the Gains from International Trade," where we discuss outsourcing and analyze government policies that affect trade; in Chapter 14, "Monopoly and Antitrust Policy," where we examine the effect of market power on economic efficiency; and in Chapter 15, "Pricing Strategy," where we examine the effect of firm pricing policy on economic efficiency.) In Chapter 7, "Firms, the Stock Market, and Corporate Governance," we provide students with a basic understanding of how firms are organized, how they raise funds, and how they provide information to investors. We also illustrate how in a market system entrepreneurs meet consumer wants and efficiently organize production.

- **EARLY COVERAGE OF POLICY ISSUES.** To expose students to policy issues early in the course, we discuss immigration in Chapter 1, "Economics: Foundations and Models," rent control and the minimum wage in Chapter 4, "Economic Efficiency, Government Price Setting, and Taxes," air pollution, global warming, and whether the government should run the health care system in Chapter 5, "Externalities, Environmental Policy, and Public Goods," and government policy toward illegal drugs in Chapter 6, "Elasticity: The Responsiveness of Demand and Supply."

- **COMPLETE COVERAGE OF MONOPOLISTIC COMPETITION.** We devote a full chapter, Chapter 12, "Monopolistic Competition: The Competitive Model in a More Realistic Setting," to monopolistic competition prior to covering oligopoly and monopoly in Chapter 13, "Oligopoly: Firms in Less Competitive Markets," and Chapter 14, "Monopoly and Antitrust Policy." Although many instructors cover monopolistic competition very briefly or dispense with it entirely, we think it is an overlooked tool for reinforcing the basic message of how markets work in a context that is much more familiar to students than are the agricultural examples that dominate other discussions of perfect competition. We use the monopolistic competition model to introduce the downward-sloping demand curve material usually introduced in a monopoly chapter. This helps students grasp the important point that nearly all firms—not just monopolies—face downward-sloping demand curves. Covering monopolistic competition directly after perfect competition also allows for the early discussion of topics such as brand management and sources of competitive success. Nevertheless, we wrote the chapter so that instructors who prefer to cover monopoly (Chapter 14, "Monopoly and Antitrust Policy") directly after perfect competition (Chapter 11, "Firms in Perfectly Competitive Markets") can do so without loss of continuity.

- **EXTENSIVE, REALISTIC GAME THEORY COVERAGE.** In Chapter 13, "Oligopoly: Firms in Less Competitive Markets," we use game theory to analyze competition among oligopolists. Game theory helps students understand how companies with market power make strategic decisions in many competitive situations. We use familiar companies such as Apple, Hewlett-Packard, Coca-Cola, PepsiCo, and Dell in our game theory applications.

- **UNIQUE COVERAGE OF PRICING STRATEGY.** In Chapter 15, "Pricing Strategy," we explore how firms use pricing strategies to increase profits. Students encounter pricing strategies everywhere—when they buy a movie ticket, book a flight for spring break, or research book prices online. We use these relevant, familiar examples to illustrate how companies use strategies such as price discrimination, cost-plus pricing, and two-part tariffs.

- **A CHAPTER DEVOTED TO THE ECONOMICS OF INFORMATION.** In Chapter 17, "The Economics of Information," we explore the important fact that consumers, firms, and governments must make decisions on the basis of incomplete information. Students face uncertainty and make decisions with incomplete information when they buy used cars or health insurance, or when they search for a job. We help students analyze these familiar situations and explore the perspective of the consumer and firm. We also apply the concepts of adverse selection and moral hazard to financial markets.

# Special Features:
## A Real-World, Hands-on Approach to Learning Economics

### Business Cases and *An Inside Look* News Articles

Each chapter-opening case provides a real-world context for learning, sparks students' interest in economics, and helps to unify the chapter. The case describes an actual company facing a real situation. The company is integrated in the narrative, graphs, and pedagogical features of the chapter. Many of the chapter openers focus on the role of entrepreneurs in developing new products and bringing them to the market. For example, Chapter 3 covers Dietrich Mateschitz of Red Bull, Chapter 7 covers Mark Zuckerberg of Facebook, Chapter 9 covers Oprah Winfrey, and Chapter 12 covers Howard Schultz of Starbucks. Here are a few examples of companies we explore in the chapter openers in this new edition:

- Red Bull (Chapter 3, "Where Prices Come From: The Interaction of Demand and Supply")
- Facebook (Chapter 7, "Firms, the Stock Market, and Corporate Governance")
- Caterpillar (Chapter 8, "Comparative Advantage and the Gains from International Trade")

*An Inside Look* is a two-page feature that shows students how to apply the concepts from the chapter to the analysis of a news article. Select articles deal with policy issues and are titled *An Inside Look at Policy*. Articles are from sources such as the *Wall Street Journal*, the *Economist*, and *BusinessWeek*. The *An Inside Look* feature presents an excerpt from an article, analysis of the article, a graph(s), and critical thinking questions.

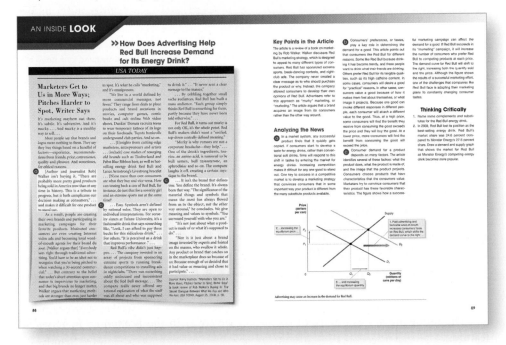

Here are some examples of the articles featured in *An Inside Look*:

- "Marketers Get to Us in More Ways; Pitches Harder to Spot, Writer Says," *USA Today* (Chapter 3, "Where Prices Come From: The Interaction of Demand and Supply")

- Facebook Founder Puts Idealism Before Profits," *The (London) Times* (Chapter 7, "Firms, the Stock Market, and Corporate Governance")

- "'Buy American' Clause Stirs Up Controversy," *USA Today* (Chapter 8, "Comparative Advantage and the Gains from International Trade")

## Economics in Your Life

After the chapter-opening real-world business case, we have added a personal dimension to the chapter opener with a feature titled *Economics in Your Life*, which asks students to consider how economics affects their own lives. The feature piques the interest of students and emphasizes the connection between the material they are learning and their own experiences.

---

### Economics in YOUR Life!

**Will You Drink Red Bull or Monster?**

Suppose you are about to buy an energy drink and that you are choosing between a Red Bull and a Monster Energy. As the more established, well-known brand, Red Bull has many advantages over a newer entrant like Monster Energy. One strategy Monster can use to overcome those advantages is to compete based on price and value. Would you choose to buy a can of Monster Energy if it had a lower price than a can of Red Bull? Would you be less likely to drink Monster Energy if your income had declined? As you read the chapter, see if you can answer these questions. You can check your answers against those we provide at the end of the chapter.

▶ Continued on page 87

---

At the end of the chapter, we use the chapter concepts to answer the questions asked at the beginning of the chapter.

---

▶ Continued from page 65

### Economics in YOUR Life!

**Will You Drink Red Bull or Monster?**

At the beginning of the chapter, we asked you to consider two questions: Would you choose to buy a can of Monster Energy if it had a lower price than a can of Red Bull? and Would you be less likely to drink Monster Energy if your income had declined? To determine the answer to the first question, you have to recognize that Red Bull and Monster Energy are substitutes. If you consider the two drinks to be very close substitutes, then you are likely to buy the one with the lower price. In the market, if consumers generally believe that Red Bull and Monster Energy are close substitutes, a fall in the price of Monster Energy will increase the quantity of Monster Energy demanded and decrease the demand for Red Bull. Suppose that you are currently buying Red Bull, despite its higher price, because you prefer its taste. If you switch to Monster Energy when your income declines—perhaps because you have lost your job during a recession—then Monster Energy is an inferior good for you.

---

The following are examples of the topics we cover in the *Economics in Your Life* feature:

- Will you buy a Red Bull or a Monster? (Chapter 3, "Where Prices Come From: The Interaction of Demand and Supply")

- Does rent control make it easier to find an affordable apartment? (Chapter 4, "Economic Efficiency, Government Price Setting, and Taxes")

- Do corporate managers act in the best interests of shareholders? (Chapter 7, "Firms, the Stock Market, and Corporate Governance.")

## Solved Problems

As we all know, many students have great difficulty handling applied economics problems. We help students overcome this hurdle by including two or three worked-out problems tied to select chapter-opening learning objectives. Our goals are to keep students focused on the main ideas of each chapter and to give students a model of how to solve an economic problem by breaking it down step by step. Additional exercises in the end-of-chapter *Problems and Applications* section are tied to every *Solved Problem*.

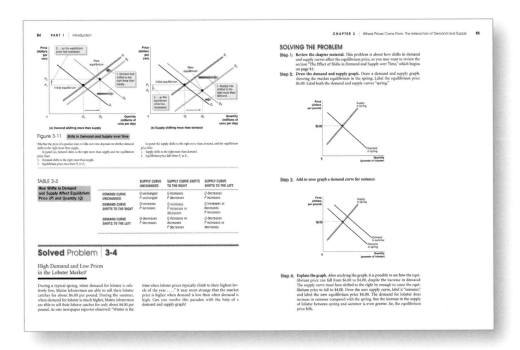

Additional *Solved Problems* appear in the following areas:

- The *Instructor's Manual*
- PowerPoint® slides
- The *Study Guide*

In addition, the Test Item Files includes problems tied to the *Solved Problems* in the main book.

## Don't Let This Happen to You!

We know from many years of teaching which concepts students find most difficult. Each chapter contains a box feature called *Don't Let This Happen to You!* that alerts students to the most common pitfalls in that chapter's material. We follow up with a related question in the end-of-chapter *Problems and Applications* section.

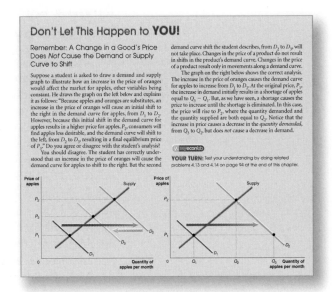

## Making the Connection

Each chapter includes two to four *Making the Connection* features that present real-world reinforcement of key concepts and help students learn how to interpret what they read on the Web and in newspapers. Most *Making the Connection* features use relevant, stimulating, and provocative news stories focused on businesses and policy issues. One-third of the *Making the Connection* features are new to this edition, and most others have been updated. Several *Making the Connection* features discuss health care, which remains a pressing policy issue. Each *Making the Connection* has at least one supporting end-of-chapter problem to allow students to test their understanding of the topic discussed. Here are some of the new *Making the Connection* features:

- Chapter 2: "Facing the Trade-offs in Health Care Spending"
- Chapter 3: "The Aging of the Baby Boom Generation"
- Chapter 8: "How Caterpillar Depends on International Trade"
- Chapter 9: "A Blogger Who Understands the Importance of Ignoring Sunk Costs"
- Chapter 12: "The Rise and Decline of Starbucks"
- Chapter 14: "Have Google and Microsoft Violated Antitrust Laws?"
- Chapter 16: "Are U.S. Firms Handicapped by Paying Their Employees' Health Insurance?"

## Graphs and Summary Tables

Graphs are an indispensable part of the principles of economics course but are a major stumbling block for many students. Every chapter except Chapter 1 includes end-of-chapter problems that require students to draw, read, and interpret graphs. Interactive graphing exercises appear on the book's supporting Web site. We use four devices to help students read and interpret graphs:

1. Detailed captions
2. Boxed notes
3. Color-coded curves
4. Summary tables with graphs

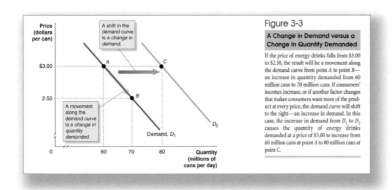

Figure 3-3

**A Change in Demand versus a Change in Quantity Demanded**

If the price of energy drinks falls from $3.00 to $2.50, the result will be a movement along the demand curve from point A to point B—an increase in quantity demanded from 60 million cans to 70 million cans. If consumers' incomes increase, or if another factor changes that makes consumers want more of the product at every price, the demand curve will shift to the right—an increase in demand. In this case, the increase in demand from $D_1$ to $D_2$ causes the quantity of energy drinks demanded at a price of $3.00 to increase from 60 million cans at point A to 80 million cans at point C.

## Review Questions and Problems and Applications— Grouped by Learning Objective to Improve Assessment

All the end-of-chapter material—*Summary*, *Review Questions*, and *Problems and Applications*—is grouped under learning objectives. The goals of this organization are to make it easier for instructors to assign problems based on learning objectives, both in the book and in MyEconLab, and to help students efficiently review material that they find difficult. If students have difficulty with a particular learning objective, an instructor can easily identify which end-of-chapter questions and problems support that objective and assign them as homework or discuss them in class. Every exercise in a chapter's *Problems and Applications* section is available in MyEconLab. Using MyEconLab, students can complete these and many other exercises online, get tutorial help, and receive instant feedback and assistance on exercises they answer incorrectly. Also, student learning will be enhanced by having the summary material and problems grouped together by learning objective, which will allow students to focus on the parts of the chapter they found most challenging. Each major section of the chapter, paired with a learning objective, has at least two review questions and three problems.

As in the first and second editions, we include one or more end-of-chapter problems that test students' understanding of the content presented in the *Solved Problem*, *Making the*

*Connection*, and *Don't Let This Happen to You!* special features in the chapter. Instructors can cover a feature in class and assign the corresponding problem for homework. The Test Item Files also include test questions that pertain to these special features.

# Integrated Supplements

The authors and Pearson Education have worked together to integrate the text, print, and media resources to make teaching and learning easier.

MyEconLab is a unique online course management, testing, and tutorial resource.

## For the Instructor

Instructors can choose how much or how little time to spend setting up and using MyEconLab. Here is a snapshot of what instructors are saying about MyEconLab:

> "MyEconLab offers [students] a way to practice every week. They receive immediate feedback and a feeling of personal attention. As a result, my teaching has become more targeted and efficient." —Kelly Blanchard, Purdue University

> "Students tell me that offering them MyEconLab is almost like offering them individual tutors." —Jefferson Edwards, Cypress Fairbanks College

> "MyEconLab's eText is great—particularly in that it helps offset the skyrocketing cost of textbooks. Naturally, students love that." —Doug Gehrke, Moraine Valley Community College

Each chapter contains two preloaded homework exercise sets that can be used to build an individualized study plan for each student. These study plan exercises contain tutorial resources, including instant feedback, links to the appropriate learning objective in the eText, pop-up definitions from the text, learning objective summaries, and step-by-step guided solutions, where appropriate. Student use of these materials requires no initial instructor setup. The online gradebook records each student's performance and time spent on the tests and study plan and generates reports by student or by chapter.

Alternatively, instructors can fully customize MyEconLab to match their course exactly, including reading assignments, homework assignments, video assignments, current news assignments, and quizzes and tests. Assignable resources include:

- Preloaded homework exercise sets for each chapter that include the student tutorial resources mentioned above
- Preloaded quizzes for each chapter that are unique to the text and not repeated in the study plan or homework exercise sets
- Study plan problems that are similar to the end-of-chapter problems and numbered exactly like the book to make assigning homework easier
- *Economics in the News* articles that are updated weekly with appropriate exercises
- ABC News clips, which explore current economic applications and policy issues, along with exercises
- Test Item File questions that allow you to assign quizzes or homework that will look just like your exams
- Econ Exercise Builder, which allows you to build your own customized exercises

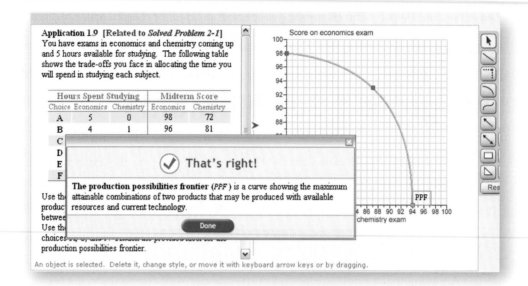

Exercises include multiple-choice, graph drawing, and free-response items, many of which are generated algorithmically so that each time a student works them, a different variation is presented.

MyEconLab grades every problem, even problems with graphs. When working homework exercises, students receive immediate feedback, with links to additional learning tools.

### Customization and Communication

MyEconLab in CourseCompass provides additional optional customization and communication tools. Instructors who teach distance-learning courses or very large lecture sections find the CourseCompass format useful because they can upload course documents and assignments, customize the order of chapters, and use communication features such as Digital Dropbox and Discussion Board.

### For the Student

MyEconLab puts students in control of their learning through a collection of testing, practice, and study tools tied to the online, interactive version of the textbook and other medial resources. Here is a snapshot of what students are saying about MyEconLab:

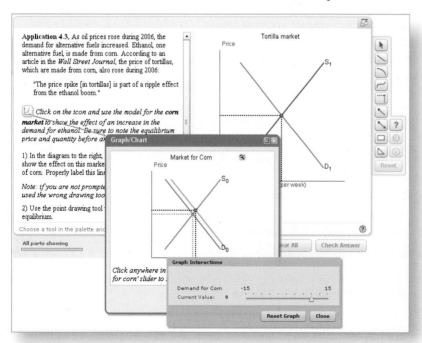

"It was very useful because it had EVERYTHING, from practice exams to exercises to reading. Very helpful."
—student, Northern Illinois University

"I would recommend taking the quizzes on MyEconLab because it gives you a true account of whether or not you understand the material."
—student, Montana Tech

"It made me look through the book to find answers, so I did more reading."
—student, Northern Illinois University

Students can study on their own, or they can complete assignments created by their instructor. Within MyEconLab's structured environment, students practice what they learn, test their understanding, and pursue a personalized study plan generated from their performance on sample tests and from quizzes created by their instructors. In Homework or Study Plan mode, students have access to a wealth of tutorial features, including:

- Instant feedback on exercises that helps students understand and apply the concepts

- Links to the eText to promote reading of the text just when the student needs to revisit a concept or explanation

- Step-by-step guided solutions that force students to break down a problem in much the same way an instructor would do during office hours

- Pop-up summaries of the appropriate learning objective to remind students of key ideas while studying

- Pop-up key term definitions from the eText to help students master the vocabulary of economics

- Links to the important features of the eText, such as *Solved Problems*, *Making the Connection*, *An Inside Look*, and *Don't Let This Happen to You!*

- A graphing tool that is integrated into the various exercises to enable students to build and manipulate graphs so that students better understand how concepts, numbers, and graphs connect

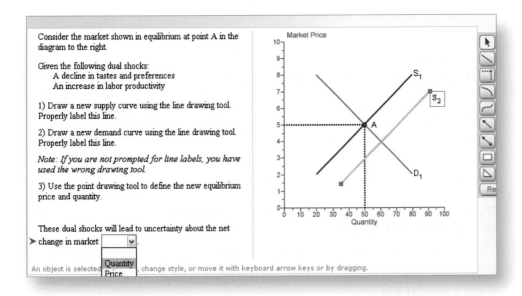

## Additional MyEconLab Tools

MyEconLab includes the following additional features:

- **eText**—In addition to the portions of eText available as pop-ups or links, a fully searchable eText is available for students who wish to read and study in a fully electronic environment.

- **Glossary flashcards**—Every key term is available as a flashcard, allowing students to quiz themselves on vocabulary from one or more chapters at a time.

MyEconLab content has been created through the efforts of Chris Annala, State University of New York–Geneseo; Charles Baum, Middle Tennessee State University; Sarah Ghosh, University of Scranton; Woo Jung, University of Colorado; Katherine McCann, University of Delaware; Chris Kauffman, University of Tennessee–Knoxville; Russell Kellogg, University of Colorado–Denver; Noel Lotz, Pearson Education; Christine Polek, University of Massachusetts–Boston; Douglas A. Ruby, Pearson Education; Leonie L. Stone, State University of New York–Geneseo; and Bert G. Wheeler, Cedarville University.

## Other Resources for the Instructor

### Instructor's Manual

Edward Scahill of the University of Scranton prepared the *Instructor's Manual* for *Microeconomics*. The *Instructor's Manual* includes chapter-by-chapter summaries, learning objectives, extended examples and class exercises, teaching outlines incorporating key terms and definitions, teaching tips, topics for class discussion, new *Solved Problems*, new *Making the Connections*, new *Economics in Your Life* scenarios, and solutions to all review questions and problems in the book. The *Instructor's Manual* is available for download from the Instructor's Resource Center (www.pearsonglobaleditions.com/hubbard). The authors and Randy Methenitis of Richland College prepared the solutions to the end-of-chapter review questions and problems.

### Two Test Item Files

Randy Methenitis of Richland College prepared two *Test Item Files*. Each *Test Item File* includes 2,000 multiple-choice, true/false, short-answer, and graphing questions. There are questions to support each key feature in the book. The *Test Item Files* are available for download from the Instructor's Resource Center (www.pearsonglobaleditions.com/hubbard). Test questions are annotated with the following information:

- **Difficulty:** 1 for straight recall, 2 for some analysis, 3 for complex analysis
- **Type:** multiple-choice, true/false, short-answer, essay
- **Topic:** the term or concept the question supports
- **Learning objective**
- **AACSB** (see description that follows)
- **Page number**
- **Special feature in the main book:** chapter-opening business example, *Economics in Your Life*, *Solved Problem*, *Making the Connection*, *Don't Let this Happen to You!* and *An Inside Look*

The *Test Item Files* were checked for accuracy by Fatma Abdel-Raouf of Goldey-Beacom College.

### The Association to Advance Collegiate Schools of Business (AACSB)

The Test Item File authors have connected select questions to the general knowledge and skill guidelines found in the AACSB Assurance of Learning Standards.

### What is the AACSB?

AACSB is a not-for-profit corporation of educational institutions, corporations, and other organizations devoted to the promotion and improvement of higher education in business administration and accounting. A collegiate institution offering degrees in business administration or accounting may volunteer for AACSB accreditation review. The AACSB makes initial accreditation decisions and conducts periodic reviews to promote continuous quality improvement in management education. Pearson Education is a proud member of the AACSB and is pleased to provide advice to help you apply AACSB Assurance of Learning Standards.

### What are AACSB Assurance of Learning Standards?

One of the criteria for AACSB accreditation is the quality of curricula. Although no specific courses are required, the AACSB expects a curriculum to include learning experiences in the following categories of Assurance of Learning Standards:

- Communication
- Ethical Reasoning

- Analytic Skills
- Use of Information Technology
- Multicultural and Diversity
- Reflective Thinking

Questions that test skills relevant to these standards are tagged with the appropriate standard. For example, a question testing the moral questions associated with externalities would receive the Ethical Reasoning tag.

### How Can Instructors Use the AACSB Tags?

Tagged questions help you measure whether students are grasping the course content that aligns with the AACSB guidelines noted above. This in turn may suggest enrichment activities or other educational experiences to help students achieve these skills.

## TestGen

The computerized TestGen package allows instructors to customize, save, and generate classroom tests. The test program permits instructors to edit, add, or delete questions from the Test Item Files; edit existing graphics and create new graphics; analyze test results; and organize a database of tests and student results. This software allows for extensive flexibility and ease of use. It provides many options for organizing and displaying tests, along with search and sort features. The software and the Test Item Files can be downloaded from the Instructor's Resource Center (www.pearsonglobaleditions.com/hubbard).

## PowerPoint® Lecture Presentation

Three sets of PowerPoint® slides, prepared by Fernando Quijano and Yvonn Quijano, are available:

1. A comprehensive set of PowerPoint® slides can be used by instructors for class presentations or by students for lecture preview or review. These slides include all the graphs, tables, and equations in the textbook. Two versions are available—step-by-step mode, in which you can build graphs as you would on a blackboard, and automated mode, in which you use a single click per slide.

2. A student version of the PowerPoint® slides is available as .pdf files. This version allows students to print the slides and bring them to class for note taking. Instructors can download these PowerPoint® presentations from the Instructor's Resource Center (www.pearsonglobaleditions.com/hubbard).

## Blackboard and WebCT Course Content

Pearson Education offers fully customizable course content for the Blackboard and WebCT Course Management Systems.

# Other Resources for the Student

In addition to MyEconLab, Pearson provides the following resources.

## Study Guides

Kelly Blanchard of Purdue University prepared the study guide, which reinforces the textbook and provides students with the following:

- Chapter summary
- Discussion of each learning objective
- Section-by-section review of the concepts presented
- Helpful study hints

- Additional *Solved Problems* to supplement those in the text
- Key terms with definitions
- A self-test, including 40 multiple-choice questions plus a number of short-answer and true/false questions, with accompanying answers and explanations

## PowerPoint® Slides

For student use as a study aid or note-taking guide, PowerPoint® slides, prepared by Fernando Quijano and Yvonn Quijano, can be downloaded from MyEconLab or the Instructor's Resource Center and made available to students. The slides include:

- All graphs, tables, and equations in the text
- Figures in step-by-step, automated mode, using a single click per graph curve
- End-of-chapter key terms with hyperlinks to relevant slides

# Consultant Board, Accuracy Review Board, and Reviewers

The guidance and recommendations of the following instructors helped us develop the revision plans for the third edition and the supplements package. While we could not incorporate every suggestion from every consultant board member, reviewer, or accuracy checker, we do thank each and every one of you and acknowledge that your feedback was indispensable in developing this text. We greatly appreciate your assistance in making this the best text it could be; you have helped teach a whole new generation of students about the exciting world of economics.

## Consultant Board

Kelly Blanchard, Purdue University
Robert Godby, University of Wyoming
William Goffe, State University of New York–Oswego
David Mitch, University of Maryland–Baltimore County
Edward Scahill, University of Scranton
Robert Whaples, Wake Forest University

## Accuracy Review Board

Our accuracy checkers did a particularly painstaking and thorough job of helping us proof the graphs, equations, and features of the text and the supplements. We are grateful for their time and commitment:

Fatma Abdel-Raouf, Goldey-Beacom College
Anne Alexander, University of Wyoming
Kelly Blanchard, Purdue University
Charles Callahan III, State University of New York–Brockport
Marc Fusaro, Arkansas Tech University
Robert Godby, University of Wyoming
William Goffe, State University of New York–Oswego
Tony Lima, California State University–East Bay
Randy Methenitis, Richland College
David Mitch, University of Maryland–Baltimore County
James Moreno, Blinn College
Edward Scahill, University of Scranton
Ed Steinberg, New York University
Arlena Sullivan, Jones County Junior College
Robert Whaples, Wake Forest University

## Reviewers

The guidance and thoughtful recommendations of many instructors helped us develop and implement a revision plan that expanded the book's content, improved the figures, and strengthened assessment features. We extend special thanks to

Edward Scahill of the University of Scranton and Marc Fusaro of Arkansas Tech University for helping us revise the chapter openers and *An Inside Look* features, and to Randy Methenitis of Richland College for helping us revise and update the end-of-chapter problems. In the macroeconomics volume, Bill Goffe of State University of New York–Oswego helped us update the macro data, based on the new base year of 2005. We are grateful for the comments and many helpful suggestions received from the following reviewers:

**ALABAMA**
Edward Merkel, Troy University

**ARKANSAS**
Jerry Crawford, Arkansas State University
Marc Fusaro, Arkansas Tech University
Randall Kesselring, Arkansas State University
Dan Marburger, Arkansas State University

**CALIFORNIA**
Ercument Aksoy, Los Angeles Valley College
Kate Antonovics, University of California–San Diego
Asatar Bair, City College of San Francisco
Diana Bajrami, College of Alameda
Anoshua Chaudhuri, San Francisco State University
Craig Gallet, California State University–Sacramento
Julie Gonzalez, University of California–Santa Cruz
Lisa Grobar, California State University–Long Beach
Jessica Howell, California State University–Sacramento
John Ifcher, Santa Clara University
Leland Kempe, California State University–Fresno
David Lang, California State University–Sacramento
Tony Lima, California State University–East Bay
Solina Lindahl, California Polytechnic State University–San Luis Obispo
Roger Mack, DeAnza College
Michael Marlow, California Polytechnic State University
Nivedita Mukherji, Oakland University
Andrew Narwold, University of San Diego
Hanna Paulson, West Los Angeles College
Mary Pranzo, California State University–Fresno
Sasha Radisich, Glendale Community College

Jonathan Silberman, Oakland University
Martha Stuffler, Irvine Valley College
Va Nee Van Vleck, California State University–Fresno
Steven Yamarik, California State University–Long Beach
Guy Yamashiro, California State University–Long Beach

COLORADO
Mohammed Akacem, Metropolitan State College of Denver
Karen Gebhardt, Colorado State University
Nancy Jianakoplos, Colorado State University

CONNECTICUT
Mark Gius, Quinnipiac University
Robert Martel, University of Connecticut
Christian Zimmermann, University of Connecticut

DELAWARE
Fatma Abdel-Raouf, Goldey–Beacom College

DISTRICT OF COLUMBIA
Colleen Callahan, American University
Robert Feinberg, American University
Walter Park, American University

FLORIDA
Herman Baine, Broward College
Thomas McCaleb, Florida State University
Nora Underwood, University of Central Florida

GEORGIA
Greg Brock, Georgia Southern University
Donna Fisher, Georgia Southern University
Shelby Frost, Georgia State University
John King, Georgia Southern University
Michael Reksulak, Georgia Southern University
Bill Yang, Georgia Southern University

IDAHO
Cynthia Hill, Idaho State University
Tesa Stegner, Idaho State University

ILLINOIS
Rosa Lea Danielson, College of DuPage
Kevin Dunagan, Oakton Community College
Dennis Shannon, Southwestern Illinois College

INDIANA
Kelly Blanchard, Purdue University
John Pomery, Purdue University
Rob Rude, Ivy Tech Community College

IOWA
Jennifer Fuhrman, University of Iowa
Ken McCormick, University of Northern Iowa
Andy Schuchart, Iowa Central Community College
John Solow, University of Iowa

KANSAS
Amanda Freeman, Kansas State University

KENTUCKY
Bob Gillette, University of Kentucky
Gail Hoyt, University of Kentucky

LOUISIANA
Lara Gardner, Southeastern Louisiana University
Jay Johnson, Southeastern Louisiana University
Sung No, Southern University and A&M College
Nancy Rumore, University of Louisiana at Lafayette

MARYLAND
Marsha Goldfarb, University of Maryland–Baltimore City
Henry Terrell, University of Maryland–College Park

MASSACHUSETTS
Gerald Friedman, University of Massachusetts
Jay Zagorsky, Boston University

MICHIGAN
Jared Boyd, Henry Ford Community College
Steven Hayworth, Eastern Michigan University
James Luke, Lansing Community College
Norman Obst, Michigan State University

MINNESOTA
Philip Grossman, Saint Cloud State University
Matthew Hyle, Winona State University
Artatrana Ratha, Saint Cloud State University
Katherine Schmeiser, University of Minnesota

MISSISSIPPI
Randall Campbell, Mississippi State University
Becky Campbell Smith, Mississippi State University
Arlena Sullivan, Jones County Junior College

MISSOURI
Chris Azevedo, University of Central Missouri
Kermit Clay, Ozarks Technical Community College
Mark Karscig, University of Central Missouri

NEVADA
Bill Robinson, University of Nevada–Las Vegas

NEW JERSEY
Jeff Rubin, Rutgers University
Henry Ryder, Gloucester County College

NEW YORK
Charles Callahan III, State University of New York–Brockport
Michael Carew, Baruch College
Bill Goffe, State University of New York–Oswego
Nancy Howe, Hudson Valley Community College
Ghassan Karam, Pace University
Anna Musatti, Columbia University
Theodore Muzio, St. John's University, New York
Emre Ozsoz, Fashion Institute of Technology
Ed Steinberg, New York University

NORTH CAROLINA
Michael Goode, Central Piedmont Community College
Jonathan Phillips, North Carolina State University
Robert Shoffner, Central Piedmont Community College
Eric Taylor, Central Piedmont Community College
Hui-Kuan Tseng, University of North Carolina at Charlotte

Rick Zuber, University of North Carolina at Charlotte
John Whitehead, Appalachian State University

OHIO

James D'Angelo, University of Cincinnati
Timothy Fuerst, Bowling Green State University
Daniel Horton, Cleveland State University
Jay Mutter, University of Akron
Charles Reichheld, Cuyahoga Community College
Teresa Riley, Youngstown State University
Richard Stratton, University of Akron
Albert Sumell, Youngstown State University
Yaqin Wang, Youngstown State University
Sourushe Zandvakili, University of Cincinnati

OKLAHOMA

Bill McLean, Oklahoma State University
Denny Myers, Oklahoma City Community College
Ed Price, Oklahoma State University

OREGON

Tim Duy, University of Oregon
B. Starr McMullen, Oregon State University
Ted Scheinman, Mount Hood Community College

PENNSYLVANIA

Cynthia Benzing, West Chester University
Steven Husted, University of Pittsburgh
Katherine McCann, Penn State
Nicole Sadowski, York College of Pennsylvania
Edward Scahill, University of Scranton
Ken Slaysman, York College of Pennsylvania

RHODE ISLAND

Jongsung Kim, Bryant University

SOUTH CAROLINA

Calvin Blackwell, College of Charleston

TENNESSEE

Sindy Abadie, Southwest Tennessee Community College
John Brassel, Southwest Tennessee Community College
Michael J. Gootzeit, University of Memphis
Christopher Klein, Middle Tennessee State University
Leila Pratt, University of Tennessee at Chattanooga

TEXAS

Klaus Becker, Texas Tech University
Alex Brown, Texas A&M University

Steven Craig, University of Houston
Patrick Crowley, Texas A&M University–Corpus Christi
Richard Croxdale, Austin Community College
Harry Ellis, University of North Texas
Jim Holcomb, University of Texas–El Paso
Jim Lee, Texas A&M University–Corpus Christi
Randy Methenitis, Richland College
Carl Montano, Lamar University
James Moreno, Blinn College
Camille Nelson, Texas A & M University
Michael Nelson, Texas A&M University
David Schutte, Mountain View College
David Torres, University of Texas–El Paso
Ross vanWassenhove, University of Houston
Inske Zandvliet, Brookhaven College

UTAH

Chris Fawson, Utah State University

VIRGINIA

Janelle Davenport, Hampton University
Bob Subrick, James Madison University
Susanne Toney, Hampton University

WASHINGTON

Andrew Ewing, University of Washington

WEST VIRGINIA

Jacqueline Agesa, Marshall University
Richard Agesa, Marshall University

WYOMING

Robert Godby, University of Wyoming

## International Contributors

Sayed Bozorgnia, Abu Dhabi University
Alex Lum, Singapore Polytechnic University

## International Reviewers

Manuchehr Irandoust, UAE University
Dr. Lawrence Khoo, City University of Hong Kong
Joyce Chai Hui Ming, Temasek Polytechnic
Ahmed A. Salama, British University of Egypt

# Previous Edition Class Testers, Accuracy Reviewers, and Consultants

## Class Testers

We are grateful to both the instructors who class tested manuscript of the first edition and their students for providing clear-cut recommendations on how to make chapters interesting, relevant, and comprehensive:

Charles A. Bennett, Gannon University
Anne E. Bresnock, University of California, Los Angeles and California State Polytechnic University–Pomona
Linda Childs-Leatherbury, Lincoln University, Pennsylvania
John Eastwood, Northern Arizona University
David Eaton, Murray State University
Paul Elgatian, St. Ambrose University
Patricia A. Freeman, Jackson State University
Robert Godby, University of Wyoming
Frank Gunter, Lehigh University
Ahmed Ispahani, University of LaVerne
Brendan Kennelly, Lehigh University and National University of Ireland–Galway
Ernest Massie, Franklin University
Carol McDonough, University of Massachusetts–Lowell
Shah Mehrabi, Montgomery College
Sharon Ryan, University of Missouri–Columbia
Bruce G. Webb, Gordon College
Madelyn Young, Converse College
Susan Zumas, Lehigh University

## Accuracy Review Boards

We are grateful to the following first edition and second edition accuracy checkers for their hard work on the book and supplements:

Fatma Abdel-Raouf, Goldey–Beacom College
Mohammad Bajwa, Northampton Community College
Hamid Bastin, Shippensburg University
Kelly Hunt Blanchard, Purdue University
Don Bumpass, Sam Houston State University
Mark S. Chester, Reading Area Community College
Kenny Christianson, Binghamton University
Ishita Edwards, Oxnard College
Harold Elder, University of Alabama
Harry Ellis, University of North Texas
Can Erbil, Brandeis University
Marc Fusaro, East Carolina University
Robert Gillette, University of Kentucky
William L. Goffe, State University of New York–Oswego
Sarah Ghosh, University of Scranton

Maria Giuili, Diablo Valley College
Travis Hayes, University of Tennessee–Chattanooga
Carol Hogan, University of Michigan–Dearborn
Anisul M. Islam, University of Houston–Downtown
Aaron Jackson, Bentley College
Faik A. Koray, Louisiana State University
Nancy Jianakoplos, Colorado State University
Thomas C. Kinnaman, Bucknell University
Mary K. Knudson, University of Iowa
Stephan Kroll, California State University–Sacramento
Tony Lima, California State University–East Bay
Randy Methenitis, Richland College
Normal C. Miller, Miami University
James A. Moreno, Blinn College
Michael Potepan, San Francisco State University
Mary L. Pranzo, California State University–Fresno
Matthew Rafferty, Quinnipiac University
Jeff Reynolds, Northern Illinois University
Brian Rosario, University of California, Davis
Joseph M. Santos, South Dakota State University
Edward Scahill, University of Scranton
Mark V. Siegler, California State University–Sacramento
Rachel Small, University of Colorado–Boulder
Stephen Smith, Bakersfield College
Rajeev Sooreea, Pennsylvania State University–Altoona
Rebecca Stein, University of Pennsylvania
Wendine Thompson–Dawson, University of Utah
Robert Whaples, Wake Forest University

## Consultant Boards

We received guidance during the first and second edition development at several critical junctures from a dedicated consultant board. We relied on the board for input on content, figure treatment, and design:

Kate Antonovics, University of California–San Diego
Robert Beekman, University of Tampa
Valerie Bencivenga, University of Texas–Austin
Kelly Blanchard, Purdue University
Susan Dadres, Southern Methodist University
Harry Ellis, Jr., University of North Texas
Robert Gillette, University of Kentucky
Robert Godby, University of Wyoming
William L. Goffe, State University of New York–Oswego
Jane S. Himarios, University of Texas–Arlington
Donn M. Johnson, Quinnipiac University

Mark Karscig, Central Missouri State University
Jenny Minier, University of Kentucky
Nicholas Noble, Miami University
Michael Potepan, San Francisco State University
Matthew Rafferty, Quinnipiac University
Helen Roberts, University of Illinois–Chicago
Robert Rosenman, Washington State University
Joseph M. Santos, South Dakota State University
Martin C. Spechler, Indiana University–Purdue University Indianapolis
Robert Whaples, Wake Forest University
Jonathan B. Wight, University of Richmond

## Reviewers

The guidance and recommendations of the following instructors helped us shape the first and second editions over the course of three years.

**ALABAMA**
Doris Bennett, Jacksonville State University
Harold W. Elder, University of Alabama–Tuscaloosa
Wanda Hudson, Alabama Southern Community College
James L. Swofford, University of Southern Alabama

**ARIZONA**
Doug Conway, Mesa Community College
John Eastwood, Northern Arizona University
Price Fishback, University of Arizona

**ARKANSAS**
Jerry Crawford, Arkansas State University

**CALIFORNIA**
Renatte Adler, San Diego State University
Maneeza Aminy, Golden Gate University
Becca Arnold, Mesa College
Robert Bise, Orange Coast Community College
Victor Brajer, California State University–Fullerton
Anne E. Bresnock, University of California, Los Angeles and California State Polytechnic University–Pomona
David Brownstone, University of California, Irvine
Maureen Burton, California State Polytechnic University–Pomona
Anoshua Chaudhuri, San Francisco State University
James G. Devine, Loyola Marymount University
Jose Esteban, Palomar College
Roger Frantz, San Diego State University
Craig Gallet, California State University–Sacramento
Andrew Gill, California State University–Fullerton
Maria Giuili, Diablo Valley College
Lisa Grobar, California State University–Long Beach
Steve Hamilton, California State University–Fullerton
Dewey Heinsma, Mt. San Jacinto Community College
Jessica Howell, California State University–Sacramento
Greg Hunter, California State University–Pomona

Ahmed Ispahani, University of LaVerne
George A. Jouganatos, California State University–Sacramento
Jonathan Kaplan, California State University–Sacramento
Philip King, San Francisco State University
Lori Kletzer, University of California, Santa Cruz
Stephan Kroll, California State University–Sacramento
David Lang, California State University–Sacramento
Carsten Lange, California State Polytechnic University–Pomona
Don Leet, California State University–Fresno
Rose LeMont, Modesto Junior College
Solina Lindahl, California Polytechnic State University–San Luis Obispo
Kristen Monaco, California State University–Long Beach
W. Douglas Morgan, University of California, Santa Barbara
Joseph M. Pogodzinksi, San Jose State University
Michael J. Potepan, San Francisco State University
Mary L. Pranzo, California State University–Fresno
Ratha Ramoo, Diablo Valley College
Scott J. Sambucci, California State University–East Bay
Ariane Schauer, Marymount College
Frederica Shockley, California State University–Chico
Mark Siegler, California State University–Sacramento
Lisa Simon, California Polytechnic State University–San Louis Obispo
Stephen Smith, Bakersfield College
Rodney B. Swanson, University of California, Los Angeles
Lea Templer, College of the Canyons
Kristin A. Van Gaasbeck, California State University–Sacramento
Michael Visser, Sonoma State University
Kevin Young, Diablo Valley College
Anthony Zambelli, Cuyamaca College

**COLORADO**
Rhonda Corman, University of Northern Colorado
Dale DeBoer, University of Colorado–Colorado Springs
Murat Iyigun, University of Colorado at Boulder
Nancy Jianakoplos, Colorado State University
Jay Kaplan, University of Colorado–Boulder
William G. Mertens, University of Colorado–Boulder
Rachael Small, University of Colorado–Boulder
Stephen Weiler, Colorado State University

**CONNECTICUT**
Christopher P. Ball, Quinnipiac University
Donn M. Johnson, Quinnipiac University
Judith Mills, Southern Connecticut State University
Matthew Rafferty, Quinnipiac University

**DELAWARE**
Fatma Abdel-Raouf, Goldey–Beacom College
Ali Ataiifar, Delaware County Community College
Andrew T. Hill, University of Delaware

**FLORIDA**

Herman Baine, Broward Community College
Robert L. Beekman, University of Tampa
Eric P. Chiang, Florida Atlantic University
Martine Duchatelet, Barry University
Hadley Hartman, Santa Fe Community College
Richard Hawkins, University of West Florida
Brad Kamp, University of South Florida
Brian Kench, University of Tampa
Barbara A. Moore, University of Central Florida
Augustine Nelson, University of Miami
Jamie Ortiz, Florida Atlantic University
Deborah Paige, Santa Fe Community College
Robert Pennington, University of Central Florida
Bob Potter, University of Central Florida
Jerry Schwartz, Broward Community College–North
William Stronge, Florida Atlantic University
Nora Underwood, University of Central Florida
Zhiguang Wang, Florida International University
Joan Wiggenhorn, Barry University

**GEORGIA**

Constantin Ogloblin, Georgia Southern University
Dr. Greg Okoro, Georgia Perimeter College–Clarkston

**IDAHO**

Don Holley, Boise State University

**ILLINOIS**

Teshome Abebe, Eastern Illinois University
Ali Akarca, University of Illinois–Chicago
Zsolt Becsi, Southern Illinois University–Carbondale
James Bruehler, Eastern Illinois University
Louis Cain, Loyola University Chicago and Northwestern University
Rosa Lea Danielson, College of DuPage
Scott Gilbert, Southern Illinois University
Rajeev K. Goel, Illinois State University
David Gordon, Illinois Valley Community College
Alan Grant, Eastern Illinois University
Rik Hafer, Southern Illinois University–Edwardsville
Alice Melkumian, Western Illinois University
Christopher Mushrush, Illinois State University
Jeff Reynolds, Northern Illinois University
Helen Roberts, University of Illinois–Chicago
Thomas R. Sadler, Western Illinois University
Eric Schulz, Northwestern University
Charles Sicotte, Rock Valley Community College
Neil T. Skaggs, Illinois State University
Kevin Sylwester, Southern Illinois University–Carbondale
Wendine Thompson-Dawson, Monmouth College
Mark Witte, Northwestern University
Laurie Wolff, Southern Illinois University–Carbondale
Paula Worthington, Northwestern University

**INDIANA**

Kelly Blanchard, Purdue University
Cecil Bohanon, Ball State University
Thomas Gresik, University of Notre Dame
Robert B. Harris, Indiana University–Purdue University Indianapolis
Fred Herschede, Indiana University–South Bend
James K. Self, Indiana University–Bloomington
Esther-Mirjam Sent, University of Notre Dame
Virginia Shingleton, Valparaiso University
Martin C. Spechler, Indiana University–Purdue University Indianapolis
Arun K. Srinivasan, Indiana University–Southeast Campus
Geetha Suresh, Purdue University–West Lafayette

**IOWA**

Terry Alexander, Iowa State University
Paul Elgatian, St. Ambrose University
John Solow, University of Iowa
Jonathan Warner, Dordt College

**KANSAS**

Guatam Bhattacharya, University of Kansas
Dipak Ghosh, Emporia State University
Alan Grant, Baker University
Wayne Oberle, St. Ambrose University
Jodi Messer Pelkowski, Wichita State University
Martin Perline, Wichita State University
Joel Potter, Kansas State University
Joshua Rosenbloom, University of Kansas
Shane Sanders, Kansas State University
Bhavneet Walia, Kansas State University

**KENTUCKY**

Tom Cate, Northern Kentucky University
Nan-Ting Chou, University of Louisville
David Eaton, Murray State University
Ann Eike, University of Kentucky
Robert Gillette, University of Kentucky
Barry Haworth, University of Louisville
Donna Ingram, Eastern Kentucky University
Waithaka Iraki, Kentucky State University
Hak Youn Kim, Western Kentucky University
Martin Milkman, Murray State University
Jenny Minier, University of Kentucky
David Shideler, Murray State University
John Vahaly, University of Louisville

**LOUISIANA**

Faik Koray, Louisiana State University
Paul Nelson, University of Louisiana–Monroe
Sung Chul No, Southern University and A&M College
Tammy Parker, University of Louisiana–Monroe
Wesley A. Payne, Delgado Community College

MARYLAND

Carey Borkoski, Anne Arundel Community College

Kathleen A. Carroll, University of Maryland–Baltimore County

Jill Caviglia-Harris, Salisbury University

Dustin Chambers, Salisbury University

Karl Einolf, Mount Saint Mary's University

Bruce Madariaga, Montgomery College

Shah Mehrabi, Montgomery College

Gretchen Mester, Anne Arundel Community College

David Mitch, University of Maryland–Baltimore County

John Neri, University of Maryland

Henry Terrell, University of Maryland

MASSACHUSETTS

William L. Casey, Jr., Babson College

Arthur Schiller Casimir, Western New England College

Michael Enz, Western New England College

Can Erbil, Brandeis University

Lou Foglia, Suffolk University

Todd Idson, Boston University

Aaron Jackson, Bentley College

Russell A. Janis, University of Massachusetts–Amherst

Anthony Laramie, Merrimack College

Carol McDonough, University of Massachusetts–Lowell

William O'Brien, Worcester State College

Ahmad Saranjam, Bridgewater State College

Howard Shore, Bentley College

Janet Thomas, Bentley College

Gregory H. Wassall, Northeastern University

Bruce G. Webb, Gordon College

Gilbert Wolpe, Newbury College

MICHIGAN

Eric Beckman, Delta College

Jared Boyd, Henry Ford Community College

Victor Claar, Hope College

Dr. Sonia Dalmia, Grand Valley State University

Daniel Giedeman, Grand Valley State University

Gregg Heidebrink, Washtenaw Community College

Carol Hogan, University of Michigan–Dearborn

Marek Kolar, Delta College

Susan J. Linz, Michigan State University

James Luke, Lansing Community College

Ilir Miteza, University of Michigan–Dearborn

John Nader, Grand Valley State University

Norman P. Obst, Michigan State University

Laudo M. Ogura, Grand Valley State University

Robert J. Rossana, Wayne State University

Michael J. Ryan, Western Michigan University

Charles A. Stull, Kalamazoo College

Michael J. Twomey, University of Michigan–Dearborn

Mark Wheeler, Western Michigan University

Wendy Wysocki, Monroe County Community College

MINNESOTA

Mary Edwards, Saint Cloud State University

Phillip J. Grossman, Saint Cloud State University

Monica Hartman, University of St. Thomas

David J. O'Hara, Metropolitan State University–Minneapolis

Kwang Woo (Ken) Park, Minnesota State University–Mankato

Ken Rebeck, Saint Cloud State University

MISSISSIPPI

Becky Campbell, Mississippi State University

Randall Campbell, Mississippi State University

Patricia A. Freeman, Jackson State University

MISSOURI

Chris Azevedo, University of Central Missouri

Ariel Belasen, Saint Louis University

Catherine Chambers, University of Central Missouri

Paul Chambers, University of Central Missouri

Ben Collier, Northwest Missouri State University

John R. Crooker, University of Central Missouri

Jo Durr, Southwest Missouri State University

Julie H. Gallaway, Southwest Missouri State University

Terrel Gallaway, Southwest Missouri State University

Mark Karscig, Central Missouri State University

Nicholas D. Peppes, Saint Louis Community College–Forest Park

Steven T. Petty, College of the Ozarks

Sharon Ryan, University of Missouri–Columbia

Ben Young, University of Missouri–Kansas City

MONTANA

Agnieszka Bielinska-Kwapisz, Montana State University–Bozeman

Jeff Bookwalter, University of Montana–Missoula

NEBRASKA

Allan Jenkins, University of Nebraska–Kearney

James Knudsen, Creighton University

Craig MacPhee, University of Nebraska–Lincoln

Kim Sosin, University of Nebraska–Omaha

Mark E. Wohar, University of Nebraska–Omaha

NEVADA

Bernard Malamud, University of Nevada–Las Vegas

NEW HAMPSHIRE

Evelyn Gick, Dartmouth College

Neil Niman, University of New Hampshire

NEW JERSEY

Len Anyanwu, Union County College

Maharuk Bhiladwalla, Rutgers University–New Brunswick

Giuliana Campanelli-Andreopoulos, William Paterson University

Gary Gigliotti, Rutgers University–New Brunswick

John Graham, Rutgers University–Newark

Berch Haroian, William Paterson University

Paul Harris, Camden County College

Donna Thompson, Brookdale Community College

**NEW MEXICO**

Donald Coes, University of New Mexico

Kate Krause, University of New Mexico

Curt Shepherd, University of New Mexico

**NEW YORK**

Seemi Ahmad, Dutchess Community College

Chris Annala, State University of New York–Geneseo

Erol Balkan, Hamilton College

John Bockino, Suffolk County Community College–Ammerman

Sean Corcoran, New York University

Ranjit S. Dighe, City University of New York–Bronx Community College

Debra Dwyer, Stony Brook University

Glenn Gerstner, Saint John's University–Queens

Susan Glanz, Saint John's University–Queens

William L. Goffe, State University of New York–Oswego

Wayne A. Grove, LeMoyne College

Christopher Inya, Monroe Community College

Clifford Kern, State University of New York–Binghamton

Mary Lesser, Iona College

Howard Ross, Baruch College

Leonie Stone, State University of New York–Geneseo

Ganti Subrahmanyam, University of Buffalo

Jogindar S. Uppal, State University of New York–Albany

Susan Wolcott, Binghamton University

**NORTH CAROLINA**

Otilia Boldea, North Carolina State University

Robert Burrus, University of North Carolina–Wilmington

Lee A. Craig, North Carolina State University

Kathleen Dorsainvil, Winston–Salem State University

Marc Fusaro, East Carolina University

Salih Hakeem, North Carolina Central University

Melissa Hendrickson, North Carolina State University

Haiyong Liu, East Carolina University

Kosmas Marinakis, North Carolina State University

Todd McFall, Wake Forest University

Shahriar Mostashari, Campbell University

Jeff Sarbaum, University of North Carolina–Greensboro

Peter Schuhmann, University of North Carolina–Wilmington

Catherine Skura, Sandhills Community College

Carol Stivender, University of North Carolina–Charlotte

Vera Tabakova, East Carolina University

Robert Whaples, Wake Forest University

Gary W. Zinn, East Carolina University

**OHIO**

John P. Blair, Wright State University

Bolong Cao, Ohio University–Athens

Kyongwook Choi, Ohio University

Darlene DeVera, Miami University

Tim Fuerst, Bowling Green University

Harley Gill, Ohio State University

Leroy Gill, Ohio State University

Steven Heubeck, Ohio State University

Ernest Massie, Franklin University

Ida A. Mirzaie, Ohio State University

Mike Nelson, University of Akron

Nicholas Noble, Miami University

Dennis C. O'Neill, University of Cincinnati

Joseph Palardy, Youngstown State University

Rochelle Ruffer, Youngstown State University

Kate Sheppard, University of Akron

Steve Szheghi, Wilmington College

Melissa Thomasson, Miami University

Yaqin Wang, Youngstown State University

Bert Wheeler, Cedarville University

Kathryn Wilson, Kent State University

Sourushe Zandvakili, University of Cincinnati

**OKLAHOMA**

David Hudgins, University of Oklahoma

Ed Price, Oklahoma State University

Abdulhamid Sukar, Cameron University

**OREGON**

Bill Burrows, Lane Community College

Tom Carroll, Central Oregon Community College

Larry Singell, University of Oregon

Ayca Tekin-Koru, Oregon State University

**PENNSYLVANIA**

Bradley Andrew, Juniata College

Mohammad Bajwa, Northampton Community College

Gustavo Barboza, Mercyhurst College

Charles A. Bennett, Gannon University

Howard Bodenhorn, Lafayette College

Milica Bookman, St. Joseph's University

Robert Brooker, Gannon University

Eric Brucker, Widener University

Linda Childs-Leatherbury, Lincoln University

Scott J. Dressler, Villanova University

Satyajit Ghosh, University of Scranton

Anthony Gyapong, Pennsylvania State University–Abington

Mehdi Haririan, Bloomsburg University

Andrew Hill, Federal Reserve Bank of Philadelphia

James Jozefowicz, Indiana University of Pennsylvania

Stephanie Jozefowicz, Indiana University of Pennsylvania

Nicholas Karatjas, Indiana University of Pennsylvania

Mary Kelly, Villanova University

Brendan Kennelly, Lehigh University

Thomas C. Kinnaman, Bucknell University

Christopher Magee, Bucknell University

Judy McDonald, Lehigh University
Ranganath Murthy, Bucknell University
Hong V. Nguyen, University of Scranton
Cristian Pardo, Saint Joseph's University
Iordanis Petsas, University of Scranton
Adam Renhoff, Drexel University
Edward Scahill, University of Scranton
Rajeev Sooreea, Pennsylvania State University–Altoona
Rebecca Stein, University of Pennsylvania
Sandra Trejos, Clarion University
Peter Zaleski, Villanova University
Ann Zech, Saint Joseph's University
Lei Zhu, West Chester University of Pennsylvania
Susan Zumas, Lehigh University

**RHODE ISLAND**

Leonard Lardaro, University of Rhode Island
Nazma Latif-Zaman, Providence College

**SOUTH CAROLINA**

Calvin Blackwell, College of Charleston
Ward Hooker, Orangeburg–Calhoun Technical College
Woodrow W. Hughes, Jr., Converse College
John McArthur, Wofford College
Chad Turner, Clemson University
Madelyn Young, Converse College

**SOUTH DAKOTA**

Joseph M. Santos, South Dakota State University
Jason Zimmerman, South Dakota State University

**TENNESSEE**

Charles Baum, Middle Tennessee State University
Bichaka Fayissa, Middle Tennessee State University
Michael J. Gootzeit, University of Memphis
Travis Hayes, University of Tennessee–Chattanooga
Christopher C. Klein, Middle Tennessee State University
Millicent Sites, Carson-Newman College

**TEXAS**

Carlos Aguilar, El Paso Community College
Rashid Al-Hmoud, Texas Tech University
William Beaty, Tarleton State University
Klaus Becker, Texas Tech University
Jack A. Bucco, Austin Community College–Northridge and Saint Edward's University
Don Bumpass, Sam Houston State University
Marilyn M. Butler, Sam Houston State University
Mike Cohick, Collin County Community College
Cesar Corredor, Texas A&M University
Patrick Crowley, Texas A&M University–Corpus Christi
Susan Dadres, Southern Methodist University
Harry Ellis, Jr., University of North Texas
Paul Emberton, Texas State University
Diego Escobari, Texas A&M University
Nicholas Feltovich, University of Houston–Main
Charles Harold Fifield, Baylor University

Mark Frank, Sam Houston State University
Richard Gosselin, Houston Community College–Central
Sheila Amin Gutierrez de Pineres, University of Texas–Dallas
Tina J. Harvell, Blinn College–Bryan Campus
James W. Henderson, Baylor University
Jane S. Himarios, University of Texas–Arlington
James Holcomb, University of Texas–El Paso
Jamal Husein, Angelo State University
Ansul Islam, University of Houston–Downtown
Karen Johnson, Baylor University
Kathy Kelly, University of Texas–Arlington
Thomas Kemp, Tarrant County College–Northwest
Jim Lee, Texas A&M University–Corpus Christi
Ronnie W. Liggett, University of Texas–Arlington
Akbar Marvasti, University of Houston–Downtown
James Mbata, Houston Community College
Kimberly Mencken, Baylor University
Randy Methenitis, Richland College
Carl Montano, Lamar University
James Moreno, Blinn College
Charles Newton, Houston Community College–Southwest College
John Pisciotta, Baylor University
Sara Saderion, Houston Community College–Southwest College
George E. Samuels, Sam Houston State University
Ivan Tasic, Texas A&M University
Roger Wehr, University of Texas–Arlington
Jim Wollscheid, Texas A&M University–Kingsville
J. Christopher Wreh, North Central Texas College
David W. Yoskowitz, Texas A&M University–Corpus Christi
Inske Zandvliet, Brookhaven College

**UTAH**

Lowell Glenn, Utah Valley State College
Aric Krause, Westminster College
Arden Pope, Brigham Young University

**VERMONT**

Nancy Brooks, University of Vermont

**VIRGINIA**

Lee Badgett, Virginia Military Institute
Lee A. Coppock, University of Virginia
Philip Heap, James Madison University
George E. Hoffer, Virginia Commonwealth University
Oleg Korenok, Virginia Commonwealth University
Frances Lea, Germanna Community College
Carrie Meyer, George Mason University
John Min, Northern Virginia Community College
James Roberts, Tidewater Community College–Virginia Beach
Araine A. Schauer, Mary Mount College

Sarah Stafford, The College of William & Mary
Susanne Toney, Hampton University
Michelle Vachris, Christopher Newport University
James Wetzel, Virginia Commonwealth University
George Zestos, Christopher Newport University

WASHINGTON

Stacey Jones, Seattle University
Dean Peterson, Seattle University
Robert Rosenman, Washington State University

WISCONSIN

Marina Karabelas, Milwaukee Area Technical College
Elizabeth Sawyer Kelly, University of Wisconsin–Madison

Pascal Ngoboka, University of Wisconsin–River Falls
Kevin Quinn, St. Norbert College
John R. Stoll, University of Wisconsin–Green Bay

WYOMING

Robert Godby, University of Wyoming

DISTRICT OF COLUMBIA

Leon Battista, American Enterprise Institute
Michael Bradley, George Washington University
Colleen M. Callahan, American University

INTERNATIONAL

Minh Quang Dao, Carleton University–Ottawa, Canada

# A Word of Thanks

Once again, we benefited greatly from the dedication and professionalism of the Pearson Economics team. Executive Editor David Alexander's energy and support were indispensable. David helped mold the presentation and provided words of encouragement whenever our energy flagged. Developmental Editor Lena Buonanno worked tirelessly to ensure that this text was as good as it could be and to coordinate the many moving parts involved in a project of this magnitude. We remain astonished at the amount of time, energy, and unfailing good humor she brings to this project. As we worked on the first edition, Director of Key Markets David Theisen provided invaluable insight into how best to structure a principles text. His advice helped shape nearly every chapter. Executive Marketing Manager Lori DeShazo developed a unique and innovative marketing plan. Steve Deitmer, Director of Development, brought sound judgment to the many decisions required to create this book. Alison Eusden and Rachel Mattison managed the extensive supplement package that accompanies the book. Heidi Allgair, Kathryn Dinovo, and Anthony Gemmellaro turned our manuscript pages into a beautiful published book. Rachel Lucas located photographs that captured the essence of key concepts. We received excellent research assistance from Ed Timmons, David Van Der Goes, and Jason Hockenberry. We thank Pam Smith and Elena Zeller for their careful proofreading of first- and second-round page proofs.

A good part of the burden of a project of this magnitude is borne by our families. We appreciate the patience, support, and encouragement of our wives and children.

# Microeconomics

Global Edition

# CHAPTER 1

# Economics:
## Foundations and Models

## Chapter Outline and Learning Objectives

# >> Microsoft Versus the U.S. Congress on Worker Visas

The number of jobs requiring technical education and training continues to increase. Many U.S. firms, particularly those involved with information technology, have had difficulty filling all their available job openings with U.S. citizens. U.S. law restricts the number of foreign "specialty workers" who may enter the United States under the H-1B visa program to just 65,000 per year. This visa program covers a very broad range of workers—from software engineers to fashion models. Bill Gates, chairman of Microsoft, testified before Congress in 2008 that limiting the number of foreign technical workers allowed into the United States was resulting in a "critical shortage of scientific talent" and hindering the ability of U.S. firms to compete with foreign firms. Gates noted that foreign students make up more than half of enrollments in computer science programs at leading U.S. universities:

> We provide the world's best universities . . . and the students are not allowed to stay and work in the country. The . . . smartest people want to come here, and that's a huge advantage to us, and in a sense, we're turning them away.

In 2009, though, Congress tightened rather than loosened restrictions on the immigration of technical workers to the United States. As part of the 2009 Recovery and Reinvestment Act, a bill intended to stimulate the U.S. economy during the recession, Congress put strict limits on the ability of banks and other firms receiving government aid to hire foreign workers. Economists and policymakers have debated how restrictions on the immigration of technical workers affect the U.S. economy. In this chapter and the remainder of this book, we will see how economics provides us with tools to analyze many important questions, including the economic effect of the immigration of skilled workers.

**AN INSIDE LOOK AT POLICY** on **page 18** discusses arguments for and against restricting the number of H-1B visas for highly skilled workers.

Sources: "Turning Away Talent," *Wall Street Journal*, March 10, 2009; Mehul Srivastava, "Anger Grows in India over U.S. Visa Rules," *BusinessWeek*, February 24, 2009; and Grant Gross, "Gates Repeats Request for More H-1B Visas," *InfoWorld*, March 12, 2008.

## Economics in YOUR LIFE!

**Will You Be Competing with Immigrant Workers for Your Next Job?**

Immigrant workers holding H-1B visas compete with U.S. workers for many high-paying jobs. For example, the average salary of H-1B visa holders working in the social sciences—including economics—is over $60,000. Managers with H-1B visas and a professional degree earn $107,500, and computer scientists earn $71,200. Suppose you plan on working as a software engineer, a financial analyst, an accountant, a lawyer, or in another industry where a high level of education is required. Is it likely that during your career, you will be competing for a job with immigrant workers from China, India, or some other foreign country? As you read the chapter, see if you can answer this question. You can check your answer against the one we provide at the end of the chapter.

▶ Continued on page 16

In this book, we use economics to answer questions such as the following:

- How are the prices of goods and services determined?
- How does pollution affect the economy, and how should government policy deal with these effects?
- Why do firms engage in international trade, and how do government policies affect international trade?
- Why does government control the prices of some goods and services, and what are the effects of those controls?

Economists do not always agree on the answers to every question. In fact, as we will see, economists engage in lively debate on some issues. In addition, new problems and issues are constantly arising. So, economists are always at work developing new methods to analyze economic issues.

All the issues we discuss in this book illustrate a basic fact of life: People must make choices as they try to attain their goals. We must make choices because we live in a world of **scarcity**, which means that although our wants are unlimited, the resources available to fulfill those wants are limited. You might like to own five BMWs and spend three months each summer in five-star European hotels, but unless Bill Gates is a close relative, you probably lack the money to fulfill these dreams. Every day, you make choices as you spend your limited income on the many goods and services available. The finite amount of time you have also limits your ability to attain your goals. If you spend an hour studying for your economics midterm, you have one less hour to study for your history midterm. Firms and the government are in the same situation as you: They also must attain their goals with limited resources. **Economics** is the study of the choices consumers, business managers, and government officials make to attain their goals, given their scarce resources.

We begin this chapter by discussing three important economic ideas that we will return to many times in this book: *People are rational, people respond to incentives, and optimal decisions are made at the margin.* Then we consider the three fundamental questions that any economy must answer: *What* goods and services will be produced? *How* will the goods and services be produced? and *Who* will receive the goods and services produced? Next, we consider the role of *economic models* in analyzing economic issues. **Economic models** are simplified versions of reality used to analyze real-world economic situations. We will explore why economists use models and how they construct them. Finally, we will discuss the difference between microeconomics and macroeconomics, and we will preview some important economic terms.

**Scarcity** A situation in which unlimited wants exceed the limited resources available to fulfill those wants.

**Economics** The study of the choices people make to attain their goals, given their scarce resources.

**Economic model** A simplified version of reality used to analyze real-world economic situations.

**1.1 LEARNING** OBJECTIVE

Explain these three key economic ideas: People are rational. People respond to incentives. Optimal decisions are made at the margin.

**Market** A group of buyers and sellers of a good or service and the institution or arrangement by which they come together to trade.

# Three Key Economic Ideas

As you try to achieve your goals, whether they are buying a new computer or finding a part-time job, you will interact with other people in *markets*. A **market** is a group of buyers and sellers of a good or service and the institution or arrangement by which they come together to trade. Most of economics involves analyzing what happens in markets. Throughout this book, as we study how people make choices and interact in markets, we will return to three important ideas:

1. People are rational.
2. People respond to economic incentives.
3. Optimal decisions are made at the margin.

## People Are Rational

Economists generally assume that people are rational. This assumption does *not* mean that economists believe everyone knows everything or always makes the "best" decision. It means that economists assume that consumers and firms use all available information as they act to achieve their goals. Rational individuals weigh the benefits and costs of each action, and they choose an action only if the benefits outweigh the costs. For example, if Microsoft charges a price of $239 for a copy of Windows, economists assume that the managers at Microsoft have estimated that a price of $239 will earn Microsoft the most profit. The managers may be wrong; perhaps a price of $265 would be more profitable, but economists assume that the managers at Microsoft have acted rationally on the basis of the information available to them in choosing the price. Of course, not everyone behaves rationally all the time. Still, the assumption of rational behavior is very useful in explaining most of the choices that people make.

## People Respond to Economic Incentives

Human beings act from a variety of motives, including religious belief, envy, and compassion. Economists emphasize that consumers and firms consistently respond to *economic* incentives. This fact may seem obvious, but it is often overlooked. For example, according to an article in the *Wall Street Journal*, the FBI couldn't understand why banks were not taking steps to improve security in the face of an increase in robberies: "FBI officials suggest that banks place uniformed, armed guards outside their doors and install bullet-resistant plastic, known as a 'bandit barrier,' in front of teller windows." FBI officials were surprised that few banks took their advice. But the article also reported that installing bullet-resistant plastic costs $10,000 to $20,000, and a well-trained security guard receives $50,000 per year in salary and benefits. The average loss in a bank robbery is only about $1,200. The economic incentive to banks is clear: It is less costly to put up with bank robberies than to take additional security measures. FBI agents may be surprised by how banks respond to the threat of robberies—but economists are not.

In each chapter, the *Making the Connection* feature discusses a news story or another application related to the chapter material. Read the following *Making the Connection* for a discussion of whether people respond to economic incentives even when making the decision to have children.

Making
the
Connection

## Will Women Have More Babies if the Government Pays Them To?

The populations of the United States, Japan, and most European countries are aging as birthrates decline and the average person lives longer. The governments of these countries have programs to pay money to retired workers, such as the Social Security system in the United States. Most of the money for these programs comes from taxes paid by people currently working. As the population ages, there are fewer workers paying taxes relative to the number of retired people receiving government payments. The result is a funding crisis that countries can solve only by either reducing government payments to retired workers or by raising the taxes paid by current workers.

In some European countries, birthrates have fallen so low that the total population will soon begin to decline, which will make the funding crisis for government retirement programs even worse. For the population of a country to be stable, the average woman must have 2.1 children, which is enough to replace both parents and account for children who die before reaching adulthood. In recent years, the birthrates in a number of countries, including France, Germany, and Italy, have fallen below this replacement level. The concern about falling birthrates has been particularly strong in the small European country of Estonia. In 2001, the United Nations issued a report in which it forecast that, given its current birthrate, by 2050, the population of Estonia would decline from 1.4 million to only about 700,000. The Estonian government responded by using economic incentives in an attempt to increase the birthrate. Beginning in 2007, the government began paying working women who take time off after having a baby their entire salary for up to 15 months. Women who have a baby but who do not work receive $200 per month, which is a substantial amount, given that the average income in Estonia is only $650 per month.

Will women actually have more babies as a result of this economic incentive? As the graph below shows, the birthrate in Estonia has increased from 1.3 children per woman in the late 1990s to 1.7 children per woman in 2008. This is still below the replacement level birthrate of 2.1 children, and it is too early to tell whether the increased birthrate is due to the economic incentives. But the Estonian government is encouraged by the results and is looking for ways to provide additional economic incentives to raise the birthrate further. And Estonia is not alone; more than 45 other countries in Europe and Asia have taken steps to try to raise their birthrates. These policies suggest that people may respond to economic incentives even when making the very personal decision of how many children to have.

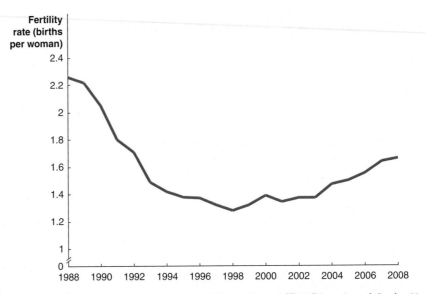

Source: Marcus Walker, "In Estonia, Paying Women to Have Babies Is Paying Off," *Wall Street Journal*, October 20, 2006; Sharon Lerner, "The Motherhood Experiment," *New York Times*, March 4, 2007; and Statistics Estonia, Population Reference Bureau.

 **YOUR TURN:** Test your understanding by doing related problem 1.4 on page 20 at the end of this chapter.

## Optimal Decisions Are Made at the Margin

Some decisions are "all or nothing": For instance, when an entrepreneur decides whether to open a new restaurant, he or she either starts the new restaurant or doesn't. When you decide whether to enter graduate school or to take a job, you either enter graduate school or you don't. But rather than being all or nothing, most decisions in life involve doing a little more or a little less. If you are trying to decrease your spending and increase your saving, the decision is not really between saving all the money you earn or spending it all. Rather, many small choices are involved, such as whether to buy a caffè mocha at Starbucks every day or just three times per week.

Economists use the word *marginal* to mean "extra" or "additional." Should you watch another hour of TV or spend that hour studying? The *marginal benefit* (or, in symbols, *MB*) of watching more TV is the additional enjoyment you receive. The *marginal cost* (or *MC*) is the lower grade you receive from having studied a little less. Should Apple produce an additional 300,000 iPhones? Firms receive *revenue* from selling goods. Apple's marginal benefit is the additional revenue it receives from selling 300,000 more iPhones. Apple's marginal cost is the additional cost—for wages, parts, and so forth—of producing 300,000 more iPhones. *Economists reason that the optimal decision is to continue any activity up to the point where the marginal benefit equals the marginal cost*—in symbols, where MB = MC. Often we apply this rule without consciously thinking about it. Usually you will know whether the additional enjoyment from watching a television program is worth the additional cost involved in not spending that hour studying, without giving the decision a lot of thought. In business situations, however, firms often have to make careful calculations to determine, for example, whether the additional revenue received from increasing production is greater or less than the additional cost of the production. Economists refer to analysis that involves comparing marginal benefits and marginal costs as **marginal analysis**.

**Marginal analysis** Analysis that involves comparing marginal benefits and marginal costs.

# The Economic Problem That Every Society Must Solve

**1.2 LEARNING** OBJECTIVE

Discuss how an economy answers these questions: What goods and services will be produced? How will the goods and services be produced? Who will receive the goods and services produced?

Because we live in a world of scarcity, any society faces the *economic problem* that it has only a limited amount of economic resources—such as workers, machines, and raw materials—and so can produce only a limited amount of goods and services. Therefore, every society faces **trade-offs**: Producing more of one good or service means producing less of another good or service. In fact, the best way to measure the cost of producing a good or service is the value of what has to be given up to produce it. The **opportunity cost** of any activity—such as producing a good or service—is the highest-valued alternative that must be given up to engage in that activity. The concept of opportunity cost is very important in economics and applies to individuals as much as it does to firms or to society as a whole. Consider the example of someone who could receive a salary of $80,000 per year working as a manager at Microsoft but decides to open her own consulting firm instead. In that case, the opportunity cost of her managerial services to her own firm is the $80,000 she gives up by not working for Microsoft, even if she does not explicitly pay herself a salary.

**Trade-off** The idea that because of scarcity, producing more of one good or service means producing less of another good or service.

**Opportunity cost** The highest-valued alternative that must be given up to engage in an activity.

Trade-offs force society to make choices when answering the following three fundamental questions:

1. *What* goods and services will be produced?
2. *How* will the goods and services be produced?
3. *Who* will receive the goods and services produced?

Throughout this book, we will return to these questions many times. For now, we briefly introduce each question.

## What Goods and Services Will Be Produced?

How will society decide whether to produce more economics textbooks or more Blu-ray players? More daycare facilities or more football stadiums? Of course, "society" does not make decisions; only individuals make decisions. The answer to the question of what will be produced is determined by the choices that consumers, firms, and the government make. Every day, you help decide which goods and services firms will produce when you choose to buy an iPhone instead of a BlackBerry or a caffè mocha rather than a chai tea. Similarly, Apple must choose whether to devote its scarce resources to making more iPhones or more MacBook laptop computers. The federal government must choose whether to spend more of its limited budget on breast cancer research or on homeland security. In each case, consumers, firms, and the government face the problem of scarcity by trading off one good or service for another. And each choice made comes with an opportunity cost, measured by the value of the best alternative given up.

## How Will the Goods and Services Be Produced?

Firms choose how to produce the goods and services they sell. In many cases, firms face a trade-off between using more workers or using more machines. For example, a local service station has to choose whether to provide car repair services using more diagnostic computers and fewer auto mechanics or more auto mechanics and fewer diagnostic computers.

Similarly, movie studios have to choose whether to produce animated films using highly skilled animators to draw them by hand or fewer animators and more computers. In deciding whether to move production offshore to China, firms may need to choose between a production method in the United States that uses fewer workers and more machines and a production method in China that uses more workers and fewer machines.

## Who Will Receive the Goods and Services Produced?

In the United States, who receives the goods and services produced depends largely on how income is distributed. Individuals with the highest income have the ability to buy the most goods and services. Often, people are willing to give up some of their income—and, therefore, some of their ability to purchase goods and services—by donating to charities to increase the incomes of poorer people. Each year, Americans donate more than $300 billion to charity, or an average donation of $2,750 for each household in the country. An important policy question, however, is whether the government should intervene to make the distribution of income more equal. Such intervention already occurs in the United States, because people with higher incomes pay a larger fraction of their incomes in taxes and because the government makes payments to people with low incomes. There is disagreement over whether the current attempts to redistribute income are sufficient or whether there should be more or less redistribution.

## Centrally Planned Economies versus Market Economies

**Centrally planned economy** An economy in which the government decides how economic resources will be allocated.

**Market economy** An economy in which the decisions of households and firms interacting in markets allocate economic resources.

To answer the three questions—what, how, and who—societies organize their economies in two main ways. A society can have a **centrally planned economy** in which the government decides how economic resources will be allocated. Or a society can have a **market economy** in which the decisions of households and firms interacting in markets allocate economic resources.

From 1917 to 1991, the most important centrally planned economy in the world was that of the Soviet Union, which was established when Vladimir Lenin and the Communist Party staged a revolution and took over the Russian Empire. In the Soviet Union, the government decided what goods to produce, how the goods would be produced, and who would receive the goods. Government employees managed factories and stores. The objective of these managers was to follow the government's orders rather than to satisfy the wants of consumers. Centrally planned economies like the Soviet Union have not been successful in producing low-cost, high-quality goods and services. As a result, the standard of living of the average person in a centrally planned economy tends to be low. All centrally planned economies have also been political dictatorships. Dissatisfaction with low living standards and political repression finally led to the collapse of the Soviet Union in 1991. Today, only a few small countries, such as Cuba and North Korea, still have completely centrally planned economies.

All the high-income democracies, such as the United States, Canada, Japan, and the countries of western Europe, are market economies. Market economies rely primarily on privately owned firms to produce goods and services and to decide how to produce them. Markets, rather than the government, determine who receives the goods and services produced. In a market economy, firms must produce goods and services that meet the wants of consumers, or the firms will go out of business. In that sense, it is ultimately consumers who decide what goods and services will be produced. Because firms in a market economy compete to offer the highest-quality products at the lowest price, they are under pressure to use the lowest-cost methods of production. For example, in the past 10 years, some U.S. firms, particularly in the electronics and furniture industries, have been under pressure to reduce their costs to meet competition from Chinese firms.

In a market economy, the income of an individual is determined by the payments he receives for what he has to sell. If he is a civil engineer, and firms are willing to pay a salary of $85,000 per year for engineers with his training and skills, that is the amount of income he will have to purchase goods and services. If the engineer also owns a house that he rents out, his income will be even higher. One of the attractive features of markets is that they reward hard work. Generally, the more extensive the training a person has received and the longer the hours the person works, the higher the person's income will be. Of course, luck—both good and bad—also plays a role here, as elsewhere in life. We can conclude that market economies respond to the question "Who receives the goods and services produced?" with the answer "Those who are most willing and able to buy them."

In each chapter of this book, you will see the special feature *Solved Problem*. This feature will increase your understanding of the material by leading you through the steps of solving an applied economic problem. After reading the problem, you can test your understanding by working the related problems that appear at the end of the chapter and in the study guide that accompanies this book. You can also complete Solved Problems on www.myeconlab.com and receive tutorial help.

# Solved Problem | 1-2

## Giving Advice to New Government Leaders

Suppose that a developing nation experienced a change in government leadership. Prior to this change, the nation employed a centrally planned economy to allocate its resources. The new leaders are willing to try a different system if they can be convinced that it will yield better results. They hire an economist to advise them and will order their citizens to follow this advisor's recommendations for change. The economist suggests that a market economy replace central planning to answer the nation's economic questions (*what*, *how*, and *who*?):

**a.** What will the economist suggest the leaders order their citizens to do?

**b.** Do you believe the leaders and citizens will accept the economist's suggestions?

## SOLVING THE PROBLEM

**Step 1:** **Review the chapter material.** This problem is about economic systems, so you may want to review the section "Centrally Planned Economies versus Market Economies," which begins on page 8.

**Step 2:** **What will the economist suggest the leaders order their citizens to do?** Because market economies allow members of households to employ self-interest to select occupations and purchase goods and services and for production of goods and services to be done by privately owned firms that respond to their own self-interest, the rulers would be told to not issue any orders. Government officials should have no influence over individual decisions made in markets.

**Step 3:** **Do you believe the leaders and citizens will accept the economist's suggestions?** Even democratically elected rulers, especially those with previous experience with significant government involvement in the nation's resource allocation, will find it difficult to accept the new system. They may wonder how self-interested individuals will produce and distribute goods and services so as to promote the welfare of the entire nation. This new system requires a significant reduction in government influence in people's lives; history has shown that government officials are often reluctant to give up this influence. Acceptance is most likely when the rulers have some knowledge and experience with the successful operation of a market economy in other countries. Ordinary citizens are more likely to accept the economist's suggestions because they will have more freedom to pursue their own economic goals.

**YOUR TURN:** For more practice, do related problem 2.8 on page 21 at the end of this chapter.

## The Modern "Mixed" Economy

In the nineteenth and early twentieth centuries, the U.S. government engaged in relatively little regulation of markets for goods and services. Beginning in the middle of the twentieth century, government intervention in the economy dramatically increased in the United States and other market economies. This increase was primarily caused by the high rates of unemployment and business bankruptcies during the Great Depression of the 1930s. Some government intervention was also intended to raise the incomes of the elderly, the sick, and people with limited skills. For example, in the 1930s, the United States established the Social Security system, which provides government payments to retired and disabled workers, and minimum wage legislation, which sets a floor on the wages employers can pay workers in many occupations. In more recent years, government intervention in the economy has also expanded to meet such goals as protection of the environment and the promotion of civil rights.

**Mixed economy** An economy in which most economic decisions result from the interaction of buyers and sellers in markets but in which the government plays a significant role in the allocation of resources.

Some economists argue that the extent of government intervention makes it no longer accurate to refer to the U.S., Canadian, Japanese, and western European economies as pure market economies. Instead, they should be referred to as *mixed economies*. A **mixed economy** is still primarily a market economy because most economic decisions result from the interaction of buyers and sellers in markets. However, the government plays a significant role in the allocation of resources. As we will see in later chapters, economists continue to debate the role government should play in a market economy.

One of the most important developments in the international economy in recent years has been the movement of China from being a centrally planned economy to being a more mixed economy. The Chinese economy had suffered decades of economic stagnation following the takeover of the government in 1949 by Mao Zedong and the Communist Party. Although China remains a political dictatorship, production of most goods and services is now determined in the market rather than by the government. The result has been rapid economic growth that in the near future may lead to total production of goods and services in China surpassing total production in the United States.

## Efficiency and Equity

**Productive efficiency** A situation in which a good or service is produced at the lowest possible cost.

**Allocative efficiency** A state of the economy in which production is in accordance with consumer preferences; in particular, every good or service is produced up to the point where the last unit provides a marginal benefit to society equal to the marginal cost of producing it.

**Voluntary exchange** A situation that occurs in markets when both the buyer and seller of a product are made better off by the transaction.

Market economies tend to be more efficient than centrally planned economies. There are two types of efficiency: *productive efficiency* and *allocative efficiency*. **Productive efficiency** occurs when a good or service is produced at the lowest possible cost. **Allocative efficiency** occurs when production is in accordance with consumer preferences. Markets tend to be efficient because they promote competition and facilitate voluntary exchange. With **voluntary exchange**, both the buyer and seller of a product are made better off by the transaction. We know that the buyer and seller are both made better off because, otherwise, the buyer would not have agreed to buy the product or the seller would not have agreed to sell it. Productive efficiency is achieved when competition among firms in markets forces the firms to produce goods and services at the lowest cost. Allocative efficiency is achieved when the combination of competition among firms and voluntary exchange between firms and consumers results in firms producing the mix of goods and services that consumers prefer most. Competition will force firms to continue producing and selling goods and services as long as the additional benefit to consumers is greater than the additional cost of production. In this way, the mix of goods and services produced will match consumer preferences.

Although markets promote efficiency, they don't guarantee it. Inefficiency can arise from various sources. To begin with, it may take some time to achieve an efficient outcome. When Blu-ray players were introduced, for example, firms did not instantly achieve productive efficiency. It took several years for firms to discover the lowest-cost method of producing this good. As we will discuss in Chapter 4, governments sometimes reduce efficiency by interfering with voluntary exchange in markets. For example, many governments limit the imports of some goods from foreign countries. This limitation reduces efficiency by keeping goods from being produced at the lowest cost. The production of some goods damages the environment. In this case, government intervention can increase efficiency because without such intervention, firms may ignore the costs of environmental damage and thereby fail to produce the goods at the lowest possible cost.

An economically efficient outcome is not necessarily a desirable one. Many people prefer economic outcomes that they consider fair or equitable, even if those outcomes are less efficient. **Equity** is harder to define than efficiency, but it usually involves a fair distribution of economic benefits. For some people, equity involves a more equal distribution of economic benefits than would result from an emphasis on efficiency alone. For example, some people support taxing people with higher incomes to provide the funds for programs that aid the poor. Although governments may increase equity by reducing the incomes of high-income people and increasing the incomes of the poor, efficiency may be reduced. People have less incentive to open new businesses, to supply labor, and to save if the government takes a significant amount of the income they earn from working or saving. The result is that fewer goods and services are produced, and less saving takes place. As this example illustrates, *there is often a trade-off between efficiency and equity*. Government policymakers often confront this trade-off.

**Equity** The fair distribution of economic benefits.

# Economic Models

**1.3 LEARNING** OBJECTIVE

Understand the role of models in economic analysis.

Economists rely on economic theories, or *models* (the words *theory* and *model* are used interchangeably), to analyze real-world issues, such as the economic effects of immigration. As mentioned earlier, economic models are simplified versions of reality. Economists are certainly not alone in relying on models: An engineer may use a computer model of a bridge to help test whether it will withstand high winds, or a biologist may make a physical model of a nucleic acid to better understand its properties. One purpose of economic models is to make economic ideas sufficiently explicit and concrete so that individuals, firms, or the government can use them to make decisions. For example, we will see in Chapter 3 that the model of demand and supply is a simplified version of how the prices of products are determined by the interactions among buyers and sellers in markets.

Economists use economic models to answer questions. For example, consider the question from the chapter opener: What effect does immigration of technical workers have on the U.S. economy? For a complicated question like this one, economists often use several models to examine different aspects of the issue. For example, they may use a model of how wages are determined to analyze the effect of the immigration of technical workers on wages in particular industries. Economists may use a model of international trade to analyze how labor costs affect the competitiveness of high-technology firms. Sometimes economists use an existing model to analyze an issue, but in other cases, they must develop a new model. To develop a model, economists generally follow these steps:

1. Decide on the assumptions to use in developing the model.
2. Formulate a testable hypothesis.
3. Use economic data to test the hypothesis.
4. Revise the model if it fails to explain well the economic data.
5. Retain the revised model to help answer similar economic questions in the future.

## The Role of Assumptions in Economic Models

Any model is based on making assumptions because models have to be simplified to be useful. We cannot analyze an economic issue unless we reduce its complexity. For example, economic models make *behavioral assumptions* about the motives of consumers and firms. Economists assume that consumers will buy the goods and services that will maximize their well-being or their satisfaction. Similarly, economists assume that firms act to maximize their profits. These assumptions are simplifications because they do not describe the motives of every consumer and every firm. How can we know if the assumptions in a model are too simplified or too limiting? We discover this when we form hypotheses based on these assumptions and test these hypotheses using real-world information.

## Forming and Testing Hypotheses in Economic Models

An **economic variable** is something measurable that can have different values, such as the wages paid to software programmers. A *hypothesis* in an economic model is a statement that may be either correct or incorrect about an economic variable. An example of

**Economic variable** Something measurable that can have different values, such as the wages of software programmers.

a hypothesis in an economic model is the statement that immigration of technical workers reduces wages paid to software programmers in the United States. An economic hypothesis is usually about a *causal relationship*; in this case, the hypothesis states that immigration causes, or leads to, lower wages for U.S. software programmers.

We have to test a hypothesis before we can accept it. To test a hypothesis, we analyze statistics on the relevant economic variables. In our H1-B visas example, we would gather statistics on the wages paid to software programmers and perhaps on other variables as well. Testing a hypothesis can be tricky. For example, showing that the wages paid to software programmers fell at a time when immigration was increasing would not be enough to demonstrate that immigration *caused* the wage fall. Just because two things are *correlated*—that is, they happen at the same time—does not mean that one caused the other. For example, suppose that the U.S. economy went into a recession at the same time that immigration of software engineers was increasing. In that case, the recession, rather than the immigration of foreign engineers, might have caused the fall in wages paid to software engineers in the United States. Over a period of time, many economic variables change, which complicates the testing of hypotheses. In fact, when economists disagree about a hypothesis, such as the effect of immigration on wages, it is often because of disagreements over interpreting the statistical analysis used to test the hypothesis.

Note that hypotheses must be statements that could, in principle, turn out to be incorrect. Statements such as "Immigration is good" or "Immigration is bad" are value judgments rather than hypotheses because it is not possible to disprove them.

Economists accept and use an economic model if it leads to hypotheses that are confirmed by statistical analysis. In many cases, the acceptance is tentative, however, pending the gathering of new data or further statistical analysis. In fact, economists often refer to a hypothesis having been "not rejected," rather than having been "accepted," by statistical analysis. But what if statistical analysis clearly rejects a hypothesis? For example, what if a model leads to a hypothesis that immigration lowers wages of U.S. software programmers but the data reject this hypothesis? In that case, the model must be reconsidered. It may be that an assumption used in the model was too simplified or too limiting. For example, perhaps the model used to determine the effect of immigration on wages paid to software programmers assumed that foreign software programmers entering the United States had the same training and experience as software programmers in the United States. If, in fact, U.S. software programmers have more training and experience than immigrant programmers, this difference may explain why the data rejected our hypothesis.

The process of developing models, testing hypotheses, and revising models occurs not just in economics but also in disciplines such as physics, chemistry, and biology. This process is often referred to as the *scientific method*. Economics is a *social science* because it applies the scientific method to the study of the interactions among individuals.

## Normative and Positive Analysis

Throughout this book, as we build economic models and use them to answer questions, we need to bear in mind the distinction between *positive analysis* and *normative analysis*. **Positive analysis** is concerned with *what is*, and **normative analysis** is concerned with *what ought to be*. Economics is about positive analysis, which measures the costs and benefits of different courses of action.

**Positive analysis**  Analysis concerned with what is.

**Normative analysis**  Analysis concerned with what ought to be.

We can use the federal government's minimum wage law to compare positive and normative analysis. In 2009, under this law, it was illegal for an employer to hire a worker at a wage less than $7.25 per hour. Without the minimum wage law, some firms and some workers would voluntarily agree to a lower wage. Because of the minimum wage law, some workers have difficulty finding jobs, and some firms end up paying more for labor than they otherwise would have. A positive analysis of the federal minimum wage law uses an economic model to estimate how many workers have lost their jobs because of the law, its impact on the costs and profits of businesses, and the gains to workers receiving the minimum wage. After economists complete this positive analysis, the decision as to whether the minimum wage law is a good idea or a bad idea is a normative one and depends on how people evaluate the trade-off involved.

# Don't Let This Happen to **YOU!**

## Don't Confuse Positive Analysis with Normative Analysis

"Economic analysis has shown that the minimum wage law is a bad idea because it causes unemployment." Is this statement accurate? As of 2009, the federal minimum wage law prevents employers from hiring workers at a wage of less than $7.25 per hour. This wage is higher than some employers are willing to pay some workers. If there were no minimum wage law, some workers who currently cannot find any firm willing to hire them at $7.25 per hour would be able to find employment at a lower wage. Therefore, positive economic analysis indicates that the minimum wage law causes unemployment (although economists disagree about how much unemployment the minimum wage causes). *But*, those workers who still have jobs benefit from the minimum wage because they are paid a higher wage than they otherwise would be. In other words, the minimum wage law creates both losers (the workers who become unemployed and the firms that have to pay higher wages) and winners (the workers who receive higher wages).

Should we value the gains to the winners more than we value the losses to the losers? The answer to this question involves normative analysis. Positive economic analysis can show the consequences of a particular policy, but it cannot tell us whether the policy is "good" or "bad." So, the statement at the beginning of this box is inaccurate.

**YOUR TURN:** Test your understanding by doing related problem 3.9 on page 22 at the end of this chapter.

Supporters of the law believe that the losses to employers and to workers who are unemployed as a result of the law are more than offset by the gains to workers who receive higher wages than they would without the law. Opponents of the law believe the losses are greater than the gains. The assessment by any individual depends, in part, on that person's values and political views. The positive analysis an economist provides would play a role in the decision but can't by itself decide the issue one way or the other.

In each chapter, you will see a *Don't Let This Happen to You!* box like the one above. These boxes alert you to common pitfalls in thinking about economic ideas. After reading this box, test your understanding by working the related problem that appears at the end of the chapter.

## Economics as a Social Science

Because economics studies the actions of individuals, it is a social science. Economics is therefore similar to other social science disciplines, such as psychology, political science, and sociology. As a social science, economics considers human behavior—particularly decision-making behavior—in every context, not just in the context of business. Economists have studied such issues as how families decide the number of children to have, why people have difficulty losing weight or attaining other desirable goals, and why people often ignore relevant information when making decisions. Economics also has much to contribute to questions of government policy. As we will see throughout this book, economists have played an important role in formulating government policies in areas such as the environment, health care, and poverty.

## Making the Connection | Should the Host Governments Protect the Migrant Workers?

Each year millions of unskilled workers from India, Pakistan, Bangladesh, Indonesia, and elsewhere leave their homes and families in search of jobs and a better future. Their search often leads them to the oil rich Gulf Cooperation Council (GCC) countries of Saudi Arabia, the United Arab Emirates (UAE), Kuwait, Qatar, Bahrain, and Oman. These migrant workers come from regions with high levels of unemployment, low wages and poor living conditions. They come in search of jobs hoping for a better future for themselves and their families. Through hard work, they expect to be able to support their families back home and

*Should host governments protect migrant workers?*

accumulate sufficient savings to return home one day to buy a house or set up a business.

The host countries are in need of laborers to fill thousands of jobs created annually as a consequence of the investment of oil revenues in construction, agriculture, manufacturing, and services. While many of these counties have their own pool of able local laborers, they often find it difficult to fulfill these vacancies. The lack of a minimum wage level and other labor laws make salaries and employment conditions unattractive to the local population. In addition, the stigma attached to certain employment, especially manual work, causes the local laborers to shy away from available vacancies. As a result, thousands of jobs are regularly filled by "guest" workers from Southeast Asian countries.

Most workers who take these jobs are recruited in their home country by local employment agencies. They are promised high salaries, accommodation, insurance benefits, and long-term employment contracts. The workers that are hired are mostly illiterate. Those that are able to read and write can seldom comprehend the complex terms and conditions of their employment contracts. Once they arrive in the host country, their dream of better jobs and a higher standard of living is quickly shattered. Many find themselves housed in cramped labor camps, working long hours for wages that are barely enough to cover food and other basic necessities. For the first few years of their contract deductions are made from their meagre wages to cover the cost of their air travel to the host country, visa fees, insurance, and other outlays made by their employer. As security against the migrants absconding, their passports are confiscated and held until completion of their contracts. Local laws prohibit them from changing employment until fulfillment of their contractual obligation. Any violation is grounds for dismissal and the placement of a life time ban on their return to the host country. Organized demands for better wages or working conditions are also causes for discharge, deportation, and banishment.

Many international human rights organizations have criticized the GCC countries for their labor laws and their treatment of guest workers. The GCC governments, however, believe that the present conditions actually *help* workers by providing employment to otherwise unemployed people. They accuse the international organizations of interference in local laws and the free flow of labor.

**YOUR TURN:** Test your understanding by doing related problem 3.7 on page 22 at the end of this chapter.

---

**1.4 LEARNING** OBJECTIVE

Distinguish between microeconomics and macroeconomics.

**Microeconomics** The study of how households and firms make choices, how they interact in markets, and how the government attempts to influence their choices.

**Macroeconomics** The study of the economy as a whole, including topics such as inflation, unemployment, and economic growth.

# Microeconomics and Macroeconomics

Economic models can be used to analyze decision making in many areas. We group some of these areas together as *microeconomics* and others as *macroeconomics*. **Microeconomics** is the study of how households and firms make choices, how they interact in markets, and how the government attempts to influence their choices. Microeconomic issues include explaining how consumers react to changes in product prices and how firms decide what prices to charge for the products they sell. Microeconomics also involves policy issues, such as analyzing the most efficient way to reduce teenage smoking, analyzing the costs and benefits of approving the sale of a new prescription drug, and analyzing the most efficient way to reduce air pollution.

**Macroeconomics** is the study of the economy as a whole, including topics such as inflation, unemployment, and economic growth. Macroeconomic issues include explaining why economies experience periods of recession and increasing unemployment and why, over the long run, some economies have grown much faster than others. Macroeconomics also involves policy issues, such as whether government intervention can reduce the severity of recessions.

The division between microeconomics and macroeconomics is not hard and fast. Many economic situations have *both* a microeconomic and a macroeconomic aspect. For example, the level of total investment by firms in new machinery and equipment helps to determine how rapidly the economy grows—which is a macroeconomic issue. But to understand how much new machinery and equipment firms decide to purchase, we have to analyze the incentives individual firms face—which is a microeconomic issue.

# A Preview of Important Economic Terms

**1.5 LEARNING** OBJECTIVE

Become familiar with important economic terms.

In the following chapters, you will encounter certain important terms again and again. Becoming familiar with these terms is a necessary step in learning economics. Here we provide a brief introduction to some of these terms. We will discuss them all in greater depth in later chapters:

- *Entrepreneur.* An entrepreneur is someone who operates a business. In a market system, entrepreneurs decide what goods and services to produce and how to produce them. An entrepreneur starting a new business puts his or her own funds at risk. If an entrepreneur is wrong about what consumers want or about the best way to produce goods and services, the entrepreneur's funds can be lost. This is not an unusual occurrence: In the United States, about half of new businesses close within four years. Without entrepreneurs willing to assume the risk of starting and operating businesses, economic progress would be impossible in a market system.

- *Innovation.* There is a distinction between an *invention* and *innovation.* An invention is the development of a new good or a new process for making a good. An innovation is the practical application of an invention. (*Innovation* may also be used more broadly to refer to any significant improvement in a good or in the means of producing a good.) Much time often passes between the appearance of a new idea and its development for widespread use. For example, the Wright brothers first achieved self-propelled flight at Kitty Hawk, North Carolina, in 1903, but the Wright brothers' plane was very crude, and it wasn't until the introduction of the DC-3 by Douglas Aircraft in 1936 that regularly scheduled intercity airline flights became common in the United States. Similarly, the first digital electronic computer—the ENIAC—was developed in 1945, but the first IBM personal computer was not introduced until 1981, and widespread use of computers did not have a significant effect on the productivity of U.S. business until the 1990s.

- *Technology.* A firm's technology is the processes it uses to produce goods and services. In the economic sense, a firm's technology depends on many factors, such as the skill of its managers, the training of its workers, and the speed and efficiency of its machinery and equipment.

- *Firm, company, or business.* A firm is an organization that produces a good or service. Most firms produce goods or services to earn profits, but there are also nonprofit firms, such as universities and some hospitals. Economists use the terms *firm*, *company*, and *business* interchangeably.

- *Goods.* Goods are tangible merchandise, such as books, computers, or Blu-ray players.

- *Services.* Services are activities done for others, such as providing haircuts or investment advice.

- *Revenue.* A firm's revenue is the total amount received for selling a good or service. It is calculated by multiplying the price per unit by the number of units sold.

- *Profit.* A firm's profit is the difference between its revenue and its costs. Economists distinguish between *accounting profit* and *economic profit*. In calculating accounting profit, we exclude the cost of some economic resources that the firm does not pay for explicitly. In calculating economic profit, we include the opportunity cost of all resources used by the firm. When we refer to *profit* in this book, we mean economic profit. It is important not to confuse *profit* with *revenue*.

- *Household.* A household consists of all persons occupying a home. Households are suppliers of factors of production—particularly labor—used by firms to make goods and services. Households also demand goods and services produced by firms and governments.

- *Factors of production or economic resources.* Firms use factors of production to produce goods and services. The main factors of production are labor, capital, natural resources—including land—and entrepreneurial ability. Households earn income by supplying to firms the factors of production.

- *Capital.* The word *capital* can refer to *financial capital* or to *physical capital*. Financial capital includes stocks and bonds issued by firms, bank accounts, and holdings of money. In economics, though, *capital* refers to physical capital, which includes manufactured goods that are used to produce other goods and services. Examples of physical capital are computers, factory buildings, machine tools, warehouses, and trucks. The total amount of physical capital available in a country is referred to as the country's *capital stock*.

- *Human capital.* Human capital refers to the accumulated training and skills that workers possess. For example, college-educated workers generally have more skills and are more productive than workers who have only high school degrees.

▶ Continued from page 3

## Economics in YOUR LIFE!

At the beginning of the chapter, we posed the question "Is it likely that during your career, you will be competing for a job with immigrant workers from China, India, or some other foreign country?" Some information helpful in answering this question appears in the chapter opener. Supporters of restrictions on H-1B visas for highly skilled workers argue that reducing the ability of firms to hire foreign workers would increase the jobs and wages available to U.S. workers. The chapter opener points out, however, that the total number of H-1B visas is limited to 65,000 per year and that this category of visas covers a broad range of "skilled workers," from computer programmers to fashion models. In 2009, Congress placed additional restrictions on the ability of banks and other firms receiving government aid to hire foreign workers. Is 65,000 workers a large number? To put the number in perspective, between June 2007 and June 2008, the U.S. economy created 29.4 *million* new jobs, even though part of the period was during an economic recession. So, although you may encounter difficulty finding a job and you may lose your job one or more times during your career, competition from foreign workers will probably not be the reason.

## Conclusion

The best way to think of economics is as a group of useful ideas about how individuals make choices. Economists have put these ideas into practice by developing economic models. Consumers, business managers, and government policymakers use these models every day to help make choices. In this book, we explore many key economic models and give examples of how to apply them in the real world.

Most students taking an introductory economics course do not major in economics or become professional economists. Whatever your major, the economic principles you will learn in this book will improve your ability to make choices in many aspects of your life. These principles will also improve your understanding of how decisions are made in business and government.

Reading newspapers and other periodicals is an important part of understanding the current business climate and learning how to apply economic concepts to a variety of real-world events. At the end of each chapter, you will see a two-page feature titled *An Inside Look*. This feature consists of an excerpt of an article that relates to the company or economic issue introduced at the start of the chapter and also to the concepts discussed in the chapter. A summary and an analysis and supporting graphs highlight the key economic points of the article. Read *An Inside Look at Policy* on the next page to explore arguments for and against restricting or reducing the number of H-1B visas for highly skilled workers. Test your understanding by answering the *Thinking Critically about Policy* questions.

# >> Do Immigrants Displace or Complement Domestic Workers?

## THE ECONOMIST

## Give Me Your Scientists . . .

JOE BIDEN, America's new vice-president, is prone to gaffes. In 2006 it was the turn of some Americans of Asian descent to take offence at his comment about needing "a slight Indian accent" to go to a 7-Eleven or a Dunkin' Donuts in Delaware. Mr Biden's defence was that he was trying to compliment the immigrant group on its entrepreneurial zeal.

(a) Many Americans are less favourably disposed towards immigrants. And rising unemployment is hardening attitudes. In the hubbub over the insertion of "Buy American" provisions into President Obama's fiscal-stimulus package, the Grassley-Sanders amendment was largely overlooked. This restricts the freedom of recipients of federal bail-out money to hire high-skilled foreign workers under the government's H-1B visa programme. Some people were delighted at what they saw as a significant, if small, first step in cracking down on those who they fear crowd skilled American workers out of the workplace. But others contend that such restrictions could dull America's edge in innovation, just when it is needed to help revive the economy.

Mr Obama says that part of the solution to America's economic problems should come from its universities and research laboratories. Yet these institutions in America are now manned disproportionately by immigrants, who made up 47% of scientists and engineers in America with PhDs, according to the 2000 census. Immigrants accounted for two-thirds of the net addition to America's stock of such workers between 1995 and 2006. Their role in innovation may seem obvious: the more clever people there are, the more ideas are likely to flourish, especially if they can be commercialised. But although contemporary theories of growth emphasise the importance of ideas, they assign no special role to immigration. Economists have tended to think of innovation as driven by the demand for better goods, which generates a need for skilled innovators. People's choices of career and education should respond to the labour market's demands, encouraging more of them to become innovators if needed. But because career choices cannot be expected to adjust instantly, there might be scope for skilled immigrants to fill the gap.

(b) Addressing these issues requires data on just how inventive immigrants are, a question that until recently was the province of educated guesswork. But William Kerr, an economist at Harvard Business School, used name-matching software to identify the ethnicity of each of the 8m scientists who had acquired an American patent since 1975. He found that the share of patents awarded to scientists born in America fell between 1975 and 2004. The share of all patents given to scientists of Chinese and Indian descent living in America more than tripled, from 4.1% in the second half of the 1970s to 13.9% in the years between 2000 and 2004. Nearly 40% of patents filed in 2005 by Intel, a silicon-chip maker, were for work done by people of Chinese or Indian origin. Some of these patents may have been awarded to American-born children of earlier migrants, but Mr Kerr reckons that most changes over time arise from fresh immigration.

(c) What of the criticism that these workers are displacing native scientists who would have been just as inventive? To address this, Mr Kerr and William Lincoln, an economist at the University of Michigan, used data on how patents responded to periodic changes in the number of H-1B entrants. If immigrants were merely displacing natives, increases in the H-1B quota should not have led to increases in innovation. But Messrs Kerr and Lincoln found that when the federal government increased the number of people allowed in under the programme by 10%, total patenting increased by around 2% in the short run. This was driven mainly by more patenting by immigrant scientists. But even patenting by native scientists increased slightly, rather than decreasing as proponents of crowding out would have predicted.

If anything, immigrants seemed to "crowd in" native innovation, perhaps because ideas feed off each other. Economists think of knowledge, unlike physical goods, as "non-rival": use by one person does not necessarily preclude use by others . . .

*Source: "Give Me Your Scientists. . . ," The Economist, March 5, 2009.*

## Key Points in the Article

This article discusses the possibility that as highly skilled Chinese, Indian, and other immigrants are restricted from working in the United States, U.S. firms will become less competitive with foreign companies. Restricting the number of highly-skilled workers in the United States could undermine economic growth and reduce increases in living standards. The article argues that one strength of the United States is that it attracts the best and brightest from all around the world.

## Analyzing the News

**a** Figure 1 shows that the fraction of scientists and engineers in the United States who are foreign born has been slowly increasing. Figure 2 shows the countries of origin of foreign-born students receiving Ph.D.s in science and engineering. The article states that some people are in favor of restricting the number of H-1B visas for highly skilled workers, while other people would prefer that more of these visas be granted. In this chapter, we learned

that people are rational. So, how can rational people come to different conclusions about such a fundamental question? Being rational means that people have goals and pursue actions that further those goals. U.S. firms argue that if more skilled workers are not allowed to immigrate to the United States, the firms will have difficulty competing with foreign companies that do not face restriction on whom they can hire. On the other hand, skilled workers who were born in the United States prefer not to have competition from foreign workers for the jobs that are available. Reduced competition would drive up wages. So, each party to the debate is advocating pursuing policies according to its own interests.

**b** We have seen in this chapter that economists use models to analyze economic questions. When studying an economic question, economists form a hypothesis that can be tested using available data. In this case, the issue is how many innovations are attributed to immigrant scientists and engineers. William Kerr of the Harvard Business School attempted to answer the question by calculating how

many patents had been granted to scientists whose names indicated that they were of Chinese or Indian descent. He discovered that the percentage of innovations discovered by scientists of Chinese and Indian descent increased from 4.1 percent in the late 1970s to 13.9 percent by the early 2000s.

**c** One key aspect of the debate over H-1B visas concerns whether new immigrants are displacing native workers or whether they are adding to the productive capacity of the economy by increasing the total amount of innovation. The study by William Kerr and William Lincoln mentioned in the article indicates that new immigrants increase the total amount of innovation, as measured by increases in the number of patents granted. In fact, the authors show that both native workers and foreign workers increase their patenting when the number of H-1B visas increases. This study will not end the debate over the value of immigration. But it does provide some evidence that immigrant scientists appear to be complementing domestic workers rather than displacing them.

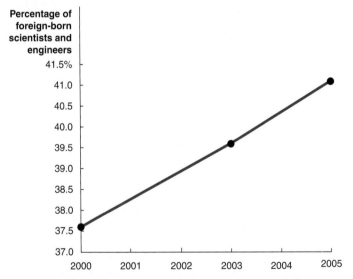

Figure 1  Foreign-Born Scientists and Engineers as a Percentage of All Scientists and Engineers in the United States

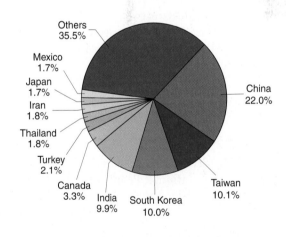

Figure 2  Foreign Recipients of U.S. Science and Engineering Doctorates, 1985–2005

Source: National Science Foundation, Division of Science Resources Statistics, *Science and Engineering Indicators: 2008*, NSF 08-01 (Arlington, VA, February 2008).

## Thinking Critically
*About Policy*

1. According to the article, many Americans would like the government to further restrict the number of H-1B work visas. What evidence from the article indicates that further limits on the immigration of

highly-skilled workers would create job vacancies that firms would have difficulty filling using only native-born scientists and engineers?

2. The article points out that when the number of immigrant scientists and engineers increases 10 percent, the number of patents increases by 2 percent and

that both immigrant and native-born scientists and engineers were responsible for this increase. Why would patenting by native-born scientists increase at the same time that the number of foreign-born scientists and engineers was increasing?

## Key Terms

---

 **1.1**

### Three Key Economic Ideas, pages 4–7

LEARNING OBJECTIVE: Explain these three key economic ideas: People are rational. People respond to incentives. Optimal decisions are made at the margin.

## Summary

**Economics** is the study of the choices consumers, business managers, and government officials make to attain their goals, given their scarce resources. We must make choices because of **scarcity**, which means that although our wants are unlimited, the resources available to fulfill those wants are limited. Economists assume that people are rational in the sense that consumers and firms use all available information as they take actions intended to achieve their goals. Rational individuals weigh the benefits and costs of each action and choose an action only if the benefits outweigh the costs. Although people act from a variety of motives, ample evidence indicates that they respond to economic incentives. Economists use the word **marginal** to mean extra or additional. The optimal decision is to continue any activity up to the point where the marginal benefit equals the marginal cost.

 Visit **www.myeconlab.com** to complete these exercises online and get instant feedback.

## Review Questions

1.1 Briefly discuss each of the following economic ideas: People are rational. People respond to incentives. Optimal decisions are made at the margin.

1.2 What is scarcity? Why is scarcity central to the study of economics?

## Problems and Applications

1.3 Bank robberies are on the rise in New Jersey, and according to the FBI, this increase has little to do with the economic downturn. The FBI claims that banks have allowed themselves to become easy targets by refusing to install clear acrylic partitions, called "bandit barriers," which separate bank tellers from the public. Of the 193 banks robbed in New Jersey in 2008, only 23 had these barriers, and of the 40 banks robbed in the first 10 weeks of 2009, only 1 had a bandit barrier. According to a special agent with the FBI, "Bandit barriers are a great deterrent. We've talked to guys who rob banks, and as soon as they see a bandit barrier, they go find another bank." Despite this finding, many banks have been reluctant to install these barriers. Wouldn't banks have a strong incentive to install bandit barriers to deter robberies? Why, then, do so many banks not do so?

Source: Richard Cowen, "FBI: Banks Are to Blame for Rise in Robberies," *NorthJersey.com*, March 10, 2009.

1.4 (Related to the *Making the Connection* on page 5) The country of Estonia has attempted to increase its birthrate by making payments to women who have babies. According to an article in the *Wall Street Journal*, "Some demographers argue that paying people to have a baby simply makes them have one earlier; it doesn't necessarily make them have more." Reread the description of Estonia's programs. Could the program be changed in ways that might make it more likely that Estonian women will have more children rather than simply changing the timing of when they have children? What information would we need to have to resolve the question of whether Estonian women are responding to the government's incentives by having more children or simply by having them earlier?

Source: Marcus Walker, "In Estonia, Paying Women to Have Babies Is Paying Off," *Wall Street Journal*, October 20, 2006, p. A1.

1.5 In a paper written by Bentley College economists Patricia M. Flynn and Michael A. Quinn, the authors state, "We find evidence that Economics is a good choice of major for those aspiring to become a CEO [chief executive officer]. When adjusting for size of the pool of graduates, those with undergraduate degrees in Economics are shown to have had a greater likelihood of becoming an S&P 500 CEO than any other major." A list of famous economics majors published by Marietta College includes business leaders Warren Buffet, Donald Trump, Ted Turner, and Sam Walton, as well as former presidents George H.W. Bush, Gerald Ford, and Ronald Reagan. Why might studying economics be particularly good preparation for being the top manager of a corporation or a leader in government?

Sources: Patricia M. Flynn and Michael A. Quinn, "Economics: A Good Choice of Major for Future CEOs," *Social Science Research Network*, November 28, 2006; and "Econ 360: Law and Economics," *Famous Economics Majors*, Marietta College, September 27, 2008.

**>> End Learning Objective 1.1**

## 1.2 The Economic Problem That Every Society Must Solve, pages 7–11

LEARNING OBJECTIVE: Discuss how an economy answers these questions: What goods and services will be produced? How will the goods and services be produced? Who will receive the goods and services produced?

## Summary

Society faces **trade-offs**: Producing more of one good or service means producing less of another good or service. The **opportunity cost** of any activity—such as producing a good or service—is the highest-valued alternative that must be given up to engage in that activity. The choices of consumers, firms, and governments determine what goods and services will be produced. Firms choose how to produce the goods and services they sell. In the United States, who receives the goods and services produced depends largely on how income is distributed in the marketplace. In a **centrally planned economy**, most economic decisions are made by the government. In a **market economy**, most economic decisions are made by consumers and firms. Most economies, including that of the United States, are **mixed economies** in which most economic decisions are made by consumers and firms but in which the government also plays a significant role. There are two types of efficiency: productive efficiency and allocative efficiency. **Productive efficiency** occurs when a good or service is produced at the lowest possible cost. **Allocative efficiency** occurs when production is in accordance with consumer preferences. **Voluntary exchange** is a situation that occurs in markets when both the buyer and seller of a product are made better off by the transaction. **Equity** is more difficult to define than efficiency, but it usually involves a fair distribution of economic benefits. Government policymakers often face a trade-off between equity and efficiency.

 Visit **www.myeconlab.com** to complete these exercises online and get instant feedback.

## Review Questions

2.1 What are the three economic questions that every society must answer? Briefly discuss the differences in how centrally planned, market, and mixed economies answer these questions.

2.2 What is the difference between productive efficiency and allocative efficiency?

2.3 What is the difference between efficiency and equity? Why do government policymakers often face a trade-off between efficiency and equity?

## Problems and Applications

2.4 Does Bill Gates, one of the richest people in the world, face scarcity? Does everyone? Are there any exceptions?

2.5 Would you expect new and better machinery and equipment to be adopted more rapidly in a market economy or in a centrally planned economy? Briefly explain.

2.6 Centrally planned economies have been less efficient than market economies.
   a. Has this happened by chance, or is there some underlying reason?
   b. If market economies are more economically efficient than centrally planned economies, would there ever be a reason to prefer having a centrally planned economy rather than a market economy?

2.7 Leonard Fleck, a philosophy professor at Michigan State University, has written, "When it comes to health care in America, we have limited resources for unlimited health care needs. We want everything contemporary medical technology can offer that will improve the length or quality of our lives as we age. But as presently healthy taxpayers, we want costs controlled." Why is it necessary for all economic systems to limit services such as health care? How does a market system prevent people from getting as many goods and services as they want?
   Source: Leonard Fleck, *Just Caring: Health Care Rationing and Democratic Deliberation*, New York: Oxford University Press, 2009.

2.8 (Related to *Solved Problem 1-2* on page 9) Define *equity*. What type of economic system is most equitable?

2.9 Suppose that your local police department recovers 100 tickets to a big NASCAR race in a drug raid. It decides to distribute these to residents and announces that tickets will be given away at 10 A.M. Monday at City Hall.

a. What groups of people will be most likely to try to get the tickets? Think of specific examples and then generalize.

b. What is the opportunity cost of distributing the tickets this way?

c. Productive efficiency occurs when a good or service (such as the distribution of tickets) is produced at the lowest possible cost. Is this an efficient way to distribute the tickets? If possible, think of a more efficient method of distributing the tickets.

d. Is this an equitable way to distribute the tickets? Explain.

**>> End Learning Objective 1.2**

---

**1.3** **Economic Models, pages 11-14**

LEARNING OBJECTIVE: Understand the role of models in economic analysis.

## Summary

Economists rely on economic models when they apply economic ideas to real-world problems. **Economic models** are simplified versions of reality used to analyze real-world economic situations. Economists accept and use an economic model if it leads to hypotheses that are confirmed by statistical analysis. In many cases, the acceptance is tentative, however, pending the gathering of new data or further statistical analysis. Economics is a *social science* because it applies the scientific method to the study of the interactions among individuals. Economics is concerned with positive analysis rather than normative analysis. **Positive analysis** is concerned with what is. **Normative analysis** is concerned with what ought to be. Because economics is based on studying the actions of individuals, it is a social science. As a social science, economics considers human behavior in every context of decision making, not just in business.

 Visit **www.myeconlab.com** to complete these exercises online and get instant feedback.

## Review Questions

3.1 Why do economists use models? How are economic data used to test models?

3.2 Describe the five steps by which economists arrive at a useful economic model.

3.3 What is the difference between normative analysis and positive analysis? Is economics concerned mainly with normative analysis or with positive analysis? Briefly explain.

## Problems and Applications

3.4 Do you agree or disagree with the following assertion: "The problem with economics is that it assumes that consumers and firms always make the correct decision. But we know everyone's human, and we all make mistakes."

3.5 Suppose an economist develops an economic model and finds that "it works great in theory, but it fails in practice." What should the economist do next?

3.6 Dr. Strangelove's theory is that the price of mushrooms is determined by the activity of subatomic particles that exist in another universe parallel to ours. When the subatomic particles are emitted in profusion, the price of mushrooms is high. When subatomic particle emissions are low, the price of mushrooms also is low. How would you go about testing Dr. Strangelove's theory? Discuss whether this theory is useful.

3.7 (Related to the *Making the Connection* on page 13) The *Making the Connection* explores the debate over the immigration of skilled workers. What is the impact of labor law on local workers employment, wages, and working conditions? How will changes to the minimum wage and other labor laws affect the flow of migrant workers to the host country? Think about some local labor laws in your own home country. Do they encourage local employment? Do they help attract workers to your country?

3.8 (Related to the *Chapter Opener* on page 3) Many U.S. firms have had difficulty filling available jobs with U.S. citizens. U.S. law restricts the number of foreign "specialty workers" who may enter the United States under the H-1B visa program to just 65,000 per year. In 2009, Congress tightened these restrictions even more.

a. Why have U.S. firms had difficulty filling available jobs with U.S. citizens?

b. What affect might the tightening of restrictions on immigration of foreign workers have on the U.S. economy?

3.9 (Related to the *Don't Let This Happen to You!* on page 13) Explain which of the following statements represent positive analysis and which represent normative analysis.

a. A 50-cent-per-pack tax on cigarettes will lead to a 12 percent reduction in smoking by teenagers.

b. The federal government should spend more on AIDS research.

c. Rising paper prices will increase textbook prices.

d. The price of coffee at Starbucks is too high.

3.10 In Australia, anyone providing financial advice must be licensed through the Australia Securities and

Investment Commission (ASIC). ASIC chairman Jeffrey Lucy reminded consumers of this law after receiving complaints that people were continuing to invest large sums of money with people who were not authorized to provide financial advice. This law applies to financial advice from the Internet in the same way it applies to financial advice in any other medium.

a. How would this law help protect consumers?

b. How might this law protect financial advisors more than consumers?

c. Briefly discuss whether you consider this law to be a good law.

Sources: Australian Services and Investment Commission, "06-162: Has your financial adviser got a license?" May 24, 2006; and "Securities Advice," *Oz NetLaw*, 2008.

**≫ End Learning Objective 1.3**

---

**1.4**  **Microeconomics and Macroeconomics, pages 14–15**
LEARNING OBJECTIVE: Distinguish between microeconomics and macroeconomics.

## Summary

**Microeconomics** is the study of how households and firms make choices, how they interact in markets, and how the government attempts to influence their choices. **Macroeconomics** is the study of the economy as a whole, including topics such as inflation, unemployment, and economic growth.

 Visit www.myeconlab.com to complete these exercises online and get instant feedback.

## Review Question

4.1 Briefly discuss the difference between microeconomics and macroeconomics.

## Problems and Applications

4.2 Briefly explain whether each of the following is primarily a microeconomic issue or a macroeconomic issue.

a. The effect of higher cigarette taxes on the quantity of cigarettes sold

b. The effect of higher income taxes on the total amount of consumer spending

c. The reasons for the economies of East Asian countries growing faster than the economies of sub-Saharan African countries

d. The reasons for low rates of profit in the airline industry

4.3 Briefly explain whether you agree with the following assertion: "Microeconomics is concerned with things that happen in one particular place, such as the unemployment rate in one city. In contrast, macroeconomics is concerned with things that affect the country as a whole, such as how the rate of teenage smoking in the United States would be affected by an increase in the tax on cigarettes."

**≫ End Learning Objective 1.4**

---

**1.5**  **A Preview of Important Economic Terms, pages 15–16**
LEARNING OBJECTIVE: Become familiar with important economic terms.

## Summary

Becoming familiar with important terms is a necessary step in learning economics. These important economic terms include *capital, entrepreneur, factors of production, firm, goods, household, human capital, innovation, profit, revenue,* and *technology.*

**≫ End Learning Objective 1.5**

# Appendix

## Using Graphs and Formulas

Graphs are used to illustrate key economic ideas. Graphs appear not just in economics textbooks but also on Web sites and in newspaper and magazine articles that discuss events in business and economics. Why the heavy use of graphs? Because they serve two useful purposes: (1) They simplify economic ideas, and (2) they make the ideas more concrete so they can be applied to real-world problems. Economic and business issues can be complicated, but a graph can help cut through complications and highlight the key relationships needed to understand the issue. In that sense, a graph can be like a street map.

For example, suppose you take a bus to New York City to see the Empire State Building. After arriving at the Port Authority Bus Terminal, you will probably use a map similar to the one shown below to find your way to the Empire State Building.

Maps are very familiar to just about everyone, so we don't usually think of them as being simplified versions of reality, but they are. This map does not show much more than the streets in this part of New York City and some of the most important buildings. The names, addresses, and telephone numbers of the people who live and work in the area aren't given. Almost none of the stores and buildings those people work and live in are shown either. The map doesn't indicate which streets allow curbside parking and which don't. In fact, the map shows almost nothing about the messy reality of life in this section of New York City, except how the streets are laid out, which is the essential information you need to get from the Port Authority to the Empire State Building.

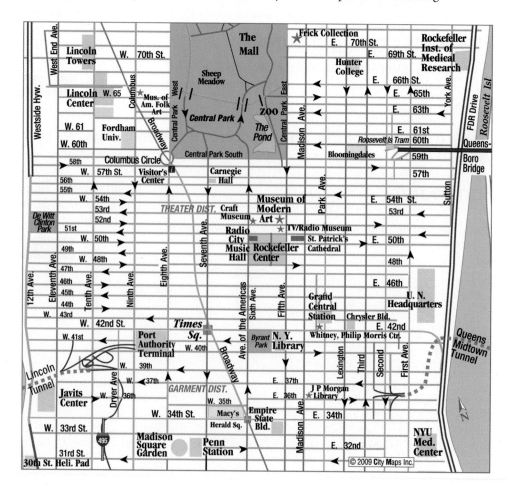

Think about someone who says, "I know how to get around in the city, but I just can't figure out how to read a map." It certainly is possible to find your destination in a city without a map, but it's a lot easier with one. The same is true of using graphs in economics. It is possible to arrive at a solution to a real-world problem in economics and business without using graphs, but it is usually a lot easier if you do use them.

Often, the difficulty students have with graphs and formulas is a lack of familiarity. With practice, all the graphs and formulas in this text will become familiar to you. Once you are familiar with them, you will be able to use them to analyze problems that would otherwise seem very difficult. What follows is a brief review of how graphs and formulas are used.

# Graphs of One Variable

Figure 1A-1 displays values for *market shares* in the U.S. automobile market, using two common types of graphs. Market shares show the percentage of industry sales accounted for by different firms. In this case, the information is for groups of firms: the "Big Three"—Ford, General Motors, and Chrysler—as well as Japanese firms, European firms, and Korean firms. Panel (a) displays the information on market shares as a *bar graph*, where the market share of each group of firms is represented by the height of its bar. Panel (b) displays the same information as a *pie chart*, with the market share of each group of firms represented by the size of its slice of the pie.

Information on economic variables is also often displayed in *time-series graphs*. Time-series graphs are displayed on a coordinate grid. In a coordinate grid, we can measure the value of one variable along the vertical axis (or *y*-axis), and the value of another variable along the horizontal axis (or *x*-axis). The point where the vertical axis intersects the horizontal axis is called the *origin*. At the origin, the value of both variables is zero. The points on a coordinate grid represent values of the two variables. In Figure 1A-2, we measure the number of automobiles and trucks sold worldwide by Ford Motor Company on the vertical axis, and we measure time on the horizontal axis. In time-series graphs, the height of the line at each date shows the value of the variable measured on the vertical axis. Both panels of Figure 1A-2 show Ford's worldwide sales

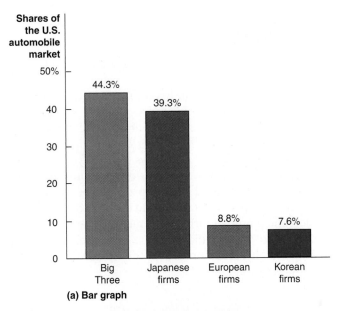

(a) Bar graph

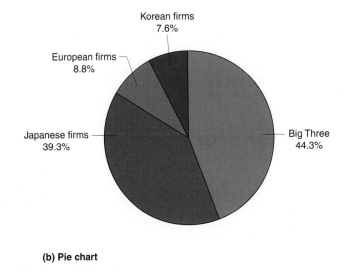

(b) Pie chart

Figure 1A-1    Bar Graphs and Pie Charts

Values for an economic variable are often displayed as a bar graph or as a pie chart. In this case, panel (a) shows market share data for the U.S. automobile industry as a bar graph, where the market share of each group of firms is represented by the height of its bar. Panel (b) displays the same information as a pie chart, with the market share of each group of firms represented by the size of its slice of the pie.

Source: "Auto Sales," *Wall Street Journal*, March 3, 2009.

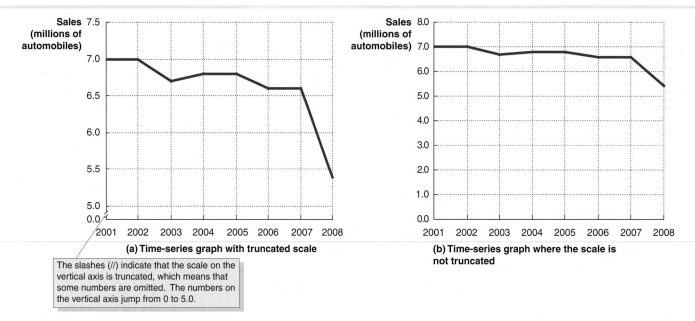

(a) Time-series graph with truncated scale

The slashes (//) indicate that the scale on the vertical axis is truncated, which means that some numbers are omitted. The numbers on the vertical axis jump from 0 to 5.0.

(b) Time-series graph where the scale is not truncated

## Figure 1A-2    Time-Series Graphs

Both panels present time-series graphs of Ford Motor Company's worldwide sales during each year from 2001 to 2008. Panel (a) has a truncated scale on the vertical axis, and panel (b) does not. As a result, the fluctuations in Ford's sales appear smaller in panel (b) than in panel (a).

Source: Ford Motor Company, *Annual Report*, various years.

during each year from 2001 to 2008. The difference between panel (a) and panel (b) illustrates the importance of the scale used in a time-series graph. In panel (a), the scale on the vertical axis is truncated, which means that it does not start with zero. The slashes (//) near the bottom of the axis indicate that the scale is truncated. In panel (b), the scale is not truncated. In panel (b), the decline in Ford's sales during 2008 appears smaller than in panel (a). (Technically, the horizontal axis is also truncated because we start with the year 2001, not the year 0.)

## Graphs of Two Variables

We often use graphs to show the relationship between two variables. For example, suppose you are interested in the relationship between the price of a pepperoni pizza and the quantity of pizzas sold per week in the small town of Bryan, Texas. A graph showing the relationship between the price of a good and the quantity of the good demanded at each price is called a *demand curve*. (As we will discuss later, in drawing a demand curve for a good, we have to hold constant any variables other than price that might affect the willingness of consumers to buy the good.) Figure 1A-3 shows the data you have collected on price and quantity. The figure shows a two-dimensional grid on which we measure the price of pizza along the *y*-axis and the quantity of pizza sold per week along the *x*-axis. Each point on the grid represents one of the price and quantity combinations listed in the table. We can connect the points to form the demand curve for pizza in Bryan, Texas. Notice that the scales on both axes in the graph are truncated. In this case, truncating the axes allows the graph to illustrate more clearly the relationship between price and quantity by excluding low prices and quantities.

## Slopes of Lines

Once you have plotted the data in Figure 1A-3, you may be interested in how much the quantity of pizza sold increases as the price decreases. The *slope* of a line tells us how much the variable we are measuring on the *y*-axis changes as the variable we are measuring on the *x*-axis changes. We can use the Greek letter delta (Δ) to stand for the

| Price (dollars per pizza) | Quantity (pizzas per week) | Points |
|---|---|---|
| $15 | 50 | A |
| 14 | 55 | B |
| 13 | 60 | C |
| 12 | 65 | D |
| 11 | 70 | E |

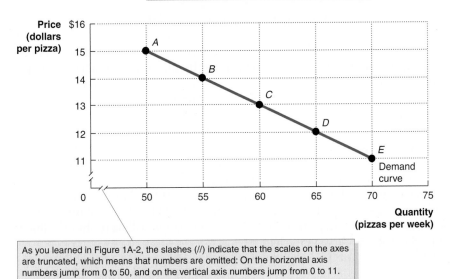

As you learned in Figure 1A-2, the slashes (//) indicate that the scales on the axes are truncated, which means that numbers are omitted: On the horizontal axis numbers jump from 0 to 50, and on the vertical axis numbers jump from 0 to 11.

## Figure 1A-3

### Plotting Price and Quantity Points in a Graph

The figure shows a two-dimensional grid on which we measure the price of pizza along the vertical axis (or $y$-axis) and the quantity of pizza sold per week along the horizontal axis (or $x$-axis). Each point on the grid represents one of the price and quantity combinations listed in the table. By connecting the points with a line, we can better illustrate the relationship between the two variables.

change in a variable. The slope is sometimes referred to as the rise over the run. So, we have several ways of expressing slope:

$$\text{Slope} = \frac{\text{Change in value on the vertical axis}}{\text{Change in value on the horizontal axis}} = \frac{\Delta y}{\Delta x} = \frac{\text{Rise}}{\text{Run}}.$$

Figure 1A-4 reproduces the graph from Figure 1A-3. Because the slope of a straight line is the same at any point, we can use any two points in the figure to calculate the slope of the line. For example, when the price of pizza decreases from $14 to $12, the quantity of pizza sold increases from 55 per week to 65 per week. Therefore, the slope is:

$$\text{Slope} = \frac{\Delta \text{Price of pizza}}{\Delta \text{Quantity of pizza}} = \frac{(\$12 - \$14)}{(65 - 55)} = \frac{-2}{10} = -0.2.$$

The slope of this line gives us some insight into how responsive consumers in Bryan, Texas, are to changes in the price of pizza. The larger the value of the slope

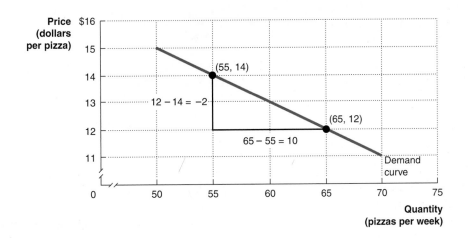

## Figure 1A-4

### Calculating the Slope of a Line

We can calculate the slope of a line as the change in the value of the variable on the $y$-axis divided by the change in the value of the variable on the $x$-axis. Because the slope of a straight line is constant, we can use any two points in the figure to calculate the slope of the line. For example, when the price of pizza decreases from $14 to $12, the quantity of pizza demanded increases from 55 per week to 65 per week. So, the slope of this line equals −2 divided by 10, or −0.2.

(ignoring the negative sign), the steeper the line will be, which indicates that not many additional pizzas are sold when the price falls. The smaller the value of the slope, the flatter the line will be, which indicates a greater increase in pizzas sold when the price falls.

## Taking into Account More Than Two Variables on a Graph

The demand curve graph in Figure 1A-4 shows the relationship between the price of pizza and the quantity of pizza sold, but we know that the quantity of any good sold depends on more than just the price of the good. For example, the quantity of pizza sold in a given week in Bryan, Texas, can be affected by such other variables as the price of hamburgers, whether an advertising campaign by local pizza parlors has begun that week, and so on. Allowing the values of any other variables to change will cause the position of the demand curve in the graph to change.

Suppose, for example, that the demand curve in Figure 1A-4 was drawn holding the price of hamburgers constant at $1.50. If the price of hamburgers rises to $2.00, then some consumers will switch from buying hamburgers to buying pizza, and more pizzas will be sold at every price. The result on the graph will be to shift the line representing the demand curve to the right. Similarly, if the price of hamburgers falls from $1.50 to $1.00, some consumers will switch from buying pizza to buying hamburgers, and fewer pizzas will be sold at every price. The result on the graph will be to shift the line representing the demand curve to the left.

The table in Figure 1A-5 shows the effect of a change in the price of hamburgers on the quantity of pizza demanded. For example, suppose that at first we are on the line labeled *Demand curve₁*. If the price of pizza is $14 (point A), an increase in the price of hamburgers from $1.50 to $2.00 increases the quantity of pizzas demanded from 55 to 60 per week (point B) and shifts us to *Demand curve₂*. Or, if we start on *Demand curve₁* and the price of pizza is $12 (point C), a decrease in the price of hamburgers from $1.50

## Figure 1A-5

### Showing Three Variables on a Graph

The demand curve for pizza shows the relationship between the price of pizzas and the quantity of pizzas demanded, *holding constant other factors that might affect the willingness of consumers to buy pizza.* If the price of pizza is $14 (point *A*), an increase in the price of hamburgers from $1.50 to $2.00 increases the quantity of pizzas demanded from 55 to 60 per week (point *B*) and shifts us to *Demand curve₂*. Or, if we start on *Demand curve₁* and the price of pizza is $12 (point *C*), a decrease in the price of hamburgers from $1.50 to $1.00 decreases the quantity of pizza demanded from 65 to 60 per week (point *D*) and shifts us to *Demand curve₃*.

| Price (dollars per pizza) | Quantity (pizzas per week) | | |
|---|---|---|---|
| | When the Price of Hamburgers = $1.00 | When the Price of Hamburgers = $1.50 | When the Price of Hamburgers = $2.00 |
| $15 | 45 | 50 | 55 |
| 14 | 50 | 55 | 60 |
| 13 | 55 | 60 | 65 |
| 12 | 60 | 65 | 70 |
| 11 | 65 | 70 | 75 |

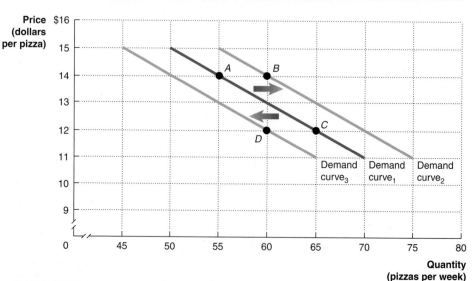

to $1.00 decreases the quantity of pizzas demanded from 65 to 60 per week (point *D*) and shifts us to *Demand curve₃*. By shifting the demand curve, we have taken into account the effect of changes in the value of a third variable—the price of hamburgers. We will use this technique of shifting curves to allow for the effects of additional variables many times in this book.

## Positive and Negative Relationships

We can use graphs to show the relationships between any two variables. Sometimes the relationship between the variables is *negative*, meaning that as one variable increases in value, the other variable decreases in value. This was the case with the price of pizza and the quantity of pizzas demanded. The relationship between two variables can also be *positive*, meaning that the values of both variables increase or decrease together. For example, when the level of total income—or *disposable personal income*—received by households in the United States increases, the level of total *consumption spending*, which is spending by households on goods and services, also increases. The table in Figure 1A-6 shows the values for income and consumption spending for the years 2005–2008 (the values are in billions of dollars). The graph plots the data from the table, with disposable personal income measured along the horizontal axis and consumption spending measured along the vertical axis. Notice that the four points do not all fall exactly on the line. This is often the case with real-world data. To examine the relationship between two variables, economists often use the straight line that best fits the data.

## Determining Cause and Effect

When we graph the relationship between two variables, we often want to draw conclusions about whether changes in one variable are causing changes in the other variable. Doing so, however, can lead to incorrect conclusions. For example, suppose you graph the number of homes in a neighborhood that have a fire burning in the fireplace and the number of leaves on trees in the neighborhood. You would get a relationship like that shown in panel (a) of Figure 1A-7: The more fires burning in the neighborhood, the fewer leaves the trees have. Can we draw the conclusion from this graph that using a fireplace causes trees to lose their leaves? We know, of course, that such a conclusion would be incorrect. In spring and summer, there are relatively few fireplaces being used, and the trees are full of leaves. In the fall, as trees begin to lose their leaves, fireplaces are used more frequently. And in winter, many

## Figure 1A-6

**Graphing the Positive Relationship between Income and Consumption**

In a positive relationship between two economic variables, as one variable increases, the other variable also increases. This figure shows the positive relationship between disposable personal income and consumption spending. As disposable personal income in the United States has increased, so has consumption spending.

Source: U.S. Department of Commerce, Bureau of Economic Analysis.

| Year | Disposable Personal Income (billions of dollars) | Consumption Spending (billions of dollars) |
|---|---|---|
| 2005 | $9,277 | $8,819 |
| 2006 | 9,916 | 9,323 |
| 2007 | 10,403 | 9,826 |
| 2008 | 10,806 | 10,130 |

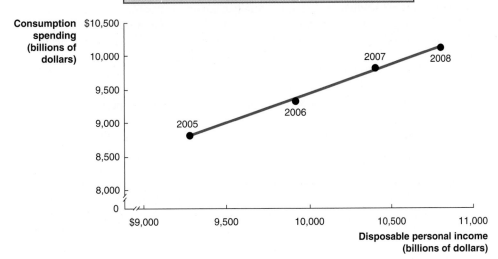

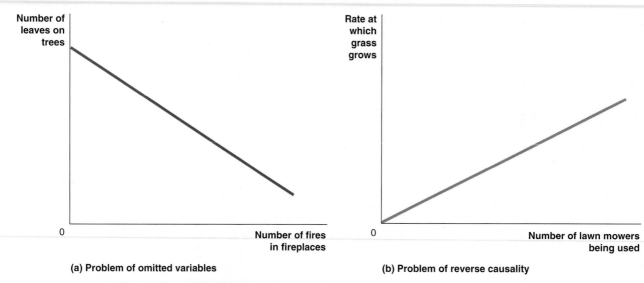

**(a) Problem of omitted variables**

**(b) Problem of reverse causality**

Figure 1A-7   Determining Cause and Effect

Using graphs to draw conclusions about cause and effect can be hazardous. In panel (a), we see that there are fewer leaves on the trees in a neighborhood when many homes have fires burning in their fireplaces. We cannot draw the conclusion that the fires cause the leaves to fall because we have an *omitted variable*—the season of the year. In panel (b), we see that more lawn mowers are used in a neighborhood during times when the grass grows rapidly and fewer lawn mowers are used when the grass grows slowly. Concluding that using lawn mowers *causes* the grass to grow faster would be making the error of *reverse causality*.

fireplaces are being used and many trees have lost all their leaves. The reason that the graph in Figure 1A-7 is misleading about cause and effect is that there is obviously an *omitted variable* in the analysis—the season of the year. An omitted variable is one that affects other variables, and its omission can lead to false conclusions about cause and effect.

Although in our example the omitted variable is obvious, there are many debates about cause and effect where the existence of an omitted variable has not been clear. For instance, it has been known for many years that people who smoke cigarettes suffer from higher rates of lung cancer than do nonsmokers. For some time, tobacco companies and some scientists argued that there was an omitted variable—perhaps a failure to exercise or a poor diet—that made some people more likely to smoke and more likely to develop lung cancer. If this omitted variable existed, then the finding that smokers were more likely to develop lung cancer would not have been evidence that smoking *caused* lung cancer. In this case, however, nearly all scientists eventually concluded that the omitted variable did not exist and that, in fact, smoking does cause lung cancer.

A related problem in determining cause and effect is known as *reverse causality*. The error of reverse causality occurs when we conclude that changes in variable *X* cause changes in variable *Y* when, in fact, it is actually changes in variable *Y* that cause changes in variable *X*. For example, panel (b) of Figure 1A-7 plots the number of lawn mowers being used in a neighborhood against the rate at which grass on lawns in the neighborhood is growing. We could conclude from this graph that using lawn mowers *causes* the grass to grow faster. We know, however, that in reality, the causality is in the other direction: Rapidly growing grass during the spring and summer causes the increased use of lawn mowers. Slowly growing grass in the fall or winter or during periods of low rainfall causes decreased use of lawn mowers.

Once again, in our example, the potential error of reverse causality is obvious. In many economic debates, however, cause and effect can be more difficult to determine. For example, changes in the money supply, or the total amount of money in the economy, tend to occur at the same time as changes in the total amount of income people in the economy earn. A famous debate in economics was about whether the changes in the money supply caused the changes in total income or whether the changes in total income caused the changes in the money supply. Each side in the debate accused the other side of committing the error of reverse causality.

# Are Graphs of Economic Relationships Always Straight Lines?

The graphs of relationships between two economic variables that we have drawn so far have been straight lines. The relationship between two variables is *linear* when it can be represented by a straight line. Few economic relationships are actually linear. For example, if we carefully plot data on the price of a product and the quantity demanded at each price, holding constant other variables that affect the quantity demanded, we will usually find a curved—or *nonlinear*—relationship rather than a linear relationship. In practice, however, it is often useful to approximate a nonlinear relationship with a linear relationship. If the relationship is reasonably close to being linear, the analysis is not significantly affected. In addition, it is easier to calculate the slope of a straight line, and it also is easier to calculate the area under a straight line. So, in this textbook, we often assume that the relationship between two economic variables is linear, even when we know that this assumption is not precisely correct.

## Slopes of Nonlinear Curves

In some situations, we need to take into account the nonlinear nature of an economic relationship. For example, panel (a) of Figure 1A-8 shows the hypothetical relationship between Apple's total cost of producing iPods and the quantity of iPods produced. The relationship is curved rather than linear. In this case, the cost of production is increasing

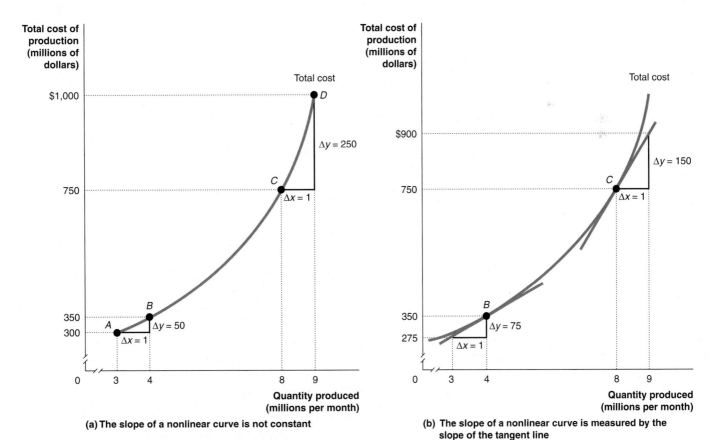

(a) The slope of a nonlinear curve is not constant

(b) The slope of a nonlinear curve is measured by the slope of the tangent line

Figure 1A-8 | **The Slope of a Nonlinear Curve**

The relationship between the quantity of iPods produced and the total cost of production is curved rather than linear. In panel (a), in moving from point *A* to point *B*, the quantity produced increases by 1 million iPods, while the total cost of production increases by $50 million. Farther up the curve, as we move from point *C* to point *D*, the change in quantity is the same—1 million iPods—but the change in the total cost of production is now much larger: $250 million.

Because the change in the *y* variable has increased, while the change in the *x* variable has remained the same, we know that the slope has increased. In panel (b), we measure the slope of the curve at a particular point by the slope of the tangent line. The slope of the tangent line at point *B* is 75, and the slope of the tangent line at point *C* is 150.

at an increasing rate, which often happens in manufacturing. Put a different way, as we move up the curve, its slope becomes larger. (Remember that with a straight line, the slope is always constant.) To see this effect, first remember that we calculate the slope of a curve by dividing the change in the variable on the $y$-axis by the change in the variable on the $x$-axis. As we move from point $A$ to point $B$, the quantity produced increases by 1 million iPods, while the total cost of production increases by $50 million. Farther up the curve, as we move from point $C$ to point $D$, the change in quantity is the same—1 million iPods—but the change in the total cost of production is now much larger: $250 million. Because the change in the $y$ variable has increased, while the change in the $x$ variable has remained the same, we know that the slope has increased.

To measure the slope of a nonlinear curve at a particular point, we must measure the slope of the *tangent line* to the curve at that point. A tangent line will touch the curve only at that point. We can measure the slope of the tangent line just as we would the slope of any other straight line. In panel (b), the tangent line at point $B$ has a slope equal to:

$$\frac{\Delta \text{Cost}}{\Delta \text{Quantity}} = \frac{75}{1} = 75.$$

The tangent line at point $C$ has a slope equal to:

$$\frac{\Delta \text{Cost}}{\Delta \text{Quantity}} = \frac{150}{1} = 150.$$

Once again, we see that the slope of the curve is larger at point $C$ than at point $B$.

# Formulas

We have just seen that graphs are an important economic tool. In this section, we will review several useful formulas and show how to use them to summarize data and to calculate important relationships.

## Formula for a Percentage Change

One important formula is the percentage change. The *percentage change* is the change in some economic variable, usually from one period to the next, expressed as a percentage. An important macroeconomic measure is the real gross domestic product (GDP). *GDP* is the value of all the final goods and services produced in a country during a year. "Real" GDP is corrected for the effects of inflation. When economists say that the U.S. economy grew 0.4 percent during 2008, they mean that real GDP was 0.4 percent higher in 2008 than it was in 2007. The formula for making this calculation is:

$$\left( \frac{\text{GDP}_{2008} - \text{GDP}_{2007}}{\text{GDP}_{2007}} \right) \times 100$$

or, more generally, for any two periods:

$$\text{Percentage change} = \frac{\text{Value in the second period} - \text{Value in the first period}}{\text{Value in the first period}} \times 100.$$

In this case, real GDP was $13,254 billion in 2007 and $13,312 billion in 2008. So, the growth rate of the U.S. economy during 2008 was:

$$\left( \frac{\$13,312 - \$13,254}{\$13,254} \right) \times 100 = 0.4\%.$$

Notice that it doesn't matter that in using the formula, we ignored the fact that GDP is measured in billions of dollars. In fact, when calculating percentage changes, *the units don't matter*. The percentage increase from $13,254 billion to $13,312 billion is exactly the same as the percentage increase from $13,254 to $13,312.

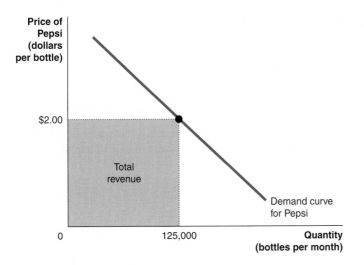

The area of a rectangle is equal to its base multiplied by its height. Total revenue is equal to quantity multiplied by price. Here, total revenue is equal to the quantity of 125,000 bottles times the price of $2.00 per bottle, or $250,000. The area of the green-shaded rectangle shows the firm's total revenue.

## Formulas for the Areas of a Rectangle and a Triangle

Areas that form rectangles and triangles on graphs can have important economic meaning. For example, Figure 1A-9 shows the demand curve for Pepsi. Suppose that the price is currently $2.00 and that 125,000 bottles of Pepsi are sold at that price. A firm's *total revenue* is equal to the amount it receives from selling its product, or the quantity sold multiplied by the price. In this case, total revenue will equal 125,000 bottles times $2.00 per bottle, or $250,000.

The formula for the area of a rectangle is:

$$\text{Area of a rectangle} = \text{base} \times \text{height}.$$

In Figure 1A-9, the green-shaded rectangle also represents the firm's total revenue because its area is given by the base of 125,000 bottles multiplied by the price of $2.00 per bottle.

We will see in later chapters that areas that are triangles can also have economic significance. The formula for the area of a triangle is:

$$\text{Area of a triangle} = \tfrac{1}{2} \times \text{base} \times \text{height}.$$

The blue-shaded area in Figure 1A-10 is a triangle. The base equals 150,000 − 125,000, or 25,000. Its height equals $2.00 − $1.50, or $0.50. Therefore, its area equals ½ × 25,000 × $0.50, or $6,250. Notice that the blue area is a triangle only if the demand curve is a straight line, or linear. Not all demand curves are linear. However, the formula for the area of a triangle will usually still give a good approximation, even if the demand curve is not linear.

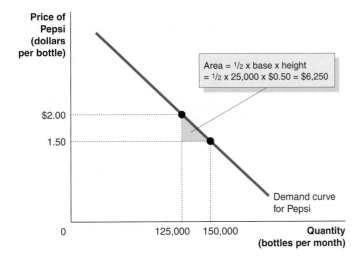

The area of a triangle is equal to ½ multiplied by its base multiplied by its height. The area of the blue-shaded triangle has a base equal to 150,000 − 125,000, or 25,000, and a height equal to $2.00 − $1.50, or $0.50. Therefore, its area equals ½ × 25,000 × $0.50, or $6,250.

## Summary of Using Formulas

You will encounter several other formulas in this book. Whenever you must use a formula, you should follow these steps:

1. Make sure you understand the economic concept that the formula represents.

2. Make sure you are using the correct formula for the problem you are solving.

3. Make sure that the number you calculate using the formula is economically reasonable. For example, if you are using a formula to calculate a firm's revenue and your answer is a negative number, you know you made a mistake somewhere.

---

| 1A | **Using Graphs and Formulas,** pages 24–34 |
|----|----|
|    | LEARNING OBJECTIVE: Review the use of graphs and formulas. |

  Visit **www.myeconlab.com** to complete these exercises online and get instant feedback.

# Problems and Applications

**1A.1** The following table shows the relationship between the price of custard pies and the number of pies Jacob buys per week.

| PRICE | QUANTITY OF PIES | WEEK |
|-------|------------------|------|
| $3.00 | 6 | July 2 |
| 2.00 | 7 | July 9 |
| 5.00 | 4 | July 16 |
| 6.00 | 3 | July 23 |
| 1.00 | 8 | July 30 |
| 4.00 | 5 | August 6 |

    **a.** Is the relationship between the price of pies and the number of pies Jacob buys a positive relationship or a negative relationship?

    **b.** Plot the data from the table on a graph similar to Figure 1A-3 on page 27. Draw a straight line that best fits the points.

    **c.** Calculate the slope of the line.

**1A.2** The following table gives information on the quantity of glasses of lemonade demanded on sunny and overcast days. Plot the data from the table on a graph similar to Figure 1A-5 on page 28. Draw two straight lines representing the two demand curves—one for sunny days and one for overcast days.

| PRICE (DOLLARS PER GLASS) | QUANTITY (GLASSES OF LEMONADE PER DAY) | WEATHER |
|---------------------------|----------------------------------------|---------|
| $0.80 | 30 | Sunny |
| 0.80 | 10 | Overcast |
| 0.70 | 40 | Sunny |
| 0.70 | 20 | Overcast |
| 0.60 | 50 | Sunny |
| 0.60 | 30 | Overcast |
| 0.50 | 60 | Sunny |
| 0.50 | 40 | Overcast |

**1A.3** Using the information in Figure 1A-2 on page 26, calculate the percentage change in auto sales from one year to the next. Between which years did sales fall at the fastest rate?

**1A.4** Real GDP in 1981 was $5,292 billion. Real GDP in 1982 was $5,189 billion. What was the percentage change in real GDP from 1981 to 1982? What do economists call the percentage change in real GDP from one year to the next?

**1A.5** Assume that the demand curve for Pepsi passes through the following two points:

| PRICE PER BOTTLE OF PEPSI | NUMBER OF BOTTLES SOLD |
|---------------------------|------------------------|
| $2.50 | 100,000 |
| 1.25 | 200,000 |

    **a.** Draw a graph with a linear demand curve that passes through these two points.

    **b.** Show on the graph the areas representing total revenue at each price. Give the value for total revenue at each price.

**1A.6** What is the area of the blue triangle shown in the following figure?

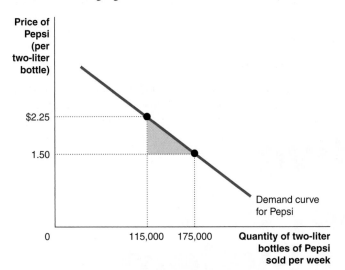

**1A.7** Calculate the slope of the total cost curve at point *A* and at point *B* in the following figure.

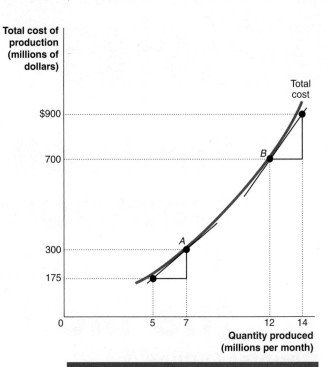

**>> End Appendix Learning Objective**

# CHAPTER 2

# Trade-offs, Comparative Advantage, and the Market System

## Chapter Outline and Learning Objectives

## >> Managers Making Choices at BMW

When you think of cars that combine fine engineering, high performance, and cutting-edge styling, you are likely to think of BMW. Founded in Germany in 1916, BMW today has 23 factories in 15 countries and worldwide sales of more than 1.4 million cars.

To compete in the automobile market, the managers of BMW must make many strategic decisions, such as whether to introduce new car models. BMW has begun selling a hydrogen-powered version of the 7-Series sedan and is also working on fuel cell–powered cars. Another strategic decision BMW's managers face is where to advertise. Although some of BMW's managers did not believe the company could sell cars in China, BMW decided to advertise heavily there. The advertising paid off: China has become the company's fifth-largest market, with sales increasing by more than 23 percent in 2008 alone.

BMW's managers have also faced the strategic decision of whether to concentrate production in factories in Germany or to build new factories in overseas markets. Keeping production in Germany makes it eas-

ier for BMW's managers to supervise production and to employ German workers, who generally have high levels of technical training. By building factories in other countries, BMW can benefit from paying lower wages and can reduce political friction by producing vehicles in the same country in which it sells them. BMW opened a plant at Shenyang, in northeast China, and a U.S. factory in Spartanburg, South Carolina, which currently produces the Z4 roadster and X5 sport-utility vehicle (SUV) for sale both in the United States and worldwide.

Managers also face smaller-scale—or tactical—business decisions. For instance, in scheduling production at BMW's Spartanburg plant, managers must decide each month the quantity of Z4 and the X5 models to produce. Like other decisions managers make, this one involves a trade-off: Producing more Z4s means producing fewer X5s.

**AN INSIDE LOOK** on **page 56** discusses how managers decide between producing hybrid cars or improving existing conventional gasoline-powered cars.

## Economics in YOUR Life!

### The Trade-offs When You Buy a Car

When you buy a car, you probably consider factors such as safety and fuel efficiency. To increase fuel efficiency, automobile manufacturers make cars small and light. Large cars absorb more of the impact of an accident than do small cars. As a result, people are usually safer driving large cars than small cars. What can we conclude from these facts about the relationship between safety and fuel efficiency? Under what circumstances would it be possible for automobile manufacturers to make cars safer and more fuel efficient? As you read the chapter, see if you can answer these questions. You can check your answers against those provided at the end of the chapter.

▶ Continued on page 54

**Scarcity** A situation in which unlimited wants exceed the limited resources available to fulfill those wants.

I n a market system, managers at most firms must make decisions like those made by BMW's managers. The decisions managers face reflect a key fact of economic life: *Scarcity requires trade-offs.* **Scarcity** exists because we have unlimited wants but only limited resources available to fulfill those wants. Goods and services are scarce. So, too, are the economic resources, or *factors of production*—workers, capital, natural resources, and entrepreneurial ability—used to make goods and services. Your time is scarce, which means you face trade-offs: If you spend an hour studying for an economics exam, you have one less hour to spend studying for a psychology exam or going to the movies. If your university decides to use some of its scarce budget to buy new computers for the computer labs, those funds will not be available to buy new books for the library or to resurface the student parking lot. If BMW decides to devote some of the scarce workers and machinery in its Spartanburg assembly plant to producing more Z4 roadsters, those resources will not be available to produce more X5 SUVs.

Households and firms make many of their decisions in markets. Trade is a key activity that takes place in markets. Trade involves the decisions of millions of households and firms spread around the world. By engaging in trade, people can raise their standard of living. In this chapter, we provide an overview of how the market system coordinates the independent decisions of these millions of households and firms. We begin our analysis of the economic consequences of scarcity and the working of the market system by introducing an important economic model: the *production possibilities frontier*.

Use a production possibilities frontier to analyze opportunity costs and trade-offs.

**Production possibilities frontier** (*PPF*) A curve showing the maximum attainable combinations of two products that may be produced with available resources and current technology.

# Production Possibilities Frontiers and Opportunity Costs

As we saw in the chapter opener, BMW operates an automobile factory in Spartanburg, South Carolina, where it assembles Z4 roadsters and X5 SUVs. Because the firm's resources—workers, machinery, materials, and entrepreneurial skills—are limited, BMW faces a trade-off: Resources devoted to producing Z4s are not available for producing X5s and vice versa. Chapter 1 explained that economic models can be useful in analyzing many questions. We can use a simple model called the *production possibilities frontier* to analyze the trade-offs BMW faces in its Spartanburg plant. A **production possibilities frontier** (*PPF*) is a curve showing the maximum attainable combinations of two products that may be produced with available resources and current technology. In BMW's case, the two products are Z4 roadsters and X5 SUVs, and the resources are BMW's workers, materials, robots, and other machinery.

## Graphing the Production Possibilities Frontier

Figure 2-1 uses a production possibilities frontier to illustrate the trade-offs that BMW faces. The numbers from the table are plotted in the graph. The line in the graph is BMW's production possibilities frontier. If BMW uses all its resources to produce roadsters, it can produce 800 per day—point *A* at one end of the production possibilities frontier. If BMW uses all its resources to produce SUVs, it can produce 800 per day—point *E* at the other end of the production possibilities frontier. If BMW devotes resources to producing both vehicles, it could be at a point like *B*, where it produces 600 roadsters and 200 SUVs.

All the combinations either on the frontier—like *A*, *B*, *C*, *D*, and *E*—or inside the frontier—like point *F*—are *attainable* with the resources available. Combinations on the frontier are *efficient* because all available resources are being fully utilized, and the fewest possible resources are being used to produce a given amount of output. Combinations inside the frontier—like point *F*—are *inefficient* because maximum output is not being obtained from the available resources—perhaps because the assembly line is not operating at capacity. BMW might like to be beyond the frontier—at a point like *G*, where it would be producing 600 roadsters and 500 SUVs—but points beyond the production possibilities frontier are *unattainable*, given the firm's current resources. To produce the combination at *G*, BMW would need more machines or more workers.

| BMW's Production Choices at Its Spartanburg Plant | | |
|---|---|---|
| Choice | Quantity of Roadsters Produced | Quantity of SUVs Produced |
| A | 800 | 0 |
| B | 600 | 200 |
| C | 400 | 400 |
| D | 200 | 600 |
| E | 0 | 800 |

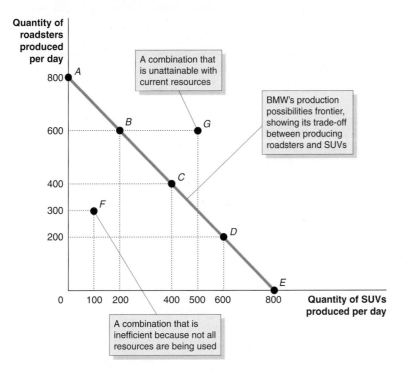

## Figure 2-1

**BMW's Production Possibilities Frontier**

BMW faces a trade-off: To build one more roadster, it must build one less SUV. The production possibilities frontier illustrates the trade-off BMW faces. Combinations on the production possibilities frontier—like points *A, B, C, D,* and *E*—are *technically efficient* because the maximum output is being obtained from the available resources. Combinations inside the frontier—like point *F*—are *inefficient* because some resources are not being used. Combinations outside the frontier—like point *G*—are *unattainable* with current resources.

Notice that if BMW is producing efficiently and is on the production possibilities frontier, the only way to produce more of one vehicle is to produce fewer of the other vehicle. Recall from Chapter 1 that the **opportunity cost** of any activity is the highest-valued alternative that must be given up to engage in that activity. For BMW, the opportunity cost of producing one more SUV is the number of roadsters the company will not be able to produce because it has shifted those resources to producing SUVs. For example, in moving from point *B* to point *C*, the opportunity cost of producing 200 more SUVs per day is the 200 fewer roadsters that can be produced.

What point on the production possibilities frontier is best? We can't tell without further information. If consumer demand for SUVs is greater than the demand for roadsters, the company is likely to choose a point closer to *E.* If demand for roadsters is greater than demand for SUVs, the company is likely to choose a point closer to *A.*

**Opportunity cost** The highest-valued alternative that must be given up to engage in an activity.

## Making the Connection | Facing the Trade-offs in Health Care Spending

Households have limited incomes. If the price of health care rises, households have to choose whether to buy less health care or spend less on other goods and services. The same is true of the federal government's expenditures on health care. The government provides health insurance to about one-quarter of the population through programs such as Medicare for people over age 65 and Medicaid for low-income people. If the price of health care rises, the government has to either cut back on the services provided through Medicare and Medicaid or cut spending in another part of the government's budget. (Of course, both households and the government can borrow to pay for some of their spending, but ultimately the funds they can borrow are also limited.)

*Spending more on health care means spending less on other goods and services.*

About two-thirds of the population has private health insurance, often provided by an employer. When the fees doctors charge, the cost of prescription drugs, and the cost of hospital stays rise, the cost to employers of providing health insurance increases. As a result, employers will typically increase the amount they withhold from employees' paychecks to pay for the insurance. Some employers—particularly small firms—will even stop offering health insurance to their employees. In either case, the price employees pay for health care will rise. How do people respond to rising health care costs? Isn't health care a necessity that people continue to consume the same amount of no matter how much its price increases? In fact, studies have shown that rising health care costs cause people to cut back their spending on medical services, just as people cut back their spending on other goods and services when their prices rise. One study indicates that for every 1 percent increase in the amount employers charge employees for insurance, 164,000 people become uninsured. Of course, people without health insurance can still visit the doctor and obtain prescriptions, but they have to pay higher prices than do people with insurance. Although the consequences of being uninsured can be severe, particularly if someone develops a serious illness, economists are not surprised that higher prices for health insurance lead to less health insurance being purchased: Faced with limited incomes, people have to make choices among the goods and services they buy.

The Congressional Budget Office estimates that as the U.S. population ages and medical costs continue to rise, federal government spending on Medicare will more than double over the next 10 years. Many policymakers are concerned that this rapid increase in Medicare spending will force a reduction in spending on other government programs. Daniel Callahan, a researcher at the Hastings Center for Bioethics, has argued that policymakers should consider taking some dramatic steps, such as having Medicare stop paying for open-heart surgery and other expensive treatments for people over 80 years of age. Callahan argues that the costs of open-heart surgery and similar treatments for the very old exceed the benefits, and the funds would be better spent on treatments for younger patients where the benefits would exceed the costs. Spending less on prolonging the lives of the very old in order to save resources that can be used for other purposes is a very painful trade-off to consider. But in a world of scarcity, trade-offs of some kind are inevitable.

Sources: Daniel Callahan, "The Economic Woes of Medicare," *New York Times*, November 13, 2008; Ezekiel J. Emanuel, "The Cost–Coverage Trade-off," *Journal of the American Medical Association*, Vol. 299, No. 8, February 27, 2008, pp. 947–949; and Congressional Budget Office, *A Preliminary Analysis of the President's Budget and an Update of CBO's Budget and Economic Outlook*, March 2009.

 **YOUR TURN:** Test your understanding by doing related problems 1.9, 1.10, 1.11, and 1.12 on page 59 at the end of this chapter.

## Increasing Marginal Opportunity Costs

We can use the production possibilities frontier to explore issues concerning the economy as a whole. For example, suppose we divide all the goods and services produced in the economy into just two types: military goods and civilian goods. In Figure 2-2, we let tanks represent military goods and automobiles represent civilian goods. If all the country's resources are devoted to producing military goods, 400 tanks can be produced in one year. If all resources are devoted to producing civilian goods, 500 automobiles can be produced in one year. Devoting resources to producing both goods results in the economy being at other points along the production possibilities frontier.

Notice that this production possibilities frontier is bowed outward rather than being a straight line. Because the curve is bowed out, the opportunity cost of automobiles in terms of tanks depends on where the economy currently is on the production possibilities frontier. For example, to increase automobile production from 0 to 200—moving from point *A* to point *B*—the economy has to give up only 50 tanks. But to increase automobile production by another 200 vehicles—moving from point *B* to point *C*—the economy has to give up 150 tanks.

As the economy moves down the production possibilities frontier, it experiences *increasing marginal opportunity costs* because increasing automobile production by a

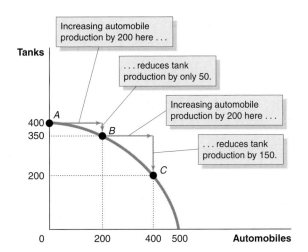

## Figure 2-2

**Increasing Marginal Opportunity Costs**

As the economy moves down the production possibilities frontier, it experiences *increasing marginal opportunity costs* because increasing automobile production by a given quantity requires larger and larger decreases in tank production. For example, to increase automobile production from 0 to 200—moving from point *A* to point *B*—the economy has to give up only 50 tanks. But to increase automobile production by another 200 vehicles—moving from point *B* to point *C*—the economy has to give up 150 tanks.

given quantity requires larger and larger decreases in tank production. Increasing marginal opportunity costs occur because some workers, machines, and other resources are better suited to one use than to another. At point *A*, some resources that are well suited to producing automobiles are forced to produce tanks. Shifting these resources into producing automobiles by moving from point *A* to point *B* allows a substantial increase in automobile production, without much loss of tank production. But as the economy moves down the production possibilities frontier, more and more resources that are better suited to tank production are switched into automobile production. As a result, the increases in automobile production become increasingly smaller, while the decreases in tank production become increasingly larger. We would expect in most situations that production possibilities frontiers will be bowed outward rather than linear, as in the BMW example discussed earlier.

The idea of increasing marginal opportunity costs illustrates an important economic concept: *The more resources already devoted to an activity, the smaller the payoff to devoting additional resources to that activity.* For example, the more hours you have already spent studying economics, the smaller the increase in your test grade from each additional hour you spend—and the greater the opportunity cost of using the hour in that way. The more funds a firm has devoted to research and development during a given year, the smaller the amount of useful knowledge it receives from each additional dollar—and the greater the opportunity cost of using the funds in that way. The more funds the federal government spends cleaning up the environment during a given year, the smaller the reduction in pollution from each additional dollar—and, once again, the greater the opportunity cost of using the funds in that way.

## Economic Growth

At any given time, the total resources available to any economy are fixed. Therefore, if the United States produces more automobiles, it must produce less of something else—tanks in our example. Over time, though, the resources available to an economy may increase. For example, both the labor force and the capital stock—the amount of physical capital available in the country—may increase. The increase in the available labor force and the capital stock shifts the production possibilities frontier outward for the U.S. economy and makes it possible to produce both more automobiles and more tanks. Panel (a) of Figure 2-3 shows that the economy can move from point *A* to point *B*, producing more tanks and more automobiles.

Similarly, technological change makes it possible to produce more goods with the same number of workers and the same amount of machinery, which also shifts the production possibilities frontier outward. Technological change need not affect all sectors equally. Panel (b) of Figure 2-3 shows the results of technological change in the automobile industry that increases the quantity of automobiles workers can produce per year while leaving unchanged the quantity of tanks that can be produced.

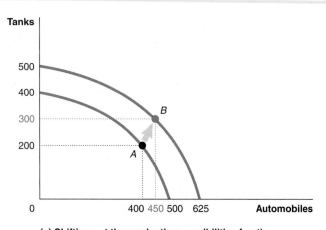

(a) Shifting out the production possibilities frontier

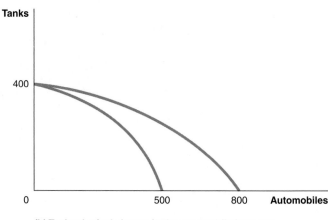

(b) Technological change in the automobile industry

## Figure 2-3   Economic Growth

Panel (a) shows that as more economic resources become available and technological change occurs, the economy can move from point *A* to point *B*, producing more tanks and more automobiles. Panel (b) shows the results of technological change in the automobile industry that increases the quantity of vehicles workers can produce per year while leaving unchanged the maximum quantity of tanks that can be produced. Shifts in the production possibilities frontier represent *economic growth*.

**Economic growth** The ability of the economy to increase the production of goods and services.

Shifts in the production possibilities frontier represent **economic growth** because they allow the economy to increase the production of goods and services, which ultimately raises the standard of living. In the United States and other high-income countries, the market system has aided the process of economic growth, which over the past 200 years has greatly increased the well-being of the average person.

**2.2 LEARNING** OBJECTIVE

Understand comparative advantage and explain how it is the basis for trade.

**Trade** The act of buying and selling.

# Comparative Advantage and Trade

We can use the ideas of production possibilities frontiers and opportunity costs to understand the basic economic activity of *trade*. Markets are fundamentally about **trade**, which is the act of buying and selling. Sometimes we trade directly, as when children trade one baseball card for another baseball card. But often we trade indirectly: We sell our labor services as, say, an accountant, a salesperson, or a nurse for money, and then we use the money to buy goods and services. Although in these cases, trade takes place indirectly, ultimately the accountant, salesperson, or nurse is trading his or her services for food, clothing, and other goods and services. One of the great benefits of trade is that it makes it possible for people to become better off by increasing both their production and their consumption.

## Specialization and Gains from Trade

Consider the following situation: You and your neighbor both have fruit trees on your property. Initially, suppose you have only apple trees and your neighbor has only cherry trees. In this situation, if you both like apples and cherries, there is an obvious opportunity for both of you to gain from trade: You trade some of your apples for some of your neighbor's cherries, making you both better off. But what if there are apple and cherry trees growing on both of your properties? In that case, there can still be gains from trade. For example, your neighbor might be very good at picking apples, and you might be very good at picking cherries. It would make sense for your neighbor to concentrate on picking apples and for you to concentrate on picking cherries. You can then trade some of the cherries you pick for some of the apples your neighbor picks. But what if your neighbor is actually better at picking both apples and cherries than you are?

We can use production possibilities frontiers (*PPF*s) to show how your neighbor can benefit from trading with you *even though she is better than you are at picking both apples and cherries*. (For simplicity, and because it will not have any effect on the conclusions we draw, we will assume that the *PPF*s in this example are straight lines.) The table in Figure 2-4 shows how many apples and how many cherries you and your neighbor can pick in one week. The graph in the figure uses the data from the table to construct

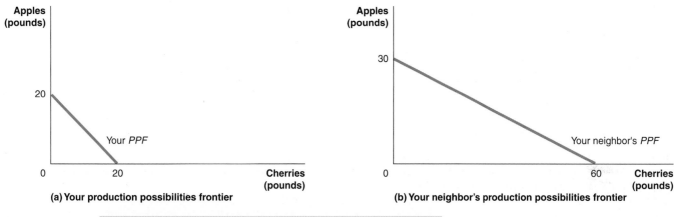

|  | You | | Your Neighbor | |
| --- | --- | --- | --- | --- |
|  | Apples | Cherries | Apples | Cherries |
| Devote all time to picking apples | 20 pounds | 0 pounds | 30 pounds | 0 pounds |
| Devote all time to picking cherries | 0 pounds | 20 pounds | 0 pounds | 60 pounds |

**(a) Your production possibilities frontier**

**(b) Your neighbor's production possibilities frontier**

Figure 2-4    Production Possibilities for You and Your Neighbor, without Trade

The table in this figure shows how many pounds of apples and how many pounds of cherries you and your neighbor can each pick in one week. The graphs in the figure use the data from the table to construct production possibilities frontiers (*PPFs*) for you and your neighbor. Panel (a) shows your *PPF*. If you devote all your time to pick-ing apples and none of your time to picking cherries, you can pick 20 pounds. If you devote all your time to picking cherries, you can pick 20 pounds. Panel (b) shows that if your neighbor devotes all her time to picking apples, she can pick 30 pounds. If she devotes all her time to picking cherries, she can pick 60 pounds.

*PPF*s. Panel (a) shows your *PPF*. If you devote all your time to picking apples, you can pick 20 pounds of apples per week. If you devote all your time to picking cherries, you can pick 20 pounds per week. Panel (b) shows that if your neighbor devotes all her time to picking apples, she can pick 30 pounds. If she devotes all her time to picking cherries, she can pick 60 pounds.

The production possibilities frontiers in Figure 2-4 show how many apples and cherries you and your neighbor can consume, *without trade*. Suppose that when you don't trade with your neighbor, you pick and consume 8 pounds of apples and 12 pounds of cherries per week. This combination of apples and cherries is represented by point *A* in panel (a) of Figure 2-5. When your neighbor doesn't trade with you, she picks and consumes 9 pounds of apples and 42 pounds of cherries per week. This com-bination of apples and cherries is represented by point *C* in panel (b) of Figure 2-5.

After years of picking and consuming your own apples and cherries, suppose your neighbor comes to you one day with the following proposal: She offers to trade you 15 pounds of her cherries for 10 pounds of your apples next week. Should you accept this offer? You should accept because you will end up with more apples and more cherries to consume. To take advantage of her proposal, you should specialize in picking only apples rather than splitting your time between picking apples and picking cherries. We know this will allow you to pick 20 pounds of apples. You can trade 10 pounds of apples to your neighbor for 15 pounds of her cherries. The result is that you will be able to consume 10 pounds of apples and 15 pounds of cherries (point *B* in panel (a) of Fig-ure 2-5). You are clearly better off as a result of trading with your neighbor: You now can consume 2 more pounds of apples and 3 more pounds of cherries than you were consuming without trading. You have moved beyond your *PPF*!

Your neighbor has also benefited from the trade. By specializing in picking only cherries, she can pick 60 pounds. She trades 15 pounds of cherries to you for 10 pounds of apples. The result is that she can consume 10 pounds of apples and 45 pounds of cherries (point *D* in panel (b) of Figure 2-5). This is 1 more pound of apples and 3 more pounds of cherries than she was consuming before trading with you. She also has moved beyond her *PPF*.

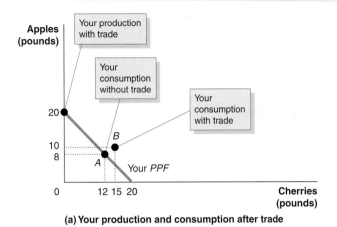

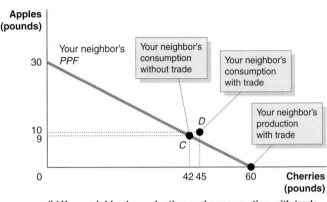

(a) Your production and consumption after trade

(b) Your neighbor's production and consumption with trade

## Figure 2-5    Gains from Trade

When you don't trade with your neighbor, you pick and consume 8 pounds of apples and 12 pounds of cherries per week—point *A* in panel (a). When your neighbor doesn't trade with you, she picks and consumes 9 pounds of apples and 42 pounds of cherries per week—point *C* in panel (b). If you specialize in picking apples, you can pick 20 pounds. If your neighbor specializes in picking cherries, she can pick 60

pounds. If you trade 10 pounds of your apples for 15 pounds of your neighbor's cherries, you will be able to consume 10 pounds of apples and 15 pounds of cherries—point *B* in panel (a). Your neighbor can now consume 10 pounds of apples and 45 pounds of cherries—point *D* in panel (b). You and your neighbor are both better off as a result of trade.

Table 2-1 summarizes the changes in production and consumption that result from your trade with your neighbor. (In this example, we chose one specific rate of trading cherries for apples—15 pounds of cherries for 10 pounds of apples. There are, however, many other rates of trading cherries for apples that would also make you and your neighbor better off.)

## Absolute Advantage versus Comparative Advantage

Perhaps the most remarkable aspect of the preceding example is that your neighbor benefits from trading with you even though she is better than you at picking both apples and cherries. **Absolute advantage** is the ability of an individual, a firm, or a country to produce more of a good or service than competitors, using the same amount of resources. Your neighbor has an absolute advantage over you in producing both apples and cherries because she can pick more of each fruit than you can in the same amount of time. Although it seems that your neighbor should pick her own apples *and* her own cherries, we have just seen that she is better off specializing in cherry picking and leaving the apple picking to you.

We can consider further why both you and your neighbor benefit from specializing in picking only one fruit. First, think about the opportunity cost to each of you of picking the two fruits. We saw from the *PPF* in Figure 2-4 that if you devoted all your time to picking apples, you would be able to pick 20 pounds of apples per week. As you move down your *PPF* and shift time away from picking apples to picking cherries, you have to give up 1 pound of apples for each pound of cherries you pick (the slope of your *PPF* is −1). (For a review of calculating slopes, see the appendix to Chapter 1.) Therefore, your opportunity cost of picking 1 pound of cherries is 1 pound of apples. By the same reasoning, your opportunity cost of picking 1 pound of apples is 1 pound of cherries. Your neighbor's *PPF*

**Absolute advantage** The ability of an individual, a firm, or a country to produce more of a good or service than competitors, using the same amount of resources.

## TABLE 2-1

### A Summary of the Gains from Trade

| | YOU | | YOUR NEIGHBOR | |
| --- | --- | --- | --- | --- |
| | **APPLES (IN POUNDS)** | **CHERRIES (IN POUNDS)** | **APPLES (IN POUNDS)** | **CHERRIES (IN POUNDS)** |
| Production *and* consumption *without* trade | 8 | 12 | 9 | 42 |
| Production *with* trade | 20 | 0 | 0 | 60 |
| Consumption *with* trade | 10 | 15 | 10 | 45 |
| Gains from trade (increased consumption) | 2 | 3 | 1 | 3 |

| | OPPORTUNITY COST OF PICKING 1 POUND OF APPLES | OPPORTUNITY COST OF PICKING 1 POUND OF CHERRIES | **TABLE 2-2** |
|---|---|---|---|
| **YOU** | 1 pound of cherries | 1 pound of apples | **Opportunity Costs of Picking Apples and Cherries** |
| **YOUR NEIGHBOR** | 2 pounds of cherries | 0.5 pound of apples | |

has a different slope, so she faces a different trade-off: As she shifts time from picking apples to picking cherries, she has to give up 0.5 pound of apples for every 1 pound of cherries she picks (the slope of your neighbor's *PPF* is –0.5). As she shifts time from picking cherries to picking apples, she gives up 2 pounds of cherries for every 1 pound of apples she picks. Therefore, her opportunity cost of picking 1 pound of apples is 2 pounds of cherries, and her opportunity cost of picking 1 pound of cherries is 0.5 pound of apples.

Table 2-2 summarizes the opportunity costs for you and your neighbor of picking apples and cherries. Note that even though your neighbor can pick more apples in a week than you can, the *opportunity cost* of picking apples is higher for her than for you because when she picks apples, she gives up more cherries than you do. So, even though she has an absolute advantage over you in picking apples, it is more costly for her to pick apples than it is for you. The table also shows that her opportunity cost of picking cherries is lower than your opportunity cost of picking cherries. **Comparative advantage** is the ability of an individual, a firm, or a country to produce a good or service at a lower opportunity cost than competitors. In apple picking, your neighbor has an *absolute advantage* over you, but you have a *comparative advantage* over her. Your neighbor has both an absolute and a comparative advantage over you in picking cherries. As we have seen, you are better off specializing in picking apples, and your neighbor is better off specializing in picking cherries.

**Comparative advantage** The ability of an individual, a firm, or a country to produce a good or service at a lower opportunity cost than competitors.

## Comparative Advantage and the Gains from Trade

We have just derived an important economic principle: *The basis for trade is comparative advantage, not absolute advantage.* The fastest apple pickers do not necessarily do much apple picking. If the fastest apple pickers have a comparative advantage in some other activity—picking cherries, playing major league baseball, or being industrial engineers—they are better off specializing in that other activity. Individuals, firms, and countries are better off if they specialize in producing goods and services for which they have a comparative advantage and obtain the other goods and services they need by trading. We will return to the important concept of comparative advantage in Chapter 8, which is devoted to the subject of international trade.

# Don't Let This Happen to **YOU!**

### Don't Confuse Absolute Advantage and Comparative Advantage

First, make sure you know the definitions:

- **Absolute advantage.** The ability of an individual, a firm, or a country to produce more of a good or service than competitors, using the same amount of resources. In our example, your neighbor has an absolute advantage over you in both picking apples and picking cherries.

- **Comparative advantage.** The ability of an individual, a firm, or a country to produce a good or service at a lower opportunity cost than competitors. In our example, your neighbor has a comparative advantage in picking cherries, but you have a comparative advantage in picking apples.

Keep these two key points in mind:

1. It is possible to have an absolute advantage in producing a good or service without having a comparative advantage. This is the case with your neighbor picking apples.

2. It is possible to have a comparative advantage in producing a good or service without having an absolute advantage. This is the case with you picking apples.

**myeconlab**

**YOUR TURN:** Test your understanding by doing related problem 2.7 on page 61 at the end of this chapter.

# Solved Problem | 2-2

## Comparative Advantage and the Gains from Trade

Suppose that Canada and the United States both produce maple syrup and honey. These are the combinations of the two goods that each country can produce in one day:

| CANADA | | UNITED STATES | |
|---|---|---|---|
| HONEY (IN TONS) | MAPLE SYRUP (IN TONS) | HONEY (IN TONS) | MAPLE SYRUP (IN TONS) |
| 0 | 60 | 0 | 50 |
| 10 | 45 | 10 | 40 |
| 20 | 30 | 20 | 30 |
| 30 | 15 | 30 | 20 |
| 40 | 0 | 40 | 10 |
| | | 50 | 0 |

a. Who has a comparative advantage in producing maple syrup? Who has a comparative advantage in producing honey?

b. Suppose that Canada is currently producing 30 tons of honey and 15 tons of maple syrup, and the United States is currently producing 10 tons of honey and 40 tons of maple syrup. Demonstrate that Canada and the United States can both be better off if they specialize in producing only one good and engage in trade.

c. Illustrate your answer to question (b) by drawing a *PPF* for the United States and a *PPF* for Canada. Show on your *PPF*s the combinations of honey and maple syrup produced and consumed in each country before and after trade.

## SOLVING THE PROBLEM:

**Step 1:** **Review the chapter material.** This problem is about comparative advantage, so you may want to review the section "Absolute Advantage versus Comparative Advantage," which begins on page 44.

**Step 2:** **Answer part (a) by calculating who has a comparative advantage in each activity.** Remember that a country has a comparative advantage in producing a good if it can produce the good at the lowest opportunity cost. When Canada produces 1 more ton of honey, it produces 1.5 fewer tons of maple syrup. When the United States produces 1 more ton of honey, it produces 1 ton less of maple syrup. Therefore, the United States's opportunity cost of producing honey—1 ton of maple syrup—is lower than Canada's—1.5 tons of maple syrup. When Canada produces 1 more ton of maple syrup, it produces 0.67 ton less of honey. When the United States produces 1 more ton of maple syrup, it produces 1 ton less of honey. Therefore, Canada's opportunity cost of producing maple syrup—0.67 ton of honey—is lower than that of the United States—1 ton of honey. We can conclude that the United States has a comparative advantage in the production of honey and Canada has a comparative advantage in the production of maple syrup.

**Step 3:** **Answer part (b) by showing that specialization makes Canada and the United States better off.** We know that Canada should specialize where it has a comparative advantage and the United States should specialize where it has a comparative advantage. If both countries specialize, Canada will produce 60 tons of maple syrup and 0 tons of honey, and the United States will produce 0 tons of maple syrup and 50 tons of honey. After both countries specialize, the United States could then trade 30 tons of honey to Canada in exchange for 40 tons of maple syrup. (Other mutually beneficial trades are possible as well.) We can summarize the results in a table:

| | BEFORE TRADE | | AFTER TRADE | |
|---|---|---|---|---|
| | HONEY (IN TONS) | MAPLE SYRUP (IN TONS) | HONEY (IN TONS) | MAPLE SYRUP (IN TONS) |
| **CANADA** | 30 | 15 | 30 | 20 |
| **UNITED STATES** | 10 | 40 | 20 | 40 |

The United States is better off after trade because it can consume the same amount of maple syrup and 10 more tons of honey. Canada is better off after trade because it can consume the same amount of honey and 5 more tons of maple syrup.

**Step 4:** **Answer part (c) by drawing the *PPF*s.**

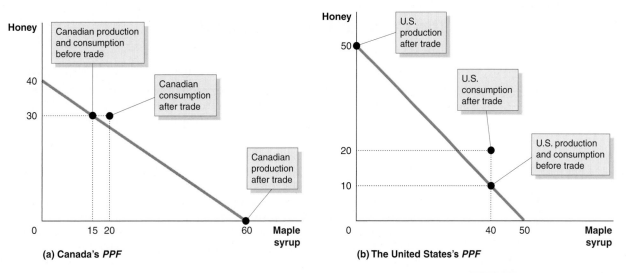

(a) Canada's *PPF*

(b) The United States's *PPF*

**YOUR TURN:** For more practice, do related problems 2.5 and 2.6 on pages 60–61 at the end of this chapter.

# The Market System

**2.3 LEARNING** OBJECTIVE

Explain the basic idea of how a market system works.

We have seen that households, firms, and the government face trade-offs and incur opportunity costs because resources are scarce. We have also seen that trade allows people to specialize according to their comparative advantage. By engaging in trade, people can raise their standard of living. Of course, trade in the modern world is much more complex than the examples we have considered so far. Trade today involves the decisions of millions of people around the world. But how does an economy make trade possible, and how are the decisions of these millions of people coordinated? In the United States and most other countries, trade is carried out in markets. Markets also determine the answers to the three fundamental questions discussed in Chapter 1: What goods and services will be produced? How will the goods and services be produced? and Who will receive the goods and services produced?

Recall that the definition of **market** is a group of buyers and sellers of a good or service and the institution or arrangement by which they come together to trade. Markets take many forms: They can be physical places, such as a local pizza parlor or the New York Stock Exchange, or virtual places, such as eBay. In a market, the buyers are demanders of goods or services, and the sellers are suppliers of goods or services. Households and firms interact in two types of markets: *product markets* and *factor markets*. **Product markets** are markets for goods—such as computers—and services—such as medical treatment. In product markets, households are demanders and firms are suppliers. **Factor markets** are markets for the *factors of production*. **Factors of production** are the inputs used to make goods and services. Factors of production are divided into four broad categories:

- *Labor* includes all types of work, from the part-time labor of teenagers working at McDonald's to the work of top managers in large corporations.

- *Capital* refers to physical capital, such as computers and machine tools, that is used to produce other goods.

**Market** A group of buyers and sellers of a good or service and the institution or arrangement by which they come together to trade.

**Product markets** Markets for goods—such as computers—and services—such as medical treatment.

**Factor markets** Markets for the factors of production, such as labor, capital, natural resources, and entrepreneurial ability.

**Factors of production** The inputs used to make goods and services.

- *Natural resources* include land, water, oil, iron ore, and other raw materials (or "gifts of nature") that are used in producing goods.

- An *entrepreneur* is someone who operates a business. *Entrepreneurial ability* is the ability to bring together the other factors of production to successfully produce and sell goods and services.

## The Circular Flow of Income

Two key groups participate in markets:

- A *household* consists of all the individuals in a home. Households are suppliers of factors of production—particularly labor—employed by firms to make goods and services. Households use the income they receive from selling the factors of production to purchase the goods and services supplied by firms. We are familiar with households as suppliers of labor because most people earn most of their income by going to work, which means they are selling their labor services to firms in the labor market. But households own the other factors of production as well, either directly or indirectly, by owning the firms that have these resources. All firms are owned by households. Small firms, like a neighborhood restaurant, might be owned by one person. Large firms, like Microsoft or BMW, are owned by millions of households that own shares of stock in them. (We discuss the stock market in Chapter 7.) When firms pay profits to the people who own them, the firms are paying for using the capital and natural resources that are supplied to them by those owners. So, we can generalize by saying that in factor markets, households are suppliers and firms are demanders.

- *Firms* are suppliers of goods and services. Firms use the funds they receive from selling goods and services to buy the factors of production needed to make the goods and services.

**Circular-flow diagram** A model that illustrates how participants in markets are linked.

We can use a simple economic model called the **circular-flow diagram** to see how participants in markets are linked. Figure 2-6 shows that in factor markets, households supply labor and other factors of production in exchange for wages and other payments from firms. In product markets, households use the payments they earn in factor markets to purchase the goods and services supplied by firms. Firms produce these goods and services using the factors of production supplied by households. In the figure, the blue arrows show the flow of factors of production from households through factor markets to firms. The red arrows show the flow of goods and services from firms through product markets to households. The green arrows show the flow of funds from firms through factor markets to households and the flow of spending from households through product markets to firms.

Like all economic models, the circular-flow diagram is a simplified version of reality. For example, Figure 2-6 leaves out the important role of government in buying goods from firms and in making payments, such as Social Security or unemployment insurance payments, to households. The figure also leaves out the roles played by banks, the stock and bond markets, and other parts of the *financial system* in aiding the flow of funds from lenders to borrowers. Finally, the figure does not show that some goods and services purchased by domestic households are produced in foreign countries and some goods and services produced by domestic firms are sold to foreign households. (The government, the financial system, and the international sector are explored further in later chapters.) Despite these simplifications, the circular-flow diagram in Figure 2-6 is useful for seeing how product markets, factor markets, and their participants are linked together. One of the great wonders of the market system is that it manages to successfully coordinate the independent activities of so many households and firms.

## The Gains from Free Markets

**Free market** A market with few government restrictions on how a good or service can be produced or sold or on how a factor of production can be employed.

A **free market** exists when the government places few restrictions on how a good or a service can be produced or sold or on how a factor of production can be employed. Governments in all modern economies intervene more than is consistent with a fully

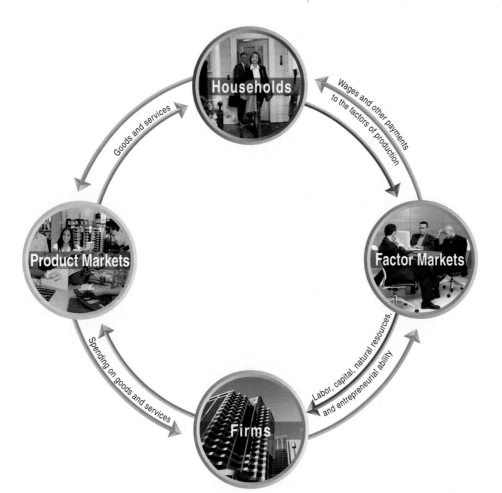

## Figure 2-6

### The Circular-Flow Diagram

Households and firms are linked together in a circular flow of production, income, and spending. The blue arrows show the flow of the factors of production. In factor markets, households supply labor, entrepreneurial ability, and other factors of production to firms. Firms use these factors of production to make goods and services that they supply to households in product markets. The red arrows show the flow of goods and services from firms to households. The green arrows show the flow of funds. In factor markets, households receive wages and other payments from firms in exchange for supplying the factors of production. Households use these wages and other payments to purchase goods and services from firms in product markets. Firms sell goods and services to households in product markets, and they use the funds to purchase the factors of production from households in factor markets.

free market. In that sense, we can think of the free market as being a benchmark against which we can judge actual economies. There are relatively few government restrictions on economic activity in the United States, Canada, the countries of western Europe, Hong Kong, Singapore, and Estonia. So these countries come close to the free market benchmark. In countries such as Cuba and North Korea, the free market system has been rejected in favor of centrally planned economies with extensive government control over product and factor markets. Countries that come closest to the free market benchmark have been more successful than countries with centrally planned economies in providing their people with rising living standards.

The Scottish philosopher Adam Smith is considered the father of modern economics because his book *An Inquiry into the Nature and Causes of the Wealth of Nations*, published in 1776, was an early and very influential argument for the free market system. Smith was writing at a time when extensive government restrictions on markets were still very common. In many parts of Europe, the *guild system* still prevailed. Under this system, governments would give guilds, or organizations of producers, the authority to control the production of a good. For example, the shoemakers' guild controlled who was allowed to produce shoes, how many shoes they could produce, and what price they could charge. In France, the cloth makers' guild even dictated the number of threads in the weave of the cloth.

Smith argued that such restrictions reduced the income, or wealth, of a country and its people by restricting the quantity of goods produced. Some people at the time supported the restrictions of the guild system because it was in their financial interest to do so. If you were a member of a guild, the restrictions served to reduce the competition you faced. But other people sincerely believed that the alternative to the guild system was economic chaos. Smith argued that these people were wrong and that a country could enjoy a smoothly functioning economic system if firms were freed from guild restrictions.

# **Solved** Problem | **2-3**

## Adam Smith's "Invisible Hand"

Alan Krueger, an economist at Princeton University, has argued that Adam Smith "worried that if merchants and manufacturers pursued their self-interest by seeking government regulation and privilege, the invisible hand would not work its magic."

Source: Alan B. Krueger, "Rediscovering the Wealth of Nations," *New York Times*, August 16, 2001.

**a.** What types of regulation and privilege might merchants and manufacturers seek from the government?

**b.** How might these regulations and privileges keep the invisible hand from working?

### SOLVING THE PROBLEM

**Step 1:** **Review the chapter material.** This problem is about how goods and services are produced and sold and how factors of production are employed in a free market economic system, as described by Adam Smith in *An Inquiry into the Nature and Causes of the Wealth of Nations,* so you may want to review the section "The Gains from Free Markets," which begins on page 48.

**Step 2:** **Answer question (a) by noting the economic system in place in Europe in 1776.** At the time, governments gave guilds—associations of producers—the authority to control production. The production controls limited the amount of output of goods such as shoes and clothing, as well as the number of producers of these items. Limiting production and competition led to higher prices and fewer choices for consumers. Instead of catering to the wants of consumers, producers sought the favor of government officials.

**Step 3:** **Answer question (b) by contrasting the behavior of merchants and manufacturers under a guild system and a market system.** The regulations ceded to guilds by government meant that producers did not have to respond to consumers' demands for better quality, better variety, and lower prices. Under a market system, producers that sell goods of poor quality at high prices suffer economic losses; producers that provide better-quality goods at low prices are rewarded with profits. Therefore, it is in the self-interest of producers to address consumer wants. This is how the invisible hand works in a free market economy, but it did not work this way in Europe in the eighteenth century.

**YOUR TURN:** For more practice, do related problem 3.8 on page 62 at the end of this chapter.

## The Market Mechanism

In Smith's day, defenders of the guild system worried that if, for instance, the shoemakers' guild did not control shoe production, either too many or too few shoes would be produced. Smith argued that prices would do a better job of coordinating the activities of buyers and sellers than the guilds could. A key to understanding Smith's argument is the assumption that *individuals usually act in a rational, self-interested way.* In particular, individuals take those actions most likely to make themselves better off financially. This assumption of rational, self-interested behavior underlies nearly all economic analysis. In fact, economics can be distinguished from other fields that study human behavior—such as sociology and psychology—by its emphasis on the assumption of self-interested behavior. Adam Smith understood—as economists today understand—that people's motives can be complex. But in analyzing people in the act of buying and selling, the motivation of financial reward usually provides the best explanation for the actions people take.

For example, suppose that a significant number of consumers switch from buying regular gasoline-powered cars to buying gasoline/electric-powered hybrid cars, such as the Toyota Prius, as in fact happened in the United States during the 2000s. Firms will find that they can charge relatively higher prices for hybrid cars than they can for regular cars. The self-interest of these firms will lead them to respond to consumers' wishes by producing more hybrids and fewer regular cars. Or suppose that consumers decide that they want to eat less bread, pasta, and other foods high in carbohydrates, as many did following the increase in popularity of the Atkins and South Beach diets. Then the prices firms can charge for bread and pasta will fall. The self-interest of firms will lead them to produce less bread and pasta, which in fact is what happened.

In the case where consumers want more of a product, and in the case where they want less of a product, the market system responds without a guild or the government giving orders about how much to produce or what price to charge. In a famous phrase, Smith said that firms would be led by the "invisible hand" of the market to provide consumers with what they wanted. Firms would respond to changes in prices by making decisions that ended up satisfying the wants of consumers.

| Making the Connection | **A Story of the Market System in Action: How Do You Make an iPod?** |

Apple produces the iPod. Because Apple's headquarters is in Cupertino, California, it seems reasonable to assume that iPods are also manufactured in that state. In fact, Apple produces none of the components of the iPod, nor does it assemble the components into a finished product. Far from being produced entirely by one company in one place, the iPod requires the coordinated activities of thousands of workers and dozens of firms spread around the world.

Several Asian firms, including Asustek, Inventec Appliances, and Foxconn, assemble the iPod, which is then shipped to Apple for sale in the United States. But the firms doing final assembly don't make any of the components. For example, the iPod's hard drive is manufactured by the Japanese firm Toshiba, although Toshiba actually assembles the hard drive in factories in China and the Philippines. Apple purchases the controller chip that manages the iPod's functions from PortalPlayer, which is based in Santa Clara, California. But PortalPlayer actually has the chip manufactured for it by Taiwan Semiconductor Manufacturing Corporation, and the chip's processor core was designed by ARM, a British company. Taiwan Semiconductor Manufacturing Corporation's factories are for the most part not in Taiwan but in mainland China and eastern Europe.

All told, an iPod contains about 450 parts, designed and manufactured by firms around the world. Many of these firms are not even aware of which other firms are also producing components for the iPod. Few of the managers of these firms have met managers of the other firms or shared knowledge of how their particular components are produced. In fact, no one person from Steve Jobs, the head of Apple, on down possesses the knowledge of how to produce all the components that are assembled into an iPod. Instead, the invisible hand of the market has led these firms to contribute their knowledge and resources to the process that ultimately results in an iPod available for sale in a store in the United States. Apple has so efficiently organized the process of producing the iPod that you can order a custom iPod with a personal engraving and have it delivered from an assembly plant in China to your doorstep in the United States in as little as three days.

Hal Varian, an economist at the University of California, Berkeley, has summarized the iPod story: "Those clever folks at Apple figured out how to combine 451 mostly generic parts into a valuable product. They may not make the iPod, but they created it."

*The market coordinates the activities of the many people spread around the world who contribute to the making of an iPod.*

Sources: Hal Varian, "An iPod Has Global Value. Ask the (Many) Countries That Make It," *New York Times*, June 28, 2007; and Greg Linden, Kenneth L. Kraemer, and Jaon Dedrick, "Who Captures Value in a Global Innovation System? The Case of Apple's iPod," Personal Computing Industry Center, June 2007.

**YOUR TURN:** Test your understanding by doing related problem 3.9 on page 62 at the end of this chapter.

## The Role of the Entrepreneur

**Entrepreneur** Someone who operates a business, bringing together the factors of production—labor, capital, and natural resources—to produce goods and services.

*Entrepreneurs* are central to the working of the market system. An **entrepreneur** is someone who operates a business. Entrepreneurs must first determine what goods and services they believe consumers want, and then they must decide how to produce those goods and services most profitably. Entrepreneurs bring together the factors of production—labor, capital, and natural resources—to produce goods and services. They put their own funds at risk when they start businesses. If they are wrong about what consumers want or about the best way to produce goods and services, they can lose those funds. In fact, it is not unusual for entrepreneurs who eventually achieve great success to fail at first. For instance, early in their careers, both Henry Ford and Sakichi Toyoda, who eventually founded the Toyota Motor Corporation, started companies that quickly failed.

## The Legal Basis of a Successful Market System

In a free market, government does not restrict how firms produce and sell goods and services or how they employ factors of production, but the absence of government intervention is not enough for the market system to work well. Government has to take active steps to provide a *legal environment* that will allow the market system to succeed.

**Protection of Private Property** For the market system to work well, individuals must be willing to take risks. Someone with $250,000 can be cautious and keep it safely in a bank—or even in cash, if the person doesn't trust banks. But the market system won't work unless a significant number of people are willing to risk their funds by investing them in businesses. Investing in businesses is risky in any country. Many businesses fail every year in the United States and other high-income countries. But in high-income countries, someone who starts a new business or invests in an existing business doesn't have to worry that the government, the military, or criminal gangs might decide to seize the business or demand payments for not destroying the business. Unfortunately, in many poor countries, owners of businesses are not well protected from having their businesses seized by the government or from having their profits taken by criminals. Where these problems exist, opening a business can be extremely risky. Cash can be concealed easily, but a business is difficult to conceal and difficult to move.

**Property rights** The rights individuals or firms have to the exclusive use of their property, including the right to buy or sell it.

**Property rights** are the rights individuals or firms have to the exclusive use of their property, including the right to buy or sell it. Property can be tangible, physical property, such as a store or factory. Property can also be intangible, such as the right to an idea.

Two amendments to the U.S. Constitution guarantee property rights: The 5th Amendment states that the federal government shall not deprive any person "of life, liberty, or property, without due process of law." The 14th Amendment extends this guarantee to the actions of state governments: "No state ... shall deprive any person of life, liberty, or property, without due process of law." Similar guarantees exist in every high-income country. Unfortunately, in many developing countries, such guarantees do not exist or are poorly enforced.

In any modern economy, *intellectual property rights* are very important. Intellectual property includes books, films, software, and ideas for new products or new ways of producing products. To protect intellectual property, the federal government grants a *patent* that gives an inventor—which is often a firm—the exclusive right to produce and sell a new product for a period of 20 years from the date the product was invented. For instance, because Microsoft has a patent on the Windows operating system, other firms cannot sell their own versions of Windows. The government grants patents to encourage firms to spend money on the research and development necessary to create new products. If other companies could freely copy Windows, Microsoft would not have spent the funds necessary to develop it. Just as a new product or a new method of making a product receives patent protection, books, films, and software receive *copyright* protection. Under U.S. law, the creator of a book, film, or piece of music has the exclusive right to use the creation during the creator's lifetime. The creator's heirs retain this exclusive right for 50 years after the death of the creator.

*Some recording artists worry that the copyrights for their songs are not being protected on the Internet.*

## Making the Connection

## Property Rights in Cyberspace: YouTube, Facebook, and MySpace

The development of the Internet led to new problems in protecting intellectual property rights. People can copy and e-mail songs, newspaper and magazine articles, and even entire motion pictures and television programs or post them on Web sites. Controlling unauthorized copying is more difficult today than it was when "copying" meant making a physical copy of a book, CD, or DVD. The popularity of YouTube and MySpace highlights the problem of unauthorized copying of videos and music. YouTube, founded in 2005, quickly became an enormous success because it provides an easy way to upload videos, which can then be viewed by anyone who has an Internet connection. By 2009, thousands of new videos were being uploaded each day, and the site was receiving more than 70 million visitors per month. YouTube has earned substantial profits from selling online advertising. Unfortunately, many of the videos on the site contain copyrighted material.

At first, YouTube's policy was to remove any video containing unauthorized material if the holder of the copyright complained. Then YouTube began to negotiate with the copyright holders to pay a fee in return for allowing the copyrighted material to remain on the site. But some copyright issues are in dispute. For instance, a high school student uploaded a video of herself singing the Christmas song "Winter Wonderland." When Warner Music Group, owner of the copyright to the song, insisted that the video be removed from the site, YouTube complied, even though some lawyers argue that it is legal to use copyrighted music in a nonprofessional video. The willingness of YouTube's owners to sell their company to Google in 2006 was motivated at least partly by the expectation that Google had the resources to help resolve the copyright problems.

MySpace has had similar problems because many Web pages on the site contain copyrighted music or videos. Universal Music sued MySpace after music from one of rapper Jay-Z's CDs started appearing on the site even before it was released. In its lawsuit, Universal claimed that the illegal use of its copyrighted music had "created hundreds of millions of dollars of value for the owners of MySpace." Facebook encountered a somewhat different problem when it began requiring members to grant it the right to license or copy anything posted to a member's page. Facebook believed this was necessary to guard against members later claiming that Facebook had violated their copyrights by disseminating material posted to their pages.

Music, television, and movie companies believe that the failure to give the full protection of property rights to the online use of their material reduces their ability to sell CDs and DVDs.

Sources: Tim Arango, "As Rights Clash on YouTube, Some Music Vanishes," *New York Times*, March 22, 2009; Brad Stone, "Is Facebook Growing Up Too Fast?" *New York Times*, March 28, 2009; and Ethan Smith and Julia Angwin, "Universal Music Sues MySpace Claiming Copyright Infringement," *Wall Street Journal*, November 18, 2006, p. A3.

**YOUR TURN:** Test your understanding by doing related problem 3.15 on page 62 at the end of this chapter.

myeconlab

---

**Enforcement of Contracts and Property Rights** Business activity often involves someone agreeing to carry out some action in the future. For example, you may borrow $20,000 to buy a car and promise the bank—by signing a loan contract—that you will pay back the money over the next five years. Or Microsoft may sign a licensing agreement with a small technology company, agreeing to use that company's technology for a period of several years in return for a fee. Usually these agreements take the form of legal contracts. For the market system to work, businesses and individuals have to rely on these contracts being carried out. If one party to a legal contract does not fulfill its obligations—perhaps the small company had promised Microsoft exclusive use of its technology but then began licensing it to other companies—the other party can go to court to have the agreement enforced. Similarly, if property owners in the United States believe that the federal or state government has violated their rights under the 5th or 14th Amendments, they can go to court to have their rights enforced.

But going to court to enforce a contract or private property rights will be successful only if the court system is independent and judges are able to make impartial decisions on the basis of the law. In the United States and other high-income countries, the court systems have enough independence from other parts of the government and enough protection from intimidation by outside forces—such as criminal gangs—that they are able to make their decisions based on the law. In many developing countries, the court systems lack this independence and will not provide a remedy if the government violates private property rights or if a person with powerful political connections decides to violate a business contract.

If property rights are not well enforced, fewer goods and services will be produced. This reduces economic efficiency, leaving the economy inside its production possibilities frontier.

▶ **Continued from page 37**

## Economics in YOUR Life!

At the beginning of the chapter, we asked you to think about two questions: When buying a new car, what is the relationship between safety and fuel efficiency? and Under what circumstances would it be possible for automobile manufacturers to make cars safer and more fuel efficient? To answer the first question, you have to recognize that there is a trade-off between safety and fuel efficiency. With the technology available at any particular time, an automobile manufacturer can increase fuel efficiency by making a car smaller and lighter. But driving a lighter car increases your chances of being injured if you have an accident. The trade-off between safety and fuel efficiency would look much like the relationship in Figure 2-1 on page 39. To get more of both safety and gas mileage, automobile makers would have to discover new technologies that allow them to make cars lighter and safer at the same time. Such new technologies would make points like *G* in Figure 2-1 attainable.

# Conclusion

We have seen that by trading in markets, people are able to specialize and pursue their comparative advantage. Trading on the basis of comparative advantage makes all participants in trade better off. The key role of markets is to facilitate trade. In fact, the market system is a very effective means of coordinating the decisions of millions of consumers, workers, and firms. At the center of the market system is the consumer. To be successful, firms must respond to the desires of consumers. These desires are communicated to firms through prices. To explore how markets work, we must study the behavior of consumers and firms. We continue this exploration of markets in Chapter 3, when we develop the model of demand and supply.

Before moving on to Chapter 3, read *An Inside Look* on the next page to learn how managers decide between producing hybrid cars and improving conventional gasoline-powered cars.

## >> Detroit Challenges Hybrids with New Technology

*WALL STREET JOURNAL*

## Gas Engines Get Upgrade in Challenge to Hybrids

Hybrids and electric cars are generating the buzz this week at Detroit's North American International Auto Show. But thanks to new technology, the century-old internal-combustion engine appears poised to make a significant leap in fuel efficiency.

While car makers are showcasing gas-electric hybrids, plug-in hybrids and concept cars powered by fuel-cell batteries, they also are rolling out vehicles with advanced gasoline engines that rely on a technology known as direct fuel injection.

Analysts say sales of vehicles with such engines—which deliver greater fuel economy and power than today's similarly sized gas engines—will far exceed those of hybrids and electrics for years to come.

**(a)** U.S. sales of hybrids will rise to 578,000 by 2014 from 353,000 this year, according to CSM Worldwide. But the forecasting firm projects that sales of vehicles using direct-injection gas engines will jump to 5.1 million by 2014 from 585,000 this year. Globally, hybrid, plug-in and battery-only vehicles will capture about 14% of the automotive market by 2020, according to HIS Global Insight, another forecasting firm.

"Leaping to a new technology is really a big risk," said Eric Fedewa, CSM's vice president of global powertrain forecasting. "It's much more cost effective and much less risky to do something to an existing, proven technology."

All auto makers are under pressure to boost fuel economy to meet stricter governmental standards. But consumers are fickle when it comes to buying superefficient vehicles.

**(b)** Sales of Toyota Motor Corp.'s Prius, the best-known hybrid, zoomed last year when gas prices hit $4 a gallon in the U.S. But now, with gas costing less than half that, Toyota has seen Prius sales slow dramatically and it recently mothballed a U.S. factory slated to build the model. One big hurdle hybrids face is higher sticker prices, often thousands of dollars more than the same model with a traditional engine. It takes years for a customer to earn back this cost through gas savings.

Early this decade, car makers looked to the diesel engine for better mileage. But in the U.S., many turned away from that strategy for passenger cars as the cost of making diesel engines "clean" increased by thousands of dollars per vehicle after federal environmental regulations tightened. Also, diesel fuel costs more than gasoline.

The internal-combustion engine "will likely remain the backbone of mobility for the foreseeable future,"

said Daimler AG Chief Executive Dieter Zetsche. He said his company has been able to improve the efficiency of gas and diesel engines by about 23% and "there is still further to go."

**(c)** At the car show, BMW AG displayed hybrid concepts of its 7-Series and X6 models that combine V8 engines with a two-mode hybrid to deliver a 20% improvement in fuel economy. But the German maker also expects it could still get up to a 10% improvement in fuel economy with tweaks to its existing lineup of gasoline engines, said Klaus Draeger, a member of BMW's executive board.

Leading the way are direct-injection engines, which take highly pressurized fuel and thrust it squarely into the combustion chamber of each cylinder. By contrast, traditional engines first mix fuel with incoming air before reaching the combustion chamber, which is less efficient. Car makers say the advantages of direct injection are lower emissions, better performance and greater fuel efficiency. . . .

*Source:* Matthew Dolan, "Gas Engines Get Upgrade in Challenge to Hybrids," *Wall Street Journal*, January 14, 2009, p B1.

## Key Points in the Article

This article discusses the trade-offs managers at BMW, Toyota, and other car manufacturers face as they attempt to increase the fuel efficiency of vehicles. In recent years, car makers have focused on hybrid cars that use electric batteries or batteries in combination with conventional gasoline-powered engines. But the article indicates that car makers have also been developing new cars that will use advanced gasoline engines. Because the resources available to firms are limited, they face a trade-off in deciding which of these approaches to more fuel-efficient cars to pursue.

## Analyzing the News

(a) In 2009, the auto industry produced 353,000 hybrid cars and 585,000 fuel-efficient direct-injection gasoline engine cars. One industry forecast projects that by 2014, production of hybrids will have increased only to 578,000 cars, while production of direct-injection cars will have soared to 5.1 million. If we assume that in any one year the resources available to produce fuel-efficient cars are fixed, then car manufacturers must decide how to allocate these resources between hybrids and direct-injection cars. In the figure below, we illustrate the trade-off car manufacturers face

with a production possibilities frontier. In 2009, car manufacturers are at point A. By 2014, car manufacturers will have allocated additional resources to the production of fuel-efficient cars, and the production possibilities frontier will have shifted out, allowing manufacturers to reach point B.

(b) Car manufacturers alter production at their assembly plants in response to changes in sales. For example, Toyota produced more hybrid cars when gas prices were high in 2008 but produced far fewer when gas prices declined during 2009. By deciding to close a plant previously intended to produce hybrid Priuses, Toyota was able to reallocate resources to producing other models for which the demand was stronger. Notice that consumers also face a trade-off. When gas prices are high, a consumer is more likely to pay the additional thousands of dollars that a hybrid costs relative to a comparable non-hybrid vehicle. But spending thousands of dollars in this way has an opportunity cost—namely, the other goods and services that a consumer has to give up in order to buy a hybrid. When gas prices fall, consumers reallocate these funds away from hybrids and towards other goods and services.

(c) Improvements in technology cause an outward shift of the production possibilities frontier by increasing the ability of

firms to produce goods using the same number of workers and amount of capital. Improvements in technology occur when scientists and engineers develop entirely new technologies. But they can also occur when existing technologies are improved. In this case, BMW expects to both introduce new hybrid engines and to tweak its existing gasoline engines to improve their mileage.

## Thinking Critically

1. Continuing to produce traditional gasoline-powered cars will mean that BMW can produce fewer hybrids than if it switches all its production to hybrids. Because hybrids promise 20 percent better fuel economy and improvements in traditional gasoline-powered cars promise 10 percent better fuel economy, why would BMW continue producing traditional gasoline-powered cars?

2. Hybrids are less expensive to operate and produce less pollution than traditional gasoline-powered cars. If the U.S. government wants to encourage the production of hybrid cars, should it restrict production of traditional gasoline-powered cars?

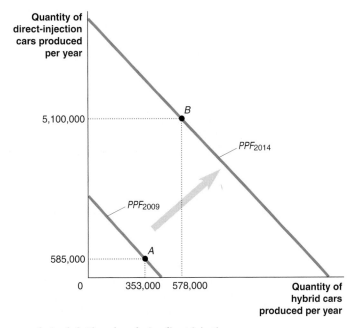

Choosing between producing hybrids and producing direct-injection cars.

## Key Terms

---

**2.1** **Production Possibilities Frontiers and Opportunity Costs,** pages 38–42

LEARNING OBJECTIVE: Use a production possibilities frontier to analyze opportunity costs and trade-offs

## Summary

The **production possibilities frontier** (***PPF***) is a curve that shows the maximum attainable combinations of two products that may be produced with available resources. The *PPF* is used to illustrate the trade-offs that arise from **scarcity**. Points on the frontier are technically efficient. Points inside the frontier are inefficient, and points outside the frontier are unattainable. The **opportunity cost** of any activity is the highest-valued alternative that must be given up to engage in that activity. Because of increasing marginal opportunity costs, production possibilities frontiers are usually bowed out rather than straight lines. This illustrates the important economic concept that the more resources that are already devoted to any activity, the smaller the payoff from devoting additional resources to that activity is likely to be. **Economic growth** is illustrated by shifting a production possibilities frontier outward.

 Visit www.myeconlab.com to complete these exercises online and get instant feedback.

## Review Questions

1.1 What do economists mean by *scarcity*? Can you think of anything that is not scarce according to the economic definition?

1.2 What is a production possibilities frontier? How can we show economic efficiency on a production possibilities frontier? How can we show inefficiency? What causes a production possibilities frontier to shift outward?

1.3 What does increasing marginal opportunity costs mean? What are the implications of this idea for the shape of the production possibilities frontier?

## Problems and Applications

1.4 Draw a production possibilities frontier that shows the trade-off between the production of cotton and the production of soybeans.

   a. Show the effect that a prolonged drought would have on the initial production possibilities frontier.

   b. Suppose genetic modification makes soybeans resistant to insects, allowing yields to double. Show the effect of this technological change on the initial production possibilities frontier.

1.5 (Related to the *Chapter Opener* on page 37) One of the trade-offs BMW faces is between safety and gas mileage. For example, adding steel to a car makes it safer but also heavier, which results in lower gas mileage. Draw a hypothetical production possibilities frontier that BMW engineers face that shows this trade-off.

1.6 Suppose you win free tickets to a movie plus all you can eat at the snack bar for free. Would there be a cost to you to attend this movie? Explain.

1.7 Suppose we can divide all the goods produced by an economy into two types: consumption goods and capital goods. Capital goods, such as machinery, equipment, and computers, are goods used to produce other goods.

   a. Use a production possibilities frontier graph to illustrate the trade-off to an economy between producing consumption goods and producing capital goods. Is it likely that the production possibilities frontier in this situation would be a straight line (as in Figure 2-1 on page 39) or bowed out (as in Figure 2-2 on page 41)? Briefly explain.

   b. Suppose a technological change occurs that has a favorable effect on the production of capital goods but not consumption goods. Show the effect on the production possibilities frontier.

   c. Suppose that country A and country B currently have identical production possibilities frontiers but that country A devotes only 5 percent of its resources to producing capital goods over each of the next 10 years, whereas country B devotes 30 percent. Which country is likely to experience more rapid economic growth in the future? Illustrate using a production possibilities frontier graph. Your graph should include production possibilities frontiers for country A today and in 10 years and production possibilities frontiers for country B today and in 10 years.

**1.8** Use the following production possibilities frontier for a country to answer the questions.

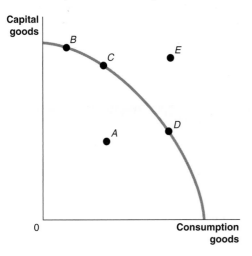

a. Which point or points are unattainable? Briefly explain why.

b. Which point or points are efficient? Briefly explain why.

c. Which point or points are inefficient? Briefly explain why.

d. At which point is the country's future growth rate likely to be the highest? Briefly explain why.

**1.9** (Related to the *Making the Connection* on page 39) Suppose the U.S. president is attempting to decide whether the federal government should spend more on research to find a cure for heart disease. He asks you, one of his economic advisors, to prepare a report discussing the relevant factors he should consider. Use the concepts of opportunity cost and trade-offs to discuss some of the main issues you would deal with in your report.

**1.10** (Related to the *Making the Connection* on page 39) Uwe Reinhardt, an economist at Princeton University, wrote the following in a column in the *New York Times*:

> [Cost-effectiveness analysis] seeks to establish which of several alternative strategies capable of achieving a given therapeutic goal is the least-cost strategy. It seems a sensible form of inquiry in a nation that is dismayed over the rising cost of health care. . . . Opponents of cost-effectiveness analysis includes individuals who sincerely believe that health and life are "priceless." . . .

Are health and life priceless? Are there any decisions you make during your everyday life that indicate whether you consider health and life to be priceless?

Source: Uwe E. Reinhardt, "'Cost-Effectiveness Analysis' and U.S. Health Care," *New York Times*, March 13, 2009.

**1.11** (Related to the *Making the Connection* on page 39) Suppose that the federal government is deciding which of two cancer treatment therapies it will allow Medicare funds to be used to pay for (assume that only one treatment therapy will be funded): Therapy A, which will prolong the average lifespan of patients receiving the treatment by 24 months and will cost $750,000 per patient treated; and Therapy B, which will prolong the average lifespan of patients receiving the treatment by 20 months and will cost $25,000 per patient treated. What factors should the federal government take into account in making its decision?

**1.12** (Related to the *Making the Connection* on page 39) Lawrence Summers served as secretary of the treasury in the Clinton administration and as director of National Economic Council in the Obama administration. He has been quoted as giving the following moral defense of the economic approach:

> There is nothing morally unattractive about saying: We need to analyze which way of spending money on health care will produce more benefit and which less, and using our money as efficiently as we can. I don't think there is anything immoral about seeking to achieve environmental benefits at the lowest possible costs.

Would it be more moral to reduce pollution without worrying about the cost or by taking the cost into account? Briefly explain.

Source: David Wessel, "Precepts from Professor Summers," *Wall Street Journal*, October 17, 2002.

**1.13** In *The Wonderful Wizard of Oz* and his other books about the Land of Oz, L. Frank Baum observed that if people's wants were modest enough, most goods would not be scarce. According to Baum, this was the case in Oz:

> There were no poor people in the Land of Oz, because there was no such thing as money. . . . Each person was given freely by his neighbors whatever he required for his use, which is as much as anyone may reasonably desire. Some tilled the lands and raised great crops of grain, which was divided equally among the whole population, so that all had enough. There were many tailors and dressmakers and shoemakers and the like, who made things that any who desired them might wear. Likewise there were jewelers who made ornaments for the person, which pleased and beautified the people, and these ornaments also were free to those who asked for them. Each man and woman, no matter what he or she produced for the good of the community, was supplied by the neighbors with food and clothing and a

house and furniture and ornaments and games. If by chance the supply ever ran short, more was taken from the great storehouses of the Ruler, which were afterward filled up again when there was more of any article than people needed. . . .

You will know, by what I have told you here, that the Land of Oz was a remark-

able country. I do not suppose such an arrangement would be practical with us.

Do you agree with Baum that the economic system in Oz wouldn't work in the contemporary United States? Briefly explain why or why not.

Source: L. Frank Baum, *The Emerald City of Oz*, New York: HarperCollins, 1993, pp. 30–31. First edition published in 1910.

>> **End Learning Objective 2.1**

---

## 2.2 Comparative Advantage and Trade, pages 42–47

LEARNING OBJECTIVE: Understand comparative advantage and explain how it is the basis for trade

## Summary

Fundamentally, markets are about **trade**, which is the act of buying or selling. People trade on the basis of comparative advantage. An individual, a firm, or a country has a **comparative advantage** in producing a good or service if it can produce the good or service at the lowest opportunity cost. People are usually better off specializing in the activity for which they have a comparative advantage and trading for the other goods and services they need. It is important not to confuse comparative advantage with absolute advantage. An individual, a firm, or a country has an **absolute advantage** in producing a good or service if it can produce more of that good or service from the same amount of resources. It is possible to have an absolute advantage in producing a good or service without having a comparative advantage.

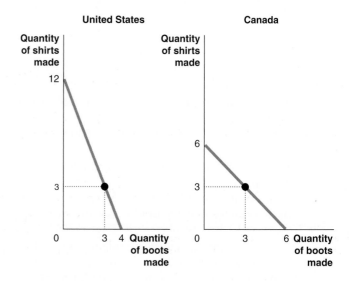

 Visit **www.myeconlab.com** to complete these exercises online and get instant feedback.

## Review Questions

2.1 What is absolute advantage? What is comparative advantage? Is it possible for a country to have a comparative advantage in producing a good without also having an absolute advantage? Briefly explain.

2.2 What is the basis for trade? What advantages are there to specialization?

## Problems and Applications

2.3 Look again at the information in Figure 2-4 on page 43. Choose a rate of trading cherries for apples different than the rate used in the text (15 pounds of cherries for 10 pounds of apples) that will allow you and your neighbor to benefit from trading apples and cherries. Prepare a table like Table 2-1 on page 44 to illustrate your answer.

2.4 Using the same amount of resources, the United States and Canada can both produce lumberjack shirts and lumberjack boots, as shown in the following production possibilities frontiers.

a. Who has a comparative advantage in producing lumberjack boots? Who has a comparative advantage in producing lumberjack shirts? Explain your reasoning.

b. Does either country have an absolute advantage in producing both goods? Explain.

c. Suppose that both countries are currently producing three pairs of boots and three shirts. Show that both can be better off if they each specialize in producing one good and then engage in trade.

2.5 (Related to *Solved Problem 2-2* on page 46) Suppose Iran and Iraq both produce oil and olive oil. The following table shows combinations of both goods that each country can produce in a day, measured in thousands of barrels.

| IRAQ | | IRAN | |
|---|---|---|---|
| OIL | OLIVE OIL | OIL | OLIVE OIL |
| 0 | 8 | 0 | 4 |
| 2 | 6 | 1 | 3 |
| 4 | 4 | 2 | 2 |
| 6 | 2 | 3 | 1 |
| 8 | 0 | 4 | 0 |

a. Who has the comparative advantage in producing oil? Explain.
b. Can these two countries gain from trading oil and olive oil? Explain.

2.6 (Related to *Solved Problem 2-2* on page 46) Suppose that France and Germany both produce schnitzel and wine. The following table shows combinations of the goods that each country can produce in a day.

| FRANCE | | GERMANY | |
|---|---|---|---|
| WINE (BOTTLES) | SCHNITZEL (POUNDS) | WINE (BOTTLES) | SCHNITZEL (POUNDS) |
| 0 | 8 | 0 | 15 |
| 1 | 6 | 1 | 12 |
| 2 | 4 | 2 | 9 |
| 3 | 2 | 3 | 6 |
| 4 | 0 | 4 | 3 |
| | | 5 | 0 |

a. Who has a comparative advantage in producing wine? Who has a comparative advantage in producing schnitzel?
b. Suppose that France is currently producing 1 bottle of wine and 6 pounds of schnitzel, and Germany is currently producing 3 bottles of wine and 6 pounds of schnitzel. Demonstrate that France and Germany can both be better off if they specialize in producing only one good and then engage in trade.

2.7 (Related to *Don't Let This Happen to You!* on page 45) In the 1950s, the economist Bela Balassa compared 28 manufacturing industries in the United States and Britain. In every one of the 28 industries, Balassa found that the United States had an absolute advantage. In these circumstances, would there have been any gain to the United States from importing any of these products from Britain? Explain.

2.8 In colonial America, the population was spread thinly over a large area, and transportation costs were very high because it was difficult to ship products by road for more than short distances. As a result, most of the free population lived on small farms, where they not only grew their own food but also usually made their own clothes and very rarely bought or sold anything for money. Explain why the incomes of these farmers were likely to rise as transportation costs fell. Use the concept of comparative advantage in your answer.

2.9 During the 1928 presidential election campaign, Herbert Hoover, the Republican candidate, argued that the United States should import only products that could not be produced here. Do you believe that this would be a good policy? Explain.

>> **End Learning Objective 2.2**

---

| 2.3 | **The Market System, pages 47–55** |
|---|---|
| | LEARNING OBJECTIVE: Explain the basic idea of how a market system works |

## Summary

A **market** is a group of buyers and sellers of a good or service and the institution or arrangement by which they come together to trade. **Product markets** are markets for goods and services, such as computers and medical treatment. **Factor markets** are markets for the **factors of production**, such as labor, capital, natural resources, and entrepreneurial ability. A **circular-flow diagram** shows how participants in product markets and factor markets are linked. Adam Smith argued in his 1776 book *The Wealth of Nations* that in a **free market**, where the government does not control the production of goods and services, changes in prices lead firms to produce the goods and services most desired by consumers. If consumers demand more of a good, its price will rise. Firms respond to rising prices by increasing production. If consumers demand less of a good, its price will fall. Firms respond to falling prices by producing less of a good. An **entrepreneur** is someone who operates a business. In the market system, entrepreneurs are responsible for organizing the production of goods and services. The market system will work well only if there is protection for **property rights**, which are the rights of individuals and firms to use their property.

 Visit www.myeconlab.com to complete these exercises online and get instant feedback.

## Review Questions

3.1 What is a circular-flow diagram, and what does it demonstrate?
3.2 What are the two main categories of participants in markets? Which participants are of greatest importance in determining what goods and services are produced?
3.3 What is a free market? In what ways does a free market economy differ from a centrally planned economy?
3.4 What is an entrepreneur? Why do entrepreneurs play a key role in a market system?
3.5 Under what circumstances are firms likely to produce more of a good or service? Under what circumstances are firms likely to produce less of a good or service?
3.6 What are private property rights? What role do they play in the working of a market system? Why are

independent courts important for a well-functioning economy?

## Problems and Applications

**3.7** Identify whether each of the following transactions will take place in the factor market or in the product market and whether households or firms are supplying the good or service or demanding the good or service:
   a. George buys a BMW X5 SUV.
   b. BMW increases employment at its Spartanburg plant.
   c. George works 20 hours per week at McDonald's.
   d. George sells land he owns to McDonald's so it can build a new restaurant.

**3.8** **(Related to *Solved Problem* 2-3 on page 50)** Alan Krueger, an economist at Princeton University, has argued that Adam Smith "worried that if merchants and manufacturers pursued their self-interest by seeking government regulation and privilege, the invisible hand would not work its magic."

Source: Alan B. Krueger, "Rediscovering the Wealth of Nations," New York Times, August 16, 2001.

If the government's regulating competition and granting privileges keeps the invisible hand from working properly, is all government intervention in the marketplace bad for the economy?

**3.9** **(Related to the *Making the Connection* on page 51)** In *The Wealth of Nations*, Adam Smith wrote the following (Book I, Chapter II): "It is not from the benevolence of the butcher, the brewer, or the baker, that we expect our dinner, but from their regard to their own interest." Briefly discuss what he meant by this.

**3.10** In a speech at the New York University Law School, Federal Reserve Chairman Ben Bernanke stated:

> Writing in the eighteenth century, Adam Smith conceived of the free-market system as an "invisible hand" that harnesses the pursuit of private interest to promote the public good. Smith's conception remains relevant today, notwithstanding the enormous increase in economic complexity since the Industrial Revolution.

Briefly explain the idea of the invisible hand. What's so important about the idea of the invisible hand?

Source: Ben S. Bernanke, "Financial Regulation and the Invisible Hand," speech made at the New York University Law School, New York, New York, April 11, 2007.

**3.11** Evaluate the following argument: "Adam Smith's analysis is based on a fundamental flaw: He assumes that people are motivated by self-interest. But this isn't true. I'm not selfish, and most people I know aren't selfish."

**3.12** Writing in the *New York Times*, Michael Lewis argued that "a market economy is premised on a system of incentives designed to encourage an ignoble human trait: self-interest." Do you agree that self-interest is an "ignoble human trait"? What incentives does a market system provide to encourage self-interest?

Source: Michael Lewis, "In Defense of the Boom," New York Times, October 27, 2002.

**3.13** Jason Bordoff, policy director of the Hamilton Project at the Brookings Institution, argues that "economic performance should be measured by . . . 'a rising standard of living for the great majority of citizens.'" Briefly discuss whether you agree.

Source: Jason Bordoff, "Lifting Our Economy," Brookings, January 23, 2009.

**3.14** The 2009 International Property Rights Index study states:

> Data shows that countries that protect the physical and intellectual property of their people enjoy nearly nine times higher [income per person] . . . than countries ranking lowest in property rights protections. The study . . . compared the protections of physical and intellectual property to economic stability in 115 countries. . . .

How would the creation of property rights be likely to affect the economic opportunities available to citizens of those countries ranking lowest in property rights protections?

Source: Kelsey Zahourek, "Report: Property Rights Linked to Economic Security," International Property Rights Index 2009 Report, February 23, 2009.

**3.15** **(Related to the *Making the Connection* on page 53)** In a commentary written for the basketball information Web site The Hoop Doctors, the author, who goes by the handle "Dr. Anklesnap," discussed the removal of a video clip The Hoop Doctors had posted to YouTube:

> CBS has decided to file a copyright complaint against The Hoop Doctors' YouTube account because we uploaded a video clip of Blake Griffin during yesterday's matchup between Oklahoma and Morgan State

from a CBS broadcast. Bloggers beware . . . CBS is on the hunt . . . !! What a joke, do you really think you can regulate and control the web, CBS?

Do you think that CBS should be compensated by anyone posting clips of its copyrighted material to the Internet? Do all copyright holders suffer significant financial damage from having their material posted to YouTube? Is there any way copyright holders might benefit from having their material posted, without approval or compensation, on sites such as YouTube?

Source: Dr. Anklesnap, "CBS Files Copyright Complaint Against The Hoop Doctors YouTube Account," *TheHoopDoctors.com*, March 20, 2009.

**>> End Learning Objective 2.3**

# Where Prices Come From: The Interaction of Demand and Supply

## Chapter Outline and Learning Objectives

# >> Red Bull and the Market for Energy Drinks

Markets for some products suddenly explode. This was the case in recent years with energy drinks. Red Bull was developed in Austria by Dietrich Mateschitz, who based it on a drink he discovered being sold in pharmacies in Thailand. Red Bull entered the U.S. market in 1997. At that time, only a few energy drinks, such as Jolt Cola, were available, and they made up only a sliver of the soft drink market. By 2009, however, sales of energy drinks were growing by 10 percent per year, which was a rate faster than sales of other soft drinks, even though energy drinks sell for three times as much per ounce as soda. The market for energy drinks has found a particularly valuable niche with students wanting an extra boost of energy while engaging in sports or studying. One report predicts that energy drinks might replace coffee for the current generation of teens and young adults.

The success of Red Bull, Monster Energy, and Rockstar attracted the notice of the large beverage firms, as well as entrepreneurs looking to introduce new products into a hot market. Coca-Cola signed an agreement to distribute Monster Energy in 20 U.S. states,

Canada, and six western European countries. Pepsi signed an agreement with Rockstar to distribute the drink throughout North America. New, mostly small, startup companies also appeared nearly every month. By 2009, 210 different energy drinks were for sale in North America.

The intense competition among firms selling energy drinks is a striking example of how the market responds to changes in consumer tastes. Although intense competition is not always good news for firms trying to sell products, it is a boon to consumers because it increases the available choice of products and lowers the prices consumers pay for those products.

**AN INSIDE LOOK** on **page 88** discusses Red Bull's use of advertising to increase demand.

Sources: Betsy McKay, "Pepsi Fortifies Position in Energy-Drink Market," *Wall Street Journal*, February 20, 2009; Kristi E. Swartz, "Coke Signs Deal to Distribute Monster Energy Drinks," *Atlanta Journal Constitution*, October 6, 2008; and Canadean, "Bottled Water Growth Slows as Consumers Turn on the Tap," *Global Beverage Forecast*, March 18, 2009.

## Economics in YOUR Life!

### Will You Drink Red Bull or Monster?

Suppose you are about to buy an energy drink and that you are choosing between a Red Bull and a Monster Energy. As the more established, well-known brand, Red Bull has many advantages over a newer entrant like Monster Energy. One strategy Monster can use to overcome those advantages is to compete based on price and value. Would you choose to buy a can of Monster Energy if it had a lower price than a can of Red Bull? Would you be less likely to drink Monster Energy if your income had declined? As you read the chapter, see if you can answer these questions. You can check your answers against those we provide at the end of the chapter.

▶ Continued on page 86

I n Chapter 1, we explored how economists use models to predict human behavior. In Chapter 2, we used the model of production possibilities frontiers to analyze scarcity and trade-offs. In this chapter and the next, we explore the model of demand and supply, which is the most powerful tool in economics, and use it to explain how prices are determined.

Recall from Chapter 1 that because economic models rely on assumptions, the models are simplifications of reality. In some cases, the assumptions of the model may not seem to describe exactly the economic situation being analyzed. For example, the model of demand and supply assumes that we are analyzing a *perfectly competitive market*. In a **perfectly competitive market**, there are many buyers and sellers, all the products sold are identical, and there are no barriers to new firms entering the market. These assumptions are very restrictive and apply exactly to only a few markets, such as the markets for wheat and other agricultural products. Experience has shown, however, that the model of demand and supply can be very useful in analyzing markets where competition among sellers is intense, even if there are relatively few sellers and the products being sold are not identical. In fact, in recent studies, the model of demand and supply has been successful in analyzing markets with as few as four buyers and four sellers. In the end, the usefulness of a model depends on how well it can predict outcomes in a market. As we will see in this chapter, the model of demand and supply is often very useful in predicting changes in quantities and prices in many markets.

We begin considering the model of demand and supply by discussing consumers and the demand side of the market, before turning to firms and the supply side. As you will see, we will apply this model throughout this book to understand business, the economy, and economic policy.

**Perfectly competitive market**
A market that meets the conditions of (1) many buyers and sellers, (2) all firms selling identical products, and (3) no barriers to new firms entering the market.

**3.1 LEARNING** OBJECTIVE

Discuss the variables that influence demand.

# The Demand Side of the Market

Chapter 2 explained that in a market system, consumers ultimately determine which goods and services will be produced. The most successful businesses are the ones that respond best to consumer demand. But what determines consumer demand for a product? Certainly, many factors influence the willingness of consumers to buy a particular product. For example, consumers who are considering buying an energy drink, such as Red Bull or Monster Energy, will make their decisions based on, among other factors, the income they have available to spend and the effectiveness of the advertising campaigns of the companies that sell energy drinks. The main factor in consumer decisions, though, will be the price of the energy drink. So, it makes sense to begin with price when analyzing the decisions of consumers to buy a product. It is important to note that when we discuss demand, we are considering not what a consumer *wants* to buy but what the consumer is both willing and *able* to buy.

## Demand Schedules and Demand Curves

**Demand schedule** A table showing the relationship between the price of a product and the quantity of the product demanded.

**Quantity demanded** The amount of a good or service that a consumer is willing and able to purchase at a given price.

**Demand curve** A curve that shows the relationship between the price of a product and the quantity of the product demanded.

**Market demand** The demand by all the consumers of a given good or service.

Tables that show the relationship between the price of a product and the quantity of the product demanded are called **demand schedules**. The table in Figure 3-1 shows the number of cans of energy drinks consumers would be willing to buy over the course of a day at five different prices. The amount of a good or a service that a consumer is willing and able to purchase at a given price is referred to as the **quantity demanded**. The graph in Figure 3-1 plots the numbers from the table as a **demand curve**, a curve that shows the relationship between the price of a product and the quantity of the product demanded. (Note that for convenience, we made the demand curve in Figure 3-1 a straight line, or linear. There is no reason that all demand curves need to be straight lines.) The demand curve in Figure 3-1 shows the **market demand**, or the demand by all the consumers of a given good or service. The market for a product, such as restaurant meals, that is purchased locally would include all the consumers in a city or a rela-

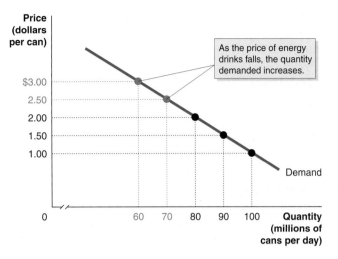

| Demand Schedule | |
| --- | --- |
| Price (dollars per can) | Quantity (millions of cans per day) |
| $3.00 | 60 |
| 2.50 | 70 |
| 2.00 | 80 |
| 1.50 | 90 |
| 1.00 | 100 |

As the price of energy drinks falls, the quantity demanded increases.

## Figure 3-1

### A Demand Schedule and Demand Curve

As the price changes, consumers change the quantity of energy drinks they are willing to buy. We can show this as a *demand schedule* in a table or as a *demand curve* on a graph. The table and graph both show that as the price of energy drinks falls, the quantity demanded rises. When the price of energy drinks is $3.00, consumers buy 60 million cans per day. When the price drops to $2.50, consumers buy 70 million cans. Therefore, the demand curve for energy drinks is downward sloping.

tively small area. The market for a product that is sold internationally, such as energy drinks, would include all the consumers in the world.

The demand curve in Figure 3-1 slopes downward because consumers will buy more cans as the price falls. When the price of a can is $3.00, consumers buy 60 million cans per day. If the price of a can falls to $2.50, consumers buy 70 million cans. Buyers demand a larger quantity of a product as the price falls because the product becomes less expensive relative to other products and because they can afford to buy more at a lower price.

## The Law of Demand

The inverse relationship between the price of a product and the quantity of the product demanded is known as the **law of demand**: Holding everything else constant, when the price of a product falls, the quantity demanded of the product will increase, and when the price of a product rises, the quantity demanded of the product will decrease. The law of demand holds for any market demand curve. Economists have found only a very few exceptions to it.

**Law of demand** The rule that, holding everything else constant, when the price of a product falls, the quantity demanded of the product will increase, and when the price of a product rises, the quantity demanded of the product will decrease.

## What Explains the Law of Demand?

It makes sense that consumers will buy more of a good when the price falls and less of a good when the price rises, but let's look more closely at why this is true. When the price of energy drinks falls, consumers buy a larger quantity because of the *substitution effect* and the *income effect*.

**Substitution Effect** The **substitution effect** refers to the change in the quantity demanded of a good that results from a change in price, making the good more or less expensive *relative* to other goods that are *substitutes*. When the price of energy drinks falls, consumers will substitute buying energy drinks for buying other goods, such as sports drinks or coffee.

**Substitution effect** The change in the quantity demanded of a good that results from a change in price, making the good more or less expensive relative to other goods that are substitutes.

**The Income Effect** The **income effect** of a price change refers to the change in the quantity demanded of a good that results from the effect of a change in the good's price on consumers' purchasing power. Purchasing power is the quantity of goods a consumer can buy with a fixed amount of income. When the price of a good falls, the increased purchasing power of consumers' incomes will usually lead them to purchase a larger quantity of the good. When the price of a good rises, the decreased purchasing power of consumers' incomes will usually lead them to purchase a smaller quantity of the good.

**Income effect** The change in the quantity demanded of a good that results from the effect of a change in the good's price on consumers' purchasing power.

Note that although we can analyze them separately, the substitution effect and the income effect happen simultaneously whenever a price changes. Thus, a fall in the price of energy drinks leads consumers to buy more energy drinks, both because the cans are now less expensive relative to substitute products and because the purchasing power of the consumers' incomes has increased.

## Holding Everything Else Constant: The *Ceteris Paribus* Condition

Notice that the definition of the law of demand contains the phrase *holding everything else constant*. In constructing the market demand curve for energy drinks, we focused only on the effect that changes in the price of energy drinks would have on the quantity consumers would be willing and able to buy. We were holding constant other variables that might affect the willingness of consumers to buy energy drinks. Economists refer to the necessity of holding all variables other than price constant in constructing a demand curve as the **ceteris paribus condition**; *ceteris paribus* is Latin for "all else equal."

What would happen if we allowed a change in a variable—other than price—that might affect the willingness of consumers to buy energy drinks? Consumers would then change the quantity they demanded at each price. We can illustrate this effect by shifting the market demand curve. A shift of a demand curve is *an increase or a decrease in demand*. A movement along a demand curve is *an increase or a decrease in the quantity demanded*. As Figure 3-2 shows, we shift the demand curve to the right if consumers decide to buy more of the good at each price, and we shift the demand curve to the left if consumers decide to buy less at each price.

## Variables That Shift Market Demand

Many variables other than price can influence market demand. These five are the most important:

- Income

- Prices of related goods

- Tastes

- Population and demographics

- Expected future prices

We next discuss how changes in each of these variables affect the market demand curve.

*Ceteris paribus* ("all else equal") condition   The requirement that when analyzing the relationship between two variables—such as price and quantity demanded—other variables must be held constant.

## Figure 3-2

### Shifting the Demand Curve

When consumers increase the quantity of a product they want to buy at a given price, the market demand curve shifts to the right, from $D_1$ to $D_2$. When consumers decrease the quantity of a product they want to buy at a given price, the demand curve shifts to the left, from $D_1$ to $D_3$.

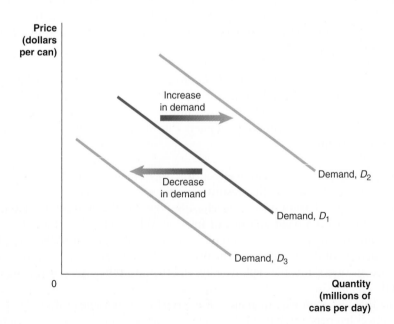

**Income** The income that consumers have available to spend affects their willingness and ability to buy a good. Suppose that the market demand curve in Figure 3-1 on page 67 represents the willingness of consumers to buy energy drinks when average household income is $43,000. If household income rises to $45,000, the demand for energy drinks will increase, which we show by shifting the demand curve to the right. A good is a **normal good** when demand increases following a rise in income and decreases following a fall in income. Most goods are normal goods, but the demand for some goods falls when income rises and rises when income falls. For instance, as your income rises, you might buy less canned tuna or fewer hot dogs and buy more shrimp or prime rib. A good is an **inferior good** when demand decreases following a rise in income and increases following a fall in income. So, for you canned tuna and hot dogs would be examples of inferior goods—not because they are of low quality but because you buy less of them as your income increases.

**Normal good**   A good for which the demand increases as income rises and decreases as income falls.

**Inferior good**   A good for which the demand increases as income falls and decreases as income rises.

## Making the Connection | Are Big Macs an Inferior Good?

In recent years, as American families juggle busy schedules, they have increasingly relied on eating out rather than preparing meals at home. According to a survey by *Restaurants and Institutions* magazine, adults eat an average of nearly four meals per week outside the home. Nearly one-third of consumers frequently eat lunch away from home, and on weekdays more than 15 percent frequently eat dinner away from home, a proportion that rises to more than 35 percent on weekends.

Does this behavior change during a recession? We might expect that it would because recessions result in declining incomes as some people lose their jobs and others are forced to work fewer hours or have their wages reduced. Dining out is more expensive than preparing meals at home, so one way to save during a recession is to cut back on restaurant meals. In fact, during the 2007–2009 recession many restaurants had a difficult time. Particularly hard hit were "casual dining" restaurants that provide table service and serve moderately priced food. Among other restaurants, Ruby Tuesday, Olive Garden, Red Lobster, and LongHorn Steakhouse all experienced declining demand, while Bennigan's and Steak and Ale filed for bankruptcy.

*McDonald's restaurants experienced increased sales during 2008 and 2009, despite the recession.*

However, the recession did not hurt all restaurants. McDonald's restaurants experienced increased sales during 2008 and 2009. Why did demand for Big Macs increase as incomes fell? As one report put it: "Analysts said [McDonald's] strength . . . shows that Americans still want to eat out and are heading to quick-service restaurants to stretch their dollars further." So, Big Macs seem to fit the economic definition of an inferior good because demand increased as income fell. But remember that inferior goods are not necessarily of low quality, they are just goods for which consumers increase their demand as their incomes fall.

Source: Janet Adamy, "McDonald's Seeks Ways to Keep Sizzling," *Wall Street Journal*, March 10, 2009; Mike Barris, "McDonald's Same Store Sales Rise," *Wall Street Journal*, March 9, 2009; Carl Gutierrez, "McDonald's Recession-Proof Menu," *Forbes*, November 10, 2008; and "The New American Diner," *Restaurants and Institutions*, January 1, 2008.

**YOUR TURN:** For more practice, do related problem 1.8 on page 91 at the end of this chapter.

**Prices of Related Goods** The prices of other goods can also affect consumers' demand for a product. Goods and services that can be used for the same purpose—such as energy drinks and caffè lattes—are **substitutes**. When two goods are substitutes, the

**Substitutes**   Goods and services that can be used for the same purpose.

more you buy of one, the less you will buy of the other. A decrease in the price of a substitute causes the demand curve for a good to shift to the left. An increase in the price of a substitute causes the demand curve for a good to shift to the right.

Suppose that the market demand curve in Figure 3-1 represents the willingness and ability of consumers to buy energy drinks during a week when the average price of a caffè latte is $3.00. If the average price of lattes falls to $2.50, how will the market demand for energy drinks change? Consumers will demand fewer cans at every price. We show this by shifting the demand curve for energy drinks to the left.

**Complements**   Goods and services that are used together.

Goods and services that are used together—such as hot dogs and hot dog buns— are **complements**. When two goods are complements, the more consumers buy of one, the more they will buy of the other. A decrease in the price of a complement causes the demand curve for a good to shift to the right. An increase in the price of a complement causes the demand curve for a good to shift to the left.

Many people drink Red Bull or Monster Energy when working out at a gym. So, for many people, energy drinks and a gym membership are complements. Suppose the market demand curve in Figure 3-1 represents the willingness of consumers to buy energy drinks at a time when the average price of a gym membership is $40 per month. If the price of gym memberships drops to $30 per month, consumers will buy more gym memberships *and* more energy drinks: The demand curve for energy drinks will shift to the right.

**Tastes**   Consumers can be influenced by an advertising campaign for a product. If the firms making Red Bull, Monster Energy, Rockstar, and other energy drinks begin to advertise heavily online, consumers are more likely to buy cans at every price, and the demand curve will shift to the right. An economist would say that the advertising campaign has affected consumers' *taste* for energy drinks. Taste is a catchall category that refers to the many subjective elements that can enter into a consumer's decision to buy a product. A consumer's taste for a product can change for many reasons. Sometimes trends play a substantial role. For example, the popularity of low-carbohydrate diets caused a decline in demand for some goods, such as bread and donuts, and an increase in demand for beef. In general, when consumers' taste for a product increases, the demand curve will shift to the right, and when consumers' taste for a product decreases, the demand curve for the product will shift to the left.

**Demographics**   The characteristics of a population with respect to age, race, and gender.

**Population and Demographics**   Population and demographic factors can affect the demand for a product. As the population of the United States increases, so will the number of consumers, and the demand for most products will increase. The **demographics** of a population refers to its characteristics, with respect to age, race, and gender. As the demographics of a country or region change, the demand for particular goods will increase or decrease because different categories of people tend to have different preferences for those goods. For instance, Hispanics are expected to increase from 16 percent of the U.S. population in 2010 to 19 percent in 2020. This increase will expand demand for Spanish-language DVDs and cable television channels, as well as other goods and services.

Making
the
Connection

## The Aging of the Baby Boom Generation

The average age of the U.S. population is increasing. After World War II in 1945, the United States experienced a "baby boom" as birthrates rose and remained high through the early 1960s. Falling birthrates after 1965 mean that the baby boom generation is larger than the generation before it and the generations after it. The figure on the next page uses projections from the U.S. Census Bureau to show that as boomers age they are increasing the fraction of the U.S. population that is older than 65.

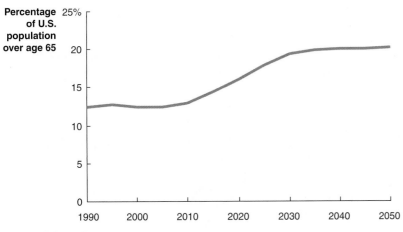

Source: U.S. Census Bureau

What effects will the aging of the baby boom generation have on the economy? Older people have a greater demand for medical care than do younger people. So, in coming years, the demand for doctors, nurses, and hospital facilities should all increase. The increasing demand for health care is so strong that during 2009, as the U.S. economy suffered from its worst recession since the Great Depression of the 1930s and the total number of jobs declined, jobs in health care continued to increase. As we mentioned in Chapter 2, the increased demand for medical care will also drive up the federal government's costs under the Medicare program, which pays part of the medical bills of people who are 65 and older.

Aging boomers will also have an effect on the housing market. Older people often "downsize" their housing by moving from large, single-family homes, whose maintenance can be difficult and expensive, to smaller homes, condominiums, or apartments. Hence, in coming years, the demand for large homes may decrease, while the demand for smaller homes and apartments may increase.

Sources: Kendra Marr, "The Economy's Steady Pulse—Health-Care Sector Is Poised to Keep Expanding, but So Are Its Costs," *Washington Post*, June 13, 2008; Peter Francese, "The Changing Face of the U.S. Consumer," *Advertising Age*, July 7, 2008; and U.S. Bureau of Labor Statistics.

**YOUR TURN:** For more practice, do related problem 1.9 on page 91 at the end of this chapter.

**Expected Future Prices** Consumers choose not only which products to buy but also when to buy them. For instance, if enough consumers become convinced that houses will be selling for lower prices in three months, the demand for houses will decrease now, as some consumers postpone their purchases to wait for the expected price decrease. Alternatively, if enough consumers become convinced that the price of houses will be higher in three months, the demand for houses will increase now, as some consumers try to beat the expected price increase.

Table 3-1 on page 72 summarizes the most important variables that cause market demand curves to shift. Note that the table shows the shift in the demand curve that results from an *increase* in each of the variables. A *decrease* in these variables would cause the demand curve to shift in the opposite direction.

## A Change in Demand versus a Change in Quantity Demanded

It is important to understand the difference between a *change in demand* and a *change in quantity demanded*. A change in demand refers to a shift of the demand curve. A shift occurs if there is a change in one of the variables, *other than the price of the product*, that affects the willingness of consumers to buy the product. A change in quantity demanded

## TABLE 3-1

**Variables That Shift Market Demand Curves**

| AN INCREASE IN... | SHIFTS THE DEMAND CURVE... | BECAUSE... |
|---|---|---|
| income (and the good is normal) | | consumers spend more of their higher incomes on the good. |
| income (and the good is inferior) | | consumers spend less of their higher incomes on the good. |
| the price of a substitute good | | consumers buy less of the substitute good and more of this good. |
| the price of a complementary good | | consumers buy less of the complementary good and less of this good. |
| taste for the good | | consumers are willing to buy a larger quantity of the good at every price. |
| population | | additional consumers result in a greater quantity demanded at every price. |
| the expected price of the good in the future | | consumers buy more of the good today to avoid the higher price in the future. |

refers to a movement along the demand curve as a result of a change in the product's price. Figure 3-3 illustrates this important distinction. If the price of energy drinks falls from $3.00 to $2.50 per can, the result will be a movement along the demand curve from point *A* to point *B*—an increase in quantity demanded from 60 million to 70 million. If consumers' incomes increase, or if another factor changes that makes consumers want more of the product at every price, the demand curve will shift to the right—an

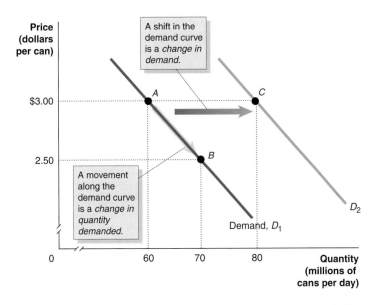

Figure 3-3

**A Change in Demand versus a Change in Quantity Demanded**

If the price of energy drinks falls from $3.00 to $2.50, the result will be a movement along the demand curve from point $A$ to point $B$—an increase in quantity demanded from 60 million cans to 70 million cans. If consumers' incomes increase, or if another factor changes that makes consumers want more of the product at every price, the demand curve will shift to the right—an increase in demand. In this case, the increase in demand from $D_1$ to $D_2$ causes the quantity of energy drinks demanded at a price of $3.00 to increase from 60 million cans at point $A$ to 80 million cans at point $C$.

increase in demand. In this case, the increase in demand from $D_1$ to $D_2$ causes the quantity of energy drinks demanded at a price of $3.00 to increase from 60 million at point $A$ to 80 million at point $C$.

## Red Bull and the Future Demand for Energy Drinks

**Making the Connection**

It is important for managers to accurately forecast the demand for their products because it helps them determine how much of a good to produce. Firms typically set manufacturing schedules at least a month ahead of time. Failing to foresee a decline in demand can lead to a firm producing more of a good than it can sell, which is a particular problem for a good such as Red Bull that can spoil if stored for too long. Up through 2009, Red Bull had few concerns about declining demand, because energy drinks were a very hot product, even during the 2007–2009 recession. For instance, during 2008, while sales of conventional sodas declined by 5 percent, sales of energy drinks increased by nearly 8 percent. Red Bull also had a strong position in the market, accounting for about 25 percent of industry sales, second only to Monster Energy's 30 percent share.

In a rapidly growing market such as energy drinks, firms need to increase productive capacity quickly enough. Firms that fail to produce enough goods to keep pace with increasing demand can lose out to competitors. But will the demand for energy drinks continue to grow at such a rapid pace? Certainly, the 40 percent increase in sales during 2006 and the 30 percent increase during 2007 were not sustainable over the long run, even without the impact of the 2007–2009 recession. Richard Tedlow of the Harvard Business School has developed a theory of the "three phases of marketing" that can provide some insight into how the markets for many consumer products develop over time. In the first phase, there are often a very large number of firms, each producing a relatively small volume of goods and charging high prices. This phase corresponds to the conventional soft drink industry in the late nineteenth century, the automobile industry in the early twentieth century, and the personal computer industry in the late 1970s. In the second phase, the market consolidates, with one or a few brands attaining high market shares by selling a large number of units at lower prices. This phase corresponds to the soft drink industry during the middle of the twentieth century, the automobile industry during the 1920s, and the personal computer industry during the 1980s. The third phase of marketing involves a rapid multiplication of products introduced by the dominant firms. Conventional soft drinks, automobiles, and personal computers are all currently in this phase. For instance, Coca-Cola and Pepsi are the dominant firms in the conventional soft drink industry, but they offer an incredible

*Will Red Bull continue to grow its share of the energy drink market?*

variety of products, from basic Coke and Pepsi to caffeine-free, Diet Cherry Coke, and Black Cherry French Vanilla Diet Pepsi Jazz.

The energy drink industry is probably in the second phase of marketing, with Monster Energy, Red Bull, and Rockstar having 15 percent or more of the market; Amp, Full Throttle, and SoBe each having around 5 percent; and dozens of smaller companies making up the remainder of the market. If energy drinks end up becoming a significant fraction of the overall beverage market, then the industry will probably enter the third phase of marketing, with Red Bull and the remaining firms competing by offering a variety of different products.

Sources: Barbara Grondin Francella, "Energy Drink Sales Growth Running Out of Steam," *Convenience Store News*, April 3, 2009; Betsey McKay, "Pepsi Fortifies Position in Energy-Drink Market," *Wall Street Journal*, February 20, 2009; and Richard Tedlow, *New and Improved: The Story of Mass Marketing in America*, Cambridge, MA: Harvard Business School Press, 1996.

**myeconlab**   **YOUR TURN:** For more practice, do related problem 1.11 on page 91 at the end of this chapter.

**3.2** LEARNING OBJECTIVE

Discuss the variables that influence supply.

**Quantity supplied**   The amount of a good or service that a firm is willing and able to supply at a given price.

# The Supply Side of the Market

Just as many variables influence the willingness and ability of consumers to buy a particular good or service, many variables also influence the willingness and ability of firms to sell a good or service. The most important of these variables is price. The amount of a good or service that a firm is willing and able to supply at a given price is the **quantity supplied**. Holding other variables constant, when the price of a good rises, producing the good is more profitable, and the quantity supplied will increase. When the price of a good falls, the good is less profitable, and the quantity supplied will decrease. In addition, as we saw in Chapter 2, devoting more and more resources to the production of a good results in increasing marginal costs. If, for example, Red Bull, Monster Energy, and Rockstar increase production of energy drinks during a given time period, they are likely to find that the cost of producing additional cans increases as they run existing factories for longer hours and pay higher prices for ingredients and higher wages for workers. With higher marginal costs, firms will supply a larger quantity only if the price is higher.

**Supply schedule**   A table that shows the relationship between the price of a product and the quantity of the product supplied.

**Supply curve**   A curve that shows the relationship between the price of a product and the quantity of the product supplied.

## Supply Schedules and Supply Curves

A **supply schedule** is a table that shows the relationship between the price of a product and the quantity of the product supplied. The table in Figure 3-4 is a supply schedule showing the quantity of energy drinks that firms would be willing to supply per day at different prices. The graph in Figure 3-4 plots the numbers from the supply schedule as a *supply curve*. A **supply curve** shows the relationship between the price of a product

## Figure 3-4

**A Supply Schedule and Supply Curve**

As the price changes, Red Bull, Monster Energy, Rockstar, and the other firms producing energy drinks change the quantity they are willing to supply. We can show this as a *supply schedule* in a table or as a *supply curve* on a graph. The supply schedule and supply curve both show that as the price of energy drinks rises, firms will increase the quantity they supply. At a price of $2.50 per can, firms will supply 90 million cans. At a price of $3.00, firms will supply 100 million cans.

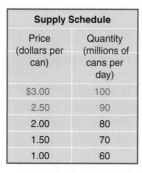

| Supply Schedule | |
| --- | --- |
| Price (dollars per can) | Quantity (millions of cans per day) |
| $3.00 | 100 |
| 2.50 | 90 |
| 2.00 | 80 |
| 1.50 | 70 |
| 1.00 | 60 |

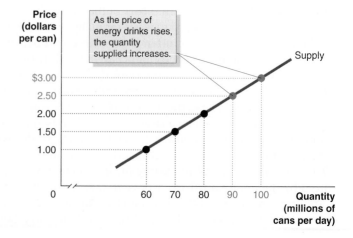

and the quantity of the product supplied. The supply schedule and supply curve both show that as the price of energy drinks rises, firms will increase the quantity they supply. At a price of $2.50 per can, firms will supply 90 million cans per day. At the higher price of $3.00, firms will supply 100 million. (Once again, we are assuming for convenience that the supply curve is a straight line, even though not all supply curves are actually straight lines.)

## The Law of Supply

The *market supply curve* in Figure 3-4 is upward sloping. We expect most supply curves to be upward sloping according to the **law of supply**, which states that, holding everything else constant, increases in price cause increases in the quantity supplied, and decreases in price cause decreases in the quantity supplied. Notice that the definition of the law of supply—like the definition of the law of demand—contains the phrase *holding everything else constant*. If only the price of the product changes, there is a movement along the supply curve, which is *an increase or a decrease in the quantity supplied*. As Figure 3-5 shows, if any other variable that affects the willingness of firms to supply a good changes, the supply curve will shift, which is *an increase or a decrease in supply*. When firms increase the quantity of a product they want to sell at a given price, the supply curve shifts to the right. The shift from $S_1$ to $S_3$ represents *an increase in supply*. When firms decrease the quantity of a product they want to sell at a given price, the supply curve shifts to the left. The shift from $S_1$ to $S_2$ represents *a decrease in supply*.

**Law of supply**   The rule that, holding everything else constant, increases in price cause increases in the quantity supplied, and decreases in price cause decreases in the quantity supplied.

## Variables That Shift Market Supply

The following are the most important variables that shift market supply:

- Prices of inputs
- Technological change
- Prices of substitutes in production
- Number of firms in the market
- Expected future prices

We next discuss how each of these variables affects the market supply curve.

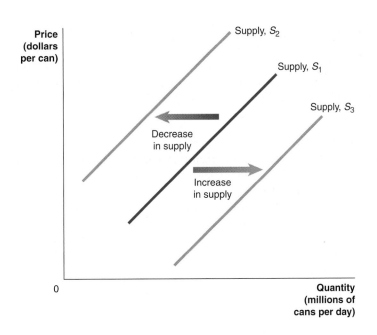

## Figure 3-5

### Shifting the Supply Curve

When firms increase the quantity of a product they want to sell at a given price, the supply curve shifts to the right. The shift from $S_1$ to $S_3$ represents an *increase in supply*. When firms decrease the quantity of a product they want to sell at a given price, the supply curve shifts to the left. The shift from $S_1$ to $S_2$ represents a *decrease in supply*.

**Prices of Inputs** The factor most likely to cause the supply curve for a product to shift is a change in the price of an *input*. An input is anything used in the production of a good or service. For instance, if the price of an ingredient in energy drinks, such as guarana (which is the source of caffeine in many drinks), rises, the cost of producing energy drinks will increase, and energy drinks will be less profitable at every price. The supply of energy drinks will decline, and the market supply curve for energy drinks will shift to the left. Similarly, if the price of an input declines, the supply of energy drinks will increase, and the supply curve will shift to the right.

**Technological Change** A second factor that causes a change in supply is *technological change*. **Technological change** is a positive or negative change in the ability of a firm to produce a given level of output with a given quantity of inputs. Positive technological change occurs whenever a firm is able to produce more output using the same amount of inputs. This shift will happen when the *productivity* of workers or machines increases. If a firm can produce more output with the same amount of inputs, its costs will be lower, and the good will be more profitable to produce at any given price. As a result, when positive technological change occurs, the firm will increase the quantity supplied at every price, and its supply curve will shift to the right. Normally, we expect technological change to have a positive effect on a firm's willingness to supply a product.

Negative technological change is relatively rare, although it could result from a natural disaster or a war that reduces a firm's ability to supply as much output with a given amount of inputs. Negative technological change will raise a firm's costs, and the good will be less profitable to produce. Therefore, negative technological change causes a firm's supply curve to shift to the left.

**Prices of Substitutes in Production** Firms often choose which good or service they will produce. Alternative products that a firm could produce are called *substitutes in production*. A number of companies produce both energy drinks and non-energy drinks. For instance, the Coca-Cola company produces the energy drink Full Throttle in addition to many varieties of Coke, and Pepsi produces the energy drink Amp. If the price of colas falls, colas will become less profitable, and Coca-Cola, Pepsi, and other companies will shift some of their productive capacity away from colas and toward energy drinks. The companies will offer more cans of energy drinks for sale at every price, so the supply curve for energy drinks will shift to the right.

**Number of Firms in the Market** A change in the number of firms in the market will change supply. When new firms *enter* a market, the supply curve shifts to the right, and when existing firms leave, or *exit*, a market, the supply curve shifts to the left. For instance, when Coca-Cola introduced Full Throttle in 2004, the market supply curve for energy drinks shifted to the right.

**Expected Future Prices** If a firm expects that the price of its product will be higher in the future than it is today, it has an incentive to decrease supply now and increase it in the future. For instance, if Red Bull believes that prices for energy drinks are temporarily low—perhaps because of a recession—it may store some of its production today to sell later on, when it expects prices to be higher, provided the period of time is not so long that the drinks will spoil.

Table 3-2 summarizes the most important variables that cause market supply curves to shift. Note that the table shows the shift in the supply curve that results from an *increase* in each of the variables. A *decrease* in these variables would cause the supply curve to shift in the opposite direction.

**Technological change**  A positive or negative change in the ability of a firm to produce a given level of output with a given quantity of inputs.

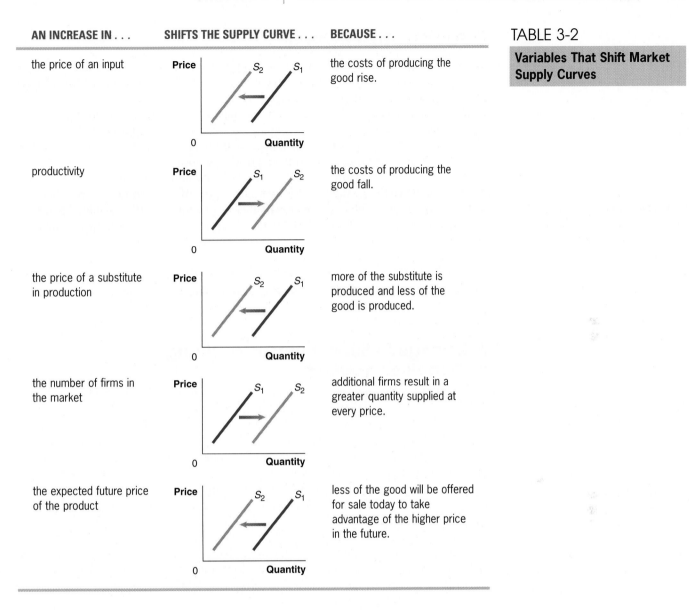

| AN INCREASE IN... | SHIFTS THE SUPPLY CURVE... | BECAUSE... | TABLE 3-2 |
|---|---|---|---|
| the price of an input | | the costs of producing the good rise. | **Variables That Shift Market Supply Curves** |
| productivity | | the costs of producing the good fall. | |
| the price of a substitute in production | | more of the substitute is produced and less of the good is produced. | |
| the number of firms in the market | | additional firms result in a greater quantity supplied at every price. | |
| the expected future price of the product | | less of the good will be offered for sale today to take advantage of the higher price in the future. | |

# Solved Problem | 3-2

## To (Soy)bean or Not to (Soy)bean?

Television programming in Illinois features many commercials directed at farmers. Ads for fertilizer, seed, and farm equipment are as common as commercials for laundry soap and soft drinks. Much of the nation's corn is grown in Illinois, but the climate and soil conditions in the state are well suited for growing soybeans as well. Farmers face a choice each year to plant corn or soybeans or a combination of the two crops.

a. If both crops can be grown on the same land, why would a farmer choose to produce corn rather than soybeans?

b. Which of the variables that influence supply would explain a farmer's choice to produce soybeans or corn?

## SOLVING THE PROBLEM:

**Step 1:** **Review the chapter material.** This problem is about variables that shift supply, so you may want to review the section "Variables That Shift Market Supply," which begins on page 75.

**Step 2:** **Answer question (a).** Among the factors that would influence a farmer's choice is the expected profitability of the two crops. A farmer will grow corn rather than soybeans if he expects that the profits from growing corn will be greater than those earned from growing soybeans.

**Step 3:** **Answer question (b).** Other things being equal, as the price of soybeans falls relative to the price of corn, the supply of corn would increase. Because corn and soybeans are substitutes in production, the variable "prices of substitutes in production" is the variable that would explain the farmer's choice.

**YOUR TURN:** For more practice, do related problem 2.6 on page 92 at the end of this chapter.

## A Change in Supply versus a Change in Quantity Supplied

We noted earlier the important difference between a change in demand and a change in quantity demanded. There is a similar difference between a *change in supply* and a *change in quantity supplied*. A change in supply refers to a shift of the supply curve. The supply curve will shift when there is a change in one of the variables, *other than the price of the product*, that affects the willingness of suppliers to sell the product. A change in quantity supplied refers to a movement along the supply curve as a result of a change in the product's price. Figure 3-6 illustrates this important distinction. If the price of energy drinks rises from $2.00 to $2.50 per can, the result will be a movement up the supply curve from point *A* to point *B*—an increase in quantity supplied from 80 million cans to 90 million cans. If the price of an input decreases or another factor makes sellers supply more of the product at every price change, the supply curve will shift to the right—an increase in supply. In this case, the increase in supply from $S_1$ to $S_2$ causes the quantity of energy drinks supplied at a price of $2.50 to increase from 90 million at point *B* to 110 million at point *C*.

### Figure 3-6

**A Change in Supply versus a Change in Quantity Supplied**

If the price of energy drinks rises from $2.00 to $2.50 per can, the result will be a movement up the supply curve from point *A* to point *B*—an increase in quantity supplied by Red Bull, Monster Energy, Rockstar, and the other firms from 80 million to 90 million cans. If the price of an input decreases or another factor changes that makes sellers supply more of the product at every price, the supply curve will shift to the right—an increase in supply. In this case, the increase in supply from $S_1$ to $S_2$ causes the quantity of energy drinks supplied at a price of $2.50 to increase from 90 million cans at point *B* to 110 million cans at point *C*.

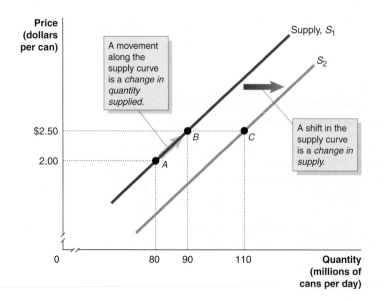

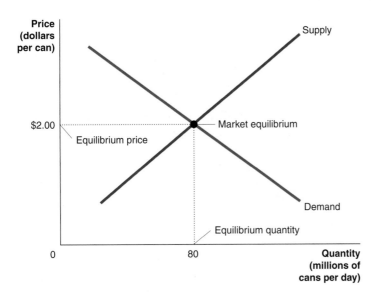

Figure 3-7

**Market Equilibrium**

Where the demand curve crosses the supply curve determines market equilibrium. In this case, the demand curve for energy drinks crosses the supply curve at a price of $2.00 and a quantity of 80 million cans. Only at this point is the quantity of energy drinks consumers are willing to buy equal to the quantity that Red Bull, Monster Energy, Rockstar, and the other firms are willing to sell: The quantity demanded is equal to the quantity supplied.

# Market Equilibrium: Putting Demand and Supply Together

The purpose of markets is to bring buyers and sellers together. As we saw in Chapter 2, instead of being chaotic and disorderly, the interaction of buyers and sellers in markets ultimately results in firms being led to produce the goods and services that consumers want most. To understand how this process happens, we first need to see how markets work to reconcile the plans of buyers and sellers.

In Figure 3-7, we bring together the market demand curve for energy drinks and the market supply curve. Notice that the demand curve crosses the supply curve at only one point. This point represents a price of $2.00 and a quantity of 80 million cans. Only at this point is the quantity of cans consumers are willing to buy equal to the quantity of cans firms are willing to sell. This is the point of **market equilibrium**. Only at market equilibrium will the quantity demanded equal the quantity supplied. In this case, the *equilibrium price* is $2.00, and the *equilibrium quantity* is 80 million. As we noted at the beginning of the chapter, markets that have many buyers and many sellers are competitive markets, and equilibrium in these markets is a **competitive market equilibrium**. In the market for energy drinks, there are many buyers but only about 80 firms. Whether 80 firms is enough for our model of demand and supply to apply to this market is a matter of judgment. In this chapter, we are assuming that the market for energy drinks has enough sellers to be competitive.

## How Markets Eliminate Surpluses and Shortages

A market that is not in equilibrium moves toward equilibrium. Once a market is in equilibrium, it remains in equilibrium. To see why, consider what happens if a market is not in equilibrium. For instance, suppose that the price in the market for energy drinks was $2.50, rather than the equilibrium price of $2.00. As Figure 3-8 shows, at a price of $2.50, the quantity of cans supplied would be 90 million, and the quantity of cans demanded would be 70 million. When the quantity supplied is greater than the quantity demanded, there is a **surplus** in the market. In this case, the surplus is equal to 20 million cans (90 million − 70 million = 20 million). When there is a surplus, firms have unsold goods piling up, which gives them an incentive to increase their sales by cutting the price. Cutting the price will simultaneously increase the quantity demanded and decrease the quantity supplied. This adjustment will reduce the surplus, but as long as the price is above $2.00, there will be a surplus, and downward pressure on the price will continue. Only when the price has fallen to $2.00 will the market be in equilibrium.

If, however, the price was $1.00, the quantity supplied would be 60 million, and the quantity demanded would be 100 million, as shown in Figure 3-8. When the quantity demanded is greater than the quantity supplied, there is a **shortage** in the market. In this

**3.3** LEARNING OBJECTIVE

Use a graph to illustrate market equilibrium.

**Market equilibrium** A situation in which quantity demanded equals quantity supplied.

**Competitive market equilibrium** A market equilibrium with many buyers and many sellers.

**Surplus** A situation in which the quantity supplied is greater than the quantity demanded.

**Shortage** A situation in which the quantity demanded is greater than the quantity supplied.

## Figure 3-8

**The Effect of Surpluses and Shortages on the Market Price**

When the market price is above equilibrium, there will be a *surplus*. In the figure, a price of $2.50 for energy drinks results in 90 million cans being supplied but only 70 million cans being demanded, or a surplus of 20 million. As Red Bull, Monster Energy, Rockstar, and the other firms cut the price to dispose of the surplus, the price will fall to the equilibrium of $2.00. When the market price is below equilibrium, there will be a *shortage*. A price of $1.00 results in 100 million cans being demanded but only 60 million cans being supplied, or a shortage of 40 million cans. As consumers who are unable to buy energy drinks offer to pay higher prices, the price will rise to the equilibrium of $2.00.

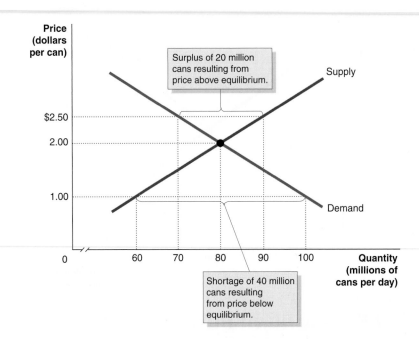

case, the shortage is equal to 40 million cans (100 million − 60 million = 40 million). When a shortage occurs, some consumers will be unable to buy energy drinks at the current price. In this situation, firms will realize that they can raise the price without losing sales. A higher price will simultaneously increase the quantity supplied and decrease the quantity demanded. This adjustment will reduce the shortage, but as long as the price is below $2.00, there will be a shortage, and upward pressure on the price will continue. Only when the price has risen to $2.00 will the market be in equilibrium.

At a competitive market equilibrium, all consumers willing to pay the market price will be able to buy as much of the product as they want, and all firms willing to accept the market price will be able to sell as much of the product as they want. As a result, there will be no reason for the price to change unless either the demand curve or the supply curve shifts.

### Demand and Supply Both Count

Keep in mind that the interaction of demand and supply determines the equilibrium price. Neither consumers nor firms can dictate what the equilibrium price will be. No firm can sell anything at any price unless it can find a willing buyer, and no consumer can buy anything at any price without finding a willing seller.

**3.4 LEARNING OBJECTIVE**

Use demand and supply graphs to predict changes in prices and quantities.

# The Effect of Demand and Supply Shifts on Equilibrium

We have seen that the interaction of demand and supply in markets determines the quantity of a good that is produced and the price at which it sells. We have also seen that several variables cause demand curves to shift, and other variables cause supply curves to shift. As a result, demand and supply curves in most markets are constantly shifting, and the prices and quantities that represent equilibrium are constantly changing. In this section, we look at how shifts in demand and supply curves affect equilibrium price and quantity.

## The Effect of Shifts in Supply on Equilibrium

When Coke started selling Full Throttle, the market supply curve for energy drinks shifted to the right. Figure 3-9 shows the supply curve shifting from $S_1$ to $S_2$. When the supply curve shifts to the right, there will be a surplus at the original equilibrium price, $P_1$. The surplus is eliminated as the equilibrium price falls to $P_2$, and the equilibrium quantity rises from $Q_1$ to $Q_2$. If existing firms exit the market, the supply curve will shift to the left, causing the equilibrium price to rise and the equilibrium quantity to fall.

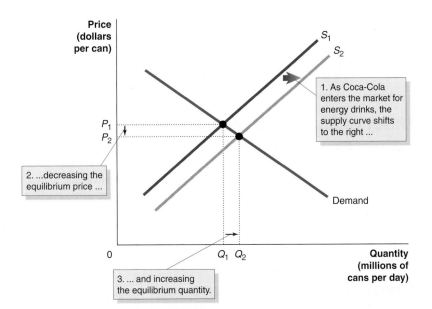

1. As Coca-Cola enters the market for energy drinks, the supply curve shifts to the right ...

2. ...decreasing the equilibrium price ...

3. ... and increasing the equilibrium quantity.

## Figure 3-9

### The Effect of an Increase in Supply on Equilibrium

If a firm enters a market, as Coca-Cola entered the market for energy drinks when it launched Full Throttle, the equilibrium price will fall, and the equilibrium quantity will rise:

1. As Coca-Cola enters the market for energy drinks, a larger quantity of energy drinks will be supplied at every price, so the market supply curve shifts to the right, from $S_1$ to $S_2$, which causes a surplus of cans at the original price, $P_1$.
2. The equilibrium price falls from $P_1$ to $P_2$.
3. The equilibrium quantity rises from $Q_1$ to $Q_2$.

## Making the Connection | The Falling Price of LCD Televisions

Research on flat-screen televisions using liquid crystal displays (LCDs) began in the 1960s. However, it was surprisingly difficult to use this research to produce a television with a low enough price for many consumers to purchase. One researcher noted, "In the 1960s, we used to say 'In ten years, we're going to have the TV on the wall.' We said the same thing in the seventies and then in the eighties." A key technical problem in manufacturing LCD televisions was making glass sheets large enough, thin enough, and clean enough to be used as LCD screens. Finally, in 1999, Corning, Inc., developed a process to manufacture glass that was less than 1 millimeter thick and very clean because it was produced without being touched by machinery.

Corning's breakthrough led to what the *Wall Street Journal* described as a "race to build new, better factories." For years, the leading firms were Korea's Samsung Electronics and LG Phillips LCD, Taiwan's AU Optronics, and Japan's Sharp Corporation. But in recent years, new firms, such as Vizio, headquartered in Irvine, California, have entered the market, and existing firms, such as Matsushita, which sells televisions under the Panasonic brand, have greatly expanded production. Matsushita's new Japanese factory will be able to produce as many as 15 million LCD screens a year by 2010. The figure below shows that an increase in supply drove the price of a typical large LCD television from $4,000 in fall 2004 to $1,000 at the end of 2008, increasing the quantity demanded worldwide from 8 million to 105 million.

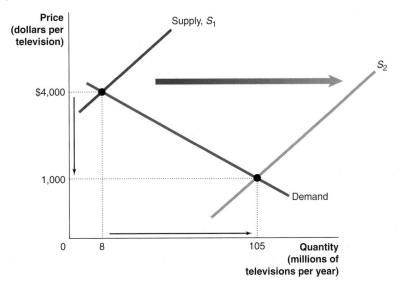

Sources: Daisuke Wakabayashi and Christopher Lawton, "TV Makers Confront a Shakeout," *Wall Street Journal*, January 20, 2009; David Richards, "Sony and Panasonic Flat Screen Kings," *Smarthouse.com*, February 13, 2007; and Evan Ramstad, "Big Display: Once a Footnote, Flat Screens Grow into Huge Industry," *Wall Street Journal*, August 30, 2004.

 **YOUR TURN:** For more practice, do related problem 4.7 on page 93 at the end of this chapter.

## The Effect of Shifts in Demand on Equilibrium

Because energy drinks are a normal good, when incomes increase, the market demand curve for energy drinks shifts to the right. Figure 3-10 shows the effect of a demand curve shifting to the right, from $D_1$ to $D_2$. This shift causes a shortage at the original equilibrium price, $P_1$. To eliminate the shortage, the equilibrium price rises to $P_2$, and the equilibrium quantity rises from $Q_1$ to $Q_2$. In contrast, if the price of a substitute good, such as colas, were to fall, the demand for energy drinks would decrease, shifting the demand curve for energy drinks to the left. When the demand curve shifts to the left, the equilibrium price and quantity will both decrease.

## The Effect of Shifts in Demand and Supply over Time

Whenever only demand or only supply shifts, we can easily predict the effect on equilibrium price and quantity. But what happens if *both* curves shift? For instance, in many markets, the demand curve shifts to the right over time, as population and income grow. The supply curve also often shifts to the right as new firms enter the market and positive technological change occurs. Whether the equilibrium price in a market rises or falls over time depends on whether demand shifts to the right more than does supply. Panel (a) of Figure 3-11 shows that when demand shifts to the right more than supply, the equilibrium price rises. But, as panel (b) shows, when supply shifts to the right more than demand, the equilibrium price falls.

Table 3-3 summarizes all possible combinations of shifts in demand and supply over time and the effects of the shifts on equilibrium price ($P$) and quantity ($Q$). For example, the entry in red in the table shows that if the demand curve shifts to the right and the supply curve also shifts to the right, the equilibrium quantity will increase, while the equilibrium price may increase, decrease, or remain unchanged. To make sure you understand each entry in the table, draw demand and supply graphs to check whether you can reproduce the predicted changes in equilibrium price and quantity. If the entry in the table says the predicted change in equilibrium price or quantity can be either an increase or a decrease, draw two graphs similar to panels (a) and (b) of Figure 3-11, one showing the equilibrium price or quantity increasing and the other showing it decreasing. Note also that in the ambiguous cases where either price or quantity might increase or decrease, it is also possible that price or quantity might remain unchanged. Be sure you understand why this is true.

## Figure 3-10

**The Effect of an Increase in Demand on Equilibrium**

Increases in income will cause the equilibrium price and quantity to rise:
1. Because energy drinks are a normal good, as income grows, the quantity demanded increases at every price, and the market demand curve shifts to the right, from $D_1$ to $D_2$, which causes a shortage of energy drinks at the original price, $P_1$.
2. The equilibrium price rises from $P_1$ to $P_2$.
3. The equilibrium quantity rises from $Q_1$ to $Q_2$.

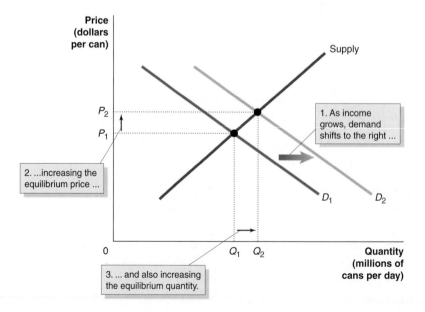

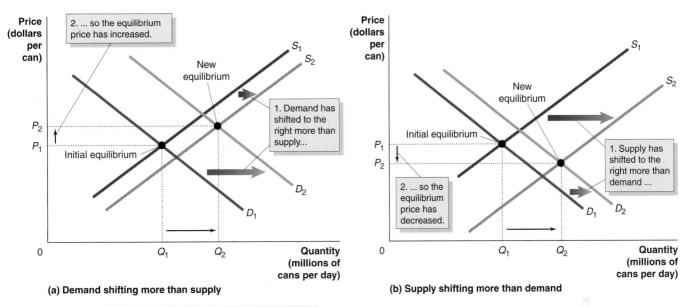

### Figure 3-11 | Shifts in Demand and Supply over Time

Whether the price of a product rises or falls over time depends on whether demand shifts to the right more than supply.

In panel (a), demand shifts to the right more than supply, and the equilibrium price rises:
1. Demand shifts to the right more than supply.
2. Equilibrium price rises from $P_1$ to $P_2$.

In panel (b), supply shifts to the right more than demand, and the equilibrium price falls:
1. Supply shifts to the right more than demand.
2. Equilibrium price falls from $P_1$ to $P_2$.

### TABLE 3-3

**How Shifts in Demand and Supply Affect Equilibrium Price (P) and Quantity (Q)**

|  | SUPPLY CURVE UNCHANGED | SUPPLY CURVE SHIFTS TO THE RIGHT | SUPPLY CURVE SHIFTS TO THE LEFT |
|---|---|---|---|
| **DEMAND CURVE UNCHANGED** | $Q$ unchanged<br>$P$ unchanged | $Q$ increases<br>$P$ decreases | $Q$ decreases<br>$P$ increases |
| **DEMAND CURVE SHIFTS TO THE RIGHT** | $Q$ increases<br>$P$ increases | $Q$ increases<br>$P$ increases or decreases | $Q$ increases or decreases<br>$P$ increases |
| **DEMAND CURVE SHIFTS TO THE LEFT** | $Q$ decreases<br>$P$ decreases | $Q$ increases or decreases<br>$P$ decreases | $Q$ decreases<br>$P$ increases or decreases |

# Solved Problem | 3-4

## High Demand and Low Prices in the Lobster Market?

During a typical spring, when demand for lobster is relatively low, Maine lobstermen are able to sell their lobster catches for about $6.00 per pound. During the summer, when demand for lobster is much higher, Maine lobstermen are able to sell their lobster catches for only about $4.00 per pound. As one

newspaper reporter observed: "Winter is the time when lobster prices typically climb to their highest levels of the year . . . ." It may seem strange that the market price is higher when demand is low than when demand is high. Can you resolve this paradox with the help of a demand and supply graph?

## SOLVING THE PROBLEM

**Step 1:** **Review the chapter material.** This problem is about how shifts in demand and supply curves affect the equilibrium price, so you may want to review the section "The Effect of Shifts in Demand and Supply over Time," which begins on page 82.

**Step 2:** **Draw the demand and supply graph.** Draw a demand and supply graph, showing the market equilibrium in the spring. Label the equilibrium price $6.00. Label both the demand and supply curves "spring."

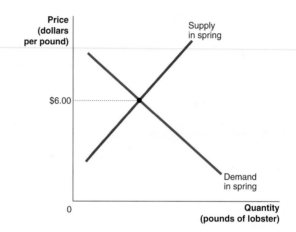

**Step 3:** **Add to your graph a demand curve for summer.**

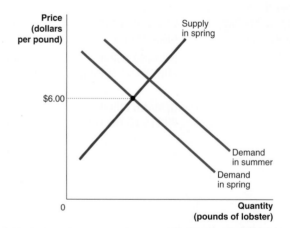

**Step 4:** **Explain the graph.** After studying the graph, it is possible to see how the equilibrium price can fall from $6.00 to $4.00, despite the increase in demand: The supply curve must have shifted to the right by enough to cause the equilibrium price to fall to $4.00. Draw the new supply curve, label it "summer," and label the new equilibrium price $4.00. The demand for lobster does increase in summer compared with the spring. But the increase in the supply of lobster between spring and summer is even greater. So, the equilibrium price falls.

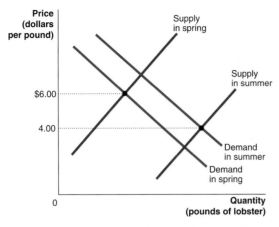

Source: Clarke Canfield, "Maine Lobster Prices Rebound," *Associated Press*, January 8, 2009.

**YOUR TURN:** For more practice, do related problems 4.5 and 4.6 on page 93 at the end of this chapter.

# Don't Let This Happen to **YOU!**

## Remember: A Change in a Good's Price Does *Not* Cause the Demand or Supply Curve to Shift

Suppose a student is asked to draw a demand and supply graph to illustrate how an increase in the price of oranges would affect the market for apples, other variables being constant. He draws the graph on the left below and explains it as follows: "Because apples and oranges are substitutes, an increase in the price of oranges will cause an initial shift to the right in the demand curve for apples, from $D_1$ to $D_2$. However, because this initial shift in the demand curve for apples results in a higher price for apples, $P_2$, consumers will find apples less desirable, and the demand curve will shift to the left, from $D_2$ to $D_3$, resulting in a final equilibrium price of $P_3$." Do you agree or disagree with the student's analysis?

You should disagree. The student has correctly understood that an increase in the price of oranges will cause the demand curve for apples to shift to the right. But the second

demand curve shift the student describes, from $D_2$ to $D_3$, will not take place. Changes in the price of a product do not result in shifts in the product's demand curve. Changes in the price of a product result only in movements along a demand curve.

The graph on the right below shows the correct analysis. The increase in the price of oranges causes the demand curve for apples to increase from $D_1$ to $D_2$. At the original price, $P_1$, the increase in demand initially results in a shortage of apples equal to $Q_3 - Q_1$. But, as we have seen, a shortage causes the price to increase until the shortage is eliminated. In this case, the price will rise to $P_2$, where the quantity demanded and the quantity supplied are both equal to $Q_2$. Notice that the increase in price causes a decrease in the *quantity demanded*, from $Q_3$ to $Q_2$, but does *not* cause a decrease in demand.

**YOUR TURN:** Test your understanding by doing related problems 4.13 and 4.14 on page 94 at the end of this chapter.

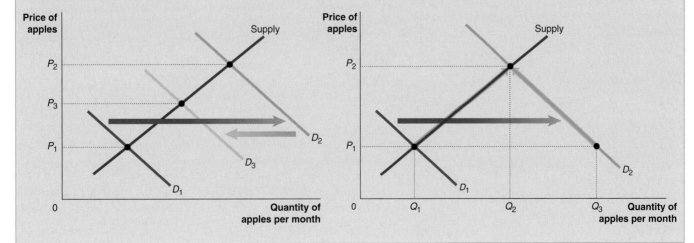

## Shifts in a Curve versus Movements along a Curve

When analyzing markets using demand and supply curves, it is important to remember that *when a shift in a demand or supply curve causes a change in equilibrium price, the change in price does not cause a further shift in demand or supply.* For instance, suppose an increase in supply causes the price of a good to fall, while everything else that affects the willingness of consumers to buy the good is constant. The result will be an increase in the quantity demanded but not an increase in demand. For demand to increase, the whole curve must shift. The point is the same for supply: If the price of the good falls but everything else that affects the willingness of sellers to supply the good is constant, the quantity supplied decreases, but the supply does not. For supply to decrease, the whole curve must shift.

▶ Continued from page 65

## Economics in YOUR Life!

### Will You Drink Red Bull or Monster?

At the beginning of the chapter, we asked you to consider two questions: Would you choose to buy a can of Monster Energy if it had a lower price than a can of Red Bull? and Would you be less likely to drink Monster Energy if your income had declined? To determine the answer to the first question, you have to recognize that Red Bull and Monster Energy are substitutes. If you consider the two drinks to be very close substitutes, then you are likely to buy the one with the lower price. In the market, if consumers generally believe that Red Bull and Monster Energy are close substitutes, a fall in the price of Monster Energy will increase the quantity of Monster Energy demanded and decrease the demand for Red Bull. Suppose that you are currently buying Red Bull, despite its higher price, because you prefer its taste. If you switch to Monster Energy when your income declines—perhaps because you have lost your job during a recession—then Monster Energy is an inferior good for you.

# Conclusion

The interaction of demand and supply determines market equilibrium. The model of demand and supply is a powerful tool for predicting how changes in the actions of consumers and firms will cause changes in equilibrium prices and quantities. As we have seen in this chapter, we can use the model to analyze markets that do not meet all the requirements for being perfectly competitive. As long as there is intense competition among sellers, the model of demand and supply can often successfully predict changes in prices and quantities. We will use the model in the next chapter to analyze economic efficiency and the results of government-imposed price floors and price ceilings.

Before moving on to Chapter 4, read *An Inside Look* on the next page to learn how Red Bull uses advertising to increase demand.

## >> How Does Advertising Help Red Bull Increase Demand for Its Energy Drink?

*USA TODAY*

### Marketers Get to Us in More Ways; Pitches Harder to Spot, Writer Says

It's marketing mayhem out there. It's subtle. It's subversive. And it's murky. . . . And murky is a stealthy way to sell. . . .

Most people say that brands and logos mean nothing to them. They say they buy things based on a handful of factors—experience, recommendations from friends, price, convenience, quality and pleasure. And sometimes, for ethical reasons.

[a] [Author and journalist Rob] Walker isn't buying it. "There are probably more pretty good products being sold in America now than at any time in history. This is a tribute to progress, but it both complicates our decision making as consumers," . . . and makes it difficult for one product to stand out.

As a result, people are creating their own brands and participating in marketing campaigns for their favorite products. Motivated consumers are even creating Internet video ads and becoming loyal word-of-mouth agents for their brand du jour. [Walker argues that] "Everybody sees right through traditional advertising. You'd have to be an idiot not to recognize that you're being pitched to when watching a 30-second commercial." . . . But contrary to the belief that today's short-attention-span consumer is impervious to marketing, and that big brands no longer matter, Walker argues that marketing methods are stronger than ever, just harder

to spot. It's what he calls "murketing," and it's omnipresent.

"We live in a world defined by more commercial messages, not fewer." They range from deals to place products and brand mentions in movies, computer games, comic books and cult online Web video shows. Dunkin' Donuts recruits teens to wear temporary tattoos of its logo on their foreheads. Toyota bankrolls underground club parties. And so on.

. . . [I]nsights from cutting-edge marketers, entrepreneurs and artists . . . [include] case studies of resurging old brands such as Timberland and Pabst Blue Ribbon beer, as well as hot-selling energy drink Red Bull and Lance Armstrong's Livestrong bracelet . . . [N]ow more than ever consumers are what they buy and vice versa. How can tossing back a can of Red Bull, for instance, do just that for a sorority girl and an extreme sports nut at the same time?

[b] . . . Easy. Symbols aren't defined by rational rules. They are open to individual interpretations. For sorority sisters at Tulane University, it's a fashionable drink that says something like, "Look, I can afford to pay three bucks for this ridiculous drink." . . . For others, "It is perceived as a drink that improves performance ." . . .

Red Bull's vibe didn't just happen. . . . The company invested in an array of projects from sponsoring extreme sports to running break-dance competitions to installing ads in nightclubs. "There was something oddly unfocused and inconsistent about the Red Bull message. . . . The company really never offered any rational explanation of what the stuff was all about and who was supposed

to drink it." . . . "It never sent a clear message to the masses."

. . . By cobbling together small niche audiences, Red Bull has built a mass audience. "Each group simply thinks Red Bull is something for them, partly because they have never been told otherwise." . . .

For Red Bull, it turns out murky is not only OK, it's the whole point. Red Bull's makers didn't want a "unified, top-down centrally defined meaning."

"Murky is why rumors are not a corporate headache—they help." . . . One of the drink's ingredients, taurine, an amino acid, is rumored to be bull semen, bull testosterone, an aphrodisiac and so on. The company laughs it off, creating a certain mystique to the brand.

[c] . . . It isn't the brand that defines you. You define the brand. It's always been that way. "The significance of the material things and symbols that mean the most has always flowed from us to the object, not the other way around," he concludes. We give meaning and values to symbols. "You surround yourself with who you are."

"It's not just about what a product is made of or what it's supposed to do." . . .

"Nor is it just about a brand image invented by experts and foisted on the masses, who swallow it whole. Any product or brand that catches on in the marketplace does so because of us: Because enough of us decided that it had value or meaning and chose to participate." . . .

*Source:* Kerry Hannon, "Marketers Get to Us in More Ways; Pitches Harder to Spot, Writer Says" (a book review of Rob Walker's *Buying In: The Secret Dialogue Between What We Buy and Who We Are*), *USA TODAY*, August 25, 2008, p. 5B.

## Key Points in the Article

The article is a review of a book on marketing by Rob Walker. Walker discusses Red Bull's marketing strategy, which is designed to appeal to many different types of consumers. Red Bull has sponsored extreme sports, break-dancing contests, and nightclub ads. The company never created a clear message as to who should purchase the product or why. Instead, the company allowed consumers to develop their own opinions of Red Bull. Advertisers refer to this approach as "murky" marketing, or "murketing." The article argues that a brand acquires an image from its consumers rather than the other way around.

## Analyzing the News

(a) In a market system, any successful product finds that it quickly gets copied. If consumers start to develop a taste for energy drinks, rather than conventional soft drinks, firms will respond to this shift in tastes by entering the market for energy drinks. Increasing competition makes it difficult for any one good to stand out. One key to success in a competitive market is to develop a marketing strategy that convinces consumers that in some important way your product is different from the many substitute products available.

(b) Consumers' preferences, or tastes, play a key role in determining the demand for a good. This article points out that consumers like Red Bull for different reasons. Some like Red Bull because drinking it has become trendy, and these people want to drink what their friends are drinking. Others prefer Red Bull for its tangible qualities, such as its high caffeine content. In some cases, consumers will desire a good for "practical" reasons. In other cases, consumers value a good because of how it makes them feel about themselves, or what image it projects. Because one good can invoke different responses in different people, each consumer will attach a different value to the good. Thus, at a high price, some consumers will find the benefit they receive from consuming the good exceeds the price and they will buy the good. At a lower price, more consumers will find the benefit from consuming the good will exceed the price.

(c) Consumer demand for a product depends on many factors. The article identifies several of these factors: what the product does, what the product is made of, and the image that the product projects. Consumers choose products that have characteristics that the consumers value. Marketers try to convince consumers that their product has these favorable characteristics. The figure shows how a success-

ful marketing campaign can affect the demand for a good. If Red Bull succeeds in its "murketing" campaign, it will increase the number of consumers who prefer Red Bull to competing products at each price. The demand curve for Red Bull will shift to the right, increasing both the quantity sold and the price. Although the figure shows the results of a successful marketing effort, one of the challenges that companies like Red Bull face is adapting their marketing plans to constantly changing consumer tastes.

## Thinking Critically

1. Name some complements and substitutes for the Red Bull energy drink.
2. In 2008, Red Bull lost its position as the best-selling energy drink. Red Bull's market share was 24.6 percent compared to Monster Energy's 27.6 percent share. Draw a demand and supply graph that shows the market for Red Bull as Monster Energy's competing energy drink becomes more popular.

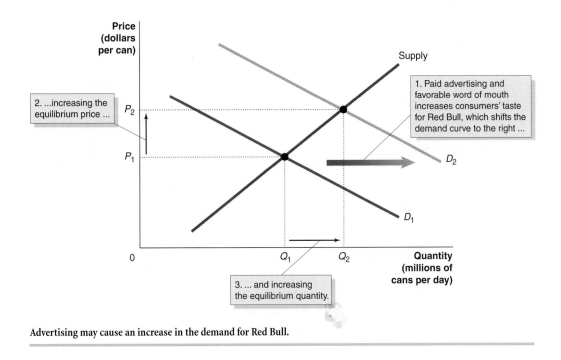

Advertising may cause an increase in the demand for Red Bull.

## Key Terms

*Ceteris paribus* ("all else equal") condition, p. 68

Competitive market equilibrium, p. 79

Complements, p. 70

Demand curve, p. 66

Demand schedule, p. 66

Demographics, p. 70

Income effect, p. 67

Inferior good, p. 69

Law of demand, p. 67

Law of supply, p. 75

Market demand, p. 66

Market equilibrium, p. 79

Normal good, p. 69

Perfectly competitive market, p. 66

Quantity demanded, p. 66

Quantity supplied, p. 74

Shortage, p. 79

Substitutes, p. 69

Substitution effect, p. 67

Supply curve, p. 74

Supply schedule, p. 74

Surplus, p. 79

Technological change, p. 76

---

**3.1**    **The Demand Side of the Market, pages 66–74**
LEARNING OBJECTIVE: Discuss the variables that influence demand.

## Summary

The model of demand and supply is the most powerful in economics. The model applies exactly only to **perfectly competitive markets**, where there are many buyers and sellers, all the products sold are identical, and there are no barriers to new sellers entering the market. But the model can also be useful in analyzing markets that don't meet all these requirements. The **quantity demanded** is the amount of a good or service that a consumer is willing and able to purchase at a given price. A **demand schedule** is a table that shows the relationship between the price of a product and the quantity of the product demanded. A **demand curve** is a graph that shows the relationship between the price of a good and the quantity of the good demanded. **Market demand** is the demand by all consumers of a given good or service. The **law of demand** states that *ceteris paribus*—holding everything else constant—the quantity of a product demanded increases when the price falls and decreases when the price rises. Demand curves slope downward because of the **substitution effect**, which is the change in quantity demanded that results from a price change making one good more or less expensive relative to another good, and the income effect, which is the change in quantity demanded of a good that results from the effect of a change in the good's price on consumer purchasing power. Changes in income, the prices of related goods, tastes, population and demographics, and expected future prices all cause the demand curve to shift. **Substitutes** are goods that can be used for the same purpose. **Complements** are goods that are used together. A **normal good** is a good for which demand increases as income increases. An **inferior good** is a good for which demand decreases as income increases. **Demographics** are the characteristics of a population with respect to age, race, and gender. A change in demand refers to a shift of the demand curve. A change in quantity demanded refers to a movement along the demand curve as a result of a change in the product's price.

 Visit **www.myeconlab.com** to complete these exercises online and get instant feedback.

## Review Questions

1.1 What is a demand schedule? What is a demand curve?

1.2 What do economists mean when they use the Latin expression *ceteris paribus*?

1.3 What is the difference between a change in demand and a change in quantity demanded?

1.4 What is the law of demand? What are the main variables that will cause the demand curve to shift? Give an example of each.

## Problems and Applications

1.5 For each of the following pairs of products, state which are complements, which are substitutes, and which are unrelated.
   a. Pepsi and Coke
   b. Oscar Mayer hot dogs and Wonder hot dog buns
   c. Jif peanut butter and Smucker's strawberry jam
   d. iPods and Texas Instruments financial calculators

1.6 **(Related to the *Chapter Opener* on page 65)** When Red Bull entered the U.S. market in 1997, it was one of the very few energy drinks available. Now, dozens of energy drinks are being sold. Discuss the effect on Red Bull's demand curve from the entry of these new energy drinks. Will your answer be different if it turns out that the advertising of these new drinks has increased consumers' taste for energy drinks in general? Briefly explain.

1.7 State whether each of the following events will result in a movement along the demand curve for McDonald's Big Mac hamburgers or whether it will cause the curve to shift. If the demand curve shifts, indicate whether it will shift to the left or to the right and draw a graph to illustrate the shift.
   a. The price of Burger King's Whopper hamburger declines.

b. McDonald's distributes coupons for $1.00 off the purchase of a Big Mac.

c. Because of a shortage of potatoes, the price of French fries increases.

d. KFC raises the price of a bucket of fried chicken.

e. The U.S. economy enters a period of rapid growth in incomes.

1.8 **(Related to the *Making the Connection* on page 69)** According to an article in the *New York Times*:

> The recession seems to have a sweet tooth. As unemployment has risen ... Americans, particularly adults, have been consuming growing volumes of candy, from Mary Janes and Tootsie Rolls to Gummy Bears and cheap chocolates, say candy makers, store owners and industry experts.

If the article is accurate, is candy a normal good or an inferior good? Briefly explain what characteristics of candy relative to related goods might make it a normal good or an inferior good.

Source: Christine Haughney, "When Economy Sours, Tootsie Rolls Soothe Souls," *New York Times*, March 24, 2009.

1.9 **(Related to the *Making the Connection* on page 70)** Name three products whose demand is likely to increase rapidly if the following demo-graphic groups increase at a faster rate than the population as a whole:

a. Teenagers

b. Children under age five

c. Recent immigrants

1.10 Suppose the following table shows the price of a base model Toyota Prius hybrid and the quantity of Priuses sold for three years. Do these data indicate that the demand curve for Priuses is upward sloping? Explain.

| YEAR | PRICE | QUANTITY |
|------|-------|----------|
| 2008 | $24,880 | 35,265 |
| 2009 | 24,550 | 33,250 |
| 2010 | 25,250 | 36,466 |

1.11 **(Related to the *Making the Connection* on page 73)** In early 2009, some analysts of the beverage industry believed that sales of energy drinks might increase by only 5 percent during the year. What factors could affect the accuracy of this forecast? Are forecasts of energy drink sales likely to be more or less accurate than forecasts of cola drink sales during the same time period? Briefly explain.

**>> End Learning Objective 3.1**

---

## 3.2 | The Supply Side of the Market, pages 74–78

LEARNING OBJECTIVE: Discuss the variables that influence supply.

## Summary

The **quantity supplied** is the amount of a good that a firm is willing and able to supply at a given price. A **supply schedule** is a table that shows the relationship between the price of a product and the quantity of the product supplied. A **supply curve** shows on a graph the relationship between the price of a product and the quantity of the product supplied. When the price of a product rises, producing the product is more profitable, and a greater amount will be supplied. The **law of supply** states that, holding everything else constant, the quantity of a product supplied increases when the price rises and decreases when the price falls. Changes in the prices of inputs, technology, the prices of substitutes in production, expected future prices, and the number of firms in a market all cause the supply curve to shift. **Technological change** is a positive or negative change in the ability of a firm to produce a given level of output with a given quantity of inputs. A change in supply refers to a shift of the supply curve. A change in quantity supplied refers to a movement along the supply curve as a result of a change in the product's price.

 Visit **www.myeconlab.com** to complete these exercises online and get instant feedback.

## Review Questions

2.1 What is a supply schedule? What is a supply curve?

2.2 What is the law of supply? What are the main variables that will cause a supply curve to shift? Give an example of each.

## Problems and Applications

2.3 Briefly explain whether each of the following statements describes a change in supply or a change in the quantity supplied.

a. To take advantage of high prices for snow shovels during a very snowy winter, Alexander Shovels, Inc., decides to increase output.

b. The success of Red Bull leads more firms to begin producing energy drinks.

c. In the six months following Hurricane Katrina in 2005, production of oil in the Gulf of Mexico declined by 25 percent.

**2.4** Will each firm in a given industry always supply the same quantity as every other firm at each price? What factors might cause the quantity of energy drinks supplied by each firm at each price to be different?

**2.5** If the price of a good increases, is the increase in the quantity of the good supplied likely to be smaller or larger, the longer the time period being considered? Briefly explain.

**2.6** (Related to *Solved Problem 3-2* on page 77) Television programming in Illinois features many commercials directed at farmers. Ads for fertilizer, seed, and farm equipment are as common as commercials for laundry soap and soft drinks. Much of the nation's corn is grown in Illinois, but the climate and soil conditions in the state are well suited for growing soybeans as well. Farmers face a choice each year to plant corn or soybeans or a combination of the two crops.

a. What effect will an increase in the price of soybeans have on the supply curve for corn?

b. What effect will an increase in the price of soybeans have on the supply curve for soybeans?

>> **End Learning Objective 3.2**

---

 **3.3**   **Market Equilibrium: Putting Demand and Supply Together**, pages 79–80
LEARNING OBJECTIVE: Use a graph to illustrate market equilibrium.

## Summary

**Market equilibrium** occurs where the demand curve intersects the supply curve. A **competitive market equilibrium** has a market equilibrium with many buyers and many sellers. Only at this point is the quantity demanded equal to the quantity supplied. Prices above equilibrium result in **surpluses**, with the quantity supplied being greater than the quantity demanded. Surpluses cause the market price to fall. Prices below equilibrium result in **shortages**, with the quantity demanded being greater than the quantity supplied. Shortages cause the market price to rise.

 Visit **www.myeconlab.com** to complete these exercises online and get instant feedback.

## Review Questions

**3.1** What do economists mean by *market equilibrium*?

**3.2** What happens in a market if the current price is above the equilibrium price? What happens if the current price is below the equilibrium price?

## Problems and Applications

**3.3** Briefly explain whether you agree with the following statement: "When there is a shortage of a good, consumers eventually give up trying to buy it, so the demand for the good declines, and the price falls until the market is finally in equilibrium."

**3.4** If a market is in equilibrium, is it necessarily true that all buyers and all sellers are satisfied with the market price? Briefly explain.

>> **End Learning Objective 3.3**

---

 **3.4**   **The Effect of Demand and Supply Shifts on Equilibrium, pages 80–87**
LEARNING OBJECTIVE: Use demand and supply graphs to predict changes in prices and quantities.

## Summary

In most markets, demand and supply curves shift frequently, causing changes in equilibrium prices and quantities. Over time, if demand increases more than supply, equilibrium price will rise. If supply increases more than demand, equilibrium price will fall.

 Visit **www.myeconlab.com** to complete these exercises online and get instant feedback.

## Review Questions

**4.1** Draw a demand and supply graph to show the effect on the equilibrium price in a market in the following two situations:
a. The demand curve shifts to the right.
b. The supply curve shifts to the left.

**4.2** If, over time, the demand curve for a product shifts to the right more than the supply curve does, what will happen to the equilibrium price? What will happen to the equilibrium price if the supply curve shifts to the right more than the demand curve? For each case, draw a demand and supply graph to illustrate your answer.

## Problems and Applications

**4.3** As oil prices rose during 2006, the demand for alternative fuels increased. Ethanol, one alternative fuel, is made from corn. According to an article in the *Wall Street Journal*, the price of tortillas, which are made from corn, also rose during 2006: "The price spike [in tortillas] is part of a ripple effect from the ethanol boom."

    a. Draw a demand and supply graph for the corn market and use it to show the effect on this market of an increase in the demand for ethanol. Be sure to indicate the equilibrium price and quantity before and after the increase in the demand for ethanol.

    b. Draw a demand and supply graph for the tortilla market and use it to show the effect on this market of an increase in the price of corn. Once again, be sure to indicate the equilibrium price and quantity before and after the increase in the demand for ethanol.

    c. During 2009, the demand for gasoline had fallen, lowering its price. The demand for ethanol had declined as well. Ethanol producers, though, were asking the Environmental Protection Agency (EPA) to raise the allowable amount of ethanol in gasoline blends from 10 percent to 15 percent. If the EPA were to agree to this proposal, what would be the likely effect on tortilla prices?

Source: Stephen Power, "Industry Seeks to Raise Ethanol Levels in Fuel," *Wall Street Journal*, March 7, 2009; and Mark Gongloff, "Tortilla Soup," *Wall Street Journal*, January 25, 2007.

**4.4** A recent study indicated that "stricter college alcohol policies, such as raising the price of alcohol, or banning alcohol on campus, decrease the number of students who use marijuana."

    a. On the basis of this information, are alcohol and marijuana substitutes or complements?

    b. Suppose that campus authorities reduce the supply of alcohol on campus. Use demand and supply graphs to illustrate the impact on the campus alcohol and marijuana markets.

Source: Jenny Williams, Rosalie Pacula, Frank Chaloupka, and Henry Wechsler, "Alcohol and Marijuana Use Among College Students: Economic Complements or Substitutes?" *Health Economics*, Volume 13, Issue 9, September 2005, pp. 825–843.

**4.5** (Related to *Solved Problem 3-4* on page 83) The demand for watermelons is highest during summer and lowest during winter. Yet watermelon prices are normally lower in summer than in winter. Use a demand and supply graph to demonstrate how this is possible. Be sure to carefully label the curves in your graph and to clearly indicate the equilibrium summer price and the equilibrium winter price.

**4.6** (Related to *Solved Problem 3-4* on page 83) According to one observer of the lobster market: "After Labor Day, when the vacationers have gone home, the lobstermen usually have a month or more of good fishing conditions, except for the occasional hurricane." Use a demand and supply graph to explain whether lobster prices are likely to be higher or lower during the fall than during the summer.

Source: Jay Harlow, "Lobster: An Affordable Luxury," *Sallybernstein.com*.

**4.7** (Related to the *Making the Connection* on page 81) During 2009, the demand for LCD televisions appeared to be falling. At the same time, some industry observers expected that several smaller television manufacturers might exit the market. Use a demand and supply graph to analyze the effects of these factors on the equilibrium price and quantity of LCD televisions. Clearly show on your graph the old equilibrium price and quantity and the new equilibrium price and quantity. Can you tell for certain whether the new equilibrium price will be higher or lower than the old equilibrium price? Briefly explain.

**4.8** According to an article in the *Wall Street Journal*, in early 2009, the prices of airline tickets in the United States had dropped by 40 percent at the same time that U.S. airlines had reduced the number of planes they had in service, thereby reducing the supply of airline seats. Use a demand and supply graph to illustrate how it is possible for the supply of airline seats available at every price to have declined at the same time that the equilibrium price fell.

Source: Mike Esterl, "Airlines Slash Fares to Fill Up Empty Seats," *Wall Street Journal*, March 4, 2009.

**4.9** An article in the *Wall Street Journal* notes that during early 2009 the demand for Internet advertising was declining at the same time that the number of Internet sites accepting advertising was increasing. After reading the article, a student argues: "From this information, we know that the price of Internet ads should fall, but we don't know whether the total quantity of Internet ads will increase or decrease." Is the student's analysis correct? Illustrate your answer with a demand and supply graph.

Source: Martin Peers, "Future Shock for Internet Ads?" *Wall Street Journal*, February 17, 2009.

**4.10** Richard Polsky is an art dealer and the author of annual guides to the art market. In one article, Polsky speculated on the market for 50 heavily traded artists' works. Listing each artist's works as "buy," "sell," or "hold," Polsky gave his opinions on the state of the auction market for the works of these artists. The following table lists three of the artists mentioned in the article. The table contains each artist's name, date of birth and (if applicable) death, Polsky's recommended action, and his comments about the market for each of the listed artist's works. Use the information contained in the table to draw a demand and supply graph for the works of each of the three artists listed, based on the author's comments and recommendations to buy, sell, or hold.

| ARTIST | ACTION | COMMENTS |
|---|---|---|
| Roy Lichtenstein (1923–1997) | Buy | "The highest batting average of any artist over the last 50 years—Lichtenstein rarely faltered. If the art market ever blows up, the three safest bets will be Warhol, Calder and Lichtenstein." |
| Cindy Sherman (1954–) | Hold | "From a market perspective, she is historically important as the first photographer that the auction houses grouped with painters in a sale. She paved the way for the large-scale picture takers who went on to bring painter-like money (Gursky, Struth, etc). However, Sherman's color prints will probably never command the big bucks until she pumps up the size." |
| Marlene Dumas (1953–) | Sell | "Ridiculous. I don't care what 'insiders' tell me about the significance of her work. If she can paint, I haven't seen evidence of it. And at $1 million–$3 million per picture at auction, there better be something happening there that goes beyond talk." |

Source: Richard Polsky, "Art Market Guide 2007," *artnet Magazine*, October 9, 2007.

**4.11** Historically, the production of many perishable foods, such as dairy products, was highly seasonal. Thus, as the supply of those products fluctuated, prices tended to fluctuate tremendously—typically by 25 to 50 percent or more—over the course of the year. One impact of mechanical refrigeration, which was commercialized on a large scale in the last decade of the nineteenth century, was that suppliers could store perishables from one season to the next. Economists have estimated that as a result of refrigerated storage, wholesale prices rose by roughly 10 percent during peak supply periods, while they fell by almost the same amount during the off season. Use a demand and supply graph for each season to illustrate how refrigeration affected the market for perishable food.

Source: Lee A. Craig, Barry Goodwin, and Thomas Grennes, "The Effect of Mechanical Refrigeration on Nutrition in the U.S.," *Social Science History*, Vol. 28, No. 2, Summer 2004, pp. 327–328.

**4.12** Briefly explain whether each of the following statements is true or false.
   a. If the demand and supply for a product both increase, the equilibrium quantity of the product must also increase.
   b. If the demand and supply for a product both increase, the equilibrium price of the product must also increase.

   c. If the demand for a product decreases and the supply of the product increases, the equilibrium price of the product may increase or decrease, depending on whether supply or demand has shifted more.

**4.13** (Related to the *Don't Let This Happen to You!* on page 85) A student writes the following: "Increased production leads to a lower price, which in turn increases demand." Do you agree with his reasoning? Briefly explain.

**4.14** (Related to the *Don't Let This Happen to You!* on page 85) A student was asked to draw a demand and supply graph to illustrate the effect on the laptop computer market of a fall in the price of computer hard drives, *ceteris paribus*. She drew the graph at the top of the column on the next page and explained it as follows:

> Hard drives are an input to laptop computers, so a fall in the price of hard drives will cause the supply curve for personal computers to shift to the right (from $S_1$ to $S_2$). Because this shift in the supply curve results in a lower price ($P_2$), consumers will want to buy more laptops, and the demand curve will shift to the right (from $D_1$ to $D_2$). We know that more laptops will be sold, but we can't be sure whether the price of laptops will rise or fall. That depends on whether the supply curve or the demand curve has shifted farther to the right. I assume that the effect on supply is greater than the effect on demand, so I show the final equilibrium price ($P_3$) as being lower than the initial equilibrium price ($P_1$).

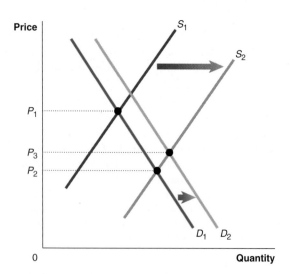

Explain whether you agree or disagree with the student's analysis. Be careful to explain exactly what—if anything—you find wrong with her analysis.

**4.15** Following are four graphs and four market scenarios, each of which would cause either a movement along the supply curve for Pepsi or a shift of the supply curve. Match each scenario with the appropriate graph.
  **a.** A decrease in the supply of Coke
  **b.** A drop in the average household income in the United States from $44,000 to $43,000

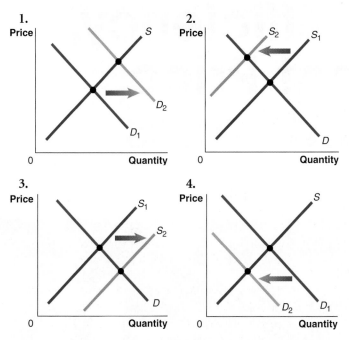

  **c.** An improvement in soft drink bottling technology
  **d.** An increase in the prices of sugar and high-fructose corn syrup

**4.16** David Surdam, an economist at Loyola University of Chicago, made the following observation about the world cotton market at the beginning of the Civil War:

> As the supply of American-grown raw cotton decreased and the price of raw cotton increased, there would be a *movement along* the supply curve of non-American raw cotton suppliers, and the quantity supplied by these producers would increase.

Illustrate this observation with one demand and supply graph for the market for American-grown cotton and another demand and supply graph for the market for non-American cotton. Make sure your graphs clearly show (1) the initial equilibrium before the decrease in the supply of American-grown cotton and (2) the final equilibrium. Also clearly show any shifts in the demand and supply curves for each market.

Source: David G. Surdam, "King Cotton: Monarch or Pretender? The State of the Market for Raw Cotton on the Eve of the American Civil War," *The Economic History Review*, Vol. 51, No. 1, February 1998, p. 116.

**4.17** Proposals have been made to increase government regulation of firms providing childcare services by, for instance, setting education requirements for childcare workers. Suppose that these regulations increase the quality of childcare and cause the demand for childcare services to increase. At the same time, assume that complying with the new government regulations increases the costs of firms providing childcare services. Draw a demand and supply graph to illustrate the effects of these changes in the market for childcare services. Briefly explain whether the total quantity of childcare services purchased will increase or decrease as a result of regulation.

**4.18** Below are the supply and demand functions for two markets. One of the markets is for BMW automobiles, and the other is for a cancer-fighting drug, without which lung cancer patients will die. Briefly explain which graph most likely represents which market.

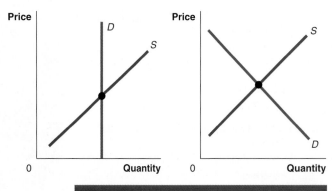

>> **End Learning Objective 3.4**

# CHAPTER 4

# Economic Efficiency, Government Price Setting, and Taxes

## Chapter Outline and Learning Objectives

## >> Should the Government Control Apartment Rents?

Robert F. Moss owns an apartment building in New York City. Unlike most other business owners, he is not free to charge the prices he would like for the service he offers. In New York, San Francisco, Los Angeles, and nearly 200 smaller cities, apartments are subject to rent control by the local government. Rent control puts a legal limit on the rent that landlords can charge for an apartment.

New York City has 2 million apartments, about 70 percent of which are subject to rent control. The other 1 million apartments have their rents determined in the market by the demand and supply for apartments. Mr. Moss's building includes apartments that are rent controlled and apartments that are not. The market-determined rents are usually far above the controlled rents. The government regulations that determine what Mr. Moss can charge for a rent-controlled apartment are very complex. The following is Mr. Moss's description:

> When [an apartment] is vacated, state rent laws entitle landlords to raise rents in three primary ways: a vacancy increase of 20 percent for a new tenant's two-year lease (a bit less for a one-year lease); one-fortieth per month of the cost of any improvements, and a "longevity bonus" for longtime residents (calculated at six-tenths of 1 percent times the tenant's last legal rent multiplied by the number of years of residency beyond eight). . . . Apartments renting for $2,000 a month are automatically deregulated if they are vacant. Occupied apartments whose rent reaches that figure can be deregulated if the income of the tenants has been $175,000 or more for two years.

As this description shows, someone earning a living by renting out apartments in New York City has to deal with much more complex government regulation of prices than someone who owns, for instance, a McDonald's restaurant.

Tenants in rent-controlled apartments in New York are very reluctant to see rent control end because rents for those apartments are much lower than rents for apartments that aren't rent controlled. As we will see in this chapter, however, rent control can also cause significant problems for renters.

**AN INSIDE LOOK AT POLICY** on **page 118** explores the debate over rent control laws in New York.

Source: Robert F. Moss, "A Landlord's Lot Is Sometimes Not an Easy One," *New York Times*, August 3, 2003, Section 11, p. 1.

---

## Economics in YOUR LIFE!

### Does Rent Control Make It Easier for You to Find an Affordable Apartment?

Suppose you have job offers in two cities. One factor in deciding which job to accept is whether you can find an affordable apartment. If one city has rent control, are you more likely to find an affordable apartment in that city, or would you be better off looking for an apartment in a city without rent control? As you read the chapter, see if you can answer this question. You can check your answer against the one we provide at the end of the chapter.

▶ Continued on page 117

W e saw in Chapter 3 that, in a competitive market, the price adjusts to ensure that the quantity demanded equals the quantity supplied. Stated another way, in equilibrium, every consumer willing to pay the market price is able to buy as much of the product as the consumer wants, and every firm willing to accept the market price can sell as much as it wants. Even so, consumers would naturally prefer to pay a lower price, and sellers would prefer to receive a higher price. Normally, consumers and firms have no choice but to accept the equilibrium price if they wish to participate in the market. Occasionally, however, consumers succeed in having the government impose a **price ceiling**, which is a legally determined maximum price that sellers may charge. Rent control is an example of a price ceiling. Firms also sometimes succeed in having the government impose a **price floor**, which is a legally determined minimum price that sellers may receive. In markets for farm products such as milk, the government has been setting price floors that are above the equilibrium market price since the 1930s.

Another way the government intervenes in markets is by imposing taxes. The government relies on the revenue raised from taxes to finance its operations. Unfortunately, whenever the government imposes a price ceiling, a price floor, or a tax, there are predictable negative economic consequences. It is important for government policymakers and voters to understand the negative consequences when evaluating these policies. Economists have developed the concepts of *consumer surplus*, *producer surplus*, and *economic surplus* to analyze the economic effects of price ceilings, price floors, and taxes.

**Price ceiling** A legally determined maximum price that sellers may charge.

**Price floor** A legally determined minimum price that sellers may receive.

**4.1 LEARNING** OBJECTIVE

Distinguish between the concepts of consumer surplus and producer surplus.

# Consumer Surplus and Producer Surplus

Consumer surplus measures the dollar benefit consumers receive from buying goods or services in a particular market. Producer surplus measures the dollar benefit firms receive from selling goods or services in a particular market. Economic surplus in a market is the sum of consumer surplus plus producer surplus. As we will see, *when the government imposes a price ceiling or a price floor, the amount of economic surplus in a market is reduced*—in other words, price ceilings and price floors reduce the total benefit to consumers and firms from buying and selling in a market. To understand why this is true, we need to understand how consumer surplus and producer surplus are determined.

## Consumer Surplus

**Consumer surplus** is the difference between the highest price a consumer is willing to pay for a good or service and the price the consumer actually pays. For example, suppose you are in Wal-Mart, and you see a DVD of *Star Trek* on the rack. No price is indicated on the package, so you take it over to the register to check the price. As you walk to the register, you think to yourself that $20 is the highest price you would be willing to pay. At the register, you find out that the price is actually $12, so you buy the DVD. Your consumer surplus in this example is $8: the difference between the $20 you were willing to pay and the $12 you actually paid.

We can use the demand curve to measure the total consumer surplus in a market. Demand curves show the willingness of consumers to purchase a product at different prices. Consumers are willing to purchase a product up to the point where the marginal benefit of consuming a product is equal to its price. The **marginal benefit** is the additional benefit to a consumer from consuming one more unit of a good or service. As a simple example, suppose there are only four consumers in the market for chai tea: Theresa, Tom, Terri, and Tim. Because these four consumers have different tastes for tea and different incomes, the marginal benefit each of them receives from consuming a cup of tea will be different. Therefore, the highest price each is willing to pay for a cup of tea is also different. In Figure 4-1, the information from the table is used to construct a demand curve for chai tea. For prices above $6 per cup, no tea is sold because $6 is the highest price any of the consumers is willing to pay. At a price of $5, both Theresa and Tom are willing to buy, so two cups are sold. At prices of $3 and below, all four consumers are willing to buy, and four cups are sold.

**Consumer surplus** The difference between the highest price a consumer is willing to pay for a good or service and the price the consumer actually pays.

**Marginal benefit** The additional benefit to a consumer from consuming one more unit of a good or service.

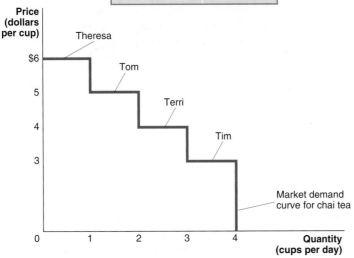

| Consumer | Highest Price Willing to Pay |
|---|---|
| Theresa | $6 |
| Tom | 5 |
| Terri | 4 |
| Tim | 3 |

## Figure 4-1

**Deriving the Demand Curve for Chai Tea**

With four consumers in the market for chai tea, the demand curve is determined by the highest price each consumer is willing to pay. For prices above $6, no tea is sold because $6 is the highest price any consumer is willing to pay. For prices of $3 and below, every one of the four consumers is willing to buy a cup of tea.

Suppose the market price of tea is $3.50 per cup. As Figure 4-2 shows, the demand curve allows us to calculate the total consumer surplus in this market. In panel (a), we can see that the highest price Theresa is willing to pay is $6, but because she pays only $3.50, her consumer surplus is $2.50 (shown by the area of rectangle *A*). Similarly, Tom's consumer surplus is $1.50 (rectangle *B*), and Terri's consumer surplus is $0.50 (rectangle *C*). Tim is unwilling to buy a cup of tea at a price of $3.50, so he doesn't participate in this market and receives no consumer surplus. In this simple example, the total consumer surplus is equal to $2.50 + $1.50 + $0.50 = $4.50 (or the sum of the areas of rectangles *A*, *B*, and *C*). Panel (b) shows that a lower price will increase consumer surplus. If the price of

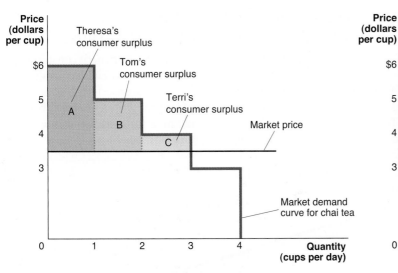

**(a) Consumer surplus with a market price of $3.50**

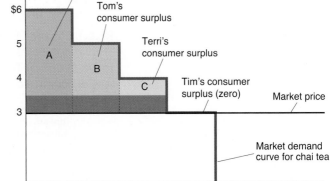

**(b) Consumer surplus with a market price of $3.00**

## Figure 4-2    Measuring Consumer Surplus

Panel (a) shows the consumer surplus for Theresa, Tom, and Terri when the price of tea is $3.50 per cup. Theresa's consumer surplus is equal to the area of rectangle *A* and is the difference between the highest price she would pay—$6—and the market price of $3.50. Tom's consumer surplus is equal to the area of rectangle *B*, and Terri's

consumer surplus is equal to the area of rectangle *C*. Total consumer surplus in this market is equal to the sum of the areas of rectangles *A*, *B*, and *C*, or the total area below the demand curve and above the market price. In panel (b), consumer surplus increases by the shaded area as the market price declines from $3.50 to $3.00.

## Figure 4-3

### Total Consumer Surplus in the Market for Chai Tea

The demand curve tells us that most buyers of chai tea would have been willing to pay more than the market price of $2.00. For each buyer, consumer surplus is equal to the difference between the highest price he or she is willing to pay and the market price actually paid. Therefore, the total amount of consumer surplus in the market for chai tea is equal to the area below the demand curve and above the market price. Consumer surplus represents the benefit to consumers in excess of the price they paid to purchase the product.

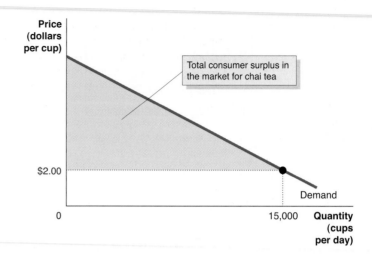

tea drops from $3.50 per cup to $3.00, Theresa, Tom, and Terri each receive $0.50 more in consumer surplus (shown by the shaded areas), so total consumer surplus in the market rises to $6.00. Tim now buys a cup of tea but doesn't receive any consumer surplus because the price is equal to the highest price he is willing to pay. In fact, Tim is indifferent between buying the cup or not—his well-being is the same either way.

The market demand curves shown in Figures 4-1 and 4-2 do not look like the smooth curves we saw in Chapter 3. This is because this example uses a small number of consumers, each consuming a single cup of tea. With many consumers, the market demand curve for chai tea will have the normal smooth shape shown in Figure 4-3. In this figure, the quantity demanded at a price of $2.00 is 15,000 cups per day. We can calculate total consumer surplus in Figure 4-3 the same way we did in Figures 4-1 and 4-2: by adding up the consumer surplus received on each unit purchased. Once again, we can draw an important conclusion: *The total amount of consumer surplus in a market is equal to the area below the demand curve and above the market price.* Consumer surplus is shown as the blue area in Figure 4-3 and represents the benefit to consumers in excess of the price they paid to purchase the product—in this case, chai tea.

## Making the Connection | The Consumer Surplus from Broadband Internet Service

Consumer surplus allows us to measure the benefit consumers receive in excess of the price they paid to purchase a product. Recently, Shane Greenstein and Ryan McDevitt, economists at Northwestern University, estimated the consumer surplus that households receive from subscribing to broadband Internet service. To do this, they estimated the demand curve for broadband Internet service and then computed the shaded area shown in the graph.

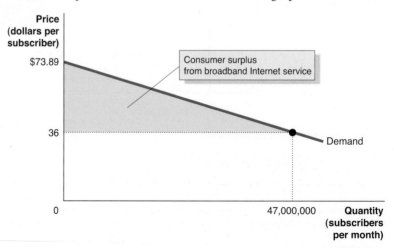

In 2006, 47 million consumers paid an average price of $36 per month to subscribe to a broadband Internet service. The demand curve shows the marginal benefit consumers receive from subscribing to a broadband Internet service rather than using dialup or doing without access to the Internet. The area below the demand curve and above the $36 price line represents the difference between the price consumers would have paid rather than do without broadband service and the $36 they did pay. The shaded area on the graph represents the total consumer surplus in the market for broadband Internet service. Greenstein and McDevitt estimate that the value of this area is $890.5 million. This is one month's benefit to the consumers who subscribe to a broadband Internet service.

Source: Shane Greenstein and Ryan C. McDevitt, "The Broadband Bonus: Accounting for Broadband Internet's Impact on U.S. GDP," National Bureau of Economic Research Working Paper 14758, February 2009.

**YOUR TURN:** Test your understanding by doing related problem 1.8 on page 120 at the end of this chapter.

## Producer Surplus

Just as demand curves show the willingness of consumers to buy a product at different prices, supply curves show the willingness of firms to supply a product at different prices. The willingness to supply a product depends on the cost of producing it. Firms will supply an additional unit of a product only if they receive a price equal to the additional cost of producing that unit. **Marginal cost** is the additional cost to a firm of producing one more unit of a good or service. Consider the marginal cost to the firm Heavenly Tea of producing one more cup: In this case, the marginal cost includes the ingredients to make the tea and the wages paid to the worker preparing the tea. Often, the marginal cost of producing a good increases as more of the good is produced during a given period of time. This is the key reason—as we saw in Chapter 3—that supply curves are upward sloping.

Panel (a) of Figure 4-4 shows Heavenly Tea's producer surplus. For simplicity, we show Heavenly producing only a small quantity of tea. The figure shows that Heavenly's

> **Marginal cost** The additional cost to a firm of producing one more unit of a good or service.

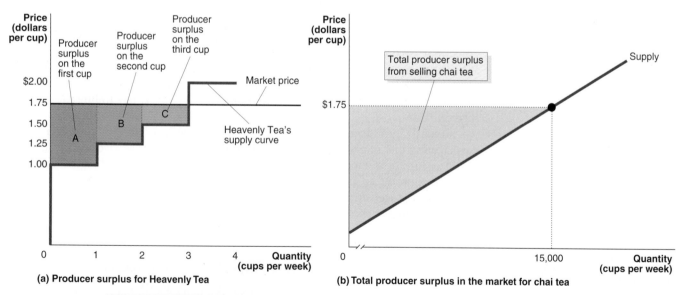

**(a) Producer surplus for Heavenly Tea**

**(b) Total producer surplus in the market for chai tea**

Figure 4-4 | Measuring Producer Surplus

Panel (a) shows Heavenly Tea's producer surplus. Producer surplus is the difference between the lowest price a firm would be willing to accept and the price it actually receives. The lowest price Heavenly Tea is willing to accept to supply a cup of tea is equal to its marginal cost of producing that cup. When the market price of tea is $1.75, Heavenly receives producer surplus of $0.75 on the first cup (the area of rectangle A), $0.50 on the second cup (rectangle B), and $0.25 on the third cup (rectangle C). In panel (b), the total amount of producer surplus tea sellers receive from selling chai tea can be calculated by adding up for the entire market the producer surplus received on each cup sold. In the figure, total producer surplus is equal to the area above the supply curve and below the market price, shown in red.

marginal cost of producing the first cup of tea is $1.00. Its marginal cost of producing the second cup is $1.25, and so on. The marginal cost of each cup of tea is the lowest price Heavenly is willing to accept to supply that cup. The supply curve, then, is also a marginal cost curve. Suppose the market price of tea is $1.75 per cup. On the first cup of tea, the price is $0.75 higher than the lowest price Heavenly is willing to accept. **Producer surplus** is the difference between the lowest price a firm would be willing to accept for a good or service and the price it actually receives. Therefore, Heavenly's producer surplus on the first cup is $0.75 (shown by the area of rectangle *A*). Its producer surplus on the second cup is $0.50 (rectangle *B*). Its producer surplus on the third cup is $0.25 (rectangle *C*). Heavenly will not be willing to supply the fourth cup because the marginal cost of producing it is greater than the market price. Heavenly Tea's total producer surplus is equal to $0.75 + $0.50 + $0.25 = $1.50 (or the sum of rectangles *A*, *B*, and *C*). A higher price will increase producer surplus. For example, if the market price of chai tea rises from $1.75 to $2.00, Heavenly Tea's producer surplus will increase from $1.50 to $2.25. (Make sure you understand how the new level of producer surplus was calculated.)

> **Producer surplus** The difference between the lowest price a firm would be willing to accept for a good or service and the price it actually receives.

The supply curve shown in panel (a) of Figure 4-4 does not look like the smooth curves we saw in Chapter 3 because this example uses a single firm producing only a small quantity of tea. With many firms, the market supply curve for chai tea will have the normal smooth shape shown in panel (b) of Figure 4-4. In panel (b), the quantity supplied at a price of $2.00 is 15,000 cups per day. We can calculate total producer surplus in panel (b) the same way we did in panel (a): by adding up the producer surplus received on each cup sold. Therefore, *the total amount of producer surplus in a market is equal to the area above the market supply curve and below the market price.* The total producer surplus tea sellers receive from selling chai tea is shown as the red area in panel (b) of Figure 4-4.

## What Consumer Surplus and Producer Surplus Measure

We have seen that consumer surplus measures the benefit to consumers from participating in a market, and producer surplus measures the benefit to producers from participating in a market. It is important, however, to be clear what this means. In a sense, consumer surplus measures the *net* benefit to consumers from participating in a market rather than the *total* benefit. That is, if the price of a product were zero, the consumer surplus in a market would be all of the area under the demand curve. When the price is not zero, consumer surplus is the area below the demand curve and above the market price. So, consumer surplus in a market is equal to the total benefit received by consumers minus the total amount they must pay to buy the good or service.

Similarly, producer surplus measures the *net* benefit received by producers from participating in a market. If producers could supply a good or service at zero cost, the producer surplus in a market would be all of the area below the market price. When cost is not zero, producer surplus is the area below the market price and above the supply curve. So, producer surplus in a market is equal to the total amount firms receive from consumers minus the cost of producing the good or service.

**4.2 LEARNING** OBJECTIVE

Understand the concept of economic efficiency.

## The Efficiency of Competitive Markets

In Chapter 3, we defined a *competitive market* as a market with many buyers and many sellers. An important advantage of the market system is that it results in efficient economic outcomes. But what do we mean by *economic efficiency*? The concepts we have developed so far in this chapter give us two ways to think about the economic efficiency of competitive markets. We can think in terms of marginal benefit and marginal cost. We can also think in terms of consumer surplus and producer surplus. As we will see,

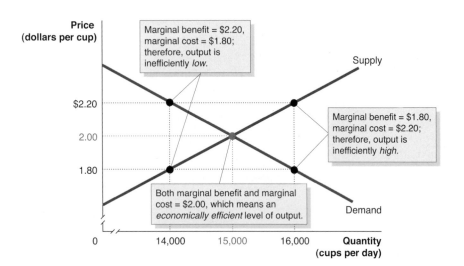

Figure 4-5

**Marginal Benefit Equals Marginal Cost Only at Competitive Equilibrium**

In a competitive market, equilibrium occurs at a quantity of 15,000 cups and a price of $2.00 per cup, where marginal benefit equals marginal cost. This is the economically efficient level of output because every cup has been produced where the marginal benefit to buyers is greater than or equal to the marginal cost to producers.

these two approaches lead to the same outcome, but using both can increase our understanding of economic efficiency.

## Marginal Benefit Equals Marginal Cost in Competitive Equilibrium

Figure 4-5 again shows the market for chai tea. Recall from our discussion that the demand curve shows the marginal benefit received by consumers, and the supply curve shows the marginal cost of production. To achieve economic efficiency in this market, the marginal benefit from the last unit sold should equal the marginal cost of production. The figure shows that this equality occurs at competitive equilibrium where 15,000 cups per day are produced and marginal benefit and marginal cost are both equal to $2.00. Why is this outcome economically efficient? Because every cup of chai tea has been produced where the marginal benefit to buyers is greater than or equal to the marginal cost to producers.

Another way to see why the level of output at competitive equilibrium is efficient is to consider what the situation would be if output were at a different level. For instance, suppose that output of chai tea were 14,000 cups per day. Figure 4-5 shows that at this level of output, the marginal benefit from the last cup sold is $2.20, whereas the marginal cost is only $1.80. This level of output is not efficient because 1,000 more cups could be produced for which the additional benefit to consumers would be greater than the additional cost of production. Consumers would willingly purchase those cups, and tea sellers would willingly supply them, making both consumers and sellers better off. Similarly, if the output of chai tea were 16,000 cups per day, the marginal cost of the 16,000th cup is $2.20, whereas the marginal benefit is only $1.80. Tea sellers would only be willing to supply this cup at a price of $2.20, which is $0.40 higher than consumers would be willing to pay. In fact, consumers would not be willing to pay the price tea sellers would need to receive for any cup beyond the 15,000th.

To summarize, we can say this: *Equilibrium in a competitive market results in the economically efficient level of output, where marginal benefit equals marginal cost.*

## Economic Surplus

**Economic surplus** in a market is the sum of consumer surplus and producer surplus. In a competitive market, with many buyers and sellers and no government restrictions, economic surplus is at a maximum when the market is in equilibrium. To see this, let's look one more time at the market for chai tea shown in Figure 4-6. The consumer surplus in this market is the blue area below the demand curve and above the line indicating the equilibrium price of $2.00. The producer surplus is the red area above the supply curve and below the price line.

**Economic surplus** The sum of consumer surplus and producer surplus.

## Figure 4-6

**Economic Surplus Equals the Sum of Consumer Surplus and Producer Surplus**

The economic surplus in a market is the sum of the blue area, representing consumer surplus, and the red area, representing producer surplus.

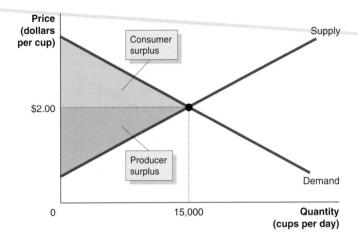

# Deadweight Loss

To show that economic surplus is maximized at equilibrium, consider a situation in which the price of chai tea is *above* the equilibrium price, as shown in Figure 4-7. At a price of $2.20 per cup, the number of cups consumers are willing to buy per day drops from 15,000 to 14,000. At competitive equilibrium, consumer surplus is equal to the sum of areas *A*, *B*, and *C*. At a price of $2.20, fewer cups are sold at a higher price, so consumer surplus declines to just the area of *A*. At competitive equilibrium, producer surplus is equal to the sum of areas *D* and *E*. At the higher price of $2.20, producer surplus changes to be equal to the sum of areas *B* and *D*. The sum of consumer and producer surplus—economic surplus—has been reduced to the sum of areas *A*, *B*, and *D*. Notice that this is less than the original economic surplus by an amount equal to areas *C* and *E*. Economic surplus has declined because at a price of $2.20, all the cups between the 14,000th and the 15,000th, which would have been produced in competitive equilibrium, are not being produced. These "missing" cups are not providing any consumer or producer surplus, so economic surplus has declined. The reduction in economic surplus resulting from a market not being in competitive equilibrium is called the **deadweight loss**. In the figure, it is equal to the sum of areas *C* and *E*.

**Deadweight loss** The reduction in economic surplus resulting from a market not being in competitive equilibrium.

## Figure 4-7

**When a Market Is Not in Equilibrium, There Is a Deadweight Loss**

Economic surplus is maximized when a market is in competitive equilibrium. When a market is not in equilibrium, there is a deadweight loss. When the price of chai tea is $2.20, instead of $2.00, consumer surplus declines from an amount equal to the sum of areas *A*, *B*, and *C* to just area *A*. Producer surplus increases from the sum of areas *D* and *E* to the sum of areas *B* and *D*. At competitive equilibrium, there is no deadweight loss. At a price of $2.20, there is a deadweight loss equal to the sum of areas *C* and *E*.

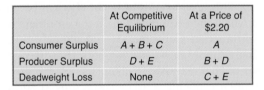

|  | At Competitive Equilibrium | At a Price of $2.20 |
| --- | --- | --- |
| Consumer Surplus | *A + B + C* | *A* |
| Producer Surplus | *D + E* | *B + D* |
| Deadweight Loss | None | *C + E* |

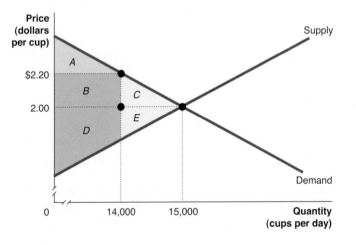

## Economic Surplus and Economic Efficiency

Consumer surplus measures the benefit to consumers from buying a particular product, such as chai tea. Producer surplus measures the benefit to firms from selling a particular product. Therefore, economic surplus—which is the sum of the benefit to firms plus the benefit to consumers—is the best measure we have of the benefit to society from the production of a particular good or service. This gives us a second way of characterizing the economic efficiency of a competitive market: *Equilibrium in a competitive market results in the greatest amount of economic surplus, or total net benefit to society, from the production of a good or service.* Anything that causes the market for a good or service not to be in competitive equilibrium reduces the total benefit to society from the production of that good or service.

Now we can give a more general definition of *economic efficiency* in terms of our two approaches: **Economic efficiency** is a market outcome in which the marginal benefit to consumers of the last unit produced is equal to its marginal cost of production and in which the sum of consumer surplus and producer surplus is at a maximum.

**Economic efficiency** A market outcome in which the marginal benefit to consumers of the last unit produced is equal to its marginal cost of production and in which the sum of consumer surplus and producer surplus is at a maximum.

# Solved Problem 4-2

## The Loss to the American Colonies from Being Part of the British Empire

Before the American Revolution, the British required the American colonies to follow certain rules, known as the Navigation Acts. One of the rules required that all imports to the colonies from outside the British Empire had to be shipped first to Great Britain. For instance, a colonial business in New York importing wine from France had to have the wine shipped first from France to Great Britain before it could be shipped to New York. This requirement increased the cost of importing goods into the colonies.

Draw a graph to show the loss in economic efficiency from the Navigation Act on importation of wine into New York.

## SOLVING THE PROBLEM:

**Step 1:** **Review the chapter material.** This problem is about economic efficiency, so you may want to review the section "The Efficiency of Competitive Markets," which begins on page 102.

**Step 2:** **Draw a demand and supply graph that illustrates the equilibrium price and quantity of imported wine to the Colonies with and without the trade restrictions imposed by the Navigation Acts.**

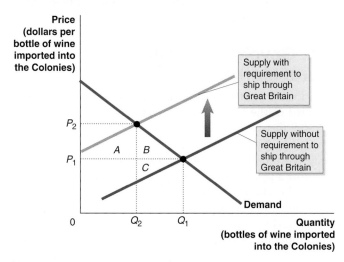

**Step 3:** **Estimate the loss of consumer surplus and deadweight loss.** The imposition of the Navigation Acts restrictions on trade caused the supply curve to shift to the left. As a result, the equilibrium price was greater and the equilibrium

quantity less than they would have been in the absence of the restrictions. Areas $A$ and $B$ represent the loss of consumer surplus. Part of this area—area $A$—is transferred to producers in the form of higher revenue from selling $Q_2$: $(P_2 - eaP_1) \times Q_2$. There is an overall gain in producer surplus (that is, area $A$ is larger than area $C$). But areas $B$ and $C$ indicate the deadweight loss, a net efficiency loss compared to the competitive equilibrium price and quantity ($P_1$ and $Q_1$). Robert Paul Thomas has estimated that loss of consumer surplus was \$605,000 in 1770. Because the total income of the colonies was only \$130 million in 1770, the loss of consumer surplus was the equivalent of about \$47 billion in today's economy.

Source: Robert Paul Thomas, "A Quantitative Approach to the Study of the Effects of British Imperial Policy on Colonial Welfare," *Journal of Economic History*, Vol. 25, No. 4, December 1965, pp. 615–638.

**YOUR TURN:** For more practice, do related problem 2.8 on pages 121–122 at the end of this chapter.

**4.3 LEARNING** OBJECTIVE

Explain the economic effect of government-imposed price floors and price ceilings.

# Government Intervention in the Market: Price Floors and Price Ceilings

Notice that we have *not* concluded that every *individual* is better off if a market is at competitive equilibrium. We have only concluded that economic surplus, or the *total* net benefit to society, is greatest at competitive equilibrium. Any individual producer would rather receive a higher price, and any individual consumer would rather pay a lower price, but usually producers can sell and consumers can buy only at the competitive equilibrium price.

Producers or consumers who are dissatisfied with the competitive equilibrium price can lobby the government to legally require that a different price be charged. In the United States, the government only occasionally overrides the market outcome by setting prices. When the government does intervene, it can either attempt to aid sellers by requiring that a price be above equilibrium—a price floor—or aid buyers by requiring that a price be below equilibrium—a price ceiling. To affect the market outcome, the government must set a price floor that is above the equilibrium price, or set a price ceiling that is below the equilibrium price. Otherwise, the price ceiling or price floor will not be *binding* on buyers and sellers. The preceding section demonstrates that moving away from competitive equilibrium will reduce economic efficiency. We can use the concepts of consumer surplus, producer surplus, and deadweight loss to see more clearly the economic inefficiency of price floors and price ceilings.

## Price Floors: Government Policy in Agricultural Markets

The Great Depression of the 1930s was the worst economic disaster in U.S. history, affecting every sector of the U.S. economy. Many farmers were unable to sell their products or could sell them only at very low prices. Farmers were able to convince the federal government to set price floors for many agricultural products. Government intervention in agriculture—often referred to as the *farm program*—has continued ever since. To see how a price floor in an agricultural market works, suppose that the equilibrium price in the wheat market is \$3.00 per bushel, but the government decides to set a price floor of \$3.50 per bushel. As Figure 4-8 shows, the price of wheat rises from \$3.00 to \$3.50, and the quantity of wheat sold falls from 2.0 billion bushels per year to 1.8 billion. Initially, suppose that production of wheat also falls to 1.8 billion bushels.

Just as we saw in the earlier example of the market for chai tea (refer to Figure 4-7), the producer surplus received by wheat farmers increases by an amount equal to the area of the red rectangle $A$ and falls by an amount equal to the area of the yellow

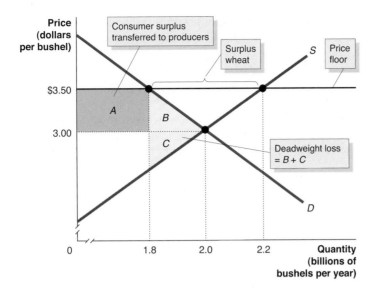

## Figure 4-8

### The Economic Effect of a Price Floor in the Wheat Market

If wheat farmers convince the government to impose a price floor of $3.50 per bushel, the amount of wheat sold will fall from 2.0 billion bushels per year to 1.8 billion. If we assume that farmers produce 1.8 billion bushels, producer surplus then increases by the red rectangle *A*— which is transferred from consumer surplus— and falls by the yellow triangle *C*. Consumer surplus declines by the red rectangle *A* plus the yellow triangle *B*. There is a deadweight loss equal to the yellow triangles *B* and *C*, representing the decline in economic efficiency due to the price floor. In reality, a price floor of $3.50 per bushel will cause farmers to expand their production from 2.0 billion to 2.2 billion bushels, resulting in a surplus of wheat.

triangle *C*. The area of the red rectangle *A* represents a transfer from consumer surplus to producer surplus. The total fall in consumer surplus is equal to the area of the red rectangle *A* plus the area of the yellow triangle *B*. Wheat farmers benefit from this program, but consumers lose. There is also a deadweight loss equal to the areas of the yellow triangles *B* and *C*, which represents the decline in economic efficiency due to the price floor. There is a deadweight loss because the price floor has reduced the amount of economic surplus in the market for wheat. Or, looked at another way, the price floor has caused the marginal benefit of the last bushel of wheat to be greater than the marginal cost of producing it. We can conclude that a price floor reduces economic efficiency.

We assumed initially that farmers reduce their production of wheat to the amount consumers are willing to buy. In fact, as Figure 4-8 shows, a price floor will cause the quantity of wheat that farmers want to supply to increase from 2.0 billion to 2.2 billion bushels. Because the higher price also reduces the amount of wheat consumers want to buy, the result is a surplus of 0.4 billion bushels of wheat (the 2.2 billion bushels supplied minus the 1.8 billion demanded).

The federal government's farm programs have often resulted in large surpluses of wheat and other agricultural products. In response, the government has usually either bought the surplus food or paid farmers to restrict supply by taking some land out of cultivation. Because both of these options are expensive, Congress passed the Freedom to Farm Act of 1996. The intent of the act was to phase out price floors and government purchases of surpluses and return to a free market in agriculture. To allow farmers time to adjust, the federal government began paying farmers *subsidies*, or cash payments based on the number of acres planted. Although the subsidies were originally scheduled to be phased out, Congress has continued to pay them.

## Making the Connection | Price Floors in Labor Markets: The Debate over Minimum Wage Policy

The minimum wage may be the most controversial "price floor." Supporters see the minimum wage as a way of raising the incomes of low-skilled workers. Opponents argue that it results in fewer jobs and imposes large costs on small businesses.

Since July 2009, the national minimum wage as set by Congress is $7.25 per hour for most occupations. It is illegal for an employer to pay less than this wage in those occupations. For most workers, the minimum wage is irrelevant because it is well below the wage employers are voluntarily willing to pay them. But for low-skilled workers— such as workers in fast-food restaurants—the minimum wage is above the wage they would otherwise receive. The following figure shows the effect of the minimum wage on employment in the market for low-skilled labor.

Without a minimum wage, the equilibrium wage would be $W_1$, and the number of workers hired would be $L_1$. With a minimum wage set above the equilibrium wage, the

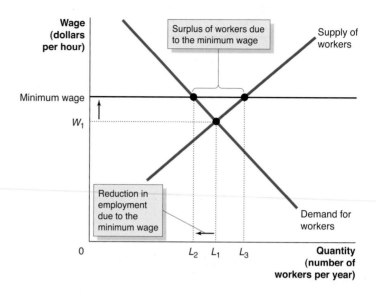

number of workers demanded by employers declines from $L_1$ to $L_2$, and the quantity of labor supplied increases to $L_3$, leading to a surplus of workers unable to find jobs equal to $L_3 - L_2$. The quantity of labor supplied increases because the higher wage attracts more people to work. For instance, some teenagers may decide that working after school is worthwhile at the minimum wage of $7.25 per hour but would not be worthwhile at a lower wage.

This analysis is very similar to our analysis of the wheat market in Figure 4-8. Just as a price floor in the wheat market leads to less wheat being consumed, a price floor in the labor market should lead to fewer workers being hired. Views differ sharply among economists, however, concerning how large a reduction in employment the minimum wage causes. For instance, David Card of the University of California, Berkeley, and Alan Krueger of Princeton University conducted a study of fast-food restaurants in New Jersey and Pennsylvania. Their study indicated that the effect of minimum wage increases on employment is very small. This study has been very controversial, however. Other economists have examined similar data and have come to the different conclusion that the minimum wage leads to a significant decrease in employment.

Whatever the extent of employment losses from the minimum wage, because it is a price floor, it will cause a deadweight loss, just as a price floor in the wheat market does. Therefore, many economists favor alternative policies for attaining the goal of raising the incomes of low-skilled workers. One policy many economists support is the *earned income tax credit*. The earned income tax credit reduces the amount of tax that low-income wage earners would otherwise pay to the federal government. Workers with very low incomes who do not owe any tax receive a payment from the government. Compared with the minimum wage, the earned income tax credit can increase the incomes of low-skilled workers without reducing employment. The earned income tax credit also places a lesser burden on the small businesses that employ many low-skilled workers, and it may cause a smaller loss of economic efficiency.

Sources: David Card and Alan B. Krueger, *Myth and Measurement: The New Economics of the Minimum Wage*, Princeton, NJ: Princeton University Press, 1995; David Neumark and William Wascher, "Minimum Wages and Employment: A Case Study of the Fast-Food Industry in New Jersey and Pennsylvania: Comment," *American Economic Review*, Vol. 90, No. 5, December 2000, pp. 1362–1396; and David Card and Alan B. Krueger, "Minimum Wages and Employment: A Case Study of the Fast-Food Industry in New Jersey and Pennsylvania: Reply," *American Economic Review*, Vol. 90, No. 5, December 2000, pp. 1397–1420.

 **YOUR TURN:** Test your understanding by doing related problem 3.12 on page 123 at the end of this chapter.

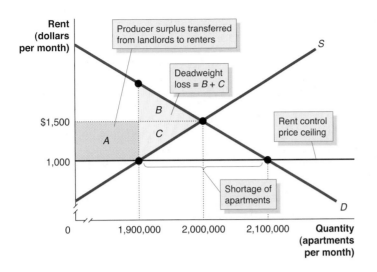

Figure 4-9

**The Economic Effect of a Rent Ceiling**

Without rent control, the equilibrium rent is $1,500 per month. At that price, 2,000,000 apartments would be rented. If the government imposes a rent ceiling of $1,000, the quantity of apartments supplied falls to 1,900,000, and the quantity of apartments demanded increases to 2,100,000, resulting in a shortage of 200,000 apartments. Producer surplus equal to the area of the blue rectangle *A* is transferred from landlords to renters, and there is a deadweight loss equal to the areas of yellow triangles *B* and *C*.

# Price Ceilings: Government Rent Control Policy in Housing Markets

Support for governments setting price floors typically comes from sellers, and support for governments setting price ceilings typically comes from consumers. For example, when there is a sharp increase in gasoline prices, there are often proposals for the government to impose a price ceiling on the market for gasoline. As we saw in the chapter opener, New York is one of a number of cities that impose rent control, which puts a ceiling on the maximum rent that landlords can charge for an apartment. Figure 4-9 shows the market for apartments in a city that has rent control.

Without rent control, the equilibrium rent would be $1,500 per month, and 2,000,000 apartments would be rented. With a maximum legal rent of $1,000 per month, landlords reduce the quantity of apartments supplied to 1,900,000. The fall in the quantity of apartments supplied can be the result of landlords converting some apartments into offices, selling some off as condominiums, or converting some small apartment buildings into single-family homes. Over time, landlords may even abandon some apartment buildings. At one time in New York City, rent control resulted in landlords abandoning whole city blocks because they were unable to cover their costs with the rents the government allowed them to charge. In London, when rent controls were applied to rooms and apartments located in a landlord's own home, the quantity of these apartments supplied dropped by 75 percent.

In Figure 4-9, with the rent ceiling of $1,000, the quantity of apartments demanded rises to 2,100,000. There is a shortage of 200,000 apartments. Consumer surplus increases by rectangle *A* and falls by triangle *B*. Rectangle *A* would have been part of producer surplus if rent control were not in place. With rent control, it is part of consumer surplus. Rent control causes the producer surplus received by landlords to fall by rectangle *A* plus triangle *C*. Triangles *B* and *C* represent the deadweight loss. There is a deadweight loss because rent control has reduced the amount of economic surplus in the market for apartments. Rent control has caused the marginal benefit of the last apartment rented to be greater than the marginal cost of supplying it. We can conclude that a price ceiling, such as rent control, reduces economic efficiency. The appendix to this chapter shows how we can make quantitative estimates of the deadweight loss, and it provides an example of the changes in consumer surplus and producer surplus that can result from rent control.

Renters as a group benefit from rent controls—total consumer surplus is larger—but landlords lose. Because of the deadweight loss, the total loss to landlords is greater than the gain to renters. Notice also that although renters as a group benefit, the number of renters is reduced, so some renters are made worse off by rent controls because they are unable to find an apartment at the legal rent.

# Don't Let This Happen to **YOU!**

## Don't Confuse "Scarcity" with a "Shortage"

At first glance, the following statement seems correct: "There is a shortage of every good that is scarce." In everyday conversation, we describe a good as "scarce" if we have trouble finding it. For instance, if you are looking for a present for a child, you might call the latest hot toy "scarce" if you are willing to buy it at its listed price but can't find it online or in any store. But recall from Chapter 2 that economists have a broad definition of *scarce*. In the economic sense, almost everything—except undesirable things like garbage—is scarce. A shortage of a good occurs only if the quantity demanded is greater than the quantity supplied at the current price. Therefore, the preceding statement— "There is a shortage of every good that is scarce"—is incorrect. In fact, there is no shortage of most scarce goods.

**YOUR TURN:** Test your understanding by doing related problem 3.16 on page 124 at the end of this chapter.

## Black Markets

**Black market** A market in which buying and selling take place at prices that violate government price regulations.

To this point, our analysis of rent controls is incomplete. In practice, renters may be worse off and landlords may be better off than Figure 4-9 makes it seem. We have assumed that renters and landlords actually abide by the price ceiling, but sometimes they don't. Because rent control leads to a shortage of apartments, renters who would otherwise not be able to find apartments have an incentive to offer landlords rents above the legal maximum. When governments try to control prices by setting price ceilings or price floors, buyers and sellers often find a way around the controls. The result is a **black market** where buying and selling take place at prices that violate government price regulations.

In a housing market with rent controls, the total amount of consumer surplus received by renters may be reduced and the total amount of producer surplus received by landlords may be increased if apartments are being rented at prices above the legal price ceiling.

# **Solved** Problem | **4-3**

## What's the Economic Effect of a Black Market for Apartments?

In many cities that have rent controls, the actual rents paid can be much higher than the legal maximum. Because rent controls cause a shortage of apartments, desperate tenants are often willing to pay landlords rents that are higher than the law allows, perhaps by writing a check for the legally allowed rent and paying an additional amount in cash. Look again at Figure 4-9 on page 109.

Suppose that competition among tenants results in the black market rent rising to $2,000 per month. At this rent, tenants demand 1,900,000 apartments. Use a graph showing the market for apartments to compare this situation with the one shown in Figure 4-9. Be sure to note any differences in consumer surplus, producer surplus, and deadweight loss.

## SOLVING THE PROBLEM:

**Step 1:** **Review the chapter material.** This problem is about price controls in the market for apartments, so you may want to review the section "Price Ceilings: Government Rent Control Policy in Housing Markets," which begins on page 109.

**Step 2:** **Draw a graph similar to Figure 4-9, with the addition of the black market price.**

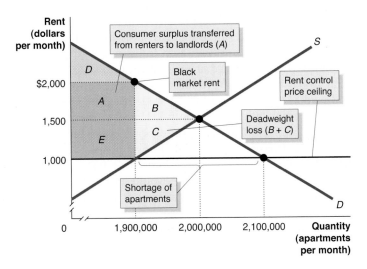

**Step 3:** **Analyze the changes from Figure 4-9.** The black market rent is now $2,000—even higher than the original competitive equilibrium rent shown in Figure 4-9. So, consumer surplus declines by an amount equal to the red rectangle *A* plus the red rectangle *E*. The remaining consumer surplus is the blue triangle *D*. Note that the rectangle *A*, which would have been part of consumer surplus without rent control, represents a transfer from renters to landlords. Compared with the situation shown in Figure 4-9, producer surplus has increased by an amount equal to rectangles *A* and *E*, and consumer surplus has declined by the same amount. Deadweight loss is equal to triangles *B* and *C*, the same as in Figure 4-9.

**EXTRA CREDIT:** This analysis leads to a surprising result: With an active black market in apartments, rent control may leave renters as a group worse off—with less consumer surplus—than if there were no rent control. There is one more possibility to consider, however. If enough landlords become convinced that they can get away with charging rents above the legal ceiling, the quantity of apartments supplied will increase. Eventually, the market could even end up at the competitive equilibrium, with an equilibrium rent of $1,500 and equilibrium quantity of 2,000,000 apartments. In that case, the rent control price ceiling becomes nonbinding, not because it was set below the equilibrium price but because it was not legally enforced.

**YOUR TURN:** For more practice, do related problems 3.14 on page 124 and 3.23 on page 125 at the end of this chapter.

---

Rent controls can also lead to an increase in racial and other types of discrimination. With rent controls, more renters are looking for apartments than there are apartments to rent. Landlords can afford to indulge their prejudices by refusing to rent to people they don't like. In cities without rent controls, landlords face more competition, which makes it more difficult to turn down tenants on the basis of irrelevant characteristics, such as race.

**Making** | **Does Holiday Gift Giving Have**
*the*
**Connection** | **a Deadweight Loss?**

The deadweight loss that results from rent control occurs, in part, because consumers rent fewer apartments than they would in a competitive equilibrium. Their choices are *constrained* by government. When you receive a gift, you are also constrained because the person who gave the gift has already chosen the product. In many cases, you would have chosen a different gift for yourself. Economist Joel Waldfogel of the University of Pennsylvania argues that gift

*Gift giving may lead to deadweight loss.*

giving results in a deadweight loss. The amount of the deadweight loss is equal to the difference between the gift's price and the dollar value the recipient places on the gift. Waldfogel surveyed his students, asking them to list every gift they had received for Christmas, to estimate the retail price of each gift, and to state how much they would have been willing to pay for each gift. Waldfogel's students estimated that their families and friends had paid $438 on average for the students' gifts. The students themselves, however, would have been willing to pay only $313 to buy the presents. If we extrapolate the deadweight losses Waldfogel's students experienced to the whole population, the deadweight loss of Christmas gift giving could be as much as $13 billion.

If the gifts had been cash, the people receiving the gifts would not have been constrained by the gift givers' choices, and there would have been no deadweight loss. If your sister had given you cash instead of that sweater you didn't like, you could have bought whatever you wanted. Why then do people continue giving presents rather than cash? One answer is that most people receive more satisfaction from giving or receiving a present than from giving or receiving cash. If we take this satisfaction into account, the deadweight loss from gift giving will be lower than in Waldfogel's calculations. In fact, a later study by economists John List of the University of Chicago and Jason Shogren of the University of Wyoming showed that as much as half the value of a gift to a recipient was its sentimental value. As Professor Shogren concluded, "People get a whole heck of a lot of value out of doing something for others and other people doing something for them. Aunt Helga gave you that ugly scarf, but hey, it's Aunt Helga."

Sources: Mark Whitehouse, "How Christmas Brings Out the Grinch in Economists," *Wall Street Journal*, December 23, 2006, p. A1; Joel Waldfogel, "The Deadweight Loss of Christmas," *American Economic Review*, Vol. 83, No. 4, December 1993, pp. 328–336; and John A. List and Jason F. Shogren, "The Deadweight Loss of Christmas: Comment," *American Economic Review*, Vol. 88, No. 5, 1998, pp. 1350–1355.

**YOUR TURN:** Test your understanding by doing related problem 3.15 on page 124 at the end of this chapter.

## The Results of Government Price Controls: Winners, Losers, and Inefficiency

When the government imposes price floors or price ceilings, three important results occur:

- Some people win.

- Some people lose.

- There is a loss of economic efficiency.

The winners with rent control are the people who are paying less for rent because they live in rent-controlled apartments. Landlords may also gain if they break the law by charging rents above the legal maximum for their rent-controlled apartments, provided that those illegal rents are higher than the competitive equilibrium rents would be. The losers from rent control are the landlords of rent-controlled apartments who abide by the law and renters who are unable to find apartments to rent at the controlled price. Rent control reduces economic efficiency because fewer apartments are rented than would be rented in a competitive market (refer again to Figure 4-9, on page 109). The resulting deadweight loss measures the decrease in economic efficiency.

## Positive and Normative Analysis of Price Ceilings and Price Floors

Are rent controls, government farm programs, and other price ceilings and price floors bad? As we saw in Chapter 1, questions of this type have no right or wrong answers. Economists are generally skeptical of government attempts to interfere with competitive market equilibrium. Economists know the role competitive markets have played in raising the average person's standard of living. They also know that too much government intervention has the potential to reduce the ability of the market system to produce similar increases in living standards in the future.

But recall from Chapter 1 the difference between positive and normative analysis. Positive analysis is concerned with *what is*, and normative analysis is concerned with *what should be*. Our analysis of rent control and of the federal farm programs in this chapter is positive analysis. We discussed the economic results of these programs. Whether these programs are desirable or undesirable is a normative question. Whether the gains to the winners more than make up for the losses to the losers and for the decline in economic efficiency is a matter of judgment and not strictly an economic question. Price ceilings and price floors continue to exist partly because people who understand their downside still believe they are good policies and therefore support them. The policies also persist because many people who support them do not understand the economic analysis in this chapter and so do not understand the drawbacks to these policies.

# The Economic Impact of Taxes

**4.4 LEARNING** OBJECTIVE

Analyze the economic impact of taxes.

Supreme Court Justice Oliver Wendell Holmes once remarked, "Taxes are what we pay for a civilized society." When the government taxes a good or service, however, it affects the market equilibrium for that good or service. Just as with a price ceiling or price floor, one result of a tax is a decline in economic efficiency. Analyzing taxes is an important part of the field of economics known as *public finance*. In this section, we will use the model of demand and supply and the concepts of consumer surplus, producer surplus, and deadweight loss to analyze the economic impact of taxes.

## The Effect of Taxes on Economic Efficiency

Whenever a government taxes a good or service, less of that good or service will be produced and consumed. For example, a tax on cigarettes will raise the cost of smoking and reduce the amount of smoking that takes place. We can use a demand and supply graph to illustrate this point. Figure 4-10 shows the market for cigarettes.

Without the tax, the equilibrium price of cigarettes would be $4.00 per pack, and 4 billion packs of cigarettes would be sold per year (point *A*). If the federal government requires sellers of cigarettes to pay a $1.00-per-pack tax, then their cost of selling cigarettes will increase by $1.00 per pack. This causes the supply curve for cigarettes to shift up by $1.00 because sellers will now require a price that is $1.00 greater to supply the same quantity of cigarettes. In Figure 4-10, the supply curve shifts up by $1.00 to show the effect of the tax, and there is a new equilibrium price of $4.90 and a new equilibrium quantity of 3.7 billion packs (point *B*).

## Figure 4-10

**The Effect of a Tax on the Market for Cigarettes**

Without the tax, market equilibrium occurs at point *A*. The equilibrium price of cigarettes is $4.00 per pack, and 4 billion packs of cigarettes are sold per year. A $1.00-per-pack tax on cigarettes will cause the supply curve for cigarettes to shift up by $1.00, from $S_1$ to $S_2$. The new equilibrium occurs at point *B*. The price of cigarettes will increase by $0.90, to $4.90 per pack, and the quantity sold will fall to 3.7 billion packs. The tax on cigarettes has increased the price paid by consumers from $4.00 to $4.90 per pack. Producers receive a price of $4.90 per pack (point *B*), but after paying the $1.00 tax, they are left with $3.90 (point *C*). The government will receive tax revenue equal to the green shaded box. Some consumer surplus and some producer surplus will become tax revenue for the government and some will become deadweight loss, shown by the yellow-shaded area.

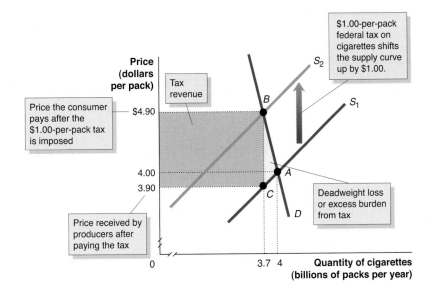

The federal government will collect tax revenue equal to the tax per pack multiplied by the number of packs sold, or $3.7 billion. The area shaded in green in Figure 4-10 represents the government's tax revenue. Consumers will pay a higher price of $4.90 per pack. Although sellers appear to be receiving a higher price per pack, once they have paid the tax, the price they receive falls from $4.00 per pack to $3.90 per pack. There is a loss of consumer surplus because consumers are paying a higher price. The price producers receive falls, so there is also a loss of producer surplus. Therefore, the tax on cigarettes has reduced *both* consumer surplus and producer surplus. Some of the reduction in consumer and producer surplus becomes tax revenue for the government. The rest of the reduction in consumer and producer surplus is equal to the deadweight loss from the tax, shown by the yellow-shaded triangle in the figure.

We can conclude that the true burden of a tax is not just the amount consumers and producers pay the government but also includes the deadweight loss. The deadweight loss from a tax is referred to as the *excess burden* of the tax. *A tax is efficient if it imposes a small excess burden relative to the tax revenue it raises.* One contribution economists make to government tax policy is to advise policymakers on which taxes are most efficient.

## Tax Incidence: Who Actually Pays a Tax?

The answer to the question "Who pays a tax?" seems obvious: Whoever is legally required to send a tax payment to the government pays the tax. But there can be an important difference between who is legally required to pay the tax and who actually *bears the burden* of the tax. The actual division of the burden of a tax between buyers and sellers is referred to as **tax incidence**. The federal government currently levies an excise tax of 18.4 cents per gallon of gasoline sold. Gas station owners collect this tax and forward it to the federal government, but who actually bears the burden of the tax?

**Tax incidence** The actual division of the burden of a tax between buyers and sellers in a market.

**Determining Tax Incidence on a Demand and Supply Graph** Suppose that currently the federal government does not impose a tax on gasoline. In Figure 4-11, equilibrium in the retail market for gasoline occurs at the intersection of the demand curve and supply curve, $S_1$. The equilibrium price is $3.00 per gallon, and the equilibrium quantity is 144 billion gallons. Now suppose that the federal government imposes a 10-cents-per-gallon tax. As a result of the tax, the supply curve for gasoline will shift up by 10 cents per gallon. At the new equilibrium, where the demand curve intersects the supply curve, $S_2$, the price has risen by 8 cents per gallon, from $3.00 to $3.08. Notice that only in the extremely unlikely case that demand is a vertical line will the market price rise by the full amount of the tax. Consumers are paying 8 cents more per gallon. Sellers of gasoline receive a new higher price of $3.08 per gallon, but after paying

## Figure 4-11

### The Incidence of a Tax on Gasoline

With no tax on gasoline, the price would be $3.00 per gallon, and 144 billion gallons of gasoline would be sold each year. A 10-cents-per-gallon excise tax shifts up the supply curve from $S_1$ to $S_2$, raises the price consumers pay from $3.00 to $3.08, and lowers the price sellers receive from $3.00 to $2.98. Therefore, consumers pay 8 cents of the 10-cents-per-gallon tax on gasoline, and sellers pay 2 cents.

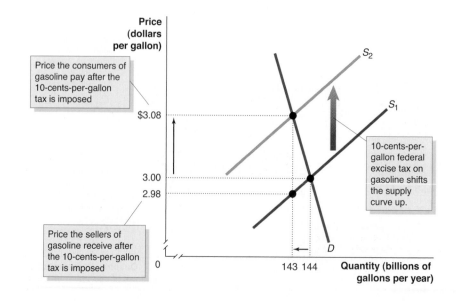

the 10-cents-per-gallon tax, they are left with $2.98 per gallon, or 2 cents less than they were receiving in the old equilibrium.

Although the sellers of gasoline are responsible for collecting the tax and sending the tax receipts to the government, they do not bear most of the burden of the tax. In this case, consumers pay 8 cents of the tax because the market price has risen by 8 cents, and sellers pay 2 cents of the tax because after sending the tax to the government, they are receiving 2 cents less per gallon of gasoline sold. Expressed in percentage terms, consumers pay 80 percent of the tax, and sellers pay 20 percent of the tax.

### Does It Matter Whether the Government Collects a Tax from Buyers or Sellers?
We have already seen the important distinction between the true burden of a tax and whether buyers or sellers are legally required to pay a tax. We can reinforce this point by noting explicitly that the incidence of a tax does *not* depend on whether the government collects a tax from the buyers of a good or from the sellers. Figure 4-12 illustrates this point by showing the effect on equilibrium in the market for gasoline if a 10-cents-per-gallon tax is imposed on buyers rather than on sellers. That is, we are now assuming that instead of sellers having to collect the 10-cents-per-gallon tax at the pump, buyers are responsible for keeping track of how many gallons of gasoline they purchase and sending the tax to the government. (Of course, it would be very difficult for buyers to keep track of their purchases or for the government to check whether they were paying all of the taxes they owe. That is why the government collects the tax on gasoline from sellers.)

Figure 4-12 is similar to Figure 4-11 except that it shows the gasoline tax being imposed on buyers rather than sellers. In Figure 4-12, the supply curve does not shift because nothing has happened to change the quantity of gasoline sellers are willing to supply at any given price. The demand curve has shifted, however, because consumers now have to pay a 10-cent tax on every gallon of gasoline they buy. Therefore, at every quantity, they are willing to pay a price 10 cents less than they would have without the tax. In the figure, we indicate the effect of the tax by shifting the demand curve down by 10 cents, from $D_1$ to $D_2$. Once the tax has been imposed and the demand curve has shifted down, the new equilibrium quantity of gasoline is 140 billion gallons, which is exactly the same as in Figure 4-11.

The new equilibrium price after the tax is imposed appears to be different in Figure 4-12 than in Figure 4-11, but if we include the tax, buyers will pay the same price and sellers will receive the same price in both figures. To see this, notice that in Figure 4-11, buyers paid sellers a price of $3.08 per gallon. In Figure 4-12, they pay sellers only $2.98, but they must also pay the government a tax of 10 cents per gallon. So, the total price buyers pay remains $3.08 per gallon. In Figure 4-11, sellers receive $3.08 per gallon from buyers, but after they pay the tax of 10 cents per gallon, they are left with $2.98, which is the same amount they receive in Figure 4-12.

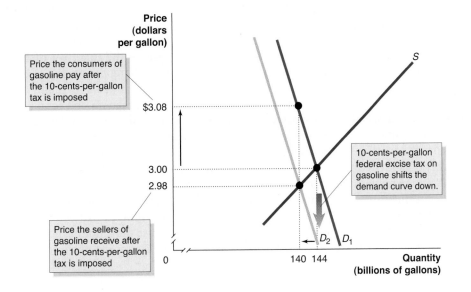

### Figure 4-12

#### The Incidence of a Tax on Gasoline Paid by Buyers

With no tax on gasoline, the demand curve is $D_1$. If a 10-cents-per-gallon tax is imposed that consumers are responsible for paying, the demand curve shifts down by the amount of the tax, from $D_1$ to $D_2$. In the new equilibrium, consumers pay a price of $3.08 per gallon, including the tax. Producers receive $2.98 per gallon. This is the same result we saw when producers were responsible for paying the tax.

*How much FICA do you think this employee pays?*

## Making the Connection | Is the Burden of the Social Security Tax Really Shared Equally between Workers and Firms?

Most people who receive paychecks have several different taxes withheld from them by their employers, who forward these taxes directly to the government. In fact, many people are shocked after getting their first job, when they discover the gap between their gross pay and their net pay after taxes have been deducted. The largest tax many people of low or moderate income pay is FICA, which stands for the Federal Insurance Contributions Act. FICA funds the Social Security and Medicare programs, which provide income and health care to the elderly and disabled. FICA is sometimes referred to as the *payroll tax*. When Congress passed the act, it wanted employers and workers to equally share the burden of the tax. Currently, FICA is 15.3 percent of wages, with 7.65 percent paid by workers by being withheld from their paychecks and the other 7.65 percent paid by employers.

But does requiring workers and employers to each pay half the tax mean that the burden of the tax is also shared equally? Our discussion in this chapter shows us that the answer is no. In the labor market, employers are buyers, and workers are sellers. As we saw in the example of the federal tax on gasoline, whether the tax is collected from buyers or from sellers does not affect the incidence of the tax. Most economists believe, in fact, that the burden of FICA falls almost entirely on workers. The following figure, which shows the market for labor, illustrates why.

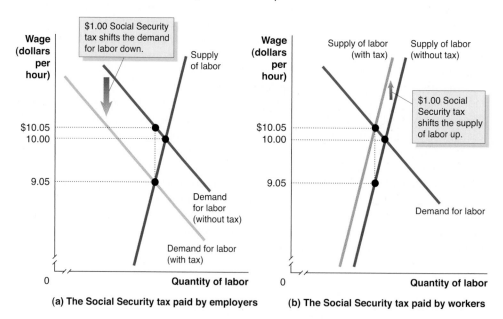

**(a) The Social Security tax paid by employers**    **(b) The Social Security tax paid by workers**

In the market for labor, the demand curve represents the quantity of labor demanded by employers at various wages, and the supply curve represents the quantity of labor supplied by workers at various wages. The intersection of the demand curve and the supply curve determines the equilibrium wage. In both panels, the equilibrium wage without a Social Security payroll tax is $10 per hour. For simplicity, let's assume that the payroll tax equals $1 per hour of work. In panel (a), we assume that employers must pay the tax. The tax causes the demand for labor curve to shift down by $1 at every quantity of labor because firms now must pay a $1 tax for every hour of labor they hire. We have drawn the supply curve for labor as being very steep because most economists believe the quantity of labor supplied by workers does not change much as the wage rate changes. Workers pay $0.95 of the tax because their wages fall from $10 before the tax to $9.05 after the tax. Firms pay only $0.05 of the tax because the amount they pay for an hour of labor increases from $10 before the tax to $10.05 after the tax. In panel (a), after the tax is imposed, the equilibrium wage declines from $10 per hour to $9.05 per hour. Firms are now paying a total of $10.05 for every hour of work they hire: $9.05 in wages to workers and $1 in tax to the government. In other words, workers have paid $0.95 of the $1 tax, and firms have paid only $0.05.

Panel (b) shows that this result is exactly the same if the tax is imposed on workers rather than on firms. In this case, the tax causes the supply curve for labor to shift up by $1 at every quantity of labor because workers must now pay a tax of $1 for every hour they work. After the tax is imposed, the equilibrium wage increases to $10.05 per hour. But workers receive only $9.05 after they have paid the $1.00 tax. Once again, workers have paid $0.95 of the $1 tax, and firms have paid only $0.05.

Although the figure presents a simplified analysis, it reflects the conclusion of most economists who have studied the incidence of FICA: Even though Congress requires employers to pay half the tax and workers to pay the other half, in fact, the burden of the tax falls almost entirely on workers. This conclusion would not be changed even if Congress revised the law to require either employers or workers to pay all of the tax. The forces of demand and supply working in the labor market, and not Congress, determine the incidence of the tax.

**YOUR TURN:** Test your understanding by doing related problem 4.5 on page 126 at the end of this chapter.

▶ **Continued from page 97**

## Economics in YOUR LIFE!

At the beginning of the chapter, we posed the following question: If you have two job offers in different cities, one with rent control and one without, will you be more likely to find an affordable apartment in the city with rent control? In answering the question, this chapter has shown that although rent control can keep rents lower than they might otherwise be, it can also lead to a permanent shortage of apartments. You may have to search for a long time to find a suitable apartment, and landlords may even ask you to give them payments "under the table," which would make your actual rent higher than the controlled rent. Finding an apartment in a city without rent control should be much easier, although the rent may be higher.

## Conclusion

The model of demand and supply introduced in Chapter 3 showed that markets free from government intervention eliminate surpluses and shortages and do a good job of responding to the wants of consumers. We have seen in this chapter that both consumers and firms sometimes try to use the government to change market outcomes in their favor. The concepts of consumer and producer surplus and deadweight loss allow us to measure the benefits consumers and producers receive from competitive market equilibrium. They also allow us to measure the effects of government price floors and price ceilings and the economic impact of taxes.

Read *An Inside Look at Policy* on the next page for a discussion of the debate over rent control in New York.

## >> Is Rent Control a Lifeline or Stranglehold?

### WALL STREET JOURNAL

## Rent Control Is the Real New York Scandal

This week Charlie Rangel—the New York Democrat and powerful chairman of the House Ways and Means Committee—gave a news conference in Washington where he admitted failing to report on his taxes $75,000 in rental income from a villa he owns in the Dominican Republic.

Just a few months ago Mr. Rangel admitted that he occupies four rent-stabilized apartments in a posh New York City building. It turns out that in a city with a very tight housing market, Mr. Rangel has wrangled himself a pretty good deal, thanks to rent-control laws that are ostensibly aimed at helping the poor and middle class.

But don't cluck too loudly at Mr. Rangel alone. Lots of well-connected New Yorkers have good deals.

New York City has had rent control laws since 1947, on grounds that they were necessary to protect people from rising rents. New York State expanded the regime in 1969, creating a rent stabilization program to cover apartments built after 1947 and before 1974—allowable rent increases are set by the City's Rent Guidelines Board.

The restrictions were loosened somewhat in 1971 and again in 1997 because of the realization that the system was benefiting wealthy renters. Under today's rules, landlords can move apartments renting for more than $2,000 a month with occupants making more than $175,000 a year onto the free market.

Today, there are 43,317 apartments where tenants (or their heirs) pay rents first frozen in 1947. There are another 1,043,677 units covered by rent stabilization. All told, about 70% of the city's rental apartments are either rent controlled or rent stabilized. And because the system has been in place for more than six decades, many residents see their below-market rents as an entitlement.

The regime has also incentivized builders to put up more luxury units—a result met with policy gimmicks such as tax incentives for builders of affordable housing and landlords who keep units in rent stabilization.

This is the world in which Mr. Rangel lives. He uses three adjacent rent-stabilized apartments in Harlem's Lenox Terrace as his "primary" residence. He has a fourth apartment that he has used as an office and which he is giving up. He pays a total of $3,864 a month in rent, which is less than what he would pay for the same apartments on the open market.

His defense, that "They didn't give me anything. I'm paying the highest legal rent I can," is actually true. And that's precisely the problem. Rent control and rent stabilization have increasingly become a tool of the well-heeled and the well-connected. New York Gov. David Paterson, for example, also keeps a rent-stabilized apartment in the Lenox.

According to the New York City Rent Guidelines Board annual report, "Housing NYC: Rents, Markets and Trends," across the city there are 87,358 New York households reporting income of more than $100,000 a year which pay below-market rent thanks to the city's rent control and stabilization laws. A full 35% of all the city's apartments covered by the rent control regimes are rented by tenants who make more than $50,000 a year.

This system is destructive to the city's housing stock, because landlords who own rent-controlled apartments have less incentive to pay for repairs and upkeep. It also warps the housing market, and forces many new arrivals to occupy the least desirable apartments. New York has a city-wide vacancy rate of just 3%—and when good rent-stabilized apartments come on the market, you have to either know someone or pay someone (a broker, for example) to get it.

The result is that many renters who pay below-market rents are reluctant to move—because it's too difficult to get as good a deal elsewhere in the city. Thus, economists Ed Glaeser and Erzo Luttmer estimate that 21% of the city's renters live in apartments that are bigger or smaller than they would otherwise occupy. The controlled rents certainly don't increase the number of affordable apartments. . . .

*Source:* Eileen Norcross, "Rent Control Is the Real New York Scandal," *Wall Street Journal,* September 13, 2008, p. A11.

## Key Points in the Article

This is an opinion column (or, "op-ed") written by an opponent of rent control. As such, it is intended to help make a case against rent control by highlighting some of its more questionable aspects, such as Representative Charles Rangel of New York City renting four apartments at controlled rates. As we saw in the chapter opener, many apartments in New York City are subject to rent control. The stated purpose of rent control laws is to ensure that low-income people can find affordable housing. Rent control can have some unintended consequences, however, as this opinion column points out.

## Analyzing the News

**a** Rent control was first enacted in New York City in 1947 to deal with the post-World War II housing shortage. Few new apartment houses were built during the Great Depression of the 1930s or during World War II, so the increased demand for apartments immediately after the end of the war in 1945 caused rents to soar. Policymakers were afraid that low and moderate-income people would be unable to continue to live in the city if rents remained at their market levels. Even after the immediate postwar housing shortage passed, rent controls have remained in place down to the present, although the details of the laws have been changed. As the chapter opener discusses, current rent control laws in New York City are quite complex.

**b** Although rent control laws are typically meant to help low- and moderate-income people find affordable housing, rent-controlled apartments are often occupied by people with higher incomes who would be able to afford higher rents. The column focuses on Charles Rangel, who as a member of the U.S. House of Representatives had a base salary of $174,000 in 2009. Higher-income tenants end up in rent-controlled apartments for a couple reasons: (1) In New York, as in most other cities with rent control, there were no limits on the incomes of tenants occupying rent-controlled apartments. (Currently, as the column notes, landlords can free an apartment from rent control if the apartment has a rent of more than $2,000 per month and the tenant has an income of more than $175,000.) (2) Because rent control leads to a shortage of apartments, landlords will often favor renting to high-income tenants than to low-income tenants.

**c** The column argues that one unintended consequence of New York City's rent control laws has been a reduction in the number of apartment buildings with affordable apartments—which would be subject to rent control—and an increase in the number of apartment buildings with luxury apartments—which are not subject to rent control. In fact, rent control provides landlords and developers with an incentive to convert low and moderate-income housing to luxury housing in order to escape from the controls. Although the city has responded with tax incentives for builders of affordable housing, the net effect of rent control has been to reduce the supply of affordable housing. The figure shows the market for affordable apartments in New York City. In the absence of rent controls, the equilibrium would be $Rent_{Market}$, where demand curve $D$ intersects supply curve $S_1$. With rent control, the rent is $Rent_{Controlled}$. As we have seen in this chapter, one consequence of rent control is a shortage of apartments, which in the figure is equal to $Q_1 - Q_2$. But if rent control also leads to a reduction in the supply of affordable apartments, then the supply curve will shift from $S_1$ to $S_2$. This reduction in supply increases the shortage of apartments to $Q_1 - Q_3$.

## Thinking Critically
### *About Policy*

1. The article describes the significant costs associated with rent control laws. Despite these costs, rent control laws are very popular with tenants and local politicians. Why would some tenants support rent control laws? Do all tenants in the market gain from rent control laws?

2. Economists are often critical of rent control laws for several reasons. One reason is that the laws create a deadweight loss. The magnitude of the deadweight loss depends on the slopes of the demand and supply curves. Look at the figure for Solved Problem 4-3 on page 110. The deadweight loss equals $B + C$, which is the yellow area. What causes the deadweight loss? What would the supply curve have to look like for the deadweight loss to equal zero?

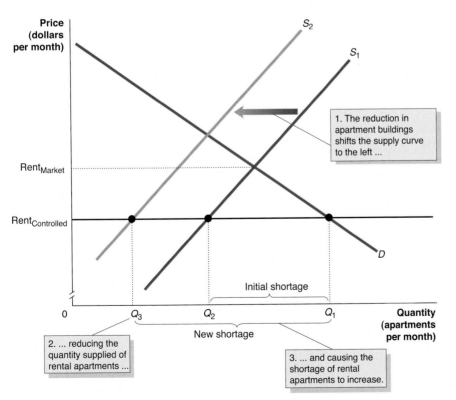

1. The reduction in apartment buildings shifts the supply curve to the left ...

2. ... reducing the quantity supplied of rental apartments ...

3. ... and causing the shortage of rental apartments to increase.

Initial shortage

New shortage

The effect of rent control laws on the supply of affordable apartments.

# Key Terms

---

**4.1**   **Consumer Surplus and Producer Surplus, pages 98–102**
LEARNING OBJECTIVE: Distinguish between the concepts of consumer surplus and producer surplus.

## Summary

Although most prices are determined by demand and supply in markets, the government sometimes imposes *price ceilings* and *price floors*. A **price ceiling** is a legally determined maximum price that sellers may charge. A **price floor** is a legally determined minimum price that sellers may receive. Economists analyze the effects of price ceilings and price floors using *consumer surplus* and *producer surplus*. **Marginal benefit** is the additional benefit to a consumer from consuming one more unit of a good or service. The demand curve is also a marginal benefit curve. **Consumer surplus** is the difference between the highest price a consumer is willing to pay for a good or service and the price the consumer actually pays. The total amount of consumer surplus in a market is equal to the area below the demand curve and above the market price. **Marginal cost** is the additional cost to a firm of producing one more unit of a good or service. The supply curve is also a marginal cost curve. **Producer surplus** is the difference between the lowest price a firm is willing to accept for a good or service and the price it actually receives. The total amount of producer surplus in a market is equal to the area above the supply curve and below the market price.

  Visit www.myeconlab.com to complete these exercises online and get instant feedback.

## Review Questions

1.1  What is marginal benefit? Why is the demand curve referred to as a marginal benefit curve?

1.2  What is marginal cost? Why is the supply curve referred to as a marginal cost curve?

1.3  What is consumer surplus? How does consumer surplus change as the equilibrium price of a good rises or falls?

1.4  What is producer surplus? How does producer surplus change as the equilibrium price of a good rises or falls?

## Problems and Applications

1.5  Suppose that a frost in Florida reduces the size of the orange crop, which causes the supply curve for oranges to shift to the left. Briefly explain whether

each of the following will increase or decrease. Use demand and supply to illustrate your answers.
a. Consumer surplus
b. Producer surplus

1.6  A student makes the following argument: "When a market is in equilibrium, there is no consumer surplus. We know this because in equilibrium, the market price is equal to the price consumers are willing to pay for the good." Briefly explain whether you agree with the student's argument.

1.7  The following graph illustrates the market for a breast cancer–fighting drug, without which breast cancer patients cannot survive. What is the consumer surplus in this market? How does it differ from the consumer surplus in the markets you have studied up to this point?

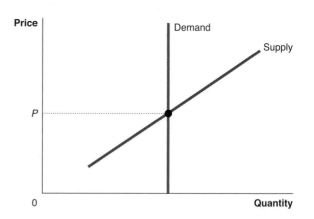

1.8  (Related to the *Making the Connection* on page 100) The *Making the Connection* states that the value of the area representing consumer surplus from broadband Internet service is $890.5 million. Use the information from the graph in the *Making the Connection* to show how this value was calculated. (For a review of how to calculate the area of a triangle, see the appendix to Chapter 1.)

1.9  The graph at the top of the next page shows the market for tickets to a concert that will be held in a local arena that seats 15,000 people. What is the producer surplus in this market? How does it differ from the producer surplus in the markets you have studied up to this point?

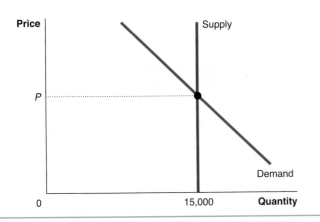

1.10 A study estimates that the total consumer surplus gained by people participating in auctions on eBay in a recent year was $7 billion. Is it likely that the total consumer surplus for the items bought in these auctions was higher or lower than it would have been if the items had been purchased for fixed prices in retail stores?

Source: Ravi Bapna, Wolfgang Jank, and Galit Shmueli, "Consumer Surplus in Online Auctions," *Information Systems Research*, Vol. 19, No. 4, December 2008, pp. 400–416.

>> **End Learning Objective 4.1**

---

**4.2** **The Efficiency of Competitive Markets, pages 102–106**
LEARNING OBJECTIVE: Understand the concept of economic efficiency.

## Summary

Equilibrium in a competitive market is **economically efficient**. **Economic surplus** is the sum of consumer surplus and producer surplus. Economic efficiency is a market outcome in which the marginal benefit to consumers from the last unit produced is equal to the marginal cost of production and where the sum of consumer surplus and producer surplus is at a maximum. When the market price is above or below the equilibrium price, there is a reduction in economic surplus. The reduction in economic surplus resulting from a market not being in competitive equilibrium is called the **deadweight loss**.

 Visit www.myeconlab.com to complete these exercises online and get instant feedback.

## Review Questions

2.1 Define *economic surplus* and *deadweight loss*.
2.2 What is economic efficiency? Why do economists define *efficiency* in this way?

## Problems and Applications

2.3 Suppose you were assigned the task of coming up with a single number that would allow someone to compare the economic activity in one country to that in another country. How might such a number be related to economic efficiency and consumer and producer surplus?
2.4 Briefly explain whether you agree with the following statement: "If at the current quantity marginal benefit is greater than marginal cost, there will be a deadweight loss in the market. However, there is no deadweight loss when marginal cost is greater than marginal benefit."

2.5 Briefly explain whether you agree with the following statement: "If consumer surplus in a market increases, producer surplus must decrease."
2.6 Does an increase in economic surplus in a market always mean that economic efficiency in the market has increased? Briefly explain.
2.7 Using the graph below, explain why economic surplus would be smaller if $Q_1$ or $Q_3$ were the quantity produced than if $Q_2$ is the quantity produced.

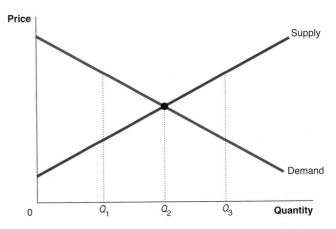

2.8 (Related to *Solved Problem 4-2* on page 105) In the United States, the Food and Drug Administration (FDA) regulates prescription drugs. Before a new prescription drug can be marketed in the U.S. market, the FDA must approve its use. Approval involves a long process of clinical testing and bureaucratic processing. Many people argue that the FDA is overly conservative, taking too long to approve new drugs. Often these drugs are available in other countries for years before they gain FDA approval in the United States. The extra time it takes for drugs to be approved for the U.S. market adds to the drug companies' development and production costs. Assuming that this criticism of the FDA's drug approval process is correct, draw a graph to show the loss in economic efficiency.

Why might the FDA approval process be slower than the approval processes for new drugs in other countries?

**» End Learning Objective 4.2**

**4.3  Government Intervention in the Market: Price Floors and Price Ceilings, pages 106–113**

LEARNING OBJECTIVE: Explain the economic effect of government-imposed price floors and price ceilings.

## Summary

Producers or consumers who are dissatisfied with the market outcome can attempt to convince the government to impose price floors or price ceilings. Price floors usually increase producer surplus, decrease consumer surplus, and cause a deadweight loss. Price ceilings usually increase consumer surplus, reduce producer surplus, and cause a deadweight loss. The results of the government imposing price ceilings and price floors are that some people win, some people lose, and a loss of economic efficiency occurs. Price ceilings and price floors can lead to a **black market**, where buying and selling take place at prices that violate government price regulations. Positive analysis is concerned with what is, and normative analysis is concerned with what should be. Positive analysis shows that price ceilings and price floors cause deadweight losses. Whether these policies are desirable or undesirable, though, is a normative question.

 Visit www.myeconlab.com to complete these exercises online and get instant feedback.

## Review Questions

3.1  Why do some consumers tend to favor price controls while others tend to oppose them?

3.2  Do producers tend to favor price floors or price ceilings? Why?

3.3  What is a black market? Under what circumstances do black markets arise?

3.4  Can economic analysis provide a final answer to the question of whether the government should intervene in markets by imposing price ceilings and price floors? Why or why not?

## Problems and Applications

3.5  The graph below shows the market for apples. Assume that the government has imposed a price floor of $10 per crate.

a. How many crates of apples will be sold after the price floor has been imposed?

b. Will there be a shortage or a surplus? If there is a shortage or a surplus, how large will it be?

c. Will apple producers benefit from the price floor? If so, explain how they will benefit.

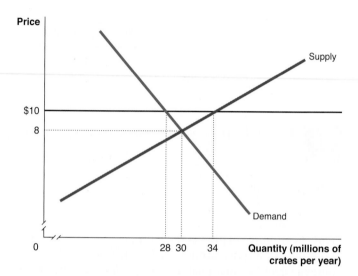

3.6  Use the information on the kumquat market in the table to answer the following questions.

a. What are the equilibrium price and quantity? How much revenue do kumquat producers receive when the market is in equilibrium? Draw a graph showing the market equilibrium and the area representing the revenue received by kumquat producers.

| PRICE (PER CRATE) | QUANTITY DEMANDED (MILLIONS OF CRATES PER YEAR) | QUANTITY SUPPLIED (MILLIONS OF CRATES PER YEAR) |
|---|---|---|
| $10 | 120 | 20 |
| 15 | 110 | 60 |
| 20 | 100 | 100 |
| 25 | 90 | 140 |
| 30 | 80 | 180 |
| 35 | 70 | 220 |

b. Suppose the federal government decides to impose a price floor of $30 per crate. Now how many crates of kumquats will consumers purchase? How much revenue will kumquat producers receive? Assume that the government does not purchase any surplus kumquats. On your graph from question (a), show the price floor, the change in the quantity of kumquats purchased, and the revenue received by kumquat producers after the price floor is imposed.

c. Suppose the government imposes a price floor of $30 per crate and purchases any surplus kumquats from producers. Now how much revenue will kumquat producers receive? How much will the government spend on purchasing surplus kumquats? On your graph from question (a), show the area representing the amount the government spends to purchase the surplus kumquats.

**3.7** Suppose that the government sets a price floor for milk that is above the competitive equilibrium price.

a. Draw a graph showing this situation. Be sure your graph shows the competitive equilibrium price, the price floor, the quantity that would be sold in competitive equilibrium, and the quantity that would be sold with the price floor.

b. Compare the economic surplus in this market when there is a price floor and when there is no price floor.

**3.8** During 2007, the Venezuelan government allowed consumers to buy only a limited quantity of sugar. The government also imposed a ceiling on the price of sugar. As a result, both the quantity of sugar consumed and the market price of sugar were below the competitive equilibrium price and quantity. Draw a graph to illustrate this situation. On your graph, be sure to indicate the areas representing consumer surplus, producer surplus, and deadweight loss.

**3.9** Refer to problem 3.8. An article in the *New York Times* contained the following (Hugo Chávez is the president of Venezuela):

> José Vielma Mora, the chief of Seniat, the government's tax agency, oversaw a raid this month on a warehouse here where officials seized about 165 tons of sugar. Mr. Vielma said the raid exposed hoarding by vendors who were unwilling to sell the sugar at official prices. He and other officials in Mr. Chávez's government have repeatedly blamed the shortages on producers, intermediaries and grocers.

Do you agree that the shortages in the Venezuelan sugar market are the fault of "producers, intermediaries and grocers"? Briefly explain.

Source: Simon Romero, "Chavez Threatens to Jail Price Control Violators," *New York Times*, February 17, 2007.

**3.10** To drive a taxi legally in New York City, you must have a medallion issued by the city government. City officials have issued only 13,200 medallions. Let's assume that this puts an absolute limit on the number of taxi rides that can be supplied in New York City on any day because no one breaks the law by driving a taxi without a medallion. Let's also assume that each taxi can provide 6 trips per day. In that case, the supply of taxi rides is fixed at 79,200 (or 6 rides per taxi × 13,200 taxis). We show this in the following graph, with a vertical line at this quantity. *Assume*

*that there are no government controls on the prices that drivers can charge for rides.* Use the graph below to answer the following questions.

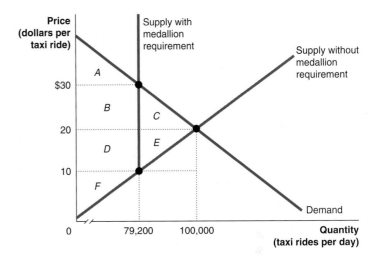

a. What would the equilibrium price and quantity be in this market if there were no medallion requirement?

b. What are the price and quantity with the medallion requirement?

c. Indicate on the graph the areas representing consumer surplus and producer surplus if there were no medallion requirement.

d. Indicate on the graph the areas representing consumer surplus, producer surplus, and deadweight loss with the medallion requirement.

**3.11** In 2008, the government of Ukraine imposed price controls on imports into the country of prescription drugs. Was this action likely to help or hurt consumers of prescription drugs in Ukraine? Briefly explain.

Source: "Currency Collapse in Ukraine," *Economist*, December 1, 2008.

**3.12** (Related to the *Making the Connection* on page 107) Some economists studying the effects of the minimum wage law have found that it tends to reduce the employment of black teenagers relative to white teenagers. Does the graph in the *Making the Connection* on page 108 help you understand why black teenagers may have been disproportionately affected by the minimum wage law? Briefly explain.

**3.13** (Related to the *Chapter Opener* on page 97) Suppose the competitive equilibrium rent for a standard two-bedroom apartment in Lawrence is $600. Now suppose the city council passes a rent control law, imposing a price ceiling of $500. Use a demand and supply graph to illustrate the impact of the rent control law. Suppose that shortly after the law is passed, a large employer in the area announces that it will close a plant in Lawrence and lay off 5,000 workers. Show on your graph how this will affect the market for rental property in Lawrence.

**3.14** (Related to *Solved Problem 4-3* on page 110) Use the information on the market for apartments in Bay City in the table below to answer the following questions.

| RENT | QUANTITY DEMANDED | QUANTITY SUPPLIED |
|------|-------------------|-------------------|
| $ 500 | 375,000 | 225,000 |
| 600 | 350,000 | 250,000 |
| 700 | 325,000 | 275,000 |
| 800 | 300,000 | 300,000 |
| 900 | 275,000 | 325,000 |
| 1,000 | 250,000 | 350,000 |

a. In the absence of rent control, what is the equilibrium rent, and what is the equilibrium quantity of apartments rented? Draw a demand and supply graph of the market for apartments to illustrate your answer. In equilibrium, will there be any renters who are unable to find an apartment to rent or any landlords who are unable to find a renter for an apartment?

b. Suppose the government sets a ceiling on rents of $600 per month. What is the quantity of apartments demanded, and what is the quantity of apartments supplied?

c. Assume that all landlords abide by the law. Use a demand and supply graph to illustrate the impact of this price ceiling on the market for apartments. Be sure to indicate on your graph each of the following: (i) the area representing consumer surplus after the price ceiling has been imposed, (ii) the area representing producer surplus after the price ceiling has been imposed, and (iii) the area representing the deadweight loss after the ceiling has been imposed.

d. Assume that the quantity of apartments supplied is the same as you determined in (b). But now assume that landlords ignore the law and rent this quantity of apartments for the highest rent they can get. Briefly explain what this rent will be.

**3.15** (Related to the *Making the Connection* on page 111) Joel Waldfogel argues that there is a deadweight loss to holiday gift giving. An article in the *Wall Street Journal* suggests that retail stores might be better off if the tradition of holiday gift giving ended: "In theory, smoother sales throughout the year would be better for retailers, enabling them to avoid the extra costs of planning and stocking up for the holidays." Owners of many stores disagree, however. The owner of a store in New York City was quoted in the article as arguing, "Christmas is the lifeblood of the retail business. It's a time of year when people don't have a choice. They *have* to spend." Do you believe the efficiency of the economy would be improved if the tradition of holiday gift giving ended? Briefly explain your reasoning.

Source: Mark Whitehouse, "How Christmas Brings Out the Grinch in Economists," *Wall Street Journal*, December 23, 2006, p. A1.

**3.16** (Related to the *Don't Let This Happen to You!* on page 110) Briefly explain whether you agree or disagree with the following statement: "If there is a shortage of a good, it must be scarce, but there is not a shortage of every scarce good."

**3.17** A student makes the following argument:

A price floor reduces the amount of a product that consumers buy because it keeps the price above the competitive market equilibrium. A price ceiling, on the other hand, increases the amount of a product that consumers buy because it keeps the price below the competitive market equilibrium.

Do you agree with the student's reasoning? Use a demand and supply graph to illustrate your answer.

**3.18** An advocate of medical care system reform makes the following argument:

The 15,000 kidneys that are transplanted in the United States each year are received for free from organ donors. Despite this, because of hospital and doctor fees, the average price of a kidney transplant is $250,000. As a result, only rich people or people with very good health insurance can afford these transplants. The government should put a ceiling of $100,000 on the price of kidney transplants. That way, middle-income people will be able to afford them, the demand for kidney transplants will increase, and more kidney transplants will take place.

Do you agree with the advocate's reasoning? Use a demand and supply graph to illustrate your answer.

**3.19** (Related to the *Chapter Opener* on page 97) The cities of Peabody and Woburn are five miles apart. Woburn enacts a rent control law that puts a ceiling on rents well below their competitive market value. Predict the impact of this law on the competitive equilibrium rent in Peabody, which does not have a rent control law. Illustrate your answer with a demand and supply graph.

**3.20** (Related to the *Chapter Opener* on page 97) According to an article in *The Economist*, because of rent controls in the Indian city of Mumbai, "landlords have left an estimated 40,000 properties vacant." Briefly explain why rent controls might result in landlords leaving properties vacant.

Source: "Creaking, Groaning," *Economist*, December 11, 2008.

**3.21** (Related to the *Chapter Opener* on page 97) The competitive equilibrium rent in the city of Lowell is currently $1,000 per month. The government decides to enact rent control and to establish a price ceiling for apartments of $750 per month. Briefly explain whether rent control is likely to make each of the following people better or worse off.

a. Someone currently renting an apartment in Lowell

b. Someone who will be moving to Lowell next year and who intends to rent an apartment

c. A landlord who intends to abide by the rent control law

d. A landlord who intends to ignore the law and illegally charge the highest rent possible for his apartments

**3.22** (Related to the *Chapter Opener* on page 97) The following is from a newspaper article:

> About ten years ago, a lawyer suggested that I withhold my rent because my landlord had consistently failed to provide adequate heat, and my building was infested with mice and roaches. When the landlord took me to court for not paying rent, his attorney offered no defense to my complaints about conditions in the building. I won an abatement and did not have to pay any rent for six months.
>
> Little did I know at the time that allowing the landlord to take me to Housing Court would make it almost impossible for me to rent another apartment, not only here in New York City, but anywhere in the United States.

Is it more likely that a tenant will be "blacklisted" in a city with rent control or one without rent control? Briefly explain.

Source: Susan Lippman, "Blacklist Blues: Landlords Use Dodgy Database to Fend Off Feisty Tenants," *The Indypendent*, December 12, 2008.

**3.23** (Related to *Solved Problem 4-3* on page 110) Suppose that initially the gasoline market is in equilibrium, at a price of $3.00 per gallon and a quantity of 45 million gallons per month. Then a war in the Middle East disrupts imports of oil into the United States, shifting the supply curve for gasoline from $S_1$ to $S_2$. The price of gasoline begins to rise, and consumers protest. The federal government responds

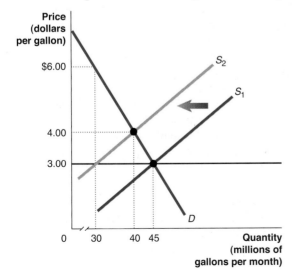

by setting a price ceiling of $3.00 per gallon. Use the graph to answer the following questions.

a. If there were no price ceiling, what would be the equilibrium price of gasoline, the quantity of gasoline demanded, and the quantity of gasoline supplied? Now assume that the price ceiling is imposed and that there is no black market in gasoline. What are the price of gasoline, the quantity of gasoline demanded, and the quantity of gasoline supplied? How large is the shortage of gasoline?

b. Assume that the price ceiling is imposed, and there is no black market in gasoline. Show on the graph the areas representing consumer surplus, producer surplus, and deadweight loss.

c. Now assume that there is a black market, and the price of gasoline rises to the maximum that consumers are willing to pay for the amount supplied by producers at $3.00 per gallon. Show on the graph the areas representing producer surplus, consumer surplus, and deadweight loss.

d. Are consumers made better off with the price ceiling than without it? Briefly explain.

**3.24** In the United States, Amazon.com, BarnesandNoble.com, and many other retailers sell books, DVDs, and music CDs for less than the price marked on the package. In Japan, retailers are not allowed to discount prices in this way. In what ways is this Japanese regulation similar to a price floor? Who benefits and who loses from this Japanese law?

**3.25** An editorial in the *Economist* magazine discusses the fact that in most countries—including the United States—it is illegal for individuals to buy or sell body parts, such as kidneys.

a. Draw a demand and supply graph for the market for kidneys. Show on your graph the legal maximum price of zero and indicate the quantity of kidneys supplied at this price. (*Hint:* Because we know that some kidneys are donated, the quantity supplied will not be zero.)

b. The editorial argues that buying and selling kidneys should be legalized:

> With proper regulation, a kidney market would be a big improvement over the current sorry state of affairs. Sellers could be checked for disease and drug use, and cared for after operations. . . . Buyers would get better kidneys, faster. Both sellers and buyers would do better than in the illegal market, where much of the money goes to middlemen.

Do you agree with this argument? Should the government treat kidneys like other goods and allow the market to determine the price?

Source: "Psst, Wanna Buy a Kidney?" *Economist*, November 18, 2006, p. 15.

**>> End Learning Objective 4.3**

## **The Economic Impact of Taxes,** pages 113–117

**4.4**

LEARNING OBJECTIVE: Analyze the economic impact of taxes.

## Summary

Most taxes result in a loss of consumer surplus, a loss of producer surplus, and a deadweight loss. The true burden of a tax is not just the amount paid to government by consumers and producers but also includes the deadweight loss. The deadweight loss from a tax is the excess burden of the tax. **Tax incidence** is the actual division of the burden of a tax. In most cases, consumers and firms share the burden of a tax levied on a good or service.

 Visit **www.myeconlab.com** to complete these exercises online and get instant feedback.

## Review Questions

4.1 What is meant by tax incidence?
4.2 Does who is legally responsible for paying a tax—buyers or sellers—make a difference in the amount of tax each pays? Briefly explain.

## Problems and Applications

4.3 Suppose the current equilibrium price of cheese pizzas is $10, and 10 million pizzas are sold per month. After the federal government imposes a $0.50 per pizza tax, the equilibrium price of pizzas rises to $10.40, and the equilibrium quantity falls to 9 million. Illustrate this situation with a demand and supply graph. Be sure your graph shows the equilibrium price before and after the tax, the equilibrium quantity before and after the tax, and the areas representing consumer surplus after the tax, producer surplus after the tax, tax revenue collected by the government, and deadweight loss.

4.4 Use the graph of the market for cigarettes below to answer the following questions.

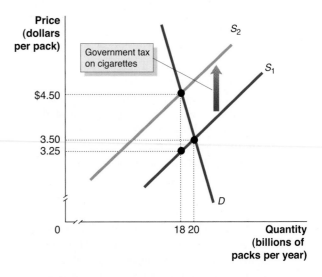

a. According to the graph, how much is the government tax on cigarettes?
b. What price do producers receive after paying the tax?
c. How much tax revenue does the government collect?
Illustrate your answer with a graph.
4.5 **(Related to the** *Making the Connection* **on page 116)** If the price consumers pay and the price sellers receive are not affected by whether consumers or sellers collect a tax on a good or service, why does the government usually require sellers and not consumers to collect a tax?

**>> End Learning Objective 4.4**

# Appendix

## Quantitative Demand and Supply Analysis

Graphs help us understand economic change *qualitatively*. For instance, a demand and supply graph can tell us that if household incomes rise, the demand curve for a normal good will shift to the right, and its price will rise. Often, though, economists, business managers, and policymakers want to know more than the qualitative direction of change; they want a *quantitative estimate* of the size of the change.

In this chapter, we carried out a qualitative analysis of rent controls. We saw that imposing rent controls involves a trade-off: Renters as a group gain, but landlords lose, and the market for apartments becomes less efficient, as shown by the deadweight loss. To better evaluate rent controls, we need to know more than just that these gains and losses exist; we need to know how large they are. A quantitative analysis of rent controls will tell us how large the gains and losses are.

## Demand and Supply Equations

The first step in a quantitative analysis is to supplement our use of demand and supply curves with demand and supply *equations*. We noted briefly in Chapter 3 that economists often statistically estimate equations for demand curves. Supply curves can also be statistically estimated. For example, suppose that economists have estimated that the demand for apartments in New York City is:

$$Q^D = 3,000,000 - 1,000P,$$

and the supply of apartments is:

$$Q^S = -450,000 + 1,300P.$$

We have used $Q^D$ for the quantity of apartments demanded per month, $Q^S$ for the quantity of apartments supplied per month, and $P$ for the apartment rent in dollars per month. In reality, both the quantity of apartments demanded and the quantity of apartments supplied will depend on more than just the rental price of apartments in New York City. For instance, the demand for apartments in New York City will also depend on the average incomes of families in the New York area and on the rents of apartments in surrounding cities. For simplicity, we will ignore these other factors.

With no government intervention, we know that at competitive market equilibrium, the quantity demanded must equal the quantity supplied, or:

$$Q^D = Q^S.$$

We can use this equation, which is called an *equilibrium condition*, to solve for the equilibrium monthly apartment rent by setting the demand equation equal to the supply equation:

$$3,000,000 - 1,000P = -450,000 + 1,300P$$

$$3,450,000 = 2,300P$$

$$P = \frac{3,450,000}{2,300} = \$1,500.$$

We can then substitute this price back into either the supply equation or the demand equation to find the equilibrium quantity of apartments rented:

$$Q^D = 3,000,000 - 1,000P = 3,000,000 - 1,000(1,500) = 1,500,000$$

$$Q^S = -450,000 + 1,300P = -450,000 + 1,300(1,500) = 1,500,000.$$

Figure 4A-1 illustrates the information from these equations in a graph. The figure shows the values for rent when the quantity supplied is zero and when the quantity demanded is zero. These values can be calculated from the demand equation and the supply equation by setting $Q^D$ and $Q^S$ equal to zero and solving for price:

$$Q^D = 0 = 3,000,000 - 1,000P$$

$$P = \frac{3,000,000}{1,000} = \$3,000$$

and:

$$Q^S = 0 = -450,000 + 1,300P$$

$$P = \frac{-450,000}{-1,300} = \$346.15.$$

# Calculating Consumer Surplus and Producer Surplus

Figure 4A-1 shows consumer surplus and producer surplus in this market. Recall that the sum of consumer surplus and producer surplus equals the net benefit that renters and landlords receive from participating in the market for apartments. We can use the values from the demand and supply equations to calculate the value of consumer surplus and producer surplus. Remember that consumer surplus is the area below the demand curve and above the line representing market price. Notice that this area forms a right triangle because the demand curve is a straight line—it is *linear*. As we noted in the appendix to Chapter 1, the area of a triangle is equal to ½ × Base × Height. In this case, the area is:

$$\tfrac{1}{2} \times (1,500,000) \times (3,000 - 1,500) = \$1,125,000,000.$$

So, this calculation tells us that the consumer surplus in the market for rental apartments in New York City would be about $1.125 billion.

## Figure 4A-1

### Graphing Supply and Demand Equations

After statistically estimating supply and demand equations, we can use the equations to draw supply and demand curves. In this case, the equilibrium rent for apartments is $1,500 per month, and the equilibrium quantity of apartments rented is 1,500,000. The supply equation tells us that at a rent of $346, the quantity of apartments supplied will be zero. The demand equation tells us that at a rent of $3,000, the quantity of apartments demanded will be zero. The areas representing consumer surplus and producer surplus are also indicated on the graph.

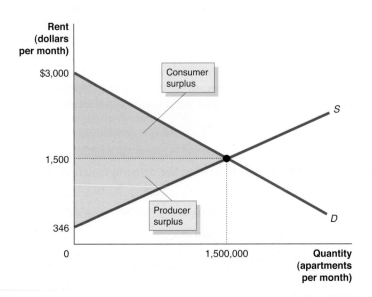

We can calculate producer surplus in a similar way. Remember that producer surplus is the area above the supply curve and below the line representing market price. Because our supply curve is also a straight line, producer surplus on the figure is equal to the area of the right triangle:

$$\frac{1}{2} \times 1,500,000 \times (1,500 - 346) = \$865,500,000.$$

This calculation tells us that the producer surplus in the market for rental apartments in New York City is about $865 million.

We can use this same type of analysis to measure the impact of rent control on consumer surplus, producer surplus, and economic efficiency. For instance, suppose the city imposes a rent ceiling of $1,000 per month. Figure 4A-2 can help guide us as we measure the impact.

First, we can calculate the quantity of apartments that will actually be rented by substituting the rent ceiling of $1,000 into the supply equation:

$$Q^S = -450,000 + (1,300 \times 1,000) = 850,000.$$

We also need to know the price on the demand curve when the quantity of apartments is 850,000. We can do this by substituting 850,000 for quantity in the demand equation and solving for price:

$$850,000 = 3,000,000 - 1,000P$$

$$P = \frac{-2,150,000}{-1,000} = \$2,150.$$

Compared with its value in competitive equilibrium, consumer surplus has been reduced by a value equal to the area of the yellow triangle *B* but increased by a value equal to the area of the blue rectangle *A*. The area of the yellow triangle *B* is:

$$\frac{1}{2} \times (1,500,000 - 850,000) \times (2,150 - 1,500) = \$211,250,000,$$

and the area of the blue rectangle *A* is Base × Height, or:

$$(\$1,500 - \$1,000) \times (850,000) = \$425,000,000.$$

The value of consumer surplus in competitive equilibrium was $1,125,000,000. As a result of the rent ceiling, it will be increased to:

$$(\$1,125,000,000 + \$425,000,000) - \$211,250,000 = \$1,338,750,000.$$

Compared with its value in competitive equilibrium, producer surplus has been reduced by a value equal to the area of the yellow triangle *C* plus a value equal to the area of the blue rectangle. The area of the yellow triangle *C* is:

$$\frac{1}{2} \times (1,500,000 - 850,000) \times (1,500 - 1,000) = \$162,500,000.$$

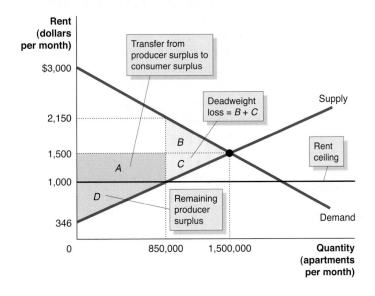

### Figure 4A-2

**Calculating the Economic Effect of Rent Controls**

Once we have estimated equations for the demand and supply of rental housing, a diagram can guide our numeric estimates of the economic effects of rent control. Consumer surplus falls by an amount equal to the area of the yellow triangle *B* and increases by an amount equal to the area of the blue rectangle *A*. The difference between the values of these two areas is $213,750,000. Producer surplus falls by an amount equal to the area of the blue rectangle *A* plus the area of the yellow triangle *C*. The value of these two areas is $587,500,000. The remaining producer surplus is equal to the area of triangle *D*, or $278,000,000. Deadweight loss is equal to the area of triangle *B* plus the area of triangle *C*, or $373,750,000.

We have already calculated the area of the blue rectangle *A* as $425,000,000. The value of producer surplus in competitive equilibrium was $865,500,000. As a result of the rent ceiling, it will be reduced to:

$$\$865,500,000 - \$162,500,000 - \$425,000,000 = \$278,000,000.$$

The loss of economic efficiency, as measured by the deadweight loss, is equal to the value represented by the areas of the yellow triangles *B* and *C*, or:

$$\$211,250,000 + \$162,500,000 = \$373,750,000.$$

The following table summarizes the results of the analysis (the values are in millions of dollars).

| CONSUMER SURPLUS | | PRODUCER SURPLUS | | DEADWEIGHT LOSS | |
|---|---|---|---|---|---|
| COMPETITIVE EQUILIBRIUM | RENT CONTROL | COMPETITIVE EQUILIBRIUM | RENT CONTROL | COMPETITIVE EQUILIBRIUM | RENT CONTROL |
| $1,125 | $1,338.75 | $865.50 | $278 | $0 | $373.75 |

Qualitatively, we know that imposing rent controls will make consumers better off, make landlords worse off, and decrease economic efficiency. The advantage of the analysis we have just gone through is that it puts dollar values on the qualitative results. We can now see how much consumers have gained, how much landlords have lost, and how great the decline in economic efficiency has been. Sometimes the quantitative results can be surprising. Notice, for instance, that after the imposition of rent control, the deadweight loss is actually greater than the remaining producer surplus.

Economists often study issues where the qualitative results of actions are apparent, even to non-economists. You don't have to be an economist to understand who wins and who loses from rent control or that if a company cuts the price of its product, its sales will increase. Business managers, policymakers, and the general public do, however, need economists to measure quantitatively the effects of different actions—including policies such as rent control—so that they can better assess the results of these actions.

---

**4A**   **Quantitative Demand and Supply Analysis, pages 127–130**

LEARNING OBJECTIVE: Use quantitative demand and supply analysis.

  Visit **www.myeconlab.com** to complete these exercises online and get instant feedback.

## Review Questions

**4A.1** In a linear demand equation, what economic information is conveyed by the intercept on the price axis?

**4A.2** Suppose you were assigned the task of choosing a price that maximized economic surplus in a market. What price would you choose? Why?

**4A.3** Consumer surplus is used as a measure of a consumer's net benefit from purchasing a good or service. Explain why consumer surplus is a measure of net benefit.

**4A.4** Why would economists use the term *deadweight loss* to describe the impact on consumer surplus and producer surplus from a price control?

## Problems and Applications

**4A.5** Suppose that you have been hired to analyze the impact on employment from the imposition of a minimum wage in the labor market. Further suppose that you estimate the supply and demand functions for labor, where *L* stands for the quantity of labor (measured in thousands of workers) and *W* stands for the wage rate (measured in dollars per hour):

Demand:     $L^D = 100 - 4W$
Supply:     $L^S = 6W$

First, calculate the free-market equilibrium wage and quantity of labor. Now suppose the proposed minimum wage is $12. How large will the surplus of labor in this market be?

**4A.6** The following graphs illustrate the markets for two different types of labor. Suppose an identical minimum wage is imposed in both markets. In which market will the minimum wage have the largest impact on employment? Why?

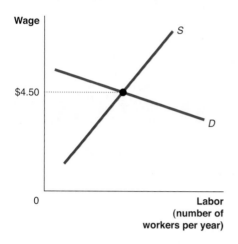

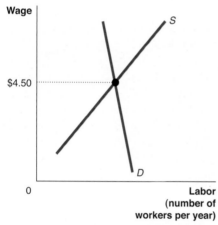

**4A.7** Suppose that you are the vice president of operations of a manufacturing firm that sells an industrial lubricant in a competitive market. Further suppose that your economist gives you the following supply and demand functions:

Demand: $Q^D = 45 - 2P$
Supply: $Q^S = -15 + P$

What is the consumer surplus in this market? What is the producer surplus?

**4A.8** The following graph shows a market in which a price floor of $3.00 per unit has been imposed. Calculate the values of each of the following.

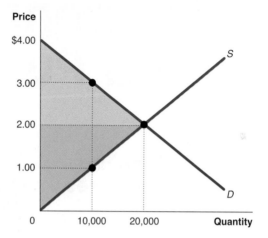

a. The deadweight loss
b. The transfer of producer surplus to consumers or the transfer of consumer surplus to producers
c. Producer surplus after the price floor is imposed
d. Consumer surplus after the price floor is imposed

**4A.9** Construct a table like the one in this appendix on page 130, but assume that the rent ceiling is $1,200 rather than $1,000.

**>> End Appendix Learning Objective**

CHAPTER **5**

# Externalities, Environmental Policy, and Public Goods

## Chapter Outline and Learning Objectives

# >> Economic Policy and the Environment

Pollution is a part of economic life. Consumers create air pollution by burning gasoline to power their cars and natural gas to heat their homes. Firms create air pollution when they produce electricity, pesticides, or plastics, among other products. Utilities produce sulfur dioxide when they burn coal to generate electricity. Sulfur dioxide contributes to acid rain, which can damage trees, crops, and buildings. The burning of fossil fuels generates carbon dioxide and other greenhouse gases that can increase global warming.

How should government policy deal with the problem of pollution? Can economic analysis help in formulating more efficient pollution policies? In the past, Congress frequently employed policies that ordered firms to use particular methods to reduce pollution. But many economists are critical of this approach—known as *command and control*—because some companies are able to reduce their emissions much more inexpensively if they are allowed to choose the method. Many economists argue that a more efficient way to deal with pollution is through a *market-based approach*. For instance, a tax on carbon dioxide emissions would give utilities and other firms an incentive to reduce pollution efficiently.

In 2009, President Barack Obama proposed a market-based policy known as *cap-and-trade*. Under this system, the federal government would distribute allowances to produce a given amount of carbon dioxide emissions. Firms would buy and sell allowances, although they must end up with allowances equal to the amount of carbon dioxide they emit. James Rogers, the chief executive officer of Duke Energy, a North Carolina–based utility, was among the critics of the plan. Rogers argued that the proposed cap-and-trade system would result in electric utility rates rising as much as 40 percent.

As we will see in this chapter, economic analysis can play a significant role in evaluating the effects of environmental policies.

**AN INSIDE LOOK AT POLICY** on **page 158** discusses the views of an energy company executive who favors using a cap-and-trade policy to reduce emissions of carbon dioxide.

Sources: Stephen Power, "Duke Energy CEO: Cap-and-Trade Plan Would Raise Electric Rates 40%," *Wall Street Journal*, February 27, 2009; and Darren Samuelson, "Obama Erred on Key Cap-and-Trade Features, Economists Say," *New York Times*, March 13, 2009.

## Economics in YOUR LIFE!

### What's the "Best" Level of Pollution?

Carbon taxes and a cap-and-trade policy are alternative approaches for achieving the goal of reducing carbon dioxide emissions. But how do we know the "best" level of carbon emissions? If carbon dioxide emissions hurt the environment, should the government take action to eliminate them completely? As you read the chapter, see if you can answer these questions. You can check your answers against those we provide at the end of the chapter.

▶ Continued on page 157

**Externality** A benefit or cost that affects someone who is not directly involved in the production or consumption of a good or service.

Pollution is just one example of an *externality*. An **externality** is a benefit or cost that affects someone who is not directly involved in the production or consumption of a good or service. In the case of air pollution, there is a *negative externality* because, for example, people with asthma may bear a cost even though they were not involved in the buying or selling of the electricity that caused the pollution. *Positive externalities* are also possible. For instance, medical research can provide a positive externality because people who are not directly involved in producing it or paying for it can benefit. A competitive market usually does a good job of producing the economically efficient amount of a good or service. This may not be true, though, if there is an externality in the market. When there is a negative externality, the market may produce a quantity of the good that is greater than the efficient amount. When there is a positive externality, the market may produce a quantity that is less than the efficient amount. In Chapter 4, we saw that government interventions in the economy—such as price floors on agricultural products or price ceilings on rents—can reduce economic efficiency. But when there are externalities, government intervention may actually increase economic efficiency and enhance the well-being of society. The way in which government intervenes is important, however. Economists can help policymakers ensure that government programs are as efficient as possible.

In this chapter, we explore how best to deal with the problem of pollution and other externalities. We also look at *public goods*, which are goods that may not be produced at all unless the government produces them.

**5.1 LEARNING** OBJECTIVE

Identify examples of positive and negative externalities and use graphs to show how externalities affect economic efficiency.

# Externalities and Economic Efficiency

When you consume a Big Mac, only you benefit, but when you consume a college education, other people also benefit. College-educated people are less likely to commit crimes and, by being better-informed voters, more likely to contribute to better government policies. So, although you capture most of the benefits of your college education, you do not capture all of them.

When you buy a Big Mac, the price you pay covers all McDonald's costs of producing the Big Mac. When you buy electricity from a utility that burns coal and generates acid rain, the price you pay for the electricity does not cover the cost of the damage caused by the acid rain.

So, there is a *positive externality* in the production of college educations because people who do not pay for college educations will nonetheless benefit from them. There is a *negative externality* in the generation of electricity because, for example, people with homes on a lake from which fish and wildlife have disappeared because of acid rain have incurred a cost, even though they might not have bought their electricity from the polluting utility.

## The Effect of Externalities

**Private cost** The cost borne by the producer of a good or service.

**Social cost** The total cost of producing a good or service, including both the private cost and any external cost.

**Private benefit** The benefit received by the consumer of a good or service.

**Social benefit** The total benefit from consuming a good or service, including both the private benefit and any external benefit.

Externalities interfere with the *economic efficiency* of a market equilibrium. We saw in Chapter 4 that a competitive market achieves economic efficiency by maximizing the sum of consumer surplus and producer surplus. *But that result holds only if there are no externalities in production or consumption.* An externality causes a difference between the *private cost* of production and the *social cost*, or the *private benefit* from consumption and the *social benefit*. The **private cost** is the cost borne by the producer of a good or service. The **social cost** is the total cost of producing a good or service, and is equal to the private cost plus any external cost, such as the cost of pollution. Unless there is an externality, the private cost and the social cost are equal. The **private benefit** is the benefit received by the consumer of a good or service. The **social benefit** is the total benefit from consuming a good or service, and is equal to the private benefit plus any external benefit, such as the benefit to others resulting from your college education. Unless there is an externality, the private benefit and the social benefit are equal.

## How a Negative Externality in Production Reduces Economic Efficiency

Consider how a negative externality in production affects economic efficiency. In Chapters 3 and 4, we assumed that the producer of a good or service must bear all the costs of production. We now know that this observation is not always true. In producing electricity, private costs are borne by the utility, but some external costs of pollution are borne by people who are not customers of the utility. The social cost of producing electricity is the sum of the private cost plus the external cost. Figure 5-1 shows the effect on the market for electricity of a negative externality in production.

$S_1$ is the market supply curve and represents only the private costs that utilities have to bear in generating electricity. As we saw in Chapter 4, firms will supply an additional unit of a good or service only if they receive a price equal to the additional cost of producing that unit, so a supply curve represents the *marginal cost* of producing a good or service. If utilities also had to bear the cost of pollution, the supply curve would be $S_2$, which represents the true marginal social cost of generating electricity. The equilibrium with price $P_{Efficient}$ and quantity $Q_{Efficient}$ is efficient. The equilibrium with price $P_{Market}$ and quantity $Q_{Market}$ is not efficient. To see why, remember from Chapter 4 that an equilibrium is economically efficient if economic surplus—which is the sum of consumer surplus plus producer surplus—is at a maximum. When economic surplus is at a maximum, the net benefit to society from the production of the good or service is at a maximum. With an equilibrium quantity of $Q_{Efficient}$, economic surplus is at a maximum, so this equilibrium is efficient. But with an equilibrium quantity of $Q_{Market}$, economic surplus is reduced by the deadweight loss, shown in Figure 5-1 by the yellow triangle, and the equilibrium is not efficient. The deadweight loss occurs because the supply curve is above the demand curve for the production of the units of electricity between $Q_{Efficient}$ and $Q_{Market}$. That is, the additional cost—including the external cost—of producing these units is greater than the marginal benefit to consumers, as represented by the demand curve. In other words, because of the cost of the pollution, economic efficiency would be improved if less electricity were produced.

We can conclude the following: *When there is a negative externality in producing a good or service, too much of the good or service will be produced at market equilibrium.*

## How a Positive Externality in Consumption Reduces Economic Efficiency

We have seen that a negative externality interferes with achieving economic efficiency. The same holds true for a positive externality. In Chapters 3 and 4, we assumed that the demand curve represents all the benefits that come from consuming a good. But we have seen that a college education generates benefits that are not captured by the student receiving the education and so are not represented in the market demand curve for

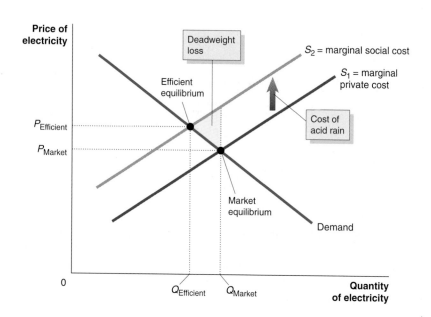

## Figure 5-1

### The Effect of Pollution on Economic Efficiency

Because utilities do not bear the cost of acid rain, they produce electricity beyond the economically efficient level. Supply curve $S_1$ represents just the marginal private cost that the utility has to pay. Supply curve $S_2$ represents the marginal social cost, which includes the costs to those affected by acid rain. The figure shows that if the supply curve were $S_2$, rather than $S_1$, market equilibrium would occur at price $P_{Efficient}$ and quantity $Q_{Efficient}$, the economically efficient level of output. But when the supply curve is $S_1$, the market equilibrium occurs at price $P_{Market}$ and quantity $Q_{Market}$, where there is a deadweight loss equal to the area of the yellow triangle. Because of the deadweight loss, this equilibrium is not efficient.

## Figure 5-2

**The Effect of a Positive Externality on Efficiency**

People who do not consume college educations can still benefit from them. As a result, the marginal social benefit from a college education is greater than the marginal private benefit seen by college students. Because only the marginal private benefit is represented in the market demand curve $D_1$, the quantity of college educations produced, $Q_{Market}$, is too low. If the market demand curve were $D_2$ instead of $D_1$, the level of college educations produced would be $Q_{Efficient}$, which is the efficient level. At the market equilibrium of $Q_{Market}$, there is a deadweight loss equal to the area of the yellow triangle.

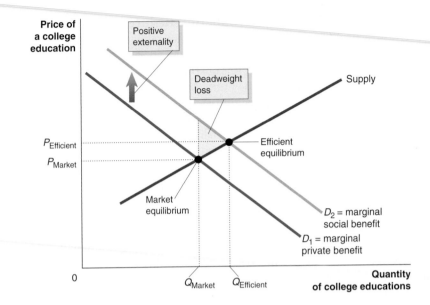

college educations. Figure 5-2 shows the effect of a positive externality in consumption on the market for college educations.

If students receiving a college education could capture all its benefits, the demand curve would be $D_2$, which represents the marginal social benefits. The actual demand curve is $D_1$, however, which represents only the marginal private benefits received by students. The efficient equilibrium would come at price $P_{Efficient}$ and quantity $Q_{Efficient}$. At this equilibrium, economic surplus is maximized. The market equilibrium, at price $P_{Market}$ and quantity $Q_{Market}$, will not be efficient because the demand curve is above the supply curve for production of the units between $Q_{Market}$ and $Q_{Efficient}$. That is, the marginal benefit—including the external benefit—for producing these units is greater than the marginal cost. As a result, there is a deadweight loss equal to the area of the yellow triangle. Because of the positive externality, economic efficiency would be improved if more college educations were produced. We can conclude the following: *When there is a positive externality in consuming a good or service, too little of the good or service will be produced at market equilibrium.*

# Solved Problem | 5-1

## Finding a Cure for Malaria

Malaria is a serious disease caused by a parasite. Patients with malaria typically suffer from high fevers, chills, and other flu-like symptoms. The World Health Organization estimates that 300 million to 500 million cases of malaria occur each year. For more than 1 million people each year, the disease is fatal. Only about 1,300 cases of malaria are diagnosed in the United States; most of these cases involve people who contracted the disease after traveling abroad to malaria-risk areas. The disease is usually transmitted through a bite from an infected *Anopheles* mosquito.

Draw a graph that illustrates the impact associated with research directed at finding a cure for malaria. Assume that all research efforts are funded through private markets.

### SOLVING THE PROBLEM:

**Step 1:  Review the chapter material.** This problem is about externalities and efficiency, so you may want to review the section "Externalities and Economic Efficiency," which begins on page 134.

**Step 2:  Draw a graph to illustrate the externality associated with privately funded research to cure malaria.**

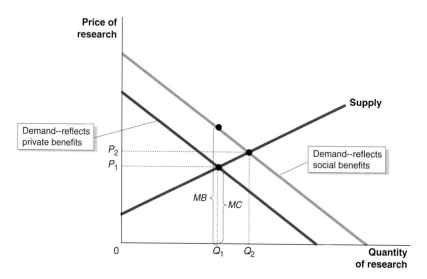

**Step 3:** **Describe how the externality causes a deviation from economic efficiency.**
There is a positive externality associated with malaria research because of the external benefits it generates. Assume that researchers were to find a cure for malaria. Using the World Health Organization's figures, 300 million to 500 million people (per year) could be cured of malaria. Even if the benefits to these people were very conservatively estimated at $2 each, the external benefits would be $600 million to $1 billion. Of course, the research is by nature uncertain, and doctors and other scientists can work many years without finding a cure. Private hospitals and research laboratories are likely to receive a relatively small amount of the social benefit from their efforts. As a result, the private demand for malaria research will be less than the demand that reflects social benefits. The private market equilibrium price and quantity would be $P_1$ and $Q_1$; at this point, the marginal social benefit ($MSB$) would exceed the marginal cost ($MC$). The economically efficient level price and quantity would be $P_2$ and $Q_2$, where marginal social benefit is equal to marginal cost.

*Source*: Centers for Disease Control and Prevention. *Malaria: Frequently Asked Questions.* www.cdc.gov/malaria/faq.htm.

**YOUR TURN:** For more practice, do related problem 1.12 on page 161 at the end of this chapter.

## Externalities and Market Failure

We have seen that because of externalities, the efficient level of output may not occur in either the market for electricity or the market for college educations. These are examples of **market failure**: situations in which the market fails to produce the efficient level of output. Later, we will discuss possible solutions to problems of externalities. But first we need to consider why externalities occur.

**Market failure** A situation in which the market fails to produce the efficient level of output.

## What Causes Externalities?

We saw in Chapter 2 that governments need to guarantee *property rights* in order for a market system to function well. **Property rights** refers to the rights individuals or businesses have to the exclusive use of their property, including the right to buy or sell it. Property can be tangible, physical property, such as a store or factory. Property can also be intangible, such as the right to an idea. Most of the time, the U.S. government and the governments of other high-income countries do a good job of enforcing property rights, but in certain situations, property rights do not exist or cannot be legally enforced.

Consider the following situation: Lee owns land that includes a lake. A paper company wants to lease some of Lee's land to build a pulp and paper mill. The paper mill will discharge pollutants into Lee's lake. Because Lee owns the lake, he can charge the paper

**Property rights** The rights individuals or businesses have to the exclusive use of their property, including the right to buy or sell it.

company the cost of cleaning up the pollutants. The result is that the cost of the pollution is a private cost to the paper company and is included in the price of the paper it sells. There is no externality, the efficient level of paper is produced, and there is no market failure.

Now suppose that the paper company builds its paper mill on privately owned land on the banks of a lake that is owned by the state. In the absence of any government regulations, the company will be free to discharge pollutants into the lake. The cost of the pollution will be external to the company because it doesn't have to pay the cost of cleaning it up. More than the economically efficient level of paper will be produced, and a market failure will occur. Or, suppose that Lee owns the lake, but the pollution is caused by acid rain generated by an electric utility hundreds of miles away. The law does not allow Lee to charge the electric utility for the damage caused by the acid rain. Even though someone is damaging Lee's property, the law does not allow him to enforce his property rights in this situation. Once again, there is an externality, and the market failure will result in too much electricity being produced.

Similarly, if you buy a house, the government will protect your right to exclusive use of that house. No one else can use the house without your permission. Because of your property rights in the house, your private benefit from the house and the social benefit are the same. When you buy a college education, however, other people are, in effect, able to benefit from your college education. You have no property right that will enable you to prevent them from benefiting or to charge them for the benefits they receive. As a result, there is a positive externality, and the market failure will result in too few college educations being supplied.

We can conclude the following: *Externalities and market failures result from incomplete property rights or from the difficulty of enforcing property rights in certain situations.*

**5.2 LEARNING** OBJECTIVE

Discuss the Coase theorem and explain how private bargaining can lead to economic efficiency in a market with an externality.

# Private Solutions to Externalities: The Coase Theorem

As noted at the beginning of this chapter, government intervention may actually increase economic efficiency and enhance the well-being of society when externalities are present. It is also possible, however, for people to find private solutions to the problem of externalities.

Can the market cure market failure? In an important article written in 1960, Ronald Coase of the University of Chicago, winner of the 1991 Nobel Prize in Economics, argued that under some circumstances, private solutions to the problem of externalities will occur. To understand Coase's argument, it is important to recognize that completely eliminating an externality usually is not economically efficient. Consider pollution, for example. There is, in fact, an *economically efficient level of pollution reduction*. At first, this seems paradoxical. Pollution is bad, and you might think the efficient amount of a bad thing is zero. But it isn't zero.

## The Economically Efficient Level of Pollution Reduction

Chapter 1 introduced the important idea that the optimal decision is to continue any activity up to the point where the marginal benefit equals the marginal cost. This applies to reducing pollution just as much as it does to other activities. Sulfur dioxide emissions contribute to smog and acid rain. As sulfur dioxide emissions—or any other type of pollution—decline, society benefits: Fewer trees die, fewer buildings are damaged, and fewer people suffer breathing problems. But a key point is that the additional benefit—that is, the *marginal benefit*—received from eliminating another ton of sulfur dioxide declines as sulfur dioxide emissions are reduced. To see why this is true, consider what happens with no reduction in sulfur dioxide emissions. In this situation, many smoggy days will occur in the cities of the Midwest and Northeast. Even healthy people may experience breathing problems. As sulfur dioxide emissions are reduced, the number of smoggy days will fall, and healthy people will no longer experience breathing problems. Eventually, if emissions of sulfur dioxide fall to low levels, even people with asthma will no longer be affected. Further reductions in sulfur dioxide will have little additional benefit. The same will be true of the other benefits from reducing sulfur dioxide emissions: As the reductions increase, the additional benefits from fewer buildings and trees being damaged and lakes polluted will decline.

## Making the Connection | The Clean Air Act: How a Government Policy Reduced Infant Mortality

The following bar graphs show that the United States has made tremendous progress in reducing air pollution since Congress passed the Clean Air Act in 1970: Total emissions of the six main air pollutants have fallen by more than half. Over the same period, real U.S. gross domestic product—which measures the value, corrected for inflation, of all the final goods and services produced in the country—almost doubled, energy consumption increased by half, and the number of miles traveled by all vehicles almost doubled.

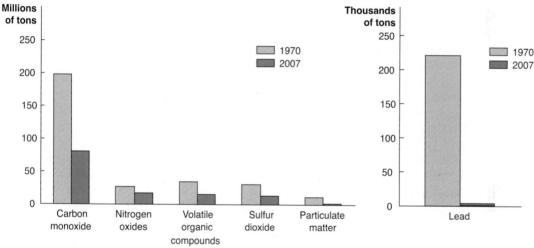

Source: U.S. Environmental Protection Agency, "Air Trends," November 21, 2008.

As we have seen, when levels of pollution are high, the marginal benefit of reducing pollution is also high. We would expect, then, that the benefit of reducing air pollution in 1970 was much higher than the benefit from a proportional reduction in air pollution would be today, when the level of pollution is much lower. Kenneth Y. Chay of Brown University and Michael Greenstone of MIT have shown that the benefits from the air pollution reductions that occurred in the period immediately after passage of the Clean Air Act were indeed high. Chay and Greenstone argue that the exposure of pregnant women to high levels of air pollution can be damaging to their unborn fetuses, possibly by retarding lung functioning. This damage would increase the chance that the infant would die in the first weeks after being born. In the two years following passage of the Clean Air Act, there was a sharp reduction in air pollution and also a reduction in infant mortality. The decline in infant mortality was mainly due to a reduction in deaths within one month of birth. Of course, other factors also may have been responsible for the decline in infant mortality, but Chay and Greenstone use statistical analysis to isolate the effect of the decline in air pollution. They conclude that "1,300 fewer infants died in 1972 than would have in the absence of the Clean Air Act."

Source: Kenneth Y. Chay and Michael Greenstone, "Air Quality, Infant Mortality, and the Clean Air Act of 1970," National Bureau of Economic Research Working Paper 10053, October 2003.

**Your Turn:** Test your understanding by doing related problem 2.8 on page 162 at the end of this chapter.

What about the marginal cost to electric utilities of reducing pollution? To reduce sulfur dioxide emissions, utilities have to switch from burning high-sulfur coal to burning more costly fuel, or they have to install pollution control devices, such as scrubbers. As the level of pollution falls, further reductions become increasingly costly. Reducing emissions or other types of pollution to very low levels can require complex and expensive new technologies. For example, Arthur Fraas, formerly of the federal Office of Management and Budget, and Vincent Munley, of Lehigh University, have shown that the marginal cost of removing 97 percent of pollutants from municipal wastewater is more than twice as high as the marginal cost of removing 95 percent.

The *net benefit* to society from reducing pollution is equal to the difference between the benefit of reducing pollution and the cost. To maximize the net benefit to society, sulfur dioxide emissions—or any other type of pollution—should be reduced up to the point where the marginal benefit from another ton of reduction is equal to the marginal cost. Figure 5-3 illustrates this point.

In Figure 5-3, we measure *reductions* in sulfur dioxide emissions on the horizontal axis. We measure the marginal benefit and marginal cost in dollars from eliminating another ton of sulfur dioxide emissions on the vertical axis. As reductions in pollution increase, the marginal benefit declines and the marginal cost increases. The economically efficient amount of pollution reduction occurs where the marginal benefit equals the marginal cost. The figure shows that in this case, the economically efficient reduction of sulfur dioxide emissions is 8.5 million tons per year. In a program begun in 1990, this is the amount of reduction Congress decided should occur by 2010. At that level of emission reduction, the marginal benefit and the marginal cost of the last ton of sulfur dioxide emissions eliminated are both $200 per ton. Suppose instead that the emissions target were only 7.0 million tons. The figure shows that, at that level of reduction, the last ton of reduction has added $250 to the benefits received by society, but it has added only $175 to the costs of utilities. There has been a net benefit to society from this ton of pollution reduction of $75. In fact, the figure shows a net benefit to society from pollution reduction for every ton from 7.0 million to 8.5 million. Only when sulfur dioxide emissions are reduced by 8.5 million tons per year will marginal benefit fall enough and marginal cost rise enough that the two are equal.

## Figure 5-3

### The Marginal Benefit from Pollution Reduction Should Equal the Marginal Cost

If the reduction of sulfur dioxide emissions is at 7.0 million tons per year, the marginal benefit of $250 per ton is greater than the marginal cost of $175 per ton. Further reductions in emissions will increase the net benefit to society. If the reduction of sulfur dioxide emissions is at 10.0 million tons, the marginal cost of $225 per ton is greater than the marginal benefit of $150 per ton. An increase in sulfur dioxide emissions will increase the net benefit to society. Only when the reduction is at 8.5 million tons is the marginal benefit equal to the marginal cost. This level is the economically efficient level of pollution reduction.

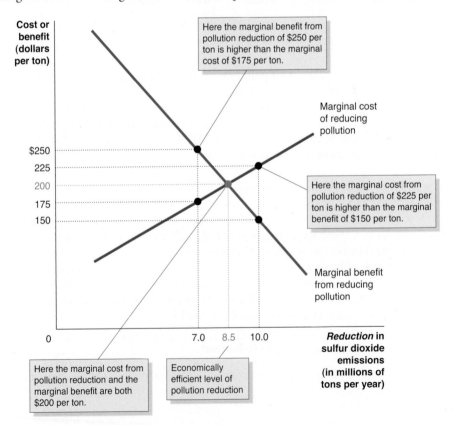

Now suppose Congress had set the target for sulfur dioxide emissions reduction at 10 million tons per year. The figure shows that the marginal benefit at that level of reduction has fallen to only $150 per ton and the marginal cost has risen to $225 per ton. The last ton of reduction has actually *reduced* the net benefit to society by $75 per ton. In fact, every ton of reduction beyond 8.5 million reduces the net benefit to society.

To summarize: If the marginal benefit of reducing sulfur dioxide emissions is greater than the marginal cost, further reductions will make society better off. But if the marginal cost of reducing sulfur dioxide emissions is greater than the marginal benefit, reducing sulfur dioxide emissions will actually make society worse off.

## The Basis for Private Solutions to Externalities

In arguing that private solutions to the problem of externalities were possible, Ronald Coase emphasized that when more than the optimal level of pollution is occurring, the benefits from reducing the pollution to the optimal level are greater than the costs. Figure 5-4 illustrates this point.

The marginal benefit curve shows the additional benefit from each reduction in a ton of sulfur dioxide emissions. The area under the marginal benefit curve between the two emission levels is the *total* benefit received from reducing emissions from one level to another. For instance, in Figure 5-4, the total benefit from increasing the reduction in sulfur dioxide emissions from 7.0 million tons to 8.5 million tons is the sum of the areas of A and B. The marginal cost curve shows the additional cost from each reduction in a ton of emissions. The *total* cost of reducing emissions from one level to another is the area under the marginal cost curve between the two emissions levels. The total cost from increasing the reduction in emissions from 7.0 million tons to 8.5 million tons is the

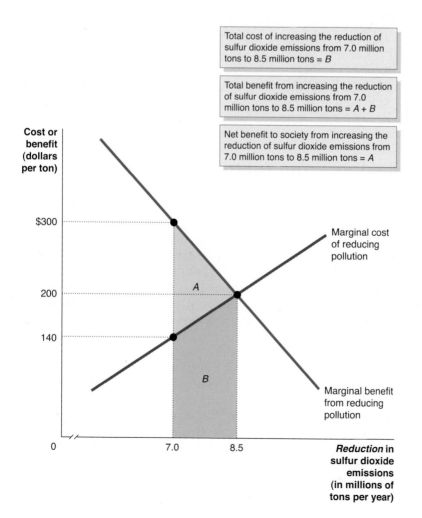

Total cost of increasing the reduction of sulfur dioxide emissions from 7.0 million tons to 8.5 million tons = B

Total benefit from increasing the reduction of sulfur dioxide emissions from 7.0 million tons to 8.5 million tons = A + B

Net benefit to society from increasing the reduction of sulfur dioxide emissions from 7.0 million tons to 8.5 million tons = A

### Figure 5-4

**The Benefits of Reducing Pollution to the Optimal Level Are Greater Than the Costs**

Increasing the reduction in sulfur dioxide emissions from 7.0 million tons to 8.5 million tons results in total benefits equal to the sum of the areas A and B under the marginal benefits curve. The total cost of this decrease in pollution is equal to the area B under the marginal cost curve. The total benefits are greater than the total costs by an amount equal to the area of triangle A. Because the total benefits from reducing pollution are greater than the total costs, it's possible for those receiving the benefits to arrive at a private agreement with polluters to pay them to reduce pollution.

# Don't Let This Happen to **YOU!**

### Remember That It's the *Net* Benefit That Counts

Why would we not want to *completely* eliminate anything unpleasant? As long as any person suffers any unpleasant consequences from air pollution, the marginal benefit of reducing air pollution will be positive. So, removing every particle of air pollution results in the largest *total* benefit to society. But removing every particle of air pollution is not optimal for the same reason that it is not optimal to remove every particle of dirt or dust from a room when cleaning it. The cost of cleaning your room is not just the price of the cleaning products but also the opportunity cost of your time. The more time you devote to cleaning your room, the less time you have for other activities. As

you devote more and more additional hours to cleaning your room, the alternative activities you have to give up are likely to increase in value, raising the opportunity cost of cleaning: Cleaning instead of watching TV may not be too costly, but cleaning instead of eating any meals or getting any sleep is very costly. Optimally, you should eliminate dirt in your room up to the point where the marginal benefit of the last dirt removed equals the marginal cost of removing it. Society should take the same approach to air pollution. The result is the largest *net* benefit to society.

**(X) myeconlab**

**YOUR TURN:** Test your understanding by doing related problem 2.6 on page 162 at the end of this chapter.

---

area *B*. The net benefit from reducing emissions is the difference between the total cost and the total benefit, which is equal to the area of triangle *A*.

In Figure 5-4, the benefits from further reductions in sulfur dioxide emissions are much greater than the costs. In the appendix to Chapter 1, we reviewed the formula for calculating the area of a triangle, which is ½ × Base × Height, and the formula for the area of a rectangle, which is Base × Height. Using these formulas, we can calculate the value of the total benefits from the reduction in emissions and the value of the total costs. The value of the benefits (*A* + *B*) is $375 million. The value of the costs (*B*) is $255 million. If the people who would benefit from a reduction in pollution could get together, they could offer to pay the electric utilities $255 million to reduce the pollution to the optimal level. After making the payment, they would still be left with a net benefit of $120 million. In other words, a private agreement to reduce pollution to the optimal level is possible, without any government intervention.

*Some apple growers and beekeepers make private arrangements to arrive at an economically efficient outcome.*

### Making the Connection | **The Fable of the Bees**

Apple trees must be pollinated by bees in order to bear fruit. Bees need the nectar from apple trees (or other plants) to produce honey. In an important article published in the early 1950s, the British economist James Meade, winner of the 1977 Nobel Prize in Economics, argued that there were positive externalities in both apple growing and bee-keeping. The more apple trees growers planted, the more honey would be produced in the hives of local beekeepers. And the more hives beekeepers kept, the larger the apple crops in neighboring apple orchards. Meade assumed that beekeepers were not being compensated by apple growers for the pollination services they were providing to apple growers and that apple growers were not being compensated by beekeepers for the use of their nectar in honey making. Therefore, he concluded that unless the government intervened, the market would not supply enough apple trees and beehives.

Steven Cheung of the University of Washington showed, however, that government intervention was not necessary because beekeepers and apple growers had long since arrived at private agreements. In fact, in Washington State, farmers with fruit orchards had been renting beehives to pollinate their trees since at least as early as World War I. According to Cheung, "Pollination contracts usually include stipulations regarding the number and strength of the [bee] colonies, the rental fee per hive, the time of delivery and removal of hives, the protection of bees from pesticide sprays, and the strategic placing of hives."

Today, honeybees pollinate more than $14 billion worth of crops annually, from blueberries in Maine all the way to almonds in California. Increasing demand for almonds has expanded the crop in California until it now stretches for 300 miles, across 580,000 acres. Currently, more than 1 million beehives are required to pollinate the California almond crop. Beehives are shipped into the state in February and March to pollinate the almond trees, and then they are shipped to Oregon and Washington to pollinate the cherry, pear, and apple orchards in those states during April and May.

Sources: J. E. Meade, "External Economies and Diseconomies in a Competitive Situation," *Economic Journal*, Vol. 62, March 1952, pp. 54–67; Steven N. S. Cheung, "The Fable of the Bees: An Economic Investigation," *Journal of Law and Economics*, Vol. 16, 1973, pp. 11–33; and Aaron E. Hirsh, "A Low-Tech Treatment for Bee Plague," *New York Times*, January 27, 2009.

**YOUR TURN:** Test your understanding by doing related problem 2.9 on page 162 at the end of this chapter.

## Do Property Rights Matter?

In discussing the bargaining between the electric utilities and the people suffering the effects of the utilities' pollution, we assumed that the electric utilities were not legally liable for the damage they were causing. In other words, the victims of pollution could not legally enforce the right of their property not to be damaged, so they would have to pay the utilities to reduce the pollution. But would it make any difference if the utilities were legally liable for the damages? Surprisingly, as Coase was the first to point out, it does not matter for the amount of pollution reduction. The only difference would be that now the electric utilities would have to pay the victims of pollution for the right to pollute rather than the victims having to pay the utilities to reduce pollution. Because the marginal benefits and marginal costs of pollution reduction would not change, the bargaining should still result in the efficient level of pollution reduction—in this case, 8.5 million tons.

In the absence of the utilities being legally liable, the victims of pollution have an incentive to pay the utilities to reduce pollution up to the point where the marginal benefit of the last ton of reduction is equal to the marginal cost. If the utilities are legally liable, they have an incentive to pay the victims of pollution to allow them to pollute up to the same point.

## The Problem of Transactions Costs

Unfortunately, there are frequently practical difficulties in the way of a private solution to the problem of externalities. In cases of pollution, for example, there are often both many polluters and many people suffering from the negative effects of pollution. Bringing together all those suffering from pollution with all those causing the pollution and negotiating an agreement often fails due to *transactions costs*. **Transactions costs** are the costs in time and other resources that parties incur in the process of agreeing to and carrying out an exchange of goods or services. In this case, the transactions costs would include the time and other costs of negotiating an agreement, drawing up a binding contract, purchasing insurance, and monitoring the agreement. Unfortunately, when many people are involved, the transactions costs are often higher than the net benefits from reducing the externality. Thus, the cost of transacting ends up exceeding the gain from the transaction. In such cases, a private solution to an externality problem is not feasible.

**Transactions costs** The costs in time and other resources that parties incur in the process of agreeing to and carrying out an exchange of goods or services.

## The Coase Theorem

Coase's argument that private solutions to the problem of externalities are possible is summed up in the **Coase theorem**: If transactions costs are low, private bargaining will result in an efficient solution to the problem of externalities. We have seen the basis for the Coase theorem in the preceding example of pollution by electric utilities: Because

**Coase theorem** The argument of economist Ronald Coase that if transactions costs are low, private bargaining will result in an efficient solution to the problem of externalities.

the benefits from reducing an externality are often greater than the costs, private bargaining can arrive at an efficient outcome. But we have also seen that this outcome will occur only if transactions costs are low, and in the case of pollution, they usually are not. In general, private bargaining is most likely to reach an efficient outcome if the number of parties bargaining is small.

In practice, we must add a couple of other qualifications to the Coase theorem. In addition to low transactions costs, private solutions to the problem of externalities will occur only if all parties to the agreement have full information about the costs and benefits associated with the externality, and all parties must be willing to accept a reasonable agreement. For example, if those suffering from the effects of pollution do not have information on the costs of reducing pollution, it is unlikely that the parties can reach an agreement. Unreasonable demands can also hinder an agreement. For instance, in the example of pollution by electric utilities, we saw that the total benefit of reducing sulfur dioxide emissions was $375 million. Even if transactions costs are very low, if the utilities insist on being paid more than $375 million to reduce emissions, no agreement will be reached because the amount paid exceeds the value of the reduction to those suffering from the emissions.

**5.3 LEARNING** OBJECTIVE

Analyze government policies to achieve economic efficiency in a market with an externality.

# Government Policies to Deal with Externalities

When private solutions to externalities are not feasible, how should the government intervene? The first economist to analyze market failure systematically was A. C. Pigou, a British economist at Cambridge University. Pigou argued that to deal with a negative externality in production, the government should impose a tax equal to the cost of the externality. The effect of such a tax is shown in Figure 5-5, which reproduces the negative externality from acid rain shown in Figure 5-1.

By imposing on the production of electricity a tax equal to the cost of acid rain, the government will cause electric utilities to *internalize* the externality. As a consequence, the cost of the acid rain will become a private cost borne by the utilities, and the supply curve for electricity will shift from $S_1$ to $S_2$. The result will be a decrease in the equilibrium output of electricity from $Q_{Market}$ to the efficient level, $Q_{Efficient}$. The price consumers pay for electricity will rise from $P_{Market}$—which does not include the cost of acid rain—to $P_{Efficient}$—which does include the cost. Producers will receive a price $P$, which is equal to $P_{Efficient}$ minus the amount of the tax.

## Figure 5-5

**When There Is a Negative Externality, a Tax Can Bring about the Efficient Level of Output**

Because utilities do not bear the cost of acid rain, they produce electricity beyond the economically efficient level. If the government imposes a tax equal to the cost of acid rain, the utilities will internalize the externality. As a consequence, the supply curve will shift up, from $S_1$ to $S_2$. The market equilibrium quantity changes from $Q_{Market}$, where an inefficiently high level of electricity is produced, to $Q_{Efficient}$, the economically efficient equilibrium quantity. The price of electricity will rise from $P_{Market}$—which does not include the cost of acid rain—to $P_{Efficient}$—which does include the cost. Consumers pay the price $P_{Efficient}$, while producers receive a price $P$, which is equal to $P_{Efficient}$ minus the amount of the tax.

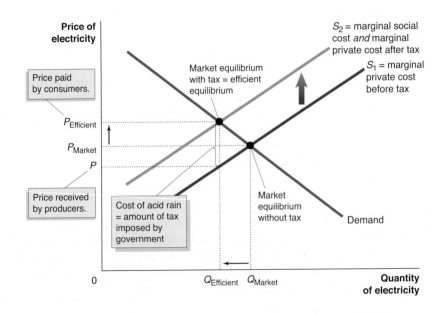

Figure 5-6

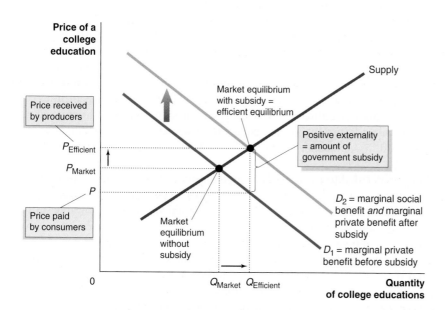

People who do not consume college educations can benefit from them. As a result, the social benefit from a college education is greater than the private benefit seen by college students. If the government pays a subsidy equal to the external benefit, students will internalize the externality. The subsidy will cause the demand curve to shift up, from $D_1$ to $D_2$. The result will be that market equilibrium quantity shifts from $Q_{Market}$, where an inefficiently low level of college educations is supplied, to $Q_{Efficient}$, the economically efficient equilibrium quantity.

Producers receive the price $P_{Efficient}$, while consumers pay a price $P$, which is equal to $P_{Efficient}$ minus the amount of the subsidy.

Pigou also argued that the government can deal with a positive externality in consumption by giving consumers a subsidy, or payment, equal to the value of the externality. The effect of the subsidy is shown in Figure 5-6, which reproduces the positive externality from college education shown in Figure 5-2.

By paying college students a subsidy equal to the external benefit from a college education, the government will cause students to *internalize* the externality. That is, the external benefit from a college education will become a private benefit received by college students, and the demand curve for college educations will shift from $D_1$ to $D_2$. The equilibrium number of college educations supplied will increase from $Q_{Market}$ to the efficient level, $Q_{Efficient}$. Producers receive the price $P_{Efficient}$, while consumers pay a price $P$, which is equal to $P_{Efficient}$ minus the amount of the subsidy. In fact, the government does heavily subsidize college educations. All states have government-operated universities that charge tuitions well below the cost of providing the education. The state and federal governments also provide students with grants and low-interest loans that subsidize college educations. The economic justification for these programs is that college educations provide an external benefit to society.

Because A. C. Pigou was the first economist to propose using government taxes and subsidies to deal with externalities, they are sometimes referred to as **Pigovian taxes and subsidies**. Note that a Pigovian tax eliminates deadweight loss and improves economic efficiency. This situation is the opposite of the one we saw in Chapter 4, in which we discussed how most taxes reduce consumer surplus and producer surplus and create a deadweight loss. In fact, one reason that economists support Pigovian taxes as a way to deal with negative externalities is that the government can use the revenues raised by Pigovian taxes to lower other taxes that reduce economic efficiency.

**Pigovian taxes and subsidies**
Government taxes and subsidies intended to bring about an efficient level of output in the presence of externalities.

# Command and Control versus Market-Based Approaches

Although the federal government has sometimes used taxes and subsidies to deal with externalities, in dealing with pollution, it has traditionally used a *command-and-control approach* with firms that pollute. A **command-and-control approach** to reducing pollution involves the government imposing quantitative limits on the amount of pollution firms are allowed to generate or requiring firms to install specific pollution control devices. For example, in 1983, the federal government required auto manufacturers

**Command-and-control approach**
An approach that involves the government imposing quantitative limits on the amount of pollution firms are allowed to emit or requiring firms to install specific pollution control devices.

such as Ford and General Motors to install catalytic converters to reduce auto emissions on all new automobiles.

Congress could have used direct pollution controls to deal with the problem of acid rain. To achieve its objective of a reduction of 8.5 million tons per year in sulfur dioxide emissions by 2010, Congress could have required every utility to reduce sulfur dioxide emissions by the same specified amount. However, this approach would not have been an economically efficient solution to the problem because utilities can have very different costs of reducing sulfur dioxide emissions. Some utilities, such as Duke Energy, that already use low-sulfur coal can reduce emissions further only at a high cost. Other utilities, particularly those in the Midwest, are able to reduce emissions at a lower cost.

Congress decided to use a market-based approach to reducing sulfur dioxide emissions by setting up a cap-and-trade system of tradable emissions allowances. The federal government gave utilities allowances equal to the total amount of allowable sulfur dioxide emissions. The utilities were then free to buy and sell the allowances. An active market where the allowances can be bought and sold is conducted on the Chicago Mercantile Exchange. Utilities that could reduce emissions at low cost have done so and have sold their allowances. Utilities that could only reduce emissions at high cost have bought allowances. Using tradable emissions allowances to reduce acid rain has been a great success and has made it possible for utilities to meet Congress's emissions goal at a much lower cost than expected. Just before Congress enacted the allowances program in 1990, the Edison Electric Institute estimated that the cost to utilities of complying with the program would be $7.4 billion by 2010. By 1994, the federal government's General Accounting Office estimated that the cost would be less than $2 billion. In practice, the cost appears likely to be almost 90 percent less than the initial estimate, or only about $870 *million*.

## Are Tradable Emissions Allowances Licenses to Pollute?

Some environmentalists have criticized tradable emissions allowances, labeling them "licenses to pollute." They argue that just as the government does not issue licenses to rob banks or to drive drunk, it should not issue licenses to pollute. But this criticism ignores one of the central lessons of economics: Resources are scarce, and trade-offs exist. Resources that are spent reducing one type of pollution are not available to reduce other types of pollution or for any other use. Because reducing acid rain using tradable emissions allowances has cost utilities $870 million, rather than $7.4 billion, as originally estimated, society has saved more than $6.5 billion.

## Making the Connection | Can a Cap-and-Trade System Reduce Global Warming?

In the past 25 years, the global surface temperature has increased about 0.75 degree Fahrenheit (or 0.40 degree Centigrade) compared with the average for the previous 30 years. The following graph shows changes in temperature over the years since 1880.

Global temperatures have gone through many periods of warming and cooling. In fact, the below-normal temperatures that prevailed before 1970 led some scientists to predict the eventual arrival of a new ice age. Nevertheless, many scientists are convinced that the recent warming is not part of the natural fluctuations in temperature but is instead due to the burning of fossil fuels, such as coal, natural gas, and petroleum. Burning these fuels releases $CO_2$ (carbon dioxide), which accumulates in the atmosphere as a "greenhouse gas." Greenhouse gases cause some of the heat released from the earth to be reflected back, increasing temperatures.

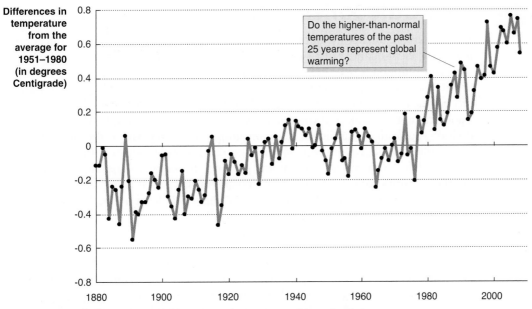

Differences in temperature from the average for 1951–1980 (in degrees Centigrade)

Do the higher-than-normal temperatures of the past 25 years represent global warming?

Source: NASA, Goddard Institute for Space Studies, http://data.giss.nasa.gov/gistemp/graphs/.

If greenhouse gases continue to accumulate in the atmosphere, according to some estimates, global temperatures could increase by 3 degrees Fahrenheit or more during the next 100 years. Such increases in temperature could lead to significant changes in climate, which might result in more storms and flooding, as well as other problems. By 1995, a number of nations had concluded that the threat of global warming was significant enough to take steps toward reducing emissions of $CO_2$ and other greenhouse gases. The result was the 1997 Kyoto Treaty, which, if accepted, would have required the high-income countries to reduce their $CO_2$ emissions by more than 5 percent compared with their 1990 levels. However, President George W. Bush was not willing to commit the United States to the treaty. He argued that the costs to the United States of complying with the treaty were too high, particularly because some scientists were still skeptical that $CO_2$ emissions actually were causing the increase in temperature. Even scientists who believed that $CO_2$ emissions contribute to rising temperatures were skeptical that the Kyoto Treaty would have much effect on global warming. President Bush also argued that developing countries should be included in any agreement. Some developing countries, such as China and India, are experiencing rapid economic growth, which in turn has led to rapid increases in $CO_2$ emissions. European countries that ratified the Kyoto Treaty have had difficulty fulfilling their commitments to reduce $CO_2$ emissions to the levels indicated by the treaty. Of the larger European countries, only Great Britain and Germany, which have reduced their emissions by more than 15 percent since 1990, seem likely to succeed in fulfilling their commitments by 2012.

Policymakers and economists have debated the mechanism by which reductions in $CO_2$ emissions should occur. The United States has favored a global system of tradable emission permits for $CO_2$ that would be similar to the system for sulfur dioxide discussed earlier in this chapter. In 2009, President Barack Obama proposed a cap-and-trade system for the United States that would result in gradually reducing $CO_2$ emissions to their 1990 level by 2020 and to 80 percent below their 1990 level by 2050. The debate over the costs and benefits of reducing $CO_2$ emissions will likely continue for many years.

Sources: Darren Samuelsohn, "Climate Bill Needed to 'Save Our Planet,' Says Obama," *New York Times*, February 25, 2009; and United Nations Framework Convention on Climate Change, *National Greenhouse Gas Inventory Data for the Period 1990–2006*, November 17, 2008.

**YOUR TURN:** Test your understanding by doing related problem 3.10 on page 163 at the end of this chapter.

Explain how goods can be categorized on the basis of whether they are rival or excludable, and use graphs to illustrate the efficient quantities of public goods and common resources.

**Rivalry** The situation that occurs when one person's consuming a unit of a good means no one else can consume it.

**Excludability** The situation in which anyone who does not pay for a good cannot consume it.

**Private good** A good that is both rival and excludable.

**Public good** A good that is both nonrivalrous and nonexcludable.

**Free riding** Benefiting from a good without paying for it.

**Common resource** A good that is rival but not excludable.

# Four Categories of Goods

We can explore further the question of when the market is likely to succeed in supplying the efficient quantity of a good by noting that goods differ on the basis of whether their consumption is *rival* and *excludable*. **Rivalry** occurs when one person's consuming a unit of a good means no one else can consume it. If you consume a Big Mac, for example, no one else can consume it. **Excludability** means that anyone who does not pay for a good cannot consume it. If you don't pay for a Big Mac, for example, MacDonald's can exclude you from consuming it. The consumption of a Big Mac is therefore rival and excludable. The consumption of some goods, however, can be either *nonrival* or *nonexcludable*. Nonrival means that one person's consumption does not interfere with another person's consumption. Nonexcludable means that it is impossible to exclude others from consuming the good, whether they have paid for it or not. Figure 5-7 shows four possible categories into which goods can fall.

We next consider each of the four categories:

1. *Private goods.* A good that is both rival and excludable is a **private good**. Food, clothing, haircuts, and many other goods and services fall into this category. One person's consuming a unit of these goods precludes other people from consuming that unit, and no one can consume these goods without buying them. Although we didn't state it explicitly, when we analyzed the demand and supply for goods and services in Chapter 3, we assumed that the goods and services were all private goods.

2. *Public goods.* A **public good** is both nonrivalrous and nonexcludable. Public goods are often, although not always, supplied by a government rather than by private firms. The classic example of a public good is national defense. Your consuming national defense does not interfere with your neighbor's consuming it, so consumption is nonrivalrous. You also cannot be excluded from consuming it, whether you pay for it or not. No private firm would be willing to supply national defense because everyone can consume national defense without paying for it. The behavior of consumers in this situation is referred to as *free riding*. **Free riding** involves individuals benefiting from a good—in this case, the provision of national defense—without paying for it.

3. *Quasi-public goods.* Some goods are excludable but not rival. An example is cable television. People who do not pay for cable television do not receive it, but one person's watching it doesn't affect other people's watching it. The same is true of a toll road. Anyone who doesn't pay the toll doesn't get on the road, but one person using the road doesn't interfere with someone else using the road (unless so many people are using the road that it becomes congested). Goods that fall into this category are called *quasi-public goods*.

4. *Common resources.* If a good is rival but not excludable, it is a **common resource**. Forest land in many poor countries is a common resource. If one person cuts down a tree, no one else can use the tree. But if no one has a property right to the forest, no one can be excluded from using it. As we will discuss in more detail later, people often overuse common resources.

## Figure 5-7

### Four Categories of Goods

Goods and services can be divided into four categories on the basis of whether people can be excluded from consuming them and whether they are rival in consumption. A good or service is rival in consumption if one person consuming a unit of a good means that another person cannot consume that unit.

|  | Excludable | Nonexcludable |
|---|---|---|
| **Rival** | **Private Goods** <br> *Examples:* <br> *Big Macs* <br> *Running shoes* | **Common Resources** <br> *Examples:* <br> *Tuna in the ocean* <br> *Public pasture land* |
| **Nonrival** | **Quasi-Public Goods** <br> *Examples:* <br> *Cable TV* <br> *Toll road* | **Public Goods** <br> *Examples:* <br> *National defense* <br> *Court system* |

# Making the Connection

## Should the Government Run the Health Care System?

In many countries, such as Canada, Japan, the United Kingdom, and France, the government either supplies health care directly by operating hospitals and employing doctors and nurses, or pays for most health care expenses, even if hospitals are not government owned and doctors are not government employees. In the United States, the federal government supplies health care to veterans of the armed forces through the Veterans Administration (VA) system and pays for the health care of people over age 65 under the Medicare program. The federal government also contributes to the Medicaid program, under which state governments pay for health care for some poor people. Most medium and large-size firms provide health insurance as a fringe benefit to their employees. About 88 percent of individuals who have private health insurance receive it as part of a benefits package from their employers. Those individuals not covered by health insurance plans and not eligible for government aid must pay for their own health care bills out of pocket, just as they pay their other bills, or receive charity care. The chart shows that in 2008, government spending on Medicare, Medicaid, and other government health care programs was about 47 percent of total health care spending.

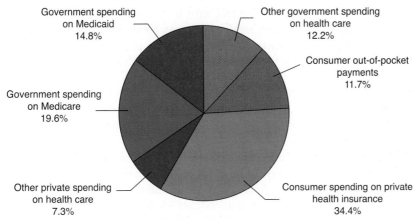

Source: Andrea Sisko, et al., "Health Spending Projections Through 2018: Recession Effects Add Uncertainty to the Outlook," *Health Affairs*, Vol. 28, No. 2, March/April 2009, pp. w346–w357.

In 2009, President Barack Obama proposed expanding the federal government's role in health care by requiring more firms to offer health insurance to their employees and by offering a government health insurance plan as an alternative to private plans. What should be the government's role in health care? Is health care a public good that government should supply—or, at least, pay for? Is it a private good, like furniture, clothing, or television sets, that private firms should supply and consumers should pay for without government aid? Should private firms supply most health care, subject to some government regulation? Economists differ in their answers to these questions because the delivery of health care involves a number of complex issues. But we can consider briefly some of the most important points. We have seen that a public good is both nonrivalrous and nonexcludable. In this sense, health care does not qualify as a public good. More than one person cannot simultaneously consume the same surgical operation, for example. And someone who will not pay for an operation can be excluded from consuming it. (Most states require hospitals to treat patients who are too poor to pay for treatment, and many doctors will treat poor people at a reduced price. But because there is nothing in the nature of health care that keeps people who do not pay for it from being excluded from consuming it, health care does not fit the definition of a public good.)

There are aspects of the delivery of health care that have convinced some economists that government intervention is justified, however. For example, consuming certain types of health care generates positive externalities. In particular, being vaccinated against a communicable disease, such as influenza or chicken pox, not only reduces the chance that the person vaccinated will catch the disease but also reduces the probability that an epidemic of the disease will occur. Therefore, the market may supply an inefficiently small quantity of vaccinations unless vaccinations receive a government subsidy. *Information problems* can also be important in the market for private health insurance. Consumers as buyers of health insurance often know much more about the state of their health than do the companies selling health insurance. This information problem may raise costs to insurance companies when the pool of people being insured is small, making insurance companies less willing to offer health insurance to consumers the companies suspect may file too many claims. Economists debate how important information problems are in health care markets and whether government intervention is required to reduce them. We will consider this question further in Chapter 17, when we discuss the economics of information.

Many economists believe that market-based solutions are the best approach to improving the health care system. Currently, the U.S. health care system is a world leader in innovation in medical technology and prescription drugs. The market-oriented approach to reforming health care starts with the goal of preserving incentives for U.S. firms to continue with innovations in medical screening equipment, surgical procedures, and prescription drugs. Presently, markets are delivering inaccurate signals to consumers because when buying health care, unlike when buying most other goods and services, consumers pay a price well *below* the true cost of providing the service. Consumers usually pay less than the true cost of medical treatment because a third party—typically, an insurance company—often pays most of the bill. For example, consumers who have health insurance provided by their employers usually pay only a small amount—perhaps $20—for a visit to a doctor's office, when the true cost of the visit might be $80 or $90. The result is that consumers demand a larger quantity of health care services than they would if they paid a price that better represented the cost of providing the services. Doctors and other health care providers also have a reduced incentive to control costs because they know that an insurance company will pick up most of the bill.

Under current tax laws, individuals do not pay taxes on health insurance benefits they receive from their employers, and this encourages them to want very generous coverage that reduces incentives to control costs. But individuals get no tax break for buying insurance on their own or for out-of-pocket medical spending. Some economists have proposed making the tax treatment of health insurance and health spending more uniform, a change that might significantly reduce spending on health care without reducing the effectiveness of the health care received. Such tax law changes would make it more likely that company-provided health insurance would focus on large medical bills—such as those resulting from hospitalizations—while consumers would pay prices closer to the costs of providing routine medical care.

Because health care is so important to consumers and because health care spending looms so large in the U.S. economy, the role of the government in the health care system is likely to be the subject of intense debate for some time to come.

Sources: To read more on the role of the government in the market for health care, see Sherman Folland, Allen C. Goodman, and Miron Stano, *The Economics of Health and Health Care*, 6th ed., Upper Saddle River, NJ: Prentice Hall, 2010, Chapter 19; and John F. Coogan, R. Glenn Hubbard, and Daniel P. Kessler, *Healthy, Wealthy, and Wise: Five Steps to a Better Health Care System*, Washington, DC: The AEI Press, 2005.

**myeconlab** **YOUR TURN:** Test your understanding by doing related problem 4.9 on page 165 at the end of this chapter.

We discussed the demand and supply for private goods in Chapter 3. For the remainder of this chapter, we focus on the categories of public goods and common resources. To determine the optimal quantity of a public good, we have to modify the demand and supply analysis of Chapter 3 to take into account that a public good is both nonrivalrous and nonexcludable.

# The Demand for a Public Good

We can determine the market demand curve for a good or service by adding up the quantity of the good demanded by each consumer at each price. To keep things simple, let's consider the case of a market with only two consumers. Figure 5-8 shows that the market demand curve for hamburgers depends on the individual demand curves of Jill and Joe.

At a price of $4.00, Jill demands 2 hamburgers per week and Joe demands 4. Adding horizontally, the combination of a price of $4.00 per hamburger and a quantity demanded of 6 hamburgers will be a point on the market demand curve for hamburgers. Similarly, adding horizontally at a price of $1.50, we have a price of $1.50 and a quantity demanded of 11 as another point on the market demand curve. A consumer's demand curve for a good represents the marginal benefit the consumer receives from the good, so when we add together the consumers' demand curves, we not only have the market demand curve but also the marginal social benefit curve for this good, assuming that there is no externality in consumption.

How can we find the demand curve or marginal social benefit curve for a public good? Once again, for simplicity, assume that Jill and Joe are the only consumers. Unlike with a private good, where Jill and Joe can end up consuming different quantities, with a public good, they will consume *the same quantity*. Suppose that Jill owns a service station on an isolated rural road, and Joe owns a car dealership next door. These are the only two businesses around for miles. Both Jill and Joe are afraid that unless they hire a security guard at night, their businesses may be burgled. Like national defense, the services of a security guard are in this case a public good: Once hired, the guard will be able to protect both businesses, so the good is nonrival. It also will not be possible to exclude either business from being protected, so the good is nonexcludable.

To arrive at a demand curve for a public good, we don't add quantities at each price, as with a private good. Instead, we add the price each consumer is willing to pay for each quantity of the public good. This value represents the total dollar amount consumers as a group would be willing to pay for that quantity of the public good. Put another way, to find the demand curve, or marginal social benefit curve, for a private good, we add the demand curves of individual consumers horizontally, while for public goods, we add individual demand curves vertically. Figure 5-9 shows how the marginal social benefit curve for security guard services depends on the individual demand curves of Jill and Joe.

The figure shows that Jill is willing to pay $8 per hour for the guard to provide 10 hours of protection per night. Joe would suffer a greater loss from a burglary, so he is

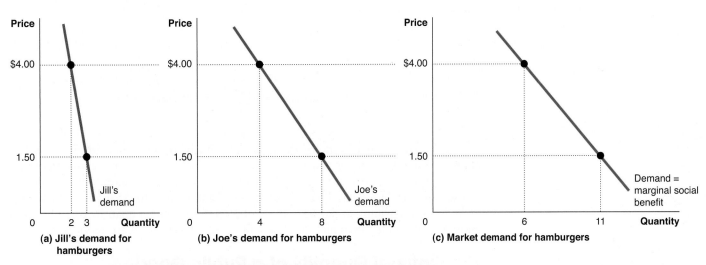

Figure 5-8     **Constructing the Market Demand Curve for a Private Good**

The market demand curve for private goods is determined by adding horizontally the quantity of the good demanded at each price by each consumer. For instance, in panel (a), Jill demands 2 hamburgers when the price is $4.00, and in panel (b), Joe demands 4 hamburgers when the price is $4.00. So, a quantity of 6 hamburgers and a price of $4.00 is a point on the market demand curve in panel (c).

## Figure 5-9

**Constructing the Market Demand Curve for a Public Good**

To find the demand curve for a public good, we add up the price at which each consumer is willing to purchase each quantity of the good. In panel (a), Jill is willing to pay $8 per hour for a security guard to provide 10 hours of protection. In panel (b), Joe is willing to pay $10 for that level of protection. Therefore, in panel (c), the price of $18 per hour and the quantity of 10 hours will be a point on the market demand curve for security guard services.

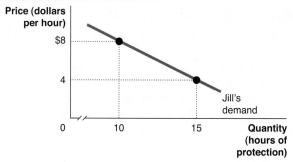

**(a) Jill's demand for security guard services**

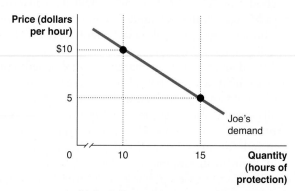

**(b) Joe's demand for security guard services**

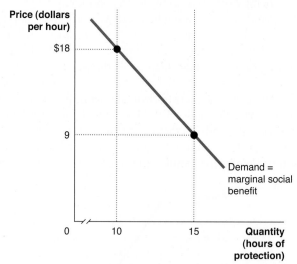

**(c) Market demand for security guard services**

willing to pay $10 per hour for the same amount of protection. Adding the dollar amount that each is willing to pay gives us a price of $18 per hour and a quantity of 10 hours as a point on the marginal social benefit curve for security guard services. The figure also shows that because Jill is willing to spend $4 per hour for 15 hours of guard services and Joe is willing to pay $5, a price of $9 per hour and a quantity of 15 hours is another point on the marginal social benefit curve for security guard services.

## The Optimal Quantity of a Public Good

We know that to achieve economic efficiency, a good or service should be produced up to the point where the sum of consumer surplus and producer surplus is maximized, or, alternatively, where the marginal social cost equals the marginal social benefit. Therefore, the optimal quantity of security guard services—or any other public

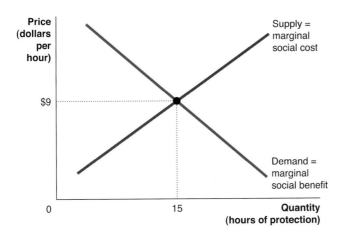

Figure 5-10

**The Optimal Quantity of a Public Good**

The optimal quantity of a public good is produced where the sum of consumer surplus and producer surplus is maximized, which occurs where the demand curve intersects the supply curve. In this case, the optimal quantity of security guard services is 15 hours, at a price of $9 per hour.

good—will occur where the marginal social benefit curve intersects the supply curve. As with private goods, in the absence of an externality in production, the supply curve represents the marginal social cost of supplying the good. Figure 5-10 shows that the optimal quantity of security guard services supplied is 15 hours, at a price of $9 per hour.

Will the market provide the economically efficient quantity of security guard services? One difficulty is that the individual preferences of consumers, as shown by their demand curves, are not revealed in this market. This difficulty does not arise with private goods because consumers must reveal their preferences in order to purchase private goods. If the market price of Big Macs is $3.50, Joe either reveals that he is willing to pay that much by buying it or he does without it. In our example, neither Jill nor Joe can be excluded from consuming the services provided by a security guard once either hires one, and, therefore, neither has an incentive to reveal her or his preferences. In this case, though, with only two consumers, it is likely that private bargaining will result in an efficient quantity of the public good. This outcome is not likely for a public good—such as national defense—that is supplied by the government to millions of consumers.

Governments sometimes use *cost–benefit analysis* to determine what quantity of a public good should be supplied. For example, before building a dam on a river, the federal government will attempt to weigh the costs against the benefits. The costs include the opportunity cost of other projects the government cannot carry out if it builds the dam. The benefits include improved flood control or new recreational opportunities on the lake formed by the dam. However, for many public goods, including national defense, the government does not use a formal cost–benefit analysis. Instead, the quantity of national defense supplied is determined by a political process involving Congress and the president. Even here, of course, Congress and the president realize that trade-offs are involved: The more resources used for national defense, the fewer resources available for other public goods or for private goods.

# Solved Problem | 5-4

## Determining the Optimal Level of Public Goods

Suppose, once again, that Jill and Joe run isolated businesses that are next door to each other and in need of the services of a security guard. Their demand schedules for security guard services are as follows:

### JOE

| PRICE (DOLLARS PER HOUR) | QUANTITY (HOURS OF PROTECTION) |
|---|---|
| $20 | 0 |
| 18 | 1 |
| 16 | 2 |
| 14 | 3 |
| 12 | 4 |
| 10 | 5 |
| 8 | 6 |
| 6 | 7 |
| 4 | 8 |
| 2 | 9 |

### JILL

| PRICE (DOLLARS PER HOUR) | QUANTITY (HOURS OF PROTECTION) |
|---|---|
| $20 | 1 |
| 18 | 2 |
| 16 | 3 |
| 14 | 4 |
| 12 | 5 |
| 10 | 6 |
| 8 | 7 |
| 6 | 8 |
| 4 | 9 |
| 2 | 10 |

The supply schedule for security guard services is as follows:

| PRICE (DOLLARS PER HOUR) | QUANTITY (HOURS OF PROTECTION) |
|---|---|
| $ 8 | 1 |
| 10 | 2 |
| 12 | 3 |
| 14 | 4 |
| 16 | 5 |
| 18 | 6 |
| 20 | 7 |
| 22 | 8 |
| 24 | 9 |

**a.** Draw a graph that shows the optimal level of security guard services. Be sure to label the curves on the graph.

**b.** Briefly explain why 8 hours of security guard protection is not an optimal quantity.

## SOLVING THE PROBLEM:

**Step 1:** **Review the chapter material.** This problem is about the determination of the optimal level of public goods, so you may want to review the section "The Optimal Quantity of a Public Good," which begins on page 152.

**Step 2:** **Begin by deriving the demand curve or marginal social benefit curve for security guard services.** To calculate the marginal social benefit of guard services, we need to add the prices that Jill and Joe are willing to pay at each quantity:

### DEMAND OR MARGINAL SOCIAL BENEFIT

| PRICE (DOLLARS PER HOUR) | QUANTITY (HOURS OF PROTECTION) |
|---|---|
| $38 | 1 |
| 34 | 2 |
| 30 | 3 |
| 26 | 4 |
| 22 | 5 |
| 18 | 6 |
| 14 | 7 |
| 10 | 8 |
| 6 | 9 |

**Step 3:** **Answer part (a) by plotting the demand (marginal social benefit) and supply (marginal social cost) curves.** The graph shows that the optimal level of security guard services is 6 hours.

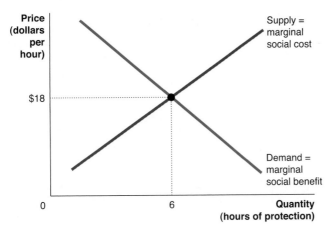

**Step 4:** **Answer part (b) by explaining why 8 hours of security guard protection is not an optimal quantity.** For each hour beyond 6, the supply curve is above the demand curve. Therefore, the marginal social benefit received will be less than the marginal social cost of supplying these hours. This results in a dead-weight loss and a reduction in economic surplus.

**YOUR TURN:** For more practice, do related problem 4.4 on page 164 at the end of this chapter.   [myeconlab]

# Common Resources

In England during the Middle Ages, each village had an area of pasture, known as a *commons*, on which any family in the village was allowed to graze its cows or sheep without charge. Of course, the grass one family's cow ate was not available for another family's cow, so consumption was rival. But every family in the village had the right to use the commons, so it was nonexcludable. Without some type of restraint on usage, the commons would end up overgrazed. To see why, consider the economic incentives facing a family that was thinking of buying another cow and grazing it on the commons. The family would gain the benefits from increased milk production, but adding another cow to the commons would create a negative externality by reducing the amount of grass available for the cows of other families. Because this family—and the other families in the village—did not take this negative externality into account when deciding whether to add another cow to the commons, too many cows would be added. The grass on the commons would eventually be depleted, and no family's cow would get enough to eat.

**The Tragedy of the Commons** The tendency for a common resource to be overused is called the **tragedy of the commons**. The forests in many poor countries are a modern example. When a family chops down a tree in a public forest, it takes into account the benefits of gaining firewood or wood for building, but it does not take into account the costs of deforestation. Haiti, for example, was once heavily forested. Today, 80 percent of the country's forests have been cut down, primarily to be burned to create charcoal, which is used for heating and cooking. Because the mountains no longer have tree roots to hold the soil, heavy rains lead to devastating floods. The following is from a newspaper account of tree cutting in Haiti:

> "No Tree Cutting" signs hang over the park entrance, but without money and manpower, there is no way to enforce that. Loggers make nightly journeys, hacking away at trees until they fall. The next day, they're on a truck out. Days later, they've been chopped up, burned and packaged in white bags offered for sale by soot-covered women. "This is the only way I can feed my four kids," said Vena Verone, one of the vendors. "I've heard about the floods and deforestation that caused them, but there's nothing I can do about that."

**Tragedy of the commons** The tendency for a common resource to be overused.

## Figure 5-11

### Overuse of a Common Resource

For a common resource such as wood from a forest, the efficient level of use, $Q_{Efficient}$, is determined by the intersection of the demand curve—which represents the marginal benefit received by consumers—and $S_2$, which represents the marginal social cost of cutting the wood. Because each individual tree cutter ignores the external cost, the equilibrium quantity of wood cut is $Q_{Actual}$, which is greater than the efficient quantity. At the equilibrium level of output, there is a deadweight loss, as shown by the yellow triangle.

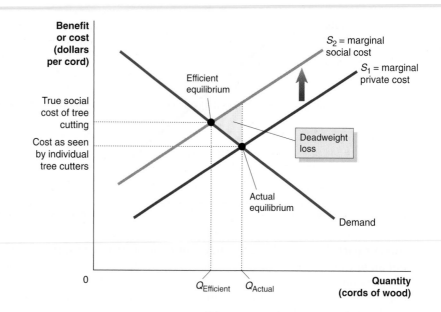

Figure 5-11 shows that with a common resource such as wood from a forest, the efficient level of use, $Q_{Efficient}$, is determined by the intersection of the demand curve—which represents the marginal social benefit received by consumers—and $S_2$, which represents the marginal social cost of cutting the wood. As in our discussion of negative externalities, the social cost is equal to the private cost of cutting the wood plus the external cost. In this case, the external cost represents the fact that the more wood each person cuts, the less wood there is available for others, and the greater the deforestation, which increases the chances of floods. Because each individual tree cutter ignores the external cost, the equilibrium quantity of wood cut is $Q_{Actual}$, which is greater than the efficient quantity. At the equilibrium level of output, there is a deadweight loss, as shown in Figure 5-11 by the yellow triangle.

**Is There a Way Out of the Tragedy of the Commons?** Notice that our discussion of the tragedy of the commons is very similar to our earlier discussion of negative externalities. The source of the tragedy of the commons is the same as the source of negative externalities: lack of clearly defined and enforced property rights. For instance, suppose that instead of being held as a collective resource, a piece of pastureland is owned by one person. That person will take into account the effect of adding another cow on the food available to cows already using the pasture. As a result, the optimal number of cows will be placed on the pasture. Over the years, most of the commons lands in England were converted to private property. Most of the forest land in Haiti and other developing countries is actually the property of the government. The failure of the government to protect the forests against trespassers or convert them to private property is the key to their overuse.

In some situations, though, enforcing property rights is not feasible. An example is the oceans. Because no country owns the oceans beyond its own coastal waters, the fish and other resources of the ocean will remain a common resource. In situations in which enforcing property rights is not feasible, two types of solutions to the tragedy of the commons are possible. If the geographic area involved is limited and the number of people involved is small, access to the commons can be restricted through community norms and laws. If the geographic area or the number of people involved is large, legal restrictions on access to the commons are required. As an example of the first type of solution, the tragedy of the commons was avoided in the Middle Ages by traditional limits on the number of animals each family was allowed to put on the common pasture. Although these traditions were not formal laws, they were usually enforced adequately by social pressure.

With the second type of solution, the government imposes restrictions on access to the common resources. These restrictions can take several different forms, of which taxes, quotas, and tradable permits are the most common. By setting a tax equal to the external cost, governments can ensure that the efficient quantity of a resource is used.

Quotas, or legal limits, on the quantity of the resource that can be taken during a given time period have been used in the United States to limit access to pools of oil when the pool is beneath property owned by many different persons. The governments of Canada, New Zealand, and Iceland have used a system of tradable permits to restrict access to ocean fisheries. Under this system, a total allowable catch (TAC) limits the number of fish that fishermen can catch during a season. The fishermen are then assigned permits called individual transferable quotas (ITQs) that are equal to the total allowable catch. This system operates like the tradable emissions allowances described earlier in this chapter. The fishermen are free to use the ITQs or to sell them, which ensures that the fishermen with the lowest costs use the ITQs. The use of ITQs has sometimes proven controversial, which has limited their use in managing fisheries along the coastal United States. Critics argue that allowing trading of ITQs can result in their concentration in the hands of a relatively few large commercial fishing firms. Such a concentration may, though, be economically efficient if these firms have lower costs than smaller, family-based firms.

▶ Continued from page 133

## Economics in YOUR LIFE!

At the beginning of the chapter, we asked you to think about what the "best" level of carbon emissions is. Conceptually, this is a straightforward question to answer: The efficient level of carbon emissions is the level for which the marginal benefit of reducing carbon emissions exactly equals the marginal cost of reducing carbon emissions. In practice, however, this is a very difficult question to answer. Scientists disagree about how much carbon emissions are contributing to climate change and what the damage from climate change will be. In addition, the cost of reducing carbon emissions depends on the method of reduction used. As a result, neither the marginal cost curve nor the marginal benefit curve for reducing carbon emissions is known with certainty. This uncertainty makes it difficult for policymakers to determine the economically efficient level of carbon emissions and is the source of much of the current debate. In any case, economists agree that the total cost of *completely* eliminating carbon emissions is much greater than the total benefit.

## Conclusion

In Chapter 4, we saw that government intervention in the economy can reduce economic efficiency. In this chapter, however, we have seen that the government plays an indispensable role in the economy when the absence of well-defined and enforceable property rights keeps the market from operating efficiently. For instance, because no one has a property right for clean air, in the absence of government intervention, firms will produce too great a quantity of products that generate air pollution. We have also seen that public goods are nonrivalrous and nonexcludable and are, therefore, often supplied directly by the government.

Read *An Inside Look at Policy* on the next page for a discussion of the views of an energy company executive who favors using a cap-and-trade policy to reduce emissions of carbon dioxide.

## *WALL STREET JOURNAL*

# Entergy's CEO on the Politics and Economics of Tackling Global Warming

J. Wayne Leonard, chairman and CEO of Entergy Corp., one of the largest U.S. energy companies and the No. 2 generator of nuclear power . . . [has a] deep-seated concern about climate change. . . . Leonard thinks like an economist. He talks about "efficiency" and "maximizing consumer surplus" the same way other utility executives talk about rate schedules and voltage. The most important thing the government can do on climate change, in Leonard's estimation, is to change the incentives for producing—or not producing—carbon. . . . Set the price, and market forces, not government, will make the decisions.

"We see ourselves as a market economy, and that's created great wealth for society over time," he says, "but we're a market economy that doesn't have price signals for $CO_2$."

**(a)** Entergy belongs to the swarm of major energy companies that are—contrary to type—practically begging Washington to create a cap-and-trade program. . . . It sounds strange: Lobbying the government to tax your products is generally not taught in business school.

Once Congress puts a ceiling on emissions, and then allows businesses to sell any of its extra allowances that stand for the right to emit, it is essentially creating the world's largest commodity market—in carbon-backed securities. These will be extremely valuable, and everything comes down to how the government chooses to distribute them.

Mr. Leonard thinks the allowances should be auctioned off, rather than given away. . . . Then the billions in new revenues . . . should be returned to the public. "Ideally you want to recycle it all, give all the money back," he says.

That . . . view . . . puts him at odds with many of his peers at big coal-fired utilities like Duke Energy and American Electric Power that emit the most carbon . . . [and who want] the allowances handed out at no charge. . . .

**(b)** On pure economic grounds, Mr. Leonard seems to prefer a straight carbon tax, which would be simpler and more efficient than cap and trade. But he also notes that "the political will to go the tax route . . . is just not there. Nonexistent" . . . The key, he says, is to design a cap-and-trade program that will "simulate the same thing a tax would do." . . .

Mr. Leonard does evince a certain . . . uneasiness with the direction of climate politics. "The old adage of 'think globally, act locally'—it still works," he says. "But with climate change, for it to really be effective, we have to take that thought much more completely and much more deeply than probably we've ever really thought about an issue."

**(c)** He notes China's breakneck construction of conventional coal plants. China has already surpassed U.S. coal capacity and is on pace to double it sometime in the middle of the next decade. The U.S., he says, "could close down every single coal plant immediately. . . . But that wouldn't do much good in the scheme of things," because atmospheric $CO_2$ concentrations would continue to rise as China continues to expand.

"We go to zero emissions in this country, and if China doesn't follow us, we're nowhere. . . . We've just ruined our economy, and we're nowhere," Leonard says. "We make mistakes here," meaning a poorly designed carbon system, "and we have a real problem." He goes on, "We talk about that we should lead, then people will follow, but that's kind of"—he pauses—"silly. China's not going to follow us because we're the United States. . . . You say, 'Shut down your plants'—well, that's going to be a short conversation. They've got $2 trillion invested in their plants and they still aren't feeding all their people." He adds that "If we were China, we wouldn't shut our plants down either."

"The focus," Mr. Leonard reiterates, "should be on developing the cap-and-trade program: Setting the amount of reductions, . . . setting the price signal that works so that it's not so high that it shuts down coal plants prematurely, and that's not so low that it becomes a loophole and people don't end up doing anything . . .

Still, the government is not exactly run by omniscient technocrats. Does he believe that Congress—with its entrenched constituencies, its own self-interest, its many antibusiness biases—can actually create a climate system that is as sensitive and efficient as he envisions? That is, can the political class actually write the same bill that economists would write? . . . We may find out.

*Source:* Joseph Rago, "The Carbon Cap Dilemma, Entergy's CEO on the Politics and Economics of Tackling Global Warming," *Wall Street Journal*, March 28, 2009.

## Key Points in the Article

This article presents an interview by a reporter for the *Wall Street Journal* with J. Wayne Leonard, the chairman and chief executive officer of Entergy Corp., a major electric utility. Entergy Corp. primarily uses nuclear energy, rather than coal, to generate electricity. In the interview, Leonard gives his views on the best way to reduce $CO_2$ emissions. Leonard favors market-based approaches to reducing $CO_2$. He argues that the most straightforward approach would be to tax the use of carbon-based fuels. This tax would be similar to the Pigovian taxes discussed in this chapter. He also discusses the cap-and-trade system the Obama Administration has proposed. Under this system, the government determines how much carbon dioxide utilities and firms can emit and issues a corresponding number of permits. Firms would then buy and sell the permits. Utilities that are heavily reliant on burning coal would be buyers, and utilities that are less reliant would be sellers.

## Analyzing the News

(a) The goal of the carbon trading program is to raise the price of energy sources such as coal that emit more $CO_2$ than energy sources such as nuclear power. Each year, the federal government will reduce the total amount of $CO_2$ that can be emitted by reducing the number of permits. This will force up the price of the permits and make generating electricity by burning

coal increasingly expensive. The prices utilities charge their residential and business customers will rise, reducing the quantity of electricity demanded. In addition, utilities will have an economic incentive to reduce their $CO_2$ emissions by using new technologies that allow coal to be burned more cleanly or by switching to other means of generating electricity. There is a debate over how the government should distribute the emission permits. Many utilities argue that they should be given away for free. Leonard argues that the government should auction them off. That way, the funds raised could be redistributed to utilities' customers, thereby offsetting some of the economic hardship that might otherwise result from higher electricity bills.

(b) The most straightforward way to reduce use of a product that causes a negative externality is to tax it. The figure below (which is very similar to Figure 5-5 on page 144) shows the effects of a carbon tax. The supply curve faced by electricity producers, labeled $S_1$, represents only the firms' private costs, not including the external cost from $CO_2$ emissions. Imposing a tax on carbon emissions equal to the external cost shifts the supply curve from $S_1$ to $S_2$. Businesses and households that purchase electricity will experience an increase in price from $P_{Market}$ to $P_{Efficient}$. The higher price reflects the external cost of $CO_2$ emissions. Utilities receive the lower price, $P$, equal to the price paid by consumers minus the amount of the carbon tax.

(c) Leonard points out that while the United States and other high-income countries are taking steps to reduce carbon emissions, most developing countries are not. In particular, China has been experiencing very rapid economic growth and a correspondingly rapid growth in demand for electricity. Most of the new plants being built in China burn coal to generate electricity. Even if the United States reduces its own emissions of $CO_2$ to an economically efficient level, world–wide emissions would continue to be far above the efficient levels if China and other developing countries do not take action to control their emissions. It's possible to think of reducing carbon emissions as being like a public good. If the United States and other developed nations pay the cost of reducing carbon emissions, developing nations such as China could benefit from the reduction while not contributing to it.

## Thinking Critically
### *About Policy*

1. The article points out some of the difficulties with carbon trading programs. If the number of permits is set too high, the program will not provide a strong incentive to switch from coal to natural gas. As a result, it is likely that firms will use too much coal. Would a carbon tax result in similar difficulties?

2. The government raises no revenue from tradable permits if it gives the permits to firms at no charge. In the event that tradable permits raise no government revenue—which might be used to reduce other taxes that result in deadweight losses—some economists and policymakers favor carbon taxes over carbon trading. What is an alternative means of allocating the initial carbon permits that would raise revenue for the government?

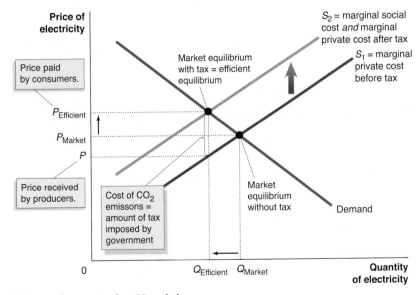

Using a carbon tax to reduce $CO_2$ emissions.

# Key Terms

Coase theorem, p. 143

Command-and-control approach, p. 145

Common resource, p. 148

Excludability, p. 148

Externality, p. 134

Free riding, p. 148

Market failure, p. 137

Pigovian taxes and subsidies, p. 145

Private benefit, p. 134

Private cost, p. 134

Private good, p. 148

Property rights, p. 137

Public good, p. 148

Rivalry, p. 148

Social benefit, p. 134

Social cost, p. 134

Tragedy of the commons, p. 155

Transactions costs, p. 143

**5.1** | **Externalities and Economic Efficiency, pages 134–138**
LEARNING OBJECTIVE: Identify examples of positive and negative externalities and use graphs to show how externalities affect economic efficiency.

## Summary

An **externality** is a benefit or cost to parties who are not involved in a transaction. Pollution and other externalities in production cause a difference between the **private cost** borne by the producer of a good or services and the **social cost**, which includes any external cost, such as the cost of pollution. An externality in consumption causes a difference between the **private benefit** received by the consumer and the **social benefit**, which includes any external benefit. If externalities exist in production or consumption, the market will not produce the optimal level of a good or service. This outcome is referred to as **market failure**. Externalities arise when property rights do not exist or cannot be legally enforced. **Property rights** are the rights individuals or businesses have to the exclusive use of their property, including the right to buy or sell it.

 Visit www.myeconlab.com to complete these exercises online and get instant feedback.

## Review Questions

**1.1** What is an externality? Give an example of a positive externality and give an example of a negative externality.

**1.2** When will the private cost of producing a good differ from the social cost? Give an example. When will the private benefit from consuming a good differ from the social benefit? Give an example.

**1.3** What is economic efficiency? How do externalities affect the economic efficiency of a market equilibrium?

**1.4** What is market failure? When is market failure likely to arise?

**1.5** Briefly discuss the relationship between property rights and the existence of externalities.

## Problems and Applications

**1.6** The chapter states that your consuming a Big Mac does not create an externality. But suppose you arrive at your favorite McDonald's at lunchtime and get in a long line to be served. By the time you reach the counter, there are 10 people in line behind you. Because you decided to have a Big Mac for lunch—instead of, say, a pizza—each of those 10 people must wait in line an additional 2 minutes. Or suppose that after a lifetime of consuming Big Macs, you develop heart disease. Because you are now over age 65, the government must pay most of your medical bills through the Medicare system. Is it still correct to say that your consuming a Big Mac created no externalities? Might there be a justification here for the government to intervene in the market for Big Macs? Explain.

**1.7** The chapter discusses the cases of consumption generating a positive externality and production generating a negative externality. Is it possible for consumption to generate a negative externality? If so, give an example. Is it possible for production to generate a positive externality? If so, give an example.

**1.8** In a study at a large state university, students were randomly assigned roommates. Researchers found that, on average, males assigned to roommates who reported drinking alcohol in the year before entering college had GPAs one-quarter point lower than those assigned to non-drinking roommates. For males who drank frequently before college, being assigned to a roommate who also drank frequently before college reduced their GPAs by two-thirds of a point. Draw a graph showing the price of alcohol and the quantity of alcohol consumption on college campuses. Include in the graph the private and social costs of drinking. Label any deadweight loss that arises in this market.
Source: Michael Kremer and Dan M. Levy, "Peer Effects and Alcohol Use Among College Students," *Journal of Economic Perspectives*, Vol. 22, No. 3, Summer 2008, pp. 189–206.

**1.9** Tom and Jacob are college students. Each of them will probably get married later and have two or three children. Each knows that if he studies more in college, he'll get a better job and earn more than if he doesn't study. Earning more means the ability to spend more on their future families—things like orthodontia, nice clothes, admission to an expensive college, and travel. Tom thinks about the potential benefits to his potential children when he decides how much studying to do. Jacob doesn't.

a. What type of externality arises from studying?

b. Draw a graph showing this externality, contrasting the responses of Tom and Jacob. Who studies more? Who acts more efficiently? Why?

**1.10** The following information regarding cable television is from the Federal Communications Commission (FCC) Web site:

> In general, a cable television operator has the right to select the channels and services that are available on its cable system. With the exception of certain channels like local broadcast television channels which are required to be carried by federal law, the cable operator has broad discretion in choosing which channels will be available and how those channels will be packaged and marketed to subscribers. With the exception of programming that is required to be carried on the basic tier, the cable operator and the entity that owns the channel or programming service negotiate the terms and conditions for carriage on the cable system. Terms may include whether the channel or service will be offered in a package with other programming or whether the channel or service will be offered on a per-channel or pay-per-view basis.

Suppose you are a fan of *The Daily Show* with Jon Stewart and *The Colbert Report*, both on the Comedy Central cable channel, but the only way you can get Comedy Central from your local cable provider is to subscribe to a package that includes 30 other channels. Is there an externality involved here? If so, is it an externality in production or consumption, and is it positive or negative? If there is an externality, discuss possible solutions.

Source: Consumer and Government Affairs Bureau, "Choosing Cable Channels," www.fcc.gov/cgb/consumerfacts/cablechannels.html, November 6, 2008.

**1.11** In an article in the agriculture magazine *Choices*, Oregon State University economist JunJie Wu made the following observation about the conversion of farmland to urban development:

> Land use provides many economic and social benefits, but often comes at a substantial cost to the environment. Although most economic costs are figured into land use decisions, most environmental externalities are not. These environmental "externalities" cause a divergence between private and social costs for some land uses, leading to an inefficient land allocation. For example, developers may not bear all the environmental and infrastructural costs generated by their projects. Such "market failures" provide a justification for private conservation efforts and public land use planning and regulation.

What does the author mean by *market failures* and *inefficient land allocation*? Explain why the author describes inefficient land allocation as a market failure. Illustrate your argument with a graph showing the market for land to be used for urban development.

Source: JunJie Wu, "Land Use Changes: Economic, Social, and Environmental Impacts," *Choices*, Vol. 23, No. 4, Fourth Quarter 2008, pp. 6–10.

**1.12** (Related to *Solved Problem 5-1* on page 136) Tuberculosis is a disease caused by a bacterium. The disease is contagious through the air. It is particularly likely to spread in a closed atmosphere, such as an airplane. Travel benefits those who consume it. But when people with tuberculosis travel, they impose costs on their fellow travelers. Draw a graph that illustrates the impact associated with infected persons traveling.

**>> End Learning Objective 5.1**

---

**5.2** **Private Solutions to Externalities: The Coase Theorem**, pages 138–144

LEARNING OBJECTIVE: Discuss the Coase theorem and explain how private bargaining can lead to economic efficiency in a market with an externality.

## Summary

Externalities and market failures result from incomplete property rights or from the difficulty of enforcing property rights in certain situations. When an externality exists, and the efficient quantity of a good is not being produced, the total cost of reducing the externality is usually less than the total benefit. According to the **Coase theorem**, if **transactions costs** are low, private bargaining will result in an efficient solution to the problem of externalities.

  Visit **www.myeconlab.com** to complete these exercises online and get instant feedback.

## Review Questions

**2.1** What do economists mean by "an economically efficient level of pollution"?

**2.2** What is the Coase theorem? What are transactions costs? When are we likely to see private solutions to the problem of externalities?

## Problems and Applications

**2.3** Is it ever possible for an *increase* in pollution to make society better off? Briefly explain, using a graph like Figure 5-3 on page 140.

**2.4** If the marginal cost of reducing a certain type of pollution is zero, should all that type of pollution be eliminated? Briefly explain.

**2.5** Discuss the factors that determine the marginal cost of reducing crime. Discuss the factors that determine the marginal benefit of reducing crime. Would it be economically efficient to reduce the amount of crime to zero? Briefly explain.

**2.6** (Related to the *Don't Let This Happen to You!* on page 142) Briefly explain whether you agree or disagree with the following statement: "Sulfur dioxide emissions cause acid rain and breathing difficulties for people with respiratory problems. The total benefit to society is greatest if we completely eliminate sulfur dioxide emissions. Therefore, the economically efficient level of emissions is zero."

**2.7** In discussing the reduction of air pollution in the developing world, Richard Fuller of the Blacksmith Institute, an environmental organization, observed, "It's the 90/10 rule. To do 90 percent of the work only costs 10 percent of the money. It's the last 10 percent

of the cleanup that costs 90 percent of the money." Why should it be any more costly to clean up the last 10 percent of polluted air than to clean up the first 90 percent? What trade-offs would be involved in cleaning up the final 10 percent?

Source: Tiffany M. Luck, "The World's Dirtiest Cities," *Middle East Times*, February 28, 2008.

**2.8** (Related to the *Making the Connection* on page 139) In the first years following the passage of the Clean Air Act in 1970, air pollution declined sharply, and there were important health benefits, including a decline in infant mortality. Should the government take action to reduce air pollution further? How should government go about deciding this question?

**2.9** (Related to the *Making the Connection* on page 142) We know that owners of apple orchards and owners of beehives are able to negotiate private agreements. Is it likely that as a result of these private agreements, the market supplies the efficient quantities of apple trees and beehives? Are there any real-world difficulties that might stand in the way of achieving this efficient outcome?

>> **End Learning Objective 5.2**

---

 ### 5.3 Government Policies to Deal with Externalities, pages 144–147

LEARNING OBJECTIVE: Analyze government policies to achieve economic efficiency in a market with an externality.

## Summary

When private solutions to externalities are unworkable, the government sometimes intervenes. One way to deal with a negative externality in production is to impose a tax equal to the cost of the externality. The tax causes the producer of the good to internalize the externality. The government can deal with a positive externality in consumption by giving consumers a subsidy, or payment, equal to the value of the externality. Government taxes and subsidies intended to bring about an efficient level of output in the presence of externalities are called **Pigovian taxes and subsidies**. Although the federal government has sometimes used subsidies and taxes to deal with externalities, in dealing with pollution, it has more often used a command-and-control approach. A **command-and-control approach** involves the government imposing quantitative limits on the amount of pollution allowed or requiring firms to install specific pollution control devices. Direct pollution controls of this type are not economically efficient, however. As a result, Congress decided to use a system of tradable emissions allowances to reduce sulfur dioxide emissions.

 Visit www.myeconlab.com to complete these exercises online and get instant feedback.

## Review Questions

**3.1** What is a Pigovian tax? At what level must a Pigovian tax be set to achieve efficiency?

**3.2** Why do most economists prefer tradable emissions allowances rather than the command-and-control approach to pollution?

## Problems and Applications

**3.3** Why does the government subsidize the purchase of college educations but not the purchase of hamburgers?

**3.4** Writing in the *New York Times*, Michael Lewis argued: "Good new technologies are a bit like good new roads: Their social benefits far exceed what any one person or company can get paid for creating them." Does this observation justify the government subsidizing the production of new technologies? If so, how might the government do this?

Source: Michael Lewis, "In Defense of the Boom," *New York Times*, October 27, 2002.

**3.5** In 2007, Governor Deval Patrick of Massachusetts proposed that criminals would have to pay a "safety fee" to the government. The size of the fee would be based on the seriousness of the crime (that is, the fee would be larger for more serious crimes).

**a.** Is there an economically efficient amount of crime? Briefly explain.

**b.** Briefly explain whether the "safety fee" is a Pigovian tax of the type discussed in this chapter.

Source: Michael Levenson, "Patrick Proposes New Fee on Criminals," *Boston Globe*, January 14, 2007.

**3.6** In a paper written for the Harvard Project on International Climate Agreements, the authors state that while a majority of developed nations are enacting significant regulations to mitigate climate change, "Developing countries typically place greater priority on economic development than on environmental protection, despite being vulnerable to the potential adverse effects of continued warming." Recall the definition of *normal goods* given in Chapter 3. Is environmental protection a normal good? If so, is there any connection between this fact and the observation of the authors of the above statement? Briefly explain. How do the marginal cost and marginal benefit of environmental protection change with economic development?

Source: Daniel S. Hall, Michael A. Levi, William A. Pizer, and Takahiro Ueno, "Policies for Developing Country Engagement," Discussion Paper 08-15, Harvard Project on International Climate Agreements, Belfer Center for Science and International Affairs, Harvard Kennedy School, October 2008.

**3.7** The following graph illustrates the situation in the dry cleaning market. The marginal social cost of the pollution rises as the quantity of items cleaned per week increases. In addition, there are two demand curves, one for a smaller city, $D_S$, and the other for a larger city, $D_L$.

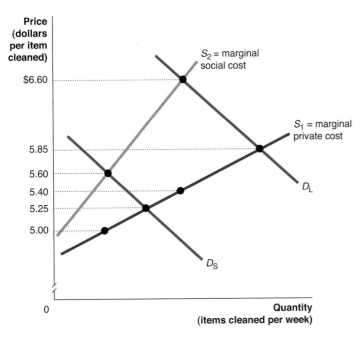

**a.** Explain why the marginal social cost curve has a different slope than the marginal private cost curve.

**b.** What tax per item cleaned will achieve economic efficiency in the smaller city? In the larger city? Explain why the efficient tax is different in the two cities.

**3.8** Negative externalities can exist in consumption. Writing in the *New England Journal of Medicine*, Kelly Brownell of Yale and Thomas Frieden, health commissioner of New York City, argue that consuming sugar-sweetened soft drinks involves a significant externality. They argue that this externality exists because consuming soft drinks can lead to medical problems whose treatment is paid for partly by taxpayers through the government Medicare and Medicaid programs, and because these medical problems can also reduce school performance and work productivity.

**a.** Assuming that this analysis is correct, use a graph to illustrate the externality in the market for sugar-sweetened soft drinks. Be sure to label on your graph the points representing the market equilibrium and the efficient equilibrium.

**b.** If the government decides to tax soft drinks to deal with the externality, is it likely to require firms producing soft drinks to pay the tax or consumers of soft drinks to pay the tax? Assuming that the government can collect the tax as easily from consumers as from firms, will it matter which group pays the tax? Illustrate your answer with a graph showing the effect of the tax if consumers are required to pay it and the effect of the tax if firms are required to pay it.

Source: Kelly D. Brownell and Thomas R. Frieden, "Ounces of Prevention—The Public Policy Case for Taxes on Sugared Beverages," *New England Journal of Medicine*, April 30, 2009, pp. 1805–1808.

**3.9** (Related to the *Chapter Opener* on page 133) As mentioned in the chapter opener, James Rogers, the chief executive officer of Duke Energy, argued against President Obama's proposed cap-and-trade system for reducing $CO_2$ emissions, on the grounds that it could result in electric utility rates rising by as much as 40 percent.

**a.** Is the fact that the cap-and-trade system for reducing $CO_2$ emissions would raise electric utility rates a good argument against this way of reducing emissions? Briefly explain.

**b.** Under President Obama's original proposal, permits to emit $CO_2$ would have been auctioned off, and the funds raised would have been used to finance tax cuts for low- and middle-income people. Would the emission permits being auctioned off affect your answer to part a?

**3.10** (Related to the *Making the Connection* on page 146) As discussed in this chapter, a system of tradable permits was very successful in efficiently reducing emissions of sulfur dioxide in the United States. Why have some economists proposed a similar system of tradable permits to reduce carbon dioxide emissions? Briefly discuss similarities and differences

between the problem of reducing sulfur dioxide emissions and the problem of reducing carbon dioxide emissions.

>> **End Learning Objective 5.3**

**5.4**  **Four Categories of Goods**, pages 148–157
LEARNING OBJECTIVE: Explain how goods can be categorized on the basis of whether they are rival or excludable, and use graphs to illustrate the efficient quantities of public goods and common resources.

## Summary

There are four categories of goods: private goods, public goods, quasi-public goods, and common resources. **Private goods** are both rival and excludable. **Rivalry** means that when one person consumes a unit of a good, no one else can consume that unit. **Excludability** means that anyone who does not pay for a good cannot consume it. **Public goods** are both nonrivalrous and nonexcludable. Private firms are usually not willing to supply public goods because of free riding. **Free riding** involves benefiting from a good without paying for it. **Quasi-public goods** are excludable but not rival. **Common resources** are rival but not excludable. The **tragedy of the commons** refers to the tendency for a common resource to be overused. The tragedy of the commons results from a lack of clearly defined and enforced property rights. We find the market demand curve for a private good by adding the quantity of the good demanded by each consumer at each price. We find the demand curve for a public good by adding vertically the price each consumer would be willing to pay for each quantity of the good. The optimal quantity of a public good occurs where the demand curve intersects the curve representing the marginal cost of supplying the good.

 Visit **www.myeconlab.com** to complete these exercises online and get instant feedback.

## Review Questions

4.1  Define *rivalry* and *excludability* and use these terms to discuss the four categories of goods.
4.2  What is a public good? What is free riding? How is free riding related to the tendency of a public good to create market failure?
4.3  What is the tragedy of the commons? How can it be avoided?

## Problems and Applications

4.4  **(Related to *Solved Problem 5-4* on page 153)** Suppose that Jill and Joe are the only two people in the small town of Andover. Andover has land available to build a park of no more than 9 acres. Jill and Joe's demand schedules for the park are as follows:

| JOE | |
|---|---|
| PRICE PER ACRE | NUMBER OF ACRES |
| $10 | 0 |
| 9 | 1 |
| 8 | 2 |
| 7 | 3 |
| 6 | 4 |
| 5 | 5 |
| 4 | 6 |
| 3 | 7 |
| 2 | 8 |
| 1 | 9 |

| JILL | |
|---|---|
| PRICE PER ACRE | NUMBER OF ACRES |
| $15 | 0 |
| 14 | 1 |
| 13 | 2 |
| 12 | 3 |
| 11 | 4 |
| 10 | 5 |
| 9 | 6 |
| 8 | 7 |
| 7 | 8 |
| 6 | 9 |

The supply curve is as follows:

| PRICE | NUMBER OF ACRES |
|---|---|
| $11 | 1 |
| 13 | 2 |
| 15 | 3 |
| 17 | 4 |
| 19 | 5 |
| 21 | 6 |
| 23 | 7 |
| 25 | 8 |
| 27 | 9 |

a. Draw a graph showing the optimal size of the park. Be sure to label the curves on the graph.

b. Briefly explain why a park of 2 acres is not optimal.

4.5 Commercial whaling has been described as a modern example of the tragedy of the commons. Briefly explain whether you agree or disagree.

4.6 Nancy Folbre, an economist at the University of Massachusetts, Amherst, argued: "We must take responsibility for governing the commons—not just the quaint old-fashioned village green, but things that cannot easily be privatized—[such as] clean air. . . ." Do you agree that clean air is like a common pasture in England in the Middle Ages? Briefly explain.

Source: Nancy Folbre, "Taking Responsibility for the Commons," *New York Times*, February 26, 2009.

4.7 The more frequently bacteria are exposed to antibiotics, the more quickly the bacteria will develop resistance to the antibiotics. An article from MayoClinic.com includes the following statement regarding the responsibility of antibiotic users:

> Antibiotic resistance is a pressing, global health problem. Nearly all significant bacterial infections in the world are becoming resistant to commonly used antibiotics. When you abuse antibiotics, the resistant microorganisms that you help create can become widely established, causing new and hard-to-treat infections. That's why the decisions you make about antibiotic

use—unlike almost any other medicine you take—extend far beyond your reach. Responsible antibiotic use protects the health of your family, neighbors and ultimately the global community.

Briefly discuss in what sense antibiotics can be considered a common resource.

Source: Mayo Clinic staff, "Antibiotics: Use Them Wisely," *MayoClinic.com*, February 13, 2008.

4.8 Put each of these goods or services into one of the boxes in Figure 5-7 on page 148. That is, categorize them as private goods, public goods, quasi-public goods, or common resources.

a. A television broadcast of the World Series

b. Home mail delivery

c. Education in a public school

d. Education in a private school

e. Hiking in a park surrounded by a fence

f. Hiking in a park not surrounded by a fence

g. An apple

4.9 (Related to the *Making the Connection* on page 149) Explain whether you agree or disagree with the following statement: "Providing health care is obviously a public good. If one person becomes ill and doesn't receive treatment, that person may infect many other people. If many people become ill, then the output of the economy will be negatively affected. Therefore, providing health care is a public good that should be supplied by the government."

**>> End Learning Objective 5.4**

# CHAPTER 6

# Elasticity:
## The Responsiveness of Demand and Supply

## Chapter Outline and Learning Objectives

## >> Do People Respond to Changes in the Price of Gasoline?

Some people have argued that consumers don't vary the quantity of gas they buy as the price changes because the number of miles they need to drive to get to work or school or to run errands is roughly constant. During the spring and summer of 2008, however, as the price of gasoline soared to $4.00 per gallon in many parts of the country, consumers certainly responded. For instance, during July 2008, when the average price of gasoline was $4.09, U.S. consumers bought nearly 6 percent less gasoline than they had during July 2007, when the average price of gasoline had been $2.96 per gallon.

Service station owners were definitely aware that consumers were responding to higher gas prices. In the spring of 2008, a service station owner on Staten Island, New York, was trying to avoid losing customers by keeping his price below $4.00 per gallon, even if it meant making very little profit. A newspaper article quoted him as saying:

> That gasoline costs me $3.78 cents. . . . If you take the $3.78 and you pay with an American Express card [the charge to the service station owner is] about 11 cents. Plus there's a 2 or 3 cents . . . sales tax extra that we don't charge. So now you're talking a cost of about $3.92 to me. And I'm charging $3.99.

But he was afraid that raising his prices would cause the quantity of gasoline he sold to fall by so much that he would be in an even worse situation.

In this chapter, we will explore what determines the responsiveness of the quantity demanded and the quantity supplied to changes in the market price. **AN INSIDE LOOK** on **page 192** discusses the effect of higher gas prices on the demand for public transportation.

Sources: Glenn Collins, "Gas Station Owners Try to Hold a Psychological Line," *New York Times*, May 3, 2008; and data on gasoline prices and consumption from the U.S. Energy Information Administration.

## Economics in YOUR LIFE!

### How Much Do Gas Prices Matter to You?

What factors would make you more or less responsive to price when purchasing gasoline? Have you responded differently to price changes during different periods of your life? Why do consumers seem to respond more to changes in gas prices at a particular service station but seem less sensitive when gas prices rise or fall at all service stations? As you read the chapter, see if you can answer these questions. You can check your answers against those we provide at the end of the chapter.

▶ Continued on page 190

Whether you are managing a service station, a bookstore, or a coffee shop, you need to know how an increase or a decrease in the price of your products will affect the quantity consumers are willing to buy. We saw in Chapter 3 that cutting the price of a good increases the quantity demanded and that raising the price reduces the quantity demanded. But the critical question is this: *How much* will the quantity demanded change as a result of a price increase or decrease? Economists use the concept of **elasticity** to measure how one economic variable—such as the quantity demanded—responds to changes in another economic variable—such as the price. For example, the responsiveness of the quantity demanded of a good to changes in its price is called the *price elasticity of demand*. Knowing the price elasticity of demand allows you to compute the effect of a price change on the quantity demanded.

We also saw in Chapter 3 that the quantity of a good that consumers demand depends not just on the price of the good but also on consumer income and on the prices of related goods. As a manager, you would also be interested in measuring the responsiveness of demand to these other factors. As we will see, we can use the concept of elasticity here as well. We are also interested in the responsiveness of the quantity supplied of a good to changes in its price, which is called the *price elasticity of supply*.

Elasticity is an important concept not just for business managers but for policymakers as well. If the government wants to discourage teenage smoking, it can raise the price of cigarettes by increasing the tax on them. If we know the price elasticity of demand for cigarettes, we can calculate how many fewer packs of cigarettes will be demanded at a higher price. In this chapter, we will also see how policymakers use the concept of elasticity.

**Elasticity**  A measure of how much one economic variable responds to changes in another economic variable.

**6.1 LEARNING** OBJECTIVE

Define price elasticity of demand and understand how to measure it.

# The Price Elasticity of Demand and its Measurement

We know from the law of demand that when the price of a product falls, the quantity demanded of the product increases. But the law of demand tells firms only that the demand curves for their products slope downward. More useful is a measure of the responsiveness of the quantity demanded to a change in price. This measure is called the **price elasticity of demand**.

**Price elasticity of demand**  The responsiveness of the quantity demanded to a change in price, measured by dividing the percentage change in the quantity demanded of a product by the percentage change in the product's price.

## Measuring the Price Elasticity of Demand

We might measure the price elasticity of demand by using the slope of the demand curve because the slope of the demand curve tells us how much quantity changes as price changes. Using the slope of the demand curve to measure price elasticity has a drawback, however: The measurement of slope is sensitive to the units chosen for quantity and price. For example, suppose a $1 per gallon decrease in the price of gasoline leads to an increase in the quantity demanded from 10.1 million gallons to 10.2 million gallons per day. The change in quantity is 0.1 million gallons, and the change in price is −$1, so the slope is 0.1/−1 = −0.1. But if we measure price in cents, rather than dollars, the slope is 0.1/−100 = −0.001. If we measure price in dollars and gallons in thousands, instead of millions, the slope is 100/−1 = −100. Clearly, the value we compute for the slope can change dramatically, depending on the units we use for quantity and price.

To avoid this confusion over units, economists use *percentage changes* when measuring the price elasticity of demand. Percentage changes are not dependent on units of measurement. (For a review of calculating percentage changes, see the appendix to Chapter 1.) No matter what units we use to measure the quantity of gasoline, 10 percent more gasoline is 10 percent more gasoline. Therefore, the price elasticity of demand is measured by dividing the percentage change in the quantity demanded by the percentage change in the price. Or:

$$\text{Price elasticity of demand} = \frac{\text{Percentage change in quantity demanded}}{\text{Percentage change in price}}.$$

It's important to remember that *the price elasticity of demand is not the same as the slope of the demand curve.*

If we calculate the price elasticity of demand for a price cut, the percentage change in price will be negative, and the percentage change in quantity demanded will be positive. Similarly, if we calculate the price elasticity of demand for a price increase, the percentage change in price will be positive, and the percentage change in quantity demanded will be negative. Therefore, the price elasticity of demand is always negative. In comparing elasticities, though, we are usually interested in their relative size. So, we often drop the minus sign and compare their *absolute values*. In other words, although −3 is actually a smaller number than −2, a price elasticity of −3 is larger than a price elasticity of −2.

## Elastic Demand and Inelastic Demand

If the quantity demanded is responsive to changes in price, the percentage change in quantity demanded will be *greater* than the percentage change in price, and the price elasticity of demand will be greater than 1 in absolute value. In this case, demand is **elastic**. For example, if a 10 percent decrease in the price of bagels results in a 20 percent increase in the quantity of bagels demanded, then:

$$\text{Price elasticity of demand} = \frac{20\%}{-10\%} = -2,$$

and we can conclude that the demand for bagels is elastic.

When the quantity demanded is not very responsive to price, however, the percentage change in quantity demanded will be *less* than the percentage change in price, and the price elasticity of demand will be less than 1 in absolute value. In this case, demand is **inelastic**. For example, if a 10 percent decrease in the price of wheat results in a 5 percent increase in the quantity of wheat demanded, then:

$$\text{Price elasticity of demand} = \frac{5\%}{-10\%} = -0.5,$$

and we can conclude that the demand for wheat is inelastic.

In the special case in which the percentage change in the quantity demanded is equal to the percentage change in price, the price elasticity of demand equals −1 (or 1 in absolute value). In this case, demand is **unit elastic**.

## An Example of Computing Price Elasticities

Suppose you own a service station and you are trying to decide whether to cut the price you are charging for a gallon of gas. You are currently at point *A* in Figure 6-1: selling 1,000 gallons per day at a price of $3.00 per gallon. How many more gallons you will sell by cutting the price to $2.70 depends on the price elasticity of demand for gasoline at your service station. Let's consider two possibilities: If $D_1$ is the demand curve for gasoline at your station, your sales will increase to 1,200 gallons per day, point *B*. But if $D_2$ is your demand curve, your sales will increase only to 1,050 gallons per day, point *C*. We might expect—correctly, as we will see—that between these points, demand curve $D_1$ is *elastic*, and demand curve $D_2$ is *inelastic*.

To confirm that $D_1$ is elastic between these points and that $D_2$ is inelastic, we need to calculate the price elasticity of demand for each curve. In calculating price elasticity between two points on a demand curve, though, we run into a problem because we get a different value for price increases than for price decreases. For example, suppose we

**Elastic demand** Demand is elastic when the percentage change in quantity demanded is *greater* than the percentage change in price, so the price elasticity is *greater* than 1 in absolute value.

**Inelastic demand** Demand is inelastic when the percentage change in quantity demanded is *less* than the percentage change in price, so the price elasticity is *less* than 1 in absolute value.

**Unit-elastic demand** Demand is unit elastic when the percentage change in quantity demanded is *equal to* the percentage change in price, so the price elasticity is equal to 1 in absolute value.

## Figure 6-1

**Elastic and Inelastic Demand Curves**

Along $D_1$, cutting the price from $3.00 to $2.70 increases the number of gallons sold from 1,000 per day to 1,200 per day, so demand is elastic between point A and point B. Along $D_2$, cutting the price from $3.00 to $2.70 increases the number of gallons sold from 1,000 per day only to 1,050 per day, so demand is inelastic between point A and point C.

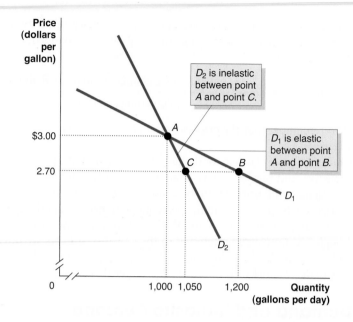

calculate the price elasticity for $D_1$ as the price is cut from $3.00 to $2.70. This reduction is a 10 percent price cut that increases the quantity demanded from 1,000 gallons to 1,200 gallons, or by 20 percent. Therefore, the price elasticity of demand between points A and B is 20/−10 = −2.0. Now let's calculate the price elasticity for $D_1$ as the price is *increased* from $2.70 to $3.00. This is an 11.1 percent price increase that decreases the quantity demanded from 1,200 gallons to 1,000 gallons, or by 16.7 percent. So, now our measure of the price elasticity of demand between points A and B is −16.7/11.1 = −1.5. It can be confusing to have different values for the price elasticity of demand between the same two points on the same demand curve. As we will see in the next section, to avoid this confusion, economists often use a particular formula when calculating elasticities.

## The Midpoint Formula

We can use the *midpoint formula* to ensure that we have only one value of the price elasticity of demand between the same two points on a demand curve. The midpoint formula uses the *average* of the initial and final quantities and the initial and final prices. If $Q_1$ and $P_1$ are the initial quantity and price and $Q_2$ and $P_2$ are the final quantity and price, the midpoint formula is:

$$\text{Price elasticity of demand} = \frac{(Q_2 - Q_1)}{\left(\frac{Q_1 + Q_2}{2}\right)} \div \frac{(P_2 - P_1)}{\left(\frac{P_1 + P_2}{2}\right)}.$$

The midpoint formula may seem challenging at first, but the numerator is just the change in quantity divided by the average of the initial and final quantities, and the denominator is just the change in price divided by the average of the initial and final prices.

Let's apply the formula to calculating the price elasticity of $D_1$ in Figure 6-1. Between point A and point B on $D_1$, the change in quantity is 200, and the average of the two quantities is 1,100. Therefore, there is an 18.2 percent change in quantity. The change in price is −$0.30, and the average of the two prices is $2.85. Therefore, there is a −10.5 percent change in price. So, the price elasticity of demand is 18.2/−10.5 = −1.7. Notice these three results from calculating the price elasticity of demand using the midpoint formula: First, as we suspected from examining Figure 6-1, demand curve $D_1$ is elastic between points A and B. Second, our value for the price elasticity calculated using the midpoint formula is between the two values we calculated earlier. Third, the midpoint formula will give us the same value whether we are moving from the higher price to the lower price or from the lower price to the higher price.

We can also use the midpoint formula to calculate the elasticity of demand between point $A$ and point $C$ on $D_2$. In this case, there is a 4.9 percent change in quantity and a $-10.5$ percent change in price. So, the elasticity of demand is $4.9/-10.5 = -0.5$. Once again, as we suspected, demand curve $D_2$ is price inelastic between points $A$ and $C$.

# Solved Problem | 6-1

## Calculating the Price Elasticity of Demand

Suppose you own a service station and you are currently selling gasoline for $2.50 per gallon. At this price you can sell 2,000 gallons per day. You are considering cutting the price to $2.30 to attract drivers who have been buying their gas at competing stations. The graph below shows two possible increases in the quantity sold as a result of your price cut. Use the information in the graph to calculate the price elasticity between these two prices on each of the demand curves. Use the midpoint formula in your calculations. State whether each demand curve is elastic or inelastic between these two prices.

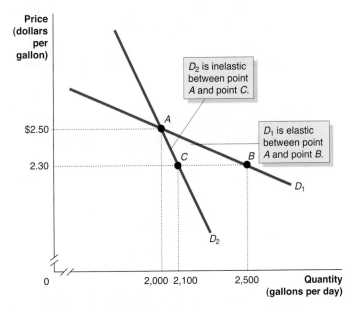

## SOLVING THE PROBLEM:

**Step 1:** **Review the chapter material.** This problem requires calculating the price elasticity of demand, so you may want to review the material in the section "The Midpoint Formula," which begins on page 170.

**Step 2:** **To begin using the midpoint formula, calculate the average quantity and the average price for demand curve $D_1$.**

$$\text{Average quantity} = \frac{2,000 + 2,500}{2} = 2,250$$

$$\text{Average price} = \frac{\$2.50 + \$2.30}{2} = \$2.40$$

**Step 3:** **Now calculate the percentage change in the quantity demanded and the percentage change in price for demand curve $D_1$.**

$$\text{Percentage change in quantity demanded} = \frac{2,500 - 2,000}{2,250} \times 100 = 22.2\%$$

$$\text{Percentage change in price} = \frac{\$2.30 - \$2.50}{\$2.40} \times 100 = -8.3\%$$

**Step 4:** **Divide the percentage change in the quantity demanded by the percentage change in price to arrive at the price elasticity for demand curve $D_1$.**

$$\text{Price elasticity of demand} = \frac{22.2\%}{-8.3\%} = -2.7$$

Because the elasticity is greater than 1 in absolute value, $D_1$ is price *elastic* between these two prices.

**Step 5:** **Calculate the price elasticity of demand curve $D_2$ between these two prices.**

$$\text{Percentage change in quantity demanded} = \frac{2,100 - 2,000}{2,050} \times 100 = 4.9\%$$

$$\text{Percentage change in price} = \frac{\$2.30 - \$2.50}{\$2.40} \times 100 = -8.3\%$$

$$\text{Price elasticity of demand} = \frac{4.9\%}{-8.3\%} = -0.6$$

Because the elasticity is less than 1 in absolute value, $D_2$ is price *inelastic* between these two prices.

 **YOUR TURN:** For more practice, do related problem 1.6 on page 194 at the end of this chapter.

## When Demand Curves Intersect, the Flatter Curve Is More Elastic

Remember that elasticity is not the same thing as slope. While slope is calculated using changes in quantity and price, elasticity is calculated using percentage changes. But it *is* true that if two demand curves intersect, the one with the smaller slope (in absolute value)—the flatter demand curve—is more elastic, and the one with the larger slope (in absolute value)—the steeper demand curve—is less elastic. In Figure 6-1, for a given change in price, demand curve $D_1$ is more elastic than demand curve $D_2$.

## Polar Cases of Perfectly Elastic and Perfectly Inelastic Demand

**Perfectly inelastic demand** The case where the quantity demanded is completely unresponsive to price, and the price elasticity of demand equals zero.

Although they do not occur frequently, you should be aware of the extreme, or polar, cases of price elasticity. If a demand curve is a vertical line, it is **perfectly inelastic**. In this case, the quantity demanded is completely unresponsive to price, and the price elasticity of demand equals zero. No matter how much price may increase or decrease, the quantity remains the same. For only a very few products will the quantity demanded be completely unresponsive to the price, making the demand curve a vertical line. The drug insulin is an example. Diabetics must take a certain amount of insulin each day. If the price of insulin declines, it will not affect the required dose and thus will not increase the quantity demanded. Similarly, a price increase will not affect the required dose or decrease the quantity demanded. (Of course, some diabetics will not be able to afford insulin at a higher price. If so, even in this case, the demand curve may not be completely vertical and, therefore, not perfectly inelastic.)

**Perfectly elastic demand** The case where the quantity demanded is infinitely responsive to price, and the price elasticity of demand equals infinity.

If a demand curve is a horizontal line, it is **perfectly elastic**. In this case, the quantity demanded is infinitely responsive to price, and the price elasticity of demand equals infinity. If a demand curve is perfectly elastic, an increase in price causes the quantity demanded to fall to zero. Once again, perfectly elastic demand curves are rare, and it is important not to confuse *elastic* with *perfectly elastic*. Table 6-1 summarizes the different price elasticities of demand.

TABLE 6-1

**Summary of the Price Elasticities of Demand**

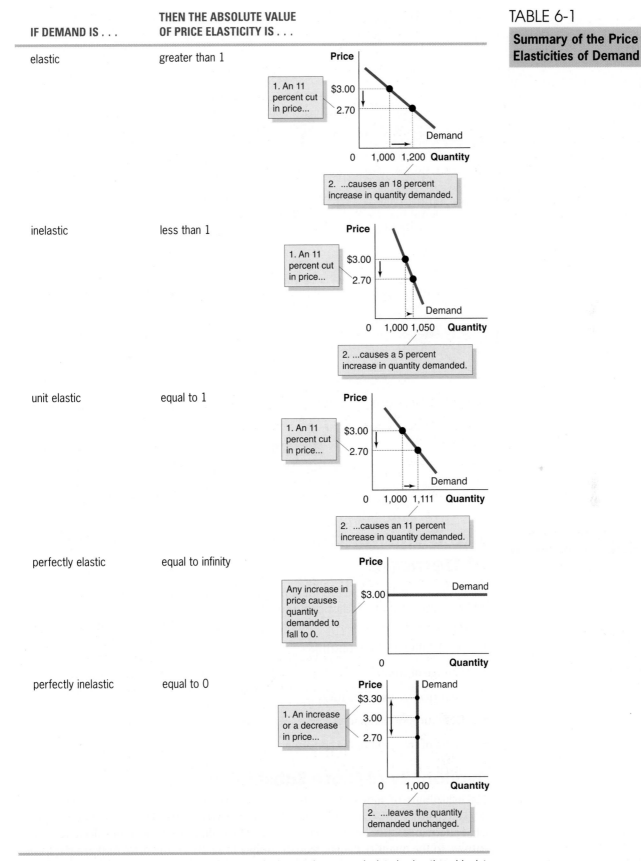

| IF DEMAND IS . . . | THEN THE ABSOLUTE VALUE OF PRICE ELASTICITY IS . . . |
| --- | --- |
| elastic | greater than 1 |
| inelastic | less than 1 |
| unit elastic | equal to 1 |
| perfectly elastic | equal to infinity |
| perfectly inelastic | equal to 0 |

*Note:* The percentage increases shown in the boxes in the graphs were calculated using the midpoint formula, given on page 170.

# Don't Let This Happen to **YOU!**

## Don't Confuse Inelastic with *Perfectly* Inelastic

You may be tempted to simplify the concept of elasticity by assuming that any demand curve described as being inelastic is *perfectly* inelastic. You should never assume this because perfectly inelastic demand curves are rare. For example, consider the following problem: "Use a demand and supply graph to show how a decrease in supply affects the equilibrium quantity of gasoline. Assume that the demand for gasoline is inelastic." The following graph would be an *incorrect* answer to this problem.

The demand for gasoline is inelastic, but it is not *perfectly* inelastic. When the price of gasoline rises, the quantity demanded falls. So, the graph that would be the correct answer to this problem would show a typical downward-sloping demand curve rather than a vertical demand curve.

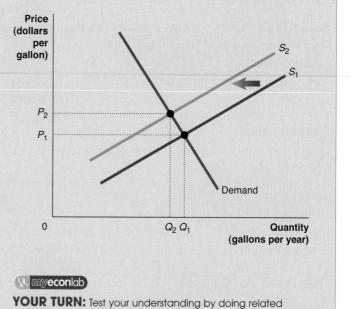

**YOUR TURN:** Test your understanding by doing related problem 1.11 on page 195 at the end of this chapter.

---

**6.2 LEARNING** OBJECTIVE

Understand the determinants of the price elasticity of demand.

# The Determinants of the Price Elasticity of Demand

We have seen that the demand for some products may be elastic, while the demand for other products may be inelastic. In this section, we examine why price elasticities differ among products. The key determinants of the price elasticity of demand are as follows:

- Availability of close substitutes

- Passage of time

- Luxuries versus necessities

- Definition of the market

- Share of the good in the consumer's budget

## Availability of Close Substitutes

The availability of substitutes is the most important determinant of price elasticity of demand because how consumers react to a change in the price of a product depends on what alternatives they have. When the price of gasoline rises, consumers have few alternatives, so the quantity demanded falls only a little. But if the price of pizza rises, consumers have many alternatives, so the quantity demanded is likely to fall quite a lot. In fact, a key constraint on a firm's pricing policies is how many close substitutes exist for its product. In general, *if a product has more substitutes available, it will have more elastic demand. If a product has fewer substitutes available, it will have less elastic demand.*

## Passage of Time

It usually takes consumers some time to adjust their buying habits when prices change. If the price of chicken falls, for example, it takes a while before consumers decide to change from eating chicken for dinner once per week to eating it twice per week. If the price of gasoline increases, it also takes a while for consumers to decide to begin taking public transportation, to buy more fuel-efficient cars, or to find new jobs closer to where they live. *The more time that passes, the more elastic the demand for a product becomes.*

## Luxuries versus Necessities

Goods that are luxuries usually have more elastic demand curves than goods that are necessities. For example, the demand for bread is inelastic because bread is a necessity, and the quantity that people buy is not very dependent on its price. Tickets to a concert are a luxury, so the demand for concert tickets is much more elastic than the demand for bread. *The demand curve for a luxury is more elastic than the demand curve for a necessity.*

## Definition of the Market

In a narrowly defined market, consumers have more substitutes available. At the beginning of this chapter, we saw that a service station owner on Staten Island, New York, worried that if he raised the price he was charging for gasoline, many of his customers would switch to buying from a competitor. So, the demand for gasoline at his particular station is likely to be elastic. The demand for gasoline as a product, on the other hand, is inelastic because consumers have few alternatives (in the short run) to buying it. *The more narrowly we define a market, the more elastic demand will be.*

## Share of a Good in a Consumer's Budget

Goods that take only a small fraction of a consumer's budget tend to have less elastic demand than goods that take a large fraction. For example, most people buy table salt infrequently and in relatively small quantities. The share of the average consumer's budget that is spent on salt is very low. As a result, even a doubling of the price of salt is likely to result in only a small decline in the quantity of salt demanded. "Big-ticket items," such as houses, cars, and furniture, take up a larger share in the average consumer's budget. Increases in the prices of these goods are likely to result in significant declines in quantity demanded. In general, *the demand for a good will be more elastic the larger the share of the good in the average consumer's budget.*

## Some Estimated Price Elasticities of Demand

Table 6-2 shows some estimated short-run price elasticities of demand. It's important to remember that estimates of the price elasticity of different goods can vary, depending on the data used and the time period over which the estimates were made. The results given in the table are consistent with our discussion of the determinants of price elasticity. Goods for which there are few substitutes, such as cigarettes and gasoline, are price inelastic, as are broadly defined goods, such as bread or beer. Particular brands of products, such as Coca-Cola or Post Raisin Bran, are price elastic. (This point is discussed further in the *Making the Connection* on the price elasticity of breakfast cereal.)

The demand for books or DVDs bought from a particular retailer is typically price elastic. Note, though, that demand for books from Amazon is inelastic. This estimate would indicate that at least in the early 2000s, when the estimate was made, consumers did not consider ordering from other online sites to be good substitutes for ordering from Amazon.

An increase in the price of grapes will lead some consumers to substitute other fruits, so demand for grapes is price elastic. Similarly, an increase in the price of new automobiles will lead some consumers to buy used automobiles or to continue driving their current cars, so demand for automobiles is also price elastic. Necessities, such as natural gas and water, are also price inelastic.

## TABLE 6-2

**Estimated Real-World Price Elasticities of Demand**

| PRODUCT | ESTIMATED ELASTICITY | PRODUCT | ESTIMATED ELASTICITY |
|---|---|---|---|
| Books (Barnes&Noble) | −4.00 | Water (residential use) | −0.38 |
| Books (Amazon) | −0.60 | Chicken | −0.37 |
| DVDs (Amazon) | −3.10 | Cocaine | −0.28 |
| Post Raisin Bran | −2.50 | Cigarettes | −0.25 |
| Automobiles | −1.95 | Beer | −0.23 |
| Coca-Cola | −1.22 | Residential natural gas | −0.09 |
| Grapes | −1.18 | Gasoline | −0.06 |
| Restaurant meals | −0.67 | Milk | −0.04 |
| Bread | −0.40 | Sugar | −0.04 |

Sources: Kelly D. Brownell and Thomas R. Frieden, "Ounces of Prevention—The Public Policy Case for Taxes on Sugared Beverages," *New England Journal of Medicine*, April 30, 2009; Sheila M. Olmstead and Robert N. Stavins, "Comparing Price and Non-Price Approaches to Urban Water Conservation," Resources for the Future, Discussion paper 08-22, June 2008; Jonathan E. Hughes, Christopher R. Knittel, and Daniel Sperling, *Evidence of a Shift in the Short-Run Price Elasticity of Gasoline Demand,* Research Report UCD-ITS-RR-06-16 (University of California, Davis: Institute of Transportation Studies, 2006); Robert P. Trost, Frederick Joutz, David Shin, and Bruce McDonwell, "Using Shrinkage Estimators to Obtain Regional Short-Run and Long-Run Price Elasticities of Residential Natural Gas Demand in the U.S." George Washington University Working Paper, March 13, 2009; Lesley Chiou, "Empirical Analysis of Competition between Wal-Mart and Other Retail Channels", *Journal of Economics and Management Strategy*, forthcoming; Judith Chevalier, and Austan Goolsbee, "Price Competition Online: Amazon versus Barnes and Noble", *Quantitative Marketing and Economics*, Vol. 1, no. 2, June, 2003; Henry Saffer and Frank Chaloupka, "The Demand for Illicit Drugs," *Economic Inquiry*, Vol. 37, No. 3, July 1999; "Response to Increases in Cigarette Prices by Race/Ethnicity, Income, and Age Groups—United States, 1976–1993," *Morbidity and Mortality Weekly Report*, July 31, 1998; James Wetzel and George Hoffer, "Consumer Demand for Automobiles: A Disaggregated Market Approach," *Journal of Consumer Research*, Vol. 9, No. 2, September 1982; Jerry A. Hausman, "The Price Elasticity of Demand for Breakfast Cereal," in Timothy F. Bresnahan and Robert J. Gordon, eds., *The Economics of New Goods*, Chicago: University of Chicago Press, 1997; X. M. Gao, Eric J. Wailes, and Gail L. Cramer, "A Microeconometric Model Analysis of U.S. Consumer Demand for Alcoholic Beverages," *Applied Economics*, January 1995; and U.S. Department of Agriculture, Economic Research Service.

*What happens when the price of Post Raisin Bran increases?*

## Making the Connection

### The Price Elasticity of Demand for Breakfast Cereal

MIT economist Jerry Hausman has estimated the price elasticity of demand for breakfast cereal. He divided breakfast cereals into three categories: children's cereals, such as Trix and Froot Loops; adult cereals, such as Special K and Grape-Nuts; and family cereals, such as Corn Flakes and Raisin Bran. Some of the results of his estimates are given in the following table.

| CEREAL | PRICE ELASTICITY OF DEMAND |
|---|---|
| Post Raisin Bran | −2.5 |
| All family breakfast cereals | −1.8 |
| All types of breakfast cereals | −0.9 |

Source: Jerry A. Hausman, "The Price Elasticity of Demand for Breakfast Cereal," in Timothy F. Bresnahan and Robert J. Gordon, eds., *The Economics of New Goods*, Chicago: University of Chicago Press, 1997. Used with permission of The University of Chicago Press.

Just as we would expect, the price elasticity for a particular brand of raisin bran was larger in absolute value than the elasticity for all family cereals, and the elasticity for all family cereals was larger than the elasticity for all types of breakfast cereals. If Post increases the price of its Raisin Bran by 10 percent, sales will decline by 25 percent, as many consumers switch to another brand of raisin bran. If the prices of all family breakfast cereals rise by 10 percent, sales will decline by 18 percent, as consumers switch to child or adult cereals. In both of these cases, demand is elastic. But if the prices of all types of breakfast cereals rise by 10 percent, sales will decline by only 9 percent. Demand for all breakfast cereals is inelastic.

Source: Jerry A. Hausman, "Valuation of New Goods under Perfect and Imperfect Competition," in Timothy F. Bresnahan and Robert J. Gordon, eds., *The Economics of New Goods*, Chicago: University of Chicago Press, 1997.

**YOUR TURN:** Test your understanding by doing related problems 2.4 and 2.5 on page 196 at the end of this chapter.

# The Relationship between Price Elasticity of Demand and Total Revenue

A firm is interested in price elasticity because it allows the firm to calculate how changes in price will affect its **total revenue**, which is the total amount of funds it receives from selling a good or service. Total revenue is calculated by multiplying price per unit by the number of units sold. When demand is inelastic, price and total revenue move in the same direction: An increase in price raises total revenue, and a decrease in price reduces total revenue. When demand is elastic, price and total revenue move inversely: An increase in price reduces total revenue, and a decrease in price raises total revenue.

To understand the relationship between price elasticity and total revenue, consider Figure 6-2. Panel (a) shows a demand curve for gasoline (as in Figure 6-1 on page 170). This demand curve is inelastic between point *A* and point *B*. The total revenue received

**6.3 LEARNING** OBJECTIVE

Understand the relationship between the price elasticity of demand and total revenue.

**Total revenue** The total amount of funds received by a seller of a good or service, calculated by multiplying price per unit by the number of units sold.

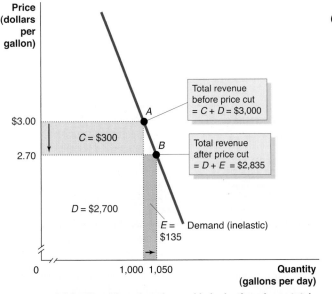

**(a) Cutting price when demand is inelastic reduces total revenue.**

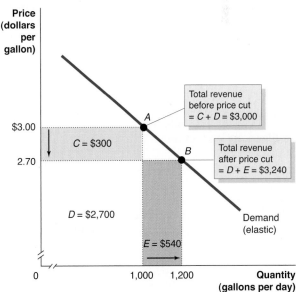

**(b) Cutting price when demand is elastic increases total revenue.**

Figure 6-2 **The Relationship between Price Elasticity and Total Revenue**

When demand is inelastic, a cut in price will decrease total revenue. In panel (a), at point *A*, the price is $3.00, 1,000 gallons are sold, and total revenue received by the service station equals $3.00 × 1,000 gallons, or $3,000. At point *B*, cutting price to $2.70 increases the quantity demanded to 1,050 gallons, but the fall in price more than offsets the increase in quantity. As a result, revenue falls to $2.70 × 1,050 gallons, or $2,835. When demand is elastic, a cut in price will increase total revenue. In panel (b), at point *A*, the area of rectangles *C* and *D* is still equal to $3,000. But at point *B*, the area of rectangles *D* and *E* is equal to $2.70 × 1,200 gallons, or $3,240. In this case, the increase in the quantity demanded is large enough to offset the fall in price, so total revenue increases.

by the service station owner at point A equals the price of $3.00 multiplied by the 1,000 gallons sold, or $3,000. This amount equals the areas of the rectangles C and D in the figure because together the rectangles have a height of $3.00 and a base of 1,000 gallons. Because this demand curve is inelastic between point A and point B (it was demand curve $D_2$ in Figure 6-1), cutting the price to $2.70 (point B ) reduces total revenue. The new total revenue is shown by the areas of rectangles D and E, and it is equal to $2.70 multiplied by 1,050 gallons, or $2,835. Total revenue falls because the increase in the quantity demanded is not large enough to make up for the decrease in price. As a result, the $135 increase in revenue gained as a result of the price cut—dark-green rectangle E—is less than the $300 in revenue lost—light-green rectangle C.

Panel (b) of Figure 6-2 shows a demand curve that is elastic between point A and point B (it was demand curve $D_1$ in Figure 6-1). In this case, cutting the price increases total revenue. At point A, the areas of rectangles C and D are still equal to $3,000, but at point B, the areas of rectangles D and E are equal to $2.70 multiplied by 1,200 gallons, or $3,240. Here, total revenue rises because the increase in the quantity demanded is large enough to offset the lower price. As a result, the $540 increase in revenue gained as a result of the price cut—dark-green rectangle E—is greater than the $300 in revenue lost—light-green rectangle C.

The third, less common, possibility is that demand is unit elastic. In that case, a small change in price is exactly offset by a proportional change in quantity demanded, leaving revenue unaffected. Therefore, when demand is unit elastic, neither a decrease in price nor an increase in price affects revenue. Table 6-3 summarizes the relationship between price elasticity and revenue.

## Elasticity and Revenue with a Linear Demand Curve

Along most demand curves, elasticity is not constant at every point. For example, a straight-line, or linear, demand curve for rentals of DVDs is shown in panel (a) of Figure 6-3. The numbers from the table are plotted in the graphs. The demand curve shows that when the price drops by $1, consumers always respond by renting 2 more DVDs per month. When the price is high and the quantity demanded is low, demand is elastic. Demand is elastic because a $1 drop in price is a smaller percentage change when the price is high, and an increase of 2 DVD rentals is a larger percentage change when the quantity of DVD rentals is small. By similar reasoning, we can see why demand is inelastic when the price is low and the quantity demanded is high.

**TABLE 6-3**

**The Relationship between Price Elasticity and Revenue**

| IF DEMAND IS . . . | THEN . . . | BECAUSE . . . |
|---|---|---|
| elastic | an increase in price reduces revenue | the decrease in quantity demanded is proportionally *greater* than the increase in price. |
| elastic | a decrease in price increases revenue | the increase in quantity demanded is proportionally *greater* than the decrease in price. |
| inelastic | an increase in price increases revenue | the decrease in quantity demanded is proportionally *smaller* than the increase in price. |
| inelastic | a decrease in price reduces revenue | the increase in quantity demanded is proportionally *smaller* than the decrease in price. |
| unit elastic | an increase in price does not affect revenue | the decrease in quantity demanded is proportionally *the same as* the increase in price. |
| unit elastic | a decrease in price does not affect revenue | the increase in quantity demanded is proportionally *the same as* the decrease in price. |

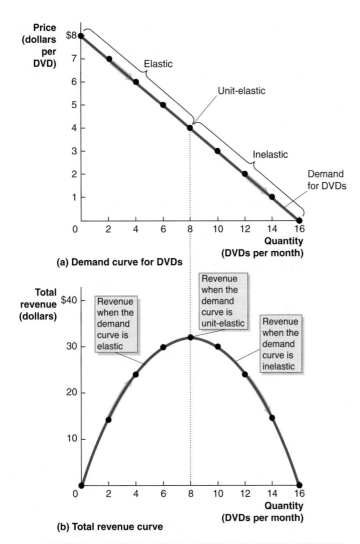

| Price | Quantity Demanded | Total Revenue |
|-------|-------------------|---------------|
| $8 | 0 | $0 |
| 7 | 2 | 14 |
| 6 | 4 | 24 |
| 5 | 6 | 30 |
| 4 | 8 | 32 |
| 3 | 10 | 30 |
| 2 | 12 | 24 |
| 1 | 14 | 14 |
| 0 | 16 | 0 |

**Figure 6-3**   | **Elasticity Is Not Constant Along a Linear Demand Curve**

The data from the table are plotted in the graphs. Panel (a) shows that as we move down the demand curve for DVD rentals, the price elasticity of demand declines. In other words, at higher prices, demand is elastic, and at lower prices, demand is inelastic. Panel

(b) shows that as the quantity of DVDs rented increases from zero, revenue will increase until it reaches a maximum of $32 when 8 DVDs are rented. As rentals increase beyond 8 DVDs, revenue falls because demand is inelastic on this portion of the demand curve.

Panel (a) in Figure 6-3 shows that when rental price is between $8 and $4 and quantity demanded is between 0 and 8, demand is elastic. Panel (b) shows that over this same range, total revenue will increase as price falls. For example, in panel (a), as price falls from $7 to $6, quantity demanded increases from 2 to 4, and in panel (b), total revenue increases from $14 to $24. Similarly, when price is between $4 and zero and quantity demanded is between 8 and 16, demand is inelastic. Over this same range, total revenue will decrease as price falls. For example, as price falls from $3 to $2 and quantity demanded increases from 10 to 12, total revenue decreases from $30 to $24.

## Estimating Price Elasticity of Demand

To estimate the price elasticity of demand, economists need to know the demand curve for a product. To calculate the price elasticity of demand for new products, firms often rely on market experiments. With market experiments, firms try different prices and observe the change in quantity demanded that results.

*Apple initially misjudged the price elasticity of iPhones.*

Making
the
Connection

## Determining the Price Elasticity of Demand through Market Experiments

Firms usually have a good idea of the price elasticity of demand for products that have been on the market for at least a few years. For new products, however, firms will often experiment with different prices to determine the price elasticity. For example, Apple introduced the first-generation iPhone in June 2007, at a price of $599. But demand for the iPhone was more elastic than Apple had expected, and when sales failed to reach Apple's projections, the company cut the price to $399 just two months later. (People who had bought the phone at the higher price were so upset at the price cut that Steve Jobs, Apple's chairman, felt obliged to offer them a $100 credit for purchases of other Apple products.)

Similarly, as each new format for recorded films has been introduced—first VHS tapes, then DVDs, and, most recently, Blu-ray discs—firms have experimented with different prices in trying to determine the relevant price elasticity. The table below is from 2001, when DVDs had been recently introduced. It compares the prices that film studios suggested retailers charge for four films that were available in both DVD and VHS tape formats. The prices of DVDs were much less standardized than the prices of VHS tapes because the studios were unsure of their price elasticities.

| FILM | DVD PRICE | VHS PRICE |
|------|-----------|-----------|
| *Rugrats in Paris* | $22.46 | $22.99 |
| *The Mummy Returns* | 26.98 | 22.98 |
| *Miss Congeniality* | 16.69 | 22.98 |
| *The Perfect Storm* | 24.98 | 22.99 |

Both the film studios and retailers, such as Amazon.com and Wal-Mart, engaged in similar experimentation after the introduction of Blu-ray discs in 2006. At first, the studios were convinced that consumers would pay substantially more for Blu-ray discs than for DVDs in order to obtain the superior image quality of the discs. By the end of 2008, it had become clear that the price elasticity of demand for Blu-ray discs was significantly higher than had been expected. At that point, Blu-ray discs had captured only 8 percent of the market, with conventional DVDs accounting for the other 92 percent. By 2009, Blu-ray discs, which had been typically priced at $28 to $30 in 2008, were selling for $26 or less. Some industry analysts expected prices to fall even further. Russ Crupnick of NPD, a market research firm, argued, "Consumers were saying a year ago that the price was high and that they were much more comfortable at $22 or $23. . . . But the consumers do get that Blu-ray is a premium, but it's the extent of that premium where they are resistant." One reason that the price elasticity of demand for Blu-ray discs turned out to be higher than the film studios had expected is that many consumers considered downloads of high-definition movies to be a good substitute for buying discs.

Sources: Susanne Ault, "Blu-Ray Prices Drop at Retail," videobusiness.com, March 13, 2009; Kate Hafner and Brad Stone, "iPhone Owners Crying Foul Over Price Cut," *New York Times*, September 7, 2007; and prices from Amazon.com.

**YOUR TURN:** Test your understanding by doing related problem 3.11 on page 198 at the end of this chapter.

---

**6.4 LEARNING** OBJECTIVE

Define cross-price elasticity of demand and income elasticity of demand and understand their determinants and how they are measured.

## Other Demand Elasticities

Elasticity is an important concept in economics because it allows us to quantify the responsiveness of one economic variable to changes in another economic variable. In addition to price elasticity, two other demand elasticities are important: *cross-price elasticity of demand* and *income elasticity of demand*.

# Cross-Price Elasticity of Demand

Suppose you work at Apple and you need to predict the effect of an increase in the price of Microsoft's Zune on the quantity of iPods demanded, holding other factors constant. You can do this by calculating the **cross-price elasticity of demand**, which is the percentage change in the quantity of iPods demanded divided by the percentage change in the price of Zunes—or, in general:

$$\text{Cross-price elasticity of demand} = \frac{\text{Percentage change in quantity demanded of one good}}{\text{Percentage change in price of another good}}.$$

**Cross-price elasticity of demand**
The percentage change in quantity demanded of one good divided by the percentage change in the price of another good.

The cross-price elasticity of demand is positive or negative, depending on whether the two products are substitutes or complements. Recall that substitutes are products that can be used for the same purpose, such as two brands of digital music players. Complements are products that are used together, such as digital music players and song downloads from online music sites. An increase in the price of a substitute will lead to an increase in quantity demanded, so the cross-price elasticity of demand will be positive. An increase in the price of a complement will lead to a decrease in the quantity demanded, so the cross-price elasticity of demand will be negative. Of course, if the two products are unrelated—such as digital music players and peanut butter—the cross-price elasticity of demand will be zero. Table 6-4 summarizes the key points concerning the cross-price elasticity of demand.

Cross-price elasticity of demand is important to firm managers because it allows them to measure whether products sold by other firms are close substitutes for their products. For example, Amazon.com and Barnesandnoble.com are the leading online booksellers. We might predict that if Amazon raises the price of a new John Grisham novel, many consumers will buy it from Barnesandnoble.com instead. But Jeff Bezos, Amazon's chief executive officer, has argued that because of Amazon's reputation for good customer service and because more customers are familiar with the site, ordering a book from Barnesandnoble.com is not a good substitute for ordering a book from Amazon. In effect, Bezos is arguing that the cross-price elasticity between Amazon's books and Barnesandnoble.com's books is low. Economists Judith Chevalier of Yale University and Austan Goolsbee of the University of Chicago used data on prices and quantities of books sold on these Web sites to estimate the cross-price elasticity. They found that the cross-price elasticity of demand between books at Amazon and books at Barnesandnoble.com was 3.5. This estimate means that if Amazon raises its prices by 10 percent, the quantity of books demanded on Barnesandnoble.com will increase by 35 percent. This result indicates that, contrary to Jeff Bezos's argument, consumers do consider books sold on the two Web sites to be close substitutes.

## TABLE 6-4

**Summary of Cross-Price Elasticity of Demand**

| IF THE PRODUCTS ARE . . . | THEN THE CROSS-PRICE ELASTICITY OF DEMAND WILL BE . . . | EXAMPLE |
| --- | --- | --- |
| substitutes | positive | Two brands of digital music players |
| complements | negative | Digital music players and song downloads from online music stores |
| unrelated | zero | Digital music players and peanut butter |

**TABLE 6-5**

**Summary of Income Elasticity of Demand**

| IF THE INCOME ELASTICITY OF DEMAND IS . . . | THEN THE GOOD IS . . . | EXAMPLE |
| --- | --- | --- |
| positive but less than 1 | normal and a necessity. | Bread |
| positive and greater than 1 | normal and a luxury. | Caviar |
| negative | inferior. | High-fat meat |

## Income Elasticity of Demand

**Income elasticity of demand** A measure of the responsiveness of quantity demanded to changes in income, measured by the percentage change in quantity demanded divided by the percentage change in income.

The **income elasticity of demand** measures the responsiveness of quantity demanded to changes in income. It is calculated as follows:

$$\text{Income elasticity of demand} = \frac{\text{Percentage change in quantity demanded}}{\text{Percentage change in income}}.$$

As we saw in Chapter 3, if the quantity demanded of a good increases as income increases, then the good is a *normal good*. Normal goods are often further subdivided into *luxury goods* and *necessity goods*. A good is a luxury if the quantity demanded is very responsive to changes in income, so that a 10 percent increase in income results in more than a 10 percent increase in quantity demanded. Expensive jewelry and vacation homes are examples of luxuries. A good is a necessity if the quantity demanded is not very responsive to changes in income, so that a 10 percent increase in income results in less than a 10 percent increase in quantity demanded. Food and clothing are examples of necessities. A good is *inferior* if the quantity demanded falls when income increases. Ground beef with a high fat content is an example of an inferior good. We should note that *normal good*, *inferior good*, *necessity*, and *luxury* are just labels economists use for goods with different income elasticities; the labels are not intended to be value judgments about the worth of these goods.

Because most goods are normal goods, during periods of economic expansion, when consumer income is rising, most firms can expect—holding other factors constant—that the quantity demanded of their products will increase. Sellers of luxuries can expect particularly large increases. During recessions, falling consumer income can cause firms to experience increases in demand for inferior goods. For example, the demand for bus trips increases as consumers cut back on air travel, and supermarkets find that the demand for hamburger increases relative to the demand for steak. Table 6-5 summarizes the key points about the income elasticity of demand.

# Solved Problem | 6-4

## A Subway Fare Increase and an Economic Boom Affect the Taxi Business

Assume that two separate events affect the market for taxi rides in New York City:

1. There is a 20 percent increase in New York subway fares. As a result, the number of taxi rides increases 5 percent.

2. An economic expansion causes a 5 percent increase in the incomes of tourists visiting New York City. The number of taxi rides increases 2 percent.

Describe the cross-price and income elasticity formulas and use these formulas to determine the values of these elasticities for taxi rides.

## SOLVING THE PROBLEM:

**Step 1:** **Review the chapter material.** This problem is about the determinants of the cross-price elasticity and income elasticity of demand, so you may want to review the section "Other Demand Elasticities," which begins on page 180.

**Step 2:** **State the cross-price elasticity formula and determine the value of this elasticity for taxi rides.** The cross-price elasticity formula is:

$$\text{Cross-price elasticity of demand} = \frac{\text{Percentage change in quantity demanded of one good}}{\text{Percentage change in price of another good}}.$$

Because a 20 percent increase in subway fares raised the quantity demanded of taxi rides by 5 percent, the value of the cross-price elasticity is:

$$\frac{5 \text{ percent}}{20 \text{ percent}} = 0.25.$$

Subway and taxi rides are substitutes, so the elasticity is positive.

**Step 2:** **State the income elasticity formula and determine the value of this elasticity for taxi rides.** The income elasticity is:

$$\text{Income elasticity of demand} = \frac{\text{Percentage change in quantity demanded}}{\text{Percentage change in income}}$$

Because a 5 percent increase in income led to a 2 percent increase in taxi rides, the value of the income elasticity is:

$$2 \text{ percent}/5 \text{ percent} = 0.4$$

The elasticity is positive but less than 1. Therefore, a taxi ride is a normal good and a necessity.

**YOUR TURN:** For more practice, do related problem 4.9 on page 199 at the end of this chapter.

---

**Making the Connection** | **Price Elasticity, Cross-Price Elasticity, and Income Elasticity in the Market for Alcoholic Beverages**

Many public policy issues are related to the consumption of alcoholic beverages. These issues include underage drinking, drunk driving, and the possible beneficial effects of red wine in lowering the risk of heart disease. X. M. Gao, an economist who works at American Express, and two colleagues have estimated statistically the following elasticities. (*Spirits* refers to all beverages that contain alcohol, other than beer and wine.)

| | |
|---|---|
| Price elasticity of demand for beer | −0.23 |
| Cross-price elasticity of demand between beer and wine | 0.31 |
| Cross-price elasticity of demand between beer and spirits | 0.15 |
| Income elasticity of demand for beer | −0.09 |
| Income elasticity of demand for wine | 5.03 |
| Income elasticity of demand for spirits | 1.21 |

The demand for beer is inelastic. A 10 percent increase in the price of beer will result in a 2.3 percent decline in the quantity of beer demanded. Not surprisingly, both wine and spirits are substitutes for beer. A 10 percent increase in the price of wine will result in a 3.1 percent *increase* in the quantity of beer demanded. A 10 percent increase in income will result in a little less than a 1 percent *decline* in the quantity of beer demanded. So, beer is an inferior good. Both wine and spirits are categorized as luxuries because their income elasticities are greater than 1.

Source: X. M. Gao, Eric J. Wailes, and Gail L. Cramer, "A Microeconometric Model Analysis of U.S. Consumer Demand for Alcoholic Beverages," *Applied Economics*, January 1995.

**myeconlab**

**YOUR TURN:** Test your understanding by doing related problem 4.8 on page 199 at the end of this chapter.

---

**6.5 LEARNING** OBJECTIVE

Use price elasticity and income elasticity to analyze economic issues.

# Using Elasticity to Analyze the Disappearing Family Farm

The concepts of price elasticity and income elasticity can help us understand many economic issues. For example, some people are concerned that the family farm is becoming an endangered species in the United States. Although food production continues to grow rapidly, the number of farms and the number of farmers continue to dwindle. In 1950, the United States was home to more than 5 million farms, and more than 23 million people lived on farms. By 2009, only about 2 million farms remained, and fewer than 3 million people lived on them. In Chapter 4, we discussed several federal government programs designed to aid farmers. Many of these programs have been aimed at helping small, family-operated farms, but rapid growth in farm production, combined with low price and income elasticities for most food products, has made family farming difficult in the United States.

Productivity measures the ability of firms to produce goods and services with a given amount of economic inputs, such as workers, machines, and land. Productivity has grown very rapidly in U.S. agriculture. In 1950, the average U.S. wheat farmer harvested about 17 bushels from each acre of wheat planted. By 2009, because of the development of superior strains of wheat and improvements in farming techniques, the average American wheat farmer harvested 45 bushels per acre. So, even though the total number of acres devoted to growing wheat declined from about 62 million to about 56 million, total wheat production rose from about 1.0 billion bushels to about 2.5 billion.

Unfortunately for U.S. farmers, this increase in wheat production resulted in a substantial decline in wheat prices. Two key factors explain this decline in wheat prices: (1) The

## Figure 6-4

**Elasticity and the Disappearing Family Farm**

In 1950, U.S. farmers produced 1.0 billion bushels of wheat at a price of $17.65 per bushel. Over the next 60 years, rapid increases in farm productivity caused a large shift to the right in the supply curve for wheat. The income elasticity of demand for wheat is low, so the demand for wheat increased relatively little over this period. Because the demand for wheat is also inelastic, the large shift in the supply curve and the small shift in the demand curve resulted in a sharp decline in the price of wheat, from $17.65 per bushel in 1950 to $5.33 per bushel in 2009.

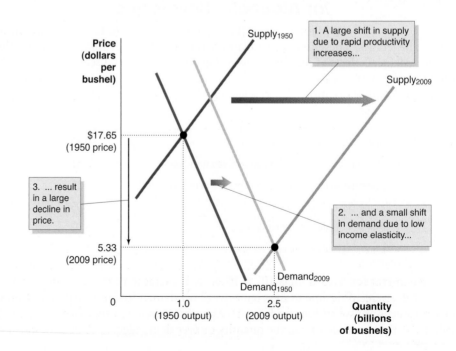

demand for wheat is inelastic and (2) the income elasticity of demand for wheat is low. Even though the U.S. population has increased greatly since 1950 and the income of the average American is much higher than it was in 1950, the demand for wheat has increased only moderately. For all of the additional wheat to be sold, the price has had to decline. Because the demand for wheat is inelastic, the price decline has been substantial. Figure 6-4 illustrates these points.

A large shift in supply, a small shift in demand, and an inelastic demand curve combined to drive down the price of wheat from $17.65 per bushel in 1950 to $5.33 per bushel in 2009. (The 1950 price is measured in terms of prices in 2009, to adjust for the general increase in prices since 1950.) With low prices, only the most efficiently run farms have been able to remain profitable. Smaller, family-run farms have found it difficult to survive, and many of these farms have disappeared. The markets for most other food products are similar to the market for wheat. They are characterized by rapid output growth and low income and price elasticities. The result is the paradox of American farming: ever more abundant and cheaper food, supplied by fewer and fewer farms. American consumers have benefited, but most family farmers have not.

# The Price Elasticity of Supply and its Measurement

**6.6 LEARNING** OBJECTIVE

Define price elasticity of supply and understand its main determinants and how it is measured.

We can use the concept of elasticity to measure the responsiveness of firms to a change in price, just as we used it to measure the responsiveness of consumers. We know from the law of supply that when the price of a product increases, the quantity supplied increases. To measure how much the quantity supplied increases when price increases, we use the *price elasticity of supply*.

## Measuring the Price Elasticity of Supply

Just as with the price elasticity of demand, we calculate the **price elasticity of supply** using percentage changes:

$$\text{Price elasticity of supply} = \frac{\text{Percentage change in quantity supplied}}{\text{Percentage change in price}}.$$

**Price elasticity of supply** The responsiveness of the quantity supplied to a change in price, measured by dividing the percentage change in the quantity supplied of a product by the percentage change in the product's price.

Notice that because supply curves are upward sloping, the price elasticity of supply will be a positive number. We categorize the price elasticity of supply the same way we categorized the price elasticity of demand: If the price elasticity of supply is less than 1, then supply is *inelastic*. For example, the price elasticity of supply of gasoline from U.S. oil refineries is about 0.20, and so it is inelastic; a 10 percent increase in the price of gasoline will result in only a 2 percent increase in the quantity supplied. If the price elasticity of supply is greater than 1, then supply is *elastic*. If the price elasticity of supply is equal to 1, then supply is *unit elastic*. As with other elasticity calculations, when we calculate the price elasticity of supply, we hold the values of other factors constant.

## Determinants of the Price Elasticity of Supply

Whether supply is elastic or inelastic depends on the ability and willingness of firms to alter the quantity they produce as price increases. Often, firms have difficulty increasing the quantity of the product they supply during any short period of time. For example, a pizza parlor cannot produce more pizzas on any one night than is possible using the ingredients on hand. Within a day or two it can buy more ingredients, and within a few months it can hire more cooks and install additional ovens. As a result, the supply curve for pizza and most other products will be inelastic if we measure it over a short period of time, but the supply curve will be increasingly elastic the longer the period of time over which we measure it. Products that require resources that are themselves in fixed supply are an exception to this rule. For example, a French winery may rely on a particular variety of grape. If all the land on which that grape can be grown is already planted in vineyards, then the supply of that wine will be inelastic even over a long period.

## Making
the
## Connection

## Why Are Oil Prices So Unstable?

Bringing oil to market is a long process. Oil companies hire geologists to locate fields for exploratory oil well drilling. If significant amounts of oil are present, the company begins full-scale development of the field. The process from exploration to pumping significant amounts of oil can take years. This long process is why the price elasticity of supply for oil is very low.

During the period from 2003 to mid-2008, the worldwide demand for oil increased rapidly as India, China, and some other developing countries increased both their manufacturing production and their use of automobiles. As the graph shows, when supply is inelastic, an increase in demand can cause a large increase in price. The shift in the demand curve from $D_1$ to $D_2$ causes the equilibrium quantity of oil to increase only by 5 percent, from 80 million barrels per day to 84 million, but the equilibrium price rises by 75 percent, from $80 per barrel to $140 per barrel.

The world oil market is heavily influenced by the Organization of Petroleum Exporting Countries (OPEC). OPEC has 11 members, including Saudi Arabia, Kuwait, Iran, Venezuela, and Nigeria. Together these countries own 75 percent of the world's proven oil reserves. Periodically, OPEC has attempted to force up the price of oil by reducing the quantity of oil its members supply. As we will discuss further in Chapter 13, since the 1970s, the attempts by OPEC to reduce the quantity of oil on world markets have been successful only sporadically. As a result, the supply curve for oil shifts fairly frequently. Combined with the low price elasticities of oil supply and demand, these shifts in supply have caused the price of oil to fluctuate significantly over the past 30 years, from as low as $10 per barrel to more than $140 per barrel.

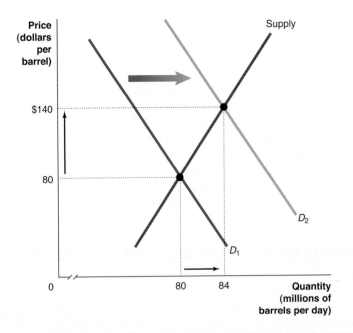

Beginning in mid-2008, the financial crisis that had begun in the United States had spread to other countries, resulting in a severe recession. As production and incomes fell during the recession, the worldwide demand for oil declined sharply. Over the space of a few months, the equilibrium price of oil fell from $140 per barrel to $40 per barrel. As the graph below shows, once again, the extent of the price change reflected not only the size of the decline in demand but also oil's low price elasticity of supply.

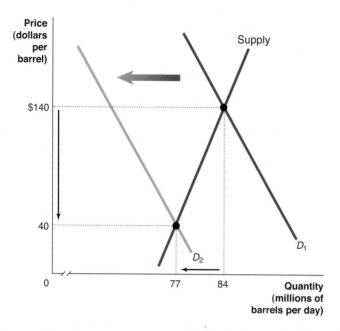

**YOUR TURN** Test your understanding by doing related problem 6.3 on page 201 at the end of this chapter.

# Solved Problem | 6-6

## The Supply of Medallions and the Supply of Taxis

The number of taxi licenses in New York City has been limited since 1937, when there were fewer than 14,000 outstanding licenses. These licenses are also called *medallions*. Because some cab owners allowed their licenses to expire, the number of licenses fell to the current number of 11,787. The New York City Council created the Taxi and Limousine Commission in 1971 to regulate taxi and livery service. Despite the great demand for taxi service, with more than 220 million passengers per year, no new taxis are allowed to operate without one of the existing medallions. License holders are allowed to sell their medallions. In 2004, the average price paid for a medallion was over $275,000.

**a.** Use the price elasticity of supply formula to calculate the elasticity of supply for taxi medallions in New York City.

**b.** Assume that the Taxi and Limousine Commission doubles the number of available medallions. Describe the likely impact on the quantity supplied and the elasticity of supply of taxis.

## SOLVING THE PROBLEM:

**Step 1:** **Review the chapter material.** This problem is about the determinants of the elasticity of supply, so you may want to review the section "The Price Elasticity of Supply and Its Measurement," which begins on page 185.

**Step 2:** **State the price elasticity of supply formula and determine the value of this elasticity for taxi medallions.** The price elasticity of supply formula is:

$$\text{Price elasticity of supply} = \frac{\text{Percentage change in quantity supplied}}{\text{Percentage change in price}}$$

Because the quantity supplied of medallions is fixed, the percentage change in quantity supplied is zero, the value of the elasticity of supply is zero, and the supply curve is vertical at the existing quantity of 11,787 medallions, no matter how much the price of medallions changes.

**Step 3:**  **Determine the impact of a doubling of medallions.** The high price of existing medallions suggests that current, and possibly new, taxi companies would bid for the new medallions. But the number of taxis in service would not rise immediately because companies would have to acquire new vehicles and hire and train new drivers. As the market period lengthens (from one day to one month, to one year, and so on), the quantity supplied of taxis in service and the elasticity of supply of taxis would increase; the supply curve would become increasingly flatter.

Sources: Bruce Schaller, *The New York City Taxicab Fact Book*, 3rd ed., 2006, www.schallerconsult.com/taxi/taxifb.pdf. New York City Taxi & Limousine Commission Medallion Sale Information, www.nyc.gov/html/tlc/medallion/html/home/home.shtml.

**YOUR TURN:** For more practice, do related problem 6.6 on page 201 at the end of this chapter.

## Polar Cases of Perfectly Elastic and Perfectly Inelastic Supply

Although it occurs infrequently, it is possible for supply to fall into one of the polar cases of price elasticity. If a supply curve is a vertical line, it is *perfectly inelastic*. In this case, the quantity supplied is completely unresponsive to price, and the price elasticity of supply equals zero. Regardless of how much price may increase or decrease, the quantity remains the same. Over a brief period of time, the supply of some goods and services may be perfectly inelastic. For example, a parking lot may have only a fixed number of parking spaces. If demand increases, the price to park in the lot may rise, but no more spaces will become available. Of course, if demand increases permanently, over a longer period of time the owner of the lot may buy more land to add additional spaces.

If a supply curve is a horizontal line, it is *perfectly elastic*. In this case, the quantity supplied is infinitely responsive to price, and the price elasticity of supply equals infinity. If a supply curve is perfectly elastic, a very small increase in price causes a very large increase in quantity supplied. Just as with demand curves, it is important not to confuse a supply curve being elastic with its being perfectly elastic and not to confuse a supply curve being inelastic with its being perfectly inelastic. Table 6-6 summarizes the different price elasticities of supply.

## Using Price Elasticity of Supply to Predict Changes in Price

Figure 6-5 illustrates the important point that, when demand increases, the amount that price increases depends on the price elasticity of supply. The figure shows the demand and supply for parking spaces at a beach resort. In panel (a), on a typical summer weekend, equilibrium occurs at point *A*, where Demand$_{\text{Typical}}$ intersects a supply curve that is inelastic. The increase in demand for parking spaces on the Fourth of July shifts the demand curve to the right, moving the equilibrium to point *B*. Because the supply curve is inelastic, the increase in demand results in a large increase in price—from $2.00 per hour to $4.00—but only a small increase in the quantity of spaces supplied—from 1,200 to 1,400.

In panel (b), supply is elastic, perhaps because the resort has vacant land that can be used for parking during periods of high demand. As a result, the shift in equilibrium from point *A* to point *B* results in a smaller increase in price and a larger increase in the quantity supplied. An increase in price from $2.00 per hour to $2.50 is sufficient to increase the quantity of parking spaces supplied from 1,200 to 2,100. Knowing the price

TABLE 6-6

**Summary of the Price Elasticities of Supply**

| IF SUPPLY IS . . . | THEN THE VALUE OF PRICE ELASTICITY IS . . . | |
|---|---|---|
| elastic | greater than 1 | |
| inelastic | less than 1 | |
| unit elastic | equal to 1 | |
| perfectly elastic | equal to infinity | |
| perfectly inelastic | equal to 0 | |

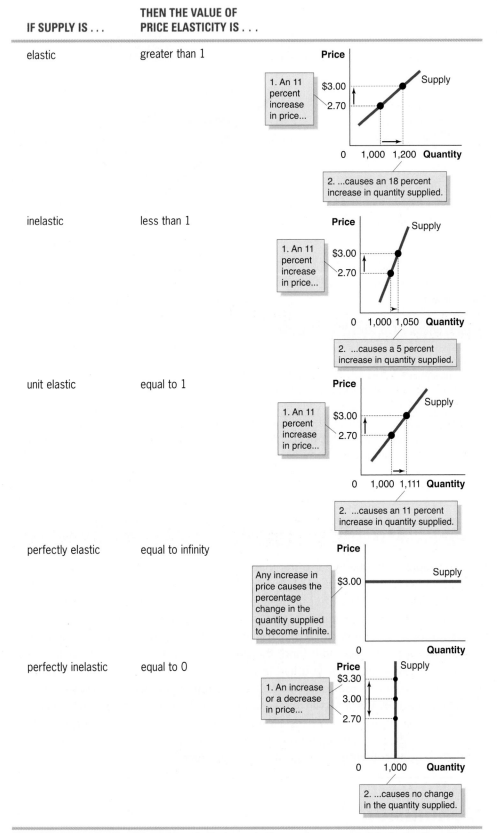

*Note:* The percentage increases shown in the boxes in the graphs were calculated using the midpoint formula, given on page 170.)

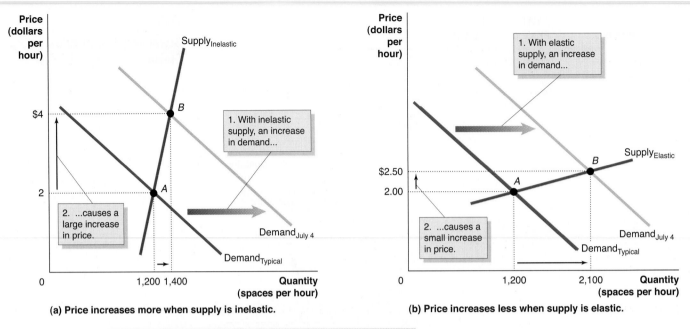

**(a) Price increases more when supply is inelastic.**

**(b) Price increases less when supply is elastic.**

## Figure 6-5 | Changes in Price Depend on the Price Elasticity of Supply

In panel (a), Demand_Typical represents the typical demand for parking spaces on a summer weekend at a beach resort. Demand_July 4 represents demand on the Fourth of July. Because supply is inelastic, the shift in equilibrium from point A to point B results in a large increase in price—from $2.00 per hour to $4.00—but only a small increase in the quantity of spaces supplied—from 1,200 to 1,400. In panel (b), sup-

ply is elastic. As a result, the shift in equilibrium from point A to point B results in a smaller increase in price and a larger increase in the quantity supplied. An increase in price from $2.00 per hour to $2.50 is sufficient to increase the quantity of parking supplied from 1,200 to 2,100.

elasticity of supply makes it possible to predict more accurately how much price will change following an increase or a decrease in demand.

▶ Continued from page 167

## Economics in YOUR LIFE!

At the beginning of the chapter, we asked you to think about three questions: What factors would make you more or less sensitive to price when purchasing gasoline? Have you responded differently to price changes during different periods of your life? and Why do consumers seem to respond more to changes in gas prices at a particular service station but seem less sensitive when gas prices rise or fall at all service stations? A number of factors are likely to affect your sensitivity to changes in gas prices, including how high your income is (and, therefore, how large a share of your budget is taken up by gasoline purchases), whether you live in an area with good public transportation (which can be a substitute for having to use your own car), and whether you live within walking distance of your school or job. Each of these factors may change over the course of your life, making you more or less sensitive to changes in gas prices. Finally, consumers respond to changes in the price of gas at a particular service station because gas at other service stations is a good substitute. But there are presently few good substitutes for gasoline as a product.

## Conclusion

In this chapter, we have explored the important concept of elasticity. Table 6-7 summarizes the various elasticities we discussed. Computing elasticities is important in economics because it allows us to measure how one variable changes in response to changes in another variable. For example, by calculating the price elasticity of demand for its product, a firm can make a quantitative estimate of the effect of a price change on the revenue

**PRICE ELASTICITY OF DEMAND**

TABLE 6-7

**Summary of Elasticities**

Formula: $\dfrac{\text{Percentage change in quantity demanded}}{\text{Percentage change in price}}$

Midpoint Formula: $\dfrac{(Q_2 - Q_1)}{\left(\dfrac{Q_2 + Q_1}{2}\right)} \div \dfrac{(P_2 - P_1)}{\left(\dfrac{P_1 + P_2}{2}\right)}$

|  | ABSOLUTE VALUE OF PRICE ELASTICITY | EFFECT ON TOTAL REVENUE OF AN INCREASE IN PRICE |
|---|---|---|
| Elastic | Greater than 1 | Total revenue falls |
| Inelastic | Less than 1 | Total revenue rises |
| Unit elastic | Equal to 1 | Total revenue unchanged |

**CROSS-PRICE ELASTICITY OF DEMAND**

Formula: $\dfrac{\text{Percentage change in quantity demanded of one good}}{\text{Percentage change in price of another good}}$

| TYPES OF PRODUCTS | VALUE OF CROSS-PRICE ELASTICITY |
|---|---|
| Substitutes | Positive |
| Complements | Negative |
| Unrelated | Zero |

**INCOME ELASTICITY OF DEMAND**

Formula: $\dfrac{\text{Percentage change in quantity demanded}}{\text{Percentage change in income}}$

| TYPES OF PRODUCTS | VALUE OF INCOME ELASTICITY |
|---|---|
| Normal and a necessity | Positive but less than 1 |
| Normal and a luxury | Positive and greater than 1 |
| Inferior | Negative |

**PRICE ELASTICITY OF SUPPLY**

Formula: $\dfrac{\text{Percentage change in quantity supplied}}{\text{Percentage change in price}}$

|  | VALUE OF PRICE ELASTICITY |
|---|---|
| Elastic | Greater than 1 |
| Inelastic | Less than 1 |
| Unit elastic | Equal to 1 |

it receives. Similarly, by calculating the price elasticity of demand for cigarettes, the government can better estimate the effect of an increase in cigarette taxes on smoking.

Before going further in analyzing how firms decide on the prices to charge and the quantities to produce, we need to look at how firms are organized. We do this in the next chapter. Read *An Inside Look* on pages 192–193 for a discussion of the effect of higher gas prices on the demand for public transportation.

## >> Consumers Change Their Behavior in Response to the Gas Prices

**NEW YORK TIMES**

## Politics Failed, but Fuel Prices Cut Congestion

Soaring gas prices and higher tolls seem to be doing for traffic in New York what Mayor Michael R. Bloomberg's ambitious congestion pricing was supposed to do: reducing the number of cars clogging the city's streets and pushing more people to use mass transit.

**(a)** In May, with gasoline at more than $4 a gallon, traffic at the Metropolitan Transportation Authority's bridges and tunnels dropped 4.7 percent compared with the same month the previous year. Preliminary data for June shows a similar decrease in traffic, and officials say the change is largely because of higher prices at the pump. The Port Authority of New York and New Jersey has recorded a similar decline in travel across its bridges and tunnels since early March, when it raised tolls. The greatest decline was in April, when traffic fell by 4.2 percent.

. . .

**(b)** At the same time, subway, bus and commuter rail ridership has increased. Weekday subway ridership was up 6.5 percent in April, compared with the same month a year ago. April ridership increased 5.5 percent on the Long Island Rail Road, 4.3 percent on the Metro-North Railroad and almost 9 percent on PATH trains between Manhattan and New Jersey. Use of the subways and rail lines also increased in May, compared with the previous

year, but in most cases by smaller amounts. New Jersey Transit ridership, including bus, commuter rail and light rail, was up about 4.6 percent in April and May combined.

"We're at the point where people really are changing habits," said Sam Schwartz, a transportation consultant. He said that if gas prices stayed high, the result could be . . . to reduce traffic in much of Manhattan by 6.3 percent. "If we start eclipsing $5 a gallon, which we might over the summer, I think we might get very close," Mr. Schwartz said.

. . .

"It shows that pricing matters and that people respond to it," said Jeffrey M. Zupan, a senior fellow for transportation at the Regional Plan Association. It is hard to say exactly what the impact of lighter bridge and tunnel traffic has been on the streets of Manhattan—or other boroughs— since the city does not take traffic measurements that show changes from month to month. But there are other indications.

The Metropolitan Parking Association, which represents garage and parking lot owners, said that its members had seen about a 10 percent decrease in daily customers. And gas station managers interviewed in Brooklyn, Queens and New Jersey said that the number of drivers buying gas had also declined. . . . Commuter trains have also become more crowded, riders say.

. . .

At the Secaucus Junction train station of New Jersey Transit, Brian Simmons, 30, said that it had become much harder to get a seat on the train in recent months. "It's like the New York City subway," he said.

. . .

**(c)** . . . The current reduction in traffic at bridges and tunnels could actually take money away from transit, because a large portion of the tolls collected at the transportation authority's crossings helps to finance the subways, buses and commuter railroads. In May, toll revenues were more than $4 million below budget projections, and Gary J. Dellaverson, the authority's chief financial officer, said that June toll revenues appeared to be down even further.

. . .

While some drivers have given up and switched to trains or buses, those who are sticking with their cars say they are driving less. Singh Bridgemohan, 50, was putting some gas, at $4.35 a gallon, in his red 1996 Jeep Grand Cherokee on a recent morning at an Exxon station in Bay Terrace, Queens. Mr. Bridgemohan, who runs a small construction company, said he used to drive his wife, a nanny, from their home in Jamaica to her work in Bayside every day. Now he does it rarely, to save on gas, while she makes a much longer commute by bus.

. . .

*Source:* William Neuman, "Politics Failed, but Fuel Prices Cut Congestion," *New York Times*, July 3, 2008.

## Key Points in the Article

The article discusses the effects that high gas prices have on the choice of consumers in the New York City area to drive or take public transportation. As gas prices rose during early 2008, more consumers decided to take public transportation rather than drive into the city. The number of motorists crossing bridges into the city declined, as did the number of cars parked in city lots. At the same time, ridership of buses, subways, and commuter rail lines increased. The decline in travel across bridges was also due to an increase in bridge tolls. Revenue from commuters traveling across the bridges decreased following the increase in tolls.

## Analyzing the News

(a) This chapter discusses the price elasticity of demand, which measures the responsiveness of quantity demanded to a change in price. This article shows an example of elasticity in action. During 2008, when gas prices rose above $4.00 per gallon, the quantity of gasoline demanded declined as consumers cut back on driving. For people who live near a bus, subway, or commuter line, public transportation provides a substitute to driving their own cars. So, the cross-price elasticity of demand between gasoline and public transportation is positive: An increase in the price of gasoline will result in an increase in the quantity of bus or subway rides demanded.

(b) The chapter discusses the fact that the price elasticity of demand for a product will be larger (in absolute value) the longer the period of time involved. It takes time for buyers to adjust their routines as a result of a change in price. As gasoline prices increased through 2007 and early 2008—finally reaching $4.00 or more per gallon—consumers began to explore alternatives to driving their cars. The result was more people using public transportation. The figure below illustrates the effect of price elasticity increasing over time. Suppose that initially the price of gasoline is $2.00 per gallon, and $Q_1$ gallons of gasoline are being purchased. If the price of gasoline increases to $4.00 per gallon, then at first consumers will move up the demand curve, $D_{\text{Short period}}$, and the quantity of gasoline demanded will decline only to $Q_2$. But if high gasoline prices persist, consumers will make adjustments, such as driving less and taking public transportation more. The demand for gasoline will become the more elastic curve, $D_{\text{Longer period}}$. (Remember that if two demand curves pass through the same point, the flatter curve is more elastic.) As demand becomes more elastic over the longer period of time, the quantity of gasoline demanded will decline further, to $Q_3$.

(c) The article also notes that in the spring of 2008, tolls on the bridges leading into New York City were raised. Following the increase in tolls, both the number of cars crossing the bridges and the total revenue collected from the tolls declined. We learned in the chapter that an increase in the price of

a product will increase the revenue from the product if demand is price inelastic and decrease the revenue if demand is price elastic. So, can we conclude that the demand by motorists to use the bridges into New York City must be price elastic because revenues fell when the tolls were increased? Possibly, but in this case we have a complicating factor. We could draw a conclusion about price elasticity only if all other factors that might affect the demand by motorists to use the bridges had remained constant. In fact, though, during this time another factor affecting the demand for bridge crossings had changed because gasoline prices had been rising. The fact that the quantity of bridge crossings declined by more than enough to offset the increase in tolls might indicate that the demand for bridge crossings is price elastic, but it also might indicate that during this period the demand for bridge crossings shifted to the left as gasoline prices increased.

## Thinking Critically

1. Joe Ferris owns Joe's Gas-and-Go service station. Joe reads a newspaper article in which an economist describes the demand for gasoline as price inelastic. Remembering his principles of economics course from college, Joe comes to the following conclusion: "Because the demand for gasoline is inelastic, if I increase the price I charge, I will lose a few customers, but the price increase will more than compensate for the fact that I will be selling a smaller quantity of gasoline. Therefore, the revenue I earn from gasoline sales will increase." Briefly explain whether you agree with Joe's reasoning.

2. Suppose that initially the only sellers of gasoline in a town are conventional service stations. Then Wal-Mart and Sam's Club decide to begin selling gasoline. They install service islands near their stores and sell gasoline for lower prices than the conventional service stations. What effect do these new gasoline sellers have on the demand curves faced by the conventional service stations?

The demand for gasoline becomes more elastic over time.

# Key Terms

---

**6.1** | ## The Price Elasticity of Demand and Its Measurement, pages 168–174
LEARNING OBJECTIVE: Define price elasticity of demand and understand how to measure it.

## Summary

**Elasticity** measures how much one economic variable responds to changes in another economic variable. The **price elasticity of demand** measures how responsive quantity demanded is to changes in price. The price elasticity of demand is equal to the percentage change in quantity demanded divided by the percentage change in price. If the quantity demanded changes more than proportionally when price changes, the price elasticity of demand is greater than 1 in absolute value, and demand is **elastic**. If the quantity demanded changes less than proportionally when price changes, the price elasticity of demand is less than 1 in absolute value, and demand is **inelastic**. If the quantity demanded changes proportionally when price changes, the price elasticity of demand is equal to 1 in absolute value, and demand is **unit elastic**. **Perfectly inelastic demand** curves are vertical lines, and **perfectly elastic demand** curves are horizontal lines. Relatively few products have perfectly elastic or perfectly inelastic demand curves.

 Visit www.myeconlab.com to complete these exercises online and get instant feedback.

## Review Questions

1.1 Write the formula for the price elasticity of demand. Why isn't elasticity just measured by the slope of the demand curve?

1.2 If a 10 percent increase in the price of Cap'n Crunch cereal causes a 25 percent reduction in the number of boxes of cereal demanded, what is the price elasticity of demand for Cap'n Crunch cereal? Is demand for Cap'n Crunch elastic or inelastic?

1.3 What is the midpoint method for calculating price elasticity of demand? How else can you calculate the price elasticity of demand? What is the advantage of the midpoint method?

1.4 Draw a graph of a perfectly inelastic demand curve. Think of a product that would have a perfectly inelastic demand curve. Explain why demand for this product would be perfectly inelastic.

## Problems and Applications

1.5 Suppose the following table gives data on the price of rye and the number of bushels of rye sold in 2009 and 2010.

| YEAR | PRICE (DOLLARS PER BUSHEL) | QUANTITY (BUSHELS) |
|------|----------------------------|--------------------|
| 2009 | $3.00 | 8 million |
| 2010 | 2.00 | 12 million |

a. Calculate the change in the quantity of rye demanded divided by the change in the price of rye. Measure the quantity of rye in bushels.

b. Calculate the change in the quantity of rye demanded divided by the change in the price of rye, but this time measure the quantity of rye in millions of bushels. Compare your answer to the one you computed in a.

c. Assuming that the demand curve for rye did not shift between 2009 and 2010, use the information in the table to calculate the price elasticity of demand for rye. Use the midpoint formula in your calculation. Compare the value for the price elasticity of demand to the values you calculated in a and b.

1.6 (Related to *Solved Problem 6-1* on page 171) You own a hot dog stand that you set up outside the student union every day at lunch time. Currently, you are selling hot dogs for a price of $3, and you sell 30 hot dogs a day. You are considering cutting the price to $2. The following graph shows two possible increases in the quantity sold as a result of your price cut. Use the information in the graph to calculate the price elasticity between these two prices on each of the demand curves. Use the midpoint formula to calculate the price elasticities.

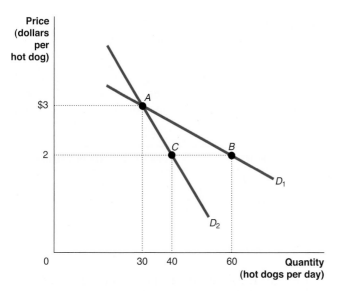

1.7 In fall 2006, Pace University in New York raised its annual tuition from $24,751 to $29,454. Freshman enrollment declined from 1,469 in the fall of 2005 to 1,131 in the fall of 2006. Assuming that the demand curve for places in the freshman class at Pace did not shift between 2005 and 2006, use this information to calculate the price elasticity of demand. Use the midpoint formula in your calculation. Is the demand for places in Pace's freshman class elastic or inelastic? Did the total amount of tuition Pace received from its freshman class rise or fall in 2006 compared with 2005?

Source: Karen W. Arenson, "At Universities, Plum Post at Top Is Now Shaky," *New York Times*, January 9, 2007.

1.8 Consider the following excerpt from a newspaper story on increases in college tuition:

> Facing stiff competition, Hendrix College, a small liberal arts institution in Conway, Ark., decided two years ago to bolster its academic offerings, promising students at least three hands-on experiences outside the classroom, including research, internships and service projects. It also raised tuition and fees 29 percent, to $21,636. . . . As a result, 409 students enrolled in the freshman class this year, a 37 percent increase. "What worked was the buzz," said J. Timothy Cloyd, the Hendrix president.

> "Students saw that they were going to get an experience that had value, and the price positioning conveyed to them the value of the experience."

Does this excerpt provide enough information to calculate the price elasticity of demand for places in Hendrix College's freshman class? Briefly explain.

Source: Jonathan D. Glater and Alan Finder, "In New Twist on Tuition Game, Popularity Rises with the Price," *New York Times*, December 12, 2006.

1.9 In the fall of 2008, analyst Charlie Wolf of the investment banking firm Needham & Company argued that if Apple cut the price of its 8GB iPhone from $199 to $99, its sales would double or triple. Calculate the price elasticity of demand for iPhones if the price cut would lead to a *doubling* of iPhone sales. Use the midpoint formula in your calculation. Now calculate the price elasticity of demand for iPhones if the price would lead to a *tripling* of iPhone sales.

Source: Jesus Diaz, "iPhone Could Hit $99, Analyst Says," Gizmodo. com, October 27, 2008.

1.10 In 1916, the Ford Motor Company sold 500,000 Model T Fords at a price of $440 each. Henry Ford believed that he could increase sales of the Model T by 1,000 cars for every dollar he cut the price. Use this information to calculate the price elasticity of demand for Model T Fords. Use the midpoint formula in your calculation.

1.11 **(Related to the *Don't Let This Happen to You!* on page 174)** The publisher of a magazine gives his staff the following information:

| Current price | $2.00 per issue |
|---|---|
| Current sales | 150,000 copies per month |
| Current total costs | $450,000 per month |

He tells the staff, "Our costs are currently $150,000 more than our revenues each month. I propose to eliminate this problem by raising the price of the magazine to $3.00 per issue. This will result in our revenue being exactly equal to our cost." Do you agree with the publisher's analysis? Explain. (*Hint:* Remember that a firm's revenue is equal to the price of the product multiplied by the quantity sold.)

>> **End Learning Objective 6.1**

**6.2**  ## The Determinants of the Price Elasticity of Demand, pages 174–177
LEARNING OBJECTIVE: Understand the determinants of the price elasticity of demand.

## Summary

The main determinants of the price elasticity of demand for a product are the availability of close substitutes, the passage of time, whether the good is a necessity or a luxury, how narrowly the market for the good is defined, and the share of the good in the consumer's budget.

 Visit www.myeconlab.com to complete these exercises online and get instant feedback.

## Review Questions

2.1  Is the demand for most agricultural products elastic or inelastic? Why?

2.2  What are the key determinants of the price elasticity of demand for a product? Which determinant is the most important?

## Problems and Applications

2.3  Briefly explain whether the demand for each of the following products is likely to be elastic or inelastic.
   a. Milk
   b. Frozen cheese pizza
   c. Cola
   d. Prescription medicine

2.4  (Related to the *Making the Connection* on page 176) One study found that the price elasticity of demand for soda is −0.78, while the price elasticity of demand for Coca-Cola is −1.22. Coca-Cola is a type of soda, so why isn't its price elasticity the same as the price elasticity for soda as a product?
   Source: Kelly D. Brownell and Thomas R. Frieden, "Ounces of Prevention—The Public Policy Case for Taxes on Sugared Beverages," *New England Journal of Medicine*, April 30, 2009, pp. 1805–1808.

2.5  (Related to the *Making the Connection* on page 176) A study of the price elasticities of products sold in supermarkets contained the following data:

| PRODUCT | PRICE ELASTICITY OF DEMAND |
|---|---|
| Soft drinks | −3.18 |
| Canned soup | −1.62 |
| Cheese | −0.72 |
| Toothpaste | −0.45 |

   a. For which products is the demand inelastic? Discuss reasons why the demand for each product is either elastic or inelastic.
   b. Use the information in the table to predict the change in the quantity demanded for each product following a 10 percent price increase.
   Source: Stephen J. Hoch, Byung-do Kim, Alan L. Montgomery, and Peter E. Rossi, "Determinants of Store-Level Price Elasticity," *Journal of Marketing Research*, Vol. 32, February 1995, pp. 17–29.

2.6  According to an article in the *Wall Street Journal*, in 1999 when the average price of a gallon of gasoline was $1.19, the average household spent 4.0 percent of its income on gasoline. In 2008, when the average price of gasoline had risen to $4.06 per gallon, the average household spent 11.5 percent of its income on gasoline. During which year was the price elasticity of gasoline likely to have been higher? Briefly explain.
   Source: "Income vs. Gas Prices, an Update," *Wall Street Journal*, August 4, 2008.

>> **End Learning Objective 6.2**

**6.3**  ## The Relationship between Price Elasticity of Demand and Total Revenue, pages 177–180
LEARNING OBJECTIVE: Understand the relationship between the price elasticity of demand and total revenue.

## Summary

**Total revenue** is the total amount of funds received by a seller of a good or service. When demand is inelastic, a decrease in price reduces total revenue, and an increase in price increases total revenue. When demand is elastic, a decrease in price increases total revenue, and an increase in price decreases total revenue. When demand is unit elastic, an increase or a decrease in price leaves total revenue unchanged.

 Visit www.myeconlab.com to complete these exercises online and get instant feedback.

## Review Questions

3.1  If the demand for orange juice is inelastic, will an increase in the price of orange juice increase or decrease the revenue received by orange juice sellers?

3.2  The price of organic apples falls, and apple growers find that their revenue increases. Is the demand for organic apples elastic or inelastic?

# Problems and Applications

**3.3** Economists' estimates of price elasticities can differ somewhat, depending on the time period and on the markets in which the price and quantity data used in the estimates were gathered. An article in the *New York Times* contained the following statement from the Centers for Disease Control and Prevention: "A 10 percent increase in the price of cigarettes reduces consumption by 3 percent to 5 percent." Given this information, compute the range of price elasticity of demand for cigarettes. Explain whether the demand for cigarettes is elastic, inelastic, or unit elastic. If cigarette manufacturers raise prices, will their revenue increase or decrease? Briefly explain.

Source: Shaila Dewan, "States Look at Tobacco to Balance the Budget," *New York Times*, March 20, 2009.

**3.4** Use the following graph for Yolanda's Frozen Yogurt Stand to answer the questions that follow.

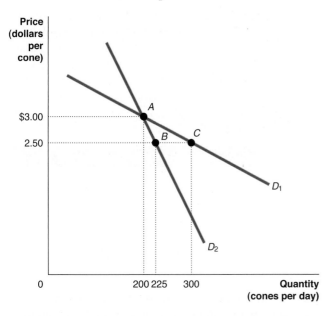

**a.** Use the midpoint formula to calculate the price elasticity of demand for $D_1$ between point *A* and point *C* and the price elasticity of demand for $D_2$ between point *A* and point *B*. Which demand curve is more elastic, $D_1$ or $D_2$? Briefly explain.
**b.** Suppose Yolanda is initially selling 200 cones per day at a price of $3.00 per cone. If she cuts her price to $2.50 per cone and her demand curve is $D_1$, what will be the change in her revenue? What will be the change in her revenue if her demand curve is $D_2$?

**3.5** A sportswriter makes the following observation: "The Yankees slashed some ticket prices. . . . Only the Yankees know exactly how much money this will cost them, but it makes sense that they're working to fill the empty seats around home plate." Is this sportswriter correct that the Yankees will lose money if they cut ticket prices? Briefly explain.

Source: Buster Olney, "Steroids Talk Kept Alive By More Than Just Media," Espn.com, April 29, 2009.

**3.6** Consider the following description of a pricing decision by an academic book publisher:

> A publisher may have issued a monograph several years ago, when both costs and book prices were lower, and priced it at $14.95. The book is still selling reasonably well and would continue to do so at $19.95. Why not, then, raise the price? The only danger is miscalculation: By raising the price you may reduce sales to the point where you make less money overall, even while making more per copy.

Assume that the situation described in the last sentence happens. What does this tell us about the price elasticity of demand for that book? Briefly explain.

Source: Beth Luey, *Handbook for Academic Authors*, 4th ed., Cambridge, UK: Cambridge University Press, 2002, p. 250.

**3.7** In November 2008, parking rates were increased substantially for the "Big Blue Deck" at Detroit's Metro Airport. According to an article in a local newspaper, "In December, . . . after parking rates jumped from $10 to $16 a day . . . fewer cars used the Big Blue Deck compared to the previous year. . . . Still, the move at the North Terminal structure brought in about $61,000 more than the previous December. . . ." Use the information in the following table to calculate the price elasticity of demand for parking spaces at the Big Blue Deck using the midpoint formula. Assume that nothing happened between December 2007 and December 2008 to shift the demand curve for parking places. Be sure to state whether demand is elastic or inelastic.

| MONTH | RATE | REVENUE |
| --- | --- | --- |
| December 2007 | $10 | $1,387,000 |
| December 2008 | 16 | 1,448,000 |

Sources: Mary Francis Masson, "Metro Airport Parking Rate Hikes Worry Employees," *Detroit Free Press*, February 14, 2009; and Tanveer Ali, "Parking Dips; Revenue Soars," *Detroit News*, February 13, 2009.

**3.8** An article about the newspaper industry that appeared in the *Wall Street Journal* noted the following: "Declining circulation hasn't stopped Knight Ridder papers from raising subscription prices. Such increases, while boosting revenue per copy, almost always trigger a readership decline."
**a.** What is a newspaper's "circulation"?
**b.** To what is "revenue per copy" equal?
**c.** Why would a newspaper's management increase its subscription price if the result was a decline in the quantity of newspapers sold?

Source: Patricia Callahan and Kevin Helliker, "Subscriptions Fall, but Knight Ridder Lifts Advertising Rates," *Wall Street Journal*, June 18, 2001.

**3.9** Stephen Rubin, who is an executive vice-president at Random House, once made the following argument about book prices: "I am just convinced that there is no difference between $22 and $23. Let's face it. If you want a book in translation from a Czech writer, you are going to buy the book—price is not a factor if it is a book that you really want." Doubleday, which is part of Random House, is selling John Grisham's novel *The Associate* at a price of $27.95.

   **a.** Assume that the demand for this book is perfectly inelastic. Draw a demand curve showing the effect on the quantity demanded of raising the price from $27.95 to $39.95. Assume that sales are 500,000 at a price of $27.95. What is the change in revenue as a result of the price change?

   **b.** Now assume that the price elasticity of demand is −2. Draw a demand curve showing the effect of raising the price from $27.95 to $39.95. Be sure to show the quantity demanded at each price. Now what is the change in revenue as a result of the price change?

   **c.** In the quote from Stephen Rubin at the beginning of this question, does it matter that he was referring to "a book in translation from a Czech writer" rather than a book by a popular author such as John Grisham?

   Source: Virginia Postrel, "Often, Basic Concepts in Economics Are Taken for Granted," *New York Times*, January 3, 2002.

**3.10** The Delaware River Joint Toll Bridge Commission increased the toll on the bridges on Route 22 and Interstate 78 from New Jersey to Pennsylvania from $0.50 to $1.00. Use the information in the table to answer the questions. (Assume that besides the toll change, nothing occurred during the months that would affect consumer demand.)

| | | NUMBER OF VEHICLES CROSSING THE BRIDGE | |
|---|---|---|---|
| MONTH | TOLL | ROUTE 22 BRIDGE | INTERSTATE 78 BRIDGE |
| November | $0.50 | 519,337 | 728,022 |
| December | 1.00 | 433,691 | 656,257 |

   **a.** Calculate the price elasticity of demand for each bridge, using the midpoint formula.

   **b.** How much total revenue did the commission collect from these bridges in November? How much did it collect in December? Relate your answer to your answer in part a.

   Source: Garrett Therolf, "Frugal Drivers Flood Free Bridge," (*Allentown, Pennsylvania*) *Morning Call*, January 20, 2003.

**3.11** **(Related to the *Making the Connection* on page 180)** Suppose you check out the prices of two products on Amazon.com: conventional DVD players and Blu-ray players. For which type of players would you expect manufacturers to be offering similar players at about the same prices and for which type of players would you expect prices to be more spread out? Briefly explain.

>> **End Learning Objective 6.3**

---

**6.4** **Other Demand Elasticities, pages 180–182**
LEARNING OBJECTIVE: Define cross-price elasticity of demand and income elasticity of demand and understand their determinants and how they are measured.

## Summary

In addition to the elasticities already discussed, other important demand elasticities are the **cross-price elasticity of demand**, which is equal to the percentage change in quantity demanded of one good divided by the percentage change in the price of another good, and the **income elasticity of demand**, which is equal to the percentage change in the quantity demanded divided by the percentage change in income.

 Visit www.myeconlab.com to complete these exercises online and get instant feedback.

## Review Questions

**4.1** Define the cross-price elasticity of demand. What does it mean if the cross-price elasticity of demand is negative? What does it mean if the cross-price elasticity of demand is positive?

**4.2** Define the income elasticity of demand. Use income elasticity to distinguish a normal good from an inferior good. Is it possible to tell from the income elasticity of demand whether a product is a luxury good or a necessity good?

## Problems and Applications

**4.3** In the spring of 2002, lettuce prices doubled, from about $1.50 per head to about $3.00. The reaction of one consumer was quoted in a newspaper article: "I will not buy [lettuce] when it's $3 a head," she said, adding that other green vegetables can fill in for lettuce. "If bread were $5 a loaf we'd still have to buy it. But lettuce is not that important in our family."

   **a.** For this consumer's household, which product has the higher price elasticity of demand: bread or lettuce? Briefly explain.

b. Is the cross-price elasticity of demand between lettuce and other green vegetables positive or negative for this consumer? Briefly explain.

Source: Justin Bachman, "Sorry, Romaine Only," Associated Press, March 29, 2002.

**4.4** In the following graph, the demand for hot dog buns has shifted outward because the price of hot dogs has fallen from $2.20 to $1.80 per package. Calculate the cross-price elasticity of demand between hot dogs and hot dog buns.

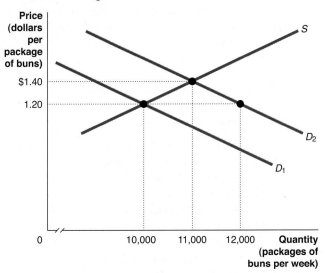

**4.5** Are the cross-price elasticities of demand between the following pairs of products likely to be positive or negative? Briefly explain.
   a. Pepsi and Coca-Cola
   b. French fries and ketchup
   c. Steak and chicken
   d. Blu-ray players and Blu-ray discs
**4.6** **(Related to the** *Chapter Opener* **on page 167)** During the spring of 2008, gasoline prices increased sharply in the United States. According to a newspaper article, rising gas prices had the following impact in the car market:

> Sales of Toyota's subcompact Yaris increased 46 percent, and Honda's tiny Fit had a record month. Ford's compact Focus model jumped 32 percent in April from a year earlier. All those models are rated at more than 30 miles per gallon for highway driving. . . .

> Sales of traditional S.U.V.'s are down more than 25 percent this year. In April, for example, sales of G.M.'s Chevrolet Tahoe fell 35 percent. Full-size pickup sales have fallen more than 15 percent this year, with Ford's industry-leading F-Series pickup dropping 27 percent in April alone.

   a. Is the cross-price elasticity of demand between gasoline and high-mileage subcompact cars positive or negative? Is the cross-price elasticity of demand between gasoline and low-mileage SUVs and full-size pickups positive or negative? Briefly explain.
   b. How can we best think of the relationships among gasoline, subcompact cars, and SUVs? Briefly discuss which can be thought of as substitutes and which can be thought of as complements.

Source: Bill Vlasic, "As Gas Costs Soar, Buyers Are Flocking to Small Cars," *New York Times*, May 2, 2008.

**4.7** Rank the following four goods from lowest income elasticity of demand to highest income elasticity of demand. Briefly explain your ranking.
   a. Bread
   b. Pepsi
   c. Mercedes-Benz automobiles
   d. Personal computers
**4.8** **(Related to the** *Making the Connection* **on page 183)** Is the cross-price elasticity of demand between wine and spirits likely to be positive or negative? Can you think of reasons why the income elasticity of demand for wine is so much higher than the income elasticity of demand for spirits?
**4.9** **(Related to** *Solved Problem 6-4* **on page 182)** Suppose two separate events occur that affect the demand for train tickets:
   1. There is a 15 percent increase in the price of taxi fares. As a result, sales of train tickets increase by 30 percent.
   2. An economic expansion causes a 3 percent increase in income. Sales of train tickets increase by 5 percent.
   Give the cross-price and income elasticities formulas and use these formulas to determine the value of these elasticities for train tickets.

**>> End Learning Objective 6.4**

## 6.5 Using Elasticity to Analyze the Disappearing Family Farm, pages 184–185

LEARNING OBJECTIVE: Use price elasticity and income elasticity to analyze economic issues.

## Summary

Price elasticity and income elasticity can be used to analyze many economic issues. One example is the disappearance of the family farm in the United States. Because the income elasticity of demand for food is low, the demand for food has not increased proportionally as incomes in the United States have grown. As farmers have become more productive, they have increased the supply of most foods. Because the price elasticity of demand for food is low, increasing supply has resulted in continually falling food prices.

 Visit www.myeconlab.com to complete these exercises online and get instant feedback.

## Review Questions

5.1 The demand for agricultural products is inelastic, and the income elasticity of demand for agricultural products is low. How do these facts help explain the disappearing family farm?

## Problems and Applications

5.2 Corruption has been a significant problem in Iraq. Opening and running a business in Iraq usually requires paying multiple bribes to government officials. We can think of there being a demand and supply for bribes, with the curves having the usual shapes: The demand for bribes will be downward sloping because the smaller the bribe, the more business owners will be willing to pay it. The supply of bribes will be upward sloping because the larger the bribe, the more government officials will be willing to run the risk of breaking the law by accepting the bribe. Suppose that the Iraqi government introduces a new policy to reduce corruption that raises the cost to officials of accepting bribes—perhaps by increasing the jail term for accepting a bribe. As a result, the supply curve for bribes will shift to the left. If we measure the burden on the economy from corruption by the total value of the bribes paid, what must be true of the demand for bribes if the government policy is to be effective? Illustrate your answer with a demand and supply graph. Be sure to show on your graph the areas representing the burden of corruption before and after the government policy is enacted.

Source: Frank Gunter, "Corruption in Iraq: Poor Data, Questionable Policies," Working Paper, March 2009.

5.3 The head of the United Kumquat Growers Association makes the following statement:

> The federal government is considering implementing a price floor in the market for kumquats. The government will not be able to buy any surplus kumquats produced at the price floor or to pay us any other subsidy. Because the demand for kumquats is elastic, I believe this program will make us worse off, and I say we should oppose it.

Explain whether you agree or disagree with this reasoning.

5.4 Review the concept of economic efficiency from Chapter 4 before answering the following question: Will there be a greater loss of economic efficiency from a price ceiling when demand is elastic or inelastic? Illustrate your answer with a demand and supply graph.

**>> End Learning Objective 6.5**

## 6.6 The Price Elasticity of Supply and Its Measurement, pages 185–190

LEARNING OBJECTIVE: Define price elasticity of supply and understand its main determinants and how it is measured.

## Summary

The **price elasticity of supply** is equal to the percentage change in quantity supplied divided by the percentage change in price. The supply curves for most goods are inelastic over a short period of time, but they become increasingly elastic over longer periods of time. Perfectly inelastic supply curves are vertical lines, and perfectly elastic supply curves are horizontal lines. Relatively few products have perfectly elastic or perfectly inelastic supply curves.

 Visit www.myeconlab.com to complete these exercises online and get instant feedback.

## Review Questions

6.1 Write the formula for the price elasticity of supply. If an increase of 10 percent in the price of frozen pizzas results in a 9 percent increase in the quantity of frozen pizzas supplied, what is the price elasticity of supply for frozen pizzas? Is the supply of pizzas elastic or inelastic?

**6.2** What is the main determinant of the price elasticity of supply?

## Problems and Applications

**6.3** **(Related to the *Making the Connection* on page 186)** Refer again to the first graph in the *Making the Connection* on page 186. Suppose that demand had stayed at the level indicated in the graph, with the equilibrium price of oil remaining at $140 per barrel. Over long periods of time, high oil prices lead to greater increases in the quantity of oil supplied. In other words, the price elasticity of supply for oil increases. This happens because higher prices provide an economic incentive to recover oil from more costly sources, such as under the oceans, from tar sands, or at greater depths in the earth. If the supply of oil becomes more elastic, explain how the increase in demand shown in the figure will result in a lower equilibrium price than $140 per barrel and a higher equilibrium quantity than 84 million barrels per day. Illustrate your answer with a demand and supply graph.

**6.4** Use the midpoint formula for calculating elasticity to calculate the price elasticity of supply between point *A* and point *B* for each panel of Figure 6-5 on page 190.

**6.5** Briefly explain whether you agree with the following statement: "The longer the period of time following an increase in the demand for apples, the greater the increase in the equilibrium quantity of apples and the smaller the increase in the equilibrium price."

**6.6** **(Related to *Solved Problem 6-6* on page 187)** In New York City, the government sets the fares that taxi drivers can charge. The number of taxi licenses

in New York City has been limited since 1937, when there were fewer than 14,000 outstanding licenses. These licenses are also called *medallions*. Because some cab owners allowed their licenses to expire, the number of licenses fell to the current number of 11,787. The New York City Council created the Taxi and Limousine Commission in 1971 to regulate taxi service. Despite the great demand for taxi service, with more than 220 million passengers per year, no new taxis are allowed to operate without one of the existing medallions. License holders are allowed to sell their medallions. In 2004, the average price paid for a medallion was over $275,000. Suppose that the New York City Taxi and Limousine Commission decides that if the price of medallions rises to $350,000 from its current level, the commission will increase the number of medallions to 13,000. What is the elasticity of supply in this case? If the elasticity of supply remains constant, how high will the price need to rise in order for the commission to issue another 1,000 medallions, bringing the total back to the 1937 level of 14,000?

**6.7** On most days, the price of a rose is $1, and 8,000 roses are purchased. On Valentine's Day, the price of a rose jumps to $2, and 30,000 roses are purchased.

   **a.** Draw a demand and supply diagram that shows why the price jumps.

   **b.** Based on this information, what do we know about the price elasticity of demand for roses? What do we know about the price elasticity of supply for roses? Calculate values for the price elasticity of demand and the price elasticity of supply or explain why you can't calculate these values.

>> **End Learning Objective 6.6**

# Firms, the Stock Market, and Corporate Governance

## Chapter Outline and Learning Objectives

# >> Facebook: From Dorm Room to Wall Street

When Mark Zuckerberg started Facebook in 2004, he was still a sophomore in college. Just five years later, Facebook had 150 million users. By contrast, it took cell phone companies 15 years to reach 150 million users and 7 years for Apple's iPod to reach that many users. Although other social networking sites, such as MySpace, already existed when Zuckerberg started Facebook, he believed those sites were based on a flawed assumption. Zuckerberg argued that people were less interested in meeting new friends online—the assumption built into other sites—than they were in finding a better way of staying in touch with the friends they already had. On Facebook, pages would typically be visible only to people the user had linked to, or "friended," which helped to reduce the problem of fake identities that plagued other sites.

Any business experiencing the runaway success of Facebook quickly develops a need to raise money to finance its expansion. Some businesses raise the funds they need by borrowing from banks. Firms such as Facebook that have the potential to become large and profitable relatively quickly can turn for financing to venture capital firms, which raise funds from investors. Several venture capital firms invested more than $100 million in Facebook. By 2009, Facebook was becoming increasingly costly to run as users uploaded more than 850 million photos and 8 million videos per day, and the company was considering new sources of funds.

Facebook is an example of a private firm. Private firms are typically smaller than public firms, such as Microsoft, Apple, or General Electric. As we will see in this chapter, public firms can raise funds by selling stocks and bonds in financial markets. Like many private firms, as of 2009, Facebook was still controlled by its founder. Once a firm grows very large, its founders often do not continue to manage it. Large corporations are owned by millions of individual investors who have purchased the firms' stock. As **AN INSIDE LOOK** on **page 220** discusses how disagreements about goals and strategies can exist even for a private firm such as Facebook that is run by its founder.

Sources: Jessi Hempel, "How Facebook Is Taking Over Our Lives," *Fortune*, March 11, 2009; Felix Salmon, "Facebook Eyes Additional Funding," Reuters.com, April 30, 2009; and Fred Vogelstein, "How Mark Zuckerberg Turned Facebook into the Web's Hottest Platform," *Wired*, September 6, 2007.

## Economics in YOUR LIFE!

### Do Corporate Managers Act in the Best Interests of Shareholders?

Although stockholders legally own corporations, managers often have a great deal of freedom in deciding how corporations are run. As a result, managers can make decisions, such as spending money on large corporate headquarters or decorating their offices with expensive paintings, that are in their interests but not in the interests of the shareholders. If managers make decisions that waste money and lower the profits of a firm, the price of the firm's stock will fall, which hurts the investors who own the stock. Suppose you own stock in a corporation. Why is it difficult to get the managers to act in your interest rather than in their own? Given this problem, should you ever take on the risk of buying stock? As you read the chapter, see if you can answer these questions. You can check your answers against those we provide at the end of the chapter.

▶ Continued on page 219

I n this chapter, we look at the firm: how it is organized, how it raises funds, and the information it provides to investors. As we have already discussed, firms in a market system are responsible for organizing the factors of production to produce goods and services. Firms are the vehicles entrepreneurs use to earn profits. To succeed, entrepreneurs must meet consumer wants by producing new or better goods and services or by finding ways of producing existing goods and services at a lower cost so they can be sold at a lower price. Entrepreneurs also need access to sufficient funds, and they must be able to efficiently organize production. As the typical firm in many industries has become larger during the past 100 years, the task of efficiently organizing production has become more difficult. Toward the end of this chapter, we look at problems of corporate governance, which occurred during the 2000s. We also look at the steps firms and the government have taken to avoid similar problems in the future.

Categorize the major types of firms in the United States.

**Sole proprietorship** A firm owned by a single individual and not organized as a corporation.

**Partnership** A firm owned jointly by two or more persons and not organized as a corporation.

**Corporation** A legal form of business that provides owners with protection from losing more than their investment should the business fail.

**Asset** Anything of value owned by a person or a firm.

**Limited liability** The legal provision that shields owners of a corporation from losing more than they have invested in the firm.

# Types of Firms

In studying a market economy, it is important to understand the basics of how firms operate. In the United States, there are three legal categories of firms: *sole proprietorships*, *partnerships*, and *corporations*. A **sole proprietorship** is a firm owned by a single individual. Although most sole proprietorships are small, some employ many workers and earn large profits. **Partnerships** are firms owned jointly by two or more—sometimes many—persons. Most law and accounting firms are partnerships. Some of these can be quite large. For instance, in 2009, the Baker & McKenzie law firm in Chicago had more than 1,100 partners. Most large firms, though, are organized as *corporations*. A **corporation** is a legal form of business that provides owners with protection from losing more than their investment should the business fail.

## Who Is Liable? Limited and Unlimited Liability

A key distinction among the three types of firms is that the owners of sole proprietorships and partnerships have unlimited liability. Unlimited liability means there is no legal distinction between the personal assets of the owners of the firm and the assets of the firm. An **asset** is anything of value owned by a person or a firm. If a sole proprietorship or a partnership owes a lot of money to the firm's suppliers or employees, the suppliers and employees have a legal right to sue the firm for payment, even if this requires the firm's owners to sell some of their personal assets, such as stocks or bonds. In other words, with sole proprietorships and partnerships, the owners are not legally distinct from the firms they own.

It may only seem fair that the owners of a firm be responsible for a firm's debts. But early in the nineteenth century, it became clear to many state legislatures in the United States that unlimited liability was a significant problem for any firm that was attempting to raise funds from large numbers of investors. An investor might be interested in making a relatively small investment in a firm but be unwilling to become a partner in the firm for fear of placing at risk all of his or her personal assets if the firm were to fail. To get around this problem, state legislatures began to pass *general incorporation laws*, which allowed firms to be organized as corporations. Under the corporate form of business, the owners of a firm have **limited liability**, which means that if the firm fails, the owners can never lose more than the amount they have invested in the firm. The personal assets of the owners of the firm are not affected by the failure of the firm. In fact, in the eyes of the law, a corporation is a legal "person," separate from its owners. Limited liability has made it possible for corporations to raise funds by issuing shares of stock to large numbers of investors. For example, if you buy a share of Google stock, you are a part owner of the firm, but even if Google were to go bankrupt, you would not be personally responsible for any of Google's debts. Therefore, you could not lose more than the amount you paid for the stock.

|  | SOLE PROPRIETORSHIP | PARTNERSHIP | CORPORATION |
|---|---|---|---|
| **ADVANTAGES** | • Control by owner<br>• No layers of management | • Ability to share work<br>• Ability to share risks | • Limited personal liability<br>• Greater ability to raise funds |
| **DISADVANTAGES** | • Unlimited personal liability<br>• Limited ability to raise funds | • Unlimited personal liability<br>• Limited ability to raise funds | • Costly to organize<br>• Possible double taxation of income |

**TABLE 7-1**

**Differences among Business Organizations**

Corporate organizations also have some disadvantages. In the United States, corporate profits are taxed twice—once at the corporate level and again when investors receive a share of corporate profits. Corporations generally are larger than sole proprietorships and partnerships and therefore more difficult to organize and run. Table 7-1 reviews the advantages and disadvantages of different forms of business organization.

## Corporations Earn the Majority of Revenue and Profits

Figure 7-1 gives basic statistics on the three types of business organizations. Panel (a) shows that almost three-quarters of all firms are sole proprietorships. Panels (b) and (c) show that although only 19 percent of all firms are corporations, corporations account for a large majority of the revenue and profits earned by all firms. *Profit* is the difference between revenue and the total cost to a firm of producing the goods and services it offers for sale.

There are more than 5.6 million corporations in the United States, but only 32,000 have annual revenues of more than $50 million. We can think of these 32,000 firms—including Microsoft, General Electric, and Google—as representing "big business." These large firms earn more than 85 percent of the total profits of all corporations in the United States.

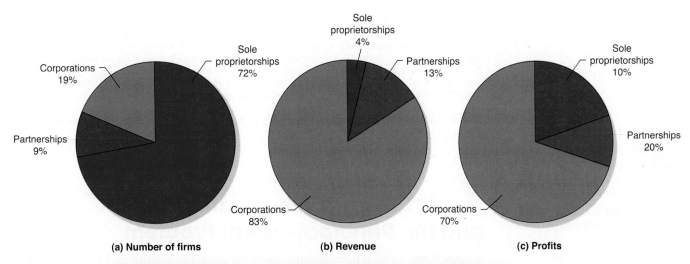

**(a) Number of firms**  **(b) Revenue**  **(c) Profits**

**Figure 7-1**  **Business Organizations: Sole Proprietorships, Partnerships, and Corporations**

The three types of firms in the United States are sole proprietorships, partnerships, and corporations. Panel (a) shows that only 19 percent of all firms are corporations.

Yet, as panels (b) and (c) show, corporations account for a large majority of the total revenue and profits earned by all firms.

Source: U.S. Census Bureau, *The 2009 Statistical Abstract of the United States.*

*In a typical year, 40 percent of new jobs are created by small firms like Yelp.com, which is a community-based review and directory website founded by Jeremy Stoppelman, left, and Russel Simmons.*

## Making the Connection | How Important Are Small Businesses to the U.S. Economy?

We have seen that although a large majority of all firms are sole proprietorships, they account for only a small fraction of total revenues and profits earned by all firms. And while 85 percent of all firms employ fewer than 20 workers, fewer than 20 percent of all workers are employed by these firms. Does this mean that small businesses are unimportant to the U.S. economy?

To the contrary, most economists would argue that small firms are vital to the health of the economy. Starting a small firm provides an entrepreneur with a vehicle for bringing a new product or process to market. While anyone starting a new firm hopes to become successful, perhaps even wealthy, the act of founding a company can also provide employment opportunities for workers and new goods and services for consumers. In a typical year, more than 600,000 new firms open in the United States, of which more than 95 percent employ fewer than 20 workers. In a typical year, 40 percent of new jobs are created by small firms, and in some years more than half are. Strikingly, more than 85 percent of all jobs created by new firms are created by small firms.

Although, on average, jobs at small firms pay lower wages than jobs at large firms and are less likely to provide fringe benefits, such as health insurance and retirement accounts, workers at small firms tend to be younger and, in fact, the first job for many workers is often with a small firm. Small firms are also less likely to lay off workers during a recession than are large firms.

Entrepreneurs founding small firms have been the source of many of the most important new goods and services available to consumers. This is true despite the fact that large firms spend much more on research and development than do small firms. Some economists have argued that although spending on research and development by large firms often leads to important improvements in existing products, innovative new products are often introduced by small firms. For instance, during the late nineteenth and early twentieth centuries, Thomas Edison, Henry Ford, and the Wright Brothers were all responsible for introducing important products shortly after starting what were initially very small firms. In more recent years, Bill Gates, Steve Jobs, and Michael Dell decided that the best way to develop their ideas was by founding Microsoft, Apple, and Dell Computer rather than by going to work for large corporations. These firms all began with a handful of employees, and the key products and processes they pioneered were developed long before they evolved into the large corporations they are today.

Sources: Amar Bhidé, *The Origins and Evolution of New Businesses*, New York: Oxford University Press, 2003; Giuseppe Moscarini and Fabien Postel-Vinay, "Large Employers Are More Cyclically Sensitive," National Bureau of Economic Research, Working Paper 14740, February 2009; data are from the *2009 Statistical Abstract of the United States*, the U.S. Small Business Administration, and the U.S. Bureau of Labor Statistics; some of the difficulties in measuring the link between firm size and employment are discussed in David Neumark, Brandon Wall, and Junfu Zhang, "Do Small Businesses Create More Jobs?" National Bureau of Economic Research Working Paper 13818, February 2008.

**(myeconlab)**   **YOUR TURN:** Test your understanding by doing related problem 1.6 on page 222 at the end of this chapter.

---

**7.2 LEARNING** OBJECTIVE

Describe the typical management structure of corporations and understand the concepts of separation of ownership from control and the principal–agent problem.

**Corporate governance** The way in which a corporation is structured and the effect a corporation's structure has on the firm's behavior.

## The Structure of Corporations and the Principal-Agent Problem

Because large corporations account for most sales and profits in the economy, it is important to know how they are managed. Most large corporations have a similar management structure. The way in which a corporation is structured and the effect a corporation's structure has on the firm's behavior is referred to as **corporate governance**.

## Corporate Structure and Corporate Governance

Corporations are legally owned by their *shareholders*, the owners of the corporation's stock. Unlike with a sole proprietorship, a corporation's shareholders, although they are the firm's owners, do not manage the firm directly. Instead, they elect a *board of directors* to represent their interests. The board of directors appoints a *chief executive officer* (CEO) to run the day-to-day operations of the corporation. Sometimes the board of directors also appoints other members of *top management*, such as the *chief financial officer* (CFO). At other times, the CEO appoints other members of top management. Members of top management, including the CEO and CFO, often serve on the board of directors. Members of management serving on the board of directors are referred to as *inside directors*. Members of the board of directors who do not have a direct management role in the firm are referred to as *outside directors*. The outside directors are intended to act as checks on the decisions of top managers, but the distinction between an outside director and an inside director is not always clear. For example, the CEO of a firm that sells a good or service to a large corporation may sit on the board of directors of that corporation. Although technically an outside director, this person may be reluctant to oppose the top managers because the top managers have the power to stop purchasing from his or her firm. In some instances, top managers have effectively controlled their firms' boards of directors.

Unlike the owners of family businesses or private firms such as Facebook, the top management of a large corporation does not generally own a large share of the firm's stock, so large corporations have a **separation of ownership from control**. Although the shareholders actually own the firm, top management controls the firm's day-to-day operations. Because top managers do not own the entire firm, they may decrease the firm's profits by spending money to purchase private jets or schedule management meetings at luxurious resorts. Economists refer to the conflict between the interests of shareholders and the interests of top management as a **principal–agent problem**. This problem occurs when agents—in this case, a firm's top management—pursue their own interests rather than the interests of the principal who hired them—in this case, the shareholders of the corporation. To reduce the impact of the principal–agent problem, many boards of directors in the 1990s began to tie the salaries of top managers to the profits of the firm or to the price of the firm's stock. They hoped this would give top managers an incentive to make the firm as profitable as possible, thereby benefiting its shareholders.

> **Separation of ownership from control** A situation in a corporation in which the top management, rather than the shareholders, control day-to-day operations.
>
> **Principal–agent problem** A problem caused by an agent pursuing his own interests rather than the interests of the principal who hired him.

---

# Solved Problem | 7-2

## Does the Principal–Agent Problem Apply to the Relationship between Managers and Workers?

Briefly explain whether you agree with the following argument:

> The principal–agent problem applies not just to the relationship between shareholders and top managers. It also applies to the relationship between managers and workers. Just as shareholders have trouble monitoring whether top managers are earning as much profit as possible, managers have trouble monitoring whether workers are working as hard as possible.

## SOLVING THE PROBLEM:

**Step 1: Review the chapter material.** This problem concerns the principal–agent problem, so you may want to review the section "Corporate Structure and Corporate Governance," which appears above.

**Step 2: Evaluate the argument.** You should agree with the argument. A corporation's shareholders have difficulty monitoring the activities of top managers. In practice, they attempt to do so indirectly through the corporation's board of directors. But the firm's top managers may influence—or even control—the firm's board of directors. Even if top managers do not control a board of directors, it may be difficult for the board to know whether actions managers take—say, opening a branch office in Paris—will increase the profitability of the firm or just increase the enjoyment of the top managers.

To answer the problem, we must extend this analysis to the relationship between managers and workers: Managers would like workers to work as hard as possible. Workers would often rather not work hard, particularly if they do not see a direct financial reward for doing so. Managers can have trouble monitoring whether workers are working hard or goofing off. Is that worker in his cubicle diligently staring at a computer screen because he is hard at work on a report or because he is surfing the Web for sports scores or writing a long e-mail to his girlfriend? So, the principal–agent problem does apply to the relationship between managers and workers.

**EXTRA CREDIT:** Boards of directors try to reduce the principal–agent problem by designing compensation policies for top managers that give them financial incentives to increase profits. Similarly, managers try to reduce the principal–agent problem by designing compensation policies that give workers an incentive to work harder. For example, some manufacturers pay factory workers on the basis of how much they produce rather than on the basis of how many hours they work.

 **YOUR TURN:** For more practice, do related problems 2.4 and 2.5 on page 223 at the end of this chapter.

---

**7.3 LEARNING** OBJECTIVE

Explain how firms raise the funds they need to operate and expand.

# How Firms Raise Funds

Owners and managers of firms try to earn a profit. To earn a profit, a firm must raise funds to pay for its operations, including paying its employees and buying machines. Indeed, a central challenge for anyone running a firm, whether that person is a sole proprietor or a top manager of a large corporation, is raising the funds needed to operate and expand the business. Suppose you decide to open an online trading service using $100,000 you have saved in a bank. You use the $100,000 to rent a building for your firm, to buy computers, and to pay other start-up expenses. Your firm is a great success, and you decide to expand by moving to a larger building and buying more computers. As the owner of a small business, you can raise the funds for this expansion in three ways:

1. If you are making a profit, you could reinvest the profits back into your firm. Profits that are reinvested in a firm rather than taken out of a firm and paid to the firm's owners are *retained earnings*.
2. You could raise funds by recruiting additional owners to invest in the firm. This arrangement would increase the firm's *financial capital*. As we have seen, Mark Zuckerberg took this approach when he sold part ownership of Facebook to venture capital firms.
3. Finally, you could borrow the funds from relatives, friends, or a bank.

The managers of a large, public firm have some additional ways to raise funds, as we will see in the next section.

## Sources of External Funds

Unless firms rely on retained earnings, they have to raise the *external funds* they need from others who have funds available to invest. It is the role of an economy's *financial system* to transfer funds from savers to borrowers—directly through financial markets or indirectly through financial intermediaries such as banks.

Most firms raise external funds in two ways. The first relies on financial intermediaries such as banks and is called **indirect finance**. If you put $1,000 in a checking account or a savings account, or if you put money in a $1,000 certificate of deposit (CD), the bank will loan most of those funds to borrowers. The bank will combine your funds with those of other depositors and, for example, make a $100,000 loan to a local business. Small businesses rely heavily on bank loans as their primary source of external funds.

A second way for firms to acquire external funds is through *financial markets*. Raising funds in these markets, such as the New York Stock Exchange on Wall Street in New York, is called **direct finance**. Direct finance usually takes the form of the borrower selling the lender a *financial security*. A financial security is a document—sometimes in electronic form—that states the terms under which the funds have passed from the buyer of the security (who is lending funds) to the borrower. *Bonds* and *stocks* are the two main types of financial securities. Typically, only large corporations are able to sell bonds and stocks on financial markets. Investors are generally unwilling to buy securities issued by small and medium-sized firms because the investors lack sufficient information on the financial health of smaller firms.

**Bonds** **Bonds** are financial securities that represent promises to repay a fixed amount of funds. When General Electric (GE) sells a bond to raise funds, it promises to pay the purchaser of the bond an interest payment each year for the term of the bond, as well as a final payment of the amount of the loan, or the *principal*, at the end of the term. GE may need to raise many millions of dollars to build a factory, but each individual bond has a principal, or *face value*, of $1,000, which is the amount each bond purchaser is lending GE. So, GE must sell many bonds to raise all the funds it needs. Suppose GE promises it will pay interest of $60 per year to anyone who will buy one of its bonds. The interest payments on a bond are referred to as **coupon payments**. The **interest rate** is the cost of borrowing funds, usually expressed as a percentage of the amount borrowed. If we express the coupon as a percentage of the face value of the bond, we find the interest rate on the bond, called the *coupon rate*. In this case, the interest rate is:

$$\frac{\$60}{\$1,000} = 0.06, \text{ or } 6\%$$

Many bonds that corporations issue have terms, or *maturities*, of 30 years. For example, if you bought a bond from GE, GE would pay you $60 per year for 30 years, and at the end of the thirtieth year, GE would pay you back the $1,000 principal.

**Stocks** When you buy a newly issued bond from a firm, you are lending funds to that firm. When you buy **stock** issued by a firm, you are actually buying part ownership of the firm. When a corporation sells stock, it is doing the same thing the owner of a small business does when she takes on a partner: The firm is increasing its financial capital by bringing additional owners into the firm. Any individual shareholder usually owns only a small fraction of the total shares of stock issued by a corporation.

A shareholder is entitled to a share of the corporation's profits, if there are any. Corporations generally keep some of their profits—known as retained earnings—to finance future expansion. The remaining profits are paid to shareholders as **dividends**. Investors hope that the firm will earn economic profits on its retained earnings, causing the firm's share price to rise, and providing a *capital gain* for investors. If a corporation is unable to make a profit, it usually does not pay a dividend. Under the law, corporations must make payments on any debt they have before making payments to their owners. That is, a corporation must make promised payments to bondholders before it can make any dividend payments to shareholders. In addition, when firms sell stock, they acquire from investors an open-ended commitment of funds to the firm.

Unlike bonds, stocks do not have a maturity date, so the firm is not obliged to return the investor's funds at any particular date.

---

**Indirect finance** A flow of funds from savers to borrowers through financial intermediaries such as banks. Intermediaries raise funds from savers to lend to firms (and other borrowers).

**Direct finance** A flow of funds from savers to firms through financial markets, such as the New York Stock Exchange.

**Bond** A financial security that represents a promise to repay a fixed amount of funds.

**Coupon payment** An interest payment on a bond.

**Interest rate** The cost of borrowing funds, usually expressed as a percentage of the amount borrowed.

**Stock** A financial security that represents partial ownership of a firm.

**Dividends** Payments by a corporation to its shareholders.

## Stock and Bond Markets Provide Capital— and Information

The original purchasers of stocks and bonds may resell them to other investors. In fact, most of the buying and selling of stocks and bonds that takes place each day involves investors reselling existing stocks and bonds to each other rather than corporations selling new stocks and bonds to investors. The buyers and sellers of stocks and bonds together make up the *stock and bond markets.* There is no single place where stocks and bonds are bought and sold. Some trading of stocks and bonds takes place in buildings known as *exchanges,* such as the New York Stock Exchange or the Tokyo Stock Exchange. In the United States, the stocks and bonds of the largest corporations are traded on the New York Stock Exchange. The development of computer technology has spread the trading of stocks and bonds outside exchanges to *securities dealers* linked by computers. These dealers comprise the *over-the-counter market.* The stocks of many computer and other high-technology firms—including Apple, Google, and Microsoft—are traded in the most important of the over-the-counter markets, the *National Association of Securities Dealers Automated Quotations* system, which is referred to by its acronym, NASDAQ.

Shares of stock represent claims on the profits of the firms that issue them. Therefore, as the fortunes of the firms change and they earn more or less profit, the prices of the stock the firms have issued should also change. Similarly, bonds represent claims to receive coupon payments and one final payment of principal. Therefore, a particular bond that was issued in the past may have its price go up or down, depending on whether the coupon payments being offered on newly issued bonds are higher or lower than on existing bonds. If you hold a bond with a coupon of $80 per year, and newly issued bonds have coupons of $100 per year, the price of your bond will fall because it is less attractive to investors. The price of a bond will be affected by changes in investors' perceptions of the issuing firm's ability to make the coupon payments. For example, if investors begin to believe that a firm may soon go out of business and stop making coupon payments to its bondholders, the price of the firm's bonds will fall to very low levels.

# Don't Let This Happen to **YOU!**

### When Google Shares Change Hands, Google Doesn't Get the Money

Google is a popular investment, with investors buying and selling shares often as their views about the value of the firm shift. That's great for Google, right? Think of all that money flowing into Google's coffers as shares change hands and the stock price goes up. *Wrong.* Google raises funds in a primary market, but shares change hands in a secondary market. Those trades don't put money into Google's hands, but they do give important information to the firm's managers. Let's see why.

*Primary markets* are those in which newly issued claims are sold to initial buyers by the issuer. Businesses can raise funds in a primary financial market in two ways—by borrowing (selling bonds) or by selling shares of stock—which result in different types of claims on the borrowing firm's future income. Although you hear about the stock market fluctuations each night on the evening news, bonds actually account for more of the funds raised by borrowers. The total value of bonds in the United States is typically about twice the value of stocks.

In *secondary markets,* stocks and bonds that have already been issued are sold by one investor to another. If Google sells shares to the public, it is turning to a primary market for new funds. Once Google shares are issued, investors trade the shares in the secondary market. Google does not receive any new funds when Google shares are traded on secondary markets. The initial seller of a stock or bond raises funds from a lender only in the primary market. Secondary markets convey information to firms' managers and to investors by determining the price of stocks and bonds. For example, a major increase in Google's stock price conveys the market's good feelings about the firm, and the firm may decide to raise funds to expand. Hence, secondary markets are valuable sources of information for corporations that are considering raising funds.

Primary and secondary markets are both important, but they play different roles. As an investor, you principally trade stocks and bonds in a secondary market. As a corporate manager, you may help decide how to raise new funds to expand the firm where you work.

**YOUR TURN:** Test your understanding by doing related problem 3.10 on page 224 at the end of this chapter.

Changes in the value of a firm's stocks and bonds offer important information for a firm's managers, as well as for investors. An increase in the stock price means that investors are more optimistic about the firm's profit prospects, and the firm's managers might want to expand the firm's operations as a result. By contrast, a decrease in the firm's stock price indicates that investors are less optimistic about the firms' profit prospects, so management may want to shrink the firm's operations. Likewise, changes in the value of the firm's bonds imply changes in the cost of external funds to finance the firm's investment in research and development or in new factories. A higher bond price indicates a lower cost of new external funds, while a lower bond price indicates a higher cost of new external funds.

# Solved Problem | 7-3

## Building a Better and Bigger Lemonade Stand

Many children learn their first business lessons when they sell cold drinks outside their homes to family members and neighbors. For some of these children, the urge to start their own businesses carries over into their adult lives, when they start what they hope will be more permanent businesses. Nearly all new businesses start on a small scale. If successful, business owners must decide whether to expand their operations. Business expansion carries with it new risks for business owners. Because few budding entrepreneurs are independently wealthy, most need to obtain financial support from others for their expanded operations.

List and compare the main sources owners can use to expand their businesses.

## SOLVING THE PROBLEM:

**Step 1:** **Review the chapter material.** This problem is about firms raising funds, so you may want to review the section "How Firms Raise Funds," which begins on page 208.

**Step 2:** **List and compare the options available to firms to finance expansion of their operations.** Assume that a firm is initially a sole proprietorship.

**Internal Funds**
1. Retained earnings: Profits are reinvested.

**External Funds**
2. Borrowing from relatives, friends, or a bank: Interest is paid on the borrowed amount; a business plan may be required to outline the purpose of the loan.
3. Changing the firm to a partnership: Adding one or more partners increases financial capital but dilutes control of the business among the partners.
4. Changing the firm to a corporation: Becoming a publicly owned firm allows the firm to raise financial capital by selling ownership shares to stockholders and to borrow through bond issues. But owners lose some control over the firm to shareholders and must make regular public disclosures of the firm's financial condition.

**YOUR TURN:** For more practice, do related problem 3.12 on page 225 at the end of this chapter.

# Why Do Stock Prices Fluctuate So Much?

The performance of the U.S. stock market is often measured using *stock market indexes*. Stock market indexes are averages of stock prices with the value of the index set equal to 100 in a particular year, called the *base year*. Because the stock indexes are intended to show movements in prices from one year to the next, rather than the actual dollar values of the underlying stocks, the year chosen for the base year is unimportant. Figure 7-2 shows movements from 1995 to mid-2009 in the three most widely followed stock indexes:

- The Dow Jones Industrial Average, which is an index of the stock prices of 30 large U.S. corporations.

- The S&P 500, which is an index prepared by the Standard and Poor's company and includes the stock prices of 500 large U.S. firms.

- The NASDAQ composite index, which includes the stock prices of the more than 4,000 firms whose shares are traded in the NASDAQ stock market, which is named for the National Association of Securities Dealers. NASDAQ is an "over-the-counter" market, meaning that buying and selling on NASDAQ are carried out between dealers who are linked together by computer. The listings on NASDAQ are dominated by high-tech firms such as Apple, Microsoft, and Google.

As we have seen, ownership of a firm's stock represents a claim on the firm's profits. So, the larger the firm's profits are, the higher its stock price will be. When the overall economy is expanding, incomes, employment, and spending will all increase, as will corporate profits. When the economy is in a recession, incomes, employment, and spending will fall, as will corporate profits. We would expect that stock prices will rise when the economy is expanding, and fall when the economy is in recession. We see this pattern reflected in the three stock markets indexes in Figure 7-2. All three indexes follow a roughly similar pattern: Increases in stock prices during the economic expansion of the late 1990s, declines after the "dot-com crash" of 2000 and the recession of 2001, increases from late 2001 to late 2007, and then declines as the U.S. economy entered a recession at the end of 2007.

The stock prices of many early Internet companies had soared in the late 1990s as some analysts made what turned out to be overly optimistic predictions about how rapidly online retailing would grow. In 2000, when investors came to believe that many dot-coms would never be profitable, their stock prices crashed. Because the NASDAQ is dominated by high tech stocks, it experienced greater swings during the dot-com boom and bust of the late-1990s and early 2000s than did the other two indexes. The sharp declines in all three indexes beginning in late 2007 reflected the severity of recession that began in December of that year. The severity of the recession was due in part to problems with financial firms, which we will discuss later in this chapter.

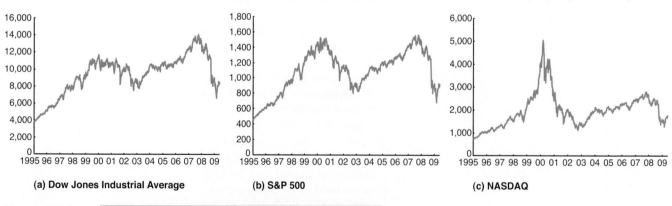

**(a) Dow Jones Industrial Average**    **(b) S&P 500**    **(c) NASDAQ**

## Figure 7-2    Movements in Stock Market Indexes, 1995–mid-2009

The performance of the U.S. stock market is often measured by market indexes, which are averages of stock prices. The three most important indexes are the Dow Jones Industrial Average, the S&P 500, and the NASDAQ. During the period from 1995 to mid-2009, the three indexes followed similar patterns, rising when the U.S. economy was expanding and falling when the economy was in recession.

## Making the Connection

## Following Abercrombie & Fitch's Stock Price in the Financial Pages

If you read the online stock listings at the *Wall Street Journal* or another site, you will notice that the listings pack into a small space a lot of information about what happened to stocks during the previous day's trading. The figure on the next page reproduces a small portion of the listings from the *Wall Street Journal* from May 12, 2009, for stocks listed on the New York Stock Exchange. The listings provide information on the buying and selling of the stock of five firms during the previous day. Let's focus on the highlighted listing for Abercrombie & Fitch, the clothing store, and examine the information in each column:

- The first column gives the name of the company.

- The second column gives the firm's "ticker" symbol (ANF), which you may have seen scrolling along the bottom of the screen on cable financial news channels.

- The third column (Open) gives the price (in dollars) of the stock at the time that trading began, which is 9:30 A.M. on the New York Stock Exchange. Abercrombie & Fitch opened for trading at a price of $25.90.

- The fourth column (High) and the fifth column (Low) give the highest price and the lowest price the stock sold for during the day.

- The sixth column (Close) gives the price the stock sold for the last time it was traded before the close of trading (4:30 P.M.), which in this case was $25.43.

- The seventh column (Net Chg) gives the amount by which the closing price changed from the closing price the day before. In this case, the price of Abercrombie & Fitch's stock had fallen by $1.10 per share from its closing price the day before. Changes in Abercrombie & Fitch's stock price give the firm's managers a signal that they may want to expand or contract the firm's operations.

- The eighth column (%Chg) gives the change in the price in percentage terms rather than in dollar terms.

- The ninth column (Vol) gives the number of shares of stock traded on the previous day.

- The tenth column (52 Week High) and the eleventh column (52 Week Low) give the highest price the stock has sold for and the lowest price the stock has sold for during the previous year. These numbers tell how *volatile* the stock price is—that is, how much it fluctuates over the course of the year. In this case, Abercrombie's stock had been quite volatile, rising as high as $77.25 per share and falling as low as $13.66 per share. These large fluctuations in price are an indication of how risky investing in the stock market can be.

- The twelfth column (Div) gives the dividend, expressed in dollars. In this case, 0.70 means that Abercrombie paid a dividend of $0.70 per share.

- The thirteenth column (Yield) gives the *dividend yield*, which is calculated by dividing the dividend by the *closing price* of the stock—that is, the price at which Abercrombie's stock last sold before the close of trading on the previous day.

- The fourteenth column (PE) gives the *P-E ratio* (or *price–earnings ratio*), which is calculated by dividing the price of the firm's stock by its earnings per share. (Remember that because firms retain some earnings, earnings per share is not necessarily the same as dividends per share.) Abercrombie's P-E ratio was 8, meaning that its price per share was 8 times its earnings per share. So, you would have to pay $8 to buy $1 of Abercrombie & Fitch's earnings.

- The final column (Year-To-Date %Chg) gives the percentage change in the price of the stock from the beginning of the year to the previous day. In this case, the price of Abercrombie's stock had risen by 10.2 percent since the beginning of 2009.

| | Symbol | Open | High | Low | Close | Net Chg | %Chg | Vol | 52 Week High | 52 Week Low | Div | Yield | PE | Year-To-Date %Chg |
|---|---|---|---|---|---|---|---|---|---|---|---|---|---|---|
| ABB LTD ADS | ABB | 15.99 | 16.17 | 15.91 | 16.02 | -0.50 | -3.03 | 3,299,629 | 33.39 | 9.11 | 0.47 | 2.9 | 13 | 6.7 |
| ABBOTT LABORATORIES | ABT | 44.96 | 45.43 | 44.52 | 44.87 | -0.06 | -0.13 | 6,137,718 | 60.78 | 41.27 | 1.60 | 3.6 | 15 | -15.9 |
| ABERCROMBIE & FITCH CO. | ANF | 25.90 | 26.00 | 25.16 | 25.43 | -1.10 | -4.15 | 2,720,831 | 77.25 | 13.66 | 0.70 | 2.8 | 8 | 10.2 |
| ACADIA REALTY TRUST SBI | AKR | 14.00 | 14.14 | 13.61 | 13.66 | -0.73 | -5.07 | 535,181 | 25.10 | 8.50 | 0.84 | 6.1 | 24 | -4.3 |
| ACCENTURE LTD. CL A | ACN | 28.98 | 29.72 | 28.92 | 29.47 | 0.07 | 0.24 | 4,375,552 | 43.04 | 24.76 | 0.50 | 1.7 | 11 | -10.1 |

Source: *Wall Street Journal* Eastern Edition [staff-produced copy only] by *Wall Street Journal*. Copyright 2009 by Dow Jones & Co Inc. Reproduced with permission of Dow Jones & Co. Inc. in the format Textbook via Copyright Clearance Center.

 **YOUR TURN:** Test your understanding by doing related problem 3.11 on page 224 at the end of this chapter.

---

**7.4 LEARNING** OBJECTIVE

Understand the information provided in corporations' financial statements.

# Using Financial Statements to Evaluate a Corporation

To raise funds, a firm's managers must persuade banks or buyers of its stocks or bonds that it will be profitable. Before a firm can sell new issues of stocks or bonds, it must first provide investors and financial regulators with information about its finances. To borrow from a bank or another financial intermediary, the firm must disclose financial information to the lender as well.

In most high-income countries, government agencies require firms to disclose specific financial information to the public before they are allowed to sell securities such as stocks or bonds in financial markets. In the United States, the Securities and Exchange Commission requires publicly owned firms to report their performance in financial statements prepared using standard accounting methods, often referred to as *generally accepted accounting principles*. Such disclosure reduces information costs, but it doesn't eliminate them—for two reasons. First, some firms may be too young to have much information for potential investors to evaluate. Second, managers may try to present the required information in the best possible light so that investors will overvalue their securities.

Private firms also collect information on business borrowers and sell the information to lenders and investors. If the information-gathering firm does a good job, lenders and investors purchasing the information will be better able to judge the quality of borrowing firms. Firms specializing in information—including Moody's Investors Service, Standard & Poor's Corporation, Value Line, and Dun & Bradstreet—collect information from businesses and sell it to subscribers. Buyers include individual investors, libraries, and financial intermediaries. You can find some of these publications in your college library or through online information services.

What kind of information do investors and firm managers need? A firm must answer three basic questions: What to produce? How to produce it? and What price to charge? To answer these questions, a firm's managers need two pieces of information: The first is the firm's revenues and costs, and the second is the value of the property and other assets the firm owns and the firm's debts, or other **liabilities**, that it owes to other persons and firms. Potential investors in the firm also need this information to decide whether to buy the firm's stocks or bonds. This information is contained in the firm's *financial statements*, principally its income statement and balance sheet, which we discuss next.

**Liability** Anything owed by a person or a firm.

# The Income Statement

A firm's **income statement** sums up its revenues, costs, and profit over a period of time. Corporations issue annual income statements, although the 12-month *fiscal year* covered may be different from the calendar year to better represent the seasonal pattern of the business. We explore income statements in greater detail in the appendix to this chapter.

**Getting to Accounting Profit** An income statement shows a firm's revenue, costs, and profit for the firm's fiscal year. To determine profitability, the income statement starts with the firm's revenue and subtracts its operating expenses and taxes paid. The remainder, *net income*, is the **accounting profit** of the firm.

**. . . And Economic Profit** Accounting profit provides information on a firm's current net income, measured according to accepted accounting standards. Accounting profit is not, however, the ideal measure of a firm's profits because it neglects some of the firm's costs. By taking into account all costs, *economic profit* provides a better indication than accounting profit of how successful a firm is. Firms making an economic profit will remain in business and may even expand. Firms making an *economic loss* are unlikely to remain in business in the long run. To understand how economic profit is calculated, remember that economists always measure cost as *opportunity cost*. The **opportunity cost** of any activity is the highest-valued alternative that must be given up to engage in that activity. Costs are either *explicit* or *implicit*. When a firm spends money, an **explicit cost** results. If a firm incurs an opportunity cost but does not spend money, an **implicit cost** results. For example, firms incur an explicit labor cost when they pay wages to employees. Firms have many other explicit costs as well, such as the cost of the electricity used to light their buildings or the costs of advertising or insurance.

Some costs are implicit, however. The most important of these is the opportunity cost to investors of the funds they have invested in the firm. Economists refer to the minimum amount that investors must earn on the funds they invest in a firm, expressed as a percentage of the amount invested, as a *normal rate of return*. If a firm fails to provide investors with at least a normal rate of return, it will not be able to remain in business over the long run because investors will not continue to invest their funds in the firm. For example, Bethlehem Steel was once the second-leading producer of steel in the United States and a very profitable firm with stock that sold for more than $50 per share. By 2002, investors became convinced that the firm's uncompetitive labor costs in world markets meant that the firm would never be able to provide investors with a normal rate of return. Many investors expected that the firm would eventually have to declare bankruptcy, and as a result, the price of Bethlehem Steel's stock plummeted to $1 per share. Shortly thereafter, the firm declared bankruptcy, and its remaining assets were sold off to a competing steel firm. The return (in dollars) that investors require to continue investing in a firm is a true cost to the firm and should be subtracted from the firm's revenues to calculate its profits.

The necessary rate of return that investors must receive to continue investing in a firm varies from firm to firm. If the investment is risky—as would be the case with a biotechnology start-up—investors may require a high rate of return to compensate them for the risk. Investors in firms in more established industries, such as electric utilities, may require lower rates of return. The exact rate of return investors require to invest in any particular firm is difficult to calculate, which also makes it difficult for an accountant to include the return as a cost on an income statement. Firms have other implicit costs besides the return investors require that can also be difficult to calculate. As a result, the rules of accounting generally require that only explicit costs be included in the firm's financial records. *Economic costs* include both explicit costs *and* implicit costs. **Economic profit** is equal to a firm's revenues minus its economic costs. Because accounting profit excludes some implicit costs, it is larger than economic profit.

**Income statement** A financial statement that sums up a firm's revenues, costs, and profit over a period of time.

**Accounting profit** A firm's net income, measured by revenue minus operating expenses and taxes paid.

**Opportunity cost** The highest-valued alternative that must be given up to engage in an activity.

**Explicit cost** A cost that involves spending money.

**Implicit cost** A nonmonetary opportunity cost.

**Economic profit** A firm's revenues minus all of its implicit and explicit costs.

## The Balance Sheet

**Balance sheet** A financial statement that sums up a firm's financial position on a particular day, usually the end of a quarter or year.

A firm's **balance sheet** sums up its financial position on a particular day, usually the end of a quarter or year. Recall that an asset is anything of value that a firm owns, and a liability is a debt or an obligation owed by a firm. Subtracting the value of a firm's liabilities from the value of its assets leaves its *net worth*. We can think of the net worth as what the firm's owners would be left with if the firm were closed, its assets were sold, and its liabilities were paid off. Investors can determine a firm's net worth by inspecting its balance sheet. We analyze a balance sheet in more detail in the appendix to this chapter, which begins on page 227.

which begins on page 227.

**7.5 LEARNING** OBJECTIVE

Understand the role of government in corporate governance.

# Corporate Governance Policy

A firm's financial statements provide important information on the firm's ability to create value for investors and the economy. Accurate and easy-to-understand financial statements are inputs to decisions by the firm's managers and by investors. Indeed, the information in accounting statements helps guide resource allocation in the economy.

Firms disclose financial statements in periodic filings to the federal government and in *annual reports* to shareholders. An investor is more likely to buy a firm's stock if the firm's income statement shows a large after-tax profit and if its balance sheet shows a large net worth. The top management of a firm has at least two reasons to attract investors and keep the firm's stock price high. First, a higher stock price increases the funds the firm can raise when it sells a given amount of stock. Second, to reduce the principal–agent problem, boards of directors often tie the salaries of top managers to the firm's stock price or to the profitability of the firm.

Top managers clearly have an incentive to maximize the profits reported on the income statement and the net worth reported on the balance sheet. If top managers make good decisions, the firm's profits will be high, and the firm's assets will be large relative to its liabilities. Problems that surfaced during the early 2000s, however, revealed that some top managers have inflated profits and hidden liabilities that should have been listed on their balance sheets. At other firms, managers took on more risk than they disclosed to investors. We will explore recent problems with corporate governance, and the government's reaction to these problems, by discussing the accounting scandals of the early 2000s and problems with many financial firms several years later.

## The Accounting Scandals of the Early 2000s

In the early 2000s, the top managers of several large and well-known firms, including Enron, an energy trading firm, and WorldCom, a telecommunications firm, were shown to have falsified the firm's financial statements in order to mislead investors about how profitable the firms actually were. Several top managers were sentenced to long jail terms, and some of the firms, including Enron, went out of business.

How was it possible for corporations such as Enron and WorldCom to falsify their financial statements? The federal government regulates how financial statements are prepared, but this regulation cannot by itself guarantee the accuracy of the statements. All firms that issue stock to the public have certified public accountants *audit* their financial statements. Unfortunately, as the Enron and WorldCom scandals revealed, top managers who are determined to deceive investors about the true financial condition of their firms can also deceive outside auditors.

To guard against future scandals, new federal legislation was enacted in 2002. The landmark *Sarbanes-Oxley Act of 2002* requires that CEOs personally certify the accuracy of financial statements. The Sarbanes-Oxley Act also requires that financial analysts and auditors disclose whether any conflicts of interest might exist that would limit their independence in evaluating a firm's financial condition. On balance, most observers acknowledge that the Sarbanes-Oxley Act increased confidence in the U.S. corporate governance system, though, as we will discuss in the next section, problems in the late 2000s at financial firms again raised questions of whether corporations were adequately disclosing information to investors.

## The Financial Meltdown of the Late 2000s

Beginning in 2007 and lasting into 2009, the U.S. economy suffered through the worst financial crisis since the Great Depression of the 1930s. At the heart of the crisis was a problem in the market for home mortgages. When people buy houses, they typically borrow the money by taking out a mortgage loan from a bank or another financial institution. The house they are buying is pledged as collateral for the loan, meaning that the bank can take possession of the house and sell it if the borrower defaults by failing to make the payments on the loan.

For many years, the bank or other financial institution granting the mortgage would keep the loan until the borrower had paid it off. Beginning in the 1970s, financial institutions began *securitizing* some mortgage loans, which means that groups of mortgages were bundled together and sold to investors. These *mortgage-backed securities* are very similar to bonds in that the investor who buys one receives regular interest payments, which in this case come from the payments being made on the original mortgage loans. At first, the securitization process was carried out by the Federal National Mortgage Association ("Fannie Mae") and the Federal Home Loan Mortgage Corporation ("Freddie Mac"), which had been established by Congress to help increase the volume of lending in the home mortgage market. Fannie and Freddie would buy mortgages granted to credit-worthy borrowers and bundle them into securities that were then sold to investors.

Beginning in the 1990s, private financial firms, primarily investment banks, became involved in securitizing mortgages. By the early 2000s, many mortgages were being granted by banks and other financial institutions to "subprime" borrowers, who are borrowers whose credit histories include failures to make payments on bills, and "Alt-A" borrowers, who failed to document that their incomes were high enough to afford their mortgage payments. Both subprime and Alt-A borrowers were more likely to default on loans than were conventional borrowers. Fueled by the ease of obtaining a mortgage, housing prices in the United States soared before beginning a sharp downturn in mid-2006. By 2007, many borrowers—particularly subprime and Alt-A borrowers—began to default on their mortgages. This was bad news for anyone owning mortgage-backed securities because the value of these securities depended on steady payments being made on the underlying mortgages. As prices of these securities plunged, many financial institutions suffered heavy losses, and some of the largest remained in business only because they received aid from the federal government.

During the financial crisis, many investors complained that they weren't aware of how risky some of the assets—particularly mortgage-backed securities—on the balance sheets of financial firms were. Some observers believed that the managers of many financial firms had intentionally misled investors about the riskiness of these assets. Others argued that the managers themselves had not understood how risky the assets were. As of mid-2009, the federal government was considering a number of steps to increase the regulation of financial firms in the wake of the crisis. In fall 2008, Fannie Mae and Freddie Mac were brought under direct control of the government. Other policy changes under consideration included tighter oversight of the types of assets that banks and other financial firms could hold and increases in the net worth, or capital, they would be required to maintain. Many economists were concerned about policymakers striking the right balance with new regulations. Regulations that were too restrictive would threaten the access of households to the credit necessary to finance purchases of homes, cars, and college educations, as well as the ability of firms to borrow the funds needed to finance their current operations and their future growth.

## Making the Connection

# Was the Principal–Agent Problem at the Heart of the Financial Crisis?

As we have seen, the process of securitizing mortgages played an important role in the financial crisis of 2007–2009. Beginning in the 1990s, private investment banks began to become involved in securitizing mortgages. Unlike commercial banks, whose main activities are accepting deposits and making loans, investment banks had traditionally concentrated on providing advice to corporations on selling new stocks and bonds and on *underwriting* the issuance of stocks and bonds by guaranteeing a price to the firm selling them. Investment banking is considered more risky than commercial banking because investment banks can suffer heavy losses on underwriting. To address this greater risk, Congress passed the Glass-Steagall Act in 1933. The act prevented financial firms from being both commercial banks and investment banks.

*Did principal–agent problems lay low this Wall Street bull?*

Some economists and policymakers argued that Glass-Steagall reduced competition for investment banking services by prohibiting commercial banks from offering these services. Congress repealed the Glass-Steagall Act in 1999, after which some commercial banks began engaging in investment banking. Many of the largest, best-known investment banks, such as Lehman Brothers, Bear Stearns, Goldman Sachs, Merrill Lynch, and Morgan Stanley, remained exclusively investment banks. The mortgage-backed securities originated by the investment banks were mostly sold to investors, but some were retained as investments by these firms. As a result, when the prices of these securities declined beginning in 2007, the investment banks suffered heavy losses. Lehman Brothers was forced to declare bankruptcy, Merrill Lynch and Bear Stearns were sold to commercial banks in deals arranged by the U.S. government, and Goldman Sachs and Morgan Stanley became bank holding companies, which allowed them to engage in commercial banking activity. With these developments, the era of the large Wall Street investment bank came to an end.

Why did the investment banks take on so much risk by originating securities backed by mortgages granted to borrowers who had a high likelihood of defaulting on the loans? Michael Lewis, a financial journalist and former Wall Street bond trader, has argued that a key reason was a change in how the investment banks were organized. Traditionally, Wall Street investment banks had been organized as partnerships, but by 2000 they had all converted to being publicly traded corporations. As we have seen, in a partnership the funds of the relatively small group of owners are put directly at risk, and the principal–agent problem is reduced because there is little separation of ownership from control. With a publicly traded corporation, on the other hand, the principal–agent problem can be severe. Lewis argues:

> No investment bank owned by its employees would have . . . bought and held $50 billion in [exotic mortgage-backed securities]. . . . or even allow [these securities] to be sold to its customers. The hoped-for short-term gain would not have justified the long-term hit.

Issues of corporate governance will clearly continue to be a concern for economists, policymakers, and investors.

Source: Michael Lewis, "The End," *Portfolio*, December 2008.

**myeconlab**   **YOUR TURN:** Test your understanding by doing related problem 5.6 on page 226 at the end of this chapter.

▶ Continued from page 203

## Economics in YOUR LIFE!

At the beginning of the chapter, we asked you to consider two questions: Why is it difficult to get the managers of a firm to act in your interest rather than in their own? and Given this problem, should you ever take on the risk of buying stock? The reason managers may not act in shareholders' interest is that in large corporations, there is separation of ownership from control: The shareholders own the firm, but the top managers actually control it. This results in the principal–agent problem discussed in the chapter. The principal–agent problem clearly adds to the risk you would face by buying stock rather than doing something safe with your money, such as putting it in the bank. But the rewards to owning stock can also be substantial, potentially earning you far more over the long run than a bank account will. Buying the stock of well-known firms, such as Google, that are closely followed by Wall Street investment analysts helps to reduce the principal–agent problem. It is less likely that the managers of these firms will take actions that are clearly not in the best interests of shareholders because the managers' actions are difficult to conceal. Buying the stock of large, well-known firms certainly does not completely eliminate the risk from the principal–agent problem, however. Enron, WorldCom, and some of the other firms that were involved in the scandals discussed in this chapter were all well known and closely followed by Wall Street analysts, as were the large financial firms that ran into difficulties in the late 2000s, but their stock turned out to be very poor investments.

# Conclusion

In a market system, firms make independent decisions about which goods and services to produce, how to produce them, and what prices to charge. In modern high-income countries, such as the United States, large corporations account for a majority of the sales and profits earned by firms. Generally, the managers of these corporations do a good job of representing the interests of stockholders, while providing the goods and services demanded by consumers. As the business scandals of the early 2000s and the problems with financial firms in the late 2000s showed, however, the principal–agent problem can sometimes become severe. Economists debate the costs and benefits of regulations proposed to address these problems.

*An Inside Look* on the next page discusses the possible principal–agent problem at Facebook.

## >> The Principal-Agent Problem at Facebook

### *THE (LONDON) TIMES*

## Facebook Founder Puts Idealism Before Profits

Mark Zuckerberg is dog-tired and perhaps a little grumpy. The 24-year-old founder of Facebook is in London towards the end of a week-long tour of Europe and has been averaging less than five hours' sleep a night.

Being the "face" of Facebook is not his favourite part of the job and he has had some tricky questions to fend off from the European media about Facebook and its future development, particularly the niggling doubt over exactly how and when the social networking site is going to make money.

The technology blogs in Silicon Valley have been giving Facebook a hard time recently. The phenomenal popularity of the site—which is not even five years old—is no longer enough for some analysts.

Mr Zuckerberg and three others launched the site from their Harvard dorm room in early 2004. By the end of the year it already had one million active users—now it has exploded past the 110 million mark and shows no sign of slowing down. . . .

**a** Facebook is still independent, still private, still, in fact, very much Mr Zuckerberg's baby—and that is the way he wants it to stay while he concentrates on growing the user base.

"People all over the world have friends, family, co-workers they want to stay connected to and we have found that Facebook is something everyone could use. We have just hit this big milestone—100 million active users—and in a lot of ways that is a really cool thing for us, but in a lot of ways it is really just the start."

Some have mistaken his ambition for hubris. Mr Zuckerberg's geeky, aloof style can be awkward but there is no doubting the drive of a man who happily admits that the only thing he does outside work is sleep.

**b** What about making money? Turning that huge growth into cash is proving problematic. By Mr Zuckerberg's own estimates in early 2008 Facebook will make only about $300 million (£173.5million) in revenues this year, mainly in display advertising on the site in a deal with Microsoft, and will have a negative cashflow of about $150 million. Yet Mr Zuckerberg says that he is in no hurry. For the time being, he simply wants enough income to "sustain ourselves". This attitude, especially in gloomy economic times with the prospect of an IPO disappearing over the horizon, has attracted criticism.

Mr Zuckerberg says that Facebook has a strong advertising business and it is building an international salesforce to improve it further. It is also experimenting with a new type of advertising product—"engagement ads" which encourage users to share and comment, raising brand awareness. MTV recently had a successful trial with a promotion for its video awards on the site.

**c** Yet the truth is that making money is not Mr Zuckerberg's prime motivation (he is angrily forceful on this point). He retains his youthful idealism that Facebook can and should change the way people live for the better by connecting them to each other. "The goal of the company is to help people to share more in order to make the world more open and to help promote understanding between people. The long-term belief is that if we can succeed in this mission then we also will be able to build a pretty good business and everyone can be financially rewarded."

In the meantime, in an effort to keep senior staff happy after a flurry of departures, including Dustin Moskovitz, the co-founder, Facebook is to help employees to sell their company shares privately, up to a value of $900,000 each. The private stock sales are said to be at a valuation of only $3.75 billion, a huge drop from the $15 billion valuation of a year ago when Microsoft took a 1.6 per cent stake for $246 million.

For the moment such statistics do not overly concern Facebook's chief executive. He believes that building the business is the key to success. He has been pretty good at it so far.

*Source:* Mike Harvey, "Facebook Founder Mark Zuckerberg Puts Idealism Before Profits," *The (London) Times*, October 20, 2008.

## Key Points in the Article

Facebook has been growing rapidly; the number of Facebook users is growing rapidly. And that is the goal. Profits, however, are another matter. The company has yet to make a profit. Right now, the company is still privately owned. The owners consist of the company's founder, Mark Zuckerberg, and some investors. The figure below tracks the growth of Facebook users and investors. While profit is the primary concern of most company owners, Mr Zuckerberg wants to change the world, or at least how people interact with each other. He believes that if Facebook can accomplish that, profits will follow.

## Analyzing the News

(a) Some companies are publicly traded, while others are privately held. Most large corporations are owned by stockholders—people who buy stock, or ownership, in the company. These shares of stock can be bought and sold. The managers run the day-to-day operations of the firm; however, it is the stockholders who own it. These stockholders, through their representatives, have the right to hire or fire top managers. A privately held company does not have all the formal structures of a public corporation. The article reports that Zuckerberg wants to stay in control of the company, which the article describes as "his baby." This may explain why the company is still private. If Facebook were to sell shares of stock, then Zuckerberg could be forced to give up control of "his baby."

(b) Facebook has many of the same problems as other start-up companies. Companies often lose money during their first few years. In Facebook's case, the company needed investors to provide money not just to finance the purchase of capital equipment such as servers, but also to finance salaries and other operating expenses. During the 1990s, many investors were willing to supply money to start-up Internet companies. Ultimately, many of these companies failed and their investors lost their money. So far, Facebook looks like many of those 1990s-era Internet start-up firms—building an audience but having a slow road to profitability. It's an open question how long Facebook can continue to attract investors if it does not start to turn a profit.

(c) The chapter discusses the principal–agent problem. Normally the principal–agent problem occurs in publicly traded companies, where the owners do not manage the company. Normally, in a privately held company, where the founder and majority shareholder also runs the company, there is no principal–agent problem; management and ownership do not have differing interests because management and ownership are one and the same. In the case of Facebook, Zuckerberg is not the only owner. His investors also own part of the company. These investors want the company to earn a profit. The article states that Zuckerberg is interested in changing the world—and also making himself famous. Zuckerberg believes that the profit will come later, if he can attract enough users and accomplish his goal of changing the way people interact with each other online. If he is right, his investors will be happy. If not, then we have another example of the principal–agent problem.

## Thinking Critically

1. Compensating executives with stock, or equity, is a way to solve the principal–agent problem, but the practice is not without flaws. Critics of equity compensation point out that it can create incentives for executives to take actions not in the best interests of other shareholders and may have contributed to the corporate scandals of the early 2000s discussed in the chapter. How could equity compensation have contributed to these scandals?

2. In August 2006, Microsoft and Facebook reached an important advertising deal. In October 2006, they reached a deal for Microsoft to acquire 1.6 percent of Facebook for $240 million. An executive at Facebook who knew when these deals would be announced could have earned a bundle quickly by buying Microsoft stock and then selling it at a higher price a day or so later. Such "insider trading" is illegal, however. Do you think that insider trading should be illegal? Are there benefits to other investors or to the economy as a whole associated with such trading? Are there problems associated with such trading?

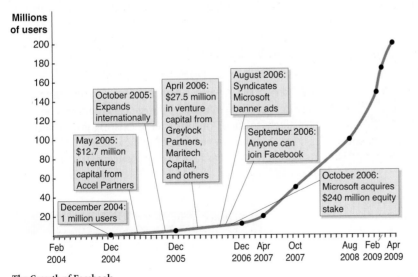

**The Growth of Facebook.**
Source: www.facebook.com/press/info.php?statistics

# Key Terms

---

**7.1** **Types of Firms, pages 204–206**

LEARNING OBJECTIVE: Categorize the major types of firms in the United States,

## Summary

There are three types of firms: A **sole proprietorship** is a firm owned by a single individual and not organized as a corporation. A **partnership** is a firm owned jointly by two or more persons and not organized as a corporation. A **corporation** is a legal form of business that provides the owners with limited liability. An **asset** is anything of value owned by a person or a firm. The owners of sole proprietorships and partners have unlimited liability, which means there is no legal distinction between the personal assets of the owners of the business and the assets of the business. The owners of corporations have **limited liability**, which means they can never lose more than their investment in the firm. Although only 20 percent of firms are corporations, they account for the majority of revenue and profit earned by all firms.

 Visit **www.myeconlab.com** to complete these exercises online and get instant feedback.

## Review Questions

**1.1** What are the three major types of firms in the United States? Briefly discuss the most important characteristics of each type.

**1.2** What is limited liability? Why does the government grant limited liability to the owners of corporations?

## Problems and Applications

**1.3** Suppose that shortly after graduating from college, you decide to start your own business. Will you be likely to organize the business as a sole proprietor-ship, a partnership, or a corporation? Explain your reasoning.

**1.4** Evaluate the following argument:

> I would like to invest in the stock market, but I think that buying shares of stock in a corporation is too risky. Suppose I buy $10,000 of General Electric stock, and the company ends up going bankrupt. Because as a stockholder I'm part owner of the company, and I might be responsible for paying hundreds of thousands of dollars of the company's debts.

**1.5** According to an article in *The Economist* magazine, historian David Faure has argued that the Chinese economy failed to grow rapidly during the nineteenth century because "family-run companies . . . could" not raise sufficient capital to exploit the large-scale opportunities tied to the rise of the steam engine, notably railways and (with limited exceptions) global shipping and automated manufacturing." How did the United States solve the problem of firms raising enough funds to operate railroads and other large-scale businesses?

Source: "The PCCW Buy-out in Court," *Economist*, April 21, 2009.

**1.6** **(Related to the *Making the Connection* on page 206)** Why might large existing firms be more likely to focus on improving existing goods and services than on introducing new ones? Why might small new firms take the opposite approach?

>> **End Learning Objective 7.1**

## 7.2 The Structure of Corporations and the Principal–Agent Problem, pages 206–208

LEARNING OBJECTIVE: Describe the typical management structure of corporations and understand the concepts of separation of ownership from control and the principal–agent problem.

## Summary

**Corporate governance** refers to the way in which a corporation is structured and the impact a corporation's structure has on the firm's behavior. Most corporations have a similar management structure: The shareholders elect a board of directors that appoints the corporation's top managers, such as the chief executive officer (CEO). Because the top management often does not own a large fraction of the stock in the corporation, large corporations have a **separation of ownership from control**. Because top managers have less incentive to increase the corporation's profits than to increase their own salaries and their own enjoyment, corporations can suffer from the **principal–agent problem**. The principal–agent problem exists when the principals—in this case, the shareholders of the corporation—have difficulty getting the agent—the corporation's top management—to carry out their wishes.

 Visit **www.myeconlab.com** to complete these exercises online and get instant feedback.

## Review Questions

2.1 What do we mean by the separation of ownership from control in large corporations?

2.2 How is the separation of ownership from control related to the principal–agent problem?

## Problems and Applications

2.3 The principal–agent problem arises almost everywhere in the business world, and it also crops up even closer to home. Discuss the principal–agent problem that exists in the college classroom. Who is the principal? Who is the agent? What is the problem between this principal and this agent?

2.4 **(Related to *Solved Problem 7-2* on page 207)** Briefly explain whether you agree or disagree with the following argument: "The separation of ownership from control in large corporations and the principal–agent problem means that top managers can work short days, take long vacations, and otherwise slack off."

2.5 **(Related to *Solved Problem 7-2* on page 207)** An economic consultant gives the board of directors of a firm the following advice:

> You can increase the profitability of the firm if you change your method of compensating top management. Instead of paying your top management a straight salary, you should pay them a salary plus give them the right to buy the firm's stock in the future at a price above the stock's current market price.

Explain the consultant's reasoning. To what difficulties might this compensation scheme lead?

2.6 The following is from an article in *BusinessWeek*:

> How do board members feel about the level of the executive compensation in the U.S.? Board members do acknowledge that CEO compensation is frequently too high. For the last 10 years more than 25% of board members have said it is generally too high, and 50% agree that it is too rich in some high-profile cases.
>
> Given this attitude, one might wonder why board members have not been more active in controlling CEO pay. Part of the answer lies in their opinions about the compensation of their own company's CEO. In our recent survey of 115 boards, 85% of board members report that their CEO's compensation program is effective. Board members tend to feel, "We're okay; it's the other guys who are the problem." Given this and that they work for the CEO, it is not surprising that boards continue to support high levels of CEO compensation.

What do you think the author meant by the statement: "Given this and that they work for the CEO, it is not surprising that boards continue to support high levels of CEO compensation"? How does this statement relate to the principal–agent problem?

Source: Edward E. Lawler III, "Fixing Executive Compensation Excesses," *BusinessWeek*, February 5, 2009.

>> **End Learning Objective 7.2**

## 7.3 How Firms Raise Funds, pages 208–214

LEARNING OBJECTIVE: Explain how firms raise the funds they need to operate and expand.

## Summary

Firms rely on retained earnings—which are profits retained by the firm and not paid out to the firm's owners—or on using the savings of households for the funds they need to operate and expand. With **direct finance**, the savings of households flow directly to businesses when investors buy **stocks** and **bonds** in financial markets. With **indirect finance**, savings flow indirectly to businesses when households deposit money in saving and checking accounts in banks and the banks lend these funds to businesses. Federal, state, and local governments also sell bonds in financial markets, and households also borrow funds from banks. When a firm sells a bond, it is borrowing money from the buyer of the bond. The firm makes a **coupon payment** to the buyer of the bond. The **interest rate** is the cost of borrowing funds, usually expressed as a percentage of the amount borrowed. When a firm sells stock, it is selling part ownership of the firm to the buyer of the stock. **Dividends** are payments by a corporation to its shareholders. The original purchasers of stocks and bonds may resell them in stock and bond markets, such as the New York Stock Exchange. The performance of the U.S. stock market is often measured using stock market indexes. The three most widely followed stock indexes are the Dow Jones Industrial Average, the S&P 500, and the NASDAQ composite index.

 Visit **www.myeconlab.com** to complete these exercises online and get instant feedback.

## Review Questions

3.1 What is the difference between direct finance and indirect finance? If you borrow money from a bank to buy a new car, are you using direct finance or indirect finance?

3.2 Why is a bond considered to be a loan but a share of stock is not? Why do corporations issue both bonds and shares of stock?

3.3 How do the stock and bond markets provide information to businesses? Why do stock and bond prices change over time?

## Problems and Applications

3.4 Suppose that a firm in which you have invested is losing money. Would you rather own the firm's stock or the firm's bonds? Explain.

3.5 Suppose you originally invested in a firm when it was small and unprofitable. Now the firm has grown considerably and is large and profitable. Would you be

better off if you had bought the firm's stock or the firm's bonds? Explain.

3.6 If you deposit $20,000 in a savings account at a bank, you might earn 3 percent interest per year. Someone who borrows $20,000 from a bank to buy a new car might have to pay an interest rate of 8 percent per year on the loan. Knowing this, why don't you just lend your money directly to the car buyer, cutting out the bank?

3.7 (Related to the *Chapter Opener* on page 203) The owners of Facebook have had several opportunities to sell the company to larger firms or to make the firm a public corporation by selling stock. In 2009, the value of Facebook was estimated to be somewhere between $2 billion and $5 billion. So, selling Facebook or making it a public corporation would make Mark Zuckerberg and its other owners very wealthy. In those circumstances, why might a firm like Facebook choose to remain a private company?

Source: Felix Salmon, "Facebook Eyes Additional Funding," Reuters.com, April 30, 2009.

3.8 What impact would the following events be likely to have on the price of Google's stock?
   a. A competitor launches a search engine that's just as good as Google's.
   b. The corporate income tax is abolished.
   c. Google's board of directors becomes dominated by close friends and relatives of its top management.
   d. The price of wireless Internet connections unexpectedly drops, so more and more people use the Internet.
   e. Google announces a huge profit of $1 billion, but everybody anticipated that Google would earn a huge profit of $1 billion.

3.9 In 2005, the French government began issuing bonds with 50-year maturities. Would such bonds be purchased only by very young investors who expect to still be alive when the bond matures? Briefly explain.

3.10 (Related to the *Don't Let This Happen to You!* on page 210) Briefly explain whether you agree or disagree with the following statement: "The total value of the shares of Microsoft stock traded on the NASDAQ last week was $250 million, so the firm actually received more revenue from stock sales than from selling software."

3.11 (Related to the *Making the Connection* on page 213) Loans from banks are the most important external source of funds to businesses because most businesses are too small to borrow in financial markets by issuing stocks or bonds. Most investors are reluctant to buy the stocks or bonds of small businesses because of the difficulty of gathering accurate information on the financial strength and profitability of the businesses. Nevertheless, news about the stock market is included in nearly every network news program and is often the lead story in the business section of most newspapers. Is there a contradiction here? Why is the average viewer of TV news or the average reader of a newspaper interested in the fluctuations in prices in the stock market?

3.12 (Related to *Solved Problem 7-3* on page 211) Assets such as stocks and bonds are traded in stock markets and bond markets. In these markets, one owner of an asset sells it to another owner. These types of markets are called *secondary markets*. Can firms raise funds through secondary markets?

>> **End Learning Objective 7.3**

---

## 7.4 | Using Financial Statements to Evaluate a Corporation, pages 214–216

LEARNING OBJECTIVE: Understand the information provided in corporations' financial statements.

## Summary

A firm's **income statement** sums up its revenues, costs, and profit over a period of time. A firm's **balance sheet** sums up its financial position on a particular day, usually the end of a quarter or year. A balance sheet records a firm's assets and liabilities. A **liability** is anything owed by a person or a firm. Firms report their **accounting profit** on their income statements. Accounting profit does not always include all of a firm's **opportunity cost**. **Explicit cost** is a cost that involves spending money. **Implicit cost** is a nonmonetary opportunity cost. Because accounting profit excludes some implicit costs, it is larger than **economic profit**.

 Visit **www.myeconlab.com** to complete these exercises online and get instant feedback.

## Review Questions

4.1 What is the difference between a firm's assets and its liabilities? Give an example of an asset and an example of a liability.

4.2 What is the difference between a firm's balance sheet and a firm's income statement?

## Problems and Applications

4.3 Paolo currently has $100,000 invested in bonds that earn him 10 percent interest per year. He wants to open a pizza restaurant and is considering either selling the bonds and using the $100,000 to start his restaurant or borrowing the $100,000 from a bank, which would charge him an annual interest rate of 7 percent. He finally decides to sell the bonds and not take out the bank loan. He reasons, "Because I already have the $100,000 invested in the bonds, I don't have to pay anything to use the money. If I take out the bank loan, I have to pay interest, so my costs of producing pizza will be higher if I take out the loan than if I sell the bonds." What do you think of Paolo's reasoning?

4.4 Paolo and Alfredo are twins who both want to open pizza restaurants. Their parents have always liked Alfredo best, and they buy two pizza ovens and give both to him. Unfortunately, Paolo must buy his own pizza ovens. Does Alfredo have a lower cost of producing pizza than Paolo does because Alfredo received his pizza ovens as a gift while Paolo had to pay for his? Briefly explain.

4.5 Dane decides to give up a job earning $100,000 per year as a corporate lawyer and converts the duplex that he owns into a UFO museum. (He had been renting out the duplex for $20,000 a year.) His direct expenses include $50,000 per year paid to his assistants and $10,000 per year for utilities. Fans flock to the museum to see his collection of extraterrestrial paraphernalia, which he could easily sell on eBay for $1,000,000. Over the course of the year, the museum brings in revenues of $100,000.

a. How much is Dane's accounting profit for the year?

b. Is Dane earning an economic profit? Explain.

4.6 The Securities and Exchange Commission requires that every firm that wishes to issue stock and bonds to the public make available its balance sheet and income statement. Briefly explain how information useful to investors can be found in these financial statements.

>> **End Learning Objective 7.4**

**7.5** **Corporate Governance Policy, pages 216–218**
LEARNING OBJECTIVE: Understand the role of government in corporate governance.

## Summary

Because their compensation often rises with the profitability of the corporation, top managers have an incentive to overstate the profits reported on their firm's income statements. During the early 2000s, it became clear that the top managers of several large corporations had done this, even though intentionally falsifying financial statements is illegal. The *Sarbanes-Oxley Act* of 2002 took several steps intended to increase the accuracy of financial statements and increase the penalties for falsifying them. During the late 2000s, the financial crisis revealed that many financial firms held assets that were far riskier than investors had realized.

 Visit **www.myeconlab.com** to complete these exercises online and get instant feedback.

## Review Questions

**5.1** What is the Sarbanes-Oxley Act? Why was it passed?

**5.2** What was the source of the problems encountered by many financial firms during the late 2000s?

## Problems and Applications

**5.3** The following is from an article in *USA Today*:

> In what some call a worldwide corporate-governance movement, shareholders are pushing for stronger corporate-governance laws, teaming with investors from different countries and negotiating behind the scenes with businesses.
>
> In earlier years, it was hard for shareholders to dig up details from thousands of global companies on their finances, their directors, executives' pay packages and other information critical to making investment moves.

What is corporate governance? Why would shareholders push for stronger corporate governance laws?

Source: Edward Iwata, "Corporate governance gets more transparent worldwide," *USA Today*, February 17, 2008.

**5.4** An article in *BusinessWeek* stated that the Allstate Corporation, a large insurance company, would now require a simple majority vote of shareholders, rather than a two-thirds majority vote, to elect members to its board of directors and to remove directors in between annual meetings when elections are held. The article also stated that the price of Allstate's stock rose following the announcement. Briefly discuss whether there may have been a possible connection between these changes in Allstate's corporate governance and the increase in the firm's stock price.

Source: "Allstate Announces Changes to Governance," *BusinessWeek*, February 20, 2007.

**5.5** According to a survey in 2007, 78 percent of corporate executives responding believed that the costs of complying with the Sarbanes-Oxley Act outweighed the benefits. The total costs of compliance were about $2.92 million per company. Is it possible to put a dollar value on the benefits to complying with Sarbanes-Oxley? Which groups are likely to receive the most benefits from Sarbanes-Oxley: investors, corporations, or some other group?

Source: Kara Scannell, "Costs to Comply with Sarbanes-Oxley Decline Again," *Wall Street Journal*, May 16, 2007, p. C7.

**5.6** **(Related to the** *Making the Connection* **on page 218)** The first Wall Street investment bank to become a publicly traded corporation was Salomon Brothers (which later became part of Citigroup). John Gutfreund was head of the firm at that time. In an interview with Michael Lewis in 2008, Gutfreund "agreed that the main effect of turning a partnership into a corporation was to transfer the financial risk to the shareholders. 'When things go wrong, it's their problem,' he said. . . . " What does it mean "to transfer financial risk to the shareholders"? How might the large investment banks have behaved differently during the 2000s if they had remained partnerships?

Source: Michael Lewis, "The End," *Portfolio*, December 2008.

>> **End Learning Objective 7.5**

# Appendix

## Tools to Analyze Firms' Financial Information

**LEARNING** OBJECTIVE

Understand the concept of present value and the information contained on a firm's income statement and balance sheet.

As we saw in the chapter, modern business organizations are not just "black boxes" transforming inputs into output. Most business revenues and profits are earned by large corporations. Unlike founder-dominated firms, the typical large corporation is run by managers who generally do not own a controlling interest in the firm. Large firms raise funds from outside investors, and outside investors seek information on firms and the assurance that the managers of firms will act in the interests of the investors.

This chapter showed how corporations raise funds by issuing stocks and bonds. This appendix provides more detail to support that discussion. We begin by analyzing *present value* as a key concept in determining the prices of financial securities. We then provide greater information on *financial statements* issued by corporations, using Google as an example.

## Using Present Value to Make Investment Decisions

Firms raise funds by selling equity (stock) and debt (bonds and loans) to investors and lenders. If you own shares of stock or a bond, you will receive payments in the form of dividends or coupons over a number of years. Most people value funds they already have more highly than funds they will receive some time in the future. For example, you would probably not trade $1,000 you already have for $1,000 you will not receive for one year. The longer you have to wait to receive a payment, the less value it will have for you. One thousand dollars you will not receive for two years is worth less to you than $1,000 you will receive after one year. The value you give today to money you will receive in the future is called the future payment's **present value**. The present value of $1,000 you will receive in one year will be less than $1,000.

Why is this true? Why is the $1,000 you will not receive for one year less valuable to you than the $1,000 you already have? The most important reason is that if you have $1,000 today, you can use that $1,000 today. You can buy goods and services with the money and receive enjoyment from them. The $1,000 you receive in one year does not have direct use to you now.

Also, prices will likely rise during the year you are waiting to receive your $1,000. So, when you finally do receive the $1,000 in one year, you will not be able to buy as much with it as you could with $1,000 today. Finally, there is some risk that you will not receive the $1,000 in one year. The risk may be very great if an unreliable friend borrows $1,000 from you and vaguely promises to pay you back in one year. The risk may be very small if you lend money to the federal government by buying a United States Treasury bond. In either case, though, there is at least some risk that you will not receive the funds promised.

When someone lends money, the lender expects to be paid back both the amount of the loan and some additional interest. Say that you decide that you are willing to lend your $1,000 today if you are paid back $1,100 one year from now. In this case, you are charging $100/$1,000 = 0.10, or 10 percent interest on the funds you have loaned. Economists would say that you value $1,000 today as equivalent to the $1,100 to be received one year in the future.

**Present value** The value in today's dollars of funds to be paid or received in the future.

Notice that $1,100 can be written as $1,000 $(1 + 0.10)$. That is, the value of money received in the future is equal to the value of money in the present multiplied by 1 plus the interest rate, with the interest rate expressed as a decimal. Or:

$$\$1,100 = 1,000(1 + 0.10).$$

Notice, also, that if we divide both sides by $(1 + 0.10)$, we can rewrite this formula as:

$$\$1,000 = \frac{\$1,100}{(1 + 0.10)}.$$

The rewritten formula states that the present value is equal to the future value to be received in one year divided by one plus the interest rate. This formula is important because you can use it to convert any amount to be received in one year into its present value. Writing the formula generally, we have:

$$\text{Present Value} = \frac{\text{Future Value}_1}{(1 + i)}.$$

The present value of funds to be received in one year—Future Value$_1$—can be calculated by dividing the amount of those funds to be received by 1 plus the interest rate. With an interest rate of 10 percent, the present value of $1,000,000 to be received one year from now is:

$$\frac{\$1,000,000}{(1 + 0.10)} = \$909,090.91.$$

This method is a very useful way of calculating the value today of funds that won't be received for one year. But financial securities such as stocks and bonds involve promises to pay funds over many years. Therefore, it would be even more useful if we could expand this formula to calculate the present value of funds to be received more than one year in the future.

This expansion is easy to do. Go back to the original example, where we assumed you were willing to loan out your $1,000 for one year, provided that you received 10 percent interest. Suppose you are asked to lend the funds for two years and that you are promised 10 percent interest per year for each year of the loan. That is, you are lending $1,000, which at 10 percent interest will grow to $1,100 after one year, and you are agreeing to loan that $1,100 out for a second year at 10 percent interest. So, after two years, you will be paid back $1,100 $(1 + 0.10)$, or $1,210. Or:

$$\$1,210 = \$1,000(1 + 0.10)(1 + 0.10),$$

or:

$$\$1,210 = \$1,000(1 + 0.10)^2.$$

This formula can also be rewritten as:

$$\$1,000 = \frac{\$1,210}{(1 + 0.10)^2}.$$

To put this formula in words, the $1,210 you receive two years from now has a present value equal to $1,210 divided by the quantity 1 plus the interest rate squared. If you were to agree to lend out your $1,000 for three years at 10 percent interest, you would receive:

$$\$1,331 = \$1,000(1 + 0.10)^3.$$

Notice, again, that:

$$\$1,000 = \frac{\$1,331}{(1 + 0.10)^3}.$$

You can probably see a pattern here. We can generalize the concept to say that the present value of funds to be received $n$ years in the future—whether $n$ is 1, 20, or 85 does not matter—equals the amount of the funds to be received divided by the quantity 1 plus the interest rate raised to the $n$th power. For instance, with an interest rate of 10 percent, the value of $1,000,000 to be received 25 years in the future is:

$$\text{Present Value} = \frac{\$1,000,000}{(1 + 0.10)^{25}} = \$92,296.$$

Or, more generally:

$$\text{Present Value} = \frac{\text{Future Value}_n}{(1 + i)^n}$$

where Future Value$_n$ represents funds that will be received in $n$ years.

# Solved Problem | 7A-1

## How to Receive Your Contest Winnings

Suppose you win a contest and are given the choice of the following prizes:

**Prize 1:** $50,000 to be received right away, with four additional payments of $50,000 to be received each year for the next four years

**Prize 2:** $175,000 to be received right away

Explain which prize you would choose and the basis for your decision.

## SOLVING THE PROBLEM:

**Step 1:** **Review the material.** This problem involves applying the concept of present value, so you may want to review the section "Using Present Value to Make Investment Decisions," which begins on page 227.

**Step 2:** **Explain the basis for choosing the prize.** Unless you need cash immediately, you should choose the prize with the highest present value.

**Step 3:** **Calculate the present value of each prize.** Prize 2 consists of one payment of $175,000 received right away, so its present value is $175,000. Prize 1 consists of five payments spread out over time. To find the present value of the prize, we must find the present value of each of these payments and add them together. To calculate present value, we must use an interest rate. Let's assume an interest rate of 10 percent. In that case, the present value of Prize 1 is:

$$\$50,000 + \frac{\$50,000}{(1 + 0.10)} + \frac{\$50,000}{(1 + 0.10)^2} + \frac{\$50,000}{(1 + 0.10)^3} + \frac{\$50,000}{(1 + 0.10)^4} =$$

$$\$50,000 + \$45,454.55 + \$41,322.31 + \$37,565.74 + \$34,150.67 = \$208,493.$$

**Step 4:** **State your conclusion.** Prize 1 has the greater present value, so you should choose it rather than Prize 2.

**YOUR TURN:** For more practice, do related problems 7A.6, 7A.8, 7A.9, and 7A.10 on pages 234–235 at the end of this appendix.

## Using Present Value to Calculate Bond Prices

Anyone who buys a financial asset, such as shares of stock or a bond, is really buying a promise to receive certain payments—dividends in the case of shares of stock or coupons in the case of a bond. The price investors are willing to pay for a financial asset should be equal to the value of the payments they will receive as a result of owning the asset. Because most of the coupon or dividend payments will be received in the future, it is their present value that matters. Put another way, we have the following important idea: *The price of a financial asset should be equal to the present value of the payments to be received from owning that asset.*

Let's consider an example. Suppose that in 1982, General Electric issued a bond with an $80 coupon that will mature in 2012. It is now 2010, and that bond has been bought and sold by investors many times. You are considering buying it. If you buy the bond, you will receive two years of coupon payments plus a final payment of the bond's principal, or face value, of $1,000. Suppose, once again, that you need an interest rate of 10 percent to invest your funds. If the bond has a coupon of $80, the present value of the payments you receive from owning the bond—and, therefore, the present value of the bond—will be:

$$\text{Present Value} = \frac{\$80}{(1 + 0.10)} + \frac{\$80}{(1 + 0.10)^2} + \frac{\$1,000}{(1 + 0.10)^2} = \$965.29.$$

That is, the present value of the bond will equal the present value of the three payments you will receive during the two years you own the bond. You should, therefore, be willing to pay $965.29 to own this bond and have the right to receive these payments from GE. This process of calculating present values of future payments is used to determine bond prices, with one qualification: The relevant interest rate used by investors in the bond market to calculate the present value and, therefore, the price of an existing bond is usually the coupon rate on comparable newly issued bonds. Therefore, the general formula for the price of a bond is:

$$\text{Bond Price} = \frac{\text{Coupon}_1}{(1 + i)} + \frac{\text{Coupon}_2}{(1 + i)^2} + \cdots + \frac{\text{Coupon}_n}{(1 + i)^n} + \frac{\text{Face Value}}{(1 + i)^n},$$

where $\text{Coupon}_1$ is the coupon payment to be received after one year, $\text{Coupon}_2$ is the coupon payment to be received after two years, up to $\text{Coupon}_n$, which is the coupon payment received in the year the bond matures. The ellipsis takes the place of the coupon payments—if any—received between the second year and the year when the bond matures. Face Value is the face value of the bond, to be received when the bond matures. The interest rate on comparable newly issued bonds is $i$.

## Using Present Value to Calculate Stock Prices

When you own a firm's stock, you are legally entitled to your share of the firm's profits. Remember that the profits a firm pays out to its shareholders are referred to as *dividends*. The price of a share of stock should be equal to the present value of the dividends investors expect to receive as a result of owning that stock. Therefore, the general formula for the price of a stock is:

$$\text{Stock Price} = \frac{\text{Dividend}_1}{(1 + i)} + \frac{\text{Dividend}_2}{(1 + i)^2} + \cdots$$

Notice that this formula looks very similar to the one we used to calculate the price of a bond, with a couple of important differences. First, unlike a bond, stock has no maturity date, so we have to calculate the present value of an infinite number of dividend payments. At first, it may seem that the stock's price must be infinite as well, but remember that dollars you don't receive for many years are worth very little today. For instance, a dividend payment of $10 that will be received 40 years in the future is worth only a little more than $0.20 today at a 10 percent interest rate. The second difference between the stock price formula and the bond price formula is that whereas the coupon payments you receive from owning the bond are known with certainty—they are written on the bond and cannot be changed—you don't know for sure what the dividend payments from owning a stock will be. How large a dividend payment you will receive depends on how profitable the company will be in the future.

Although it is possible to forecast the future profitability of a company, this cannot be done with perfect accuracy. To emphasize this point, some economists rewrite the basic stock price formula by adding a superscript *e* to each dividend term to emphasize that these are *expected* dividend payments. Because the future profitability of companies is often very difficult to forecast, it is not surprising that differences of opinion exist over what the price of a particular stock should be. Some investors will be very optimistic about the future profitability of a company and will, therefore, believe that the company's stock should have a high price. Other investors might be very pessimistic and believe that the company's stock should have a low price.

## A Simple Formula for Calculating Stock Prices

It is possible to simplify the formula for determining the price of a stock, if we assume that dividends will grow at a constant rate:

$$\text{Stock Price} = \frac{\text{Dividend}}{(i - \text{Growth Rate})}.$$

In this equation, Dividend is the dividend expected to be received one year from now, and Growth Rate is the rate at which those dividends are expected to grow. If a company pays a dividend of $1 per share to be received one year from now and Growth Rate is 10 percent, the company is expected to pay a dividend of $1.10 the following year, $1.21 the year after that, and so on.

Now suppose that IBM pays a dividend of $5 per share, the consensus of investors is that these dividends will increase at a rate of 5 percent per year for the indefinite future, and the interest rate is 10 percent. Then the price of IBM's stock should be:

$$\text{Stock Price} = \frac{\$5.00}{(0.10 - 0.05)} = \$100.00.$$

Particularly during the years 1999 and 2000, there was much discussion of whether the high prices of many Internet stocks—such as the stock of Amazon.com—were justified, given that many of these companies had not made any profit yet and so had not paid any dividends. Is there any way that a rational investor would pay a high price for the stock of a company currently not earning profits? The formula for determining stock prices shows that it is possible, provided that the investor's assumptions are optimistic enough! For example, during 1999, one stock analyst predicted that Amazon.com would soon be earning $10 per share of stock. That is, Amazon.com's total earnings divided by the number of shares of its stock outstanding would be $10. Suppose Amazon.com pays out that $10 in dividends and that the $10 will grow rapidly over the years, by, say, 7 percent per year. Then our formula indicates that the price of Amazon.com stock should be:

$$\text{Stock Price} = \frac{\$10.00}{(\$0.10 - 0.07)} = \$333.33.$$

If you are sufficiently optimistic about the future prospects of a company, a high stock price can be justified even if the company is not currently earning a profit. But investors in growth stocks must be careful. Suppose investors believe that growth prospects for Amazon are only 4 percent per year instead of 7 percent because the firm turns out not to be as profitable as initially believed. Then our formula indicates that the price of Amazon.com stock should be:

$$\text{Stock Price} = \frac{\$10.00}{(\$0.10 - 0.04)} = \$166.67.$$

This price is only half the price determined assuming a more optimistic growth rate. Hence investors use information about a firm's profitability and growth prospects to determine what the firm is worth.

# Going Deeper into Financial Statements

Corporations disclose substantial information about their business operations and financial position to actual and potential investors. Some of this information meets the demands of participants in financial markets and of information-collection agencies, such as Moody's Investors Service, which develops credit ratings that help investors judge how risky corporate bonds are. Other information meets the requirements of the U.S. Securities and Exchange Commission.

Key sources of information about a corporation's profitability and financial position are its principal financial statements—the *income statement* and the *balance sheet*. These important information sources were first introduced in the chapter. Here we go into more detail, using recent data for Google as an example.

## Analyzing Income Statements

As discussed in the chapter, a firm's income statement summarizes its revenues, costs, and profit over a period of time. Figure 7A-1 shows Google's income statement for 2008.

Google's income statement presents the results of the company's operations during the year. Listed first are the revenues it earned, largely from selling advertising on its Web site, from January 1, 2008, to December 31, 2008: $21,796 million. Listed next are Google's operating expenses, the most important of which is its *cost of revenue*—which is commonly known as *cost of sales* or *cost of goods sold*: $8,622 million. Cost of revenue is the direct cost of producing the products sold, including in this case the salaries of the

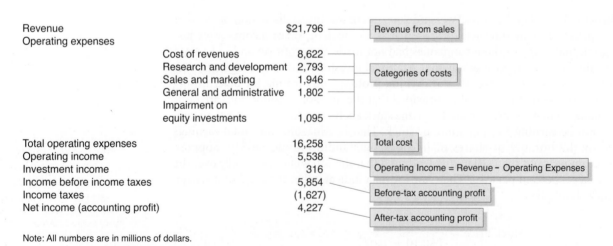

Note: All numbers are in millions of dollars.

## Figure 7A-1    Google's Income Statement for 2008

Google's income statement shows the company's revenue, costs, and profit for 2008. The difference between its revenue ($21,796 million) and its operating expenses ($16,258 million) is its operating income ($5,538 million). Most corporations also have investments, such as government or corporate bonds, that generate some income for them. In this case, Google earned $316 million, giving the firm an income before taxes of $5,854 million. After paying taxes of $1,627 million, Google was left with a net income, or accounting profit, of $4,227 million for the year.

Source: "Annual Earnings" for 2008 of Google, Inc., wsj.com.

computer programmers Google hires to write the software for its Web site. Google also has substantial costs for researching and developing its products ($2,793 million) and for advertising and marketing them ($1,946 million). General and administrative expenses ($1,802 million) include costs such as the salaries of top managers. In 2008, Google also took a significant loss on its investment in other firms ($1,095 million), which also was entered as a cost on its balance sheet.

The difference between a firm's revenue and its costs is its profit. "Profit" shows up in several forms on an income statement. A firm's *operating income* is the difference between its revenue and its operating expenses. Most corporations, including Google, also have investments, such as government and corporate bonds, that normally generate some income for them. In this case, Google earned $316 million on its investments, which increased its *income before taxes* to $5,854 million. The federal government taxes the profits of corporations. During 2008, Google paid $1,627 million—or about 28 percent of its profits—in taxes. *Net income* after taxes was $4,227 million. The net income that firms report on their income statements is referred to as their after-tax *accounting profit*.

## Analyzing Balance Sheets

As discussed in the chapter, whereas a firm's income statement reports a firm's activities for a period of time, a firm's balance sheet summarizes its financial position on a particular day, usually the end of a quarter or year. To understand how a balance sheet is organized, first recall that an asset is anything of value that the firm owns, and a liability is a debt or an obligation that the firm owes. Subtracting the value of a firm's liabilities from the value of its assets leaves its *net worth*. Because a corporation's stockholders are its owners, net worth is often listed as **stockholders' equity** on a balance sheet. Using these definitions, we can state the balance sheet equation (also called the basic accounting equation) as follows:

$$\text{Assets} - \text{Liabilities} = \text{Stockholders' Equity},$$

or:

$$\text{Assets} = \text{Liabilities} + \text{Stockholders' Equity}.$$

> **Stockholders' equity** The difference between the value of a corporation's assets and the value of its liabilities; also known as net worth.

This formula tells us that the value of a firm's assets must equal the value of its liabilities plus the value of stockholders' equity. An important accounting rule dating back to the beginning of modern bookkeeping in fifteenth-century Italy holds that balance sheets should list assets on the left side and liabilities and net worth, or stockholders' equity, on the right side. Notice that this means that *the value of the left side of the balance sheet must always equal the value of the right side.* Figure 7A-2 shows Google's balance sheet as of December 31, 2008.

A couple of the entries on the asset side of the balance sheet may be unfamiliar: *Current assets* are assets that the firm could convert into cash quickly, such as the balance in its checking account or its accounts receivable, which is money currently owed to the firm for products that have been delivered but not yet paid for. *Goodwill* represents the difference between the purchase price of a company and the market value of its assets. It represents the ability of a business to earn an economic profit from its assets. For example, if you buy a restaurant that is located on a busy intersection and you employ a chef with a reputation for preparing delicious food, you may pay more

### Figure 7A-2

**Google's Balance Sheet as of December 31, 2008**

Corporations list their assets on the left of their balance sheets and their liabilities on the right. The difference between the value of the firm's assets and the value of its liabilities equals the net worth of the firm, or stockholders' equity. Stockholders' equity is listed on the right side of the balance sheet. Therefore, the value of the left side of the balance sheet must always equal the value of the right side.

*Note:* All values are in millions of dollars.

Source: "Annual Balance Sheet" as of December 31, 2008 for Google, Inc., wsj.com.

| ASSETS | | LIABILITIES AND STOCKHOLDERS' EQUITY | |
|---|---|---|---|
| Current Assets | $20,178 | Current Liabilities | $2,302 |
| Property and Equipment | 4,003 | Long-term Liabilities | 1,227 |
| Investments | 85 | Total Liabilities | 3,529 |
| Goodwill | 4,840 | Stockholders' Equity | 24,710 |
| Other long-term assets | 2,662 | | |
| Total Assets | 31,768 | Total liabilities and stockholders' equity | 31,768 |

than the market value of the tables, chairs, ovens, and other assets. This additional amount you pay will be entered on the asset side of your balance sheet as goodwill.

*Current liabilities* are short-term debts such as accounts payable, which is money owed to suppliers for goods received but not yet paid for, or bank loans that will be paid back in less than one year. Long-term bank loans and the value of outstanding corporate bonds are *long-term liabilities*.

# Key Terms

Present value, p. 227

Stockholders' equity, p. 233

## 7A  Tools to Analyze Firms' Financial Information, pages 227–234

LEARNING OBJECTIVE: Understand the concept of present value and the information contained on a firm's income statement and balance sheet.

  Visit www.myeconlab.com to complete these exercises online and get instant feedback.

## Review Questions

**7A.1** Why is money you receive at some future date worth less than money you receive today? If the interest rate rises, what effect does this have on the present value of payments you receive in the future?

**7A.2** Give the formula for calculating the present value of a bond that will pay a coupon of $100 per year for 10 years and that has a face value of $1,000.

**7A.3** Compare the formula for calculating the present value of the payments you will receive from owning a bond to the formula for calculating the present value of the payments you will receive from owning a stock. What are the key similarities? What are the key differences?

**7A.4** How is operating income calculated? How does operating income differ from net income? How does net income differ from accounting profit?

**7A.5** What's the key difference between a firm's income statement and its balance sheet? What is listed on the left side of a balance sheet? What is listed on the right side?

## Problems and Applications

**7A.6** (Related to *Solved Problem 7A-1* on page 229) If the interest rate is 10 percent, what is the present value of a bond that matures in two years, pays $85 one year from now, and pays $1,085 two years from now?

**7A.7** The following is from an Associated Press story on the contract of baseball star Carlos Beltran:

Beltran's contract calls for his $11 million signing bonus to be paid in four installments: $5 million upon approval and $2 million each this June 15, 2005, and on Jan. 15, 2006, and Jan. 15, 2007. He gets a $10 million salary this year, $12 million in each of the following two seasons and $18.5 million in each of the final four seasons, with $8.5 million deferred annually from 2008–11. The players' association calculated the present day value of the contract at $115,726,946, using a 6 percent discount rate (the prime rate [which is the interest rate banks charge on loans to their best customers] plus 1 percent, rounded to the nearest whole number). For purposes of baseball's luxury tax, which currently uses a 3.62 percent discount rate, the contract is valued at $116,695,898.

Briefly explain why the present value of Beltran's contract is lower if a higher interest is used to make the calculation than if a lower interest rate is used.

Source: "Like Pedro, Beltran Gets Suite on Road," Associated Press, January 18, 2005.

**7A.8** (Related to *Solved Problem 7A-1* on page 229) Before the 2008 season, the New York Yankees signed second baseman Robinson Cano to a contract that would pay him the following amounts: $3 million for the 2008 season, $6 million for the 2009 season, $9 million for the 2010 season, and $10 million for the 2011 season, with an option for $14 million for the 2012 season and an option for $15 million for the 2013 season. Assume that Cano plays all six seasons for the Yankees and that he receives each of his six seasonal salaries as a lump-sum payment at the end of the season and he receives his 2008 salary one year after he signed the contract.

a. Some newspaper reports described Cano as having signed a $57 million contract with the Yankees. Do you agree that $57 million was the value of this contract? Briefly explain.

b. What was the present value of Cano's contract at the time he signed it (assuming an interest rate of 10 percent)?

c. If you use an interest rate of 5 percent, what was the present value of Cano's contract?

Source: Joel Sherman, "Robinson Cano Deal Final," *New York Post*, January 8, 2008.

**7A.9** (Related to *Solved Problem 7A-1* on page 229) A winner of the Pennsylvania Lottery was given the choice of receiving $18 million at once or $1,440,000 per year for 25 years.

a. If the winner had opted for the 25 annual payments, how much in total would she have received?

b. At an interest rate of 10 percent, what would be the present value of the 25 payments?

c. At an interest rate of 5 percent, what would be the present value of the 25 payments?

d. What interest rate would make the present value of the 25 payments equal to the one payment of $18 million? (This question is difficult and requires the use of a financial calculator or a spreadsheet. *Hint:* If you are familiar with the Excel spreadsheet program, use the RATE function. Questions (b) and (c) can be answered by using the Excel NPV [Net Present Value] function.)

**7A.10** (Related to *Solved Problem 7A-1* on page 229) Before the start of the 2000 baseball season, the New York Mets decided they didn't want Bobby Bonilla playing for them any longer. But Bonilla had a contract with the Mets for the 2000 season that would have obliged the Mets to pay him $5.9 million. When the Mets released Bonilla, he agreed to take the following payments in lieu of the $5.9 million the Mets would have paid him in the year 2000: He will receive 25 equal payments of $1,193,248.20 each July 1 from 2011 to 2035. If you were Bobby Bonilla, which would you rather have had, the lump-sum $5.9 million or the 25 payments beginning in 2011? Explain the basis for your decision.

**7A.11** Suppose that eLake, an online auction site, is paying a dividend of $2 per share. You expect this dividend to grow 2 percent per year, and the interest rate is 10 percent. What is the most you would be willing to pay for a share of stock in eLake? If the interest rate is 5 percent, what is the most you would be willing to pay? When interest rates in the economy decline, would you expect stock prices in general to rise or fall? Explain.

**7A.12** Suppose you buy the bond of a large corporation at a time when the inflation rate is very low. If the inflation rate increases during the time you hold the bond, what is likely to happen to the price of the bond?

**7A.13** Use the information in the following table for calendar year 2008 to prepare the McDonald's Corporation's income statement. Be sure to include entries for operating income and net income.

| | |
|---|---|
| Revenue from company restaurants | $16,561 million |
| Revenue from franchised restaurants | 6,961 million |
| Cost of operating company-owned restaurants | 13,653 million |
| Income taxes | 1,845 million |
| Interest expense | 523 million |
| General and administrative cost | 2,344 million |
| Cost of restaurant leases | 1,230 million |

Source: McDonalds Corporation, *Annual Report, 2008.*

**7A.14** Use the information in the following table on the financial situation of Starbucks Corporation as of September 28, 2008, to prepare the firm's balance sheet. Be sure to include an entry for stockholders' equity.

| | |
|---|---|
| Current assets | $1,748 million |
| Current liabilities | 2,188 million |
| Property and equipment | 2,956 million |
| Long-term liabilities | 992 million |
| Goodwill | 267 million |
| Other assets | 261 million |

Source: Starbucks Corporation, *Fiscal 2008 Annual Report.*

**7A.15** The *current ratio* is equal to a firm's current assets divided by its current liabilities. Use the information in Figure 7A-2 on page 233 to calculate Google's current ratio on December 31, 2008. Investors generally prefer that a firm's current ratio be greater than 1.5. What problems might a firm encounter if the value of its current assets is low relative to the value of its current liabilities?

**>> End Appendix Learning Objective**

# Comparative Advantage and the Gains from International Trade

## Chapter Outline and Learning Objectives

## >> Is a Government "Buy American" Policy a Good Idea for U.S. Firms like Caterpillar?

In early 2009, with unemployment rising and incomes falling during the recession, Congress and the Obama administration passed a stimulus bill to increase government spending. A portion of the spending would be for new highway bridges and other infrastructure. In early versions of the bill, a "Buy American" provision required all manufactured goods bought with stimulus money to be made in the United States. The intention was to increase the number of jobs the bill would create by preventing foreign companies from participating in the bridge building and other new spending projects. Several foreign countries, Canada and China in particular, protested that the United States had signed international agreements in which it had promised not to impose new barriers to foreign companies selling in the United States.

But foreign countries weren't the only ones protesting the "Buy American" provision. U.S. firms that sell products in foreign markets were also very concerned. They argued that if the United States restricted imports from foreign firms, foreign countries were likely to retaliate by limiting exports from U.S. firms. Caterpillar, Inc., which is headquartered in Peoria, Illinois, sells earthmoving, mining, and heavy construction equipment. One executive at Caterpillar was quoted as saying, "These sorts of provisions [will] backfire. The so-called Buy American

amendment is really an anti-export provision." In the final version of the stimulus bill, Congress and the administration changed the "Buy American" provision to apply only where it was consistent with the international obligations of the United States. Whether that change in wording would be enough to keep foreign countries from retaliating against U.S. exports was still unclear in mid-2009.

Are "Buy American" provisions and other attempts to protect U.S. firms from foreign competition good ideas? As we will see in this chapter, these policies create winners—the firms that are sheltered from foreign competition—but they also create losers—U.S. firms that rely on exports to foreign countries, as well as U.S. consumers and taxpayers who must pay higher prices for goods that could have been purchased at lower prices from foreign companies. In this chapter, we will explore who wins and who loses from international trade and review the political debate over whether international trade should be restricted.

**AN INSIDE LOOK AT POLICY** on **page 262** looks more closely at the debate over the "Buy American" provision in the 2009 government stimulus bill.

Source: Mark Drajem, "GE, Caterpillar Fight 'Buy American' Rule in Stimulus," Bloomberg.com, January 22, 2009.

## Economics in YOUR LIFE!

### Have You Heard of the "Buy American" Provision?

Politicians often support restrictions on trade to convince people to vote for them. The workers in the industries these restrictions protect are likely to vote for the politicians because the workers think trade restrictions will protect their jobs. But most people are not workers in industries protected from foreign competition by trade restrictions. Many people work for firms, such as Caterpillar, that sell goods in foreign markets. These workers risk losing their jobs if foreign countries retaliate against U.S. attempts to reduce imported goods. In the case of the "Buy American" provision of the stimulus bill, millions of taxpayers may have to pay higher prices for U.S.-made steel and other manufactured goods if foreign-made goods are excluded. How, then, did some U.S. companies convince Congress to include the "Buy American" provision in the stimulus bill, and why have relatively few people even heard of this provision? As you read the chapter, see if you can answer these questions. You can check your answers against those we provide at the end of the chapter.

▶ Continued on page 261

Trade is simply the act of buying or selling. Is there a difference between trade that takes place within a country and international trade? Within the United States, domestic trade makes it possible for consumers in Ohio to eat salmon caught in Alaska or for consumers in Montana to drive cars built in Michigan or Kentucky. Similarly, international trade makes it possible for consumers in the United States to drink wine from France or use Blu-ray players from Japan. But one significant difference between domestic trade and international trade is that international trade is more controversial. At one time, nearly all the televisions, shoes, clothing, and toys bought in the United States were also produced in the United States. Today, these goods are produced mainly by firms in other countries. This shift has benefited U.S. consumers because foreign-made goods have lower prices or higher quality than the U.S.-made goods they have replaced. But at the same time, many U.S. firms that produced these goods have gone out of business, and their workers have had to find other jobs. Not surprisingly, opinion polls show that many Americans favor reducing international trade because they believe doing so will preserve jobs in the United States. But is this belief accurate?

We can use the tools of demand and supply developed in Chapter 3 to analyze markets for internationally traded goods and services. We saw in Chapter 2 that trade in general—whether within a country or between countries—is based on the principle of comparative advantage. In this chapter, we look more closely at the role of comparative advantage in international trade. We also use the concepts of consumer surplus, producer surplus, and deadweight loss from Chapter 4 to analyze government policies that interfere with trade. With this background, we can return to the political debate over whether the United States benefits from international trade. We begin by looking at how large a role international trade plays in the U.S. economy.

## 8.1 LEARNING OBJECTIVE

Discuss the role of international trade in the U.S. economy.

# The United States in the International Economy

International trade has grown tremendously over the past 50 years. The increase in trade is the result of the falling costs of shipping products around the world, the spread of inexpensive and reliable communications, and changes in government policies. Firms can use large container ships to send their products across the oceans at low cost. Businesspeople today can travel to Europe or Asia, using fast, inexpensive, and reliable air transportation. The Internet, cell phones, and text messaging allow managers to communicate instantaneously and at a very low cost with customers and suppliers around the world. These and other improvements in transportation and communication have created a global marketplace that earlier generations of businesspeople could only dream of.

In addition, over the past 50 years, many governments have changed policies to facilitate international trade. For example, tariff rates have fallen. A **tariff** is a tax imposed by a government on *imports* of a good into a country. **Imports** are goods and services bought domestically but produced in other countries. In the 1930s, the United States charged an average tariff rate above 50 percent. Today, the rate is less than 2 percent. In North America, most tariffs between Canada, Mexico, and the United States were eliminated following the passage of the North American Free Trade Agreement (NAFTA) in 1994. Twenty-seven countries in Europe have formed the European Union, which has eliminated all tariffs among member countries, greatly increasing both imports and **exports**, which are goods and services produced domestically but sold in other countries.

**Tariff** A tax imposed by a government on imports.

**Imports** Goods and services bought domestically but produced in other countries.

**Exports** Goods and services produced domestically but sold in other countries.

## The Importance of Trade to the U.S. Economy

U.S. consumers buy increasing quantities of goods and services produced in other countries. At the same time, U.S. businesses sell increasing quantities of goods and services to consumers in other countries. Figure 8-1 shows that since 1950, both exports and imports have been steadily increasing as a fraction of U.S. gross domestic product

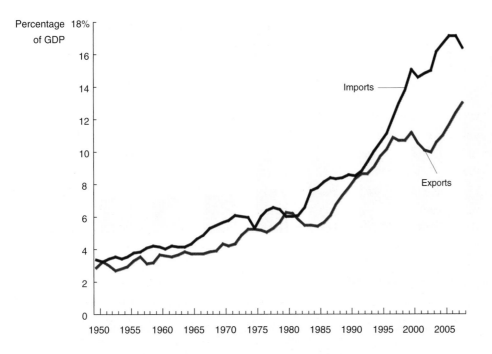

## Figure 8-1

**International Trade Is of Increasing Importance to the United States**

Exports and imports of goods and services as a percentage of total production—measured by GDP—show the importance of international trade to an economy. Since 1950, both imports and exports have been steadily rising as a fraction of U.S. GDP.

Source: U.S. Department of Commerce, Bureau of Economic Analysis.

(GDP). Recall that GDP is the value of all the goods and services produced in a country during a year. In 1950, exports and imports were both about 4 percent of GDP. In 2008, exports were about 13 percent of GDP, and imports were about 16 percent.

Not all sectors of the U.S. economy are affected equally by international trade. For example, although it's difficult to import or export some services, such as haircuts or appendectomies, a large percentage of U.S. agricultural production is exported. Each year, the United States exports about 50 percent of its wheat and rice crops, and 20 percent of its corn crop.

Many U.S. manufacturing industries also depend on trade. About 20 percent of U.S. manufacturing jobs depend directly or indirectly on exports. In some industries, such as computers, the products these workers make are directly exported. In other industries, such as steel, the products are used to make other products, such as bulldozers or machine tools, that are then exported. In all, about two-thirds of U.S. manufacturing industries depend on exports for at least 10 percent of jobs.

## U.S. International Trade in a World Context

The United States is the largest exporter in the world, as Figure 8-2 illustrates. Six of the other seven leading exporting countries are also high-income countries. Although China is still a relatively low-income country, the rapid growth of the Chinese economy over the past 30 years has resulted in its becoming the third largest exporter.

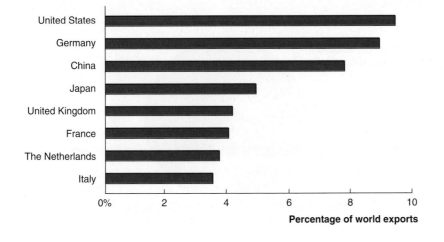

## Figure 8-2

**The Eight Leading Exporting Countries**

The United States is the leading exporting country, accounting for about 9.5 percent of total world exports. The values are the shares of total world exports of merchandise and commercial services.

Source: World Trade Organization, *International Trade Statistics*, 2008.

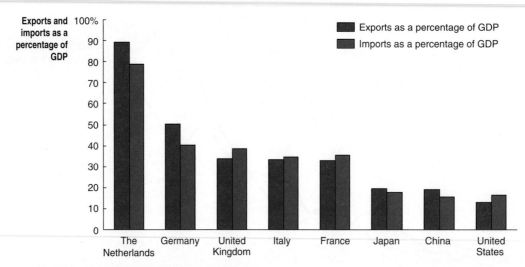

**Figure 8-3** | **International Trade as a Percentage of GDP**

International trade is still less important to the United States than to most other countries.

Source: Organization for Economic Cooperation and Development, *Country Statistical Profiles*, 2009.

International trade remains less important to the United States than it is to most other countries. Figure 8-3 shows that imports and exports remain smaller fractions of GDP in the United States than in many other countries. In some smaller countries, such as the Netherlands, imports and exports make up more than half of GDP. In the larger European economies, imports and exports make up one-third to one-half of GDP.

## Making the Connection

### How Caterpillar Depends on International Trade

We saw in the chapter opener that Caterpillar, Inc., was opposed to the "Buy American" provision in the 2009 stimulus bill. Jim Owens, Caterpillar's CEO, argued, "We need to avoid things like . . . 'Buy American.' . . . If we turn inward, it sends a terrible signal to the rest of the world, and I'm concerned that other countries will adopt even more protectionist measures for their countries." Owens had cause to be concerned because, as the graph below shows, more than half of Caterpillar sales were outside the United States. This dependence on exports made Caterpillar vulnerable if foreign governments responded to the "Buy American" provision by restricting exports from the United States.

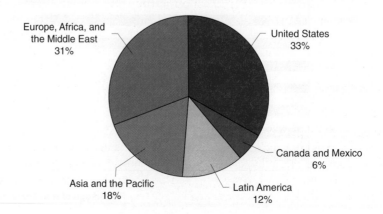

In fact, Caterpillar has become increasingly dependent over time on foreign markets. The firm's exports rose from just over half of total sales in 2004 to more than two-thirds in 2008. Because Caterpillar sells earthmoving and other construction equipment, it was severely affected by the decline in the U.S. housing market that began in 2006. Although sales in the United States declined by more than half between 2006 and 2008, increases in exports were enough to make 2008 a record sales year for Caterpillar. By 2009, however, the slowdown in the world economy had begun to affect the company. During the first three months of 2009, sales plunged 22 percent, and Caterpillar announced that it was laying off 25,000 people from its global workforce.

Although Caterpillar now sells more outside the United States than inside, it still remains a major employer in the United States. At the end of 2008, Caterpillar employed more than 53,000 workers in 278 offices and factories in the United States. In addition, Caterpillar dealers in the United States employed more than 50,000 people. Thousands of other workers are employed at the many U.S. firms that supply Caterpillar with parts and components for its products. Problems at Caterpillar result in problems in the U.S. communities where the company and its suppliers are located. Caterpillar employs more than 20,000 people in the area around Peoria, Illinois. When sales declines led to layoffs in early 2009, the local real estate market, local stores and businesses, and the tax revenues of local governments were all affected. Many Caterpillar employees hoped that further job losses wouldn't result from foreign retaliation against U.S. exports.

Sources: Bob Tita, "Caterpillar Posts Loss, Cuts Outlook," *Wall Street Journal*, April 22, 2009; Abdon Pallasch, "Caterpillar CEO, Obama Talk Stimulus," *Chicago Sun-Times*, February 12, 2009; Steven Gray, "Caterpillar Layoffs: How They're Playing in Peoria," *Time*, January 29, 2009; and Caterpillar, 2008 Annual Report.

**YOUR TURN:** Test your understanding by doing related problem 1.5 on page 264 at the end of this chapter.

# Comparative Advantage in International Trade

**8.2 LEARNING** OBJECTIVE

Understand the difference between comparative advantage and absolute advantage in international trade.

Why have businesses around the world increasingly looked for markets in other countries? Why have consumers increasingly purchased goods and services made in other countries? People trade for one reason: Trade makes them better off. Whenever a buyer and seller agree to a sale, they must both believe they are better off; otherwise, there would be no sale. This outcome must hold whether the buyer and seller live in the same city or in different countries. As we will see, governments are more likely to interfere with international trade than they are with domestic trade, but the reasons for the interference are more political than economic.

## A Brief Review of Comparative Advantage

In Chapter 2, we discussed the key economic concept of *comparative advantage*. **Comparative advantage** is the ability of an individual, a firm, or a country to produce a good or service at a lower opportunity cost than competitors. Recall that **opportunity cost** is the highest-valued alternative that must be given up to engage in an activity. People, firms, and countries specialize in economic activities in which they have a comparative advantage. In trading, we benefit from the comparative advantage of other people (or firms or countries), and they benefit from our comparative advantage.

A good way to think of comparative advantage is to recall the example in Chapter 2 of you and your neighbor picking fruit. Your neighbor is better at picking both apples and cherries than you are. Why, then, doesn't your neighbor pick both types of fruit? Because the opportunity cost to your neighbor of picking her own apples is very high: She is a particularly skilled cherry picker, and every hour spent picking apples is an hour

**Comparative advantage** The ability of an individual, a firm, or a country to produce a good or service at a lower opportunity cost than competitors.

**Opportunity cost** The highest-valued alternative that must be given up to engage in an activity.

taken away from picking cherries. You can pick apples at a much lower opportunity cost than your neighbor, so you have a comparative advantage in picking apples. Your neighbor can pick cherries at a much lower opportunity cost than you can, so she has a comparative advantage in picking cherries. Your neighbor is better off specializing in picking cherries, and you are better off specializing in picking apples. You can then trade some of your apples for some of your neighbor's cherries, and both of you will end up with more of each fruit.

## Comparative Advantage in International Trade

The principle of comparative advantage can explain why people pursue different occupations. It can also explain why countries produce different goods and services. International trade involves many countries importing and exporting many different goods and services. Countries are better off if they specialize in producing the goods for which they have a comparative advantage. They can then trade for the goods for which other countries have a comparative advantage.

We can illustrate why specializing on the basis of comparative advantage makes countries better off with a simple example involving just two countries and two products. Suppose the United States and Japan produce only cell phones and digital music players, like Apple's iPod. Assume that each country uses only labor to produce each good and that Japanese and U.S. cell phones and digital music players are exactly the same. Table 8-1 shows how much each country can produce of each good with one hour of labor.

Notice that Japanese workers are more productive than U.S. workers in making both goods. In one hour of work, Japanese workers can make six times as many cell phones and one and one-half times as many digital music players as U.S. workers. Japan has an *absolute advantage* over the United States in producing both goods. **Absolute advantage** is the ability to produce more of a good or service than competitors when using the same amount of resources. In this case, Japan can produce more of both goods using the same amount of labor as the United States.

It might seem at first that Japan has nothing to gain from trading with the United States because it has an absolute advantage in producing both goods. However, Japan should specialize and produce only cell phones and obtain the digital music players it needs by exporting cell phones to the United States in exchange for digital music players. The reason that Japan benefits from trade is that although it has an *absolute advantage* in the production of both goods, it has a *comparative advantage* only in the production of cell phones. The United States has a comparative advantage in the production of digital music players.

If it seems contrary to common sense that Japan should import digital music players from the United States even though Japan can produce more players per hour of work, think about the opportunity cost to each country of producing each good. If Japan wants to produce more digital music players, it has to switch labor away from cell phone production. Every hour of labor switched from producing cell phones to producing digital music players increases digital music player production by 6 and reduces cell phone production by 12. Japan has to give up 12 cell phones for every 6 digital music players it produces. Therefore, the opportunity cost to Japan of producing one more digital music player is 12/6, or 2 cell phones.

If the United States switches one hour of labor from cell phones to digital music players, production of cell phones falls by 2, and production of digital music players

**Absolute advantage** The ability to produce more of a good or service than competitors when using the same amount of resources.

TABLE 8-1

| An Example of Japanese Workers Being More Productive Than American Workers | OUTPUT PER HOUR OF WORK | |
|---|---|---|
| | CELL PHONES | DIGITAL MUSIC PLAYERS |
| JAPAN | 12 | 6 |
| UNITED STATES | 2 | 4 |

| OPPORTUNITY COSTS | | |
|---|---|---|
| | CELL PHONES | DIGITAL MUSIC PLAYERS |
| JAPAN | 0.5 digital music player | 2 cell phones |
| UNITED STATES | 2 digital music players | 0.5 cell phone |

TABLE 8-2

**The Opportunity Costs of Producing Cell Phones and Digital Music Players**

The table shows the opportunity cost each country faces in producing cell phones and digital music players. For example, the entry in the first row and second column shows that Japan must give up 2 cell phones for every digital music player it produces.

rises by 4. Therefore, the opportunity cost to the United States of producing one more digital music player is 2/4, or 0.5 cell phone. The United States has a lower opportunity cost of producing digital music players and, therefore, has a comparative advantage in making this product. By similar reasoning, we can see that Japan has a comparative advantage in producing cell phones. Table 8-2 summarizes the opportunity cost each country faces in producing these goods.

# Solved Problem | 8-2

## Confusion over the Basis for Trade

Historian Paul Kennedy of Yale University wrote the following regarding comparative and absolute advantage:

> How does [modernization] work when production of an item takes place not just in a specific region . . . but globally when there are 50 countries, with varying standards of wages, capable of producing soybeans, and 70 countries capable of producing steel?

> Adam Smith's famous argument in favor of free trade and specialization (that it made no economic sense for both England and Portugal to strive to produce wine and textiles when England's climate made it a better textile producer and Portugal's climate made it a better wine producer) doesn't address this reality of multiple competitive sources. Yet, that is the basis of modern,

free-market economics. What if there is nothing you can produce more cheaply or efficiently than anywhere except by constantly cutting labor costs?

**a.** Professor Kennedy explains that a well-known argument for free trade between England and Portugal was based on (1) England's favorable climate for producing textiles and (2) Portugal's favorable climate for producing wine. Is the argument for trade based on absolute advantage or comparative advantage?

**b.** Is it true that for some nations, "there is nothing you can produce more cheaply or efficiently than anywhere except by constantly cutting labor costs"?

## SOLVING THE PROBLEM:

**Step 1:** **Review the chapter material.** This problem is about comparative advantage, so you may want to review the section "Comparative Advantage in International Trade," which begins on page 241.

**Step 2:** **Is the argument for trade based on absolute or comparative advantage?** The argument for free trade is based on comparative advantage. In effect, Professor Kennedy's statements regarding the climates of England and Portugal are claims that each has an *absolute advantage*: textiles for England and wine for Portugal.

**Step 3:** **Is it true that for some nations, there is nothing they can produce more cheaply than other nations?** No. Even if a nation has an absolute disadvantage in two goods versus another nation, it will have a comparative advantage in one of them, if the opportunity cost of producing each good differs for the two countries.

P.S. It was David Ricardo, not Adam Smith, who used the wine cloth example of comparative advantage as an argument in favor of free trade.

**YOUR TURN:** For more practice, do related problem 2.8 on page 265 at the end of this chapter.

**8.3 LEARNING** OBJECTIVE

Explain how countries gain from international trade.

**Autarky** A situation in which a country does not trade with other countries.

**Terms of trade** The ratio at which a country can trade its exports for imports from other countries.

# How Countries Gain from International Trade

Can Japan really gain from producing only cell phones and trading with the United States for digital music players? To see that it can, assume at first that Japan and the United States do not trade with each other. A situation in which a country does not trade with other countries is called **autarky**. Assume that in autarky each country has 1,000 hours of labor available to produce the two goods, and each country produces the quantities of the two goods shown in Table 8-3. Because there is no trade, these quantities also represent consumption of the two goods in each country.

## Increasing Consumption through Trade

Suppose now that Japan and the United States begin to trade with each other. The **terms of trade** is the ratio at which a country can trade its exports for imports from other countries. For simplicity, let's assume that the terms of trade end up with Japan and the United States being willing to trade one cell phone for one digital music player.

Once trade has begun, the United States and Japan can exchange digital music players for cell phones or cell phones for digital music players. For example, if Japan specializes by using all 1,000 available hours of labor to produce cell phones, it will be able to produce 12,000. It then could export 1,500 cell phones to the United States in exchange for 1,500 digital music players. (Remember: We are assuming that the terms of trade are one cell phone for one digital music player.) Japan ends up with 10,500 cell phones and 1,500 digital music players. Compared with the situation before trade, Japan has the same number of digital music players but 1,500 more cell phones. If the United States specializes in producing digital music players, it will be able to produce 4,000. It could then export 1,500 digital music players to Japan in exchange for 1,500 cell phones. The United States ends up with 2,500 digital music players and 1,500 cell phones. Compared with the situation before trade, the United States has the same number of cell phones but 1,500 more digital music players. Trade has allowed both countries to increase the quantities of goods consumed. Table 8-4 summarizes the gains from trade for the United States and Japan.

By trading, Japan and the United States are able to consume more than they could without trade. This outcome is possible because world production of both goods increases after trade. (Remember that, in this example, our "world" consists of just the United States and Japan.)

Why does total production of cell phones and digital music players increase when the United States specializes in producing digital music players and Japan specializes in producing cell phones? A domestic analogy helps to answer this question: If a company shifts production from an old factory to a more efficient modern factory, its output will increase. In effect, the same thing happens in our example. Producing digital music players in Japan and cell phones in the United States is inefficient. Shifting production to the more efficient country—the one with the comparative advantage—increases total production. The key point is this: *Countries gain from specializing in producing goods in which they have a comparative advantage and trading for goods in which other countries have a comparative advantage.*

| TABLE 8-3 | PRODUCTION AND CONSUMPTION | |
|---|---|---|
| **Production without Trade** | **CELL PHONES** | **DIGITAL MUSIC PLAYERS** |
| **JAPAN** | 9,000 | 1,500 |
| **UNITED STATES** | 1,500 | 1,000 |

TABLE 8-4

**Gains from Trade for Japan and the United States**

**WITHOUT TRADE**

**Production and Consumption**

| | CELL PHONES | MP3 PLAYERS |
|---|---|---|
| JAPAN | 12,000 | 1,500 |
| UNITED STATES | 1,500 | 1,000 |

**WITH TRADE**

| | Production with Trade | | Trade | | Consumption with Trade | |
|---|---|---|---|---|---|---|
| | CELL PHONES | MP3 PLAYERS | CELL PHONES | MP3 PLAYERS | CELL PHONES | MP3 PLAYERS |
| JAPAN | 12,000 | 0 | Export 1,500 | Import 1,500 | 10,500 | 1,500 |
| UNITED STATES | 0 | 4,000 | Export 1,500 | Import 1,500 | 1,500 | 2,500 |

With trade, the United States and Japan specialize in the good they have a comparative advantage in producing . . .

. . . and export some of that good in exchange for the good the other country has a comparative advantage in producing.

**GAINS FROM TRADE**

**Increased Consumption**

| | |
|---|---|
| JAPAN | 1,500 Cell Phones |
| UNITED STATES | 1,500 MP3 Players |

The increased consumption made possible by trade represents the gains from trade.

## Why Don't We See Complete Specialization?

In our example of two countries producing only two products, each country specializes in producing one of the goods. In the real world, many goods and services are produced in more than one country. For example, the United States and Japan both produce automobiles. We do not see complete specialization in the real world for three main reasons:

- *Not all goods and services are traded internationally.* Even if, for example, Japan had a comparative advantage in the production of medical services, it would be difficult for Japan to specialize in producing medical services and then export them. There is no easy way for U.S. patients who need appendectomies to receive them from surgeons in Japan.

- *Production of most goods involves increasing opportunity costs.* Recall from Chapter 2 that production of most goods involves increasing opportunity costs. As a result, when the United States devotes more workers to producing digital music players, the opportunity cost of producing more digital music players will increase. At some point, the opportunity cost of producing digital music players in the United States may rise to the level of the opportunity cost of producing digital music players in Japan. When that happens, international trade will no longer push the United States further toward specialization. The same will be true of Japan: Increasing opportunity cost will cause Japan to stop short of complete specialization in producing cell phones.

- *Tastes for products differ.* Most products are *differentiated*. Cell phones, digital music players, cars, and televisions—to name just a few products—come with a wide variety of features. When buying automobiles, some people look for reliability and fuel efficiency, others look for room to carry seven passengers, and still others want styling and high performance. So, some car buyers prefer Toyota Prius hybrids,

# Don't Let This Happen to **YOU!**

## Remember That Trade Creates Both Winners and Losers

The following statement is from a Federal Reserve publication: "Trade is a win–win situation for all countries that participate." People sometimes interpret statements like this to mean that there are no losers from international trade. But notice that the statement refers to *countries*, not individuals. When countries participate in trade, they make their consumers better off by increasing the quantity of goods and services available to them. As we have seen, however, expanding trade eliminates the jobs of workers employed at companies that are less efficient than foreign companies. Trade also creates new jobs at companies that export to foreign markets. It may be difficult, though, for workers who lose their jobs because of trade to easily find others. That is why in the United States, the federal government uses the Trade Adjustment Assistance program to provide funds for workers who have lost their jobs due to international trade. Qualified unemployed workers can use these funds to pay for retraining, for searching for new jobs, or for relocating to areas where new jobs are available. This program—and similar programs in other countries—recognizes that there are losers from international trade as well as winners.

Source: Quote from Federal Reserve Bank of Dallas, "International Trade and the Economy," www.dallasfed.org/educate/everyday/ev7.html.

**YOUR TURN:** Test your understanding by doing related problem 3.10 on page 266 at the end of this chapter.

---

some prefer Chevy Suburbans, and others prefer BMWs. As a result, Japan, the United States, and Germany may each have a comparative advantage in producing different types of automobiles.

## Does Anyone Lose as a Result of International Trade?

In our cell phone and digital music player example, consumption increases in both the United States and Japan as a result of trade. Everyone gains, and no one loses. Or do they? In our example, we referred repeatedly to "Japan" or the "United States" producing cell phones or digital music players. But countries do not produce goods—firms do. In a world without trade, there would be cell phone and digital music player firms in both Japan and the United States. In a world with trade, there would only be Japanese cell phone firms and U.S. digital music player firms. Japanese digital music player firms and U.S. cell phone firms would close. Overall, total employment will not change and production will increase as a result of trade. Nevertheless, the owners of Japanese digital music player firms, the owners of U.S. cell phone firms, and the people who work for them are worse off as a result of trade. The losers from trade are likely to do their best to convince the Japanese and U.S. governments to interfere with trade by barring imports of the competing products from the other country or by imposing high tariffs on them.

## Where Does Comparative Advantage Come From?

Among the main sources of comparative advantage are the following:

- **Climate and natural resources.** This source of comparative advantage is the most obvious. Because of geology, Saudi Arabia has a comparative advantage in the production of oil. Because of climate and soil conditions, Costa Rica has a comparative advantage in the production of bananas, and the United States has a comparative advantage in the production of wheat.

- *Relative abundance of labor and capital.* Some countries, such as the United States, have many highly skilled workers and a great deal of machinery. Other countries, such as China, have many unskilled workers and relatively little machinery. As a result, the United States has a comparative advantage in the production of goods that require highly skilled workers or sophisticated machinery to manufacture, such as aircraft, semiconductors, and computer software. China has a comparative advantage in the production of goods, such as tools, clothing, and children's toys, that require unskilled workers and small amounts of simple machinery.

- *Technology.* Broadly defined, *technology* is the process firms use to turn inputs into goods and services. At any given time, firms in different countries do not all have access to the same technologies. In part, this difference is the result of past investments countries have made in supporting higher education or in providing support for research and development. Some countries are strong in *product technologies*, which involve the ability to develop new products. For example, firms in the United States have pioneered the development of such products as radios, televisions, digital computers, airliners, and many prescription drugs. Other countries are strong in *process technologies*, which involve the ability to improve the processes used to make existing products. For example, firms in Japan, such as Toyota and Honda, have succeeded by greatly improving the processes for designing and manufacturing automobiles.

- *External economies.* It is difficult to explain the location of some industries on the basis of climate, natural resources, the relative abundance of labor and capital, or technology. For example, why does southern California have a comparative advantage in making movies or Switzerland in making watches or New York in providing financial services? The answer is that once an industry becomes established in an area, firms that locate in that area gain advantages over firms located elsewhere. The advantages include the availability of skilled workers, the opportunity to interact with other firms in the same industry, and proximity to suppliers. These advantages result in lower costs to firms located in the area. Because these lower costs result from increases in the size of the industry in an area, economists refer to them as **external economies**.

> **External economies** Reductions in a firm's costs that result from an increase in the size of an industry.

## Making the Connection | Why Is Dalton, Georgia, the Carpet-Making Capital of the World?

Factories within a 65-mile radius of Dalton, Georgia, account for 75 percent of U.S. carpet production and more than half of world carpet production. Carpet production is highly automated and relies primarily on synthetic fibers. Dalton, a small city located in rural northwest Georgia, would not seem to have any advantages in carpet production. In fact, the location of the carpet industry in Dalton was a historical accident.

In the early 1900s, Catherine Evans Whitener started making bedspreads using a method called "tufting," in which she sewed cotton yarn through the fabric and then cut the ends of the yarn so it would fluff up. These bedspreads became very popular. By the 1930s, the process was mechanized and was then applied to carpets. In the early years, the industry used cotton grown in Georgia, but today synthetic fibers, such as nylon and olefin, have largely replaced cotton and wool in carpet manufacturing.

*Because Catherine Evans Whitener started making bedspreads by hand in Dalton, Georgia, 100 years ago, a multibillion-dollar carpet industry is now located there.*

More than 170 carpet factories are now located in the Dalton area. Supporting the carpet industry are local yarn manufacturers, machinery suppliers, and maintenance firms. Dye plants have opened solely to supply the carpet industry. Printing shops have opened to print tags and labels for carpets. Box factories have opened to produce cartons designed specifically for shipping carpets. The local workforce has developed highly specialized skills for running and maintaining the carpet-making machinery.

A company establishing a carpet factory outside the Dalton area is unable to use the suppliers or the skilled workers available to factories in Dalton. As a result, carpet factories located outside Dalton may have higher costs than factories located in Dalton. Although there is no particular reason the carpet industry should have originally located in Dalton, external economies gave the area a comparative advantage in carpet making once it began to grow there.

 **YOUR TURN:** Test your understanding by doing related problem 3.11 on page 266 at the end of this chapter.

## Comparative Advantage Over Time: The Rise and Fall—and Rise— of the U.S. Consumer Electronics Industry

A country may develop a comparative advantage in the production of a good, and then, as time passes and circumstances change, the country may lose its comparative advantage in producing that good and develop a comparative advantage in producing other goods. For several decades, the United States had a comparative advantage in the production of consumer electronic goods, such as televisions, radios, and stereos. The comparative advantage of the United States in these products was based on having developed most of the underlying technology, having the most modern factories, and having a skilled and experienced workforce. Gradually, however, other countries, particularly Japan, gained access to the technology, built modern factories, and developed skilled workforces. As mentioned earlier, Japanese firms have excelled in process technologies, which involve the ability to improve the processes used to make existing products. By the 1970s and 1980s, Japanese firms were able to produce many consumer electronic goods more cheaply and with higher quality than could U.S. firms. Japanese firms Sony, Panasonic, and Pioneer replaced U.S. firms Magnavox, Zenith, and RCA as world leaders in consumer electronics.

By 2009, however, as the technology underlying consumer electronics evolved, comparative advantage had shifted again, and several U.S. firms surged ahead of their Japanese competitors. For example, Apple had developed the iPod and iPhone; Linksys, a division of Cisco Systems, took the lead in home wireless networking technology; and TiVo pioneered the digital video recorder (DVR), which allows viewers to easily record television programs for later viewing. As pictures and music converted to digital data, process technologies became less important than the ability to design and develop new products. These new consumer electronic products required skills similar to those in computer design and software writing, where the United States had long maintained a comparative advantage.

Once a country has lost its comparative advantage in producing a good, its income will be higher and its economy will be more efficient if it switches from producing the good to importing it, as the United States did when it switched from producing televisions to importing them. As we will see in the next section, however, there is often political pressure on governments to attempt to preserve industries that have lost their comparative advantage.

# Government Policies That Restrict International Trade

**Free trade**, or trade between countries that is without government restrictions, makes consumers better off. We can expand on this idea by using the concepts of consumer surplus and producer surplus from Chapter 4. Figure 8-4 shows the market in the United States for the bio-fuel ethanol, which can be used as a substitute for gasoline. The figure shows the situation of autarky, where the United States does not trade with other countries. The equilibrium price of ethanol is $2.00 per gallon, and the equilibrium quantity is 6.0 billion gallons per year. The blue area represents consumer surplus, and the red area represents producer surplus.

Now suppose that the United States begins importing ethanol from Brazil and other countries that produce ethanol for $1.00 per gallon. Because the world market for ethanol is large, we will assume that the United States can buy as much ethanol as it wants without causing the *world price* of $1.00 per gallon to rise. Therefore, once imports of ethanol are permitted into the United States, U.S. firms will not be able to sell ethanol at prices higher than the world price of $1.00, and the U.S. price will become equal to the world price.

Figure 8-5 shows the result of allowing imports of ethanol into the United States. With the price lowered from $2.00 to $1.00, U.S. consumers increase their purchases from 6.0 billion gallons to 9.0 billion gallons. Equilibrium moves from point *F* to point *G*. In the new equilibrium, U.S. producers have reduced the quantity of ethanol they supply from 6.0 billion gallons to 3.0 billion gallons. Imports will equal 6.0 billion gallons, which is the difference between U.S. consumption and U.S. production.

Under autarky, consumer surplus would be area *A* in Figure 8-5. With imports, the reduction in price increases consumer surplus, so it is now equal to the sum of areas *A*, *B*, *C*, and *D*. Although the lower price increases consumer surplus, it reduces producer surplus. Under autarky, producer surplus was equal to the sum of the areas *B* and *E*. With imports, producer surplus is equal to only area *E*. Recall that economic surplus equals the sum of consumer surplus and producer surplus. Moving from autarky to allowing imports increases economic surplus in the United States by an amount equal to the sum of areas *C* and *D*.

**8.4 LEARNING** OBJECTIVE

Analyze the economic effects of government policies that restrict international trade.

**Free trade** Trade between countries that is without government restrictions.

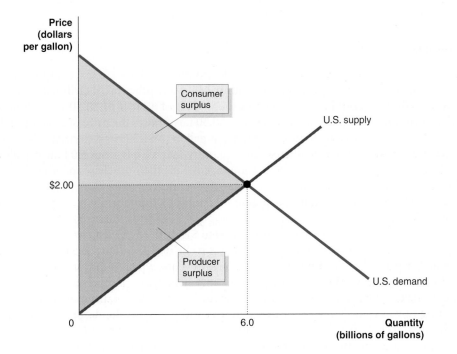

## Figure 8-4

### The U.S. Market for Ethanol under Autarky

This figure shows the market for ethanol in the United States, assuming autarky, where the United States does not trade with other countries. The equilibrium price of ethanol is $2.00 per gallon, and the equilibrium quantity is 6.0 billion gallons per year. The blue area represents consumer surplus, and the red area represents producer surplus.

# Figure 8-5

### The Effect of Imports on the U.S. Ethanol Market

When imports are allowed into the United States, the price of ethanol falls from $2.00 to $1.00. U.S. consumers increase their purchases from 6.0 billion gallons to 9.0 billion gallons. Equilibrium moves from point *F* to point *G*. U.S. producers reduce the quantity of ethanol they supply from 6.0 billion gallons to 3.0 billion gallons. Imports equal 6.0 billion gallons, which is the difference between U.S. consumption and U.S. production. Consumer surplus equals the areas *A*, *B*, *C*, and *D*. Producer surplus equals the area *E*.

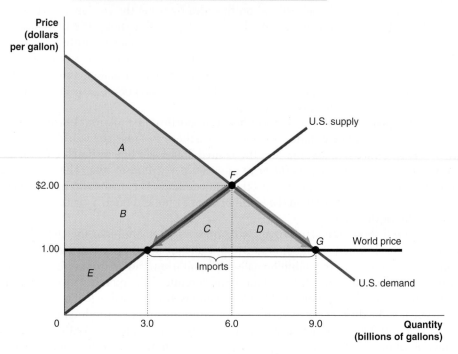

| | Under Autarky | With Imports |
|---|---|---|
| Consumer Surplus | *A* | *A + B + C + D* |
| Producer Surplus | *B + E* | *E* |
| Economic Surplus | *A + B + E* | *A + B + C + D + E* |

We can conclude that international trade helps consumers but hurts firms that are less efficient than foreign competitors. As a result, these firms and their workers are often strong supporters of government policies that restrict trade. These policies usually take one of two forms:

- Tariffs

- Quotas and voluntary export restraints

## Tariffs

The most common interferences with trade are *tariffs*, which are taxes imposed by a government on goods imported into a country. Like any other tax, a tariff increases the cost of selling a good. Figure 8-6 shows the impact of a tariff of $0.50 per gallon on ethanol imports into the United States. The $0.50 tariff raises the price of ethanol in the United States from the world price of $1.00 per gallon to $1.50 per gallon. At this higher price, U.S. ethanol producers increase the quantity they supply from 3.0 billion gallons to 4.5 billion gallons. U.S. consumers, though, cut back their purchases of ethanol from 9.0 billion gallons to 7.5 billion gallons. Imports decline from 6.0 billion gallons (9.0 billion – 3.0 billion) to 3.0 billion (7.5 billion – 4.5 billion). Equilibrium moves from point *G* to point *H*.

By raising the price of ethanol from $1.00 to $1.50, the tariff reduces consumer surplus by the sum of areas *A*, *T*, *C*, and *D*. Area *A* is the increase in producer surplus from the higher price. The government collects tariff revenue equal to the tariff of $0.50 per gallon multiplied by the 3.0 billion gallons imported. Area *T* represents the government's tariff revenue. Areas *C* and *D* represent losses to U.S. consumers that are not captured by anyone. They are deadweight loss and represent the decline in economic efficiency resulting from the ethanol tariff. Area *C* shows the effect on U.S. consumers of being forced to buy from U.S. producers who are less efficient than foreign producers, and area *D* shows the effect of U.S. consumers buying less ethanol than they would have

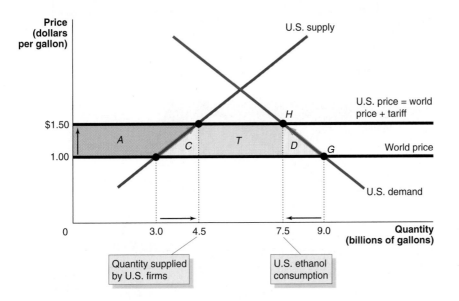

| Loss of Consumer Surplus | = | Increase in Producer Surplus | + | Government Tariff Revenue | + | Deadweight Loss |
|:---:|:---:|:---:|:---:|:---:|:---:|:---:|
| A + C + T + D | | A | | T | | C + D |

## Figure 8-6

### The Effects of a Tariff on Ethanol

Without a tariff on ethanol, U.S. producers will sell 3.0 billion gallons of ethanol, U.S. consumers will purchase 9.0 billion gallons, and imports will be 6.0 billion gallons. The U.S. price will equal the world price of $1.00 per gallon. The $0.50-per-gallon tariff raises the price of ethanol in the United States to $1.50 per gallon, and U.S. producers increase the quantity they supply to 4.5 billion gallons. U.S. consumers reduce their purchases to 7.5 billion gallons. Equilibrium moves from point *G* to point *H*. The ethanol tariff causes a loss of consumer surplus equal to the area *A* + *C* + *T* + *D*. The area *A* is the increase in producer surplus due to the higher price. The area *T* is the government's tariff revenue. The areas *C* and *D* represent deadweight loss.

at the world price. As a result of the tariff, economic surplus has been reduced by the sum of areas *C* and *D*.

We can conclude that the tariff succeeds in helping U.S. ethanol producers but hurts U.S. consumers and the efficiency of the U.S. economy.

## Quotas and Voluntary Export Restraints

A **quota** is a numeric limit on the quantity of a good that can be imported, and it has an effect similar to a tariff. A quota is imposed by the government of the importing country. A **voluntary export restraint (VER)** is an agreement negotiated between two countries that places a numerical limit on the quantity of a good that can be imported by one country from the other country. In the early 1980s, the United States and Japan negotiated a VER that limited the quantity of automobiles the United States would import from Japan. The Japanese government agreed to the VER primarily because it was afraid that if it did not, the United States would impose a tariff or quota on imports of Japanese automobiles. Quotas and VERs have similar economic effects.

The main purpose of most tariffs and quotas is to reduce the foreign competition that domestic firms face. For many years, Congress has imposed a quota on sugar imports to protect U.S. sugar producers. Figure 8-7 shows the actual statistics for the U.S. sugar market in 2008. The effect of a quota is very similar to the effect of a tariff. By limiting imports, a quota forces the domestic price of a good above the world price. In this case, the sugar quota limits sugar imports to 3.6 billion pounds (shown by the bracket in Figure 8-7), forcing the U.S. price of sugar up to $0.33 per pound, or $0.17 higher than the world price of $0.16 per pound. The U.S. price is above the world price because the quota keeps foreign sugar producers from selling the additional sugar in the United States that would drive the price down to the world price. At a price of $0.33 per pound, U.S. producers increased the quantity of sugar they supply from 3.5 billion pounds to 15.2 billion pounds, and U.S. consumers cut back their purchases of sugar from 21.7 billion pounds to 18.8 billion pounds. Equilibrium moves from point *E* to point *F*.

**Quota** A numerical limit imposed by a government on the quantity of a good that can be imported into the country.

**Voluntary export restraint (VER)** An agreement negotiated between two countries that places a numerical limit on the quantity of a good that can be imported by one country from the other country.

# Figure 8-7

**The Economic Effect of the U.S. Sugar Quota**

Without a sugar quota, U.S. sugar producers would have sold 3.5 billion pounds of sugar, U.S. consumers would have purchased 21.7 billion pounds of sugar, and imports would have been 18.2 billion pounds. The U.S. price would have equaled the world price of $0.16 per pound. Because the sugar quota limits imports to 3.6 billion pounds (the bracket in the graph), the price of sugar in the United States rises to $0.33 per pound, and U.S. producers increase the quantity of sugar they supply to 15.2 billion pounds. U.S. consumers reduce their sugar purchases to 18.8 billion pounds. Equilibrium moves from point $E$ to point $F$. The sugar quota causes a loss of consumer surplus equal to the area $A + B + C + D$. The area $A$ is the gain to U.S. sugar producers. The area $B$ is the gain to foreign sugar producers. The areas $C$ and $D$ represent deadweight loss. The total loss to U.S. consumers in 2008 was $3.44 billion.

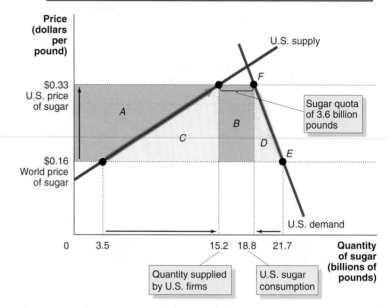

| Loss of Consumer Surplus | = | Gain to U.S. Sugar Producers | + | Gain to Foreign Sugar Producers | + | Deadweight Loss |
|---|---|---|---|---|---|---|
| $A + C + B + D$ | | $A$ | | $B$ | | $C + D$ |
| $3.44 billion | = | $1.59 billion | + | $0.61 billion | + | $1.24 billion |

## Measuring the Economic Effect of the Sugar Quota

We can use the concepts of consumer surplus, producer surplus, and deadweight loss to measure the economic impact of the sugar quota. Without a sugar quota, the world price of $0.16 per pound would also be the U.S. price. In Figure 8-7, consumer surplus equals the area above the $0.16 price line and below the demand curve. The sugar quota causes the U.S. price to rise to $0.33 and reduces consumer surplus by the area $A + B + C + D$. Without a sugar quota, producer surplus received by U.S. sugar producers would be equal to the area below the $0.16 price line and above the supply curve. The higher U.S. price resulting from the sugar quota increases the producer surplus of U.S. sugar producers by an amount equal to area $A$.

A foreign producer must have a license from the U.S. government to import sugar under the quota system. Therefore, a foreign sugar producer that is lucky enough to have an import license also benefits from the quota because it is able to sell sugar on the U.S. market at $0.33 per pound instead of $0.16 per pound. The gain to foreign sugar producers is area $B$. Areas $A$ and $B$ represent transfers from U.S. consumers of sugar to U.S. and foreign producers of sugar. Areas $C$ and $D$ represent losses to U.S. consumers that are not captured by anyone. They are deadweight losses and represent the decline in economic efficiency resulting from the sugar quota. Area $C$ shows the effect of U.S. consumers being forced to buy from U.S. producers that are less efficient than foreign producers, and area $D$ shows the effect of U.S. consumers buying less sugar than they would have at the world price.

Figure 8-7 provides enough information to calculate the dollar value of each of the four areas. The table in the figure shows the results of these calculations. The total loss to consumers from the sugar quota was $3.44 billion in 2008. About 46 percent of the loss to consumers, or $1.59 billion, was gained by U.S. sugar producers as increased producer surplus. About 18 percent, or $0.61 billion, was gained by foreign sugar producers as increased producer surplus, and about 36 percent, or $1.24 billion, was a deadweight loss to the U.S. economy. The U.S. International Trade Commission estimates that eliminating the sugar quota would result in the loss of about 3,000 jobs in the U.S. sugar industry. The cost to U.S. consumers of saving these jobs is equal to $3.44 billion/3,000, or about $1,150,000 per job. In fact, this cost is an underestimate because eliminating the sugar quota would result in new jobs being created, particularly in the candy industry. Over the years, several U.S. candy companies—including the makers of Life Savers and Star Brite mints—have moved factories to other countries to escape the impact of the sugar quota.

# Solved Problem | 8-4

## Measuring the Economic Effect of a Quota

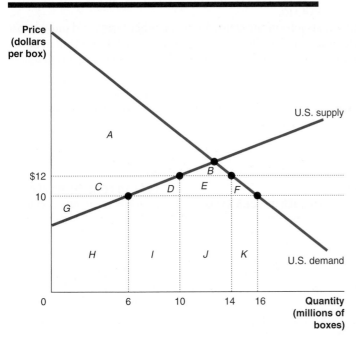

Suppose that the United States currently both produces and imports apples. The U.S. government then decides to restrict international trade in apples by imposing a quota that allows imports of only 4 million boxes of apples into the United States each year. The figure shows the results of imposing the quota.

Fill in the following table, using the prices, quantities, and letters in the figure:

| | WITHOUT QUOTA | WITH QUOTA |
|---|---|---|
| World price of apples | _____ | _____ |
| U.S. price of apples | _____ | _____ |
| Quantity supplied by U.S. firms | _____ | _____ |
| Quantity demanded by U.S. consumers | _____ | _____ |
| Quantity imported | _____ | _____ |
| Area of consumer surplus | _____ | _____ |
| Area of producer surplus | _____ | _____ |
| Area of deadweight loss | _____ | _____ |

## SOLVING THE PROBLEM:

**Step 1:** **Review the chapter material.** This problem is about measuring the economic effects of a quota, so you may want to review the section "Quotas and Voluntary Export Restraints," which begins on page 251, and "Measuring the Economic Effect of the Sugar Quota," which begins on page 252.

**Step 2:** **Fill in the table.** After studying Figure 8-7, you should be able to fill in the table. Remember that consumer surplus is the area below the demand curve and above the market price.

| | WITHOUT QUOTA | WITH QUOTA |
|---|---|---|
| World price of apples | $10 | $10 |
| U.S. price of apples | $10 | $12 |
| Quantity supplied by U.S. firms | 6 million boxes | 10 million boxes |
| Quantity demanded by U.S. consumers | 16 million boxes | 14 million boxes |
| Quantity imported | 10 million boxes | 4 million boxes |
| Area of consumer surplus | A + B + C + D + E + F | A + B |
| Area of domestic producer surplus | G | G + C |
| Area of deadweight loss | No deadweight loss | D + F |

**YOUR TURN:** For more practice, do related problem 4.14 on page 268 at the end of this chapter.

## The High Cost of Preserving Jobs with Tariffs and Quotas

The sugar quota is not alone in imposing a high cost on U.S. consumers to save jobs at U.S. firms. Table 8-5 shows, for several industries, the costs tariffs and quotas impose on U.S. consumers per year for each job saved.

Many countries besides the United States also use tariffs and quotas to try to protect jobs. Table 8-6 shows the cost to Japanese consumers per year for each job saved as a result of tariffs and quotas in the listed industries. Note the staggering cost of $51 million for each job saved that is imposed on Japanese consumers by the Japanese government's restrictions on imports of rice.

Just as the sugar quota costs jobs in the candy industry, other tariffs and quotas cost jobs outside the industries immediately affected. For example, in 1991, the United States imposed tariffs on flat-panel displays used in laptop computers. This was good news for U.S. producers of these displays but bad news for companies producing laptop computers. Toshiba, Sharp, and Apple all closed their U.S. laptop production facilities and moved production overseas. In fact, whenever one industry receives tariff or quota protection, jobs are lost in other domestic industries.

**TABLE 8-5**

**Preserving U.S. Jobs with Tariffs and Quotas Is Expensive**

| PRODUCT | NUMBER OF JOBS SAVED | COST TO CONSUMERS PER YEAR FOR EACH JOB SAVED |
|---|---|---|
| Benzenoid chemicals | 216 | $1,376,435 |
| Luggage | 226 | 1,285,078 |
| Softwood lumber | 605 | 1,044,271 |
| Dairy products | 2,378 | 685,323 |
| Frozen orange juice | 609 | 635,103 |
| Ball bearings | 146 | 603,368 |
| Machine tools | 1,556 | 479,452 |
| Women's handbags | 773 | 263,535 |
| Canned tuna | 390 | 257,640 |

Source: Federal Reserve Bank of Dallas, *2002 Annual Report*, Exhibit 11.

**TABLE 8-6**

**Preserving Japanese Jobs with Tariffs and Quotas Is Also Expensive**

| PRODUCT | COST TO CONSUMERS PER YEAR FOR EACH JOB SAVED |
|---|---|
| Rice | $51,233,000 |
| Natural gas | 27,987,000 |
| Gasoline | 6,329,000 |
| Paper | 3,813,000 |
| Beef, pork, and poultry | 1,933,000 |
| Cosmetics | 1,778,000 |
| Radio and television sets | 915,000 |

Source: Yoko Sazabami, Shujiro Urata, and Hiroki Kawai, *Measuring the Cost of Protection in Japan*, Washington, DC: Institute for International Economics, 1995. Used with permission.

## Gains from Unilateral Elimination of Tariffs and Quotas

Some politicians argue that eliminating U.S. tariffs and quotas would help the U.S. economy only if other countries eliminate their tariffs and quotas in exchange. It is easier to gain political support for reducing or eliminating tariffs or quotas if it is done as part of an agreement with other countries that involves their eliminating some of their tariffs or quotas. But as the example of the sugar quota shows, *the U.S. economy would gain from the elimination of tariffs and quotas even if other countries do not reduce their tariffs and quotas.*

## Other Barriers to Trade

In addition to tariffs and quotas, governments sometimes erect other barriers to trade. For example, all governments require that imports meet certain health and safety requirements. Sometimes, however, governments use these requirements to shield domestic firms from foreign competition. This can be true when a government imposes stricter health and safety requirements on imported goods than on goods produced by domestic firms.

Many governments also restrict imports of certain products on national security grounds. The argument is that in time of war, a country should not be dependent on imports of critical war materials. Once again, these restrictions are sometimes used more to protect domestic companies from competition than to protect national security. For example, for years, the U.S. government would buy military uniforms only from U.S. manufacturers, even though uniforms are not a critical war material.

# The Arguments Over Trade Policies and Globalization

**8.5 LEARNING** OBJECTIVE

Evaluate the arguments over trade policies and globalization.

The argument over whether the U.S. government should regulate international trade dates back to the early days of the country. One particularly controversial attempt to restrict trade took place during the Great Depression of the 1930s. At that time, the United States and other countries attempted to help domestic firms by raising tariffs on foreign imports. The United States started the process by passing the Smoot-Hawley Tariff in 1930, which raised average tariff rates to more than 50 percent. As other countries retaliated by raising their tariffs, international trade collapsed.

By the end of World War II in 1945, government officials in the United States and Europe were looking for a way to reduce tariffs and revive international trade. To help achieve this goal, they set up the General Agreement on Tariffs and Trade (GATT) in 1948. Countries that joined GATT agreed not to impose new tariffs or import quotas. In addition, a series of *multilateral negotiations*, called *trade rounds*, took place, in which countries agreed to reduce tariffs from the very high levels of the 1930s.

In the 1940s, most international trade was in goods, and the GATT agreement covered only goods. In the following decades, trade in services and in products incorporating *intellectual property*, such as software programs and movies, grew in importance. Many GATT members pressed for a new agreement that would cover services and intellectual property, as well as goods. A new agreement was negotiated, and in January 1995, GATT was replaced by the **World Trade Organization (WTO)**, headquartered in Geneva, Switzerland. More than 150 countries are currently members of the WTO.

**World Trade Organization (WTO)** An international organization that oversees international trade agreements.

## Why Do Some People Oppose the World Trade Organization?

During the years immediately after World War II, many low-income, or developing, countries erected high tariffs and restricted investment by foreign companies. When these policies failed to produce much economic growth, many of these countries decided during the 1980s to become more open to foreign trade and investment. This process became known as **globalization**. Most developing countries joined the WTO and began to follow its policies.

**Globalization** The process of countries becoming more open to foreign trade and investment.

During the 1990s, opposition to globalization began to increase. In 1999, this opposition took a violent turn at a meeting of the WTO in Seattle, Washington. A large number of protestors assembled in Seattle to meet the WTO delegates. Protests started peacefully but quickly became violent. Protesters looted stores and burned cars, and many delegates were unable to leave their hotel rooms. Similar incidents have occurred at most WTO meetings in the years since.

Why would attempts to reduce trade barriers with the objective of increasing income around the world cause such a furious reaction? The opposition to the WTO comes from three sources. First, some opponents are specifically against the globalization process that began in the 1980s and became widespread in the 1990s. Second, other opponents have the same motivation as the supporters of tariffs in the 1930s—to erect trade barriers to protect domestic firms from foreign competition. Third, some critics of the WTO support globalization in principle but believe that the WTO favors the interests of the high-income countries at the expense of the low-income countries. Let's look more closely at the sources of opposition to the WTO.

**Anti-Globalization** Many of those who protest at WTO meetings distrust globalization. Some believe that free trade and foreign investment destroy the distinctive cultures of many countries. As developing countries began to open their economies to imports from the United States and other high-income countries, these imports of food, clothing, movies, and other goods began to replace the equivalent local products. So, a teenager in Thailand might be sitting in a McDonald's restaurant, wearing Levi's jeans and a Ralph Lauren shirt, listening to a recording by U2 on his iPod, before going to the local movie theater to watch *Star Trek*. Globalization has increased the variety of products available to consumers in developing countries, but some people argue that this is too high a price to pay for what they see as damage to local cultures.

Globalization has also allowed multinational corporations to relocate factories from high-income countries to low-income countries. These new factories in Indonesia, Malaysia, Pakistan, and other countries pay much lower wages than are paid in the United States, Europe, and Japan and often do not meet the environmental or safety regulations that are imposed in high-income countries. Some factories use child labor, which is illegal in high-income countries. Some people have argued that firms with factories in developing countries should pay workers wages as high as those paid in high-income countries. They also believe these firms should abide by the health, safety, and environmental regulations that exist in the high-income countries.

The governments of most developing countries have resisted these proposals. They argue that when the currently rich countries were poor, they also lacked environmental or safety standards, and their workers were paid low wages. They argue that it is easier for rich countries to afford high wages and environmental and safety regulations than it is for poor countries. They also point out that many jobs that seem to have very low wages based on high-income country standards are often better than the alternatives available to workers in low-income countries.

## Making the Connection | The Unintended Consequences of Banning Goods Made with Child Labor

In many developing countries, such as Indonesia, Thailand, and Peru, children as young as seven or eight work 10 or more hours a day. Reports of very young workers laboring long hours, producing goods for export, have upset many people in high-income countries. In the United States, boycotts have been organized against stores that stock goods made in developing countries with child labor. Many people assume that if child workers in developing countries weren't working in factories making clothing, toys, and other products, they would be in school, as are children in high-income countries.

In fact, children in developing countries usually have few good alternatives to work. Schooling is frequently available for only a few months each year, and even children who attend school rarely do so for more than a few years. Poor families are often unable to afford even the small costs of sending their children to school. Families may even rely on the earnings of very young children to survive, as poor families once did in the United States, Europe, and Japan. There is substantial evidence that as incomes begin to rise in poor countries, families rely less on child labor. The United States eventually outlawed child labor, but not until 1938. In developing countries where child labor is common today, jobs producing export goods are usually better paying and less hazardous than the alternatives.

As preparations began in France for the 1998 World Cup, there were protests that Baden Sports—the main supplier of soccer balls—was purchasing the balls from suppliers in Pakistan that used child workers. France decided to ban all use of soccer balls made by child workers. Bowing to this pressure, Baden Sports moved production from Pakistan, where the balls were hand-stitched by child workers, to China, where the balls were machine-stitched by adult workers in factories. There was some criticism of the boycott of hand-stitched soccer balls at the time. In a broad study of child labor, three economists argued:

> Of the array of possible employment in which impoverished children might engage, soccer ball stitching is probably one of the most benign. . . . [In Pakistan] children generally work alongside other family members in the home or in small workshops. . . . Nor are the children exposed to toxic chemicals, hazardous tools or brutal working conditions. Rather, the only serious criticism concerns the length of the typical child stitcher's work-day and the impact on formal education.

In fact, the alternatives to soccer ball stitching for child workers in Pakistan turned out to be extremely grim. According to Keith Maskus, an economist at the University of Colorado and the World Bank, a "large proportion" of the children who lost their jobs stitching soccer balls ended up begging or in prostitution.

Sources: Drusilla K. Brown, Alan V. Deardorff, and Robert M. Stern, "U.S. Trade and Other Policy Options to Deter Foreign Exploitation of Child Labor," in Magnus Blomstrom and Linda S. Goldberg, eds., *Topics in Empirical International Economics: A Festschrift in Honor of Bob Lipsey*, Chicago: University of Chicago Press, 2001; Tomas Larsson, *The Race to the Top: The Real Story of Globalization*, Washington, DC: Cato Institute, 2001, p. 48; and Eric V. Edmonds and Nina Pavcnik, "Child Labor in the Global Economy," *Journal of Economic Perspectives*, Vol. 19, No. 1, Winter 2005, pp. 199–220.

**YOUR TURN:** Test your understanding by doing related problem 5.5 on page 269 at the end of this chapter.

*Would eliminating child labor, such as stitching soccer balls, improve the quality of children's lives?*

**Protectionism** The use of trade barriers to shield domestic firms from foreign competition.

**"Old-Fashioned" Protectionism** The anti-globalization argument against free trade and the WTO is relatively new. Another argument against free trade, called *protectionism*, has been around for centuries. **Protectionism** is the use of trade barriers to shield domestic firms from foreign competition. For as long as international trade has existed, governments have attempted to restrict it to protect domestic firms. As we saw with the analysis of the sugar quota, protectionism causes losses to consumers and eliminates jobs in the domestic industries that buy the protected product. In addition, by reducing the ability of countries to produce according to comparative advantage, protectionism reduces incomes.

Why, then, does protectionism attract support? Protectionism is usually justified on the basis of one of the following arguments:

- *Saving jobs.*   Supporters of protectionism argue that free trade reduces employment by driving domestic firms out of business. It is true that when more-efficient foreign firms drive less-efficient domestic firms out of business, jobs are lost, but jobs are also lost when more-efficient domestic firms drive less-efficient domestic firms out of business. These job losses are rarely permanent. In the U.S. economy, jobs are lost and new jobs are created continually. No economic study has ever found a long-term connection between the total number of jobs available and the level of tariff protection for domestic industries. In addition, trade restrictions destroy jobs in some industries at the same time that they preserve jobs in others. The U.S. sugar quota may have saved jobs in the U.S. sugar industry, but it has also destroyed jobs in the U.S. candy industry.

- *Protecting high wages.*   Some people worry that firms in high-income countries will have to start paying much lower wages to compete with firms in developing countries. This fear is misplaced, however, because free trade actually raises living standards by increasing economic efficiency. When a country practices protectionism and produces goods and services it could obtain more inexpensively from other countries, it reduces its standard of living. The United States could ban imports of coffee and begin growing it domestically. But this would entail a very high opportunity cost because coffee could only be grown in the continental United States in greenhouses and would require large amounts of labor and equipment. The coffee would have to sell for a very high price to cover these costs. Suppose the United States did ban coffee imports: Eliminating the ban at some future time would eliminate the jobs of U.S. coffee workers, but the standard of living in the United States would rise as coffee prices declined and labor, machinery, and other resources moved out of coffee production and into production of goods and services for which the United States has a comparative advantage.

- *Protecting infant industries.*   It is possible that firms in a country may have a comparative advantage in producing a good, but because the country begins production of the good later than other countries, its firms initially have higher costs. In producing some goods and services, substantial "learning by doing" occurs. As workers and firms produce more of the good or service, they gain experience and become more productive. Over time, costs and prices will fall. As the firms in the "infant industry" gain experience, their costs will fall, and they will be able to compete successfully with foreign producers. Under free trade, however, they may not get the chance. The established foreign producers can sell the product at a lower price and drive domestic producers out of business before they gain enough experience to compete. To economists, this is the most persuasive of the protectionist arguments. It has a significant drawback, however. Tariffs used to protect an infant industry eliminate the need for the firms in the industry to become productive enough to compete with foreign firms. After World War II, the governments of many developing countries used the "infant industry" argument to justify high tariff rates. Unfortunately, most of their infant industries never grew up, and they continued for years as inefficient drains on their economies.

- *Protecting national security.* As already discussed, a country should not rely on other countries for goods that are critical to its military defense. For example, the United States would probably not want to import all its jet fighter engines from China. The definition of which goods are critical to military defense is a slippery one, however. In fact, it is rare for an industry to ask for protection without raising the issue of national security, even if its products have mainly nonmilitary uses.

## Dumping

In recent years, the United States has extended protection to some domestic industries by using a provision in the WTO agreement that allows governments to impose tariffs in the case of *dumping*. **Dumping** is selling a product for a price below its cost of production. Although allowable under the WTO agreement, using tariffs to offset the effects of dumping is very controversial.

In practice, it is difficult to determine whether foreign companies are dumping goods because the true production costs of a good are not easy for foreign governments to calculate. As a result, the WTO allows countries to determine that dumping has occurred if a product is exported for a lower price than it sells for on the home market. There is a problem with this approach, however. Often there are good business reasons for a firm to sell a product for different prices to different consumers. For example, the airlines charge business travelers higher ticket prices than leisure travelers. Firms also use "loss leaders"—products that are sold below cost, or even given away free—when introducing a new product or, in the case of retailing, to attract customers who will also buy full-price products. For example, when Sun Microsystems attempted to establish StarOffice as a competitor to Microsoft Office, Sun offered the software as a free download on its Web site. During the Christmas season, Wal-Mart sometimes offers toys at prices below what they pay to buy them from manufacturers. It's unclear why these normal business practices should be unacceptable when used in international trade.

**Dumping** Selling a product for a price below its cost of production.

## Positive versus Normative Analysis (Once Again)

Economists emphasize the burden on the economy imposed by tariffs, quotas, and other government restrictions on free trade. Does it follow that these interferences are bad? Remember from Chapter 1 the distinction between *positive analysis* and *normative analysis*. Positive analysis concerns what *is*. Normative analysis concerns what *ought to be*. Measuring the impact of the sugar quota on the U.S. economy is an example of positive analysis. Asserting that the sugar quota is bad public policy and should be eliminated is normative analysis. The sugar quota—like all other interferences with trade—makes some people better off and some people worse off, and it reduces total income and consumption. Whether increasing the profits of U.S. sugar companies and the number of workers they employ justifies the costs imposed on consumers and the reduction in economic efficiency is a normative question.

Most economists do not support interferences with trade, such as the sugar quota. Few people become economists if they don't believe that markets should usually be as free as possible. But the opposite view is certainly intellectually respectable. It is possible for someone to understand the costs of tariffs and quotas but still believe that tariffs and quotas are a good idea, perhaps because they believe unrestricted free trade would cause too much disruption to the economy.

The success of industries in getting the government to erect barriers to foreign competition depends partly on some members of the public knowing full well the costs of trade barriers but supporting them anyway. However, two other factors are also at work:

1. The costs tariffs and quotas impose on consumers are large in total but relatively small per person. For example, the sugar quota imposes a total burden of about $3.44 billion per year on consumers. Spread across 310 million Americans, the burden is

only about $11 per person: too little for most people to worry about, even if they know the burden exists.

**2.** The jobs lost to foreign competition are easy to identify, but the jobs created by foreign trade are less easy to identify.

In other words, the industries that benefit from tariffs and quotas benefit a lot—the sugar quota increases the profits of U.S. sugar producers by more than $1.5 billion—whereas each consumer loses relatively little. This concentration of benefits and widely spread burdens makes it easy to understand why members of Congress receive strong pressure from some industries to enact tariffs and quotas and relatively little pressure from the general public to reduce them.

## Making the Connection | The Obama Administration Develops a Trade Policy

During the 2008 presidential election, Barack Obama argued that some existing trade agreements, such as the North American Free Trade Agreement (NAFTA), which went into effect in 1994, were flawed. NAFTA eliminated most tariffs on products shipped between the United States, Canada, and Mexico. Supporters of NAFTA argue that the treaty had made it possible for each of these countries to better pursue its comparative advantage. For example, before NAFTA, the Mexican government had used tariffs to protect its domestic automobile industry, but that industry was much less efficient than the U.S. automobile industry. When tariffs were removed, Mexican consumers could take advantage of the efficiency of the U.S. industry, and U.S. exports of motor vehicles to Mexico soared.

Similarly, Canadian consumers could take advantage of lower-priced U.S. beef, and U.S. consumers could take advantage of lower-priced Canadian lumber. As we would expect, expanding trade increased consumption in all three countries. Some early opponents of NAFTA argued that it would lead to a loss of jobs in the United States. Although employment in some industries did decline following the passage of NAFTA, overall employment in the United States increased by more than 23 million between the time NAFTA took effect and 2008.

Obama argued, though, that NAFTA and other trade agreements, such as the Central American Free Trade Agreement (CAFTA), were flawed because they failed to require that U.S. trading partners enact labor regulations and environmental protections similar to those in the United States. In some countries, workers are denied the right to join unions, and they sometimes work in unsafe conditions. Obama pledged that as president, he would "use trade agreements to spread good labor and environmental standards around the world."

*Would a free trade agreement with Colombia benefit the United States?*

Once in office, though, Obama found that the governments of Canada and Mexico were reluctant to renegotiate NAFTA. With unemployment rising through 2009, the president also faced political pressure to pursue protectionist policies. As we have seen, Congress included a "Buy American" provision in the 2009 stimulus bill. But Obama came out against the stricter provision included in the original version of the bill, declaring: "We can't send a protectionist message . . . that somehow we're just looking after ourselves and not concerned with world trade." In April 2009, Ron Kirk, the president's trade representative, announced that the administration would attempt to gain congressional approval for trade agreements with Panama and Colombia. Kirk argued, "At this moment of economic uncertainty, we should make our best effort to create the strong global trading system of tomorrow. Now is not the time to turn inward."

As the administration attempted to develop a trade policy, it was faced with the politically difficult task of trying to preserve and extend the efficiency gains from freer trade in the face of often popular efforts to protect jobs in favored industries at a time of rising unemployment.

Sources: David E. Sanger, "Senate Agrees to Dilute 'Buy America' Provisions," *New York Times*, February 4, 2009; Mark Drajem, "Obama to Pursue Trade Deals, Avoid Turning 'Inward,'" Bloomberg.com, April 23, 2009; and "A Friendly Visit," *Economist*, February 20, 2009.

**YOUR TURN:** Test your understanding by doing related problems 5.7 and 5.8 on page 270 at the end of this chapter.

▶ Continued from page 237

## Economics in YOUR LIFE!

At the beginning of the chapter, we asked you to consider how some U.S. companies convinced Congress to include the "Buy American" provision in the stimulus bill and why relatively few people have heard of this provision. In the chapter, we saw that trade restrictions tend to preserve relatively few jobs in the protected industries, while leading to job losses in other industries and costing consumers billions per year in higher prices. This might seem to increase the mystery of why Congress enacted the "Buy American" provision. We have also seen, though, that *per person*, the burden of specific trade restrictions can be small. The sugar quota, for instance, imposes a per-person cost on consumers of only about $11 per year. Not many people will take the trouble of writing a letter to their member of Congress or otherwise make their views known in the hope of saving $11 per year. In fact, few people will even spend the time to become aware that a specific trade restriction exists. So, if before you read this chapter you had never heard of the "Buy American" provision, you are certainly not alone.

# Conclusion

There are few issues economists agree upon more than the economic benefits of free trade. However, there are few political issues as controversial as government policy toward trade. Many people who would be reluctant to see the government interfere with domestic trade are quite willing to see it interfere with international trade. The damage high tariffs inflicted on the world economy during the 1930s shows what can happen when governments around the world abandon free trade. Whether future episodes of that type can be avoided is by no means certain.

Read *An Inside Look at Policy* on the next page for a closer look at the debate over the "Buy American" provision in the 2009 government stimulus bill.

## >> Caterpillar and Other Exporters Oppose "Buy American" Provision

### USA TODAY

## "Buy American" Clause Stirs Up Controversy

A contentious debate over a "Buy American" provision in the economic stimulus package poses an early test for President Obama on both domestic politics and foreign policy. The Senate this week is considering an $885 billion bill designed to help mend the ailing economy, which requires all "manufactured goods" purchased with stimulus money to be made in the United States. The House already has approved a narrower bill mandating the use of domestic iron and steel.

**(a)** To supporters, including labor unions that helped the Democrats retake the White House last year, a "Buy American" requirement is just common sense at a time of economic crisis and rising unemployment. . . . If Congress doesn't insist upon the use of U.S.-made materials, taxpayer funds could line the pockets of European or Chinese workers rather than hard-hit Americans.

"If we're gonna spend many billions of taxpayer dollars in an effort to get the economy up and moving again, it's obvious that money should be spent in our economy," said . . . a United Steelworkers (USW) official . . .

**(b)** Opponents, however, say the new language could breach U.S. trade commitments and ignite a disastrous round of beggar-thy-neighbor retaliation like that which worsened the Great Depression. Both the European Union and Canada already warned the administration against the consequences of resurgent economic nationalism. If other countries enact similar limits, U.S. exporters such as Caterpillar and Boeing would lose lucrative foreign sales.

### Obama's view

In an interview Tuesday with Fox News, Obama cast doubt on the measure, saying, "We can't send a protectionist message." . . .

From Indonesia to Sweden, countries have carved out protected turf for favored industries. . . . "The real problem here is not the legality. It's that it will undoubtedly trigger retaliatory actions," said Stanley Marcuss, a partner at the law firm Bryan Cave. . . .

**(c)** The new provisions would expand to more products existing laws dating to 1933 and 1982 giving preference to domestic goods in government programs such as highway building. The president could waive the domestic content rule with a finding that "the public interest" required the use of foreign material or if buying at home was 25% more expensive than abroad. . . .

Gary Huffbauer, an economist at the Peterson Institute for International Economics, says the "Buy American" requirement could violate U.S. treaty commitments if applied to Canada, Mexico or the 37 countries that signed the World Trade Organization agreement on government procurement. And he disputes claims that steering more stimulus cash to domestic suppliers will dramatically boost employment. The Alliance for American Manufacturing, for example, says "Buy American" language would create 77,000 more jobs. But only 4% of federal procurement spending on manufactured goods goes to foreign companies, says Huffbauer. Based on that, he says the extra steel industry jobs spawned by domestic content requirement could be as few as 1,000 and would be swamped by the export jobs lost in any new trade war.

### Community interests

The stakes can be seen in individual communities. Steel plants across the rust belt are feeling the effects of the depressed economy and auto industry meltdown. An ArcelorMittal plant in Burns Harbor, Ind., is representative. Last year, the company and USW agreed on a plan to avoid involuntary layoffs of up to 2,400 workers with some voluntary pink slips and a shortened workweek.

"These plants certainly can produce the steel necessary for infrastructure," says Robinson, . . . of the USW. . . . ArcelorMittal spokesman Bill Steers declined comment on the "Buy American" measure's impact.

About 200 miles southwest of Burns Harbor is a Caterpillar factory where roughly 3,500 other Midwesterners could be hurt by the potential boomerang effect of new domestic content legislation. The company's Decatur, Ill., plant produces heavy equipment for customers all over the world. About 80% of its output is exported, including massive mining trucks used in Canada's Alberta oil sands development.

"The world economy is at a tipping point. If the U.S. embraces protectionism, it will send a signal that will be hard for anyone to resist," says Bill Lane, Caterpillar's head of governmental affairs.

Source: David J. Lynch, "'Buy American' Clause Stirs Up Controversy," *USA Today*, February 6, 2009, p. 9A.

## Key Points in the Article

This article discusses the debate over the "Buy American" provision in the 2009 economic stimulus bill. The bill was intended to use increases in federal government spending to stimulate the economy during the 2007–2009 recession. By funding construction of highway bridges and other infrastructure projects, supporters of the bill hoped to increase demand for steel and other goods, thereby raising production and employment. (The bill also increased federal spending on other, non-infrastructure, projects.) The "Buy American" provision would require that the money be spent only on U.S.-made goods. Supporters of the provision argued that if money was spent on steel and other goods produced in Canada or other countries, then the impact on U.S. production and employment would be reduced. Opponents of the measure, such as Caterpillar, argued that excluding foreign-produced goods from the stimulus program would violate international trade agreements and invite foreign governments to retaliate against U.S.-made goods.

## Analyzing the News

**(a)** In this chapter, we have seen that firms support restrictions on trade in an effort to reduce the competition they face. In this case, U.S. steel companies and their workers were attempting to reduce competition from foreign steel companies. The figure shows the effect of the "Buy American" provision on the steel market in the United States. (For simplicity, we assume that there are no barriers to foreign steel producers selling to the United States, apart from the "Buy American" provision. We also assume that the figure represents the whole market for steel in the United States, not just the market for steel to be used in projects funded by the stimulus bill.) In the absence of the "Buy American" provision, the price of steel in the United States is $P_1$, which is both the U.S. price and the world price. By limiting the amount of steel that can be imported into the United States, the "Buy American" provision raises the price of steel in the United States to $P_2$, which is above the world price, and equilibrium moves from point $E$ to point $F$. U.S. consumption of steel falls from $Q_4$ to $Q_3$, the quantity of steel supplied by U.S. steel producers increases from $Q_1$ to $Q_2$, and imports of foreign steel decline from $Q_4 - Q_1$ to $Q_3 - Q_2$. The area of $A$ represents a transfer of consumer surplus to producer surplus received by U.S. steel companies. The area of $B$ represents a transfer of consumer surplus to producer surplus received by foreign steel companies. Areas $C$ and $D$ represent a conversion of consumer surplus to deadweight loss. U.S. steel companies—and their workers—gain from the provision, as do foreign steel companies still able to sell in the United States because they receive a price higher than the world price. U.S. consumers—and taxpayers—lose because they must now pay a price above the world price

**(b)** The chapter mentions the Smoot-Hawley Tariff, which Congress passed at the beginning of the Great Depression of the 1930s. Then, as in 2009, production, incomes, and employment were falling, and Congress hoped to increase spending on domestically produced goods by raising tariffs on foreign imports to record levels. Other countries countered quickly, however, by raising tariffs on U.S. goods. As a result, world trade declined, and all economies sank deeper into the Depression. In 2009, during the debate over the "Buy American" provision, companies such as Caterpillar and Boeing, which rely heavily on exports, were concerned about foreign retaliation. Although, as was discussed in the chapter, Congress eventually modified the provision to make it consistent with U.S. obligations under international trade agreements, foreign governments continued during 2009 to express their concerns, and the possibility of retaliation still existed.

**(c)** Critics of the "Buy American" provisions also raised a concern that paying more for U.S.-produced steel would drive up the cost of some of the projects being funded. Bridges and other projects that use a lot of steel would become particularly more costly. Because the total amount of spending under the stimulus bill was fixed, the more costly each project was, the fewer projects that would be able to be funded. Earlier experience with projects forced to rely primarily on U.S.-produced steel—such as the extensive reconstruction of the San Francisco–Oakland Bay Bridge during the 1990s—shows that the increase in cost can be substantial.

## Thinking Critically
### *About Policy*

1. "Buy American" provisions, as well as tariffs and quotas on foreign imports, are intended to save jobs in the United States. Do they, in fact, save jobs? Do you support these trade restrictions? Why or why not?

2. In which goods mentioned in the article does the United States have a comparative advantage? In which goods do other countries have a comparative advantage? Explain your reasoning.

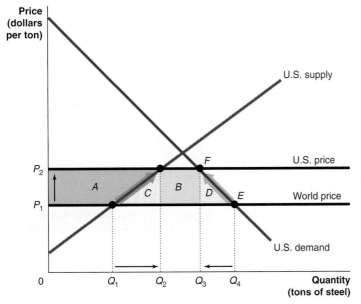

The effect of the "Buy American" provision on the steel market in the United States.

# Key Terms

Absolute advantage, p. 242

Autarky, p. 244

Comparative advantage, p. 241

Dumping, p. 259

Exports, p. 238

External economies, p. 247

Free trade, p. 249

Globalization, p. 256

Imports, p. 238

Opportunity cost, p. 241

Protectionism, p. 258

Quota, p. 251

Tariff, p. 238

Terms of trade, p. 244

Voluntary export restraint (VER), p. 251

World Trade Organization (WTO), p. 255

---

> **8.1** **The United States in the International Economy,** pages 238–241
> LEARNING OBJECTIVE: Discuss the role of international trade in the U.S. economy.

## Summary

International trade has been increasing in recent decades, in part because of reductions in *tariffs* and other barriers to trade. A **tariff** is a tax imposed by a government on imports. The quantity of goods and services the United States imports and exports has been continually increasing. **Imports** are goods and services bought domestically but produced in other countries. **Exports** are goods and services produced domestically and sold to other countries. Today, the United States is the leading exporting country in the world, and about 20 percent of U.S. manufacturing jobs depend on exports.

 Visit **www.myeconlab.com** to complete these exercises online and get instant feedback.

## Review Questions

1.1 Briefly explain whether the value of U.S. exports is typically larger or smaller than the value of U.S. imports.

1.2 Briefly explain whether you agree with the following statement: "International trade is more important to the U.S. economy than to most other economies."

## Problems and Applications

1.3 If the United States were to stop trading goods and services with other countries, which U.S. industries would be likely to see their sales decline the most? Briefly explain.

1.4 Briefly explain whether you agree with the following statement: "Japan has always been much more heavily involved in international trade than are most other nations. In fact, today Japan exports a larger fraction of its GDP than Germany, Great Britain, or the United States."

1.5 **(Related to the *Making the Connection* on page 240)** Douglas Irwin, a professor of economics at Dartmouth College, wrote the following in a column in the *New York Times*:

> General Electric and Caterpillar have opposed the Buy American provision because they fear it will hurt their ability to win contracts abroad. . . . Once we get through the current economic mess, China, India and other countries are likely to continue their large investments in building projects. If such countries also adopt our preferences for domestic producers, then America will be at a competitive disadvantage in bidding for those contracts.

What are "preferences for domestic producers"? Why would these preferences put U.S. firms at a "competitive disadvantage"? Why might having difficulty making sales in China and India be a particular problem for Caterpillar?

Source: Douglas A. Irwin, "If We Buy American, No One Else Will," *New York Times*, January 31, 2009.

**>> End Learning Objective 8.1**

**8.2** **Comparative Advantage in International Trade,** pages 241–243

LEARNING OBJECTIVE: Understand the difference between comparative advantage and absolute advantage in international trade.

## Summary

**Comparative advantage** is the ability of an individual, a business, or a country to produce a good or service at the lowest **opportunity cost**. **Absolute advantage** is the ability to produce more of a good or service than competitors when using the same amount of resources. Countries trade on the basis of comparative advantage, not on the basis of absolute advantage.

 Visit **www.myeconlab.com** to complete these exercises online and get instant feedback.

## Review Questions

**2.1** A WTO publication calls comparative advantage "arguably the single most powerful insight in economics." What is comparative advantage? What makes it such a powerful insight?

Source: World Trade Organization, "Understanding the WTO," www.wto.org/english/thewto_e/whatis_e/tif_e/fact3_e.htm.

**2.2** What is the difference between absolute advantage and comparative advantage? Will a country always be an exporter of a good where it has an absolute advantage in production?

## Problems and Applications

**2.3** Why do the goods that countries import and export change over time? Use the concept of comparative advantage in your answer.

**2.4** Briefly explain whether you agree with the following argument: "Unfortunately, Bolivia does not have a comparative advantage with respect to the United States in the production of any good or service." (*Hint:* You do not need any specific information about the economies of Bolivia or the United States to be able to answer this question.)

**2.5** In January 2008, the Bank of France published a report, stating that in 2006, hourly labor productivity in the United States was higher than the productivity in Japan. If U.S. workers can produce more goods and services per hour than Japanese workers, why does the United States continue to import from Japan some products it could produce at home?

Source: Gilbert Cette, Yusuf Kocoglu, and Jacques Mairesse, "A Comparison of Productivity in France, Japan, The United Kingdom and the United States over the Past Century," Banque de France, January 8, 2008.

**2.6** Patrick J. Buchanan, a former presidential candidate, argued in his book on the global economy that there

is a flaw in David Ricardo's theory of comparative advantage:

> Classical free trade theory fails the test of common sense. According to Ricardo's law of comparative advantage . . . if America makes better computers and textiles than China does, but our advantage in computers is greater than our advantage in textiles, we should (1) focus on computers, (2) let China make textiles, and (3) trade U.S. computers for Chinese textiles. . . .
>
> The doctrine begs a question. If Americans are more efficient than Chinese in making clothes . . . why surrender the more efficient American industry? Why shift to a reliance on a Chinese textile industry that will take years to catch up to where American factories are today?

Do you agree with Buchanan's argument? Briefly explain.

Source: Patrick J. Buchanan, *The Great Betrayal: How American Sovereignty and Social Justice Are Being Sacrificed to the Gods of the Global Economy,* Boston: Little, Brown, 1998, p. 66.

**2.7** In a 2007 debate among Democratic presidential candidates, Barack Obama made the following statement: "Well, look, people don't want a cheaper T-shirt if they're losing a job in the process." What did Obama mean by the phrase "losing a job in the process"? Using the economic concept of comparative advantage, explain under what circumstances it would make sense for the United States to produce all of the T-shirts purchased in the United States. Do you agree with Obama's statement? Briefly explain.

Source: James Pethokoukis, "Democratic Debate Spawns Weird Economics," *U.S. News & World Report,* August 8, 2007.

**2.8** (Related to *Solved Problem 8-2* on page 243) Consider a simple economy with two traded goods and two countries. The country of Calabria can produce a bushel of corn with 10 hours of labor input or a mobile phone with 10 hours of labor. The country of Nerranova can produce a bushel of corn with 5 hours of labor or a mobile phone with 7 hours of labor.

a. Which country has an absolute advantage in the production of corn? Which country has an absolute advantage in the production of mobile phones?

b. Which country has a comparative advantage in the production of corn? Which country has a comparative advantage in the production of mobile phones?

**>> End Learning Objective 8.2**

## 8.3 How Countries Gain from International Trade, pages 244–248

LEARNING OBJECTIVE: Explain how countries gain from international trade.

## Summary

**Autarky** is a situation in which a country does not trade with other countries. The **terms of trade** is the ratio at which a country can trade its exports for imports from other countries. When a country specializes in producing goods where it has a comparative advantage and trades for the other goods it needs, the country will have a higher level of income and consumption. We do not see complete specialization in production for three reasons: Not all goods and services are traded internationally, production of most goods involves increasing opportunity costs, and tastes for products differ across countries. Although the population of a country as a whole benefits from trade, companies—and their workers—that are unable to compete with lower-cost foreign producers lose. Among the main sources of comparative advantage are climate and natural resources, relative abundance of labor and capital, technology, and *external economies*. **External economies** are reductions in a firm's cost that result from an increase in the size of an industry. A country may develop a comparative advantage in the production of a good, and then as time passes and circumstances change, the country may lose its comparative advantage in producing that good and develop a comparative advantage in producing other goods.

 Visit **www.myeconlab.com** to complete these exercises online and get instant feedback.

## Review Questions

3.1 Briefly explain how international trade increases a country's consumption.

3.2 What is meant by a country specializing in the production of a good? Is it typical for countries to be completely specialized? Briefly explain.

3.3 What are the main sources of comparative advantage?

## Problems and Applications

3.4 Demonstrate how the opportunity costs of producing cell phones and digital music players in Japan and the United States were calculated in Table 8-2 on page 243.

3.5 Briefly explain whether you agree with the following statement: "Most countries exhaust their comparative advantage in producing a good or service before they reach complete specialization."

3.6 Is free trade likely to benefit a large, populous country more than a small country with fewer people? Briefly explain.

3.7 An article in the *New Yorker* magazine states, "the main burden of trade-related job losses and wage declines has fallen on middle- and lower-income Americans. But . . . the very people who suffer most from free trade are often, paradoxically, among its biggest beneficiaries." Explain how it is possible that middle- and lower-income Americans are both the biggest losers and at the same time the biggest winners from free trade.
Source: James Surowiecki, "The Free-Trade Paradox," *New Yorker*, May 26, 2008.

3.8 Hal Varian, an economist at the University of California, Berkeley, has made two observations about international trade:
a. Trade allows a country "to produce more with less."
b. There is little doubt who wins [from trade] in the long run: consumers.

Briefly explain whether you agree with either or both of these observations.
Source: Hal R. Varian, "The Mixed Bag of Productivity," *New York Times*, October 23, 2003.

3.9 In a recent public opinion poll, 41 percent of people responding believed that free trade hurts the U.S. economy, while only 28 percent believed that it helps the economy. (The remaining people were uncertain about the effects of free trade.) What is "free trade"? Do you believe it helps or hurts the economy? (Be sure to define what you mean by "helps" or "hurts.") Why do you think that more Americans appear to believe that free trade hurts the economy than believe that it helps the economy?
Source: Matthew Benjamin, "Americans Souring on Free Trade Amid Optimism About Economy," *Bloomberg News*, January 19, 2007.

3.10 (Related to the *Don't Let This Happen to You!* on page 246) Briefly explain whether you agree with the following statement: "I can't believe that anyone opposes expanding international trade. After all, when international trade expands, everyone wins."

3.11 (Related to the *Making the Connection* on page 247) Explain why there are advantages to a movie studio operating in southern California, rather than in, say, Florida.

**>> End Learning Objective 8.3**

## 8.4 Government Policies That Restrict International Trade, pages 249–255

LEARNING OBJECTIVE: Analyze the economic effects of government policies that restrict international trade.

## Summary

**Free trade** is trade between countries without government restrictions. Government policies that interfere with trade usually take the form of *tariffs*, *quotas*, or *voluntary export restraints* (VERs). A **tariff** is a tax imposed by a government on imports. A **quota** is a numeric limit imposed by a government on the quantity of a good that can be imported into the country. A **voluntary export restraint (VER)** is an agreement negotiated between two countries that places a numerical limit on the quantity of a good that can be imported by one country from the other country. The federal government's sugar quota costs U.S. consumers $3.44 billion per year, or about $1,150,000 per year for each job saved in the sugar industry. Saving jobs by using tariffs and quotas is often very expensive.

 Visit **www.myeconlab.com** to complete these exercises online and get instant feedback.

## Review Questions

**4.1** What is a tariff? What is a quota? Give an example of a non-tariff barrier to trade.

**4.2** Who gains and who loses when a country imposes a tariff or a quota on imports of a good?

## Problems and Applications

**4.3** The G20 is a group of central bankers and finance ministers from 19 countries and the European Union who have a common goal of promoting global economic stability. In a letter to the editor of the *New York Times*, Victor K. Fung, the chairman of the International Chamber of Commerce, comments on the 2009 G20 summit in London: "While global leaders promise to fight protectionism when they gather at summit meetings, they must also resist intense pressure back home to adopt populist policies that will most certainly protract the recession." What does Fung mean by "fighting protectionism"? What does he mean by "populist policies"? How might populist trade policies extend a period of high unemployment and low production, such as the 2007–2009 recession?
Source: Victor K. Fung, "Resist Protectionism," Letter to the Editor, *New York Times*, March 30, 2009.

**4.4** Political commentator B. Bruce-Biggs once wrote the following in the *Wall Street Journal*: "This is not to say that the case for international free trade is invalid; it is just irrelevant. It is an 'if only everybody . . .' argument. . . . In the real world almost everybody sees benefits in economic nationalism." What do you think he means by "economic nationalism"? Do you agree that a country benefits from free trade only if every other country also practices free trade? Briefly explain.
Source: B. Bruce-Biggs, "The Coming Overthrow of Free Trade," *Wall Street Journal*, February 24, 1983, p. 28.

**4.5** Two U.S. senators make the following argument against allowing free trade: "Fewer and fewer Americans support our government's trade policy. They see a shrinking middle class, lost jobs and exploding trade deficits. Yet supporters of free trade continue to push for more of the same—more job-killing trade agreements. . . ." Do you agree with these senators that reducing barriers to trade reduces the number of jobs available to workers in the United States? Briefly explain.
Source: Byron Dorgan and Sherrod Brown, "How Free Trade Hurts," *Washington Post*, December 23, 2006, p. A21.

**4.6** The United States produces beef and also imports beef from other countries.
  a. Draw a graph showing the supply and demand for beef in the United States. Assume that the United States can import as much as it wants at the world price of beef without causing the world price of beef to increase. Be sure to indicate on the graph the quantity of beef imported.
  b. Now show on your graph the effect of the United States imposing a tariff on beef. Be sure to indicate on your graph the quantity of beef sold by U.S. producers before and after the tariff is imposed, the quantity of beef imported before and after the tariff, and the price of beef in the United States before and after the tariff.
  c. Discuss who benefits and who loses when the United States imposes a tariff on beef.

**4.7** (Related to the *Chapter Opener* on page 237) Which firms are most likely to be unfavorably affected by a provision that states that only U.S. firms can participate in programs financed by federal spending? Suppose such a provision drives up the price of steel in the United States. Would any firms outside the steel industry be hurt? Would any industries be helped? (*Hint:* Think about what steel is used for and whether substitutes exist for these uses.)

**4.8** When Congress was considering a bill to impose quotas on imports of textiles, shoes, and other products, Milton Friedman, a Nobel Prize–winning economist, made the following comment: "The consumer will be forced to spend several extra dollars to subsidize the producers [of these goods] by one dollar. A straight handout would be far cheaper." Why would a quota result in consumers paying much more than domestic producers receive? Where do the other dollars go? What does Friedman mean by a "straight handout"? Why would this be cheaper than a quota?

Source: Milton Friedman, "Free Trade," *Newsweek*, August 27, 1970.

**4.9** The United States has about 9,000 rice farmers. In 2006, these rice farmers received $780 million in subsidy payments from the U.S. government (or nearly $87,000 per farmer). These payments result in U.S. farmers producing much more rice than they otherwise would, a substantial amount of which is exported. According to an article in the *Wall Street Journal*, Kpalagim Mome, a farmer in the African country of Ghana, can no longer find buyers in Ghana for his rice:

> "We can't sell our rice anymore. It gets worse every year," Mr. Mome says. . . . Years of economic hardship have driven three of his brothers to walk and hitchhike 2,000 miles across the Sahara to reach the Mediterranean and Europe. His sister plans to leave next year. Mr. Mome's plight is repeated throughout farm communities in Africa and elsewhere in the developing world.

Why would subsidies paid by the U.S. government to U.S. rice farmers reduce the incomes of rice farmers in Africa?

Source: Juliane von Reppert-Bismarck, "How Trade Barriers Keep Africans Adrift," *Wall Street Journal*, December 27, 2006.

**4.10** An economic analysis of a proposal to impose a quota on steel imports into the United States indicated that the quota would save 3,700 jobs in the steel industry but cost about 35,000 jobs in other U.S. industries. Why would a quota on steel imports cause employment to fall in other industries? Which other industries are likely to be most affected?

Source: Study cited in Douglas A. Irwin, *Free Trade Under Fire*, Princeton, NJ: Princeton University Press, 2002, p. 82.

**4.11** A student makes the following argument:

> Tariffs on imports of foreign goods into the United States will cause the foreign companies to add the amount of the tariff to the prices they charge in the United States for those goods. Instead of putting a tariff on imported goods, we should ban importing them. Banning imported goods is better than putting tariffs on them because U.S. producers benefit from the reduced competition, and U.S. consumers don't have to pay the higher prices caused by tariffs.

Briefly explain whether you agree with the student's reasoning.

**4.12** Suppose China decides to pay large subsidies to any Chinese company that exports goods or services to the United States. As a result, these companies are able to sell products in the United States at far below their cost of production. In addition, China decides to bar all imports from the United States. The dollars that the United States pays to import Chinese goods are left in banks in China. Will this strategy raise or lower the standard of living in China? Will it raise or lower the standard of living in the United States? Briefly explain. Be sure to provide a definition of "standard of living" in your answer.

**4.13** According to an editorial in the *New York Times*, because of the sugar quota:

> Sugar growers in this country, long protected from global competition, have had a great run at the expense of just about everyone else—refineries, candy manufacturers, other food companies, individual consumers and farmers in the developing world.

Briefly explain how each group mentioned in this editorial is affected by the sugar quota.

Source: "America's Sugar Daddies," *New York Times*, November 29, 2003.

**4.14** (Related to *Solved Problem 8-4* on page 253) Suppose that the United States currently both produces kumquats and imports them. The U.S. government then decides to restrict international trade in kumquats by imposing a quota that allows imports of only 6 million pounds of kumquats into the United States each year. The figure shows the results of imposing the quota.

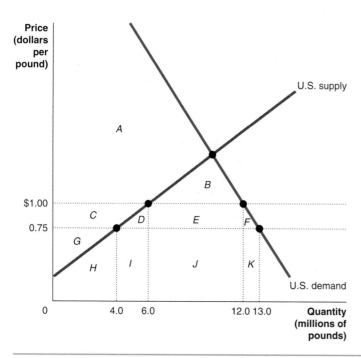

Fill in the table below using the letters in the figure.

| | WITHOUT QUOTA | WITH QUOTA |
|---|---|---|
| World price of kumquats | _____ | _____ |
| U.S. price of kumquats | _____ | _____ |
| Quantity supplied by U.S. firms | _____ | _____ |
| Quantity demanded | _____ | _____ |
| Quantity imported | _____ | _____ |
| Area of consumer surplus | _____ | _____ |
| Area of domestic producer surplus | _____ | _____ |
| Area of deadweight loss | _____ | _____ |

**>> End Learning Objective 8.4**

---

**8.5** | ## The Arguments over Trade Policies and Globalization, pages 255–261
LEARNING OBJECTIVE: Evaluate the arguments over trade policies and globalization.

## Summary

The **World Trade Organization (WTO)** is an international organization that enforces international trade agreements. The WTO has promoted **globalization**, the process of countries becoming more open to foreign trade and investment. Some critics of the WTO argue that globalization has damaged local cultures around the world. Other critics oppose the WTO because they believe in **protectionism**, which is the use of trade barriers to shield domestic firms from foreign competition. The WTO allows countries to use tariffs in cases of **dumping**, when an imported product is sold for a price below its cost of production. Economists can point out the burden imposed on the economy by tariffs, quotas, and other government interferences with free trade. But whether these policies should be used is a normative decision.

 Visit **www.myeconlab.com** to complete these exercises online and get instant feedback.

## Review Questions

5.1 What events led to the General Agreement on Tariffs and Trade? Why did the WTO eventually replace GATT?
5.2 What is globalization? Why are some people opposed to globalization?

5.3 What is protectionism? Who benefits and who loses from protectionist policies? What are the main arguments people use to justify protectionism?
5.4 What is dumping? Who benefits and who loses from dumping? What problems arise when anti-dumping laws are implemented?

## Problems and Applications

5.5 (Related to the *Making the Connection* on page 257) The following excerpt is from a newspaper story on President Bill Clinton's proposals for changes in the WTO. The story was published just before the 1999 WTO meeting in Seattle that ended in rioting:

> [President Clinton] suggested that a working group on labor be created within the WTO to develop core labor standards that would become "part of every trade agreement. And ultimately I would favor a system in which sanctions would come for violating any provision of a trade agreement. . . ." But the new U.S. stand is sure to meet massive resistance from developing countries, which make up more than 100 of the 135 countries in the WTO. They are not interested in adopting tougher U.S. labor standards.

What did Clinton mean by "core labor standards"? Why would developing countries resist adopting these standards?

Source: Terence Hunt, "Salute to Trade's Benefits Turns into 'Kind of Circus,'" Associated Press, December 2, 1999.

5.6 Steven Landsburg, an economist at the University of Rochester, wrote the following in an article in the *New York Times*:

> Free trade is not only about the right of American consumers to buy at the cheapest possible price; it's also about the right of foreign producers to earn a living. Steelworkers in West Virginia struggle hard to make ends meet. So do steelworkers in South Korea. To protect one at the expense of the other, solely because of where they happened to be born, is a moral outrage.

How does the U.S. government protect steelworkers in West Virginia at the expense of steelworkers in South Korea? Is Landsburg making a positive or a normative statement? A few days later, Tom Redburn published an article disagreeing with Landsburg:

> It is not some evil character flaw to care more about the welfare of people nearby than about that of those far away—it's human nature. And it is morally—and economically—defensible. . . . A society that ignores the consequences of economic disruption on those among its citizens who come out at the short end of the stick is not only heartless, it also undermines its own cohesion and adaptability.

Which of the two arguments do you find most convincing?

Sources: Steven E. Landsburg, "Who Cares if the Playing Field Is Level?" *New York Times*, June 13, 2001; and Tom Redburn, "Economic View: Of Politics, Free Markets, and Tending to Society," *New York Times*, June 17, 2001.

5.7 **(Related to the *Chapter Opener* on page 237 and the *Making the Connection* on page 260)** In a forum in the *New York Times* on the "Buy American" provision in the stimulus bill, the editors posed the following question: "Why is the buy-American idea objectionable, or, alternatively, under what circumstances should it be promoted?" Roger Simmermaker, the author of *How Americans Can Buy American*, responded:

> The buy-American provision in the economic stimulus bill isn't as much about a return to protectionism as it is about a return to the American virtues and values—

self-sufficiency, self-reliance and independence—that this country was founded on. Workers in foreign countries don't pay taxes to America. Only American workers pay taxes to America. We need to employ American steelworkers, ironworkers and autoworkers so we need to . . . keep and create American jobs. . . .

Burton Folsom Jr., a professor at Hillsdale College, offered an opposing view:

> "Slap a tariff on China and save American jobs," the protectionists say. This tempting line of reasoning is flawed for two reasons. First, if Americans pay more for, say, American-made shoes or shirts, then they have less to spend for other things they might need—they are simply subsidizing inefficient local producers. And those American manufacturers, who are protected from foreign competitors, have little incentive to innovate and cut prices. Second, if we refuse to buy China's imports, China will refuse to buy our exports, including our first-rate computers and iPods. Our export market collapses.

Which of the two arguments do you find the most convincing?

Source: "That 'Buy American' Provision," *New York Times*, February 11, 2009.

5.8 **(Related to the *Making the Connection* on page 260)** In April 2009, when the Obama administration announced it was going to push for ratifying trade agreements with Colombia and Panama, Representative Phil Hare of Illinois was quoted as saying: "At a time when American workers need a life raft, passage of these two trade agreements would be like throwing them anchors." Is it likely that trade agreements that reduce tariffs and quotas will decrease the number of jobs available to U.S. workers? Briefly explain.

Source: Mark Drajem, "Obama to Pursue Trade Deals, Avoid Turning 'Inward,'" Bloomberg.com, April 23, 2009.

5.9 The following appeared in an article in *BusinessWeek* that argued against free trade: "The U.S. is currently in a precarious position. In addition to geopolitical threats, we face a severe economic shock. We have already lost trillions of dollars and millions of jobs to foreigners." If a country engages in free trade, is the total number of jobs in the country likely to decline? Briefly explain.

Source: Vladimir Masch, "A Radical Plan to Manage Globalization," *BusinessWeek*, February 14, 2007.

**>> End Learning Objective 8.5**

# Appendix
## Multinational Firms

Most large corporations are multinational. **Multinational enterprises** are firms that conduct operations in more than one country—as opposed to simply trading with other countries. For example, the U.S. firm General Electric employs more than 300,000 people in more than 100 countries. Toyota Motor Corporation of Japan has invested more than $10 billion in factories and other facilities in the United States and assembles more than a million cars and trucks in North American factories. (Almost two-thirds of the cars and trucks Toyota sells in the United States are assembled in North American factories.) The Nestlé Company is headquartered in the small city of Vevey, Switzerland, but it produces and sells food products in practically every country in the world. It has more than 500 factories worldwide, employing about 260,000 people.

Table 8A-1 shows the top 25 multinational corporations, ranked by the value of their revenues in 2009. Large corporations based in the United States generally established multinational operations earlier than did firms based in other countries. Today, 4 of the 10 largest multinational corporations in the world are based in the United States. The table shows that large corporations in the petroleum refining, banking, insurance, and motor vehicle industries are most likely to have extensive multinational operations.

## A Brief History of Multinational Enterprises

From at least 2500 B.C., companies have traded over long distances. Well-developed systems of long-distance trade existed in the eastern Mediterranean by 1500 B.C. By the Middle Ages, a number of multinational firms had been established in Europe. For example, the Medici bank was based in Florence, Italy, but had branches in France, Switzerland, and England. Some multinational companies founded during these years still exist. The Austrian freight forwarding firm Gebrüder Weiss, which had offices in several countries in the fourteenth century, continues to operate today. Before the twentieth century, multinational firms were still relatively rare, however.

In the late nineteenth and early twentieth centuries, a few large U.S. corporations began to expand their operations beyond the domestic market. Two key technological innovations made it possible for these firms to coordinate operations on several continents. The first innovation was the successful completion of the transatlantic cable in 1866, which made possible instant communication by telegraph between the United States and Europe. The second innovation was the development of more efficient steam engines, which reduced the cost and increased the speed of long ocean voyages. U.S. firms such as Standard Oil, the Singer Sewing Machine Company, and the American Tobacco Company took advantage of these innovations to establish factories and distribution networks around the world. When firms build or buy facilities in foreign countries, they are engaging in **foreign direct investment**. When individuals or firms buy stocks or bonds issued in another country, they are engaging in **foreign portfolio investment**. In the early twentieth century, most U.S. firms expanded abroad through foreign direct investment because the stock and bond markets in other countries were often too poorly developed to make foreign portfolio investment practical.

## TABLE 8A-1

**Top 25 Multinational Corporations, 2009**

| RANK | CORPORATION | HOME COUNTRY | INDUSTRY |
|---|---|---|---|
| 1 | Royal Dutch Shell | The Netherlands/ United Kingdom | Petroleum refining |
| 2 | Exxon Mobil | United States | Petroleum refining |
| 3 | Wal-Mart Stores | United States | Retailing |
| 4 | BP | United Kingdom | Petroleum refining |
| 5 | Chevron | United States | Petroleum refining |
| 6 | Total | France | Petroleum refining |
| 7 | ConocoPhillips | United States | Petroleum refining |
| 8 | ING Group | The Netherlands | Insurance |
| 9 | Sinopec | China | Petroleum refining |
| 10 | Toyota Motors | Japan | Motor vehicles |
| 11 | Japan Post Holdings | Japan | Postal service |
| 12 | General Electric | United States | Diversified financials |
| 13 | China National Petroleum | China | Petroleum refining |
| 14 | Volkswagen | Germany | Motor vehicles |
| 15 | State Grid | China | Power generation |
| 16 | Dexia Group | Belgium | Banking |
| 17 | ENI | Italy | Petroleum refining |
| 18 | General Motors | United States | Motor vehicles |
| 19 | Ford Motor | United States | Motor vehicles |
| 20 | Allianz | Germany | Insurance |
| 21 | HSBC Holdings | United Kingdom | Banking |
| 22 | Gazprom | Russia | Natural gas |
| 23 | Daimler | Germany | Motor vehicles |
| 24 | BNP Paribas | France | Banking |
| 25 | Carrefour | France | Retailing |

Source: "Fortune Global 500," *Fortune*, July 20, 2009. © 2009 Time Inc. All rights reserved. Reprinted by permission.
*Note:* Corporations are ranked by their revenue

# Strategic Factors in Moving from Domestic to Foreign Markets

Today, most large U.S. corporations have established factories and other facilities overseas. Corporations expand their operations outside the United States when they expect to increase their profitability by doing so. Firms might expect to increase their profits through overseas operations for five main reasons:

- ***To avoid tariffs or the threat of tariffs.***  As we saw in this chapter, tariffs are taxes imposed by countries on imports from other countries. Sometimes firms establish factories in other countries to avoid having to pay tariffs. At other times, a firm establishes a factory in a country to which it is exporting because it fears the other country's government will impose a tariff or some other restriction on its product. Governments often are less concerned about domestic production by foreign-owned companies than they are about imports. As we also saw in this chapter, government restrictions on imports frequently result from a fear that imports will cause job losses in domestic industries. For example, in the 1970s and 1980s, many Americans feared that imports of Japanese automobiles would reduce employment in the U.S. automobile industry. Members of Congress threatened to increase tariffs or impose quotas on imports of Japanese automobiles. In fact, beginning in 1981, a voluntary export restraint reduced imports of Japanese automobiles. In response to this political pressure, the Japanese automobile companies established assembly plants in the United States. Now that a majority of Japanese automobiles sold in the United States are also assembled in the United States by U.S. workers, the Japanese share of the U.S. automobile market is a less heated political issue than it was during the 1970s and 1980s.

- *To gain access to raw materials.* Some U.S. firms have expanded abroad to secure supplies of raw materials. U.S. oil firms—beginning with Standard Oil in the late nineteenth century—have had extensive overseas operations aimed at discovering, recovering, and refining crude oil. In early 2001, one of Standard Oil's successor firms, ChevronTexaco, headquartered in San Francisco, opened its largest oil field in Kazakhstan, in the former Soviet Union. ChevronTexaco also constructed a 990-mile pipeline to bring the oil from this field on the Caspian Sea across Russia to a port on the Black Sea.

- *To gain access to low-cost labor.* In the past 20 years, some U.S. firms have located factories or other facilities in countries such as China, India, Malaysia, and El Salvador to take advantage of the lower wages paid to workers in those countries. Most economists believe that this *outsourcing* ultimately improves the efficiency of the economy and raises the consumption of U.S. households, but it can also disrupt the lives of U.S. workers who lose their jobs. For this reason, outsourcing has caused political controversy.

- *To minimize exchange-rate risk.* The exchange rate tells us how many units of foreign currency are received in exchange for a unit of domestic currency. Fluctuations in exchange rates can reduce the profits of a firm that exports goods to other countries. The J. M. Smucker Company, headquartered in Orrville, Ohio, ships jams, ice cream toppings, peanut butter, and other products to more than 70 other countries. Suppose Smucker's has contracted to sell 200,000 cases of jam to a British importer. The British importer will be paying for the shipment in British currency, the pound (the symbol for the pound is £). The importer will pay Smucker's £21 million in 60 days. It is currently possible to exchange $1 for £0.7, so Smucker's expects to receive $30 million (£21 million/£0.70 per dollar) in 60 days. But if the value of the pound falls against the dollar during the next 60 days, the amount Smucker's receives in dollars could be significantly reduced. For example, if the value of the pound falls to £0.80 per $1, then Smucker's will receive only $26.25 million (£21 million/£0.80 per dollar).

  Firms like Smucker's that have extensive international operations are exposed to significant risk to their profits from fluctuations in the values of international currencies. This risk is known as *exchange-rate risk*. If Smucker's began producing jam in Britain, it would reduce its exposure to exchange-rate risk.

- *To respond to industry competition.* In some instances, companies expand overseas as a competitive response to an industry rival. The worldwide competition for markets between Pepsi and Coke is an example of this kind of expansion. Coke began expanding overseas before World War II, and by the 1970s it was earning more from its foreign sales than from its sales in the United States. It became clear to Pepsi's management that the firm needed to compete with Coke in foreign as well as domestic markets. In 1972, Pepsi had a major success when it signed an agreement with the Soviet Union to become the first foreign product sold in that country. Coke and Pepsi continue to compete vigorously in many countries, with their shares of the market often fluctuating significantly.

*Many U.S. jobs require technical training and pay higher wages.*

Making
the
Connection

## Have Multinational Corporations Reduced Employment and Lowered Wages in the United States?

During the 1990s, some U.S. corporations responded to the greater economic openness of many poorer countries by relocating manufacturing operations to those countries. For example, most U.S. toy firms, such as Mattel, now produce nearly all their toys in factories in China. Most U.S. clothing manufacturers now produce the bulk of their goods in factories in Central America or Asia. These firms have reduced their production costs by paying much lower wages in their overseas factories than they were paying in the United States. The workers who lost their jobs in U.S. factories have often experienced periods of unemployment and have sometimes had to accept lower wages when they find new jobs. Towns and cities where factories have closed have also been hurt by losses of tax revenues to support schools and other local services.

Most economists do not believe that relocating jobs abroad has reduced either total employment in the United States or the average wage paid to U.S. workers. The overall level of employment in the United States in the long run is not affected by job losses in particular industries, however painful the losses may be to those experiencing them. The U.S. economy creates more than 2 million additional new jobs during a typical year. Nearly all workers who lose jobs at one firm eventually find new ones at other firms.

Competition from low-wage foreign workers has not reduced the average wages of U.S. workers. Wages are determined by the ability of workers to produce goods and services. This ability depends in part on the workers' education and training and in part on the machinery and equipment available to them. American workers have high wages because, on average, they are well trained and because of the quantity and quality of the machinery and equipment they work with. Low-wage foreign workers are generally less well trained and work with smaller amounts of machinery and equipment than do American workers.

Beginning in the late 1970s and continuing through the 2000s, the gap in the United States between the wages of skilled workers and the wages of unskilled workers has increased. It has been suggested that competition from low-wage foreign workers forced unskilled U.S. workers to accept lower wages to keep their jobs. To a small extent, the increase in the wage gap in the United States may have been due to this cause. But careful economic studies by Daron Acemoglu of MIT, Thomas Lemieux of the University of British Columbia, and others, have shown that most of the increase in the wage gap is attributable to developments within the U.S. economy—such as the increasing number of jobs that require technical training—rather than to competition from low-wage foreign workers.

Sources: Thomas Lemieux, "Increasing Residual Wage Inequality: Composition Effects, Noisy Data, or Rising Demand for Skill?" *American Economic Review*, Vol. 96, No. 3, June 2006, pp. 461–498; and Daron Acemoglu, "Technical Change, Inequality, and the Labor Market," *Journal of Economic Literature*, Vol. 40, No. 1, March 2002, pp. 7–72.

**YOUR TURN:** Test your understanding by doing related problem 8A.12 on page 277 at the end of this appendix.

---

Most U.S. firms have followed similar steps in expanding their operations overseas: Newly established firms usually begin by selling only within the United States. If successful in the domestic market, they begin to export. They initially use foreign firms to market and distribute their products. If sales are good in these foreign markets, U.S. firms establish their own overseas marketing and distribution networks. Finally, firms establish their own production facilities in these foreign countries. Since World War II, many U.S. firms have switched from building their own production facilities to a strategy of acquiring local firms that were already producing the good. Some firms have first licensed production to local firms, later acquiring the firms. U.S.-based Colgate-Palmolive, for example, typically has entered a foreign market first by licensing a foreign soap manufacturer to produce its brands, while keeping control over marketing and distribution. Typically, Colgate-Palmolive has eventually acquired ownership of the foreign firm.

## Challenges to U.S. Firms in Foreign Markets

It seems obvious that any successful firm will want to expand into foreign markets. After all, it is always better to have more customers than fewer customers. In fact, however, expanding into foreign markets can often be quite difficult, and the additional costs incurred may end up being greater than the additional revenue gained. One problem encountered by U.S. firms is differences in tastes between U.S. and foreign consumers. Although products such as Coke seem to appeal to consumers everywhere in the world, other products run into problems because of cultural differences among countries. For example, Singapore banned Janet Jackson's album *All for You* because, according to a government spokesman, its "sexually explicit lyrics" were "not acceptable to our society." After several years of trying to operate in Japan, eBay closed its online auction site there. Although eBay is successful at selling collectibles and other goods in the United States, many Japanese consumers do not like to buy used goods. In 2006, Wal-Mart sold its 85 stores in Germany, taking a loss of $1 billion. German consumers were not as receptive as U.S. consumers to buying groceries, clothes, consumer electronics, and other products in one very large store. For similar reasons, Wal-Mart sold its stores in South Korea.

Some U.S. companies have had difficulty adapting their employment practices to deal with the differences between U.S. and foreign labor markets. Many countries have much stronger labor unions than does the United States, and many foreign governments regulate labor markets much more than does the U.S. government. For example, government regulations in most European countries make it much more difficult than it is in the United States to lay off workers.

## Competitive Advantages of U.S. Firms

Some U.S. firms have successful foreign operations because of the strength of their brand names. Many producers of soft drinks and many fast-food restaurants can be found in nearly every foreign country, but Coca-Cola and McDonald's have such strong name recognition that their appeal extends around the world. Other firms have developed a significant technological edge over foreign rivals. Microsoft, the software giant, and Hewlett-Packard, the computer and printer firm, are examples. Some U.S. firms, such as Dell Computer and Boeing, have advantages over foreign manufacturers based on having developed the most efficient and lowest-cost way of producing a good.

A U.S. firm's global competitive advantage changes over time. This change is illustrated dramatically by the experience of U.S. semiconductor firms. The semiconductor industry originated in the United States, with the invention of the transistor at Bell Telephone Laboratories in 1947. U.S. predominance in the industry was enhanced further in 1959, with the invention of the integrated circuit, which contains multiple transistors on a single silicon chip. Through 1980, U.S. firms held between 60 and 80 percent of the global market for semiconductors. Beginning in the 1970s, the Japanese government moved to establish a strong domestic semiconductor industry by subsidizing domestic firms and by limiting imports of semiconductors from the United States. The Japanese policy was very successful with respect to DRAM—dynamic random access memory—the most basic chip. By the mid-1980s, Japanese firms dominated the global market, and nearly all U.S. chipmakers had abandoned DRAM manufacture. Many observers predicted the collapse of the U.S. semiconductor industry. Even Intel Corporation, the most successful U.S. semiconductor firm, appeared to be close to bankruptcy.

From this low point, U.S. semiconductor firms rebounded to regain global predominance by the 1990s. The key to the rebound of U.S. firms was the decreasing demand for simple memory chips and the increasing demand for two products: microprocessors—such as the Intel chips used in personal computers—and ASICs—application-specific integrated circuits—which are used in many electronic products. In manufacturing microprocessors and ASICs, a firm's ability to rapidly design and develop new products is more important than using low-cost production processes. U.S. firms, such as Intel, have proven to be much better at designing and rapidly bringing to market advanced microprocessors and ASICs than have competing firms in Japan, South Korea, and elsewhere.

## Key Terms

Foreign direct investment, p. 271

Foreign portfolio investment, p. 271

Multinational enterprise, p. 271

---

**8A**  **Multinational Firms, pages 271-277**
LEARNING OBJECTIVE: Understand why firms operate in more than one country.

    Visit **www.myeconlab.com** to complete these exercises online and get instant feedback.

## Review Questions

**8A.1** When did large U.S. corporations first begin to operate internationally? What key technological changes made it easier for U.S. corporations to operate overseas?

**8A.2** What is the difference between foreign direct investment and foreign portfolio investment? Is the Camry assembly plant that Toyota operates in Kentucky an example of foreign direct investment or foreign portfolio investment?

**8A.3** What are the five main reasons firms expand their operations overseas? Which of these reasons explains why U.S.-based oil companies have extensive overseas operations?

**8A.4** What are the main reasons U.S. firms succeed overseas?

## Problems and Applications

**8A.5** Suppose it is 1850, and you are operating a large factory, manufacturing cotton cloth. You are considering

expanding your operations overseas. What technical problems are you likely to encounter in coordinating your overseas and domestic operations?

**8A.6** The Ford Motor Company and the International Harvester Company were two of the first U.S. firms to establish extensive manufacturing operations overseas. Why might a producer of automobiles and a producer of farm machinery find it particularly advantageous to manufacture their products in countries in which they have substantial sales?

**8A.7** Why might many U.S. firms that were expanding their operations overseas after World War II have been more likely to acquire an existing firm in the market they were entering rather than build new facilities there?

**8A.8** Would a firm based in the United States ever produce a good in another country if it cost less to produce it in the United States and ship it to the other country? Explain.

**8A.9** Is expanding a firm's operations internationally really any different from expanding within a nation? For example, if a firm is based in Texas, what's the difference between its expanding operations to Mexico, Canada, Singapore, or Germany rather than to North Carolina or Pennsylvania?

**8A.10** Is expanding a firm's operations internationally really any different than expanding into a new product market? For example, is Whirlpool's expanding into Europe different than Whirlpool's expanding by making a new line of appliances, such as humidifiers?

**8A.11** If you ran a successful U.S. firm like Wal-Mart, IBM, or Hershey's, into which countries would you first expand? Why?

**8A.12** (Related to the *Making the Connection* on page 274) Suppose that the U.S. government wants to help textile workers who have lost their jobs as U.S. clothing manufacturers have moved to Central America and Asia. To do this, the government imposes a tariff on imported textiles. What would be the effects of this policy on employment in the U.S. textile industry? Would the policy increase total employment in the United States? What would happen to employment in U.S. industries other than the textile industry?

>> **End Appendix Learning Objective**

# CHAPTER 9

# Consumer Choice and Behavioral Economics

## Chapter Outline and Learning Objectives

## >> Can Oprah Get You to Buy a Kindle?

Are paper books, newspapers, and magazines going to become things of the past? Maybe not, but several e-readers—devices for reading electronic books and magazines—have become popular in the past few years. In November 2007, Amazon entered the market with the Kindle. Unlike other e-readers, such as Sony's Reader, which have to be connected to a computer to download books, the Kindle can download books wirelessly. The Kindle experienced steady sales in the months following its introduction, and then it received a huge boost from talk-show host Oprah Winfrey.

In an episode of her show broadcast in October 2008, Oprah revealed that she had been given a Kindle as a present that summer. It was a gift she said had changed her life: "It's absolutely my new favorite favorite thing in the world." Almost instantly the Kindle sold out. On the strength of this success, Amazon introduced a new model, Kindle 2, in February 2009, and the Kindle DX, capable of displaying full pages of magazines and textbooks, in the summer of 2009. By 2009, Amazon had 275,000 books available for download. For books that were available in both paper and electronic form, 35 percent of sales were of the electronic version. Amazon CEO Jeff Bezos proclaimed his goal: "Every book ever printed in any language, all available in less than 60 seconds."

Why did Oprah's endorsement have such a big impact on the Kindle's sales? Why should consumers buy more of a product just because a celebrity endorses it? In this chapter, we will examine how consumers make decisions about which products to buy. Firms must understand consumer behavior to determine what strategies are likely to be most effective in selling their products.

**AN INSIDE LOOK** on **page 302** discusses some of the details of Oprah's endorsement of the Kindle.

Sources: Joseph Galante, "Oprah Turns Amazon Kindle Reader into $1,500 Hot Gift," bloomberg.com, December 18, 2008; Brad Stone, "Live Blog of Amazon.com Introducing the New Kindle," nytimes.com, May 6, 2009; and Oprah.com: www.oprah.com/slideshow/oprahshow/20081024_tows_kindle.

## Economics in YOUR LIFE!

### Do You Make Rational Decisions?

Economists generally assume that people make decisions in a rational, consistent way. But are people actually as rational as economists assume? Consider the following situation: You bought a concert ticket for $75, which is the most you were willing to pay. While you are in line to enter the concert hall, someone offers you $90 for the ticket. Would you sell the ticket? Would an economist think it is rational to sell the ticket? As you read the chapter, see if you can answer these questions. You can check your answers against those we provide at the end of the chapter.

▶ Continued on page 301

We begin this chapter by exploring how consumers make decisions. In Chapter 1, we saw that economists usually assume that people act in a rational, self-interested way. In explaining consumer behavior, this means economists believe consumers make choices that will leave them as satisfied as possible, given their *tastes*, their *incomes*, and the *prices* of the goods and services available to them. We will see how the downward-sloping demand curves we encountered in Chapters 3 through 5 result from the economic model of consumer behavior. We will also see that in certain situations, knowing which decision is the best one can be difficult. In these cases, economic reasoning provides a powerful tool for consumers to improve their decision making. Finally, we will see that *experimental economics* has shown that factors such as social pressure and notions of fairness can affect consumer behavior. We will look at how businesses take these factors into account when setting prices. In the appendix to this chapter, we extend the analysis by using indifference curves and budget lines to understand consumer behavior.

**9.1 LEARNING** OBJECTIVE

Define utility and explain how consumers choose goods and services to maximize their utility.

# Utility and Consumer Decision Making

We saw in Chapter 3 that the model of demand and supply is a powerful tool for analyzing how prices and quantities are determined. We also saw that, according to the *law of demand*, whenever the price of a good falls, the quantity demanded increases. In this section, we will show how the economic model of consumer behavior leads to the law of demand.

## The Economic Model of Consumer Behavior in a Nutshell

Imagine walking through a shopping mall, trying to decide how to spend your clothing budget. If you had an unlimited budget, your decision would be easy: Just buy as much of everything as you want. Given that you have a limited budget, what do you do? Economists assume that consumers act so as to make themselves as well off as possible. Therefore, you should choose the one combination of clothes that makes you as well off as possible from among those combinations that you can afford. Stated more generally, the economic model of consumer behavior predicts that consumers will choose to buy the combination of goods and services that makes them as well off as possible from among all the combinations that their budgets allow them to buy.

This prediction may seem obvious and not particularly useful. But as we explore the implication of this prediction, we will see that it leads to conclusions that are both useful and not obvious.

## Utility

Ultimately, how well off you are from consuming a particular combination of goods and services depends on your tastes, or preferences. There is an old saying—"There's no accounting for tastes"—and economists don't try to. If you buy Red Bull instead of Monster Energy, even though Monster Energy has a lower price, you must receive more enjoyment or satisfaction from drinking Red Bull. Economists refer to the enjoyment or satisfaction people receive from consuming goods and services as **utility**. So we can say that the goal of a consumer is to spend available income so as to maximize utility. But utility is a difficult concept to measure because there is no way of knowing exactly how much enjoyment or satisfaction someone receives from consuming a product. Similarly, it is not possible to compare utility across consumers. There is no way of knowing for sure whether Jill receives more or less satisfaction than Jack from drinking a can of Red Bull.

Two hundred years ago, economists hoped to measure utility in units called *utils*. The util would be an objective measure in the same way that temperature is: If it is 70 degrees

**Utility** The enjoyment or satisfaction people receive from consuming goods and services.

in New York and 70 degrees in Los Angeles, it is just as warm in both cities. These economists wanted to say that if Jack's utility from drinking a can of Red Bull is 10 utils and Jill's utility is 5 utils, then Jack receives exactly twice the satisfaction from drinking a can of Red Bull as Jill does. In fact, it is *not* possible to measure utility across people. It turns out that none of the important conclusions of the economic model of consumer behavior depend on utility being directly measurable (a point we demonstrate in the appendix to this chapter). Nevertheless, the economic model of consumer behavior is easier to understand if we assume that utility is something directly measurable, like temperature.

## The Principle of Diminishing Marginal Utility

To make the model of consumer behavior more concrete, let's see how a consumer makes decisions in a case involving just two products: pepperoni pizza and Coke. To begin, consider how the utility you receive from consuming a good changes with the amount of the good you consume. For example, suppose that you have just arrived at a Super Bowl party, where the hosts are serving pepperoni pizza, and you are very hungry. In this situation, you are likely to receive quite a lot of enjoyment, or utility, from consuming the first slice of pizza. Suppose this satisfaction is measurable and is equal to 20 units of utility, or *utils*. After eating the first slice, you decide to have a second slice. Because you are no longer as hungry, the satisfaction you receive from eating the second slice of pizza is less than the satisfaction you received from eating the first slice. Consuming the second slice increases your utility by only an *additional* 16 utils, which raises your *total* utility from eating the 2 slices to 36 utils. If you continue eating slices, each additional slice gives you less and less additional satisfaction.

The table in Figure 9-1 shows the relationship between the number of slices of pizza you consume while watching the Super Bowl and the amount of utility you receive. The second column in the table shows the total utility you receive from eating a particular number of slices. The third column shows the additional utility, or **marginal utility** (*MU*), you receive from consuming one additional slice. (Remember that in economics, *marginal* means *additional*.) For example, as you increase your consumption from 2 slices to 3 slices, your total utility increases from 36 to 46, so your marginal utility from consuming the third slice is 10 utils. As the table shows, by the time you eat the fifth slice of pizza that evening, your marginal utility is very low: only 2 utils. If you were to eat a sixth slice, you would become slightly nauseated, and your marginal utility would actually be a *negative* 3 utils.

Figure 9-1 also plots the numbers from the table as graphs. Panel (a) shows how your total utility rises as you eat the first 5 slices of pizza and then falls as you eat the sixth slice. Panel (b) shows how your marginal utility declines with each additional slice you eat and finally becomes negative when you eat the sixth slice. The height of the marginal utility line at any quantity of pizza in panel (b) represents the change in utility as a result of consuming that additional slice. For example, the change in utility as a result of consuming 4 slices instead of 3 is 6 utils, so the height of the marginal utility line in panel (b) is 6 utils.

The relationship illustrated in Figure 9-1 between consuming additional units of a product during a period of time and the marginal utility received from consuming each additional unit is referred to as the **law of diminishing marginal utility**. For nearly every good or service, the more you consume during a period of time, the less you increase your total satisfaction from each additional unit you consume.

## The Rule of Equal Marginal Utility per Dollar Spent

The key challenge for consumers is to decide how to allocate their limited incomes among all the products they wish to buy. Every consumer has to make trade-offs: If you have $100 to spend on entertainment for the month, then the more DVDs you buy, the fewer movies you can see in the theater. Economists refer to the limited amount of income you have available to spend on goods and services as your **budget constraint**. The principle of diminishing marginal utility helps us understand how consumers can best spend their limited incomes on the products available to them.

Suppose you attend a Super Bowl party at a restaurant, and you have $10 to spend on refreshments. Pizza is selling for $2 per slice, and Coke is selling for $1 per cup.

**Marginal utility (*MU*)** The change in total utility a person receives from consuming one additional unit of a good or service.

**Law of diminishing marginal utility** The principle that consumers experience diminishing additional satisfaction as they consume more of a good or service during a given period of time.

**Budget constraint** The limited amount of income available to consumers to spend on goods and services.

## Figure 9-1

**Total and Marginal Utility from Eating Pizza on Super Bowl Sunday**

The table shows that for the first 5 slices of pizza, the more you eat, the more your total satisfaction, or utility, increases. If you eat a sixth slice, you start to feel ill from eating too much pizza, and your total utility falls. Each additional slice increases your utility by less than the previous slice, so your marginal utility from each slice is less than the one before. Panel (a) shows your total utility rising as you eat the first 5 slices and falling with the sixth slice. Panel (b) shows your marginal utility falling with each additional slice you eat and becoming negative with the sixth slice. The height of the marginal utility line at any quantity of pizza in panel (b) represents the change in utility as a result of consuming that additional slice. For example, the change in utility as a result of consuming 4 slices instead of 3 is 6 utils, so the height of the marginal utility line in panel (b) for the fourth slice is 6 utils.

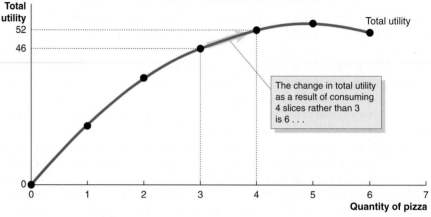

| Number of Slices | Total Utility from Eating Pizza | Marginal Utility from the Last Slice Eaten |
|---|---|---|
| 0 | 0 | -- |
| 1 | 20 | 20 |
| 2 | 36 | 16 |
| 3 | 46 | 10 |
| 4 | 52 | 6 |
| 5 | 54 | 2 |
| 6 | 51 | -3 |

The change in total utility as a result of consuming 4 slices rather than 3 is 6 . . .

**(a) Total utility**

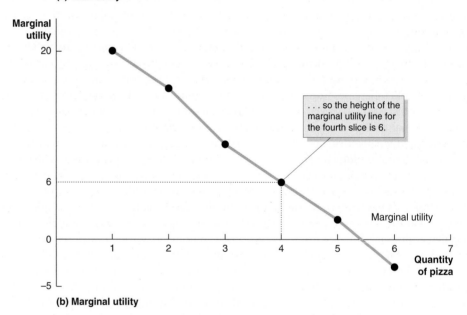

. . . so the height of the marginal utility line for the fourth slice is 6.

**(b) Marginal utility**

Table 9-1 shows the relationship between the amount of pizza you eat, the amount of Coke you drink, and the amount of satisfaction, or utility, you receive. The values for pizza are repeated from the table in Figure 9-1. The values for Coke also follow the principle of diminishing marginal utility.

How many slices of pizza and how many cups of Coke do you buy if you want to maximize your utility? If you did not have a budget constraint, you would buy 5 slices of pizza and 5 cups of Coke because that would give you total utility of 107 (54 + 53), which is the maximum utility you can achieve. Eating another slice of pizza or drinking another cup of Coke during the evening would lower your utility. Unfortunately, you do have a budget constraint: You have only $10 to spend. To buy 5 slices of pizza (at $2 per slice) and 5 cups of Coke (at $1 per cup), you would need $15.

To select the best way to spend your $10, remember this key economic principle: *Optimal decisions are made at the margin.* That is, most of the time, economic decision

| NUMBER OF SLICES OF PIZZA | TOTAL UTILITY FROM EATING PIZZA | MARGINAL UTILITY FROM THE LAST SLICE | NUMBER OF CUPS OF COKE | TOTAL UTILITY FROM DRINKING COKE | MARGINAL UTILITY FROM THE LAST CUP |
|---|---|---|---|---|---|
| 0 | 0 | — | 0 | 0 | — |
| 1 | 20 | 20 | 1 | 20 | 20 |
| 2 | 36 | 16 | 2 | 35 | 15 |
| 3 | 46 | 10 | 3 | 45 | 10 |
| 4 | 52 | 6 | 4 | 50 | 5 |
| 5 | 54 | 2 | 5 | 53 | 3 |
| 6 | 51 | −3 | 6 | 52 | −1 |

**TABLE 9-1**

**Total Utility and Marginal Utility from Eating Pizza and Drinking Coke**

makers—consumers, firms, and the government—are faced with decisions about whether to do a little more of one thing or a little more of an alternative. In this case, you are choosing to consume a little more pizza or a little more Coke. BMW chooses to manufacture more roadsters or more SUVs in its South Carolina factory. Congress and the president choose to spend more for research on heart disease or more for research on breast cancer. Every economic decision maker faces a budget constraint, and every economic decision maker faces trade-offs.

The key to making the best consumption decision is to maximize utility by following the *rule of equal marginal utility per dollar spent*. As you decide how to spend your income, you should buy pizza and Coke up to the point where the last slice of pizza purchased and the last cup of Coke purchased give you equal increases in utility *per dollar*. By doing this, you will have maximized your total utility.

It is important to remember that to follow this rule, you must equalize your marginal utility per dollar spent, *not* your marginal utility from each good. Buying season tickets for your favorite NFL team or for the opera or buying a BMW may give you a lot more satisfaction than drinking a cup of Coke, but the NFL tickets may well give you less satisfaction *per dollar spent*. To decide how many slices of pizza and how many cups of Coke to buy, you must convert the values for marginal utility in Table 9-1 into marginal utility per dollar. You can do this by dividing marginal utility by the price of each good, as shown in Table 9-2.

In column (3), we calculate marginal utility per dollar spent on pizza. Because the price of pizza is $2 per slice, the marginal utility per dollar from eating 1 slice of pizza equals 20 divided by $2, or 10 utils per dollar. Similarly, we show in column (6) that because the price of Coke is $1 per cup, the marginal utility per dollar from drinking 1 cup of Coke equals 20 divided by $1, or 20 utils per dollar. To maximize the total utility you receive, you must make sure that the utility per dollar of pizza for the last slice of pizza is equal to the utility per dollar of Coke for the last cup of Coke. Table 9-2 shows that there

| (1) SLICES OF PIZZA | (2) MARGINAL UTILITY ($MU_{Pizza}$) | (3) MARGINAL UTILITY PER DOLLAR $\left(\dfrac{MU_{Pizza}}{P_{Pizza}}\right)$ | (4) CUPS OF COKE | (5) MARGINAL UTILITY ($MU_{Coke}$) | (6) MARGINAL UTILITY PER DOLLAR $\left(\dfrac{MU_{Coke}}{P_{Coke}}\right)$ |
|---|---|---|---|---|---|
| 1 | 20 | 10 | 1 | 20 | 20 |
| 2 | 16 | 8 | 2 | 15 | 15 |
| 3 | 10 | 5 | 3 | 10 | 10 |
| 4 | 6 | 3 | 4 | 5 | 5 |
| 5 | 2 | 1 | 5 | 3 | 3 |
| 6 | −3 | −1.5 | 6 | −1 | −1 |

**TABLE 9-2**

**Converting Marginal Utility to Marginal Utility per Dollar**

TABLE 9-3

**Equalizing Marginal Utility per Dollar Spent**

| COMBINATIONS OF PIZZA AND COKE WITH EQUAL MARGINAL UTILITIES PER DOLLAR | MARGINAL UTILITY PER DOLLAR (MARGINAL UTILITY/PRICE) | TOTAL SPENDING | TOTAL UTILITY |
|---|---|---|---|
| 1 slice of pizza and 3 cups of Coke | 10 | $2 + $3 = $5 | 20 + 45 = 65 |
| 3 slices of pizza and 4 cups of Coke | 5 | $6 + $4 = $10 | 46 + 50 = 96 |
| 4 slices of pizza and 5 cups of Coke | 3 | $8 + $5 = $13 | 52 + 53 = 105 |

are three combinations of slices of pizza and cups of Coke where marginal utility per dollar is equalized. Table 9-3 lists the combinations, the total amount of money needed to buy each combination, and the total utility received from consuming each combination.

If you buy 4 slices of pizza, the last slice gives you 3 utils per dollar. If you buy 5 cups of Coke, the last cup also gives you 3 utils per dollar, so you have equalized your marginal utility per dollar. Unfortunately, as the third column in the table shows, to buy 4 slices and 5 cups, you would need $13, and you have only $10. You could also equalize your marginal utility per dollar by buying 1 slice and 3 cups, but that would cost just $5, leaving you with $5 to spend. Only when you buy 3 slices and 4 cups have you equalized your marginal utility per dollar and spent neither more nor less than the $10 available.

We can summarize the two conditions for maximizing utility:

1. $\dfrac{MU_{Pizza}}{P_{Pizza}} = \dfrac{MU_{Coke}}{P_{Coke}}$

2. Spending on pizza + Spending on Coke = Amount available to be spent

The first condition shows that the marginal utility per dollar spent must be the same for both goods. The second condition is the budget constraint, which states that total spending on both goods must equal the amount available to be spent. Of course, these conditions for maximizing utility apply not just to pizza and Coke but to any two pairs of goods.

# Solved Problem | 9-1

## Finding the Optimal Level of Consumption

The following table shows Lee's utility from consuming ice cream cones and cans of Lime Fizz soda.

| NUMBER OF ICE CREAM CONES | TOTAL UTILITY FROM ICE CREAM CONES | MARGINAL UTILITY FROM LAST CONE | NUMBER OF CANS OF LIME FIZZ | TOTAL UTILITY FROM CANS OF LIME FIZZ | MARGINAL UTILITY FROM LAST CAN |
|---|---|---|---|---|---|
| 0 | 0 | — | 0 | 0 | — |
| 1 | 30 | 30 | 1 | 40 | 40 |
| 2 | 55 | 25 | 2 | 75 | 35 |
| 3 | 75 | 20 | 3 | 101 | 26 |
| 4 | 90 | 15 | 4 | 119 | 18 |
| 5 | 100 | 10 | 5 | 134 | 15 |
| 6 | 105 | 5 | 6 | 141 | 7 |

a. Ed inspects this table and concludes, "Lee's optimal choice would be to consume 4 ice cream cones and 5 cans of Lime Fizz because with that combination, his marginal utility from ice cream cones is equal to his marginal utility from Lime Fizz." Do you agree with Ed's reasoning? Briefly explain.

b. Suppose that Lee has an unlimited budget to spend on ice cream cones and cans of Lime Fizz. Under these circumstances, how many ice cream cones and how many cans of Lime Fizz will he consume? (Assume Lee cannot consume more than 6 ice cream cones or 6 cans of Lime Fizz.)

c. Suppose that Lee has $7 per week to spend on ice cream cones and Lime Fizz. The price of an ice cream cone is $2, and the price of a can of Lime Fizz is $1. If

Lee wants to maximize his utility, how many ice cream cones and how many cans of Lime Fizz should he buy?

## SOLVING THE PROBLEM:

**Step 1:** **Review the chapter material.** This problem involves finding the optimal consumption of two goods, so you may want to review the section "The Rule of Equal Marginal Utility per Dollar Spent," which begins on page 281.

**Step 2:** **Answer part (a) by analyzing Ed's reasoning.** Ed's reasoning is incorrect. To maximize utility, Lee needs to equalize marginal utility per dollar for the two goods.

**Step 3:** **Answer part (b) by determining how Lee would maximize utility with an unlimited budget.** With an unlimited budget, consumers maximize utility by continuing to buy each good as long as their utility is increasing. In this case, Lee will maximize utility by buying 6 ice cream cones and 6 cans of Lime Fizz, given that we are assuming he can't buy more than 6 units of either good.

**Step 4:** **Answer part (c) by determining Lee's optimal combination of ice cream cones and cans of Lime Fizz.** Lee will maximize his utility if he spends his $7 per week so that the marginal utility of ice cream cones divided by the price of ice cream cones is equal to the marginal utility of Lime Fizz divided by the price of Lime Fizz. We can use the following table to solve this part of the problem:

| | ICE CREAM CONES | | | CANS OF LIME FIZZ | |
|---|---|---|---|---|---|
| QUANTITY | MU | $\frac{MU}{P}$ | | MU | $\frac{MU}{P}$ |
| 1 | 30 | 15 | | 40 | 40 |
| 2 | 25 | 12.5 | | 35 | 35 |
| 3 | 20 | 10 | | 26 | 26 |
| 4 | 15 | 7.5 | | 18 | 18 |
| 5 | 10 | 5 | | 15 | 15 |
| 6 | 5 | 2.5 | | 7 | 7 |

Lee will maximize his utility by buying 1 ice cream cone and 5 cans of Lime Fizz. At this combination, the marginal utility of each good divided by its price equals 15. He has also spent all of his $7.

**YOUR TURN:** For more practice, do related problems 1.7 and 1.8 on pages 304–305 at the end of this chapter.

---

## What if the Rule of Equal Marginal Utility per Dollar Does Not Hold?

The idea of getting the maximum utility by equalizing the ratio of marginal utility to price for the goods you are buying can be difficult to grasp, so it is worth thinking about in another way. Suppose that instead of buying 3 slices of pizza and 4 cups of Coke, you buy 4 slices and 2 cups. Four slices and 2 cups cost $10, so you would meet your budget constraint by spending all the money available to you, but would you have gotten the maximum amount of utility? No, you wouldn't have. From the information in Table 9-1 on page 283, we can list the additional utility per dollar you are getting from the last slice and the last cup and the total utility from consuming 4 slices and 2 cups:

    Marginal utility per dollar for the fourth slice of pizza = 3 utils per dollar

    Marginal utility per dollar for the second cup of Coke = 15 utils per dollar

    Total utility from 4 slices of pizza and 2 cups of Coke = 87 utils

# Don't Let This Happen to **YOU!**

### Equalize Marginal Utilities *per Dollar*

Consider the information in the following table, which gives Harry's utility from buying CDs and DVDs.

**HARRY'S UTILITY FROM BUYING CDS AND DVDS**

| QUANTITY OF CDs | TOTAL UTILITY FROM CDs | MARGINAL UTILITY FROM LAST CDs | QUANTITY OF DVDs | TOTAL UTILITY FROM DVDs | MARGINAL UTILITY FROM LAST DVD |
|---|---|---|---|---|---|
| 0 | 0 | — | 0 | 0 | — |
| 1 | 50 | 50 | 1 | 60 | 60 |
| 2 | 85 | 35 | 2 | 105 | 45 |
| 3 | 110 | 25 | 3 | 145 | 40 |
| 4 | 130 | 20 | 4 | 175 | 30 |
| 5 | 140 | 10 | 5 | 195 | 20 |
| 6 | 145 | 5 | 6 | 210 | 15 |

Can you determine from this information the optimal combination of CDs and DVDs for Harry? It is very tempting to say that Harry should buy 4 CDs and 5 DVDs because his marginal utility from CDs is equal to his marginal utility from DVDs with that combination. In fact, we can't be sure this is the best combination because we are lacking some critical information: Harry's budget constraint—how much he has available to spend on CDs and DVDs—and the prices of CDs and DVDs.

Let's say that Harry has $100 to spend this month, the price of a CD is $10, and the price of a DVD is $20. Using the information from the first table, we can now calculate Harry's marginal utility per dollar for both goods, as shown in the following table.

**HARRY'S MARGINAL UTILITY AND MARGINAL UTILITY PER DOLLAR FROM BUYING CDs AND DVDs**

| QUANTITY OF CDs | MARGINAL UTILITY FROM LAST CD $(MU_{CD})$ | MARGINAL UTILITY PER DOLLAR $\left(\dfrac{MU_{CD}}{P_{CD}}\right)$ | QUANTITY OF DVDs | MARGINAL UTILITY FROM LAST DVD $(MU_{DVD})$ | MARGINAL UTILITY PER DOLLAR $\left(\dfrac{MU_{DVD}}{P_{DVD}}\right)$ |
|---|---|---|---|---|---|
| 1 | 50 | 5 | 1 | 60 | 3 |
| 2 | 35 | 3.5 | 2 | 45 | 2.25 |
| 3 | 25 | 2.5 | 3 | 40 | 2 |
| 4 | 20 | 2 | 4 | 30 | 1.5 |
| 5 | 10 | 1 | 5 | 20 | 1 |
| 6 | 5 | 0.5 | 6 | 15 | 0.75 |

Harry's marginal utility per dollar is the same for two combinations of CDs and DVDs, as shown in the following table.

| COMBINATIONS OF CDs AND DVDs WITH EQUAL MARGINAL UTILITIES PER DOLLAR | MARGINAL UTILITY PER DOLLAR (MARGINAL UTILITY/PRICE) | TOTAL SPENDING | TOTAL UTILITY |
|---|---|---|---|
| 5 CDs and 5 DVDs | 1 | $50 + $100 = $150 | 140 + 195 = 335 |
| 4 CDs and 3 DVDs | 2 | $40 + $60 = $100 | 130 + 145 = 275 |

Unfortunately, 5 CDs and 5 DVDs would cost Harry $150, and he has only $100. The best Harry can do is to buy 4 CDs and 3 DVDs. This combination provides him with the maximum amount of utility attainable, given his budget constraint.

The key point, which we also saw in Solved Problem 9-1, is that consumers maximize their utility when they equalize marginal utility *per dollar* for every good they buy, not when they equalize marginal utility.

**YOUR TURN:** Test your understanding by doing related problem 1.10 on page 305 at the end of this chapter.

Obviously, the marginal utilities per dollar are not equal. The last cup of Coke gave you considerably more satisfaction per dollar than did the last slice of pizza. You could raise your total utility by buying less pizza and more Coke. Buying 1 less slice of pizza frees up $2 that will allow you to buy 2 more cups of Coke. Eating 1 less slice of pizza reduces your utility by 6 utils, but drinking 2 additional cups of Coke raises your utility by 15 utils (make sure you see this), for a net increase of 9. You end up equalizing your marginal utility per dollar (5 utils per dollar for both the last slice and the last cup) and raising your total utility from 87 utils to 96 utils.

## The Income Effect and Substitution Effect of a Price Change

We can use the rule of equal marginal utility per dollar to analyze how consumers adjust their buying decisions when a price changes. Suppose you are back at the restaurant for the Super Bowl party, but this time the price of pizza is $1.50 per slice, rather than $2. You still have $10 to spend on pizza and Coke.

When the price of pizza was $2 per slice and the price of Coke was $1 per cup, your optimal choice was to consume 3 slices of pizza and 4 cups of Coke. The fall in the price of pizza to $1.50 per slice has two effects on the quantity of pizza you consume: the *income effect* and the *substitution effect*. First, consider the income effect. When the price of a good falls, you have more purchasing power. In our example, 3 slices of pizza and 4 cups of Coke now cost a total of only $8.50 instead of $10.00. An increase in purchasing power is essentially the same thing as an increase in income. The change in the quantity of pizza you will demand because of this increase in purchasing power—holding all other factors constant—is the **income effect** of the price change. Recall from Chapter 3 that if a product is a *normal good*, a consumer increases the quantity demanded as the consumer's income rises, but if a product is an *inferior good*, a consumer decreases the quantity demanded as the consumer's income rises. So, if we assume that for you pizza is a normal good, the income effect of a fall in price causes you to consume more pizza. If pizza was an inferior good for you, the income effect of a fall in the price would have caused you to consume less pizza.

The second effect of the price change is the substitution effect. When the price of pizza falls, pizza becomes cheaper *relative* to Coke, and the marginal utility per dollar for each slice of pizza you consume increases. If we hold constant the effect of the price change on your purchasing power and just focus on the effect of the price being lower relative to the price of the other good, we have isolated the **substitution effect** of the price change. The lower price of pizza relative to the price of Coke has lowered the *opportunity cost* to you of consuming pizza because now you have to give up less Coke to consume the same quantity of pizza. Therefore, the substitution effect from the fall in the price of pizza relative to the price of Coke causes you to eat more pizza and drink less Coke. In this case, both the income effect and the substitution effect of the fall in price cause you to eat more pizza. If the price of pizza had risen, both the income effect and the substitution effect would have caused you to eat less pizza. Table 9-4 summarizes the effect of a price change on the quantity demanded.

**Income effect** The change in the quantity demanded of a good that results from the effect of a change in price on consumer purchasing power, holding all other factors constant.

**Substitution effect** The change in the quantity demanded of a good that results from a change in price making the good more or less expensive relative to other goods, holding constant the effect of the price change on consumer purchasing power.

**TABLE 9-4**

**Income Effect and Substitution Effect of a Price Change**

| | | **INCOME EFFECT** | | **SUBSTITUTION EFFECT** |
|---|---|---|---|---|
| **PRICE DECREASE** | Increases the consumer's purchasing power, which . . . | causes the quantity demanded to increase, if a normal good. | causes the quantity demanded to decrease, if an inferior good. | Lowers the opportunity cost of consuming the good, which causes the quantity of the good demanded to increase. |
| **PRICE INCREASE** | Decreases the consumer's purchasing power, which . . . | causes the quantity demanded to decrease, if a normal good. | causes the quantity demanded to increase, if an inferior good. | Raises the opportunity cost of consuming the good, which causes the quantity of the good demanded to decrease. |

**TABLE 9-5**

**Adjusting Optimal Consumption to a Lower Price of Pizza**

| NUMBER OF SLICES OF PIZZA | MARGINAL UTILITY FROM LAST SLICE ($MU_{Pizza}$) | MARGINAL UTILITY PER DOLLAR ($\frac{MU_{Pizza}}{P_{Pizza}}$) | NUMBER OF CUPS OF COKE | MARGINAL UTILITY FROM LAST CUP ($MU_{Coke}$) | MARGINAL UTILITY PER DOLLAR ($\frac{MU_{Coke}}{P_{Coke}}$) |
|---|---|---|---|---|---|
| 1 | 20 | 13.33 | 1 | 20 | 20 |
| 2 | 16 | 10.67 | 2 | 15 | 15 |
| 3 | 10 | 6.67 | 3 | 10 | 10 |
| 4 | 6 | 4 | 4 | 5 | 5 |
| 5 | 2 | 1.33 | 5 | 3 | 3 |
| 6 | −3 | — | 6 | −1 | — |

We can use Table 9-5 to determine the effect of the fall in the price of pizza on your optimal consumption. Table 9-5 has the same information as Table 9-2, with one change: The marginal utility per dollar from eating pizza has been changed to reflect the new lower price of $1.50 per slice. Examining the table, we can see that the fall in the price of pizza will result in your eating 1 more slice of pizza, so your optimal consumption now becomes 4 slices of pizza and 4 cups of Coke. You will be spending all of your $10, and the last dollar you spend on pizza will provide you with about the same marginal utility per dollar as the last dollar you spend on Coke. You will not be receiving exactly the same marginal utility per dollar spent on the two products. As Table 9-5 shows, the last slice of pizza gives you 4 utils per dollar, and the last cup of Coke gives you 5 utils per dollar. But this is as close as you can come to equalizing marginal utility per dollar for the two products, unless you can buy a fraction of a slice of pizza or a fraction of a cup of Coke.

**9.2 LEARNING** OBJECTIVE

Use the concept of utility to explain the law of demand.

# Where Demand Curves Come From

We saw in Chapter 3 that, according to the *law of demand*, whenever the price of a product falls, the quantity demanded increases. Now that we have covered the concepts of total utility, marginal utility, and the budget constraint, we can look more closely at why the law of demand holds.

In our example of optimal consumption of pizza and Coke at the Super Bowl party, we found the following:

Price of pizza = $2 per slice ⟹ Quantity of pizza demanded = 3 slices

Price of pizza = $1.50 per slice ⟹ Quantity of pizza demanded = 4 slices

In panel (a) of Figure 9-2, we plot the two points showing the optimal number of pizza slices you choose to consume at each price. In panel (b) of Figure 9-2, we draw a line connecting the two points. This downward-sloping line represents your demand curve for pizza. We could find more points on the line by changing the price of pizza and using the information in Table 9-2 to find the new optimal number of slices of pizza you would demand at each price.

To this point in this chapter, we have been looking at an individual demand curve. As we saw in Chapter 3, however, economists are typically interested in market demand curves. We can construct the market demand curve from the individual demand curves for all the consumers in the market. To keep things simple, let's assume that there are only three consumers in the market for pizza: you, David, and Lori. The table in Figure 9-3 shows the individual demand schedules for the three consumers.

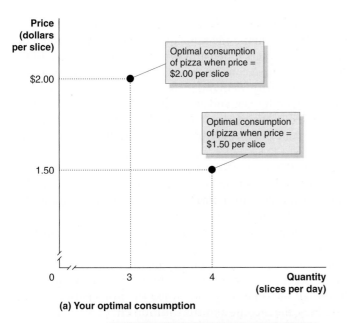

(a) Your optimal consumption

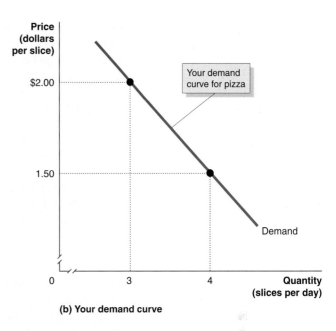

(b) Your demand curve

**Figure 9-2** | **Deriving the Demand Curve for Pizza**

A consumer responds optimally to a fall in the price of a product by consuming more of that product. In panel (a), the price of pizza falls from $2 per slice to $1.50, and the optimal quantity of slices consumed rises from 3 to 4. When we graph this result in panel (b), we have the consumer's demand curve.

| | Quantity (slices per day) | | | |
| Price (dollars per slice) | You | David | Lori | Market |
| --- | --- | --- | --- | --- |
| $2.50 | 2 | 4 | 1 | 7 |
| 2.00 | 3 | 5 | 3 | 11 |
| 1.50 | 4 | 6 | 5 | 15 |
| 1.00 | 5 | 7 | 7 | 19 |
| 0.50 | 6 | 8 | 9 | 23 |

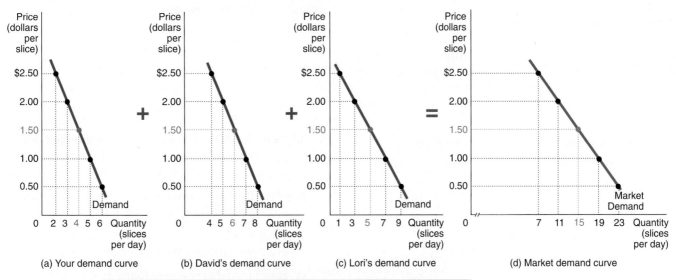

(a) Your demand curve  (b) David's demand curve  (c) Lori's demand curve  (d) Market demand curve

**Figure 9-3** | **Deriving the Market Demand Curve from Individual Demand Curves**

The table shows that the total quantity demanded in a market is the sum of the quantities demanded by each buyer. We can find the market demand curve by adding horizontally the individual demand curves in parts (a), (b), and (c). For instance, at a price of $1.50, your quantity demanded is 4 slices, David's quantity demanded is 6 slices, and Lori's quantity demanded is 5 slices. Therefore, part (d) shows a price of $1.50, and a quantity demanded of 15 is a point on the market demand curve.

Because consumers differ in their incomes and their preferences for products, we would not expect every consumer to demand the same quantity of a given product at each price. The final column gives the market demand, which is simply the sum of the quantities demanded by each of the three consumers at each price. For example, at a price of $1.50 per slice, your quantity demanded is 4 slices, David's quantity demanded is 6 slices, and Lori's quantity demanded is 5 slices. So, at a price of $1.50, a quantity of 15 slices is demanded in the market. The graphs in the figure show that we can obtain the market demand curve by adding horizontally the individual demand curves.

Remember that according to the law of demand, market demand curves always slope downward. We now know that this is true because the income and substitution effects of a fall in price cause consumers to increase the quantity of the good they demand. There is a complicating factor, however. As we discussed earlier, only for normal goods will the income effect result in consumers increasing the quantity of the good they demand when the price falls. If the good is an inferior good, the income effect leads consumers to *decrease* the quantity of the good they demand. The substitution effect, on the other hand, results in consumers increasing the quantity they demand of both normal and inferior goods when the price falls. So, when the price of an inferior good falls, the income and substitution effects work in opposite directions: The income effect causes consumers to decrease the quantity of the good they demand, whereas the substitution effect causes consumers to increase the quantity of the good they demand. Is it possible, then, that consumers might actually buy less of a good when the price falls? If this happened, the demand curve would be upward sloping.

# Solved Problem | 9-2

## Of Jake, Wings, and Dogs

The rule of equal marginal utility per dollar (*MU/P*) can be used to analyze how consumers adjust their buying decisions in response to price changes. The following table shows Jake's utility from his two favorite foods, chicken wings (with each order containing 10 wings) and chili dogs:

| CHICKEN WINGS | | CHILI DOGS | |
|---|---|---|---|
| ORDERS | *MU* PER ORDER | CHILI DOGS | *MU* PER CHILI DOG |
| 1 | 120 | 1 | 80 |
| 2 | 80 | 2 | 64 |
| 3 | 40 | 3 | 40 |
| 4 | 20 | 4 | 20 |
| 5 | 8 | 5 | 8 |

Assume that Jake has $20. Assume also that the price of chicken wings is $4 per order and that the price of chili dogs is initially $2. The following table shows the *MU/P* for wings and chili dogs at their initial prices as well as the *MU/P* of chili dogs after the price increases to $4:

| ORDERS | *MU/P* (PRICE = $4) | CHILI DOGS | *MU/P* (PRICE = $2) | *MU/P* (PRICE = $4) |
|---|---|---|---|---|
| 1 | 30 | 1 | 40 | 20 |
| 2 | 20 | 2 | 32 | 16 |
| 3 | 10 | 3 | 20 | 10 |
| 4 | 5 | 4 | 10 | 5 |
| 5 | 2 | 5 | 4 | 2 |

a. Using the rule of equal marginal utility per dollar, how many orders of wings and chili dogs will Jake consume when the price of chili dogs is $2?

b. How many wings and chili dogs will Jake consume when the price of chili dogs is $4?

c. What is the substitution effect of the change in the price of chili dogs? What is the income effect?

d. How does Jake's response to the increase in the price of chili dogs illustrate the law of demand?

# SOLVING THE PROBLEM:

**Step 1:** **Review the chapter material.** This problem is about the concept of utility and the law of demand, so you may want to review the section "The Income Effect and Substitution Effect of a Price Change," which begins on page 287.

**Step 2:** **Answer question (a).** Jake will first consume two chili dogs because the *MU/P* of the first and second chili dogs is greater than the *MU/P* of the first order of wings. Jake will then consume one order of wings. Because the *MU/P* for the second order of wings and a third chili dog are equal (20), Jake will consume one more of each. At this point, Jake will have spent $14. With his remaining $6, he will consume a third order of wings and a fourth chili dog. Jake will now have spent his $20, and the *MU/P* of both goods will be equal (10).

**Step 3:** **Answer question (b).** After the price of chili dogs rises, the *MU/P* for this good falls. Jake will spend $16 on two chili dogs (2 × $4 = $8) and two orders of wings (2 × $4 = $8). Because the *MU/P* for the third chili dog and third order of wings is the same (10), Jake will be indifferent between these two choices. Assume that he buys a third chili dog.

**Step 4:** **Answer question (c).** When the *MU/P* for chili dogs falls because of the price increase, the opportunity cost of consuming each chili dog rises. As a result, Jake will substitute toward wings, holding constant the effect on his purchasing power. This is the substitution effect. After the price increase, it would require $28 for Jake to buy the same number of chicken wings (3 × $4 = $12) and chili dogs (4 × $4 = $16) as he bought before the price increase. Because his purchasing power, or real income, has declined, he will buy fewer chili dogs because of the income effect if chili dogs are a normal good. He would buy more chili dogs because of the income effect if chili dogs were inferior goods; this would require Jake to buy fewer wings. Because the income effect is small, the net effect of the price increase is to decrease the quantity demanded of chili dogs.

**Step 5:** **Answer question (d).** The change in the price caused a reduction in the quantity demanded of chili dogs. According to the law of the demand, as the price of a product increases, the quantity demanded will decrease. Jake's response to the price increase for chili dogs is consistent with this law:

| PRICE | QUANTITY DEMANDED OF CHILI DOGS |
|---|---|
| $4 | 3 |
| $2 | 4 |

**YOUR TURN:** For more practice, do related problem 2.8 on page 306 at the end of this chapter.

---

Making the Connection

## Are There Any Upward-Sloping Demand Curves in the Real World?

For a demand curve to be upward sloping, the good would have to be an inferior good and the income effect would have to be larger than the substitution effect. Economists have understood the conditions for an upward-sloping demand curve since the possibility was first discussed by the British economist Alfred Marshall in the 1890s. Marshall wrote that his friend, Sir Robert Giffen, had told him that when the price of bread rose, very poor people in British cities would actually buy more bread rather than less. Since that time, goods with upward-sloping demand curves have been referred to as *Giffen goods*.

For more than a century, finding an actual Giffen good proved impossible. A close examination of the data showed that Giffen had been mistaken and that poor people in British cities bought less bread when prices rose, so their demand curves were downward sloping. Other possible candidates for being Giffen goods were also found to actually have downward-sloping demand curves. Finally, in 2006 Robert Jensen of Brown University and Nolan Miller of Harvard discovered two Giffen goods. Jensen and Miller

*Rice is a Giffen good in poor parts of China.*

reasoned that to be a Giffen good, with an income effect larger than its substitution effect, a good must be inferior and make up a very large portion of consumers' budgets. Jensen and Miller knew that very poor people in the Hunan region of China spent most of their incomes on rice, while in the Gansu province, very poor people spent most of their income on wheat-based foods, such as buns and noodles. In both places, poor people ate meat when their incomes allowed it because they preferred the taste of meat even though it did not supply as many calories as the rice or wheat they could purchase for the same price.

Jensen and Miller carried out the following experiment: In Hunan, for a five-month period they gave a selected number of poor families coupons that would allow them to buy rice at a lower price. Families could not use the coupons for any other purpose. In Gansu, Jensen and Miller gave a selected number of poor families coupons to buy wheat at a lower price. Jensen and Miller then observed the purchases of the families during the time they received the coupons and during the period immediately thereafter. In Hunan, during the months they received the coupons, the families bought less rice and more meat, and in Gansu, they bought less wheat and more meat. Because in Hunan families bought less rice when the price was lower, their demand curves for rice were upward sloping. Similarly, in Gansu, families bought less wheat when the price was lower, so their demand curves for wheat were upward sloping. After more than a century of searching, economists had finally discovered examples of a Giffen good.

Source: Robert T. Jensen and Nolan H. Miller, "Giffen Behavior and Subsistence Consumption," *American Economic Review*, Vol. 98, No. 4, September 2008, pp. 1553–1577.

 **YOUR TURN:** Test your understanding by doing related problem 2.7 on page 306 at the end of this chapter.

Test your understanding by doing related problem 2.7 on page 306 at the end of this chapter.

---

**9.3 LEARNING** OBJECTIVE

Explain how social influences can affect consumption choices.

# Social Influences on Decision Making

Sociologists and anthropologists have argued that social factors such as culture, customs, and religion are very important in explaining the choices consumers make. Economists have traditionally seen such factors as being relatively unimportant, if they take them into consideration at all. Recently, however, some economists have begun to study how social factors influence consumer choice.

For example, people seem to receive more utility from consuming goods they believe are popular. As the economists Gary Becker and Kevin Murphy put it:

> The utility from drugs, crime, going bowling, owning a Rolex watch, voting Democratic, dressing informally at work, or keeping a neat lawn depends on whether friends and neighbors take drugs, commit crimes, go bowling, own Rolex watches, vote Democratic, dress informally, or keep their lawns neat.

This reasoning can help to explain why one restaurant is packed, while another restaurant that serves essentially the same food and has a similar décor has many fewer customers. Consumers decide which restaurant to go to partly on the basis of food and décor but also on the basis of the restaurant's popularity. People receive utility from being seen eating at a popular restaurant because they believe it makes them appear knowledgeable and fashionable. Whenever consumption takes place publicly, many consumers base their purchasing decisions on what other consumers are buying. Examples of public consumption include eating in restaurants, attending sporting events, wearing clothes or jewelry, and driving cars. In all these cases, the decision to buy a product depends partly on the characteristics of the product and partly on how many other people are buying the product.

## The Effects of Celebrity Endorsements

In many cases, it is not just the number of people who use a product that makes it desirable but the types of people who use it. If consumers believe that media stars or professional athletes use a product, demand for the product will often increase. This may be partly because consumers believe public figures are particularly knowledgeable about products: "Tiger Woods knows more about razors than I do, so I'll shave with the same razor he shaves with." But many consumers also feel more fashionable and closer to famous people if they use the same products. These considerations help to explain why companies are willing to pay millions of dollars to have celebrities endorse their products. Some companies, such as Coca-Cola, have been using celebrities in their advertising for decades.

*Tiger Woods earns much more from product endorsements than from playing golf.*

### Making the Connection | Why Do Firms Pay Tiger Woods to Endorse Their Products?

Tiger Woods may be the best golfer who's ever lived. In his first five years as a professional, he won 27 tournaments on the Professional Golfers' Association (PGA) tour. When he won the Masters tournament in 2001, he became the first golfer ever to win all four major professional golf championships in a row. By 2009, he had won 14 major championships and 66 total tournaments. Tiger Woods is a great golfer, but should consumers care what products he uses? A number of major companies apparently believe consumers do care. To endorse Gillette razors, Nike clothing and golf balls, Gatorade sports drinks, American Express charge cards, and Rolex watches, among other products, companies pay him more than $100 million per year, which is more than twice the amount earned by any other athlete from product endorsements.

There seems little doubt that consumers care what products Tiger uses, but *why* do they care? It might be that they believe Tiger has better information than they do about the products he endorses. The average weekend golfer might believe that if Tiger endorses Nike golf balls, maybe Nike balls are better than other golf balls. But it seems more likely that people buy products associated with Tiger Woods or other celebrities because using these products makes them feel closer to the celebrity endorser or because it makes them appear to be fashionable.

Source: Tim Arango, "Top 10 Celebrity Endorsers," CNNMoney.com, December 31, 2008.

**YOUR TURN:** Test your understanding by doing related problem 3.9 on page 307 at the end of this chapter.

## Network Externalities

Technology can play a role in explaining why consumers buy products that many other consumers are already buying. There is a **network externality** in the consumption of a product if the usefulness of the product increases with the number of consumers who use it. For example, if you owned the only phone in the world, it would not be very useful. The usefulness of phones increases as the number of people who own them increases. Similarly, your willingness to buy an Amazon Kindle depends in part on the number of other people who own Kindles. The more people who own Kindles, the more novels, textbooks, newspapers, and magazines that will be available for download and the more useful a Kindle is to you.

Some economists have suggested the possibility that network externalities may have a significant downside because they might result in consumers buying products that contain inferior technologies. This outcome could occur because network externalities can create significant *switching costs* related to changing products: When a product

**Network externality** A situation in which the usefulness of a product increases with the number of consumers who use it.

becomes established, consumers may find it too costly to switch to a new product that contains a better technology. The selection of products may be *path dependent*. This means that because of switching costs, the technology that was first available may have advantages over better technologies that were developed later. In other words, the path along which the economy has developed in the past is important.

One example of path dependence and the use of an inferior technology is the QWERTY order of the letters along the top row of most computer keyboards. This order became widely used when manual typewriters were developed in the late nineteenth century. The metal keys on manual typewriters would stick together if a user typed too fast, and the QWERTY keyboard was designed to slow down typists and minimize the problem of the keys sticking together. With computers, the problem that QWERTY was developed to solve no longer exists, so keyboards could be changed to have letters in a more efficient layout. But because the overwhelming majority of people have learned to use keyboards with the QWERTY layout, there might be significant costs to them if they had to switch, even if a new layout ultimately made them faster typists.

Other products that supposedly embodied inferior technologies are VHS video recorders—supposedly inferior to Sony Betamax recorders—and the Windows computer operating system—supposedly inferior to the Macintosh operating system. Some economists have argued that because of path dependence and switching costs, network externalities can result in *market failures*. As we saw in Chapter 5, a market failure is a situation in which the market fails to produce the efficient level of output. If network externalities result in market failure, government intervention in these markets might improve economic efficiency. Many economists are skeptical, however, that network externalities really do lead to consumers being locked into products with inferior technologies. In particular, economists Stan Leibowitz of the University of Texas, Dallas, and Stephen Margolis of North Carolina State University have argued that, in practice, the gains from using a superior technology are larger than the losses due to switching costs. After carefully studying the cases of the QWERTY keyboard, VHS video recorders, and the Windows computer operating system, they have concluded that there is no good evidence that the alternative technologies were actually superior. The implications of network externalities for economic efficiency remain controversial among economists.

## Does Fairness Matter?

If people were only interested in making themselves as well off as possible in a material sense, they would not be concerned with fairness. There is a great deal of evidence, however, that people like to be treated fairly and that they usually attempt to treat others fairly, even if doing so makes them worse off financially. Tipping servers in restaurants is an example. In the United States, diners in restaurants typically add 15 to 20 percent to their food bills as tips to their servers. Tips are not *required*, but most people see it as very unfair not to tip, unless the service has been exceptionally bad. You could argue that people leave tips not to be fair but because they are afraid that if they don't leave a tip the next time they visit the restaurant they will receive poor service. Studies have shown, however, that most people leave tips at restaurants even while on vacation or in other circumstances where they are unlikely to visit the restaurant again.

There are many other examples where people willingly part with money when they are not required to do so and when they receive nothing material in return. The most obvious example is making donations to charity. Apparently, donating money to charity or leaving tips in restaurants that they will never visit again gives people more utility than they would receive from keeping the money and spending it on themselves.

### A Test of Fairness in the Economic Laboratory: The Ultimatum Game Experiment Economists have used experiments to increase their understanding of the role that fairness plays in consumer decision making. Experimental economics has been

widely used during the past two decades, and a number of experimental economics laboratories exist in the United States and Europe. Economists Maurice Allais, Reinhard Selten, and Vernon Smith were awarded the Nobel Prize in Economics in part because of their contributions to experimental economics. Experiments make it possible to focus on a single aspect of consumer behavior. The *ultimatum game*, first popularized by Werner Güth of the Max Planck Institute of Economics, is an experiment that tests whether fairness is important in consumer decision making. Various economists have conducted the ultimatum game experiment under slightly different conditions, but with generally the same result. In this game, a group of volunteers—often college students—are divided into pairs. One member of each pair is the "allocator," and the other member of the pair is the "recipient."

Each pair is given an amount of money, say $20. The allocator decides how much of the $20 each member of the pair will get. There are no restrictions on how the allocator divides up the money. He or she could keep it all, give it all to the recipient, or anything in between. The recipient must then decide whether to accept the allocation or reject it. If the recipient decides to accept the allocation, each member of the pair gets to keep his or her share. If the recipient decides to reject the allocation, both members of the pair receive nothing.

If neither the allocator nor the recipient cared about fairness, optimal play in the ultimatum game is straightforward: The allocator should propose a division of the money in which the allocator receives $19.99 and the recipient receives $0.01. The allocator has maximized his or her gain. The recipient should accept the division because the alternative is to reject the division and receive nothing at all: Even a penny is better than nothing.

In fact, when the ultimatum game experiment is carried out, both allocators and recipients act as if fairness is important. Allocators usually offer recipients at least a 40 percent share of the money, and recipients almost always reject offers of less than a 10 percent share. Why do allocators offer recipients more than a negligible amount? It might be that allocators do not care about fairness but fear that recipients do care and will reject offers they consider unfair. This possibility was tested in an experiment known as the *dictator game* carried out by Daniel Kahneman (a psychologist who shared the Nobel Prize in Economics), Jack Knetsch, and Richard Thaler, using students at Cornell University. In this experiment, the allocators were given only two possible divisions of $20: either $18 for themselves and $2 for the recipient or an even division of $10 for themselves and $10 for the recipient. One important difference from the ultimatum game was that *the recipient was not allowed to reject the division*. Of the 161 allocators, 122 chose the even division of the $20. Because there was no possibility of the $18/$2 split being rejected, the allocators must have chosen the even split because they valued acting fairly.

Why would recipients in the ultimatum game ever reject any division of the money in which they receive even a very small amount, given that even a small amount of money is better than nothing? Apparently, most people value fairness enough that they will refuse to participate in transactions they consider unfair, even if they are worse off financially as a result.

**Business Implications of Fairness** If consumers value fairness, how does that affect firms? One consequence is that firms will sometimes not raise prices of goods and services, even when there is a large increase in demand, because they are afraid their customers will consider the price increases unfair and may buy elsewhere.

For example, the Broadway play *The Producers* was extremely popular during its first year in production. Even though ticket prices were an average of $75, on most nights, many more people wanted to buy tickets at that price than could be accommodated in the St. James Theater, where the play was running. Figure 9-4 illustrates this situation.

Notice that the supply curve in Figure 9-4 is a vertical line, which indicates that the capacity of the St. James Theater is fixed at 1,644 seats. At a price of $75 per ticket, there

## Figure 9-4

### The Market for Tickets to *The Producers*

The St. James Theater could have raised prices for the Broadway musical *The Producers* to $125 per ticket and still sold all of the 1,644 tickets available. Instead, the theater kept the price of tickets at $75, even though the result was a shortage of more than 400 seats. Is it possible that this strategy maximized profits?

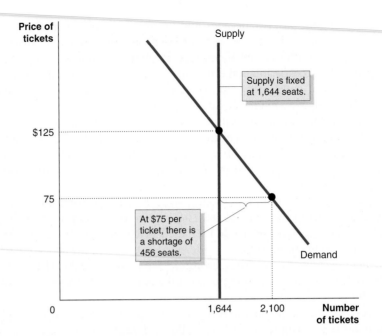

was a shortage of more than 400 tickets. Why didn't the theater raise ticket prices to $125, where the quantity supplied would have equaled the quantity demanded?

Before answering, let's look at two other examples where it seems that businesses could increase their profits by raising prices. First, each year, many more people would like to buy tickets to see the Super Bowl than there are tickets for them to buy at the price the National Football League charges. Why doesn't the National Football League raise prices? Second, at very popular restaurants, there are often long lines of people waiting to be served. Some of the people will wait hours to be served, and some won't be served at all before the restaurant closes. Why doesn't the restaurant raise prices high enough to eliminate the lines?

In each of these cases, it appears that a firm could increase its profits by raising prices. The seller would be selling the same quantity—of seats in a theater or a football stadium or meals in a restaurant—at a higher price, so profits should increase. Economists have provided two explanations why firms sometimes do not raise prices in these situations. Gary Becker, winner of the Nobel Prize in Economics, has suggested that the products involved—theatrical plays, football games, or restaurant meals—are all products that buyers consume together with other buyers. In those situations, the amount consumers wish to buy may be related to how much of the product other people are consuming. People like to consume, and be seen consuming, a popular product. In this case, a popular restaurant that increased its prices enough to eliminate lines might find that it had also eliminated its popularity.

Daniel Kahneman, Jack Knetsch, and Richard Thaler have offered another explanation for why firms don't always raise prices when doing so would seem to increase their profits. In surveys of consumers, these researchers found that most people considered it fair for firms to raise their prices following an increase in costs but unfair to raise prices following an increase in demand. For example, Kahneman, Knetsch, and Thaler conducted a survey in which people were asked their opinion of the following situation: "A hardware store has been selling snow shovels for $15. The morning after a large snowstorm, the store raises the price to $20." Eighty-two percent of those surveyed responded that they considered the hardware store's actions to be unfair. Kahneman, Knetsch, and Thaler have concluded that firms may sometimes not raise their prices even when the quantity demanded of their product is greater than the quantity supplied out of fear that in the long run, they will lose customers who believe the price increases were unfair.

These explanations share the same basic idea: Sometimes firms will give up some profits in the short run to keep their customers happy and increase their profits in the long run.

## Making the Connection | Professor Krueger Goes to the Super Bowl

Economist Alan Krueger of Princeton University has studied the question of why the National Football League does not charge a price for Super Bowl tickets that is high enough to make the quantity of tickets demanded equal to the quantity of tickets available. The prices may seem high—in 2009, they were $1,000 for the best seats and $800 for most of the rest—but the quantity demanded still greatly exceeds the quantity supplied. Most Super Bowl tickets are allocated to the two teams playing in the game or to the league's corporate sponsors. To give ordinary fans a chance to attend the game, in 2001, the NFL set aside 500 pairs of tickets and then held a lottery for the opportunity to buy these tickets at $325 or $400 each. More than 36,000 people applied. Some fans were willing to pay as much as $5,000 to buy a ticket from ticket scalpers. (Scalpers buy tickets at their face value and then resell them at much higher prices, even though in Florida, where the 2001 Super Bowl was held, ticket scalping was illegal.)

*Should the NFL raise the price of Super Bowl tickets?*

Why didn't the NFL simply raise the price of tickets to clear the market? Krueger decided to survey football fans attending the game to see if their views could help explain this puzzle. Krueger's survey provides support for the Kahneman, Knetsch, and Thaler explanation of why companies do not always raise prices when the quantity demanded is greater than the quantity supplied. When asked whether it would "be fair for the NFL to raise the [price of tickets] to $1,500 if that is still less than the amount most people are willing to pay for tickets," 92 percent of the fans surveyed answered "no." Even 83 percent of the fans who had paid more than $1,500 for their tickets answered "no." Krueger concluded that whatever the NFL might gain in the short run from raising ticket prices, it would more than lose in the long run by alienating football fans.

Source: Alan B. Krueger, "Supply and Demand: An Economist Goes to the Super Bowl," *Milken Institute Review*, Second Quarter 2001.

**YOUR TURN:** Test your understanding by doing related problems 3.11 and 3.12 on page 307 at the end of this chapter.

---

# Behavioral Economics: Do People Make Their Choices Rationally?

**9.4 LEARNING** OBJECTIVE

Describe the behavioral economics approach to understanding decision making.

When economists say that consumers and firms are behaving "rationally," they mean that consumers and firms are taking actions that are appropriate to reach their goals, given the information available to them. In recent years, some economists have begun studying situations in which people do not appear to be making choices that are economically rational. This new area of economics is called **behavioral economics**. Why might consumers or businesses not act rationally? The most obvious reason would be that they do not realize that their actions are inconsistent with their goals. As we discussed in Chapter 1, one of the objectives of economics is to suggest ways to make better decisions. In this section, we discuss ways in which consumers can improve their decisions by avoiding some common pitfalls.

**Behavioral economics** The study of situations in which people make choices that do not appear to be economically rational.

Consumers commonly commit the following three mistakes when making decisions:

- They take into account monetary costs but ignore nonmonetary opportunity costs.

- They fail to ignore sunk costs.

- They are unrealistic about their future behavior.

## Ignoring Nonmonetary Opportunity Costs

**Opportunity cost** The highest-valued alternative that must be given up to engage in an activity.

Remember from Chapter 2 that the **opportunity cost** of any activity is the highest-valued alternative that must be given up to engage in that activity. For example, if you own something you could sell, using it yourself involves an opportunity cost. It is often difficult for people to think of opportunity costs in these terms.

Consider the following example: Some of the fans at the 2001 Super Bowl participated in a lottery run by the National Football League that allowed the winners to purchase tickets at their face value, which was either $325 or $400, depending on where in the stadium the seats were located. Alan Krueger surveyed the lottery winners, asking them two questions:

*Question 1:* If you had not won the lottery, would you have been willing to pay $3,000 for your ticket?
*Question 2:* If after winning your ticket (and before arriving in Florida for the Super Bowl) someone had offered you $3,000 for your ticket, would you have sold it?

In answer to the first question, 94 percent said that if they had not won the lottery, they would not have paid $3,000 for a ticket. In answer to the second question, 92 percent said they would not have sold their ticket for $3,000. But these answers are contradictory! If someone offers you $3,000 for your ticket, then by using the ticket rather than selling it, you incur an opportunity cost of $3,000. There really is a $3,000 cost involved in using that ticket, even though you do not pay $3,000 in cash. The two alternatives—either paying $3,000 or not receiving $3,000—amount to exactly the same thing.

If the ticket is really not worth $3,000 to you, you should sell it. If it is worth $3,000 to you, you should be willing to pay $3,000 in cash to buy it. Not being willing to sell a ticket you already own for $3,000, while at the same time not being willing to buy a ticket for $3,000 if you didn't already own one is inconsistent behavior. The inconsistency comes from a failure to take into account nonmonetary opportunity costs. Behavioral economists believe this inconsistency is caused by the **endowment effect**, which is the tendency of people to be unwilling to sell a good they already own even if they are offered a price that is greater than the price they would be willing to pay to buy the good if they didn't already own it.

**Endowment effect** The tendency of people to be unwilling to sell a good they already own even if they are offered a price that is greater than the price they would be willing to pay to buy the good if they didn't already own it.

The failure to take into account opportunity costs is a very common error in decision making. Suppose, for example, that a friend is in a hurry to have his room cleaned—it's the Friday before parents' weekend—and he offers you $50 to do it for him. You turn him down and spend the time cleaning your own room, even though you know somebody down the hall who would be willing to clean your room for $20. Leave aside complicating details—the guy who asked you to clean his room is a real slob, or you don't want the person who offered to clean your room for $20 to go through your stuff—and you should see the point we are making. The opportunity cost of cleaning your own room is $50—the amount your friend offered to pay you to clean his room. It is inconsistent to turn down an offer from someone else to clean your room for $20 when you are doing it for yourself at a cost of $50. The key point here is this: *Nonmonetary opportunity costs are just as real as monetary costs and should be taken into account when making decisions.*

There are many examples of businesses taking advantage of the tendency of consumers to ignore nonmonetary costs. For example, many film processing companies have a policy of printing every picture on a roll of film, even if the picture is very fuzzy. Customers are allowed to ask for refunds on pictures they don't like. Once again, the companies are relying on the fact that passing up a refund once you have already paid for a picture is a nonmonetary opportunity cost rather than a direct monetary cost. In fact, customers rarely ask for refunds.

## Failing to Ignore Sunk Costs

**Sunk cost** A cost that has already been paid and cannot be recovered.

A **sunk cost** is a cost that has already been paid and cannot be recovered. Once you have paid money and can't get it back, you should ignore that money in any later decisions you make. Consider the following two situations:

*Situation 1:* You bought a ticket to a play for $75. The ticket is nonrefundable and must be used on Tuesday night, which is the only night the play will be performed. On Monday, a friend calls and invites you to a local comedy club to see a comedian you both like who is appearing only on Tuesday night. Your friend offers to pay the cost of going to the club.

*Situation 2:* It's Monday night, and you are about to buy a ticket for the Tuesday night performance of the same play as in situation 1. As you are leaving to buy the ticket, your friend calls and invites you to the comedy club.

Would your decision to go to the play or to the comedy club be different in situation 1 than in situation 2? Most people would say that in situation 1, they would go to the play, because otherwise they would lose the $75 they had paid for the ticket. In fact, though, the $75 is "lost" no matter what you do because the ticket is not refundable. The only real issue for you to decide is whether you would prefer to see the play or prefer to go with your friend to the comedy club. If you would prefer to go to the club, the fact that you have already paid $75 for the ticket to the play is irrelevant. Your decision should be the same in situation 1 as in situation 2.

Psychologists Daniel Kahneman and Amos Tversky explored the tendency of consumers to not ignore sunk costs by asking two samples of people the following questions:

*Question 1:* One sample of people was asked: "Imagine that you have decided to see a play and have paid the admission price of $10 per ticket. As you enter the theater, you discover that you have lost the ticket. The seat was not marked, and the ticket cannot be recovered. Would you pay $10 for another ticket?" Of those asked, 46 percent answered "yes," and 54 percent answered "no."

*Question 2:* A different sample of people was asked: "Imagine that you have decided to see a play where admission is $10 per ticket. As you enter the theater, you discover that you have lost a $10 bill. Would you still pay $10 for a ticket to the play?" Of those asked, 88 percent answered "yes," and 12 percent answered "no."

The situations presented in the two questions are actually the same and should have received the same fraction of yes and no responses. Many people, though, have trouble seeing that in question 1, when deciding whether to see the play, they should ignore the $10 already paid for a ticket because it is a sunk cost.

## Making the Connection | A Blogger Who Understands the Importance of Ignoring Sunk Costs

*Would you give up being a surgeon to start your own blog?*

In recent years, many people have started blogs—or, "Web logs"—where they record their thoughts on politics, sports, their favorite hobbies, or anything else that interests them. Some bloggers can spend hours a day writing up their latest ideas and providing links to relevant material on the Web. A few blogs become so successful that they attract paid advertising and earn their owners a good income. Arnold Kim began blogging about Apple products in 2000, during his fourth year of medical school. He continued blogging on his site, MacRumors.com, over the next eight years while pursuing a medical career as a nephrologist—a doctor who treats kidney problems.

By 2008, Kim's site had become very successful, attracting 4.4 million people and more than 40 million page views each month. Kim was earning more than $100,000 per year from paid advertising by companies such as Verizon, Audible.com, and CDW. But compiling rumors about new Apple products, keeping an Apple buying guide up to date, and monitoring multiple discussion boards on the site became more than he could handle as a part-time job. Kim enjoyed working on the Web site and believed that ultimately it could earn him more than he was earning as a doctor. Still, he hesitated to abandon his medical career because he had invested nearly $200,000 in his education.

But the $200,000, as well as the years he had spent in medical school, completing a residency in internal medicine, and completing a fellowship in nephrology, were sunk costs. Kim realized he needed to ignore these sunk costs in order to make a rational decision about whether to continue in medicine or to become a full-time blogger. After calculating that he would make more from his Web site than from his medical career—and taking into account that by working from home he could spend more time with his young daughter—he decided to blog full time. He was quoted as saying, "on paper it was an easy decision."

Knowing that it is rational to ignore sunk costs can be important in making key decisions in life.

Source: Brian Stelter, "My Son, the Blogger: An M.D. Trades Medicine for Apple Rumors," *New York Times*, July 21, 2008; and Dan Frommer, "Nephrologist to Mac Blogger: The Unlikely Career Path of MacRumors' Arnold Kim," businessinsider.com, July 13, 2008.

 **YOUR TURN:** Test your understanding by doing related problems 4.7, 4.8, and 4.9 on page 308 at the end of this chapter.

*If the payoff to studying is so high, why don't students study more?*

## Making the Connection | Why Don't Students Study More?

Government statistics show that students who do well in college earn at least $10,000 more per year than students who fail to graduate or who graduate with low grades. So, over the course of a career of 40 years or more, students who do well in college will have earned upwards of $400,000 more than students who failed to graduate or who received low grades. Most colleges advise that students study at least two hours outside class for every hour they spend in class. Surveys show that students often ignore this advice.

If the opportunity cost of not studying is so high, why do many students choose to study relatively little? Some students have work or family commitments that limit the amount of time they can study. But many other students study less than they would if they were more realistic about their future behavior. On any given night, a student has to choose between studying and other activities—such as watching television, going to a movie, or going to a party—that may seem to provide higher utility in the short run. Many students choose one of these activities over studying because they expect to study tomorrow or the next day, but tomorrow they face the same choices and make similar decisions. As a result, they do not study enough to meet their long-run goal of graduating with high grades. If they were more realistic about their future behavior, they would not make the mistake of overvaluing the utility from activities such as watching television or partying because they would realize that those activities can endanger their long-run goal of graduating with honors.

 **YOUR TURN:** Test your understanding by doing related problems 4.10 and 4.11 on page 309 at the end of this chapter.

Taking into account nonmonetary opportunity costs, ignoring sunk costs, and being more realistic about future behavior are three ways in which consumers are able to improve the decisions they make.

▶ Continued from page 279

## Economics in YOUR LIFE!

At the beginning of the chapter, we asked you to consider a situation in which you had paid $75 for a concert ticket, which is the most you would be willing to pay. Just before you enter the concert hall, someone offers you $90 for the ticket. We posed two questions: Would you sell the ticket? and Would an economist think it is rational to sell the ticket? If you answered that you would sell, then your answer is rational in the sense in which economists use the term. The cost of going to see the concert is what you have to give up for the ticket. Initially, the cost was just $75—the dollar price of the ticket. This amount was also the most you were willing to pay. However, once someone offers you $90 for the ticket, the cost of seeing the concert rises to $90. The reason the cost of the concert is now $90 is that once you turn down an offer of $90 for the ticket, you have incurred a nonmonetary opportunity cost of $90 if you use the ticket yourself. The endowment effect explains why some people would not sell the ticket. People seem to value things that they have more than things that they do not have. Therefore, a concert ticket you already own may be worth more to you than a concert ticket you have yet to purchase. Behavioral economists study situations like this where people make choices that do not appear to be economically rational.

## Conclusion

In a market system, consumers are in the driver's seat. Goods are produced only if consumers want them to be. Therefore, how consumers make their decisions is an important area for economists to study, a fact that was highlighted when Daniel Kahneman—whose research was mentioned several times in this chapter—shared the Nobel Prize in Economics. Economists expect that consumers will spend their incomes so that the last dollar spent on each good provides them with equal additional amounts of satisfaction, or utility. In practice, there are significant social influences on consumer decision making, particularly when a good or service is consumed in public. Fairness also seems to be an important consideration for most consumers. Finally, many consumers could improve the decisions they make if they would take into account nonmonetary opportunity costs and ignore sunk costs.

In this chapter, we studied consumers' choices. In the next several chapters, we will study firms' choices. Before moving on to the next chapter, read *An Inside Look* on the next page for a discussion of the effects of Oprah Winfrey's endorsement of Amazon's Kindle e-reader.

## >> The Power of Oprah's Kindle Endorsement

### THE TECH HERALD

# Oprah Endorsement to Dramatically Increase Exposure for Amazon Kindle

Sitting on the periphery of book-reading culture looking like some kind of ominous smoke and mirrors parlour trick, the Amazon Kindle electronic book reader has not yet won the widespread support of those keen to hold on to the printed page. However, that stubborn reticence could be about to change.

More pointedly, Oprah Winfrey, talk-show figurehead and one of the media world's most powerful women, has officially endorsed the Amazon Kindle on her hugely popular show, which could well catapult electronic reading into mainstream consciousness.

*Time* magazine quotes *Publishers Weekly* business editor Jim Milliot as saying that endorsement exposure through the Oprah book club can see individual titles benefiting from "a minimum of 500,000 additional sales." And that's a potential audience boost not to be taken lightly.

**a** Clearly viewed in the publishing world as having a Midas touch, an on-air endorsement of the lightweight and portable Kindle device by Oprah could well turn the ebook reader into an overnight success.

And that endorsement was certainly forthcoming when an enthusiastic and animated Oprah recently revealed on her show that she'd received a Kindle electronic book reader during the summer and it had changed her life. "When I get something this great I have to share it with everybody," Winfrey gushed. "I'm really not a gadget person at all, but I have fallen in love with this thing."

**b** Not alone in her excitement, Oprah was joined on stage by Amazon CEO Jeff Bezos, who then helped walk audience members through the Kindle's abilities after everyone in the studio was gifted with a free unit. With Oprah openly making a play to watching technophobes regarding the Kindle's user-friendly functionality, it was down to Bezos to reinforce that enjoyment is not dependent on computer knowledge and that the Kindle quickly downloads its publications by creating a wireless connection to the Internet.

**c** While obviously enthralled by the technology's portability, connectivity and onboard storage for hundreds of books, Oprah was also keen to point out that she has absolutely "no stake" in the Kindle, and is merely an amazed consumer looking to share her lucky discovery with others.

And, in so doing, Amazon is building on the endorsement by hacking a solid $50 USD from the Kindle price for every Oprah viewer . . . through to November 01 of this year.

*Source: Stevie Smith, "Oprah Endorsement to Dramatically Increase Exposure for Amazon Kindle," The Tech Herald, October 27, 2008.*

## Key Points in the Article

This article from the online magazine *The Tech Herald* was published just after Oprah Winfrey endorsed the Amazon Kindle e-reader in October 2008. (We also discussed this endorsement in the chapter opener.) The article correctly forecast that Oprah's endorsement would have a major positive effect on demand for the Kindle. The article notes that the business editor of *Publishers Weekly* magazine believed that Oprah's endorsement of a book by selecting it for her book club was enough to increase sales of the book by 500,000 copies. It seemed reasonable to expect that Oprah's viewers might react in a similarly positive way to her endorsement of the Kindle. Consumers might purchase the Kindle because they value Oprah's judgment or because doing so makes them feel closer to Oprah.

However, celebrity endorsements do come with risks. There are many examples of celebrities getting in trouble, much to the embarrassment of companies whose products the celebrities had endorsed. Singer Chris Brown was dropped from the "Got Milk?" campaign after he assaulted his girlfriend, singer Rihanna. Similarly, Wheaties dropped Olympic gold-medalist Michael Phelps from its advertisements after he was photographed apparently using an illegal drug. Once a firm is associated with a celebrity, consumers associate the product with the celebrity. This association can be a good or a bad thing, depending on the celebrity's actions.

## Analyzing the News

**a** Amazon CEO Jeff Bezos was happy to appear on Oprah's television show the day she endorsed the Kindle. He clearly hoped that her endorsement would lead to an increase in demand for the e-reader. In the chapter opener, we saw that Oprah's endorsement had a large effect, and Amazon quickly sold out of Kindles. In fact, the effect of the endorsement may have been greater than Amazon wanted because the Kindle remained out of stock during the 2008 holiday season, thereby disappointing many would-be buyers.

We saw in Chapter 3 that when consumers' taste for a product increases, the demand curve shifts to the right, and when consumers' taste for a product decreases, the demand curve for the product shifts to the left. When a firm receives a celebrity endorsement for one of its products, the firm hopes the endorsement will increase consumers' taste for the product. The figure shows that if the endorsement is successful, the demand curve for the Kindle shifts from $D_1$ to $D_2$. The increase in demand allows the firm to sell more Kindle readers at every price. For example, at a price of $P_1$, it could sell $Q_1$ e-readers without the endorsement but $Q_2$ e-readers with the endorsement.

**b** The chapter notes that one reason that celebrity endorsements attract customers is that public figures are perceived to be particularly knowledgeable about products. Oprah, having founded the Oprah book club, may have particular credibility with her audience in matters related to reading. The article states that Oprah described some of the features of the product. She showed her audience what it does, how easy it is to use, and how quickly readers can download new books. Celebrities do not need to have this level of knowledge about the products they endorse. However, sometimes consumers might listen more closely if this information is delivered by a celebrity they trust or find knowledgeable.

**c** The chapter also notes that one reason that celebrity endorsements are effective is that some consumers feel fashionable and closer to famous people if they use the same products that these people use. Thus, when Oprah told her audience that she is a satisfied customer, this endorsement sent the message that Oprah now uses the Kindle to read books, and if you want to be cool like Oprah, you should also use the Kindle to read books.

## Thinking Critically

1. Celebrity endorsements may be rewarding to firms, but they can also be risky. By appearing on Oprah's program, Amazon CEO Jeff Bezos tied the image of the Kindle to Oprah's image in the minds of the public. What do you think would happen to the demand curve for the Kindle if Oprah were to get involved in an embarrassing scandal?

2. Amazon did not pay Oprah to endorse the Kindle. She devoted time to the Kindle on her television show because she thought it was a good product that would be interesting to her viewers. Many companies pay celebrities considerable sums to endorse their products. Should a firm whose celebrity endorser was just arrested make a decision about whether to cancel its ad campaign based on the amount of money it has already spent on making the ads? Briefly explain.

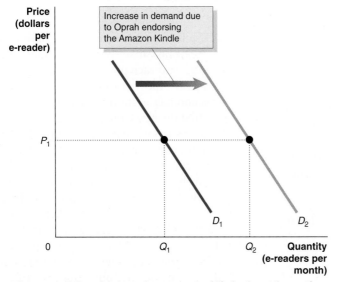

When successful, a celebrity endorsement can shift the demand curve for a product to the right, from $D_1$ to $D_2$.

# Key Terms

**9.1** **Utility and Consumer Decision Making, pages 280–288**

LEARNING OBJECTIVE: Define utility and explain how consumers choose goods and services to maximize their utility.

## Summary

**Utility** is the enjoyment or satisfaction that people receive from consuming goods and services. The goal of a consumer is to spend available income so as to maximize utility. **Marginal utility** is the change in total utility a person receives from consuming one additional unit of a good or service. The **law of diminishing marginal utility** states that consumers receive diminishing additional satisfaction as they consume more of a good or service during a given period of time. The **budget constraint** is the amount of income consumers have available to spend on goods and services. To maximize utility, consumers should make sure they spend their income so that the last dollar spent on each product gives them the same marginal utility. The **income effect** is the change in the quantity demanded of a good that results from the effect of a change in the price on consumer purchasing power. The **substitution effect** is the change in the quantity demanded of a good that results from a change in price making the good more or less expensive relative to other goods, holding constant the effect of the price change on consumer purchasing power.

 Visit **www.myeconlab.com** to complete these exercises online and get instant feedback.

## Review Questions

**1.1** What is the economic definition of *utility*? Is utility measurable?

**1.2** What is the definition of *marginal utility*? What is the law of diminishing marginal utility? Why is marginal utility more useful than total utility in consumer decision making?

**1.3** What is meant by a consumer's *budget constraint*? What is the rule of equal marginal utility per dollar spent?

## Problems and Applications

**1.4** Does the law of diminishing marginal utility hold true in every situation? Is it possible to think of goods for which consuming additional units will result in increasing marginal utility?

**1.5** If consumers should allocate their income so that the last dollar spent on every product gives them the same amount of additional utility, how should they decide the amount of their income to save?

**1.6** You have six hours to study for two exams tomorrow. The following table shows the relationship between hours of study and test scores.

| ECONOMICS | | PSYCHOLOGY | |
|---|---|---|---|
| HOURS | SCORE | HOURS | SCORE |
| 0 | 54 | 0 | 54 |
| 1 | 62 | 1 | 60 |
| 2 | 69 | 2 | 65 |
| 3 | 75 | 3 | 69 |
| 4 | 80 | 4 | 72 |
| 5 | 84 | 5 | 74 |
| 6 | 87 | 6 | 75 |

a. Use the rule for determining optimal purchases to decide how many hours you should study each subject. Treat each point on an exam as 1 unit of utility and assume that you consider an extra point on an economics exam to have the same value as an extra point on a psychology exam.

b. Now suppose that you are a psychology major and that you value each point you earn on a psychology exam as being worth three times as much as each point you earn on an economics exam. Now how many hours will you study each subject?

**1.7** (Related to *Solved Problem 9-1* on page 284) Joe has $16 to spend on Twinkies and Ho-Hos. Twinkies have a price of $1 per pack, and Ho-Hos have a price of $2 per pack. Use the information in the graphs on the following page to determine the number of Twinkies packs and the number of Ho-Hos packs Joe should buy to maximize his utility. Briefly explain your reasoning.

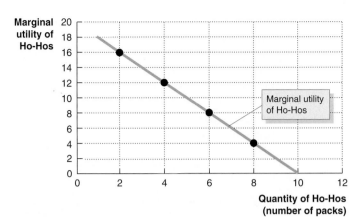

Marginal utility of Ho-Hos

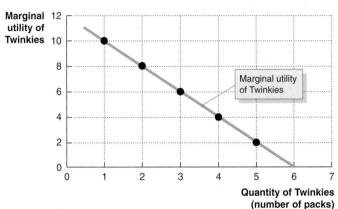

Marginal utility of Twinkies

| PRODUCT | PRICE | QUANTITY | TOTAL UTILITY | MARGINAL UTILITY OF LAST UNIT |
|---|---|---|---|---|
| Apples | $0.50 | 50 | 1,000 | 20 |
| Oranges | $0.75 | 40 | 500 | 30 |

**1.9** Suppose the price of a bag of Frito's corn chips declines from $0.69 to $0.59. Which is likely to be larger: the income effect or the substitution effect? Briefly explain.

**1.10** (Related to the *Don't Let This Happen to You!* on page 286) Mary is buying corn chips and soda. She has 4 bags of corn chips and 5 bottles of soda in her shopping cart. The marginal utility of the fourth bag of corn chips is 10, and the marginal utility of the fifth bottle of soda is also 10. Is Mary maximizing utility? Briefly explain.

**1.11** When the price of pizza falls in the Super Bowl example on pages 287–288, both the income and the substitution effect cause you to want to consume more pizza. If pizza were an inferior good, how would the analysis be changed? In this case, is it possible that a lower price for pizza might lead you to buy less pizza? Briefly explain.

**1.8** (Related to *Solved Problem 9-1* on page 284) Joe has $55 to spend on apples and oranges. Given the information in the following table, is Joe maximizing utility? Briefly explain.

**≫ End Learning Objective 9.1**

---

**9.2** | **Where Demand Curves Come From, pages 288–292**
LEARNING OBJECTIVE: Use the concept of utility to explain the law of demand.

## Summary

When the price of a good declines, the ratio of the marginal utility to price rises. This leads consumers to buy more of that good. As a result, whenever the price of a product falls, the quantity demanded increases. We saw in Chapter 1 that this is known as the *law of demand*. The market demand curve can be constructed from the individual demand curves for all the consumers in the market.

 Visit www.myeconlab.com to complete these exercises online and get instant feedback.

## Review Questions

**2.1** Explain how a downward-sloping demand curve results from consumers adjusting their consumption choices to changes in price.

**2.2** What would need to be true for a demand curve to be upward sloping?

## Problems and Applications

**2.3** Considering only the income effect, if the price of an inferior good declines, would a consumer want to buy a larger quantity or a smaller quantity of the good? Does this mean that the demand curves for inferior goods should slope upward? Briefly explain.

**2.4** The chapter states that "when the price of an inferior good falls, the income and substitution effects work in opposite directions." Explain what this statement means.

**2.5** Suppose the market for ice cream cones is made up of three consumers: Josh, Daisuke, and Tim. Use the information in the following table to construct the market demand curve for ice cream cones. Show the information in a table and in a graph.

**2.6** Suppose the wage you are being paid increases. Is there an income and substitution effect involved? If so, what is being substituted for what?

| PRICE | JOSH QUANTITY DEMANDED (CONES PER WEEK) | DAISUKE QUANTITY DEMANDED (CONES PER WEEK) | TIM QUANTITY DEMANDED (CONES PER WEEK) |
|---|---|---|---|
| $1.75 | 2 | 1 | 0 |
| 1.50 | 4 | 3 | 2 |
| 1.25 | 6 | 4 | 3 |
| 1.00 | 7 | 6 | 4 |
| 0.75 | 9 | 7 | 5 |

**2.7** (Related to the *Making the Connection* on page 291) In studying the consumption of very poor families in China, Robert Jensen and Nolan Miller found that in both Hunan and Gansu "Giffen behavior is most likely to be found among a range of households that are poor (but not too poor or too rich)."

   **a.** What do Jensen and Miller mean by "Giffen behavior"?

   **b.** Why would the poorest of the poor be less likely than people with slightly higher incomes to exhibit this behavior?

Source: Robert T. Jensen and Nolan H. Miller, "Giffen Behavior and Subsistence Consumption," *American Economic Review*, Vol. 98, No. 4, September 2008, p. 1569.

**2.8** (Related to *Solved Problem 9-2* on page 290) Anna lives in Germany and loves chocolate. The following table shows Anna's utility (*MU*) from her two favorite desserts, chocolate bars and chocolate ice cream:

| BARS | CHOCOLATE BARS *MU* PER BAR | CONES | CHOCOLATE ICE CREAM *MU* PER CONE |
|---|---|---|---|
| 1 | 340 | 1 | 420 |
| 2 | 280 | 2 | 330 |
| 3 | 240 | 3 | 300 |
| 4 | 220 | 4 | 240 |
| 5 | 208 | 5 | 120 |

Assume that Anna has €14 to spend on chocolate. Assume also that the price of a chocolate bar is €2 and that the price of an ice cream cone is initially €2 but then increases to €3. The following table shows the *MU/P* for chocolate bars and chocolate ice cream at their initial prices as well as the *MU/P* of chocolate ice cream after the price changes to €3.

| BARS | CHOCOLATE BARS *MU/P* P = €2 | CONES | CHOCOLATE ICE CREAM *MU/P* P = €2 | *MU/P* P = €3 |
|---|---|---|---|---|
| 1 | 170 | 1 | 210 | 140 |
| 2 | 140 | 2 | 165 | 110 |
| 3 | 120 | 3 | 150 | 110 |
| 4 | 110 | 4 | 120 | 80 |
| 5 | 104 | 5 | 60 | 40 |

   **a.** Using the rule of equal marginal utility per euro, how many chocolate bars and how many ice cream cones will Anna consume when the price of ice cream is €2?

   **b.** How many chocolate bars and how many chocolate ice cream cones will Anna consume when the price of ice cream rises to €3?

   **c.** What is the substitution effect of the change in the price of ice cream? What is the income effect?

   **d.** How does Anna's response to the increase in the price of ice cream illustrate the law of demand?

>> **End Learning Objective 9.2**

---

**9.3**  **Social Influences on Decision Making, pages 292–297**

LEARNING OBJECTIVE: Explain how social influences can affect consumption choices.

# Summary

Social factors can have an effect on consumption. For example, the amount of utility people receive from consuming a good often depends on how many other people they know who also consume the good. There is a **network externality** in the consumption of a product if the usefulness of the product increases with the number of consumers who use it. There is also evidence that people like to be treated fairly and that they usually attempt to treat others fairly, even if doing so makes them worse off financially. This result has been demonstrated in laboratory experiments, such as the ultimatum game. When firms set prices, they take into account consumers' preference for fairness. For example, hardware stores often do not increase the price of snow shovels to take advantage of a temporary increase in demand following a snowstorm.

 Visit **www.myeconlab.com** to complete these exercises online and get instant feedback.

## Review Questions

**3.1** In which of the following situations are social influences on consumer decision making likely to be greater: choosing a restaurant for dinner or choosing a brand of toothpaste to buy? Briefly explain.

**3.2** Why do consumers pay attention to celebrity endorsements of products?

**3.3** What are network externalities? For what types of products are network externalities likely to be important? What is path dependence?

**3.4** What is the ultimatum game? What insight does it provide into consumer decision making?

**3.5** How does the fact that consumers apparently value fairness affect the decisions that businesses make?

## Problems and Applications

**3.6** Which of the following products are most likely to have significant network externalities? Explain.
a. Fax machines
b. Dog food
c. Board games
d. Conventional (CRT) televisions
e. LCD televisions

**3.7** Speaking about a recent trip to Switzerland, Daniel Hamermesh made the following comment in the *New York Times*:

> A waste of time! After arriving at our hotel in Switzerland at 7 p.m., my wife and I had both hoped to work on our computers—but we couldn't. Although we had bought universal plug adapters (which convert American plugs to European, Australian, and English outlets), it turns out that Switzerland has its own unique three-prong plug. Why? This kind of plug adapter is not sold with standard adapter sets. Why does Switzerland renounce the network externalities that would come with using standard European plugs with their standard 220-volt electricity?

How is Switzerland "renouncing network externalities" by not using standard European plugs?

Source: Daniel Hamermesh, "If Switzerland Would Only Change Its Plugs," *New York Times*, September 23, 2008.

**3.8** (Related to the *Chapter Opener* on page 279) In endorsing the Kindle, Oprah said: "If you're like me and a little computer challenged, do not be afraid of the Kindle—do not be afraid—because you don't even have to have a computer for it to work. That's the brilliant thing about it." Why might an endorsement from Oprah be more valuable to Amazon than an endorsement from a young singer or movie star?

Source: Oprah.com: www.oprah.com/slideshow/oprahshow/20081024_tows_kindle/2

**3.9** (Related to the *Making the Connection* on page 293) Tiger Woods is a professional golfer who knows more than most consumers about golfing and golf-related products. However, he does not necessarily know more than consumers about Gillette razors, Rolex watches, and American Express products. Consider the model of utility-maximizing behavior described in this chapter. For Gillette's use of Tiger Woods as a celebrity endorser to make economic sense, how must Woods's endorsement affect the marginal utility that at least some consumers receive from shaving with Gillette razors? What will this do to the demand curve for Gillette razors?

**3.10** Las Vegas is one of the most popular tourist destinations in the United States. In November 2008, the Rio Hotel and Casino in Las Vegas dropped the price of its breakfast buffet to $5.99 for local residents, while keeping the regular price of $14.99 for nonlocals. When setting the price for a meal, why would it matter to the restaurant if the customer is a local resident?

Source: *Las Vegas Advisor*, November, 2008.

**3.11** (Related to the *Making the Connection* on page 297) Suppose the rock band U2 can sell out a concert at Madison Square Garden with tickets priced at $85 each. U2's manager estimates that the band could still sell out the Garden at $125 per ticket. Why might U2 and their manager want to keep the ticket price at $85?

**3.12** (Related to the *Making the Connection* on page 297) Suppose that *Spider-Man 4* comes out, and hundreds of people arrive at a theater and discover that the movie is already sold out. Meanwhile, the theater is also showing a boring movie in its third week of release in a mostly empty theater. Why would this firm charge the same $7.50 for a ticket to either movie, when the quantity of tickets demanded is much greater than the quantity supplied for one movie, and the quantity of tickets demanded is much less than the quantity supplied for the other?

>> **End Learning Objective 9.3**

**9.4**   **Behavioral Economics: Do People Make Their Choices Rationally?**
pages 297–300

LEARNING OBJECTIVE: Describe the behavioral economics approach to understanding decision making.

## Summary

**Behavioral economics** is the study of situations in which people act in ways that are not economically rational. **Opportunity cost** is the highest-valued alternative that must be given up to engage in an activity. People would improve their decision making if they took into account nonmonetary opportunity costs. People sometimes ignore nonmonetary opportunity costs because of the **endowment effect**—the tendency of people to be unwilling to sell something they already own even if they are offered a price that is greater than the price they would be willing to pay to buy the good if they didn't already own it. People would also improve their decision making if they ignored *sunk costs*. A **sunk cost** is a cost that has already been paid and cannot be recovered. Finally, people would improve their decision making if they were more realistic about their future behavior.

 Visit **www.myeconlab.com** to complete these exercises online and get instant feedback.

## Review Questions

**4.1**  What does it mean to be economically rational?

**4.2**  Define *behavioral economics* and give an example of three common mistakes that consumers often make.

## Problems and Applications

**4.3**  Suppose your little brother tells you on Tuesday that one of his friends offered him $80 for his Albert Pujols rookie baseball card, but your brother decided not to sell the card. On Wednesday, your brother loses the card. Your parents feel sorry for him and give him $80 to make up the loss. Instead of buying another Albert Pujols card with the money (which we will assume he could have done), your brother uses the money to buy an iPod shuffle. Explain your brother's actions by using the concepts in this chapter.

**4.4**  Richard Thaler, an economist at the University of Chicago, is the person who first used the term *endowment effect* to describe placing a higher value on something already owned than would be placed on the object if not currently owned. According to an article in the *Economist*:

> Dr Thaler, who recently had some expensive bottles of wine stolen, observes that he is "now confronted with precisely one of my own experiments: these are bottles I

wasn't planning to sell and now I'm going to get a cheque from an insurance company and most of these bottles I will not buy. I'm a good enough economist to know there's a bit of an inconsistency there."

Based on Thaler's statement, how do his stolen bottles of wine illustrate the endowment effect, and why does he make the statement: "I'm a good enough economist to know there's a bit of an inconsistency there"?

Source: "It's mine, I tell you," *Economist*, June 19, 2008.

**4.5**  Oldies 93 has a promotion in which it announces that a local gas station will sell gasoline at 93 cents per gallon beginning in 30 minutes. Jack hops in his car and drives to the station to fill up his half-empty tank. He pays only $9.30 for 10 gallons instead of the going price of $19.30. Did Jack save $10.00? Is the radio station doing its listeners a favor by offering this promotion? Briefly explain.

**4.6**  You have tickets to see Bruce Springsteen in concert at a stadium 50 miles away. A severe thunderstorm on the night of the concert makes driving hazardous. Will your decision to attend the concert be different if you paid $70 for the tickets than if you received the tickets for free? Explain your answer.

**4.7**  **(Related to the *Making the Connection* on page 299)** Rob Neyer is a baseball writer for ESPN.com. He described attending a Red Sox game at Fenway Park in Boston and having a seat in the sun on a hot, humid day: "Granted, I could have moved under the overhang and enjoyed today's contest from a nice, cool, shady seat. But when you paid forty-five dollars for a ticket in the fourth row, it's tough to move back to the twenty-fourth [row]." Evaluate Neyer's reasoning.

Source: Rob Neyer, *Feeding the Green Monster*, New York: iPublish.com, 2001, p. 50.

**4.8**  **(Related to the *Making the Connection* on page 299)** After owning a used car for two years, you start having problems with it. You take it into the shop, and a mechanic tells you that repairs will cost $4,000. What factors will you take into account in deciding whether to have the repairs done or to junk the car and buy another one? Will the price you paid for the car be one of those factors? Briefly explain.

**4.9**  **(Related to the *Making the Connection* on page 299)** The following excerpt is from a letter sent to a financial advice columnist: "My wife and I are trying to decide how to invest a $250,000 windfall. She wants to pay off our $114,000 mortgage, but I'm not eager to do that because we refinanced only nine months ago, paying $3,000 in fees and costs." Briefly discuss what effect the $3,000 refinancing cost should have on this couple's investment decision.

Source: Liz Pulliam, *Los Angeles Times* advice column, March 24, 2004.

**4.10** (Related to the *Making the Connection* on page 300) In a blog posting on msn.com, J.D. Roth recalls his desire get in better physical condition:

> To goad myself into action, I paid about $100 (nonrefundable, nontransferable) to sign up for the Portland Marathon. For a while, this seemed like a brilliant idea. Having paid for the marathon in advance, I was motivated to train so that my money didn't go to waste. At the end of May,

however, I hurt myself, so I took some time off. But when I tried to return to running, the pain persisted. I went to a physical therapist. June turned to July turned to August. Eventually I decided that maybe I could walk the marathon. I'd paid $100 for it, and I wasn't going to let that money go to waste.

Roth goes on to say that he eventually realized his reasoning about letting the $100 go to waste was flawed. Why was his reasoning flawed?

Source: J.D. Roth, "The Sunk-Cost Fallacy Revisited," msn.com, November 3, 2008.

**4.11** (Related to the *Making the Connection* on page 300) Briefly explain whether you agree with the following statement: "If people were more realistic about their future behavior, the demand curve for potato chips would shift to the left."

**>> End Learning Objective 9.4**

# Appendix

**LEARNING** OBJECTIVE

Use indifference curves and budget lines to understand consumer behavior.

# Using Indifference Curves and Budget Lines to Understand Consumer Behavior

## Consumer Preferences

In this chapter, we analyzed consumer behavior, using the assumption that satisfaction, or *utility*, is measurable in utils. Although this assumption made our analysis easier to understand, it is unrealistic. In this appendix we use the more realistic assumption that consumers are able to *rank* different combinations of goods and services in terms of how much utility they provide. In other words, a consumer is able to determine whether he or she prefers 2 slices of pizza and 1 can of Coke or 1 slice of pizza and 2 cans of Coke, even if the consumer is unsure exactly how much utility he or she would receive from consuming these goods. This approach has the advantage that it allows us to actually draw a map of a consumer's preferences.

To begin with, suppose that a consumer is presented with the following alternatives, or *consumption bundles:*

| CONSUMPTION BUNDLE A | CONSUMPTION BUNDLE B |
|---|---|
| 2 slices of pizza and 1 can of Coke | 1 slice of pizza and 2 cans of Coke |

We assume that the consumer will always be able to decide which of the following is true:

- The consumer prefers bundle A to bundle B.

- The consumer prefers bundle B to bundle A.

- The consumer is indifferent between bundle A and bundle B. That is, the consumer would be equally happy to receive either bundle, so we can say the consumer receives equal utility from the two bundles.

For consistency, we also assume that the consumer's preferences are *transitive*. For example, if a consumer prefers pepperoni pizza to mushroom pizza and prefers mushroom pizza to anchovy pizza, the consumer must prefer pepperoni pizza to anchovy pizza.

## Indifference Curves

**Indifference curve** A curve that shows the combinations of consumption bundles that give the consumer the same utility.

Given the assumptions in the preceding section, we can draw a map of a consumer's preferences by using indifference curves. An **indifference curve** shows combinations of consumption bundles that give the consumer the same utility. In reality, consumers choose among consumption bundles containing many goods and services, but to make

| Consumption Bundle | Slices of Pizza | Cans of Coke |
|---|---|---|
| A | 1 | 2 |
| B | 3 | 4 |
| C | 4 | 5 |
| D | 1 | 6 |
| E | 2 | 8 |
| F | 5 | 2 |

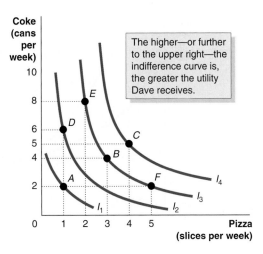

## Figure 9A-1

### Plotting Dave's Preferences for Pizza and Coke

Every possible combination of pizza and Coke will have an indifference curve passing through it, although in the graph we show just four of Dave's indifference curves. Dave is indifferent among all the consumption bundles that are on the same indifference curve. So, he is indifferent among bundles $E$, $B$, and $F$ because they all lie on indifference curve $I_3$. Moving to the upper right in the graph increases the quantities of both goods available for Dave to consume. Therefore, the further to the upper right the indifference curve is, the greater the utility Dave receives.

the discussion easier to follow, we will assume that only two goods are involved. Nothing important would change if we expanded the discussion to include many goods instead of just two.

The table in Figure 9A-1 gives Dave's preferences for pizza and Coke. The graph plots the information from the table. Every possible combination of pizza and Coke will have an indifference curve passing through it, although in the figure we have shown only four of Dave's indifference curves. Dave is indifferent among all the consumption bundles that are on the same indifference curve. So, he is indifferent among bundles $E$, $B$, and $F$ because they all lie on indifference curve $I_3$. Even though Dave has 4 fewer cans of Coke with bundle $B$ than with bundle $E$, the additional slice of pizza he has in bundle $B$ means he has the same amount of utility at both points.

Even without looking at Dave's indifference curves, we know he will prefer consumption bundle $D$ to consumption bundle $A$ because in $D$ he receives the same quantity of pizza as in $A$ but 4 additional cans of Coke. But we need to know Dave's preferences, as shown by his indifference curves, to know how he will rank bundle $B$ and bundle $D$. Bundle $D$ contains more Coke but less pizza than bundle $B$, so Dave's ranking will depend on how much pizza he would be willing to give up to receive more Coke. The higher the indifference curve—that is, the further to the upper right on the graph—the greater the amounts of both goods that are available for Dave to consume and the greater his utility. In other words, Dave receives more utility from the consumption bundles on indifference curve $I_2$ than from the consumption bundles on indifference curve $I_1$, more utility from the bundles on $I_3$ than from the bundles on $I_2$, and so on.

## The Slope of an Indifference Curve

Remember that the slope of a curve is the ratio of the change in the variable on the vertical axis to the change in the variable on the horizontal axis. Along an indifference curve, the slope tells us the rate at which the consumer is willing to trade off one product for another while keeping the consumer's utility constant. Economists call this rate the **marginal rate of substitution** (*MRS*).

We expect that the *MRS* will change as we move down an indifference curve. In Figure 9A-1, at a point like $E$ on indifference curve $I_3$, Dave's indifference curve is relatively steep. As we move down the curve, it becomes less steep, until it becomes relatively flat at a point like $F$. This is the usual shape of indifference curves: They are bowed in, or convex. A consumption bundle like $E$ contains a lot of Coke and not much pizza. We would expect that Dave could give up a significant quantity of Coke for a smaller quantity of additional pizza and still have the same level of utility. Thus, the *MRS* will be high. As we move down the indifference curve, Dave moves to bundles, like $B$ and $F$, that have more pizza and less Coke. As a result, Dave is willing to trade less Coke for pizza, and the *MRS* declines.

**Marginal rate of substitution (MRS)** The rate at which a consumer would be willing to trade off one good for another.

## Figure 9A-2

**Indifference Curves Cannot Cross**

Because bundle $X$ and bundle $Z$ are both on indifference curve $I_1$, Dave must be indifferent between them. Similarly, because bundle $X$ and bundle $Y$ are on indifference curve $I_2$, Dave must be indifferent between them. The assumption of transitivity means that Dave should also be indifferent between bundle $Z$ and bundle $Y$. We know that this is not true, however, because bundle $Y$ contains more pizza and more Coke than bundle $Z$. So Dave will definitely prefer bundle $Y$ to bundle $Z$, which violates the assumption of transitivity. *Therefore, none of Dave's indifference curves can cross.*

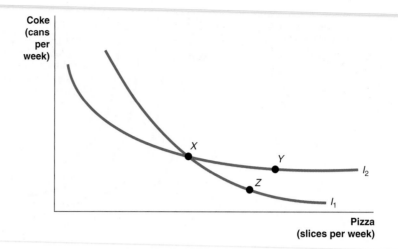

## Can Indifference Curves Ever Cross?

Remember that we assume that consumers have transitive preferences. That is, if Dave prefers consumption bundle $X$ to consumption bundle $Y$ and he prefers consumption bundle $Y$ to consumption bundle $Z$, he must prefer bundle $X$ to bundle $Z$. If indifference curves cross, this assumption is violated. To understand why, look at Figure 9A-2, which shows two of Dave's indifference curves crossing.

Because bundle $X$ and bundle $Z$ are both on indifference curve $I_1$, Dave must be indifferent between them. Similarly, because bundle $X$ and bundle $Y$ are on indifference curve $I_2$, Dave must be indifferent between them. The assumption of transitivity means that Dave should also be indifferent between bundle $Z$ and bundle $Y$. We know that this is not true, however, because bundle $Y$ contains more pizza and more Coke than bundle $Z$. So, Dave will definitely prefer bundle $Y$ to bundle $Z$, which violates the assumption of transitivity. Therefore, none of Dave's indifference curves can cross.

## The Budget Constraint

Remember that a consumer's *budget constraint* is the amount of income he or she has available to spend on goods and services. Suppose that Dave has $10 per week to spend on pizza and Coke. The table in Figure 9A-3 shows the combinations that he can afford to buy if the price of pizza is $2 per slice and the price of Coke is $1 per can. As you can see, all the points lie on a straight line. This line represents Dave's budget constraint. The line intersects the vertical axis at the maximum number of cans of Coke Dave can afford to buy with $10, which is consumption bundle G. The line intersects the horizontal axis at the maximum number of slices of pizza Dave can afford to buy with $10, which is consumption bundle L. As he moves down his budget constraint from bundle G, he gives up 2 cans of Coke for every slice of pizza he buys.

Any consumption bundle along the line or inside the line is *affordable* for Dave because he has the income to buy those combinations of pizza and Coke. Any bundle that lies outside the line is *unaffordable* because those bundles cost more than the income Dave has available to spend.

The slope of the budget constraint is constant because the budget constraint is a straight line. The slope of the line equals the change in the number of cans of Coke divided by the change in the number of slices of pizza. In this case, moving down the budget constraint from one point to another point, the change in the number of cans of Coke equals −2, and the change in the number of slices of pizza equals 1, so the slope equals −2/1, or −2. Notice that with the price of pizza equal to $2 per slice and the price of Coke equal to $1 per can, the slope of the budget constraint is equal to the ratio of

| Combinations of Pizza and Coke Dave Can Buy with $10 | | | |
|---|---|---|---|
| Consumption Bundle | Slices of Pizza | Cans of Coke | Total Spending |
| G | 0 | 10 | $10.00 |
| H | 1 | 8 | 10.00 |
| I | 2 | 6 | 10.00 |
| J | 3 | 4 | 10.00 |
| K | 4 | 2 | 10.00 |
| L | 5 | 0 | 10.00 |

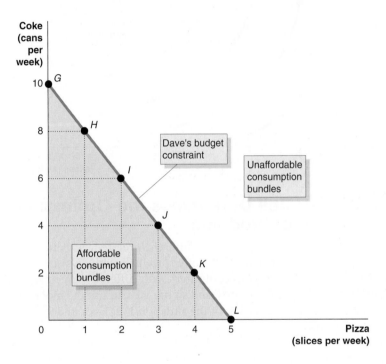

## Figure 9A-3

**Dave's Budget Constraint**

Dave's budget constraint shows the combinations of slices of pizza and cans of Coke he can buy with $10. The price of Coke is $1 per can, so if he spends all of his $10 on Coke, he can buy 10 cans (bundle *G*). The price of pizza is $2 per slice, so if he spends all of his $10 on pizza, he can buy 5 slices (bundle *L*). As he moves down his budget constraint from bundle *G*, he gives up 2 cans of Coke for every slice of pizza he buys. Any consumption bundles along the line or inside the line are affordable. Any bundles that lie outside the line are unaffordable.

the price of pizza to the price of Coke (multiplied by −1). In fact, this result will always hold: *The slope of the budget constraint is equal to the ratio of the price of the good on the horizontal axis divided by the price of the good on the vertical axis, multiplied by −1.*

## Choosing the Optimal Consumption of Pizza and Coke

Dave would like to be on the highest possible indifference curve because higher indifference curves represent more pizza and more Coke. But Dave can only buy the bundles that lie on or inside his budget constraint. In other words, *to maximize utility, a consumer needs to be on the highest indifference curve, given his budget constraint.*

Figure 9A-4 plots the consumption bundles from Figure 9A-1 along with the budget constraint from Figure 9A-3. The figure also shows the indifference curves that pass through each consumption bundle. In Figure 9A-4, the highest indifference curve shown is $I_4$. Unfortunately, Dave lacks the income to purchase consumption bundles—such as *C*—that lie on $I_4$. He has the income to purchase bundles such as *A* and *D*, but he can do better. If he consumes bundle *B*, he will be on the highest indifference curve he can reach, given his budget constraint of $10. The resulting combination of 3 slices of pizza and 4 cans of Coke represents optimal consumption of pizza and Coke, given Dave's preferences and given his budget constraint. Notice that at point *B*, Dave's budget constraint just touches—or is *tangent* to—$I_3$. In fact, bundle *B* is the only bundle on $I_3$ that Dave is able to purchase for $10.

## Figure 9A-4

**Finding Optimal Consumption**

Dave would like to be on the highest possible indifference curve, but he cannot reach indifference curves such as $I_4$ that are outside his budget constraint. Dave's optimal combination of slices of pizza and cans of Coke comes at point *B*, where his budget constraint just touches—or is *tangent* to—the highest indifference curve he can reach. At point *B*, he buys 3 slices of pizza and 4 cans of Coke.

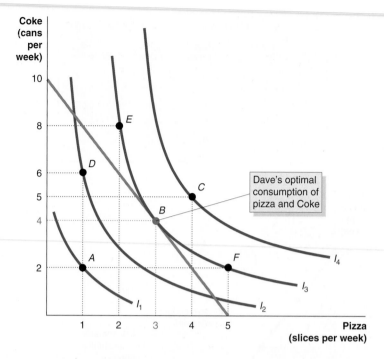

## Making the Connection

# Dell Determines the Optimal Mix of Products

Consumers have different preferences, which helps explain why many firms offer products with a variety of characteristics. For example, Dell sells laptop computers with different screen sizes, processor speeds, hard drive sizes, graphics cards, and so on. We can use the model of consumer choice to analyze a simplified version of the situation Dell faces in deciding which features to offer consumers.

Assume that consumers have $1,000 each to spend on laptops and that they are concerned with only two laptop characteristics: screen size and processor speed. Because larger screens and faster processors increase Dell's cost of producing laptops, consumers face a trade-off: The larger the screen, the slower the processor speed. Consumers in panel (a) of the figure prefer screen size to processor speed. For this group, the point of tangency between a typical consumer's indifference curve and the budget constraint shows an optimal choice of a 17-inch screen and a 1.5-gigahertz processor. Consumers

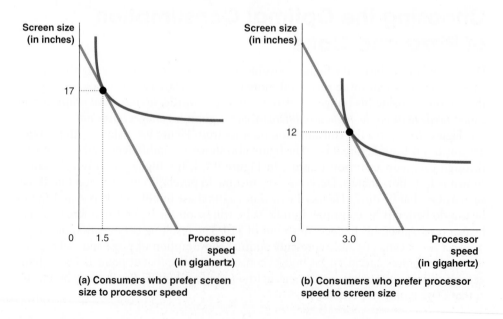

(a) Consumers who prefer screen size to processor speed

(b) Consumers who prefer processor speed to screen size

in panel (b) prefer processor speed to screen size. For this group, the point of tangency between a typical consumer's indifference curve and the budget constraint shows an optimal choice of a 12-inch screen and 3.0-gigahertz processor.

Companies such as Dell use surveys and other means to gather information about consumer preferences. With knowledge of consumers' preferences and data on the costs of producing different laptop components, Dell can determine the mix of components to offer consumers.

**YOUR TURN:** Test your understanding by doing related problem 9A.8 on page 323 at the end of this appendix.

## Deriving the Demand Curve

Suppose the price of pizza falls from $2 per slice to $1 per slice. How will this affect Dave's decision about which combination of pizza and Coke is optimal? First, notice what happens to Dave's budget constraint when the price of pizza falls. As Figure 9A-5 shows, when the price of pizza is $2 per slice, the maximum number of slices Dave can buy is 5. After the price of pizza falls to $1 per slice, Dave can buy a maximum of 10 slices. His budget constraint rotates outward from point *A* to point *B* to represent this. (Notice that the fall in the price of pizza does not affect the maximum number of cans of Coke Dave can buy with his $10.)

When his budget constraint rotates outward, Dave is able to purchase consumption bundles that were previously unaffordable. Panel (a) of Figure 9A-6 shows that the combination of 3 slices of pizza and 4 cans of Coke was optimal when the price of pizza was $2 per slice, but the combination of 7 slices of pizza and 3 cans of Coke is optimal when the price of pizza falls to $1. The lower price of pizza causes Dave to consume more pizza and less Coke and to end up on a higher indifference curve.

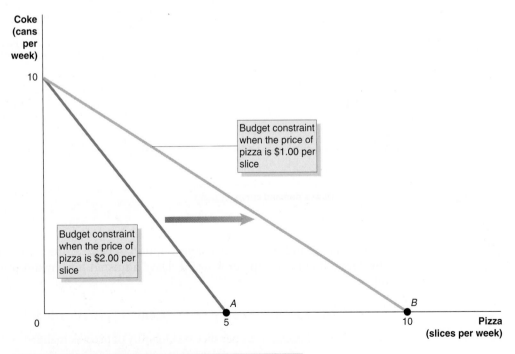

Figure 9A-5   **How a Price Decrease Affects the Budget Constraint**

A fall in the price of pizza from $2 per slice to $1 per slice increases the maximum number of slices Dave can buy with $10 from 5 to 10. The budget constraint rotates outward from point *A* to point *B* to show this.

# Figure 9A-6

## How a Price Change Affects Optimal Consumption

In panel (a), a fall in the price of pizza results in Dave's consuming less Coke and more pizza.

1. A fall in the price of pizza rotates the budget constraint outward because Dave can now buy more pizza with his $10.
2. In the new optimum on indifference curve $I_2$, Dave changes the quantities he consumes of both goods. His consumption of Coke falls from 4 cans to 3 cans.
3. In the new optimum, Dave's consumption of pizza increases from 3 slices to 7 slices.

In panel (b) Dave responds optimally to the fall in the price of pizza from $2 per slice to $1, by increasing the quantity of slices he consumes from 3 slices to 7 slices. When we graph this result, we have Dave's demand curve for pizza.

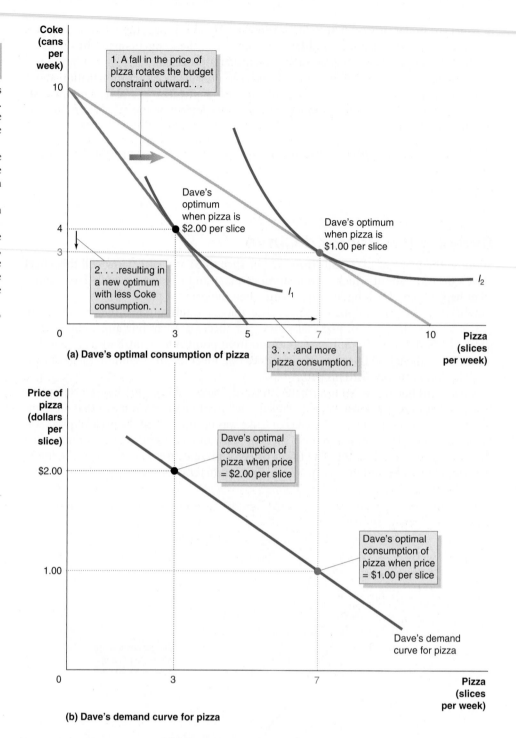

(a) Dave's optimal consumption of pizza

(b) Dave's demand curve for pizza

The change in Dave's optimal consumption of pizza as the price changes explains why demand curves slope downward. Dave adjusted his consumption of pizza as follows:

Price of pizza = $2 per slice ⇒ Quantity of pizza demanded = 3 slices

Price of pizza = $1 per slice ⇒ Quantity of pizza demanded = 7 slices

In panel (b) of Figure 9A-6, we plot the two points of optimal consumption, and draw a line connecting the points. This downward-sloping line is Dave's demand curve for pizza. We could find more points on the demand curve by changing the price of pizza and finding the new optimal number of slices of pizza Dave would demand.

Remember that according to the law of demand, demand curves always slope downward. We have just shown that the law of demand results from the optimal adjustment by consumers to changes in prices. A fall in the price of a good will rotate *outward* the budget constraint and make it possible for a consumer to reach higher indifference curves. As a result, the consumer will increase the quantity of the good demanded. An increase in price will rotate *inward* the budget constraint and force the consumer to a lower indifference curve. As a result, the consumer will decrease the quantity of the good demanded.

# Solved Problem | 9A-1

## When Does a Price Change Make a Consumer Better Off?

Dave has $300 to spend each month on DVDs and CDs. DVDs and CDs both currently have a price of $10, and Dave is maximizing his utility by buying 20 DVDs and 10 CDs. Suppose Dave still has $300 to spend, but the price of a CD rises to $20, while the price of a DVD drops to $5. Is Dave better or worse off than he was before the price change? Use a budget constraint–indifference curve graph to illustrate your answer.

## SOLVING THE PROBLEM:

**Step 1:** **Review the chapter material.** This problem concerns the effect of price changes on optimal consumption, so you may want to review the section "Deriving the Demand Curve" which begins on page 315.

**Step 2:** **Answer the problem by drawing the appropriate graph.** We begin by drawing the budget constraint, indifference curve, and point of optimal consumption for the original prices:

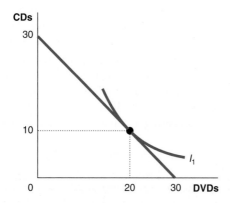

Now draw a graph that shows the results of the price changes. Notice that in this problem, the prices of *both* goods change. However, you can determine the position of the new budget constraint by calculating the maximum quantity of DVDs and CDs Dave can buy after the price changes. You should also note that after the price changes, Dave can still buy his original optimal consumption bundle—20 DVDs and 10 CDs—by

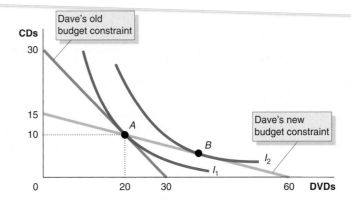

spending all of his $300, so his new budget constraint must pass through this point.

At the new prices, Dave can buy a maximum of 60 DVDs or 15 CDs. Both his old and his new budget constraints pass through the consumption bundle at point *A*. This consumption bundle is no longer optimal, however, because with the new prices, it is possible for him to reach an indifference curve that is higher than $I_1$. We can draw in the new highest indifference curve he can reach—$I_2$—and show the new optimal consumption bundle—point *B*.

Because Dave can now reach a higher indifference curve, we can conclude that he is better off as a result of the price change.

 **YOUR TURN:** For more practice, do related problem 9A.10 on page 323 at the end of this appendix.

## The Income Effect and the Substitution Effect of a Price Change

We saw in this chapter that a price change has two effects on the quantity of a good consumed: the *income effect* and the *substitution effect*. The income effect is the change in the quantity demanded of a good that results from the effect of a change in price on consumer purchasing power, holding all other factors constant. The substitution effect is the change in the quantity demanded of a good that results from a change in price making the good more or less expensive relative to other goods, holding constant the effect of the price change on consumer purchasing power. We can use indifference curves and budget constraints to analyze these two effects more exactly.

Figure 9A-7 illustrates the same situation as Figure 9A-6: The price of pizza has fallen from $2 per slice to $1 per slice, and Dave's budget constraint has rotated outward. As before, Dave's optimal consumption of pizza increases from 3 slices (point *A* in Figure 9A-7) per week to 7 slices per week (point *C*). We can think of this movement from point *A* to point *C* as taking place in two steps: The movement from point *A* to point *B* represents the substitution effect, and the movement from point *B* to point *C* represents the income effect. To isolate the substitution effect, we have to hold constant the effect of the price change on Dave's income. We do this by changing the price of pizza relative to the price of Coke *but at the same time holding his utility constant by keeping Dave on the same indifference curve*. In Figure 9A-7, in moving from point *A* to point *B*, Dave remains on indifference curve $I_1$. Point *A* is a point of tangency between $I_1$ and Dave's original budget constraint. Point *B* is a point of tangency

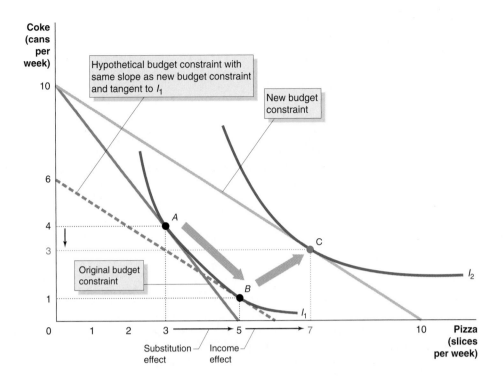

Coke (cans per week)

Hypothetical budget constraint with same slope as new budget constraint and tangent to $I_1$

New budget constraint

Original budget constraint

Substitution effect   Income effect

$I_1$

$I_2$

Pizza (slices per week)

**Figure 9A-7**

**Income and Substitution Effects of a Price Change**

Following a decline in the price of pizza, Dave's optimal consumption of pizza increases from 3 slices (point $A$) per week to 7 slices per week (point $C$). We can think of this movement from point $A$ to point $C$ as taking place in two steps: The movement from point $A$ to point $B$ along indifference curve $I_1$ represents the substitution effect, and the movement from point $B$ to point $C$ represents the income effect. Dave increases his consumption of pizza from 3 slices per week to 5 slices per week because of the substitution effect of a fall in the price of pizza and from 5 slices per week to 7 slices per week because of the income effect.

between $I_1$ and a new, *hypothetical* budget constraint that has a slope equal to the new ratio of the price of pizza to the price of Coke. At point $B$, Dave has increased his consumption of pizza from 3 slices to 5 slices. Because we are still on indifference curve $I_1$, we know that this increase is Dave's response only to the change in the relative price of pizza and, therefore, that the increase represents the substitution effect of the fall in the price of pizza.

At point $B$, Dave has not spent all his income. Remember that the fall in the price of pizza has increased Dave's purchasing power. In Figure 9A-7, we illustrate the additional pizza Dave consumes because of the income effect of increased purchasing power by the movement from point $B$ to point $C$. Notice that in moving from point $B$ to point $C$, the price of pizza relative to the price of Coke is constant because the slope of the new budget constraint is the same as the slope of the hypothetical budget constraint that is tangent to $I_1$ at point $B$.

We can conclude that Dave increases his consumption of pizza from 3 slices per week to 5 slices per week because of the substitution effect of a fall in the price of pizza and from 5 slices per week to 7 slices per week because of the income effect. Recall from our discussion of income and substitution effects in this chapter that the income effect of a price decline causes consumers to buy more of a normal good and less of an inferior good. Because the income effect causes Dave to increase his consumption of pizza, pizza must be a normal good for him.

## How a Change in Income Affects Optimal Consumption

Suppose that the price of pizza remains at $2 per slice, but the income Dave has to spend on pizza and Coke increases from $10 to $20. Figure 9A-8 shows how this affects his budget constraint. With an income of $10, Dave could buy a maximum of 5 slices of pizza or 10 cans of Coke. With an income of $20, he can buy 10 slices of pizza or 20 cans of Coke. The additional income allows Dave to increase his consumption of both pizza and Coke and to move to a higher indifference curve. Figure 9A-9 shows Dave's new optimum. Dave is able to increase his consumption of pizza from 3 slices per week to 7 and his consumption of Coke from 4 cans per week to 6.

## Figure 9A-8

**How a Change in Income Affects the Budget Constraint**

When the income Dave has to spend on pizza and Coke increases from $10 to $20, his budget constraint shifts outward. With $10, Dave could buy a maximum of 5 slices of pizza or 10 cans of Coke. With $20, he can buy a maximum of 10 slices of pizza or 20 cans of Coke.

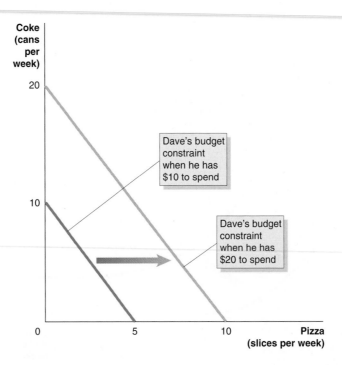

# The Slope of the Indifference Curve, the Slope of the Budget Line, and the Rule of Equal Marginal Utility Per Dollar Spent

In this chapter, we saw that consumers maximize utility when they consume each good up to the point where the marginal utility per dollar spent is the same for every good. This condition seems different from the one we stated earlier in this appendix that to

## Figure 9A-9

**How a Change in Income Affects Optimal Consumption**

An increase in income leads Dave to consume more Coke and more pizza.

1. An increase in income shifts Dave's budget constraint outward because he can now buy more of both goods.
2. In the new optimum on indifference curve $I_2$, Dave changes the quantities he consumes of both goods. His consumption of Coke increases from 4 cans to 6 cans.
3. In the new optimum, Dave's consumption of pizza increases from 3 slices to 7 slices.

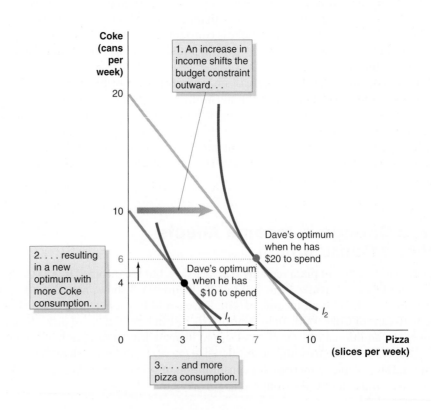

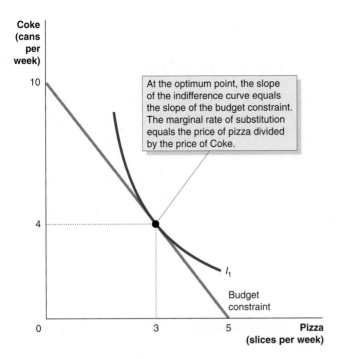

**Coke (cans per week)**

At the optimum point, the slope of the indifference curve equals the slope of the budget constraint. The marginal rate of substitution equals the price of pizza divided by the price of Coke.

$I_1$

Budget constraint

**Pizza (slices per week)**

## Figure 9A-10

**At the Optimum Point, the Slopes of the Indifference Curve and Budget Constraint Are the Same**

At the point of optimal consumption, the marginal rate of substitution is equal to the ratio of the price of the product on the horizontal axis to the price of the product on the vertical axis.

maximize utility, a consumer needs to be on the highest indifference curve, given his budget constraint. In fact, though, the two conditions are equivalent. To see this, begin by looking at Figure 9A-10, which again combines Dave's indifference curve and budget constraint. Remember that at the point of optimal consumption, the indifference curve and the budget constraint are tangent, so they have the same slope. Therefore: *At the point of optimal consumption, the marginal rate of substitution* (MRS) *is equal to the ratio of the price of the product on the horizontal axis to the price of the product on the vertical axis.*

The slope of the indifference curve tells us the rate at which a consumer is *willing* to trade off one good for the other. The slope of the budget constraint tells us the rate at which a consumer is *able* to trade off one good for the other. Only at the point of optimal consumption is the rate at which a consumer is willing to trade off one good for the other equal to the rate at which he can trade off one good for the other.

## The Rule of Equal Marginal Utility per Dollar Spent Revisited

Recall from this chapter the *rule of equal marginal utility per dollar*, which states that to maximize utility, consumers should spend their income so that the last dollar spent on each product gives them the same marginal utility. We can use our indifference curve and budget constraint analysis to see why this rule holds. When we move from one point on an indifference curve to another, we end up with more of one product and less of the other product but the same amount of utility. For example, as Dave moves down an indifference curve, he consumes less Coke and more pizza, but he has the same amount of utility.

Remember that marginal utility (*MU*) tells us how much additional utility a consumer gains (or loses) from consuming more (or less) of a good. So when Dave consumes less Coke by moving down an indifference curve, he loses utility equal to:

$$-\text{Change in the quantity of Coke} \times MU_{Coke}$$

but he consumes more pizza, so he gains utility equal to:

$$\text{Change in the quantity of pizza} \times MU_{Pizza}.$$

We know that the gain in utility from the additional pizza is equal to the loss from the smaller quantity of Coke because Dave's total utility remains the same along an indifference curve. Therefore, we can write:

$$-(\text{Change in the quantity of Coke} \times MU_{Coke}) = (\text{Change in the quantity of pizza} \times MU_{Pizza}).$$

Loss in utility from consuming less Coke

Gain in utility from consuming more pizza

If we rearrange terms, we have:

$$\frac{-\text{Change in the quantity of Coke}}{\text{Change in the quantity of pizza}} = \frac{MU_{Pizza}}{MU_{Coke}}$$

because the:

$$\frac{-\text{Change in the quantity of Coke}}{\text{Change in the quantity of pizza}}$$

is the slope of the indifference curve, it is equal to the marginal rate of substitution (multiplied by negative 1). So, we can write:

$$\frac{-\text{Change in the quantity of Coke}}{\text{Change in the quantity of pizza}} = MRS = \frac{MU_{Pizza}}{MU_{Coke}}.$$

The slope of Dave's budget constraint equals the price of pizza divided by the price of Coke. We saw earlier in this appendix that at the point of optimal consumption, the *MRS* equals the ratio of the prices of the two goods. Therefore:

$$\frac{MU_{Pizza}}{MU_{Coke}} = \frac{P_{Pizza}}{P_{Coke}}.$$

We can rewrite this to show that at the point of optimal consumption:

$$\frac{MU_{Pizza}}{P_{Pizza}} = \frac{MU_{Coke}}{P_{Coke}}.$$

This last expression is the rule of equal marginal utility per dollar that we first developed in this chapter. So we have shown how this rule follows from the indifference curve and budget constraint approach to analyzing consumer choice.

## Key Terms

Indifference curve, p. 310

Marginal rate of substitution (*MRS*), p. 311

**9A** **Using Indifference Curves and Budget Lines to Understand Consumer Behavior, pages 310–322**

LEARNING OBJECTIVE: Use indifference curves and budget lines to understand consumer behavior.

 Visit www.myeconlab.com to complete these exercises online and get instant feedback.

## Review Questions

**9A.1** What are the two assumptions economists make about consumer preferences?

**9A.2** What is an indifference curve? What is a budget constraint?

**9A.3** How do consumers choose the optimal consumption bundle?

## Problems and Applications

**9A.4** Jacob receives an allowance of $5 per week. He spends all his allowance on ice cream cones and cans of Lemon Fizz soda.
  a. If the price of ice cream cones is $0.50 per cone and the price of Lemon Fizz is $1 per can, draw a graph showing Jacob's budget constraint. Be sure to indicate on the graph the maximum number of ice cream cones and the maximum number of cans of Lemon Fizz that Jacob can buy.
  b. Jacob buys 8 cones and 1 can of Lemon Fizz. Draw an indifference curve representing Jacob's choice, assuming that he has chosen the optimal combination.
  c. Suppose that the price of ice cream cones rises to $1 per cone. Draw Jacob's new budget constraint and his new optimal consumption of ice cream cones and Lemon Fizz.

**9A.5** Suppose that Jacob's allowance in problem 9A.4 climbs from $5 per week to $10 per week.
  a. Show how the increased allowance alters Jacob's budget constraint.
  b. Draw a set of indifference curves showing how Jacob's choice of cones and Lemon Fizz changes when his allowance increases. Assume that both goods are normal.
  c. Draw a set of indifference curves showing how Jacob's choice of cones and Lemon Fizz changes when his allowance increases. Assume that Lemon Fizz is normal but cones are inferior.

**9A.6** Suppose that Calvin considers Pepsi and Coke to be perfect substitutes. They taste the same to him, and he gets exactly the same amount of enjoyment from drinking a can of Pepsi or a can of Coke.
  a. Will Calvin's indifference curves showing his trade-off between Pepsi and Coke have the same curvature as the indifference curves drawn in the figures in this appendix? Briefly explain.

  b. How will Calvin decide whether to buy Pepsi or to buy Coke?

**9A.7** In the following budget constraint–indifference curve graph, Nikki has $200 to spend on blouses and skirts.
  a. What is the price of blouses? What is the price of skirts?

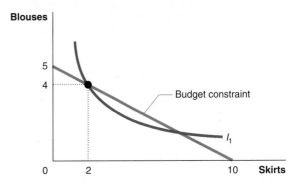

  b. Is Nikki making the optimum choice if she buys 4 blouses and 2 skirts? Explain how you know this.

**9A.8** **(Related to the** *Making the Connection* **on page 314)** Marilou and Hunter both purchase milk and doughnuts at the same Quik Mart. They have different tastes for milk and doughnuts and different incomes. They both buy some milk and some doughnuts, but they buy considerably different quantities of the two goods. Can we conclude that their marginal rate of substitution between milk and doughnuts is the same? Draw a graph showing their budget constraints and indifference curves and explain.

**9A.9** Sunsweet decides that prune juice has a bad image, so it launches a slick advertising campaign to convince young people that prune juice is very hip. The company hires Eminem, Jay-Z, and Trick Daddy to endorse its product. The campaign works! Prune juice sales soar, even though Sunsweet hasn't cut the price. Draw a budget constraint and indifference curve diagram with Sunsweet prune juice on one axis and other drinks on the other axis and show how the celebrity endorsements have changed things.

**9A.10** **(Related to** *Solved Problem 9A-1* **on page 317)** Dave has $300 to spend each month on DVDs and CDs. DVDs and CDs both currently have a price of $10, and Dave is maximizing his utility by buying 20 DVDs and 10 CDs. Suppose Dave still has $300 to spend, but the price of a DVD rises to $12, while the price of a CD drops to $6. Is Dave better or worse off than he was before the price change? Use a budget constraint–indifference curve graph to illustrate your answer.

CHAPTER 10

# Technology, Production, and Costs

## Chapter Outline and Learning Objectives

## >> Sony Uses a Cost Curve to Determine the Price of Radios

Technological change leads to new products and lower production costs. How do firms take costs into account when setting prices? This is an important question that we will explore in the next few chapters, and it is a question that Sony Corporation, the Japanese electronics giant, must answer every day. Sony manufactures computers, televisions, and game consoles, among other products.

Sony's early success resulted from the vision and energy of two young entrepreneurs, Akio Morita and Masaru Ibuka. In 1953, Sony purchased a license that allowed it to use transistor technology developed in the United States at Bell Laboratories. Sony used the technology to develop a transistor radio that was far smaller than any other radio then available. In 1955, Akio Morita arrived in New York, hoping to convince one of the U.S. department store chains to carry the Sony radios.

Morita offered to sell one department store chain 5,000 radios at a price of $29.95 each. If the chain wanted more than 5,000 radios, the price would change. As Morita described it years later:

> I sat down and drew a curve that looked something like a lopsided letter U. The price for five thousand would be our regular price. That would be the beginning of the curve. For ten thousand there would be a discount, and that was at the bottom of the curve. For thirty thousand the price would begin to climb. For fifty thousand the price per unit would be higher than for five thousand, and for one hundred thousand units the price per unit would have to be much higher than for the first five thousand.

Morita offered prices that followed a U shape because Sony's cost per unit, or *average cost*, of manufacturing the radios had the same shape. Curves that show the relationship between the level of output and per-unit cost are called *average total cost curves.* Average total cost curves typically have the U shape of Morita's curve. As we explore the relationship between production and costs in this chapter, we will see why average total cost curves have this shape.

**AN INSIDE LOOK** on **page 346** discusses the effect of lower production costs on the prices of flat-panel televisions.

Source: Akio Morita, with Edwin M. Reingold and Mitsuko Shimomura, *Made in Japan: Akio Morita and Sony*, New York: Signet Books, 1986, p. 94.

## Economics in YOUR LIFE!

### Using Cost Concepts in Your Own Business

Suppose that you have the opportunity to open a store selling recliners. You learn that you can purchase the recliners from the manufacturer for $300 each. Bob's Big Chairs is an existing store that is the same size as your new store will be. Bob's sells the same recliners you plan to sell and also buys them from the manufacturer for $300 each. Your plan is to sell the recliners for a price of $500. After studying how Bob's is operated, you find that Bob's is selling more recliners per month than you expect to be able to sell and that it is selling them for $450. You wonder how Bob's makes a profit at the lower price. Are there any reasons to expect that because Bob's sells more recliners per month, its costs will be lower than your store's costs? You can check your answer against the one we provide at the end of the chapter.

▶ Continued on page 344

In Chapter 9, we looked behind the demand curve to better understand consumer decision making. In this chapter, we look behind the supply curve to better understand firm decision making. Earlier chapters showed that supply curves are upward sloping because marginal cost increases as firms increase the quantity of a good that they supply. In this chapter, we look more closely at why this is true. In the appendix to this chapter, we extend the analysis by using isoquants and isocost lines to understand the relationship between production and costs. Once we have a good understanding of production and cost, we can proceed in the following chapters to understand how firms decide what level of output to produce and what price to charge.

**Technology**  The processes a firm uses to turn inputs into outputs of goods and services.

**Technological change**  A change in the ability of a firm to produce a given level of output with a given quantity of inputs.

# Technology: An Economic Definition

The basic activity of a firm is to use *inputs*, such as workers, machines, and natural resources, to produce *outputs* of goods and services. A pizza parlor, for example, uses inputs such as pizza dough, pizza sauce, cooks, and ovens to produce pizza. A firm's **technology** is the processes it uses to turn inputs into outputs of goods and services. Notice that this economic definition of technology is broader than the everyday definition. When we use the word *technology* in everyday language, we usually refer only to the development of new products. In the economic sense, a firm's technology depends on many factors, such as the skills of its managers, the training of its workers, and the speed and efficiency of its machinery and equipment. The technology of pizza production, for example, includes not only the capacity of the pizza ovens and how quickly they bake the pizza but also how quickly the cooks can prepare the pizza for baking, how well the manager motivates the workers, and how well the manager has arranged the facilities to allow the cooks to quickly prepare the pizzas and get them in the ovens.

Whenever a firm experiences positive **technological change**, it is able to produce more output using the same inputs or the same output using fewer inputs. Positive technological change can come from many sources. A firm's managers may rearrange the factory floor or the layout of a retail store in order to increase production and sales. The firm's workers may go through a training program. The firm may install faster or more reliable machinery or equipment. It is also possible for a firm to experience negative technological change. If a firm hires less-skilled workers or if a hurricane damages its facilities, the quantity of output it can produce from a given quantity of inputs may decline.

*Better inventory controls have helped reduce firms' costs.*

### Making the Connection | Improving Inventory Control at Wal-Mart

Inventories are goods that have been produced but not yet sold. For a retailer such as Wal-Mart, inventories at any point in time include the goods on the store shelves as well as goods in warehouses. Inventories are an input into Wal-Mart's output of goods sold to consumers. Having money tied up in holding inventories is costly, so firms have an incentive to hold as few inventories as possible and to *turn over* their inventories as rapidly as possible by ensuring that goods do not remain on the shelves long. Holding too few inventories, however, results in *stockouts*—that is, sales being lost because the goods consumers want to buy are not on the shelf.

Improvements in inventory control meet the economic definition of positive technological change because they allow firms to produce the same output with fewer inputs. In recent years, many firms have adopted *just-in-time* inventory systems in which firms accept shipments from suppliers as close as possible to the time they will be needed. The just-in-time system was pioneered by Toyota, which used it to reduce the inventories of parts in its automobile assembly plants. Wal-Mart has been a pioneer in using similar inventory control systems in its stores.

Wal-Mart actively manages its *supply chain*, which stretches from the manufacturers of the goods it sells to its retail stores. Entrepreneur Sam Walton, the company founder, built a series of distribution centers spread across the country to supply goods to the retail stores. As goods are sold in the stores, this *point-of-sale* information is sent electronically to the firm's distribution centers to help managers determine what products will be shipped to each store. Depending on a store's location relative to a distribution center, managers can use Wal-Mart's trucks to ship goods overnight. This distribution system allows Wal-Mart to minimize its inventory holdings without running the risk of many stockouts occurring. Because Wal-Mart sells 15 percent to 25 percent of all the toothpaste, disposable diapers, dog food, and many other products sold in the United States, it has been able to involve many manufacturers closely in its supply chain. For example, a company such as Procter & Gamble, which is one of the world's largest manufacturers of toothpaste, laundry detergent, toilet paper, and other products, receives Wal-Mart's point-of-sale and inventory information electronically. Procter & Gamble uses that information to help determine its production schedules and the quantities it should ship to Wal-Mart's distribution centers.

Technological change has been a key to Wal-Mart's becoming one of the largest firms in the world, with 2.1 million employees and revenue of more than $405 billion in 2009.

**YOUR TURN:** Test your understanding by doing related problem 1.5 on page 348 at the end of this chapter.

# **Solved** Problem | **10-1**

## Technological Change: Wright and Wrong

Decades can pass before a new idea is developed to the point where it can be widely used. For instance, the Wright brothers first achieved self-propelled flight at Kitty Hawk, North Carolina, in 1903. But the Wright brothers' plane was very crude, and it wasn't until the introduction of the DC-3 by Douglas Aircraft in 1936 that regularly scheduled intercity flights became common in the United States. Similarly, the development of the first digital electronic computer—the ENIAC—occurred in 1945. But the first IBM personal computer was not introduced until 1981. It wasn't until the 1990s that widespread use of computers began to have a significant effect on the productivity of U.S. business.

In 1999, Hershey Foods, manufacturer of Hershey's bars and Reese's Peanut Butter Cups, installed a new software program designed by the German company SAP to coordinate almost all of the company's operations. Unfortunately, it took Hershey many months to get the software to work properly. During the period when the software was not working well, Hershey failed to send out some shipments, and some of the shipments it did send contained less candy than they were supposed to. Software problems made it difficult for Hershey to keep track of

what was shipped out and to whom it had been shipped. The company lost $150 million worth of sales before the problem was corrected and the software began to work as it was intended.

Sources: For DC-3 and ENIAC, David Mowery and Nathan Rosenberg, "Twentieth Century Technological Change," in Stanley L. Engerman and Robert Gallman, eds., *The Cambridge Economic History of the United States, Vol. III: The Twentieth Century*, Cambridge: Cambridge University Press, 2000. For Hershey: Emily Nelson and Evan Ramstad, "Trick or Treat: Hershey's Biggest Dud Has Turned out to Be Its New Technology," *Wall Street Journal*, October 29, 1999; and "Hershey Foods Warns 1999 Earnings Will Be Worse Than Initially Feared," *Dow Jones Business News*, December 28, 1999.

**a.** Define technology and technological change.

**b.** Was the Wright brothers' 1903 flight at Kitty Hawk an example of technological change? Was the development of the ENIAC computer an example of technological change?

**c.** Explain why the widespread use of computers in the 1990s resulted in positive technological change.

**d.** Did Hershey's use of a new software program in 1999 result in positive or negative technological change?

## SOLVING THE PROBLEM:

**Step 1:** **Review the chapter material.** This problem is about technology and technological change, so you may want to review the section "Technology: An Economic Definition," which begins on page 326.

**Step 2:** **Answer question (a): Define *technology and technological change.*** A firm's technology is the process it uses to turn inputs into outputs of goods and services. Technological change is the change in the ability to produce a given level of output with a given quantity of inputs.

**Step 3:** **Answer question (b): Solve both of these questions.** Neither of these represents technological change because there was no impact on the ability of firms to produce output with a different quantity of inputs.

**Step 4:** **Answer question (c).** This led to a widespread improvement in productivity. Many firms were able to produce the same output of goods and services with fewer inputs or more output with the same quantity of inputs.

**Step 5:** **Answer question (d).** The initial use of the software produced negative technological change because Hershey's output was less with the same quantity of inputs. After the "bugs" were eliminated, the use of this software produced a positive technological change.

**YOUR TURN:** For more practice, do related problem 1.6 on page 348 at the end of this chapter.

---

**10.2 LEARNING** OBJECTIVE

Distinguish between the economic short run and the economic long run.

**Short run** The period of time during which at least one of a firm's inputs is fixed.

**Long run** The period of time in which a firm can vary all its inputs, adopt new technology, and increase or decrease the size of its physical plant.

**Total cost** The cost of all the inputs a firm uses in production.

**Variable costs** Costs that change as output changes.

**Fixed costs** Costs that remain constant as output changes.

# The Short Run and the Long Run in Economics

When firms analyze the relationship between their level of production and their costs, they separate the time period involved into the short run and the long run. In the **short run**, at least one of the firm's inputs is fixed. In particular, in the short run, the firm's technology and the size of its physical plant—its factory, store, or office—are both fixed, while the number of workers the firm hires is variable. In the **long run**, the firm is able to vary all its inputs and can adopt new technology and increase or decrease the size of its physical plant. Of course, the actual length of calendar time in the short run will be different from firm to firm. A pizza parlor may be able to increase its physical plant by adding another pizza oven and some tables and chairs in just a few weeks. BMW, in contrast, may take more than a year to increase the capacity of one of its automobile assembly plants by installing new equipment.

## The Difference between Fixed Costs and Variable Costs

**Total cost** is the cost of all the inputs a firm uses in production. We have just seen that in the short run, some inputs are fixed and others are variable. The costs of the fixed inputs are *fixed costs*, and the costs of the variable inputs are *variable costs*. We can also think of **variable costs** as the costs that change as output changes. Similarly, **fixed costs** are costs that remain constant as output changes. A typical firm's variable costs include its labor costs, raw material costs, and costs of electricity and other utilities. Typical fixed costs include lease payments for factory or retail space, payments for fire insurance, and payments for newspaper and television advertising. All of a firm's costs are either fixed or variable, so we can state the following:

$$\text{Total Cost} = \text{Fixed Cost} + \text{Variable Cost}$$

or, using symbols:

$$TC = FC + VC$$

## Making the Connection

## Fixed Costs in the Publishing Industry

An editor at Cambridge University Press gives the following estimates of the annual fixed cost for a medium-size academic book publisher.

| COST | AMOUNT |
| --- | --- |
| Salaries and benefits | $437,500 |
| Rent | 75,000 |
| Utilities | 20,000 |
| Supplies | 6,000 |
| Postage | 4,000 |
| Travel | 8,000 |
| Subscriptions, etc. | 4,000 |
| Miscellaneous | 5,000 |
| Total | $559,500 |

*Publishers consider the salaries of editors to be a fixed cost.*

Academic book publishers hire editors, designers, and production and marketing managers who help prepare books for publication. Because these employees work on several books simultaneously, the number of people the company hires does not go up and down with the quantity of books the company publishes during any particular year. Publishing companies therefore consider the salaries and benefits of people in these job categories to be fixed costs.

In contrast, for a company that *prints* books, the quantity of workers varies with the quantity of books printed. The wages and benefits of the workers operating the printing presses, for example, would be a variable cost.

The other costs listed in the preceding table are typical of fixed costs at many firms.

Source: Beth Luey, *Handbook for Academic Authors*, 4th ed., Cambridge, UK: Cambridge University Press, 2002, p. 244.

**YOUR TURN:** Test your understanding by doing related problems 2.4, 2.5, and 2.6 on page 349 at the end of this chapter.

## Implicit Costs versus Explicit Costs

It is important to remember that economists always measure costs as *opportunity costs*. The **opportunity cost** of any activity is the highest-valued alternative that must be given up to engage in that activity. As we saw in Chapter 7, costs are either *explicit* or *implicit*. When a firm spends money, it incurs an **explicit cost**. When a firm experiences a non-monetary opportunity cost, it incurs an **implicit cost**.

For example, suppose that Jill Johnson owns a pizza restaurant. In operating her store, Jill has explicit costs, such as the wages she pays her workers and the payments she makes for rent and electricity. But some of Jill's most important costs are implicit. Before opening her own restaurant, Jill earned a salary of $30,000 per year managing a restaurant for someone else. To start her restaurant, Jill quit her job, withdrew $50,000 from her bank account—where it earned her interest of $3,000 per year—and used the funds to equip her restaurant with tables, chairs, a cash register, and other equipment. To open her own business, Jill had to give up the $30,000 salary and the $3,000 in interest. This $33,000 is an implicit cost because it does not represent payments that Jill has to make. All the same, giving up this $33,000 per year is a real cost to Jill. In addition, during the course of the year, the $50,000 worth of tables, chairs, and other physical capital in Jill's store will lose some of its value due partly to wear and tear and partly to better furniture, cash registers, and so forth becoming available. *Economic depreciation* is the difference between what Jill paid for her capital at the beginning of the year and what she could sell the capital for at the end of the year. If Jill could sell the capital for $40,000 at the end of the year, then the $10,000 in economic depreciation represents another implicit cost.

**Opportunity cost** The highest-valued alternative that must be given up to engage in an activity.

**Explicit cost** A cost that involves spending money.

**Implicit cost** A nonmonetary opportunity cost.

## TABLE 10-1

**Jill Johnson's Costs per Year**

| | |
|---|---:|
| Pizza dough, tomato sauce, and other ingredients | $20,000 |
| Wages | 48,000 |
| Interest payments on loan to buy pizza ovens | 10,000 |
| Electricity | 6,000 |
| Lease payment for store | 24,000 |
| Foregone salary | 30,000 |
| Foregone interest | 3,000 |
| Economic depreciation | 10,000 |
| Total | $151,000 |

(Note that the whole $50,000 she spent on the capital is not a cost because she still has the equipment at the end of the year, although it is now worth only $40,000.)

Table 10-1 lists Jill's costs. The entries in red are explicit costs, and the entries in blue are implicit costs. As we saw in Chapter 7, the rules of accounting generally require that only explicit costs be used for purposes of keeping the company's financial records and for paying taxes. Therefore, explicit costs are sometimes called *accounting costs*. *Economic costs* include both accounting costs and implicit costs.

## The Production Function

Let's look at the relationship between the level of production and costs in the short run for Jill Johnson's restaurant. To keep things simpler than in the more realistic situation in Table 10-1, let's assume that Jill uses only labor—workers—and one type of capital—pizza ovens—to produce a single good: pizzas. Many firms use more than two inputs and produce more than one good, but it is easier to understand the relationship between output and cost by focusing on the case of a firm using only two inputs and producing only one good. In the short run, Jill doesn't have time to build a larger restaurant, install additional pizza ovens, or redesign the layout of her restaurant. So, in the short run, she can increase or decrease the quantity of pizzas she produces only by increasing or decreasing the quantity of workers she employs.

The first three columns of Table 10-2 show the relationship between the quantity of workers and ovens Jill uses per week and the quantity of pizzas she can produce. The relationship between the inputs employed by a firm and the maximum output it can produce with those inputs is called the firm's **production function**. Because a firm's technology is the processes it uses to turn inputs into output, the production function represents the firm's technology. In this case, Table 10-2 shows Jill's *short-run* production function

**Production function** The relationship between the inputs employed by a firm and the maximum output it can produce with those inputs.

## TABLE 10-2   Short-Run Production and Cost at Jill Johnson's Restaurant

| QUANTITY OF WORKERS | QUANTITY OF PIZZA OVENS | QUANTITY OF PIZZAS PER WEEK | COST OF PIZZA OVENS (FIXED COST) | COST OF WORKERS (VARIABLE COST) | TOTAL COST OF PIZZAS PER WEEK | COST PER PIZZA (AVERAGE TOTAL COST) |
|---|---|---|---|---|---|---|
| 0 | 2 | 0 | $800 | $0 | $800 | — |
| 1 | 2 | 200 | 800 | 650 | 1,450 | $7.25 |
| 2 | 2 | 450 | 800 | 1,300 | 2,100 | 4.67 |
| 3 | 2 | 550 | 800 | 1,950 | 2,750 | 5.00 |
| 4 | 2 | 600 | 800 | 2,600 | 3,400 | 5.67 |
| 5 | 2 | 625 | 800 | 3,250 | 4,050 | 6.48 |
| 6 | 2 | 640 | 800 | 3,900 | 4,700 | 7.34 |

because we are assuming that the time period is too short for Jill to increase or decrease the quantity of ovens she is using.

## A First Look at the Relationship between Production and Cost

Table 10-2 gives us information on Jill Johnson's costs. We can determine the total cost of producing a given quantity of pizzas if we know how many workers and ovens are required to produce that quantity of pizzas and what Jill has to pay for those workers and pizzas. Suppose Jill has taken out a bank loan to buy two pizza ovens. The cost of the loan is $800 per week. Therefore, her fixed costs are $800 per week. If Jill pays $650 per week to each worker, her variable costs depend on how many workers she hires. In the short run, Jill can increase the quantity of pizzas she produces only by hiring more workers. The table shows that if she hires 1 worker, she produces 200 pizzas during the week; if she hires 2 workers, she produces 450 pizzas; and so on. For a particular week, Jill's total cost of producing pizzas is equal to the $800 she pays on the loan for the ovens plus the amount she pays to hire workers. If Jill decides to hire 4 workers and produce 600 pizzas, her total cost is $3,400: $800 to lease the ovens and $2,600 to hire the workers. Her cost per pizza is equal to her total cost of producing pizzas divided by the quantity of pizzas produced. If she produces 600 pizzas at a total cost of $3,400, her cost per pizza, or *average total cost*, is $3,400/600 = $5.67. A firm's **average total cost** is always equal to its total cost divided by the quantity of output produced.

**Average total cost** Total cost divided by the quantity of output produced.

Panel (a) of Figure 10-1 uses the numbers in the next-to-last column of Table 10-2 to graph Jill's total cost. Panel (b) uses the numbers in the last column to graph her average total cost. Notice in panel (b) that Jill's average cost has roughly the same U shape as the

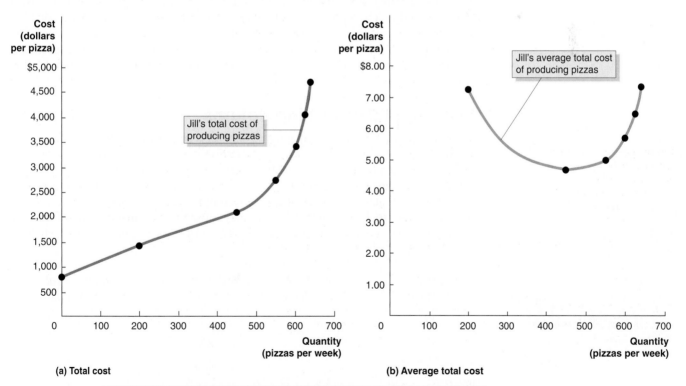

(a) Total cost

(b) Average total cost

Figure 10-1    Graphing Total Cost and Average Total Cost at Jill Johnson's Restaurant

We can use the information from Table 10-2 to graph the relationship between the quantity of pizzas Jill produces and her total cost and average total cost. Panel (a) shows that total cost increases as the level of production increases. In panel (b), we see that the average total cost is roughly U-shaped: As production increases from low levels, average cost falls before rising at higher levels of production. To understand why average cost has this shape, we must look more closely at the technology of producing pizzas, as shown by the production function.

average cost curve we saw Akio Morita calculate for Sony transistor radios at the beginning of this chapter. As production increases from low levels, average cost falls. Average cost then becomes fairly flat, before rising at higher levels of production. To understand why average cost has this U shape, we first need to look more closely at the technology of producing pizzas, as shown by the production function for Jill's restaurant. Then we need to look at how this technology determines the relationship between production and cost.

Understand the relationship between the marginal product of labor and the average product of labor.

# The Marginal Product of Labor and the Average Product of Labor

To better understand the choices Jill faces, given the technology available to her, think first about what happens if she hires only one worker. That one worker will have to perform several different activities, including taking orders from customers, baking the pizzas, bringing the pizzas to the customers' tables, and ringing up sales on the cash register. If Jill hires two workers, some of these activities can be divided up: One worker could take the orders and ring up the sales, and one worker could bake the pizzas. With this division of tasks, Jill will find that hiring two workers actually allows her to produce more than twice as many pizzas as she could produce with just one worker.

**Marginal product of labor** The additional output a firm produces as a result of hiring one more worker.

The additional output a firm produces as a result of hiring one more worker is called the **marginal product of labor**. We can calculate the marginal product of labor by determining how much total output increases as each additional worker is hired. We do this for Jill's restaurant in Table 10-3.

When Jill hires only 1 worker, she produces 200 pizzas per week. When she hires 2 workers, she produces 450 pizzas per week. Hiring the second worker increases her production by 250 pizzas per week. So, the marginal product of labor for 1 worker is 200 pizzas. For 2 workers, the marginal product of labor rises to 250 pizzas. This increase in marginal product results from the *division of labor* and from *specialization*. By dividing the tasks to be performed—the division of labor—Jill reduces the time workers lose moving from one activity to the next. She also allows them to become more specialized at their tasks. For example, a worker who concentrates on baking pizzas will become skilled at doing so quickly and efficiently.

## The Law of Diminishing Returns

**Law of diminishing returns** The principle that, at some point, adding more of a variable input, such as labor, to the same amount of a fixed input, such as capital, will cause the marginal product of the variable input to decline.

In the short run, the quantity of pizza ovens Jill leases is fixed, so as she hires more workers, the marginal product of labor eventually begins to decline. This happens because at some point, Jill uses up all the gains from the division of labor and from specialization and starts to experience the effects of the **law of diminishing returns**. This law states that adding more of a variable input, such as labor, to the same amount of a fixed input, such as capital, will eventually cause the marginal product of the variable input to decline. For Jill, the marginal product of labor begins to decline when she

TABLE 10-3

**The Marginal Product of Labor at Jill Johnson's Restaurant**

| QUANTITY OF WORKERS | QUANTITY OF PIZZA OVENS | QUANTITY OF PIZZAS | MARGINAL PRODUCT OF LABOR |
|---|---|---|---|
| 0 | 2 | 0 | — |
| 1 | 2 | 200 | 200 |
| 2 | 2 | 450 | 250 |
| 3 | 2 | 550 | 100 |
| 4 | 2 | 600 | 50 |
| 5 | 2 | 625 | 25 |
| 6 | 2 | 640 | 15 |

hires the third worker. Hiring three workers raises the quantity of pizzas she produces from 450 per week to 550. But the increase in the quantity of pizzas—100—is less than the increase when she hired the second worker—250.

If Jill kept adding more and more workers to the same quantity of pizza ovens, eventually workers would begin to get in each other's way, and the marginal product of labor would actually become negative. When the marginal product is negative, the level of total output declines. No firm would actually hire so many workers as to experience a negative marginal product of labor and falling total output.

## Graphing Production

Panel (a) in Figure 10-2 shows the relationship between the quantity of workers Jill hires and her total output of pizzas, using the numbers from Table 10-3. Panel (b) shows the marginal product of labor. In panel (a), output increases as more workers are hired, but the increase in output does not occur at a constant rate. Because of specialization and

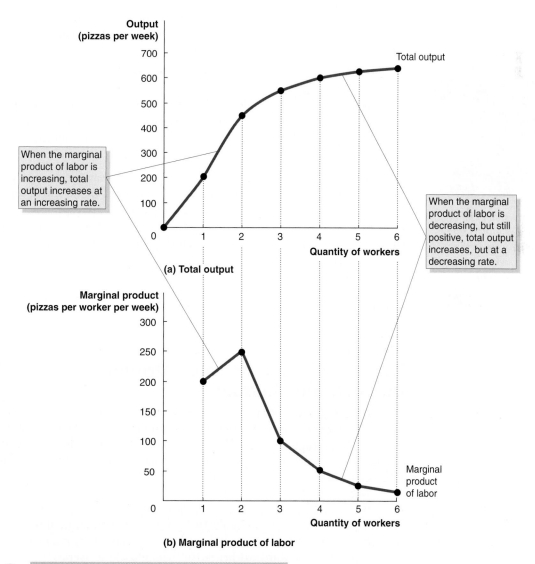

(a) Total output

(b) Marginal product of labor

### Figure 10-2 | Total Output and the Marginal Product of Labor

In panel (a), output increases as more workers are hired, but the increase in output does not occur at a constant rate. Because of specialization and the division of labor, output at first increases at an increasing rate, with each additional worker hired causing production to increase by a *greater* amount than did the hiring of the previous worker. After the third worker has been hired, hiring more workers while keeping the number of pizza ovens constant results in diminishing returns. When the point of diminishing returns is reached, production increases at a decreasing rate. Each additional worker hired after the third worker causes production to increase by a *smaller* amount than did the hiring of the previous worker. In panel (b), the *marginal product of labor* is the additional output produced as a result of hiring one more worker. The marginal product of labor rises initially because of the effects of specialization and division of labor, and then it falls due to the effects of diminishing returns.

the division of labor, output at first increases at an increasing rate, with each additional worker hired causing production to increase by a *greater* amount than did the hiring of the previous worker. But after the second worker has been hired, hiring more workers while keeping the quantity of ovens constant results in diminishing returns. When the point of diminishing returns is reached, production increases at a decreasing rate. Each additional worker hired after the second worker causes production to increase by a *smaller* amount than did the hiring of the previous worker. In panel (b), the marginal product of labor curve rises initially because of the effects of specialization and division of labor, and then it falls due to the effects of diminishing returns.

<table>
<tr>
<td>Making<br>the<br>Connection</td>
<td>**Adam Smith's Famous Account<br>of the Division of Labor<br>in a Pin Factory**</td>
</tr>
</table>

In *The Wealth of Nations*, Adam Smith uses production in a pin factory as an example of the gains in output resulting from the division of labor. The following is an excerpt from his account of how pin making was divided into a series of tasks:

> One man draws out the wire, another straightens it, a third cuts it, a fourth points it, a fifth grinds it at the top for receiving the head; to make the head requires two or three distinct operations; to put it on is a [distinct operation], to whiten the pins is another; it is even a trade by itself to put them into the paper; and the important business of making a pin is, in this manner, divided into eighteen distinct operations.

Because the labor of pin making was divided up in this way, the average worker was able to produce about 4,800 pins per day. Smith speculated that a single worker using the pin-making machinery alone would make only about 20 pins per day. This lesson from more than 225 years ago, showing the tremendous gains from division of labor and specialization, remains relevant to most business situations today.

Source: Adam Smith, *An Inquiry into the Nature and Causes of the Wealth of Nations*, Vol. I, Oxford, UK: Oxford University Press, 1976 [original edition, 1776], pp. 14–15.

 **YOUR TURN:** Test your understanding by doing related problem 3.6 on page 350 at the end of this chapter.

The gains from division of labor and specialization are as important to firms today as they were in the eighteenth century, when Adam Smith first discussed them.

## The Relationship between Marginal and Average Product

The marginal product of labor tells us how much total output changes as the quantity of workers hired changes. We can also calculate how many pizzas workers produce on average. The **average product of labor** is the total output produced by a firm divided by the quantity of workers. For example, using the numbers in Table 10-3 on page 331, if Jill hires 4 workers to produce 600 pizzas, the average product of labor is 600/4 = 150.

We can state the relationship between the marginal and average products of labor this way: *The average product of labor is the average of the marginal products of labor.* For example, the numbers from Table 10-3 show that the marginal product of the first worker Jill hires is 200, the marginal product of the second worker is 250, and the marginal product of the third worker is 100. Therefore, the average product of labor for three workers is 183.3:

**Average product of labor** The total output produced by a firm divided by the quantity of workers.

$$183.3 = (200 + 250 + 100) / 3$$

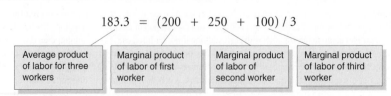

| Average product of labor for three workers | Marginal product of labor of first worker | Marginal product of labor of second worker | Marginal product of labor of third worker |

By taking the average of the marginal products of the first three workers, we have the average product of the three workers.

Whenever the marginal product of labor is greater than the average product of labor, the average product of labor must be increasing. This statement is true for the same reason that a person 6 feet, 2 inches tall entering a room where the average height is 5 feet, 9 inches raises the average height of people in the room. Whenever the marginal product of labor is less than the average product of labor, the average product of labor must be decreasing. The marginal product of labor equals the average product of labor for the quantity of workers where the average product of labor is at its maximum.

## An Example of Marginal and Average Values: College Grades

The relationship between the marginal product of labor and the average product of labor is the same as the relationship between the marginal and average values of any variable. To see this more clearly, think about the familiar relationship between a student's grade point average (GPA) in one semester and his overall, or cumulative, GPA. The table in Figure 10-3 shows Paul's college grades for each semester, beginning with fall 2007. The graph in Figure 10-3 plots the grades from the table. Just as each

|  | Semester GPA (Marginal GPA) | Cumulative GPA (Average GPA) |
|---|---|---|
| *Freshman Year* |  |  |
| Fall | 1.50 | 1.50 |
| Spring | 2.00 | 1.75 |
| *Sophomore Year* |  |  |
| Fall | 2.20 | 1.90 |
| Spring | 3.00 | 2.18 |
| *Junior Year* |  |  |
| Fall | 3.20 | 2.38 |
| Spring | 3.00 | 2.48 |
| *Senior Year* |  |  |
| Fall | 2.40 | 2.47 |
| Spring | 2.00 | 2.41 |

Average GPA continues to rise, although marginal GPA falls.

With the marginal GPA below the average, the average GPA falls.

### Figure 10-3

**Marginal and Average GPAs**

The relationship between marginal and average values for a variable can be illustrated using GPAs. We can calculate the GPA Paul earns in a particular semester (his "marginal GPA"), and we can calculate his cumulative GPA for all the semesters he has completed so far (his "average GPA"). Paul's GPA is only 1.50 in the fall semester of his freshman year. In each following semester through the fall of his junior year, his GPA for the semester increases—raising his cumulative GPA. In Paul's junior year, even though his semester GPA declines from fall to spring, his cumulative GPA rises. Only in the fall of his senior year, when his semester GPA drops below his cumulative GPA, does his cumulative GPA decline.

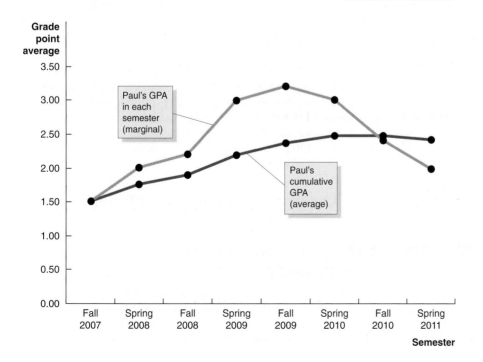

additional worker hired adds to a firm's total production, each additional semester adds to Paul's total grade points. We can calculate what each individual worker hired adds to total production (marginal product), and we can calculate the average production of the workers hired so far (average product).

Similarly, we can calculate the GPA Paul earns in a particular semester (his "marginal GPA"), and we can calculate his cumulative GPA for all the semesters he has completed so far (his "average GPA"). As the table shows, Paul gets off to a weak start in the fall semester of his freshman year, earning only a 1.50 GPA. In each subsequent semester through the fall of his junior year, his GPA for the semester increases from the previous semester—raising his cumulative GPA. As the graph shows, however, his cumulative GPA does not increase as rapidly as his semester-by-semester GPA because his cumulative GPA is held back by the low GPAs of his first few semesters. Notice that in Paul's junior year, even though his semester GPA declines from fall to spring, his cumulative GPA rises. Only in the fall of his senior year, when his semester GPA drops below his cumulative GPA, does his cumulative GPA decline.

**10.4 LEARNING** OBJECTIVE

Explain and illustrate the relationship between marginal cost and average total cost.

# The Relationship Between Short-Run Production and Short-Run Cost

We have seen that technology determines the values of the marginal product of labor and the average product of labor. In turn, the marginal and average products of labor affect the firm's costs. Keep in mind that the relationships we are discussing are *short-run* relationships: We are assuming that the time period is too short for the firm to change its technology or the size of its physical plant.

At the beginning of this chapter, we saw how Akio Morita used an average total cost curve to determine the price of radios. The average total cost curve Morita used and the average total cost curve in Figure 10-1 on page 331 for Jill Johnson's restaurant both have a U shape. As we will soon see, the U shape of the average total cost curve is determined by the shape of the curve that shows the relationship between *marginal cost* and the level of production.

## Marginal Cost

**Marginal cost** The change in a firm's total cost from producing one more unit of a good or service.

As we saw in Chapter 1, one of the key ideas in economics is that optimal decisions are made at the margin. Consumers, firms, and government officials usually make decisions about doing a little more or a little less. As Jill Johnson considers whether to hire additional workers to produce additional pizzas, she needs to consider how much she will add to her total cost by producing the additional pizzas. **Marginal cost** is the change in a firm's total cost from producing one more unit of a good or service. We can calculate marginal cost for a particular increase in output by dividing the change in cost by the change in output. We can express this idea mathematically (remembering that the Greek letter delta, $\Delta$, means "change in"):

$$MC = \frac{\Delta TC}{\Delta Q}.$$

In the table in Figure 10-4, we use this equation to calculate Jill's marginal cost of producing pizzas.

## Why Are the Marginal and Average Cost Curves U-Shaped?

Notice in the graph in Figure 10-4 that Jill's marginal cost of producing pizzas declines at first and then increases, giving the marginal cost curve a U shape. The table in Figure 10-4 also shows the marginal product of labor. This table helps us see the important relationship between the marginal product of labor and the marginal cost of production: The marginal

| Quantity of Workers | Quantity of Pizzas | Marginal Product of Labor | Total Cost of Pizzas | Marginal Cost of Pizzas | Average Total Cost of Pizzas |
|---|---|---|---|---|---|
| 0 | 0 | – | $800 | – | – |
| 1 | 200 | 200 | 1,450 | $3.25 | $7.25 |
| 2 | 450 | 250 | 2,100 | 2.60 | 4.67 |
| 3 | 550 | 100 | 2,750 | 6.50 | 5.00 |
| 4 | 600 | 50 | 3,400 | 13.00 | 5.67 |
| 5 | 625 | 25 | 4,050 | 26.00 | 6.48 |
| 6 | 640 | 15 | 4,700 | 43.33 | 7.34 |

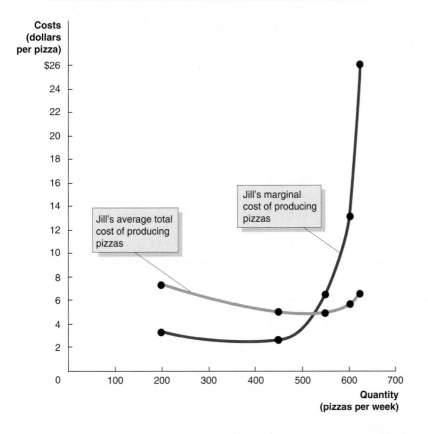

## Figure 10-4

### Jill Johnson's Marginal Cost and Average Total Cost of Producing Pizzas

We can use the information in the table to calculate Jill's marginal cost and average total cost of producing pizzas. For the first two workers hired, the marginal product of labor is increasing. This increase causes the marginal cost of production to fall. For the last four workers hired, the marginal product of labor is falling. This causes the marginal cost of production to increase. Therefore, the marginal cost curve falls and then rises—that is, has a U shape—because the marginal product of labor rises and then falls. As long as marginal cost is below average total cost, average total cost will be falling. When marginal cost is above average total cost, average total cost will be rising. The relationship between marginal cost and average total cost explains why the average total cost curve also has a U shape.

product of labor is *rising* for the first two workers, but the marginal cost of the pizzas produced by these workers is *falling*. The marginal product of labor is *falling* for the last four workers, but the marginal cost of pizzas produced by these workers is *rising*. To summarize this point: *When the marginal product of labor is rising, the marginal cost of output is falling. When the marginal product of labor is falling, the marginal cost of production is rising.*

One way to understand why this point is true is first to notice that the only additional cost to Jill from producing more pizzas is the additional wages she pays to hire more workers. She pays each new worker the same $650 per week. So the marginal cost of the additional pizzas each worker makes depends on that worker's additional output, or marginal product. As long as the additional output from each new worker is rising, the marginal cost of that output is falling. When the additional output from each new worker is falling, the marginal cost of that output is rising. *We can conclude that the marginal cost of production falls and then rises—forming a U shape—because the marginal product of labor rises and then falls.*

The relationship between marginal cost and average total cost follows the usual relationship between marginal and average values. As long as marginal cost is below average total cost, average total cost falls. When marginal cost is above average total cost, average total cost rises. Marginal cost equals average total cost when average total cost is at its lowest point. Therefore, the average total cost curve has a U shape because the marginal cost curve has a U shape.

Graph average total cost, average variable cost, average fixed cost, and marginal cost.

**Average fixed cost**  Fixed cost divided by the quantity of output produced.

**Average variable cost**  Variable cost divided by the quantity of output produced.

# Graphing Cost Curves

We have seen that we calculate average total cost by dividing total cost by the quantity of output produced. Similarly, we can calculate **average fixed cost** by dividing fixed cost by the quantity of output produced. And we can calculate **average variable cost** by dividing variable cost by the quantity of output produced. Or, mathematically, with $Q$ being the level of output, we have:

$$\text{Average total cost} = ATC = \frac{TC}{Q}$$

$$\text{Average fixed cost} = AFC = \frac{FC}{Q}$$

$$\text{Average variable cost} = AVC = \frac{VC}{Q}.$$

Finally, notice that average total cost is the sum of average fixed cost plus average variable cost:

$$ATC = AFC + AVC.$$

The only fixed cost Jill incurs in operating her restaurant is the $800 per week she pays on the bank loan for her pizza ovens. Her variable costs are the wages she pays her workers. The table and graph in Figure 10-5 show Jill's costs.

We will use graphs like the one in Figure 10-5 in the next several chapters to analyze how firms decide the level of output to produce and the price to charge. Before going further, be sure you understand the following three key facts about Figure 10-5:

1. The marginal cost ($MC$), average total cost ($ATC$), and average variable cost ($AVC$) curves are all U-shaped, and the marginal cost curve intersects the average variable cost and average total cost curves at their minimum points. When marginal cost is less than either average variable cost or average total cost, it causes them to decrease. When marginal cost is above average variable cost or average total cost, it causes them to increase. Therefore, when marginal cost equals average variable cost or average total cost, they must be at their minimum points.

2. As output increases, average fixed cost gets smaller and smaller. This happens because in calculating average fixed cost, we are dividing something that gets larger and larger—output—into something that remains constant—fixed cost. Firms often refer to this process of lowering average fixed cost by selling more output as "spreading the overhead" (where "overhead" refers to fixed costs).

3. As output increases, the difference between average total cost and average variable cost decreases. This happens because the difference between average total cost and average variable cost is average fixed cost, which gets smaller as output increases.

Understand how firms use the long-run average cost curve in their planning.

# Costs in the Long Run

The distinction between fixed cost and variable cost that we just discussed applies to the short run but *not* to the long run. For example, in the short run, Jill Johnson has fixed costs of $800 per week because she signed a loan agreement with a bank when she bought her pizza ovens. In the long run, the cost of purchasing more pizza ovens becomes variable because Jill can choose whether to expand her business by buying more ovens. The same would be true of any other fixed costs a company like Jill's might have. Once a company has purchased a fire insurance policy, the cost of the policy is fixed. But when the policy expires, the company must decide whether to renew it, and

| Quantity of Workers | Quantity of Ovens | Quantity of Pizzas | Cost of Ovens (Fixed cost) | Cost of Workers (Variable cost) | Total Cost of Pizzas | ATC | AFC | AVC | MC |
|---|---|---|---|---|---|---|---|---|---|
| 0 | 2 | 0 | $800 | $0 | $800 | – | – | – | – |
| 1 | 2 | 200 | 800 | 650 | 1,450 | $7.25 | $4.00 | $3.25 | $3.25 |
| 2 | 2 | 450 | 800 | 1,300 | 2,100 | 4.67 | 1.78 | 2.88 | 2.60 |
| 3 | 2 | 550 | 800 | 1,950 | 2,750 | 5.00 | 1.45 | 3.54 | 6.50 |
| 4 | 2 | 600 | 800 | 2,600 | 3,400 | 5.67 | 1.33 | 4.33 | 13.00 |
| 5 | 2 | 625 | 800 | 3,250 | 4,050 | 6.48 | 1.28 | 5.20 | 26.00 |
| 6 | 2 | 640 | 800 | 3,900 | 4,700 | 7.34 | 1.25 | 6.09 | 43.33 |

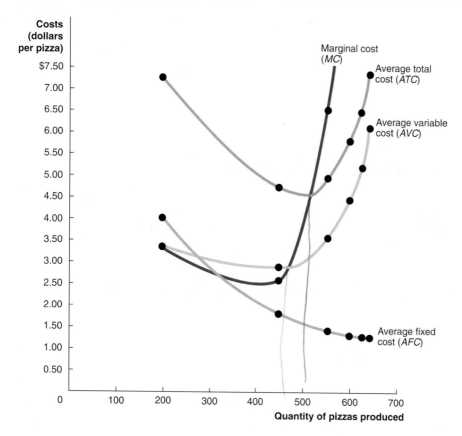

## Figure 10-5

### Costs at Jill Johnson's Restaurant

Jill's costs of making pizzas are shown in the table and plotted in the graph. Notice three important facts about the graph: (1) The marginal cost (*MC*), average total cost (*ATC*), and average variable cost (*AVC*) curves are all U-shaped, and the marginal cost curve intersects both the average variable cost curve and average total cost curve at their minimum points. (2) As output increases, average fixed cost (*AFC*) gets smaller and smaller. (3) As output increases, the difference between average total cost and average variable cost decreases. Make sure you can explain why each of these three facts is true. You should spend time becoming familiar with this graph because it is one of the most important graphs in microeconomics.

the cost becomes variable. The important point here is this: *In the long run, all costs are variable. There are no fixed costs in the long run.* In other words, in the long run, total cost equals variable cost, and average total cost equals average variable cost.

Managers of successful firms simultaneously consider how they can most profitably run their current store, factory, or office and also whether in the long run they would be more profitable if they became larger or, possibly, smaller. Jill must consider how to run her current restaurant, which has only two pizza ovens, and she must also plan what to do when her current bank loan is paid off and the lease on her store ends. Should she buy more pizza ovens? Should she lease a larger restaurant?

## Economies of Scale

Short-run average cost curves represent the costs a firm faces when some input, such as the quantity of machines it uses, is fixed. The **long-run average cost curve** shows the lowest cost at which a firm is able to produce a given level of output in the long run, when no inputs are fixed. A firm may experience **economies of scale**, which means the firm's long-run average costs fall as it increases the quantity of output it produces. We can see the effects of economies of scale in Figure 10-6, which shows the relationship between short-run and long-run average cost curves. Managers can use long-run average cost

**Long-run average cost curve** A curve showing the lowest cost at which a firm is able to produce a given quantity of output in the long run, when no inputs are fixed.

**Economies of scale** The situation when a firm's long-run average costs fall as it increases output.

## Figure 10-6

**The Relationship between Short-Run Average Cost and Long-Run Average Cost**

If a small bookstore expects to sell only 1,000 books per month, then it will be able to sell that quantity of books at the lowest average cost of $22 per book if it builds the small store represented by the *ATC* curve on the left of the figure. A larger bookstore will be able to sell 20,000 books per month at a lower cost of $18 per book. A bookstore selling 20,000 books per month and a bookstore selling 40,000 books per month will experience constant returns to scale and have the same average cost. A bookstore selling 20,000 books per month will have reached minimum efficient scale. Very large bookstores will experience diseconomies of scale, and their average costs will rise as sales increase beyond 40,000 books per month.

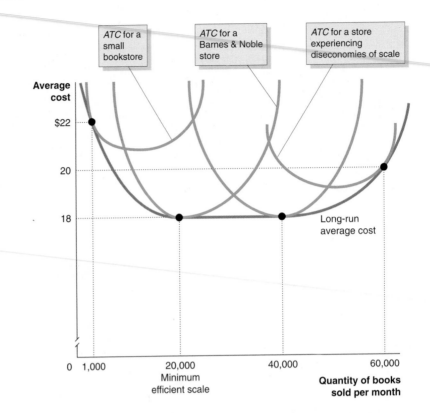

**Constant returns to scale** The situation when a firm's long-run average costs remain unchanged as it increases output.

**Minimum efficient scale** The level of output at which all economies of scale are exhausted.

curves for planning because they show the effect on cost of expanding output by, for example, building a larger factory or store.

## Long-Run Average Total Cost Curves for Bookstores

Figure 10-6 shows long-run average cost in the retail bookstore industry. If a small bookstore expects to sell only 1,000 books per month, then it will be able to sell that quantity of books at the lowest average cost of $22 per book if it builds the small store represented by the *ATC* curve on the left of the figure. A much larger bookstore, such as one run by a national chain like Barnes & Noble, will be able to sell 20,000 books per month at a lower average cost of $18 per book. This decline in average cost from $22 to $18 represents the economies of scale that exist in bookselling. Why would the larger bookstore have lower average costs? One important reason is that the Barnes & Noble store is selling 20 times as many books per month as the small store but might need only six times as many workers. This saving in labor cost would reduce Barnes & Noble's average cost of selling books.

Firms may experience economies of scale for several reasons. First, as in the case of Barnes & Noble, the firm's technology may make it possible to increase production with a smaller proportional increase in at least one input. Second, both workers and managers can become more specialized, enabling them to become more productive, as output expands. Third, large firms, like Barnes & Noble, Wal-Mart, and General Motors, may be able to purchase inputs at lower costs than smaller competitors. In fact, as Wal-Mart expanded, its bargaining power with its suppliers increased, and its average costs fell. Finally, as a firm expands, it may be able to borrow money at a lower interest rate, thereby lowering its costs.

Economies of scale do not continue forever. The long-run average cost curve in most industries has a flat segment that often stretches over a substantial range of output. As Figure 10-6 shows, a bookstore selling 20,000 books per month and a bookstore selling 40,000 books per month have the same average cost. Over this range of output, firms in the industry experience **constant returns to scale**. As these firms increase their output, they have to increase their inputs, such as the size of the store and the quantity of workers, proportionally. The level of output at which all economies of scale are exhausted is known as **minimum efficient scale**. A bookstore selling 20,000 books per month has reached minimum efficient scale.

Very large bookstores experience increasing average costs as managers begin to have difficulty coordinating the operation of the store. Figure 10-6 shows that for sales above 40,000 books per month, firms in the industry experience **diseconomies of scale**. Firms in the auto industry can also experience diseconomies of scale. For instance, Toyota found that as it expanded production at its Georgetown, Kentucky, plant and its plants in China, its managers had difficulty keeping average cost from rising. The president of Toyota's Georgetown plant was quoted as saying, "Demand for . . . high volumes saps your energy. Over a period of time, it eroded our focus . . . [and] thinned out the expertise and knowledge we painstakingly built up over the years." One analysis of the problems Toyota faced in expanding production concluded: "It is the kind of paradox many highly successful companies face: Getting bigger doesn't always mean getting better."

**Diseconomies of scale** The situation when a firm's long-run average costs rise as the firm increases output.

---

# Solved Problem | 10-6

## Using Long-Run Average Cost Curves to Understand Business Strategy

A few years ago, Motorola and Siemens were each manufacturing both mobile phone handsets and wireless infrastructure—the base stations needed to operate a wireless communications network. The firms discussed the following arrangement: Motorola would give Siemens its wireless infrastructure business in exchange for Siemens giving Motorola its mobile phone handsets business. The main factor motivating the trade was the hope of taking advantage of economies of scale in each business. Use long-run average total cost curves to explain why this trade might have made sense for Motorola and Siemens.

## SOLVING THE PROBLEM:

**Step 1:** **Review the chapter material.** This problem is about the long-run average cost curve, so you may want to review the material in the section "Costs in the Long Run," which begins on page 338.

**Step 2:** **Draw long-run average cost graphs for Motorola and Siemens.** The problem does not provide us with the details of the quantity of each product each firm is producing before the trade or the firms' average costs of production. If economies of scale were an important reason for the trade, we can assume that Motorola and Siemens were not yet at minimum efficient scale in the wireless infrastructure and phone handset businesses. Therefore, we can draw the following graphs:

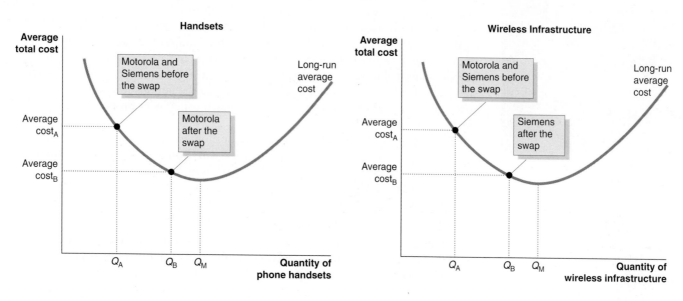

**Step 3:** **Explain the curves in the graphs.** Before the proposed trade, Motorola and Siemens are producing both products at less than the minimum efficient scale, which is $Q_M$ in both graphs. After the trade, Motorola's production of handsets will increase, moving it from $Q_A$ to $Q_B$ in the first graph. This increase in production will allow it to take advantage of economies of scale and reduce its average cost from Average cost$_A$ to Average cost$_B$. Similarly, production of wireless infrastructure by Siemens will increase from $Q_A$ to $Q_B$, lowering its average cost from Average cost$_A$ to Average cost$_B$. As drawn, the graphs show that both firms will still be short of minimum efficient scale after the trade, although their average costs will have fallen.

**EXTRA CREDIT:** These were new technologies at the time Motorola and Siemens discussed the trade. As a result, companies making these products were only beginning to understand how large minimum efficient scale was. To survive in the industry, the managements of both companies wanted to lower their costs by taking advantage of economies of scale. As one industry analyst put it: "Motorola and Siemens may be driven by the conviction that they have little choice. Most observers believe consolidation in both the [wireless] networking and handset areas is inevitable."

Source for quote: Ray Hegarty, *Rumored Motorola–Siemens Business Unit Swap? A Compelling M&A Story*, thefeature.

 **YOUR TURN:** For more practice, do related problems 6.5, 6.6, 6.7, and 6.8 on pages 353 and 354 at the end of this chapter.

---

Over time, most firms in an industry will build factories or stores that are at least as large as the minimum efficient scale but not so large that diseconomies of scale occur. In the bookstore industry, stores will sell between 20,000 and 40,000 books per month. However, firms often do not know the exact shape of their long-run average cost curves. As a result, they may mistakenly build factories or stores that are either too large or too small.

*Was Ford's River Rouge plant too big?*

**Making** the **Connection** | **The Colossal River Rouge: Diseconomies of Scale at Ford Motor Company**

When Henry Ford started the Ford Motor Company in 1903, automobile companies produced cars in small workshops, using highly skilled workers. Ford introduced two new ideas that allowed him to take advantage of economies of scale. First, Ford used identical—or, interchangeable—parts so that unskilled workers could assemble the cars. Second, instead of having groups of workers moving from one stationary automobile to the next, he had the workers remain stationary while the automobiles moved along an assembly line. Ford built a large factory at Highland Park, outside Detroit, where he used these ideas to produce the famous Model T at an average cost well below what his competitors could match using older production methods in smaller factories.

Ford believed that he could produce automobiles at an even lower average cost by building a still larger plant along the River Rouge in Dearborn, Michigan. Unfortunately, Ford's River Rouge plant was too large and suffered from diseconomies of scale. Ford's managers had great difficulty coordinating the production of automobiles in such a large plant. The following description of the River Rouge comes from a biography of Ford by Allan Nevins and Frank Ernest Hill:

A total of 93 separate structures stood on the [River Rouge] site. . . . Railroad trackage covered 93 miles, conveyors 27 [miles]. About 75,000 men worked in the great plant. A force of 5000 did nothing but keep it clean, wearing out 5000 mops and 3000 brooms a month, and using 86 tons of soap on the floors, walls, and 330 acres of windows. The Rouge was an industrial city, immense, concentrated, packed with power. . . . By its very massiveness and complexity, it denied men at the top contact with and understanding of those beneath, and gave those beneath a sense of being lost in inexorable immensity and power.

Beginning in 1927, Ford produced the Model A—its only car model at that time—at the River Rouge plant. Ford failed to achieve economies of scale and actually *lost money* on each of the four Model A body styles.

Ford could not raise the price of the Model A to make it profitable because at a higher price, the car could not compete with similar models produced by competitors such as General Motors and Chrysler. He eventually reduced the cost of making the Model A by constructing smaller factories spread out across the country. These smaller factories produced the Model A at a lower average cost than was possible at the River Rouge plant.

Source for quote: Allan Nevins and Frank Ernest Hill, *Ford: Expansion and Challenge, 1915–1933*, New York: Scribner, 1957, pp. 293, 295.

**YOUR TURN:** Test your understanding by doing related problems 6.9 and 6.10 on page 354 at the end of this chapter.

# Don't Let This Happen to **YOU!**

## Don't Confuse Diminishing Returns with Diseconomies of Scale

The concepts of diminishing returns and diseconomies of scale may seem similar, but, in fact, they are unrelated. Diminishing returns applies only to the short run, when at least one of the firm's inputs, such as the quantity of machinery it uses, is fixed. The law of diminishing returns tells us that in the short run, hiring more workers will, at some point, result in less additional output. Diminishing returns explains why marginal cost curves eventually slope upward. Diseconomies of scale apply only in the long run, when the firm is free to vary all its inputs, can adopt new technology, and can vary the amount of machinery it uses and the size of its facility. Diseconomies of scale explain why long-run average cost curves eventually slope upward.

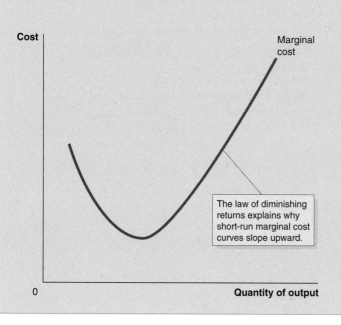

The law of diminishing returns explains why short-run marginal cost curves slope upward.

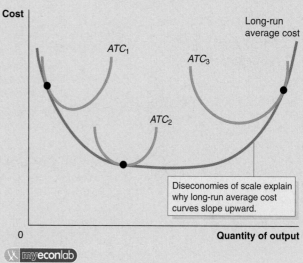

Diseconomies of scale explain why long-run average cost curves slope upward.

**YOUR TURN:** Test your understanding by doing related problem 6.12 on page 354 at the end of this chapter.

▶ **Continued from page 325**

## Economics in YOUR LIFE!

At the beginning of the chapter, we asked you to suppose that you are about to open a store to sell recliners. Both you and a competing store, Bob's Big Chairs, can buy recliners from the manufacturer for $300 each. But because Bob's sells more recliners per month than you expect to be able to sell, his costs per recliner are lower than yours. We asked you to think about why this might be true. In this chapter, we have seen that firms often experience declining average costs as the quantity they sell increases. A key reason Bob's average cost might be lower than yours has to do with fixed costs. Because your store is the same size as Bob's store, you may be paying about the same amount to lease the store space. You may also be paying about the same amounts for utilities, insurance, and advertising. All these are fixed costs because they do not change as the quantity of recliners you sell changes. Because Bob's fixed costs are the same as yours, but he is selling more recliners, his average fixed costs are lower than yours, and, therefore, so are his average total costs. With lower average total costs, he can sell his recliners for a lower price than you do and still make a profit.

# Conclusion

In this chapter, we discussed the relationship between a firm's technology, production, and costs. In the discussion, we encountered a number of definitions of costs. Because we will use these definitions in later chapters, it is useful to bring them together in Table 10-4 for you to review.

We have seen the important relationship between a firm's level of production and its costs. Just as this information was vital to Akio Morita in deciding which price to charge for his transistor radios, so it remains vital today to all firms as they attempt to decide the optimal level of production and the optimal prices to charge for their products. We will explore this point further in Chapter 11. Before moving on to that chapter, read *An Inside Look* on pages 346–347 to see how we can use long-run average cost curves to understand the effect of lower costs of production on the pricing of flat-panel TVs.

| TERM | DEFINITION | SYMBOLS AND EQUATIONS |
|---|---|---|
| Total cost | The cost of all the inputs used by a firm, or fixed cost plus variable cost | $TC$ |
| Fixed costs | Costs that remain constant when a firm's level of output changes | $FC$ |
| Variable costs | Costs that change when the firm's level of output changes | $VC$ |
| Marginal cost | Increase in total cost resulting from producing another unit of output | $MC = \dfrac{\Delta TC}{\Delta Q}$ |
| Average total cost | Total cost divided by the quantity of output produced | $ATC = \dfrac{TC}{Q}$ |
| Average fixed cost | Fixed cost divided by the quantity of output produced | $AFC = \dfrac{FC}{Q}$ |
| Average variable cost | Variable cost divided by the quantity of output produced | $AVC = \dfrac{VC}{Q}$ |
| Implicit cost | A nonmonetary opportunity cost | — |
| Explicit cost | A cost that involves spending money | — |

**TABLE 10-4**

**A Summary of Definitions of Cost**

## >> Sony Gambles on the Future Cost of the Next Generation of TVs

## USA TODAY

# Will Thin Be In, or Will Sony Be Out?

About $2,500 will buy a 50-inch, high-end Panasonic flat-panel TV . . .

Or it will buy an 11-inch Sony (SNE), smaller than most laptop screens.

. . . When this tiny television makes its U.S. debut Monday at the Consumer Electronics trade show in Las Vegas, people are expected to line up to see it. . . .

"It's beautiful," says electronics analyst Rosemary Abowd with researcher Pacific Media Associates. "It has a crystal-clear picture," agrees tech analyst Tim Bajarin. . . .

(a) Sony uses a new flat-panel technology, called organic light-emitting diode (OLED), to produce a brilliant picture on a screen only 3 millimeters thick. The technology is so new that Sony is barely breaking even on the pricey sets. And the company could lose millions if OLED flounders. . . .

That's the risk of coming to a market early, says independent tech analyst Rob Enderle. It can be worse than arriving too late, because it allows a company's rivals to learn from its mistakes.

Bajarin and other analysts who are more optimistic about OLED's potential say it is always risky to bring out a new technology. "OLED is on track to become the next major flat-panel technology," he says . . .

. . . Sony has a lot to lose. The Japanese electronics giant has invested more than $78 million in OLED, which it thinks may eventually replace plasma and liquid crystal display (LCD) as the dominant TV technology. . . If all goes as expected over the next five years, 2.8 million OLED TVs will be sold in 2013, says tech analyst Paul Semenza at researcher iSuppli. That's a promising opportunity for Sony, which has lost market share in music players, video game systems and other types of TVs in recent years. "Sony desperately needs a new (television) technology," Semenza says . . .

But Sony's bet could be a disaster, since there's a chance OLED will flop, Abowd says . . . Plasma and LCD televisions are getting better and cheaper so quickly that OLED may not be able to catch up, she says . . .

Rivals have decided that the risk isn't worth it. Samsung, Sharp and others are experimenting with the technology but aren't yet planning to bring any products to market . . .

## Wowing the crowd

Sony's first hurdle will be to win over the crowds at the Consumer Electronics Show, one of the world's largest gatherings of electronics makers and sellers . . .

(b) Sony's OLED won't be the only one. Samsung will be demonstrating two prototype models, a 14-inch and a 31-inch. "OLED is probably the best technology we see out there in terms of picture quality," says S.I. Lee, a Samsung senior vice president.

But Samsung isn't ready to bring the sets to market. If the 31-inch were commercially available, it would cost $15,000 to $20,000, Lee says. There isn't enough high-definition programming to make such a pricey set worth it, he says. "We want to continue to work on this, to bring the price down to a level that makes sense," he says.

All new products take time and money to develop, but television technology is particularly difficult. It's complicated and tough to manufacture in large quantities . . .

(c) OLED . . . is used in a few tiny products today . . . But the technology can't yet produce a TV screen size "at a price that will be accepted by the consumer," says Bob Scaglione, senior vice president at TV maker Sharp.

That's why Sharp is betting on LCD . . . the company is showing off an experimental, 52-inch LCD that's less than 1 inch thick . . .

And LCD has more room to improve. The sets will get at least 40% better than they are today as the technology is refined, Scaglione says. Such improvements are a moving target that OLED manufacturers must constantly chase, Abowd says. And quickly producing larger OLED TVs is crucial, because, "Everyone is looking for the biggest TV they can afford," she says. "I just don't know that (OLED) can get there fast enough."

. . . Even if OLED does do well, it will be years before it will really take on plasma and LCD. Sizes won't be comparable until 2012 at the earliest, Bajarin says . . .

Source: Michelle Kessler, "Will Thin Be In, or Will Sony Be Out?" *USA Today*, January 8, 2008.

## Key Points in the Article

This article describes Sony's efforts to develop a flat-panel technology, organic light-emitting diode (OLED), that the company hopes will replace plasma and liquid crystal display (LCD) technology as the industry standard. But there is no guarantee that Sony's nearly $80 million investment in OLED will be successful. The first televisions with OLED technology were not profitable, despite their high prices, and many consumers in the market for televisions chose larger and less expensive plasma or LCD models. Sony is counting on the average cost and price of OLED TVs falling over time enough for them to become the industry standard by 2013. Sony's task will be especially difficult because of future improvements in the technology used to produce plasma and LCD TVs.

## Analyzing the News

Ⓐ Analysts agree that the clarity of the picture produced by TV sets with OLED technology is superior to the picture produced by plasma and LCD sets. But in 2008, OLED technology was brand new, and Sony did not produce and sell enough OLED sets to realize economies of scale. In the figure, we see that the average total cost of producing OLED sets in 2008 was high because the number of sets produced

by Sony was low. The average total cost was so high that Sony was not able to earn a profit (Sony was "barely breaking even") from the small number of OLED sets it sold, despite the high prices it charged. If Sony is not able to convince consumers that the quality of OLED TVs is worth the premium prices, it must lower its prices in order to increase quantity demanded and incur what it hopes will be temporary losses until economies of scale are realized. The long-run average total cost curve in the figure shows how the average total cost can decrease if Sony can produce 2.8 million OLED TVs in 2013. This is the number of TVs analyst Paul Semenza believes Sony will sell "if all goes as expected." Sony executives believe that they will be able to lower the price the firm charges consumers for OLED TVs in the future and still earn a profit if the long-run average total cost decreases.

Ⓑ Sony is betting that the demand for OLED sets will expand enough by 2013 that the average total cost will fall and a profit will be earned. But firms that produce LCD and plasma TVs expect to lower their average costs as well. Improvements in current technology "are a moving target that OLED manufacturers must constantly chase." In addition to achieving lower average costs for its OLED sets, Sony faces the challenge of competing with ever-larger LCD TV sets, such as Sharp's 52-inch

model with a screen less than 1 inch thick. Sony executives must believe that consumers will prefer OLED TVs to the improved LCD TVs its competitors will be producing in the future.

Ⓒ Sony's rivals were reluctant to adopt OLED technology. Although a Samsung executive admitted that "OLED is probably the best technology . . . in terms of picture quality," Samsung was not ready to market OLED TVs. To be "commercially viable" (that is, profitable) OLED sets would have had to be sold for much higher prices—as much as $20,000 for a 31-inch set—than consumers would pay for plasma and LCD sets. Samsung is concerned that the current amount of high-definition programming is not enough to convince consumers that the new technology is worth the high prices they would have to charge.

## Thinking Critically

1. LCD and plasma TVs have been very popular with consumers. Why would Sony risk investing in a new, unproven—and more expensive—technology rather than continue to sell TVs with a proven technology and lower prices?

2. Sony risked $78 million on its investment in OLED technology. Rival firms Samsung and Sharp experimented with the technology but decided not to market OLED TVs. The article quoted an analyst who referred to ". . . the risk of coming to a market early. . . . It can be worse than arriving too late, because it allows a company's rivals to learn from its mistakes." If Sony's investment is successful, what advantages would it have over other firms from being the first to market OLED TVs?

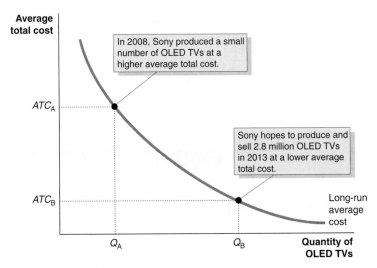

Economies of scale will result in a lower average total cost of production in 2013 if Sony can sell 2.8 million OLED TVs.

# Key Terms

---

**10.1** **Technology: An Economic Definition,** pages 326–327

LEARNING OBJECTIVE: Define technology and give examples of technological change.

## Summary

The basic activity of a firm is to use inputs, such as workers, machines, and natural resources, to produce goods and services. The firm's **technology** is the processes it uses to turn inputs into goods and services. **Technological change** refers to a change in the ability of a firm to produce a given level of output with a given quantity of inputs.

 Visit **www.myeconlab.com** to complete these exercises online and get instant feedback.

## Review Questions

1.1 What is the difference between technology and technological change?

1.2 Is it possible for technological change to be negative? If so, give an example.

## Problems and Applications

1.3 Briefly explain whether you agree with the following observation: "Technological change refers only to the introduction of new products, so it is not relevant to the operations of most firms."

1.4 Which of the following are examples of a firm experiencing positive technological change?
   a. A firm is able to cut each worker's wage rate by 10 percent and still produce the same level of output.

b. A training program makes a firm's workers more productive.

c. An exercise program makes a firm's workers more healthy and productive.

d. A firm cuts its workforce and is able to maintain its initial level of output.

e. A firm rearranges the layout of its factory and finds that by using its initial set of inputs, it can produce exactly as much as before.

1.5 **(Related to the** *Making the Connection* **on page 326)** The 7-Eleven chain of convenience stores in Japan reorganized its system for supplying its stores with food. This led to a sharp reduction in the number of trucks the company had to use, while increasing the amount of fresh food on store shelves. Someone discussing 7-Eleven's new system argues, "This is not an example of technological change because it did not require the use of new machinery or equipment." Briefly explain whether you agree with this argument.

1.6 **(Related to** *Solved Problem 10-1* **on page 327)** Indicate which of the following are examples of technological change. For each that is not, explain why.
   a. The invention of the iPhone
   b. The invention of the software that helps airlines schedule and reschedule flights
   c. The invention of the fuel cell–powered automobile

>> **End Learning Objective 10.1**

---

**10.2** **The Short Run and the Long Run in Economics,** pages 328–332

LEARNING OBJECTIVE: Distinguish between the economic short run and the economic long run.

## Summary

In the **short run**, a firm's technology and the size of its factory, store, or office are fixed. In the **long run**, a firm is able to adopt new technology and to increase or decrease the size of its physical plant. **Total cost** is the cost of all the inputs a firm uses in production. **Variable costs** are costs that change as output changes. **Fixed costs** are costs that remain constant as output changes. **Opportunity cost** is the highest-valued alternative that must be given up to engage in an activity. An **explicit cost** is a cost that involves spending money. An **implicit cost** is a nonmonetary opportunity cost.

The relationship between the inputs employed by a firm and the maximum output it can produce with those inputs is called the firm's **production function**.

 Visit **www.myeconlab.com** to complete these exercises online and get instant feedback.

## Review Questions

**2.1** What is the difference between the short run and the long run? Is the amount of time that separates the short run from the long run the same for every firm?

**2.2** What are implicit costs? How are they different from explicit costs?

## Problems and Applications

**2.3** An article in *BusinessWeek* discussed Apple's cost to produce the iPod shuffle: "All told, the cost of the shuffle's components, the headphones, and the packaging it ships in comes to $21.77. . . . That's about 28% of the device's retail price [of $79]." Can we conclude from this information that Apple is making a profit of about $57 per shuffle? Briefly explain.

Source: Arik Hesseldahl, "Deconstructing Apple's Tiny iPod Shuffle," *BusinessWeek*, April 13, 2009.

**2.4** (Related to the *Making the Connection* on page 329) Many firms consider their wage costs to be variable costs. Why do publishers usually consider their wage and salary costs to be fixed costs? Are the costs of utilities always fixed, are they always variable, or can they be both? Briefly explain.

**2.5** (Related to the *Making the Connection* on page 329) For Jill Johnson's pizza restaurant, explain whether each of the following is a fixed cost or a variable cost.
   a. The payment she makes on her fire insurance policy
   b. The payment she makes to buy pizza dough
   c. The wages she pays her workers
   d. The lease payment she makes to the landlord who owns the building where her store is located
   e. The $300-per-month payment she makes to her local newspaper for running her weekly advertisements

**2.6** (Related to the *Making the Connection* on page 329) The *Statistical Abstract of the United States* is published each year by the U.S. Census Bureau. It provides a summary of business, economic, social, and political statistics. It is available for free online, and a printed copy can also be purchased from the U.S. Government Printing Office for $37. Because government documents are not copyrighted, anyone can print copies of the *Statistical Abstract* and sell them. Each year, one or two companies typically will print and sell copies for a significantly lower price than the Government Printing Office does. The copies of the *Statistical Abstract* that these companies sell are usually identical to those sold by the government, except for having different covers. How can these companies sell the same book for a lower price than the government and still cover their costs?

**2.7** In 2008, Clay Bennett, the owner of the Seattle Supersonics basketball team, estimated that if the team remained in Seattle, he would suffer a loss of about $63 million over the following two seasons. If the team were allowed to move to Oklahoma City, he estimated that he would earn a profit of $19 million. What was the opportunity cost to Bennett of his team playing in Seattle rather than Oklahoma City? Briefly explain.

Source: Jim Brunner, "New Details Emerge from Sonics Owner's Combative Deposition," *Seattle Times*, June 7, 2008.

**2.8** Suppose Jill Johnson operates her pizza restaurant in a building she owns in the center of the city. Similar buildings in the neighborhood rent for $4,000 per month. Jill is considering selling her building and renting space in the suburbs for $3,000 per month. Jill decides not to make the move. She reasons, "I would like to have a restaurant in the suburbs, but I pay no rent for my restaurant now, and I don't want to see my costs rise by $3,000 per month." What do you think of Jill's reasoning?

**2.9** When the DuPont chemical company first attempted to enter the paint business, it was not successful. According to a company report, in one year it "lost nearly $500,000 in actual cash in addition to an expected return on investment of nearly $500,000, which made a total loss of income to the company of nearly a million." Why did this report include as part of the company's loss the amount it had expected to earn—but didn't—on its investment in manufacturing paint?

Source: Alfred D. Chandler, Jr., Thomas K. McCraw, and Richard Tedlow, *Management Past and Present*, Cincinnati: South-Western, 2000, pp. 3–92.

>> **End Learning Objective 10.2**

---

**10.3** | **The Marginal Product of Labor and the Average Product of Labor, pages 332–336**
LEARNING OBJECTIVE: Understand the relationship between the marginal product of labor and the average product of labor.

## Summary

The **marginal product of labor** is the additional output produced by a firm as a result of hiring one more worker. Specialization and division of labor cause the marginal product of labor to rise for the first few workers hired. Eventually, the **law of diminishing returns** causes the marginal product of labor to decline. The **average product of labor** is the total amount of output produced by a firm divided by the quantity of workers hired. When the marginal product of labor is greater than the average product of labor, the average product of labor increases. When the marginal product of labor is less than the average product of labor, the average product of labor decreases.

 Visit **www.myeconlab.com** to complete these exercises online and get instant feedback.

## Review Questions

**3.1** Draw a graph showing the usual relationship between the marginal product of labor and the average product of labor. Why do the marginal product of labor and the average product of labor have the shapes you drew?

**3.2** What is the law of diminishing returns? Does it apply in the long run?

## Problems and Applications

**3.3** Fill in the missing values in the following table.

| QUANTITY OF WORKERS | TOTAL OUTPUT | MARGINAL PRODUCT OF LABOR | AVERAGE PRODUCT OF LABOR |
|---|---|---|---|
| 0 | 0 | | |
| 1 | 400 | | |
| 2 | 900 | | |
| 3 | 1,500 | | |
| 4 | 1,900 | | |
| 5 | 2,200 | | |
| 6 | 2,400 | | |
| 7 | 2,300 | | |

**3.4** Use the numbers from problem 3.3 to draw one graph showing how total output increases with the quantity of workers hired and a second graph showing the marginal product of labor and the average product of labor.

**3.5** A student looks at the data in Table 10-3 on page 332 and draws this conclusion: "The marginal product of labor is increasing for the first two workers hired, and then it declines for the next four workers. I guess each of the first two workers must have been hard workers. Then Jill must have had to settle for increasingly poor workers." Do you agree with the student's analysis? Briefly explain.

**3.6** (Related to the *Making the Connection* on page 334) Briefly explain whether you agree with the following argument:

> Adam Smith's idea of the gains to firms from the division of labor makes a lot of sense when the good being manufactured is something complex like automobiles or computers, but it doesn't apply in the manufacturing of less complex goods or in other sectors of the economy, such as retail sales.

**3.7** Sally looks at her college transcript and says to Sam, "How is this possible? My grade point average for this semester's courses is higher than my grade point average for last semester's courses, but my cumulative grade point average still went down from last semester to this semester." Explain to Sally how this is possible.

**3.8** Is it possible for a firm to experience a technological change that would increase the marginal product of labor while leaving the average product of labor unchanged? Explain.

**>> End Learning Objective 10.3**

---

**10.4** **The Relationship between Short-Run Production and Short-Run Cost,** pages 336–337

LEARNING OBJECTIVE: Explain and illustrate the relationship between marginal cost and average total cost.

## Summary

The **marginal cost** of production is the increase in total cost resulting from producing another unit of output. The marginal cost curve has a U shape because when the marginal product of labor is rising, the marginal cost of output is falling. When the marginal product of labor is falling, the marginal cost of output is rising. When marginal cost is less than average total cost, average total cost falls. When marginal cost is greater than average total cost, average total cost rises.

 Visit **www.myeconlab.com** to complete these exercises online and get instant feedback.

## Review Questions

**4.1** If the marginal product of labor is rising, is the marginal cost of production rising or falling? Briefly explain.

**4.2** Explain why the marginal cost curve intersects the average total cost curve at the level of output where average total cost is at a minimum.

# Problems and Applications

**4.3** Is it possible for average total cost to be decreasing over a range of output where marginal cost is increasing? Briefly explain.

**4.4** Suppose a firm has no fixed costs, so all its costs are variable, even in the short run.

  **a.** If the firm's marginal costs are continually increasing (that is, marginal cost is increasing from the first unit of output produced), will the firm's average total cost curve have a U shape?

  **b.** If the firm's marginal costs are $5 at every level of output, what shape will the firm's average total cost have?

**>> End Learning Objective 10.4**

---

**10.5** **Graphing Cost Curves, page 338**
LEARNING OBJECTIVE: Graph average total cost, average variable cost, average fixed cost, and marginal cost.

## Summary

**Average fixed cost** is equal to fixed cost divided by the level of output. **Average variable cost** is equal to variable cost divided by the level of output. Figure 10-5 on page 339 shows the relationship among marginal cost, average total cost, average variable cost, and average fixed cost. It is one of the most important graphs in microeconomics.

 Visit **www.myeconlab.com** to complete these exercises online and get instant feedback.

## Review Questions

**5.1** As the level of output increases, what happens to the value of average fixed cost?

**5.2** As the level of output increases, what happens to the difference between the value of average total cost and average variable cost?

## Problems and Applications

**5.3** Suppose the total cost of producing 10,000 tennis balls is $30,000, and the fixed cost is $10,000.

  **a.** What is the variable cost?

  **b.** When output is 10,000, what are the average variable cost and the average fixed cost?

  **c.** Assuming that the cost curves have the usual shape, is the dollar difference between the average total cost and the average variable cost greater when the output is 10,000 tennis balls or when the output is 30,000 tennis balls? Explain.

**5.4** One description of the costs of operating a railroad makes the following observation: "The fixed ... expenses which attach to the operation of railroads ... are in the nature of a tax upon the business of the road; the smaller the [amount of] business, the larger the tax." Briefly explain why fixed costs are like a tax. In what sense is this tax smaller when the amount of business is larger?

Source for quote: Alfred D. Chandler, Jr., Thomas K. McCraw, and Richard Tedlow, *Management Past and Present*, Cincinnati: South-Western, 2000, pp. 2–27.

**5.5** In the ancient world, a book could be produced either on a scroll or as a codex, which was made of folded sheets glued together, something like a modern book. One scholar has estimated the following variable costs (in Greek drachmas) of the two methods:

|  | SCROLL | CODEX |
|---|---|---|
| Cost of writing (wage of a scribe) | 11.33 drachmas | 11.33 drachmas |
| Cost of paper | 16.50 drachmas | 9.25 drachmas |

Another scholar points out that a significant fixed cost was involved in producing a codex:

> In order to copy a codex . . . the amount of text and the layout of each page had to be carefully calculated in advance to determine the exact number of sheets . . . needed. No doubt, this is more time-consuming and calls for more experimentation than the production of a scroll would. But for the next copy, these calculations would be used again.

  **a.** Suppose that the fixed cost of preparing a codex was 58 drachmas and that there was no similar fixed cost for a scroll. Would an ancient book publisher who intended to sell 5 copies of a book be likely to publish it as a scroll or as a codex? What if he intended to sell 10 copies? Briefly explain.

  **b.** Although most books were published as scrolls in the first century A.D., by the third century, most were published as codices. Considering only the factors mentioned in this problem, explain why this change may have taken place.

Sources: T. C. Skeat, "The Length of the Standard Papyrus Roll and the Cost-Advantage of the Codex," *Zeitschrift fur Papyrologie and Epigraphik*, 1982, p. 175; and David Trobisch, *The First Edition of the New Testament*, New York: Oxford University Press, 2000, p. 73.

5.6 Use the information in the following graph to find the values for the following at an output level of 1,000.
   a. Marginal cost
   b. Total cost
   c. Variable cost
   d. Fixed cost

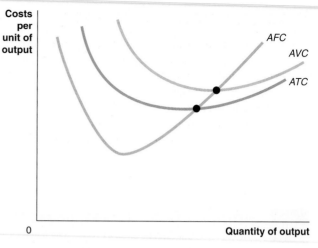

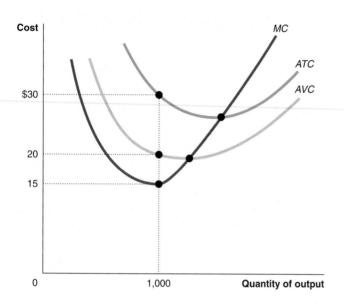

5.7 List the errors in the following graph. Carefully explain why the curves drawn this way are wrong. In other words, why can't these curves be as they are shown in the graph?

5.8 Explain how the listed events (a–d) would affect the following at Southwest Airlines:
   i. Marginal cost
   ii. Average variable cost
   iii. Average fixed cost
   iv. Average total cost
   a. Southwest signs a new contract with the Transport Workers Union that requires the airline to increase wages for its flight attendants.
   b. The federal government starts to levy a $20 per passenger carbon emissions tax on all commercial air travel.
   c. Southwest decides on an across-the-board 10 percent cut in executive salaries.
   d. Southwest decides to double its television advertising budget.

>> End Learning Objective 10.5

---

**10.6** **Costs in the Long Run,** pages 338–343

LEARNING OBJECTIVE: Understand how firms use the long-run average cost curve in their planning.

## Summary

The **long-run average cost curve** shows the lowest cost at which a firm is able to produce a given level of output in the long run. For many firms, the long-run average cost curve falls as output expands because of **economies of scale. Minimum efficient scale** is the level of output at which all economies of scale have been exhausted. After economies of scale have been exhausted, firms experience **constant returns to scale**, where their long-run average cost curve is flat. At high levels of output, the long-run average cost curve turns up as the firm experiences **diseconomies of scale.**

 Visit **www.myeconlab.com** to complete these exercises online and get instant feedback.

## Review Questions

6.1 What is the difference between total cost and variable cost in the long run?
6.2 What is minimum efficient scale? What is likely to happen in the long run to firms that do not reach minimum efficient scale?
6.3 What are economies of scale? What are diseconomies of scale? What is the main reason that a firm eventually encounters diseconomies of scale as it keeps increasing the size of its store or factory?

# Problems and Applications

**6.4** Factories for producing computer chips are called "fabs." As the semiconductors used in computer chips have become smaller and smaller, the cost of the machines necessary to make them have become more and more expensive. According to an article in the *Economist* magazine:

> To reach the economies of scale needed to make such investments pay, chipmakers must build bigger fabs. . . . In 1966 a new fab cost $14 million. By 1995 the price had risen to $1.5 billion. Today, says Intel, the cost of a leading-edge fab exceeds $6 billion.

Why would the rising costs of chipmaking machines lead chipmaking companies, such as Intel, to build larger factories?

Source: "Under New Management," *Economist*, April 2, 2009.

**6.5** (Related to *Solved Problem 10-6* on page 341) Suppose that Jill Johnson has to choose between building a smaller restaurant and a larger restaurant. In the following graph, the relationship between costs and output for the smaller restaurant is represented by the curve $ATC_1$, and the relationship between costs and output for the larger restaurant is represented by the curve $ATC_2$.

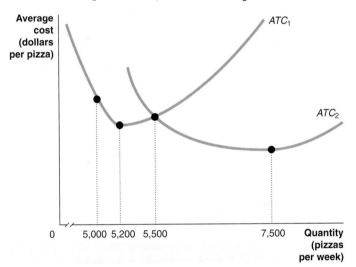

a. If Jill expects to produce 5,100 pizzas per week, should she build a smaller restaurant or a larger restaurant? Briefly explain.

b. If Jill expects to produce 6,000 pizzas per week, should she build a smaller restaurant or a larger restaurant? Briefly explain.

c. A student asks, "If the average cost of producing pizzas is lower in the larger restaurant when Jill produces 7,500 pizzas per week, why isn't it also lower when Jill produces 5,200 pizzas per week?" Give a brief answer to the student's question.

**6.6** (Related to *Solved Problem 10-6* on page 341) Consider the following description of U.S. manufacturing in the late nineteenth century:

> When . . . Standard Oil . . . reorganized its refinery capacity in 1883 and concentrated almost two-fifths of the nation's refinery production in three huge refineries, the unit cost dropped from 1.5 cents a gallon to 0.5 cents. A comparable concentration of two-fifths of the nation's output of textiles or shoes in three plants would have been impossible, and in any case would have brought huge diseconomies of scale and consequently higher prices.

a. Use this information to draw a long-run average cost curve for an oil-refining firm and a long-run average cost curve for a firm manufacturing shoes.

b. Is it likely that there were more oil refineries or more shoe factories in the United States in the late nineteenth century? Briefly explain.

c. Why would concentrating two-fifths of total shoe output in three factories have led to higher shoe prices?

Source: Alfred D. Chandler, Jr., Thomas K. McCraw, and Richard Tedlow, *Management Past and Present*, Cincinnati: South-Western, 2000, pp. 4–53.

**6.7** (Related to *Solved Problem 10-6* on page 341) An account of the difficulties of Japanese mobile-phone manufacturers argues that these firms made a mistake by concentrating on selling in high-income countries, while making little effort to sell in low-income countries:

> The main growth in the wireless industry overall is in emerging markets, which need cheap phones. The world's top three makers—Nokia, Samsung and Motorola—focus on this segment. . . . Japanese firms are caught in a vicious circle: because they are not selling to poor countries, their volume stays low, which keeps prices high, which makes selling to poor countries infeasible.

Why would the price of Japanese mobile phones be high because Japanese firms are producing these phones in low volumes? Use a graph like Figure 10-6 on page 340 to illustrate your answer.

Source: "Dropped Call," *Economist*, May 7, 2008.

**6.8** (Related to *Solved Problem 10-6* on page 341) In 2003, Time Warner and the Walt Disney Company discussed merging their news operations. Time Warner owns the Cable News Network (CNN), and Disney owns ABC News. After analyzing the situation, the companies decided that a combined news operation would have higher average costs than either CNN or ABC News had separately. Use a long-run average cost curve graph to illustrate why the companies did not merge their news operations.

Source: Martin Peers and Joe Flint, "AOL Calls Off CNN–ABC Deal, Seeing Operating Difficulties," *Wall Street Journal*, February 14, 2003.

**6.9** **(Related to the *Making the Connection* on page 342)** Suppose that Henry Ford had continued to experience increasing returns to scale, no matter how large an automobile factory he built. Discuss what the implications of this would have been for the automobile industry.

**6.10** **(Related to the *Making the Connection* on page 342)** According to one account of the problems DuPont had in entering the paint business, "the du Ponts had assumed that large volume would bring profits through lowering unit costs." In fact, according to one company report, "The more paint and varnish we sold, the more money we lost." Draw an average cost curve graph showing the relationship between paint output and the average cost DuPont expected. Draw another graph that explains the result that the more paint the company sold, the more money it lost.

Source: Alfred D. Chandler, Jr., Thomas K. McCraw, and Richard Tedlow, *Management Past and Present*, Cincinnati: South-Western, 2000, pp. 3–88.

**6.11** Online booksellers have captured a very large portion of the retail book market over the past several years. Companies such as Amazon, Barnes & Noble, and Borders, which all have a large online presence, now dominate this market. According to the American Booksellers Association, over the past 15 years, the number of independent booksellers has fallen from 4,700 to 1,600. Briefly explain what role costs may have played in explaining the large decline in independent booksellers.

Source: Alex Beam, "Where Have All the Bookstores Gone?" *New York Times*, February 20, 2009.

**6.12** **(Related to the *Don't Let This Happen to You!* on page 343)** Explain whether you agree with the following statement: "Henry Ford expected to be able to produce cars at a lower average cost at his River Rouge plant. Unfortunately, because of diminishing returns, his costs were actually higher."

**6.13** **(Related to the *Chapter Opener* on page 325)** Review the discussion at the beginning of the chapter of Akio Morita selling transistor radios in the United States. Suppose that Morita became convinced that Sony would be able to sell more than 75,000 transistor radios each year in the United States. What steps would he have taken?

**6.14** TIAA-CREF is a retirement system for people who work at colleges and universities. For some years, TIAA-CREF also offered long-term care insurance to its customers before deciding to sell that business to MetLife, a large insurance company. TIAA-CREF's chairman and chief executive officer explained the decision this way:

> In recent years, the long-term care insurance market has experienced significant consolidation. A few large insurance companies now own most of the business. MetLife has 428,000 policies, for example—nearly 10 times the number we have—and can achieve economies of scale that we can't. Over time, we would have had difficulty holding down premium rates.

Briefly explain what economies of scale have to do with the premiums (that is, the prices buyers have to pay for insurance policies) that insurance companies can charge for their policies.

Source: "Long-Term Care Sale in Best Interest of Policyholders," *Advance*, Spring 2004, p. 6.

**6.15** In January, 2009, the U.S. Department of Agriculture released a report on the changing dynamics of the U.S. livestock industry. It concluded that: "U.S. livestock production is shifting to much larger enterprises, in part because of scale economies." What are "scale economies"? What would scale economies have to do with livestock production shifting to much larger operations?

Source: James M. MacDonald and William D. McBride, *The Transformation of U.S. Livestock Agriculture: Scale, Efficiency, and Risks*, Economic Information Bulletin No. (EIB-43), Economic Research Service, U.S. Department of Agriculture, January 2009.

>> **End Learning Objective 10.6**

# Appendix

## Using Isoquants and Isocosts to Understand Production and Cost

**LEARNING** OBJECTIVE

Use isoquants and isocost lines to understand production and cost.

## Isoquants

In this chapter, we studied the important relationship between a firm's level of production and its costs. In this appendix, we will look more closely at how firms choose the combination of inputs to produce a given level of output. Firms usually have a choice of how they will produce their output. For example, Jill Johnson is able to produce 5,000 pizzas per week by using 10 workers and 2 ovens or by using 6 workers and 3 ovens. We will see that firms search for the *cost-minimizing* combination of inputs that will allow them to produce a given level of output. The cost-minimizing combination of inputs depends on two factors: technology—which determines how much output a firm receives from employing a given quantity of inputs—and input prices—which determine the total cost of each combination of inputs.

## An Isoquant Graph

We begin by graphing the levels of output that Jill can produce using different combinations of two inputs: labor—the quantity of workers she hires per week—and capital—the quantity of ovens she uses per week. In reality, of course, Jill uses more than just these two inputs to produce pizzas, but nothing important would change if we expanded the discussion to include many inputs instead of just two. Figure 10A-1 measures capital along the vertical axis and labor along the horizontal axis. The curves in the graph are **isoquants**, which show all the combinations of two inputs, in this case capital and labor, that will produce the same level of output.

**Isoquant** A curve that shows all the combinations of two inputs, such as capital and labor, that will produce the same level of output.

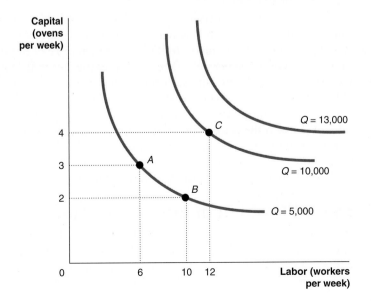

## Figure 10A-1

**Isoquants**

Isoquants show all the combinations of two inputs, in this case capital and labor, that will produce the same level of output. For example, the isoquant labeled $Q = 5,000$ shows all the combinations of ovens and workers that enable Jill to produce that quantity of pizzas per week. At point $A$, she produces 5,000 pizzas using 3 ovens and 6 workers, and at point $B$, she produces the same output using 2 ovens and 10 workers. With more ovens and workers, she can move to a higher isoquant. For example, with 4 ovens and 12 workers, she can produce at point $C$ on the isoquant $Q = 10,000$. With even more ovens and workers, she could move to the isoquant $Q = 13,000$.

The isoquant labeled $Q = 5,000$ shows all the combinations of workers and ovens that enable Jill to produce that quantity of pizzas per week. For example, at point $A$, she produces 5,000 pizzas using 6 workers and 3 ovens, and at point $B$, she produces the same output using 10 workers and 2 ovens. With more workers and ovens, she can move to a higher isoquant. For example, with 12 workers and 4 ovens, she can produce at point $C$ on the isoquant $Q = 10,000$. With even more workers and ovens, she could move to the isoquant $Q = 13,000$. The higher the isoquant—that is, the further to the upper right on the graph—the more output the firm produces. Although we have shown only three isoquants in this graph, there are, in fact, an infinite number of isoquants—one for every level of output.

### The Slope of an Isoquant

**Marginal rate of technical substitution** (*MRTS*) The rate at which a firm is able to substitute one input for another while keeping the level of output constant.

Remember that the slope of a curve is the ratio of the change in the variable on the vertical axis to the change in the variable on the horizontal axis. Along an isoquant, the slope tells us the rate at which a firm is able to substitute one input for another while keeping the level of output constant. This rate is called the **marginal rate of technical substitution** (*MRTS*).

We expect that the *MRTS* will change as we move down an isoquant. In Figure 10A-1, at a point like $A$ on isoquant $Q = 5,000$, the isoquant is relatively steep. As we move down the curve, it becomes less steep at a point like $B$. This shape is the usual one for isoquants: They are bowed in, or convex. The reason isoquants have this shape is that as we move down the curve, we continue to substitute labor for capital. As the firm produces the same quantity of output using less capital, the additional labor it needs increases because of diminishing returns. Remember from the chapter that, as a consequence of diminishing returns, for a given decline in capital, increasing amounts of labor are necessary to produce the same level of output. Because the *MRTS* is equal to the change in capital divided by the change in labor, it will become smaller (in absolute value) as we move down an isoquant.

## Isocost Lines

**Isocost line** All the combinations of two inputs, such as capital and labor, that have the same total cost.

Any firm wants to produce a given quantity of output at the lowest possible cost. We can show the relationship between the quantity of inputs used and the firm's total cost by using an *isocost* line. An **isocost line** shows all the combinations of two inputs, such as capital and labor, that have the same total cost.

### Graphing the Isocost Line

Suppose Jill has $6,000 per week to spend on capital and labor. Suppose, to simplify the analysis, that Jill can rent pizza ovens by the week. The table in Figure 10A-2 shows the combinations of capital and labor available to her if the rental price of ovens is $1,000 per week and the wage rate is $500 per week. The graph uses the data in the table to construct an isocost line. The isocost line intersects the vertical axis at the maximum number of ovens Jill can rent per week, which is shown by point $A$. The line intersects the horizontal axis at the maximum number of workers Jill can hire per week, which is point $G$. As Jill moves down the isocost line from point $A$, she gives up renting 1 oven for every 2 workers she hires. Any combination of inputs along the line or inside the line can be purchased with $6,000. Any combination that lies outside the line cannot be purchased because it would have a total cost to Jill of more than $6,000.

### The Slope and Position of the Isocost Line

The slope of the isocost line is constant and equals the change in the quantity of ovens divided by the change in the quantity of workers. In this case, in moving from any point on the isocost line to any other point, the change in the quantity of ovens equals $-1$, and the change in the quantity of workers equals 2, so the slope equals $-1/2$. Notice that with

**Combinations of Workers and Ovens with a Total Cost of $6,000**

| Point | Ovens | Workers | Total Cost |
|-------|-------|---------|------------|
| A | 6 | 0 | (6 x $1,000) + (0 x $500) = $6,000 |
| B | 5 | 2 | (5 x $1,000) + (2 x $500) = 6,000 |
| C | 4 | 4 | (4 x $1,000) + (4 x $500) = 6,000 |
| D | 3 | 6 | (3 x $1,000) + (6 x $500) = 6,000 |
| E | 2 | 8 | (2 x $1,000) + (8 x $500) = 6,000 |
| F | 1 | 10 | (1 x $1,000) + (10 x $500) = 6,000 |
| G | 0 | 12 | (0 x $1,000) + (12 x $500) = 6,000 |

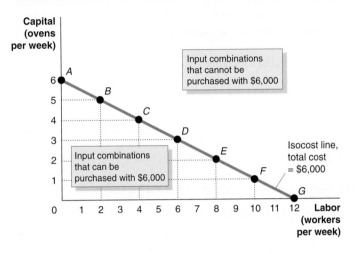

## Figure 10A-2

### An Isocost Line

The isocost line shows the combinations of inputs with a total cost of $6,000. The rental price of ovens is $1,000 per week, so if Jill spends the whole $6,000 on ovens, she can rent 6 ovens (point A). The wage rate is $500 per week, so if Jill spends the whole $6,000 on workers, she can hire 12 workers. As she moves down the isocost line, she gives up renting 1 oven for every 2 workers she hires. Any combinations of inputs along the line or inside the line can be purchased with $6,000. Any combinations that lie outside the line cannot be purchased with $6,000.

a rental price of ovens of $1,000 per week and a wage rate for labor of $500 per week, the slope of the isocost line is equal to the ratio of the wage rate divided by the rental price of capital, multiplied by −1: −$500/$1,000 = −1/2. In fact, this result will always hold, whatever inputs are involved and whatever their prices may be: *The slope of the isocost line is equal to the ratio of the price of the input on the horizontal axis divided by the price of the input on the vertical axis, multiplied by −1.*

The position of the isocost line depends on the level of total cost. Higher levels of total cost shift the isocost line outward, and lower levels of total cost shift the isocost line inward. This can be seen in Figure 10A-3, which shows isocost lines for total costs of $3,000, $6,000, and $9,000. We have shown only three isocost lines in the graph, but there is, in fact, a different isocost line for every level of total cost.

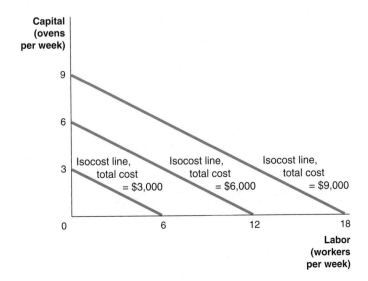

## Figure 10A-3

### The Position of the Isocost Line

The position of the isocost line depends on the level of total cost. As total cost increases from $3,000 to $6,000 to $9,000 per week, the isocost line shifts outward. For each isocost line shown, the rental price of ovens is $1,000 per week, and the wage rate is $500 per week.

# Choosing the Cost-Minimizing Combination of Capital and Labor

Suppose Jill wants to produce 5,000 pizzas per week. Figure 10A-1 shows that there are many combinations of ovens and workers that will allow Jill to produce this level of output. There is only one combination of ovens and workers, however, that will allow her to produce 5,000 pizzas *at the lowest total cost.* Figure 10A-4 shows the isoquant $Q = 5,000$ along with three isocost lines. Point $B$ is the lowest-cost combination of inputs shown in the graph, but this combination of 1 oven and 4 workers will produce fewer than the 5,000 pizzas needed. Points $C$ and $D$ are combinations of ovens and workers that will produce 5,000 pizzas, but their total cost is $9,000. The combination of 3 ovens and 6 workers at point $A$ produces 5,000 pizzas at the lowest total cost of $6,000.

Figure 10A-4 shows that moving to an isocost line with a total cost of less than $6,000 would mean producing fewer than 5,000 pizzas. Being at any point along the isoquant $Q = 5,000$ other than point $A$ would increase total cost above $6,000. In fact, the combination of inputs at point $A$ is the only one on isoquant $Q = 5,000$ that has a total cost of $6,000. All other input combinations on this isoquant have higher total costs. Notice also that at point $A$, the isoquant and the isocost lines are tangent, so the slope of the isoquant is equal to the slope of the isocost line at that point.

## Different Input Price Ratios Lead to Different Input Choices

Jill's cost-minimizing choice of 3 ovens and 6 workers is determined jointly by the technology available to her—as represented by her firm's isoquants—and by input prices—as represented by her firm's isocost lines. If the technology of making pizzas changes, perhaps because new ovens are developed, her isoquants will be affected, and her choice of inputs may change. If her isoquants remain unchanged but input prices change, then her choice of inputs may also change. This fact can explain why firms in different countries that face different input prices may produce the same good using different combinations of capital and labor, even though they have the same technology available.

For example, suppose that in China, pizza ovens are higher priced and labor is lower priced than in the United States. In our example, Jill Johnson pays $1,000 per week to rent pizza ovens and $500 per week to hire workers. Suppose a businessperson

## Figure 10A-4

### Choosing Capital and Labor to Minimize Total Cost

Jill wants to produce 5,000 pizzas per week at the lowest total cost. Point $B$ is the lowest-cost combination of inputs shown in the graph, but this combination of 1 oven and 4 workers will produce fewer than the 5,000 pizzas needed. Points $C$ and $D$ are combinations of ovens and workers that will produce 5,000 pizzas, but their total cost is $9,000. The combination of 3 ovens and 6 workers at point $A$ produces 5,000 pizzas at the lowest total cost of $6,000.

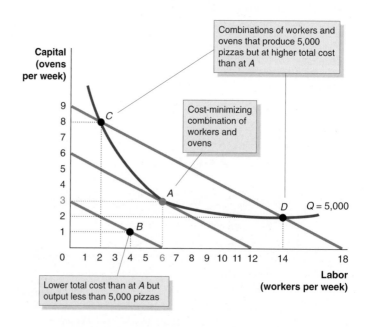

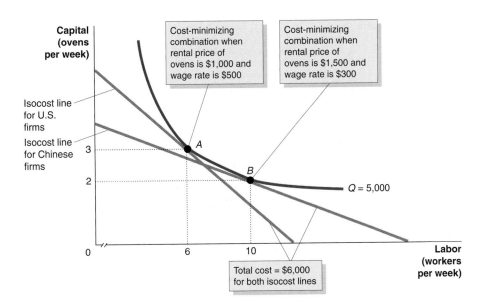

### Figure 10A-5

**Changing Input Prices Affects the Cost-Minimizing Input Choice**

As the graph shows, the input combination at point *A*, which was optimal for Jill, is not optimal for a businessperson in China. Using the input combination at point *A* would cost businesspeople in China more than $6,000. Instead, the Chinese isocost line is tangent to the isoquant at point *B*, where the input combination is 2 ovens and 10 workers. Because ovens cost more in China but workers cost less, a Chinese firm will use fewer ovens and more workers than a U.S. firm, even if it has the same technology as the U.S. firm.

in China must pay a price of $1,500 per week to rent the identical pizza ovens but can hire Chinese workers who are as productive as U.S. workers at a wage of $300 per week. Figure 10A-5 shows how the cost-minimizing input combination for the businessperson in China differs from Jill's.

Remember that the slope of the isocost line equals the wage rate divided by the rental price of capital, multiplied by −1. The slope of the isocost line that Jill and other U.S. firms face is −$500/$1,000, or −1/2. Firms in China, however, face an isocost line with a slope of −$300/$1,500, or −1/5. As Figure 10A-5 shows, the input combination at point *A*, which was optimal for Jill, is not optimal for a firm in China. Using the input combination at point *A* would cost a firm in China more than $6,000. Instead, the Chinese isocost line is tangent to the isoquant at point *B*, where the input combination is 2 ovens and 10 workers. This result makes sense: Because ovens cost more in China, but workers cost less, a Chinese firm will use fewer ovens and more workers than a U.S. firm, even if it has the same technology as the U.S. firm.

<table>
<tr><td>Making the Connection</td><td>

## The Changing Input Mix in Walt Disney Film Animation

</td></tr>
</table>

The inputs used to make feature-length animated films have changed dramatically in the past 15 years. Prior to the early 1990s, the Walt Disney Company dominated the market for animated films. Disney's films were produced using hundreds of animators drawing most of the film by hand. Each film would contain as many as 170,000 individual drawings. Then, two developments dramatically affected how animated films are produced. First, in 1994, Disney had a huge hit with *The Lion King*, which cost only $50 million but earned the company more than $1 billion in profit. As a result of this success, Disney and other film studios began to produce more animated films, increasing the demand for animators and more than doubling their salaries. The second development came in 1995, when Pixar Animation Studios released the film *Toy Story*. This was the first successful feature-length film produced using computers, with no hand-drawn animation. In the following years, technological advance continued to reduce the cost of the computers and software necessary to produce an animated film.

As a result of these two developments, the price of capital—computers and software—fell relative to the price of labor—animators. As the figure shows, the change in the price of computers relative to animators changed the slope of the isocost line and resulted in film studios now producing animated films using many more computers and many

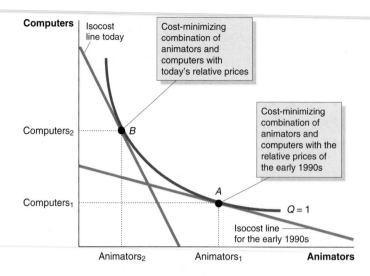

fewer animators than in the early 1990s. In 2006, Disney bought Pixar, and by 2009, all the major film studios had converted to computer animation, now referred to as CGI animation.

Source: "Magic Restored," *Economist*, April 17, 2008; and Bruce Orwall, "Disney Delivers 'Lilo and Stitch' on Competition-Driven Budget," *Wall Street Journal*, June 18, 2002, p. A1.

 **YOUR TURN:** Test your understanding by doing related problem 10A.8 on page 365 at the end of this appendix.

---

## Another Look at Cost Minimization

In Chapter 9, we saw that consumers maximize utility when they consume each good up to the point where the marginal utility per dollar spent is the same for every good. We can derive a very similar cost-minimization rule for firms. Remember that at the point of cost minimization, the isoquant and the isocost line are tangent, so they have the same slope. Therefore, *at the point of cost minimization, the marginal rate of technical substitution (MRTS) is equal to the wage rate divided by the rental price of capital.*

The slope of the isoquant tells us the rate at which a firm is able to substitute labor for capital, *given existing technology*. The slope of the isocost line tells us the rate at which a firm is able to substitute labor for capital, *given current input prices*. Only at the point of cost minimization are these two rates the same.

When we move from one point on an isoquant to another, we end up using more of one input and less of the other input, but the level of output remains the same. For example, as Jill moves down an isoquant, she uses fewer ovens and more workers but produces the same quantity of pizzas. In this chapter, we defined the *marginal product of labor* ($MP_L$) as the additional output produced by a firm as a result of hiring one more worker. Similarly, we can define the *marginal product of capital* ($MP_K$) as the additional output produced by a firm as a result of using one more machine. So, when Jill uses fewer ovens by moving down an isoquant, she loses output equal to:

$$-\text{Change in the quantity of ovens} \times MP_K.$$

But she uses more workers, so she gains output equal to:

$$\text{Change in the quantity of workers} \times MP_L.$$

We know that the gain in output from the additional workers is equal to the loss from the smaller quantity of ovens because total output remains the same along an isoquant. Therefore, we can write:

$-$Change in the quantity of ovens $\times MP_K =$ Change in the quantity of workers $\times MP_L.$

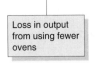

Loss in output from using fewer ovens

Gain in output from using more workers

If we rearrange terms, we have the following:

$$\frac{-\text{Change in the quantity of ovens}}{\text{Change in the quantity of workers}} = \frac{MP_L}{MP_K}.$$

Because the

$$\frac{-\text{Change in the quantity of ovens}}{\text{Change in the quantity of workers}}$$

is the slope of the isoquant, it is equal to the marginal rate of technical substitution (multiplied by negative 1). So, we can write:

$$\frac{-\text{Change in the quantity of ovens}}{\text{Change in the quantity of workers}} = MRTS = \frac{MP_L}{MP_K}.$$

The slope of the isocost line equals the wage rate ($w$) divided by the rental price of capital ($r$). We saw earlier in this appendix that at the point of cost minimization, the *MRTS* equals the ratio of the prices of the two inputs. Therefore:

$$\frac{MP_L}{MP_K} = \frac{w}{r}.$$

We can rewrite this to show that at the point of cost minimization:

$$\frac{MP_L}{w} = \frac{MP_K}{r}.$$

This last expression tells us that to minimize cost for a given level of output, a firm should hire inputs up to the point where the last dollar spent on each input results in the same increase in output. If this equality did not hold, a firm could lower its costs by using more of one input and less of the other. For example, if the left side of the equation were greater than the right side, a firm could rent fewer ovens, hire more workers, and produce the same output at lower cost.

# Solved Problem | 10A-1

## Determining the Optimal Combination of Inputs

Consider the information in the following table for Jill Johnson's restaurant.

| | |
|---|---|
| Marginal product of capital | 3,000 pizzas per oven |
| Marginal product of labor | 1,200 pizzas per worker |
| Wage rate | $300 per week |
| Rental price of ovens | $600 per week |

Briefly explain whether Jill is minimizing costs. If she is not minimizing costs, explain whether she should rent more ovens and hire fewer workers or rent fewer ovens and hire more workers.

## SOLVING THE PROBLEM:

**Step 1:** **Review the chapter material.** This problem is about determining the optimal choice of inputs by comparing the ratios of the marginal products of inputs to their prices, so you may want to review the section "Another Look at Cost Minimization," which begins on page 360.

**Step 2:** **Compute the ratios of marginal product to input price to determine whether Jill is minimizing costs.** If Jill is minimizing costs, the following relationship should hold:

$$\frac{MP_L}{w} = \frac{MP_K}{r}.$$

In this case, we have:

$$MP_L = 1{,}200$$
$$MP_K = 3{,}000$$
$$w = \$300$$
$$r = \$600.$$

So:

$$\frac{MP_L}{w} = \frac{1{,}200}{\$300} = 4 \text{ pizzas per dollar, and } \frac{MP_K}{r} = \frac{3{,}000}{\$600} = 5 \text{ pizzas per dollar.}$$

Because the two ratios are not equal, Jill is not minimizing cost.

**Step 3:** **Determine how Jill should change the mix of inputs she uses.** Jill produces more pizzas per dollar from the last oven than from the last worker. This indicates that she has too many workers and too few ovens. Therefore, to minimize cost, Jill should use more ovens and hire fewer workers.

  **YOUR TURN:** For more practice, do related problems 10A.6 and 10A.7 on page 365 at the end of this appendix.

---

*Are the Detroit Lions paying Matt Stafford too much?*

Making
the
Connection

## Do National Football League Teams Behave Efficiently?

In the National Football League (NFL), the "salary cap" is the maximum amount each team can spend each year on salaries for football players. Each year's salary cap results from negotiations between the league and the union representing the players. To achieve efficiency, an NFL team should distribute salaries among players so as to maximize the level of output—in this case, winning football games—given the constant level of cost represented by the salary cap. (Notice that maximizing the level of output for a given level of cost is equivalent to minimizing cost for a given level of output. To see why, think about the situation where an isocost line is tangent to an isoquant. At the point of tangency, the firm has simultaneously minimized the cost of producing the level of output represented by the isoquant and maximized the output produced at the level of cost represented by the isocost line.) In distributing salaries, teams should equalize the marginal productivity of players as represented by their contribution to winning games to the salaries paid. Just as a firm may not use a machine that has a very high marginal product if its rental price is very high, a football team may not want to hire a superstar player if the salary the team would need to pay is too high.

Economists Cade Massey, of Duke University, and Richard Thaler, of the University of Chicago, have analyzed whether NFL teams distribute their salaries efficiently. NFL teams obtain their players either by signing free agents—who are players whose contracts with other teams have expired—or by signing players chosen in the annual draft of eligible college players. The college draft consists of seven rounds, with the teams with the worst records the previous year choosing first. Massey and Thaler find that, in fact, NFL teams do not allocate salaries efficiently. In particular, the players chosen with the first few picks of the first round of the draft tend to be paid salaries that are much higher relative to their marginal products than is true for players taken later in the first round. A typical team with a high draft pick would increase its ability to win football games at the constant cost represented by the salary cap if it traded for lower draft picks. Why do NFL teams apparently make the error of not efficiently distributing salaries? Massey and Thaler argue that general managers of NFL teams tend to be overconfident in their ability to forecast how well a college player is likely to perform in the NFL.

General managers of NFL teams are not alone in suffering from overconfidence. Studies have shown that, in general, people tend to overestimate their ability to forecast an uncertain outcome. Because NFL teams tend to overestimate the future marginal productivity of high draft picks, they pay them salaries that are inefficiently high when compared to salaries other draft picks receive.

This example shows that the concepts developed in this chapter provide powerful tools for analyzing whether firms are operating efficiently.

Source: Cade Massey and Richard Thaler, "Overconfidence versus Market Efficiency in the National Football League," Cambridge, MA: National Bureau of Economic Research Working Paper 11270, April 2005.

**YOUR TURN:** Test your understanding by doing related problem 10A.14 on page 365 at the end of this appendix.

---

# The Expansion Path

We can use isoquants and isocost lines to examine what happens as a firm expands its level of output. Figure 10A-6 shows three isoquants for a firm that produces bookcases. The isocost lines are drawn under the assumption that the machines used in producing bookcases can be rented for $100 per day and the wage rate is $25 per day. The point where each isoquant is tangent to an isocost line determines the cost-minimizing combination of capital and labor for producing that level of output. For example, 10 machines and 40 workers is the cost-minimizing combination of inputs for producing 50 bookcases per day. The cost-minimizing points *A*, *B*, and *C* lie along the firm's **expansion path,** which is a curve that shows the cost-minimizing combination of inputs for every level of output.

An important point to note is that the expansion path represents the least-cost combination of inputs to produce a given level of output *in the long run*, when the firm is able to vary the levels of all of its inputs. We know, though, that in the short run, at

**Expansion path** A curve that shows a firm's cost-minimizing combination of inputs for every level of output.

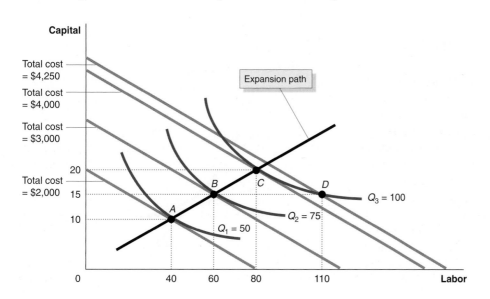

## Figure 10A-6

### The Expansion Path

The tangency points *A*, *B*, and *C* lie along the firm's expansion path, which is a curve that shows the cost-minimizing combination of inputs for every level of output. In the short run, when the quantity of machines is fixed, the firm can expand output from 75 bookcases per day to 100 bookcases per day at the lowest cost only by moving from point *B* to point *D* and increasing the number of workers from 60 to 110. In the long run, when it can increase the quantity of machines it uses, the firm can move from point *D* to point *C*, thereby reducing its total costs of producing 100 bookcases per day from $4,250 to $4,000.

least one input is fixed. We can use Figure 10A-6 to show that as the firm expands in the short run, its costs will be higher than in the long run. For example, suppose that the firm is currently at point B, using 15 machines and 60 workers to produce 75 bookcases per day. The firm wants to expand its output to 100 bookcases per day, but in the short run, it is unable to increase the quantity of machines it uses. Therefore, to expand output, it must hire more workers. The figure shows that in the short run, to produce 100 bookcases per day using 15 machines, the lowest costs it can attain are at point D, where it employs 110 workers. With a rental price of machines of $100 per day and a wage rate of $25 per day, in the short run, the firm will have total costs of $4,250 to produce 100 bookcases per day. In the long run, though, the firm can increase the number of machines it uses from 15 to 20 and reduce the number of workers from 110 to 80. This change allows it to move from point D to point C on its expansion path and to lower its total costs of producing 100 bookcases per day from $4,250 to $4,000. The firm's minimum total costs of production are lower in the long run than in the short run.

# Key Terms

**Using isoquants and isocosts to understand production and cost,** pages 355–364

LEARNING OBJECTIVE: Use isoquants and isocost lines to understand production and cost.

 Visit **www.myeconlab.com** to complete these exercises online and get instant feedback.

## Review Questions

**10A.1** What is an isoquant? What is the slope of an isoquant?

**10A.2** What is an isocost line? What is the slope of an isocost line?

**10A.3** How do firms choose the optimal combination of inputs?

## Problems and Applications

**10A.4** Draw an isoquant–isocost line graph to illustrate the following situation: Jill Johnson can rent pizza ovens for $400 per week and hire workers for $200 per week. She is currently using 5 ovens and 10 workers to produce 20,000 pizzas per week and has total costs of $4,000. Make sure to label your graph showing the cost-minimizing input combination and the maximum quantity of labor and capital she can use with total costs of $4,000.

**10A.5** Use the following graph to answer the questions.
a. If the wage rate and the rental price of machines are both $100 and total cost is $2,000, is the cost-minimizing point *A*, *B*, or *C*? Briefly explain.

b. If the wage rate is $25, the rental price of machines is $100, and total cost is $1,000, is the cost-minimizing point *A*, *B*, or *C*? Briefly explain.

c. If the wage rate and the rental price of machines are both $100 and total cost is $4,000, is the cost-minimizing point *A*, *B*, or *C*? Briefly explain.

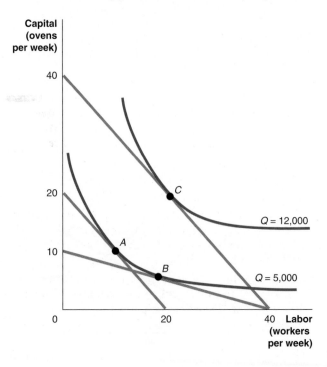

**10A.6** (Related to *Solved Problem 10A-1* on page 361) Consider the information in the following table for Jill Johnson's restaurant.

| | |
|---|---|
| Marginal product of capital | 4,000 |
| Marginal product of labor | 100 |
| Wage rate | $10 |
| Rental price of pizza ovens | $500 |

Briefly explain whether Jill is minimizing costs. If she is not minimizing costs, explain whether she should rent more ovens and hire fewer workers or rent fewer ovens and hire more workers.

**10A.7** (Related to *Solved Problem 10A-1* on page 361) Draw an isoquant–isocost line graph to illustrate the following situation: Jill Johnson can rent pizza ovens for $200 per week and hire workers for $100 per week. Currently, she is using 5 ovens and 10 workers to produce 20,000 pizzas per week and has total costs of $2,000. Jill's marginal rate of technical substitution (*MRTS*) equals −1. Explain why this means that she's not minimizing costs and what she could do to minimize costs.

**10A.8** (Related to the *Making the Connection* on page 359) During the eighteenth century, the American colonies had much more land per farmer than did Europe, with the result that the price of labor in the colonies was much higher relative to the price of land than was true in Europe. Assume that Europe and the colonies had access to the same technology for producing food. Use an isoquant–isocost line graph to illustrate why the combination of land and labor used in producing food in the colonies would have been different than the combination used to produce food in Europe.

**10A.9** Draw an isoquant–isocost line graph to illustrate the following situation and the change that occurs: Jill Johnson can rent pizza ovens for $2,000 per week and hire workers for $1,000 per week. Currently, she is using 5 ovens and 10 workers to produce 20,000 pizzas per week and has total costs of $20,000. Then Jill reorganizes the way things are done in her business and achieves positive technological change.

**10A.10** Use the following graph to answer the following questions about Jill Johnson's isoquant curve.

   **a.** Which combination of inputs yields more output: combination *A* (3 ovens and 2 workers) or combination *B* (2 ovens and 3 workers)?

   **b.** What will determine whether Jill selects *A*, *B*, or some other point along this isoquant curve?

   **c.** Is the marginal rate of technical substitution (*MRTS*) greater at point *A* or point *B*?

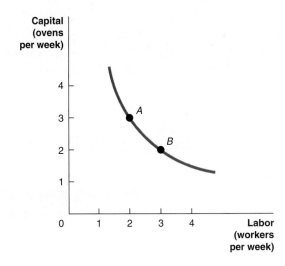

**10A.11** Draw an isoquant–isocost line graph to illustrate the following situation: Jill Johnson can rent pizza ovens for $2,000 per week and hire workers for $1,000 per week. She can minimize the cost of producing 20,000 pizzas per week by using 5 ovens and 10 workers, at a total cost of $20,000. She can minimize the cost of producing 45,000 pizzas per week by using 10 ovens and 20 workers, at a total cost of $40,000. And she can minimize the cost of producing 60,000 pizzas per week by using 15 ovens and 30 workers, at a total cost of $60,000. Now draw Jill's long-run average cost curve and discuss its economies and diseconomies of scale.

**10A.12** In Brazil, a grove of oranges is picked using 20 workers, ladders, and baskets. In Florida, a grove of oranges is picked using 1 worker and a machine that shakes the oranges off the trees and scoops up the fallen oranges. Using an isoquant–isocost line graph, illustrate why these two different methods are used to pick the same number of oranges per day in these two locations.

**10A.13** Jill Johnson is minimizing the costs of producing pizzas. The rental price of one of her ovens is $2,000 per week, and the wage rate is $600 per week. The marginal product of capital in her business is 12,000 pizzas. What must be the marginal product of her workers?

**10A.14** (Related to the *Making the Connection* on page 362) If Massey and Thaler are correct, should the team that has the first pick in the draft keep the pick or trade it to another team for a lower pick? Explain.

**>> End Appendix Learning Objective**

# CHAPTER 11

# Firms in Perfectly Competitive Markets

## Chapter Outline and Learning Objectives

# >> Perfect Competition in the Market for Organic Apples

The market for organically grown food has expanded rapidly in the United States. By the 2000s, sales of organic foods were growing at a rate of more than 20 percent per year. According to U.S. Department of Agriculture (USDA) standards, a firm can label and advertise food as "organic" only if that food is "produced without using most conventional pesticides; fertilizers made with synthetic ingredients or sewage sludge; bioengineering; or ionizing radiation." The growing methods required for organic apples are about 15 percent more costly than traditional methods.

In 1997, farmers in the Yakima Valley of Washington State sold organically grown apples for a price 50 percent higher than the price of regular apples, more than offsetting their higher costs. This price difference made organically grown apples considerably more profitable than apples grown using traditional methods. As a result, many apple farmers switched from traditional to organic growing methods, rapidly increasing the production of organically grown apples. The additional supply of organically grown apples forced down prices and made them no more profitable than apples grown using traditional methods. As one farmer in the Yakima Valley put it, "It's like anything else in agriculture. If people see an economic opportunity, usually it only lasts for a few years."

What the organic apple farmers in the Yakima Valley experienced is not unique to agriculture. Throughout the economy, entrepreneurs are continually introducing new products, which—when successful—enable them to earn economic profits in the short run. But in the long run, competition among firms forces prices to the level where they just cover the costs of production. This process of competition is at the heart of the market system and is the focus of this chapter.

**AN INSIDE LOOK AT POLICY** on **page 392** discusses the difficulty and cost of having a product certified as "organic."

Sources: Data from National Agricultural Statistics Service, USDA, www.nass.usda.gov; quote from farmer is from *All Things Considered*, National Public Radio, www.npr.org, April 18, 2001.

## Economics in YOUR LIFE!

### Are You an Entrepreneur?

Were you an entrepreneur during your high school years? Perhaps you didn't have your own store, but you may have worked as a babysitter, or perhaps you mowed lawns for families in your neighborhood. While you may not think of these jobs as being small businesses, that is exactly what they are. How did you decide what price to charge for your services? You may have wanted to charge $25 per hour to babysit or mow lawns, but you probably charged much less. As you read the chapter, think about the competitive situation you faced as a teenaged entrepreneur and try to determine why the prices received by most people who babysit and mow lawns are so low. You can check your answers against those we provide at the end of the chapter.

▶ Continued on page 391

Organic apple growing is an example of a *perfectly competitive* industry. Firms in perfectly competitive industries are unable to control the prices of the products they sell and are unable to earn an economic profit in the long run for two main reasons: Firms in these industries sell identical products, and it is easy for new firms to enter these industries. Studying how perfectly competitive industries operate is the best way to understand how markets answer the fundamental economic questions discussed in Chapter 1:

* What goods and services will be produced?

* How will the goods and services be produced?

* Who will receive the goods and services produced?

In fact, though, most industries are not perfectly competitive. In most industries, firms do *not* produce identical products, and in some industries, it may be difficult for new firms to enter. There are thousands of industries in the United States. Although in some ways each industry is unique, industries share enough similarities that economists group them into four market structures. In particular, any industry has three key characteristics:

* The number of firms in the industry

* The similarity of the good or service produced by the firms in the industry

* The ease with which new firms can enter the industry

Economists use these characteristics to classify industries into the four market structures listed in Table 11-1.

Many industries, including restaurants, clothing stores, and other retailers, have a large number of firms selling products that are differentiated, rather than identical, and fall into the category of *monopolistic competition*. Some industries, such as computers and automobiles, have only a few firms and are *oligopolies*. Finally, a few industries, such as the delivery of first-class mail by the U.S. Postal Service, have only one firm and are *monopolies*. After discussing perfect competition in this chapter, we will devote a chapter to each of these other market structures.

## TABLE 11-1    The Four Market Structures

| | MARKET STRUCTURE | | | |
| CHARACTERISTIC | PERFECT COMPETITION | MONOPOLISTIC COMPETITION | OLIGOPOLY | MONOPOLY |
| --- | --- | --- | --- | --- |
| Number of firms | Many | Many | Few | One |
| Type of product | Identical | Differentiated | Identical or differentiated | Unique |
| Ease of entry | High | High | Low | Entry blocked |
| Examples of industries | • Growing wheat<br>• Growing apples | • Clothing stores<br>• Restaurants | • Manufacturing computers<br>• Manufacturing automobiles | • First-class mail delivery<br>• Tap water |

# Perfectly Competitive Markets

Why are firms in a **perfectly competitive market** unable to control the prices of the goods they sell, and why are the owners of these firms unable to earn economic profit in the long run? We can begin our analysis by listing the three conditions that make a market perfectly competitive:

1. There must be many buyers and many firms, all of which are small relative to the market.
2. The products sold by all firms in the market must be identical.
3. There must be no barriers to new firms entering the market.

All three of these conditions hold in the market for organic apples. No single consumer or producer of organic apples buys or sells more than a tiny fraction of the total apple crop. The apples sold by each apple grower are identical, and there are no barriers to a new firm entering the organic apple market by purchasing land and planting apple trees. As we will see, it is the existence of many firms, all selling the same good, that keeps any single organic apple farmer from affecting the price of organic apples.

Although the market for organic apples meets the conditions for perfect competition, the markets for most goods and services do not. In particular, the second and third conditions are very restrictive. In most markets that have many buyers and sellers, firms do not sell identical products. For example, not all restaurant meals are the same, nor is all women's clothing the same. In Chapter 12, we will explore the common situation of monopolistic competition where many firms are selling similar but not identical products. In Chapters 13 and 14, we will analyze industries that are oligopolies or monopolies, where it is difficult for new firms to enter. In this chapter, we concentrate on perfectly competitive markets so we can use them as a benchmark to analyze how firms behave when facing the maximum possible competition.

## A Perfectly Competitive Firm Cannot Affect the Market Price

Prices in perfectly competitive markets are determined by the interaction of demand and supply. The actions of any single consumer or any single firm have no effect on the market price. Consumers and firms have to accept the market price if they want to buy and sell in a perfectly competitive market.

Because a firm in a perfectly competitive market is very small relative to the market and because it is selling exactly the same product as every other firm, it can sell as much as it wants without having to lower its price. But if a perfectly competitive firm tries to raise its price, it won't sell anything at all because consumers will switch to buying the product from the firm's competitors. Therefore, the firm will be a **price taker** and will have to charge the same price as every other firm in the market. Although we don't usually think of firms as being too small to affect the market price, consumers are often in the position of being price takers. For instance, suppose your local supermarket is selling bread for $1.50 per loaf. You can load up your shopping cart with 10 loaves of bread, and the supermarket will gladly sell them all to you for $1.50 per loaf. But if you go to the cashier and offer to buy the bread for $1.49 per loaf, he or she will not sell it to you at that price. As a buyer, you are too small relative to the bread market to have any effect on the equilibrium price. Whether you leave the supermarket and buy no bread or you buy 10 loaves, you are unable to change the market price of bread by even 1 cent.

The situation you face as a bread buyer is the same one a wheat farmer faces as a wheat seller. In 2009, roughly 167,000 farmers grew wheat in the United States. The market price of wheat is determined not by any individual wheat farmer but by the interaction in the wheat market of all the buyers and all the sellers. If any one wheat farmer has the best crop the farmer has ever had, or if any one wheat farmer stops growing wheat altogether, the market price of wheat will not be affected *because the market supply curve for wheat will not shift by enough to change the equilibrium price by even 1 cent.*

**11.1 LEARNING** OBJECTIVE

Explain what a perfectly competitive market is and why a perfect competitor faces a horizontal demand curve.

**Perfectly competitive market** A market that meets the conditions of (1) many buyers and sellers, (2) all firms selling identical products, and (3) no barriers to new firms entering the market.

**Price taker** A buyer or seller that is unable to affect the market price.

## Figure 11-1

**A Perfectly Competitive Firm Faces a Horizontal Demand Curve**

A firm in a perfectly competitive market is selling exactly the same product as many other firms. Therefore, it can sell as much as it wants at the current market price, but it cannot sell anything at all if it raises the price by even 1 cent. As a result, the demand curve for a perfectly competitive firm's output is a horizontal line. In the figure, whether the wheat farmer sells 6,000 bushels per year or 15,000 bushels has no effect on the market price of $4.

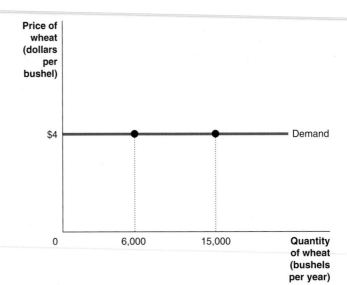

## The Demand Curve for the Output of a Perfectly Competitive Firm

Suppose Bill Parker grows wheat on a 250-acre farm in Washington state. Farmer Parker is selling wheat in a perfectly competitive market, so he is a price taker. Because he can sell as much wheat as he chooses at the market price—but can't sell any wheat at all at a higher price—the demand curve for his wheat has an unusual shape: It is horizontal, as shown in Figure 11-1. With a horizontal demand curve, Farmer Parker must accept the market price, which in this case is $4 per bushel. Whether Farmer Parker sells 6,000 bushels per year or 15,000 has no effect on the market price.

The demand curve for Farmer Parker's wheat is very different from the market demand curve for wheat. Panel (a) of Figure 11-2 shows the market for wheat. The demand curve in panel (a) is the *market demand curve for wheat* and has the normal downward slope we are familiar with from the market demand curves in Chapter 3. Panel (b) of Figure 11-2 shows the demand curve for Farmer Parker's wheat, which is a horizontal line. By viewing these graphs side by side, you can see that the price Farmer Parker receives for his wheat in panel (b) is determined by the interaction of all sellers and all

# Don't Let This Happen to **YOU!**

## Don't Confuse the Demand Curve for Farmer Parker's Wheat with the Market Demand Curve for Wheat

The demand curve for wheat has the normal downward-sloping shape. If the price of wheat goes up, the quantity of wheat demanded goes down, and if the price of wheat goes down, the quantity of wheat demanded goes up. But the demand curve for the output of a single wheat farmer is *not* downward sloping: It is a horizontal line. If an individual wheat farmer tries to increase the price he charges for his wheat, the quantity demanded falls to zero because buyers will purchase from one of the other 167,000 wheat farmers. But any one farmer can sell as much wheat as the farmer can produce without needing to cut the price. Both of these things are true because each wheat farmer is very small relative to the overall market for wheat.

When we draw graphs of the wheat market, we usually show the market equilibrium quantity in millions or billions of bushels. When we draw graphs of the demand for wheat produced by one farmer, we usually show the quantity produced in smaller units, such as thousands of bushels. It is important to remember this difference in scale when interpreting these graphs.

Finally, it is not just wheat farmers who have horizontal demand curves for their products; any firm in a perfectly competitive market faces a horizontal demand curve.

**YOUR TURN:** Test your understanding by doing related problem 1.6 on page 394 at the end of this chapter.

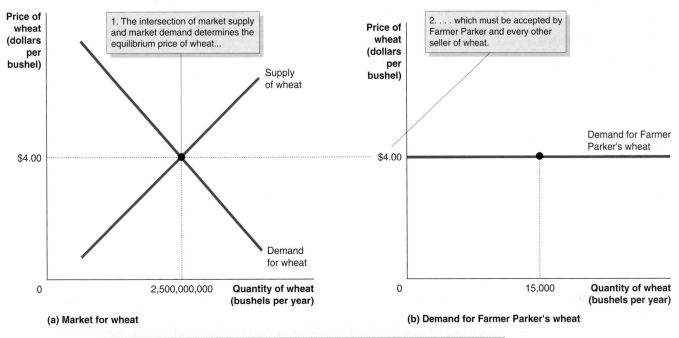

**Figure 11-2**    The Market Demand for Wheat versus the Demand for One Farmer's Wheat

In a perfectly competitive market, price is determined by the intersection of market demand and market supply. In panel (a), the demand and supply curves for wheat intersect at a price of $4 per bushel. An individual wheat farmer like Farmer Parker cannot affect the market price for wheat. Therefore, as panel (b) shows, the demand curve for Farmer Parker's wheat is a horizontal line. To understand this figure, it is important to notice that the scales on the horizontal axes in the two panels are very different. In panel (a), the equilibrium quantity of wheat is 2.5 *billion* bushels, and in panel (b), Farmer Parker is producing only 15,000 bushels of wheat.

buyers of wheat in the wheat market in panel (a). Keep in mind, however, that the scales on the horizontal axes in the two panels are very different. In panel (a), the equilibrium quantity of wheat is 2.5 *billion* bushels. In panel (b), Farmer Parker is producing only 15,000 bushels, or less than 0.001 percent of market output. We need to use different scales in the two panels so we can display both of them on one page. Keep in mind this key point: Farmer Parker's output of wheat is very small relative to the total market output.

# How a Firm Maximizes Profit in a Perfectly Competitive Market

We have seen that Farmer Parker cannot control the price of his wheat. In this situation, how does he decide how much wheat to produce? We assume that Farmer Parker's objective is to maximize profit. This is a reasonable assumption for most firms, most of the time. Remember that **profit** is the difference between total revenue (*TR*) and total cost (*TC*):

$$\text{Profit} = TR - TC.$$

**Profit** Total revenue minus total cost.

To maximize his profit, Farmer Parker should produce the quantity of wheat where the difference between the total revenue he receives and his total cost is as large as possible.

## Revenue for a Firm in a Perfectly Competitive Market

To understand how Farmer Parker maximizes profits, let's first consider his revenue. To keep the numbers simple, we will assume that he owns a very small farm and produces at most 10 bushels of wheat per year. Table 11-2 shows the revenue Farmer Parker will earn from selling various quantities of wheat if the market price for wheat is $4.

The third column in Table 11-2 shows that Farmer Parker's *total revenue* rises by $4 for every additional bushel he sells because he can sell as many bushels as he wants at the market price of $4 per bushel. The fourth and fifth columns in the table show Farmer Parker's *average revenue* and *marginal revenue* from selling wheat. His **average revenue** (**AR**) is his total revenue divided by the quantity of bushels he sells. For example, if he

**Average revenue** (**AR**) Total revenue divided by the quantity of the product sold.

TABLE 11-2

**Farmer Parker's Revenue from Wheat Farming**

| NUMBER OF BUSHELS (Q) | MARKET PRICE (PER BUSHEL) (P) | TOTAL REVENUE (TR) | AVERAGE REVENUE (AR) | MARGINAL REVENUE (MR) |
|:---:|:---:|:---:|:---:|:---:|
| 0 | $4 | $0 | — | — |
| 1 | 4 | 4 | $4 | $4 |
| 2 | 4 | 8 | 4 | 4 |
| 3 | 4 | 12 | 4 | 4 |
| 4 | 4 | 16 | 4 | 4 |
| 5 | 4 | 20 | 4 | 4 |
| 6 | 4 | 24 | 4 | 4 |
| 7 | 4 | 28 | 4 | 4 |
| 8 | 4 | 32 | 4 | 4 |
| 9 | 4 | 36 | 4 | 4 |
| 10 | 4 | 40 | 4 | 4 |

sells 5 bushels for a total of $20, his average revenue is $20/5 = $4. Notice that his average revenue is also equal to the market price of $4. In fact, for any level of output, a firm's average revenue is always equal to the market price. One way to see this is to note that total revenue equals price times quantity ($TR = P \times Q$), and average revenue equals total revenue divided by quantity ($AR = TR/Q$). So, $AR = TR/Q = (P \times Q)/Q = P$.

Farmer Parker's **marginal revenue (MR)** is the change in his total revenue from selling one more bushel:

**Marginal revenue (MR)** The change in total revenue from selling one more unit of a product.

$$\text{Marginal Revenue} = \frac{\text{Change in total revenue}}{\text{Change in quantity}}, \text{ or } MR = \frac{\Delta TR}{\Delta Q}.$$

Because for each additional bushel sold Farmer Parker always adds $4 to his total revenue, his marginal revenue is $4. Farmer Parker's marginal revenue is $4 per bushel because he is selling wheat in a perfectly competitive market and can sell as much as he wants at the market price. In fact, Farmer Parker's marginal revenue and average revenue are both equal to the market price. This is an important point: *For a firm in a perfectly competitive market, price is equal to both average revenue and marginal revenue.*

## Determining the Profit-Maximizing Level of Output

To determine how Farmer Parker can maximize profit, we have to consider his costs as well as his revenue. A wheat farmer has many costs, including the cost of seed and fertilizer, and the wages of farm workers. In Table 11-3, we bring together the revenue data from Table 11-2 with cost data for Farmer Parker's farm. Recall from Chapter 10 that a firm's *marginal cost* is the increase in total cost resulting from producing another unit of output.

We calculate profit in the fourth column by subtracting total cost in the third column from total revenue in the second column. The fourth column shows that as long as Farmer Parker produces between 2 and 8 bushels of wheat, he will earn a profit. His maximum profit is $7.50, which he will earn by producing 6 bushels of wheat. Because Farmer Parker wants to maximize his profits, we would expect him to produce 6 bushels of wheat. Producing more than 6 bushels reduces his profit. For example, if he produces 7 bushels of wheat, his profit will decline from $7.50 to $6.50. The values for marginal cost given in the last column of the table help us understand why Farmer Parker's profits will decline if he produces more than 6 bushels of wheat: After the sixth bushel of wheat, rising marginal cost causes Farmer Parker's profits to fall.

In fact, comparing the marginal cost and marginal revenue at each level of output is an alternative method of calculating Farmer Parker's profits. We illustrate the two methods of calculating profits in Figure 11-3. We show the total revenue and total cost approach in panel (a) and the marginal revenue and marginal cost approach in panel (b). Total revenue

| QUANTITY (BUSHELS) (Q) | TOTAL REVENUE (TR) | TOTAL COST (TC) | PROFIT (TR−TC) | MARGINAL REVENUE (MR) | MARGINAL COST (MC) |
|---|---|---|---|---|---|
| 0 | $0.00 | $2.00 | −$2.00 | — | — |
| 1 | 4.00 | 5.00 | −1.00 | $4.00 | $3.00 |
| 2 | 8.00 | 7.00 | 1.00 | 4.00 | 2.00 |
| 3 | 12.00 | 8.50 | 3.50 | 4.00 | 1.50 |
| 4 | 16.00 | 10.50 | 5.50 | 4.00 | 2.00 |
| 5 | 20.00 | 13.00 | 7.00 | 4.00 | 2.50 |
| 6 | 24.00 | 16.50 | 7.50 | 4.00 | 3.50 |
| 7 | 28.00 | 21.50 | 6.50 | 4.00 | 5.00 |
| 8 | 32.00 | 28.50 | 3.50 | 4.00 | 7.00 |
| 9 | 36.00 | 38.00 | −2.00 | 4.00 | 9.50 |
| 10 | 40.00 | 50.50 | −10.50 | 4.00 | 12.50 |

**TABLE 11-3**

**Farmer Parker's Profits from Wheat Farming**

is a straight line on the graph in panel (a) because total revenue increases at a constant rate of $4 for each additional bushel sold. Farmer Parker's profits are maximized when the vertical distance between the line representing total revenue and the total cost curve is as large as possible. Just as we saw in Table 11-3, this occurs at an output of 6 bushels.

The last two columns of Table 11-3 show the marginal revenue (*MR*) Farmer Parker receives from selling another bushel of wheat and his marginal cost (*MC*) of producing another bushel of wheat. Panel (b) of Figure 11-3 is a graph of Farmer Parker's marginal revenue and marginal cost. Because marginal revenue is always equal to $4, it is a horizontal line at the market price. We have already seen that the demand curve for a perfectly competitive firm is also a horizontal line at the market price. *Therefore, the*

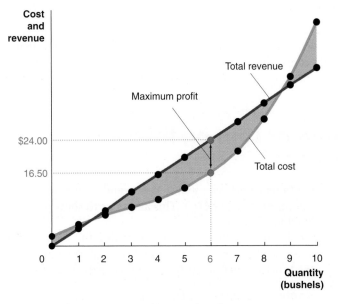

(a) Total revenue, total cost, and profit

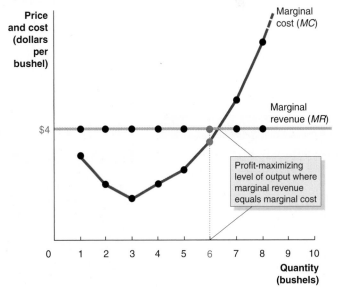

(b) Marginal revenue and marginal cost

**Figure 11-3** The Profit-Maximizing Level of Output

In panel (a), Farmer Parker maximizes his profit where the vertical distance between total revenue and total cost is the largest. This happens at an output of 6 bushels. Panel (b) shows that Farmer Parker's marginal revenue (*MR*) is equal to a constant $4 per bushel. Farmer Parker maximizes profits by producing wheat up to the point where the marginal revenue of the last bushel produced is equal to its marginal cost, or *MR* = *MC*.

In this case, at no level of output does marginal revenue exactly equal marginal cost. The closest Farmer Parker can come is to produce 6 bushels of wheat. He will not want to continue to produce once marginal cost is greater than marginal revenue because that would reduce his profits. Panels (a) and (b) show alternative ways of thinking about how Farmer Parker can determine the profit-maximizing quantity of wheat to produce.

*marginal revenue curve for a perfectly competitive firm is the same as its demand curve.* Farmer Parker's marginal cost of producing wheat first falls and then rises, following the usual pattern we discussed in Chapter 10.

We know from panel (a) that profit is at a maximum at 6 bushels of wheat. In panel (b), profit is also at a maximum at 6 bushels of wheat. To understand why profit is maximized at the level of output where marginal revenue equals marginal cost, remember a key economic principle that we discussed in Chapter 1: *Optimal decisions are made at the margin.* Firms use this principle to decide the quantity of a good to produce. For example, in deciding how much wheat to produce, Farmer Parker needs to compare the marginal revenue he earns from selling another bushel of wheat to the marginal cost of producing that bushel. The difference between the marginal revenue and the marginal cost is the additional profit (or loss) from producing one more bushel. As long as marginal revenue is greater than marginal cost, Farmer Parker's profits are increasing, and he will want to expand production. For example, he will not stop producing at 5 bushels of wheat because producing and selling the sixth bushel adds $4.00 to his revenue but only $3.50 to his cost, so his profit increases by $0.50. He wants to continue producing until the marginal revenue he receives from selling another bushel is equal to the marginal cost of producing it. At that level of output, he will make no *additional* profit by selling another bushel, so he will have maximized his profits.

By inspecting Table 11–3 on page 373, we can see that there is no level of output at which marginal revenue exactly equals marginal cost. The closest Farmer Parker can come is to produce 6 bushels of wheat. He will not want to produce additional wheat once marginal cost is greater than marginal revenue because that would reduce his profits. For example, the seventh bushel of wheat adds $5.00 to his cost but only $4.00 to his revenue, so producing the seventh bushel *reduces* his profit by $1.00.

From the information in Table 11-3 and Figure 11-3, we can draw the following conclusions:

1. The profit-maximizing level of output is where the difference between total revenue and total cost is the greatest.

2. The profit-maximizing level of output is also where marginal revenue equals marginal cost, or *MR = MC.*

Both of these conclusions are true for any firm, whether or not it is in a perfectly competitive industry. We can draw one other conclusion about profit maximization that is true only of firms in perfectly competitive industries: For a firm in a perfectly competitive industry, price is equal to marginal revenue, or *P = MR.* So, we can restate the *MR = MC* condition as *P = MC.*

**11.3 LEARNING** OBJECTIVE

Use graphs to show a firm's profit or loss.

# Illustrating Profit or Loss on the Cost Curve Graph

We have seen that profit is the difference between total revenue and total cost. We can also express profit in terms of *average total cost* (*ATC*). This allows us to show profit on the cost curve graph we developed in Chapter 10.

To begin, we need to work through several steps to determine the relationship between profit and average total cost. Because profit is equal to total revenue minus total cost (*TC*) and total revenue is price times quantity, we can write the following:

$$\text{Profit} = (P \times Q) - TC.$$

If we divide both sides of this equation by Q, we have:

$$\frac{\text{Profit}}{Q} = \frac{(P \times Q)}{Q} - \frac{TC}{Q},$$

or:

$$\frac{\text{Profit}}{Q} = P - ATC,$$

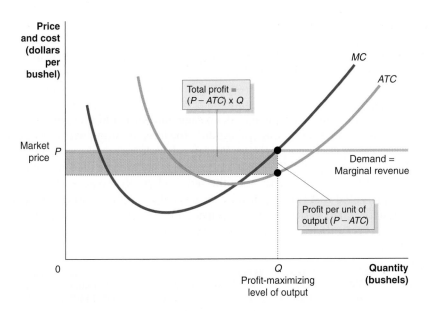

## Figure 11-4

**The Area of Maximum Profit**

A firm maximizes profit at the level of output at which marginal revenue equals marginal cost. The difference between price and average total cost equals profit per unit of output. Total profit equals profit per unit multiplied by the number of units produced. Total profit is represented by the area of the green-shaded rectangle, which has a height equal to $(P - ATC)$ and a width equal to $Q$.

because $TC/Q$ equals $ATC$. This equation tells us that profit per unit (or average profit) equals price minus average total cost. Finally, we obtain the equation for the relationship between total profit and average total cost by multiplying again by $Q$:

$$\text{Profit} = (P - ATC) \times Q.$$

This equation tells us that a firm's total profit is equal to the quantity produced multiplied by the difference between price and average total cost.

## Showing a Profit on the Graph

Figure 11-4 shows the relationship between a firm's average total cost and its marginal cost that we discussed in Chapter 10. In this figure, we also show the firm's marginal revenue curve (which is the same as its demand curve) and the area representing total profit. Using the relationship between profit and average total cost that we just determined, we can say that the area representing total profit has a height equal to $(P - ATC)$ and a base equal to $Q$. This area is shown by the green-shaded rectangle.

---

# Solved Problem | 11-3

## Determining Profit-Maximizing Price and Quantity

Suppose that Andy sells basketballs in the perfectly competitive basketball market. His output per day and his costs are as follows:

| OUTPUT PER DAY | TOTAL COST |
|---|---|
| 0 | $10.00 |
| 1 | 20.50 |
| 2 | 24.50 |
| 3 | 28.50 |
| 4 | 34.00 |
| 5 | 43.00 |
| 6 | 55.50 |
| 7 | 72.00 |
| 8 | 93.00 |
| 9 | 119.00 |

**a.** Suppose the current equilibrium price in the basketball market is $12.50. To maximize profit, how many basketballs will Andy produce, what price will he charge, and how much profit (or loss) will he make? Draw a graph to illustrate your answer. Your graph should be labeled clearly and should include Andy's demand, $ATC$, $AVC$, $MC$, and $MR$ curves; the price he is charging; the quantity he is producing; and the area representing his profit (or loss).

**b.** Suppose the equilibrium price of basketballs falls to $6.00. Now how many basketballs will Andy produce, what price will he charge, and how much profit (or loss) will he make? Draw a graph to illustrate this situation, using the instructions in question (a).

## SOLVING THE PROBLEM:

**Step 1:**  **Review the chapter material.** This problem is about using cost curve graphs to analyze perfectly competitive firms, so you may want to review the section "Illustrating Profit or Loss on the Cost Curve Graph," which begins on page 374.

**Step 2:**  **Calculate Andy's marginal cost, average total cost, and average variable cost.** To maximize profit, Andy will produce the level of output where marginal revenue is equal to marginal cost. We can calculate marginal cost from the information given in the table. We can also calculate average total cost and average variable cost in order to draw the required graph. Average total cost ($ATC$) equals total cost ($TC$) divided by the level of output ($Q$). Average variable cost ($AVC$) equals variable cost ($VC$) divided by output ($Q$). To calculate variable cost, recall that total cost equals variable cost plus fixed cost. When output equals zero, total cost equals fixed cost. In this case, fixed cost equals $10.00.

| OUTPUT PER DAY (Q) | TOTAL COST (TC) | FIXED COST (FC) | VARIABLE COST (VC) | AVERAGE TOTAL COST (ATC) | AVERAGE VARIABLE COST (AVC) | MARGINAL COST (MC) |
|---|---|---|---|---|---|---|
| 0 | $10.00 | $10.00 | $0.00 | — | — | — |
| 1 | 20.50 | 10.00 | 10.50 | $20.50 | $10.50 | $10.50 |
| 2 | 24.50 | 10.00 | 14.50 | 12.25 | 7.25 | 4.00 |
| 3 | 28.00 | 10.00 | 18.00 | 9.33 | 6.00 | 3.50 |
| 4 | 34.00 | 10.00 | 24.00 | 8.50 | 6.00 | 6.00 |
| 5 | 43.00 | 10.00 | 33.00 | 8.60 | 6.60 | 9.00 |
| 6 | 55.50 | 10.00 | 45.50 | 9.25 | 7.58 | 12.50 |
| 7 | 72.00 | 10.00 | 62.00 | 10.29 | 8.86 | 16.50 |
| 8 | 93.00 | 10.00 | 83.00 | 11.63 | 10.38 | 21.00 |
| 9 | 119.00 | 10.00 | 109.00 | 13.22 | 12.11 | 26.00 |

**Step 3:**  **Use the information from the table in step 2 to calculate how many basketballs Andy will produce, what price he will charge, and how much profit he will earn if the market price of basketballs is $12.50.** Andy's marginal revenue is equal to the market price of $12.50. Marginal revenue equals marginal cost when Andy produces 6 basketballs per day. So, Andy will produce 6 basketballs per day and charge a price of $12.50 per basketball. Andy's profits are equal to his total revenue minus his total costs. His total revenue equals the 6 basketballs he sells multiplied by the $12.50 price, or $75.00. So, his profits equal $75.00 − $55.50 = $19.50.

**Step 4:**  **Use the information from the table in step 2 to illustrate your answer to question (a) with a graph.**

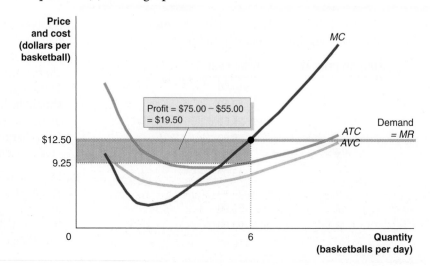

**Step 5:** **Calculate how many basketballs Andy will produce, what price he will charge, and how much profit he will earn when the market price of basketballs is $6.00.** Referring to the table in step 2, we can see that marginal revenue equals marginal cost when Andy produces 4 basketballs per day. He charges the market price of $6.00 per basketball. His total revenue is only $24.00, while his total costs are $34.00, so he will have a loss of $10.00. (Can we be sure that Andy will continue to produce even though he is operating at a loss? We answer this question in the next section.)

**Step 6:** **Illustrate your answer to question (b) with a graph.**

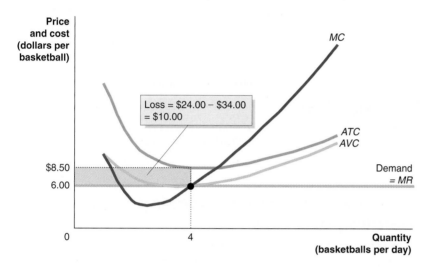

**YOUR TURN:** For more practice, do related problems 3.3 and 3.4 on pages 395–396 at the end of this chapter.

# Don't Let This Happen to **YOU!**

## Remember That Firms Maximize Their Total Profits, Not Their Profits per Unit

A student examines the following graph and argues, "I believe that a firm will want to produce at $Q_1$, not $Q_2$. At $Q_1$, the distance between price and average total cost is the greatest. Therefore, at $Q_1$, the firm will be maximizing its profits per unit." Briefly explain whether you agree with the student's argument.

The student's argument is incorrect because firms are interested in maximizing their *total* profits, not their profits per unit. We know that profits are not maximized at $Q_1$ because at that level of output, marginal revenue is greater than marginal cost. A firm can always increase its profits by producing any unit that adds more to its revenue than it does to its costs. Only when the firm has expanded production to $Q_2$ will it have produced every unit for which marginal revenue is greater than marginal cost. At that point, it will have maximized profit.

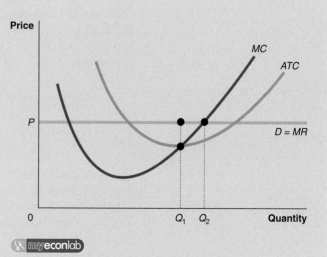

**YOUR TURN:** Test your understanding by doing related problem 3.5 on page 396 at the end of this chapter.

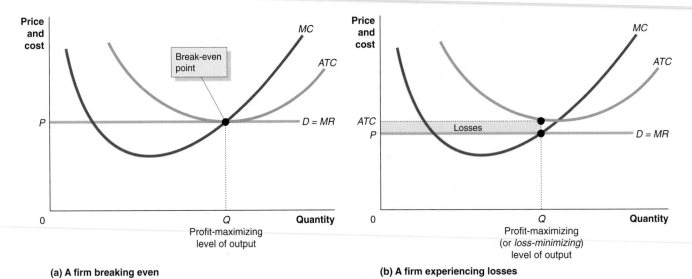

**(a) A firm breaking even**                    **(b) A firm experiencing losses**

Figure 11-5 | **A Firm Breaking Even and a Firm Experiencing Losses**

In panel (a), price equals average total cost, and the firm breaks even because its total revenue will be equal to its total cost. In this situation, the firm makes zero economic profit. In panel (b), price is below average total cost, and the firm experiences a loss.

The loss is represented by the area of the red-shaded rectangle, which has a height equal to ($ATC - P$) and a width equal to $Q$.

## Illustrating When a Firm Is Breaking Even or Operating at a Loss

We have already seen that to maximize profit, a firm produces the level of output where marginal revenue equals marginal cost. But will the firm actually make a profit at that level of output? It depends on the relationship of price to average total cost. There are three possibilities:

1. $P > ATC$, which means the firm makes a profit
2. $P = ATC$, which means the firm *breaks even* (its total cost equals its total revenue)
3. $P < ATC$, which means the firm experiences losses

Figure 11-4 on page 375 shows the first possibility, where the firm makes a profit. Panels (a) and (b) of Figure 11-5 show the situations where a firm breaks even or experiences losses. In panel (a) of Figure 11-5, at the level of output at which $MR = MC$, price is equal to average total cost. Therefore, total revenue is equal to total cost, and the firm will break even, making zero economic profit. In panel (b), at the level of output at which $MR = MC$, price is less than average total cost. Therefore, total revenue is less than total cost, and the firm has losses. In this case, maximizing profits amounts to *minimizing* losses.

Making
the
Connection

## Losing Money in the Medical Screening Industry

In a market system, a good or service becomes available to consumers only if an entrepreneur brings the product to market. Thousands of new businesses open every week in the United States. Each new business represents an entrepreneur risking his or her funds, trying to earn a profit by offering a good or service to consumers. Of course, there are no guarantees of success, and many new businesses experience losses rather than earn the profits their owners hoped for.

In the early 2000s, technological advance reduced the price of computed tomography (CT) scanning equipment. For years, doctors and hospitals have prescribed CT scans to diagnose patients showing symptoms of heart disease, cancer, and other disorders. The declining price of CT scanning equipment convinced many entrepreneurs that it would be profitable to offer preventive body scans to apparently healthy people. The idea was that the scans would provide early detection of diseases before the customers had begun experiencing symptoms. Unfortunately, the new firms offering this service ran into several difficulties: First, because the CT scan was a voluntary procedure, it was not covered under most medical insurance plans. Second, very few consumers used the service more than once, so there was almost no repeat business. Finally, as with any other medical test, some false positives occurred, where the scan appeared to detect a problem that did not actually exist. Negative publicity from people who had expensive additional—and unnecessary—medical procedures as a result of false-positive CT scans also hurt these new businesses.

As a result of these difficulties, the demand for CT scans was less than most of these entrepreneurs had expected, and the new businesses operated at a loss. For example, the owner of California HeartScan would have broken even if the market price had been $495 per heart scan, but he suffered losses because the actual market price was only $250. The following graphs show the owner's situation.

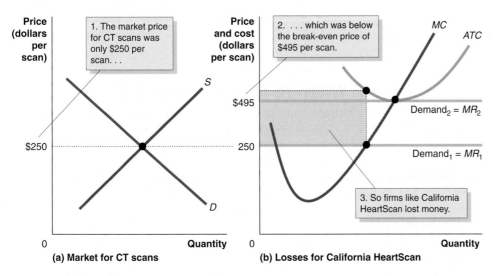

(a) Market for CT scans

1. The market price for CT scans was only $250 per scan...

$250

(b) Losses for California HeartScan

2. ... which was below the break-even price of $495 per scan.

MC

ATC

$495

250

Demand₂ = MR₂

Demand₁ = MR₁

3. So firms like California HeartScan lost money.

Why didn't California HeartScan and other medical clinics just raise the price to the level they needed to break even? We have already seen that any firm that tries to raise the price it charges above the market price loses customers to competing firms. By fall 2003, many scanning businesses began to close. Most of the entrepreneurs who had started these businesses lost their investments.

Source: Patricia Callahan, "Scanning for Trouble," *Wall Street Journal*, September 11, 2003, p. B1.

**YOUR TURN:** Test your understanding by doing related problem 3.8 on page 396 at the end of this chapter.

# Deciding Whether to Produce or to Shut Down in the Short Run

In panel (b) of Figure 11-5, we assumed that the firm would continue to produce, even though it was operating at a loss. In fact, in the short run, a firm experiencing losses has two choices:

1. Continue to produce
2. Stop production by shutting down temporarily

In many cases, a firm experiencing losses will consider stopping production temporarily. Even during a temporary shutdown, however, a firm must still pay its fixed costs. For example, if the firm has signed a lease for its building, the landlord will expect

**11.4 LEARNING** OBJECTIVE

Explain why firms may shut down temporarily.

to receive a monthly rent payment, even if the firm is not producing anything that month. Therefore, if a firm does not produce, it will suffer a loss equal to its fixed costs. This loss is the maximum the firm will accept. The firm will shut down if producing would cause it to lose an amount greater than its fixed costs.

A firm can reduce its loss below the amount of its total fixed cost by continuing to produce, provided that the total revenue it receives is greater than its variable cost. A firm can use the revenue over and above variable cost to cover part of its fixed cost. In this case, a firm will have a smaller loss by continuing to produce than if it shut down.

In analyzing the firm's decision to shut down, we are assuming that its fixed costs are *sunk costs*. Remember from Chapter 9 that a **sunk cost** is a cost that has already been paid and cannot be recovered. We assume, as is usually the case, that the firm cannot recover its fixed costs by shutting down. For example, if a farmer has taken out a loan to buy land, the farmer is legally required to make the monthly loan payment whether he grows any wheat that season or not. The farmer has to spend those funds and cannot get them back, *so the farmer should treat his sunk costs as irrelevant to his decision making.* For any firm, whether total revenue is greater or less than *variable costs* is the key to deciding whether to shut down. As long as a firm's total revenue is greater than its variable costs, it should continue to produce no matter how large or small its fixed costs are.

**Sunk cost** A cost that has already been paid and that cannot be recovered.

*Keeping a business open even when suffering losses can sometimes be the best decision for an entrepreneur in the short run.*

## Making the Connection | When to Close a Laundry

An article in the *Wall Street Journal* describes what happened to Robert Kjelgaard when he quit his job writing software code at Microsoft and bought a laundry by paying the previous owner $80,000. For this payment, he received 76 washers and dryers and the existing lease on the building. The lease had six years remaining and required a monthly payment of $3,300. Unfortunately, Mr. Kjelgaard had difficulty operating the laundry at a profit. His explicit costs were $4,000 per month more than his revenue.

He tried but failed to sell the laundry. As he told a reporter, "It's hard to sell a business that's losing money." He considered closing the laundry, but as a sole proprietor, he would be responsible for the remainder of the lease. At $3,300 per month for six years, he would be responsible for paying almost $200,000 out of his personal savings. Closing the laundry would still seem to be the better choice because his $3,300 per month in sunk costs were less than the $4,000 per month plus the opportunity cost of his time that he was losing from operating the laundry.

Mr. Kjelgaard finally decided to reorganize his business and hire a professional manager. This change allowed him to return to Microsoft and still reduce his losses to $2,000 per month. Because this amount was less than the $3,300 per month he would lose by shutting down, it made sense for him to continue to operate the laundry. But he was still suffering losses and, according to the article, his wife was "counting the days until the lease runs out."

Source: G. Pascal Zachary, "How a Success at Microsoft Washed Out at a Laundry," *Wall Street Journal*, May 30, 1995.

 **YOUR TURN:** Test your understanding by doing related problems 4.5 and 4.6 on page 397 at the end of this chapter.

---

One option not available to a firm with losses in a perfectly competitive market is to raise its price. If the firm did raise its price, it would lose all its customers, and its sales would drop to zero. For example, in a recent year, the price of wheat in the United States was $3.16 per bushel. At that price, the typical U.S. wheat farmer lost $9,500. At a price of about $4.25 per bushel, the typical wheat farmer would have broken even. But any wheat farmer who tried to raise his price to $4.25 per bushel would have seen his sales quickly disappear because buyers could purchase all the wheat they wanted at $3.16 per bushel from the thousands of other wheat farmers.

## The Supply Curve of a Firm in the Short Run

Remember that the supply curve for a firm tells us how many units of a product the firm is willing to sell at any given price. Notice that the marginal cost curve for a firm in a perfectly competitive market tells us the same thing. The firm will produce at the level of output where $MR = MC$. Because price equals marginal revenue for a firm in a perfectly competitive market, the firm will produce where $P = MC$. For any given price, we can determine from the marginal cost curve the quantity of output the firm will supply. *Therefore, a perfectly competitive firm's marginal cost curve also is its supply curve.* There is, however, an important qualification to this. We have seen that if a firm is experiencing losses, it will shut down if its total revenue is less than its variable cost:

$$\text{Total Revenue} < \text{Variable Cost},$$

or, in symbols:

$$(P \times Q) < VC.$$

If we divide both sides by $Q$, we have the result that the firm will shut down if:

$$P < AVC.$$

If the price drops below average variable cost, the firm will have a smaller loss if it shuts down and produces no output. *So, the firm's marginal cost curve is its supply curve only for prices at or above average variable cost.* The red line in Figure 11-6 shows the supply curve for the firm in the short run.

Recall that the marginal cost curve intersects the average variable cost where the average variable cost curve is at its minimum point. Therefore, the firm's supply curve is its marginal cost curve above the minimum point of the average variable cost curve. For prices below minimum average variable cost ($P_{MIN}$), the firm will shut down, and its output will fall to zero. The minimum point on the average variable cost curve is called the **shutdown point** and occurs in Figure 11-6 at output level $Q_{SD}$.

## The Market Supply Curve in a Perfectly Competitive Industry

We saw in Chapter 9 that the market demand curve is determined by adding up the quantity demanded by each consumer in the market at each price. Similarly, the market supply curve is determined by adding up the quantity supplied by each firm in the market at each price. Each firm's marginal cost curve tells us how much that firm will supply at each price. So, the market supply curve can be derived directly from the marginal cost curves of the firms in the market. Panel (a) of Figure 11-7 shows the marginal cost curve

**Shutdown point** The minimum point on a firm's average variable cost curve; if the price falls below this point, the firm shuts down production in the short run.

## Figure 11-6

**The Firm's Short-Run Supply Curve**

The firm will produce at the level of output at which $MR = MC$. Because price equals marginal revenue for a firm in a perfectly competitive market, the firm will produce where $P = MC$. For any given price, we can determine the quantity of output the firm will supply from the marginal cost curve. In other words, the marginal cost curve is the firm's supply curve. But remember that the firm will shut down if the price falls below average variable cost. The marginal cost curve crosses the average variable cost at the firm's shutdown point. This point occurs at output level $Q_{SD}$. For prices below $P_{MIN}$, the supply curve is a vertical line along the price axis, which shows that the firm will supply zero output at those prices. The red line in the figure is the firm's short-run supply curve.

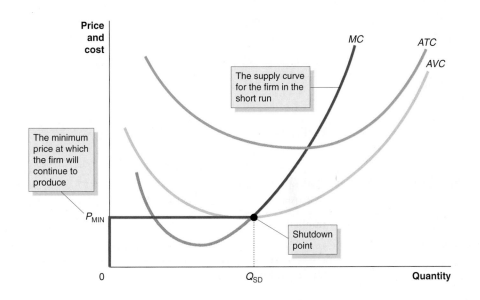

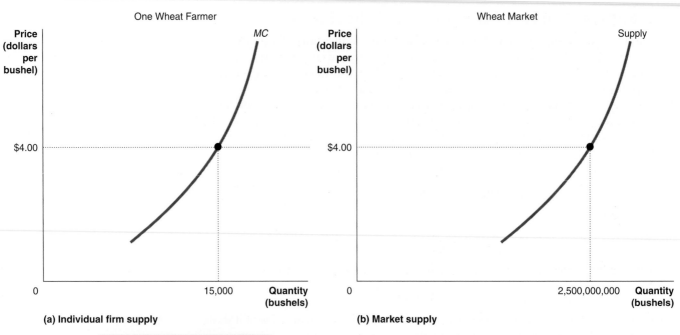

**(a) Individual firm supply**

**(b) Market supply**

## Figure 11-7   Firm Supply and Market Supply

We can derive the market supply curve by adding up the quantity that each firm in the market is willing to supply at each price. In panel (a), one wheat farmer is willing to supply 15,000 bushels of wheat at a price of $4 per bushel. If every wheat farmer supplies the same amount of wheat at this price and if there are 167,000 wheat farmers, the total amount of wheat supplied at a price of $4 will equal 15,000 bushels

per farmer × 167,000 farmers = 2.5 billion bushels of wheat. This is one point on the market supply curve for wheat shown in panel (b). We can find the other points on the market supply curve by determining how much wheat each farmer is willing to supply at each price.

for one wheat farmer. At a price of $4, this wheat farmer supplies 15,000 bushels of wheat. If every wheat farmer supplies the same amount of wheat at this price and if there are 167,000 wheat farmers, the total amount of wheat supplied at a price of $4 will be:

$$15,000 \text{ bushels per farmer} \times 167,000 \text{ farmers} = 2.5 \text{ billion bushels of wheat.}$$

Panel (b) shows a price of $4 and a quantity of 2.5 billion bushels as a point on the market supply curve for wheat. In reality, of course, not all wheat farms are alike. Some wheat farms supply more at the market price than the typical farm; other wheat farms supply less. The key point is that we can derive the market supply curve by adding up the quantity that each firm in the market is willing and able to supply at each price.

# Solved Problem | 11-4

Jill Ditto operates a photocopy store near a university campus. It is the end of May, and Jill is trying to decide whether she should remain open in June, when the student population at the university is at its lowest level of the year. She gathers the following information:

| Expected sales during June | 50,000 copies |
| Price | $0.10 per copy |

**Explicit Costs**

| | |
| --- | --- |
| Lease payment for rent of store | $1,200 |
| Lease payment for copy machines | $1,000 |
| Wages for two employees | $1,200 |
| Paper | $2,500 |

**Implicit Costs**

| | |
| --- | --- |
| Income Jill could earn managing another store | $3,000 |

Should Jill remain open for business in June?

## SOLVING THE PROBLEM:

**Step 1:** **Review the chapter material.** This problem is about whether a firm should shut down, so you may want to review the section "Deciding Whether to Produce or to Shut Down in the Short Run," which begins on page 379.

**Step 2:** **Should Jill Ditto continue producing?** Jill should remain open for business as long as the loss she makes is no greater than what she would lose if she shut down. So, we first need to calculate her loss if she shuts down. Assume that Jill would be able to manage another store during the month her store would be shut down. If Jill shuts down, she will have no revenue, and she will have the following fixed costs:

| | |
|---|---|
| Lease payment for rent of store | $1,200 |
| Lease payment for copy machines | $1,000 |
| Total | $2,200 |

**Step 3:** **Calculate Jill's loss if she operates during June.** Jill's loss will equal her total revenue minus her total cost:

| | |
|---|---|
| Total revenue: 50,000 × $0.10 per copy | $5,000 |
| Explicit cost | $5,900 |
| Implicit cost | $3,000 |
| Total costs | $8,900 |
| Loss | $3,900 |

Because she will lose less by shutting down than by operating, Jill should shut down her store in June.

**YOUR TURN:** For more practice, do related problem 4.7 on page 397 at the end of this chapter.

---

# "If Everyone Can Do It, You Can't Make Money at It": The Entry and Exit of Firms in the Long Run

**11.5 LEARNING** OBJECTIVE

Explain how entry and exit ensure that perfectly competitive firms earn zero economic profit in the long run.

In the long run, unless a firm can cover all its costs, it will shut down and exit the industry. In a market system, firms continually enter and exit industries. In this section, we will see how profits and losses provide signals to firms that lead to entry and exit.

## Economic Profit and the Entry or Exit Decision

To begin, let's look more closely at how economists characterize the profits earned by the owners of a firm. Suppose Anne Moreno decides to start her own business. After considering her interests and preparing a business plan, she decides to start an organic apple farm rather than open a restaurant or gift shop. After 10 years of effort, Anne has saved $100,000 and borrowed another $900,000 from a bank. With these funds, she has bought the land, apple trees, and farm equipment necessary to start her organic apple business. As we saw in Chapter 10, when someone invests her own funds in her firm, the opportunity cost to the firm is the return the funds would have earned in their best alternative use. If Farmer Moreno could have earned a 10 percent return on her $100,000 in savings in their best alternative use—which might have been, for example, to buy a small restaurant—then her apple business incurs a $10,000 opportunity cost. We can also think of this $10,000 as being the minimum amount that Farmer Moreno needs to earn on her $100,000 investment in her farm to remain in the industry in the long run.

Table 11-4 lists Farmer Moreno's costs. In addition to her explicit costs, we assume that she has two implicit costs: the $10,000 that represents the opportunity cost of the funds she invested in her farm and the $30,000 salary she could have earned managing

## TABLE 11-4

**Farmer Moreno's Costs per Year**

| EXPLICIT COSTS | |
| --- | --- |
| Water | $10,000 |
| Wages | $15,000 |
| Organic fertilizer | $10,000 |
| Electricity | $5,000 |
| Payment on bank loan | $45,000 |

| IMPLICIT COSTS | |
| --- | --- |
| Foregone salary | $30,000 |
| Opportunity cost of the $100,000 she has invested in her farm | $10,000 |
| **Total cost** | **$125,000** |

**Economic profit** A firm's revenues minus all its costs, implicit and explicit.

someone else's farm instead of her own. Her total costs are $125,000. If the market price of organic apples is $15 per box and Farmer Moreno sells 10,000 boxes, her total revenue will be $150,000, and her economic profit will be $25,000 (total revenue of $150,000 minus total costs of $125,000). Recall from Chapter 7 that **economic profit** equals a firm's revenues minus all its costs, implicit and explicit. So, Farmer Moreno is covering the $10,000 opportunity cost of the funds invested in her firm, and she is also earning an additional $25,000 in economic profit.

**Economic Profit Leads to Entry of New Firms** Unfortunately, Farmer Moreno is unlikely to earn an economic profit for very long. Suppose other apple farmers are just breaking even by growing apples using conventional methods. In that case, they will have an incentive to convert to organic growing methods so they can begin earning an economic profit. Remember that the more firms there are in an industry, the further to the right the market supply curve is. Panel (a) of Figure 11-8 shows that more farmers entering the market for organically grown apples will cause the market supply curve to shift to the right. Farmers will continue entering the market until the market supply curve has shifted from $S_1$ to $S_2$.

With the supply curve at $S_2$, the market price will have fallen to $10 per box. Panel (b) shows the effect on Farmer Moreno, whom we assume has the same costs as other organic apple farmers. As the market price falls from $15 to $10 per box, Farmer Moreno's demand curve shifts down, from $D_1$ to $D_2$. In the new equilibrium, Farmer Moreno is selling 8,000 boxes at a price of $10 per box. She and the other organic apple growers are no longer earning any economic profit. They are just breaking even, and the return on their investment is just covering the opportunity cost of these funds. New farmers will stop entering the market for organic apples because the rate of return is no better than they can earn elsewhere.

Will Farmer Moreno continue to grow organic apples even though she is just breaking even? She will because growing organic apples earns her as high a return on her investment as she could earn elsewhere. It may seem strange that new firms will continue to enter a market until all economic profits are eliminated and that established firms remain in a market despite not earning any economic profit. It only seems strange because we are used to thinking in terms of accounting profits, rather than *economic* profits. Remember that accounting rules generally require that only explicit costs be included on a firm's financial statements. The opportunity cost of the funds Farmer Moreno invested in her firm—$10,000—and her foregone salary—$30,000— are economic costs, but neither of them is an accounting cost. So, although an accountant would see Farmer Moreno as earning a profit of $40,000, an economist would see her as just breaking even. Farmer Moreno must pay attention to her accounting profit when preparing her financial statements and when paying her income tax. But because

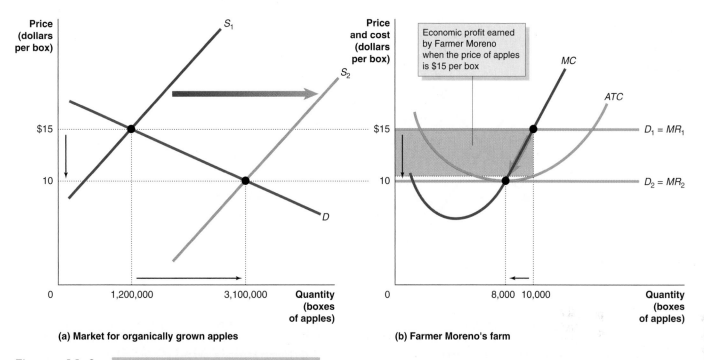

**Figure 11-8** | **The Effect of Entry on Economic Profits**

We assume that Farmer Moreno's costs are the same as the costs of other organic apple growers. Initially, she and other producers of organically grown apples are able to charge $15 per box and earn an economic profit. Farmer Moreno's economic profit is represented by the area of the green box. Panel (a) shows that as other farmers begin to grow apples using organic methods, the market supply curve shifts to the right, from $S_1$ to $S_2$, and the market price drops to $10 per box. Panel (b) shows that

the falling price causes Farmer Moreno's demand curve to shift down from $D_1$ to $D_2$, and she reduces her output from 10,000 boxes to 8,000. At the new market price of $10 per box, organic apple growers are just breaking even: Their total revenue is equal to their total cost, and their economic profit is zero. Notice the difference in scale between the graph in panel (a) and the graph in panel (b).

economic profit takes into account all her costs, it gives a truer indication of the financial health of her farm.

**Economic Losses Lead to Exit of Firms** Suppose some consumers decide that there are no important benefits from eating organically grown apples, and they switch back to buying conventionally grown apples. Panel (a) of Figure 11-9 shows that the demand curve for organically grown apples will shift to the left, from $D_1$ to $D_2$, and the market price will fall from $10 per box to $7. Panel (b) shows that as the price falls, a typical organic apple farmer, like Anne Moreno, will move down her marginal cost curve to a lower level of output. At the lower level of output and lower price, she will be suffering an **economic loss** because she will not cover all her costs. As long as price is above average variable cost, she will continue to produce in the short run, even when suffering losses. But in the long run, firms will exit an industry if they are unable to cover all their costs. In this case, some organic apple growers will switch back to growing apples using conventional methods.

Panel (c) of Figure 11-9 shows that firms exiting the organic apple industry will cause the market supply curve to shift to the left. Firms will continue to exit, and the supply curve will continue to shift to the left until the price has risen back to $10 and the market supply curve is at $S_2$. Panel (d) shows that when the price is back to $10, the remaining firms in the industry will be breaking even.

**Economic loss** The situation in which a firm's total revenue is less than its total cost, including all implicit costs.

## Long-Run Equilibrium in a Perfectly Competitive Market

We have seen that economic profits attract firms to enter an industry. The entry of firms forces down the market price until the typical firm is breaking even. Economic losses cause firms to exit an industry. The exit of firms forces up the equilibrium market price until the typical firm is breaking even. This process of entry and exit results

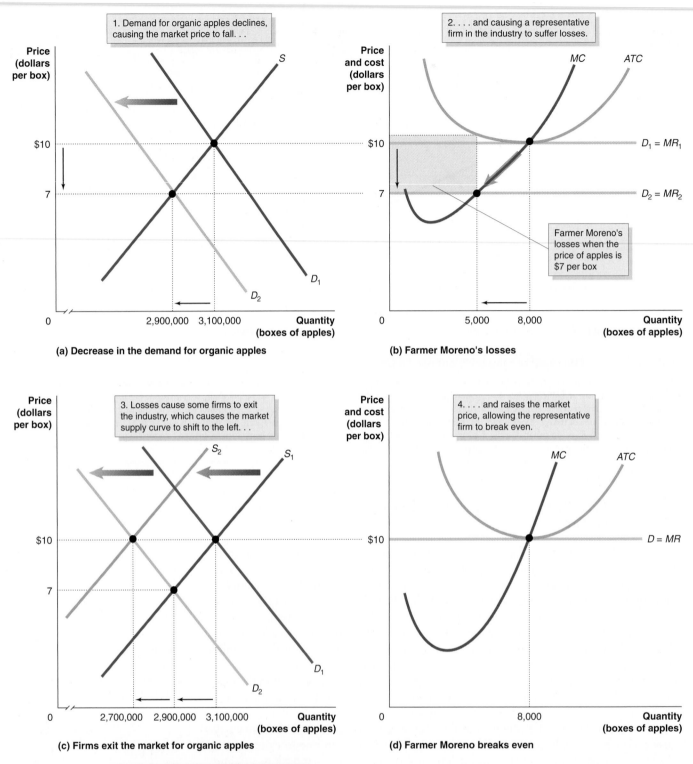

(a) Decrease in the demand for organic apples

(b) Farmer Moreno's losses

(c) Firms exit the market for organic apples

(d) Farmer Moreno breaks even

## Figure 11-9  The Effect of Exit on Economic Losses

When the price of apples is $10 per box, Farmer Moreno and other producers of organically grown apples are breaking even. A total quantity of 3,100,000 boxes is sold in the market. Farmer Moreno sells 8,000 boxes. Panel (a) shows a decline in the demand for organically grown apples from $D_1$ to $D_2$ that reduces the market price to $7 per box. Panel (b) shows that the falling price causes Farmer Moreno's demand curve to shift down from $D_1$ to $D_2$ and her output to fall from 8,000 to 5,000 boxes. At a market price of $7 per box, farmers have economic losses, represented by the area of the red box. As a result, some farmers will exit the market, which shifts the market supply curve to the left. Panel (c) shows that exit continues until the supply curve has shifted from $S_1$ to $S_2$ and the market price has risen from $7 back to $10. Panel (d) shows that with the price back at $10, Farmer Moreno will break even. In the new market equilibrium, total production of organic apples has fallen from 3,100,000 to 2,700,000 boxes.

in *long-run competitive equilibrium*. In **long-run competitive equilibrium**, entry and exit have resulted in the typical firm breaking even. We saw in Chapter 10 that in the long run firms can also vary their scale by becoming larger or smaller. The *long-run average cost curve* shows the lowest cost at which a firm is able to produce a given quantity of output in the long run. So, we would expect that in the long run, competition drives the market price to the minimum point on the typical firm's long-run average cost curve.

**Long-run competitive equilibrium** The situation in which the entry and exit of firms has resulted in the typical firm breaking even.

The long run in the organic apple market is three to four years, which is the amount of time it takes farmers to convert from conventional growing methods to organic growing methods. As discussed at the beginning of this chapter, only during the years from 1997 to 2001 was it possible for organic apple farmers to earn economic profits. By 2002, the entry of new firms had eliminated economic profits in the industry.

Firms in perfectly competitive markets are in a constant struggle to stay one step ahead of their competitors. They are always looking for new ways to provide a product, such as growing apples organically. It is possible for firms to find ways to earn an economic profit for a while, but to repeat the quote from a Yakima Valley organic apple farmer at the beginning of this chapter, "It's like anything else in agriculture. If people see an economic opportunity, usually it only lasts for a few years." This observation is not restricted to agriculture. In any perfectly competitive market, an opportunity to make economic profits never lasts long. As Sharon Oster, an economist at Yale University, has put it, "If everyone can do it, you can't make money at it."

## The Long-Run Supply Curve in a Perfectly Competitive Market

If the typical organic apple grower breaks even at a price of $10 per box, in the long run, the market price will always return to this level. If an increase in demand causes the market price to rise above $10, farmers will be earning economic profits. These profits will attract additional farmers into the market, and the market supply curve will shift to the right until the price is back to $10. Panel (a) in Figure 11-10 illustrates the long-run effect of an increase in demand. An increase in demand from $D_1$ to $D_2$ causes the market price to temporarily rise from $10 per box to $15. At this price, farmers are making economic profits growing organic apples, but these profits attract entry of new farmers' organic apples. The result is an increase in supply from $S_1$ to $S_2$, which forces the price back down to $10 per box and eliminates the economic profits.

Similarly, if a decrease in demand causes the market price to fall below $10, farmers will experience economic losses. These losses will cause some farmers to exit the market, the supply curve will shift to the left, and the price will return to $10. Panel (b) in Figure 11-10 illustrates the long-run effect of a decrease in demand. A decrease in demand from $D_1$ to $D_2$ causes the market price to fall temporarily from $10 per box to $7. At this price, farmers are suffering economic losses growing organic apples, but these losses cause some farmers to exit the market for organic apples. The result is a decrease in supply from $S_1$ to $S_2$, which forces the price back up to $10 per box and eliminates the losses.

The **long-run supply curve** shows the relationship in the long run between market price and the quantity supplied. In the long run, the price in the organic apple market will be $10 per box, no matter how many boxes of apples are produced. So, as Figure 11-10 shows, the long-run supply curve ($S_{LR}$) for organic apples is a horizontal line at a price of $10. Remember that the reason the price returns to $10 in the long run is that this is the price at which the typical firm in the industry just breaks even. The typical firm breaks even at this price because it is at the minimum point on the firm's average total cost curve. We can draw the important conclusion that *in the long run, a perfectly competitive market will supply whatever amount of a good consumers demand at a price determined by the minimum point on the typical firm's average total cost curve.*

**Long-run supply curve** A curve that shows the relationship in the long run between market price and the quantity supplied.

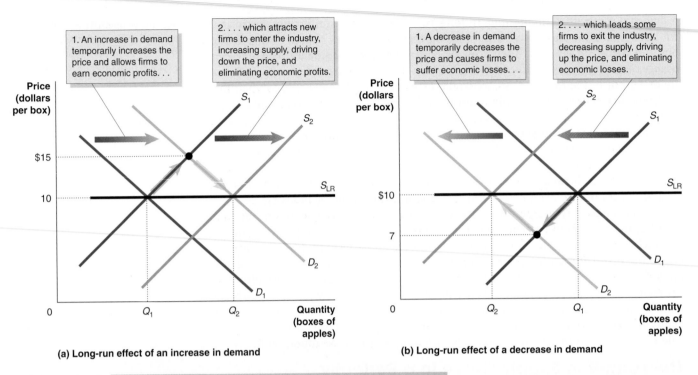

| 1. An increase in demand temporarily increases the price and allows firms to earn economic profits. . . | 2. . . . which attracts new firms to enter the industry, increasing supply, driving down the price, and eliminating economic profits. | 1. A decrease in demand temporarily decreases the price and causes firms to suffer economic losses. . . | 2. . . . which leads some firms to exit the industry, decreasing supply, driving up the price, and eliminating economic losses. |

**(a) Long-run effect of an increase in demand**          **(b) Long-run effect of a decrease in demand**

## Figure 11-10   The Long-Run Supply Curve in a Perfectly Competitive Industry

Panel (a) shows that an increase in demand for organic apples will lead to a temporary increase in price from $10 to $15 per box, as the market demand curve shifts to the right, from $D_1$ to $D_2$. The entry of new firms shifts the market supply curve to the right, from $S_1$ to $S_2$, which will cause the price to fall back to its long-run level of $10. Panel (b) shows that a decrease in demand will lead to a temporary decrease in price

from $10 to $7 per box, as the market demand curve shifts to the left, from $D_1$ to $D_2$. The exit of firms shifts the market supply curve to the left, from $S_1$ to $S_2$, which causes the price to rise back to its long-run level of $10. The long-run supply curve ($S_{LR}$) shows the relationship between market price and the quantity supplied in the long run. In this case, the long-run supply curve is a horizontal line.

Because the position of the long-run supply curve is determined by the minimum point on the typical firm's average total cost curve, anything that raises or lowers the costs of the typical firm in the long run will cause the long-run supply curve to shift. For example, if a disease infects apple trees and the costs of treating the disease adds $2 per box to the cost of producing apples, the long-run supply curve will shift up by $2.

**Making the Connection**

## Easy Entry Makes the Long Run Pretty Short in the Apple iPhone Apps Store

*Economic profits are rapidly competed away in the iPhone apps store.*

Apple introduced the first version of the iPhone in June 2007. Although popular, the original iPhone had some drawbacks, including a slow connection to the Internet and an inability to run any applications except those written by Apple. The iPhone 3G, released in July 2008, could connect to the Internet more quickly and easily, had a faster processor, and had a larger capacity. But perhaps most importantly, with the release of the iPhone 3G, Apple announced that a section of its immensely popular iTunes music and video store would be devoted to applications (or "apps") for the iPhone. Independent software programmers would write these iPhone apps. Apple would approve the apps and make them available in the iTunes app store in exchange for receiving 30 percent of the purchase price. Major software companies, as well as individuals writing their first software programs, have posted games, calendars, dictionaries, and many other types of apps to the iTunes store.

Apple sold more than 3 million iPhones within a month of launching the iPhone 3G. Demand for apps from the iTunes store soared along with sales of the iPhone. Ethan Nicholas, who in August 2008 was a programmer at Sun Microsystems but had never written a game before, decided to teach himself the coding language used in iPhone apps. His game, iShoot, with an initial price of $4.99, was a great success. Within five months, enough people had downloaded iShoot to earn Nicholas $800,000.

But could Nicholas's success last? As we have seen, when firms earn economic profits in a market, other firms have a strong economic incentive to enter that market. This is exactly what happened with iPhone apps, and by April 2009, more than 25,000 apps were available in the iTunes store. The cost of entering this market was very small. Anyone with the programming skills and the available time could write an app and have it posted in the store. As a result of this enhanced competition, the ability to get rich quick with a killer app was quickly fading. As an article in the *New York Times* put it: "The chances of hitting the iPhone jackpot keep getting slimmer: the Apple store is already crowded with look-alike games . . . and fresh inventory keeps arriving daily. Many of the simple but clever concepts that sell briskly . . . are already taken."

To try to maintain sales, Ethan Nicholas was forced to drop the price of iShoot from $4.99 in October 2008 to $2.99 in April 2009 and to $1.99 in May 2009. But his profits from the game continued to decline. In a competitive market, earning an economic profit in the long run is extremely difficult. And the ease of entering the market for iPhone apps has made the long run pretty short.

Sources: Jenna Wortham, "The iPhone Gold Rush," *New York Times*, April 5, 2009; and Bruce X. Chen, "Coder's Half-Million-Dollar Baby Proves iPhone Gold Rush Is Still On," wired.com, February 12, 2009.

**YOUR TURN:** Test your understanding by doing related problem 6.4 on page 399 at the end of this chapter.

## Increasing-Cost and Decreasing-Cost Industries

Any industry in which the typical firm's average costs do not change as the industry expands production will have a horizontal long-run supply curve, like the one in Figure 11-10. Industries, like the apple industry, where this holds true are called *constant-cost industries*. It's possible, however, for the typical firm's average costs to change as an industry expands.

For example, if an input used in producing a good is available in only limited quantities, the cost of the input will rise as the industry expands. If only a limited amount of land is available on which to grow the grapes to make a certain variety of wine, an increase in demand for wine made from these grapes will result in competition for the land and will drive up its price. As a result, more of the wine will be produced in the long run only if the price rises to cover the higher average costs of the typical firm. In this case, the long-run supply curve will slope upward. Industries with upward-sloping long-run supply curves are called *increasing-cost industries*.

Finally, in some cases, the typical firm's costs may fall as the industry expands. Suppose that someone invents a new microwave that uses as an input a specialized memory chip that is currently produced only in small quantities. If demand for the microwave increases, firms that produce microwaves will increase their orders for the memory chip. We saw in Chapter 10 that if there are economies of scale in producing a good, its average cost will decline as output increases. If there are economies of scale in producing this memory chip, the average cost of producing it will fall, and competition will result in its price falling as well. This price decline, in turn, will lower the average cost of producing the new microwave. In the long run, competition will force the price of the microwave to fall to the level of the new lower average cost of the typical firm. In this case, the long-run supply curve will slope downward. Industries with downward-sloping long-run supply curves are called *decreasing-cost industries*.

**11.6 LEARNING** OBJECTIVE

Explain how perfect
competition leads to
economic efficiency.

# Perfect Competition and Efficiency

Notice how powerful consumers are in a market system. If consumers want more organic apples, the market will supply them. This happens not because a government bureaucrat in Washington, DC, or an official in an apple growers' association gives orders. The additional apples are produced because an increase in demand results in higher prices and a higher rate of return on investments in organic growing techniques. Apple growers, trying to get the highest possible return on their investment, begin to switch from using conventional growing methods to using organic growing methods. If consumers lose their taste for organic apples and demand falls, the process works in reverse.

## Productive Efficiency

**Productive efficiency** The situation in which a good or service is produced at the lowest possible cost.

In the market system, consumers get as many apples as they want, produced at the lowest average cost possible. The forces of competition will drive the market price to the minimum average cost of the typical firm. **Productive efficiency** refers to the situation in which a good or service is produced at the lowest possible cost. As we have seen, perfect competition results in productive efficiency.

The managers of every firm strive to earn an economic profit by reducing costs. But in a perfectly competitive market, other firms quickly copy ways of reducing costs, so that in the long run, only the consumer benefits from cost reductions.

## Allocative Efficiency

Not only do perfectly competitive firms produce goods and services at the lowest possible cost, they also produce the goods and services that consumers value most. Firms will produce a good up to the point where the marginal cost of producing another unit is equal to the marginal benefit consumers receive from consuming that unit. In other words, firms will supply all those goods that provide consumers with a marginal benefit at least as great as the marginal cost of producing them. We know this is true because:

1. The price of a good represents the marginal benefit consumers receive from consuming the last unit of the good sold.
2. Perfectly competitive firms produce up to the point where the price of the good equals the marginal cost of producing the last unit.
3. Therefore, firms produce up to the point where the last unit provides a marginal benefit to consumers equal to the marginal cost of producing it.

**Allocative efficiency** A state of the economy in which production represents consumer preferences; in particular, every good or service is produced up to the point where the last unit provides a marginal benefit to consumers equal to the marginal cost of producing it.

These statements are another way of saying that entrepreneurs in a market system efficiently *allocate* labor, machinery, and other inputs to produce the goods and services that best satisfy consumer wants. In this sense, perfect competition achieves **allocative efficiency**. As we will explore in the next few chapters, many goods and services sold in the U.S. economy are not produced in perfectly competitive markets. Nevertheless, productive efficiency and allocative efficiency are useful benchmarks against which to compare the actual performance of the economy.

▶ Continued from page 367

## Economics in YOUR LIFE!

At the beginning of the chapter, we asked you to think about why you can charge only a relatively low price for performing services such as babysitting or lawn mowing. In the chapter, we saw that firms selling products in competitive markets can't charge prices higher than those being charged by competing firms. The market for babysitting and lawn mowing is very competitive. In most neighborhoods, there are many teenagers willing to supply these services. The price you can charge for babysitting may not be worth your while at age 20 but is enough to cover the opportunity cost of a 14-year-old eager to enter the market. (Or, as we put it in Table 11-1 on page 368, the ease of entry into babysitting and lawn mowing is high.) So, in your career as a teenage entrepreneur, you may have become familiar with one of the lessons of this chapter: A firm in a competitive market has no control over price.

## Conclusion

The competitive forces of the market impose relentless pressure on firms to produce new and better goods and services at the lowest possible cost. Firms that fail to adequately anticipate changes in consumer tastes or that fail to adopt the latest and most efficient technology do not survive in the long run. In the nineteenth century, the biologist Charles Darwin developed a theory of evolution based on the idea of the "survival of the fittest." Only those plants and animals that are best able to adapt to the demands of their environment are able to survive. Darwin first realized the important role that the struggle for existence plays in the natural world after reading early nineteenth-century economists' descriptions of the role it plays in the economic world. Just as "survival of the fittest" is the rule in nature, so it is in the economic world.

At the start of this chapter, we saw that there are four market structures: perfect competition, monopolistic competition, oligopoly, and monopoly. Now that we have studied perfect competition, in the following chapters we move on to the other three market structures. Before turning to those chapters, read *An Inside Look at Policy* on the next page for a discussion of the costs of having a product certified as organic.

## >> It Isn't Easy—or Cheap— to Be Green

WALL STREET JOURNAL

## As Eco-Seals Proliferate, So Do Doubts

. . . "If you want green certification bad enough, you can get it," says Mr. Owsley . . .

(a) Some label programs . . . require independent verification of product manufacturers' green claims. But many others don't . . .

## The Organic-Food Model

. . . [The] government now sets labeling and certification standards. But with food, it took decades . . . before the federal government came up with standards . . . acceptable to the myriad interested parties . . .

(b) "To date, there is no universal standard on this, and we are trying to make sense of it," says Yalmaz Siddiqui, director of environmental strategy for Office Depot.

At the heart of the dilemma: What does it really mean to be green? Is having some recycled content enough . . . is something biodegradable still green if it travels a thousand miles to reach shelves? And if a green product doesn't perform as well as its nongreen peers, is it really preferable?

Equally important: . . . Who, if anyone, should ensure green claims are valid? A soon-to-be-released study of more than 3,900 consumer products sold . . . in the U.S., Canada, the U.K. and Australia found that in every

product category, there was "green-washing"—ranging from outright lying about green claims to simply providing no proof . . .

## Rules of the Game

"What it tells me is that it's . . . understandable why consumers are so confused . . ." says Scot Case, executive director of the EcoLogo program, which requires independent auditing of the products it certifies. . . . "consumers are being duped . . . while the truly legitimate labels are getting lost amidst the green fog."

The U.S. Federal Trade Commission can take action against unfair or deceptive marketing practices. . . . But the agency's police role is often retroactive . . .

Because . . . a national imprint could dramatically affect the marketplace, groups representing pesticide and other chemical makers already are on alert. "If there are not parameters based on sound science, a lot of things could have unintended consequences," says Joe Acker, chief executive of the Society of Chemical Manufacturers and Affiliates . . . ". . . you could end up replacing products in the marketplace that have a long history of efficacy with things that don't."

## Consumer Confidence

(c) For now, bolstering consumer confidence is at the forefront of lawmakers' and retailers' labeling efforts . . . for example, Mr. Case of the EcoLogo program bought a refrigerator made

by LG Electronics Inc. that bore the Energy Star seal. That meant it was supposed to consume at least 20% less energy than required by federal standards.

Says Mr. Case: "I plug it in, and I feel wonderful because it's going to save me money and reduce my impact on global warming."

However, in February of this year, he received a letter saying his fridge didn't actually qualify for Energy Star status because LG hadn't adhered precisely to the test standards required by the U.S. Department of Energy. Notably, appliance manufacturers currently "self-certify" that they have met Energy Star test requirements . . . That may change.

Whatever shape green labeling takes in the future, cost will remain a central issue. The EcoLogo program . . . charges a minimum of $1,200 to $1,500 for initial auditing of green claims and an annual license fee . . . (ranging from $1,200 . . .) to use its logo. Mr. Case . . . acknowledges the burden it places on small firms. "For big companies," he says, "that's peanuts; for small ones, it's significant."

Source: Gwendolyn Bounds, "As Eco-Seals Proliferate, So Do Doubts," *Wall Street Journal*, April 2, 2009, p. D1.

## Key Points in the Article

This article describes the difficulty of labeling products as "organic" and "eco-friendly." Many consumers want to buy products that have these characteristics, and firms have an incentive to acquire "eco-labels" in order to appeal to these consumers. But some firms have resorted to claiming their products are environmentally friendly without independent verification by either private groups or the federal government. Consumers can't trust the labels, so they have called for the government to set certification standards—similar to those developed for organic food—for a wide variety of products. But verifying the claims firms make is costly. The costs of certification and audit fees place a greater burden on small firms than large firms.

## Analyzing the News

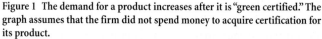 The growth of green marketing has led many firms to seek certification that their products are environmentally friendly. Suppose consumers' demand for "green" dish detergent increases. The market demand curve will shift to the right, and the equilibrium price will rise. Figure 1 shows the impact of the increase in demand for green dish detergent sold by a representative firm. The firm is initially able to charge only the original price, $P_1$, and earns no

economic profit. The increase in demand for green dish detergent allows the firm to charge the new higher market price, $P_2$, and earn an economic profit shown by the shaded area. Figure 1 assumes that firms pay no cost to obtain a certification that dish detergent is green. The article notes that some private groups do not require independent verification of manufacturers' claims. This lack of verification has led to confusion among consumers and calls by some for the federal government to establish certification standards.

**b** There is a lack of consensus about what it means to be green. The production of a good with recycled content or even the production of a biodegradable good may still result in environmental damage. Some "green" products may not perform as well as other products that are not as eco-friendly. Firms' green claims may also be exaggerated. There is evidence that some firms engage in "green-washing"—making claims that may be untrue, or at least are unproven.

**c** In practice, the acquisition of "eco-friendly" or "green" labels is costly. One firm that audits whether the green claims for a product are accurate charges a minimum of $1,200 for an initial audit and an additional annual fee for its services. These costs place a greater burden on small firms than large firms. Figure 2 shows

the case where firms have their costs increase by having their dish detergent certified as green. Figure 2 illustrates the situation where an annual certification fee shifts the firm's marginal and average cost curves up from $MC_1$ and $ATC_1$ to $MC_2$ and $ATC_2$ by just enough to eliminate the profit the firm would have earned as a result of the increase in demand if its costs had not increased. In reality, the increased costs from having a product certified as green may still allow the firm to make an economic profit, at least in the short run.

## Thinking Critically
### *About Policy*

1. Many consumers favor enacting federal "green certification" standards for a variety of products, similar to the standards the USDA established for organic food. How would the establishment of federal standards benefit consumers?

2. The article notes, "Whatever shape green labeling takes . . . cost will remain a central issue." Green labeling costs are incurred by firms that pay to have their products evaluated by a firm or an agency that can verify the products are "eco-friendly." Is it possible that the costs of certification would make consumers worse off than they would be without certification? Briefly explain.

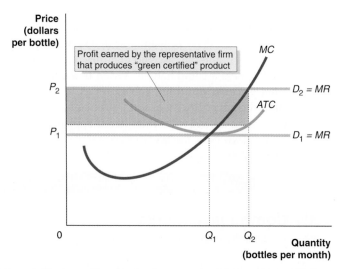

**Figure 1** The demand for a product increases after it is "green certified." The graph assumes that the firm did not spend money to acquire certification for its product.

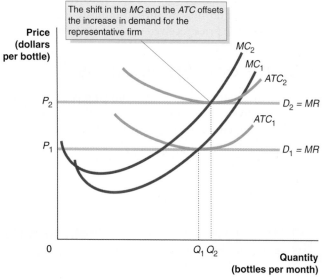

**Figure 2** The demand for a product increases after it is "green certified." The marginal cost and average total cost curves shift up due to the cost of certification.

# Key Terms

Allocative efficiency, p. 390

Average revenue (*AR*), p. 371

Economic loss, p. 385

Economic profit, p. 384

Long-run competitive equilibrium, p. 387

Long-run supply curve, p. 387

Marginal revenue (*MR*), p. 372

Perfectly competitive market, p. 369

Price taker, p. 369

Productive efficiency, p. 390

Profit, p. 371

Shutdown point, p. 381

Sunk cost, p. 380

---

 **Perfectly Competitive Markets, pages 369–371**

LEARNING OBJECTIVE: Explain what a perfectly competitive market is and why a perfect competitor faces a horizontal demand curve.

## Summary

A **perfectly competitive market** must have many buyers and sellers, firms must be producing identical products, and there must be no barriers to entry of new firms. The demand curve for a good or service produced in a perfectly competitive market is downward sloping, but the demand curve for the output of one firm in a perfectly competitive market is a horizontal line at the market price. Firms in perfectly competitive markets are **price takers** and see their sales drop to zero if they attempt to charge more than the market price.

 Visit **www.myeconlab.com** to complete these exercises online and get instant feedback.

## Review Questions

1.1 What are the three conditions for a market to be perfectly competitive?

1.2 What is a price taker? When are firms likely to be price takers?

1.3 Draw a graph showing the market demand and supply for corn and the demand for the corn produced by one corn farmer. Be sure to indicate the market price and the price received by the corn farmer.

## Problems and Applications

1.4 Explain whether each of the following is a perfectly competitive market. For each market that is not perfectly competitive, explain why it is not.
   a. Corn farming
   b. Retail bookselling
   c. Automobile manufacturing
   d. New home construction

1.5 Why are consumers usually price takers when they buy most goods and services, while relatively few firms are price takers?

1.6 (Related to the *Don't Let This Happen to You!* on page 370) Explain whether you agree or disagree with the following remark:

> According to the model of perfectly competitive markets, the demand for wheat should be a horizontal line. But this can't be true: When the price of wheat rises, the quantity of wheat demanded falls, and when the price of wheat falls, the quantity of wheat demanded rises. Therefore, the demand for wheat is not a horizontal line.

1.7 The financial writer Andrew Tobias described an incident that occurred when he was a student at the Harvard Business School: Each student in the class was given large amounts of information about a particular firm and asked to determine a pricing strategy for the firm. Most of the students spent hours preparing their answers and came to class carrying many sheets of paper with their calculations. Tobias came up with the correct answer after just a few minutes and without having made any calculations. When his professor called on him in class for an answer, Tobias stated, "The case said the XYZ Company was in a very competitive industry . . . and the case said that the company had all the business it could handle." Given this information, what price do you think Tobias argued the company should charge? Briefly explain. (Tobias says the class greeted his answer with "thunderous applause.")

Source: Andrew Tobias, *The Only Investment Guide You'll Ever Need*, San Diego: Harcourt, 2005, pp. 6–8.

**>> End Learning Objective 11.1**

---

 **How a Firm Maximizes Profit in a Perfectly Competitive Market, pages 371–374**

LEARNING OBJECTIVE: Explain how a firm maximizes profit in a perfectly competitive market.

## Summary

**Profit** is the difference between total revenue (*TR*) and total cost (*TC*). **Average revenue** (*AR*) is total revenue divided by the quantity of the product sold. A firm maximizes profit by producing the level of output where the difference between revenue and cost is the greatest. This is the same level of output where marginal revenue is equal to marginal cost. **Marginal revenue** (*MR*) is the change in total revenue from selling one more unit.

Visit **www.myeconlab.com** to complete these exercises online and get instant feedback.

## Review Questions

**2.1** Explain why it is true that for a firm in a perfectly competitive market, $P = MR = AR$.

**2.2** Explain why it is true that for a firm in a perfectly competitive market, the profit-maximizing condition $MR = MC$ is equivalent to the condition $P = MC$.

## Problems and Applications

**2.3** A student argues: "To maximize profit, a firm should produce the quantity where the difference between marginal revenue and marginal cost is the greatest. If it produces more than this quantity, then the profit made on each additional unit will be falling." Briefly explain whether you agree with this reasoning.

**2.4** Why don't firms maximize revenue rather than profit? If a firm decided to maximize revenue, would it be likely to produce a smaller or a larger quantity than if it were maximizing profit? Briefly explain.

**2.5** Refer to Table 11-2 on page 372 and Table 11-3 on page 373. Suppose the price of wheat rises to $7.00 per bushel. How many bushels of wheat will Farmer Parker produce, and how much profit will he make? Briefly explain.

**2.6** Refer to Table 11-2 and Table 11-3. Suppose that the marginal cost of wheat is $0.50 higher for every bushel of wheat produced. For example, the marginal cost of producing the eighth bushel of wheat is now $7.50. Assume that the price of wheat remains $4 per bushel. Will this increase in marginal cost change the profit-maximizing level of production for Farmer Parker? Briefly explain. How much profit will Farmer Parker make now?

>> **End Learning Objective 11.2**

---

**11.3** **Illustrating Profit or Loss on the Cost Curve Graph,** pages 374–379
LEARNING OBJECTIVE: Use graphs to show a firm's profit or loss.

## Summary

From the definitions of profit and average total cost, we can develop the following expression for the relationship between total profit and average total cost: Profit = $(P - ATC) \times Q$. Using this expression, we can determine the area showing profit or loss on a cost-curve graph: The area of profit or loss is a box with a height equal to price minus average total cost (for profit) or average total cost minus price (for loss) and a base equal to the quantity of output.

 Visit **www.myeconlab.com** to complete these exercises online and get instant feedback.

## Review Questions

**3.1** Draw a graph showing a firm in a perfectly competitive market that is making a profit. Be sure your graph includes the firm's demand curve, marginal revenue curve, marginal cost curve, average total cost curve, and average variable cost curve and make sure to indicate the area representing the firm's profits.

**3.2** Draw a graph showing a firm in a perfectly competitive market that is operating at a loss. Be sure your graph includes the firm's demand curve, marginal revenue curve, marginal cost curve, average total cost curve, and average variable cost curve and make sure to indicate the area representing the firm's losses.

## Problems and Applications

**3.3** (Related to *Solved Problem 11-3* on page 375) Frances sells earrings in the perfectly competitive earring market. Her output per day and costs are as follows:

| OUTPUT PER DAY | TOTAL COST |
|:---:|:---:|
| 0 | $1.00 |
| 1 | 2.50 |
| 2 | 3.50 |
| 3 | 4.20 |
| 4 | 4.50 |
| 5 | 5.20 |
| 6 | 6.80 |
| 7 | 8.70 |
| 8 | 10.70 |
| 9 | 13.00 |

a. If the current equilibrium price in the earring market is $1.80, how many earrings will Frances produce, what price will she charge, and how much profit (or loss) will she make? Draw a graph to illustrate your answer. Your graph should be clearly labeled and should include Frances's demand, *ATC*, *AVC*, *MC*, and *MR* curves; the price she is charging; the quantity she is producing; and the area representing her profit (or loss).

b. Suppose the equilibrium price of earrings falls to $1.00. Now how many earrings will Frances produce, what price will she charge, and how much profit (or loss) will she make? Show your work. Draw a graph to illustrate this situation, using the instructions in question (a).

c. Suppose the equilibrium price of earrings falls to $0.25. Now how many earrings will Frances produce, what price will she charge, and how much profit (or loss) will she make?

**3.4** (Related to *Solved Problem 11-3* on page 375) Review Solved Problem 11-3 and then answer the following: Suppose the equilibrium price of basketballs falls to $2.50. Now how many basketballs will Andy produce? What price will he charge? How much profit (or loss) will he make?

**3.5** (Related to the *Don't Let This Happen to You!* on page 377) A student examines the following graph and argues, "I believe that a firm will want to produce at $Q_1$, not $Q_2$. At $Q_1$, the distance between price and marginal cost is the greatest. Therefore, at $Q_1$, the firm will be maximizing its profits." Briefly explain whether you agree with the student's argument.

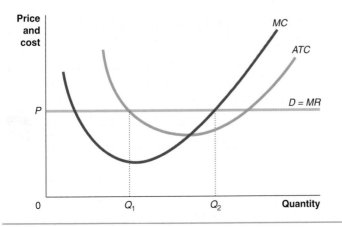

**3.6** CarMax, a nationwide retailer of used cars, announced that its total profit for the fourth quarter of 2008 fell by 10 percent, or $26.8 million, compared to the fourth quarter of 2007. At the same time, its profit per used car increased by $325. If the profit per used car increased, how could total profits fall? Illustrate your answer with a graph. Be sure to indicate profit per used car and total profit on the graph.

Source: Suzanne Ashe, "CarMax Sales Down, Net Profits Up," *CNET*, April 2, 2009.

**3.7** A report issued by the University of Illinois predicted large cost increases for inputs, including fertilizer, seed, insurance, and utilities, for soybean growers in 2009. According to the report, "Significantly higher costs will occur in 2009, leading to higher break-even prices for . . . soybeans." Draw a graph showing a farm earning a profit from soybean production before the increase in input costs. Draw a second graph showing when this same farm would shut down following the increase in input costs.

Source: Gary Schnitkey, "Dramatic Increases in Corn and Soybean Costs in 2009," Farmdoc FEFO 08-13, University of Illinois at Urbana-Champaign, July 11, 2008.

**3.8** (Related to the *Making the Connection* on page 378) Suppose the medical screening firms had run an effective advertising campaign that convinced a large number of people that yearly CT scans were critical for good health. How would this have changed the fortunes of these firms? Illustrate your answer with a graph showing the situation for a representative firm in the industry. Be sure your graph includes the firm's demand curve, marginal revenue curve, marginal cost curve, and average total cost curve.

**>> End Learning Objective 11.3**

---

**11.4**  **Deciding Whether to Produce or to Shut Down in the Short Run,** pages 379–382

LEARNING OBJECTIVE: Explain why firms may shut down temporarily.

## Summary

In deciding whether to shut down or produce during a given period, a firm should ignore its *sunk costs*. A **sunk cost** is a cost that has already been paid and that cannot be recovered. In the short run, a firm continues to produce as long as its price is at least equal to its average variable cost. A perfectly competitive firm's **shutdown point** is the minimum point on the firm's average variable cost curve. If price falls below average variable cost, the firm shuts down in the short run. For prices above the shutdown point, a perfectly competitive firm's marginal cost curve is also its supply curve.

 Visit **www.myeconlab.com** to complete these exercises online and get instant feedback.

## Review Questions

**4.1** What is the difference between a firm's shutdown point in the short run and in the long run? Why are firms willing to accept losses in the short run but not in the long run?

**4.2** What is the relationship between a perfectly competitive firm's marginal cost curve and its supply curve?

# Problems and Applications

**4.3** Edward Scahill produces table lamps in the perfectly competitive desk lamp market.
a. Fill in the missing values in the table.

| OUTPUT PER WEEK | TOTAL COSTS | AFC | AVC | ATC | MC |
|---|---|---|---|---|---|
| 0 | $100 | | | | |
| 1 | 150 | | | | |
| 2 | 175 | | | | |
| 3 | 190 | | | | |
| 4 | 210 | | | | |
| 5 | 240 | | | | |
| 6 | 280 | | | | |
| 7 | 330 | | | | |
| 8 | 390 | | | | |
| 9 | 460 | | | | |
| 10 | 540 | | | | |

b. Suppose the equilibrium price in the desk lamp market is $50. How many table lamps should Edward produce, and how much profit will he make?
c. If next week the equilibrium price of desk lamps drops to $30, should Edward shut down? Explain.

**4.4** The graph represents the situation of a perfectly competitive firm.

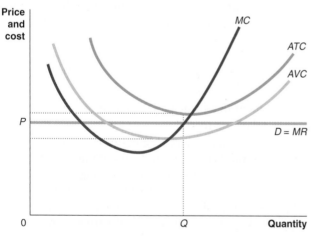

Indicate on the graph the areas that represent the following:
a. Total cost
b. Total revenue
c. Variable cost
d. Profit or loss

Briefly explain whether the firm will continue to produce in the short run.

**4.5** (Related to the *Making the Connection* on page 380) Suppose you decide to open a copy store. You rent store space (signing a one-year lease to do so), and you take out a loan at a local bank and use the money to purchase 10 copiers. Six months later, a large chain opens a copy store two blocks away from yours. As a result, the revenue you receive from your copy store, while sufficient to cover the wages of your employees and the costs of paper and utilities, doesn't cover all your rent and the interest and repayment costs on the loan you took out to purchase the copiers. Should you continue operating your business?

**4.6** (Related to the *Making the Connection* on page 380) An article in the *Wall Street Journal* discussed problems some shopping malls were having retaining stores. According to the article, some stores that were currently losing money were considering not "sticking around once their leases expire." If the owner of a store that leases space in a mall is suffering a loss at that location, why wouldn't the owner close the store right away rather than wait until the lease expires?
Source: Kris Hudson and Vanessa O'Connell, "Recession Turns Malls into Ghost Towns," *Wall Street Journal*, May 22, 2009.

**4.7** (Related to Solved Problem 11-4 on page 382) Shinji operates a bicycle rental store near a resort community in Japan. The tourist season is nearing the end, and Shinji is trying to decide whether he should remain open during the winter season, when the tourist population is at its lowest level of the year. He gathers the following information:

| | |
|---|---|
| Expected rentals during winter season | 600 bikes per month |
| Price | ¥1,000 per rental |
| **Explicit Costs** | |
| Lease payment for rent of store | ¥80,000 |
| Interest payment on loan | ¥100,000 |
| Wages for two employees | ¥130,000 |
| Bike maintenance | ¥30,000 |
| **Implicit Costs** | |
| Income Shinji could earn in a holiday job | ¥400,000 |

Should Shinji remain open for business this winter?

**>> End Learning Objective 11.4**

### 11.5  "If Everyone Can Do It, You Can't Make Money at It": The Entry and Exit of Firms in the Long Run, pages 383–389

LEARNING OBJECTIVE: Explain how entry and exit ensure that perfectly competitive firms earn zero economic profit in the long run.

## Summary

**Economic profit** is a firm's revenues minus all its costs, implicit and explicit. **Economic loss** is the situation in which a firm's total revenue is less than its total cost, including all implicit costs. If firms make economic profits in the short run, new firms enter the industry until the market price has fallen enough to wipe out the profits. If firms make economic losses, firms exit the industry until the market price has risen enough to wipe out the losses. **Long-run competitive equilibrium** is the situation in which the entry and exit of firms has resulted in the typical firm breaking even. The **long-run supply curve** shows the relationship between market price and the quantity supplied.

 Visit **www.myeconlab.com** to complete these exercises online and get instant feedback.

## Review Questions

5.1  When are firms likely to enter an industry? When are they likely to exit an industry?

5.2  Would a firm earning zero economic profit continue to produce, even in the long run?

5.3  Discuss the shape of the long-run supply curve in a perfectly competitive market. Suppose that a perfectly competitive market is initially at long-run equilibrium and then there is a permanent decrease in the demand for the product. Draw a graph showing how the market adjusts in the long run.

## Problems and Applications

5.4  Suppose an assistant professor of economics is earning a salary of $65,000 per year. One day she quits her job, sells $100,000 worth of bonds that had been earning 5 percent per year, and uses the funds to open a bookstore. At the end of the year, she shows an accounting profit of $80,000 on her income tax return. What is her economic profit?

5.5  Suppose that you and your sister both decide to open copy stores. Your parents always liked your sister better than you, so they purchase and give to her free of charge the three copiers she needs to operate her store. You, however, have to rent your copiers for $1,500 per month each. Does your sister have lower costs in operating her copy store than you have in operating your copy store because of this? Explain.

5.6  Consider the following statement: "The products for which demand is the greatest will also be the products

that are most profitable to produce." Briefly explain whether you agree with this statement.

5.7  In panel (b) of Figure 11-9 on page 386, Anne Moreno reduces her output from 8,000 to 5,000 boxes of apples when the price falls to $7. At this price and this output level, she is operating at a loss. Why doesn't she just continue charging the original $10 and continue producing 8,000 boxes of apples?

5.8  Niman Ranch, a northern California–based company that produces and distributes "all-natural" meat, announced in January 2009 that it was merging with Natural Food Holdings LLC of Chicago. According to an article in the *San Francisco Chronicle*:

> In its close to 40-year history, Niman Ranch, originally founded in Bolinas by Bill Niman, built a reputation for its high-quality meat produced by a network of small farmers and ranchers who shared Niman Ranch's commitment to humane and sustainable methods of animal rearing. But the company never turned a profit.

Why would Niman Ranch continue to operate for close to 40 years while never turning a profit rather than shut down immediately? Using revenue and cost analysis, explain when the company would shut down.

Source: Andrew S. Ross, "Niman Ranch to Merge with Chicago Investor," *San Francisco Chronicle*, January 22, 2009.

5.9  A student in a principles of economics course makes the following remark:

> The economic model of perfectly competitive markets is fine in theory but not very realistic. It predicts that in the long run, a firm in a perfectly competitive market will earn no profits. No firm in the real world would stay in business if it earned zero profits.

Do you agree with this remark?

5.10  Suppose that the laptop computer industry is perfectly competitive and that the firms that assemble laptops do not also make the displays, or screens, for them. Suppose that the laptop display industry is also perfectly competitive. Finally, suppose that because the demand for laptop displays is currently relatively small, firms in the laptop display industry have not been able to take advantage of all the economies of scale in laptop display production. Use a graph of the laptop computer market to illustrate the long-run effects on equilibrium price and quantity in the laptop computer market of a substantial and sustained increase in the demand for laptop computers. Use another graph to show the impact on the cost curves of a typical firm in the laptop computer industry. Briefly explain your graphs. Do your graphs indicate that the laptop computer industry is a constant-cost industry, an increasing-cost industry, or a decreasing-cost industry?

5.11 (Related to the *Chapter Opener* on page 367) If in the long run apple growers who use organic methods of cultivation make no greater rate of return on their investment than apple growers who use conventional methods, why did a significant number of apple growers switch from conventional to organic methods in the first place?

>> **End Learning Objective 11.5**

---

 **11.6**

## Perfect Competition and Efficiency, pages 390–391

LEARNING OBJECTIVE: Explain how perfect competition leads to economic efficiency.

## Summary

Perfect competition results in **productive efficiency**, which means that goods and services are produced at the lowest possible cost. Perfect competition also results in **allocative efficiency**, which means the goods and services are produced up to the point where the last unit provides a marginal benefit to consumers equal to the marginal cost of producing it.

 Visit **www.myeconlab.com** to complete these exercises online and get instant feedback.

## Review Questions

6.1 What is meant by allocative efficiency? What is meant by productive efficiency? Briefly discuss the difference between these two concepts.

6.2 How does perfect competition lead to allocative and productive efficiency?

## Problems and Applications

6.3 The chapter states, "Firms will supply all those goods that provide consumers with a marginal benefit at least as great as the marginal cost of producing them." A student objects to this statement and argues, "I doubt that firms will really do this. After all, firms are in business to make a profit; they don't care about what is best for consumers." Evaluate the student's argument.

6.4 (Related to the *Making the Connection* on page 388) Ethan Nicholas developed his first game

while still working as a programmer for Sun Microsystems. After his first game was a success, he quit Sun to form his own company—with himself as the only employee. How did Nicholas's quitting Sun to work full time for himself affect the cost to him of developing games?

Source: Jenna Wortham, "The iPhone Gold Rush," *New York Times*, April 5, 2009.

6.5 Although New York State is second only to Washington State in production of apples, its production has been declining during the past 20 years. The decline has been particularly steep in counties close to New York City. In 1985, there were more than 11,000 acres of apple orchards in Ulster County, which is 75 miles north of New York City. Today, only about 6,000 acres remain. As it became difficult for apple growers in the county to compete with lower-cost producers elsewhere, the resources these entrepreneurs were using to produce apples—particularly land—became more valuable in other uses. Many farmers sold their land to housing developers. Suppose a nutritionist develops a revolutionary new diet that involves eating 10 apples per day. The new diet becomes wildly popular. What effect is the new diet likely to have on the number of apple orchards within 100 miles of New York City? What effect is the diet likely to have on housing prices in New York City?

Source: Lisa W. Foderaro, "Plenty of Apples, but a Possible Shortage of Immigrant Pickers," *New York Times*, August 21, 2007.

>> **End Learning Objective 11.6**

CHAPTER 12

# Monopolistic Competition:

## The Competitive Model in a More Realistic Setting

## Chapter Outline and Learning Objectives

# >> Starbucks: The Limits to Growth through Product Differentiation

Like many other large firms, Starbucks started small. In 1971, entrepreneurs Gordon Bowker, Gerald Baldwin, and Zev Siegl opened the first Starbucks in Seattle, Washington. Current CEO Howard Schultz joined the company 10 years later. By 1993, Starbucks was opening stores on the East Coast. Today, Starbucks has stores in every state and in 38 countries. The key to the success of Starbucks was that Schultz realized that many consumers wanted a coffeehouse where they could sit, relax, read, chat, and drink higher-quality coffee than was typically served in diners or donut shops. But it was not difficult for other coffeehouses to copy the Starbucks approach. The coffeehouse market is competitive because it is inexpensive to open a new store. Hundreds of firms in the United States operate coffeehouses.

In 2008, fierce competition and a weak economy led Starbucks to close 600 coffeehouses in the United States. In 2009, Starbucks closed 300 more stores and cut prices as it tried to overcome the impression that it was the "home of the $4 coffee." Would Starbucks be able to regain its profitability and continue its expansion, or had it entered into a long-term decline?

In Chapter 11, we discussed the situation of firms in perfectly competitive markets. These markets share three key characteristics:

1. There are many firms.
2. All firms sell identical products.
3. There are no barriers to new firms entering the industry.

The market Starbucks competes in shares two of these characteristics: There are many coffeehouses, and the barriers to entering the market are very low. But the coffee at Starbucks is not identical to what competing coffeehouses offer. Selling coffee in coffeehouses is not like selling wheat: The products that Starbucks and its competitors sell are *differentiated* rather than identical. So, the coffeehouse market is *monopolistically competitive* rather than perfectly competitive. Competition from McDonald's and other firms is the main reason Starbucks faced falling sales and profits during 2008 and 2009. As we will see, most monopolistically competitive firms are unable to earn economic profits in the long run.

**AN INSIDE LOOK** on **page 420** describes how McDonald's has begun competing directly with Starbucks and other coffeehouses.

## Economics in YOUR LIFE!

### Opening Your Own Restaurant

After you graduate, you plan to realize your dream of opening your own Italian restaurant. You are confident that many people will enjoy the pasta prepared with your grandmother's secret sauce. Although your hometown already has three Italian restaurants, you are convinced that you can enter this market and make a profit.

You have many choices to make in operating your restaurant. Will it be "family style," with sturdy but inexpensive furniture, where families with small—and noisy!—children will feel welcome, or will it be more elegant, with nice furniture, tablecloths, and candles? Will you offer a full menu or concentrate on pasta dishes that use your grandmother's secret sauce? These and other choices you make will distinguish your restaurant from competitors. What's likely to happen in the restaurant market in your hometown after you open? How successful are you likely to be? See if you can answer these questions as you read this chapter. You can check your answers against those we provide at the end of the chapter.

▶ Continued on page 418

Many markets in the U.S. economy are similar to the coffeehouse market: They have many buyers and sellers, and the barriers to entry are low, but the goods and services offered for sale are differentiated rather than identical. Examples of these markets include consumer electronics stores, restaurants, movie theaters, supermarkets, and manufacturers of men's and women's clothing. In fact, the majority of the firms you patronize are competing in **monopolistically competitive** markets.

In Chapter 11, we saw how perfect competition benefits consumers and results in economic efficiency. Will these same desirable outcomes also hold for monopolistically competitive markets? This question, which we explore in this chapter, is important because monopolistically competitive markets are so common.

**Monopolistic competition** A market structure in which barriers to entry are low and many firms compete by selling similar, but not identical, products.

**12.1 LEARNING** OBJECTIVE

Explain why a monopolistically competitive firm has downward-sloping demand and marginal revenue curves.

# Demand and Marginal Revenue for a Firm in a Monopolistically Competitive Market

If the Starbucks coffeehouse located one mile from your house raises the price for a caffè latte from $3.00 to $3.25, it will lose some, but not all, of its customers. Some customers will switch to buying their coffee at another store, but other customers will be willing to pay the higher price for a variety of reasons: This store may be closer to them, or they may prefer Starbucks caffè lattes to similar coffees at competing stores. Because changing the price affects the quantity of caffè lattes sold, a Starbucks store will face a downward-sloping demand curve rather than the horizontal demand curve that a wheat farmer faces.

## The Demand Curve for a Monopolistically Competitive Firm

Figure 12-1 shows how a change in price affects the quantity of caffè lattes Starbucks sells. The increase in the price from $3.00 to $3.25 decreases the quantity of caffè lattes sold from 3,000 per week to 2,400 per week.

## Marginal Revenue for a Firm with a Downward-Sloping Demand Curve

Recall from Chapter 11 that for a firm in a perfectly competitive market, the demand curve and the marginal revenue curve are the same. A perfectly competitive firm faces a horizontal demand curve and does not have to cut the price to sell a larger quantity. A monopolistically competitive firm, on the other hand, must cut the price to sell more, so its marginal revenue curve will slope downward and will be below its demand curve.

The data in Table 12-1 illustrate this point. To keep the numbers simple, let's assume that your local Starbucks coffeehouse is very small and sells at most 10 caffè lattes per

## Figure 12-1

**The Downward-Sloping Demand for Caffè Lattes at a Starbucks**

If a Starbucks increases the price of caffè lattes, it will lose some, but not all, of its customers. In this case, raising the price from $3.00 to $3.25 reduces the quantity of caffè lattes sold from 3,000 to 2,400. Therefore, unlike a perfect competitor, a Starbucks store faces a downward-sloping demand curve.

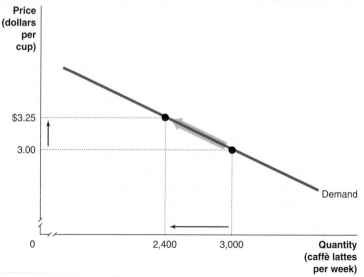

TABLE 12-1

**Demand and Marginal Revenue at a Starbucks**

| CAFFÈ LATTES SOLD PER WEEK (Q) | PRICE (P) | TOTAL REVENUE (TR = P × Q) | AVERAGE REVENUE $\left(AR = \dfrac{TR}{Q}\right)$ | MARGINAL REVENUE $\left(MR = \dfrac{\Delta TR}{\Delta Q}\right)$ |
|---|---|---|---|---|
| 0 | $6.00 | $0.00 | — | — |
| 1 | 5.50 | 5.50 | $5.50 | $5.50 |
| 2 | 5.00 | 10.00 | 5.00 | 4.50 |
| 3 | 4.50 | 13.50 | 4.50 | 3.50 |
| 4 | 4.00 | 16.00 | 4.00 | 2.50 |
| 5 | 3.50 | 17.50 | 3.50 | 1.50 |
| 6 | 3.00 | 18.00 | 3.00 | 0.50 |
| 7 | 2.50 | 17.50 | 2.50 | −0.50 |
| 8 | 2.00 | 16.00 | 2.00 | −1.50 |
| 9 | 1.50 | 13.50 | 1.50 | −2.50 |
| 10 | 1.00 | 10.00 | 1.00 | −3.50 |

week. If Starbucks charges a price of $6.00 or more, all of its potential customers will buy their coffee somewhere else. If it charges $5.50, it will sell 1 caffè latte per week. For each additional $0.50 Starbucks reduces the price, it increases the number of caffè lattes it sells by 1. The third column in the table shows how the firm's *total revenue* changes as it sells more caffè lattes. The fourth column shows the firm's revenue per unit, or its *average revenue*. Average revenue is equal to total revenue divided by quantity. Because total revenue equals price multiplied by quantity, dividing by quantity leaves just price. Therefore, *average revenue is always equal to price.* This result will be true for firms selling in any of the four market structures we discussed in Chapter 11.

The last column shows the firm's marginal revenue, or the amount that total revenue changes as the firm sells 1 more caffè latte. For a perfectly competitive firm, the additional revenue received from selling 1 more unit is just equal to the price. That will not be true for Starbucks because to sell another caffè latte, it has to reduce the price. When the firm cuts the price by $0.50, one good thing and one bad thing happen:

- **The good thing.**   It sells one more caffè latte; we can call this the *output effect.*

- **The bad thing.**   It receives $0.50 less for each caffè latte that it could have sold at the higher price; we can call this the *price effect.*

Figure 12-2 illustrates what happens when the firm cuts the price from $3.50 to $3.00. Selling the sixth caffè latte adds the $3.00 price to the firm's revenue; this is the

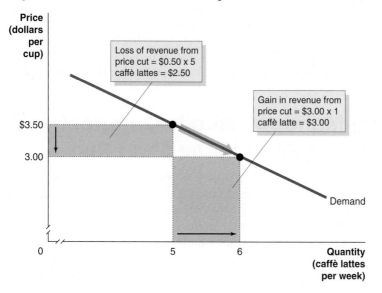

Figure 12-2

**How a Price Cut Affects a Firm's Revenue**

If the local Starbucks reduces the price of a caffè latte from $3.50 to $3.00, the number of caffè lattes it sells per week will increase from 5 to 6. Its marginal revenue from selling the sixth caffè latte will be $0.50, which is equal to the $3.00 additional revenue from selling 1 more caffè latte (the area of the green box) minus the $2.50 loss in revenue from selling the first 5 caffè lattes for $0.50 less each (the area of the red box).

## Figure 12-3

**The Demand and Marginal Revenue Curves for a Monopolistically Competitive Firm**

Any firm that has the ability to affect the price of the product it sells will have a marginal revenue curve that is below its demand curve. We plot the data from Table 12-1 to create the demand and marginal revenue curves. After the sixth caffè latte, marginal revenue becomes negative because the additional revenue received from selling 1 more caffè latte is smaller than the revenue lost from receiving a lower price on the caffè lattes that could have been sold at the original price.

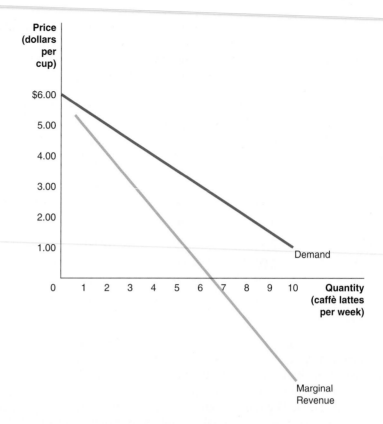

output effect. But Starbucks now receives a price of $3.00, rather than $3.50, on the first 5 caffè lattes sold; this is the price effect. As a result of the price effect, the firm's revenue on these 5 caffè lattes is $2.50 less than it would have been if the price had remained at $3.50. So, the firm has gained $3.00 in revenue on the sixth caffè latte and lost $2.50 in revenue on the first 5 caffè lattes, for a net change in revenue of $0.50. Marginal revenue is the change in total revenue from selling one more unit. Therefore, the marginal revenue of the sixth caffè latte is $0.50. Notice that the marginal revenue of the sixth unit is far below its price of $3.00. In fact, for each additional caffè latte Starbucks sells, marginal revenue will be less than price. There is an important general point: *Every firm that has the ability to affect the price of the good or service it sells will have a marginal revenue curve that is below its demand curve.* Only firms in perfectly competitive markets, which can sell as many units as they want at the market price, have marginal revenue curves that are the same as their demand curves.

Figure 12-3 shows the relationship between the demand curve and the marginal revenue curve for the local Starbucks. Notice that after the sixth caffè latte, marginal revenue becomes negative. Marginal revenue is negative because the additional revenue received from selling 1 more caffè latte is smaller than the revenue lost from receiving a lower price on the caffè lattes that could have been sold at the original price.

**12.2 LEARNING** OBJECTIVE

Explain how a monopolistically competitive firm maximizes profit in the short run.

# How a Monopolistically Competitive Firm Maximizes Profit in the Short Run

All firms use the same approach to maximize profits: They produce where marginal revenue is equal to marginal cost. For the local Starbucks, this means selling the quantity of caffè lattes for which the last caffè latte sold adds the same amount to the firm's revenue as to its costs. To begin our discussion of how monopolistically competitive firms maximize profits, let's consider the situation the local Starbucks faces in the short run. Recall from Chapter 10 that in the short run, at least one factor of production is fixed, and there is not enough time for new firms to enter the market. A Starbucks has many costs, including the cost of purchasing the ingredients for its caffè lattes and other coffees, the electricity it uses, and the wages of its employees. Recall that a firm's *marginal cost* is the increase in total cost resulting from producing another unit of output. We have seen that for many firms, marginal cost has a U shape. We will assume that the marginal cost curve for this Starbucks has the usual shape.

In the table in Figure 12-4, we bring together the revenue data from Table 12-1 with the cost data for Starbucks. The graphs in Figure 12-4 plot the data from the table. In panel (a), we see how Starbucks can determine its profit-maximizing quantity and price. As long as the marginal cost of selling one more caffè latte is less than the marginal revenue, the firm should sell additional caffè lattes. For example, increasing the quantity of caffè lattes sold from 3 per week to 4 per week increases marginal cost by $1.00 but increases marginal revenue by $2.50. So, the firm's profits are increased by $1.50 as a result of selling the fourth caffè latte.

| Caffè Lattes Sold per Week (Q) | Price (P) | Total Revenue (TR) | Marginal Revenue (MR) | Total Cost (TC) | Marginal Cost (MC) | Average Total Cost (ATC) | Profit |
|---|---|---|---|---|---|---|---|
| 0 | $6.00 | $0.00 | — | $5.00 | — | — | −$5.00 |
| 1 | 5.50 | 5.50 | $5.50 | 8.00 | $3.00 | $8.00 | −2.50 |
| 2 | 5.00 | 10.00 | 4.50 | 9.50 | 1.50 | 4.75 | 0.50 |
| 3 | 4.50 | 13.50 | 3.50 | 10.00 | 0.50 | 3.33 | 3.50 |
| 4 | 4.00 | 16.00 | 2.50 | 11.00 | 1.00 | 2.75 | 5.00 |
| 5 | 3.50 | 17.50 | 1.50 | 12.50 | 1.50 | 2.50 | 5.00 |
| 6 | 3.00 | 18.00 | 0.50 | 14.50 | 2.00 | 2.42 | 3.50 |
| 7 | 2.50 | 17.50 | −0.50 | 17.00 | 2.50 | 2.43 | 0.50 |
| 8 | 2.00 | 16.00 | −1.50 | 20.00 | 3.00 | 2.50 | −4.00 |
| 9 | 1.50 | 13.50 | −2.50 | 23.50 | 3.50 | 2.61 | −10.00 |
| 10 | 1.00 | 10.00 | −3.50 | 27.50 | 4.00 | 2.75 | −17.50 |

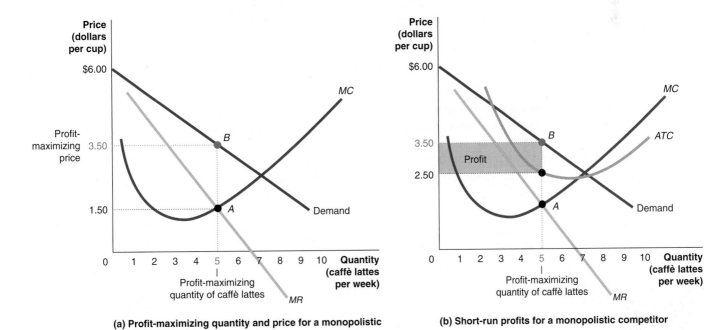

(a) Profit-maximizing quantity and price for a monopolistic competitor

(b) Short-run profits for a monopolistic competitor

## Figure 12-4    Maximizing Profit in a Monopolistically Competitive Market

To maximize profit, a Starbucks coffeehouse wants to sell caffè lattes up to the point where the marginal revenue from selling the last caffè latte is just equal to the marginal cost. As the table shows, this happens with the fifth caffè latte—point *A* in panel (a)—which adds $1.50 to the firm's costs and $1.50 to its revenues. The firm then uses the demand curve to find the price that will lead consumers to buy this

quantity of caffè lattes (point *B*). In panel (b), the green box represents the firm's profits. The box has a height equal to $1.00, which is the $3.50 price minus the average total cost of $2.50, and it has a base equal to the quantity of 5 caffè lattes. So, this Starbucks's profit equals $1 × 5 = $5.00.

As Starbucks sells more caffè lattes, rising marginal cost eventually equals marginal revenue, and the firm sells the profit-maximizing quantity of caffè lattes. Marginal cost equals marginal revenue with the fifth caffè latte, which adds $1.50 to the firm's costs and $1.50 to its revenues—point *A* in panel (a) of Figure 12-4. The demand curve tells us the price at which the firm is able to sell 5 caffè lattes per week. In Figure 12-4, if we draw a vertical line from 5 caffè lattes up to the demand curve, we can see that the price at which the firm can sell 5 caffè lattes per week is $3.50 (point *B*). We can conclude that for Starbucks the profit-maximizing quantity is 5 caffè lattes, and the profit-maximizing price is $3.50. If the firm sells more than 5 caffè lattes per week, its profits fall. For example, selling a sixth caffè latte adds $2.00 to its costs and only $0.50 to its revenues. So, its profit would fall from $5.00 to $3.50.

Panel (b) adds the average total cost curve for Starbucks. The panel shows that the average total cost of selling 5 caffè lattes is $2.50. Recall from Chapter 11 that:

$$\text{Profit} = (P - ATC) \times Q$$

In this case, profit = ($3.50 − $2.50) × 5 = $5.00. The green box in panel (b) shows the amount of profit. The box has a base equal to *Q* and a height equal to (*P* − *ATC*), so its area equals profit.

Notice that, unlike a perfectly competitive firm, which produces where *P* = *MC*, a monopolistically competitive firm produces where *P* > *MC*. In this case, Starbucks is charging a price of $3.50, although marginal cost is $1.50. For a perfectly competitive firm, price equals marginal revenue, *P* = *MR*. Therefore, to fulfill the *MR* = *MC* condition for profit maximization, a perfectly competitive firm will produce where *P* = *MC*. Because *P* > *MR* for a monopolistically competitive firm—which results from the marginal revenue curve being below the demand curve—a monopolistically competitive firm will maximize profits where *P* > *MC*.

# Solved Problem │ 12-2

## Does Minimizing Cost Maximize Profits?

Suppose Apple finds that the relationship between the average total cost of producing iPhones and the quantity of iPhones produced is as shown in the following graph.

Will Apple maximize profits if it produces 800,000 iPhones per month? Briefly explain.

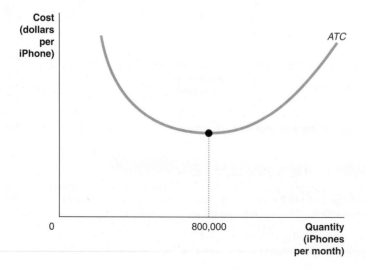

## SOLVING THE PROBLEM:

**Step 1:** **Review the chapter material.** This problem is about how monopolistically competitive firms maximize profits, so you may want to review the section "How a Monopolistically Competitive Firm Maximizes Profits in the Short Run," which begins on page 404.

**Step 2:** **Discuss the relationship between minimizing costs and maximizing profits.** Firms often talk about the steps they take to reduce costs. The figure shows that by producing 800,000 iPhones per month, Apple will minimize its average cost of production. But remember that minimizing cost is not the firm's ultimate goal; the firm's ultimate goal is to maximize profits. Depending on demand, a firm may maximize profits by producing a quantity that is either larger or smaller than the quantity that would minimize average total cost.

**Step 3:** **Draw a graph that shows Apple maximizing profit at a quantity where average cost is not minimized.** Note that in the graph, average cost reaches a minimum at a quantity of 800,000, but profits are maximized at a quantity of 600,000.

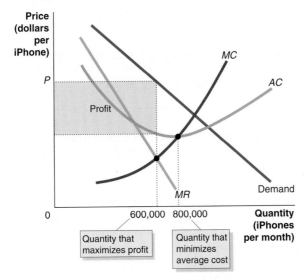

**YOUR TURN:** For more practice, do related problem 2.6 on page 423 at the end of this chapter.

---

# What Happens to Profits in the Long Run?

Remember that a firm makes an economic profit when its total revenue is greater than all of its costs, including the opportunity cost of the funds invested in the firm by its owners. Because cost curves include the owners' opportunity costs, the Starbucks coffeehouse represented in Figure 12-4 on page 405 is making an economic profit. This economic profit gives entrepreneurs an incentive to enter this market and establish new firms. If a Starbucks is earning an economic profit selling caffè lattes, new coffeehouses are likely to open in the same area.

## How Does the Entry of New Firms Affect the Profits of Existing Firms?

As new coffeehouses open near the local Starbucks, the firm's demand curve will shift to the left. The demand curve will shift because Starbucks will sell fewer caffè lattes at each price when there are additional coffeehouses in the area selling similar drinks. The

**12.3 LEARNING** OBJECTIVE

Analyze the situation of a monopolistically competitive firm in the long run.

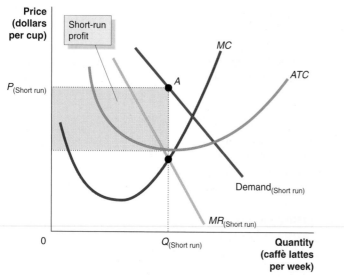

**(a) A monopolistic competitor may earn a short-run profit**

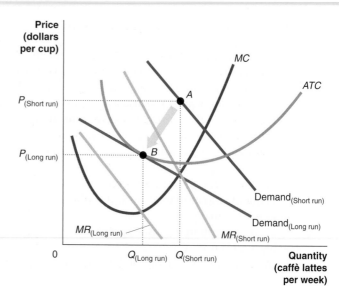

**(b) A monopolistic competitor's profits are eliminated in the long run**

## Figure 12-5 | How Entry of New Firms Eliminates Profits

Panel (a) shows that in the short run the local Starbucks faces the demand and marginal revenue curves labeled "Short run." With this demand curve, Starbucks can charge a price above average total cost (point A) and make a profit, shown by the green rectangle. But this profit attracts new firms to enter the market, which shifts the demand and marginal revenue curves to the curves labeled "Long run" in panel (b). Because price is now equal to average total cost (point B), Starbucks breaks even and no longer earns an economic profit.

demand curve will also become more elastic because consumers have additional coffeehouses from which to buy coffee, so Starbucks will lose more sales if it raises its prices. Figure 12-5 shows how the demand curve for the local Starbucks shifts as new firms enter its market.

In panel (a) of Figure 12-5, the short-run demand curve shows the relationship between the price of caffè lattes and the quantity of caffè lattes Starbucks sells per week before the entry of new firms. With this demand curve, Starbucks can charge a price above average total cost—shown as point A in panel (a)—and make a profit. But this profit attracts additional coffeehouses to the area and shifts the demand curve for the Starbucks caffè lattes to the left. As long as Starbucks is making an economic profit, there is an incentive for additional coffeehouses to open in the area, and the demand curve will continue shifting to the left. As panel (b) shows, eventually the demand curve will have shifted to the point where it is just touching—or tangent to—the average total cost curve.

In the long run, at the point at which the demand curve is tangent to the average cost curve, price is equal to average total cost (point B), the firm is breaking even, and it

# Don't Let This Happen to **YOU!**

## Don't Confuse Zero Economic Profit with Zero Accounting Profit

Remember that economists count the opportunity cost of the owner's investment in a firm as a cost. For example, suppose you invest $200,000 opening a pizza parlor, and the return you could earn on those funds each year in a similar investment—such as opening a sandwich shop—is 10 percent. Therefore, the annual opportunity cost of investing the funds in your own business is 10 percent of $200,000, or $20,000. This $20,000 is part of your profit in

the accounting sense, and you would have to pay taxes on it. But in an economic sense, the $20,000 is a cost. In long-run equilibrium, we would expect that entry of new firms would keep you from earning more than 10 percent on your investment. So, you would end up breaking even and earning zero economic profit, even though you were earning an accounting profit of $20,000.

**YOUR TURN:** Test your understanding by doing related problem 3.4 on page 425 at the end of this chapter.

no longer earns an economic profit. In the long run, the demand curve is also more elastic because the more coffeehouses there are in the area, the more sales Starbucks will lose to other coffeehouses if it raises its price.

Of course, it is possible that a monopolistically competitive firm will suffer economic losses in the short run. As a consequence, the owners of the firm will not be covering the opportunity cost of their investment. We expect that, in the long run, firms will exit an industry if they are suffering economic losses. If firms exit, the demand curve for the output of a remaining firm will shift to the right. This process will continue until the representative firm in the industry is able to charge a price equal to its average cost and break even. Therefore, in the long run, monopolistically competitive firms will experience neither economic profits nor economic losses. Table 12-2 summarizes the short run and the long run for a monopolistically competitive firm.

**TABLE 12-2**     The Short Run and the Long Run for a Monopolistically Competitive Firm

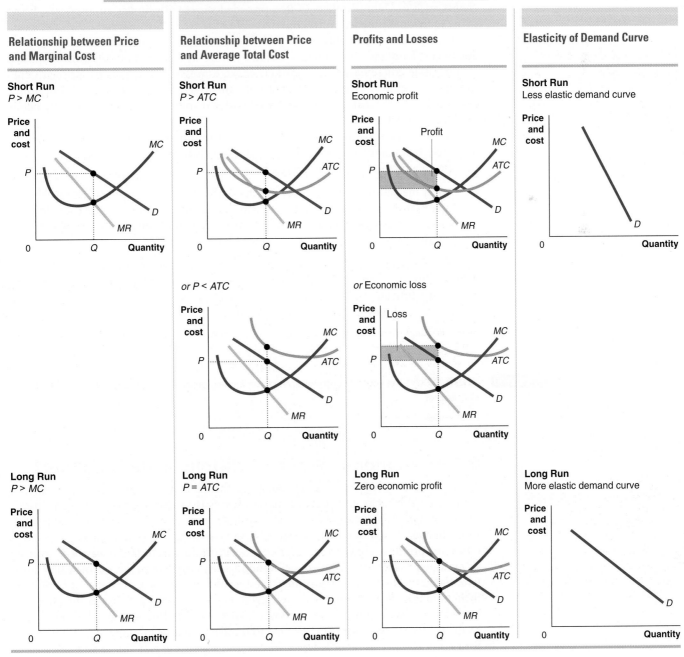

*Starbucks: No longer different enough?*

## Making the Connection | The Rise and Decline of Starbucks

In the spring of 2009, an article from Bloomberg News summed up the situation that Starbucks was in: "After more than a decade of sensational buzz, Starbucks is struggling nationwide as it faces slowing sales growth and increased competition." The initial success and later struggles of Starbucks are a familiar pattern for firms in monopolistically competitive markets.

When Starbucks began rapidly expanding, CEO Howard Schultz knew that fresh-brewed coffee was widely available in restaurants, diners, and donut shops. He believed, though, that he had a strategy that would differentiate Starbucks from competitors: Starbucks would offer a European espresso bar atmosphere, with large, comfortable chairs, music playing, and groups of friends dropping in and out during the day. From the mid-1990s through the mid-2000s, this strategy worked very well, and Starbucks had opened nearly 17,000 stores worldwide. But Starbucks's profitability attracted competitors. Other nationwide chains, such as Caribou Coffee and Diedrich Coffee, and regional chains, such as Dunn Brothers Coffee, provided stores with similar atmospheres, as did many individually owned coffeehouses.

In addition, McDonalds and Dunkin' Donuts began competing more directly with Starbucks. Dunkin' Donuts began building more upscale restaurants with "rounded granite-style coffee bars where workers make espresso drinks face-to-face with customers . . . while a carefully selected pop-music soundtrack is piped throughout." McDonald's began selling espresso-based coffee drinks for prices considerably below those at Starbucks.

Schultz was also worried that in opening thousands of coffeehouses worldwide, Starbucks had made the customer experience less distinctive and easier for competitors to copy. In a memo sent to employees, he wrote:

> Over the past ten years, in order to achieve the growth, development, and scale necessary to go from less than 1,000 stores to 13,000 stores . . . we have had to make a series of decisions that . . . have led to the watering down of the Starbucks experience.

By 2009, Starbucks was closing stores and reducing prices in an attempt to restore profitability. But in a monopolistically competitive industry, maintaining profits in the long run is very difficult. As Schultz put it, "I have said for 20 years that our success is not an entitlement and now it's proving to be a reality."

Sources: Julie Jargon, "Fan Hits a Roadblock on Drive to See Every Starbucks," *Wall Street Journal*, May 23, 2009; Andrew Harrer, "Starbucks Corporation," *Bloomberg News*, April 13, 2009; and Janet Adamy, "Brewing Battle," *Wall Street Journal*, April 8, 2006.

 **YOUR TURN:** Test your understanding by doing related problem 3.6 on page 425 at the end of this chapter.

## Is Zero Economic Profit Inevitable in the Long Run?

The economic analysis of the long run shows the effects of market forces over time. In the case of Starbucks, the effect of market forces is to eliminate the economic profit earned by a monopolistically competitive firm. Owners of monopolistically competitive firms, of course, do not have to passively accept this long-run result. The key to earning economic profits is either to sell a differentiated product or to find a way of producing an existing product at a lower cost. If a monopolistically competitive firm selling a differentiated product is earning profits, these profits will attract the entry of additional firms, and the entry of those firms will eventually eliminate the firm's profits. If a firm introduces new technology that allows it to sell a good or service at a lower cost, competing firms will eventually be able to duplicate that technology and eliminate the firm's profits. *But this result holds only if the firm stands still and fails to find new ways of differentiating its product or fails to find new ways of lowering the cost of producing its product.* Firms continually struggle to find new ways of differentiating their products as they try to stay one step ahead of other firms that are attempting to copy their success.

The owner of a competitive firm is in a position similar to that of Ebenezer Scrooge in Charles Dickens's *A Christmas Carol.* When the Ghost of Christmas Yet to Come shows Scrooge visions of his own death, he asks the ghost, "Are these the shadows of the things that Will be, or are they shadows of things that May be, only?" The shadow of the end of their profits haunts owners of every firm. Firms try to avoid losing profits by reducing costs, by improving their products, or by convincing consumers that their products are indeed different from what competitors offer. To stay one step ahead of its competitors, a firm has to offer consumers goods or services that they perceive to have greater *value* than those competing firms offer. Value can take the form of product differentiation that makes the good or service more suited to consumers' preferences, or it can take the form of a lower price.

---

# Solved Problem | 12-3

## Can It Be Profitable to Be the High-Price Seller?

During the first three months of 2009, hhgregg, an appliance and electronics retailer with stores in the Midwest, Georgia, and Florida, reported that its profits had risen 25 percent. During the same period, Best Buy's profits declined by 23 percent. Best Buy is much larger than hhgregg, so it is able to buy its appliances, televisions, and other goods from manufacturers at a low price. Because hhgregg must pay higher prices to manufacturers, it must charge higher prices to consumers. How is hhgregg able to succeed in competition with Best Buy, Wal-Mart, Amazon, and other big retailers, despite charging high prices?

According to an article in the *Wall Street Journal*: ". . . hhgregg's commissioned sales staff is an advantage over national chains with young, lower-paid hourly workers that tend to stay for shorter periods." hhgregg's CEO was quoted as saying: "We have sales people that have been with us 10 to 20 years, and customers who come in and ask for them by name."

Use this information to explain how an hhgregg store might be more profitable than a similar Best Buy store, despite the hhgregg store charging higher prices. Use a graph for hhgregg and a graph for Best Buy to illustrate your answer.

## SOLVING THE PROBLEM:

**Step 1:** **Review the chapter material.** This problem is about how a monopolistically competitive firm maximizes profits and about how firms attempt to earn economic profits in the long run, so you may want to review the section "How a Monopolistically Competitive Firm Maximizes Profits in the Short Run," which begins on page 404, and the section "Is Zero Economic Profit Inevitable in the Long Run?" which begins on page 410.

**Step 2:** **Explain how hhgregg can remain profitable despite its high costs.** If an hhgregg store has higher costs than a comparable Best Buy store, it can have greater profits only if the demand for its goods is higher. According to the *Wall Street Journal* article, hhgregg has differentiated itself from the competition, particularly from large chain stores such as Best Buy, by offering better customer service. By having salespeople who are more knowledgeable and more experienced than the salespeople hired by competitors, hhgregg has attracted consumers who need help in buying televisions and appliances. The higher demand from these consumers must be enough to offset hhgregg's higher costs.

**Step 3:** **Draw a graph to illustrate your argument.** For simplicity, we draw the graphs assuming that televisions are the product being sold. Panel (a) shows the situation for hhgregg, and panel (b) shows the situation for Best Buy. The graphs show that the hhgregg store has both greater demand and higher costs than the Best Buy store. Because the greater demand more than offsets the higher costs, the hhgregg store makes a larger profit.

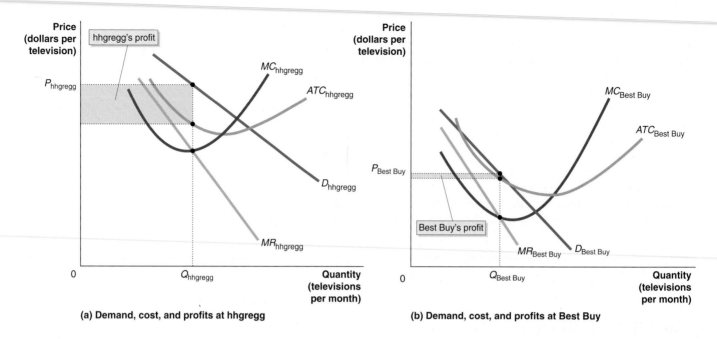

(a) Demand, cost, and profits at hhgregg

(b) Demand, cost, and profits at Best Buy

**EXTRA CREDIT:** As we have seen, firms constantly search for means of differentiating themselves from their competitors. Often, as with Starbucks, differentiation works for a while but then breaks down as competitors copy the strategy. Providing excellent customer service is more difficult to copy because it can take years to assemble an experienced sales staff and to acquire a reputation for excellent service. In fact, Best Buy, Wal-Mart, and other large chains may not want to compete for customers who are willing to pay a higher price in exchange for more help from the sales staff. In the *Wall Street Journal* article, a spokeswoman for Wal-Mart was quoted as saying: "With electronics data so readily available online today, many customers come to us looking for a particular brand or item, knowledge in hand, and may not want or feel comfortable shopping with a salesperson." If the larger firms do not compete on service, smaller firms, such as hhgregg, will have an easier time defending their market niche. For consumers in that niche, hhgregg may charge higher prices, but it still provides these consumers with greater value.

Source: Miguel Bustillo, "Small Electronics Chains Thrive in Downturn," *Wall Street Journal*, May 27, 2009.

 **YOUR TURN:** For more practice, do related problem 3.7 on page 425 at the end of this chapter.

---

# Comparing Perfect Competition and Monopolistic Competition

We have seen that monopolistic competition and perfect competition share the characteristic that in long-run equilibrium, firms earn zero economic profits. As Figure 12-6 shows, however, there are two important differences between long-run equilibrium in the two markets:

* Monopolistically competitive firms charge a price greater than marginal cost.

* Monopolistically competitive firms do not produce at minimum average total cost.

## Excess Capacity under Monopolistic Competition

Recall that a firm in a perfectly competitive market faces a perfectly elastic demand curve that is also its marginal revenue curve. Therefore, the firm maximizes profit by producing where price equals marginal cost. As panel (a) of Figure 12-6 shows, in

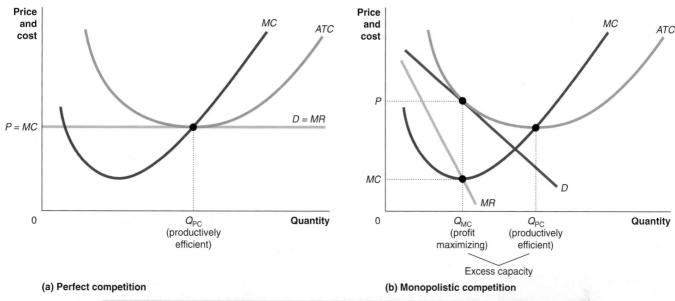

**(a) Perfect competition**    **(b) Monopolistic competition**

Figure 12-6    **Comparing Long-Run Equilibrium under Perfect Competition and Monopolistic Competition**

In panel (a), the perfectly competitive firm in long-run equilibrium produces at $Q_{PC}$, where price equals marginal cost, and average total cost is at a minimum. The perfectly competitive firm is both allocatively efficient and productively efficient. In panel (b), the monopolistically competitive firm produces at $Q_{MC}$, where price is greater than marginal cost, and average total cost is not at a minimum. As a result, the monopolistically competitive firm is neither allocatively efficient nor productively efficient. The monopolistically competitive firm has excess capacity equal to the difference between its profit-maximizing level of output and the productively efficient level of output.

long-run equilibrium, a perfectly competitive firm produces at the minimum point of its average total cost curve.

Panel (b) of Figure 12-6 shows that the profit-maximizing level of output for a monopolistically competitive firm comes at a level of output where price is greater than marginal cost, and the firm is not at the minimum point of its average total cost curve. A monopolistically competitive firm has *excess capacity*: If it increased its output, it could produce at a lower average cost.

## Is Monopolistic Competition Inefficient?

In Chapter 11, we discussed *productive efficiency* and *allocative efficiency*. Productive efficiency refers to the situation where a good is produced at the lowest possible cost. Allocative efficiency refers to the situation where every good or service is produced up to the point where the last unit provides a marginal benefit to consumers equal to the marginal cost of producing it. For productive efficiency to hold, firms must produce at the minimum point of average total cost. For allocative efficiency to hold, firms must charge a price equal to marginal cost. In a perfectly competitive market, both productive efficiency and allocative efficiency are achieved, but in a monopolistically competitive market, neither is achieved. Does it matter? Economists have debated whether monopolistically competitive markets being neither productively nor allocatively efficient results in a significant loss of well-being to society in these markets compared with perfectly competitive markets.

## How Consumers Benefit from Monopolistic Competition

Looking again at Figure 12-6, you can see that the only difference between the monopolistically competitive firm and the perfectly competitive firm is that the demand curve for the monopolistically competitive firm slopes downward, whereas the demand curve for the perfectly competitive firm is a horizontal line. The demand curve for the monopolistically competitive firm slopes downward because the good or service the firm is selling is differentiated from the goods or services being sold by competing firms. The perfectly competitive firm is selling a good or service identical to those being sold by its competitors. A key point to remember is that *firms differentiate their products to appeal to consumers*. When

Starbucks coffeehouses begin offering new flavors of coffee, when Blockbuster stores begin carrying more Blu-ray discs and fewer regular DVDs, when General Mills introduces Apple-Cinnamon Cheerios, or when PepsiCo introduces caffeine-free Diet Pepsi, they are all attempting to attract and retain consumers through product differentiation. The success of these product differentiation strategies indicates that some consumers find these products preferable to the alternatives. Consumers, therefore, are better off than they would have been had these companies not differentiated their products.

We can conclude that consumers face a trade-off when buying the product of a monopolistically competitive firm: They are paying a price that is greater than marginal cost, and the product is not being produced at minimum average cost, but they benefit from being able to purchase a product that is differentiated and more closely suited to their tastes.

*Did Abercrombie and Fitch narrow its target market too much?*

**Making** the **Connection** | **Abercrombie & Fitch: Can the Product Be Too Differentiated?**

Business managers often refer to differentiating their products as finding a "market niche." The larger the niche you have, the greater the potential profit but the more likely that other firms will be able to compete against you. Too small a niche, however, may reduce competition—but also reduce profits. Some analysts believe that the market niche chosen by the managers of the Abercrombie & Fitch clothing stores is too small. The chief executive, Mike Jeffries, argues that his store's target customer is an "18-to-22 [year old] college guy who has a good body and is aspirational." He admits that this is a narrow niche: "If I exclude people—absolutely. Delighted to do so."

But is A&F excluding too many people? One analyst argues, "they've . . . pushed a lot of people out of the brand." A&F's sales results seemed to indicate that this analyst may be correct. Managers of retail stores closely monitor "same-store sales," which measures how much sales have changed in the same stores from one year to the next. To offset the effects of inflation—or general increases in prices in the economy—same-store sales need to increase at least 2 percent to 3 percent each year. A firm whose strategy of product differentiation succeeds will experience increases in same-store sales of at least 5 percent to 6 percent each year. For several years in the early 2000s, A&F's 350 stores experienced *negative* same-store results.

Although sales increased from 2004 through early 2006, negative changes in same-store sales returned in late 2006. Particularly poor results occurred during the first part of 2009, as same-store sales declined by 30 percent. For years, Abercrombie had resisted discounting its clothing. But the poor results in early 2009 finally led them to begin cutting prices. Mike Jeffries announced that "meaningful reductions" would occur because of "a headwind where the consumer is reluctant to spend on premium brands." A&F seemed finally to be conceding that it had gone too far in narrowing its market niche.

Sources: Nicholas Casey, "After Big Loss, Abercrombie to Cut Prices," *Wall Street Journal*, May 18, 2009; and Shelly Branch, "Maybe Sex Doesn't Sell, A&F Is Discovering," *Wall Street Journal*, December 12, 2003.

**YOUR TURN:** Test your understanding by doing related problem 4.6 on page 427 at the end of this chapter.

---

**12.5 LEARNING** OBJECTIVE

Define marketing and explain how firms use it to differentiate their products.

**Marketing** All the activities necessary for a firm to sell a product to a consumer.

# How Marketing Differentiates Products

Firms can differentiate their products through marketing. **Marketing** refers to all the activities necessary for a firm to sell a product to a consumer. Marketing includes activities such as determining which product to produce, designing the product, advertising the product, deciding how to distribute the product—for example, in retail stores or through a Web site—and monitoring how changes in consumer tastes are affecting the market for the product. Peter F. Drucker, a leading business strategist, describes marketing as follows: "It is the whole business seen from the point of view of its final result, that is, from the consumer's point of view. . . . True marketing . . . does not ask, 'What do we want to sell?' It asks, 'What does the consumer want to buy?'"

As we have seen, for monopolistically competitive firms to earn economic profits and defend those profits from competitors, they must differentiate their products. Firms use two marketing tools to differentiate their products: brand management and advertising.

## Brand Management

Once a firm has succeeded in differentiating its product, it must try to maintain that differentiation over time through **brand management**. As we have seen, whenever a firm successfully introduces a new product or a significantly different version of an old product, it earns economic profits in the short run. But the success of the firm inspires competitors to copy the new or improved product and, in the long run, the firm's economic profits will be competed away. Firms use brand management to postpone the time when they will no longer be able to earn economic profits.

**Brand management** The actions of a firm intended to maintain the differentiation of a product over time.

## Advertising

An innovative advertising campaign can make even long-established and familiar products, such as Coke or McDonald's Big Mac hamburgers, seem more desirable than competing products. When a firm advertises a product, it is trying to shift the demand curve for the product to the right and to make it more inelastic. If the firm is successful, it will sell more of the product at every price, and it will be able to increase the price it charges without losing as many customers. Of course, advertising also increases a firm's costs. If the increase in revenue that results from the advertising is greater than the increase in costs, the firm's profits will rise.

| Making the Connection | ### Google Tries (and Fails) to Measure the Effectiveness of Radio Advertising |

Although the payoff to a successful advertising campaign can be substantial, so can the cost of running advertisements on television, radio, or the Internet, or buying space in newspapers and magazines. A firm's optimal level of advertising occurs where the marginal cost of advertising equals the marginal revenue earned from advertising. The marginal revenue earned from advertising is the additional revenue from the increased sales resulting from the advertising. But how can a firm calculate how much its sales increased because of advertising? For Web advertising, firms can measure how often people click on their ads and how many of those clicks lead to online sales. But the payoff to television, radio, newspaper, and magazine ads is much harder to measure.

*Does spending on radio advertising attract customers?*

Google hoped to build on its success in selling Web advertising by starting a new business that would sell radio advertising. Google's CEO Eric Schmidt predicted that within a few years the firm would employ 1,000 workers in its radio advertising business. Traditionally, firms have paid for radio commercials on the basis of the number of listeners who are estimated to have heard the commercial. Google developed a sophisticated technology that would enable it to use data obtained from retail stores and from advertisers' Web sites to determine whether commercials were leading to purchases. Google decided to auction off advertising spots, expecting that advertisers would bid up the prices of commercials once the advertisers were provided with information on how effective the commercials were rather than just on how many people listened to them. Google also planned to automate the method of distributing commercials, by sending them automatically to stations at prearranged times. Under this system, advertisers would not know ahead of time on which stations and at what times their commercials would run.

Google had difficulty selling its plan to advertisers, who were used to the traditional method of paying a fixed fee to run their commercials on specific stations at specific times. Many advertisers also questioned whether Google's new technology would accurately track sales resulting from their commercials. As a result, Google's auctions of advertising slots resulted in lower than expected prices. These low prices disappointed radio stations that believed they could obtain higher prices selling specific slots to advertisers at fixed prices. Many stations withdrew from Google's program. One station owner said, "They want me to put my faith and wallet in this?" After three years of trying to earn a profit selling radio commercials, Google announced that at the end of May 2009 it would abandon the radio advertising business. Station owners and advertisers were left to continue their search for ways to measure the effectiveness of radio commercials.

Sources: Jessica E. Vascellaro, "Radio Tunes Out Google in Rare Miss for Web Titan," *Wall Street Journal*, May 12, 2009; and Miguel Helft, "Google Ends Its Project for Selling Radio Ads," *New York Times*, February 12, 2009.

 **YOUR TURN:** Test your understanding by doing related problem 5.7 on page 428 at the end of this chapter.

## Defending a Brand Name

Once a firm has established a successful brand name, it has a strong incentive to defend it. A firm can apply for a *trademark*, which grants legal protection against other firms using its product's name.

One threat to a trademarked name is the possibility that it will become so widely used for a type of product that it will no longer be associated with the product of a specific company. Courts in the United States have ruled that when this happens, a firm is no longer entitled to legal protection of the brand name. For example, "aspirin," "escalator," and "thermos" were originally all brand names of the products of particular firms, but each became so widely used to refer to a type of product that none remains a legally protected brand name. Firms spend substantial amounts of money trying to make sure that this does not happen to them. Coca-Cola, for example, employs workers to travel to restaurants around the country and order a "Coke" with their meal. If the restaurant serves Pepsi or some other cola, rather than Coke, Coca-Cola's legal department sends the restaurant a letter reminding that "Coke" is a trademarked name and not a generic name for any cola. Similarly, Xerox Corporation spends money on advertising to remind the public that "Xerox" is not a generic term for making photocopies.

Legally enforcing trademarks can be difficult. Estimates are that each year, U.S. firms lose hundreds of billions of dollars in sales worldwide as a result of unauthorized use of their trademarked brand names. U.S. firms often find it difficult to enforce their trademarks in the courts of some foreign countries, although recent international agreements have increased the legal protections for trademarks.

Firms that sell their products through franchises rather than through company-owned stores encounter the problem that if a franchisee does not run his or her business well, the firm's brand may be damaged. Automobile firms send "roadmen" to visit their dealers to make sure the dealerships are clean and well maintained and that the service departments employ competent mechanics and are well equipped with spare parts. Similarly, McDonald's sends employees from corporate headquarters to visit McDonald's franchises to make sure the bathrooms are clean and the French fries are hot.

**12.6 LEARNING** OBJECTIVE

Identify the key factors that determine a firm's success.

## What Makes a Firm Successful?

A firm's owners and managers control some of the factors that make a firm successful and allow it to earn economic profits. The most important of these are the firm's ability to differentiate its product and to produce its product at a lower average cost than competing firms. A firm that successfully does these things creates *value* for its customers.

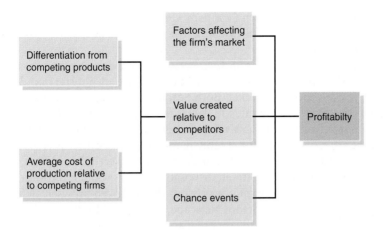

## Figure 12-7

**What Makes a Firm Successful?**

The factors under a firm's control—the ability to differentiate its product and the ability to produce it at lower cost—combine with the factors beyond its control to determine the firm's profitability.

Source: Adapted from Figure 11.3 in David Besanko, David Dranove, Mark Shanley, and Scott Schaefer, *The Economics of Strategy*, 4th ed., New York: Wiley, 2007.

Consumers will buy a product if they believe it meets a need not met by competing products or if its price is below that of competitors.

Some factors that affect a firm's profitability are not directly under the firm's control. Certain factors will affect all the firms in a market. For example, rising prices for jet fuel will reduce the profitability of all airlines. If consumers decide that rather than buy DVDs, they would prefer to watch pay-per-view movies delivered to their homes by cable or satellite, or download movies from iTunes or Amazon, the profitability of all stores selling DVDs will be reduced.

Sheer chance also plays a role in business, as it does in all other aspects of life. A struggling McDonald's franchise may see profits increase dramatically after the county unexpectedly decides to build a new road nearby. Many businesses in New York City, including restaurants, hotels, and theaters, experienced a marked drop in customers and profits following the September 11, 2001, terrorist attacks. Figure 12-7 illustrates the important point that factors within the firm's control and factors outside the firm's control interact to determine the firm's profitability.

## Making the Connection | Is Being the First Firm in the Market a Key to Success?

Some business analysts argue that the first firm to enter a market can have important *first-mover advantages*. By being the first to sell a particular good, a firm may find its name closely associated with the good in the public's mind, as, for instance, Amazon is closely associated with ordering books online or eBay is associated with online auctions. This close association may make it more difficult for new firms to enter the market and compete against the first mover.

Surprisingly, though, recent research has shown that the first firm to enter a market often does *not* have a long-lived advantage over later entrants. Consider, for instance, the market for pens. Until the 1940s, the only pens available were fountain pens that had to be refilled frequently from an ink bottle and used ink that dried slowly and smeared easily. In October 1945, entrepreneur Milton Reynolds introduced the first ballpoint pen, which never needed to be refilled. When it went on sale at Gimbel's department store in New York City, it was an instant success. Although the pen had a price of $12.00—the equivalent of about $135.00 at today's prices—hundreds of thousands were sold, and Milton Reynolds became a millionaire. Unfortunately, it didn't last. Although Reynolds had guaranteed that his pen would write for two years—later raised to five years—in fact, the pen often leaked and frequently stopped writing after only limited use. Sales began to collapse, the flood of pens returned under the company's guarantee wiped out its profits, and within a few

*Although not first to market, Bic ultimately was more successful than the firm that pioneered ballpoint pens.*

years, Reynolds International Pen Company stopped selling pens in the United States. By the late 1960s, firms such as Bic, selling inexpensive—but reliable—ballpoint pens, dominated the market.

What happened to the Reynolds International Pen Company turns out to be more the rule than the exception. For example, Apple's iPod was not the first digital music player to appear on the U.S. market. Both Seahan's MPMan and Diamond's PMP300 were released in the United States in 1998, three years before the iPod. Similarly, although Hewlett-Packard currently dominates the market for laser printers, with a market share of more than 50 percent, it did not invent the laser printer. Xerox invented the laser printer, and IBM sold the first commercial laser printers. Nor was Procter & Gamble the first firm to sell disposable diapers when it introduced Pampers in 1961. Microsoft's Internet Explorer was not the first Web browser: Before Internet Explorer, there was Netscape; before Netscape, there was Mosaic; and before Mosaic, there were several other Web browsers that for a time looked as if they might dominate the market. In all these cases, the firms that were first to introduce a product ultimately lost out to latecomers who did a better job of providing consumers with products that were more reliable, less expensive, more convenient, or otherwise provided greater value.

Sources: Steven P. Schnaars, *Managing Imitation Strategies: How Later Entrants Seize Markets from Pioneers*, New York: The Free Press, 1994; and Gerard J. Tellis and Peter N. Golder, *Will and Vision: How Latecomers Grow to Dominate Markets*, Los Angeles: Figueroa Press, 2002.

 **YOUR TURN:** Test your understanding by doing related problem 6.6 on page 429 at the end of this chapter.

▶ Continued from page 401

## Economics in YOUR LIFE!

At the beginning of the chapter, we asked you to think about how successful you are likely to be in opening an Italian restaurant in your hometown. As you learned in this chapter, if your restaurant is successful, other people are likely to open competing restaurants, and all your economic profits will eventually disappear. This occurs because economic profits attract entry of new firms into a market. The new restaurants will sell Italian food, but it won't be exactly like your Italian food—after all, they don't have your grandmother's secret sauce recipe! Each restaurant will have its own ideas on how best to appeal to people who like Italian food. Unless your food is so much different than your competitors' food—or your service is so much better—in the long run you will be unable to charge prices high enough to allow you to earn an economic profit.

In a monopolistically competitive market, free entry will reduce prices and lead to zero economic profits in the long run. In addition to lowering prices, competition benefits consumers by leading firms to offer somewhat different versions of the same product; for example, two Italian restaurants will rarely be exactly alike.

## Conclusion

In this chapter, we have applied many of the ideas about competition we developed in Chapter 11 to the more common market structure of monopolistic competition. We have seen that these ideas apply to monopolistically competitive markets, just as they do to perfectly competitive markets. At the end of Chapter 11, we concluded that "The competitive forces of the market impose relentless pressure on firms to produce new and better goods and services at the lowest possible cost. Firms that fail to adequately anticipate changes in consumer tastes or that fail to adopt the latest and most efficient production technology do not survive in the long run." These conclusions are as true for coffeehouses and firms in other monopolistically competitive markets as they are for wheat farmers or apple growers.

In Chapter 13 and Chapter 14, we discuss the remaining market structures: oligopoly and monopoly. Before moving on to those chapters, read *An Inside Look* on the next page for a discussion of how McDonald's expanded its competition with Starbucks.

## >> Starbucks Faces McCompetition

### THE ARIZONA REPUBLIC

## McDonald's Plans Frontal Attack on Starbucks

. . .

The move could give coffee giant Starbucks a kick when it's already down. The Seattle company saw its first-quarter profit tumble 77 percent as sales slipped 8 percent at locations that had been open more than a year.

On Monday, baristas stationed at McDonald's drive-through counters in Arizona will begin dispensing cappuccinos, hot chocolate and hot and cold flavored lattes and mochas . . .

(a) It's being called the biggest product change at McDonald's since it launched breakfast in 1975 with the Egg McMuffin. McDonald's hopes the McCafes will draw in non-traditional customers who will sample other products.

Deutsche Bank analyst Marc Greenberg noted in a report to clients last month that "McCafe is a game-changer in coffee." McDonald's has been slowly introducing McCafes in select markets and will roll it out nationwide next week. Eventually, all of McDonald's 14,000 U.S. restaurants . . . will offer the specialty coffee. Starbucks has about 11,500 U.S. locations . . .

The cost of store improvements and McCafe equipment is about $100,000 per location, which is mainly being paid by franchisees.

"We're getting in the beverage business in a big way," said Lee Heriaud, owner of 15 Phoenix-area McDonald's franchises.

Bill Sandweg, owner of Copper Star Coffee, an independent coffee house in central Phoenix, believes McDonald's could ultimately help his business.

"They will get the masses hooked on premium coffee," he said. "Those people will eventually come here."

Sandweg, a former Starbucks employee, sees the Seattle company as most impacted by McDonald's.

"They had it coming though," he said. "Starbucks turned coffee into fast food and that put them in the sights of McDonald's."

### Coffee bucks

(b) McDonald's and others have their sights on the $60 billion U.S. specialty-coffee market dominated by Starbucks.

On a smaller scale, Dunkin' Donuts also offers premium coffee that it serves hot and cold.

The challengers are making inroads.

. . . "The threat is real, and it has yellow arches," Deutsche Bank's Greenberg wrote to clients. "We expect McDonald's will extract a significant toll on Starbucks' performance, beginning this summer in earnest."

McDonald's sees the coffee drinks not only boosting revenue, but also drawing new customers to the stores.

"There are a lot of people who have never had an Egg McMuffin," Heriaud said. "We're hoping customers going through the drive-through for a cappuccino in the morning will also try our food."

He estimated that the specialty-coffee drinks will boost revenue 3 percent to 5 percent at his restaurant . . . in central Phoenix. He declined to say what the location grosses each year, but noted the average McDonald's franchise has sales of $2.2 million.

### Long-range plan

McDonald's has been preparing to launch McCafe in the U.S. for some time . . .

Three years ago, it upgraded the coffee at its U.S. locations to a bold roast similar to Starbucks. Later, it began customizing hot and cold coffee drinks with sweeteners and milk products.

"McCafe is the next step," Heriaud said.

The new blend got positive reviews from consumers . . .

(c) A recent taste test conducted by Quick Service Restaurant News & Trends reported that consumers believed McDonald's cappuccinos, vanilla lattes and mochas were superior to similar drinks at Starbucks.

McDonald's initially approached Starbucks about supplying coffee to its McCafes, but was turned down because it was "not a good fit." . . .

Heriaud said the "relaxed cafè-lounge ambiance" is more in-synch with consumers and better reflects its healthier offerings and its new coffee drinks.

"McDonald's continues to strive to be relevant to our customers," he said.

Source: Max Jarman, "McDonald's Plans Frontal Attack on Starbucks," *Arizona Republic*, May 23, 2009.

## Key Points in the Article

McDonald's began competing with Starbucks nationwide at a time when the Seattle company's sales and profits had already been falling. First, McDonald's began offering cappuccinos, hot chocolate, and hot and cold flavored lattes and mochas at select locations. Then, it began offering these premium coffee drinks nationwide.

As we have seen in this chapter, successful firms such as Starbucks's continually face competition from other firms. Though McDonald's, Dunkin' Donuts, and other firms threaten to reduce Starbucks's revenue and profits, they are offering consumers greater variety and more choices. In the market for premium coffee, product differentiation continues to be the key to success.

## Analyzing the News

(a) The demand for Starbucks coffee, which had declined in 2008 due to recession and competition from Dunkin' Donuts and other firms, could be reduced further by additional competition from 14,000 McDonald's restaurants. The figure assumes that an existing Starbucks coffeehouse is earning an economic profit from selling $Q_1$ cups of coffee and charging a price of $P_1$ dollars. The profit-maximizing quantity is found at the point where the marginal revenue curve, $MR_1$, intersects the

marginal cost curve, $MC$. The price is determined by the demand curve, $D_1$. The firm earns an economic profit equal to the shaded area. The economic profit earned by coffeehouses like Starbucks explains why McDonald's and other firms decided to enter the market for premium coffees.

(b) McDonald's hopes that customers who buy its new coffee products will also buy some of its other menu items, such as Egg McMuffins. This is an example of how a firm can gain from product differentiation. If McDonald's is successful, it will be at the expense of some of Starbucks's coffeehouses. As the figure shows, the entry of the McCafe coffee bars will take some of the demand away from current firms in the market. This causes the demand curve to shift to the left, from $D_1$ to $D_2$. The marginal revenue curve also shifts to the left, from $MR_1$ to $MR_2$.

The profit-maximizing level of output is now $Q_2$, where the new marginal revenue curve intersects the marginal cost curve, $MC$. The new profit-maximizing price is $P_2$. Notice that at this point, the demand curve, $D_2$, is tangent to the average total cost curve, $ATC$, and the firm is earning zero profit. At equilibrium, all firms in the market will earn zero profit. This is shown as point $E$ in the figure.

(c) This section illustrates how McDonald's McCafes use product differentiation to appeal to some Starbucks customers. There

is evidence that the quality of the coffee drinks sold at McDonald's and Starbucks is comparable, and McDonald's hopes that the ambiance at its locations will draw some of Starbucks's regular customers.

## Thinking Critically

1. Suppose that the federal government required a license to open a *new* coffeehouse (existing coffeehouses would not require a license) and that the number of licenses was limited. How would this affect the equilibrium price and quantity in the coffeehouse market? Who would gain from this requirement, and who would lose?

2. Suppose that McDonald's is successful in its efforts to attract a significant number of former Starbucks customers who regularly buy Egg McMuffins and other breakfast items with their coffee. How might Starbucks respond to this change in tastes?

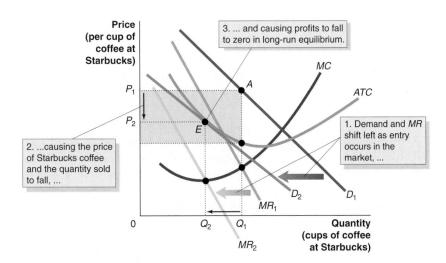

The effect of entry on price, quantity, and profits at Starbucks.

# Key Terms

Brand management, p. 415

Marketing, p. 414

Monopolistic competition,
p. 402

---

**12.1** **Demand and Marginal Revenue for a Firm in a Monopolistically Competitive Market,** pages 402–404

LEARNING OBJECTIVE: Explain why a monopolistically competitive firm has downward-sloping demand and marginal revenue curves.

## Summary

A firm competing in a **monopolistically competitive** market sells a differentiated product. Therefore, unlike a firm in a perfectly competitive market, it faces a downward-sloping demand curve. When a monopolistically competitive firm cuts the price of its product, it sells more units but must accept a lower price on the units it could have sold at the higher price. As a result, its marginal revenue curve is downward sloping. Every firm that has the ability to affect the price of the good or service it sells will have a marginal revenue curve that is below its demand curve.

| DVDs RENTED PER WEEK (Q) | PRICE (P) | TOTAL REVENUE (TR = P × Q) | AVERAGE REVENUE (AR = TR/Q) | MARGINAL REVENUE (MR = ΔTR/ΔQ) |
|---|---|---|---|---|
| 0 | $8.00 | | | |
| 1 | 7.50 | | | |
| 2 | 7.00 | | | |
| 3 | 6.50 | | | |
| 4 | 6.00 | | | |
| 5 | 5.50 | | | |
| 6 | 5.00 | | | |
| 7 | 4.50 | | | |
| 8 | 4.00 | | | |

 Visit **www.myeconlab.com** to complete these exercises online and get instant feedback.

## Review Questions

**1.1** What are the most important differences between perfectly competitive markets and monopolistically competitive markets? Give two examples of products sold in perfectly competitive markets and two examples of products sold in monopolistically competitive markets.

**1.2** Why does the local McDonald's face a downward-sloping demand curve for Big Macs? If it raises the price it charges for Big Macs above the prices charged by other McDonald's stores, won't it lose all its customers?

**1.3** Explain the differences between total revenue, average revenue, and marginal revenue.

## Problems and Applications

**1.4** Complete the following table:

**1.5** A student makes the following argument:

> When a firm sells another unit of a good, the additional revenue the firm receives is equal to the price: If the price is $10, then the additional revenue is also $10. Therefore, this chapter is incorrect when it says that marginal revenue is less than price for a monopolistically competitive firm.

Briefly explain whether you agree with this argument.

**1.6** There are many wheat farms in the world, but there are also many Starbucks coffeehouses. Why, then, does a Starbucks coffeehouse face a downward-sloping demand curve, while a wheat farmer faces a horizontal demand curve?

**1.7** Is it possible for marginal revenue to be negative for a firm selling in a perfectly competitive market? Is it possible for marginal revenue to be negative for a firm selling in a monopolistically competitive market? Briefly explain.

**>> End Learning Objective 12.1**

**12.2** **How a Monopolistically Competitive Firm Maximizes Profit in the Short Run,** pages 404–407

LEARNING OBJECTIVE: Explain how a monopolistically competitive firm maximizes profit in the short run.

## Summary

A monopolistically competitive firm maximizes profits at the level of output where marginal revenue equals marginal cost. Price equals marginal revenue for a perfectly competitive firm, but price is greater than marginal revenue for a monopolistically competitive firm. Therefore, unlike a perfectly competitive firm, which produces where $P = MC$, a monopolistically competitive firm produces where $P > MC$.

 Visit **www.myeconlab.com** to complete these exercises online and get instant feedback.

## Review Questions

**2.1** Sally runs a McDonald's franchise. She is selling 350 Big Macs per week at a price of $3.25. If she lowers the price to $3.20, she will sell 351 Big Macs. What is the marginal revenue of the 351st Big Mac?

**2.2** Eugenio runs a Hollywood Video store. Eugenio is currently renting 3,525 DVDs per week. If instead of renting 3,525 DVDs, he rents 3,526 DVDs, he will add $2.95 to his costs and $2.75 to his revenues. What will be the effect on his profits of renting 3,526 DVDs instead of 3,525 DVDs?

**2.3** Should a monopolistically competitive firm take into account its fixed costs when deciding how much to produce? Briefly explain.

## Problems and Applications

**2.4** If Daniel sells 350 Big Macs at a price of $3.25, and his average cost of producing 350 Big Macs is $3.00, what is his profit?

**2.5** Maria manages a Hollywood Video store and has the following information on demand and costs:

| DVDS RENTED PER WEEK (Q) | PRICE (P) | TOTAL COST (TC) |
|---|---|---|
| 0 | $6.00 | $3.00 |
| 1 | 5.50 | 7.00 |
| 2 | 5.00 | 10.00 |
| 3 | 4.50 | 12.50 |
| 4 | 4.00 | 14.50 |
| 5 | 3.50 | 16.00 |
| 6 | 3.00 | 17.00 |
| 7 | 2.50 | 18.50 |
| 8 | 2.00 | 21.00 |

**a.** To maximize profit, how many DVDs should Maria rent, what price should she charge, and how much profit will she make?

**b.** What is the marginal revenue received by renting the profit-maximizing DVD? What is the marginal cost of renting the profit-maximizing DVD?

**2.6** (Related to *Solved Problem 12-2* on page 406) Suppose a firm producing table lamps has the following costs:

| QUANTITY | AVERAGE TOTAL COST |
|---|---|
| 1,000 | $15.00 |
| 2,000 | 9.75 |
| 3,000 | 8.25 |
| 4,000 | 7.50 |
| 5,000 | 7.75 |
| 6,000 | 8.50 |
| 7,000 | 9.75 |
| 8,000 | 10.50 |
| 9,000 | 12.00 |

Ben and Jerry are managers at the company, and they have this discussion:

**Ben:** We should produce 4,000 lamps per month because that will minimize our average costs.
**Jerry:** But shouldn't we maximize profits rather than minimize costs? To maximize profits, don't we need to take demand into account?
**Ben:** Don't worry. By minimizing average costs, we will be maximizing profits. Demand will determine how high the price we can charge will be, but it won't affect our profit-maximizing quantity.

Evaluate the discussion between the two managers.

**2.7** The following is from an article in the *New York Times*: "American Airlines, based in Fort Worth, reported a loss of $1.45 billion, or $5.77 a share, for its second quarter, compared with a profit of $317 million, or $1.08 a share, a year earlier. Revenue rose 5.1 percent, to $6.18 billion."

**a.** Briefly explain how it is possible for a firm's revenue to increase at the same time as its profits decrease.

**b.** Construct a simple numerical example of a firm that increases its revenue while moving from making a profit to making a loss. Use a graph to illustrate your example.

Source: Abha Bhattarai, "Shares Rise at 2 Carriers, Despite $1 Billion in Losses," *New York Times*, July 17, 2008.

**2.8** During the last three months of 2008, clothing retailer J.Crew cut the prices of many of its products. During that period its profits per item of clothing declined, and it suffered a loss of $13.5 million. Is this information enough to allow us to determine that J.Crew's decision to cut prices was not a profit-maximizing strategy? Briefly explain.

Source: John Kell, "Markdowns Weigh on J. Crew," *Wall Street Journal*, March 11, 2009.

**2.9** William Germano is vice president and publishing director at the Routledge publishing company. He has given the following description of how a publisher might deal with an unexpected increase in the cost of publishing a book:

> It's often asked why the publisher can't simply raise the price [if costs increase]. . . . It's likely that the editor [is already] . . . charging as much as the market will bear. . . . In other words, you might be willing to pay $50.00 for a . . . book on the Brooklyn Bridge, but if . . . production costs [increase] by 25 percent, you might think $62.50 is too much to pay, though that would be what the publisher needs to charge. And indeed the publisher may determine that $50.00 is this book's ceiling—the most you would pay before deciding to rent a movie instead.

According to what you have learned in this chapter, how do firms adjust the price of a good when there is an increase in cost? Use a graph to illustrate your answer. Does the model of monopolistic competition seem to fit Germano's description? If a publisher does not raise the price of a book following an increase in its production cost, what will be the result?

Source: William Germano, *Getting It Published: A Guide to Scholars and Anyone Else Serious about Serious Books*, Chicago: University of Chicago Press, 2001, pp. 110–111.

**2.10** In October 2008, Amazon.com announced that during the previous three months it had increased its revenue by 31 percent compared with the previous year, despite the U.S. economy being in a recession. Jeff Bezos, Amazon's chief executive, attributed the increase in revenue in part to the company having lowered prices. Bezos was quoted as saying: "I love our position today in the marketplace because we have been spending so much time making sure we are the low-cost provider."

**a.** If Amazon.com's revenue increased after it cut the price of books, DVDs, and Blu-ray discs, what must be true about the price elasticity of demand for ordering these goods online?

**b.** Suppose that before the price cut, Amazon.com was not selling the profit-maximizing quantity of books, but after the price cut, it was. Draw a graph that shows Amazon.com's situation before and after the price cut. (For simplicity, assume that Amazon charges the same price for all books.) Be sure your graph includes the price Amazon was charging and the quantity of books it was selling before the price cut; the price and quantity after the price cut; Amazon's demand, marginal revenue, average total cost, and marginal cost curves; and the areas representing Amazon's profits before and after the price cut.

Source: Brad Stone, "Amazon Posts Profit Jump and Offers Fuzzy Forecast," *New York Times*, October 22, 2008.

**2.11** In 1916, the Ford Motor Company produced 500,000 Model T Fords at a price of $440 each. The company made a profit of $60 million that year. Henry Ford told a newspaper reporter that he intended to reduce the price of the Model T to $360, and he expected to sell 800,000 cars at that price. Ford said, "Less profit on each car, but more cars, more employment of labor, and in the end we get all the total profit we ought to make."

**a.** Did Ford expect the total revenue he received from selling Model Ts to rise or fall following the price cut?

**b.** Use the information given above to calculate the price elasticity of demand for Model Ts. Use the midpoint formula to make your calculation. See Chapter 6, page 170, if you need a refresher on the midpoint formula.

**c.** What would the average total cost of producing 800,000 Model Ts have to be for Ford to make as much profit selling 800,000 Model Ts as it made selling 500,000 Model Ts? Is this smaller or larger than the average total cost of producing 500,000 Model Ts?

**d.** Assume that Ford would make the same total profit when selling 800,000 cars as when selling 500,000 cars. Was Henry Ford correct in saying he would make less profit per car when selling 800,000 cars than when selling 500,000 cars?

>> **End Learning Objective 12.2**

**12.3** **What Happens to Profits in the Long Run?** pages 407–412

LEARNING OBJECTIVE: Analyze the situation of a monopolistically competitive firm in the long run.

## Summary

If a monopolistically competitive firm is earning economic profits in the short run, entry of new firms will eliminate those profits in the long run. If a monopolistically competitive firm is suffering economic losses in the short run, exit of existing firms will eliminate those losses in the long run. Monopolistically competitive firms continually struggle to find new ways of differentiating their products as they try to stay one step ahead of other firms that are attempting to copy their success.

 Visit **www.myeconlab.com** to complete these exercises online and get instant feedback.

## Review Questions

3.1 What effect does the entry of new firms have on the economic profits of existing firms?

3.2 What is the difference between zero accounting profit and zero economic profit?

## Problems and Applications

3.3 Use this graph to answer the questions that follow.

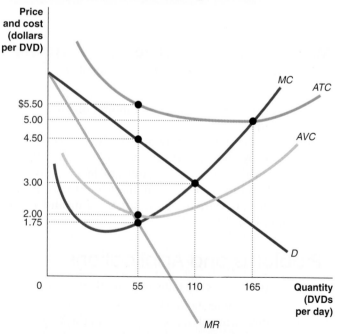

a. If the owner of this video store wants to maximize profits, how many DVDs should she rent per day, and what rental price should she charge? Briefly explain your answer.

b. How much economic profit (or loss) is she making? Briefly explain.

c. Is the owner likely to continue renting this number of DVDs in the long run? Briefly explain.

3.4 **(Related to the *Don't Let This Happen to You!* on page 408)** A student remarks:

> If firms in a monopolistically competitive industry are earning economic profits, new firms will enter the industry. Eventually, the representative firm will find that its demand curve has shifted to the left, until it is just tangent to its average cost curve and it is earning zero profit. Because firms are earning zero profit at that point, some firms will leave the industry, and the representative firm will find that its demand curve will shift to the right. In long-run equilibrium, price will be above average total cost by just enough so that each firm is just breaking even.

Briefly explain whether you agree with this analysis.

3.5 A columnist in the *Wall Street Journal* made the following observation: "The [oil] refining business is just too competitive, which is great for consumers, but not shareholders." Briefly explain why the high level of competition in the oil refining industry is good for consumers but bad for the shareholders who own these firms.

Source: James B. Stewart, "Coping with the Inevitable: The Losers in Your Portfolio," *Wall Street Journal*, December 3, 2008.

3.6 **(Related to the *Making the Connection* on page 410)** As McDonald's began to increase its competition with Starbucks in 2009, Starbucks attempted to fight back with a new advertising campaign. According to an article in the *Wall Street Journal*, one ad proclaimed: "If your coffee isn't perfect, we'll make it over. If it's still not perfect make sure you're in a Starbucks." Starbucks CEO Howard Schultz explained the purpose of the campaign: "We don't want the public to be misled that all coffee is equal, because it's not." Why would it be a problem for Starbucks if consumers came to believe that "all coffee is equal"? How might Starbucks convince consumers that all coffee is not equal?

Source: Julie Jargon, "New Ads Will Stir Up Coffee Wars," *Wall Street Journal*, May 4, 2009.

3.7 **(Related to *Solved Problem 12-3* on page 411)** hhgregg has been successful in retailing appliances and electronics by combining high prices with excellent customer service. In late 2008, Saks Fifth Avenue tried a new strategy in retailing luxury clothing. Saks decided to slash prices on designer clothing by 70 percent just before the beginning of the holiday sales season. According to an article in the *Wall Street Journal*, "Saks's risky price-cut strategy was to be one of the first to discount deeply, rather than one of the last." According to the article:

> Saks's maneuver marked an open abandonment of the longstanding unwritten pact between retailers and designers. . . . Those old rules boiled down to this: Leave the goods at full price at least two months, and don't do markdowns until the very end of the season.

Is Saks's strategy of becoming the low-priced luxury clothing retailer likely to succeed? Contrast Saks's strategy with the strategy of hhgregg in terms of how likely the two strategies are to be successful over the long run.

Source: Vanessa O'Connell and Rachel Dodes, "Saks Upends Luxury Market With Strategy to Slash Prices" *Wall Street Journal*, February 9, 2009.

3.8 Michael Korda was, for many years, editor-in-chief at the Simon & Schuster book publishing company. He has written about the many books that have become bestsellers by promising to give readers financial advice that will make them wealthy, by, for example, buying and selling real estate. Korda is skeptical about the usefulness of the advice in these books because "I have yet to meet anybody who got rich by buying a book, though quite a few people got rich by writing one." On the basis of the analysis in this chapter, discuss why it may be very difficult to become rich by following the advice found in a book.

Source: Michael Korda, *Making the List: A Cultural History of the American Bestseller, 1900–1999*, New York: Barnes & Noble Books, 2001, p. 168.

3.9 **(Related to the *Chapter Opener* on page 401)** According to an article in *Fortune* magazine, "The big question for [Starbucks' chairman] Howard Schultz is whether Starbucks can keep it up. There are those on Wall Street who say that Starbucks' game is almost over." What do you think the article means by "Starbucks' game is almost over"? Why would some people on Wall Street be making this prediction about a firm that was making substantial economic profits at the time the article was written?

Source: Andy Serwer, "Hot Starbucks to Go," *Fortune*, January 12, 2004.

3.10 Many firms that make differentiated consumer products, such as L'Oréal, which makes cosmetics, devote significant resources to developing new products and differentiating their products from those of their competitors. Suppose that L'Oréal, for instance, decided to eliminate this spending. What would be the effect on its profits in the short run? What would be the effect on its profits in the long run?

>> **End Learning Objective 12.3**

---

**12.4** ## Comparing Perfect Competition and Monopolistic Competition, pages 412–414

LEARNING OBJECTIVE: Compare the efficiency of monopolistic competition and perfect competition.

## Summary

Perfectly competitive firms produce where price equals marginal cost and at minimum average total cost. Perfectly competitive firms achieve both allocative and productive efficiency. Monopolistically competitive firms produce where price is greater than marginal cost and above minimum average total cost. Monopolistically competitive firms do not achieve either allocative or productive efficiency. Consumers face a trade-off when buying the product of a monopolistically competitive firm: They are paying a price that is greater than marginal cost, and the product is not being produced at minimum average cost, but they benefit from being able to purchase a product that is differentiated and more closely suited to their tastes.

 Visit **www.myeconlab.com** to complete these exercises online and get instant feedback.

## Review Questions

4.1 What are the differences between the long-run equilibrium of a perfectly competitive firm and the long-run equilibrium of a monopolistically competitive firm?

4.2 Does the fact that monopolistically competitive markets are not allocatively or productively efficient mean that there is a significant loss in economic well-being to society in these markets? In your answer, be sure to define what you mean by "economic well-being."

## Problems and Applications

4.3 A student asks the following question:

> I can understand why a perfectly competitive firm will not earn profits in the long run because a perfectly competitive firm charges a price equal to marginal cost. But a monopolistically competitive firm can charge a price greater than marginal cost, so why can't it continue to earn profits in the long run?

How would you answer this question?

4.4 Consider the following graph.

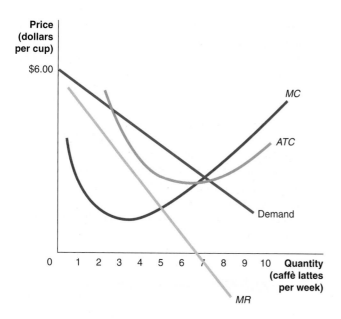

a. Is it possible to say whether this firm is a perfectly competitive firm or a monopolistically competitive firm? If so, explain how you are able to say this.

b. Does the graph show a short-run equilibrium or a long-run equilibrium? Briefly explain.

c. What quantity on the graph represents long-run equilibrium if the firm is perfectly competitive?

4.5 Before the fall of Communism, most basic consumer products in Eastern Europe and the Soviet Union were standardized. For example, government-run stores would offer for sale only one type of bar soap or one type of toothpaste. Soviet economists often argued that this system of standardizing basic consumer products avoided the waste associated with the differentiated goods and services produced in Western Europe and the United States. Do you agree with this argument?

4.6 **(Related to the *Making the Connection* on page 414)** Juicy Couture has been successful in selling women's clothing, using an unusual strategy. According to an article in the *Wall Street Journal*, the key to the firm's strategy is to "Limit distribution to maintain the brand's exclusive cachet, even if that means sacrificing sales, a brand-management technique once used only for high-end luxury brands." In 2006, Juicy clothes were sold in only four department stores: Neiman Marcus, Saks, Bloomingdale's, and Nordstrom. Although Juicy was originally known mainly for the fashion tracksuits it sold,

> Juicy Couture doesn't just make tracksuits favored by celebrities any more. With its edgy contemporary sportswear and accessories, it has become a lifestyle brand for women, men and kids with estimated annual sales of more than $300 million, up from $47 million in 2002.

a. Why would limiting the number of stores that sell your product be a successful strategy for a clothing firm? What would be likely to happen to Juicy's sales if it began to sell its clothes at Wal-Mart and similar stores?

b. Compared with the situation Apple Computer faced during the mid-1980s, is Juicy more or less likely to be able to maintain its product differentiation over a long period of time?

Source: Rachel Dodes, "From Track Suits to Fast Track," *Wall Street Journal*, September 13, 2006.

>> **End Learning Objective 12.4**

---

**12.5** | **How Marketing Differentiates Products, pages 414–416**
LEARNING OBJECTIVE: Define marketing and explain how firms use it to differentiate their products.

## Summary

**Marketing** refers to all the activities necessary for a firm to sell a product to a consumer. Firms use two marketing tools to differentiate their products: brand management and advertising. **Brand management** refers to the actions of a firm intended to maintain the differentiation of a product over time. When a firm has established a successful brand name, it has a strong incentive to defend it. A firm can apply for a *trademark*, which grants legal protection against other firms using its product's name.

 Visit www.myeconlab.com to complete these exercises online and get instant feedback.

## Review Questions

5.1 Define *marketing*. Is marketing just another name for advertising?

5.2 Why are many companies so concerned about brand management?

## Problems and Applications

5.3 Draw a graph that shows the impact on a firm's profits when it increases spending on advertising and the increased advertising has *no* effect on the demand for the firm's product.

5.4 A skeptic says, "Marketing research and brand management are redundant. If a company wants to find out what customers want, it should simply look at what they're already buying." Do you agree with this comment? Explain.

5.5 The National Football League (NFL) has a trademark on the name "Super Bowl" for its championship game. Advertisers can use the words Super Bowl in their advertising only if they pay the NFL a fee. Many companies attempt to get around this trademark by using the phrase "the big game" in their advertising. For example, just before the Super Bowl is to be played, a consumer electronics store might have an advertisement with the phrase "Watch the big game on a new HDTV." In 2007, the National Football League indicated that it might attempt legal action to have the phrase "the big game" included in its Super Bowl trademark.

a. Why does the government allow firms to trademark their products?

b. Would consumers gain or lose if the NFL were allowed to trademark the phrase "the big game"? Briefly explain.

Source: Craig S. Mende, "On Watching 'The Big Game,'" *Forbes*, February 1, 2008.

5.6 Some companies have done a poor job protecting their products' images. For example, Hormel's Spam brand name is widely ridiculed and has escaped from the company's control in cyberspace. Think of other cases of companies failing to protect their brand names. What can they do about it now? Should they re-brand their products?

5.7 **(Related to the *Making the Connection* on page 415)** In recent years, firms have increased their spending on Internet advertising while decreasing their spending on radio, television, and newspaper advertising. Why might many firms prefer to advertise on the Internet rather than in some other way? (*Hint:* Think about how firms determine the optimal amount to spend on advertising.)

>> **End Learning Objective 12.5**

---

**12.6** **What Makes a Firm Successful?** pages 416–418

LEARNING OBJECTIVE: Identify the key factors that determine a firm's success.

## Summary

A firm's owners and managers control some of the factors that determine the profitability of the firm. Other factors affect all the firms in the market or are the result of chance, so they are not under the control of the firm's owners. The interactions between factors the firm controls and factors it does not control determine its profitability.

  Visit **www.myeconlab.com** to complete these exercises online and get instant feedback.

## Review Questions

6.1 What are the key factors that determine the profitability of a firm in a monopolistically competitive market?

6.2 How might a monopolistically competitive firm continually earn economic profit greater than zero?

## Problems and Applications

6.3 According to an article in the *Wall Street Journal*:

> In early January last year, after a disappointing Christmas season and amid worries about competition from discount retailers, Zale Corp. decided to shake things up: The self-proclaimed jeweler to Middle America was going to chase upscale customers. . . . The move was a disaster. The Irving, Texas, retailer lost many of its traditional customers without winning the new ones it coveted.

Why would a firm like Zale abandon one market niche for another market niche? We know that in this case the move was not successful. Can you think of other cases where such a move has been successful?

Source: Ann Zimmerman and Kris Hudson, "Chasing Upscale Customers Tarnishes Mass-Market Jeweler," *Wall Street Journal*, June 26, 2006. p. A1.

6.4 7-Eleven, Inc., operates more than 20,000 convenience stores worldwide. Edward Moneypenny, 7-Eleven's chief financial officer, was asked to name the biggest risk the company faced. He replied, "I would say that the biggest risk that 7-Eleven faces, like all retailers, is competition . . . because that is something that you've got to be aware of in this business." In what sense is competition a "risk" to a business? Why would a company in the retail business need to be particularly aware of competition?

Source: Company Report, "CEO Interview: Edward Moneypenny—7-Eleven, Inc.," The Wall Street Transcript Corporation.

6.5 In 2006, Wal-Mart closed its stores in South Korea and Germany. According to an article in the *New York Times*:

> Wal-Mart's most successful markets, like Mexico, are those in which it started big. There, the company bought the country's largest and best-run retail chain, Cifra, and has never looked back. This year, Wal-Mart is spending more than $1 billion in Mexico to open 120 new stores.

What advantages does Wal-Mart gain from buying large retail chains, as it did in Mexico, rather than small chains, as it did in its unsuccessful attempts to enter the South Korean and German markets?

Source: Mark Landler and Michael Barbaro, "Wal-Mart Finds That Its Formula Doesn't Fit Every Culture," *New York Times*, August 2, 2006.

**6.6** (Related to the *Making the Connection* on page 417) A firm that is first to market with a new product frequently discovers that there are design flaws or problems with the product that were not anticipated. For example, the ballpoint pens made by the Reynolds International Pen Company often leaked. What effect do these problems have on the innovating firm, and how do these unexpected problems open up possibilities for other firms to enter the market?

**6.7** An article in the *New York Times* notes that in buying mutual fund shares, "Investors have ... [a] problem ...: determining whether good returns come from skill or luck." Is it ever easy to determine whether a firm making economic profits is doing so because of the skills of the firm's managers or because of luck? Briefly explain.

Source: Jeff Brown, "Hedge Funds? Only If You Like Lots of Risk," *New York Times*, August 6, 2009.

>> **End Learning Objective 12.6**

# CHAPTER 13

# Oligopoly: Firms in Less Competitive Markets

## Chapter Outline and Learning Objectives

# >> Competition in the Computer Market

Many of the largest corporations in the United States began as small businesses. In 1975, Bill Gates and Paul Allen founded Microsoft Corporation in Albuquerque, New Mexico, with themselves as the only employees. Steve Jobs and Steve Wozniak formed Apple in 1976, working at first out of Jobs's garage. Jobs and Wozniak were following in the tradition of William Hewlett and David Packard, who founded what became the Hewlett-Packard (HP) company in a garage in Palo Alto, California, in the 1930s. Michael Dell started the Dell computer company in 1984, from his dorm room at the University of Texas. Sam Walton, founder of Wal-Mart, bought his first store in 1945, with $20,000 borrowed from his father-in-law.

When each of these firms was founded, their industries included many more firms than they do now. Today, in the software and computer industries, fewer than 10 firms account for the great majority of sales. Wal-Mart accounts for a large share of several segments of retail sales.

An industry with only a few firms is an *oligopoly*. In an oligopoly, a firm's profitability depends on its interactions with other firms. In these industries, firms must develop *business strategies*, which involve not just deciding what price to charge and how many units to produce but also how much to advertise, which new technologies to adopt, how to manage relations with suppliers, and which new markets to enter.

A key part of Apple's business strategy in the computer market has been to concentrate on selling well-designed but higher-priced machines. During 2008 and 2009, the market for smaller computers, particularly "netbooks," or minimally equipped laptops, increased rapidly. Apple had to decide whether to enter this market or whether selling a low-priced netbook would damage its iMac brand and hurt sales of its desktops and laptops.

**AN INSIDE LOOK** on **page 450** discusses HP's attempts to use new technology to increase its market share in the desktop and laptop computer markets.

Source: Andrew LaVallee, "Apple Says No Netbooks, Steve Jobs Back in June," *Wall Street Journal*, April 22, 2009.

## Economics in YOUR LIFE!

### Why Can't You Find a Cheap PlayStation 3?

Final exams are over, and you and your roommate decide to treat yourselves to a PlayStation 3 game system—provided that you can find one at a relatively low price. First you check Amazon.com and find a price of $399.99. Then you check Best Buy, and the price there is also $399.99. Then you check Target; $399.99 again! Finally, you check Wal-Mart, and you find a lower price: $399.*82*, a whopping discount of $0.17. Why isn't one of these big retailers willing to charge a lower price? What happened to price competition? As you read the chapter, see if you can answer these questions. You can check your answers against those we provide at the end of the chapter.

▶ Continued on page 449

I n Chapters 11 and 12, we studied perfectly competitive and monopolistically competitive industries. Our analysis focused on the determination of a firm's profit-maximizing price and quantity. We concluded that firms maximize profit by producing where marginal revenue equals marginal cost. To determine marginal revenue and marginal cost, we used graphs that included the firm's demand, marginal revenue, and marginal cost curves. In this chapter, we will study **oligopoly**, a market structure in which a small number of interdependent firms compete. In analyzing oligopoly, we cannot rely on the same types of graphs we used in analyzing perfect competition and monopolistic competition for two reasons.

First, we need to use economic models that allow us to analyze the more complex business strategies of large oligopoly firms. Second, even in determining the profit-maximizing price and output of an oligopoly firm, demand curves and cost curves are not as useful as in the cases of perfect competition and monopolistic competition. We are able to draw the demand curves for competitive firms by assuming that the prices these firms charge have no impact on the prices other firms in their industries charge. This assumption is realistic when each firm is small relative to the market. It is not a realistic assumption, however, for firms that are as large relative to their markets as Microsoft, Apple, or Wal-Mart.

When large firms cut their prices, their rivals in the industry often—but not always—respond by also cutting their prices. Because we don't know for sure how other firms will respond to a price change, we don't know the quantity an oligopolist will sell at a particular price. In other words, it is difficult to know what an oligopolist's demand curve will look like. As we have seen, a firm's marginal revenue curve depends on its demand curve. If we don't know what an oligopolist's demand curve looks like, we also don't know what its marginal revenue curve looks like. Because we don't know marginal revenue, we can't calculate the profit-maximizing level of output and the profit-maximizing price the way we do for competitive firms.

The approach we use to analyze competition among oligopolists is called *game theory*. Game theory can be used to analyze any situation in which groups or individuals interact. In the context of economic analysis, game theory is the study of the decisions of firms in industries where the profits of each firm depend on its interactions with other firms. It has been applied to strategies for nuclear war, for international trade negotiations, and for political campaigns, among many other examples. In this chapter, we use game theory to analyze the business strategies of large firms.

**Oligopoly** A market structure in which a small number of interdependent firms compete.

## 13.1 LEARNING OBJECTIVE

Show how barriers to entry explain the existence of oligopolies.

# Oligopoly and Barriers to Entry

An *oligopoly* is an industry with only a few firms. This market structure lies between the competitive industries we studied in Chapters 11 and 12, which have many firms, and the monopolies we will study in Chapter 14, which have only a single firm. One measure of the extent of competition in an industry is the *concentration ratio*. Every five years, the U.S. Bureau of the Census publishes four-firm concentration ratios that state the fraction of each industry's sales accounted for by its four largest firms. Most economists believe that a four-firm concentration ratio greater than 40 percent indicates that an industry is an oligopoly.

The concentration ratio has some flaws as a measure of the extent of competition in an industry. For example, concentration ratios do not include sales in the United States by foreign firms. In addition, concentration ratios are calculated for the national market, even though the competition in some industries, such as restaurants or college bookstores, is mainly local. Finally, competition sometimes exists between firms in different industries. For example, Wal-Mart is included in the discount department stores industry but also competes with firms in the supermarket industry and the retail toy store industry. As we will see in Chapter 14, some economists prefer another measure of competition, known as the *Herfindahl-Hirschman Index*. Despite their shortcomings, concentration ratios can be useful in providing a general idea of the extent of competition in an industry.

Table 13-1 lists examples of oligopolies in manufacturing and retail trade. Notice that the computer industry is highly concentrated. The four largest firms—Hewlett-Packard, Dell, Acer, and Apple—sell 75 percent of all the desktops and laptops sold in the United States.

## Barriers to Entry

Why do oligopolies exist? Why aren't there many more firms in the computer industry, the discount department store industry, or the beer industry? Recall that new firms will enter industries where existing firms are earning economic profits. But new firms often have difficulty entering an oligopoly. Anything that keeps new firms from entering an industry in which firms are earning economic profits is called a **barrier to entry**. Three barriers to entry are economies of scale, ownership of a key input, and government-imposed barriers.

**Economies of Scale** The most important barrier to entry is economies of scale. Chapter 10 states that **economies of scale** exist when a firm's long-run average costs fall as it increases output. The greater the economies of scale, the smaller the number of firms that will be in the industry. Figure 13-1 illustrates this point.

If economies of scale are relatively unimportant in the industry, the typical firm's long-run average cost curve (*LRAC*) will reach a minimum at a level of output ($Q_1$ in Figure 13-1) that is a small fraction of total industry sales. The industry will have room for a large number of firms and will be competitive. If economies of scale are significant, the typical firm will not reach the minimum point on its long-run average cost curve ($Q_2$ in Figure 13-1) until it has produced a large fraction of industry sales. Then the industry will have room for only a few firms and will be an oligopoly.

Economies of scale can explain why there is much more competition in the restaurant industry than in the computer industry. Because very large restaurants do not have lower average costs than smaller restaurants, the restaurant industry has room for many firms. In contrast, large computer firms such as Apple have much lower average costs than small computer firms, partly because large firms can spread the high fixed costs of producing computers—including very large research and development costs—over a much larger quantity of computers.

**Ownership of a Key Input** If production of a good requires a particular input, then control of that input can be a barrier to entry. For many years, the Aluminum Company of America (Alcoa) controlled most of the world's supply of high-quality bauxite, the

**Barrier to entry** Anything that keeps new firms from entering an industry in which firms are earning economic profits.

**Economies of scale** The situation when a firm's long-run average costs fall as it increases output.

## TABLE 13-1

**Examples of Oligopolies in Retail Trade and Manufacturing**

| RETAIL TRADE | | MANUFACTURING | |
|---|---|---|---|
| INDUSTRY | FOUR-FIRM CONCENTRATION RATIO | INDUSTRY | FOUR-FIRM CONCENTRATION RATIO |
| Discount department stores | 95% | Cigarettes | 95% |
| Warehouse clubs and supercenters | 92% | Beer | 91% |
| Hobby, toy, and game stores | 72% | Aircraft | 81% |
| Athletic footwear stores | 71% | Breakfast cereal | 78% |
| College bookstores | 70% | Automobiles | 76% |
| Radio, television, and other electronic stores | 69% | Computers | 75% |
| Pharmacies and drugstores | 53% | Dog and cat food | 64% |

Sources: U.S. Census Bureau, *Concentration Ratios, 2002,* May 2006; and U.S. Census Bureau, *Establishment and Firm Size, 2002,* November 2005.

## Figure 13-1

### Economies of Scale Help Determine the Extent of Competition in an Industry

An industry will be competitive if the minimum point on the typical firm's long-run average cost curve ($LRAC_1$) occurs at a level of output that is a small fraction of total industry sales, such as $Q_1$. The industry will be an oligopoly if the minimum point comes at a level of output that is a large fraction of industry sales, such as $Q_2$.

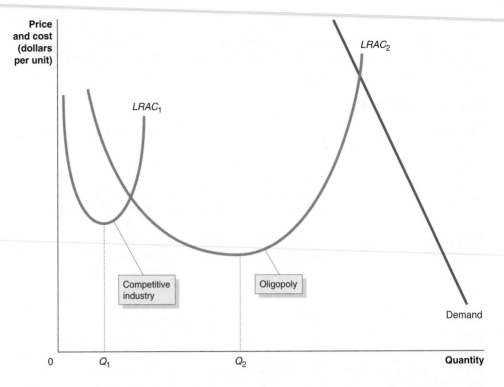

**Patent** The exclusive right to a product for a period of 20 years from the date the product is invented.

mineral needed to produce aluminum. The only way other companies could enter the industry to compete with Alcoa was to recycle aluminum. The De Beers Company of South Africa was able to block competition in the diamond market by controlling the output of most of the world's diamond mines. Until the 1990s, Ocean Spray had very little competition in the market for fresh and frozen cranberries because it controlled almost the entire supply of cranberries. Even today, it controls about 80 percent of the cranberry crop.

**Government-Imposed Barriers** Firms sometimes try to convince the government to impose barriers to entry. Many large firms employ *lobbyists* to convince state legislators and members of Congress to pass laws favorable to the economic interests of the firms. There are tens of thousands of lobbyists in Washington, DC, alone. Top lobbyists command annual salaries of $300,000 or more, which indicates the value firms place on their activities. Examples of government-imposed barriers to entry are patents, licensing requirements, and barriers to international trade.

A **patent** gives a firm the exclusive right to a new product for a period of 20 years from the date the product is invented. Governments use patents to encourage firms to carry out research and development of new and better products and better ways of producing existing products. Output and living standards increase faster when firms devote resources to research and development, but a firm that spends money to develop a new product may not earn much profit if other firms can copy the product. For example, the pharmaceutical company Merck spends more than $3 billion per year on developing new prescription drugs. If rival companies could freely produce these new drugs as soon as Merck developed them, most of the firm's investment would be wasted. Because Merck can patent a new drug, the firm can charge higher prices during the years the patent is in force and make an economic profit on its successful innovation.

Governments also restrict competition through *occupational licensing*. The United States currently has about 500 occupational licensing laws. For example, doctors and dentists in every state need licenses to practice. The justification for the laws is to protect the public from incompetent practitioners, but by restricting the number of people who can enter the licensed professions, the laws also raise prices. Studies have shown that states that make it harder to earn a dentist's license have prices for dental services that are about 15 percent higher than in other states. Similarly, states that require a license for out-of-state firms to sell contact lenses have higher prices for contact lenses.

When state licenses are required for occupations such as hair braiding, which was done several years ago in California, restricting competition is the main result.

Governments also impose barriers to entering some industries by imposing tariffs and quotas on foreign competition. As we saw in Chapter 8, a *tariff* is a tax on imports, and a *quota* limits the quantity of a good that can be imported into a country. A quota on foreign sugar imports severely limits competition in the U.S. sugar market. As a result, U.S. sugar companies can charge prices that are more than twice as high as those charged by companies outside the United States.

In summary, to earn economic profits, all firms would like to charge a price well above average cost, but earning economic profits attracts new firms to enter the industry. Eventually, the increased competition forces price down to average cost, and firms just break even. In an oligopoly, barriers to entry prevent—or at least slow down—entry, which allows firms to earn economic profits over a longer period.

# Solved Problem | 13-1

## Minimum Efficient Scale in the Automobile Industry

The U.S. automobile industry has often been cited as an example of oligopoly. The industry is an oligopoly because of the existence of economies of scale. In order to achieve minimum efficient scale of operation (MES), automobile assembly plants for light vehicles (passenger cars and light trucks, including minivans and sport-utility vehicles) must produce about 200,000 units per year. The size of the domestic market for light vehicles in the United States, including imports, has been around 16.5 million units since the late 1990s. Since 2001, the domestic production of light vehicles has been around 12 million units. To produce this number of vehicles at the lowest possible cost, there can be no more than 60 assembly plants (12,000,000 / 200,000 = 60), but the number of assembly plants can be fewer than 60 because each plant can produce more than 200,000 units at minimum unit cost. Because automobile companies own and operate multiple assembly plants, there are only three U.S. firms: DaimlerChrysler, Ford, and General Motors (the Big Three).

Toyota, Honda, Volkswagen, and other foreign-owned companies increased their share of the U.S. market for light vehicles beginning in the 1970s as higher energy prices caused many consumers to demand the smaller, more fuel-efficient models these companies specialized in producing. Subsequently, several foreign companies established manufacturing operations in the United States to better serve the market and avoid restrictions on automobile imports. By 2004, 13 foreign-owned assembly plants had been established; 6 of these plants are located south of Indiana and Ohio. These two states and Michigan are home to 44 percent of all light vehicle manufacturing plants. Further erosion of the Big Three automakers' share of the light vehicle market would have serious consequences for employment in these Midwestern states.

Source: Thomas Klier, "Caution Ahead—Challenges to the Midwest's role in the auto industry," *Chicago Fed Letter*, The Federal Reserve Bank of Chicago, February 2005.

a. Would economies of scale in the automobile industry allow for more than three U.S. firms?

b. How would additional loss of market share by the Big Three U.S. automakers affect employment in Michigan, Indiana, and Ohio?

## SOLVING THE PROBLEM:

**Step 1:** **Review the chapter material.** This problem is about barriers to entry, so you may want to review the section "Oligopoly and Barriers to Entry," which begins on page 432.

**Step 2:** **Answer question (a).** Many other firms contribute to the production of parts and services for automobiles, but the assembly of light vehicles is the part of the production process in which the Big Three specialize. The owner of a new assembly plant would have to produce and sell at least 200,000 light vehicles to compete in this market. It would be very costly for a new firm to do this because it would have to establish a distribution system, marketing campaign, and so on in addition to an assembly plant. Established firms such as Honda and Toyota that already have established markets in the United States are much more likely to be successful, but a new assembly plant would still have to produce and sell at least 200,000 vehicles to achieve the minimum efficient scale of operation. There are two sources for these sales: (1) Market share may be taken from other automakers, and (2) the annual market for light vehicles could grow beyond 16.5 million units.

**Step 3:** **Answer question (b).** As the import share of the light automobile market in the United States increases, this would reduce the demand for automobiles assembled at plants owned by Big Three firms. Because many of these assembly plants are located in Michigan, Indiana, and Ohio, it is likely that job losses would have a disproportionate effect on these states. The establishment of foreign-owned assembly plants in these states would mitigate these losses, but this would not occur if the plants were located outside these states.

YOUR TURN: For more practice, do related problem 1.11 on page 453 at the end of this chapter.

---

**13.2 LEARNING** OBJECTIVE

Use game theory to analyze the strategies of oligopolistic firms.

**Game theory** The study of how people make decisions in situations in which attaining their goals depends on their interactions with others; in economics, the study of the decisions of firms in industries where the profits of each firm depend on its interactions with other firms.

**Business strategy** Actions taken by a firm to achieve a goal, such as maximizing profits.

**Payoff matrix** A table that shows the payoffs that each firm earns from every combination of strategies by the firms.

# Using Game Theory to Analyze Oligopoly

As we noted at the beginning of the chapter, economists analyze oligopolies by using *game theory*, which was developed during the 1940s by the mathematician John von Neumann and the economist Oskar Morgenstern. **Game theory** is the study of how people make decisions in situations in which attaining their goals depends on their interactions with others. In oligopolies, the interactions among firms are crucial in determining profitability because the firms are large relative to the market.

In all games—whether poker, chess, or Monopoly—the interactions among the players are crucial in determining the outcome. In addition, games share three key characteristics:

1. *Rules* that determine what actions are allowable
2. *Strategies* that players employ to attain their objectives in the game
3. *Payoffs* that are the results of the interaction among the players' strategies

In business situations, the rules of the "game" include not just laws that a firm must obey but also other matters beyond a firm's control—at least in the short run—such as its production function. A **business strategy** is a set of actions that a firm takes to achieve a goal, such as maximizing profits. The *payoffs* are the profits a firm earns as a result of how its strategies interact with the strategies of other firms. The best way to understand the game theory approach is to look at an example.

## A Duopoly Game: Price Competition between Two Firms

In this simple example, we use game theory to analyze price competition in a *duopoly*—an oligopoly with two firms. Suppose we ignore the other firms in the industry and assume that Apple and Hewlett-Packard (HP) are the only two firms producing desktop computers. Let's focus on their sales of basic desktop computers, such as Apple's iMac or HP's "all-in-one" computer. The managers of the two firms have to decide whether to charge $1,200 or $1,000 for their computers. Which price will be more profitable depends on the price the other firm charges. The decision regarding what price to charge is an example of a business strategy. In Figure 13-2, we organize the possible outcomes that result from the actions of the two firms into a **payoff matrix**, which is a table that shows the payoffs that each firm earns from every combination of strategies by the firms.

Apple's profits are shown in red, and HP's profits are shown in blue. If Apple and HP both charge $1,200 for their computers, each firm will make a profit of $10 million per month. If Apple charges the lower price of $1,000, while HP charges $1,200, Apple will gain many of HP's customers. Apple's profits will be $15 million, and HP's will be

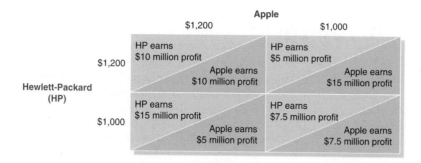

## Figure 13-2

### A Duopoly Game

HP's profits are in blue, and Apple's profits are in red. HP and Apple would each make profits of $10 million per month on sales of desktop computers if they both charged $1,200. However, each firm has an incentive to undercut the other by charging a lower price. If both firms charge $1,000, they would each make a profit of only $7.5 million per month.

only $5 million. Similarly, if HP charges $1,000, while Apple is charging $1,200, Apple's profits will be only $5 million, while HP's profits will be $15 million. If both firms charge $1,000, each will earn profits of $7.5 million per month.

Clearly, the firms will be better off if they both charge $1,200 for their computers. But will they both charge this price? One possibility is that the managers of Apple and the managers of HP will get together and *collude* by agreeing to charge the higher price. **Collusion** is an agreement among firms to charge the same price or otherwise not to compete. Unfortunately for Apple and HP—but fortunately for their customers—collusion is against the law in the United States. The government can fine companies that collude and send the managers involved to prison.

The managers of Apple can't legally discuss their pricing decision with the managers of HP, so they have to predict what the other managers will do. Suppose the Apple managers are convinced that the HP managers will charge $1,200 for their computers. In this case, the Apple managers will definitely charge $1,000 because that will increase Apple's profit from $10 million to $15 million. But suppose instead the Apple managers are convinced that the HP managers will charge $1,000. Then the Apple managers also definitely will charge $1,000 because that will increase their profit from $5 million to $7.5 million. In fact, whichever price the HP managers decide to charge, the Apple managers are better off charging $1,000. So, we know that the Apple managers will choose a price of $1,000 for their computers.

Now consider the situation of the HP managers. The HP managers are in the same position as the Apple managers, so we can expect them to make the same decision to charge $1,000 for their computers. In this situation, both firms have a *dominant strategy*. A **dominant strategy** is the best strategy for a firm, no matter what strategies other firms use. The result is an equilibrium where both firms charge $1,000 for their computers. This situation is an equilibrium because each firm is maximizing profits, *given the price chosen by the other firm*. In other words, neither firm can increase its profits by changing its price, given the price chosen by the other firm. An equilibrium where each firm chooses the best strategy, given the strategies chosen by other firms, is called a **Nash equilibrium**, named after Nobel laureate John Nash of Princeton University, a pioneer in the development of game theory.

## Firm Behavior and the Prisoner's Dilemma

Notice that the equilibrium in Figure 13-2 is not very satisfactory for either firm. The firms earn $7.5 million in profit each month by charging $1,000, but they could have earned $10 million in profit if they had both charged $1,200. By "cooperating" and charging the higher price, they would have achieved a *cooperative equilibrium*. In a **cooperative equilibrium**, players cooperate to increase their mutual payoff. We have seen, though, that the outcome of this game is likely to be a **noncooperative equilibrium**, in which each firm pursues its own self-interest.

A situation like this, in which pursuing dominant strategies results in noncooperation that leaves everyone worse off, is called a **prisoner's dilemma**. The game gets its name from the problem faced by two suspects the police arrest for a crime. If the police lack other evidence, they may separate the suspects and offer each a reduced prison sentence in exchange for confessing to the crime and testifying against the other suspect. Because each suspect has a dominant strategy to confess to the crime, they will both confess and serve a jail term, even though they would have gone free if they had both remained silent.

**Collusion** An agreement among firms to charge the same price or otherwise not to compete.

**Dominant strategy** A strategy that is the best for a firm, no matter what strategies other firms use.

**Nash equilibrium** A situation in which each firm chooses the best strategy, given the strategies chosen by other firms.

**Cooperative equilibrium** An equilibrium in a game in which players cooperate to increase their mutual payoff.

**Noncooperative equilibrium** An equilibrium in a game in which players do not cooperate but pursue their own self-interest.

**Prisoner's dilemma** A game in which pursuing dominant strategies results in noncooperation that leaves everyone worse off.

# Don't Let This Happen to **YOU!**

## Don't Misunderstand Why Each Firm Ends Up Charging a Price of $1,000

It is tempting to think that Apple and HP would each charge $1,000 rather than $1,200 for their computers because each is afraid that the other firm will charge $1,000. In fact, fear of being undercut by the other firm's charging a lower price is not the key to understanding each firm's pricing strategy. Notice that charging $1,000 is the most profitable strategy for each firm, no matter which price the other firm decides to charge. For example, even if

Apple's managers somehow knew for sure that HP's managers intended to charge $1,200, Apple would still charge $1,000 because its profits would be $15 million instead of $10 million. HP's managers are in the same situation. That is why charging $1,000 is a dominant strategy for both firms.

**YOUR TURN:** Test your understanding by doing related problem 2.14 on page 456 at the end of the chapter.

---

# **Solved** Problem | **13-2**

## Is Advertising a Prisoner's Dilemma for Coca-Cola and Pepsi?

Coca-Cola and Pepsi both advertise aggressively, but would they be better off if they didn't? Their commercials are not designed to convey new information about the products. Instead, they are designed to capture each other's customers. Construct a payoff matrix using the following hypothetical information:

- If neither firm advertises, Coca-Cola and Pepsi both earn profits of $750 million per year.

- If both firms advertise, Coca-Cola and Pepsi both earn profits of $500 million per year.

- If Coca-Cola advertises and Pepsi doesn't, Coca-Cola earns profits of $900 million and Pepsi earns profits of $400 million.

- If Pepsi advertises and Coca-Cola doesn't, Pepsi earns profits of $900 million and Coca-Cola earns profits of $400 million.

  a. If Coca-Cola wants to maximize profit, will it advertise? Briefly explain.

  b. If Pepsi wants to maximize profit, will it advertise? Briefly explain.

  c. Is there a Nash equilibrium to this advertising game? If so, what is it?

### SOLVING THE PROBLEM:

**Step 1:** **Review the chapter material.** This problem uses payoff matrices to analyze a business situation, so you may want to review the section "A Duopoly Game: Price Competition between Two Firms," which begins on page 436.

**Step 2:** **Construct the payoff matrix.**

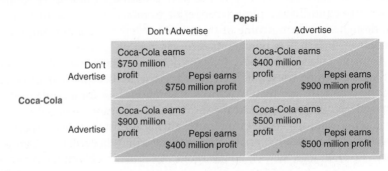

**Step 3:** **Answer part (a) by showing that Coca-Cola has a dominant strategy of advertising.** If Pepsi doesn't advertise, then Coca-Cola will make $900 million if it advertises but only $750 million if it doesn't. If Pepsi advertises, then Coca-Cola will make $500 million if it advertises but only $400 million if it doesn't. Therefore, advertising is a dominant strategy for Coca-Cola.

**Step 4:** **Answer part (b) by showing that Pepsi has a dominant strategy of advertising.** Pepsi is in the same position as Coca-Cola, so it also has a dominant strategy of advertising.

**Step 5:** **Answer part (c) by showing that there is a Nash equilibrium for this game.** Both firms advertising is a Nash equilibrium. Given that Pepsi is advertising, Coca-Cola's best strategy is to advertise. Given that Coca-Cola is advertising, Pepsi's best strategy is to advertise. Therefore, advertising is the optimal decision for both firms, *given the decision by the other firm.*

**EXTRA CREDIT:** This is another example of the prisoner's dilemma game. Coca-Cola and Pepsi would be more profitable if they both refrained from advertising, thereby saving the enormous expense of television and radio commercials and newspaper and magazine ads. Each firm's dominant strategy is to advertise, however, so they end up in an equilibrium where both advertise, and their profits are reduced.

**YOUR TURN:** For more practice, do related problems 2.11, 2.12, and 2.13 on page 455 at the end of this chapter.

---

Making the Connection

## Is There a Dominant Strategy for Bidding on eBay?

An auction is a game in which bidders compete to buy a product. The payoff in winning an auction is equal to the difference between the subjective value you place on the product being auctioned and the amount of the winning bid. On the online auction site eBay, more than 200 million items valued at more than $10 billion are auctioned each year.

eBay is run as a *second-price auction*, where the winning bidder pays an amount equal to the bid of the second-highest bidder. If the high bidder on a DVD of *Star Trek* bids $15, and the second bidder bids $10, the high bidder wins the auction and pays $10. It may seem that your best strategy when bidding on eBay is to place a bid well below the subjective value you place on the item in the hope of winning it at a low price. In fact, bidders on eBay have a dominant strategy of entering a bid equal to the maximum value they place on the item. For instance, suppose you are looking for a present for your parents' anniversary. They are U2 fans, and someone is auctioning a pair of U2 concert tickets. If the maximum value you place on the tickets is $200, that should be your bid. To see why, consider the results of strategies of bidding more or less than $200.

There are two possible outcomes of the auction: Either someone else bids more than you do, or you are the high bidder. First, suppose you bid $200 but someone else bids more than you do. If you had bid less than $200, you would still have lost. If you had bid more than $200, you might have been the high bidder, but because your bid would be for more than the value you place on the tickets, you would have a negative payoff. Second, suppose you bid $200 and you are the high bidder. If you had bid less than $200, you would have run the risk of losing the tickets to someone whose bid you would have beaten by bidding $200. You would be worse off than if you had bid $200 and won. If you had bid more than $200, you would not have affected the price you ended up paying—which, remember, is equal to the amount bid by the second-highest

*On eBay, bidding the maximum value you place on an item is a dominant strategy.*

bidder. Therefore, a strategy of bidding $200—the maximum value you place on the tickets—dominates bidding more or less than $200.

Even though making your first bid your highest bid is a dominant strategy on eBay, many bidders don't use it. After an auction is over, a link leads to a Web page showing all the bids. In many auctions, the same bidder bids several times, showing that the bidder had not understood his or her dominant strategy.

**YOUR TURN:** Test your understanding by doing related problem 2.15 on page 456 at the end of this chapter.

## Can Firms Escape the Prisoner's Dilemma?

Although the prisoner's dilemma game seems to show that cooperative behavior always breaks down, we know it doesn't. People often cooperate to achieve their goals, and firms find ways to cooperate by not competing on price. The reason the basic prisoner's dilemma story is not always applicable is that it assumes the game will be played only once. Most business situations, however, are repeated over and over. For example, consider the following situation: Suppose that in a small town, the only place to buy a PlayStation 3 game console is from either the local Target store or the local Wal-Mart store. (For simplicity, we will ignore the possibility of consumers buying the PlayStation 3 online.) We will assume that the managers will charge either $500 or $300 for the PlayStations. Panel (a) of Figure 13-3 shows the payoff matrix. Examining the matrix shows that, just as with Apple and HP pricing computers, each manager has an incentive to charge the lower price. Once again, the firms appear caught in a prisoner's dilemma. But the managers will not play this game only once because each month they will decide again what price they will charge for PlayStation 3. In the language of game theory, the managers are playing a *repeated game*. In a repeated game, the losses from

## Figure 13-3

### Changing the Payoff Matrix in a Repeated Game

Wal-Mart and Target can change the payoff matrix for selling PlayStation 3 game consoles by advertising that they will match their competitor's price. This retaliation strategy provides a signal that one store charging a lower price will be met automatically by the other store charging a lower price. In the payoff matrix in panel (a), there is no matching offer, and each store benefits if it charges $300 when the other charges $500. In the payoff matrix in panel (b), with the matching offer, the companies have only two choices: They can charge $500 and receive a profit of $10,000 per month, or they can charge $300 and receive a profit of $7,500 per month. The equilibrium shifts from the prisoner's dilemma result of both stores charging the low price and receiving low profits to both stores charging the high price and receiving high profits.

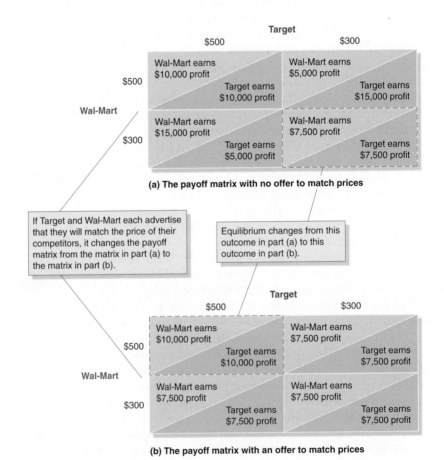

**(a) The payoff matrix with no offer to match prices**

If Target and Wal-Mart each advertise that they will match the price of their competitors, it changes the payoff matrix from the matrix in part (a) to the matrix in part (b).

Equilibrium changes from this outcome in part (a) to this outcome in part (b).

**(b) The payoff matrix with an offer to match prices**

not cooperating are greater than in a game played once, and players can also employ *retaliation strategies* against those who don't cooperate. As a result, we are more likely to see cooperative behavior.

Panel (a) of Figure 13-3 shows that Wal-Mart and Target are earning $2,500 less per month by both charging $300 instead of $500 for the PlayStation 3. Every month that passes with both stores charging $300 increases the total amount lost: Two years of charging $300 will cause each store to lose $60,000 in profit. This lost profit increases the incentive for the store managers to cooperate by *implicitly* colluding. Remember that *explicit* collusion—such as the managers meeting and agreeing to charge $500—is illegal. But if the managers can find a way to signal each other that they will charge $500, they may be within the law.

Suppose, for example, that Wal-Mart and Target both advertise that they will match the lowest price offered by any competitor—in our simple example, they are each other's only competitor. These advertisements are signals to each other that they intend to charge $500 for the PlayStation. The signal is clear because each store knows that if it charges $300, the other store will automatically retaliate by also lowering its price to $300. The offer to match prices is a good *enforcement mechanism* because it guarantees that if either store fails to cooperate and charges the lower price, the competing store will automatically punish that store by also charging the lower price. As Figure 13-3 shows, the stores have changed the payoff matrix they face.

With the original payoff matrix in panel (a), there is no matching offer, and each store makes more profit if it charges $300 when the other charges $500. The matching offer changes the payoff matrix to that shown in panel (b). Now the stores can charge $500 and receive a profit of $10,000 per month, or they can charge $300 and receive a profit of $7,500 per month. The equilibrium shifts from the prisoner's dilemma result of both stores charging the low price and receiving low profits to a result where both stores charge the high price and receive high profits. An offer to match competitors' prices might seem to benefit consumers, but game theory shows that it actually may hurt consumers by helping to keep prices high.

One form of implicit collusion occurs as a result of *price leadership*. With **price leadership**, one firm takes the lead in announcing a price change, which other firms in the industry then match. For example, through the 1970s, General Motors would announce a price change at the beginning of a model year, and Ford and Chrysler would match GM's price change. In some cases, such as in the airline industry, firms have attempted to act as price leaders but failed when other firms in the industry declined to cooperate.

> **Price leadership** A form of implicit collusion in which one firm in an oligopoly announces a price change and the other firms in the industry match the change.

## Singaporean Car Owners Experience Petrol Price Rollercoaster

Car prices in Singapore are among the highest in the world compared to the average earnings of Singaporeans. Despite this, car ownership in Singapore is relatively high with ownership at ten cars per hundred people. Hence, any changes in the price of petrol and diesel affect many Singaporeans. Car owners in Singapore thus experienced more of a rollercoaster ride than a car ride during the months of June and July in 2008 with the fluctuations in petrol and diesel prices. In fact, even the rise in pump prices during the final weeks of June 2008—with petrol going up by 5 cents a litre and diesel by 10 cents a litre—was the thirteenth consecutive rise since July 2007.

The price change effected on June 24 2008 was initiated with Shell, the petrol powerhouse, leading the way, followed by Caltex, ExxonMobil, and Singapore Petroleum Company (SPC). Not unexpectedly, within the space of 2 weeks, on July 4 2008, Shell again raised petrol and diesel prices by 5 and 10 cents respectively and again, the other petrol retailers followed suit.

Nevertheless, as motorists in Singapore were beginning to feel disgruntled at the joint increase in petrol prices, good news arrived on July 9 2008: all four petrol compa-

*Residents in Singapore experienced several fluctuations in petrol and diesel prices in June and July 2008.*

nies lowered their pump prices by 4 cents per litre for petrol to reflect current market conditions. There was no change in the diesel price, but noting that the petrol companies had increased pump prices for both petrol and diesel only days ago, motorists were generally much happier.

Even better news came about a week later. Pump prices at service stations across Singapore were adjusted downwards for both petrol and diesel on July 17 2008, with prices for all grades of petrol down by another 4 cents per litre. Then when motorists thought that it could not be better, petrol prices in Singapore fell for the third time in two weeks. A similar pattern of price leadership to that of early July 2008 emerged except this time, it was with price decreases—once again, the price change was set off with Shell leading the way and cutting prices on July 21 2008, and Caltex, ExxonMobil, and SPC also lowering their prices shortly after. They lowered prices for their petrol by 4 cents on average, and 2 cents for diesel. And in the largest price cut of the period, pump prices of petrol and diesel were adjusted down by 10 cents on July 28 2008 by all of the petrol companies.

Car owners remained pleased over the following two months as there were two further price cuts. However, by the end of 2008, petrol prices slowly crept up again. Eventually, the cycle repeated itself on July 27 2009, with Shell again leading the way with an increase in pump prices at 1pm, followed by Caltex at 3pm and ExxonMobil at 4.30pm. Within a week, on August 4 2009, Shell increased prices at 1.30pm, followed by Caltex at 3pm and ExxonMobil at 4pm.

Sources: Singapore Land Transport Authority, *The Straits Times* newspapers reports: 'Pump prices up for 13th time since last July' dated June 25 2008, *Today* newspaper report: 'Singapore petrol prices increase second time in 10 days, up 14 times in past year' dated July 5 2008; ChannelNewsAsia reports: 'Petrol companies lower pump prices in Singapore by 4 cents' dated July 9 2008, 'Petrol prices drop 4 cents for third time in two weeks' dated July 21 2008, 'Petrol and diesel down 10 cents' dated July 28 2008, 'Pump prices up at Shell, Caltex and ExxonMobil' dated July 27 2009 and 'Shell, Caltex and ExxonMobil raise pump prices' dated August 4 2009.

**YOUR TURN:** Test your understanding by doing related problem 2.17 on page 456 at the end of this chapter.

---

## Cartels: The Case of OPEC

**Cartel**  A group of firms that collude by agreeing to restrict output to increase prices and profits.

In the United States, firms cannot legally meet to agree on what prices to charge and how much to produce. But suppose they could. Would this be enough to guarantee that their collusion would be successful? The example of the Organization of Petroleum Exporting Countries (OPEC) indicates that the answer to this question is "no." OPEC has 12 members, including Saudi Arabia, Kuwait, and other Arab countries, as well as Iran, Venezuela, Nigeria, and Indonesia. Together, these countries own 75 percent of the world's proven oil reserves, although they pump a smaller share of the total oil sold each year. OPEC operates as a **cartel**, which is a group of firms that collude to restrict output to increase prices and profits. The members of OPEC meet periodically and agree on quotas, which are quantities of oil that each country agrees to produce. The quotas are intended to reduce oil production well below the competitive level in order to force up the price of oil and increase the profits of member countries.

Figure 13-4 shows oil prices from 1972 to mid-2009. The blue line shows the price of a barrel of oil in each year. Prices in general have risen since 1972, which has reduced the amount of goods and services that consumers can purchase with a dollar. The red line corrects for general price increases by measuring oil prices in terms of the dollar's purchasing power in 2009. The figure shows that OPEC had considerable success in raising the price of oil during the mid-1970s and early 1980s, although political unrest in the Middle East and other factors also affected the price of oil during these years. Oil prices, which had been below $3 per barrel in 1972, rose to more than $39 per barrel in 1980, which was more than $100 measured in dollars of 2009 purchasing power. The figure also shows that OPEC has had difficulty sustaining the high prices of 1980 in later years, although oil prices rose sharply between 2004 and mid-2008, in part due to increasing demand from China and India.

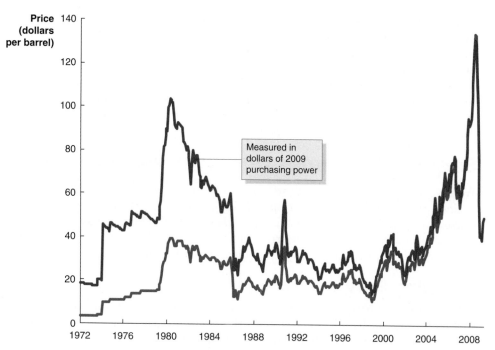

### Figure 13-4

**Oil Prices, 1972 to mid-2009**

The blue line shows the price of a barrel of oil in each year. The red line measures the price of a barrel of oil in terms of the purchasing power of the dollar in 2009. By reducing oil production, OPEC was able to raise the world price of oil in the mid-1970s and early 1980s. Sustaining high prices has been difficult over the long run, however, because members often exceed their output quotas.
Source: Federal Reserve Bank of St. Louis.

Game theory helps us understand why oil prices have fluctuated. If every member of OPEC cooperates and produces the low output level dictated by its quota, prices will be high, and the cartel will earn large profits. Once the price has been driven up, however, each member has an incentive to stop cooperating and to earn even higher profits by increasing output beyond its quota. But if no country sticks to its quota, total oil output will increase, and profits will decline. In other words, OPEC is caught in a prisoner's dilemma.

If the members of OPEC always exceeded their production quotas, the cartel would have no effect on world oil prices. In fact, the members of OPEC periodically meet and assign new quotas that, at least for a while, enable them to restrict output enough to raise prices. Two factors explain OPEC's occasional success at behaving as a cartel. First, the members of OPEC are participating in a repeated game. As we have seen, this increases the likelihood of a cooperative outcome. Second, Saudi Arabia has far larger oil reserves than any other member of OPEC. Therefore, it has the most to gain from high oil prices and a greater incentive to cooperate. To see this, consider the payoff matrix shown in Figure 13-5. To keep things simple, let's assume that OPEC has only two members: Saudi Arabia and Nigeria. In Figure 13-5, "low output" corresponds to cooperating with the OPEC-assigned output quota, and "high output" corresponds to producing at maximum capacity. The payoff matrix shows the profits received per day by each country.

We can see that Saudi Arabia has a strong incentive to cooperate and maintain its low output quota. By keeping output low, Saudi Arabia can by itself significantly raise the world price of oil, increasing its own profits as well as those of other members of OPEC. Therefore, Saudi Arabia has a dominant strategy of cooperating with the quota and producing a low output. Nigeria, however, cannot by itself have much effect on

### Figure 13-5

**The OPEC Cartel with Unequal Members**

Because Saudi Arabia can produce much more oil than Nigeria, its output decisions have a much larger effect on the price of oil. In the figure, Low Output corresponds to cooperating with the OPEC-assigned output quota, and High Output corresponds to producing at maximum capacity. Saudi Arabia has a dominant strategy to cooperate and produce a low output. Nigeria, however, has a dominant strategy not to cooperate and instead produce a high output. Therefore, the equilibrium of this game will occur with Saudi Arabia producing a low output and Nigeria producing a high output.

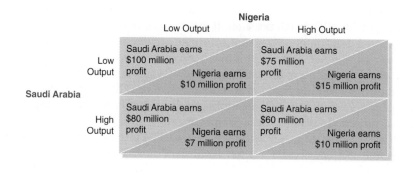

the price of oil. Therefore, Nigeria has a dominant strategy of not cooperating and instead producing a high output. The equilibrium of this game will occur with Saudi Arabia producing a low output and Nigeria producing a high output. In fact, OPEC often operates in just this way. Saudi Arabia will cooperate with the quota, while the other 11 members produce at capacity. Because this is a repeated game, however, Saudi Arabia will occasionally produce more oil than its quota to intentionally drive down the price and retaliate against the other members for not cooperating.

**13.3 LEARNING** OBJECTIVE

Use sequential games to analyze business strategies.

# Sequential Games and Business Strategy

We have been analyzing games in which both players move simultaneously. In many business situations, however, one firm will act first, and then other firms will respond. These situations can be analyzed using *sequential games*. We will use sequential games to analyze two business strategies: deterring entry and bargaining between firms. To keep things simple, we consider situations that involve only two firms.

## Deterring Entry

We saw earlier that barriers to entry are a key to firms continuing to earn economic profits. Can firms create barriers to deter new firms from entering an industry? Some recent research in game theory has focused on this question. To take a simple example, suppose once again that Apple and HP are the only makers of computers. HP has been aggressive in selling netbooks, such as the Mini 110, which it was selling for $280 in mid-2009. As we saw in the chapter opener, Apple was deciding whether to enter this market. One factor firms consider in pricing a new product is the effect different prices have on the likelihood that competitors will enter the market. A high price might lead to high profits if other firms do not enter the market, but if a high price attracts entry from other firms, it might actually result in lower profits. A low price, by deterring entry, might lead to higher profits. Assume that managers at HP have developed a netbook computer before Apple has and are considering what price to charge. To break even by covering the opportunity cost of the funds involved, netbooks must provide a minimum rate of return of 15 percent on HP's investment. If HP has the netbook market to itself and charges a price of $275, it will earn economic profits by receiving a return of 20 percent. If HP charges a price of $600 and has the market to itself, it will receive a higher return of 30 percent.

It seems clear that HP should charge $600 for its netbooks, but the managers are worried that Apple might also begin selling netbooks. If HP charges $275 and Apple enters the market, HP and Apple will divide up the market, and both will earn only 5 percent on their investments, which is below the 15 percent return necessary to break even. If HP charges $600 and Apple enters, although the market will still be divided, the higher price means that each firm will earn 16 percent on its investment.

HP and Apple are playing a sequential game, because HP makes the first move—deciding what price to charge—and Apple responds. We can analyze a sequential game by using a *decision tree*, like the one shown in Figure 13-6. The boxes in the figure represent *decision nodes*, which are points where the firms must make the decisions contained in the boxes. At the left, HP makes the initial decision of what price to charge, and then Apple responds by either entering the market or not. The decisions made are shown beside the arrows. The *terminal nodes* at the right side of the figure show the resulting rates of return.

Let's start with HP's initial decision. If HP charges $600, then the arrow directs us to the upper red decision node for Apple. If Apple decides to enter, it will earn a 16 percent rate of return on its investment, which represents an economic profit because it is above the opportunity cost of the funds involved. If Apple doesn't enter, HP will earn 30 percent, and Apple will not earn anything in this market. HP's managers can conclude that if they charge $600 for their netbooks, Apple will enter the netbook market, and both firms will earn 16 percent on their investments.

If HP decides to charge $275, then the arrow directs us to the lower red decision node for Apple. If Apple decides to enter, it will earn only a 5 percent rate of return. If it

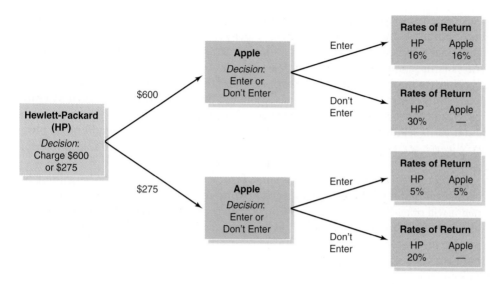

## Figure 13-6

### The Decision Tree for an Entry Game

HP earns its highest return if it charges $600 for its netbook and Apple does not enter the market. But at that price, Apple will enter the market, and HP will earn only 16 percent. If HP charges $275, Apple will not enter because Apple will suffer an economic loss by receiving only a 5 percent return on its investment. Therefore, HP's best decision is to deter Apple's entry by charging $275. HP will earn an economic profit by receiving a 20 percent return on its investment. Note that the dashes indicate the situation where Apple does not enter the market, and so makes no investment and receives no return.

doesn't enter, HP will earn 20 percent, and Apple will not earn anything in this market (indicated by the dash). HP's managers can conclude that if they charge $275, Apple will not enter, and HP will earn 20 percent on its investment.

This analysis should lead HP's managers to conclude that they can charge $600 and earn 16 percent—because Apple will enter—or they can charge $275 and earn 20 percent by deterring Apple's entry. Using a decision tree helps HP's managers to make the correct choice and charge $275 to deter Apple's entry into the netbook market.

## Bargaining

The success of many firms depends on how well they bargain with other firms. For example, firms often must bargain with their suppliers over the prices they pay for inputs. Suppose that TruImage is a small firm that has developed software that improves how pictures from a digital camera are displayed on computer screens. TruImage currently sells its software only on its Web site and earns profits of $2 million per year. Dell informs TruImage that it is considering installing the software on every new computer Dell sells. Dell expects to sell more computers at a higher price if it can install TruImage's software on its computers. The two firms begin bargaining over what price Dell will pay TruImage for its software.

The decision tree in Figure 13-7 illustrates this bargaining game. At the left, Dell makes the initial decision about what price to offer TruImage for its software, and then TruImage responds by either accepting or rejecting the contract offer. First, suppose that

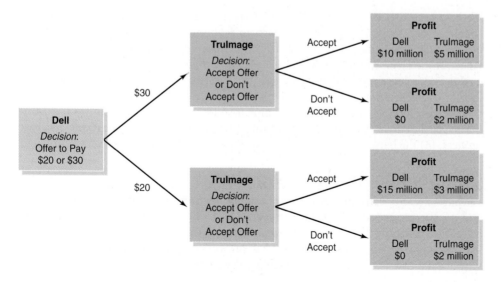

## Figure 13-7

### The Decision Tree for a Bargaining Game

Dell earns the highest profit if it offers a contract price of $20 per copy and TruImage accepts the contract. TruImage earns the highest profit if Dell offers it a contract of $30 per copy and it accepts the contract. TruImage may attempt to bargain by threatening to reject a $20-per-copy contract. But Dell knows this threat is not credible because once Dell has offered a $20-per-copy contract, TruImage's profits are higher if it accepts the contract than if it rejects it.

Dell offers TruImage a contract price of $30 per copy for its software. If TruImage accepts this contract, its profits will be $5 million per year, and Dell will earn $10 million in additional profits. If TruImage rejects the contract, its profits will be the $2 million per year it earns selling its software on its Web site, and Dell will earn zero additional profits.

Now, suppose Dell offers TruImage a contract price of $20 per copy. If TruImage accepts this contract, its profits will be $3 million per year, and Dell will earn $15 million in additional profits. If TruImage rejects this contract, its profits will be the $2 million it earns selling its software on its Web site, and Dell will earn zero additional profits. Clearly, for Dell, a contract price of $20 per copy is more profitable, while for TruImage, a contract price of $30 per copy is more profitable.

Suppose TruImage attempts to obtain a favorable outcome from the bargaining by telling Dell that it will reject a $20-per-copy contract price. If Dell believes this threat, then it will offer TruImage a $30-per-copy contract price because Dell is better off with the $10 million profit that will result from TruImage's accepting the contract than with the zero profits Dell will earn if TruImage rejects the $20-per-copy contract price. This result is a Nash equilibrium because neither firm can increase its profits by changing its choice—*provided that Dell believes TruImage's threat*. But is TruImage's threat credible? Once Dell has offered TruImage the $20 contract price, TruImage's choices are to accept the contract and earn $3 million or reject the contract and earn only $2 million. Because rejecting the contract reduces TruImage's profits, TruImage's threat to reject the contract is not credible, and Dell should ignore it.

As a result, we would expect Dell to use the strategy of offering TruImage a $20-per-copy contract price and TruImage to use the strategy of accepting the contract. Dell will earn additional profits of $15 million per year, and TruImage will earn profits of $3 million per year. This outcome is called a *subgame-perfect equilibrium*. A subgame-perfect equilibrium is a Nash equilibrium in which no player can make himself better off by changing his decision at any decision node. In our simple bargaining game, each player has only one decision to make. As we have seen, Dell's profits are highest if it offers the $20-per-copy contract price, and TruImage's profits are highest if it accepts the contract. Typically, in sequential games of this type, there is only one subgame-perfect equilibrium.

Managers use decision trees like those in Figures 13-6 and 13-7 in business planning because they provide a systematic way of thinking through the implications of a strategy and of predicting the reactions of rivals. We can see the benefits of decision trees in the simple examples we considered here. In the first example, HP's managers can conclude that charging a low price is more profitable than charging a high price. In the second example, Dell managers can conclude that TruImage's threat to reject a $20-per-copy contract is not credible.

## The Five Competitive Forces Model

**13.4 LEARNING OBJECTIVE**

Use the five competitive forces model to analyze competition in an industry.

We have seen that the number of competitors in an industry affects a firm's ability to charge a price above average cost and earn an economic profit. The number of firms is not the only determinant of the level of competition in an industry, however. Michael Porter of the Harvard Business School has drawn on the research of a number of economists to develop a model that shows how five competitive forces determine the overall level of competition in an industry. Figure 13-8 illustrates Porter's model.

We now look at each of the five competitive forces: (1) competition from existing firms, (2) the threat from potential entrants, (3) competition from substitute goods or services, (4) the bargaining power of buyers, and (5) the bargaining power of suppliers.

### Competition from Existing Firms

We have already seen that competition among firms in an industry can lower prices and profits. As another example, Educational Testing Service (ETS) produces the Scholastic Aptitude Test (SAT) and the Graduate Record Exam (GRE). High school students applying to college take the SAT, and college students applying to graduate school take the GRE. In 2009, ETS charged a price of $45 to take the SAT, and it

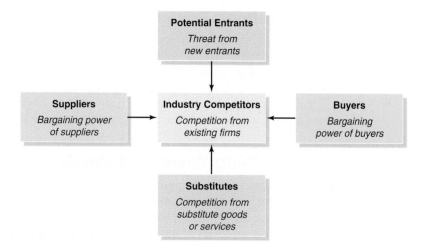

**Figure 13-8** **The Five Competitive Forces Model**

Michael Porter's model identifies five forces that determine the level of competition in an industry: (1) competition from existing firms, (2) the threat from new entrants, (3) competition from substitute goods or services, (4) the bargaining power of buyers, and (5) the bargaining power of suppliers.

Source: Reprinted with the permission of The Free Press, a Division of Simon & Schuster Adult Publishing Group, from Michael E. Porter, *Competitive Strategy: Techniques for Analyzing Industries and Competitors.* Copyright © 1980, 1998 by The Free Press. All rights reserved.

charged $140 to take the GRE. Part of the explanation for this large price difference is that ETS faces competition in the market for tests given to high school students applying to college, where the SAT competes with the ACT Assessment, produced by ACT, Inc. But there is no competition for the GRE test. As we saw earlier in this chapter, when there are only a few firms in a market, it is easier for them to implicitly collude and to charge a price close to the monopoly price. In this case, however, competition from a single firm was enough to cause ETS to keep the price of the SAT near the competitive level.

Competition in the form of advertising, better customer service, or longer warranties can also reduce profits by raising costs. For example, online booksellers Amazon.com, BarnesandNoble.com, and Buy.com have competed by offering low-cost—or free—shipping, by increasing their customer service staffs, and by building more warehouses to provide faster deliveries. These activities have raised the booksellers' costs and reduced their profits.

## The Threat from Potential Entrants

Firms face competition from companies that currently are not in the market but might enter. We have already seen how actions taken to deter entry can reduce profits. In our hypothetical example in the previous section, HP charged a lower price and earned less profit to deter Apple's entry. Business managers often take actions aimed at deterring entry. Some of these actions include advertising to create product loyalty, introducing new products—such as slightly different cereals or toothpastes—to fill market niches, and setting lower prices to keep profits at a level that would make entry less attractive.

## Competition from Substitute Goods or Services

Firms are always vulnerable to competitors introducing a new product that fills a consumer need better than their current product does. Consider the encyclopedia business. For decades, many parents bought expensive and bulky encyclopedias for their children attending high school or college. By the 1990s, computer software companies were offering electronic encyclopedias that sold for a small fraction of the price of printed encyclopedias. Encyclopedia Britannica and the other encyclopedia publishers responded by cutting prices and launching advertising campaigns aimed at showing the superiority of printed encyclopedias. Still, profits continued to decline, and by the end of the 1990s, most printed encyclopedias had disappeared.

## The Bargaining Power of Buyers

If buyers have enough bargaining power, they can insist on lower prices, higher-quality products, or additional services. Automobile companies, for example, have significant bargaining power in the tire market, which tends to lower tire prices and limit the profitability of tire manufacturers. Some retailers have significant buying power over their suppliers. For instance, Wal-Mart has required many of its suppliers to alter their distribution systems to accommodate Wal-Mart's need to control the stocks of goods in its stores.

## The Bargaining Power of Suppliers

If many firms can supply an input and the input is not specialized, the suppliers are unlikely to have the bargaining power to limit a firm's profits. For instance, suppliers of paper napkins to McDonald's restaurants have very little bargaining power. With only a single or a few suppliers of an input, the purchasing firm may face a high price. During the 1930s and 1940s, for example, the Technicolor Company was the only producer of the cameras and film that studios needed to produce color movies. Technicolor charged the studios high prices to use its cameras, and it had the power to insist that only its technicians could operate the cameras. The only alternative for the movie studios was to make black-and-white movies.

As with other competitive forces, the bargaining power of suppliers can change over time. For instance, when IBM chose Microsoft to supply the operating system for its personal computers, Microsoft was a small company with very limited bargaining power. As Microsoft's Windows operating system became standard in more than 90 percent of personal computers, this large market share increased Microsoft's bargaining power.

*Unfortunately, Circuit City's excellence as a company didn't last.*

| Making the Connection | **Can We Predict Which Firms Will Continue to Be Successful?** |

For years, economists and business strategists believed that market structure was the most important factor in explaining the ability of some firms to continue earning economic profits. For example, most economists argued that during the first few decades after World War II, steel companies in the United States earned economic profits because barriers to entry were high, there were few firms in the industry, and competition among firms was low. In contrast, restaurants were seen as less profitable because barriers to entry were low and the industry was intensely competitive. One problem with this approach to analyzing the profitability of firms is that it does not explain how firms in the same industry can have very different levels of profit.

Today, economists and business strategists put greater emphasis on the characteristics of individual firms and the strategies their managements use to continue to earn economic profits. This approach helps explain why Nucor continues to be a profitable steel company while Bethlehem Steel, at one time the second-largest steel producer in the United States, was forced into bankruptcy. It also explains why Dell, which began as a small company Michael Dell ran from his dorm room at the University of Texas, went on to become extremely profitable and an industry leader, while other computer companies have disappeared.

Is it possible to draw general conclusions about which business strategies are likely to be successful in the future? A number of business analysts have tried to identify strategies that have made firms successful and have recommended those strategies to other firms. Although books with these recommendations are often bestsellers, they have a mixed record in identifying winning strategies. For instance, in 1982, Thomas J. Peters and Robert H. Waterman, Jr., published *In Search of Excellence: Lessons from America's Best-Run Companies*. The book was favorably reviewed by business magazines and sold more than 3 million copies. Peters and Waterman identified 43 companies that were the best at using eight key strategies to "stay on top of the heap." But just two years after the book was published, an article in *BusinessWeek* pointed out that 14 of the

43 companies were experiencing significant financial difficulties. The article noted: "It comes as a shock that so many companies have fallen from grace so quickly—and it also raises some questions. Were these companies so excellent in the first place?"

In 2002, Jim Collins published *Good to Great: Why Some Companies Make the Leap . . . and Others Don't,* with the goal of determining how companies can "achieve enduring greatness." Although this book also sold 3 million copies, not all of the 11 "great companies" it identified were able to remain successful. For instance, Circuit City was forced to file for bankruptcy, and Fannie Mae avoided bankruptcy only after being largely taken over by the federal government.

These two books, and many others like them, provide useful analyses of the business strategies of successful firms. That many of the firms highlighted in these books are unable to sustain their success, though, should not be too surprising. Many successful strategies can be copied—and, often, improved on—by competitors. Even in oligopolies, competition can quickly erode profits and even turn a successful firm into an unsuccessful one. It remains difficult to predict which currently successful firms will maintain their success.

Sources: Thomas J. Peters and Robert H. Waterman, Jr., *In Search of Excellence: Lessons from America's Best-Run Companies,* New York: Harper & Row, 1982; Jim Collins, *Good to Great: Why Some Companies Make the Leap . . . and Others Don't,* New York: HarperCollins, 2001; "Who's Excellent Now?" *BusinessWeek,* November 5, 1984; and Steven D. Leavitt, "From Good to Great . . . to Below Average," *New York Times,* July 28, 2008.

**YOUR TURN:** Test your understanding by doing related problem 4.5 on page 458 at the end of this chapter.

▶ **Continued from page 431**

## Economics in YOUR LIFE!

At the beginning of this chapter, we asked you to consider why the price of the PlayStation 3 game system is almost the same at every large retailer, from Amazon.com to Wal-Mart. Why don't these retailers seem to compete on price for this type of product? In this chapter, we have seen that if big retailers were engaged in a one-time game of pricing PlayStations, they would be in a prisoner's dilemma and would probably all charge a low price. However, we have also seen that pricing PlayStations is actually a repeated game because the retailers will be selling the game system in competition over a long period of time. In this situation, it is more likely that the retailers will arrive at a cooperative equilibrium, in which they will all charge a high price—good news for the profits of the retailers, but bad news for consumers! This is one of many insights that game theory provides into the business strategies of oligopolists.

# Conclusion

Firms are locked in a never-ending struggle to earn economic profits. As noted in the two preceding chapters, competition erodes economic profits. Even in the oligopolies discussed in this chapter, firms have difficulty earning economic profits in the long run. We have seen that firms attempt to avoid the effects of competition in various ways. For example, they can stake out a secure niche in the market, they can engage in implicit collusion with competing firms, or they can attempt to have the government impose barriers to entry. *An Inside Look* on the next page discusses HP's attempts to increase its market share in the desktop and laptop computer markets.

## >> Hewlett-Packard Uses New Technology to Boost Sales of Personal Computers

### *WALL STREET JOURNAL*

## H-P Tries to Revive PC Sales with Touch Screens

Hewlett-Packard Co., seeking to revive the sagging desktop-computer business, has tried to woo consumers with sleek personal computers with glossy, touch-sensitive screens.

(a) But the touch-screen PCs, which can cost twice as much as typical machines, have been slow to catch on. H-P only sold about 400,000 of its TouchSmart desktops last year, compared with 54 million traditional desktops and laptops . . .

So H-P is embarking on a new strategy to find commercial uses for the technology . . .

In Michigan, H-P's touch screens are being put into luxury boxes in the Detroit Pistons' arena, where basketball fans can use them to access player statistics and see instant replays.

The commercial touch-screen effort is key to generating growth, since companies will "buy 10 Touch-Smarts at a time" and not just one like an individual would, said Phil McKinney, an H-P chief technology officer overseeing the touch-screen project.

. . . Desktop sales . . . have been hit hard by the recession and a consumer shift towards laptops.

. . . The deteriorating desktop PC market is a problem for H-P Chief Executive Mark Hurd, who revived the company's once money-losing PC division and helped H-P solidify its spot as the world's largest PC maker in terms of shipments.

(b) Still, H-P's PC division saw its operating margin, a measure of profitability, shrink to 5% in the January-ended quarter, down from 5.8% a year earlier.

Touch screens can help H-P combat that profit decline, analysts say. The average consumer desktop, excluding machines from Apple Inc., sold for $531 in March . . . In contrast, H-P's cheapest TouchSmart model has a list price of $1,200.

Uniguest Inc., a Nashville-based company that provides PCs with Internet access to hotels, began in January installing TouchSmart PCs in about two dozen hotels like the Nashville Airport Marriott.

"We're really pushing the new touch-screen technology," said Shawn Thomas, Uniguest's CEO. He said his company is paying between $1,200 and $1,600 per TouchSmart, but is in talks with H-P to place a large order and hopes to get a discount.

H-P isn't the only PC maker trying to boost falling desktop sales. Dell Inc. has introduced desktops in compact cases made of materials like bamboo and clear plastic, and earlier this year it also released a touch-screen desktop . . .

H-P is offering the assistance of hardware and software consultants from its services division to help customers come up with new uses for touch technology.

The strategy pits H-P against rivals like International Business Machines Corp., which has long sold touch-screen computers to do things like print out airline boarding passes.

IBM is also putting public computer kiosks into restaurants and retail stores.

Norma Wolcott, vice president of IBM's kiosk business, said IBM has tailored its touch screens, software and services for business use, arguing H-P's TouchSmart is more suited to consumers.

"It's what you want in your kitchen" and not in a high-traffic place like an airport, she said of the Touch-Smart.

(c) Bob Ducey, an H-P executive who is leading the TouchSmart's commercial marketing, said competitors like IBM are selling computers that do a single task—such as printing out movie tickets—rather than access a range of information over the Web. In contrast, Mr. Ducey said, the Touch-Smart can be used to access information much like a home PC.

At the Palace in Auburn Hills arena near Detroit, a small company called Konsyerzh LLC plans to install 35 new TouchSmart machines by June. Gregory Nasto, the company's CEO, said Konsyerzh has developed programs that let fans access instant replays and order food and merchandise.

Mr. Nasto said he could end up spending up to $1,200 per machine but he's trying to negotiate additional discounts. He expects touch-screen PC prices to drop further in the next year as more competitors enter the field . . .

Source: Justin Scheck, "H-P Tries to Revive PC Sales with Touch Screens," *Wall Street Journal*, May 15, 2009.

## Key Points in the Article

This article describes HP's plan to increase sales of personal computers with touch-sensitive screens. The market for desktop personal computers had suffered because of the recession of 2007–2009 and competition from laptop computers. Although the price of the new touch-sensitive screen computers is higher than prices of traditional desktops and laptops, HP is counting on sales to commercial buyers such as arenas and hotels that will buy multiple units. As explained in this chapter, when a market is an oligopoly, each firm must take into account the actions of its competitors. In this case, HP had to account for the likelihood that firms such as Apple and Dell would also offer high-priced touch-sensitive personal computers for their business customers.

## Analyzing the News

(a) In an oligopoly market, a firm's profits depend not only on the price it chooses but on the price its rivals choose.

HP decided to sell touch-sensitive personal computers in an effort to increase its market share. But it also decided to market the computers to commercial customers that are more likely to purchase multiple units.

(b) HP decided to charge a relatively high price for its touch-sensitive computers. The company hopes that this strategy will reverse the decline in its profits. But HP had to consider the reactions of rival firms to its strategy. The figure is helpful in analyzing whether the success of HP will depend on the reaction of a rival firm, Dell. The figure illustrates the competition between HP and Dell using two possible scenarios, shown in panel (a) and panel (b). In both panels, we assume that HP has decided to sell touch-sensitive computers for $1,200, and Dell must then decide whether it should also sell these computers for the same price. We assume that each company needs a 15 percent return on its investment in these new computers to break even. In panel (a), if Dell decides to

sell touch-sensitive computers, both companies will earn a 20 percent return. If Dell decides not to enter this market, HP will earn 30 percent and Dell will earn nothing in this market. Because 20 percent is greater than the minimum 15 percent required return, we can conclude that Dell will enter the market and both firms will earn a 20 percent return.

But suppose that HP determines that its position relative to Dell is that shown in panel (b). Now if Dell enters this market, both Dell and HP will earn 10 percent returns. If Dell does not enter the market, HP will earn a 30 percent return. Because 10 percent is below the required return of 15 percent, Dell will not enter the market. In this case, it turns out that whether panel (a) or panel (b) more accurately describes the situation in this market is not important for HP's initial decision to sell touch-sensitive computers. Whether Dell enters the market or not, HP will still earn a return greater than 15 percent. Therefore, it should sell touch-sensitive computers.

(c) Oligopoly firms often try to either (1) introduce new products that fill consumer needs that existing products do not or (2) introduce new products to fill consumer needs better than existing products can. HP is marketing its touch-sensitive computers to companies such as Konsyerzh LLC that use them to develop programs to let basketball fans at the Palace at Auburn Hills watch video replays and order food.

## Thinking Critically

1. HP is hoping that its strategy of selling high-priced touch-sensitive computers will increase its share of the personal computer market. What risks does the company face that could defeat its strategy?

2. Apply the five competitive forces model to HP. Cite one example of each of the sources of competition HP faces.

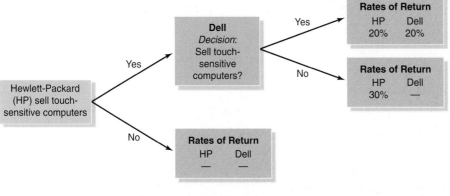

**(a) Dell should sell touch-sensitive computers**

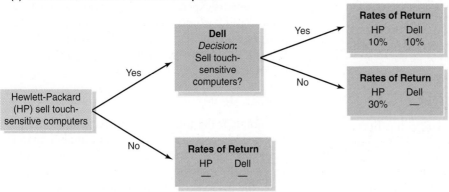

**(b) Dell should not sell touch-sensitive computers**

Dell decides whether to sell touch-sensitive personal computers.

# Key Terms

---

**13.1** **Oligopoly and Barriers to Entry, pages 432–435**
LEARNING OBJECTIVE: Show how barriers to entry explain the existence of oligopolies.

## Summary

An **oligopoly** is a market structure in which a small number of interdependent firms compete. **Barriers to entry** keep new firms from entering an industry. The three most important barriers to entry are economies of scale, ownership of a key input, and government barriers. Economies of scale are the most important barrier to entry. **Economies of scale** exist when a firm's long-run average costs fall as it increases output. Government barriers include patents, licensing, and barriers to international trade. A **patent** is the exclusive right to a product for a period of 20 years from the date the product is invented.

 Visit **www.myeconlab.com** to complete these exercises online and get instant feedback.

## Review Questions

**1.1** What is an oligopoly? Give three examples of oligopolistic industries in the United States.

**1.2** What do barriers to entry have to do with the extent of competition, or lack thereof, in an industry? What are the most important barriers to entry?

**1.3** Give an example of a government-imposed barrier to entry. Why would a government be willing to erect barriers to entering an industry?

## Problems and Applications

**1.4** Michael Porter argued, "The intensity of competition in an industry is neither a matter of coincidence nor bad luck. Rather, competition in an industry is rooted in its underlying economic structure." What does Porter mean by "economic structure"? What factors besides economic structure might be expected to determine the intensity of competition in an industry?

Source: Michael Porter, *Competitive Strategy: Techniques for Analyzing Industries and Competitors*, New York: The Free Press, 1980, p. 3.

**1.5** In 2009, some analysts of the smartphone industry argued that Apple would be likely to offer a variety of different iPhones, each with different features. One observer objected to this argument, though, arguing that: "Selling models differentiated by hardware seems unlikely. Different iPhones with very different physical specs could have far-reaching implications for Apple's production methods, volumes and costs." How would Apple's costs be affected by offering different iPhones with "very different specs"? How would this change in costs be likely to affect the prices Apple charged for the iPhone? How would this change in costs be likely to affect the ability of other firms to compete against the iPhone?

Source: James Sherwood, "Apple to Look to Software to Differentiate Multiple iPhone Models," reghardware.co.uk, May 18, 2009.

**1.6** Thomas McCraw, a professor at Harvard Business School, wrote, "Throughout American history, entrepreneurs have tried, sometimes desperately, to create big businesses out of naturally small-scale operations. It has not worked." What advantage would entrepreneurs expect to gain from creating "big businesses"? Why would entrepreneurs fail to create big businesses with "naturally small-scale operations"? Illustrate your answer with a graph showing long-run average costs.

Source: Thomas K. McCraw, ed., *Creating Modern Capitalism*, Cambridge, MA: Harvard University Press, 1997, p. 323.

**1.7** The graph at the top of the next page illustrates the average total cost curves for two automobile manufacturing firms: Little Auto and Big Auto. Under which of the following conditions would you expect to see the market composed of firms like Little Auto, and under which conditions would you expect to see the market dominated by firms like Big Auto?

a. When the market demand curve intersects the quantity axis at fewer than 1,000 units

b. When the market demand curve intersects the quantity axis at more than 1,000 units but fewer than 10,000 units

c. When the market demand curve intersects the quantity axis at more than 10,000 units

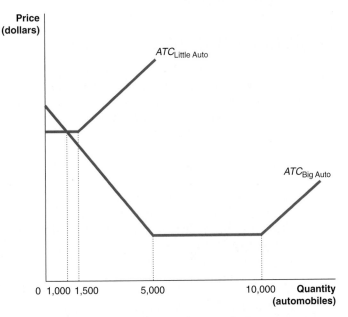

**1.8** The following graph contains two long-run average cost curves. Briefly explain which cost curve would most likely be associated with an oligopoly and which would most likely be associated with a perfectly competitive industry.

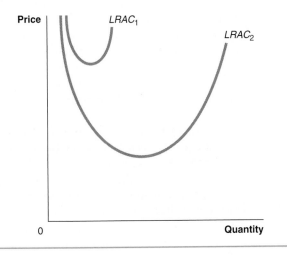

**1.9** Alfred Chandler, who was a professor at Harvard Business School, observed, "Imagine the diseconomies of scale—the great increase in unit costs—that would result from placing close to one-fourth of the world's production of shoes, or textiles, or lumber into three factories or mills!" The shoe, textiles, and lumber industries are very competitive, with many firms producing each of these products. Briefly explain whether Chandler's observation helps explain why.

Source: Alfred D. Chandler, Jr., "The Emergence of Managerial Capitalism," in Alfred D. Chandler, Jr., and Richard S. Tedlow, *The Coming of Managerial Capitalism*, New York: Irwin, 1985, p. 406.

**1.10** A historical account of the development of the cotton textile industry in England argued:

> The cotton textile industry was shaped by ruthless competition. Rapid growth in demand, low barriers to entry, frequent technological innovations, and a high rate of firm bankruptcy all combined to form an environment in which . . . oligopolistic competition became almost impossible.

Explain how each of the factors described here would contribute to making the cotton textile industry competitive rather than oligopolistic.

Source: Thomas K. McCraw, ed., *Creating Modern Capitalism*, Cambridge, MA: Harvard University Press, pp. 61–62.

**1.11** (Related to *Solved Problem 13-1* on page 435) Economic analysis predicts that when firms make a profit, new firms will enter the market, which will force down the price and reduce profits. Consider the following information on a market:

| | |
|---|---|
| Cost to open a store | $15 |
| Monthly cost to operate a store | $20 |
| Monthly revenue for all stores in the industry | $100 |
| Number of stores in the market | 4 |

Explain how barriers to entry keep a fifth firm out of the market. You may assume that the market gets split evenly between firms in the market.

**>> End Learning Objective 13.1**

**Using Game Theory to Analyze Oligopoly,** pages 436–444
LEARNING OBJECTIVE: Use game theory to analyze the strategies of oligopolistic firms.

## Summary

Because an oligopoly has only a few firms, interactions among those firms are particularly important. **Game theory** is the study of how people make decisions in situations in which attaining their goals depends on their interactions with others; in economics, it is the study of the decisions of firms in industries where the profits of each firm depend on its interactions with other firms. A **business strategy** refers to actions taken by a firm to achieve a goal, such as maximizing profits. Oligopoly games can be illustrated with a **payoff matrix**, which is a table that shows the payoffs that each firm earns from every combination of strategies by the firms. One possible outcome in oligopoly is **collusion**, which is an agreement among firms to charge the same price or otherwise not to compete. A **cartel** is a group of firms that collude by agreeing to restrict output to increase prices and profits. In a **cooperative equilibrium**, firms cooperate to increase their mutual payoff. In a **noncooperative equilibrium**, firms do not cooperate but pursue their own self-interest. A **dominant strategy** is a strategy that is the best for a firm, no matter what strategies other firms use. A **Nash equilibrium** is a situation in which each firm chooses the best strategy, given the strategies chosen by other firms. A situation in which pursuing dominant strategies results in noncooperation that leaves everyone worse off is called a **prisoner's dilemma**. Because many business situations are repeated games, firms may end up implicitly colluding to keep prices high. With **price leadership**, one firm takes the lead in announcing a price change, which is then matched by the other firms in the industry.

 Visit **www.myeconlab.com** to complete these exercises online and get instant feedback.

## Review Questions

2.1 Give brief definitions of the following concepts.
   a. Game theory
   b. Cooperative equilibrium
   c. Noncooperative equilibrium
   d. Dominant strategy
   e. Nash equilibrium
2.2 Why do economists refer to the methodology for analyzing oligopolies as game theory?
2.3 Why do economists refer to the pricing strategies of oligopoly firms as a prisoner's dilemma game?
2.4 What is the difference between explicit collusion and implicit collusion? Give an example of each.

2.5 How is the result of the prisoner's dilemma changed in a repeated game?

## Problems and Applications

2.6 Bob and Tom are two criminals who have been arrested for burglary. The police put Tom and Bob in separate cells. They offer to let Bob go free if he confesses to the crime and testifies against Tom. Bob also is told that he will serve a 15-year sentence if he remains silent while Tom confesses. If he confesses and Tom also confesses, they will each serve a 10-year sentence. Separately, the police make the same offer to Tom. Assume that Bob and Tom know that if they both remain silent, the police have only enough evidence to convict them of a lesser crime, and they will both serve 3-year sentences.
   a. Use the information provided to write a payoff matrix for Bob and Tom.
   b. Does Bob have a dominant strategy? If so, what is it?
   c. Does Tom have a dominant strategy? If so, what is it?
   d. What sentences do Bob and Tom serve? How might they have avoided this outcome?
2.7 Explain how collusion makes firms better off. Given the incentives to collude, briefly explain why every industry doesn't become a cartel.
2.8 Under "early decision" college admission plans, students apply to a college in the fall and, if they are accepted, they must enroll in that college. According to an article in *BusinessWeek*, Yale president Richard Levin argues that early decision plans put too much pressure on students to decide early in their senior years which college to attend. Levin has proposed abolishing early decision plans. But the author of the article is doubtful that this will succeed because "as long as some big-name schools offer early admissions, the others feel they must, too, or lose out on the best talent." Do you agree with this conclusion? How can game theory help analyze this situation?
2.9 Baseball players who hit the most home runs *relative to other players* usually receive the highest pay. Beginning in the mid-1990s, the typical baseball player became significantly stronger and more muscular. As one baseball announcer put it, "The players of 20 years ago look like stick figures compared with the players of today." As a result, the average number of home runs hit each year increased dramatically. Some of the increased strength that baseball players gained came from

more weight training and better conditioning and diet. As some players admitted, though, some of the increased strength came from taking steroids and other illegal drugs. Taking steroids can significantly increase the risk of developing cancer and other medical problems.

a. In these circumstances, are baseball players in a prisoner's dilemma? Carefully explain.

b. Suppose that Major League Baseball begins testing players for steroids and firing players who are caught using them (or other illegal muscle-building drugs). Will this testing make baseball players as a group better off or worse off? Briefly explain.

2.10 Soldiers in battle may face a prisoner's dilemma. If all soldiers stand and fight, the chance that the soldiers, as a unit, will survive is maximized. If there is a significant chance that the soldiers will lose the battle, an individual soldier may maximize his chance of survival by running away while the other soldiers hold off the enemy by fighting. If all soldiers run away, however, many of them are likely to be killed or captured by the enemy because no one is left to hold off the enemy. In ancient times, the Roman army practiced "decimation." If a unit of soldiers was guilty of running away during a battle or committing other cowardly acts, all would be lined up, and every tenth soldier would be killed by being run through with a sword. No attempt was made to distinguish between soldiers in the unit who had fought well and those who had been cowardly. Briefly explain under what condition the Roman system of decimation was likely to have solved the prisoner's dilemma of soldiers running away in battle.

2.11 (Related to *Solved Problem 13-2* on page 438) Would a ban on advertising beer on television be likely to increase or decrease the profits of beer companies? Briefly explain.

2.12 (Related to *Solved Problem 13-2* on page 438) Beginning in 2003, the U.S. government spent billions of dollars rebuilding the infrastructure damaged by the war in Iraq. Much of the work was carried out by construction and engineering firms that had to bid for the business. Suppose, hypothetically, that only two companies—Bechtel and Halliburton—enter the bidding and that each firm is deciding whether to bid either $4 billion or $5 billion. (Remember that in this type of bidding, the winning bid is the *low* bid because the bid represents the amount the government will have to pay to have the work done.) Each firm will have costs of $2.5 billion to do the work. If they both make the same bid, they will both be hired and will split the work and the profits. If one makes a low bid and one

makes a high bid, only the low bidder will be hired, and it will receive all the profits. The result is the following payoff matrix.

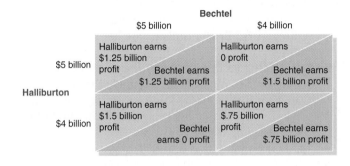

a. Is there a Nash equilibrium in this game? Briefly explain.

b. How might the situation be changed if the two companies expect to be bidding on many similar projects in future years?

2.13 (Related to *Solved Problem 13-2* on page 438) Radio frequency identification (RFID) tracking tags may ultimately replace barcodes. With this system, a radio signal will automatically record the arrival of a product in a warehouse, its shipment to a store, and its purchase by the consumer. Suppose that Wal-Mart and Target are independently deciding whether to stick with bar codes or switch to RFID tags to monitor the flow of products. Because many suppliers sell to both Wal-Mart and Target, it is much less costly for suppliers to use one system or the other rather than to use both. The following payoff matrix shows the profits per year for each company resulting from the interaction of their strategies.

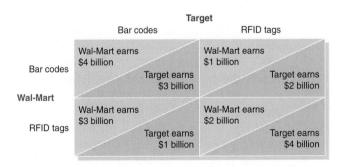

a. Briefly explain whether Wal-Mart has a dominant strategy.

b. Briefly explain whether Target has a dominant strategy.

c. Briefly explain whether there is a Nash equilibrium in this game.

**2.14** (Related to the *Don't Let This Happen to You!* on page 438) A student argues, "The prisoner's dilemma game is unrealistic. Each player's strategy is based on the assumption that the other player won't cooperate. But if each player assumes that the other player *will* cooperate, the 'dilemma' disappears." Briefly explain whether you agree with this argument.

**2.15** (Related to the *Making the Connection* on page 439) We made the argument that a bidder on an eBay auction has a dominant strategy of bidding only once, with that bid being the maximum the bidder would be willing to pay.

  a. Is it possible that a bidder might receive useful information during the auction, particularly from the dollar amounts other bidders are bidding? If so, how does that change a bidder's optimal strategy?

  b. Many people recommend the practice of "sniping," or placing your bid at the last second before the auction ends. Is there a connection between sniping and your answer to part a?

**2.16** The following appeared in an article in the *Wall Street Journal*: "Last week, true to discount roots dating to 1971, Southwest [Airlines] launched a summer fare sale on domestic flights, with one-way prices as low as $49. As in the past, major competitors were forced to follow suit." Why would other airlines be "forced" to follow Southwest's fare decrease? Does your answer change if you learn that this fare decrease took place during an economic recession, when incomes and the demand for airline travel were falling? Briefly explain.

Source: Mike Esterl, "Southwest Airlines CEO Flies Uncharted Skies," *Wall Street Journal*, March 25, 2009.

**2.17** (Related to the *Making the Connection* on page 441) Singapore residents have recently experienced fluctuations in the price of petrol and diesel.

  a. What is "price leadership"? In which other sector within the oligopolistic market structure would you expect to find similar "follow the leader" behavior?

  b. Economic theory tells us that price increases lead to lower sales. Yet, the petrol companies not only increase price, but they also raise the price in tandem. Why is this type of pricing strategy peculiar to oligopolies such as petrol companies but not other types of market structures?

**2.18** Finding dominant strategies is often a very effective way of analyzing a game. Consider the following game: Microsoft and Apple are the two firms in the market for operating systems. Each firm has two strategies: Charge a high price or charge a low price.

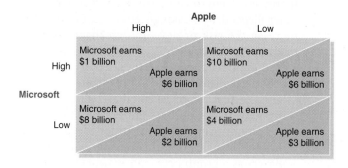

  a. What (if any) is the dominant strategy for each firm?

  b. Is there a Nash equilibrium? Briefly explain.

**2.19** One day in October 2008, the price of oil dropped to $64 a barrel, its lowest level in more than a year. This drop in price occurred on the same day that the Organization of Petroleum Exporting Countries (OPEC) announced it would cut daily oil production by 1.5 million barrels. Why would the price of oil drop at the same time that OPEC announced a cut in production? Shouldn't lower production lead to higher prices?

Source: Vivienne Walt, "What's Behind (and Ahead for) the Plunging Price of Oil," *Time*, October 24, 2008.

**2.20** In 2007, some countries that export natural gas discussed forming a cartel, modeled on the OPEC oil cartel. The head of Libya's energy sector was quoted as saying, "We are trying to strengthen the cooperation among gas producers to avoid harmful competition."

  a. What is a cartel?

  b. What is "harmful competition"? Is competition typically harmful to consumers?

  c. What factors would help the cartel succeed? What factors would reduce the cartel's chances for success?

Source: Ayesha Daya and James Herron, "Gas Exporters to Study Cartel," *Wall Street Journal*, April 10, 2007, p. A6.

**2.21** Refer to Figure 13-5 on page 443. Consider the entries in the row of the payoff matrix that correspond to Saudi Arabia choosing "low output." Suppose the numbers change so that Nigeria's profit is $15 million when Nigeria chooses "low output" and $10 million when it chooses "high output."

  a. Create the payoff matrix for this new situation, assuming that Saudi Arabia and Nigeria choose their output levels simultaneously. Is there a Nash equilibrium to this game? If so, what is it?

**b.** Draw the decision tree for this situation (using the values from the payoff matrix you created in part a), assuming that Saudi Arabia and Nigeria make their decisions sequentially: First Saudi Arabia chooses its output level, and then Nigeria responds by choosing its output level. Is there a Nash equilibrium in this game? If so, what is it?

**c.** Compare your answers to parts a and b. Briefly explain the reason for any differences in the outcomes of these two games.

>> **End Learning Objective 13.2**

---

**13.3** | **Sequential Games and Business Strategy,** pages 444–446

LEARNING OBJECTIVE: Use sequential games to analyze business strategies.

## Summary

Recent work in game theory has focused on actions firms can take to deter the entry of new firms into an industry. Deterring entry can be analyzed using a sequential game, where first one firm makes a decision and then another firm reacts to that decision. Sequential games can be illustrated using decision trees.

 Visit **www.myeconlab.com** to complete these exercises online and get instant feedback.

## Review Questions

3.1 What is a sequential game?

3.2 How are decision trees used to analyze sequential games?

## Problems and Applications

3.3 (Related to the *Chapter Opener* on page 431) The discussion of Apple and HP competing in the market for netbooks, as illustrated by Figure 13-6

on page 445, is simplified because the firms actually compete not just on the price of the netbooks but also on the features they contain. In early 2009, when asked whether Apple was considering entering the market for netbooks, Apple's chief operating officer, Tim Cook, said: "When I'm looking at what's sold in the netbook market, I see cramped keyboards, junky hardware, very small screens, bad software. Not a consumer experience that we would put the Mac brand on, quite frankly." How might HP's awareness of the importance to Apple of having the "Mac brand" associated with high-quality products have affected HP's strategy in the netbook market?

Source: www.apple.com, FY 09 Second Quarter Results Conference Call.

3.4 Suppose that in the situation shown in Figure 13-7 on page 445, TruImage's profits are $1.5 million if the firm accepts Dell's contract offer of $20 per copy. Now will Dell offer TruImage a contract of $20 per copy or a contract of $30 per copy? Briefly explain.

>> **End Learning Objective 13.3**

---

**13.4** | **The Five Competitive Forces Model,** pages 446–449

LEARNING OBJECTIVE: Use the five competitive forces model to analyze competition in an industry.

## Summary

Michael Porter of Harvard Business School argues that the state of competition in an industry is determined by five competitive forces: the degree of competition among existing firms, the threat from new entrants, competition from substitute goods or services, the bargaining power of buyers, and the bargaining power of suppliers.

 Visit **www.myeconlab.com** to complete these exercises online and get instant feedback.

## Review Questions

4.1 List the competitive forces in the five competitive forces model.

4.2 Does the strength of each of the five competitive forces remain constant over time? Briefly explain.

# Problems and Applications

**4.3** Michael Porter argued that in many industries, "strategies converge and competition becomes a series of races down identical paths that no one can win." Briefly explain whether firms in these industries will likely earn economic profits.

Source: Michael E. Porter, "What Is Strategy?" *Harvard Business Review*, November–December 1996, p. 64.

**4.4** According to an article in the *New York Times*:

> On Tuesday, Google will release a free Web browser called Chrome that the company said would challenge Microsoft's Internet Explorer, as well as the Firefox browser.
>
> The browser is a universal doorway to the Internet, and the use of Internet software and services is rapidly growing. Increasingly, the browser is also the doorway to the Web on cellphones and other mobile devices, widening the utility of the Web and Web advertising. Google, analysts say, cannot let Microsoft's dominant share of the browser market go without a direct challenge.
>
> John Lilly, chief executive of the Mozilla Corporation, which manages the Firefox project, said that Google's action would put "more competitive pressure on us to keep coming up with great browser technology."

a. What does the article mean by "competitive pressure"? Which of the five competitive forces is being referred to?

b. In the long run, will the company that first incorporates new innovations in its browser technology earn economic profits? Which group is likely to benefit the most from these innovations: the browser companies or consumers?

Source: Steve Lohr, "Microsoft Faces New Browser Foe in Google," *New York Times*, September 1, 2008.

**4.5** (Related to the *Making the Connection* on page 448) In the preface to the 2004 reprint of *In Search of Excellence*, Thomas Peters and Robert Waterman wrote: "Our main detractors point to the decline of some of the companies we featured. They miss the point.... We weren't writing *Forever Excellent*, just as it would be absurd to expect any great athlete not to age." Is the analogy the authors make between great firms and great athletes a good one? Should we expect firms to become less successful as they age, just as athletes do?

Source: Thomas Peters and Robert H. Waterman, Jr., "Authors' Note: Excellence 2003," in *In Search of Excellence: Lessons from America's Best-Run Companies*, New York: Collins, 2004 (original edition 1982).

**4.6** In a forum posting on the Web site www.startupnation.com, a contributor made the following comment regarding the advice in the business strategy book *Blue Ocean Strategy*: "The key message for me was don't try to look like, taste like, act like the competition." Briefly explain what this person meant by "look like, taste like, act like the competition." Briefly discuss whether the strategy of "look like, taste like, act like the competition" ever makes sense.

Source: "As a Small Business Owner, What Kind of Book Would You Like to Read?" "Coffee Talk" Forum, www.startupnation.com, April 25, 2007.

**4.7** The market for electronic readers consists of a relatively few firms, including Amazon, Sony, and Plastic Logic. In an interview, Walter Mossberg of the *Wall Street Journal* asked Rich Archuleta, CEO of Plastic Logic, what price the company would be charging for a new electronic reader that it was developing, aimed at business users. Archuleta declined to give a specific price, saying instead, "The market sets pricing. We don't set pricing." But Plastic Logic is competing in an oligopolistic industry, so shouldn't the firm, not the market, be setting the price? Explain why Archuleta made the statement he made.

Source: "Plastic Logic Shows New E-Book Reader," *Wall Street Journal*, May 27, 2009.

**>> End Learning Objective 13.4**

# CHAPTER 14

# Monopoly and Antitrust Policy

## Chapter Outline and Learning Objectives

# >> Is Cable Television a Monopoly?

Today most people can hardly imagine life without cable television. The first cable systems were established in the 1940s, in cities that were too small to support broadcast stations. At first, the cable industry grew slowly because the technology did not exist to rebroadcast the signals of distant stations, so cable systems offered just a few channels. By 1970, only about 7 percent of households had cable television. In addition, the Federal Communications Commission (FCC)—the U.S. government agency that regulates the television industry—placed restrictions on both rebroadcasting the signals of distant stations and the fees that cable systems could charge for "premium channels" that would show movies or sporting events. In the late 1970s, two key developments occurred: First, satellite relay technology made it feasible for local cable systems to receive signals relayed by satellite from distant broadcast stations. Second, Congress loosened regulations on rebroadcasting distant stations and charging for premium channels, which allowed cable networks such as Home Box Office (HBO) and Showtime to develop.

A firm needs a license from the city government to enter a local cable television market. Until 2008, Time Warner Cable was the only provider of cable TV in Manhattan; Time Warner had a *monopoly*. Few firms in the United States are monopolies because in a market system, whenever a firm earns economic profits, other firms will enter its market. Therefore, it is very difficult for a firm to remain the only provider of a good or service. In this chapter, we will develop an economic model of monopoly that can help analyze how such firms affect the economy.

**AN INSIDE LOOK AT POLICY** on **page 484** discusses Verizon's attempts to increase competition in the market for cable television in New York City.

## Economics in YOUR LIFE!

### Why Can't I Watch the NFL Network?

Are you a fan of the National Football League? Would you like to see more NFL-related programming on television? If so, you're not alone. The NFL concluded there was so much demand for more football programming that it began its own football network, the NFL Network.

Unfortunately for many football fans, the NFL Network is not available to most households that have cable television. Why are some of the largest cable TV systems unwilling to include the NFL Network in their channel lineups? Why are some systems requiring customers who want the NFL Network to upgrade to more expensive channel packages? As you read this chapter, see if you can answer these questions. You can check your answers against those we provide at the end of the chapter.

▶ Continued on page 482

Although few firms are monopolies, the economic model of monopoly can be quite useful. As we saw in Chapter 11, even though perfectly competitive markets are rare, this market model provides a benchmark for how a firm acts in the most competitive situation possible: when it is in an industry with many firms that all supply the same product. Monopoly provides a benchmark for the other extreme, where a firm is the only one in its market and, therefore, faces no competition from other firms supplying its product. The monopoly model is also useful in analyzing situations in which firms agree to *collude*, or not compete, and act together as if they were a monopoly. As we will discuss in this chapter, collusion is illegal in the United States, but it occasionally happens.

Monopolies pose a dilemma for the government. Should the government allow monopolies to exist? Are there circumstances in which the government should actually promote the existence of monopolies? Should the government regulate the prices monopolies charge? If so, will such price regulation increase economic efficiency? In this chapter, we will explore these public policy issues.

**14.1 LEARNING** OBJECTIVE

Define monopoly.

**Monopoly** A firm that is the only seller of a good or service that does not have a close substitute.

# Is Any Firm Ever Really a Monopoly?

A **monopoly** is a firm that is the only seller of a good or service that does not have a close substitute. Because substitutes of some kind exist for just about every product, can any firm really be a monopoly? The answer is "yes," provided that the substitutes are not "close" substitutes. But how do we decide whether a substitute is a close substitute? A narrow definition of monopoly that some economists use is that a firm has a monopoly if it can ignore the actions of all other firms. In other words, other firms must not be producing close substitutes if the monopolist can ignore the other firms' prices. For example, candles are a substitute for electric lights, but your local electric company can ignore candle prices because however low the price of candles falls, almost no customers will give up using electric lights and switch to candles. Therefore, your local electric company is clearly a monopoly.

Many economists, however, use a broader definition of monopoly. For example, suppose Donn Johnson owns the only pizza parlor in a small town. (We will consider later the question of *why* a market may have only a single firm.) Does Donn have a monopoly? Substitutes for pizza certainly exist. If the price of pizza is too high, people will switch to hamburgers or fried chicken or some other food instead. People do not have to eat at Donn's or starve. Donn is in competition with the local McDonald's and KFC, among other firms. So, Donn does not meet the narrow definition of a monopoly. But many economists would still argue that it is useful to think of Donn as having a monopoly.

Although hamburgers and fried chicken are substitutes for pizza, competition from firms selling them is not enough to keep Donn from earning economic profits. We saw in Chapter 11 that when firms earn economic profits, we can expect new firms to enter the industry, and in the long run, the economic profits are competed away. Donn's profits will not be competed away as long as he is the *only* seller of pizza. Using the broader definition, Donn has a monopoly because there are no other firms selling a substitute close enough that his economic profits are competed away in the long run.

Making
the
Connection

## Is the Xbox 360 a Close Substitute for the PlayStation 3?

In the early 2000s, Microsoft's Xbox and Sony's PlayStation 2 (PS2) were the best-selling video game consoles. In developing the Xbox, Microsoft had decided to include a hard disk and a version of the Windows computer operating system. As a result, the cost of producing the Xbox was much higher than the cost to Sony of producing the PS2. Microsoft was not concerned by the higher production cost because it believed it would be able to charge a higher price for the Xbox than Sony charged for the PS2. Unfortunately for Microsoft, consumers considered the Sony PS2 a close substitute for the Xbox. Microsoft was forced to charge the same price for the Xbox that Sony charged for the PS2. So, while Sony was able to make a substantial profit at that price, Microsoft initially lost money on the Xbox because of its higher costs.

In developing the next generation of video game consoles, both companies hoped to produce devices that could serve as multipurpose home-entertainment systems. To achieve this goal, the new systems needed to play DVDs as well as games. Sony developed a new video display system called Blu-ray. Blu-ray discs can store five times as much data as conventional DVDs and can play back high-definition (HD) video. Sony's decision to give the new PlayStation 3 (PS3) the capability to play Blu-ray discs was risky, though, because it significantly raised the cost of producing the consoles. Microsoft decided to sell its Xbox 360 with only the capability of playing older-format DVDs.

By 2009, it appeared that Microsoft may have made the better decision. Consumers seemed to consider the PS3 and the Xbox to be close substitutes, in part because Blu-ray discs had only a small share of the market, and prices of stand-alone Blu-ray players had fallen sharply. With consumers apparently viewing the two systems primarily as game consoles, the Xbox had a significant advantage because it was priced $100 less than the PS3. During 2009, sales of the Xbox 360 surged ahead of PS3 sales, and some industry analysts wondered whether with its higher price and lack of distinctive features the PS3 would be able to survive.

*To many gamers, Microsoft's Xbox is a better deal than PlayStation 3.*

Sources: Daisuke Wakabayashi and Yuzo Yamaguchi, "Sony Losses Raise Pressure on Stringer," *Wall Street Journal*, May 15, 2009; Dan Gallagher, "Video Game Sales Continue to Decline in April," marketwatch.com, May 14, 2009; and Loyd Case, "Is the PlayStation 3 in a Death Spiral?" pcmag.com, April 17, 2009.

**YOUR TURN:** Test your understanding by doing related problem 1.7 on page 486 at the end of this chapter.

# Where Do Monopolies Come From?

**14.2 LEARNING** OBJECTIVE

Explain the four main reasons monopolies arise.

Because monopolies do not face competition, every firm would like to have a monopoly. But to have a monopoly, barriers to entering the market must be so high that no other firms can enter. *Barriers to entry* may be high enough to keep out competing firms for four main reasons:

1. A government blocks the entry of more than one firm into a market.
2. One firm has control of a key resource necessary to produce a good.
3. There are important *network externalities* in supplying the good or service.
4. Economies of scale are so large that one firm has a *natural monopoly*.

## Entry Blocked by Government Action

As we will discuss later in this chapter, governments ordinarily try to promote competition in markets, but sometimes governments take action to block entry into a market. In the United States, governments block entry in two main ways:

1. By granting a *patent* or *copyright* to an individual or a firm, giving it the exclusive right to produce a product.
2. By granting a firm a *public franchise*, making it the exclusive legal provider of a good or service.

**Patents and Copyrights** The U.S. government grants patents to firms that develop new products or new ways of making existing products. A **patent** gives a firm the exclusive right to a new product for a period of 20 years from the date the product is invented. Because Microsoft has a patent on the Windows operating system, other firms cannot

**Patent** The exclusive right to a product for a period of 20 years from the date the product is invented.

sell their own versions of Windows. The government grants patents to encourage firms to spend money on the research and development necessary to create new products. If other firms could have freely copied Windows, Microsoft would have been unlikely to spend the money necessary to develop it. Sometimes a firm is able to maintain a monopoly in the production of a good without patent protection, provided that it can keep secret how the product is made.

Patent protection is of vital importance to pharmaceutical firms as they develop new prescription drugs. Pharmaceutical firms start research and development work on a new prescription drug an average of 12 years before the drug is available for sale. A firm applies for a patent about 10 years before it begins to sell the product. The average 10-year delay between the government granting a patent and the firm actually selling the drug is due to the federal Food and Drug Administration's requirements that the firm demonstrate that the drug is both safe and effective. Therefore, during the period before the drug can be sold, the firm will have substantial costs to develop and test the drug. If the drug does not successfully make it to market, the firm will have a substantial loss.

Once a drug is available for sale, the profits the firm earns from the drug will increase throughout the period of patent protection—which is usually about 10 years—as the drug becomes more widely known to doctors and patients. After the patent has expired, other firms are free to legally produce chemically identical drugs called *generic drugs*. Gradually, competition from generic drugs will eliminate the profits the original firm had been earning. For example, when patent protection expired for Glucophage, a diabetes drug manufactured by Bristol-Myers Squibb, sales of the drug declined by more than $1.5 billion in the first year due to competition from 12 generic versions of the drug produced by other firms. When the patent expired on Prozac, an antidepressant drug manufactured by Eli Lilly, sales dropped by more than 80 percent. Most economic profits from selling a prescription drug are eliminated 20 years after the drug is first offered for sale.

## Making the Connection | Monopoly on Connection

Many governments in the Middle East region have monopoly control over enterprises such as communication and transportation. In the United Arab Emirates (UAE) for example, the local telephone company Etisalat (connection) is majority owned and operated by the government. Etisalat provides landline, mobile, internet and cable services to the entire country. People often complain of high rates, poor or slow connections and long waiting times for repair and counter services. Unlike monopolies in the West, the UAE government makes no attempt to regulate Etisalat or offer operation licenses to other communication companies to compete. In 1991 the government issued law number 1 which gave Etisalat virtual control of wired and wireless telecommunication services in the UAE and between the country and the rest of the world. It also granted Etisalat the sole right to import or manufacture telecommunication equipment. While the UAE government prevents outside companies from entering its telecommunication market, Etisalat is allowed to compete in other countries. In 2009 Etisalat operated in 17 Middle East and North Africa markets and was the second largest telecommunication operator in the region by market capitalization. In October 2008, Etisalat reported net revenues of $5.204 billion and a net profit of $1.989 billion. That is a whopping return of more than 38% profit on revenue.

Companies like Etisalat serve as a source of income for the government and a means of employment for the local population. As a monopoly they are highly profitable and are often used to absorb the unemployed segment of the population. Recently, as a result of pressure by the World Trade Organization, the UAE government was forced to create a second telecommunication company, Du, to provide services to the country. Like Etisalat, Du is also majority owned by the government. It does not effectively compete with Etisalat, rather it provides the appearance of competition. The Telecommunications Regulatory Authority (TRA) in the UAE in effect prevents service price competition among these two companies and only allows for occasional promotions and discounts.

*Etisalat has monopoly control over communication in the United Arab Emirates.*

Monopoly enterprises such as Etisalat charge a high price and offer reduced services but they are highly profitable and provide both revenue and employment. In the long term though they tend to become inefficient. If faced with competition their survival would be in doubt.

Sources: Wikipedia; Gulf News September 25th, 2009.

**YOUR TURN:** Test your understanding by doing related problem 2.9 on page 487 at the end of this chapter.

Just as the government grants a new product patent protection, it grants books, films, and pieces of music **copyright** protection. U.S. law grants the creator of a book, film, or piece of music the exclusive right to use the creation during the creator's lifetime. The creator's heirs retain this exclusive right for 70 years after the creator's death. In effect, copyrights create monopolies for the copyrighted items. Without copyrights, individuals and firms would be less likely to invest in creating new books, films, and software.

> **Copyright** A government-granted exclusive right to produce and sell a creation.

**Public Franchises** In some cases, the government grants a firm a **public franchise** that allows it to be the only legal provider of a good or service. For example, state and local governments often designate one company as the sole provider of electricity, natural gas, or water.

> **Public franchise** A government designation that a firm is the only legal provider of a good or service.

Occasionally, a government may decide to provide certain services directly to consumers through a *public enterprise*. This is much more common in Europe than in the United States. For example, the governments in most European countries own the railroad systems. In the United States, many city governments provide water and sewage service themselves rather than rely on private firms.

## Control of a Key Resource

Another way for a firm to become a monopoly is by controlling a key resource. This happens infrequently because most resources, including raw materials such as oil or iron ore, are widely available from a variety of suppliers. There are, however, a few prominent examples of monopolies based on control of a key resource, such as the Aluminum Company of America (Alcoa) and the International Nickel Company of Canada.

For many years until the 1940s, Alcoa either owned or had long-term contracts to buy nearly all of the available bauxite, the mineral needed to produce aluminum. Without access to bauxite, competing firms had to use recycled aluminum, which limited the amount of aluminum they could produce. Similarly, the International Nickel Company of Canada controlled more than 90 percent of available nickel supplies. Competition in the nickel market increased when the Petsamo nickel fields in northern Russia were developed after World War II.

In the United States, a key resource for a professional sports team is a large stadium. The teams that make up the major professional sports leagues—Major League Baseball, the National Football League, and the National Basketball Association—usually have long-term leases with the stadiums in major cities. Control of these stadiums is a major barrier to new professional baseball, football, or basketball leagues forming.

## Making the Connection | Are Diamond Profits Forever? The De Beers Diamond Monopoly

The most famous monopoly based on control of a raw material is the De Beers diamond mining and marketing company of South Africa. Before the 1860s, diamonds were extremely rare. Only a few pounds of diamonds were produced each year, primarily from Brazil and India. Then in 1870, enormous deposits of diamonds were discovered along the Orange River in South Africa. It became possible to produce thousands of pounds of diamonds per year, and the owners of the new mines feared that the price of diamonds would plummet. To

*De Beers promoted the sentimental value of diamonds as a way to maintain its position in the diamond market.*

avoid financial disaster, the mine owners decided in 1888 to merge and form De Beers Consolidated Mines, Ltd.

De Beers became one of the most profitable and longest-lived monopolies in history. The company has carefully controlled the supply of diamonds to keep prices high. As new diamond deposits were discovered in Russia and Zaire, De Beers was able to maintain prices by buying most of the new supplies.

Because diamonds are rarely destroyed, De Beers has always worried about competition from the resale of stones. Heavily promoting diamond engagement and wedding rings with the slogan "A Diamond Is Forever" was a way around this problem. Because engagement and wedding rings have great sentimental value, they are seldom resold, even by the heirs of the original recipients. De Beers advertising has been successful even in some countries, such as Japan, that have had no custom of giving diamond engagement rings. As the populations in De Beers's key markets age, its advertising in recent years has focused on middle-aged men presenting diamond rings to their wives as symbols of financial success and continuing love and on professional women buying "right-hand rings" for themselves.

Over the years, competition has gradually increased in the diamond business. By 2000, De Beers directly controlled only about 40 percent of world diamond production. The company became concerned about the amount it was spending to buy diamonds from other sources to keep them off the market. It decided to abandon its strategy of attempting to control the worldwide supply of diamonds and to concentrate instead on differentiating its diamonds by relying on its name recognition. Each De Beers diamond is now marked with a microscopic brand—a "Forevermark"—to reassure consumers of its high quality. Other firms, such as BHP Billiton, which owns mines in northern Canada, have followed suit by branding their diamonds. Whether consumers will pay attention to brands on diamonds remains to be seen, although through 2009, the branding strategy had helped De Beers maintain its 40 percent share of the diamond market.

Sources: William J. Holstein, "De Beers Reworks Its Image as Rivals Multiply," *New York Times*, December 12, 2008; Edward Jay Epstein, "Have You Ever Tried to Sell a Diamond?" *Atlantic Monthly*, February 1982; and Donna J. Bergenstock, Mary E. Deily, and Larry W. Taylor, "A Cartel's Response to Cheating: An Empirical Investigation of the De Beers Diamond Empire," *Southern Economic Journal*, Vol. 73, No. 1, July 2006, pp. 173–189.

**YOUR TURN:** Test your understanding by doing related problem 2.10 on page 487 at the end of this chapter.

## Network Externalities

**Network externalities** A situation in which the usefulness of a product increases with the number of consumers who use it.

There are **network externalities** in the consumption of a product if the usefulness of the product increases with the number of people who use it. If you owned the only cell phone in the world, for example, it would not be very valuable. The more cell phones there are in use, the more valuable they become to consumers.

Some economists argue that network externalities can serve as barriers to entry. For example, in the early 1980s, Microsoft gained an advantage over other software companies by developing MS-DOS, the operating system for the first IBM personal computers. Because IBM sold more computers than any other company, software developers wrote many application programs for MS-DOS. The more people who used MS-DOS–based programs, the greater the usefulness to a consumer of using an MS-DOS–based program. By the 1990s, Microsoft had replaced MS-DOS with Windows. Today, Windows has a 90 percent share in the market for personal computer operating systems, with Apple's Mac operating system having a 9 percent share, and the open-source Linux system having less than 1 percent. If another firm introduced a new operating system, some economists argue that relatively few people would use it initially, and few applications would run on it, which would limit the operating system's value to other consumers.

eBay was the first Internet site to attract a significant number of people to its online auctions. Once a large number of people began to use eBay to buy and sell collectibles, antiques, and many other products, it became a more valuable place to buy and sell. Yahoo.com, Amazon.com, and other Internet sites eventually started online auctions, but they had difficulty attracting buyers and sellers. On eBay, a buyer expects to find more sellers, and a seller expects to find more potential buyers than on Amazon or other auction sites.

As these examples show, network externalities can set off a *virtuous cycle*: If a firm can attract enough customers initially, it can attract additional customers because its product's value has been increased by more people using it, which attracts even more customers, and so on. With products such as computer operating systems and online auctions, it might be difficult for new firms to enter the market and compete away the profits being earned by the first firm in the market.

Economists engage in considerable debate, however, about the extent to which network externalities are important barriers to entry in the business world. Some economists argue that Microsoft and eBay have dominant positions primarily because they are efficient in offering products that satisfy consumer preferences rather than because of the effects of network externalities. In this view, the advantages existing firms gain from network externalities would not be enough to protect them from competing firms offering better products. In other words, a firm entering the operating system market with a program better than Windows or a firm offering an Internet auction site better than eBay would be successful despite the effects of network externalities. (We discussed this point in more detail in Chapter 9.) In fact, the market shares of both Windows and eBay were declining during the late 2000s.

## Natural Monopoly

We saw in Chapter 10 that economies of scale exist when a firm's long-run average costs fall as it increases the quantity of output it produces. A **natural monopoly** occurs when economies of scale are so large that one firm can supply the entire market at a lower average total cost than two or more firms. In that case, there is really "room" in the market for only one firm.

Figure 14-1 shows the average total cost curve for a firm producing electricity and the total demand for electricity in the firm's market. Notice that the average total cost curve is still falling when it crosses the demand curve at point *A*. If the firm is a monopoly and produces 30 billion kilowatt-hours of electricity per year, its average total cost of production will be $0.04 per kilowatt-hour. Suppose instead that two firms are in the market, each producing half of the market output, or 15 billion kilowatt-hours per year. Assume that each firm has the same average total cost curve. The figure shows that producing 15 billion kilowatt-hours would move each firm back up its average cost curve so that the average cost of producing electricity would rise to $0.06 per kilowatt-hour (point *B*). In this case, if one of the firms expands production, it will move down the average total cost curve. With lower average costs, it will be able to offer electricity at a lower price than the other firm can offer. Eventually, the other firm

**Natural monopoly** A situation in which economies of scale are so large that one firm can supply the entire market at a lower average total cost than can two or more firms.

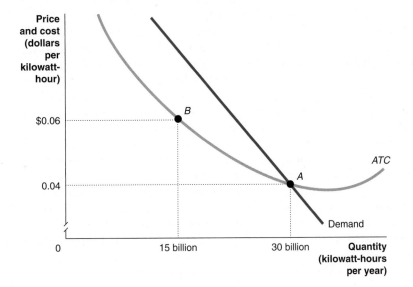

## Figure 14-1

### Average Total Cost Curve for a Natural Monopoly

With a natural monopoly, the average total cost curve is still falling when it crosses the demand curve (point *A*). If only one firm is producing electric power in the market, and it produces where average cost intersects the demand curve, average total cost will equal $0.04 per kilowatt-hour of electricity produced. If the market is divided between two firms, each producing 15 billion kilowatt-hours, the average cost of producing electricity rises to $0.06 per kilowatt-hour (point *B*). In this case, if one firm expands production, it can move down the average total cost curve, lower its price, and drive the other firm out of business.

will be driven out of business, and the remaining firm will have a monopoly. Because a monopoly would develop automatically—or *naturally*—in this market, it is a natural monopoly.

Natural monopolies are most likely to occur in markets where fixed costs are very large relative to variable costs. For example, a firm that produces electricity must make a substantial investment in machinery and equipment necessary to generate the electricity and in the wires and cables necessary to distribute it. Once the initial investment has been made, however, the marginal cost of producing another kilowatt-hour of electricity is relatively small.

**14.3 LEARNING** OBJECTIVE

Explain how a monopoly chooses price and output.

# How Does a Monopoly Choose Price and Output?

Like every other firm, a monopoly maximizes profit by producing where marginal revenue equals marginal cost. A monopoly differs from other firms in that *a monopoly's demand curve is the same as the demand curve for the product*. We emphasized in Chapter 11 that the market demand curve for wheat was very different from the demand curve for the wheat produced by any one farmer. If, however, one farmer had a monopoly on wheat production, the two demand curves would be exactly the same.

## Marginal Revenue Once Again

Recall from Chapter 11 that firms in perfectly competitive markets—such as a farmer in the wheat market—face horizontal demand curves. They are *price takers*. All other firms, including monopolies, are *price makers*. If price makers raise their prices, they will lose some, but not all, of their customers. Therefore, they face a downward-sloping demand curve and a downward-sloping marginal revenue curve as well. Let's review why a firm's marginal revenue curve slopes downward if its demand curve slopes downward.

Remember that when a firm cuts the price of a product, one good thing happens, and one bad thing happens:

- *The good thing.* It sells more units of the product.

- *The bad thing.* It receives less revenue from each unit than it would have received at the higher price.

For example, consider the table in Figure 14-2, which shows the demand curve for Time Warner Cable's basic cable package. For simplicity, we assume that the market has only 10 potential subscribers instead of the millions it actually has. If Time Warner charges a price of $60 per month, it won't have any subscribers. If it charges a price of $57, it sells 1 subscription. At $54, it sells 2 subscriptions, and so on. Time Warner's total revenue is equal to the number of subscriptions sold per month multiplied by the price. The firm's average revenue—or revenue per subscription sold—is equal to its total revenue divided by the quantity of subscriptions sold. Time Warner is particularly interested in marginal revenue because marginal revenue tells the firm how much its revenue will increase if it cuts the price to sell one more subscription.

Notice that Time Warner's marginal revenue is less than the price for every subscription sold after the first subscription. To see why, think about what happens if Time Warner cuts the price of its basic cable package from $42 to $39, which increases its subscriptions sold from 6 to 7. Time Warner increases its revenue by the $39 it receives for the seventh subscription. But it also loses revenue of $3 per subscription on the first 6 subscriptions because it could have sold them at the old price of $42. So, its marginal revenue on the seventh subscription is $39 − $18 = $21, which is the value shown in the table. The graph in Figure 14-2 plots Time Warner's demand and marginal revenue curves, based on the information given in the table.

| Subscribers per Month (Q) | Price (P) | Total Revenue (TR = P x Q) | Average Revenue (AR = TR/Q) | Marginal Revenue (MR = ΔTR/ΔQ) |
|---|---|---|---|---|
| 0 | $60 | $0 | – | – |
| 1 | 57 | 57 | $57 | $57 |
| 2 | 54 | 108 | 54 | 51 |
| 3 | 51 | 153 | 51 | 45 |
| 4 | 48 | 192 | 48 | 39 |
| 5 | 45 | 225 | 45 | 33 |
| 6 | 42 | 252 | 42 | 27 |
| 7 | 39 | 273 | 39 | 21 |
| 8 | 36 | 288 | 36 | 15 |
| 9 | 33 | 297 | 33 | 9 |
| 10 | 30 | 300 | 30 | 3 |

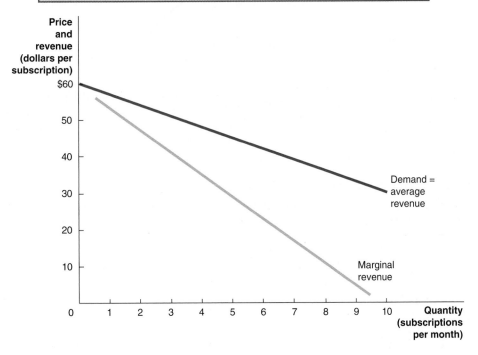

## Figure 14-2

### Calculating a Monopoly's Revenue

Time Warner Cable faces a downward-sloping demand curve for subscriptions to basic cable. To sell more subscriptions, it must cut the price. When this happens, it gains revenue from selling more subscriptions but loses revenue from selling at a lower price the subscriptions that it could have sold at a higher price. The firm's marginal revenue is the change in revenue from selling another subscription. We can calculate marginal revenue by subtracting the revenue lost as a result of a price cut from the revenue gained. The table shows that Time Warner's marginal revenue is less than the price for every subscription sold after the first subscription. Therefore, Time Warner's marginal revenue curve will be below its demand curve.

## Profit Maximization for a Monopolist

Figure 14-3 shows how Time Warner combines the information on demand and marginal revenue with information on average and marginal costs to decide how many subscriptions to sell and what price to charge. We assume that the firm's marginal cost and average total cost curves have the usual U shapes we encountered in Chapters 10 and 11. In panel (a), we see how Time Warner can calculate its profit-maximizing quantity and price. As long as the marginal cost of selling one more subscription is less than the marginal revenue, the firm should sell additional subscriptions because it is adding to its profits. As Time Warner sells more cable subscriptions, rising marginal cost will eventually equal marginal revenue, and the firm will be selling the profit-maximizing quantity of subscriptions. This happens with the sixth subscription, which adds $27 to the firm's costs and $27 to its revenues (point A in panel (a) of Figure 14-3). The demand curve tells us that Time Warner can sell 6 subscriptions for a price of $42 per month. We can conclude that Time Warner's profit-maximizing quantity of subscriptions is 6, and its profit-maximizing price is $42.

Panel (b) shows that the average total cost of 6 subscriptions is $30 and that Time Warner can sell 6 subscriptions at a price of $42 per month (point B on the demand curve). Time Warner is making a profit of $12 per subscription—the price of $42 minus the average cost of $30. Its total profit is $72 (6 subscriptions × $12 profit per subscription), which is shown by the area of the green-shaded rectangle in the figure. We could also have calculated Time Warner's total profit as the difference between its total revenue and its total cost. Its total revenue from selling 6 subscriptions is $252. Its total cost equals its average cost multiplied by the number of subscriptions sold, or $30 × 6 = $180. So, its profit is $252 − $180 = $72.

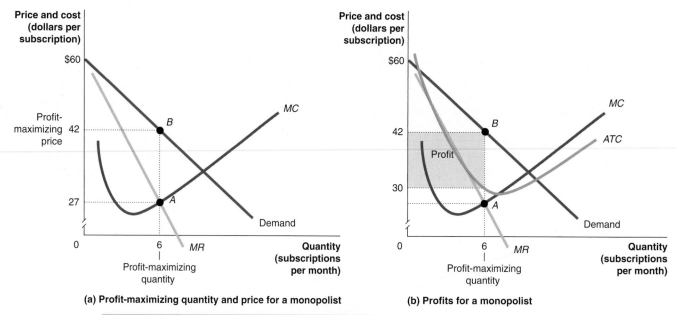

**(a) Profit-maximizing quantity and price for a monopolist**

**(b) Profits for a monopolist**

**Figure 14-3**    **Profit-Maximizing Price and Output for a Monopoly**

Panel (a) shows that to maximize profit, Time Warner should sell subscriptions up to the point where the marginal revenue from selling the last subscription equals its marginal cost (point *A*). In this case, the marginal revenue from selling the sixth subscription and the marginal cost are both $27. Time Warner maximizes profit by sell-ing 6 subscriptions per month and charging a price of $42 (point *B*). In panel (b), the green box represents Time Warner's profits. The box has a height equal to $12, which is the price of $42 minus the average total cost of $30, and a base equal to the quantity of 6 cable subscriptions. Time Warner's profit therefore equals $12 × 6 = $72.

It's important to note that even though Time Warner is earning economic profits, new firms will *not* enter the market. Because Time Warner has a monopoly, it will not face com-petition from other cable operators. Therefore, if other factors remain unchanged, Time Warner will be able to continue to earn economic profits, even in the long run.

# Solved Problem | 14-3

## Finding the Profit-Maximizing Price and Output for a Monopolist

Suppose that Comcast has a cable monopoly in Philadelphia. The following table gives Comcast's demand and costs per month for subscriptions to basic cable (for simplicity, we once again keep the number of subscribers artificially small).

| PRICE | QUANTITY | TOTAL REVENUE | MARGINAL REVENUE ($MR = \Delta TR/\Delta Q$) | TOTAL COST | MARGINAL COST ($MC = \Delta TC/\Delta Q$) |
|-------|----------|---------------|------------------|------------|----------------|
| $17 | 3 | | | $56 | |
| 16 | 4 | | | 63 | |
| 15 | 5 | | | 71 | |
| 14 | 6 | | | 80 | |
| 13 | 7 | | | 90 | |
| 12 | 8 | | | 101 | |

**a.** Fill in the missing values in the table.

**b.** If Comcast wants to maximize profits, what price should it charge and how many cable subscriptions per month should it sell? How much profit will Comcast make? Briefly explain.

**c.** Suppose the local government imposes a $2.50 per month tax on cable companies. Now what price should Comcast charge, how many subscriptions should it sell, and what will its profits be?

## SOLVING THE PROBLEM:

**Step 1: Review the chapter material.** This problem is about finding the profit-maximizing quantity and price for a monopolist, so you may want to review the section "Profit Maximization for a Monopolist," which begins on page 469.

**Step 2: Answer part (a) by filling in the missing values in the table.** Remember that to calculate marginal revenue and marginal cost, you must divide the change in total revenue or total cost by the change in quantity.

| PRICE | QUANTITY | TOTAL REVENUE | MARGINAL REVENUE $(MR = \Delta TR/\Delta Q)$ | TOTAL COST | MARGINAL COST $(MC = \Delta TC/\Delta Q)$ |
|-------|----------|---------------|----------------------------------------------|------------|--------------------------------------------|
| $17 | 3 | $51 | — | $56 | — |
| 16 | 4 | 64 | $13 | 63 | $7 |
| 15 | 5 | 75 | 11 | 71 | 8 |
| 14 | 6 | 84 | 9 | 80 | 9 |
| 13 | 7 | 91 | 7 | 90 | 10 |
| 12 | 8 | 96 | 5 | 101 | 11 |

We don't have enough information from the table to fill in the values for marginal revenue and marginal cost in the first row.

**Step 3: Answer part (b) by determining the profit-maximizing quantity and price.** We know that Comcast will maximize profits by selling subscriptions up to the point where marginal cost equals marginal revenue. In this case, that means selling 6 subscriptions per month. From the information in the first two columns, we know Comcast can sell 6 subscriptions at a price of $14 each. Comcast's profits are equal to the difference between its total revenue and its total cost: Profit = $84 − $80 = $4 per month.

**Step 4: Answer part (c) by analyzing the impact of the tax.** This tax is a fixed cost to Comcast because it is a flat $2.50, no matter how many subscriptions it sells. Because the tax has no impact on Comcast's marginal revenue or marginal cost, the profit-maximizing level of output has not changed. So, Comcast will still sell 6 subscriptions per month at a price of $14, but its profits will fall by the amount of the tax, from $4.00 per month to $1.50.

**YOUR TURN:** For more practice, do related problems 3.3 and 3.4 on pages 487–488 at the end of this chapter.

# Does Monopoly Reduce Economic Efficiency?

**14.4 LEARNING** OBJECTIVE

Use a graph to illustrate how a monopoly affects economic efficiency.

We saw in Chapter 11 that a perfectly competitive market is economically efficient. How would economic efficiency be affected if instead of being perfectly competitive, a market were a monopoly? In Chapter 4, we developed the idea of *economic surplus*. Economic surplus provides a way of characterizing the economic efficiency of a perfectly competitive market: *Equilibrium in a perfectly competitive market results in the greatest amount of economic surplus, or total benefit to society, from the production of a good or service.* What happens to economic surplus under a monopoly? We can begin

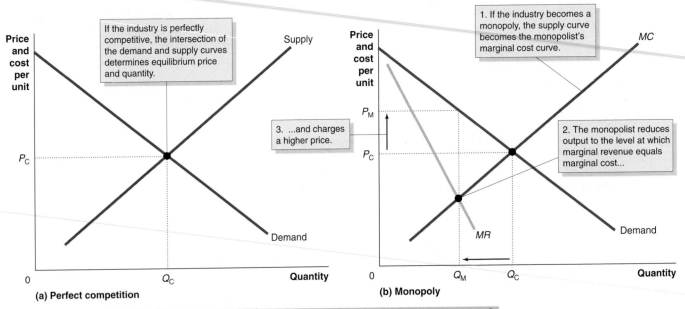

**Figure 14-4**    **What Happens If a Perfectly Competitive Industry Becomes a Monopoly?**

In panel (a), the market for television sets is perfectly competitive, and price and quantity are determined by the intersection of the demand and supply curves. In panel (b), the perfectly competitive television industry became a monopoly. As a result, the equilibrium quantity falls, and the equilibrium price rises.

1. The industry supply curve becomes the monopolist's marginal cost curve.
2. The monopolist reduces output to where marginal revenue equals marginal cost, $Q_M$.
3. The monopolist raises the price from $P_C$ to $P_M$.

the analysis by considering the hypothetical case of what would happen if the market for television sets begins as perfectly competitive and then becomes a monopoly. (In reality, the market for television sets is not perfectly competitive, but assuming that it is simplifies our analysis.)

## Comparing Monopoly and Perfect Competition

Panel (a) in Figure 14-4 illustrates the situation if the market for televisions is perfectly competitive. Price and quantity are determined by the intersection of the demand and supply curves. Remember that none of the individual firms in a perfectly

---

# Don't Let This Happen to **YOU!**

## Don't Assume That Charging a Higher Price Is Always More Profitable for a Monopolist

In answering question (c) of Solved Problem 14-3, it's tempting to argue that Comcast should increase its price to make up for the tax. After all, Comcast is a monopolist, so why can't it just pass along the tax to its customers? The reason it can't is that Comcast, like any other monopolist, must pay attention to demand. Comcast is not interested in charging high prices for the sake of charging high prices; it is interested in maximizing profits. Charging a price of $1,000 for a basic cable subscription sounds nice, but if no one will buy at that price, Comcast would hardly be maximizing profits.

To look at it another way, before the tax is imposed, Comcast has already determined that $14 is the price that will maximize its profits. After the tax is imposed, it must determine whether $14 is still the profit-maximizing price. Because the tax has not affected Comcast's marginal revenue or marginal cost (or had any effect on consumer demand), $14 is still the profit-maximizing price, and Comcast should continue to charge it. The tax reduces Comcast's profits but doesn't cause it to increase the price of cable subscriptions.

**YOUR TURN:** Test your understanding by doing related problem 3.7 on page 488 at the end of this chapter.

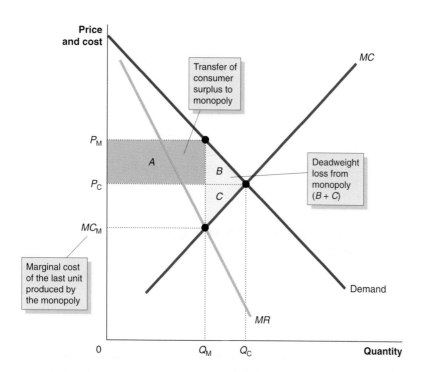

**Price and cost**

MC

Transfer of consumer surplus to monopoly

$P_M$

A

B

Deadweight loss from monopoly (B + C)

$P_C$

C

$MC_M$

Marginal cost of the last unit produced by the monopoly

Demand

MR

0   $Q_M$   $Q_C$   **Quantity**

### Figure 14-5

**The Inefficiency of Monopoly**

A monopoly charges a higher price, $P_M$, and produces a smaller quantity, $Q_M$, than a perfectly competitive industry, which charges price $P_C$ and produces $Q_C$. The higher price reduces consumer surplus by the area equal to the rectangle $A$ and the triangle $B$. Some of the reduction in consumer surplus is captured by the monopoly as producer surplus, and some becomes deadweight loss, which is the area equal to triangles $B$ and $C$.

competitive industry has any control over price. Each firm must accept the price determined by the market. Panel (b) shows what happens if the television industry becomes a monopoly. We know that the monopoly will maximize profits by producing where marginal revenue equals marginal cost. To do this, the monopoly reduces the quantity of televisions that would have been produced if the industry were perfectly competitive and increases the price. Panel (b) illustrates an important conclusion: *A monopoly will produce less and charge a higher price than would a perfectly competitive industry producing the same good.*

## Measuring the Efficiency Losses from Monopoly

Figure 14-5 uses panel (b) from Figure 14-4 to illustrate how monopoly affects consumers, producers, and the efficiency of the economy. Recall from Chapter 4 that *consumer surplus* measures the net benefit received by consumers from purchasing a good or service. We measure consumer surplus as the area below the demand curve and above the market price. The higher the price, the smaller the consumer surplus. Because a monopoly raises the market price, it reduces consumer surplus. In Figure 14-5, the loss of consumer surplus is equal to rectangle *A* plus triangle *B*. Remember that *producer surplus* measures the net benefit to producers from selling a good or service. We measure producer surplus as the area above the supply curve and below the market price. The increase in price due to monopoly increases producer surplus by an amount equal to rectangle *A* and reduces it by an amount equal to triangle *C*. Because rectangle *A* is larger than triangle *C*, we know that a monopoly increases producer surplus compared with perfect competition.

Economic surplus is equal to the sum of consumer surplus plus producer surplus. By increasing price and reducing the quantity produced, the monopolist has reduced economic surplus by an amount equal to the areas of triangles *B* and *C*. This reduction in economic surplus is called *deadweight loss* and represents the loss of economic efficiency due to monopoly.

The best way to understand how a monopoly causes a loss of economic efficiency is to recall that price is equal to marginal cost in a perfectly competitive market. As a result, a consumer in a perfectly competitive market is always able to buy a good if she is willing to pay a price equal to the marginal cost of producing it. As Figure 14-5 shows, the monopolist stops producing at a point where the price is well above marginal cost. Consumers are unable to buy some units of the good for which they would be willing to pay a price greater than the marginal cost of producing them. Why doesn't the monopolist produce this additional output? Because the monopolist's profits are greater if it restricts output and forces up the price. A monopoly produces the profit-maximizing level of output but fails to produce the efficient level of output from the point of view of society.

We can summarize the effects of monopoly as follows:

1. Monopoly causes a reduction in consumer surplus.
2. Monopoly causes an increase in producer surplus.
3. Monopoly causes a deadweight loss, which represents a reduction in economic efficiency.

## How Large Are the Efficiency Losses Due to Monopoly?

**Market power** The ability of a firm to charge a price greater than marginal cost.

We know that there are relatively few monopolies, so the loss of economic efficiency due to monopoly must be small. Many firms, though, have **market power**, which is the ability of a firm to charge a price greater than marginal cost. The analysis we just completed shows that some loss of economic efficiency will occur whenever a firm has market power and can charge a price greater than marginal cost, even if the firm is not a monopoly. The only firms that do *not* have market power are firms in perfectly competitive markets, which must charge a price equal to marginal cost. Because few markets are perfectly competitive, *some loss of economic efficiency occurs in the market for nearly every good or service.*

Is the total loss of economic efficiency due to market power large or small? It is possible to put a dollar value on the loss of economic efficiency by estimating for every industry the size of the deadweight loss triangle, as in Figure 14-5. The first economist to do this was Arnold Harberger of the University of Chicago. His estimates—largely confirmed by later researchers—indicated that the total loss of economic efficiency in the U.S. economy due to market power is small. According to his estimates, if every industry in the economy were perfectly competitive, so that price were equal to marginal cost in every market, the gain in economic efficiency would equal less than 1 percent of the value of total production in the United States, or about $450 per person.

The loss of economic efficiency is this small primarily because true monopolies are very rare. In most industries, competition keeps price much closer to marginal cost than would be the case in a monopoly. The closer price is to marginal cost, the smaller the size of the deadweight loss.

## Market Power and Technological Change

Some economists have raised the possibility that the economy may actually benefit from firms having market power. This argument is most closely identified with Joseph Schumpeter, an Austrian economist who spent many years as a professor of economics at Harvard. Schumpeter argued that economic progress depends on technological change in the form of new products. For example, the replacement of horse-drawn carriages by automobiles, the replacement of ice boxes by refrigerators, and the replacement of mechanical calculators by electronic computers all represent technological changes that significantly raised living standards. In Schumpeter's view, new products unleash a "gale of creative destruction" that drives older products—and, often, the firms that produced them—out of the market. Schumpeter was not concerned that firms with market power would charge higher prices than perfectly competitive firms:

> It is not that kind of [price] competition which counts but the competition from the new commodity, the new technology, the new source of supply, the new type of organization . . . competition which commands a decisive cost or quality advantage and which strikes not at the margins of the profits and outputs of the existing firms but at their foundations and their very lives.

Economists who support Schumpeter's view argue that the introduction of new products requires firms to spend funds on research and development. It is possible for firms to raise this money by borrowing from investors or from banks. But investors and banks are usually skeptical of ideas for new products that have not yet passed the test of consumer acceptance in the market. As a result, firms are often forced to rely on their profits to finance the research and development needed for new products. Because firms with market power are more likely to earn economic profits than are perfectly competitive firms, they are also more likely to carry out research and development and introduce new products. In this view, the higher prices firms with market power charge are unimportant compared with the benefits from the new products these firms introduce to the market.

Some economists disagree with Schumpeter's views. These economists point to the number of new products developed by smaller firms, including, for example, Steve Jobs and Steve Wozniak inventing the first Apple computer in Wozniak's garage, and Larry Page and Sergey Brin inventing the Google search engine as graduate students at Stanford. As we will see in the next section, government policymakers continue to struggle with the issue of whether, on balance, large firms with market power are good or bad for the economy.

# Solved Problem | 14-4

## Computing the Difference in Economic Surplus between Perfect Competition and Monopoly

The graph shown here illustrates a monopoly market where the firm maximizes profit by setting a price of $25 at the quantity where marginal revenue (*MR*) equals marginal cost (*MC*). The profit-maximizing quantity is 10,000. If this market were perfectly competitive, the price would equal marginal cost; therefore, the equilibrium price and quantity would be $20 and 14,000, respectively.

a. Compute the difference in consumer surplus between the equilibrium under monopoly and perfect competition.

b. Compute the difference in producer surplus between the equilibrium under monopoly and perfect competition.

c. Compute the difference in economic surplus under monopoly and perfect competition.

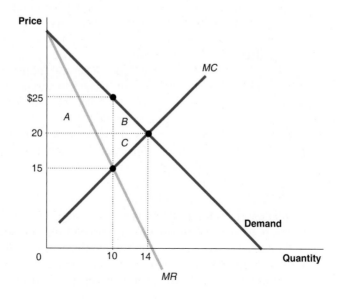

## SOLVING THE PROBLEM:

**Step 1:** **Review the chapter material.** This problem is about monopoly and efficiency, so you may want to review the section "Does Monopoly Reduce Economic Efficiency?" which begins on page 471.

**Step 2:** **Answer question (a).** Monopoly results in a loss of consumer surplus equal to the sum of areas *A* and *B* in the graph. Area *A* equals $50,000 [($25 – $20) × 10,000]. Area B equals $10,000 [1/2 × ($25 – $20) × (14,000 – 10,000)]. Therefore, there is a loss of consumer surplus equal to $60,000 from monopoly as compared to the perfectly competitive equilibrium.

**Step 3:** **Answer question (b).** Area *A* minus area *C* is the gain in producer surplus that results from the monopoly price of $25 rather than the perfectly competitive price $20. Area *A* equals $50,000. Area *C* equals $10,000 [1/2 × ($20 – $15) × (14,000 – 10,000)]. Area *A* minus area *C* equals $40,000.

**Step 4:** **Answer question (c).** Economic surplus is the total of consumer and producer surplus. Because area *A* is a transfer of surplus from consumers to producers, there is a net loss of economic surplus (a deadweight loss) equal to area *B* ($10,000) plus area *C* ($10,000), or $20,000.

**YOUR TURN:** For more practice, do related problem 4.7 on page 489 at the end of this chapter.

---

**Collusion** An agreement among firms to charge the same price or otherwise not to compete.

# Government Policy Toward Monopoly

Because monopolies reduce consumer surplus and economic efficiency, most governments have policies that regulate their behavior. Recall from Chapter 13 that **collusion** refers to an agreement among firms to charge the same price or otherwise not to compete. In the United States, *antitrust laws* are designed to prevent monopolies and collusion. Governments also regulate firms that are natural monopolies, often by controlling the prices they charge.

## Antitrust Laws and Antitrust Enforcement

The first important law regulating monopolies in the United States was the Sherman Act, which Congress passed in 1890 to promote competition and prevent the formation of monopolies. Section 1 of the Sherman Act outlaws "every contract, combination in the form of trust or otherwise, or conspiracy in restraint of trade." Section 2 states that "every person who shall monopolize, or attempt to monopolize, or combine or conspire with any other person or persons, to monopolize any part of the trade or commerce . . . shall be deemed guilty of a felony."

The Sherman Act targeted firms in several industries that had combined together during the 1870s and 1880s to form "trusts." In a trust, the firms were operated independently but gave voting control to a board of trustees. The board enforced collusive agreements for the firms to charge the same price and not to compete for each other's customers. The most notorious of the trusts was the Standard Oil Trust, organized by John D. Rockefeller. After the Sherman Act was passed, trusts disappeared, but the term **antitrust laws** has lived on to refer to the laws aimed at eliminating collusion and promoting competition among firms.

**Antitrust laws** Laws aimed at eliminating collusion and promoting competition among firms.

The Sherman Act prohibited trusts and collusive agreements, but it left several loopholes. For example, it was not clear whether it would be legal for two or more firms to merge to form a new, larger firm that would have substantial market power. A series of Supreme Court decisions interpreted the Sherman Act narrowly, and the result was a wave of mergers at the turn of the twentieth century. Included in these mergers was U.S. Steel Corporation, which was formed from dozens of smaller companies. U.S. Steel,

| LAW | DATE | PURPOSE |
|---|---|---|
| Sherman Act | 1890 | Prohibited "restraint of trade," including price fixing and collusion. Also outlawed monopolization. |
| Clayton Act | 1914 | Prohibited firms from buying stock in competitors and from having directors serve on the boards of competing firms. |
| Federal Trade Commission Act | 1914 | Established the Federal Trade Commission (FTC) to help administer antitrust laws. |
| Robinson–Patman Act | 1936 | Prohibited charging buyers different prices if the result would reduce competition. |
| Cellar–Kefauver Act | 1950 | Toughened restrictions on mergers by prohibiting any mergers that would reduce competition. |

TABLE 14-1

**Important U.S. Antitrust Laws**

organized by J. P. Morgan, was the first billion-dollar corporation, and it controlled two-thirds of steel production in the United States. The Sherman Act also left unclear whether any business practices short of outright collusion were illegal.

To address the loopholes in the Sherman Act, in 1914, Congress passed the Clayton Act and the Federal Trade Commission Act. Under the Clayton Act, a merger was illegal if its effect was "substantially to lessen competition, or to tend to create a monopoly." The Federal Trade Commission Act set up the Federal Trade Commission (FTC), which was given the power to police unfair business practices. The FTC has brought lawsuits against firms employing a variety of business practices, including deceptive advertising. In setting up the FTC, Congress divided the authority to police mergers. Currently, both the Antitrust Division of the U.S. Department of Justice and the FTC are responsible for merger policy. Table 14-1 lists the most important U.S. antitrust laws and the purpose of each.

## Mergers: The Trade-off between Market Power and Efficiency

The federal government regulates business mergers because it knows that if firms gain market power by merging, they may use that market power to raise prices and reduce output. As a result, the government is most concerned with **horizontal mergers**, or mergers between firms in the same industry. Horizontal mergers are more likely to increase market power than **vertical mergers**, which are mergers between firms at different stages of the production of a good. An example of a vertical merger would be a merger between a company making personal computers and a company making computer hard drives.

Two factors can complicate regulating horizontal mergers. First, the "market" that firms are in is not always clear. For example, if Hershey Foods wants to merge with Mars, Inc., maker of M&Ms, Snickers, and other candies, what is the relevant market? If the government looks just at the candy market, the newly merged company would have more than 70 percent of the market, a level at which the government would likely oppose the merger. What if the government looks at the broader market for "snacks"? In this market, Hershey and Mars compete with makers of potato chips, pretzels, and peanuts—and perhaps even producers of fresh fruit. Of course, if the government looked at the very broad market for "food," then both Hershey and Mars have very small market shares, and there would be no reason to oppose their merger. In practice, the government defines the relevant market on the basis of whether there are close substitutes for the products being made by the merging firms. In this case, potato chips and the other snack foods mentioned are not close substitutes for candy.

**Horizontal merger** A merger between firms in the same industry.

**Vertical merger** A merger between firms at different stages of production of a good.

So, the government would consider the candy market to be the relevant market and would oppose the merger on the grounds that the new firm would have too much market power.

The second factor that complicates merger policy is the possibility that the newly merged firm might be more efficient than the merging firms were individually. For example, one firm might have an excellent product but a poor distribution system for getting the product into the hands of consumers. A competing firm might have built a great distribution system but have an inferior product. Allowing these firms to merge might be good for both the firms and consumers. Or, two competing firms might each have an extensive system of warehouses that are only half full, but if the firms merged, they could consolidate their warehouses and significantly reduce their average costs.

Most of the mergers that come under scrutiny by the Department of Justice and the FTC are between large firms. For simplicity, though, let's consider a case in which all the firms in a perfectly competitive industry want to merge to form a monopoly. As we saw in Figure 14-5, as a result of this merger, prices will rise and output will fall, leading to a decline in consumer surplus and economic efficiency. But what if the larger, newly merged firm actually is more efficient than the smaller firms were? Figure 14-6 shows a possible result.

If costs aren't affected by the merger, we get the same result as in Figure 14-5: Price rises from $P_C$ to $P_M$, quantity falls from $Q_C$ to $Q_M$, consumer surplus is lower, and a loss of economic efficiency results. If the monopoly has lower costs than the competitive firms, it is possible for price to decline and quantity to increase. In Figure 14-6, note where $MR$ crosses $MC$ after the merger—this is the new profit-maximizing quantity, $Q_{Merge}$. The demand curve shows that the monopolist can sell this quantity at a price of $P_{Merge}$. Therefore, the price declines after the merger from $P_C$ to $P_{Merge}$, and quantity increases from $Q_C$ to $Q_{Merge}$. We have the following seemingly paradoxical result: *Although the newly merged firm has a great deal of market power, because it is more efficient, consumers are better off and economic efficiency is improved.* Of course, sometimes a merged firm will be more efficient and have lower costs, and other times it won't.

## Figure 14-6

### A Merger That Makes Consumers Better Off

This figure shows the result of all the firms in a perfectly competitive industry merging to form a monopoly. If costs are unaffected by the merger, the result is the same as in Figure 14-5 on page 473: Price rises from $P_C$ to $P_M$, quantity falls from $Q_C$ to $Q_M$, consumer surplus declines, and a loss of economic efficiency results. If, however, the monopoly has lower costs than the perfectly competitive firms, as shown by the marginal cost curve shifting to $MC$ after the merger, it is possible that the price will actually decline from $P_C$ to $P_{Merge}$ and that output will increase from $Q_C$ to $Q_{Merge}$ following the merger.

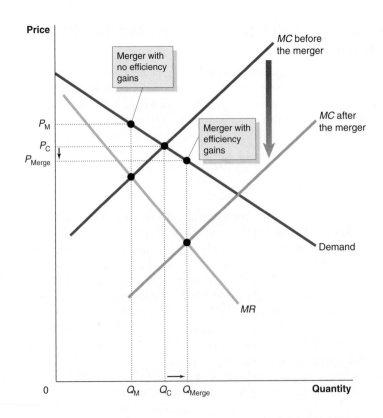

Even if a merged firm is more efficient and has lower costs, that may not offset the increased market power of the firm enough to increase consumer surplus and economic efficiency.

As you might expect, whenever large firms propose a merger, they claim that the newly merged firm will be more efficient and have lower costs. They realize that without these claims, the Department of Justice and the FTC, along with the court system, are unlikely to approve the merger.

## The Department of Justice and FTC Merger Guidelines

For many years after the passage of the Sherman Act in 1890, lawyers from the Department of Justice enforced the antitrust laws. The lawyers rarely considered economic arguments, such as the possibility that consumers might be made better off by a merger if economic efficiency were significantly improved. This began to change in 1965, when Donald Turner became the first Ph.D. economist to head the Antitrust Division of the Department of Justice. Under Turner and his successors, economic analysis shaped antitrust policy. In 1973, the Economics Section of the Antitrust Division was established and staffed with economists who evaluate the economic consequences of proposed mergers.

Economists played a major role in the development of merger guidelines by the Department of Justice and the FTC in 1982. The guidelines made it easier for firms considering a merger to understand whether the government was likely to allow the merger or to oppose it. The guidelines have three main parts:

1. Market definition
2. Measure of concentration
3. Merger standards

**Market Definition** A market consists of all firms making products that consumers view as close substitutes. We can identify close substitutes by looking at the effect of a price increase. If our definition of a market is too narrow, a price increase will cause firms to experience a significant decline in sales—and profits—as consumers switch to buying close substitutes.

Identifying the relevant market involved in a proposed merger begins with a narrow definition of the industry. For the hypothetical merger of Hershey Foods and Mars, Inc., discussed previously in this chapter, we might start with the candy industry. If all firms in the candy industry increased price by 5 percent, would their profits increase or decrease? If profits would increase, the market is defined as being just these firms. If profits would decrease, we would try a broader definition—say, by adding in potato chips and other snacks. Would a price increase of 5 percent by all firms in the broader market raise profits? If profits increase, the relevant market has been identified. If profits decrease, we consider a broader definition. We continue this process until a market has been identified.

**Measure of Concentration** A market is *concentrated* if a relatively small number of firms have a large share of total sales in the market. A merger between firms in a market that is already highly concentrated is very likely to increase market power. A merger between firms in an industry that has a very low concentration is unlikely to increase market power and can be ignored. The guidelines use the *Herfindahl-Hirschman Index (HHI)* of concentration, which squares the market shares of each firm in the industry and adds up the values of the squares. The following are some examples of calculating HHI:

- 1 firm, with 100 percent market share (a monopoly):

$$\text{HHI} = 100^2 = 10,000$$

- 2 firms, each with a 50 percent market share:

$$HHI = 50^2 + 50^2 = 5,000$$

- 4 firms, with market shares of 30 percent, 30 percent, 20 percent, and 20 percent:

$$HHI = 30^2 + 30^2 + 20^2 + 20^2 = 2,600$$

- 10 firms, each with market shares of 10 percent:

$$HHI = 10 \times (10^2) = 1,000$$

**Merger Standards** The Department of Justice and the FTC use the HHI calculation for a market to evaluate proposed horizontal mergers according to these standards:

- *Post-merger HHI below 1,000.* These markets are not concentrated, so mergers in them are not challenged.

- *Post-merger HHI between 1,000 and 1,800.* These markets are moderately concentrated. Mergers that raise the HHI by less than 100 probably will not be challenged. Mergers that raise the HHI by more than 100 may be challenged.

- *Post-merger HHI above 1,800.* These markets are highly concentrated. Mergers that increase the HHI by less than 50 points will not be challenged. Mergers that increase the HHI by 50 to 100 points may be challenged. Mergers that increase the HHI by more than 100 points will be challenged.

Increases in economic efficiency will be taken into account and can lead to approval of a merger that otherwise would be opposed, but the burden of showing that the efficiencies exist lies with the merging firms:

> The merging firms must substantiate efficiency claims so that the [Department of Justice and the FTC] can verify by reasonable means the likelihood and magnitude of each asserted efficiency. . . . Efficiency claims will not be considered if they are vague or speculative or otherwise cannot be verified by reasonable means.

**Making the Connection** | **Have Google and Microsoft Violated the Antitrust Laws?**

For as long as the antitrust laws have existed, there has been debate among economists and policymakers about how they should be enforced. Some economists and policymakers have been skeptical about the need for vigorous enforcement of the antitrust laws because they believe that firms that acquire market power and begin to make economic profits will soon face competition from other firms. In this view, market forces do a better job than the antitrust laws in dealing with inefficiently large concentrations of market power. Other economists and policymakers are more skeptical about relying on competition to reduce market power. They argue that unless the antitrust laws are vigorously enforced, some firms may be able to charge high prices for years, thereby reducing consumer surplus and causing economic inefficiency.

The disagreements among economists concerning antitrust policy are particularly strong on the question of whether the government should take action against firms that have acquired market power as a result of owning a widely used technology. For example, Microsoft has a 90 percent share in the market for personal computer operating systems not because it merged with other software firms but because it developed a technology—Windows—that consumers and firms have widely adopted. As we have seen, once a technology becomes well established, network externalities may give the firm owning the technology considerable market power. Should the government prosecute Microsoft under the Sherman Act for having monopolized the market for operating systems?

Some economists believe that Microsoft should be prosecuted. In practice, though, the federal government has not gone to court over Microsoft's dominant position in the operating system market. Instead, the Justice Department filed suit in 1998, arguing that Microsoft had attempted to use its position in the operating system market to monopolize the market for Internet browsers. Microsoft had been requiring firms that installed Windows on the computers they sold to also install Microsoft's Internet Explorer. In 2002, the lawsuit was settled when Microsoft agreed to remove the Internet Explorer icon from the Windows desktop and to allow computer manufacturers to include other companies' software icons on the desktop. The issue of Microsoft "bundling" Internet Explorer with Windows resurfaced in 2009, this time in Europe. Neelie Kroes, Europe's commissioner for competition, brought an action that would require Microsoft to include in Windows a "so-called ballot screen that would present a new computer user with a choice of browsers to install, and the option to designate one of them as a default." Microsoft contested the action, arguing that it is easy for computer users to download alternative browsers from the Internet.

*Does Google's monopoly power harm consumers?*

Google has also faced antitrust scrutiny. Google has a 64 percent share of the Internet search market. When it proposed a joint Internet advertising venture with Yahoo, which has a 21 percent share of the search market, the Justice Department threatened to intervene, and Google dropped the idea. When President Obama took office in 2009, Christine A. Varney, the new head of the Justice Department's Antitrust Division, was widely expected to bring an action against Google for monopolizing the Internet search market. Critics of the policy of prosecuting firms such as Microsoft and Google have argued that when the dominance of a firm in an industry reflects consumers choosing the firm's product over those of competing firms, the loss of economic efficiency is hard to identify. As one newspaper account of the antitrust case against Microsoft put it: "Proving that Microsoft's monopoly power harms consumers has always been a difficulty in the government's case against the company."

Whatever the outcome of the current cases, the debate over the government's role in promoting competition seems certain to continue.

Sources: Steven Lohr and Miguel Helft, "Tougher Antitrust Division May Target Google," *New York Times*, May 17, 2009; Brent Kendall, "U.S. to Toughen Antitrust Efforts," *Wall Street Journal*, May 11, 2009; Charles Forelle, "EU Plans a Fresh Strike at Microsoft," *Wall Street Journal*, May 30, 2009; and quote from Amy Harmon, "Why Gates Won't Apologize," *New York Times*, April 29, 2002.

**YOUR TURN:** Test your understanding by doing related problem 5.6 on page 490 and related problem 5.15 on page 491 at the end of this chapter.

⟨X⟩ myeconlab

# Regulating Natural Monopolies

If a firm is a natural monopoly, competition from other firms will not play its usual role of forcing price down to the level where the company earns zero economic profit. As a result, local or state *regulatory commissions* usually set the prices for natural monopolies, such as firms selling natural gas or electricity. What price should these commissions set? Recall from Chapter 11 that economic efficiency requires the last unit of a good or service produced to provide an additional benefit to consumers equal to the additional cost of producing it. We can measure the additional benefit consumers receive from the last unit by the price, and we can measure the additional

## Figure 14-7

**Regulating a Natural Monopoly**

A natural monopoly that is not subject to government regulation will charge a price equal to $P_M$ and produce $Q_M$. If government regulators want to achieve economic efficiency, they will set the regulated price equal to $P_E$, and the monopoly will produce $Q_E$. Unfortunately, $P_E$ is below average cost, and the monopoly will suffer a loss, shown by the shaded rectangle. Because the monopoly will not continue to produce in the long run if it suffers a loss, government regulators set a price equal to average cost, which is $P_R$ in the figure.

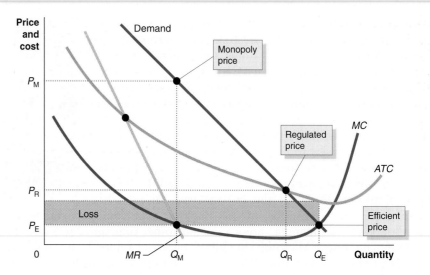

cost to the monopoly of producing the last unit by marginal cost. Therefore, to achieve economic efficiency, regulators should require that the monopoly charge a price equal to its marginal cost. There is, however, an important drawback to doing so, as illustrated in Figure 14-7, which shows the situation of a typical regulated natural monopoly.

Remember that with a natural monopoly, the average total cost curve is still falling when it crosses the demand curve. If unregulated, the monopoly will charge a price equal to $P_M$ and produce $Q_M$. To achieve economic efficiency, regulators should require the monopoly to charge a price equal to $P_E$. The monopoly will then produce $Q_E$. But here is the drawback: $P_E$ is less than average total cost, so the monopoly will be suffering a loss, shown by the area of the red-shaded rectangle. In the long run, the owners of the monopoly will not continue in business if they are experiencing losses. Realizing this, most regulators will set the regulated price, $P_R$, equal to the level of average total cost at which the demand curve intersects the $ATC$ curve. At that price, the owners of the monopoly are able to break even on their investment by producing the quantity $Q_R$.

▶ **Continued from page 461**

## Economics in YOUR LIFE

At the beginning of the chapter, we asked why many cable systems won't carry the NFL Network. You might think that the cable systems would want to televise one of the most popular sports in the nation. In most cities, a customer of a cable system can't switch to a competing cable system, so in many areas, the cable system may be the sole source of many programs. (However, some consumers have the option of switching to satellite television.) As a result, a cable system can increase its profits by, for example, not offering popular programming such as the NFL Network as part of its normal programming package, requiring instead that consumers upgrade to digital programming at a higher price.

# Conclusion

The more intense the level of competition among firms, the better a market works. In this chapter, we have seen that, compared with perfect competition, in a monopoly the price of a good or a service is higher, output is lower, and consumer surplus and economic efficiency are reduced. Fortunately, true monopolies are rare. Even though most firms resemble monopolies in being able to charge a price above marginal cost, most markets have enough competition to keep the efficiency losses from market power quite low.

We've seen that barriers to entry are an important source of market power. Read *An Inside Look at Policy* on the next page for a discussion of how Verizon's entry increased competition in the New York City cable television market.

## >> The End of the Cable TV Monopoly?

PCMAG.COM

## Verizon Launches FiOS TV in New York City

Verizon officially launched its FiOS television service in New York City Monday, rolling out the fiber-optic network to 108 neighborhoods in the five boroughs.

Only about 300,000 of the city's approximately 8 million residents will have access this week, but "by the end of this year, we'll build out fiber-optic network to service more than three million homes and businesses in New York City," Virginia Ruesterholz, president of Verizon Telecom, said during a press conference.

. . .

**(a)** Verizon also announced that FiOS TV will feature 100 high-definition channels starting Monday in all of its markets, working up to 150 channels by year's end. FiOS TV is currently available in parts of 13 states.

Verizon is expected to complete its FiOS TV build out in New York City by 2014. New York's Franchise and Concession Review Committee approved a cable franchising deal for Verizon in May that calls on the company to have FiOS availability in 57 percent of Manhattan, 13 percent of the Bronx, 15 percent of Queens, 12 percent of Brooklyn, and 98 percent of Staten Island by the end of 2008.

The company has already been installing FiOS cable in the city, but has thus far only been allowed to offer Internet service, not cable TV, because cable providers are required to reach cable franchising deals with every city in which they want to offer service.

**(b)** The nature of fiber-optic network installation also requires Verizon to reach deals with the owners of apartments and other buildings in New York City before moving in. The company has thus far installed about six million feet of fiber in New York, said Maura Breen, Verizon general manager for New York.

The company started wiring Stuyvesant Town and Peter Cooper Village, one of Manhattan's largest apartment complexes, in March and all of the residents in its 110 buildings are now wired, Breen said.

"We completed this more than 100 days ahead of schedule and today, every resident has fiber-optic capability," she said.

Verizon is currently in discussions with "hundreds of other building owners," Breen said. Residents can check Verizon's Web site to see if their neighborhood or building is FiOS-ready.

In terms of content, "we are committed to having 150 high-definition channels by year's end, and we are on track to do that," Ruesterholz said. "As the content comes in, we're ready to put it on the air, and we intend to roll that out across the country."

**(c)** Ruesterholz said Verizon's HD content "significantly" outpaces similar offerings on New York's major cable providers, Time Warner Cable and Cablevision.

"Neither of them can compete with the 100 HD channels that we're launching today," Ruesterholz said.

Cablevision on Monday added 15 HD channels to its lineup, bringing its total to 60, according to a spokesman.

"If you look at Verizon's list, at least 42 of their 100 channels are premium movie channels or premium movie multiplexes (they have a dozen Cinemax channels on there, for example), and the vast majority of our 60 channels are included in expanded basic, so they are available to customers whether they have premium movie channel subscriptions or not," the spokesman said.

Cablevision also said that renting a Verizon HD costs several more dollars per month than standard Verizon set-top boxes. "Cablevision doesn't charge anything extra for HD; our HD channels are free to our customers," he said.

A Verizon spokeswoman denied that it charges more for an HD box; the HD and standard box are both $5.95 per month for this offer, she said.

For Cablevision "to say that a larger percentage of their titles are not premium is simply based on the fact that they offer a whole lot fewer channels than we do," the spokeswoman said. "We have 54 channels, actually, that are not premium, that are included in the basic package, so very little difference there."

Time Warner Cable did not immediately respond to a request for comment.

Source: Chloe Albanesius, "Verizon Launches FiOS TV in New York City," pcmag.com, July 28, 2008.

## Key Points in the Article

The article discusses the entry of Verizon into the market for cable TV in New York City. Until 2008, Time Warner Cable and Cablevision were the sole providers of cable TV service in New York City; each company had monopoly rights to provide cable service in different parts of the city. Verizon began offering its FiOS TV service after receiving permission from New York's Franchise and Concession Review Committee. Verizon had previously begun installing a fiber-optic network and offered Internet service, services that did not require permission from local authorities. Cablevision responded to Verizon's entry by announcing the addition of 15 new high-definition channels for its subscribers.

## Analyzing the News

(a) Verizon began offering cable TV service to customers in New York City after receiving approval from the city's Franchise and Concession Review Committee. Verizon's FiOS cable service had been offered previously in about a dozen other states. Verizon planned to expand its services to the entire city by 2014.

(b) In addition to receiving permission from the city, Verizon had to reach individual agreements with owners of apartment buildings to install fiber-optic cable. These negotiations added to the time and expense incurred by Verizon.

(c) Verizon claimed that its service was superior to the services offered by Time Warner Cable and Cablevision. A spokesperson for Cablevision countered by arguing that Verizon charged a monthly rental fee that was higher than Cablevision's fee. The comments from each company's representatives demonstrate the effect that entry had in the market. As we learned in this chapter, barriers to entry enable a monopoly firm to retain the profits it earns. The figure illustrates what happens if entry results in the market becoming perfectly competitive. For simplicity, we assume that the marginal cost of providing cable services is constant, so the marginal cost curve is a horizontal line. Notice that with entry, output increases from $Q_M$ to $Q_C$, and price falls from $P_M$ to $P_C$. You can also see

that consumer surplus increases from areas $A + E$ to areas $A + E + B + C + D$, and the deadweight loss in the market (area $D$) disappears and becomes consumer surplus. In this figure, what were profits for the monopoly (areas $B + C$) are redistributed to consumers as consumer surplus. Economic profits fall to zero. In this case, in addition to paying lower prices, consumers benefit from improved services because the cable companies immediately offered more channels to their customers.

## Thinking Critically
### About Policy

1. What is the most a firm would be willing to spend to be the sole provider of cable television in a market?
2. Would entry into the cable TV market in New York ever be great enough to change the market to a perfectly competitive one (as we assume happens in the figure, with the price becoming equal to $P_C$)?

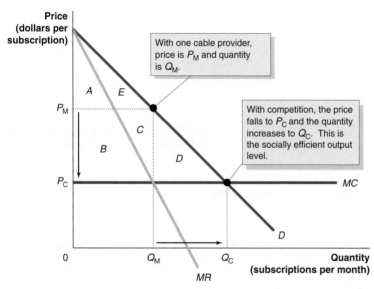

Competition lowers the price of cable TV and increases economic efficiency.

## Key Terms

Antitrust laws, p. 476

Collusion, p. 476

Copyright, p. 465

Horizontal merger, p. 477

Market power, p. 474

Monopoly, p. 462

Natural monopoly, p. 467

Network externalities, p. 466

Patent, p. 463

Public franchise, p. 465

Vertical merger, p. 477

  **14.1** | **Is Any Firm Ever Really a Monopoly?** pages 462–463
LEARNING OBJECTIVE: Define monopoly.

## Summary

A **monopoly** exists only in the rare situation in which a firm is producing a good or service for which there are no close substitutes. A narrow definition of monopoly that some economists use is that a firm has a monopoly if it can ignore the actions of all other firms. Many economists favor a broader definition of monopoly. Under the broader definition, a firm has a monopoly if no other firms are selling a substitute close enough that the firm's economic profits are competed away in the long run.

 Visit **www.myeconlab.com** to complete these exercises online and get instant feedback.

## Review Questions

1.1 What is a monopoly? Can a firm be a monopoly if close substitutes for its product exist?

1.2 If you own the only hardware store in a small town, do you have a monopoly?

1.3 Is "monopoly" a good name for the game *Monopoly*? What aspects of the game involve monopoly? Explain briefly, using the definition of monopoly.

## Problems and Applications

1.4 The great baseball player Ty Cobb was known for being very thrifty. Near the end of his life he was interviewed by a reporter who was surprised to find that Cobb used candles, rather than electricity, to light his home. From Ty Cobb's point of view, was the local electric company a monopoly?

1.5 (Related to the *Chapter Opener* on page 461) Some observers say that changes in the past few years have eroded the monopoly power of local cable TV companies, even if no other cable firms have entered their markets. What are these changes? Do these "monopoly" firms still have monopoly power?

1.6 Are there any products for which there are no substitutes? Are these the only products for which it would be possible to have a monopoly? Briefly explain.

1.7 (Related to the *Making the Connection* on page 462) Microsoft thought that the original Xbox was sufficiently different from the PS2 that it could charge a significantly higher price for the Xbox than Sony could charge for the PS2. As it turns out, Microsoft was wrong. If Microsoft had correctly forecast consumers' reponses to the two game systems, how might it have changed its strategy?

**≫ End Learning Objective 14.1**

**14.2** | **Where Do Monopolies Come From?** pages 463–468
LEARNING OBJECTIVE: Explain the four main reasons monopolies arise.

## Summary

To have a monopoly, barriers to entering the market must be so high that no other firms can enter. Barriers to entry may be high enough to keep out competing firms for four main reasons: (1) A government blocks the entry of more than one firm into a market by issuing a **patent**, which is the exclusive right to a product for 20 years, or a **copyright**, which is the exclusive right to produce and sell a creation, or giving a firm a **public franchise**, which is the right to be the only legal provider of a good or service; (2) one firm has control of a key raw material necessary to produce a good; (3) there are important *network externalities* in supplying the good or service; or (4) economies of scale are so large that one firm has a *natural monopoly*. **Network externalities** refer to the situation where the usefulness of a product increases with the number of consumers who use it. A **natural monopoly** is a situation in which economies of scale are so large that one firm can supply the entire market at a lower average cost than can two or more firms.

 Visit **www.myeconlab.com** to complete these exercises online and get instant feedback.

## Review Questions

2.1 What are the four most important ways a firm becomes a monopoly?

2.2 If patents reduce competition, why does the federal government grant them?

2.3 What is a public franchise? Are all public franchises natural monopolies?

2.4 What is "natural" about a natural monopoly?

# Problems and Applications

**2.5** The U.S. Postal Service (USPS) is a monopoly because the federal government has blocked entry into the market for delivering first-class mail. Is it also a natural monopoly? How can we tell? What would happen if the law preventing competition in this market were removed?

**2.6** Patents are granted for 20 years, but pharmaceutical companies can't use their patent-guaranteed monopoly powers for anywhere near this long because it takes several years to acquire FDA approval of drugs. Should the life of drug patents be extended to 20 years *after* FDA approval? What would be the costs and benefits of such an extension?

**2.7** Just as a new product or a new method of making a product receives patent protection from the government, books, articles, and essays receive copyright protection. Under U.S. law, authors have the exclusive right to their writings during their lifetimes—unless they sell this right, as most authors do to their publishers—and their heirs retain this exclusive right for 50 years after their death. The historian Thomas Macaulay once described the copyright law as "a tax on readers to give a bounty to authors." In what sense does the existence of the copyright law impose a tax on readers? What "bounty" do copyright laws give authors? Discuss whether the government would be doing readers a favor by abolishing the copyright law.

Source of quote: Thomas Mallon, *Stolen Words: The Classic Book on Plagiarism*, San Diego: Harcourt, 2001 (original ed. 1989), p. 59.

**2.8** The German company Koenig & Bauer has 90 percent of the world market for presses that print currency. Discuss the factors that would make it difficult for new companies to enter this market.

**2.9** (Related to the *Making the Connection* on page 464) Should money making monopolies like Etisalat be subject to competition? Do government owned monopolies act as a foreign investment tool?

**2.10** (Related to the *Making the Connection* on page 465) Why was De Beers worried that people might resell their old diamonds? How did De Beers attempt to convince consumers that used diamonds were not good substitutes for new diamonds? How did De Beers's strategy affect the demand curve for new diamonds? How were De Beers's profits affected?

>> **End Learning Objective 14.2**

---

**14.3** ## How Does a Monopoly Choose Price and Output? pages 468–471
LEARNING OBJECTIVE: Explain how a monopoly chooses price and output.

## Summary

Monopolists face downward-sloping demand and marginal revenue curves and, like all other firms, maximize profit by producing where marginal revenue equals marginal cost. Unlike a perfect competitor, a monopolist that earns economic profits does not face the entry of new firms into the market. Therefore, a monopolist can earn economic profits even in the long run.

 Visit **www.myeconlab.com** to complete these exercises online and get instant feedback.

## Review Questions

**3.1** What is the relationship between a monopolist's demand curve and the market demand curve? What is the relationship between a monopolist's demand curve and its marginal revenue curve?

**3.2** Draw a graph that shows a monopolist earning a profit. Be sure your graph includes the monopolist's demand, marginal revenue, average total cost, and marginal cost curves. Be sure to indicate the profit-maximizing level of output and price.

## Problems and Applications

**3.3** (Related to *Solved Problem 14-3* on page 470) Ed Scahill has acquired a monopoly on the production of baseballs (don't ask how) and faces the demand and cost situation shown in the following table.

| PRICE | QUANTITY (PER WEEK) | TOTAL REVENUE | MARGINAL REVENUE | TOTAL COST | MARGINAL COST |
|---|---|---|---|---|---|
| $20 | 15,000 | | | $330,000 | |
| 19 | 20,000 | | | 365,000 | |
| 18 | 25,000 | | | 405,000 | |
| 17 | 30,000 | | | 450,000 | |
| 16 | 35,000 | | | 500,000 | |
| 15 | 40,000 | | | 555,000 | |

a. Fill in the remaining values in the table.

b. If Ed wants to maximize profits, what price should he charge, and how many baseballs should he sell? How much profit will he make?

c. Suppose the government imposes a tax of $50,000 per week on baseball production. Now what price should Ed charge, how many baseballs should he sell, and what will his profits be?

**3.4** (Related to *Solved Problem 14-3* on page 470) Use the information in Solved Problem 14-3 to answer the following questions.

a. What will Comcast do if the tax is $6.00 per month instead of $2.50? (*Hint:* Will its decision be different in the long run than in the short run?)

b. Suppose that the flat per-month tax is replaced with a tax on the firm of $0.50 per cable subscriber. Now how many subscriptions should Comcast sell if it wants to maximize profit? What price should it charge? What are its profits? (Assume that Comcast will sell only the quantities listed in the table.)

3.5 Before inexpensive pocket calculators were developed, many science and engineering students used slide rules to make numerical calculations. Slide rules are no longer produced, which means nothing prevents you from establishing a monopoly in the slide rule market. Draw a graph showing the situation your slide rule firm would be in. Be sure to include on your graph your demand, marginal revenue, average total cost, and marginal cost curves. Indicate the price you would charge and the quantity you would produce. Are you likely to make a profit or a loss? Show this area on your graph.

3.6 Does a monopolist have a supply curve? Briefly explain. (*Hint:* Look again at the definition of a supply curve in Chapter 3 on page 74 and consider whether this applies to a monopolist.)

3.7 (Related to the *Don't Let This Happen to You!* on page 472) A student argues, "If a monopolist finds a way of producing a good at lower cost, he will not lower his price. Because he is a monopolist, he will keep the price and the quantity the same and just increase his profit." Do you agree? Use a graph to illustrate your answer.

3.8 When home builders construct a new housing development, they usually sell to a single cable television company the rights to lay cable. As a result, anyone buying a home in that development is not able to choose between competing cable companies. Some cities have begun to ban such exclusive agreements. Williams Township, Pennsylvania, decided to allow any cable company to lay cable in the utility trenches of new housing developments. The head of the township board of supervisors argued, "What I would like to see and do is give the consumers a choice. If there's no choice, then the price [of cable] is at the whim of the provider." In a situation in which the consumers in a housing development have only one cable company available, is the price really at the whim of the company? Would a company in this situation be likely to charge, say, $500 per month for basic cable services? Briefly explain why or why not.

Source: Sam Kennedy, "Williams Township May Ban Exclusive Cable Provider Pacts," (*Allentown, Pennsylvania*) *Morning Call*, November 5, 2004, p. D1.

3.9 Will a monopoly that maximizes profit also be maximizing revenue? Will it be maximizing production? Briefly explain.

>> **End Learning Objective 14.3**

---

**14.4** **Does Monopoly Reduce Economic Efficiency?** pages 471–476
LEARNING OBJECTIVE: Use a graph to illustrate how a monopoly affects economic efficiency.

## Summary

Compared with a perfectly competitive industry, a monopoly charges a higher price and produces less, which reduces consumer surplus and economic efficiency. Some loss of economic efficiency will occur whenever firms have **market power** and can charge a price greater than marginal cost. The total loss of economic efficiency in the U.S. economy due to market power is small, however, because true monopolies are very rare. In most industries, competition will keep price much closer to marginal cost than would be the case in a monopoly.

 Visit **www.myeconlab.com** to complete these exercises online and get instant feedback.

## Review Questions

4.1 Suppose that a perfectly competitive industry becomes a monopoly. Describe the effects of this change on consumer surplus, producer surplus, and deadweight loss.

4.2 Explain why market power leads to a deadweight loss. Is the total deadweight loss from market power for the economy large or small?

## Problems and Applications

4.3 Review Figure 14-5 on page 473 on the inefficiency of monopoly. Will the deadweight loss due to monopoly be larger if the demand is elastic or if it is inelastic? Briefly explain.

4.4 Economist Harvey Leibenstein argued that the loss of economic efficiency in industries that are not perfectly competitive has been understated. He argued that when competition is weak, firms are under less pressure to adopt the best techniques or to hold down their costs. He referred to this effect as "x-inefficiency." If x-inefficiency causes a firm's marginal costs to rise, show that the deadweight loss in Figure 14-5 understates the true deadweight loss caused by a monopoly.

4.5 In most cities, the city owns the water system that provides water to homes and businesses. Some cities charge a flat monthly fee, while other cities charge by the gallon. Which method of pricing is more likely to result in economic efficiency in the water market? Be sure to refer to the definition of economic efficiency in your answer. Why do you think the same method of pricing isn't used by all cities?

**4.6** Review the concept of externalities on page 134 in Chapter 5. If a market is a monopoly, will a negative externality in production always lead to production beyond the level of economic efficiency? Use a graph to illustrate your answer.

**4.7** (Related to *Solved Problem 14-4* on page 475) The graph shown here illustrates a monopoly market where the firm maximizes profit by setting price of $50 at the quantity where marginal revenue (*MR*) equals marginal cost (*MC*). The profit-maximizing quantity is 10,000. If this market were perfectly competitive, the price would equal marginal cost; therefore, the equilibrium price and quantity would be $40 and 14,000, respectively.

a. Compute the difference in consumer surplus between the equilibrium under monopoly and under perfect competition.

b. Compute the difference in producer surplus between the equilibrium under monopoly and under perfect competition.

c. Compute the difference in economic surplus under monopoly when compared with perfect competition.

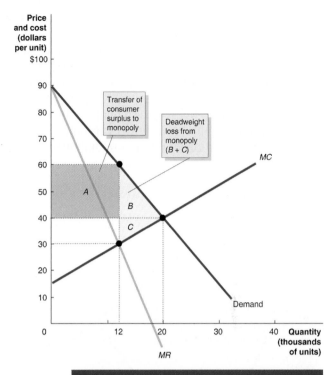

>> **End Learning Objective 14.4**

---

**14.5** **Government Policy toward Monopoly,** pages 476–482

LEARNING OBJECTIVE: Discuss government policies toward monopoly.

## Summary

Because monopolies reduce consumer surplus and economic efficiency, most governments regulate monopolies. Firms that are not monopolies have an incentive to avoid competition by **colluding**, or agreeing to charge the same price or otherwise not to compete. In the United States, **antitrust laws** are aimed at deterring monopoly, eliminating collusion, and promoting competition among firms. The Antitrust Division of the U.S. Department of Justice and the Federal Trade Commission share responsibility for enforcing the antitrust laws, including regulating mergers between firms. A **horizontal merger** is a merger between firms in the same industry. A **vertical merger** is a merger between firms at different stages of production of a good. Local governments regulate the prices charged by natural monopolies.

 Visit **www.myeconlab.com** to complete these exercises online and get instant feedback.

## Review Questions

**5.1** What is the purpose of the antitrust laws? Who is in charge of enforcing them?

**5.2** What is the difference between a horizontal merger and a vertical merger? Which type of merger is more likely to increase the market power of a newly merged firm?

**5.3** Why would it be economically efficient to require a natural monopoly to charge a price equal to marginal cost? Why do most regulatory agencies require natural monopolies to charge a price equal to average cost instead?

## Problems and Applications

**5.4** Use the following graph for a monopoly to answer the questions.

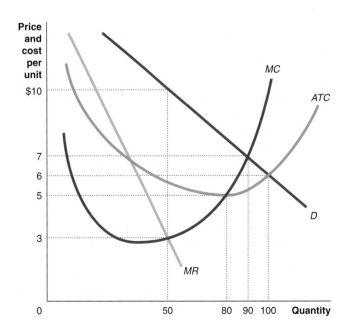

a. What quantity will the monopoly produce, and what price will the monopoly charge?

b. Suppose the monopoly is regulated. If the regulatory agency wants to achieve economic efficiency, what price should it require the monopoly to charge? How much output will the monopoly produce at this price? Will the monopoly make a profit if it charges this price? Briefly explain.

5.5 Use the following graph for a monopoly to answer the questions.

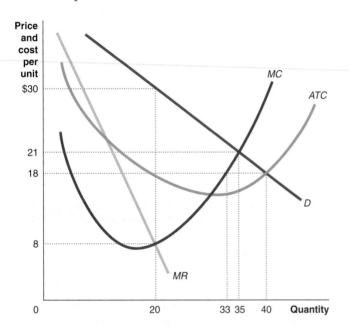

a. What quantity will the monopoly produce, and what price will the monopoly charge?

b. Suppose the government decides to regulate this monopoly and imposes a price ceiling of $18 (in other words, the monopoly can charge less than $18 but can't charge more). Now what quantity will the monopoly produce, and what price will the monopoly charge? Will every consumer who is willing to pay this price be able to buy the product? Briefly explain.

5.6 **(Related to the *Making the Connection* on page 480)** A newspaper article has the headline "Google Says It's Actually Quite Small." According to the article:

> Google rejects the idea that it's in the search advertising business, an industry in which it holds more than a 70 percent share of revenue. Instead, the company says its competition is all advertising, a category broad enough to include newspaper, radio and highway billboards.

Why does Google care whether people think it is large or small? Do highway billboards actually provide competition for Google? Briefly explain.

Source: Jeff Horwitz, "Google Says It's Actually Quite Small," *Washington Post*, June 7, 2009.

5.7 Draw a graph like Figure 14-6 on page 478. On your graph, show producer surplus and consumer surplus before a merger and consumer surplus and producer surplus after a merger.

5.8 The following phone call took place in February 1982 between Robert Crandall, the chief executive officer of American Airlines, and Howard Putnam, the chief executive officer of Braniff Airways. Although Crandall didn't know it, Putnam was recording the call:

> ***Crandall:*** I think it's dumb . . . to sit here and pound the (obscenity) out of each other and neither one of us making a (obscenity) dime . . .
> ***Putnam:*** Do you have a suggestion for me?
> ***Crandall:*** Yes, I have a suggestion for you. Raise your . . . fares 20 percent. I'll raise mine the next morning.
> ***Putnam:*** Robert, we . . .
> ***Crandall:*** You'll make more money and I will, too.
> ***Putnam:*** We can't talk about pricing.
> ***Crandall:*** Oh (obscenity), Howard. We can talk about any . . . thing we want to talk about.

Who had a better understanding of antitrust law, Crandall or Putnam? Briefly explain.

Sources: Mark Potts, "American Airlines Charged with Seeking a Monopoly," *Washington Post*, February 24, 1983; "Blunt Talk on the Phone," *New York Times*, February 24, 1983; and Thomas Petzinger, Jr., *Hard Landing: The Epic Contest for Power and Profits That Plunged the Airline Industry into Chaos*, New York: Random House, 1995, pp. 149–150.

5.9 Before they merged in 2008, Sirius Satellite Radio and XM Satellite Radio were the only two satellite radio firms. In announcing that it would not oppose the merger, the Justice Department said that "evidence developed in the investigation did not support defining a market limited to the two satellite radio firms." It believed that the two firms also competed with "other sources of audio entertainment, including traditional AM/FM radio, HD Radio, MP3 players (e.g., iPods), and audio offerings delivered through wireless telephones." Why would defining the size of the market in which the two firms competed be important to the Justice Department in deciding whether to oppose the merger?

Source: Department of Justice, "Statement of the Department of Justice Antitrust Division on Its Decision to Close Its Investigation of XM Satellite Radio Holdings Inc.'s Merger with Sirius Satellite Radio Inc.," March 24, 2008.

5.10 Look again at the section "The Department of Justice and FTC Merger Guidelines," which begins on page 479. Evaluate the following situations.

a. A market initially has 20 firms, each with a 5 percent market share. Of the firms, 4 propose to merge, leaving a total of 17 firms in the industry. Are the Department of Justice and the FTC likely to oppose the merger? Briefly explain.

b. A market initially has 5 firms, each with a 20 percent market share. Of the firms, 2 propose to merge, leaving a total of 4 firms in the industry. Are the Department of Justice and the Federal Trade Commission likely to oppose the merger? Briefly explain.

5.11 In October 2008, Delta Airlines completed its acquisition of Northwest Airlines. The newly merged company is the largest airline in the world. The following statement regarding the merger is from a Justice Department press release:

> After a thorough, six-month investigation, during which the [Antitrust] Division obtained extensive information from a wide range of market participants— including the companies, other airlines, corporate customers and travel agents— the Division has determined that the proposed merger between Delta and Northwest is likely to produce substantial and credible efficiencies that will benefit U.S. consumers and is not likely to substantially lessen competition.

What is meant by "substantial and credible efficiencies," and how might they benefit U.S. consumers? Why would a merger between two large airlines not be "likely to substantially lessen competition"?

Sources: Andrew Ross Sorkin, "Regulators Approve Delta–Northwest Merger," *New York Times*, October 30, 2008; and Department of Justice, "Statement of the Department of Justice's Antitrust Division on Its Decision to Close Its Investigation of the Merger of Delta Air Lines Inc. and Northwest Airlines Corporation," October 29, 2008.

5.12 The following table shows the market shares during the first three months of 2009 for companies in the U.S. personal computer market.

| COMPANY | MARKET SHARE |
| --- | --- |
| Hewlett-Packard | 28% |
| Dell | 26 |
| Acer | 14 |
| Apple | 7 |
| Toshiba | 7 |
| Other | 18 |

Use the information in the section "The Department of Justice and FTC Merger Guidelines," which begins on page 479, to predict whether the Department of Justice and the FTC oppose a merger between any of the five firms listed in the table. Assume that "Other" in the table consists of six firms, each of which has a 3 percent share of the market.

Source for market share data: Gartner, Inc., www.gartner.com.

5.13 The following table gives the market shares of the companies in the U.S. carbonated soft drink industry during 2008.

| COMPANY | MARKET SHARE |
| --- | --- |
| Coca-Cola | 43% |
| PepsiCo | 31 |
| Dr. Pepper Snapple | 15 |
| Other | 11 |

Use the information in the section "The Department of Justice and FTC Merger Guidelines," which begins on page 479, to predict whether the Department of Justice and the FTC would be likely to approve a merger between any two of the three companies listed. Does your answer depend on how many companies are included in the "Other" category? Briefly explain.

Source: Andrew Ross Sorkin, "Dr. Pepper Snapple Bows to Lukewarm Reception," *New York Times*, May 8, 2008.

5.14 According to a column in the *New York Times* by Austan Goolsbee of the University of Chicago, the French National Assembly approved a bill:

> . . . that would require Apple Computer to crack open the software codes of its iTunes music store and let the files work on players other than the iPod. . . . If the French gave away the codes, Apple would lose much of its rationale for improving iTunes.

a. Why would Apple no longer want to improve iTunes if its software codes were no longer secret?
b. Why would the French government believe it was a good idea to require Apple to make the codes public?

Source: Austan Goolsbee, "In iTunes War, France Has Met the Enemy. Perhaps It Is France," *New York Times*, April 27, 2006.

5.15 **(Related to the *Making the Connection* on page 480)** Are the network externalities in the market for computer operating systems likely to be larger or smaller than the network externalities in the market for Internet search engines? Should the difference play a role when the government considers bringing antitrust cases against Microsoft and Google?

**>> End Learning Objective 14.5**

# CHAPTER 15

# Pricing Strategy

## Chapter Outline and Learning Objectives

## >> Getting into Walt Disney World: One Price Does Not Fit All

When you visit Walt Disney World in Florida, your age, home address, and occupation can determine how much you pay for admission. In 2009, the price for a one-day ticket for an adult was $79.88. The same ticket for a child, aged three to nine, was $67.10. Children under three were free. Adult Florida residents paid $71.89. Adult Florida residents who were also members of Auto Club South paid $67.50. Active members of the military paid $75. Why does Disney charge so many different prices for the same product?

In previous chapters, we assumed that firms charge all consumers the same price for a given product. In reality, many firms charge customers different prices, based on differences in their willingness to pay for the product. Firms often face complicated pricing problems. For example, the Walt Disney Company faces the problem of determining the profit-maximizing prices to charge different groups of consumers for admission to its Disneyland and Walt Disney World theme parks.

In the early 1950s, most amusement parks were collections of unrelated rides, such as roller coasters and Ferris wheels. Founder Walt Disney believed that a theme park, with attractions that emphasized storytelling over thrills, would be more attractive to families

than were amusement parks. Disney hired an economist to evaluate the feasibility of the park. Managers of existing parks gave this advice to the economist: "Tell your boss . . . to stick to what he knows and leave the amusement business to people who know it." Eventually, Disney convinced the ABC television network to provide funding in exchange for his providing them with a weekly television program.

When Disneyland opened in 1955, Disney decided to charge a low price—$1 for adults and $0.50 for children—for admission into the park and also to charge for tickets to the rides. This system of separate charges for admission and for the rides continued until the early 1980s. Today, Disney charges a high price for admission to Disneyland and Walt Disney World, but once a customer is in the park, the rides are free. In this chapter, we will study some common pricing strategies, and we will see how Disney and other firms use these strategies to increase their profits.

**AN INSIDE LOOK** on **page 512** discusses the pricing strategy the Dallas Cowboys football team uses for tickets to its new stadium.

Sources: Harrison Price, *Walt's Revolution! By the Numbers*, Ripley Entertainment, Inc., 2004, p. 31; and Bruce Gordon and David Mumford, *Disneyland: The Nickel Tour*, Santa Clarita, CA: Camphor Tree Publishers, 2000, pp. 174–175.

## Economics in YOUR LIFE!

### Why So Many Prices to See a Movie?

Think about the movie theaters in your area. How much do you, as a student, pay to get into a theater? Would your parents pay the same amount? What about your grandparents? How about your little brother or sister? Is the price the same in the evening as in the afternoon? Why do you suppose movie theaters charge different prices to different groups of consumers?

If you buy popcorn at the movie theater, you pay the same price as everyone else. Why do you suppose people in certain age groups get a discount on movie admission but not on movie popcorn? As you read the chapter, see if you can answer these questions. You can check your answers against those we provide at the end of the chapter.

▶ Continued on page 511

I n previous chapters, we saw that entrepreneurs continually seek out economic profit. Using pricing strategies is one way firms can attempt to increase their economic profit. One of these strategies, called *price discrimination*, involves firms setting different prices for the same good or service, as Disney does when setting admission prices at Walt Disney World. In Chapter 14, we analyzed the situation of a monopolist who sets a single price for its product. In this chapter, we will see how a firm can increase its profits by charging a higher price to consumers who value the good more and a lower price to consumers who value the good less.

We will also analyze the widely used strategies of *odd pricing* and *cost-plus pricing*. Finally, we will analyze situations in which firms are able to charge consumers one price for the right to buy a good and a second price for each unit of the good purchased. Disney's old pricing scheme of charging for admission to Disney World and also charging for each ride is an example of a situation economists call a *two-part tariff*.

**15.1 LEARNING** OBJECTIVE

Define the law of one price and explain the role of arbitrage.

# Pricing Strategy, The Law of One Price, and Arbitrage

We saw in the chapter opener that sometimes firms can increase their profits by charging different prices for the same good. In fact, many firms rely on economic analysis to practice *price discrimination* by charging higher prices to some customers and lower prices to others. Some firms practice a sophisticated form of price discrimination in which they use technology to gather information on the preferences of consumers and their responsiveness to changes in prices. Managers use the information to rapidly adjust the prices of their goods and services. This practice of rapidly adjusting prices, called *yield management*, has been particularly important to airlines and hotels. There are limits, though, to the ability of firms to charge different prices for the same product. The key limit is the possibility in some circumstances that consumers who can buy a good at a low price will resell it to consumers who would otherwise have to buy at a high price.

## Arbitrage

According to the *law of one price*, identical products should sell for the same price everywhere. Let's explore why the law of one price usually holds true. Suppose that a Sony PlayStation Portable (PSP) handheld video game player sells for $169 in stores in Atlanta and for $109 in stores in San Francisco. Anyone who lives in San Francisco could buy PSPs for $109 and resell them for $169 in Atlanta. They could sell them on eBay or Craigslist or ship them to someone they know in Atlanta who could sell them in local flea markets. Buying a product in one market at a low price and reselling it in another market at a high price is referred to as *arbitrage*. The profits received from engaging in arbitrage are referred to as *arbitrage profits*.

As the supply of PSPs in Atlanta increases, the price of PSPs in Atlanta will decline, and as the supply of PSPs in San Francisco decreases, the price of PSPs in San Francisco will rise. Eventually the arbitrage process will eliminate most, but not all, of the price difference. Some price difference will remain because sellers must pay to list PSPs on eBay or to ship them to Atlanta. The costs of carrying out a transaction—by, for example, listing items on eBay and shipping them across the country—are called **transactions costs**. The law of one price holds exactly *only if transactions costs are zero*. As we will soon see, in cases in which it is impossible to resell a product, the law of one price will not hold, and firms will be able to practice price discrimination. Apart from this important qualification, we expect that arbitrage will result in a product selling for the same price everywhere.

**Transactions costs** The costs in time and other resources that parties incur in the process of agreeing to and carrying out an exchange of goods or services.

**PRODUCT: DAN BROWN'S *THE LOST SYMBOL***

| COMPANY | PRICE |
|---|---|
| Amazon.com | $14.83 |
| BarnesandNoble.com | 14.83 |
| WaitForeverForYourOrder.com | 13.50 |
| JustStartedinBusinessLastWednesday.com | 13.25 |

**TABLE 15-1**

**Which Internet Bookseller Would You Buy From?**

## Why Don't All Firms Charge the Same Price?

The law of one price may appear to be violated even where transactions costs are zero and a product can be resold. For example, different Internet Web sites may sell what seem to be identical products for different prices. We can resolve this apparent contradiction if we look more closely at what "product" an Internet Web site—or another business—actually offers for sale.

Suppose you want to buy a copy of Dan Brown's best-seller *The Lost Symbol*. You use Google, mySimon.com, or some other search engine to compare the book's price at various Web sites. You get the results shown in Table 15-1.

Would you automatically buy the book from one of the last two sites listed rather than from Amazon.com or BarnesandNoble.com? We can think about why you might not. Consider what these sites offer for sale. Amazon.com is not just offering *The Lost Symbol*; it is offering *The Lost Symbol* delivered quickly to your home, well packaged so it's not damaged in the mail, and charged to your credit card using a secure method that keeps your credit card number safe from computer hackers. As we discussed in Chapter 12, firms differentiate the products they sell in many ways. One way is by providing faster and more reliable delivery than competitors.

Amazon.com and BarnesandNoble.com have built reputations for fast and reliable service. New Internet booksellers who lack that reputation will have to differentiate their products on the basis of price, as the two fictitious firms listed in the table have done. So, the difference in the prices of products offered on Web sites does *not* violate the law of one price. A book Amazon.com offers for sale is not the same product as a book JustStartedinBusinessLastWednesday.com offers for sale.

# Price Discrimination: Charging Different Prices for the Same Product

We saw at the beginning of this chapter that the Walt Disney Company charges different prices for the same product: admission to Disney World. Charging different prices to different customers for the same good or service when the price differences are not due to differences in cost is called **price discrimination**. But doesn't price discrimination contradict the law of one price? Why doesn't the possibility of arbitrage profits lead people to buy at the low price and resell at the high price?

## The Requirements for Successful Price Discrimination

A successful strategy of price discrimination has three requirements:

1. A firm must possess market power.
2. Some consumers must have a greater willingness to pay for the product than other consumers, and the firm must be able to know what prices customers are willing to pay.

**15.2 LEARNING** OBJECTIVE

Explain how a firm can increase its profits through price discrimination.

**Price discrimination** Charging different prices to different customers for the same product when the price differences are not due to differences in cost.

# Don't Let This Happen to **YOU!**

## Don't Confuse Price Discrimination with Other Types of Discrimination

Don't confuse price discrimination with discrimination based on race or gender. Discriminating on the basis of arbitrary characteristics, such as race or gender, is illegal under the civil rights laws. Price discrimination is legal because it involves charging people different prices on the basis of their willingness to pay rather than on the basis of arbitrary characteristics. There is a gray area, however, when companies charge different prices on the basis of gender. For example, insurance companies usually charge women lower prices than men for automobile insurance. The courts have ruled that this is not illegal

discrimination under the civil rights laws because women, on average, have better driving records than men. Because the costs of insuring men are higher than the costs of insuring women, insurance companies are allowed to charge men higher prices. Notice that this is not actually price discrimination as we have defined it here. Price discrimination involves charging different prices for the same product *where the price differences are not due to differences in cost.*

**YOUR TURN:** Test your understanding by doing related problem 2.18 on page 516 at the end of this chapter.

---

3. The firm must be able to divide up—or *segment*—the market for the product so that consumers who buy the product at a low price are not able to resell it at a high price. In other words, price discrimination will not work if arbitrage is possible.

A firm selling in a perfectly competitive market cannot practice price discrimination because it can only charge the market price. But because most firms do not sell in perfectly competitive markets, they have market power and can set the price of the good they sell. Many firms may also be able to determine that some customers have a greater willingness to pay for a product than others. However, the third requirement—that markets be segmented so that customers buying at a low price will not be able to resell the product—can be difficult to fulfill. For example, some people really love Big Macs and would be willing to pay $10 rather than do without one. Other people would not be willing to pay a penny more than $1 for one. Even if McDonald's could identify differences in the willingness of its customers to pay for Big Macs, it would not be able to charge them different prices. Suppose McDonald's knows that Joe is willing to pay $10, whereas Jill will pay only $1. If McDonald's tries to charge Joe $10, he will just have Jill buy his Big Mac for him.

Only firms that can keep consumers from reselling a product are able to practice price discrimination. Because buyers cannot resell the product, the law of one price does not hold. For example, movie theaters know that many people are willing to pay more to see a movie in the evening than during the afternoon. As a result, theaters usually charge higher prices for tickets to evening showings than for tickets to afternoon showings. They keep these markets separate by making the tickets to afternoon showings a different color or by having the time printed on them and by having a ticket taker examine the tickets. That makes it difficult for someone to buy a lower-priced ticket in the afternoon and use the ticket to gain admission to an evening showing.

Figure 15-1 illustrates how the owners of movie theaters use price discrimination to increase their profits. The marginal cost to the movie theater owner from another person attending a showing is very small: a little more wear on a theater seat and a few more kernels of popcorn to be swept from the floor. In previous chapters, we assumed that marginal cost has a U shape. In Figure 15-1, we assume for simplicity that marginal cost is a constant $0.50, shown as a horizontal line. Panel (a) shows the demand for afternoon showings. In this segment of its market, the theater should maximize profit by selling the quantity of tickets for which marginal revenue equals marginal cost, or 450 tickets. We know from the demand curve that the theater can sell 450 tickets at a price of $7.25 per ticket. Panel (b) shows the demand for evening showings. Notice that charging $7.25 per ticket would *not* be profit maximizing in this market. At a price of $7.25, the theater sells 850 tickets, which is 225 more tickets than the profit-maximizing quantity of 625. By charging $7.25 for tickets to afternoon showings and $9.75 for tickets to evening showings, the theater has maximized profits.

Figure 15-1 also illustrates another important point about price discrimination: When firms can practice price discrimination, they will charge customers who are less sensitive to price—those whose demand for the product is *less elastic*—a higher price and charge customers who are more sensitive to price—those whose demand is *more elastic*—a lower price. In this case, the demand for tickets to evening showings is less elastic, so the price charged is higher, and the demand for tickets to afternoon showings is more elastic, so the price charged is lower.

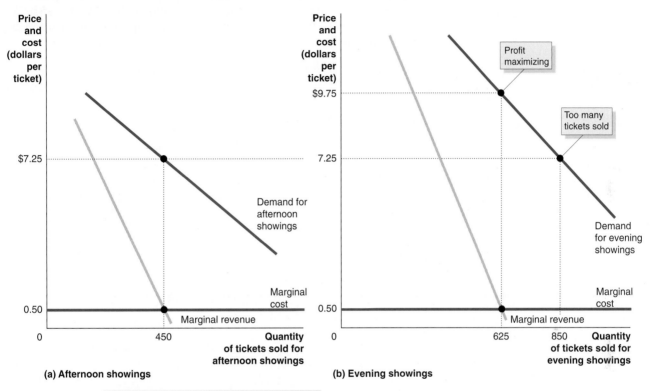

**(a) Afternoon showings**

**(b) Evening showings**

Figure 15-1 | **Price Discrimination by a Movie Theater**

Fewer people want to go to the movies in the afternoon than in the evening. In panel (a), the profit-maximizing price for a ticket to an afternoon showing is $7.25. Charging this same price for evening showings would not be profit maximizing, as

panel (b) shows. At a price of $7.25, 850 tickets would be sold to evening showings, which is more than the profit-maximizing number of 625 tickets. To maximize profits, the theater should charge $9.75 for tickets to evening showings.

# **Solved** Problem | **15-2**

## How Apple Uses Price Discrimination to Increase Profits

In mid-2009, Apple was selling an iMac desktop with a 24-inch display on its Web site and in its retail stores for $1,499. But university students and faculty members could buy the same computer from Apple for $1,399. Why would

Apple charge different prices for the same computer, depending on whether the buyer is an education customer? Draw two graphs to illustrate your answers: one for the general public and one for educational customers.

## SOLVING THE PROBLEM

**Step 1:** **Review the chapter material.** This problem is about using price discrimination to increase profits, so you may want to review the section "Price Discrimination: Charging Different Prices for the Same Product," which begins on page 495.

**Step 2:** **Explain why charging different prices to education customers and other customers will increase Apple's profits.** It makes sense for Apple to charge different prices if education customers have a different price elasticity of demand than do other customers. In that case, Apple will charge the market segment with the less elastic demand a higher price and the market segment with the more elastic demand a lower price. Because Apple is charging education customers the lower price, they must have a more elastic demand than do other customers.

**Step 3:** **Draw a graph to illustrate your answer.** Your graphs should look like the ones below, where we have chosen hypothetical quantities to illustrate the ideas. As in the case of movie theaters, you can assume for simplicity that the marginal cost is constant; in the graph we assume that the marginal cost is $400.

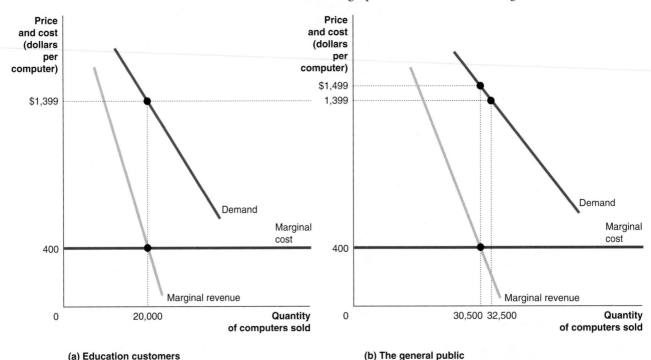

**(a) Education customers**       **(b) The general public**

Panel (a) shows that in the education customers segment of the market, marginal revenue equals marginal cost at 20,000 computers sold. Therefore, Apple should charge a price of $1,399 to maximize profits. But if Apple also charges $1,399 in the general public segment of the market, shown in panel (b), it would sell 32,500 computers, which is more than the profit-maximizing quantity. By charging $1,499 to the general public, Apple will sell 30,500 computers, the profit-maximizing quantity. We have shown that Apple maximizes its profits by charging education customers a lower price than the general public. Notice that although the demand curve in panel (a) is more elastic, it is also steeper. This reminds us of the important point from Chapter 6 that elasticity is different from slope.

ⓧ myeconlab  **YOUR TURN:** For more practice, do problem 2.12 on page 515 at the end of this chapter.

# Airlines: The Kings of Price Discrimination

Airline seats are a perishable product. Once a plane has taken off from Chicago for Los Angeles, any seat that has not been sold on that particular flight will never be sold. In addition, the marginal cost of flying one additional passenger is low. This situation gives airlines a strong incentive to manage prices so that as many seats as possible are filled on each flight.

Airlines divide their customers into two main categories: business travelers and leisure travelers. Business travelers often have inflexible schedules, can't commit until the last minute to traveling on a particular day, and, most importantly, are not very sensitive to changes in price. The opposite is true for leisure travelers: They are flexible about when they travel, willing to buy their tickets well in advance, and sensitive to changes in price. Based on what we discussed earlier in this chapter, you can see that airlines will maximize profits by charging business travelers higher ticket prices than leisure travelers, but they need to determine who is a business traveler and who is a leisure traveler. Some airlines do this by requiring people who want to buy a ticket at the leisure price to buy 14 days in advance and to stay at their destination over a Saturday night. Anyone unable to meet these requirements must pay a much higher price. Business travelers end up paying the higher ticket price because they often cannot make their plans 14 days in advance of their flight and don't want to stay over a weekend. The gap between leisure fares and business fares is often very substantial. For example, in May 2009, the price of a leisure-fare ticket between New York and San Francisco on United Airlines was $328. The price of a business-fare ticket was $1,198.

The airlines go well beyond a single leisure fare and a single business fare in their pricing strategies. Although they ordinarily charge high prices for tickets sold only a few days in advance, airlines are willing to reduce prices for seats that they expect won't sell at existing prices. Since the late 1980s, airlines have employed economists and mathematicians to construct computer models of the market for airline tickets. To calculate a suggested price each day for each seat, these models take into account factors that affect the demand for tickets, such as the season of the year, the length of the route, the day of the week, and whether the flight typically attracts primarily business or leisure travelers. This practice of continually adjusting prices to take into account fluctuations in demand is called *yield management*.

Since the late 1990s, Internet sites such as Priceline.com have helped the airlines to implement yield management. On Priceline.com, buyers commit to paying a price of their choosing for a ticket on a particular day and agree that they will fly at any time on that day. This gives airlines the opportunity to fill seats that otherwise would have gone empty, particularly on late-night or early-morning flights, even though the price may be well below the normal leisure fare. In 2001, several airlines came together to form the Internet site Orbitz, which became another means of filling seats at discount prices. In fact, in the past few years, the chance that you paid the same price for your airline ticket as the person sitting next to you has become quite small. Figure 15-2 shows an actual United Airlines flight from Chicago to Los Angeles. The 33 passengers on the flight paid 27 different prices for their tickets, including one passenger who used frequent flyer miles to obtain a free ticket.

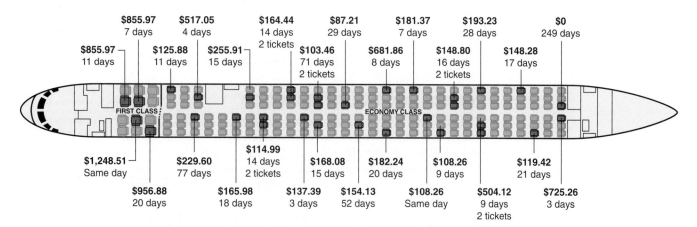

## Figure 15-2   33 Customers and 27 Different Prices

To fill as many seats on a flight as possible, airlines charge many different ticket prices. The 33 passengers on this United Airlines flight from Chicago to Los Angeles paid 27 different prices for their tickets, including one passenger who used frequent flyer miles to obtain a free ticket. The first number in the figure is the price paid for the ticket; the second number is the number of days in advance that the ticket was purchased.

Source: Matthew L. Wald, "So, How Much Did You Pay for Your Ticket?" *New York Times*, April 12, 1998. Used with permission of New York Times Agency.

*Some colleges use yield management techniques to determine financial aid.*

### Making the Connection

### How Colleges Use Yield Management

Traditionally, colleges have based financial aid decisions only on the incomes of prospective students. In recent years, however, many colleges have started using yield management techniques, first developed for the airlines, to determine the amount of financial aid they offer different students. Colleges typically use a name such as "financial aid engineering" or "student enrollment management" rather than "yield management" to describe what they are doing. There is an important difference between the airlines and colleges: Colleges are interested not just in maximizing the revenue they receive from student tuition but also in increasing the academic quality of the students who enroll.

The "price" a college charges equals the full tuition minus any financial aid it provides students. When colleges use yield management techniques, they increase financial aid offers to students who are likely to be more price sensitive, and they reduce financial aid offers to students who are likely to be less price sensitive. As Stanford economist Caroline Hoxby puts it, "Universities are trying to find the people whose decisions will be changed by these [financial aid] grants." Some of the factors colleges use to judge how sensitive to price students are likely to be include whether they applied for early admission, whether they came for an on-campus interview, their intended major, their home state, and the level of their family's income. William F. Elliot, vice president for enrollment management at Carnegie Mellon University, advises, "If finances are a concern, you shouldn't be applying any place [for] early decision" because you are less likely to receive a large financial aid offer.

Many students (and their parents) are critical of colleges that use yield management techniques in allocating financial aid. Some colleges, such as those in the Ivy League, have large enough endowments to meet all of their students' financial aid needs, so they don't practice yield management. Less well-endowed colleges defend the practice on the grounds that it allows them to recruit the best students at a lower cost in financial aid.

Sources: Jacques Steinberg, "Early Signs That College Yields Did Not Change Dramatically," *New York Times*, May 8, 2009; Jane J. Kim and Anjali Athavaley, "Colleges Seek to Address Affordability," *Wall Street Journal*, May 3, 2007; and Albert B. Crenshaw, "Price Wars on Campus: Colleges Use Discounts to Draw Best Mix of Top Students, Paying Customers," *Washington Post*, October 15, 2002.

 **YOUR TURN:** Test your understanding by doing related problem 2.14 on page 516 at the end of this chapter.

## Perfect Price Discrimination

If a firm knew every consumer's willingness to pay—and could keep consumers who bought a product at a low price from reselling it—the firm could charge every consumer a different price. In this case of *perfect price discrimination*—also known as *first-degree price discrimination*—each consumer would have to pay a price equal to the consumer's willingness to pay and, therefore, would receive no consumer surplus. To see why, remember from Chapter 4 that consumer surplus is the difference between the highest price a consumer is willing to pay for a product and the price the consumer actually pays. But if the price the consumer pays is the maximum the consumer would be willing to pay, there is no consumer surplus.

Figure 15-3 shows the effects of perfect price discrimination. To simplify the discussion, we assume that the firm is a monopoly and that it has constant marginal and average costs. Panel (a) should be familiar from Chapter 14. It shows the case of a monopolist who cannot practice price discrimination and, therefore, can charge only a single price for its product. The monopolist maximizes profits by producing the level of output where marginal revenue equals marginal cost. Recall that the economically efficient level of output occurs where price is equal to marginal cost, which is the level of output in a perfectly competitive market. Because the monopolist produces where price is greater than marginal cost, it causes a loss of economic efficiency equal to the area of the deadweight loss triangle in the figure.

Panel (b) shows the situation of a monopolist practicing perfect price discrimination. Because the firm can now charge each consumer the maximum each consumer is willing to pay, its marginal revenue from selling one more unit is equal to the price of that unit. Therefore, the monopolist's marginal revenue curve becomes equal to its demand curve, and the firm will continue to produce up to the point where price is equal to marginal cost. It may seem like a paradox, but the ability to practice perfect price discrimination causes the monopolist to produce the efficient level of output. By doing so, it converts consumer surplus *and* what is deadweight loss in panel (a) into profits. In both panel (a) and panel (b), the profit shown is also producer surplus.

Even though the result in panel (b) is more economically efficient than the result in panel (a), consumers clearly are worse off because the amount of consumer surplus has been reduced to zero. We probably will never see a case of perfect price discrimination in the real world because firms typically do not know how much each consumer is willing to pay and therefore cannot charge each consumer a different price. Still, this extreme case helps us to see the two key results of price discrimination:

1. Profits increase.
2. Consumer surplus decreases.

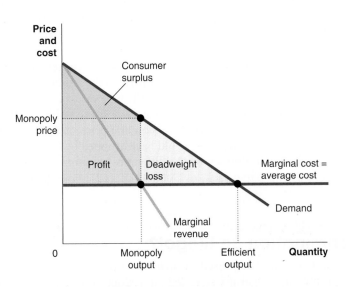

**(a) A monopolist who cannot practice price discrimination**

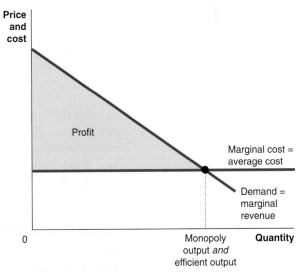

**(b) A monopolist practicing perfect price discrimination**

Figure 15-3 | **Perfect Price Discrimination**

Panel (a) shows the case of a monopolist who cannot practice price discrimination and, therefore, can charge only a single price for its product. The graph, like those in Chapter 14, shows that to maximize profits, the monopolist will produce the level of output where marginal revenue equals marginal cost. The resulting profit is shown by the area of the green rectangle. Given the monopoly price, the amount of consumer surplus in this market is shown by the area of the blue triangle. The econom-

ically efficient level of output occurs where price equals marginal cost. Because the monopolist stops production at a level of output where price is above marginal cost, there is a deadweight loss equal to the area of the yellow triangle. In panel (b), the monopolist is able to practice perfect price discrimination by charging a different price to each consumer. The result is to convert both the consumer surplus *and* the deadweight loss from panel (a) into profit.

Perfect price discrimination improves economic efficiency. Can we also say that this will be the case if price discrimination is less than perfect? Often, less-than-perfect price discrimination will improve economic efficiency. But under certain circumstances, it may actually reduce economic efficiency, so we can't draw a general conclusion.

## Price Discrimination across Time

Firms are sometimes able to engage in price discrimination over time. With this strategy, firms charge a higher price for a product when it is first introduced and a lower price later. Some consumers are *early adopters* who will pay a high price to be among the first to own certain new products. This pattern helps explain why DVD players, Blu-ray players, digital cameras, and flat-screen plasma televisions all sold for very high prices when they were first introduced. After the demand of the early adopters was satisfied, the companies reduced prices to attract more price-sensitive customers. For example, the price of DVD players dropped by 95 percent within five years of their introduction. Some of the price reductions over time for these products were also due to falling costs as companies took advantage of economies of scale, but some represented price discrimination across time.

Book publishers routinely use price discrimination across time to increase profits. Hardcover editions of novels have much higher prices and are published months before paperback editions. For example, the hardcover edition of John Grisham's novel *The Associate* was published in January 2009 at a price of $27.95. The paperback edition was published in September 2009 for $9.99. Although this difference in price might seem to reflect the higher costs of hardcover books, in fact, it does not. The marginal cost of printing another copy of the hardcover is about $1.50. The marginal cost of printing another copy of the paperback edition is only slightly less, about $1.25. So, the difference in price between the hardcover and paperback is driven primarily by differences in demand. John Grisham's most devoted fans want to read his next book at the earliest possible moment and are not very sensitive to price. Many casual readers are also interested in Grisham's books but will read something else if the price of Grisham's latest book is too high.

As Figure 15-4 shows, a publisher will maximize profits by segmenting the market—in this case across time—and by charging a higher price to the less elastic market segment and a lower price to the more elastic segment. (This example is similar to our earlier analysis of movie tickets in Figure 15-1 on page 497.) If the publisher had skipped the hardcover and issued only the paperback version at a price of $9.99 when the book was first published in January, its revenue would have dropped by the number of readers who bought the hardcover multiplied by the difference between the price of the hardcover and the price of the paperback, or $500,000 \times (\$27.95 - \$9.99) = \$8,980,000$.

## Can Price Discrimination Be Illegal?

In Chapter 14, we saw that Congress has passed *antitrust laws* to promote competition. Price discrimination may be illegal if its effect is to reduce competition in an industry. In 1936, Congress passed the Robinson–Patman Act, which outlawed price discrimination that reduced competition and which also contained language that could be interpreted as making illegal *all* price discrimination not based on differences in cost. In the 1960s, the Federal Trade Commission sued the Borden company under this act because Borden was selling the same evaporated milk for two different prices. Cans with the Borden label were sold for a high price, and cans sold to supermarkets to be repackaged as the supermarkets' private brands were sold for a much lower price. The courts ultimately ruled that Borden had not violated the law because the price differences increased, rather than reduced, competition in the market for

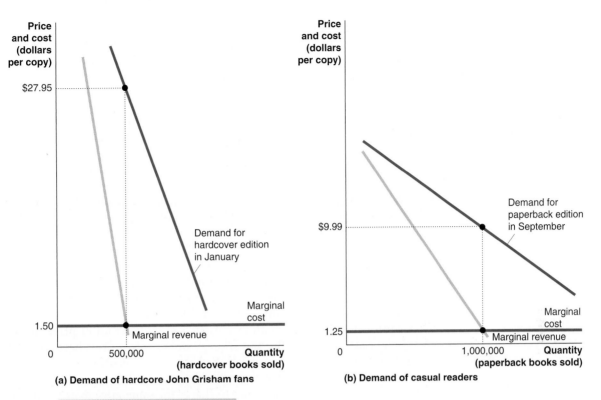

**Figure 15-4**   **Price Discrimination across Time**

Publishers issue most novels in hardcover at high prices to satisfy the demand of the novelists' most devoted fans. Later, they publish paperback editions at much lower prices to capture sales from casual readers. In panel (a), with a marginal cost of $1.50 per copy for a hardcover, the profit-maximizing level of output is 500,000 copies, which can be sold at a price of $27.95. In panel (b), the more elastic demand of casual readers and the slightly lower marginal cost result in a profit-maximizing output of 1,000,000 for the paperback edition, which can be sold at a price of $9.99.

evaporated milk. In recent years, the courts have interpreted Robinson–Patman narrowly, allowing firms to use the types of price discrimination described in this chapter.

## Making the Connection | Price Discrimination with a Twist at Netflix

Price discrimination usually refers to charging different prices to different consumers for the same good or service. But price discrimination can also involve charging the same price for goods or services of different quality. Netflix, an online DVD rental service, has apparently engaged in this second form of price discrimination. According to a newspaper story, "Netflix customers who pay the same price for the same service are often treated differently, depending on their rental patterns." Netflix subscribers pay a fixed monthly fee to rent a given number of DVDs. For instance, in 2009, Netflix was charging $16.99 per month to rent three DVDs at a time (there was an additional $4 per month charge for subscribers who wanted the option to rent Blu-ray discs). After a subscriber returns a DVD, Netflix mails that subscriber a new DVD. Subscribers can rent an unlimited number of DVDs per month, although they can have no more than three at any one time. Netflix has become very popular, with more than 10 million subscribers.

But does every Netflix subscriber receive service of the same quality? In particular, does every subscriber have an equal chance of receiving the latest movie released on DVD? Apparently not. Subscribers who rent the fewest movies per month have

*Why does renting only a few movies get you better service with Netflix?*

the best chance of receiving the latest releases and will typically receive their DVDs faster. According to Netflix's Terms of Use (the "fine print" that most subscribers don't read):

> In determining priority for shipping and inventory allocation, we may utilize many different factors. . . . For example, if all other factors are the same, we give priority to those members who receive the fewest DVDs through our service. . . . Also . . . [the service you experience] may be different from the service we provide to other members on the same membership plan.

One Netflix subscriber was quoted in a newspaper article as saying, "Sometimes it would be two or three months before I got [a movie] once it came out on DVD. The longer I was a customer, the worse it got."

Why would Netflix provide better service to subscribers who rent only a few DVDs per month and poorer service to subscribers who rent many DVDs per month? Subscribers who rent many DVDs per month are likely to have less elastic demand—they really like watching movies—than subscribers who rent only a few DVDs per month. As we have seen in this chapter, firms can increase their profits by charging higher prices to consumers with less elastic demand and lower prices to consumers with more elastic demand. But this strategy works only if firms have a way of reliably separating consumers into groups on the basis of how elastic their demand is. When they first subscribe, Netflix has no way of separating their consumers on the basis of how elastic their demand is, so it has to charge the same price to everyone. But after a few months of observing a subscriber's pattern of rentals, Netflix has enough information to determine whether the subscriber's demand is more or less elastic. By reducing the level of service to subscribers with less elastic demand, Netflix is, in effect, raising the price these consumers pay relative to consumers who receive better service. In effect, Netflix is engaging in price discrimination and increasing its profits over what they would be if every subscriber received the same service at the same price.

Sources: Robin Raskin, "The Bottom of the Netflix Totem Pole," tech.yahoo.com, March 23, 2009; Alina Tugend, "Getting Movies from a Store or a Mailbox (or Just a Box)," *New York Times*, August 5, 2006; and "Netflix Critics Slam 'Throttling,'" Associated Press, February 10, 2006.

 **YOUR TURN:** Test your understanding by doing related problem 2.17 on page 516 at the end of this chapter.

---

**15.3 LEARNING** OBJECTIVE

Explain how some firms increase their profits through the use of odd pricing, cost-plus pricing, and two-part tariffs.

# Other Pricing Strategies

In addition to price discrimination, firms use many different pricing strategies, depending on the nature of their products, the level of competition in their markets, and the characteristics of their customers. In this section, we consider three important strategies: odd pricing, cost-plus pricing, and two-part tariffs.

## Odd Pricing: Why Is the Price $2.99 Instead of $3.00?

Many firms use what is called *odd pricing*—for example, charging $4.95 instead of $5.00, or $199 instead of $200. Surveys show that 80 percent to 90 percent of the products sold in supermarkets have prices ending in "9" or "5" rather than "0." Odd pricing has a long history. In the early nineteenth century, most goods in the United States were sold in general stores and did not have fixed prices. Instead, prices were often determined by haggling, much as prices of new cars are often determined today by haggling on dealers' lots. Later in the nineteenth century, when most products began to sell for a fixed price, odd pricing became popular.

Different explanations have been given for the origin of odd pricing. One explanation is that it began because goods imported from Great Britain had a reputation for high quality. When the prices of British goods in British currency—the pound—were translated into U.S. dollars, the result was an odd price. Because customers connected odd prices with high-quality goods, even sellers of domestic goods charged odd prices. Another explanation is that odd pricing began as an attempt to guard against employee theft. An odd price forced an employee to give the customer change, which reduced the likelihood that the employee would simply pocket the customer's money without recording the sale.

Whatever the origins of odd pricing, why do firms still use it today? The most obvious answer is that an odd price, say $9.99, seems somehow significantly—more than a penny—cheaper than $10.00. But do consumers really have this illusion? To find out, three market researchers conducted a study. We saw in Chapter 3 that demand curves can be estimated statistically. If consumers have the illusion that $9.99 is significantly cheaper than $10.00, they will demand a greater quantity of goods at $9.99—and other odd prices—than the estimated demand curve predicts. The researchers surveyed consumers about their willingness to purchase six different products—ranging from a block of cheese to an electric blender—at a series of prices. Ten of the prices were either odd cent prices—99 cents or 95 cents—or odd dollar prices—$95 or $99. Nine of these 10 odd prices resulted in an odd-price effect, with the quantity demanded being greater than predicted using the estimated demand curve. The study was not conclusive because it relied on surveys rather than on observing actual purchasing behavior and because it used only a small group of products, but it does provide some evidence that using odd prices makes economic sense.

## Why Do Some Firms Use Cost-Plus Pricing?

Many firms use *cost-plus pricing*, which involves adding a percentage *markup* to average cost. With this pricing strategy, the firm first calculates average cost at a particular level of production, usually equal to the firm's expected sales. It then increases average cost by a percentage amount, say 30 percent, to arrive at the price. For example, if average cost is $100 and the percentage markup is 30 percent, the price will be $130. For a firm selling multiple products, the markup is intended to cover all costs, including those that the firm cannot assign to any particular product. Most firms have

### Making the Connection | Cost-Plus Pricing in the Publishing Industry

Book publishing companies incur substantial costs for editing, designing, marketing, and warehousing books. These costs are difficult to assign directly to any particular book. Most publishers arrive at a price for a book by applying a markup to their production costs, which are usually divided into plant costs and manufacturing costs. Plant costs include typesetting the manuscript and preparing graphics or artwork for printing. Manufacturing costs include the costs of printing, paper, and binding the book.

Consider the following example for the hypothetical new book by Adam Smith, *How to Succeed at Economics without Really Trying*. We will assume that the book is 250 pages long, the publisher expects to sell 5,000 copies, and plant and manufacturing costs are as given in the following table.

costs that are difficult to assign to one particular product. For example, the work performed by the employees in the accounting and finance departments at McDonald's applies to all of McDonald's products and can't be assigned directly to Big Macs or Happy Meals.

| PLANT COSTS | | |
| --- | --- | --- |
| | Typesetting | $3,500 |
| | Other plant costs | 2,000 |
| **MANUFACTURING COSTS** | | |
| | Printing | $5,750 |
| | Paper | 6,250 |
| | Binding | 5,000 |
| **TOTAL PRODUCTION COST** | | |
| | | $22,500 |

With total production cost of $22,500 and production of 5,000 books, the per-unit production cost is $22,500/5,000 = $4.50. Many publishers multiply the unit production cost number by 7 or 8 to arrive at the retail price they will charge customers in bookstores. In this case, multiplying by 7 results in a price of $31.50 for the book. The markup seems quite high, but publishers typically sell books to bookstores at a 40 percent discount. Although a customer in a bookstore will pay $31.50 for the book—or less, of course, if it is purchased from a bookseller that discounts the retail price—the publisher receives only $18.90. The difference between the $18.90 received from the bookstore and the $4.50 production cost equals the cost of editing, marketing, warehousing, and all other costs, including the opportunity cost of the investment in the firm by its owners, plus any economic profit the owners receive.

Source: Beth Luey, *Handbook for Academic Authors*, 4th ed., New York: Cambridge University Press, 2002.

 **YOUR TURN:** Test your understanding by doing related problem 3.8 on page 517 at the end of this chapter.

We have seen that firms maximize profit by producing the quantity where marginal revenue equals marginal cost and charging a price that will cause consumers to buy this quantity. The cost-plus approach doesn't appear to maximize profits unless the cost-plus price turns out to be the same as the price that will cause the quantity sold to be where marginal revenue is equal to marginal cost. Economists have two views of cost-plus pricing. One is that cost-plus pricing is simply a mistake that firms should avoid. The other view is that cost-plus pricing is a good way to come close to the profit-maximizing price when either marginal revenue or marginal cost is difficult to calculate.

Small firms often like cost-plus pricing because it is easy to use. Unfortunately, these firms can fall into the trap of mechanically applying a cost-plus pricing rule, which may result in charging prices that do not maximize profits. The most obvious problems with cost-plus pricing are that it ignores demand and focuses on average cost rather than marginal cost. If the firm's marginal cost is significantly different from its average cost at its current level of production, cost-plus pricing is unlikely to maximize profits.

Despite these problems, cost-plus pricing is used by some large firms that have the knowledge and resources to devise a better method of pricing if cost-plus pricing fails to maximize profits. Economists conclude that using cost-plus pricing may be the best way to determine the optimal price in two situations:

1. When marginal cost and average cost are roughly equal
2. When the firm has difficulty estimating its demand curve

In fact, most large firms that use cost-plus pricing do not just mechanically apply a markup to their estimate of average cost. Instead, they adjust the markup to reflect their best estimate of current demand. A large firm is likely to have a pricing policy committee that adjusts prices to reflect the current state of competition in the industry and the current state of the economy. If competition is strong in a weak economy, the pricing committee may decide to set price significantly below the cost-plus price.

In general, firms that take demand into account will charge lower markups on products that are more price elastic and higher markups on products that are less elastic. Supermarkets, where cost-plus pricing is widely used, have markups in the 5 percent to 10 percent range for products with more elastic demand, such as soft drinks and breakfast cereals, and markups in the 50 percent range for products with less elastic demand, such as fresh fruits and vegetables.

## Why Do Some Firms Use Two-Part Tariffs?

Some firms require consumers to pay an initial fee for the right to buy their product and an additional fee for each unit of the product purchased. For example, many golf and tennis clubs require members to buy an annual membership in addition to paying a fee each time they use the golf course or tennis court. Sam's Club requires consumers to pay a membership fee before shopping at its stores. Cellular phone companies charge a monthly fee and then have a per-minute charge after a certain number of minutes have been used. Economists refer to this situation as a **two-part tariff**.

**Two-part tariff** A situation in which consumers pay one price (or tariff) for the right to buy as much of a related good as they want at a second price.

The Walt Disney Company is in a position to use a two-part tariff by charging consumers for admission to Walt Disney World or Disneyland and also charging them to use the rides in the parks. As mentioned at the beginning of this chapter, at one time, the admission price to Disneyland was low, but people had to purchase tickets to go on the rides. Today, you must pay a high price for admission to Disneyland or Disney World, but the rides are free once you're in the park. Figure 15-5 helps us understand which of these pricing strategies is more profitable for Disney. The numbers in the figure are simplified to make the calculations easier.

Once visitors are inside the park, Disney is in the position of a monopolist: No other firm is operating rides in Disney World. So, we can draw panel (a) in Figure 15-5 to represent the market for rides at Disney World. This graph looks like the standard monopoly graph from Chapter 14. (Note that the marginal cost of another rider is quite low. We can assume that it is a constant $2 and equal to the average cost.) It seems obvious—but it will turn out to be wrong!—that Disney should determine the profit-maximizing quantity of ride tickets by setting marginal revenue equal to marginal cost. In this case, that would lead to 20,000 ride tickets sold per day at a price of $26 per ride. Disney's profit from selling *ride tickets* is shown by the area of the light-green rectangle, *B*. The area equals the difference between the $26 price and the average cost of $2, multiplied by the 20,000 tickets sold, or ($26 − $2) × 20,000 = $480,000. Disney also has a second source of profit from selling *admission tickets* to the park. Given the $26 price for ride tickets, what price would Disney be able to charge for admission tickets?

Let's assume the following for simplicity: The only reason people want admission to Disney World is to go on the rides, all consumers have the same individual demand curve for rides, and Disney knows what this demand curve is. This last assumption allows Disney to practice perfect price discrimination. More realistic assumptions would make the outcome of the analysis somewhat different but would

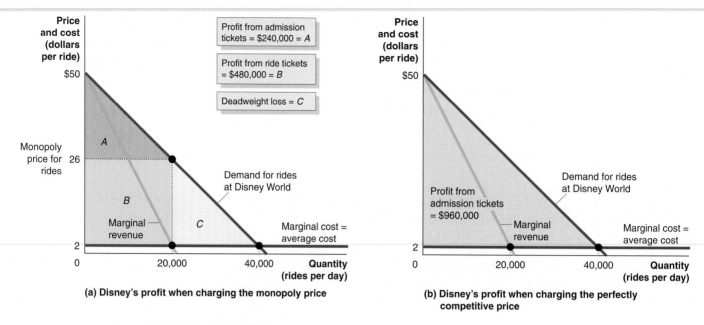

**Figure 15-5** **A Two-Part Tariff at Disney World**

In panel (a), Disney charges the monopoly price of $26 per ride ticket and sells 20,000 ride tickets. Its profit from *ride tickets* is shown by the area of the light-green rectangle, *B*, $480,000. If Disney is in the position of knowing every consumer's willingness to pay, it can also charge a price for *admission tickets* that would result in the total amount paid for admission tickets being equal to total consumer surplus from the rides. Total consumer surplus from the rides equals the area of the dark-green triangle, *A*, or $240,000. So, when charging the monopoly price, Disney's total profit equals $480,000 + $240,000, or $720,000. In panel (b), Disney charges the perfectly competitive price of $2, which results in a quantity of 40,000 ride tickets sold. At the lower ride ticket price, Disney can charge a higher price for admission tickets, which will increase its total profits from operating the park to the area of the light-green triangle, or $960,000.

not affect the main point of how Disney uses a two-part tariff to increase its profits. With these assumptions, we can use the concept of consumer surplus to calculate the maximum total amount consumers would be willing to pay for admission. Remember that consumer surplus is equal to the area below the demand curve and above the price line, shown by the dark-green triangle, *A*, in panel (a). The area represents the benefit to buyers from consuming the product. In this case, consumers would not be willing to pay more for admission to the park than the consumer surplus they receive from the rides. In panel (a) of Figure 15-5, the total consumer surplus when Disney charges a price of $26 per ride is $240,000. (This number is easy to calculate if you remember that the formula for the area of a triangle is ½ × base × height, or ½ × 20,000 × $24.) Disney can set the price of admission tickets so that the *total* amount spent by buyers would be $240,000. In other words, Disney can set the price of admission to capture the entire consumer surplus from the rides. So, Disney's total profit from Disney World would be the $240,000 it receives from admission tickets plus the $480,000 in profit from the rides, or $720,000 per day.

Is this the most profit Disney can earn from selling admission tickets and ride tickets? The answer is "no." The key to understanding why is to notice that *the lower the price Disney charges for ride tickets, the higher the price it can charge for admission tickets*. Lower-priced ride tickets increase consumer surplus from the rides and, therefore, increase the willingness of buyers to pay a higher price for admission tickets. In panel (b) of Figure 15-5, we assume that Disney acts as it would in a perfectly competitive market and charges a price for ride tickets that is equal to marginal cost, or $2. Charging this price increases consumer surplus—*and* the maximum total amount that Disney can charge for admission tickets—from $240,000 to $960,000. (Once again, we use the formula for the area of a triangle to calculate the light-green area in

| | MONOPOLY PRICE FOR RIDES | COMPETITIVE PRICE FOR RIDES | TABLE 15-2 |
|---|---|---|---|
| PROFITS FROM ADMISSION TICKETS | $240,000 | $960,000 | **Disney's Profits per Day from Different Pricing Strategies** |
| PROFITS FROM RIDE TICKETS | 480,000 | 0 | |
| TOTAL PROFIT | 720,000 | 960,000 | |

panel (b): $\frac{1}{2} \times 40,000 \times 48 = \$960,000$.) Disney's profits from the rides will decline to zero because it is now charging a price equal to average cost, *but its total profit from Disney World will rise from $720,000 per day to $960,000.* Table 15-2 summarizes this result.

What is the source of Disney's increased profit from charging a price equal to marginal cost? The answer is that Disney has converted what was deadweight loss when the monopoly price was charged—the area of triangle *C* in panel (a)—into consumer surplus. Disney then turns this consumer surplus into profit by increasing the price of admission tickets.

It is important to note the following about the outcome of a firm using an optimal two-part tariff:

1. Because price equals marginal cost at the level of output supplied, the outcome is economically efficient.
2. All consumer surplus is transformed into profit.

Notice that, in effect, Disney is practicing perfect price discrimination. As we noted in our discussion of perfect price discrimination on page 500, Disney's use of a two-part tariff has increased the amount of the product—in this case, rides at Disney World—consumers are able to purchase but has eliminated consumer surplus. Although it may seem paradoxical, consumer surplus was actually higher when consumers were being charged the monopoly price for the rides. The solution to the paradox is that although consumers pay a lower price for the rides when Disney employs a two-part tariff, the overall amount they pay to be at Disney World increases.

Disney actually does follow the profit-maximizing strategy of charging a high price for admission to the park and a very low price—zero—for the rides. It seems that Disney could increase its profits by raising the price for the rides from zero to the marginal cost of the rides. But the marginal cost is so low that it would not be worth the expense of printing ride tickets and hiring additional workers to sell the tickets and collect them at each ride. Finally, note that Disney can't convert all consumer surplus into profit because: (1) the demand curves of customers are not all the same, and (2) Disney does not know precisely what these demand curves are.

# Solved Problem | 15-3

## Tennis, Anyone?

The Topeka Racquet Club charges club members a monthly membership fee as well as an hourly fee to use its indoor tennis courts. The following graph illustrates the demand, marginal revenue, and marginal cost for the use of the courts. Because marginal cost is constant, it is also equal to average cost ($2). If the club charges a fee of $11 per hour, club members will use the tennis courts a total of 9,000 hours in a month. This is the quantity where marginal revenue equals marginal cost. The club's profit from its court fees for one month is equal to area *A* in the diagram ($11 − $2) × 9,000 = $81,000.

**a.** What is the maximum amount the club can charge as a monthly fee if it charges a court fee of $11 per hour?

**b.** Is it possible for the club to charge a different hourly court fee and increase its profit?

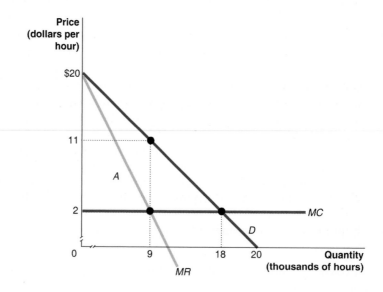

## SOLVING THE PROBLEM:

**Step 1:  Review the chapter material.** This problem is about pricing strategies, so you may want to review the section "Other Pricing Strategies," which begins on page 504.

**Step 2:  Answer question (a).** When an $11 hourly fee is charged, club members receive a total consumer surplus of [½ × ($20 − $11) × 9,000 = $40,500]. If those club members are only interested in joining the club to play tennis, total revenue from monthly fees can be as much as $40,500. If the club has no other costs, then the maximum total profit it would receive would be $81,000 + $40,500 = $121,500.

**Step 3:  Answer question (b).** Club members would receive the maximum amount of consumer surplus if there were no hourly court fee. Consumer surplus would equal the area under the demand curve: ½ × $20 × 20,000 = $200,000. This is the maximum total revenue the club could receive from monthly membership fees. If members used the courts 20,000 hours, the club's total cost would be $2 × 20,000 = $40,000. Assuming that the club received the maximum amount of revenue in the form of monthly fees, the club's profit would be $200,000 − $40,000 = $160,000. But if the club charged a court fee of $2 per hour, it would receive revenue from hourly fees plus consumer surplus equal to ½ × $18 × 18,000 = $162,000. This would yield the most profit.

**YOUR TURN:** For more practice, do related problem 3.12 on page 518 at the end of this chapter.

▶ Continued from page 493

## Economics in YOUR LIFE!

At the beginning of the chapter, we asked you to think about what you pay for a movie ticket and what people in other age groups pay. A movie theater will try to charge different prices to different consumers based on their willingness to pay. If you have two otherwise identical people, one a student and one not, you might assume that the student has less income, and thus a lower willingness to pay, than the non-student, and the movie theater would like to charge the student a lower price. The movie theater employee can ask to see a student ID to ensure that the theater is giving the discount to a student.

But why don't theaters practice price discrimination at the concession stand? It is likely that a student will also have a lower willingness to pay for popcorn, and the theater can check for a student ID at the time of purchase, but unlike with the entry ticket, the theater would have a hard time preventing the student from giving the popcorn to a non-student once inside the theater. Because it is easier to limit resale in movie admissions, we often see different prices for different groups. Because it is difficult to limit resale of popcorn and other movie concessions, all groups will typically pay the same price.

# Conclusion

Firms in perfectly competitive industries must sell their products at the market price. For firms in other industries—which means, of course, the vast majority of firms—pricing is an important part of the strategy used to maximize profits. We have seen in this chapter, for example, that if firms can successfully segment their customers into different groups on the basis of willingness to pay, they can increase their profits by charging different segments different prices.

Read *An Inside Look* on the next page for a discussion of the pricing strategy the Dallas Cowboys football team uses for tickets to its new stadium.

## >> Paying for the Right to Pay to See "America's Team"

### DALLAS STAR-TELEGRAM

# Personal Seat Licenses Should Mean Big Bucks for Cowboys Owner Jerry Jones

Dallas Cowboys owner Jerry Jones could bring in more than a $1 billion from personal seat licenses and suite sales at the [team's] new stadium.

(a) Jones could take in as much as $735 million if he sells all 55,000 licenses, which cost $2,000 to $150,000 per seat, not including the price of the game tickets. . . .

And with 200 suites already sold, the team has guaranteed itself at least $400 million in revenues based on the minimum suite price of $100,000 a year, including game tickets, with a 20-year lease. . . .

But . . . sports economist Craig Depken said the revenues from the licenses will not only help the Cowboys pay for their $750 million portion of the $1.1 billion stadium but also add to the team's bottom line.

. . .

Jones has already made $74.5 million from the sale of licenses to 497 Founders all-access seats, which are the most expensive in the house and carry a $150,000 seat license.

And as of March, the team said it had sold over half of the 15,000 club seats with licenses costing $16,000 to $50,000, which generated at least $120 million if only the cheapest club seats were sold.

About 10,000 seats in the new stadium do not have any license attached to them, but the team has already sold all of them. It has also sold all the seats in the $100,000 PSL Founders sections and $2,000 PSL sections in the upper bowl.

*Star-Telegram* analysis was based on license pricing and row-and-section information provided by the team. . . . The annual cost of tickets was not included.

The Cowboys won't get all the money upfront. The suite revenue is spread over 20 years. . . .

## On the other hand

(b) The revenue estimate has not been adjusted to account for tickets held back by the Cowboys for visiting teams, sponsors and employees. Licenses are not sold on those seats, and the lost revenue on them would be an estimated $34 million if the team held back 10 percent of its club seats and 5,000 general seats. All NFL teams hold back a portion of their available seats so they can be used by partners and visitors, but exact numbers are not released.

And although the team could make a substantial amount on the licenses, so will the tax man. NFL teams say they pay income tax on license revenues—the New York Giants say half their license revenue will go to taxes.

## More money in the bank

The Cowboys have already secured over $390 million in funds for their portion of the stadium through a parking and ticket tax, privately issued bonds and an NFL loan. Based on that, the team would have to sell about 54 percent of its licenses to cover the remaining portion of its $750 million share of stadium costs.

NFL owners are increasingly looking at seat licenses to help fund construction of stadiums. . . .

"The PSLs are a way for a team to contribute their share and their fans to contribute," said Jon Greenberg, editor at *Team Marketing Report*. "It's not like this is a publicly owned team. This isn't a nonprofit."

## Shifting the burden

(c) And with more public dollars being used to finance stadiums, sports-business experts say licenses shift the funding burden onto the people who use the stadium instead of the taxpayer who may never go to a game.

Greenberg said he is not surprised that the Cowboys, who are in a major media market and have a devoted fan base, set the highest license prices in the league so the team can build its stadium.

"Of course, [Jones] is a good businessman and he's going to figure out a way to minimize his risk," Greenberg said.

## What is a PSL?

A Dallas Cowboys personal seat license gives its holder the right to purchase season tickets for that seat in the new stadium over the next 30 years. It does not include the annual ticket price. Holders can also sell the personal seat license on the private market. . . .

PSLs for the new stadium range from $2,000 to $150,000.

2009 season ticket prices range from $59 to $340 per ticket per game for general and club seating.

Source: Andrea Ahles, "Personal Seat Licenses Should Mean Big Bucks for Cowboys Owner Jerry Jones," *Dallas Star-Telegram*, September 28, 2008.

## Key Points in the Article

This article describes an example of a two-part tariff pricing strategy the Dallas Cowboys football team uses to sell the right to watch games played in its new stadium. Although not all season tickets require the purchase of a personal seat license (PSL)—the right for the buyer to purchase season tickets for 30 years—55,000 season tickets do require the purchase of a PSL. The price for a PSL ranges from $2,000 to $150,000, which does not include the price of tickets. Ticket prices range from $59 to $340 per ticket per game. The Cowboys also sell suite licenses; the minimum price for a suite is $100,000, an amount that must be paid annually for 20 years. The Cowboys will use proceeds from ticket and PSL sales to help pay for the cost of constructing the new stadium.

## Analyzing the News

**a** The Dallas Cowboys football team is using a two-part tariff to sell season tickets to football games played at its new stadium. A fan who wants to buy a season ticket must buy a PSL—ranging in price from $2,000 to $150,000 per seat—as well as the ticket—ranging in price from $59 to $340. The figure shows how an NFL team

owner can use a two-part tariff to increase profit. Note that the diagram uses simple, hypothetical numbers rather than numbers taken from the article. The figure assumes that the profit-maximizing monopoly price for a season ticket is $2,000. This assumes that tickets to individual games are sold for $200 each (eight regular-season home games and two preseason games). Marginal cost is assumed to be zero in order to simplify the example. Therefore, the total profit earned by the team would equal area B, or $110 million ($2,000 × 55,000). If the team owner knew the maximum each season ticket buyer was willing to pay, he could charge a PSL fee that would result in a total amount paid by all season ticket buyers equal to area A—the total consumer surplus. This amount is equal to $82.5 million [½ × ($5,000 − $2,000) × 55,000].

**b** Not all of the tickets for Cowboys home games are sold to Cowboys fans. Some tickets are reserved for visiting teams and other parties. PSLs are not sold for these tickets. Revenues from PSL sales are taxed. For example, the New York Giants team pays a 50 percent tax rate on PSLs in their stadium.

**c** Many new sports stadiums are paid for with public funds, or a combina-

tion of private and public funds. Requiring season tickets holders to pay for PSLs helps shift more of the burden of paying for a stadium to those who use the stadium rather than the general public, many of whom may never visit the stadium.

## Thinking Critically

1. Many sports fans complain about the high prices professional sports teams charge to watch games played in new stadiums and arenas and argue that tickets are being increasingly sold to wealthy fans and corporations. Is it better for society for teams to charge high ticket prices than to lower prices so more fans can afford to watch their favorite teams play?

2. Suppose that local government leaders in Dallas responded to complaints from Cowboys fans by forcing the team to end sales of PSLs and placing a ceiling on ticket prices. What impact would this have on the quantity demanded and the quantity supplied of Cowboys tickets? Would the citizens of Dallas be better off as a result of these government actions?

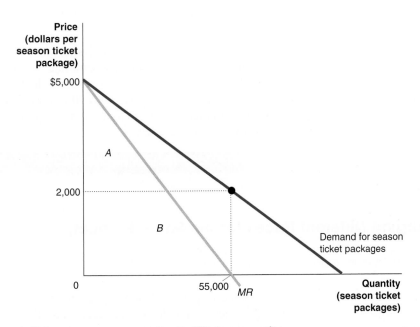

An NFL team owner can use a two-part tariff to increase profits.

# Key Terms

Price discrimination, p. 495　　Transactions costs, p. 494　　Two-part tariff, p. 507

---

## 15.1 Pricing Strategy, the Law of One Price, and Arbitrage, pages 494–495

LEARNING OBJECTIVE: Define the law of one price and explain the role of arbitrage.

## Summary

According to the *law of one price*, identical products should sell for the same price everywhere. If a product sells for different prices, it will be possible to make a profit through *arbitrage*: buying a product at a low price and reselling it at a high price. The law of one price will hold as long as arbitrage is possible. Arbitrage is sometimes blocked by high **transactions costs**, which are the costs in time and other resources incurred to carry out an exchange or because the product cannot be resold. Another apparent exception to the law of one price occurs when companies offset the higher price they charge for a product by providing superior or more reliable service to customers.

 Visit www.myeconlab.com to complete these exercises online and get instant feedback.

## Review Questions

1.1 What is the law of one price? What is arbitrage?

1.2 Does a product always have to sell for the same price everywhere? Briefly explain.

## Problems and Applications

1.3 A newspaper article contains the following description:

> For years, shoppers from New York City have played a game of retail arbitrage, traveling to the many malls in northern New Jersey, a state where there is no tax on clothing and shoes. Even accounting for tolls, gas and time, shoppers could save money by visiting the Westfield Garden State Plaza and other malls here, escaping the 8.375 percent sales tax they must pay in New York City on clothing and shoes that cost more than $110 per item.

Does this article use the word *arbitrage* correctly? Briefly explain.

Source: Ken Belson and Nate Schweber, "Sales Tax Cut in City May Dim Allure of Stores Across Hudson," *New York Times*, January 18, 2007.

1.4 The following table contains the actual prices charged by four Web sites for a DVD of the movie *The Dark Knight* in May 2009.

| | |
|---|---|
| Amazon | $17.49 |
| Wal-Mart | $17.32 |
| Fortunatus | $15.99 |
| The Good Company | $13.99 |

On Google's price comparison Web site, which allows customers to rate the seller, Amazon had 3,945 ratings, Wal-Mart had 754 ratings, Fortunatus had 2 ratings, and The Good Company had 30 ratings. Briefly explain whether the information in this table contradicts the law of one price.

>> **End Learning Objective 15.1**

---

## 15.2 Price Discrimination: Charging Different Prices for the Same Product, pages 495–504

LEARNING OBJECTIVE: Explain how a firm can increase its profits through price discrimination.

## Summary

**Price discrimination** occurs if a firm charges different prices for the same product when the price differences are not due to differences in cost. Three requirements must be met for a firm to successfully practice price discrimination: (1) A firm must possess market power; (2) some consumers must have a greater willingness to pay for the product than other consumers, and firms must be able to know what customers are willing to pay; and (3) firms must be able to divide up—or segment—the market for the product so that consumers who buy the product at a low price cannot resell it a high price. In the case of *perfect price discrimination*, each consumer pays a price equal to the consumer's willingness to pay.

 Visit www.myeconlab.com to complete these exercises online and get instant feedback.

## Review Questions

**2.1** What is price discrimination? Under what circumstances can a firm successfully practice price discrimination?

**2.2** During a particular week, US Airways charged $498 for a round-trip ticket on a flight from New York to San Francisco, provided that the ticket was purchased at least 14 days in advance. The price of the same ticket purchased two days in advance was $833. Why does US Airways use this pricing strategy?

**2.3** What is yield management? Give an example of a firm using yield management to increase profits.

**2.4** What is perfect price discrimination? Is it likely to ever occur? Explain. Is perfect price discrimination economically efficient? Explain.

**2.5** Is it possible to practice price discrimination across time? Briefly explain.

## Problems and Applications

**2.6** According to an article in the *Wall Street Journal*:

Airlines have increased restrictions on cheap fares by raising overnight requirements, upping what had commonly been only a one-night stay requirement to two and three nights. The overnights can be weeknights, so those tickets aren't as onerous as Saturday-night stay tickets. But the three-night requirement does limit the utility of discounted fares for road warriors.

What is a "road warrior"? Would a company put restrictions on a service that make the service less desirable to some of its customers?

Source: Scott McCartney, "Airlines Revive Minimum Stays on Cheap Fares," *Wall Street Journal*, August 19, 2008.

**2.7** An article on the AMC movie theater chain contained the following:

In July, [AMC] announced plans to offer steeply discounted movie tickets to shows on Friday, Saturday and Sunday mornings. "Seventy-five percent of the revenue comes from the weekend," Mr. Brown [AMC's CEO] said. His recent initiatives are attempts to address the question: "Is there a way with price that you can create opportunity, a new market?"

Why would it be profitable for AMC to sell "steeply discounted" movie tickets for movies being shown on weekend mornings? Wouldn't the firm's revenues

be higher if it charged the regular—higher—price for these showings? Briefly explain.

Source: Kate Kelly, "Box-Office Bounty Stirs Theater Deals," *Wall Street Journal*, August 10, 2006, p. C1.

**2.8** Suppose that identically equipped Kia Sportage sport-utility vehicles, all of which are imported from South Korea, sell for an average price of $22,000 in Seattle and $23,000 in Chicago. Briefly explain whether this is an example of price discrimination.

**2.9** Political columnist Michael Kinsley wrote, "The infuriating [airline] rules about Saturday night stayovers and so on are a crude alternative to administering truth serum and asking, 'So how much are you really willing to pay?'" Would a truth serum—or some other way of knowing how much people would be willing to pay for an airline ticket—really be all the airlines need to practice price discrimination? Briefly explain.

Source: Michael Kinsley, "Consuming Gets More Complicated," *Slate*, November 21, 2001.

**2.10** Microsoft offers educational discounts on its software to college students. An article in the *New York Times* mentioned the following offer from Microsoft on its Office Ultimate software, which normally sells for $680: "Actively enrolled college students with .edu e-mail addresses (and carrying at least a 0.5-credit course load) have one more day to snag a copy of Microsoft Office Ultimate for a mere $60. . . ." Why might Microsoft charge students a lower price for Office Ultimate than it charges other groups?

Source: Damon Darlin, "How to Get Microsoft Office at 91 Percent Off," *New York Times*, May 8, 2008.

**2.11** According to an article on cnet.com, in September 2008, Microsoft announced price cuts of approximately 30 percent on its Xbox 360 series in Japan but did not extend these discounts to the U.S. market. Based on this information, does Microsoft consider the demand of U.S. consumers for the Xbox 360 to be more elastic or less elastic than the demand of Japanese consumers? Briefly explain.

Source: Leslie Katz, "Xbox 360 Gets Drastic Price Cut in Japan," cnet.com, September 1, 2008.

**2.12** **(Related to *Solved Problem 15-2* on page 497)** Use the graphs at the bottom of the page to answer the following questions.

   **a.** If the firm wants to maximize profits, what price will it charge in Market 1, and what quantity will it sell?

   **b.** If the firm wants to maximize profits, what price will it charge in Market 2, and what quantity will it sell?

**2.13** When a firm offers a rebate on a product, the buyer normally has to fill out a form and mail it in to receive a rebate check in the mail. A financial columnist argued:

When a manufacturer offers a rebate, you needn't be too suspicious. The manufacturer wants to lower the price temporarily (to move an old product or combat a competitor's new low price), but doesn't have faith that the retailer will pass on the savings.

But suppose that a manufacturer wants to engage in price discrimination. Would offering rebates be a way of doing this? Briefly explain.

Source: Carol Vinzant, "The Great Rebate Scam," *Slate*, June 10, 2003.

**2.14** (Related to the *Making the Connection* on page 500) Assume that the marginal cost of admitting one more student is constant for every university. Also assume that the demand for places in the freshmen class is downward sloping at every university. Now suppose that the public becomes upset that universities charge different prices to different students. Responding to these concerns, the federal government requires universities to charge the same price to each student. Who would gain and who would lose?

**2.15** (Related to the *Chapter Opener* on page 493) Why does Walt Disney World charge a lower admission price for children aged 3 to 9 than for adults? Why does it categorize a 10-year-old as an adult for this purpose? Why does it admit children under 3 for free? Why does it charge residents of Florida a lower price than it charges residents of other states?

**2.16** Are supermarket coupons a form of price discrimination? Briefly explain why or why not.

**2.17** (Related to the *Making the Connection* on page 503) Some Netflix subscriptions have a higher price and allow more—or unlimited—movies to be rented per month. Others have a lower price and allow fewer movies to be rented per month. Is

Netflix practicing price discrimination by offering these different subscriptions? Briefly explain.

**2.18** (Related to the *Don't Let This Happen to You!* on page 496) A state law in California makes it illegal for businesses to charge men and women different prices for dry cleaning, laundry, tailoring, or hair grooming. The state legislator who introduced the law did so after a dry cleaner charged her more to have her shirts dry-cleaned than to have her husband's shirts dry-cleaned: "They charged me $1.50 for each of his, and he wears an extra large. They charged $3.50 for each of mine, and I wear a small." According to a newspaper article, "the dry cleaning proprietor told her that the price difference stemmed from the need for hand ironing her shirts because automatic presses are not made to handle small-sized women's garments." The law proved difficult to enforce, with many dry cleaners continuing to ignore it years after it was passed.

a. Was the dry cleaner practicing price discrimination, as defined in this chapter? Briefly explain.

b. Do you support laws like this one? Briefly explain.

Sources: Veronique de Turenne, "Santa Monica Sues Nine Dry Cleaners under Gender Discrimination Law," *Los Angeles Times*, May 13, 2008; and Harry Brooks, "Law Mandates Equality in Dry Cleaning, Hair Styling," *North County (California) Times*, October 7, 2001.

**2.19** Draw a graph that shows producer surplus, consumer surplus, and deadweight loss (if any) in a market where the seller practices perfect price discrimination. Profit-maximizing firms select an output at which marginal cost equals marginal revenue. Where is the marginal revenue curve in this graph?

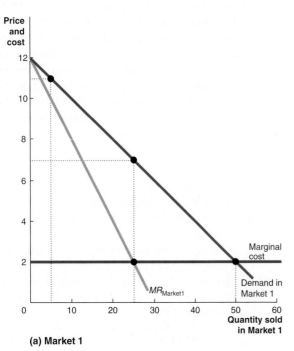

**(a) Market 1**

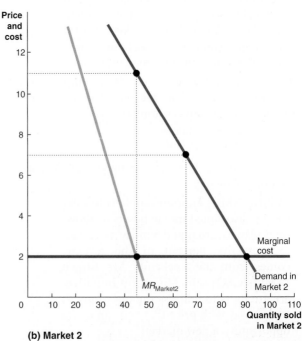

**(b) Market 2**

**» End Learning Objective 15.2**

**15.3** **Other Pricing Strategies,** pages 504–509

LEARNING OBJECTIVE: Explain how some firms increase their profits through the use of odd pricing, cost-plus pricing, and two-part tariffs.

## Summary

In addition to price discrimination, firms also use odd pricing, cost-plus pricing, and two-part tariffs as pricing strategies. Firms use *odd pricing*—for example, charging $1.99 rather than $2.00—because consumers tend to buy more at odd prices than would be predicted from estimated demand curves. With *cost-plus pricing*, firms set the price for a product by adding a percentage markup to average cost. Using cost-plus pricing may be a good way to come close to the profit-maximizing price when marginal revenue or marginal cost is difficult to measure. Some firms can require consumers to pay an initial fee for the right to buy their product and an additional fee for each unit of the product purchased. Economists refer to this situation as a **two-part tariff**. Sam's Club, cell phone companies, and many golf and tennis clubs use two-part tariffs in pricing their products.

 Visit **www.myeconlab.com** to complete these exercises online and get instant feedback.

## Review Questions

**3.1** What is odd pricing?

**3.2** What is cost-plus pricing? Is using cost-plus pricing consistent with a firm maximizing profits?

**3.3** Give an example of a firm using a two-part tariff as part of its pricing strategy.

**3.4** Why did the Walt Disney Company switch from charging for admission to Disneyland and charging for the rides to charging for admission and *not* charging for the rides?

## Problems and Applications

**3.5** One leading explanation for odd pricing is that it allows firms to trick buyers into the illusion that they're paying less than they really are. If this is true, in what types of markets and among what groups of consumers would you be most likely to find odd pricing? Should the government ban this practice and force companies to round up their prices to the nearest dollar?

**3.6** According to an article in the *Wall Street Journal*, McDonald's and Burger King have much larger markups on French fries and sodas than on hamburgers. Is it likely that the companies believe that the demand for French fries and sodas is more elastic or less elastic than the demand for hamburgers? Briefly explain.

Source: Diana Ransom, "Can They Really Make Money Off the Dollar Menu?" *Wall Street Journal*, May 21, 2009.

**3.7** An article in the *Wall Street Journal* gave the following explanation of how products were traditionally priced at Parker-Hannifin Corporation:

> For as long as anyone at the 89-year-old company could recall, Parker used the same simple formula to determine prices of its 800,000 parts—from heat-resistant seals for jet engines to steel valves that hoist buckets on cherry pickers. Company managers would calculate how much it cost to make and deliver each product and add a flat percentage on top, usually aiming for about 35%. Many managers liked the method because it was straightforward.

Is it likely that this system of pricing maximized the firm's profits? Briefly explain.

Source: Timothy Aeppel, "Changing the Formula: Seeking Perfect Prices, CEO Tears Up the Rules," *Wall Street Journal*, March 27, 2007, p. A1.

**3.8** (Related to the *Making the Connection* on page 505) Would you expect a publishing company to use a strict cost-plus pricing system for all its books? How might you find some indication as to whether a publishing company actually was using cost-plus pricing for all its books?

**3.9** Some professional sports teams charge fans a one-time lump sum for a personal seat license. The personal seat license allows a fan the right to buy season tickets each year. No one without a personal seat license can buy season tickets. After the original purchase from the team, the personal seat licenses usually can be bought and sold by fans—whoever owns the seat license in a given year can buy season tickets—but the team does not earn any additional revenue from this buying and selling. Suppose a new sports stadium has been built, and the team is trying to decide on the price to charge for season tickets.

a. Will the team make more profit from the combination of selling personal seat licenses and season tickets if it keeps the prices of the season tickets low or if it charges the monopoly price? Briefly explain.

b. After the first year, is the team's strategy for pricing season tickets likely to change?

c. Will it make a difference in the team's pricing strategy for season tickets if all the personal seat licenses are sold in the first year?

**3.10** During the nineteenth century, the U.S. Congress encouraged railroad companies to build transcontinental railways across the Great Plains by giving them land grants. At that time, the federal government owned most of the land on the Great Plains. The land grants consisted of the land on which the railway was built and alternating sections of 1 square mile each on either side of the railway to a distance of 6 to 40 miles, depending on the location. The railroad companies were free to sell this land to farmers or anyone else who wanted to buy it. The process of selling the land took decades. Some economic historians have argued that the railroad companies charged lower prices to ship freight because they owned so much land along the tracks. Briefly explain the reasoning of these economic historians.

3.11 Thomas Kinnaman, an economist at Bucknell University, has analyzed the pricing of garbage collection:

> Setting the appropriate fee for garbage collection can be tricky when there are both fixed and marginal costs of garbage collection. . . . A curbside price set equal to the average total cost of collection would have high garbage generators partially subsidizing the fixed costs of low garbage generators. For example, if the time that a truck idles outside a one-can household and a two-can household is the same, and the fees are set to cover the total cost of garbage collection, then the two-can household paying twice that of the one-can household has subsidized a portion of the collection costs of the one-can household.

Briefly explain how a city might solve this pricing problem by using a two-part tariff in setting the garbage collection fees households are charged.

Source: Thomas C. Kinnaman, "Examining the Justification for Residential Recycling," *Journal of Economic Perspectives*, Vol. 20, No. 4, Fall 2006, p. 224.

3.12 **(Related to Solved Problem 15-3 on page 509)** The following graph describes the demand, supply, and marginal revenue curves of a golf ball–making firm. The firm plans to produce at a level of 12,000 boxes of golf balls per day. Suppose that the firm has a fixed cost of $150,000.

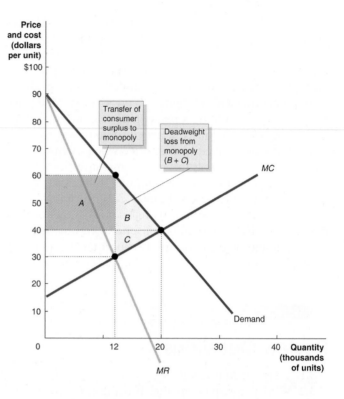

At what markup does cost-plus pricing yield the profit-maximizing price? What are the price and quantity if the firm instead chooses a markup of 44.4 percent?

>> **End Learning Objective 15.3**

# CHAPTER 16

# The Markets for Labor and Other Factors of Production

## Chapter Outline and Learning Objectives

# >> Why Are the New York Yankees Paying CC Sabathia $161 Million?

Few businesses generate as much passion as sports teams. Sports fans admire the skills of star athletes, but many question why they are paid high salaries "just for playing a game." Fans also wonder why a few teams are able to pay higher salaries than other teams. Before the 2009 baseball season, the New York Yankees signed star pitcher CC Sabathia to a seven-year contract that will pay him a total of $161 million. Although Sabathia earned $11 million in 2008 playing for the Cleveland Indians and the Milwaukee Brewers, neither team could match the Yankees's offer. The Yankees were able to offer Sabathia a better contract because of the much higher revenues the team generates from ticket sales, cable television, and broadcast television and radio.

In Chapter 3, we developed a model for analyzing the demand and supply of goods and services. We will use some of the same concepts in this chapter to analyze the demand and supply of labor and other factors of production. But the markets for factors of production are not like markets for goods and services. The most obvious difference is that in factor markets, firms are demanders, and households are suppliers.

Another difference between the labor market and the markets for goods and services is that concepts of fairness arise more frequently in labor markets. When an athlete signs a contract for millions of dollars, people often wonder: "Why should someone playing a game get paid so much more than teachers, nurses, and other people doing more important jobs?" Because people typically earn most of their income from wages and salaries, they often view the labor market as the most important market in which they participate.

**AN INSIDE LOOK** on **page 548** discusses the salaries of college basketball coaches.

Source: John Harper, "CC Sabathia Will Find Nobody Is Bigger Than the Bronx or the Yankees," *Daily News*, April 6, 2009.

## Economics in YOUR LIFE!

### How Can You Convince Your Boss to Give You a Raise?

Imagine that you have worked for a local sandwich shop for over a year and are preparing to ask for a raise. You might tell the manager that you are a good employee, with a good attitude and work ethic. You might also explain that you have learned more about your job and are now able to make sandwiches more quickly, track inventory more accurately, and work the cash register more effectively than when you were first hired. Will this be enough to convince your manager to give you a raise? How can you convince your manager that you are worth more money than you are currently being paid? As you read this chapter, see if you can answer these questions. You can check your answers against those we provide at the end of the chapter.

▶ Continued on page 547

**Factors of production** Labor, capital, natural resources, and other inputs used to produce goods and services.

Firms use **factors of production**—such as labor, capital, and natural resources—to produce goods and services. For example, the New York Yankees use labor (baseball players), capital (Yankee Stadium), and natural resources (the land on which Yankee Stadium sits) to produce baseball games. In this chapter, we will explore how firms choose the profit-maximizing quantity of labor and other factors of production. The interaction between firms' demand for labor and households' supply of labor determines the equilibrium wage rate.

Because there are many different types of labor, there are many different labor markets. The equilibrium wage in the market for baseball players is much higher than the equilibrium wage in the market for college professors. We will explore why this is true. We will also explore how factors such as discrimination, unions, and compensation for dangerous or unpleasant jobs help explain differences among wages. We will then look at *personnel economics*, which is concerned with how firms can use economic analysis to design their employee compensation plans. Finally, we will analyze the markets for other factors of production.

## The Demand for Labor

**16.1 LEARNING** OBJECTIVE

Explain how firms choose the profit-maximizing quantity of labor to employ.

**Derived demand** The demand for a factor of production; it depends on the demand for the good the factor produces.

Up until now, we have concentrated on consumer demand for final goods and services. The demand for labor is different from the demand for final goods and services because it is a *derived demand*. A **derived demand** for a factor of production depends on the demand for the good the factor produces. You demand an Apple iPod because of the utility you receive from listening to music. Apple's demand for the labor to make iPods is derived from the underlying consumer demand for iPods. As a result, we can say that Apple's demand for labor depends primarily on two factors:

1. The additional iPods Apple can produce if it hires one more worker
2. The additional revenue Apple receives from selling the additional iPods

(As we saw in Chapter 2, Apple's suppliers, rather than Apple itself, manufacture the iPod. For simplicity, we are assuming here that Apple does the manufacturing.)

### The Marginal Revenue Product of Labor

Let's consider an example. To keep the main point clear, we'll assume that in the short run, Apple can increase production of iPods only by increasing the quantity of labor it employs. The table in Figure 16-1 shows the relationship between the quantity of workers Apple hires, the quantity of iPods it produces, the additional revenue from selling the additional iPods, and the additional profit from hiring each additional worker.

For simplicity, we are keeping the scale of Apple's factory very small. We will also assume that Apple is a perfect competitor both in the market for selling digital music players and in the market for hiring labor. This means that Apple is a *price taker* in both markets. Although this is not realistic, the basic analysis would not change if we assumed that Apple can affect the price of digital music players and the wage paid to workers. Given these assumptions, suppose that Apple can sell as many iPods as it wants at a price of $200 and can hire as many workers as it wants at a wage of $600 per week. Remember from Chapter 10 that the additional output a firm produces as a result of hiring one more worker is called the **marginal product of labor**. In the table in Figure 16-1, we calculate the marginal product of labor as the change in total output as each additional worker is hired. As we saw in Chapter 10, because of *the law of diminishing returns*, the marginal product of labor declines as a firm hires more workers.

**Marginal product of labor** The additional output a firm produces as a result of hiring one more worker.

When deciding how many workers to hire, a firm is not interested in how much *output* will increase as it hires another worker but in how much *revenue* will increase as it hires another worker. In other words, what matters is how much the firm's revenue

| Number of Workers | Output of iPods per Week | Marginal Product of Labor (iPods per week) | Product Price | Marginal Revenue Product of Labor (dollars per week) | Wage (dollars per week) | Additional Profit from Hiring One More Worker (dollars per week) |
|---|---|---|---|---|---|---|
| L | Q | MP | P | MRP = P x MP | W | MRP − W |
| 0 | 0 | — | $200 | — | $600 | — |
| 1 | 6 | 6 | 200 | $1,200 | 600 | $600 |
| 2 | 11 | 5 | 200 | 1,000 | 600 | 400 |
| 3 | 15 | 4 | 200 | 800 | 600 | 200 |
| 4 | 18 | 3 | 200 | 600 | 600 | 0 |
| 5 | 20 | 2 | 200 | 400 | 600 | −200 |
| 6 | 21 | 1 | 200 | 200 | 600 | −400 |

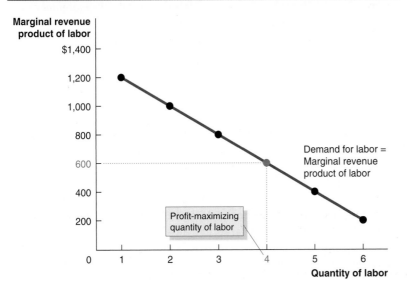

# Figure 16-1

## The Marginal Revenue Product of Labor and the Demand for Labor

The marginal revenue product of labor equals the marginal product of labor multiplied by the price of the good. The marginal revenue product curve slopes downward because diminishing returns cause the marginal product of labor to decline as more workers are hired. A firm maximizes profits by hiring workers up to the point where the wage equals the marginal revenue product of labor. The marginal revenue product of labor curve is the firm's demand curve for labor because it tells the firm the profit-maximizing quantity of workers to hire at each wage. For example, using the demand curve shown in this figure, if the wage is $600, the firm will hire 4 workers.

will rise when it sells the additional output it can produce by hiring one more worker. We can calculate this amount, which is called the **marginal revenue product of labor** (**MRP**), by multiplying the additional output produced by the product price. For example, consider what happens if Apple increases the number of workers hired from 2 to 3. The table in Figure 16-1 shows that hiring the third worker allows Apple to increase its weekly output of iPods from 11 to 15, so the marginal product of labor is 4 iPods. The price of the iPods is $200, so the marginal revenue product of the third worker is 4 × $200, or $800. In other words, Apple adds $800 to its revenue as a result of hiring the third worker. In the graph, we plot the values of the marginal revenue product of labor at each quantity of labor.

To decide how many workers to hire, Apple must compare the additional revenue it earns from hiring another worker to the increase in its costs from paying that worker. The difference between the additional revenue and the additional cost is the additional profit (or loss) from hiring one more worker. This additional profit is shown in the last column of the table in Figure 16-1 and is calculated by subtracting the wage from the marginal revenue product of labor. As long as the marginal revenue product of labor is greater than the wage, Apple's profits are increasing, and it should continue to hire more workers. When the marginal revenue product of labor is less than the wage, Apple's profits are falling, and it should hire fewer workers. When the marginal revenue product of labor is equal to the wage, Apple has maximized its profits by hiring the optimal number of workers. The values in the table show that Apple should hire 4 workers. If Apple hires a fifth worker, the marginal revenue product of $400 will be less than the wage of $600, and its profits will fall by $200. Table 16-1 summarizes the relationship between the marginal revenue product of labor and the wage.

**Marginal revenue product of labor** (**MRP**) The change in a firm's revenue as a result of hiring one more worker.

TABLE 16-1

**The Relationship between the Marginal Revenue Product of Labor and the Wage**

| WHEN . . . | THE FIRM . . . |
|---|---|
| MRP > W, | should hire more workers to increase profits. |
| MRP < W, | should hire fewer workers to increase profits. |
| MRP = W, | is hiring the optimal number of workers and is maximizing profits. |

We can see from Figure 16-1 that if Apple has to pay a wage of $600 per week, it should hire 4 workers. If the wage were to rise to $1,000, then applying the rule that profits are maximized where the marginal revenue product of labor equals the wage, Apple should hire only 2 workers. Similarly, if the wage is only $400 per week, Apple should hire 5 workers. In fact, the marginal revenue product curve tells a firm how many workers it should hire at any wage rate. In other words, *the marginal revenue product of labor curve is the demand curve for labor.*

# Solved Problem | 16-1

## Hiring Decisions by a Firm That Is a Price Maker

We have assumed that Apple can sell as many iPods as it wants to without having to cut the price. Recall from Chapter 11 that this is the case for firms in perfectly competitive markets. These firms are *price takers*. Suppose instead that a firm has market power and is a *price maker*, so that to increase sales, it must reduce the price.

Assume that Apple faces the situation shown in the following table. Fill in the blanks and then determine the profit-maximizing number of workers for Apple to hire. Briefly explain why hiring this number of workers is profit maximizing.

| (1) QUANTITY OF LABOR | (2) OUTPUT OF iPODS PER WEEK | (3) MARGINAL PRODUCT OF LABOR | (4) PRODUCT PRICE | (5) TOTAL REVENUE | (6) MARGINAL REVENUE PRODUCT OF LABOR | (7) WAGE | (8) ADDITIONAL PROFIT FROM HIRING ONE ADDITIONAL WORKER |
|---|---|---|---|---|---|---|---|
| 0 | 0 | — | $200 | | — | $500 | — |
| 1 | 6 | 6 | 180 | | | 500 | |
| 2 | 11 | 5 | 160 | | | 500 | |
| 3 | 15 | 4 | 140 | | | 500 | |
| 4 | 18 | 3 | 120 | | | 500 | |
| 5 | 20 | 2 | 100 | | | 500 | |
| 6 | 21 | 1 | 80 | | | 500 | |

## SOLVING THE PROBLEM:

**Step 1:** **Review the chapter material.** This problem is about determining the profit-maximizing quantity of labor for a firm to hire, so you may want to review the section "The Demand for Labor," which begins on page 522.

**Step 2:** **Fill in the blanks in the table.** As Apple hires more workers, it sells more iPods and earns more revenue. You can calculate how revenue increases by multiplying the number of iPods produced—shown in column 2—by the price—shown in column 4. Then you can calculate the marginal revenue product of labor as the change in revenue as each additional worker is hired. (Notice that in this case, marginal revenue product is *not* calculated by multiplying the marginal product by the product price. Because Apple is a price maker, its marginal revenue from selling additional iPods is less than the price of iPods.) Finally, you can calculate the additional profit from hiring one more worker by subtracting the wage—shown in column 7—from each worker's marginal revenue product.

| (1) QUANTITY OF LABOR | (2) OUTPUT OF iPODS PER WEEK | (3) MARGINAL PRODUCT OF LABOR | (4) PRODUCT PRICE | (5) TOTAL REVENUE | (6) MARGINAL REVENUE PRODUCT OF LABOR | (7) WAGE | (8) ADDITIONAL PROFIT FROM HIRING ONE ADDITIONAL WORKER |
|---|---|---|---|---|---|---|---|
| 0 | 0 | — | $200 | $0 | — | $500 | — |
| 1 | 6 | 6 | 180 | 1,080 | $1,080 | 500 | $580 |
| 2 | 11 | 5 | 160 | 1,760 | 680 | 500 | 180 |
| 3 | 15 | 4 | 140 | 2,100 | 340 | 500 | −160 |
| 4 | 18 | 3 | 120 | 2,160 | 60 | 500 | −440 |
| 5 | 20 | 2 | 100 | 2,000 | −160 | 500 | −660 |
| 6 | 21 | 1 | 80 | 1,680 | −320 | 500 | −820 |

**Step 3:** **Use the information in the table to determine the profit-maximizing quantity of workers to hire.** To determine the profit-maximizing quantity of workers to hire, you need to compare the marginal revenue product of labor with the wage. Column 8 makes this comparison by subtracting the wage from the marginal revenue product. As long as the values in column 8 are positive, the firm should continue to hire workers. The marginal revenue product of the second worker is $680, and the wage is $500, so column 8 shows that hiring the second worker will add $180 to Apple's profits. The marginal revenue product of the third worker is $340, and the wage is $500, so hiring the third worker would reduce Apple's profits by $160. Therefore, Apple will maximize profits by hiring 2 workers.

**YOUR TURN:** For more practice, do problem 1.5 on page 550 at the end of this chapter.

## The Market Demand Curve for Labor

We can determine the market demand curve for labor in the same way we determine a market demand curve for a good. We saw in Chapter 9 that the market demand curve for a good is determined by adding up the quantity of the good demanded by each consumer at each price. Similarly, the market demand curve for labor is determined by adding up the quantity of labor demanded by each firm at each wage, holding constant all other variables that might affect the willingness of firms to hire workers.

## Factors That Shift the Market Demand Curve for Labor

In constructing the demand curve for labor, we held constant all variables—except for the wage—that would affect the willingness of firms to demand labor. An increase or a decrease in the wage causes *an increase or a decrease in the quantity of labor demanded,* which we show by a movement along the demand curve. If any variable other than the wage changes, the result is *an increase or a decrease in the demand for labor*, which we show by a shift of the demand curve. The following are the five most important variables that cause the labor demand curve to shift:

**Human capital** The accumulated training and skills that workers possess.

1. *Increases in human capital.*   **Human capital** represents the accumulated training and skills that workers possess. For example, a worker with a college education generally has more skills and is more productive than a worker who has only a high school diploma. If workers become more educated and are therefore able to produce more output per day, the demand for their services will increase, shifting the labor demand curve to the right.

2. *Changes in technology.*   As new and better machinery and equipment are developed, workers become more productive. This effect causes the labor demand curve to shift to the right over time.

3. *Changes in the price of the product.*   The marginal revenue product of labor depends on the price a firm receives for its output. A higher price increases the marginal revenue product and shifts the labor demand curve to the right. A lower price shifts the labor demand curve to the left.

4. *Changes in the quantity of other inputs.*   Workers are able to produce more if they have more machinery and other inputs available to them. The marginal product of labor in the United States is higher than the marginal product of labor in other countries in large part because U.S. firms provide workers with more machinery and equipment. Over time, workers in the United States have had increasing amounts of other inputs available to them, and that has increased their productivity and caused the demand for labor to shift to the right.

5. *Changes in the number of firms in the market.*   If new firms enter the market, the demand for labor will shift to the right. If firms exit the market, the demand for labor will shift to the left. This effect is similar to the effect that increasing or decreasing the number of consumers in a market has on the demand for a good.

## The Supply of Labor

Having discussed the demand for labor, we can now consider the supply of labor. Of the many trade-offs each of us faces in life, one of the most important is how to divide up the 24 hours in a day between labor and leisure. Every hour spent watching television, walking on the beach, or in other forms of leisure is one hour less spent working. Because in devoting an hour to leisure we give up an hour's earnings from working, the *opportunity cost* of leisure is the wage. The higher the wage we could earn working, the higher the opportunity cost of leisure. Therefore, as the wage increases, we tend to take less leisure and work more. This relationship explains why the labor supply curve for most people is upward sloping, as Figure 16-2 shows.

Although we normally expect the labor supply curve for an individual to be upward sloping, it is possible that at very high wage levels, the labor supply curve of an individual might be *backward bending*, so that higher wages actually result in a *smaller* quantity of labor supplied, as shown in Figure 16-3. To understand why, recall the definitions of the *substitution effect* and the *income effect*, which we introduced in Chapter 3 and discussed more fully in Chapter 9. The substitution effect of a price change refers to the fact that an increase in price makes a good more expensive *relative* to other goods. In the case of a wage change, the substitution effect refers to the fact that an increase in the wage raises the opportunity cost of leisure and causes a worker to devote *more* time to working and less time to leisure.

The income effect of a price change refers to the change in the quantity demanded of a good that results from changes in consumer purchasing power as a result of a price

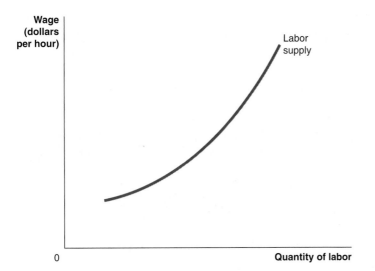

## Figure 16-2

### The Labor Supply Curve

As the wage increases, the opportunity cost of leisure increases, causing individuals to supply a greater quantity of labor. Therefore, the labor supply curve is upward sloping.

change. An increase in the wage will clearly increase a consumer's purchasing power for any given number of hours worked. For a normal good, the income effect leads to a larger quantity demanded. Because leisure is a normal good, the income effect of a wage increase will cause a worker to devote *less* time to working and more time to leisure. So, the substitution effect of a wage increase causes a worker to supply a larger quantity of labor, but the income effect causes a worker to supply a smaller quantity of labor. Whether a worker supplies more or less labor following a wage increase depends on whether the substitution effect is larger than the income effect. Figure 16-3 shows the typical case of the substitution effect being larger than the income effect at low levels of wages—so the worker supplies a larger quantity of labor as the wage rises—and the income effect being larger than the substitution effect at high levels of wages—so the worker supplies a smaller quantity of labor as the wage rises. For example, suppose an attorney has become quite successful and can charge clients very high fees. Or suppose a rock band has become very popular and receives a large payment for every concert it performs. In these cases, there is a high opportunity cost for the lawyer to turn down another client to take a longer vacation or for the band to turn down another concert. But because their incomes are already very high, they may decide to give up

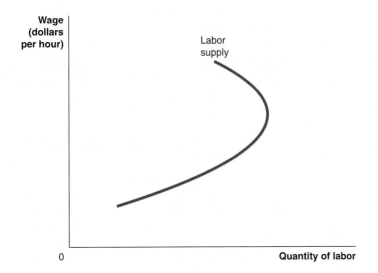

## Figure 16-3

### A Backward-Bending Labor Supply Curve

As the wage rises, a greater quantity of labor is usually supplied. As the wage climbs above a certain level, the individual is able to afford more leisure even though the opportunity cost of leisure is high. The result may be a smaller quantity of labor supplied.

additional income for more leisure. For the lawyer or the rock band, the income effect is larger than the substitution effect, and a higher wage causes them to supply *less* labor.

## The Market Supply Curve of Labor

We can determine the market supply curve of labor in the same way we determine a market supply curve of a good. We saw in Chapter 11 that the market supply curve of a good is determined by adding up the quantity of the good supplied by each firm at each price. Similarly, the market supply curve of labor is determined by adding up the quantity of labor supplied by each worker at each wage, holding constant all other variables that might affect the willingness of workers to supply labor.

## Factors That Shift the Market Supply Curve of Labor

In constructing the market supply curve of labor, we hold constant all other variables that would affect the willingness of workers to supply labor, except the wage. If any of these other variables change, the market supply curve will shift. The following are the three most important variables that cause the market supply curve of labor to shift:

1. *Increases in population.* As the population grows due to the number of births exceeding the number of deaths and due to immigration, the supply curve of labor shifts to the right. The effects of immigration on labor supply are largest in the markets for unskilled workers. In some large cities in the United States, for example, the majority of taxi drivers and workers in hotels and restaurants are immigrants. Some supporters of reducing immigration argue that wages in these jobs have been depressed by the increased supply of labor from immigrants.

2. *Changing demographics.* *Demographics* refers to the composition of the population. The more people who are between the ages of 16 and 65, the greater the quantity of labor supplied. During the 1970s and 1980s, the U.S. labor force grew particularly rapidly as members of the baby boom generation—born between 1946 and 1964—first began working. In contrast, a low birthrate in Japan has resulted in an aging population. The number of working-age people in Japan actually began to decline during the 1990s, causing the labor supply curve to shift to the left.

   A related demographic issue is the changing role of women in the labor force. In 1900, only 21 percent of women in the United States were in the labor force. By 1950, this figure had risen to 30 percent, and today, it is 60 percent. This increase in the *labor force participation* of women has significantly increased the supply of labor in the United States.

3. *Changing alternatives.* The labor supply in any particular labor market depends, in part, on the opportunities available in other labor markets. For example, the problems in the financial services industry beginning in 2007 reduced the opportunities for investment bankers, stock brokers, and other financial workers. Many workers left this industry—causing the labor supply curve to shift to the left—and entered other markets, causing the labor supply curves to shift to the right in those markets. People who have lost jobs or who have low incomes are eligible for unemployment insurance and other payments from the government. The more generous these payments are, the less pressure unemployed workers have to quickly find another job. In many European countries, it is much easier than in the United States for unemployed workers to receive a greater replacement of their wage income from government payments. Many economists believe generous unemployment benefits help explain the higher unemployment rates experienced in some European countries.

# Solved Problem 16-2

## Dear Adam: I'm Confused. Help!

The following letter was written to an advice column titled "Dear Adam." The column provides online advice to college economics students who have difficulty understanding economics concepts.

Dear Adam:

I am a college microeconomics student from Santa Fe. My hometown passed a law in 2003 that raised the minimum wage for all businesses in the city that have 25 or more workers. In 2004, the minimum wage was $8.50, and it is scheduled to rise to $10.50. My friends have expressed different opinions about this law, but what I am confused about is the effect it has had on the market for jobs. A local business owner wrote a letter to the magazine *City Journal*, complaining that the law "is driving existing businesses out of town." If this is true, it means that the higher wage will reduce the quantity supplied of jobs. But we learned in my microeconomics class that the labor supply curve is upward sloping!

After the New Mexico state court upheld the minimum wage ordinance, a lawyer who supported the law claimed that it will "benefit the low-wage workers of Sante Fe." This statement implies that the quantity demanded of jobs will rise as the minimum wage rises; I thought the demand curve for labor was downward sloping.

I have an exam on the labor market in two weeks. Help!

Yours truly,
Hopeless in Sante Fe

Sources: Brennan Center for Justice, *Court Upholds Sante Fe Wage Ordinance*, June 25, 2004. www.brennancenter.org. Ed Tinsley, "Atlas Shrugging in Sante Fe," *City Journal.* August 15, 2003. www.frontpagemag.com.

Write a reply to Hopeless in Sante Fe, explaining each of the following.

**a.** The labor supply curve for labor.

**b.** The impact of an increase in the minimum wage on Sante Fe workers.

## SOLVING THE PROBLEM:

**Step 1:** **Review the chapter material.** This problem is about the supply of labor, so you may want to review the section "The Supply of Labor," which begins on page 526.

**Step 2:** **Answer question (a).** Dear Hopeless: You made a common mistake in believing the market for labor is a market for jobs. The labor supply curve is the relationship between the quantity supplied of labor—not jobs—and the price of labor, or the wage rate. Understand, too, that the demand for labor refers to business firms' demand for workers, not for jobs. It should make sense to you that the business owner you referred to believed that the increase in the wage firms have to pay for workers would reduce the quantity demanded (of *workers*, not jobs!).

**Step 3:** **Answer question (b).** P.S. The increase in the minimum wage would increase the quantity supplied of workers because the opportunity cost of 1 hour of work is an hour spent doing something else. Let's call this "something else" leisure because the opportunity cost of working will be different for different people. At $5.15, fewer people would choose to work, or would work fewer hours, than at a wage rate of $8.50 or $10.50. But this does not mean all who are willing to work will be able to find jobs. I am sure you learned in your course that a worker will be hired only if the marginal revenue product he or she produces per hour is greater than the wage rate. Good luck on your exam! Yours truly, Adam

**YOUR TURN:** For more practice, do related problem 2.8 on page 551 at the end of this chapter.

## Figure 16-4

**Equilibrium in the Labor Market**

As in other markets, equilibrium in the labor market occurs where the demand curve for labor and the supply curve of labor intersect.

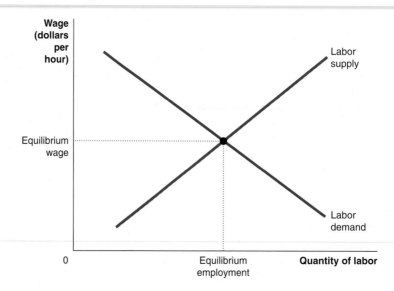

### 16.3 LEARNING OBJECTIVE

Explain how equilibrium wages are determined in labor markets.

# Equilibrium in the Labor Market

In Figure 16-4, we bring labor demand and labor supply together to determine equilibrium in the labor market. We can use demand and supply to analyze changes in the equilibrium wage and the level of employment for the entire labor market, and we can also use it to analyze markets for different types of labor, such as baseball players or college professors.

## The Effect on Equilibrium Wages of a Shift in Labor Demand

In many labor markets, increases over time in labor productivity will cause the demand for labor to increase. As Figure 16-5 shows, if labor supply is unchanged, an increase in labor demand will increase both the equilibrium wage and the number of workers employed.

## Figure 16-5

**The Effect of an Increase in Labor Demand**

Increases in labor demand will cause the equilibrium wage and the equilibrium level of employment to rise:
1. If the productivity of workers rises, the marginal revenue product increases, causing the labor demand curve to shift to the right.
2. The equilibrium wage rises from $W_1$ to $W_2$.
3. The equilibrium level of employment rises from $L_1$ to $L_2$.

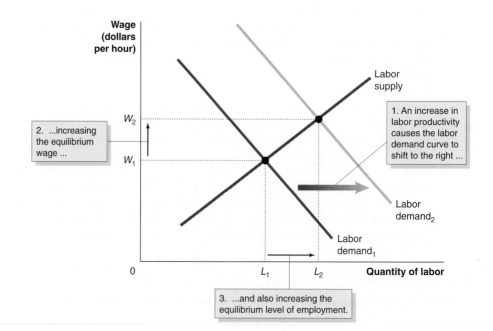

# Making the Connection

## Will Your Future Income Depend on Which Courses You Take in College?

Most people realize the value of a college education. As the following chart shows, in early 2009, full-time workers ages 25 and over with a college degree earned more per week than other workers; for example, they earned 2.5 times as much as high school dropouts.

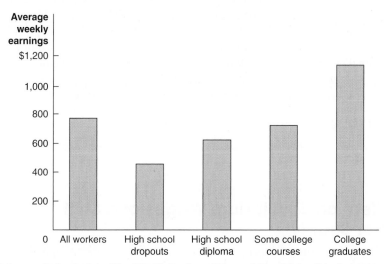

Source: U.S. Bureau of Labor Statistics, "Usual Weekly Earnings of Wage and Salary Workers," April 16, 2009.

Why do college graduates earn more than others? The obvious answer would seem to be that a college education provides skills that increase productivity. Some economists, though, advocate an alternative explanation, known as the *signaling hypothesis*, first proposed by Nobel Laureate A. Michael Spence of Stanford University. This hypothesis is based on the idea that job applicants will always have more information than will potential employers about how productive the applicants are likely to be. Although employers attempt through job interviews and background checks to distinguish "good workers" from "bad workers," they are always looking for more information.

According to the signaling hypothesis, employers see a college education as a signal that workers possess certain desirable characteristics: self-discipline, the ability to meet deadlines, and the ability to make a sustained effort. Employers value these characteristics because they usually lead to success in any activity. People generally believe that college graduates possess these characteristics, so employers often require a college degree for their best-paying jobs. In this view, the signal that a college education sends about a person's inherent characteristics—which the person presumably already possessed *before* entering college—is much more important than any skills the person may have learned in college. Or, as a college math professor of one of the authors put it (only half-jokingly), "The purpose of college is to show employers that you can succeed at something that's boring and hard."

Recently, though, several economic studies have provided evidence that the higher incomes of college graduates are due to their greater productivity rather than the signal that a college degree sends to employers. Orley Ashenfelter and Cecilia Rouse of Princeton University studied the relationship between schooling and income among 700 pairs of identical twins. Identical twins have identical genes, so differences in their inherent abilities should be relatively small. Therefore, if they have different numbers of years in school, differences in their earnings should be mainly due to the effect of schooling on their productivity. Ashenfelter and Rouse found that identical twins had returns of about 9 percent per additional year of schooling, enough to account for most of the gap in income between high school graduates and college graduates.

Daniel Hamermesh and Stephen G. Donald of the University of Texas studied the determinants of the earnings of college graduates 5 to 25 years after graduation. They collected extensive information on each person in their study, including the person's SAT scores, rank in high school graduating class, grades in every college course taken, and college major. Hamermesh and Donald discovered that, holding constant all other factors, business and engineering majors earned more than graduates with other majors. They also discovered a large impact on future earnings of taking science and math courses: "A student who takes 15 credits of upper-division science and math courses and obtains a B average in them will earn about 10% more than an otherwise identical student in the same major . . . who takes no upper-division classes in these areas." This result held even after adjusting for a student's SAT score. The study by Hamermesh and Donald contradicts the signaling hypothesis because if the signaling hypothesis is correct, the choice of courses taken in college should be of minor importance compared with the signal workers send to employers just by having completed college.

Sources: Orley Ashenfelter and Cecilia Rouse, "Income, Schooling, and Ability: Evidence from a New Sample of Identical Twins," *Quarterly Journal of Economics*, Vol. 113, No. 1, February 1998, pp. 253–284; and Daniel S. Hamermesh and Stephen G. Donald, "The Effect of College Curriculum on Earnings: An Affinity Identifier for Non-Ignorable Non-Response Bias," *Journal of Econometrics*, Vol. 144, No. 2, June 2008, pp. 479–491.

 **YOUR TURN:** Test your understanding by doing related problem 3.3 on page 552 at the end of this chapter.

## The Effect on Equilibrium Wages of a Shift in Labor Supply

What is the effect on the equilibrium wage of an increase in labor supply due to population growth? As Figure 16-6 shows, if labor demand is unchanged, an increase in labor supply will decrease the equilibrium wage but increase the number of workers employed.

Whether the wage rises in a market depends on whether demand increases faster than supply. For example, after the success of Walt Disney's animated film *The Lion King* in 1994, most movie studios increased production of animated films, increasing the demand for animators much faster than the supply of animators was increasing. The annual salary for a top animator rose from about $125,000 in 1994 to $550,000 in 1999. These high salaries led more people with artistic ability to choose to get training as film animators, causing the supply of animators to increase after 1999. Several of the animated films released between 1999 and 2001 failed to earn profits, which caused some companies to stop making these films, thereby decreasing the demand for animators. The decrease in demand for animators and the increase in supply caused the salaries of top animators to fall from $550,000 in 1999 to $225,000 in 2002.

## Figure 16-6

### The Effect of an Increase in Labor Supply

Increases in labor supply will cause the equilibrium wage to fall but the equilibrium level of employment to rise:
1. As population increases, the labor supply curve shifts to the right.
2. The equilibrium wage falls from $W_1$ to $W_2$.
3. The equilibrium level of employment increases from $L_1$ to $L_2$.

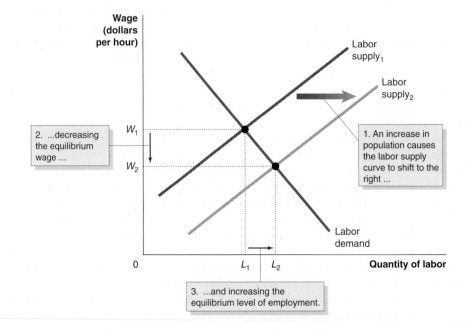

# Explaining Differences in Wages

**16.4 LEARNING** OBJECTIVE

Use demand and supply analysis to explain how compensating differentials, discrimination, and labor unions cause wages to differ.

A key conclusion of our discussion of the labor market is that the equilibrium wage equals the marginal revenue product of labor. The more productive workers are and the higher the price workers' output can be sold for, the higher the wages workers will receive. At the beginning of the chapter, we raised the question of why Major League Baseball players are paid so much more than most other workers. We are now ready to use demand and supply analysis to answer this question. Figure 16-7 shows the demand and supply curves for Major League Baseball players and the demand and supply curves for college professors.

Consider the marginal revenue product of baseball players, which is the additional revenue a team owner will receive from hiring one more player. Baseball players are hired to produce baseball games that are then sold to fans who pay admission to baseball stadiums and to radio and television stations that broadcast the games. Because a Major League Baseball team can sell each baseball game for a large amount, the marginal revenue product of baseball players is high. The supply of people with the ability to play Major League Baseball is also very limited. As a result, the average annual salary of the 750 Major League Baseball players was $3,260,000 in 2009.

The marginal revenue product of college professors is much lower than for baseball players. College professors are hired to produce college educations that are then sold to students and their parents. Although one year's college tuition is quite high at many colleges, hiring one more professor allows a college to admit at most a few more students. So, the marginal revenue product of a college professor is much lower than the marginal revenue product of a baseball player. There are also many more people who possess the skills to be a college professor than possess the skills to be a Major League Baseball player. As a result, the average annual salary of the country's 663,000 college professors was about $81,000 in 2009.

This still leaves unanswered the question raised at the beginning of this chapter: Why are the New York Yankees willing to pay CC Sabathia more than the Milwaukee Brewers were? Sabathia's marginal product—which we can think of as the extra games a team will win by employing him—should be about the same in New York as in Milwaukee. But his *marginal revenue product* will be higher in New York. Because the population of the New York metropolitan area is more than 10 times as large as the population of the Milwaukee metropolitan area, winning more games will result in a greater increase in attendance at New York Yankees games than it would at Milwaukee

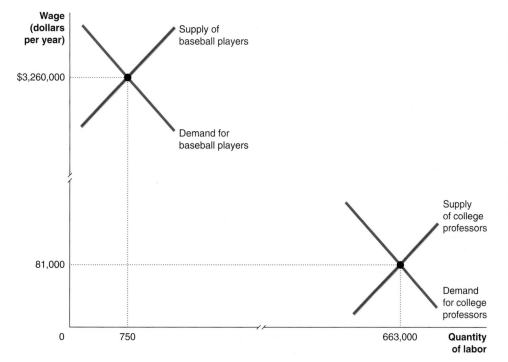

## Figure 16-7

**Baseball Players Are Paid More Than College Professors**

The marginal revenue product of baseball players is very high, and the supply of people with the ability to play Major League Baseball is low. The result is that the 750 Major League Baseball players receive an average wage of $3,260,000. The marginal revenue product of college professors is much lower, and the supply of people with the ability to be college professors is much higher. The result is that the 663,000 college professors in the United States receive an average wage of $81,000, far below the average wage of baseball players.

# Don't Let This Happen to **YOU!**

### Remember That Prices and Wages Are Determined at the Margin

You have probably heard some variation of the following remark: "We could live without baseball, but we can't live without the garbage being hauled away. In a more rational world, garbage collectors would be paid more than baseball players." This remark seems logical: The total value to society of having the garbage hauled away certainly is greater than the total value of baseball games. But wages—like prices—do not depend on total value but on *marginal* value. The *additional* baseball games the New York Yankees expect to win by signing CC Sabathia will result in millions of dollars in increased revenue. The supply of people with the ability to play Major League Baseball is very limited. The supply of people with the ability to be trash haulers is much greater. If a trash-hauling firm hires another worker, the *additional* trash-hauling services it can now offer will bring in a relatively small amount of revenue. The *total*

value of baseball games and the *total* value of trash hauling are not relevant in determining the relative salaries of baseball players and garbage collectors.

This point is related to the diamond and water paradox first noted by Adam Smith. On the one hand, water is very valuable—we literally couldn't live without it—but its price is very low. On the other hand, apart from a few industrial purposes, diamonds are used only for jewelry, yet their prices are quite high. We resolve the paradox by noting that the price of water is low because the supply is very large and the additional benefit consumers receive from the last gallon purchased is low. The price of diamonds is high because the supply is very small, and the additional benefit consumers receive from the last diamond purchased is high.

**YOUR TURN:** Test your understanding by doing related problem 4.7 on page 553 at the end of this chapter.

---

Brewers games. It will also result in a greater increase in viewers for Yankees games on television. Therefore, the Yankees are able to sell the extra wins that Sabathia produces for much more than the Milwaukee Brewers can. This difference explains why the Yankees were willing to pay Sabathia so much more than the Brewers were.

*Why does Angelina Jolie earn more today relative to the typical actor than stars did in the 1940s?*

### Making the Connection | Technology and the Earnings of "Superstars"

The gap between CC Sabathia's salary and the salary of the lowest-paid baseball players is much greater than the gap between the salaries paid during the 1950s and 1960s to top players such as Mickey Mantle and Willie Mays and the salaries of the lowest-paid players. Similarly, the gap between the $15 million Angelina Jolie is paid to star in a movie and the salary paid to an actor in a minor role is much greater than the gap between the salaries paid during the 1930s and 1940s to stars such as Clark Gable and Cary Grant and the salaries paid to bit players. In fact, in most areas of sports and entertainment, the highest-paid performers—the "superstars"—now have much higher incomes relative to other members of their professions than was true a few decades ago.

The increase in the relative incomes of superstars is mainly due to technological advances. The spread of cable television has increased the number of potential viewers of Yankees games, but many of those viewers will watch only if the Yankees are winning. This increases the value to the Yankees of winning games and, therefore, increases Sabathia's marginal revenue product and the salary he can earn.

With Blu-ray discs, DVDs, Internet streaming video, and pay-per-view cable, the value to movie studios of producing a hit movie has risen greatly. Not surprisingly, movie studios have also increased their willingness to pay large salaries to stars such as Angelina Jolie and Will Smith because they think these superstars will significantly raise the chances of a film being successful.

This process has been going on for a long time. For instance, before the invention of the motion picture, anyone who wanted to see a play had to attend the theater and see a live performance. Limits on the number of people who could see the best actors and actresses perform created an opportunity for many more people to succeed in the acting profession, and the gap between the salaries earned by the best actors and the salaries earned by average actors was relatively small. Today, when a hit movie starring Angelina Jolie appears on DVD, millions of people will buy or rent it, and they will not be forced to spend money to see a lesser actress, as their great-great-grandparents might have been.

**YOUR TURN:** Test your understanding by doing related problems 4.10 and 4.11 on page 553 at the end of this chapter.

---

Differences in marginal revenue products are the most important factor in explaining differences in wages, but they are not the whole story. To provide a more complete explanation for differences in wages, we must take into account three important aspects of labor markets: compensating differentials, discrimination, and labor unions. We begin with compensating differentials.

## Compensating Differentials

Suppose Paul runs a video rental store and acquires a reputation for being a bad boss who yells at his workers and is generally unpleasant. Two blocks away, Brendan also runs a video rental store, but Brendan is always very polite to his workers. We would expect in these circumstances that Paul will have to pay a higher wage than Brendan to attract and retain workers. Higher wages that compensate workers for unpleasant aspects of a job are called **compensating differentials**.

If working in a dynamite factory requires the same degree of training and education as working in a semiconductor factory but is much more dangerous, a larger number of workers will want to work making semiconductors than will want to work making dynamite. As a consequence, the wages of dynamite workers will be higher than the wages of semiconductor workers. We can think of the difference in wages as being the price of risk. As each worker decides on his or her willingness to assume risk and decides how much higher the wage must be to compensate for assuming more risk, wages will adjust so that dynamite factories will end up paying wages that are just high enough to compensate workers who choose to work there for the extra risk they assume. Only when workers in dynamite factories have been fully compensated with higher wages for the additional risk they assume will dynamite companies be able to attract enough workers.

One surprising implication of compensating differentials is that *laws protecting the health and safety of workers may not make workers better off.* To see this, suppose that dynamite factories pay wages of $25 per hour, and semiconductor factories pay wages of $20 per hour, with the $5 difference in wages being a compensating differential for the greater risk of working in a dynamite factory. Suppose that the government passes a law regulating the manufacture of dynamite in order to improve safety in dynamite factories. As a result of this law, dynamite factories are no longer any more dangerous than semiconductor factories. Once this happens, the wages in dynamite factories will decline to $20 per hour, the same as in semiconductor factories. Are workers in dynamite factories any better or worse off? Before the law was passed, their wages were $25 per hour, but $5 per hour was a compensating differential for the extra risk they were exposed to. Now their wages are only $20 per hour, but the extra risk has been eliminated. The conclusion seems to be that dynamite workers are no better off as a result of the safety legislation.

This conclusion is only true, though, if the compensating differential actually does compensate workers fully for the additional risk. Nobel laureate George Akerlof of the University of California, Berkeley, and William Dickens of the Brookings Institution have argued that the psychological principle known as *cognitive dissonance* might cause workers to underestimate the true risk of their jobs. According to this principle, people prefer to think of themselves as intelligent and rational and tend to reject evidence that

**Compensating differentials** Higher wages that compensate workers for unpleasant aspects of a job.

seems to contradict this image. Because working in a very hazardous job may seem irrational, workers in such jobs may refuse to believe that the jobs really are hazardous. Akerlof and Dickens present evidence that workers in chemical plants producing benzene and workers in nuclear power plants underestimate the hazards of their jobs. If this is true, the wages of these workers will not be high enough to compensate them fully for the risk they have assumed. So, in this situation, safety legislation may make workers better off.

## Making the Connection | Are U.S. Firms Handicapped by Paying for Their Employees' Health Insurance?

*Did paying for employees' health care contribute to Chrysler's bankruptcy in 2009?*

When choosing among jobs, workers consider all aspects of each job. This includes how hazardous or otherwise unpleasant a job may be. It also includes the total compensation received from a job. To this point, we have assumed that compensation takes the form of wages. But many jobs also pay fringe benefits, such as employer contributions to retirement accounts or employer-provided health insurance.

So, it would be more accurate to describe the intersection of the labor demand and labor supply curves as determining the equilibrium compensation rather than the equilibrium wage. If the demand for, say, electrical engineers increases, the equilibrium compensation will increase. This increase in compensation could be partly an increase in wages and partly an increase in employer contributions to retirement accounts or to health insurance plans.

In many countries, the government either supplies health care directly by operating hospitals and employing doctors, or it pays for most health care expenses even if hospitals are not government owned and doctors are not government employees. By contrast, in the United States about two-thirds of the population is covered by private health insurance, most of which is provided by employers. As a result, at many firms in the United States, a significant portion of the compensation workers receive is in the form of employer payments for health insurance. Does paying for health insurance put U.S. firms at a disadvantage in competing with foreign firms that do not have this expense because their workers receive government-provided health care?

Some policymakers have argued that the bankruptcies of Chrysler and General Motors in 2009 were due, in part, to their making large payments for their workers' health insurance that their foreign competitors did not have to make. Some supporters of President Barack Obama's proposals to expand the government's role in providing health care have also argued that relieving U.S. firms from paying for health care would lower their costs relative to foreign competitors. But if labor markets determine equilibrium compensation, then a reduction in employer contributions for health insurance should lead to an offsetting increase in wages, leaving the total compensation paid by firms unaffected.

The Congressional Budget Office (CBO) undertakes studies of policy issues for Congress. In an overview of proposals for reforming health insurance in the United States, the CBO addressed this question:

> Some observers have asserted that domestic producers that provide health insurance to their workers face higher costs for compensation than competitors based in countries where insurance is not employment based and that fundamental changes to the health insurance system could reduce or eliminate that disadvantage. However, such a cost reduction is unlikely to occur. . . . The equilibrium level of overall compensation in the economy is determined by the supply of and the demand for labor. Fringe benefits (such as health insurance) are just part of that compensation. Consequently, the costs of fringe benefits are borne by workers largely in the form of lower cash wages than they would receive if no such benefits were provided by their employer. Replacing employment-based health care with a government-run system could reduce employers' payments

for their workers' insurance, but the amount that they would have to pay in overall compensation would remain essentially unchanged.

This is another case where basic demand and supply analysis provides important insights into a policy issue.

Source: Congress of the United States, Congressional Budget Office, *Key Issues in Analyzing Major Health Insurance Proposals*, December 2008, p. 167.

**YOUR TURN:** Test your understanding by doing related problem 4.16 on page 554 at the end of this chapter.

# Discrimination

Table 16-2 shows that in the United States, white males on average earn more than other groups. One possible explanation for this is **economic discrimination**, which involves paying a person a lower wage or excluding a person from an occupation on the basis of an irrelevant characteristic such as race or gender.

If employers discriminated by hiring only white males for high-paying jobs or by paying white males higher wages than other groups working the same jobs, white males would have higher earnings, as Table 16-2 shows. However, excluding groups from certain jobs or paying one group more than another has been illegal in the United States since the passage of the Equal Pay Act of 1963 and the Civil Rights Act of 1964. Nevertheless, it is possible that employers are ignoring the law and practicing economic discrimination.

Most economists believe that only a small amount of the gap between the wages of white males and the wages of other groups is due to discrimination. Instead, most of the gap is explained by three main factors:

1. Differences in education
2. Differences in experience
3. Differing preferences for jobs

**Differences in Education** Some of the difference between the incomes of whites and the incomes of blacks can be explained by differences in education. Historically, African Americans have had less schooling than whites. Although the gap has closed significantly over the years, 90 percent of adult non-Hispanic white males in 2008 had graduated from high school, but only 82 percent of adult African-American males had. Thirty-one percent of white males had graduated from college, but only 16 percent of African-American males had. These statistics understate the true gap in education between blacks and whites because many blacks receive a substandard education in inner-city schools. Not surprisingly, studies have shown that differing levels of education can account for a significant part of the gap between the earnings of white and black males.

> **Economic discrimination** Paying a person a lower wage or excluding a person from an occupation on the basis of an irrelevant characteristic such as race or gender.

| GROUP | ANNUAL EARNINGS |
|---|---|
| White males | $50,364 |
| White females | 36,891 |
| Black males | 36,233 |
| Black females | 31,114 |
| Hispanic males | 30,151 |
| Hispanic females | 26,695 |

## TABLE 16-2

**Why Do White Males Earn More Than Other Groups?**

*Note:* The values are median annual earnings for persons who worked full time, year-round in 2007. Persons of Hispanic origin can be of any race.

*Source:* U.S. Bureau of the Census, Table PINC-10, "Current Population Survey," *Annual Social and Economic Supplement*, August 2008.

**Differences in Experience** Women are much more likely than men to leave their jobs for a period of time after having a child. Women with several children will sometimes have several interruptions in their careers. Some women leave the workforce for several years until their children are of school age. As a result, on average, women with children have less workforce experience than do men of the same age. Because workers with greater experience are, on average, more productive, the difference in levels of experience helps to explain some of the difference in earnings between men and women. Providing some support for this explanation is the fact that, on average, married women earn about 25 percent less than married men, but women who have never been married—and whose careers are less likely to have been interrupted—earn only about 9 percent less than men who have never been married.

**Differing Preferences for Jobs** Significant differences exist between the types of jobs held by women and men. As Table 16-3 shows, women are overrepresented in some jobs where average weekly earnings are less than $600 per week, and men are overrepresented in some jobs where weekly earnings are greater than $800 per week.

Although the patterns shown in Table 16-3 could be explained by women being excluded from some occupations, it is likely that they reflect differences in job preferences between men and women. For example, because many women interrupt their careers—at least briefly—when their children are born, they are more likely to take jobs where work experience is less important. Women may also be more likely to take jobs, such as teaching, that allow them to be home in the afternoons when their children return from school.

**TABLE 16-3**

**"Men's Jobs" Often Pay More Than "Women's Jobs"**

| "WOMEN'S JOBS" | | | "MEN'S JOBS" | | |
| --- | --- | --- | --- | --- | --- |
| OCCUPATION | WEEKLY EARNINGS | PERCENTAGE OF WORKERS WHO ARE WOMEN | OCCUPATION | WEEKLY EARNINGS | PERCENTAGE OF WORKERS WHO ARE WOMEN |
| Preschool and kindergarten teachers | $567 | 97% | Electricians | $805 | 2% |
| Dental assistants | 508 | 92 | Aircraft mechanics | 889 | 2 |
| Child care workers | 368 | 92 | Aircraft pilots | 1,358 | 4 |
| Receptionists | 482 | 92 | Fire fighters | 901 | 5 |
| Teacher assistants | 410 | 92 | Engineering managers | 1,713 | 8 |
| Hairdressers | 425 | 90 | Aerospace engineers | 1,557 | 10 |
| Health care support occupations | 454 | 88 | Civil engineers | 1,337 | 11 |
| Maids and housekeeping cleaners | 366 | 84 | Computer software engineers | 1,455 | 20 |
| Cashiers | 356 | 74 | Chief executives | 1,882 | 26 |

*Note:* Earnings are for men and women in the occupation and are "median usual weekly earnings of full-time wage and salary workers."
*Source:* U.S. Department of Labor, Bureau of Labor Statistics, *Highlights of Women's Earnings in 2007,* Report 1008, Table 2, October 2008.

**The Difficulty of Measuring Discrimination** When two people are paid different wages, discrimination may be the explanation. But differences in productivity or preferences may also be an explanation. Labor economists have attempted to measure what part of differences in wages between blacks and whites and between men and women is due to discrimination and what part is due to other factors. Unfortunately, it is difficult to precisely measure differences in productivity or in worker preferences. As a result, we can't know exactly the extent of economic discrimination in the United States today. Most economists do believe, however, that most of the differences in wages between different groups are due to factors other than discrimination.

**Does It Pay to Discriminate?** Many economists argue that economic discrimination is no longer a major factor in labor markets in the United States. One reason is that *employers who discriminate pay an economic penalty.* To see why this is true, let's consider a simplified example. Suppose that men and women are equally qualified to be airline pilots and that, initially, airlines do not discriminate. In Figure 16-8, we divide the airlines into two groups: "A" airlines and "B" airlines. If neither group of airlines discriminates, we would expect them to pay an equal wage of $1,100 per week to both men and women pilots. Now suppose that "A" airlines decide to discriminate and to fire all their women pilots. This action will reduce the supply of pilots to these airlines and, as shown in panel (a), that will force up the wage from $1,100 to $1,300. At the same time, as women fired from the jobs with "A" airlines apply for jobs with "B" airlines, the supply of pilots to "B" airlines will increase, and the equilibrium wage will fall from $1,100 to $900. All the women pilots will end up being employed at the nondiscriminating airlines and be paid a lower wage than the men who are employed by the discriminating airlines.

But this situation cannot persist for two reasons. First, male pilots employed by "B" airlines will also receive the lower wage. This lower wage gives them an incentive to quit their jobs at "B" airlines and apply at "A" airlines, which will shift the labor supply curve for "B" airlines to the left and the labor supply curve for "A" airlines to the right. Second, "A" airlines are paying $1,300 per week to hire pilots who are no more productive than the pilots being paid $900 per week by "B" airlines. As a result,

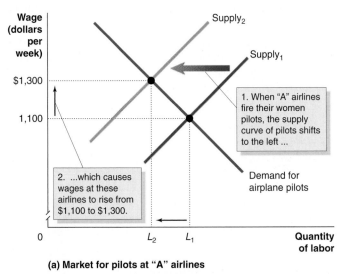

**(a) Market for pilots at "A" airlines**

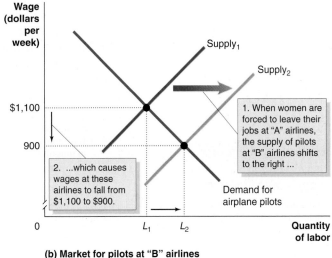

**(b) Market for pilots at "B" airlines**

## Figure 16-8 Discrimination and Wages

In this hypothetical example, we assume that initially neither "A" airlines nor "B" airlines discriminate. As a result, men and women pilots receive the same wage of $1,100 per week at both groups of airlines. We then assume that "A" airlines discriminate by firing all their women pilots. Panel (a) shows that this reduces the supply of pilots to "A" airlines and raises the wage paid by these airlines from $1,100 to $1,300.

Panel (b) shows that this increases the supply of pilots to "B" airlines and lowers the wage paid by these airlines from $1,100 to $900. All the women pilots will end up being employed at the nondiscriminating airlines and will be paid a lower wage than the men who are employed by the discriminating airlines.

"B" airlines will have lower costs and will be able to charge lower prices. Eventually, "A" airlines will lose their customers to "B" airlines and be driven out of business. The market will have imposed an economic penalty on the discriminating airlines. So, discrimination will not persist, and the wages of men and women pilots will become equal.

Can we conclude from this analysis that competition in markets will eliminate all economic discrimination? Unfortunately, this optimistic conclusion is not completely accurate. We know that until the Civil Rights Act of 1964 was passed, many firms in the United States refused to hire blacks. Even though this practice had persisted for decades, nondiscriminating competitors did not drive these firms out of business. Why not? There were three important factors:

1. *Worker discrimination.*   In many cases, white workers refused to work alongside black workers. As a result, some industries—such as the important cotton textile industry in the South—were all white. Because of discrimination by white workers, an entrepreneur who wanted to use low-cost black labor might need to hire an all-black workforce. Some entrepreneurs tried this, but because blacks had been excluded from these industries, they often lacked the skills and experience to form an effective workforce.

2. *Customer discrimination.*   Some white consumers were unwilling to buy from companies in certain industries if they employed black workers. This was not a significant barrier in manufacturing industries, where customers would not know the race of the workers producing the good. It was, however, a problem for firms in industries in which workers came into direct contact with the public.

3. *Negative feedback loops.*   Our analysis in Figure 16-8 assumed that men and women pilots were equally qualified. However, if discrimination makes it difficult for a member of a group to find employment in a particular occupation, his or her incentive to be trained to enter that occupation is reduced. Consider the legal profession as an example. In 1952, future Supreme Court Justice Sandra Day O'Connor graduated third in her class at Stanford University Law School and was an editor of the *Stanford Law Review,* but for some time she was unable to get a job as a lawyer because in those years, many law firms would not hire women. Facing such bleak job prospects, it's not surprising that relatively few women entered law school. As a result, a law firm that did not discriminate would have been unable to act like the nondiscriminating airlines in our example by hiring women lawyers at a lower salary and using this cost advantage to drive discriminating law firms out of business. In this situation, an unfortunate feedback loop was in place: Few women prepared to become lawyers because many law firms discriminated against

## Figure 16-9

### The United States is Less Unionized Than Most Other High-Income Countries

The percentage of the labor force belonging to unions is lower in the United States than in most other high-income countries.
Source: Organization for Economic Cooperation and Development.

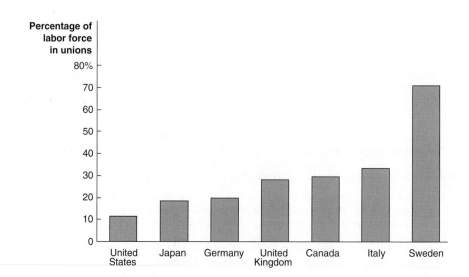

| | AVERAGE WEEKLY EARNINGS | TABLE 16-4 |
|---|---|---|
| UNION WORKERS | $886 | **Union Workers Earn More Than Nonunion Workers** |
| NONUNION WORKERS | 691 | |

*Note:* "Union workers" includes union members as well as workers who are represented by unions but who are not members of them.
Source: U.S. Bureau of Labor Statistics, *Union Members Summary*, January 28, 2009.

women, and nondiscriminating law firms were unable to drive discriminating law firms out of business because there were too few women lawyers available.

Most economists agree that the market imposes an economic penalty on firms that discriminate, but because of the factors just discussed, it may take the market a very long time to eliminate discrimination entirely. The passage of the Civil Rights Act of 1964, which outlawed hiring discrimination on the basis of race and sex, greatly sped up the process of reducing economic discrimination in the United States.

## Labor Unions

Workers' wages can differ depending on whether the workers are members of labor unions. **Labor unions** are organizations of employees that have the legal right to bargain with employers about wages and working conditions. If a union is unable to reach an agreement with a company, it has the legal right to call a *strike*, which means its members refuse to work until a satisfactory agreement has been reached. As Figure 16-9 shows, a smaller fraction of the U.S. labor force is unionized than in most other high-income countries.

As Table 16-4 shows, in the United States, workers in unions receive higher wages than workers who are not in unions. Do union members earn more than nonunion members because they are in unions? The answer might seem to be "yes," but many union workers are in industries, such as automobile manufacturing, in which their marginal revenue products are high, so their wages would be high even if they were not unionized. Economists who have attempted to estimate statistically the impact of unionization on wages have concluded that being in a union increases a worker's wages about 10 percent, holding constant other factors, such as the industry the worker is in. A related question is whether unions raise the total amount of wages received by all workers, whether unionized or not. Because the share of national income received by workers has remained roughly constant over many years, most economists do not believe that unions have raised the total amount of wages received by workers.

**Labor union** An organization of employees that has the legal right to bargain with employers about wages and working conditions.

## Personnel Economics

Traditionally, labor economists have focused on issues such as the effects of labor unions on wages or the determinants of changes in average wages over time. They have spent less time analyzing *human resources issues*, which address how firms hire, train, and promote workers and set their wages and benefits. In recent years, some labor economists, including Edward Lazear of Stanford University and William Neilson of Texas A&M University, have begun exploring the application of economic analysis to human resources issues. This new focus has become known as **personnel economics**.

Personnel economics analyzes the link between differences among jobs and differences in the way workers are paid. Jobs have different skill requirements, require more or less interaction with other workers, have to be performed in more or less unpleasant environments, and so on. Firms need to design compensation policies that take into

**16.5 LEARNING** OBJECTIVE

Discuss the role personnel economics can play in helping firms deal with human resources issues.

**Personnel economics** The application of economic analysis to human resources issues.

## Figure 16-10

**Paying Car Salespeople by Salary or by Commission**

This figure compares the compensation a car salesperson receives if she is on a straight salary of $800 per week or if she receives a commission of $200 for each car she sells. With a straight salary, she receives $800 per week, no matter how many cars she sells. This outcome is shown by the horizontal line in the figure. If she receives a commission of $200 per car, her compensation will increase with every car she sells. This outcome is shown by the upward-sloping line. If she sells fewer than 4 cars per week, she would be better off with the $800 salary. If she sells more than 4 cars per week, she would be better off with the $200-per-car commission.

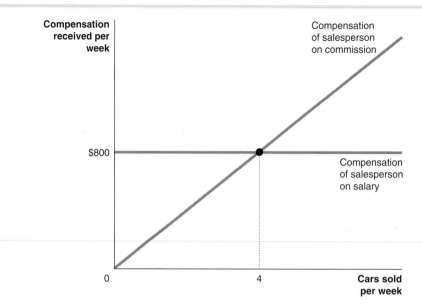

account these differences. Personnel economics also analyzes policies related to other human resources issues, such as promotions, training, and pensions. In this brief overview, we look only at compensation policies.

### Should Workers' Pay Depend on How Much They Work or on How Much They Produce?

One issue personnel economics addresses is when workers should receive *straight-time pay*—a certain wage per hour or salary per week or month—and when they should receive *commission* or *piece-rate pay*—a wage based on how much output they produce.

Suppose, for example, that Anne owns a car dealership and is trying to decide whether to pay her salespeople a salary of $800 per week or a commission of $200 on each car they sell. Figure 16-10 compares the compensation a salesperson would receive under the two systems, according to the number of cars the salesperson sells.

With a straight salary, the salesperson receives $800 per week, no matter how many cars she sells. This outcome is shown by the horizontal line in Figure 16-10. If she receives a commission of $200 per car, her compensation will increase with every car she sells. This outcome is shown by the upward-sloping line. A salesperson who sells fewer than 4 cars per week would earn more by receiving a straight salary of $800 per week. A salesperson who sells more than 4 cars per week would be better off receiving the $200-per-car commission. We can identify two advantages Anne would receive from paying her salespeople commissions rather than salaries: She would attract and retain the most productive employees, and she would provide an incentive to her employees to sell more cars.

Suppose that other car dealerships are all paying salaries of $800 per week. If Anne pays her employees on commission, any of her employees who are unable to sell at least 4 cars per week can improve their pay by going to work for one of her competitors. And any salespeople at Anne's competitors who can sell more than 4 cars per week can raise their pay by quitting and coming to work for Anne. Over time, Anne will find her least productive employees leaving, while she is able to hire new employees who are more productive.

Paying a commission also increases the incentive Anne's salespeople have to sell more cars. If Anne paid a salary, her employees would receive the same amount no matter how few cars they sold. An employee on salary might decide on a particularly hot or cold day that it was less trouble to stay inside the building than to go out on the car lot to greet potential customers. An employee on commission would know that the additional effort expended on selling more cars would be rewarded with additional compensation.

## Making the Connection

### Raising Pay, Productivity, and Profits at Safelite AutoGlass

Safelite Group, headquartered in Columbus, Ohio, is the parent company of Safelite AutoGlass, the nation's largest installer of auto glass, with 600 repair shops. In the mid-1990s, Safelite shifted from paying its glass installers hourly wages to paying them on the basis of how many windows they installed. Safelite already had in place a computer system that allowed it to easily track how many windows each worker installed per day. To make sure quality did not suffer, Safelite added a rule that if a workmanship-related defect occurred with an installed windshield, the worker would have to install a new windshield and would not be paid for the additional work.

Edward Lazear analyzed data provided by the firm and discovered that under the new piece-rate system, the number of windows installed per worker jumped 44 percent. Lazear estimates that half of this increase was due to increased productivity from workers who continued with the company and half was due to new hires being more productive than the workers they replaced who had left the company. Worker pay rose on average by about 9.9 percent. Ninety-two percent of workers experienced a pay increase, and one-quarter received an increase of at least 28 percent. Safelite's profits also increased as the cost to the company per window installed fell from $44.43 under the hourly wage system to $35.24 under the piece-rate system.

Sociologists sometimes question whether worker productivity can be increased through the use of monetary incentives. The experience of Safelite AutoGlass provides a clear example of workers reacting favorably to the opportunity to increase output in exchange for higher compensation.

*A piece-rate system at Safelite AutoGlass led to increased worker wages and firm profits.*

Source: Edward P. Lazear, "Performance Pay and Productivity," *American Economic Review*, Vol. 90, No. 5, December 2000, pp. 1346–1361.

**YOUR TURN:** Test your understanding by doing related problem 5.7 on page 555 at the end of this chapter.

## Other Considerations in Setting Compensation Systems

The discussion so far indicates that companies will find it more profitable to use a commission or piece-rate system of compensation rather than a salary system. In fact, many firms continue to pay their workers salaries, which means they are paying their workers on the basis of how long they work rather than on the basis of how much they produce. Firms may choose a salary system for several good reasons:

- *Difficulty measuring output.* Often it is difficult to attribute output to any particular worker. For example, projects carried out by an engineering firm may involve teams of workers whose individual contributions are difficult to distinguish. On assembly lines, such as those used in the automobile industry, the amount produced by each worker is determined by the speed of the line, which is set by managers rather than by workers. Managers at many firms perform such a wide variety of tasks that measuring their output would be costly, if it could be done at all.

- *Concerns about quality.* If workers are paid on the basis of the number of units produced, they may become less concerned about quality. An office assistant who is paid on the basis of the quantity of letters typed may become careless about how many typos the letters contain. In some cases, there are ways around this problem; for example, the assistant may be required to correct the mistakes on his or her own time, without pay.

- *Worker dislike of risk.* Piece-rate or commission systems of compensation increase the risk to workers because sometimes output declines for reasons not connected to the worker's effort. For example, if there is a very snowy winter, few customers may show up at Anne's auto dealership. Through no fault of their own, her salespeople may have great difficulty selling any cars. If they are paid a salary, their income will not be affected, but if they are on commission, their incomes may drop to low levels. The flip side of this is that by paying salaries, Anne assumes a greater risk. During a snowy winter, her payroll expenses will remain high even though her sales are low. With a commission system of compensation, her payroll expenses will decline along with her sales. But owners of firms are typically better able to bear risk than are workers. As a result, some firms may find that workers who would earn more under a commission system will prefer to receive a salary to reduce their risk. In these situations, paying a lower salary may reduce the firm's payroll expenses compared with what they would have been under a commission or piece-rate system.

Personnel economics is a relatively new field, but it holds great potential for helping firms deal more efficiently with human resources issues.

# The Markets for Capital and Natural Resources

The approach we have used to analyze the market for labor can also be used to analyze the markets for other factors of production. We have seen that the demand for labor is determined by the marginal revenue product of labor because the value to a firm from hiring another worker equals the increase in the firm's revenue from selling the additional output it can produce by hiring the worker. The demand for capital and natural resources is determined in a similar way.

## The Market for Capital

Physical capital includes machines, equipment, and buildings. Firms sometimes buy capital, but we will focus on situations in which firms rent capital. A chocolate manufacturer renting a warehouse and an airline leasing a plane are examples of firms renting capital. Like the demand for labor, the demand for capital is a derived demand. When a firm is considering increasing its capital by, for example, employing another machine, the value it receives equals the increase in the firm's revenue from selling the additional output it can produce by employing the machine. The *marginal revenue product of capital* is the change in the firm's revenue as a result of employing one more unit of capital, such as a machine. We have seen that the marginal revenue product of labor curve is the demand curve for labor. Similarly, the marginal revenue product of capital curve is the demand curve for capital.

Firms producing capital goods face increasing marginal costs, so the supply curve of capital goods is upward sloping, as are the supply curves for other goods and services. Figure 16-11 shows equilibrium in the market for capital. In equilibrium, suppliers of capital receive a rental price equal to the marginal revenue product of capital, just as suppliers of labor receive a wage equal to the marginal revenue product of labor.

## The Market for Natural Resources

The market for natural resources can be analyzed in the same way as the markets for labor and capital. When a firm is considering employing more natural resources, the value it receives equals the increase in the firm's revenue from selling the additional output it can produce by buying the natural resources. So, the demand for natural resources is also a derived demand. The *marginal revenue product of natural resources* is the change in the firm's revenue as a result of employing one more unit of natural resources, such as a barrel of oil. The marginal revenue product of natural resources curve is also the demand curve for natural resources.

Although the total quantity of most natural resources is ultimately fixed—as the humorist Will Rogers once remarked, "Buy land. They ain't making any more of it"—in

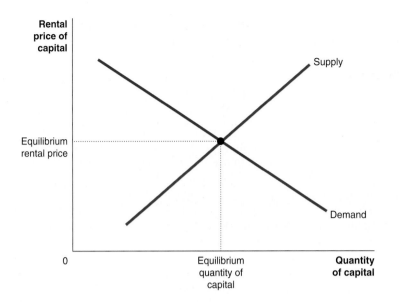

## Figure 16-11

**Equilibrium in the Market for Capital**

The rental price of capital is determined by equilibrium in the market for capital. In equilibrium, the rental price of capital is equal to the marginal revenue product of capital.

many cases, the quantity supplied still responds to the price. For example, although the total quantity of oil deposits in the world is fixed, an increase in the price of oil will result in an increase in the quantity of oil supplied during a particular period. The result, as shown in panel (a) of Figure 16-12, is an upward-sloping supply curve. In some cases, however, the quantity of a natural resource that will be supplied is fixed and will not change as the price changes. The land available at a busy intersection is fixed, for example. In panel (b) of Figure 16-12, we illustrate this situation with a supply curve that is a vertical line, or perfectly inelastic. The price received by a factor of production that is in fixed supply is called an **economic rent** (or a **pure rent**) because, in this case, the price of the factor is determined only by demand. For example, if a new highway diverts much

**Economic rent** (or **pure rent**) The price of a factor of production that is in fixed supply.

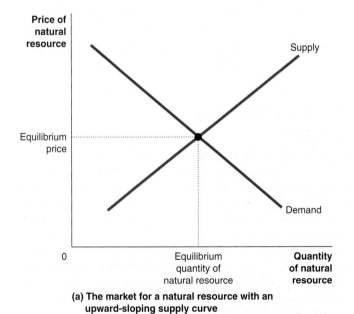

**(a) The market for a natural resource with an upward-sloping supply curve**

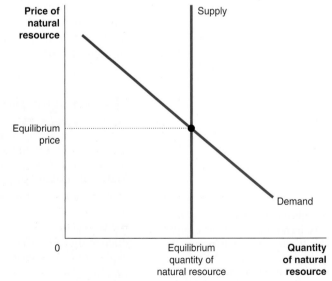

**(b) The market for a natural resource with a vertical supply curve**

## Figure 16-12 Equilibrium in the Market for Natural Resources

In panel (a), the supply curve of a natural resource is upward sloping. The price of the natural resource is determined by the interaction of demand and supply. In panel (b), the supply curve of the natural resource is a vertical line, indicating that the

quantity supplied does not respond to changes in price. In this case, the price of the natural resource is determined only by demand. The price of a factor of production with a vertical supply curve is called an *economic rent*, or a *pure rent*.

of the traffic from a previously busy intersection, the demand for the land will decline, and the price of the land will fall, but the quantity of the land will not change.

## Monopsony

**Monopsony** The sole buyer of a factor of production.

In Chapter 14, we analyzed the case of *monopoly*, where a firm is the sole *seller* of a good or service. What happens if a firm is the sole *buyer* of a factor of production? This case, which is known as **monopsony**, is comparatively rare. An example is a firm in an isolated town—perhaps a lumber mill in a small town in Washington or Oregon—that is the sole employer of labor in that location. In the nineteenth and early twentieth centuries, some coal mining firms were the sole employers in certain small towns in West Virginia, and some pineapple plantations were the sole employers on certain small islands in Hawaii. In these cases, not only would the firm own the mill, mine, or plantation, but it would also own the stores and other businesses in the town. Workers would have the choice of working for the sole employer in the town or moving to another town.

We know that a firm with a monopoly in an output market takes advantage of its market power to reduce the quantity supplied to force up the market price and increase its profits. A firm that has a monopsony in a factor market would employ a similar strategy: It would restrict the quantity of the factor demanded to force down the price of the factor and increase profits. A firm with a monopsony in a labor market will hire fewer workers and pay lower wages than would be the case in a competitive market. Because fewer workers are hired than would be hired in a competitive market, monopsony results in a deadweight loss. Monopoly and monopsony have similar effects on the economy: In both cases, a firm's market power results in a lower equilibrium quantity, a deadweight loss, and a reduction in economic efficiency compared with a competitive market.

In some cases, monopsony in labor markets is offset by worker membership in a labor union. A notable example of this is professional sports. For instance, Major League Baseball effectively has a monopsony on employing professional baseball players. (Although independent baseball leagues exist, none of the best players play for these teams, and the teams pay salaries that are a small fraction of those paid by Major League Baseball teams.) The monopsony power of the owners of Major League Baseball teams is offset by the power of the Major League Baseball Players Association, the union that represents baseball players. Bargaining between the representatives of Major League Baseball and the players' union has resulted in baseball players being paid something close to what they would be receiving in a competitive market.

## The Marginal Productivity Theory of Income Distribution

**Marginal productivity theory of income distribution** The theory that the distribution of income is determined by the marginal productivity of the factors of production that individuals own.

We have seen that in equilibrium, each factor of production receives a price equal to its marginal revenue product. We can use this fact to explain the distribution of income. Marginal revenue product represents the value of a factor's marginal contribution to producing goods and services. Therefore, individuals will receive income equal to the marginal contributions to production from the factors of production they own, including their labor. The more factors of production an individual owns and the more productive those factors are, the higher the individual's income will be. This approach to explaining the distribution of income is called the **marginal productivity theory of income distribution**. The marginal productivity theory of income distribution was developed by John Bates Clark, who taught at Columbia University in the late nineteenth and early twentieth centuries.

▶ Continued from page 521

## Economics in YOUR LIFE!

At the beginning of the chapter, we asked you to imagine that you work at a local sandwich shop and that you plan to ask your manager for a raise. One way to show the manager your worth is to demonstrate how many dollars your work earns for the sandwich shop: your marginal revenue product. You could certainly suggest that as you have become better at your job and have gained new skills, you have become a more productive employee; but, more importantly, you could say that your productivity results in increased revenue for the sandwich shop. By showing how your employment contributes to higher revenue and profit, you may be able to convince your manager to give you a raise.

# Conclusion

In this chapter, we used the demand and supply model from Chapter 3 to explain why wages differ among workers. The demand for workers depends on their productivity and on the price that firms receive for the output the workers produce. The supply of workers to an occupation depends on the wages and working conditions offered by employers and on the skills required. The demand and supply for labor can also help us analyze such issues as economic discrimination and the impact of labor unions.

Read *An Inside Look* on the next page to see how demand and supply determine the salaries of college basketball coaches.

## >> Basketball Coaches' Salaries: A March to Madness?

*WALL STREET JOURNAL*

## College Basketball's Bargains and Busts

In college basketball—and in life—the most successful people are supposed to make the most money.

It doesn't always work out that way.

(a) When University of Connecticut head basketball coach Jim Calhoun scoffed recently at a complaint about his $1.6 million guaranteed salary . . . he defended it fiercely, setting off a firestorm about a profession where a growing number of coaches are paid lavishly by taxpayer-funded schools.

At least Mr. Calhoun has two national championships, a consistent record of success and brings immeasurable exposure to the school—all of which arguably makes him worth the money. But . . . plenty of schools are getting far less for their money. "It's all about leverage over the athletic department," said Craig Fenech, a longtime agent who negotiated John Calipari's first deal with the University of Memphis—which pays him $2.5 million . . .

With more than 10% of the 343 NCAA Division 1-A basketball coaches collecting guaranteed annual compensation of more than $1 million, athletic directors are on the defensive, trying to justify paying coaches to oversee a small group of students, only about half of whom may graduate. "Do I wish these salaries were lower? Sure," said William Martin, athletic director at the University of Michigan, who gave head basketball coach John Beilein a guaranteed salary of $1.3 million two years ago. "But I'm a free-market guy. These salaries are set on a competitive basis."

The measuring stick for college basketball is the Ratings Percentage Index, or RPI, a statistic that measures a team's winning percentage against the difficulty of its schedule. . . . A 50 can usually crack the top 100, the boundary for mediocrity. The country's current top team, Pittsburgh, has an RPI of 67.7. Since universities don't pay seven figures for "OK," each school can grade their coach's performance by how much they pay in salary for every point above 50.

Among coaches who have verifiable annual salaries above $1 million and at least four years of tenure at their current schools, a *Wall Street Journal* analysis shows Georgia Tech's Paul Hewitt provided the least value. Mr. Hewitt's team caught fire during the 2004 NCAA tournament, making it all the way to the championship game. . . . That June, Georgia Tech rewarded Mr. Hewitt with a new contract that now pays him $1.3 million. . . .

(b) With an average RPI the past three years of 54.5, Georgia Tech is paying Mr. Hewitt $288,888 for each point beyond the threshold of mediocrity. By comparison, Clemson University pays Oliver Purnell $1 million, but just $97,087 for each of his 10.3 points beyond 50-point RPI threshold. Mr. Calhoun, who has his first outstanding team since 2005–06, now costs the University of Connecticut $166,667 for each point over 50.

. . . Jamie Dixon's program in Pittsburgh turned a $5 million profit, while at Syracuse Jim Boeheim's team netted $9.1 million.

. . . Mr. Hewitt is a highly respected figure who is the president of the Black Coaches Association. . . . The school's basketball program netted $6.2 million last season. . . .

(c) But no fan or booster wants to hear excuses and Mr. Radakovich has been fending off plenty of complaints about Mr. Hewitt's performance. "As long as people are communicating there is a passion for excellence," Mr. Radakovich said. "If that stops, then we have a far worse disease on our hands called apathy."

Athletic directors say the current climate puts them in a bind. Poor performances lead to dropping attendance and the loss of vital sponsorships that usually help support the rest of the athletic department. "The educator part of me says it's not fair just to judge a coach just because he's not winning," said Joel Maturi, athletic director at the University of Minnesota, who is paying Tubby Smith $2.15 million this season. "But the business side says, 'Win.'"

Source: Matthew Futterman, "College Basketball's Bargains and Busts," *Wall Street Journal*, March 13, 2009, p. W5.

## Key Points in the Article

The article describes the reasons 10 percent of the 343 NCAA Division 1-A basketball coaches are paid salaries that exceed $1 million. The high salaries have led to complaints because many Division 1-A colleges are funded by taxpayers, and many basketball players do not graduate from their schools. The high salaries are paid because many basketball programs generate large revenues and profits. But poor performances by teams can lead to low attendance and the loss of sponsorships that fund the schools' athletic departments.

## Analyzing the News

**a** Successful college basketball coaches such as Jim Calhoun and John Calipari receive high salaries because their marginal products are high, and a fixed number of schools compete for the best coaches. The labor supply curve in the figure is vertical at a quantity of 343, the number of Division 1-A college basketball programs. You can see that the demand curve $D_1$ intersects the labor supply curve at $W_1$, the equilibrium wage (or, more accurately, salary). The labor demand curve is based

on the marginal revenue product of labor ($P \times MP_L$). As William Martin, the athletic director at the University of Michigan, points out, "These salaries are set on a competitive basis."

**b** Increases in the demand for coaches occur when there are increases in the revenue generated by schools' basketball programs. One way to measure the productivity of basketball coaches is by the rating of their teams on the Ratings Percentage Index (RPI), a statistic that measures winning percentage relative to difficulty of schedule. Even coaches with salaries of $1 million and above can seem underpaid compared to other coaches. For example, Oliver Purnell of Clemson University received a $1 million salary; this equals $97,087 for each point his 2008–09 team's RPI exceeded 50, which is a benchmark figure that typically will earn a ranking among the top 100 Division 1-A teams. In contrast, Jim Calhoun of the University of Connecticut received a salary that equals $166,667 for each point that his team exceeded the RPI benchmark. If Purnell's teams continue to be successful, the demand for his coaching services will increase as other schools bid for his services. As the figure shows, as the

demand for coaches increases to $D_2$, the equilibrium salary increases to $W_2$. Schools that bid up salaries know that winning programs result in greater revenue.

**c** Not all 343 basketball programs can be successful at the same time. Athletic contests are zero-sum games with an equal number of wins and losses. Losing games can result in lower attendance, sponsorships, and revenues not only for basketball but for entire athletic programs. Ultimately, coaches are evaluated in the market for labor by their ability to win games.

## Thinking Critically

1. Why do Division 1-A college basketball coaches earn higher salaries than most of their faculty colleagues?
2. Suppose that 100 non-Division 1-A colleges became Division 1-A colleges over a three-year period, raising the total number of Division 1-A college basketball programs to 434. How would this affect the (a) demand, (b) supply, and (c) equilibrium salary for basketball coaches?

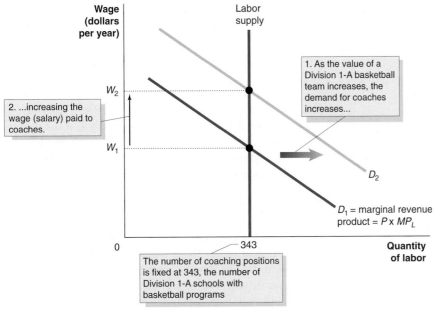

The market for NCAA Division 1-A college basketball coaches.

## Key Terms

Compensating differentials, p. 535

Derived demand, p. 522

Economic discrimination, p. 537

Economic rent (or pure rent), p. 545

Factors of production, p. 522

Human capital, p. 526

Labor union, p. 541

Marginal product of labor, p. 522

Marginal productivity theory of income distribution, p. 546

Marginal revenue product of labor (MRP), p. 523

Monopsony, p. 546

Personnel economics, p. 541

---

 **16.1** **The Demand for Labor, pages 522–526**

LEARNING OBJECTIVE: Explain how firms choose the profit-maximizing quantity of labor to employ.

## Summary

The demand for labor is a **derived demand** because it depends on the demand consumers have for goods and services. The additional output produced by a firm as a result of hiring another worker is called the **marginal product of labor**. The amount by which the firm's revenue will increase as a result of hiring one more worker is called the **marginal revenue product of labor** (**MRP**). A firm's marginal revenue product of labor curve is its demand curve for labor. Firms maximize profit by hiring workers up to the point where the wage is equal to the marginal revenue product of labor. The market demand curve for labor is determined by adding up the quantity of labor demanded by each firm at each wage, holding constant all other variables that might affect the willingness of firms to hire workers. The most important variables that shift the labor demand curve are changes in human capital, technology, the price of the product, the quantity of other inputs, and the number of firms in the market. **Human capital** is the accumulated training and skills that workers possess.

 Visit **www.myeconlab.com** to complete these exercises online and get instant feedback.

## Review Questions

1.1 What is the difference between the marginal product of labor and the marginal revenue product of labor?

1.2 Why is the demand curve for labor downward sloping?

1.3 What are the five most important variables that cause the market demand curve for labor to shift?

## Problems and Applications

1.4 Frank Gunter owns an apple orchard. He employs 87 apple pickers and pays them each $8 per hour to pick apples, which he sells for $1.60 per box. If Frank is maximizing profits, what is the marginal revenue product of the last worker he hired? What is that worker's marginal product?

1.5 **(Related to *Solved Problem 16-1* on page 524)** Replace the dashes in the following table for Terrell's Televisions.

| NUMBER OF WORKERS (L) | OUTPUT OF TELEVISIONS PER WEEK (Q) | MARGINAL PRODUCT OF LABOR (TELEVISION SETS PER WEEK) (MP) | PRODUCT PRICE (P) | MARGINAL REVENUE PRODUCT OF LABOR (DOLLARS PER WEEK) | WAGE (DOLLARS PER WEEK) (W) | ADDITIONAL PROFIT FROM HIRING ONE MORE WORKER (DOLLARS PER WEEK) |
|---|---|---|---|---|---|---|
| 0 | 0 | — | $300 | — | $1,800 | — |
| 1 | 8 | — | 300 | — | 1,800 | — |
| 2 | 15 | — | 300 | — | 1,800 | — |
| 3 | 21 | — | 300 | — | 1,800 | — |
| 4 | 26 | — | 300 | — | 1,800 | — |
| 5 | 30 | — | 300 | — | 1,800 | — |
| 6 | 33 | — | 300 | — | 1,800 | — |

a. From the information in the table, can you determine whether this firm is a price taker or a price maker? Briefly explain.

b. Use the information in the table to draw a graph like Figure 16-1 on page 523 that shows the demand for labor by this firm. Be sure to indicate the profit-maximizing quantity of labor on your graph.

1.6 State whether each of the following events will result in a movement along the market demand curve for labor in electronics factories in Japan or whether it will cause the market demand curve for labor to shift. If the demand curve shifts, indicate whether it will shift to the left or to the right and draw a graph to illustrate the shift.

a. The wage rate declines.

b. The price of televisions declines.

c. Several firms exit the television market in Japan.

d. Japanese high schools introduce new vocational courses in assembling electronic products.

1.7 Baseball writer Rany Jazayerli had this assessment of Kansas City Royal's outfielder Jose Guillen: "Guillen has negative value the way his contract stands." How could a baseball player's contract cause him to have negative value to a baseball team?

Source: Rany Jazayerli, "Radical Situations Call for Radical Solutions," ranyontheroyals.com, June 6, 2009.

>> **End Learning Objective 16.1**

**16.2** **The Supply of Labor, pages 526–528**
LEARNING OBJECTIVE: Explain how people choose the quantity of labor to supply.

## Summary

As the wage increases, the opportunity cost of leisure increases, causing individuals to supply a greater quantity of labor. Normally, the labor supply curve is upward sloping, but it is possible that at very high wage levels, the supply curve might be backward bending. This outcome occurs when someone with a high income is willing to accept a somewhat lower income in exchange for more leisure. The market labor supply curve is determined by adding up the quantity of labor supplied by each worker at each wage, holding constant all other variables that might affect the willingness of workers to supply labor. The most important variables that shift the labor supply curve are increases in population, changing demographics, and changing alternatives.

 Visit **www.myeconlab.com** to complete these exercises online and get instant feedback.

## Review Questions

2.1 How can we measure the opportunity cost of leisure? Why is the supply curve of labor usually upward sloping?

2.2 What are the three most important variables that cause the market supply curve of labor to shift?

## Problems and Applications

2.3 Daniel was earning $65 per hour and working 45 hours per week. Then Daniel's wage rose to $75 per hour, and as a result, he now works 40 hours per week. What can we conclude from this information about the income effect and the substitution effect of a wage change for Daniel?

2.4 A columnist writing in the *Wall Street Journal* during the recession of 2008–2009 made the following observation about the "price of time":

> The recession is doing funny things with the price of time.
>
> Technically it's risen in value. Although hardly anyone seems to have noticed, the government's latest figures show that hourly wages in real terms—which had pretty much stagnated for decades—have

just jumped to their highest levels since the 1970s. You can thank cheaper prices in the stores, as well as higher pay.

What is the "price of time"? Is the columnist correct that when real hourly wages rise, the price of time increases? Briefly explain.

Source: Brett Arends, "Spend Some Time, Save Some Money," *Wall Street Journal*, May 19, 2009.

2.5 Most labor economists believe that many adult males are on the vertical section of their labor supply curves. Explain when and why someone's supply of labor curve would be vertical, using the concepts of income and substitution effects.

Source: Robert Whaples, "Is There Consensus among American Labor Economists? Survey Results on Forty Propositions," *Journal of Labor Research*, Vol. 17, No. 4, Fall 1996.

2.6 Suppose that a large oil field is discovered in Michigan. By imposing a tax on the oil, the state government is able to eliminate the state income tax on wages. What is likely to be the effect on the labor supply curve in Michigan?

2.7 State whether each of the following events will result in a movement along the market supply curve of agricultural labor in the United States or whether it will cause the market supply curve of labor to shift. If the supply curve shifts, indicate whether it will shift to the left or to the right and draw a graph to illustrate the shift.
   a. The agricultural wage rate declines.
   b. Wages outside of agriculture increase.
   c. The law is changed to allow for unlimited immigration into the United States.

2.8 **(Related to Solved Problem 16-2 on page 529)** Describe how each of the following factors will affect the labor supply curve.
   a. An increase in population
   b. An increase in the wage rate
   c. A significant portion of the labor force reaches retirement age
   d. The government raises the minimum wage
   e. An increasing number of youth reach working age
   f. Local businesses expand their productive capacity by building larger factories
   g. The government makes it easier to collect unemployment compensation

**>> End Learning Objective 16.2**

## 16.3 Equilibrium in the Labor Market, pages 530–532

LEARNING OBJECTIVE: Explain how equilibrium wages are determined in labor markets.

## Summary

The intersection between labor supply and labor demand determines the equilibrium wage and the equilibrium level of employment. If labor supply is unchanged, an increase in labor demand will increase both the equilibrium wage and the number of workers employed. If labor demand is unchanged, an increase in labor supply will lower the equilibrium wage and increase the number of workers employed.

 Visit **www.myeconlab.com** to complete these exercises online and get instant feedback.

## Review Questions

**3.1** If the labor demand curve shifts to the left and the labor supply curve remains unchanged, what will happen to the equilibrium wage and the equilibrium level of employment? Illustrate your answer with a graph.

**3.2** If the labor supply curve shifts to the left and the labor demand curve remains unchanged, what will happen to the equilibrium wage and the equilibrium level of employment? Illustrate your answer with a graph.

## Problems and Applications

**3.3** (Related to the *Making the Connection* on page 531) Over time, the gap between the wages of workers with a college degree and the wages of workers without a college degree has been increasing. Shouldn't this gap have increased the incentive for workers to earn a college degree, thereby increasing

the supply of college-educated workers and reducing the size of the gap?

**3.4** Reread the discussion on page 531 of changes in the salaries of film animators. Use a graph to illustrate this situation. Make sure your graph has labor demand and supply curves for 1994, 1999, and 2002 and that the equilibrium point for each year is clearly indicated.

**3.5** Sean Astin, who played Sam in the *Lord of the Rings* movies, wrote the following about an earlier film he had appeared in: "Now I was in a movie I didn't respect, making obscene amounts of money (five times what a teacher makes, and teachers do infinitely more important work). . . ." Are salaries determined by the importance of the work being done? If not, what are they determined by?

Source: Sean Astin, with Joe Layden, *There and Back Again: An Actor's Tale,* New York: St. Martin's, 2004, p. 35.

**3.6** In 541 A.D., an outbreak of bubonic plague hit the Byzantine Empire. Because the plague was spread by flea-infested rats that often lived on ships, ports were hit particularly hard. In some ports, more than 40 percent of the population died. The emperor, Justinian, was concerned that the wages of sailors were rising very rapidly as a result of the plague. In 544 A.D., he placed a ceiling on the wages of sailors. Use a demand and supply graph of the market for sailors to show the effect of the plague on the wages of sailors. Use the same graph to show the effect of Justinian's wage ceiling. Briefly explain what is happening in your graph.

Source: Michael McCormick, *The Origins of the European Economy: Communications and Commerce,* A.D., *300–900,* New York: Cambridge University Press, 2001, p. 109.

**>> End Learning Objective 16.3**

## 16.4 Explaining Differences in Wages, pages 533–541

LEARNING OBJECTIVE: Use demand and supply analysis to explain how compensating differentials, discrimination, and labor unions cause wages to differ.

## Summary

The equilibrium wage is determined by the intersection of the labor demand and labor supply curves. Some differences in wages are explained by **compensating differentials**, which are higher wages that compensate workers for unpleasant aspects of a job. Wages can also differ because of **economic discrimination**, which involves paying a person a lower wage or excluding a person from an occupation on the basis of irrelevant characteristics, such as race or gender. **Labor unions** are organizations of employees that have the legal right to bargain with employers about wages and working conditions. Being in a union increases a worker's

wages about 10 percent, holding constant other factors, such as the industry in question.

 Visit **www.myeconlab.com** to complete these exercises online and get instant feedback.

## Review Questions

**4.1** What is a compensating differential? Give an example.

**4.2** Define *economic discrimination.* Is the fact that one group in the population has higher earnings than other groups evidence of economic discrimination? Briefly explain.

**4.3** Is the fraction of U.S. workers in labor unions larger or smaller than in other countries?

# Problems and Applications

**4.4** The journalist Michael Kinsley argued, "Free-market capitalism . . . works well for almost all by rewarding some people more than others." Discuss whether you agree.

Source: Michael Kinsley, "Curse You, Robert Caro!" *Slate*, November 21, 2002.

**4.5** Writing on the Baseball Prospectus Web site, Dan Fox argued, "What a player is really worth depends a great deal on the teams that are interested in signing him." Do you agree? Shouldn't a baseball player with a particular level of ability be worth the same to every team? Briefly explain.

Source: Dan Fox, "Schrodinger's Cat," baseballprospectus.com, May 17, 2007.

**4.6 (Related to the *Chapter Opener* on page 521)** A student remarks, "I don't think the idea of marginal revenue product really helps explain differences in wages. After all, a ticket to a baseball game costs much less than college tuition, yet baseball players are paid much more than college professors." Do you agree with the student's reasoning?

**4.7 (Related to the *Don't Let This Happen to You!* on page 534)** Joe Morgan is a sportscaster and former baseball player. After he stated that he thought the salaries of Major League Baseball players were justified, a baseball fan wrote the following to Rob Neyer, an ESPN.com columnist:

> Mr. Neyer,
> What are your feelings about Joe Morgan's comment that players are justified in being paid what they're being paid? How is it ok for A-Rod [New York Yankees infielder Alex Rodriguez] to earn $115,000 per GAME while my boss works 80 hour weeks and earns $30,000 per year?

How would you answer this fan's questions?

Source: ESPN.com, August 30, 2002.

**4.8** Buster Olney, a columnist for ESPN.com, wondered why baseball teams pay the teams' managers and general managers less than they pay most baseball players:

> About two-thirds of the players on the [New York] Mets' roster will make more money than [manager Willie] Randolph; Willie will get somewhere in the neighborhood of half of an average major league salary for 2007. But Randolph's deal is right in line with what other managers are making, and right in the range of what the highest-paid general manager are making. . . . I have a hard time believing that Randolph or general manager Omar Minaya will have less impact on the Mets than left-handed reliever Scott Schoeneweis, who will get paid more than either the manager or GM.

Provide an economic explanation of why baseball managers and general managers are generally paid less than baseball players.

Source: Buster Olney, "Managers Low on Pay Scale," ESPN.com, January 25, 2007.

**4.9** In early 2007, Nick Saban agreed to leave his job as head coach of the Miami Dolphins National Football League team to take a job as head football coach at the University of Alabama at a salary of $4 million per year for eight years. Ivan Maisel, a columnist for ESPN.com, wondered whether Saban was worth such a large salary: "Is Saban eight times better than the coach who outmaneuvered Bob Stoops of Oklahoma on Monday night? Boise State paid Chris Petersen $500,000 this season—and he still hasn't lost a game." Might Saban still be worth a salary of $4 million per year to Alabama even if he is not "eight times better" than a coach being paid $500,000 at another school? In your answer, be sure to refer to the difference between the marginal product of labor and the marginal revenue product of labor.

Source: Ivan Maisel, "Saban Will Find Crowded Pond in Tuscaloosa," ESPN.com, January 3, 2007.

**4.10 (Related to the *Making the Connection* on page 534)** According to Alan Krueger, an economist at Princeton University, the share of concert ticket revenue received by the top 1 percent of all acts rose from 26 percent in 1982 to 56 percent in 2003. Does this information indicate that the top acts in 2003 must have been much better performers relative to other acts than was the case in 1982? If not, can you think of another explanation?

Source: Eduardo Porter, "More Than Ever, It Pays to Be the Top Executive," *New York Times*, May 25, 2007.

**4.11 (Related to the *Making the Connection* on page 534)** Why are there superstar basketball players but no superstar automobile mechanics?

**4.12 (Related to the *Chapter Opener* on page 521)** The number of players on each Major League Baseball team is determined by negotiation between the players' union and the owners of major league teams. How does this fact affect the explanation given in the text of why baseball players are paid more than college professors? Briefly explain.

**4.13** Prior to the early twentieth century, a worker who was injured on the job could collect damages only by suing his employer. To sue successfully, the worker—or his family, if the worker had been killed—had to show that the injury was due to the employer's negligence, that the worker did not know the job was hazardous, and that the worker's own negligence had not contributed to the accident. These lawsuits were difficult for workers to win, and even workers who had been seriously injured on the job often were unable to collect any damages from their employers. Beginning in 1910, most states passed workers' compensation laws that required employers to purchase insurance that would compensate workers for injuries suffered on the job. A study by Price Fishback and Shawn Kantor of the University of Arizona shows that after the passage of workers' compensation laws, wages received by workers in the coal and lumber industries fell. Briefly explain why passage of workers' compensation laws would lead to a fall in wages in some industries.

Source: Price V. Fishback and Shawn Everett Kantor, "Did Workers Pay for the Passage of Workers' Compensation Laws?" *Quarterly Journal of Economics*, Vol. 100, No. 3, August 1995, pp. 713–742.

4.14 The following table is similar to Table 16-2 on page 536, except that it includes the earnings of Asian males

| GROUP | ANNUAL EARNINGS |
|---|---|
| Asian males | $51,107 |
| White males | 50,364 |
| Asian females | 40,671 |
| White females | 36,891 |
| Black males | 36,233 |
| Black females | 31,114 |
| Hispanic males | 30,151 |
| Hispanic females | 26,695 |

Source: U.S. Bureau of the Census, Current Population Survey, *Annual Social and Economic Supplement*, Table PINC-10, August 2008.

and females. Does the fact that Asian males are the highest-earning group in the table affect the likelihood that economic discrimination is the best explanation for why earnings differ among the groups listed in the table? Briefly explain your argument.

4.15 During the 1970s, many women changed their minds about whether they would leave the labor force after marrying and having children or whether they would be in the labor force most of their adult lives. In 1968, the National Longitudinal Survey asked a representative sample of women aged 14 to 24 whether they expected to be in the labor force at age 35. Twenty-nine percent of white women and 59 percent of black women responded that they expected to be in the labor force at that age. In fact, when these women were 35 years old, 60 percent of those who were married and 80 percent of those who were unmarried were in the labor force. In other words, many more women ended up being in the labor force than expected to be when they were of high school and college age. What impact did this fact have on the earnings of these women? Briefly explain.

Source: Claudia Goldin, *Explaining the Gender Gap: An Economic History of American Women*, New York: Oxford University Press, 1990, p. 155.

4.16 (Related to the *Making the Connection* on page 536) Some policymakers have proposed that all firms be required to make contributions to retirement plans for their employees. If this proposal is enacted, what is likely to happen to the wages received by workers at firms that currently do not make contributions to their employees' retirement plans? Briefly explain your reasoning.

>> **End Learning Objective 16.4**

---

**16.5** **Personnel Economics, pages 541–544**

LEARNING OBJECTIVE: Discuss the role personnel economics can play in helping firms deal with human resources issues.

## Summary

**Personnel economics** is the application of economic analysis to human resources issues. One insight of personnel economics is that the productivity of workers can often be increased if firms move from straight-time pay to commission or piece-rate pay.

  Visit **www.myeconlab.com** to complete these exercises online and get instant feedback.

## Review Questions

5.1 What is personnel economics?

5.2 If piece-rate or commission systems of compensating workers have important advantages for firms, why don't more firms use them?

## Problems and Applications

5.3 According to a recent economic study, the number of jobs in which firms used bonuses, commissions, or piece rates to tie workers' pay to their performance increased from an estimated 30 percent of all jobs in the 1970s to 40 percent in the 1990s. Why would systems that tie workers' pay to how much they produce have become increasingly popular with firms? The same study found that these pay systems were more common in higher-paid jobs than in lower-paid jobs. Briefly explain this result.

Source: Thomas Lemieux, W. Bentley MacLeod, and Daniel Parent, "Performance Pay and Wage Inequality," *Quarterly Journal of Economics*, Vol. 124, No. 1, February 2009, pp. 1–49.

5.4 Many companies that pay workers an hourly wage require some minimum level of acceptable output. Suppose a company that has been using this system decides to switch to a piece-rate system under which workers are compensated on the basis of how much output they produce. Is it likely that workers under a piece-rate system will end up choosing to produce less than the minimum output required under the hourly wage system? Briefly explain.

5.5 In most jobs, the harder you work, the more you earn. Some workers would rather work harder and earn more; others would rather work less hard, even though as a result they earn less. Suppose, though, that all workers at a company fall into the "work harder and earn more" group. Suppose also that the workers all have the same abilities. In these circumstances, would output per worker be the same under an hourly wage compensation system as under a piece-rate system? Briefly explain.

5.6 For years, the Goodyear Tire & Rubber Company compensated its sales force by paying a salesperson a salary plus a bonus, based on the number of tires he or she sold. Eventually, Goodyear made two changes to this policy: (1) The basis for the bonus was changed from the *quantity* of tires sold to the *revenue* from the tires sold, and (2) salespeople were required to get approval from corporate headquarters in Akron, Ohio, before offering to sell tires to customers at reduced prices. Explain why these changes were likely to increase Goodyear's profits.

Source: Timothy Aeppel, "Amid Weak Inflation, Firms Turn Creative to Boost Prices," *Wall Street Journal*, September 18, 2002.

5.7 **(Related to the** *Making the Connection* **on page 543)** What effect did the incentive pay system have on Safelite's marginal cost of installing replacement car windows? If all firms that replace car windows adopted an incentive pay system, what would happen to the price of replacing automobile glass? Who would ultimately benefit?

>> **End Learning Objective 16.5**

---

**16.6** **The Markets for Capital and Natural Resources, pages 544–546**

LEARNING OBJECTIVE: Show how equilibrium prices are determined in the markets for capital and natural resources.

## Summary

The approach used to analyze the market for labor can also be used to analyze the markets for other factors of production. In equilibrium, the price of capital is equal to the marginal revenue product of capital, and the price of natural resources is equal to the marginal revenue product of natural resources. The price received by a factor that is in fixed supply is called an **economic rent**, or a **pure rent**. A **monopsony** is the sole buyer of a factor of production. According to the **marginal productivity theory of income distribution**, the distribution of income is determined by the marginal productivity of the factors of production individuals own.

 Visit **www.myeconlab.com** to complete these exercises online and get instant feedback.

## Review Questions

6.1 In equilibrium, what determines the price of capital? What determines the price of natural resources? What is the marginal productivity theory of income distribution?

6.2 What is an economic rent? What is a monopsony?

## Problems and Applications

6.3 Adam operates a pin factory. Suppose Adam faces the situation shown in the following table and the cost of renting a machine is $550 per week.

a. Fill in the blanks in the table and determine the profit-maximizing number of machines for Adam

| NUMBER OF MACHINES | OUTPUT OF PINS (BOXES PER WEEK) | MARGINAL PRODUCT OF CAPITAL | PRODUCT PRICE (DOLLARS PER BOX) | TOTAL REVENUE | MARGINAL REVENUE PRODUCT OF CAPITAL | RENTAL COST PER MACHINE | ADDITIONAL PROFIT FROM RENTING ONE ADDITIONAL MACHINE |
|---|---|---|---|---|---|---|---|
| 0 | 0 | — | $100 | | — | $550 | |
| 1 | 12 | | 100 | | | 550 | |
| 2 | 21 | | 100 | | | 550 | |
| 3 | 28 | | 100 | | | 550 | |
| 4 | 34 | | 100 | | | 550 | |
| 5 | 39 | | 100 | | | 550 | |
| 6 | 43 | | 100 | | | 550 | |

to rent. Briefly explain why renting this number of machines is profit maximizing.

   **b.** Draw Adam's demand curve for capital.

**6.4** Many people have predicted, using a model like the one in panel (b) of Figure 16-12 on page 545, that the price of natural resources should rise consistently over time in comparison with the prices of other goods because the demand curve for natural resources is continually shifting to the right while the supply curve must be shifting to the left as natural resources are used up. However, the relative prices of most natural resources have not been increasing. Draw a graph that shows the demand and supply for natural resources that can explain why prices haven't risen even though demand has.

**6.5** In 1879, economist Henry George published *Progress and Poverty*, which became one of the best-selling books of the nineteenth century. In this book, George argued that all existing taxes should be replaced with a single tax on land. In Chapter 4, we discussed the concept of tax incidence, or the actual division of the burden of a tax between buyers and sellers in a market. If land is taxed, how will the burden of the tax be divided between the sellers of land and the buyers of land? Illustrate your answer with a graph of the market for land.

**6.6** The total amount of oil in the earth is not increasing. Does this mean that in the market for oil, the supply curve is perfectly inelastic? Briefly explain.

**6.7** In a competitive labor market, imposing a minimum wage should reduce the equilibrium level of employment. Will this also be true if the labor market is a monopsony? Briefly explain.

>> **End Learning Objective 16.6**

# CHAPTER 17

# The Economics of Information

## Chapter Outline and Learning Objectives

## >> Why Does State Farm Charge Young Men So Much More Than Young Women for Auto Insurance?

In 2009, a 21-year-old male in Denver, Colorado, paid State Farm Insurance $852 for automobile insurance. A 21-year-old female paid $701. A 35-year-old male paid $499, and a 68-year-old female paid just $356. Was State Farm practicing age and sex discrimination? Was the company practicing price discrimination of the type we discussed in Chapter 15? Actually, State Farm was attempting to match up the prices it charged for automobile insurance with the costs it was likely to incur on each policy.

State Farm was founded in 1922 by George J. Mecherle. Mecherle had started out as a farmer but later took a job selling insurance. The company he worked for charged the same price for automobile insurance to all drivers. Mecherle realized that farmers had far fewer accidents than did city drivers. So he started the State Farm Mutual Automobile Insurance Company to offer farmers automobile insurance policies at lower prices.

A key difficulty facing insurance companies is that drivers know more about how likely they are to have accidents than do the companies. The difficulties insurance companies face in pricing their policies are caused by *asymmetric information*, which exists when one party to an economic transaction has less information than the other party. In the market for insurance, asymmetric information leads to *adverse selection* and *moral hazard*. Adverse selection can result in an insurance company attracting more high-risk drivers than it would like, given the prices of its policies. Moral hazard occurs when people change their behavior *after* purchasing insurance.

Many companies now use sophisticated computer models to predict the chance that a driver will have an accident. The result has been an increase in the number of different prices being charged to drivers. As one executive of an insurance company put it, "Now we know a 22-year-old married woman is not as good a driving risk as a 45-year-old married woman."

**AN INSIDE LOOK AT POLICY** on **page 572** examines how pay-as-you-drive insurance policies can reduce premiums for careful drivers.

Sources: Information on State Farm pricing from the Colorado State Department of Regulatory Agencies, Division of Insurance Web site; and Denise Trowbridge, "State Farm to Lower Auto Rates," *The Columbus (Ohio) Dispatch*, March 23, 2007.

## Economics in YOUR LIFE!

### Have You Ever Tried to Sell a Car?

The classified sections of newspapers are filled with ads from people trying to sell cars. Many colleges have online bulletin boards where students can list cars for sale. Some people also list cars for sale on eBay or Craigslist. Car buyers choose between buying from individual sellers and buying from used car dealers. If you have tried to sell a car through a newspaper or an online ad, you have probably had trouble selling at a price as high as car dealers receive.

Why are used car buyers willing to pay only relatively low prices for cars they buy from individual sellers? If you found two seemingly identical cars, one at a local car dealer and the other for sale by an individual on eBay or Craigslist, would you be willing to pay the same amount for the two cars? As you read this chapter, see if you can answer these questions. You can check your answers against those we provide at the end of the chapter.

▶ Continued on page 571

I n previous chapters, we assumed that buyers and sellers in a market possess the same amount of information. In the market for insurance, as we have seen, buyers often have more information than sellers. Later in this chapter, we will see that the reverse is often true in financial markets: Firms selling stocks and bonds usually have more information than buyers. In other markets, buyers and sellers may both lack complete information. For example, when an oil company bids for the right to drill on tracts of government land, neither the company nor the government has complete information on how much oil the tracts contain. When telecommunications companies bid in U.S. Federal Communications Commission auctions for licenses to provide mobile phone services, they don't have complete information on how valuable the licenses may be.

In this chapter, we discuss the economics of information and how imperfect information can affect the decisions of both households and firms. After reading this chapter, you will better understand situations such as auctions and the markets for insurance and stocks and bonds, in which the role of imperfect information is particularly important.

**17.1 LEARNING** OBJECTIVE

Define asymmetric information and distinguish between adverse selection and moral hazard.

**Asymmetric information** A situation in which one party to an economic transaction has less information than the other party.

# Asymmetric Information

The difficulty in correctly pricing insurance policies arises from the problem of **asymmetric information**, which occurs when one party to an economic transaction has less information than the other party. As we will see, in some markets, it is difficult to understand the actions of buyers and sellers without understanding the effects of asymmetric information. In fact, guarding against the effects of asymmetric information is a major objective of sellers in the insurance market and of buyers in financial markets. The market for used automobiles was the first in which economists began to carefully study the problem of asymmetric information.

## Adverse Selection and the Market for "Lemons"

The study of asymmetric information began with an analysis of the used car market by Nobel Laureate George Akerlof, of the University of California, Berkeley. Akerlof pointed out that the seller of a used car will always have more information on the true condition of the car than will potential buyers. A car that has been poorly maintained—by, for instance, not having its oil changed regularly—may have damage that could be difficult to detect even by a trained mechanic.

If potential buyers of used cars know that they will have difficulty separating the good used cars from the bad used cars, or "lemons," they will take this into account in the prices they are willing to pay. Consider the following simple example: Suppose that half of the 2007 Volkswagen Jettas offered for sale have been well maintained and are good, reliable used cars. The other half have been poorly maintained and are lemons that will be unreliable. Suppose that potential buyers of 2007 Jettas would be willing to pay $10,000 for a reliable one but only $5,000 for an unreliable one. The sellers know how well they have maintained their cars and whether they are reliable, but the buyers do not have this information and so have no way of telling the reliable cars from the unreliable ones.

In this situation, buyers will generally offer a price somewhere between the price they would be willing to pay for a good car and the price they would be willing to pay for a lemon. In this case, with a 50–50 chance of buying a good car or a lemon, buyers might offer $7,500, which is halfway between the price they would pay if they knew for certain the car was a good one and the price they would pay if they knew it was a lemon.

Unfortunately for used car buyers, a major glitch arises at this point. From the buyers' perspective, given that they don't know whether any particular car offered for sale is a good car or a lemon, an offer of $7,500 seems reasonable. But the sellers *do* know whether the cars they are offering are good cars or lemons. To a seller of a good car, an offer of $7,500 is $2,500 below the true value of the car, and the seller will be reluctant to sell. But to a seller of a lemon, an offer of $7,500 is $2,500 *above* the true value of the car, and the seller will be quite happy to sell. As sellers of lemons take advantage of knowing more about the cars they are selling than buyers do, the used car market will fall victim to **adverse selection**: Most used cars offered for sale will be lemons. In other words, because of asymmetric information, the market has selected adversely the cars that will be offered for sale. Notice as well that the problem of adverse selection reduces the total quantity of used cars bought and sold in the market because few good cars are offered for sale. From this example we can conclude that information problems reduce economic efficiency in a market.

**Adverse selection** The situation in which one party to a transaction takes advantage of knowing more than the other party to the transaction.

## Reducing Adverse Selection in the Car Market: Warranties and Reputations

There are ways of reducing the adverse selection problem in the used car market. Car manufacturers provide warranties when cars are sold new. Such a warranty covers the costs of major repairs and can be transferred to a new owner when the car is resold. Warranties give prospective buyers some assurance that they will not be stuck with all the cost of repairs. In addition, used car dealers take steps to reassure buyers that the cars they are selling are not lemons. They do this by building a reputation for selling reliable used cars and by offering their own warranties if the manufacturer's warranty has expired or can't be transferred. If a used car dealer can convince buyers that the dealer is selling reliable cars, then, using the numbers from our earlier example, buyers would be willing to pay $10,000 rather than $7,500 for a used Jetta.

State governments have passed "lemon laws" to help reduce information problems in the car market. Most lemon laws have two main provisions:

1. New cars that need several major repairs during the first year or two after the date of the original purchase may be returned to the manufacturer for a full refund.

2. Car manufacturers must indicate whether a used car they are offering for sale was repurchased from the original owner as a lemon.

## Asymmetric Information in the Market for Insurance

Asymmetric information problems are particularly severe in the market for insurance. Buyers of insurance policies will always know more about the likelihood of the event being insured against happening than will insurance companies. For example, buyers of health insurance policies know more about the state of their health—and, therefore, how likely they are to submit medical bills to the insurance company—than will the insurance company that sells them the policies. Similarly, drivers know more about whether they are reckless drivers, homeowners know more about potential fire hazards in their homes, and so on than do the insurance companies selling them policies.

## Reducing Adverse Selection in the Insurance Market

Adverse selection problems arise because sick people are more likely to want health insurance than are healthy people, reckless drivers are more likely to want automobile insurance than are careful drivers, and people living in homes that are fire hazards are more likely to want fire insurance than are people living in safe homes. Insurance companies will cover their costs, including the opportunity cost of funds invested in them by their owners, only if they set the prices—or *premiums*—of policies at levels high enough to cover the claims for payment that insured people are likely to submit. If insurance companies have trouble determining who is healthy and who is sick or who is a reckless driver and who is a safe driver, they will set their premiums too low and will fail to cover their costs. To reduce the problem of adverse selection, insurance companies gather as much information as they can on people applying for policies. For example, people applying for individual health insurance policies or life insurance policies usually need to submit their medical records to the insurance company. Insurance companies usually also carry out their own medical examinations. People applying for automobile insurance have their driving record reviewed. Insurance companies charge higher premiums to people who have caused accidents or who have speeding tickets than to safer drivers. As we saw in the chapter opener, insurance companies such as State Farm will remain profitable only if they succeed in identifying the riskiest drivers in order to charge them higher premiums.

Sometimes the adverse selection problem leads insurance companies simply to refuse to offer policies to certain people at any price. Someone with a terminal or chronic illness, for example, may find it difficult to buy an individual health insurance or life insurance policy. The owner of a home or warehouse in an area that is prone to arson fires may have difficulty getting fire insurance. An alternative to refusing to sell policies to these people would be for insurance companies to charge very high premiums for coverage. This may make the adverse selection problem worse, however. When premiums are very high, only people who are almost certain to make a claim will purchase a policy.

The adverse selection problem can also be reduced if people are automatically covered by insurance. For example, state governments require that every driver buy automobile insurance. This policy reduces the problem of insurance being purchased primarily by bad drivers. As we saw at the beginning of the chapter, however, State Farm and other insurance companies still face the problem of determining the profit-maximizing prices to charge for their policies.

Insurance companies can reduce adverse selection problems in selling health insurance and life insurance by offering *group coverage* to large firms—including colleges and universities—or to alliances of smaller firms. With group coverage, everyone employed by a firm is automatically covered. As long as the group is large enough, the coverage is likely to represent the proportions of healthy and unhealthy people found in the general population. As a result of this *risk pooling*, it is much easier for insurance companies to estimate the average number of claims likely to be filed under a group health insurance or life insurance policy than it would be to predict the number of claims likely to be filed under an individual policy. Because everyone in the group must pay the premium—or have it paid for them by their employer—insurance companies avoid the problem of only sick people buying the insurance. Group coverage that allows healthy people not to participate is still subject to adverse selection problems, however. If healthy people don't participate, the number of claims filed per participating employee is likely to be high. This level of claims may cause the insurance company to raise the price it charges to the firm for the group policy. If the firm then raises the monthly payment required of employees, the higher price will discourage additional numbers of healthy employees from participating.

## Making the Connection | Does Adverse Selection Explain Why Some People Do Not Have Health Insurance?

Roughly 46 million people in the United States do not have health insurance. As the chart at the top of the next page shows, more than two-thirds of Americans are covered by private health insurance plans—primarily plans provided by firms to their employees—and more than one-quarter of people are covered by government health insurance plans—such as the Medicare program for people age 65 and older or the Medicaid program for poor people. But about 15 percent of people are not covered by health insurance. (Note that the percentages in the chart sum to more than 100 because some people are covered by both private health insurance and government health insurance.)

There are a number of reasons people may not have health insurance. Some healthy young adults don't expect to need medical care and so do not want to pay the monthly premiums to buy insurance they don't expect to need. As a result, although 15.3 percent of the total population lacks health insurance, the proportion of people between ages 18 and 24 who do not have insurance is almost twice as large, at 28.1 percent. And more than one-quarter of those between ages 25 and 34 do not have insurance. Many low-income people qualify for government health insurance through the Medicaid program.

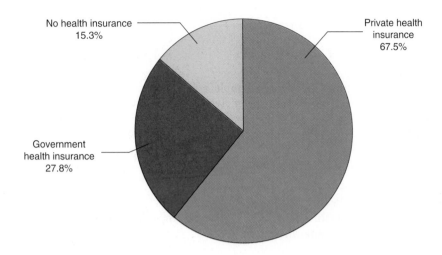

Source: Carmen DeNavas-Walt, Bernadette D. Proctor, and Jessica C. Smith, U.S. Census Bureau, Current Population Reports, P60-235, *Income, Poverty, and Health Insurance Coverage in the United States: 2007*, U.S. Government Printing Office, Washington, DC, August 2008.

But some low-income people either do not take advantage of Medicaid or are not eligible for it. For these people, their low incomes may be the main reason that they do not have insurance. However, only about 20 percent of the uninsured have incomes below the official U.S. poverty line; more than 30 percent of the uninsured have incomes more than three times greater than the poverty line. Kate Bundorf of Stanford University and Mark Pauly of the University of Pennsylvania have estimated that as many as three-quarters of the uninsured can afford to buy health insurance.

Some economists have argued that adverse selection may be an important explanation for the significant percentage of people lacking health insurance in the United States. We have seen that one effect of adverse selection in a market is that the equilibrium quantity of the good or service may be smaller than it would have been if there were no information problems. Because insurance companies are aware of the adverse selection problem, they may offer health insurance policies at prices higher than young, healthy consumers are willing to pay. Similarly, as we have already seen, insurance companies will sometimes refuse to offer insurance to people with chronic illnesses.

In recent years, state governments may have unintentionally made the adverse selection problem worse by regulating the terms of the policies insurance companies are allowed to offer small firms. These state regulations generally restrict the ability of insurance companies to offer policies that charge higher premiums to employees with existing health conditions. Research by Kosali Ilayperuma Simon of Cornell University indicates that insurance companies responded to the regulations by raising the prices of the policies they offer to small companies. When the companies, in turn, raised the prices their employees have to pay to participate in the health plans, some younger, healthier employees dropped out of the plans and became uninsured.

So, although no one factor provides a complete explanation of why some people in the United States lack health insurance, adverse selection appears to play a significant role.

Sources: M. Kate Bundorf and Mark V. Pauly, "Is Health Insurance Affordable for the Uninsured?" *Journal of Health Economics*, Vol. 25, No. 4, July 2006, pp. 650–673; and Kosali Ilayperuma Simon, "Adverse Selection in Health Insurance Markets? Evidence from State Small-Group Health Insurance Reforms," *Journal of Public Economics*, Vol. 89, Nos. 9–10, September 2005, pp. 1865–1877.

**YOUR TURN:** Test your understanding by doing related problems 1.10 and 1.11 on page 575 at the end of this chapter.

## Moral Hazard

The insurance market is subject to a second consequence of asymmetric information, called *moral hazard*. **Moral hazard** refers to actions people take after they have entered into a transaction that make the other party to the transaction worse off. Moral hazard in the insurance market occurs when people change their behavior after becoming insured. For example, once a firm has taken out a fire insurance policy on a warehouse, it may be less careful about avoiding fire hazards. Similarly, someone with health

**Moral hazard** The actions people take after they have entered into a transaction that make the other party to the transaction worse off.

# Don't Let This Happen to **YOU!**

## Don't Confuse Adverse Selection with Moral Hazard

The two key consequences of asymmetric information are adverse selection and moral hazard. It is easy to get these concepts mixed up. One way to keep the concepts straight is to remember that adverse selection refers to what happens *at the time* of entering into the transaction. An example would be an insurance company that sells a life insurance policy to a terminally ill person because the company lacks full information on the state of the person's health. Moral hazard refers to what happens *after* entering into the

transaction. For example, a nonsmoker buys a life insurance policy and then starts smoking four packs of cigarettes a day. (It may help to remember that *a* comes before *m* in the alphabet just as *a*dverse selection comes before *m*oral hazard.)

**YOUR TURN:** Test your understanding by doing related problems 1.13 on page 575 and 3.3 on page 576 at the end of this chapter.

insurance might visit the doctor for treatment of a cold or another minor illness, although he or she would not do so without the insurance.

Insurance companies can take steps to reduce moral hazard problems. For example, a fire insurance company may insist that a firm install a sprinkler system in a warehouse to offset any increased carelessness once the policy is in place, or it may reserve the right to inspect the warehouse periodically to check for fire hazards. Insurance companies also use *deductibles* and *coinsurance* to reduce moral hazard. A deductible requires the holder of the insurance policy to pay a certain dollar amount of a claim. With coinsurance, the insurance company pays only a percentage of any claim. Suppose you have a health insurance policy with a $200 deductible and 20 percent coinsurance, and you have a medical bill of $1,000. You must pay the first $200 of the bill and 20 percent of the remaining $800. Deductibles and coinsurance give the holders of insurance policies incentives to avoid filing claims.

**17.2 LEARNING** OBJECTIVE

Apply the concepts of adverse selection and moral hazard to financial markets.

# Adverse Selection and Moral Hazard in Financial Markets

Adverse selection and moral hazard pose problems for firms and investors in the markets for stocks and bonds. In Chapter 7, we saw that most firms have to raise funds by borrowing from banks. Asymmetric information is a key reason only large corporations are able to raise funds by selling stocks and bonds. Every firm knows more about its financial situation than does any potential investor. Because investors have trouble distinguishing between well-run and poorly run firms, they are reluctant to buy the stocks and bonds of firms unless a great deal of public information about those firms is available. As a result, this means only firms that are studied closely by investment analysts working for brokerage firms and investment companies are able to sell stocks and bonds to investors. The investment analysts state their opinions of the true financial health of firms in reports that are available to the investing public. A great deal of public information about Microsoft is available, and investment analysts follow the firm closely. Not much public information is available about small firms such as Anisul's Software Solutions, and no investment analysts follow the firm. As a result, Microsoft can raise funds by selling stocks and bonds, but Anisul's Software Solutions can't.

Investors also worry about moral hazard. Once a firm has sold stocks and bonds, what will it do with the funds it has raised? Of course, investors expect that the firm will use the funds in ways that will make the firm more profitable. But the possibility exists that the firm will use the funds in ways that actually reduce profits, which is obviously not in the best interests of investors. For instance, a firm might use the funds to pay high salaries to the firm's managers or to open an unneeded branch office in Paris, to which the managers can make frequent visits. In the worst case, the firm's managers might actually steal the funds.

Once again, the larger the firm is and the more carefully investment analysts follow its activities, the less likely moral hazard is to be a problem. This explains, in part, why investors are willing to buy the stocks and bonds of large firms but not of small firms. Note that we are using a broader definition of moral hazard here than we did when discussing insurance. In this case, moral hazard refers to actions taken by one party to a transaction that are different from what the other party expected at the time of the transaction.

## Reducing Adverse Selection and Moral Hazard in Financial Markets

The decline in stock prices that followed the great stock market crash of 1929 wiped out the savings of many investors. Some investors complained that firms had failed to provide them with accurate financial information. Congress responded in 1934 by establishing the *Securities and Exchange Commission (SEC)* to regulate the stock and bond markets. The SEC requires that a firm register stocks or bonds it wishes to sell. The firm must also provide potential investors with a *prospectus* that contains all relevant financial information on the firm. Although investors sometimes complain that a firm's prospectus is difficult to understand, the SEC has succeeded in increasing the amount of information available to potential investors. This additional information helps reduce the adverse selection and moral hazard problems in financial markets and increases the number of firms that are able to raise funds by selling stocks and bonds.

The failure of a number of large financial firms and the steep decline in stock prices from 2007 to 2009 made it clear that information problems still exist in financial markets. As we discussed in Chapter 7, during the housing boom of the mid-2000s, banks and other financial firms granted mortgages to subprime borrowers. The mortgages were then bundled into securities that were similar to bonds and sold to investors. Banks, insurance companies, and pension funds, as well as private investors, purchased these *mortgage-backed securities*. When the housing boom ended and housing prices began to decline beginning in 2006, many subprime borrowers defaulted on their mortgages. Because these borrowers were no longer making payments on their mortgages, mortgage-backed securities lost value, and many financial firms suffered heavy losses. The resulting financial crisis plunged the U.S. economy into the worst downturn since the Great Depression of the 1930s. During the financial crisis, many investors complained that they weren't aware of how risky some of the investments—particularly investments in mortgage-backed securities—made by financial firms had been. Some observers believed that the managers of many financial firms had intentionally misled investors about the riskiness of these assets. Others argued that the managers themselves had not understood how risky the assets were. Finally, the crisis revealed that the managers of some investment firms had been fraudulently using funds collected from investors for their own purposes rather than investing them as they had promised to do. The events of 2007–2009 served as a reminder to investors of the difficulty of overcoming adverse selection and moral hazard problems in financial markets.

## Making the Connection | Moral Hazard, Big Time: Bernie Madoff's "Ponzi" Scheme

In 2008, Bernard Madoff was 70 years old and a pillar of Wall Street: He was the widely admired head of a respected investment firm and former chairman of NASDAQ, and investors considered themselves lucky if they could convince him to manage their money. When Madoff was charged with fraud and arrested in December 2008, the news hit Wall Street like a thunderbolt. For decades, Madoff had promised investors that he would invest their money following a complex strategy that would yield steady returns of 8 to 12 percent per year, even when stock prices were declining. Although there had always been skeptics who doubted that any investment strategy could possibly succeed in providing such steady returns year in and year out, many wealthy investors competed with each other to invest with Madoff. Some spent thousands of dollars joining country clubs where Madoff was a member in the hopes of meeting him. Many charities also invested some or all of their endowments with him.

*Bernard Madoff perpetrated a Ponzi scheme that bilked investors of many billions of dollars.*

In fact, dating back to the 1970s, Madoff had been running a gigantic fraud known as a Ponzi scheme. Ponzi schemes are named after Charles Ponzi, who earned millions from investors during the 1920s by telling them he would invest their money in a way that would earn a 50 percent return in just a few months, when in fact he intended to spend their money rather than invest it. In a Ponzi scheme, the person carrying out the fraud uses funds from new investors to pay returns to existing investors and to pay off investors who want to withdraw their money. As long as Madoff was able to continually recruit new investors and as long as only a few investors withdrew all of their money, he could keep the fraud going indefinitely. In fact, from the 1970s until 2008, Madoff was able to use the scheme to finance an opulent lifestyle. The financial crisis of 2008 was his undoing. By late 2008, investors facing losses on other investments attempted to withdraw more than $7 billion from Madoff's fund, but he had less than $300 million left. At the time of his arrest, Madoff estimated that total losses to investors could be as great as $50 billion, making this by far the largest financial fraud in history.

To economists, the lesson of the Madoff case was that to cope with moral hazard, investors need to be sure they understand how their funds are being invested (many of Madoff's investors didn't) and to remember that if the return on an investment seems too good to be true, it probably is.

Sources: For an overview of the Madoff fraud, see Erin Arvedlund, *Too Good to Be True: The Rise and Fall of Bernie Madoff*, New York: Portfolio, 2009; and Amir Efrati, "Q&A on the Madoff Case," *Wall Street Journal*, January 7, 2009.

 **YOUR TURN:** Test your understanding by doing related problem 2.6 on page 575 at the end of this chapter.

# Solved Problem | 17-2

## The Fall of the House of Rigas

In early 2002, plans were unveiled for a new corporate headquarters in downtown Buffalo. The $125 million project would house 1,000 workers and serve as a catalyst for other development efforts in the city's Inner Harbor area. James Allen, executive director of the Amherst and Erie County Industrial Development Agencies, commented, "We need a signature project on the waterfront and this gives us that project." Unfortunately, the building project was proposed by Adelphia Communications. On June 24 of that same year, Adelphia filed for bankruptcy. On June 20, 2005, John Rigas, Adelphia's founder and longtime CEO, was sentenced to 15 years in prison for looting the company's finances and concealing over $2 billion in debt from investors. Rigas's son Timothy received a 20-year sentence after being convicting on the same charges as his father: conspiracy, bank fraud, and securities fraud. During the Rigases trial, U.S. attorneys accused the Rigases of using Adelphia as a "private piggy bank" to pay for such personal expenses as millions of dollars in cash advances, $13 million to build a golf course, and 100 pairs of bedroom slippers. The elder Rigas had even used a company jet to send a Christmas tree to his daughter in New York City. When he found out the tree was the wrong size, he had another tree sent—at company expense.

Despite being a publicly held firm, Adelphia was run like a family business. John Rigas and three of his sons and one son-in-law held five of the nine seats on the company's board of directors. The family's mismanagement was hidden from investors through fraudulent financial statements. After the collapse of Internet stock prices, following a rapid climb in the 1990s, and the slowdown of the overall U.S. economy in 2001, investors began looking more closely at questionable managerial and accounting practices that made debt-ridden firms such as Adelphia and Enron appear to be in better financial condition than they actually were.

Sources: James Fink, "Adelphia Picks HOK for Downtown Office Design," *Buffalo Business First*, January 16, 2002; James Fink, "John Rigas Sentenced to 15 Years in Prison," *Buffalo Business First*, June 21, 2005; and "Rigases Looted Aldelphia, Jurors Told," www.smh.com.au/articles/2004/03/02/1078191325849.html.

**a.** What characteristic(s) of the management structure of Adelphia Communications demonstrates adverse selection?

**b.** Use the Rigas family to demonstrate the consequences of moral hazard in financial markets.

## SOLVING THE PROBLEM:

**Step 1:** **Review the chapter material.** This problem is about adverse selection and moral hazard, so you may want to review the section "Adverse Selection and Moral Hazard in Financial Markets," which begins on page 564.

**Step 2:** **Answer question (a).** The strong overall performance of the U.S. economy and financial markets masked the fraudulent behavior of the Rigases during the 1990s. Perhaps most important was the fact that Rigas family members held a majority of the seats on Adelphia's board of directors. This meant that the family had effective control over the company and could prevent other board members from overruling questionable management practices.

**Step 3:** **Answer question (b).** It is critically important for investors and analysts to have access to timely and accurate information regarding a publicly owned company. Had the true financial condition of the company been known earlier, the financial markets would have penalized Adelphia with lower stock prices and credit ratings. The company could have been forced to change the composition of the board or to be sold to another company.

**YOUR TURN:** For more practice, do related problem 2.7 on page 576 at the end of this chapter.

# Adverse Selection and Moral Hazard in Labor Markets

**17.3 LEARNING** OBJECTIVE

Apply the concepts of adverse selection and moral hazard to labor markets.

We saw in Chapter 7 that economists refer to the conflict between the interests of shareholders and the interests of top management as a **principal–agent problem**. This problem occurs when agents—in this case, a firm's top management—pursue their own interests rather than the interests of the principal—in this case, the shareholders of the corporation—who hired them. There is also the potential for a principal–agent prob-lem between the managers of a firm and its workers. The moral hazard behind the principal–agent problem is that workers, once hired, may shirk their obligations and not work hard.

**Principal–agent problem** A problem caused by agents pursuing their own interests rather than the interests of the principals who hired them.

Employers can ensure that workers are doing their jobs by closely monitoring them. Telemarketing firms, for example, can monitor their employees electronically to ensure that they make the required number of telephone calls per hour. Not all firms, however, can monitor their employees so closely. Often firms must rely on workers being sufficiently motivated so they do not shirk their responsibilities. One way to motivate workers is to increase the value to them of their current jobs, relative to other jobs they might have. If you consider your current job to be more valuable than the alternatives, you will be reluctant to shirk because you won't want to risk being fired. Firms use several methods to make a worker's job seem more valuable:

- *Efficiency wages.* There is a market for every kind of labor, just as there is a market for every good and service. A firm's demand for labor is determined by how much output workers can produce for the firm—the workers' *productivity*—and by the price the firm receives when it sells the output the workers produce. The supply of labor is determined by the willingness of workers to supply a given amount of work at a particular wage. The equilibrium wage equates the quantity of labor demanded to the quantity of labor supplied. If a firm offers to pay a wage above the equilibrium wage, a worker will consider the job to be valuable and will be less likely to shirk and risk losing the job. An *efficiency wage* is a higher-than-equilibrium wage firms pay to give workers an incentive to work harder.

- *Seniority system.* Many firms use a seniority system under which workers who have been with the firm longer receive higher pay and other benefits, such as the choice of better or more interesting jobs. A worker who early in his career at a firm is fired for shirking will give up the possibility of participating in the benefits of seniority. A seniority system can have an effect similar to that of an efficiency wage in giving workers an incentive to work harder.

- *Profit sharing.* The harder employees work, the more profits a firm makes, but employees don't share in these increased profits if they are paid a fixed wage or salary. Under a profit-sharing plan, employees receive a share of the profits earned by the firm. The harder the employee works, the more profit the firm earns, and the higher the employee's income. Profit sharing increases the incentive of an employee to work hard. One problem with some profit-sharing plans is that they don't increase the incentive very much. For example, suppose you work at a firm with 100 employees, and by working harder, you can increase the firm's profits by $10,000 per year. If each employee shares equally in the increased profits, your income will rise, but only by $100 per year. This increase is probably not enough to compensate you for the additional effort required. In addition, a firm's profits can be affected by many factors, such as a slowdown in the economy, that are unrelated to how hard a particular employee works. So, you might work very hard during a given period and actually see the profits of the firm fall for reasons you can't control. In that case, your hard work would not have increased your income at all.

# Solved Problem | 17-3

## Changing Workers' Compensation to Reduce Adverse Selection and Moral Hazard

Jill runs a clothing store. She is concerned that her salespeople are not making much effort to be friendly to customers or to persuade them to buy more clothes. Because Jill has to be out of the store most of the day, it isn't easy for her to monitor the activities of her salespeople. Jill is paying her workers an hourly wage, but she is considering switching to paying them on commission: They would be compensated on the basis of how much clothing they sell.

a. What effect would this change have on the types of workers Jill attracts?

b. Briefly explain whether this change is likely to increase Jill's profits.

### SOLVING THE PROBLEM:

**Step 1:** **Review the chapter material.** This problem is about adverse selection and moral hazard in labor markets, so you may want to review the section "Adverse Selection and Moral Hazard in Labor Markets," which begins on page 567.

**Step 2:** **Use the ideas of adverse selection and moral hazard in labor markets to answer part (a).** When workers are not monitored, they have an incentive to expend as little effort as possible, which is the moral hazard problem in labor markets. When salespeople are paid an hourly wage, their compensation is determined by how many hours they are at work rather than how much they sell. If Jill switches to a system in which compensation depends on how much workers sell, she is likely to attract more workers who have the ability and interest to sell clothes. Workers who don't have much interest in selling clothes are unlikely to stay because their compensation will be reduced. Jill's new compensation scheme will reduce the adverse selection problem she faces when hiring workers.

**Step 3:** **Answer part (b) by analyzing the effect of the new compensation system on Jill's profits.** Whether Jill's profits rise under the new compensation system depends on whether she is correct that her workers are not making much effort to sell clothes. If she is correct, switching from paying hourly wages to paying commissions is likely to reduce both the adverse selection and moral hazard problems she faces. She will attract people willing to work harder, and she will provide them with an incentive to sell more clothes, so her sales and profits should increase.

**myeconlab** **YOUR TURN:** For more practice, do related problem 3.4 on page 576 at the end of this chapter.

# The Winner's Curse: When Is It Bad to Win an Auction?

**17.4 LEARNING** OBJECTIVE

Explain the winner's curse and why it occurs.

Information problems can occur in auctions. In some auctions, neither the bidder nor the seller has complete information about what is being auctioned. For example, when the government auctions off land for oil drilling, neither the government nor the oil companies bidding in the auctions know with certainty how much oil is in the land. In the 1950s and 1960s, the oil companies that won bids to drill on the North Slope of Alaska and in the Gulf of Mexico did not earn the profits they expected. Three engineers with the Atlantic Richfield oil company argued that this was not due to bad luck but was the result of a general tendency for the winners of auctions, like the ones held for the oil fields, to bid too high. This outcome, called the **winner's curse**, applies to other auctions as well. Knowledge of the winner's curse can make it possible for a savvy firm to win an auction with a high bid that is low enough to be very profitable.

**Winner's curse** The idea that the winner in certain auctions may have overestimated the value of the good, thus ending up worse off than the losers.

Why were the winning bidders in government auctions of oil fields disappointed with their profits? Three Atlantic Richfield engineers, E. C. Capen, R. V. Clapp, and W. M. Campbell, proposed an explanation. They noted that each firm participating in the auctions used geological data, data on how productive nearby wells had been, and other information to estimate how much oil was likely to be available in each tract of land up for bid. Because of the uncertainty in interpreting the information available, companies made very different bids. Figure 17-1 shows the actual bids made by seven oil companies in 1967 on a tract of land off the Louisiana coast.

Clearly, Company A, with a bid of $32.5 million, was the most optimistic about how much oil the tract contained. Company G, which bid only $3.3 million, was the least optimistic. Who was right? Capen, Clapp, and Campbell argued that as the companies bid on many tracts using the best available information, each company would overestimate the amount of oil in some tracts and underestimate the amount of oil in other tracts. Their mistakes of sometimes being too high would tend to offset their mistakes of sometimes being too low, so *on average their estimates would be correct*. For example, in the case of the tract in Figure 17-1, it was likely that the true amount of oil in the tract was worth about $11.6 million, or the average of the seven bids. The problem for Company A is that it won the auction with a bid of $32.5 million, which was much too high, given the amount of oil that was likely to actually be in the tract. Capen, Clapp, and Campbell came to two conclusions:

1. "In competitive bidding, the winner tends to be the player who most overestimates true tract value."

2. "He who bids on a parcel what he thinks it is worth will, in the long run, be taken to the cleaners."

## Figure 17-1

**Oil Company Bids to Drill Off the Louisiana Coast**

In 1967, seven oil companies bid to drill on land off the Louisiana coast. The bids by oil companies differ widely because the amount of oil contained in any particular tract of land up for bid is very uncertain. The company that has the most optimistic estimate is likely to win the auction. It is also likely to be disappointed in the profits it earns from the tract. Source: E. C. Capen, R. V. Clapp, and W. M. Campbell, "Competitive Bidding in High-Risk Situations," *Journal of Petroleum Engineering*, June 1971, p. 642.

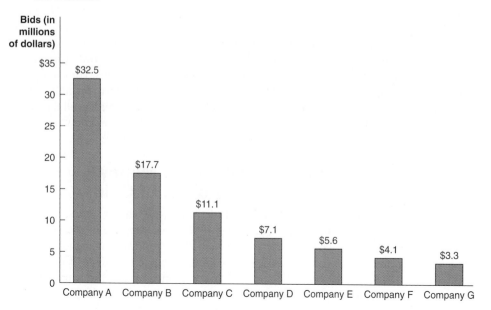

These conclusions became known as the *winner's curse* because they indicate that the winner of an auction may end up worse off than the losers. In fact, Capen, Clapp, and Campbell concluded that the oil companies would have made a greater return on their investments if they had taken the funds and put them in a savings account in a bank rather than using them to bid on oil tracts.

## Making the Connection | Is There a Winner's Curse in the Marriage Market?

In the United States, about 43 percent of all marriages end in divorce. Why the divorce rate is so high is a complicated question. But economics can provide some insight, even if it can't provide a full explanation. Economists have proposed thinking of the interactions of men and women looking for marriage partners as a *marriage market*. Of course, the marriage market is not a typical market in which a good or service is bought and sold for money. But like participants in other markets, the men and women in the marriage market are trying to make themselves as well off as possible, and they are competing against each other to find the best partners.

It's hard to tell how good a marriage partner someone will make until you are actually married to him or her. Like oil companies trying to estimate the amount of oil in a tract of land, men and women use all the information they can to estimate how good a spouse someone will be. But which potential mate are you likely to pursue most strongly? And which potential mate is most likely to find your romantic ardor greater than that of other potential marriage partners? The answer to both questions is the person whose value as a marriage partner you have most greatly overestimated. In other words, if your estimate of how desirable someone is as a marriage partner is much higher than other people's estimates, you have a good chance of marrying that person—but also a good chance of discovering later that your estimate was wrong. The idea of the winner's curse can help explain not only why oil companies can be dissatisfied with the profits from winning oil field auctions but also why many people are apparently dissatisfied with their marriages.

*A life of bliss or the winner's curse?*

**YOUR TURN:** Test your understanding by doing related problem 4.6 on page 577 at the end of this chapter.

## When Does the Winner's Curse Apply?

Does the winner's curse indicate that the winner of every auction would have been better off losing? No, because the winner's curse applies only to auctions of *common-value* assets—such as oil fields—that would be given the same value by all bidders if they had perfect information. The winner's curse does not apply to auctions of *private-value* assets where the value to each bidder depends on the bidder's own preferences. For example, if you win an auction on eBay for a Blu-ray player, you are not subject to the winner's curse if the Blu-ray player is new and the auction described it completely. You had all the information you needed to evaluate the Blu-ray player, and your bid was based on your preference for a Blu-ray player relative to other things you could have purchased.

## Making the Connection | Want to Make Some Money? Try Auctioning a Jar of Coins

A simple experiment illustrates the winner's curse. Fill a jar with coins. Let a group of people—everyone in your economics class?—inspect the jar. Then auction off the jar: Whoever makes the highest bid gets the jar. The winner will, of course, be the person with the highest estimate of how many coins are in the jar. Just as with oil companies bidding on oil fields, the winner is also likely to have *overestimated* the value of the coins in the jar. Because the high bid is likely to be greater than the value of the coins in the jar, you should end up with a profit—equal to the difference between what the high bidder pays and the value of the coins in the jar.

Will the winner's curse really apply in this situation? Max Bazerman of Harvard University and William Samuelson of Boston University tested this possibility, using MBA students enrolled in economics classes at Boston University. In each of 12 classes, they auctioned off four jars containing either coins or paper clips. The students were told that large paper clips were worth 4 cents and small paper clips were worth 2 cents. They were also told that the winning bidder would receive the value of the jar minus the value of his bid. For example, if the value of the coins or paper clips in a jar was $20, and the high bid for a jar was $15, the winner would receive $5. In addition, they asked students to submit written estimates of the value of the coins in the jars. They offered a $2 prize for the best estimate of each jar.

Although the students didn't know it, each jar contained exactly $8 worth of coins or paper clips. The students' average estimate of the value of the coins or paper clips in the jar was too low—just $5.13. Despite this, the average of the winning bids in the 48 auctions for the jars was $10.01, so on average the high bidders lost $2.01. These MBA students had fallen victim to the winner's curse.

Sources: Richard H. Thaler, *The Winner's Curse: Paradoxes and Anomalies of Economic Life*, New York: The Free Press, 1992, Chapter 5; and Max Bazerman and William Samuelson, "I Won the Auction but Don't Want the Prize," *Journal of Conflict Resolution*, Vol. 27, December 1983, pp. 618–634.

*The highest bidder on this jar of coins could lose money.*

**YOUR TURN:** Test your understanding by doing related problem 4.9 on page 577 at the end of this chapter.

▶ Continued from page 559

## Economics in YOUR LIFE!

At the beginning of the chapter, we asked you to consider why an individual will only be able to sell a used car for a much lower price than a dealer can. The key to the answer is that asymmetric information is a major problem in the used car market. Most buyers are aware that the seller of a used car knows much more about the condition of the car than the buyer does. In fact, most people get their primary information about a car from the seller of the car. The seller has some incentive to overstate the condition of the car: The better the seller makes the car sound, the higher the price the seller can hope to get. When you sell a car as an individual, the buyer is unlikely to ever buy a car from you again or to know anyone who has bought a car from you in the past. So, the buyer knows you don't have much incentive to be honest in the hopes of attracting future buyers. Car dealers, however, are hoping to continue to sell cars to many people, and their need for a good reputation keeps them from too greatly overstating the true condition of the car. So, if you have a good, well-maintained used car for sale, you may have to accept a price considerably below what a used car dealer with a good reputation could sell the car for.

## Conclusion

In this chapter, we looked at situations of asymmetric information, where either the buyer or the seller has information not available to the other. We also looked at situations where both the buyer and the seller lack full information, which can lead to outcomes such as the winner's curse. Markets, including financial markets and labor markets, are more efficient when buyers and sellers have full information. Because information problems are significant in many markets, the economics of information is an important area of study.

Read *An Inside Look at Policy* on the next page for a discussion of how pay-as-you-drive insurance policies can reduce premiums for careful drivers.

# >> Pay Less for Car Insurance! (But We'll be Watching How You Drive)

## THE SEATTLE TIMES

## Bill Would Allow Insurance to Offer Pay-as-You-Drive Plan

Polly Freeman and her husband own a car but they usually bike to get around.

So why should they pay the same car-insurance rates as someone who drives much more?

(a) Next year, people like the Freemans could get a break on their insurance if lawmakers approve legislation that would encourage insurance companies to charge rates based, in part, on the exact number of miles a customer drives.

"I would certainly be interested in learning more about that," said Freeman, a busy Seattle mom and freelance writer . . .

But the proposal raises privacy concerns . . . for so-called pay-as-you-drive insurance, companies electronically track how much people drive to help determine what they should pay. And one company that offers such coverage in other states not only tracks how far they drive, but also how they drive.

Because the exact number of miles driven are tracked, they play a more prominent role in the insurance price. . . . "The biggest concern the insurance commissioner expects to have is privacy related," said Hilary Young, spokeswoman for state Insurance Commissioner Mike Kreidler . . .

The plans would be strictly voluntary and sold as an alternative to traditional auto insurance. . . .

(b) The bill is part of a package Senate Democrats have proposed to combat global warming. The idea is to give people a financial incentive to drive less, lowering greenhouse-gas emissions and saving some money at the same time.

. . . A study by the Brookings Institution . . . estimated that if motorists nationwide switched to pay-as-you-drive insurance, driving would decrease by 8 percent and carbon-dioxide emissions would drop by 2 percent.

The bill's prospects in the House, however, are less certain. . . . Progressive Insurance offers a form of pay-as-you-drive insurance . . .

Hartford Insurance and Allstate Insurance are exploring the concept, too. The insurance company attaches a device to each customer's car that gathers information such as how you drive, when you drive and how far you drive. The data upload wirelessly to the company's computer system. Consumers are able to review their data and see what kind of discount—or price increase—they are on track to receive.

Do you drive past midnight or brake hard and accelerate fast? If so, you could be charged up to 9 percent more through the Progressive program . . . if you reduce your miles and drive more safely, your price could drop up to 15 percent.

(c) Insurance rates are fixed on a six-month basis, so consumers are able to correct their driving to receive an increased discount for the next six-month term. Before selling the insurance in Washington, Progressive wants to make sure its rating formulas and other proprietary information would be kept confidential. . . .

Unigard, a Bellevue-based insurance company, is planning a study that could lead to its own form of pay-as-you-drive insurance. The company would install devices in 5,000 customers' cars to record how much they are driving. In return for the information, customers would receive a discount on their insurance.

Participants in the study wouldn't be charged rates based on their miles driven, but the data would help Unigard design a pay-as-you-drive program that could be offered later. . . .

Chuck Ayers, president of the Cascade Bicycle Club in Seattle, said he's a fan of incentives that get people to tread lighter on the earth. "We need to be careful about stepping over the line and being big brother," Ayers said. "But if it's a voluntary thing—private industry rewarding you financially for being a better driver and driving less . . . in general, I think we would be very supportive of it."

. . . Freeman, the freelance writer, might be just the kind of driver who could benefit from pay-as-you-drive insurance. She estimates her family drives an average of 50 miles a week. Her husband occasionally drives to a poker night across town. The rest of the time they bike.

. . . Still, she doesn't sound sold on the idea of allowing someone to monitor her driving. "It seems like for being green you would have to incur a higher level of scrutiny on your driving," Freeman said. "That concerns me."

Source: Chantal Anderson, "Bill Would Allow Insurance to Offer Pay-as-You-Drive Plan," *The Seattle Times*, February 6, 2009.

## Key Points in the Article

The article describes a new program offered by automobile insurance companies to charge customers different premiums, based on when, how, and how much they drive. Washington State politicians considered legislation to permit insurance companies to allow the so-called pay-as-you-drive rates in the state. Such policies reward drivers who drive less than other drivers. Proponents of the legislation believe that it will reduce greenhouse gas emissions and global warming, but critics, as well as some supporters, are concerned that the data required for the program could intrude on drivers' privacy.

## Analyzing the News

(a) In markets where one side of the market has more information than the other, the less informed party will seek ways to gain information. If automobile insurance companies know that some of their customers drive fewer miles and drive more cautiously than other customers, they will be willing to charge those customers lower premiums. The figure shows that obtaining better information about the relative risk of insuring different drivers allows the companies to better judge the profitability of the

policies. As a result, the supply of insurance in the market should increase. You can see the increase in the figure as the supply curve shifts from $S_1$ to $S_2$. When this occurs, the market price of insurance falls from $P_1$ to $P_2$, and the quantity of insurance sold in the market increases from $Q_1$ to $Q_2$. But obtaining the information needed to offer pay-as-you-drive insurance policies requires that drivers be electronically tracked. This has raised concerns about invading drivers' privacy.

(b) Proposed legislation to offer pay-as-you-drive insurance policies was motivated by a desire to offer financial incentives to drive less, which would reduce greenhouse gas emissions. A study by the Brookings Institution estimated that a nationwide adoption of pay-as-you-drive automobile insurance could decrease driving by 8 percent and decrease carbon dioxide emissions by 2 percent.

(c) The Progressive Insurance Company offers a pay-as-you-drive insurance program that fixes the rates charged to drivers for six months. This allows consumers to alter their driving habits in order to receive increased discounts for the next six-month term. Progressive is being careful to keep proprietary information confidential before it attempts to lobby politicians in

Washington on the value of offering pay-as-you-drive insurance policies nationwide.

## Thinking Critically
### About Policy

1. Pay-as-you-drive automobile insurance policies offer consumers the option of paying lower premiums for driving fewer miles and driving more carefully. If the program is voluntary—drivers would not have to buy pay-as-you-drive policies if they did not want them—which drivers would benefit least from choosing to buy the policies? Who would be opposed to offering drivers this option?

2. In 2009, President Obama proposed that U.S. automobile manufacturers be required to meet a 35-miles-per-gallon (MPG) standard on new automobiles by 2016. An important reason for raising the required MPG to 35 is to reduce carbon dioxide emissions. Pay-as-you-drive insurance policies are also expected to reduce carbon dioxide emissions. What advantage would pay-as-you-drive insurance have relative to raising the required MPG standard as a means of reducing carbon dioxide emissions?

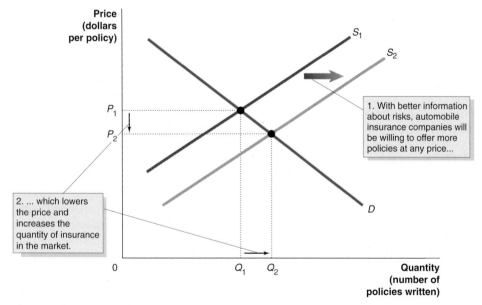

1. With better information about risks, automobile insurance companies will be willing to offer more policies at any price...

2. ... which lowers the price and increases the quantity of insurance in the market.

Information lowers price and increases quantity in the insurance market.

## Key Terms

Adverse selection, p. 561

Asymmetric information, p. 560

Moral hazard, p. 563

Principal–agent problem, p. 567

Winner's curse, p. 569

**17.1** **Asymmetric Information,** pages 560–564

LEARNING OBJECTIVE: Define asymmetric information and distinguish between adverse selection and moral hazard.

## Summary

**Asymmetric information** is a situation in which one party to an economic transaction has less information than the other party. Asymmetric information can lead to **adverse selection**, which occurs when one party to a transaction takes advantage of knowing more than the other party to the transaction. An example is the "lemons" problem, where adverse selection may lead to only unreliable used cars being offered for sale. Asymmetric information can also lead to **moral hazard**, which refers to actions people take after they have entered into a transaction that make the other party to the transaction worse off. For example, a firm that has taken out a fire insurance policy on a warehouse may be less careful in the future about avoiding fire hazards. Information problems result in the equilibrium quantity in markets being smaller than it would be if these problems did not exist. Therefore, there is a reduction in economic efficiency.

 Visit **www.myeconlab.com** to complete these exercises online and get instant feedback.

## Review Questions

1.1 What is asymmetric information? How does asymmetric information show up in the market for used cars?

1.2 What is the difference between adverse selection and moral hazard? Which is a bigger problem for consumers in the market for used cars?

1.3 Briefly discuss how adverse selection and moral hazard affect the market for insurance.

1.4 What methods do insurance companies use to reduce adverse selection and moral hazard?

## Problems and Applications

1.5 Suppose you see a 2007 Volkswagen Jetta GLS Turbo Sedan advertised in the campus newspaper for $10,000. If you knew the car was reliable, you would be willing to pay $12,000 for it. If you knew the car was unreliable, you would only be willing to pay $8,000 for it. Under what circumstances should you buy the car?

1.6 Michael Kinsley, a political columnist, observed, "The idea of insurance is to share the risks of bad outcomes." In what sense does insurance involve sharing risks? How does the problem of adverse selection affect the ability of insurance to provide the benefit of sharing risk?

Source: Michael Kinsley, "Congress on Drugs," *Slate*, August 1, 2002.

1.7 Under the Social Security retirement system, the federal government collects a tax on most people's wage income and makes payments to retired workers above a certain age who are covered by the system. (The age to receive full Social Security retirement benefits varies, based on the year the worker was born.) The Social Security retirement system is sometimes referred to as a program of social insurance. Is Social Security an insurance program in the same sense as a group life insurance or health insurance policy that a company provides to its workers? Briefly explain.

1.8 There are 10,000 houses in Lawrence. Suppose that a house there costs $100,000, and 5 percent of the houses burn down each year. Which 5 percent of houses will burn down in any particular year is impossible for anyone, including the owners, to predict. There is no fire insurance available to Lawrence residents, so you decide to start an insurance company and begin offering policies. Your policy will pay the purchaser $100,000 if his or her house burns down. You charge a premium of $22,000 per year.

a. Are the residents of Lawrence likely to buy your policies? Briefly explain.

b. Now suppose that 5 percent of the owners know with certainty that their houses will burn down and that the other 95 percent of the owners know with certainty that their houses will not burn down. You offer everyone the same insurance policy with the same $22,000 premium. What is your accounting profit likely to be for the year? Assume that you have no explicit costs except for the payments you make to people who bought your policies and had their houses burn down.

c. Now suppose that people do not know with certainty whether their houses will burn down and that some houses are significantly more likely to burn down than others. Unfortunately, the owners of the houses that are significantly more likely to burn down know it, but you do not. Is it possible for you to restructure the insurance policies you offer—that is, change the terms of how much you pay out and the premium you charge—in order to deal with this problem?

1.9 All states require that every driver have an automobile insurance policy that covers any car he or she owns and operates. Some people have such bad driving records that they are unable to find any insurance company willing to sell them a policy. These drivers are placed in an "assigned risk pool." Every insurance company that sells automobile insurance in the state is required to insure some drivers from the assigned risk pool. The state government usually sets the rates these drivers pay for insurance. Why is this system necessary? Why don't insurance companies voluntarily insure these bad drivers and charge them very high rates? Why does the state government have to force insurance companies to insure bad drivers?

**1.10** **(Related to the *Making the Connection* on page 562)** Suppose a large firm allows its employees to choose whether to participate in its health insurance plan. The firm is trying to decide whether to offer a plan with a high deductible but a low monthly premium or one with a low deductible but a high monthly premium. Under which plan is adverse selection likely to be a bigger problem? Briefly explain.

**1.11** **(Related to the *Making the Connection* on page 562)** An editorial in the *Wall Street Journal* argued that regulations imposed by state governments are responsible for making health insurance "so expensive to buy." The editorial singled out "'community rating' (insurers can't price based on differing risk factors such as age) and 'guaranteed issue' (you can wait until you're sick to buy insurance)." What problems do these regulations cause for insurance companies? How might insurance companies respond to these regulations? Do these regulations make consumers better off? The editorial concluded:

> The real scandal in American health insurance isn't that some people lack coverage for this or that treatment, but that tens of millions of Americans risk financial ruin because of [government] policies that make basic insurance difficult or impossible to buy.

Briefly explain whether you agree with this conclusion.

Source: "Why Can't You Buy Insurance?" *Wall Street Journal*, October 1, 2002.

**1.12** **(Related to the *Chapter Opener* on page 559)** Why have auto insurers such as State Farm started collecting more information on drivers and using computer models that employ thousands of variables to predict the chance that a driver will have an accident? Why didn't these firms do this sooner if these differences among drivers always existed?

**1.13** **(Related to the *Don't Let This Happen to You!* on page 564)** Briefly explain whether you agree with the following statement: "The reluctance of healthy young adults to buy medical insurance creates a moral hazard problem for insurance companies."

>> **End Learning Objective 17.1**

---

## 17.2 | Adverse Selection and Moral Hazard in Financial Markets, pages 564–566

LEARNING OBJECTIVE: Apply the concepts of adverse selection and moral hazard to financial markets.

## Summary

Adverse selection and moral hazard are serious problems in financial markets. When firms sell stocks and bonds, they know much more about their true financial condition than do potential investors. Investors are reluctant to buy stocks and bonds issued by small and medium-sized firms because they lack sufficient information about these firms. Investors also worry about the moral hazard problem of firms misusing the funds they raise through the sale of stocks and bonds. The Securities and Exchange Commission (SEC) has the authority to regulate the stock and bond markets and attempts to reduce adverse selection and moral hazard problems. The failure of financial firms and the financial frauds of the late 2000s indicate that information problems persist in financial markets.

 Visit **www.myeconlab.com** to complete these exercises online and get instant feedback.

## Review Questions

**2.1** Explain why asymmetric information makes it difficult for small firms to sell stocks and bonds.

**2.2** What is the Securities and Exchange Commission? Why was it founded?

## Problems and Applications

**2.3** In an article in the *New York Times*, Warren Buffett, one of the most successful investors of the past 30 years, wrote, "For many years, I've had little confidence in the earnings reported by corporations." Why might he be suspicious that firms were not reporting their profits accurately?

Source: Warren Buffett, "Who Really Cooks the Books?" *New York Times*, July 24, 2002.

**2.4** Many firms provide information about their plans and financial health to investment analysts who have no stake in the firm. Why would firms divulge such secrets?

**2.5** After the countries of Eastern Europe converted from Communism to the market system, they tried to set up stock and bond markets. Most of these markets have remained very small, with few firms being able to find buyers for their stocks or bonds. One economist remarked that the reason these financial markets have been unsuccessful is that "the lemons problem has been too great." Explain what the economist meant.

**2.6** **(Related to the *Making the Connection* on page 565)** Writing in the *Wall Street Journal*, the financial journalist Edward Chancellor remarked: "Boom times are always accompanied by fraud. . . . Bernard Madoff has now joined the ranks of great financial villains whose illicit activities have been exposed by market downturns." Why are frauds easier to carry out during a stock market boom and more likely to be exposed during a stock market downturn?

Source: Edward Chancellor, "A Fortune Up in Smoke," *Wall Street Journal*, April 17, 2009.

**2.7** **(Related to *Solved Problem 17-2* on page 566)** Adelphia Communications filed for bankruptcy in June 2002. In June 2005, John Rigas, Adelphia's founder and longtime CEO, was sentenced to prison for 15 years for, among other things, concealing over $2 billion in debt from investors. Rigas's son Timothy received a 20-year sentence after being convicted on the same charges as his father: conspiracy, bank fraud, and securities fraud. During the Rigas trial, U.S. attorneys accused the Rigases of using Adelphia as a "private piggy bank" to pay for such personal expenses as millions of dollars in cash advances, $13 million to build a golf course, and even 100 pairs of bedroom slippers. Despite being a publicly held firm, Adelphia was run like a family business. John Rigas and three of his sons and one son-in-law held five of the nine seats on the company's board of directors. The family's mismanagement was hidden from investors through fraudulent financial statements. After the collapse of Internet stock prices and the slowdown of the overall U.S. economy in 2001, investors began looking more closely at questionable managerial and accounting practices that made debt-ridden firms such as Adelphia and Enron appear to be in better financial condition than they actually were.

Sources: James Fink, "Adelphia Picks HOK for Downtown Office Design," *Buffalo Business First*, January 16, 2002; James Fink, "John Rigas Sentenced to 15 Years in Prison," *Buffalo Business First*, June 21, 2005; and "Rigases Looted Aldelphia, Jurors Told," www.smh.com.au/articles/2004/03/02/1078191325849.html.

Explain how shareholders can minimize or prevent the moral hazard problem.

**>> End Learning Objective 17.2**

## **17.3** Adverse Selection and Moral Hazard in Labor Markets, pages 567–568

LEARNING OBJECTIVE: Apply the concepts of adverse selection and moral hazard to labor markets.

## Summary

The potential for a **principal–agent problem** exists between employers and workers. This problem is caused by agents—workers—pursuing their own interests rather than the interests of the principals who hired them. When workers are not monitored, they may have no incentive to work hard. Employers try to avoid this moral hazard problem by increasing the value to a worker of the worker's current job. Three ways to increase the value of a worker's job are offering efficiency wages, using a seniority system, and offering profit sharing.

 Visit **www.myeconlab.com** to complete these exercises online and get instant feedback.

## Review Questions

**3.1** What problems can adverse selection and moral hazard cause in labor markets? What steps do firms take to deal with these problems?

**3.2** What are efficiency wages? What role can they play in reducing the principal–agent problem?

## Problems and Applications

**3.3** **(Related to the *Don't Let This Happen to You!* on page 564)** Briefly explain whether you agree with the following argument:

From an employer's point of view, the moral hazard problem in labor markets is that the potential employees who don't intend to work hard are the ones who are most eager for you to hire them. The adverse selection problem is that once you have hired a worker, he or she has an incentive to work hard only if monitored.

**3.4** **(Related to *Solved Problem 17-3* on page 568)** What role do tips play in dealing with the principal–agent problem in the market for restaurant servers? Suppose a law is passed that outlaws tips, and now restaurant servers just receive a wage, instead of a wage plus tips. Is the total income of servers likely to rise or fall? Briefly explain.

**3.5** Colleges and universities grant tenure to many professors, making it very difficult to fire them after they've worked there for six or seven years. Analyze this labor market strategy in light of asymmetric information, adverse selection, and moral hazard.

**3.6** The going wage for janitors is $8 per hour. The Executive Building decides to pay its janitors $12 per hour. Will this higher wage increase or decrease the firm's profits? Or could it go either way? In your answer, discuss asymmetric information and efficiency wages.

**>> End Learning Objective 17.3**

## **17.4** The Winner's Curse: When Is It Bad to Win an Auction? pages 569–571

LEARNING OBJECTIVE: Explain the winner's curse and why it occurs.

## Summary

In auctions where bidders do not know the true value of what is being auctioned, the winner, by overestimating the value of what is being bid for, can end up worse off than the losers. This is known as the **winner's curse**, and it occurs in auctions of common-value assets that would be given the same value by all bidders if they had perfect information.

 Visit **www.myeconlab.com** to complete these exercises online and get instant feedback.

# Review Questions

**4.1** What is the winner's curse? Is it a problem for the winner of every auction? Briefly explain why or why not.

**4.2** Briefly explain whether you agree or disagree with the following statement: "The more information bidders have on the true value of what is being auctioned, the less likely they are to fall victim to the winner's curse."

# Problems and Applications

**4.3** Suppose you are advising one of the oil companies involved in the oil field bidding shown in Figure 17-1 on page 569. What bidding strategy would you recommend to the company so it could avoid the winner's curse?

**4.4** After playing for six years in the major leagues, baseball players are free to sign a contract to play for any team. (Before that time, they are obligated to play for the team that first signed them.) In this situation, players often sign a contract to play for several years with the team that offers them the highest salary. Consider two players: Joe is a minor star who performs at about the same level each year. Sam's performance has been more uneven: Some years, he seems like one of the best players in baseball, but in other years, his performance has not been very good. Suppose Joe signs with the Cleveland Indians and Sam signs with the Cincinnati Reds. Three years later, is Cleveland or Cincinnati likely to be most satisfied that the player it signed played well enough to justify his salary? Briefly explain.

**4.5** A corporate takeover occurs when one firm—or a group of outside investors—buys up a majority of the stock in another firm. The usual aim of a takeover is to take advantage of the efficiencies possible with the newly merged firm or to bring in new management and run the acquired firm more profitably. In either case, the investors taking over the acquired firm are expecting to profit from the takeover. However, studies of corporate takeovers by Richard Roll of UCLA show that although the stockholders of the firm being taken over receive substantial gains—because the acquiring firm or investors bid up the price of the stock of the acquired firm as they try to take it over—the firm or investors carrying out the takeover earn small gains, if any. Relate Roll's finding to the problem of the winner's curse.

Source: Richard Roll, "The Hubris Hypothesis of Corporate Takeovers," *Journal of Business*, Vol. 59, No. 2, Pt. 1, April 1986, pp. 197–216.

**4.6** (Related to the *Making the Connection* on page 570) The winner's curse may apply to the marriage market. The winner's curse usually applies in markets with common-value assets but not in markets with private-value assets. Discuss whether it is more accurate to think of the marriage market as a market with common-value assets, private-value assets, or some combination of the two.

**4.7** An article in the *Wall Street Journal* described how many publishing companies compete for "blockbuster" books. Usually the agent for the author of a potential blockbuster will conduct an auction in which publishing companies bid for the rights to publish the book. The article described the outcome of a competition to publish a book by comedian Sarah Silverman: "HarperCollins won the rights to Sarah Silverman's book only after an intense auction with several other houses." HarperCollins agreed to an initial payment, or "advance," of $2.5 million for the right to publish the book. Give an economic explanation of the risks publishing companies take when bidding for blockbuster books.

Source: Anita Elberse, "Blockbuster or Bust," *Wall Street Journal*, January 3, 2009.

**4.8** In ancient Rome, the Praetorian Guard was a special force of personal bodyguards of the emperor. The Praetorian Guard was made up of thousands of troops, and occasionally an emperor would lose control over them. In 193 A.D., the Praetorian Guard revolted and murdered Emperor Pertinax. The guard then decided to auction off the office of emperor. The ancient historian Dio described the situation:

> Then ensued a most disgraceful business and one unworthy of Rome. For, just as if it had been in some market or auction-room, both the City and its entire empire were auctioned off. The sellers were the ones who had slain their emperor, and the would-be buyers were Sulpicianus and Julianus.

Didius Julianus won the auction with a bid that would be the equivalent of more than $1 billion today. Unfortunately, his reign was very short. The general Septimius Severus brought his army from the Danube to Rome, deposed Didius Julianus, and was proclaimed emperor. In the words of the historian Edward Gibbon, Didius Julianus was "beheaded as a common criminal, after having purchased, with an immense treasure, an anxious and precarious reign of only sixty-six days." Does the analysis in this chapter help you understand what happened to Didius Julianus?

Source: Paul Klemperer and Peter Temin, "An Early Example of the 'Winner's Curse' in an Auction," *Journal of Political Economy*, December 2001.

**4.9** (Related to the *Making the Connection* on page 570) Suppose that a $100 bill is auctioned off instead of a jar containing an unknown number of coins. Will the winner's curse still apply? Briefly explain.

**>> End Learning Objective 17.4**

# CHAPTER 18

# Public Choice, Taxes, and the Distribution of Income

## Chapter Outline and Learning Objectives

# >> Should the Government Use the Tax System to Reduce Inequality?

Taxes affect the incomes of households and the decisions made by businesses. For example, in 2003, when the federal government cut the tax on dividends—payments corporations make to stockholders—many companies responded in a big way. Before the tax cut, Microsoft, for instance, had never paid a dividend. After the tax cut, in a single year, Microsoft paid out more than $40 billion in dividends. Cutting the tax on dividends was intended to improve economic efficiency, but changing the tax code can serve other purposes as well.

When Barack Obama became president in January 2009, he proposed a number of changes to the tax system. Increased taxes on higher-income individuals and on corporations were intended to pay for part of the increases in federal government spending resulting from the economic recession of 2007–2009. Higher taxes were also intended to pay for expanding the federal government's role in the health care system, to reduce carbon dioxide emissions, and to achieve other policy goals. According to President Obama, the tax cut on dividends, as well as other tax cuts enacted during the early 2000s, had increased the burden on individuals with low and moderate incomes, while the burden on

the wealthy and on corporations had been reduced, increasing the level of income inequality. He proposed to use the tax code to help reduce this inequality. The president's critics worried that the changes he was proposing would reduce economic efficiency while having little effect on inequality.

The questions raised by the debate over President Obama's tax proposals are not new. Presidents John F. Kennedy and Ronald Reagan proposed significant cuts in income taxes that they claimed would enhance economic efficiency, while their opponents claimed that the tax cuts rewarded high-income taxpayers. The design of the tax system and the criteria to use in evaluating it are important questions. Has the tax code improved economic efficiency? Has the government, through its tax and other policies, had much impact on the distribution of income? We explore these questions in this chapter.

**AN INSIDE LOOK AT POLICY** on **page 604** describes a proposal to pay for changes in health care by imposing taxes on soda and other sugary drinks.

Sources: James Calmes and Robert Pear, "To Pay for Health Care, Obama Looks to Taxes on Affluent," *New York Times*, February 25, 2009; and "Barack Obama's Budget," *Economist*, March 5, 2009.

## Economics in YOUR LIFE!

### How Much Tax Should You Pay?

Government is ever present in your life. Just today, you likely drove on roads that the government paid for. You may attend a public college or university, paid for, at least in part, by government. Where does a government get its money? By taxing citizens. Think of the different taxes you pay. Do you think you pay more than, less than, or just about your fair share in taxes? How do you determine what your fair share is? As you read this chapter, see if you can answer these questions. You can check your answers against those we provide at the end of the chapter.

▶ Continued on page 603

W e saw in Chapter 2 that the government plays a significant role in helping the market system work efficiently by providing secure rights to private property and an independent court system to enforce contracts. We saw in Chapter 5 that the government itself must sometimes supply goods—known as *public goods*—that private firms will not supply. But how do governments decide which policies to adopt? In recent years, economists led by Nobel Laureate James Buchanan and Gordon Tullock, both of George Mason University, have developed the **public choice model**, which applies economic analysis to government decision making. In this chapter, we will explore how public choice can help us understand how policymakers make decisions.

We will also discuss the principles that governments use to create tax policy. In particular, we will see how economists identify which taxes are most economically efficient. At the end of the chapter, we will discuss the extent to which government policy—including tax policy—affects the distribution of income.

**Public choice model** A model that applies economic analysis to government decision making.

**18.1 LEARNING** OBJECTIVE

Describe the public choice model and explain how it is used to analyze government decision making.

# Public Choice

In earlier chapters, we focused on explaining the actions of households and firms. We have assumed that households and firms act to make themselves as well off as possible. In particular, we have assumed that households choose the goods they buy to maximize their utility and that firms choose the quantities and prices of the goods they sell to maximize profits. Because government policy plays an important role in the economy, it is important also to consider how government policymakers—such as senators, governors, presidents, and state legislators—arrive at their decisions. One of the key insights from the public choice model is that policymakers are no different than consumers or managers of firms: Policymakers are likely to pursue their own self-interest, even if their self-interest conflicts with the public interest. In particular, we expect that public officials will take actions that are likely to result in their being re-elected.

## How Do We Know the Public Interest? Models of Voting

It is possible to argue that, in fact, elected officials simply represent the preferences of the voters who elect them. After all, it would seem logical that voters will not re-elect a politician who fails to act in the public interest. A closer look at voting, however, makes it less clear that politicians are simply representing the views of the voters.

**The Voting Paradox** Many policy decisions involve multiple alternatives. Because the size of the federal budget is limited, policymakers face trade-offs. To take a simple example, suppose that there is $1 billion available in the budget and Congress must choose whether to spend it on *only one* of three alternatives: (1) research on breast cancer, (2) subsidies for mass transit, or (3) increased border security. Assume that the votes of members of Congress will represent the preferences of their constituents. We might expect that Congress will vote for the alternative favored by a majority of the voters. In fact, though, there are circumstances in which majority voting will fail to result in a consistent decision. For example, suppose for simplicity that there are only three voters, and they have the preferences shown at the top of Table 18-1.

In the table, we show the three policy alternatives in the first column. The remaining columns show the voters' rankings of the alternatives. For example, Lena would prefer to see the money spent on cancer research. Her second choice is mass transit, and her third choice is border security. What happens if a series of votes are taken in which each pair of alternatives is considered in turn? The bottom of Table 18-1 shows the results of these votes. If the vote is between spending the money on cancer research and spending the money on mass transit, cancer research wins because Lena and David both prefer spending the money on cancer research to spending the money on mass transit. So, if the votes of members of

| POLICY | LENA | DAVID | KATHLEEN |
|---|---|---|---|
| Cancer research | 1st | 2nd | 3rd |
| Mass transit | 2nd | 3rd | 1st |
| Border security | 3rd | 1st | 2nd |

| VOTES | OUTCOME |
|---|---|
| Cancer research versus mass transit | Cancer research wins |
| Mass transit versus border security | Mass transit wins |
| Border security versus cancer research | Border security wins |

**TABLE 18-1**

**The Voting Paradox**

Congress represent the preferences of voters, we have a clear verdict, and the money is spent on cancer research. Suppose, though, that the vote is between spending the money on mass transit and spending the money on border security. Then because Lena and Kathleen prefer spending on mass transit to spending on border security, mass transit wins. Now, finally, suppose the vote is between spending on cancer research and spending on border security. Surprisingly, border security wins because that is what David and Kathleen prefer. The outcome of this vote is surprising because if voters prefer cancer research to mass transit and mass transit to border security, we would expect that consistency in decision making would ensure that they prefer cancer research to border security. But in this example the collective preferences of the voters turn out not to be consistent. The failure of majority voting to always result in consistent choices is called the **voting paradox**.

This is an artificial example because we assumed that there were only three alternatives, there were only three voters, and a simple majority vote determined the outcomes. In fact, though, Nobel Laureate Kenneth Arrow of Stanford University has shown mathematically that the failure of majority votes to always represent voters' preferences is a very general result. The **Arrow impossibility theorem** states that no system of voting can be devised that will consistently represent the underlying preferences of voters. This theorem suggests that there is no way through democratic voting to ensure that the preferences of voters are translated into policy choices. In fact, the Arrow impossibility theorem suggests that voting might lead to shifts in policy that may not be efficient. For instance, which of the three alternatives for spending the $1 billion Congress will actually choose would depend on the order in which the alternatives happen to be voted on, which might change from one year to the next. So, with respect to economic issues, such as providing funding for public goods, we cannot count on the political process to necessarily result in an efficient outcome. In other words, the "voting market"—as represented by elections—may often do a less efficient job of representing consumer preferences than do markets for goods and services.

**The Median Voter Theorem** In practice, many political issues are decided by a majority vote. In those cases, what can we say about which voters' preferences the outcome is likely to represent? An important result known as the **median voter theorem** states that the outcome of a majority vote is likely to represent the preferences of the voter who is in the political middle. To take another simplified example, suppose there are five voters, and their preferences for spending on breast cancer research are shown in Figure 18-1. Their preferences range from Kathleen, who prefers to spend nothing on breast cancer research—preferring the funds to be spent on other programs or for federal spending to be reduced and taxes lowered—to Lena, who prefers to spend $6 billion.

In this case, David is the median voter because he is in the political middle; two voters would prefer to spend less than he does and two would prefer to spend more. To see why the median voter's preferences are likely to prevail, consider first a vote between David's preferred outcome of spending $2 billion and a proposal to spend $6 billion. Because only Lena favors $6 billion and the other voters all prefer spending less, the proposal to spend $2 billion would win four votes to one. Similarly, consider a vote between spending $2 billion and spending $1 billion. Three voters prefer spending more than

**Voting paradox** The failure of majority voting to always result in consistent choices.

**Arrow impossibility theorem** A mathematical theorem that holds that no system of voting can be devised that will consistently represent the underlying preferences of voters.

**Median voter theorem** The proposition that the outcome of a majority vote is likely to represent the preferences of the voter who is in the political middle.

## Figure 18-1

**The Median Voter Theorem**

The median voter theorem states that the outcome of a majority vote is likely to represent the preferences of the voter who is in the political middle. In this case, David is in the political middle because two voters want to spend more on breast cancer research than he does and two voters want to spend less. In any vote between a proposal to spend $2 billion and a proposal to spend a different amount, a proposal to spend $2 billion will win.

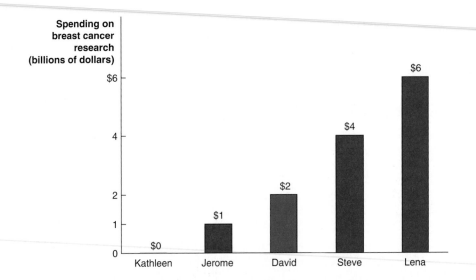

$1 billion and only two prefer spending $1 billion or less, so the proposal to spend $2 billion will win three votes to two. Only the proposal to spend $2 billion will have the support of a majority when paired with proposals to spend a different amount. Notice also that the amount spent as a result of the voting is less than the amount that would result from taking the simple average of the voter's preferences, which would be $2.6 billion.

One implication of the median voter theorem is that the political process tends to serve individuals whose preferences are in the middle, but not those individuals whose preferences are far away from the median. There is an important contrast between the political process, which results in collective actions in which everyone is obliged to participate, and the market process, in which individuals are free to participate or not. For instance, even though Kathleen would prefer not to spend government funds on breast cancer research, once a majority has voted to spend $2 billion, Kathleen is obliged to go along with the spending—and the taxes required to fund the spending. This is in contrast with the market for goods and services, where if, for instance, Kathleen disagrees with the majority of consumers who like iPods, she is under no obligation to buy one. Similarly, even though Lena and Steve might prefer to pay significantly higher taxes to fund additional spending on breast cancer research, they are obliged to go along with the lower level of spending the majority approved. If Lena would like to have her iPod gold plated, she can choose to do so, even if the vast majority of consumers would consider such spending a waste of money.

## Government Failure?

The voting models we have just looked at indicate that individuals are less likely to see their preferences represented in the outcomes of government policies than in the outcomes of markets. The public choice model goes beyond this observation to question whether the self-interest of policymakers is likely to cause them to take actions that are inconsistent with the preferences of voters, even where those preferences are clear. There are several aspects of how the political process works that might lead to this outcome.

**Rent seeking** Attempts by individuals and firms to use government action to make themselves better off at the expense of others.

**Rent seeking** Economists usually focus on analyzing the actions of individuals and firms as they attempt to make themselves better off by interacting in markets. The public choice model shifts the focus to attempts by individuals and firms to engage in **rent seeking**, which is the use of government action to make themselves better off at the expense of others. One of the benefits of the market system is that it channels self-interested behavior in a way that benefits society as a whole. Although Apple developed the iPod to make profits, its actions increased the well-being of millions of consumers. When Microsoft introduced the Zune to compete with the iPod, it also was motivated by the desire for profit, but it further increased consumer well-being by expanding the choice of digital music players available. Rent seeking, in contrast, can benefit a few individuals or firms at the expense of all other individuals and firms. For example, we saw in Chapter 8 that U.S. sugar firms have successfully convinced Congress to impose a quota on imports of sugar. The quota has benefited the owners of U.S. sugar firms and the people who work for them but has reduced consumer surplus, hurt U.S. candy companies and their workers, and reduced economic efficiency.

Because firms can benefit from government intervention in the economy, as the sugar companies benefited from the sugar quota, they are willing to spend resources attempting to secure these interventions. Members of Congress, state legislators, governors, and presidents need funds to finance their election campaigns. So, these policymakers may accept campaign contributions from rent-seeking firms and be willing to introduce *special interest legislation* in their behalf.

**Logrolling and Rational Ignorance** Two other factors help explain why rent-seeking behavior can sometimes succeed. It may seem puzzling that the sugar quota has been enacted when the number of workers and firms helped by it is so small. Why would members of Congress vote for the sugar quota if they do not have sugar producers in their districts? One possibility is logrolling. *Logrolling* refers to the situation where a member of Congress votes to approve a bill in exchange for favorable votes from other members on other bills. For example, a member of Congress from Texas might vote for the sugar quota, even though none of the member's constituents will benefit from it. In exchange, members of Congress from districts where sugar producers are located will vote for legislation the member of Congress from Texas would like to see passed. This vote trading may result in a majority of Congress supporting legislation that benefits the economic interests of a few, while harming the economic interests of a much larger group.

But if the majority of voters is harmed by rent-seeking legislation, how does it get passed, even given the effects of logrolling? In Chapter 8, we discussed one possible explanation with respect to the sugar quota. Although, collectively, consumer surplus declines by $3.44 billion per year because of the sugar quota, spread across a population of 310 million, the loss per person is only $11. Because the loss is so small, most people do not take it into account when deciding how to vote in elections, and many people are not even aware that the sugar quota exists. Other voters may be convinced to support restrictions on trade because the jobs saved by tariffs and quotas are visible and often highly publicized, while the jobs lost because of these restrictions and the reductions in consumer surplus are harder to detect. Because becoming informed on an issue may require time and effort and the economic payoff is often low, some economists argue that many voters are *rationally ignorant* of the effect of rent-seeking legislation. In this view, because voters frequently lack an economic incentive to become informed about pending legislation, the voters' preferences do not act as a constraint on legislators voting for rent-seeking legislation.

**Regulatory Capture** One way in which the government intervenes in the economy is by establishing a regulatory agency or commission that is given authority over a particular industry or type of product. For example, no firm is allowed to sell prescription drugs in the United States without first receiving authorization from the Food and Drug Administration (FDA). Ideally, regulatory agencies will make decisions in the public interest. The FDA should weigh the benefits to patients from quickly approving a new drug against the costs that the agency may overlook potentially dangerous side effects of the drug if approval is too rapid. However, because the firms being regulated are significantly affected by the regulatory agency's actions, the firms have an incentive to try to influence those actions. In extreme cases, this influence may lead the agency to make decisions that are in the best interests of the firms being regulated, even if these actions are not in the public interest. In that case, the agency has been subject to *regulatory capture* by the industry being regulated. Some economists point to the Interstate Commerce Commission (ICC) as an example of regulatory capture. Although the ICC has since been abolished by Congress, for decades it determined the prices that railroads and long-distance trucking firms could charge to haul freight. Congress originally established the ICC to safeguard the interests of consumers, but some economists have argued that for many years the ICC operated to suppress competition, which was in the interests of the railroads and trucking firms. Economists debate the extent to which regulatory capture explains the decisions of some government agencies.

In Chapter 5, we saw how the presence of externalities can lead to market failure, which is the situation where the market does not supply the economically efficient quantity of a good or service. Public choice analysis indicates that *government failure* can also occur. For the reasons we have discussed in this section, it is possible that government intervention in the economy may reduce economic efficiency rather than increase it. Economists disagree about the extent to which government failure results in serious economic inefficiency in the U.S. economy. Most economists, though, accept the basic argument of the public choice model that policymakers may have incentives to intervene in the economy in ways that do not promote efficiency and that proposals for such intervention should be evaluated with care.

## Is Government Regulation Necessary?

The public choice model raises important questions about the effect of government regulation on economic efficiency. But can we conclude that Congress should abolish agencies such as the Food and Drug Administration (FDA), the Environmental Protection Agency (EPA), and the Federal Trade Commission (FTC)? In fact, most economists agree that these agencies can serve a useful purpose. For instance, in Chapter 5 we discussed how the EPA can help correct the effects of production externalities, such as pollution. Regulatory agencies can also improve economic efficiency in markets where consumers have difficulty obtaining the information needed to make informed purchases. For example, consumers have no easy way of detecting bacteria and other contaminants in food or determining whether prescription drugs are safe and effective. The FDA was established in the early twentieth century to monitor the nation's food supply following newspaper accounts of unsanitary practices in many meatpacking plants.

Although government regulation can clearly provide important benefits to consumers, we need to take into account the costs of regulations. Recent estimates indicate that the costs of federal regulations may be several thousand dollars per taxpayer. Economics can help policymakers devise regulations that provide benefits to consumers that exceed their costs.

# The Tax System

However the size of government and the types of activities it engages in are determined, government spending has to be financed. The government primarily relies on taxes to raise the revenue it needs. Some taxes, though, such as those on cigarettes or alcohol, are intended more to discourage what society views as undesirable behavior than to raise revenue. These are the most widely used taxes:

- *Individual income taxes.* The federal government, most state governments, and some local governments tax the wages, salaries, and other income of households and the profits of firms. The individual income tax is the largest source of revenue for the federal government. In 2007 the average U.S. taxpayer earned about $59,647 and paid federal personal income taxes of $7,965.

- *Social insurance taxes.* The federal government taxes wages and salaries to raise revenue for the Social Security and Medicare systems. *Social Security* makes payments to retired workers and to disabled individuals. *Medicare* helps pay the medical expenses of people over age 65. The Social Security and Medicare taxes are often referred to as "payroll taxes." As the U.S. population has aged, payroll taxes have increased. By 2009, 75 percent of taxpayers paid more in payroll taxes than in federal income taxes. The federal government and state governments also tax wages and salaries to raise revenue for the unemployment insurance system, which makes payments to workers who have lost their jobs.

- *Sales taxes.* Most state and local governments tax retail sales of most products. More than half the states exempt food from the sales tax, and a few states also exempt clothing.

- *Property taxes.* Most local governments tax homes, offices, factories, and the land they are built on. In the United States, the property tax is the largest source of funds for public schools.

- *Excise taxes.* The federal government and some state governments levy excise taxes on specific goods, such as gasoline, cigarettes, and beer.

## An Overview of the U.S. Tax System

Panels (a) and (b) of Figure 18-2 show the revenue sources of the federal, state, and local governments. Panel (a) shows that the federal government raises more than 80 percent of its revenue from the individual income tax and from social insurance taxes. Corporate income taxes and excise taxes account for much smaller fractions of federal revenues. In 2008, federal revenues of all types amounted to almost $2.6 trillion, or about $8,300 per person. Over the past 40 years, federal revenues as a share of gross domestic product (GDP; the value of all the goods and services produced in the U.S. economy) have remained in a fairly narrow range between 17 and 23 percent.

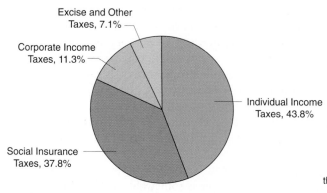

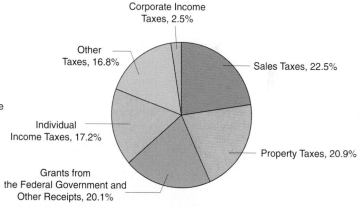

| Tax | Amount (billions) | Amount per Person | Percentage of Total Tax Receipts |
|---|---|---|---|
| Individual Income Taxes | $1,124 | $3,626 | 43.8% |
| Social Insurance Taxes | 972 | 3,135 | 37.8 |
| Corporate Income Taxes | 291 | 939 | 11.3 |
| Excise and Other Taxes | 182 | 588 | 7.1 |
| Total | $2,569 | $8,288 | 100% |

| Tax | Amount (billions) | Amount per Person | Percentage of Total Tax Receipts |
|---|---|---|---|
| Sales Taxes | $436 | $1,407 | 22.5% |
| Property Taxes | 405 | 1,305 | 20.9 |
| Grants from the Federal Government and Other Receipts | 388 | 1,253 | 20.1 |
| Individual Income Taxes | 333 | 1,075 | 17.2 |
| Other Taxes | 325 | 1,048 | 16.8 |
| Corporate Income Taxes | 48 | 154 | 2.5 |
| Total | $1,935 | $6,242 | 100% |

**(a) Sources of federal government revenue, 2008**

**(b) Sources of state and local government revenue, 2008**

Figure 18-2 | Federal, State, and Local Sources of Revenue, 2008

Individual income taxes are the most important source of revenue for the federal government, and social insurance taxes are the second most important source. State and local governments receive the most revenue from sales taxes. State and local governments also receive large transfers from the federal government, in part to help pay for federally mandated programs. Many local governments depend on property taxes to raise most of their tax revenue.

Source: U.S. Department of Commerce, Bureau of Economic Analysis, "National Income and Product Accounts of the United States," Tables 3.2 and 3.3, May 29, 2009.

**TABLE 18-2**

**Federal Income Tax Brackets and Tax Rates for Single Taxpayers, 2009**

| INCOME | TAX RATE |
|---|---|
| $0–$8,350 | 10% |
| $8,351–$33,950 | 15 |
| $33,951–$82,250 | 25 |
| $82,251–$171,550 | 28 |
| $171,551–$372,950 | 33 |
| Over $372,950 | 35 |

Source: Internal Revenue Service

Panel (b) shows that state and local governments rely on a different mix of revenue sources than does the federal government. In fact, the largest source of revenue for state and local governments is sales taxes. State and local governments also receive large grants from the federal government. These grants are intended in part to pay for programs that the federal government requires states and local governments to carry out. These programs, often called *federal mandates*, include the *Medicaid* program, which provides health care to poor people, and the Temporary Assistance for Needy Families (TANF) program, which provides financial assistance to poor families. Local governments depend heavily on property taxes. Many local school districts, in particular, rely almost entirely on revenues from property taxes.

## Progressive and Regressive Taxes

**Regressive tax** A tax for which people with lower incomes pay a higher percentage of their income in tax than do people with higher incomes.

**Progressive tax** A tax for which people with lower incomes pay a lower percentage of their income in tax than do people with higher incomes.

Economists often categorize taxes on the basis of how much tax people with different levels of income pay relative to their incomes. A tax is **regressive** if people with lower incomes pay a higher percentage of their income in tax than do people with higher incomes. A tax is **progressive** if people with lower incomes pay a lower percentage of their income in tax than do people with higher incomes. A tax is *proportional* if people with lower incomes pay the same percentage of their income in tax as do people with higher incomes.

The federal income tax is an example of a progressive tax. To see why, we must first consider the important distinction between a tax rate and a tax bracket. A *tax rate* is the percentage of income paid in taxes. A *tax bracket* refers to the income range within which a tax rate applies. Table 18-2 shows the federal income tax brackets and tax rates for single taxpayers in 2009.

We can use Table 18-2 to calculate what Matt, a single taxpayer with an income of $100,000, pays in federal income tax. This example is somewhat simplified because we are ignoring the *exemptions* and *deductions* that taxpayers can use to reduce the amount of income subject to tax. For example, taxpayers are allowed to exclude from taxation a certain amount of income, called the *personal exemption*, that represents very basic living expenses. Ignoring Matt's exemptions and deductions, he will have to make the tax payment to the federal government shown in Table 18-3. Matt's first $8,350 of income is in the 10 percent bracket, so he pays $835. His next $25,600 of income is in the 15 percent bracket, so he pays $3,840. His next $48,300 of income is in the 25 percent bracket, so he pays $12,075. His last $17,750 of income is in the 28 percent bracket, so he pays $4,970, which brings his total federal income tax bill to $21,720.

**TABLE 18-3**

**Federal Income Tax Paid on Taxable Income of $100,000**

| ON MATT'S . . . | MATT PAYS TAX OF . . . |
|---|---|
| first $8,350 of income | $ 835 |
| next $25,600 of income | 3,840 |
| next $48,300 of income | 12,075 |
| last $17,750 of income | 4,970 |
| His total federal income tax payment is | $21,720 |

## Making the Connection

## Which Groups Pay the Most in Federal Taxes?

At the beginning of this chapter, we mentioned the ongoing debate over whether to increase taxes on people with high incomes. To evaluate this debate, it's useful to know how much each income group pays of the total taxes collected by the federal government. The following table shows projections for 2009 by the Tax Policy Center, with taxpayers divided into quintiles from the 20 percent with the lowest income to the 20 percent with the highest income. The last row also shows taxpayers whose incomes put them in the top 1 percent. Column (1) shows the percentage of total income earned by each income group. Column (2) shows the percentage of all federal taxes—including Social Security and Medicare payroll taxes—paid by each income group. Column (3) shows the average federal tax rate for each group, calculated by dividing total taxes paid by total income.

| INCOME CATEGORY | PERCENTAGE OF TOTAL INCOME EARNED (1) | PERCENTAGE OF TOTAL FEDERAL TAXES PAID (2) | ALL FEDERAL TAXES PAID AS A FRACTION OF INCOME (AVERAGE FEDERAL TAX RATE) (3) |
|---|---|---|---|
| Lowest 20% | 4.0% | −0.1% | −0.3% |
| Second 20% | 9.2 | 4.0 | 7.9 |
| Third 20% | 14.9 | 12.0 | 14.5 |
| Fourth 20% | 20.8 | 19.9 | 17.2 |
| Highest 20% | 51.3 | 64.0 | 22.5 |
| **Total** | 100.0% | 100.0% | 18.0% |
| Highest 1% | 15.4 | 22.2 | 26.0 |

*Note:* Columns do not sum to precisely 100 percent due to rounding.

Source: Urban Institute and Brookings Institution, Tax Policy Center, www.taxpolicycenter.org. Used with permission.

The data in column (2) show that 64 percent of federal taxes are paid by the 20 percent of taxpayers with the highest incomes. This share is more than their share of total income earned, which is about 51 percent, as shown in column (1). Only taxpayers in the highest quintile pay a larger share of taxes than their share of income. Taxpayers whose incomes put them in the top 1 percent pay more than 22 percent of federal taxes. Many individuals in the lowest quintile of income receive tax credits from the federal government so that they in effect pay negative taxes. Column (3) indicates that average tax rates rise as income rises.

Data from the Internal Revenue Service show similar results for the federal personal income tax considered separately from the payroll tax and other federal taxes. In 2006, taxpayers in the top 1 percent of the income distribution earned 22 percent of all income while paying 40 percent of all federal personal income taxes. The top 10 percent earned 40 percent of income while paying 71 percent of taxes. The bottom 50 percent of the income distribution paid less than 3 percent of federal personal income taxes.

We can conclude that the federal taxes are progressive. Whether the federal tax system should be made more or less progressive remains a source of political debate.

Source: U.S. Department of the Treasury, Internal Revenue Service, "SOI Tax Stats—Individual Statistical Tables by Tax Rate and Income Percentile," www.irs.gov/taxstats/indtaxstats/article/0,,id=133521,00.html.

**YOUR TURN:** Test your understanding by doing related problem 2.9 on page 608 at the end of this chapter.

## Marginal and Average Income Tax Rates

The fraction of each additional dollar of income that must be paid in taxes is called the **marginal tax rate**. The **average tax rate** is the total tax paid divided by total income. When a tax is progressive, as is the federal income tax, the marginal and average tax

**Marginal tax rate** The fraction of each additional dollar of income that must be paid in taxes.

**Average tax rate** Total tax paid divided by total income.

rates differ. For example, in Table 18-3, Matt had a marginal tax rate of 28 percent because that is the rate he paid on the last dollar of his income. But his average tax rate was:

$$\left( \frac{\$21,720}{\$100,000} \right) \times 100 = 21.7\%$$

His average tax rate was lower than his marginal tax rate because the first $82,250 of his income was taxed at rates below his marginal rate of 28 percent.

When economists consider a change in tax policy, they generally focus on the marginal tax rate rather than the average tax rate because the marginal tax rate is a better indicator of how a change in a tax will affect people's willingness to work, save, and invest. For example, if Matt is considering working longer hours to raise his income, he will use his marginal tax rate to determine how much extra income he will earn after taxes. He will ignore his average tax rate because it does not reflect the taxes he must pay on the *additional* income he earns. The higher the marginal tax rate, the lower the return he receives from working additional hours and the less likely he is to work those additional hours.

## The Corporate Income Tax

The federal government taxes the profits earned by corporations under the *corporate income tax*. Like the individual income tax, the corporate income tax is progressive, with the lowest tax rate being 15 percent and the highest being 35 percent. Unlike the personal income tax, however, where relatively few taxpayers are taxed at the highest rate, most corporations are in the 35 percent tax bracket.

Economists debate the costs and benefits of a separate tax on corporate profits. The corporate income tax ultimately must be paid by a corporation's owners—which are its shareholders—or by its employees, in the form of lower wages, or by its customers, in the form of higher prices. Some economists argue that if the purpose of the corporate income tax is to tax the owners of corporations, it would be better to do so directly by taxing the owners' incomes rather than by taxing the owners indirectly through the corporate income tax. Individual taxpayers already pay income taxes on the dividends and capital gains they receive from owning stock in corporations. In effect, the corporate income tax "double taxes" earnings on individual shareholders' investments in corporations. An alternative policy that avoids this double taxation would be for corporations to calculate their total profits each year and send a notice to each shareholder, indicating the shareholder's portion of the profits. The shareholder would then be required to include this amount as taxable income on his or her personal income tax. Under another alternative, the federal government could continue to tax corporate income through the corporate income tax but allow individual taxpayers to receive corporate dividends and capital gains tax free. In 2003, Congress enacted a reduction on dividend and capital gains taxes to reduce double taxation.

## International Comparison of Corporate Income Taxes

In the past 10 years, several countries have cut corporate income taxes to increase investment spending and growth. Table 18-4 compares corporate income tax rates in several high-income countries. The tax rates given in the table include taxes at all levels of government. So, in the United States, for example, they include taxes imposed on corporate profits by state governments as well as by the federal government. The table shows that several countries, including Italy, Germany, and Ireland, significantly reduced corporate income tax rates between 2000 and 2008. Ireland, in particular, has been successful in using lower corporate income tax rates to attract foreign corporations to locate facilities there. In recent years, Microsoft, Intel, and Dell have all based some of their operations in Ireland. The table also shows that corporate income tax rates are higher in the United States than in other high-income countries, except Japan.

| COUNTRY | TAX IN 2000 | TAX IN 2008 |
|---|---|---|
| France | 37% | 33% |
| Germany | 52 | 30 |
| Ireland | 24 | 13 |
| Italy | 41 | 31 |
| Japan | 42 | 41 |
| Spain | 35 | 30 |
| Sweden | 28 | 28 |
| United Kingdom | 30 | 28 |
| United States | 40 | 40 |

TABLE 18-4

**Corporate Income Tax Rates around the World**

Source: KPMG, *KPMG's Corporate Tax Rate Survey*.

# Evaluating Taxes

We have seen that to raise revenue, governments have available a variety of taxes. In selecting which taxes to use, governments take into account the following goals and principles:

- The goal of economic efficiency
- The ability-to-pay principle
- The horizontal-equity principle
- The benefits-received principle
- The goal of attaining social objectives

**The Goal of Economic Efficiency** In Chapter 4, we analyzed the effect taxes have on economic efficiency. We briefly review that discussion here. Whenever a government taxes an activity, it raises the cost of engaging in that activity, so less of that activity will occur. Figure 18-3 uses a demand and supply graph to illustrate this point for a sales tax. As we saw in Chapter 4, a sales tax increases the cost of supplying a good, which causes the supply curve to shift up by the amount of the tax. In the figure, the equilibrium price rises from $P_1$ to $P_2$, and the equilibrium quantity falls from $Q_1$ to $Q_2$. When a good is taxed, less of it is produced.

The government collects tax revenue equal to the tax per unit multiplied by the number of units sold. The green-shaded rectangle in Figure 18-3 represents the government's tax revenue. Although sellers appear to receive a higher price for the good—$P_2$—the price they receive after paying the tax falls to $P_3$. Because the price consumers pay has risen, consumer surplus has fallen. Because the price producers receive has also

Figure 18-3

**The Efficiency Loss from a Sales Tax**

This figure reviews the discussion from Chapter 4 on the efficiency loss from a tax. A sales tax increases the cost of supplying a good, which causes the supply curve to shift up from $S_1$ to $S_2$. Without the tax, the equilibrium price of the good is $P_1$, and the equilibrium quantity is $Q_1$. After the tax is imposed, the equilibrium price rises to $P_2$, and the equilibrium quantity falls to $Q_2$. After paying the tax, producers receive $P_3$. The government receives tax revenue equal to the green-shaded rectangle. Some consumer surplus and some producer surplus become tax revenue for the government, and some become deadweight loss, shown by the yellow-shaded triangle. The deadweight loss is the *excess burden* of the tax.

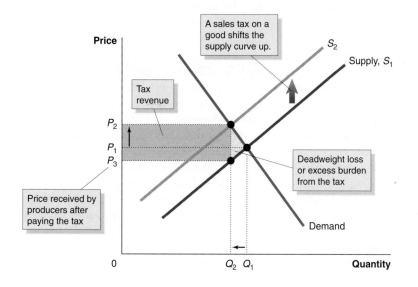

**Excess burden** A measure of the efficiency loss to the economy that results from a tax having reduced the quantity of a good produced; also known as the deadweight loss.

fallen, producer surplus has fallen. Some of the reduction in consumer surplus and producer surplus becomes tax revenue for the government. The rest of the reduction in consumer surplus and producer surplus is equal to the deadweight loss from the tax and is shown in the figure by the yellow-shaded triangle. The deadweight loss from a tax is known as the *excess burden* of the tax. The **excess burden** is a measure of the efficiency loss to the economy that results from the tax having reduced the quantity of the good produced. *A tax is efficient if it imposes a small excess burden relative to the tax revenue it raises.*

To improve the economic efficiency of a tax system, economists argue that the government should reduce its reliance on taxes that have a high deadweight loss relative to the revenue raised. The tax on interest earned from savings is an example of a tax with a high deadweight loss because savings often comes from income already taxed once. Therefore, taxing interest earned on savings from income that has already been taxed amounts to double taxation.

There are other examples of significant deadweight losses of taxation. High taxes on work can reduce the number of hours an individual works, as well as how hard the individual works or whether the individual starts a business. In each case, the reduction in the taxed activity—here, work—generates less government revenue, and individuals are worse off because the tax encourages them to change their behavior.

Taxation can have substantial effects on economic efficiency by altering incentives to work, save, or invest. A good illustration of this effect can be seen in the large differences between annual hours worked in Europe and in the United States. It is well known that Europeans now work fewer hours than do Americans. According to a recent analysis by Nobel Laureate Edward Prescott of Arizona State University, this difference was not always present. In the early 1970s, when European and U.S. tax rates on income were comparable, European and U.S. hours worked per employee were also comparable. Prescott finds that virtually all of the difference between labor supply in the United States and labor supply in France and Germany since that time is due to differences in their tax systems.

*Would a consumption tax be more efficient than an income tax?*

## Making the Connection | Should the United States Shift from an Income Tax to a Consumption Tax?

A key issue in recent debates over tax policy is whether the federal government should shift from relying on an income tax to relying on a *consumption tax*. Under the income tax, households pay taxes on all income earned. Under a consumption tax, households pay taxes only on the part of income they spend. Households pay taxes on saved income only if they spend the money at a later time.

To see how a shift from an income tax to a consumption tax can affect the economic incentives individuals face, consider the following example: Suppose a 20-year-old is deciding whether to save a $1,000 bonus paid by her employer. If she saves the $1,000 by putting it in a bank certificate of deposit (CD), the $1,000 *and* the interest she earns will both be taxed under the income tax, but neither will be taxed if the income tax is replaced by a consumption tax. Suppose she earns 6 percent per year on the CD and keeps it until she retires at age 70. With interest compounding tax-free over 50 years, she will have accumulated $18,420 at age 70. Now suppose that under the income tax she is taxed at a rate of 33 percent. As a result, she will have only $670 of her bonus left after paying the tax. In addition, if she saves the money in a CD, her after-tax return each year is only 6 percent × (1 − 0.33) = 4 percent. Now saving her bonus in a CD at age 20 yields only $4,761 at age 70. This big difference in accumulation—$13,659—is the tax burden on saving, a burden that makes saving less attractive.

Many economists argue that a taxpayer's well-being is better measured by his or her consumption (how much he or she spends) than by his or her income (how much he or she earns). Taxing consumption may therefore be more appropriate than taxing income. Also, because the income tax taxes interest and other returns to saving, it taxes *future* consumption—which is what current saving is for—more heavily than *present* consumption. That is, under an income tax, current consumption is taxed more favorably than future consumption, reducing households' willingness to save, as in the preceding example.

Some economists oppose a shift from an income tax to a consumption tax because they believe a consumption tax will be more regressive than an income tax. These economists argue that people with very low incomes are able to save little or nothing and so would not be able to benefit from the increased incentives for saving that exist under a consumption tax.

Would a shift to a consumption tax be a radical change in the tax system? For many households, the answer is, perhaps surprisingly, "no." Most taxpayers can already put part of their savings into accounts where the funds deposited and the interest received are not taxed until the funds are withdrawn for retirement spending—for example, 401(k) plans and certain types of Individual Retirement Accounts (IRAs). In effect, individuals whose savings are mainly in these retirement accounts are already paying a consumption tax rather than an income tax. And recent reductions in tax rates on dividends and capital gains—which are both returns to savings—and proposals to expand saving incentives will further increase the role of consumption taxation.

**YOUR TURN:** Test your understanding by doing related problem 2.11 on page 608 at the end of this chapter.

---

The administrative burden of a tax represents another example of the deadweight loss of taxation. Individuals spend many hours during the year keeping records for income tax purposes, and they spend many more hours prior to April 15 preparing their tax returns. The opportunity cost of this time is tens of billions of dollars each year and represents an administrative burden of the federal income tax. For corporations, complexity in tax planning arises in many areas. The federal government also has to devote resources to enforcing the tax laws. Although the government collects the revenue from taxation, the resources spent on administrative burdens benefit neither taxpayers nor the government.

Wouldn't tax simplification reduce the administrative burden and the deadweight loss of taxation? Yes. So why is the tax code complicated? In part, complexity arises because the political process has resulted in different types of income being taxed at different rates, requiring rules to limit taxpayers' ability to avoid taxes. In addition, interest groups seek benefits, while the majority of taxpayers, who do not benefit, find it difficult to organize a drive for a simpler tax system.

**The Ability-to-Pay Principle** The *ability-to-pay principle* holds that when the government raises revenue through taxes, it is fair to expect a greater share of the tax burden to be borne by people who have a greater ability to pay. Usually this principle means raising more taxes from people with high incomes than from people with low incomes, which is sometimes referred to as *vertical equity*. The federal income tax is consistent with the ability-to-pay principle. The sales tax, in contrast, is not consistent with the ability-to-pay principle because low-income people tend to spend a larger fraction of their income than do high-income people. As a result, low-income people will pay a greater fraction of their income in sales taxes than will high-income people.

**The Horizontal-Equity Principle** The *horizontal-equity principle* states that people in the same economic situation should be treated equally. Although this principle seems desirable, it is not easy to use in practice because it is sometimes difficult to determine whether two people are in the same economic situation. For example, two people with the same income are not necessarily in the same economic situation. Suppose one person does not work but receives an income of $50,000 per year entirely from interest received on bonds and another person receives an income of $50,000 per year from working at two jobs 16 hours a day. In this case, we could argue that the two people are in different economic situations and should not pay the same tax. Although policymakers and economists usually consider horizontal equity when evaluating proposals to change the tax system, it is not a principle that they can follow easily.

**The Benefits-Received Principle**  According to the *benefits-received principle*, people who receive the benefits from a government program should pay the taxes that support the program. For example, if a city operates a marina used by private boat owners, the government can raise the revenue to operate the marina by levying a tax on the boat owners. Raising the revenue through a general income tax paid both by boat owners and non–boat owners would be inconsistent with the benefits-received principle. Because the government has many programs, however, it would be impractical to identify and tax the beneficiaries of every program.

**The Goal of Attaining Social Objectives**  Taxes are sometimes used to attain social objectives. For example, the government might want to discourage smoking and drinking alcohol. Taxing cigarettes and alcoholic beverages is one way to help achieve this objective. Taxes intended to discourage certain activities are sometimes referred to as "sin taxes."

# Solved Problem | 18-2

## The Evolution of the Income Tax System

The United States did not have an income tax prior to the Civil War. Government revenue had come from such sources as excise taxes, customs duties, and the sale of public lands. The demands placed on government because of the war forced Congress to pass a law in 1862 that raised excise taxes and imposed a 3 percent tax on incomes up to $10,000 and taxed higher incomes at 5 percent. As the war ended, the government's revenue needs waned. The income tax was abolished in 1872, and from 1868 to 1913, the federal government derived most of its revenue from excise taxes and tariffs. By the early 1900s, the nation was becoming increasingly aware that tariffs and excise taxes were neither efficient nor fair, as they fell disproportionately on lower-income citizens. Proposals for a new income tax were championed by Congressmen from agricultural states who feared the possibility of a tax on land. By 1913, 36 states had ratified the 16th Amendment to the Constitution, which allowed Congress to institute a new income tax. In October, Congress passed a law that levied a tax of 1 percent on those with low incomes. The tax rose to 7 percent for those with incomes exceeding $500,000. But less than 1 percent of the population paid the tax.

The entry of the United States into World War I increased the revenue needed by the federal government. The Revenue Act of 1916 raised the lowest tax rate to 2 percent and the top rate to 15 percent for incomes in excess of $1.5 million. Other revenue acts followed. Still, in 1918, only 5 percent of the population paid income taxes. As the economy boomed in the 1920s, Congress cut tax rates five times. But after the economy plunged into the Great Depression, tax receipts fell. Congress passed the Tax Act of 1932, which raised tax rates. Another tax hike followed in 1936. The lowest tax rate was 4 percent, and the top rate reached 79 percent. Individual and corporate taxes were raised in 1940 and 1941. Once again, wartime spending led to greater tax demands. By the end of the war, taxpayers with taxable incomes of only $500 were subject to a tax rate of 23 percent, while taxpayers with incomes over $1 million faced a top rate of 94 percent. Federal taxes as a share of national income rose from 7.6 percent in 1941 to 20.4 percent in 1945.

Source: U.S. Treasury, *Fact Sheets: Taxes. History of the U.S. Tax System*, www.treas.gov/education/fact-sheets/taxes/ustax.shtml.

a.  Why did the United States first institute an income tax system?

b.  Select one goal or principle that was associated with the decision to pass the 16th Amendment to the U.S. Constitution.

## SOLVING THE PROBLEM:

Step 1:  **Review the chapter material.** This problem is about the tax system, so you may want to review the section "The Tax System," which begins on page 584.

Step 2:  **Answer question (a).** Prior to the Civil War, federal government spending was a relatively small percentage of national income. The government's revenue needs could be met through excise taxes, tariffs, and sales of public land. Many people paid little or no taxes. But wartime spending required much more revenue. The government needed a broader tax base—that is, a tax or taxes that would affect many more people.

**Step 3:** **Answer question (b).** Even before the 16th Amendment was passed, income taxes were progressive; people with lower incomes paid a lower percentage of the income in tax than people with higher incomes. Since the amendment was passed, progressive tax rates have always been a characteristic of the income tax system. This is a response to the ability-to-pay principle. One could also argue that an income tax scores higher on the benefits-received principle than the alternatives of a land tax, excise tax, or tariff. As government spending grew, especially during times of war, the benefits of government programs and services were broadly spread across the population. Hence, a broader tax was justified.

**YOUR TURN:** For more practice, do related problem 2.12 on page 608 at the end of this chapter.

# Tax Incidence Revisited: The Effect of Price Elasticity

**18.3 LEARNING** OBJECTIVE

Understand the effect of price elasticity on tax incidence.

In Chapter 4, we saw the difference between who is legally required to send a tax payment to the government and who actually bears the burden of a tax. Recall that the actual division of the burden of a tax between buyers and sellers in a market is known as **tax incidence**. We can go beyond the basic analysis of tax incidence by considering how the price elasticity of demand and price elasticity of supply affect how the burden of a tax is shared between consumers and firms.

**Tax incidence** The actual division of the burden of a tax between buyers and sellers in a market.

In Chapter 4, we discussed whether consumers or firms bear the larger share of a 10-cents-per-gallon federal excise tax on gasoline. We saw that consumers paid the majority of the tax. We can expand on this conclusion by stating that consumers of gasoline pay a larger fraction of gasoline taxes than do sellers because the elasticity of demand for gasoline is smaller than the elasticity of supply. In fact, we can draw a general conclusion: *When the demand for a product is less elastic than the supply, consumers pay the majority of the tax on the product. When demand for a product is more elastic than the supply, firms pay the majority of the tax on the product.*

## Don't Let This Happen to **YOU!**

### Remember Not to Confuse Who Pays the Tax with Who Bears the Burden of the Tax

Consider the following statement: "Of course I bear the burden of the sales tax on everything I buy. I can show you my sales receipts with the 6 percent sales tax clearly labeled. The seller doesn't bear that tax. I do."

The statement is incorrect. To understand why it is incorrect, think about what would happen to the price of a product if the sales tax on it were eliminated. Figure 18-4 shows that the price of the product would fall because the supply curve would shift down by the amount of the tax. The equilibrium price, however, would fall by less than the amount of the tax. (If you doubt that this is true, draw the graph to convince yourself.) So, the gain from eliminating

the tax would be received partly by consumers in the form of a lower price but also partly by sellers in the form of a new price that is higher than the amount they received from the old price minus the tax. Therefore, the burden from imposing a sales tax is borne partly by consumers and partly by sellers.

In determining the burden of a tax, what counts is not what is printed on the receipt for a product but what happens to the price of a product as a result of the tax.

[X] **myeconlab**

**YOUR TURN:** Test your understanding by doing related problem 3.9 on page 609 at the end of this chapter.

## Figure 18-4

**The Effect of Elasticity on Tax Incidence**

When demand is more elastic than supply, consumers bear less of the burden of a tax. When supply is more elastic than demand, firms bear less of the burden of a tax. $D_1$ is inelastic between point $A$ and point $B$, and $D_2$ is elastic between point $A$ and point $C$. With demand curve $D_1$, a 10-cents-per-gallon tax raises the equilibrium price from \$3.00 (point $A$) to \$3.08 (point $B$), so consumers pay 8 cents of the tax, and firms pay 2 cents. With $D_2$, a 10-cents-per-gallon tax on gasoline raises the equilibrium price only from \$3.00 (point $A$) to \$3.02 (point $C$), so consumers pay 2 cents of the tax. Because in this case producers receive \$2.92 per gallon after paying the tax, their share of the tax is 8 cents per gallon.

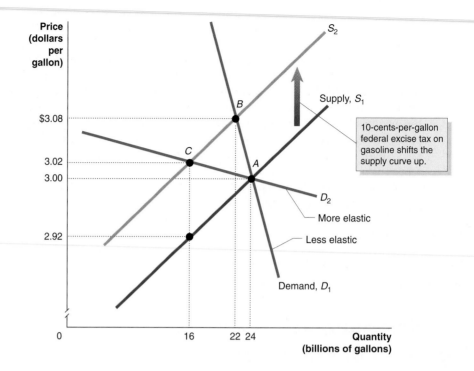

10-cents-per-gallon federal excise tax on gasoline shifts the supply curve up.

We can see why this conclusion is correct with the aid of Figure 18-4. In Figure 18-4, $D_1$ is inelastic between points $A$ and $B$, and $D_2$ is elastic between points $A$ and $C$. With demand curve $D_1$, the 10-cents-per-gallon tax raises the market price of gasoline from \$3.00 (point $A$) to \$3.08 (point $B$) per gallon, so consumers pay 8 cents of the tax, and firms pay 2 cents. With $D_2$, the market price rises only to \$3.02 (point $C$) per gallon, and consumers pay only 2 cents of the tax. With demand curve $D_2$, sellers of gasoline receive only \$2.92 per gallon after paying the tax. So, the amount they receive per gallon after taxes falls from \$3.00 to \$2.92 per gallon, and they pay 8 cents of the tax.

*Will she be paying part of Apple's corporate income tax when she buys an iPhone?*

## Making the Connection

## Do Corporations Really Bear the Burden of the Federal Corporate Income Tax?

The incidence of the corporate income tax is one of the most controversial questions in the economics of tax policy. It is straightforward to determine the incidence of the gasoline tax using demand and supply analysis. Determining the incidence of the corporate income tax is more complicated because economists disagree over how corporations respond to the tax.

A study by the Congressional Budget Office stated:

> A corporation may write its check to the Internal Revenue Service for payment of the corporate income tax, but the money must come from somewhere: from reduced returns to investors in the company, lower wages to its workers, or higher prices that consumers pay for the products the company produces.

Most economists agree that some of the burden of the corporate income tax is passed on to consumers in the form of higher prices. There is also some agreement that because the corporate income tax reduces the rates of return received by investors, it results in less investment in corporations. This reduced investment means workers have less capital available to them. As we discussed in Chapter 16, when workers have less capital, their productivity and their wages both fall. In this way, some of the burden of the corporate income tax is shifted from corporations to workers in the form of lower wages. The deadweight loss or excess burden from the corporate income tax is substantial. A study by the Congressional Budget Office estimated that this excess burden could be equal to more than half of the revenues raised by the tax. This estimate would make the corporate income tax one of the most inefficient taxes imposed by the federal government.

As a consequence, economists have long argued for reform of the system of double taxing income earned on investments that corporations finance by issuing stock. This income is taxed once by the corporate income tax and again by the individual income tax as profits are distributed to shareholders. Tax rates on dividends and capital gains were reduced in 2003, but whether to reduce double taxation further remains the subject of vigorous political debate.

Source: Congressional Budget Office, "The Incidence of the Corporate Income Tax," CBO paper, March 1996.

**YOUR TURN:** Test your understanding by doing related problem 3.7 on page 609 at the end of this chapter.

---

# Solved Problem | 18-3

## The Effect of Price Elasticity on the Excess Burden of a Tax

Explain whether you agree or disagree with the following statement: "For a given supply curve, the excess burden of a tax will be greater when demand is less elastic than when it is more elastic." Illustrate your answer with a demand and supply graph.

## SOLVING THE PROBLEM:

**Step 1:** **Review the chapter material.** This problem is about both excess burden and tax incidence, so you may want to review the section "Evaluating Taxes," which begins on page 589, and the section "Tax Incidence Revisited: The Effect of Price Elasticity," which begins on page 593.

**Step 2:** **Draw a graph to illustrate the relationship between tax incidence and excess burden.** Figure 18-4 on page 594 provides a good example of the type of graph to draw. Be sure to indicate the areas representing excess burden.

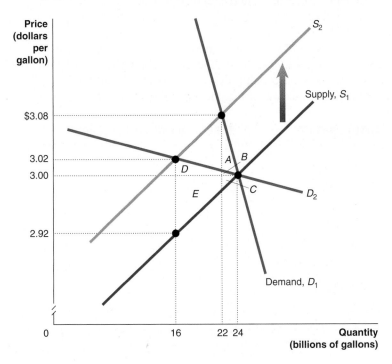

**Step 3:** **Use the graph to evaluate the statement.** The graph on page 594 is the same as Figure 18-4. As we have seen, for a given supply curve, when demand is more elastic, as with demand curve $D_2$, the fall in equilibrium quantity is greater than when demand is less elastic, as with demand curve $D_1$. The deadweight loss when demand is less elastic is shown by the area of the triangle made up of *A*, *B*, and *C*. The deadweight loss when demand is more elastic is shown by the area of the triangle made up of *B*, *C*, *D*, and *E*. The area of the deadweight loss is clearly larger when demand is more elastic than when it is less elastic. Recall that the excess burden of a tax is measured by the deadweight loss. Therefore, when demand is less elastic, the excess burden of a tax is *smaller* than when demand is more elastic. We can conclude that the statement is incorrect.

**YOUR TURN:** For more practice, do related problems 3.5 and 3.6 on pages 608–609 at the end of this chapter.

---

**18.4 LEARNING** OBJECTIVE

Discuss the distribution of income in the United States and understand the extent of income mobility.

# Income Distribution and Poverty

In practice, in most economies, some individuals will have very high incomes, and some individuals will have very low incomes. But how unequal is the distribution of income in the United States today? How does this compare with the distribution of income in the United States in the past or with the distribution of income in other countries today? What determines the distribution of income? And, to return to an issue raised at the beginning of this chapter, what impact does the tax system have on the distribution of income? These are questions we will explore in the remainder of this chapter.

## Measuring the Income Distribution and Poverty

Tables 18-5 and 18-6 show that the distribution of income clearly is unequal. Table 18-5 shows that while about 13 percent of U.S. households have annual incomes less than $15,000, the top 20 percent of households have incomes greater than $100,000. Table 18-6 divides the population of the United States into five groups, from the 20 percent with the lowest incomes to the 20 percent with the highest incomes. The fraction of total income received by each of the five groups is shown for selected years. Table 18-6 reinforces the fact that income is unequally distributed in the United States. The first row shows that in 2007, the 20 percent of Americans with the lowest incomes received only 3.4 percent of all income, while the 20 percent with the highest incomes received 49.7 percent of all income.

Table 18-6 also shows that over time, there have been some changes in the distribution of income. There was a moderate decline in inequality between 1936 and 1980, followed by some increase in inequality during the years after 1980. We will discuss some reasons for the recent increase in income inequality later in this chapter.

**TABLE 18-5**

**The Distribution of Household Income in the United States, 2007**

| ANNUAL INCOME | PERCENTAGE OF ALL HOUSEHOLDS |
|---|---|
| $0–$14,999 | 13.2% |
| $15,000–$24,999 | 11.6 |
| $25,000–$34,999 | 10.7 |
| $35,000–$49,999 | 14.1 |
| $50,000–$74,999 | 18.2 |
| $75,000–$99,999 | 11.9 |
| $100,000 and over | 20.2 |

Source: Carmen DeNavas-Walt, Bernadette D. Proctor, and Jessica C. Smith, U.S. Census Bureau, *Current Population Reports*, P60-235, *Income, Poverty, and Health Insurance Coverage in the United States: 2007*, Washington, DC: U.S. Government Printing Office, August 2008, Table A-1.

| YEAR | LOWEST 20% | SECOND 20% | THIRD 20% | FOURTH 20% | HIGHEST 20% |
|------|-----------|-----------|----------|-----------|------------|
| 2007 | 3.4% | 8.7% | 14.8% | 23.4% | 49.7% |
| 1990 | 3.9 | 9.6 | 15.9 | 24.0 | 46.6 |
| 1980 | 4.3 | 10.3 | 16.9 | 24.9 | 43.7 |
| 1970 | 4.1 | 10.8 | 17.4 | 24.5 | 43.3 |
| 1960 | 3.2 | 10.6 | 17.6 | 24.7 | 44.0 |
| 1950 | 3.1 | 10.5 | 17.3 | 24.1 | 45.0 |
| 1936 | 4.1 | 9.2 | 14.1 | 20.9 | 51.7 |

**TABLE 18-6**

**How Has the Distribution of Income Changed over Time?**

Sources: Carmen DeNavas-Walt, Bernadette D. Proctor, and Jessica C. Smith, U.S. Census Bureau, Current Population Reports, P60-235, *Income, Poverty, and Health Insurance Coverage in the United States: 2007*, Washington, DC: U.S. Government Printing Office, August 2008, Table 2; U.S. Census Bureau, *Income in the United States, 2002*, P60–221, September 2003; and U.S. Census Bureau, *Historical Statistics of the United States, Colonial Times to 1970*, Washington, DC: U.S. Government Printing Office, 1975.

**The Poverty Rate in the United States** Much of the discussion of the distribution of income focuses on poverty. The federal government has a formal definition of poverty that was first developed in the early 1960s. According to this definition, a family is below the **poverty line** if its annual income is less than three times the amount of money necessary to purchase the minimum quantity of food required for adequate nutrition. In 2007, the poverty line was $21,027 for a family of four with two children. Figure 18-5 shows the **poverty rate**, or the percentage of the U.S. population that was poor during each year between 1960 and 2007. Between 1960 and 1973, the poverty rate declined by half, falling from 22 percent of the population to 11 percent. In the past 30 years, however, the poverty rate has declined very little. In 2007, it was actually slightly higher than it was in 1973.

Different groups in the population have substantially different poverty rates. Table 18-7 shows that while the overall poverty rate in 2007 was 12.5 percent, the rate among women who head a family with no husband present, among black people, and among Hispanic people was about twice as high. The poverty rates for white and Asian people as well as for married couples were below average.

**Poverty line** A level of annual income equal to three times the amount of money necessary to purchase the minimum quantity of food required for adequate nutrition.

**Poverty rate** The percentage of the population that is poor according to the federal government's definition.

## Explaining Income Inequality

The novelists Ernest Hemingway and F. Scott Fitzgerald supposedly once had a conversation about the rich. Fitzgerald said to Hemingway, "You know, the rich are different from you and me." To which Hemingway replied, "Yes. They have more money." Although witty, Hemingway's joke doesn't help answer the question of why the rich have more money. In Chapter 16, we provided one answer to the question when we

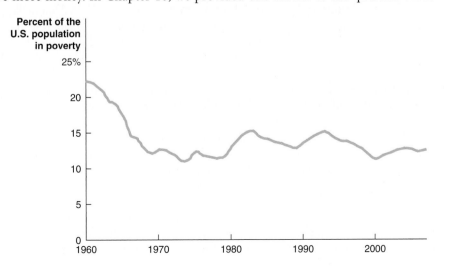

## Figure 18-5

**Poverty in the United States, 1960–2007**

The poverty rate in the United States declined from 22 percent of the population in 1960 to 11 percent in 1973. Over the past 30 years, the poverty rate has fluctuated between 11 percent and 15 percent of the population.
Source: Carmen DeNavas-Walt, Bernadette D. Proctor, and Jessica C. Smith, U.S. Census Bureau, Current Population Reports, P60-235, *Income, Poverty, and Health Insurance Coverage in the United States: 2007*, Washington, DC: U.S. Government Printing Office, August 2008.

## TABLE 18-7

**Poverty Rates Vary across Groups, 2007**

| | |
|---|---|
| All people | 12.5% |
| Female head of family, no husband present (all races) | 28.3 |
| Blacks | 24.5 |
| Hispanics | 21.5 |
| Asians | 10.2 |
| White, not Hispanic | 8.2 |
| Married couple | 4.9 |

*Note:* Hispanics can be of any race.

Source: Carmen DeNavas-Walt, Bernadette D. Proctor, and Jessica C. Smith, U.S. Census Bureau, Current Population Reports, P60-235, *Income, Poverty, and Health Insurance Coverage in the United States: 2007*, Washington, DC: U.S. Government Printing Office, August 2008, Table 3.

discussed the *marginal productivity theory of income distribution*. We saw that in equilibrium, each factor of production receives a payment equal to its marginal revenue product. The more factors of production an individual owns, and the more productive those factors are, the higher the individual's income will be.

For most people, of course, the most important factor of production they own is their labor. Therefore, the income they earn depends on how productive they are and on the prices of the goods and services their labor helps produce. Baseball player CC Sabathia earned a salary of more than $15 million in 2009 because he is a very productive player, and his employer, the New York Yankees, can sell tickets and television rights to the baseball games Sabathia plays in for a high price. Individuals who help to produce goods and services that can be sold for only a low price earn lower incomes.

Many people own other factors of production as well. For example, many people own capital by owning stock in corporations or by owning shares in mutual funds that buy the stock of corporations. Ownership of capital is not equally distributed, and income earned from capital is more unequally distributed than income earned from labor. Some people supply entrepreneurial skills by starting and managing businesses. Their income is increased by the profits from these businesses.

We saw in Table 18-6 that income inequality has increased somewhat during the past 25 years. Two factors that appear to have contributed to this increase are technological change and expanding international trade. Rapid technological change, particularly the development of information technology, has led to the substitution of computers and other machines for unskilled labor. This substitution has caused a decline in the wages of unskilled workers relative to other workers. Expanding international trade has put U.S. workers in competition with foreign workers to a greater extent than in the past. This competition has caused the wages of unskilled workers to be depressed relative to the wages of other workers. Some economists have also argued that the incomes of low-income workers have been depressed by competition with workers who have immigrated to the United States illegally.

Most economists believe that changes in tax laws have not played a major role in recent changes in income inequality. Federal income tax rates have changed dramatically during the years covered in Table 18-6. For example, the top marginal income tax rate was 91 percent in the 1950s, declining to 70 percent in the 1960s and to 28 percent in the 1980s. The rate then rose to 39.6 percent in the 1990s, before declining to 35 percent in 2003. Because tax rates changed significantly but the distribution of income has changed relatively little, it is unlikely that changes in tax rates have had a large impact on the distribution of income.

Finally, like everything else in life, earning an income is also subject to good and bad fortune. A poor person who becomes a millionaire by winning the state lottery is an obvious example, as is a person whose earning power drastically declines as a result of a debilitating illness or accident. So, we can say that as a group, the people with high incomes are likely to have greater-than-average productivity and own greater-than-average amounts of capital. They are also likely to have experienced good fortune. As a group, poor people are likely to have lower-than-average productivity and own lower-than-average amounts of capital. They are also likely to have been less fortunate.

# Showing the Income Distribution with a Lorenz Curve

Figure 18-6 presents the distribution of income using a *Lorenz curve*. A **Lorenz curve** shows the distribution of income by arraying incomes from lowest to highest on the horizontal axis and indicating the cumulative fraction of income earned by each fraction of households on the vertical axis. If the distribution of income were perfectly equal, a Lorenz curve would be a straight line because the first 20 percent of households would earn 20 percent of total income, the first 40 percent of households would earn 40 percent of total income, and so on. Panel (a) of Figure 18-6 shows a Lorenz curve for the actual distribution of income in the United States in 1980 and another curve for the distribution of income in 2007, using the data in Table 18-6. We know that income was distributed more unequally in 2007 than in 1980 because the Lorenz curve for 2007 is farther away from the line of equal distribution than is the Lorenz curve for 1980.

Panel (b) illustrates how to calculate the *Gini coefficient*, which is one way of summarizing the information provided by a Lorenz curve. The Gini coefficient is equal to the area between the line of perfect income equality and the Lorenz curve—area *A* in panel (b)—divided by the whole area below the line of perfect equality—area *A* plus area *B* in panel (b). Or:

$$\text{Gini coefficient} = \left(\frac{A}{A + B}\right).$$

If the income distribution were completely *equal*, the Lorenz curve would be the same as the line of perfect income equality, area *A* would be zero, and the Gini coefficient would be zero. If the income distribution were completely *unequal*, area *B* would be zero, and the Gini coefficient would equal 1. Therefore, the greater the degree of income inequality, the greater the value of the Gini coefficient. In 1980, the Gini coefficient for the United States was 0.403. In 2007, it was 0.463, which tells us again that income inequality increased between 1980 and 2007.

> **Lorenz curve** A curve that shows the distribution of income by arraying incomes from lowest to highest on the horizontal axis and indicating the cumulative fraction of income earned by each fraction of households on the vertical axis.

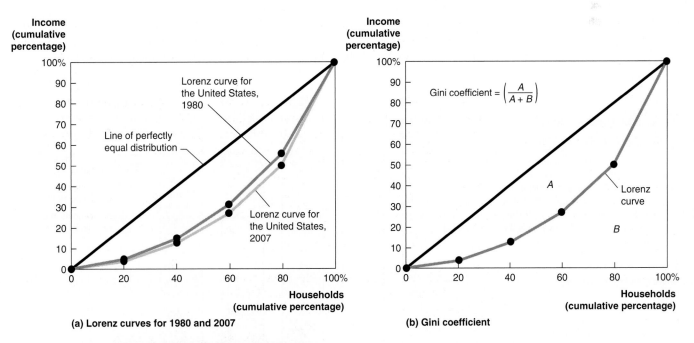

**(a) Lorenz curves for 1980 and 2007**

**(b) Gini coefficient**

## Figure 18-6 | The Lorenz Curve and Gini Coefficient

In panel (a), the Lorenz curves show the distribution of income by arraying incomes from the lowest to the highest on the horizontal axis and indicating the cumulative fraction of income by each fraction of households on the vertical axis. The straight line represents perfect income equality. Because the Lorenz curve for 1980 is closer to the line of perfect equality than the Lorenz curve for 2007, we know that income was more equally distributed in 1980 than in 2007. In panel (b), we show the Gini coefficient, which is equal to the area between the line of perfect income equality and the Lorenz curve—area *A*—divided by the whole area below the line of perfect equality—area *A* plus area *B*. The closer the Gini coefficient is to 1, the more unequal the income distribution.

## Problems in Measuring Poverty and the Distribution of Income

The measures of poverty and the distribution of income that we have discussed to this point may be misleading for two reasons. First, these measures are snapshots in time that do not take into account *income mobility*. Second, they ignore the effects of government programs meant to reduce poverty.

**Income Mobility in the United States**  We expect to see some income mobility. When you graduate from college, your income will rise as you assume a new job. A family may be below the poverty line one year because the main wage earner is unemployed but may rise well above the poverty line the next year, when that wage earner finds a job. A medical student may have a very low income for several years but a very high income after graduating and establishing a medical practice. It is also true that someone might have a high income one year—perhaps from making a very profitable investment in the stock market—and have a much lower income in future years.

Statistics on income mobility are more difficult to collect than statistics on income during a particular year because they involve following the same individuals over a number of years. A study by the U.S. Census Bureau tracked the incomes of the same households for each year from 1996 to 1999. Figure 18-7 shows the results of the study. Each column represents one quintile—or 20 percent—of households, arranged by their incomes in 1996. Reading up the column, we can see where the households that started in that quintile in 1996 ended up in 1999. For example, the bottom quintile (the first column) consists of households with incomes of $16,220 or less in 1996 (all values are measured in 1999 dollars to correct for the effects of inflation). Only 62 percent of these households were still in the bottom quintile in 1999. Only a small number—1.2 percent—had moved all the way to the top quintile, but more than one-third had moved into either the second quintile or the middle quintile. At the other end of the income distribution, of those households in the top income quintile—with incomes of $68,649 or more—in 1996, only two-thirds were still in the top quintile in 1999. Given the relatively short time period involved, this study indicates that there is significant income mobility in the United States over time.

It should be noted that the U.S. economy experienced rapid growth between 1996 and 1999, which may have increased the degree of income mobility. However, an earlier study by Peter Gottschalk of Boston College and Sheldon Danziger of the University of

### Figure 18-7

**Income Mobility in the United States, 1996–1999**

Each column represents one quintile—or 20 percent—of households, arranged by their incomes in 1996. Reading up the column, we can see where the households that started in that quintile in 1996 ended up in 1999. Only 62 percent of the households that were in the bottom quintile of income in 1996 were still in the bottom quintile in 1999. Only 66 percent of the households that were in the top quintile of income in 1996 were still in the top quintile in 1999.

*Note:* Incomes are in 1999 dollars to correct for the effects of inflation.

Source: U.S. Census Bureau, "Dynamics of Economic Well-Being: Movements in the U.S. Income Distribution, 1996–1999," *Current Population Reports*, P70–95, July 2004.

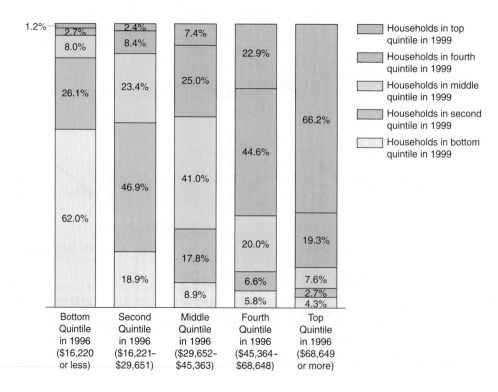

Michigan also provides evidence of significant income mobility. In that study, only 47 percent of people who were in the lowest 20 percent of incomes in 1968 were still in the lowest bracket in 1991. More than 25 percent had incomes in 1991 that put them in the middle- or higher-income brackets. Of those people who were in the highest-income bracket in 1968, only 42 percent were still in the highest bracket in 1991. Almost 8 percent of this group had fallen to the lowest-income bracket.

Another study by the U.S. Census Bureau found that of people who were poor at some time during the years 2001 to 2003, about half were in poverty for less than four months. Of the people who were poor in 2001, fewer than 60 percent were still poor in 2003. Only 2.4 percent of the U.S. population was poor every month during those three years.

**The Effect of Taxes and Transfers** A second reason the conventional statistics on poverty and income distribution may be misleading is that they omit the effects of government programs. Because of government programs, there is a difference between the income people earn and the income they actually have available to spend. The data in Tables 18-5 and 18-6 show the distribution of income before taxes are paid. We have seen that at the federal level, taxes are progressive, meaning people with high incomes pay a larger share of their incomes in taxes than do people with low incomes. Therefore, income remaining after taxes is more equally distributed than is income before taxes. The tables also do not include income from *transfer payments* individuals receive from the government, such as Social Security payments to retired and disabled people. The Social Security system has been very effective in reducing the poverty rate among people older than 65. In 1960, 35 percent of people in the United States over age 65 had incomes below the poverty line. By 2007, fewer than 10 percent of people over 65 had incomes below the poverty line.

Individuals with low incomes also receive noncash benefits, such as food stamps, free school lunches, and rent subsidies. The government's Supplemental Nutrition Assistance Program, more commonly referred to as the *food stamp program*, has been a particularly important noncash benefit. Under this program, individuals with low incomes can buy, at a discount, coupons to purchase food in supermarkets. In 2008, more than 28 million people participated in this program, at a cost to the federal government of $37.7 billion. Because individuals with low incomes are more likely to receive transfer payments and other benefits from the government than are individuals with high incomes, the distribution of income is more equal if we take these benefits into account. For example, in 2006, 12.3 percent of the U.S. population was below the poverty line, according to the official definition. Taking into account taxes paid and benefits received from government programs raises the incomes of enough people to reduce the poverty rate to 9.0 percent.

## Income Distribution and Poverty around the World

How does income inequality in the United States compare with income inequality in other countries? Table 18-8 compares the ratio of total income received by the 20 percent of the population with the lowest incomes and the 20 percent with the highest incomes in several countries. The countries are ranked from most unequal to least unequal. In Bolivia, for example, the highest-income group has $63.0/1.5 = 42.0$ times the income of the lowest-income group. In Japan, by contrast, the highest-income group has only $35.7/10.6 = 3.4$ times the income of the lowest-income group. As the table shows, poor countries, such as Bolivia and Paraguay, typically have more unequal distributions of income than does the United States. The distribution of income in the United States is more equal than in some moderate-income countries, such as Brazil and Chile, but less equal than in other moderate-income countries, such as Thailand. The United States has the most unequal distribution of income of any high-income country in the world. Of course, we must be careful with such comparisons because transfer payments are not counted in income. For example, the Social Security and Medicare systems in the United States are much more generous than the corresponding systems in Japan but less generous than those in France and Germany.

TABLE 18-8

**Income Inequality around the World**

| COUNTRY | LOWEST 20% | HIGHEST 20% | RATIO |
|---------|-----------|-------------|-------|
| Bolivia | 1.5% | 63.0% | 42.0 |
| Paraguay | 2.4 | 61.9 | 25.8 |
| Brazil | 2.8 | 61.1 | 21.8 |
| Chile | 3.8 | 60.0 | 15.8 |
| United States | 3.4 | 49.7 | 14.6 |
| Thailand | 6.3 | 49.0 | 7.8 |
| United Kingdom | 6.1 | 44.0 | 7.2 |
| Ireland | 7.4 | 42.0 | 5.7 |
| France | 7.2 | 40.2 | 5.6 |
| Canada | 7.2 | 39.9 | 5.5 |
| South Korea | 7.9 | 37.5 | 4.7 |
| Germany | 8.5 | 36.9 | 4.3 |
| Norway | 9.6 | 37.2 | 3.9 |
| Japan | 10.6 | 35.7 | 3.4 |

*Note:* Data for most countries are for the early 2000s; U.S. data are for 2007.
Source: Adapted from United Nations, *Human Development Report, 2007/2008*, New York: Palgrave Macmillan, 2007, Table 15.

Although poverty remains a problem in high-income countries, it is a much larger problem in poor countries. The level of poverty in much of Sub-Saharan Africa, in particular, is a human catastrophe. In 2007, the poverty line in the United States for a family of four was an annual income of $21,027, but economists often use a much lower threshold income of $570 per person per year (or about $1.50 per day) when calculating the rate of poverty in poor countries. As Table 18-9 shows, by this measure, poverty declined from about 20 percent of the world population in 1970 to 7 percent in 2000, the most recent year for which statistics are available. The greatest reduction in poverty has taken place in Asia. In China, the poverty rate dropped spectacularly from 32 percent in 1970 to 3.1 percent in 2000. In South Asia, which includes India, poverty rates dropped from 30.3 percent to 2.5 percent. By contrast, the poverty rate in Sub-Saharan Africa *increased* from 35.1 percent in 1970 to 48.8 percent in 2000. Why has poverty

TABLE 18-9

**Poverty in Sub-Saharan Africa Is Much Greater Than Elsewhere in the World**

| | PERCENTAGE OF THE POPULATION IN POVERTY | |
|--------|------|------|
| REGION | 1970 | 2000 |
| World | 20.2% | 7.0% |
| East Asia | 32.7 | 2.4 |
| China | 32.0 | 3.1 |
| South Asia | 30.3 | 2.5 |
| Middle East and North Africa | 10.7 | 0.6 |
| Latin America | 10.3 | 4.2 |
| Sub-Saharan Africa | 35.1 | 48.8 |

Source: Xavier Sala-i-Martin, "The World Distribution of Income: Falling Poverty and Convergence, Period," *Quarterly Journal of Economics*, Vol. 121, No. 2, May 2006, pp. 351–397.

fallen dramatically in Asia but risen in Africa? The key explanation is that the countries of Asia have had higher rates of economic growth than have the countries of Sub-Saharan Africa. Recent economic research demonstrates a positive relationship between economic growth and the incomes of lower-income people.

▶ Continued from page 579

## Economics in YOUR LIFE!

At the beginning of the chapter, we asked you to think about where government gets the money to provide goods and services and about whether you pay your fair share of taxes. After reading this chapter, you should see that you pay taxes in many different forms. When you work, you pay taxes on your income, both for individual income taxes and social insurance taxes. When you buy gasoline, you pay an excise tax, which, in part, pays for highways. When you buy goods at a local store, you pay state and local sales taxes, which the government uses to fund education and other services. Whether you are paying your fair share of taxes is a normative question. The U.S. tax system is progressive, so higher-income individuals pay more in taxes than do lower-income individuals. In fact, as we saw in the *Making the Connection* on page 587, people in the lowest 40 percent of the income distribution pay no federal income taxes at all. You may find that you will not pay much in federal income taxes in your first job after college. But as your income grows during your career, so will the percentage of your income you pay in taxes.

## Conclusion

The public choice model provides insights into how government decisions are made. The decisions of policymakers will not necessarily reflect the preferences of voters. Attempts by government to intervene in the economy may increase economic efficiency, as we saw in Chapter 5, but they may also lead to government failure and a reduction in economic efficiency.

A saying attributed to Benjamin Franklin states that "nothing in this world is certain but death and taxes." But which taxes? As we saw at the beginning of this chapter, politicians continue to debate whether the government should use the tax system and other programs to reduce the level of income inequality in the United States. The tax system represents a balance among the objectives of economic efficiency, ability to pay, paying for benefits received, and achieving social objectives. Those favoring government intervention to reduce inequality argue that it is unfair for some people to have much higher incomes than others. Others argue that income inequality largely reflects higher incomes resulting from greater skills and from entrepreneurial ability and that higher taxes reduce work, saving, and investment.

Many economists are skeptical of tax policy proposals to reduce income inequality very significantly. They argue that a market system relies on individuals being willing to work hard and take risks, with the promise of high incomes if they are successful. Taking some of that income from them in the name of reducing income inequality reduces the incentives to work hard and take risks. Ultimately, whether policies to reduce income inequality should be pursued is a normative question. Economics alone cannot decide the issue.

Read *An Inside Look at Policy* on the next page for a discussion of a proposal to pay for changes in health care by imposing a tax on soda.

## >> Should the Government Use a Tax on Soda to Pay For an Overhaul of Health Care?

### WALL STREET JOURNAL

## Soda Tax Weighed to Pay for Health Care

(a) Senate leaders are considering new federal taxes on soda and other sugary drinks to help pay for an overhaul of the nation's health-care system.

The taxes would pay for only a fraction of the cost to expand health-insurance coverage to all Americans and would face strong opposition from the beverage industry. They also could spark a backlash from consumers who would have to pay several cents more for a soft drink.

On Tuesday, the Senate Finance Committee is set to hear proposals from about a dozen experts about how to pay for the comprehensive health-care overhaul that President Barack Obama wants to enact this year. Early estimates put the cost of the plan at around $1.2 trillion. The administration has so far only ear-marked funds for about half of that amount.

The Center for Science in the Public Interest, a Washington-based watchdog group that pressures food companies to make healthier products, plans to propose a federal excise tax on soda, certain fruit drinks, energy drinks, sports drinks and ready-to-drink teas. It would not include most diet beverages. Excise taxes are levied on goods and manufacturers typically pass them on to consumers.

(b) . . . The Congressional Budget Office, which is providing lawmakers with cost estimates for each potential change in the health overhaul, included the option in a broad report on health-system financing in December. The office estimated that adding a tax of three cents per 12-ounce serving to these types of sweetened drinks would generate $24 billion over the next four years. So far, lawmakers have not indicated how big a tax they are considering.

Proponents of the tax cite research showing that consuming sugar-sweetened drinks can lead to obesity, diabetes and other ailments. They say the tax would lower consumption, reduce health problems and save medical costs. At least a dozen states already have some type of taxes on sugary beverages, said Michael Jacobson, executive director of the Center for Science in the Public Interest.

"Soda is clearly one of the most harmful products in the food supply, and it's something government should discourage the consumption of," Mr. Jacobson said.

The main beverage lobby that represents Coca-Cola Co., PepsiCo Inc., Kraft Foods Inc. and other companies said such a tax would unfairly hit lower-income Americans and wouldn't deter consumption.

"Taxes are not going to teach our children how to have a healthy lifestyle," said Susan Neely, president of the American Beverage Association. Instead, the association says it's backing programs that limit sugary beverage consumption in schools.

. . . The beverage-tax proposal would apply to drinks that many Americans don't consider unhealthy—such as PepsiCo's Gatorade and Kraft's Capri Sun—based on their calorie content.

Health advocates are floating other so-called sin tax proposals and food regulations as part of the government's health-care overhaul. Mr. Jacobson also plans to propose Tuesday that the government sharply raise taxes on alcohol, move to largely eliminate artificial trans fat from food and move to reduce the sodium content in packaged and restaurant food.

(c) The beverage tax is just one of hundreds of ideas that lawmakers are weighing to finance the health-care plans. They're expected to narrow the list in coming weeks.

The White House, meanwhile, is pulling together private health groups to identify cost savings that will help fund the health overhaul. Mr. Obama on Monday held a White House meeting with groups that represent doctors, hospitals, insurers, pharmaceutical companies and medical-device makers. They pledged to help restrain cost increases in the health-care system in an effort to save $2 trillion over the next decade.

"When it comes to health-care spending, we are on an unsustainable course that threatens the financial stability of families, businesses and government itself," Mr. Obama told reporters.

Source: Janet Adamy, "Soda Tax Weighed to Pay for Health Care," *Wall Street Journal*, May 12, 2009, p. A4.

## Key Points in the Article

This article describes a proposal to provide some funds for President Obama's overhaul of the health care system. An early estimate put the cost of the president's health care plan at $1.2 trillion. The Center for Science in the Public Interest proposed a federal excise tax on soda, certain fruit drinks, energy drinks, sports drinks, and ready-to-drink teas to cover part of this cost. Proponents of the tax cited research showing that consuming sugar-sweetened drinks can lead to obesity, diabetes, and other health problems. The tax would lower consumption of soft drinks, reduce health problems, and save medical costs. Some manufacturers of soft drinks argued that it would unfairly harm low-income Americans and would not reduce consumption.

## Analyzing the News

(a) The U.S. Senate prepared to hear proposals to impose a federal sales tax on sugary soft drinks. The tax would raise a small amount of the revenue needed to pay for a proposed overhaul of the nation's health care system. Opposition to the tax comes from the beverage industry and from consumers.

(b) The Congressional Budget Office (CBO) estimated that a 3-cent tax on a 12-ounce serving of a sweetened drink could generate $24 billion over four years. The figure shows how an excise tax would affect the market for sweetened soft drinks. The original equilibrium is at point $A$. The tax would shift the supply curve for soft drinks to the left, from $S_1$ to $S_2$. The equilibrium price would increase from $P_1$ to $P_2$, and the equilibrium quantity would decrease from $Q_1$ to $Q_2$. Point $B$ is the new equilibrium point. The actual amount by which price and quantity would change depends on the elasticity of the demand and supply of soft drinks, as we saw in this chapter. The article does not report on the elasticity assumptions the CBO made in computing its estimate of the revenue that could be raised by the tax. We do know, though, that the tax is expected to raise $24 billion over four years, so the amount raised each year must be $6 billion. If the price of a 12-ounce soft drink is $1, then the quantity sold each year must be 200 billion (because $0.03 \times 200$ billion = $6 billion). In the figure, the revenue from the tax equals the area of the green rectangle.

The beverage industry argued that the tax would not reduce consumption and that it would unfairly harm lower-income consumers.

(c) Washington lawmakers are considering other ways to finance health care, including some suggested by doctors, hospitals, insurers, pharmaceutical companies, and medical-device makers. These groups have pledged to restrain future cost increases.

## Thinking Critically
### *About Policy*

1. The article states that the lobby that represents beverage companies ". . . said such a tax would unfairly hit lower-income Americans and wouldn't deter consumption." Draw a demand and supply graph that represents the market for sugary soft drinks, assuming that the tax "wouldn't deter consumption." How does this assumption affect the equilibrium price and quantity of the drinks and the incidence of the tax?

2. Assume that the demand for sugary soft drinks is perfectly elastic. Draw a demand and supply graph that represents this assumption. How does this assumption affect the equilibrium price and quantity of the drinks and the incidence of the tax?

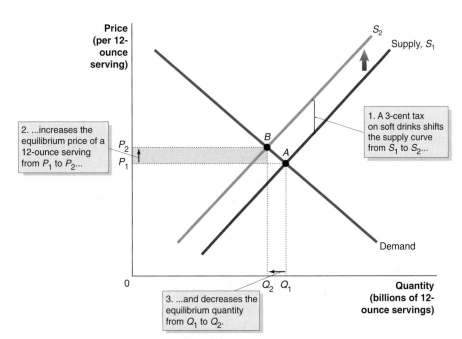

2. ...increases the equilibrium price of a 12-ounce serving from $P_1$ to $P_2$...

1. A 3-cent tax on soft drinks shifts the supply curve from $S_1$ to $S_2$...

3. ...and decreases the equilibrium quantity from $Q_1$ to $Q_2$.

A tax decreases the supply of sugary soft drinks. The amount of revenue raised by the tax depends on the elasticity of the demand and the elasticity of supply of the drinks.

## Key Terms

### 18.1 Public Choice, pages 580–584

LEARNING OBJECTIVE: Describe the public choice model and explain how it is used to analyze government decision making.

## Summary

The **public choice model** applies economic analysis to government decision making. The observation that majority voting may not always result in consistent choices is called the **voting paradox**. The **Arrow impossibility theorem** states that no system of voting can be devised that will consistently represent the underlying preferences of voters. The **median voter theorem** states that the outcome of a majority vote is likely to represent the preferences of the voter who is in the political middle. Individuals and firms sometimes engage in **rent seeking**, which is the use of government action to make themselves better off at the expense of others. Although government intervention can sometimes improve economic efficiency, public choice analysis indicates that *government failure* can also occur, reducing economic efficiency.

 Visit www.myeconlab.com to complete these exercises online and get instant feedback.

## Review Questions

1.1 What is the public choice model?

1.2 What is the difference between the voting paradox and the Arrow impossibility theorem?

1.3 What is rent seeking, and how is it related to regulatory capture?

1.4 What is the relationship between market failure and government failure?

## Problems and Applications

1.5 Will the preferences shown in the following table lead to a voting paradox? Briefly explain.

| POLICY | LENA | DAVID | KATHLEEN |
|---|---|---|---|
| Cancer research | 1st | 2nd | 3rd |
| Mass transit | 2nd | 1st | 1st |
| Border security | 3rd | 3rd | 2nd |

1.6 Many political observers have noted that Republican presidential candidates tend to emphasize their conservative positions on policy issues while running for their party's nomination, and Democratic presidential candidates tend to emphasize their liberal positions on policy issues while running for their party's nomination. In the general election, though, Republican candidates tend to downplay their conservative positions and Democratic candidates tend to downplay their liberal positions. Can the median voter theorem help explain this pattern? Briefly explain.

1.7 Briefly explain whether you agree with the following argument: "The median voter theorem will be an accurate predictor of the outcomes of elections when a majority of voters have preferences very similar to those of the median voter. When the majority of voters have preferences very different from those of the median voter, the median voter theorem will not lead to accurate predictions of the outcomes of elections."

1.8 An article in the *Economist* magazine made the following observation:

> People often complain that it is simplistic for economics to assume that individuals are rational and self-interested. Of course this is a simplification, but it is an enlightening one, and not flatly contradicted in the real world. The corresponding assumption about government—that the state aims to maximize social welfare—is contradicted by the real world about as flatly as you could wish.

What does it mean for the state to "maximize the social welfare"? If policymakers are not attempting to maximize the social welfare, what are they attempting to do?

Source: "The Grabbing Hand," *Economist*, February 11, 1999.

1.9 Is the typical person likely to gather more information when buying a new car or when voting for a member of the House of Representatives? Briefly explain.

**1.10** James Buchanan, who is one of the key figures in developing the public choice model, wrote: "The relevant difference between markets and politics does not lie in the kinds of values/interests that persons pursue, but in the conditions under which they pursue their various interests." Do you agree with this statement? Are there significant ways in which the business marketplace differs from the political marketplace?

Source: James M. Buchanan, "The Constitution of Economic Policy," *American Economic Review*, Vol. 77, No. 3, June 1987, p. 246.

>> **End Learning Objective 18.1**

---

**18.2** **The Tax System, pages 584–592**

LEARNING OBJECTIVE: Understand the tax system in the United States, including the principles that governments use to create tax policy.

## Summary

Governments raise the funds they need through taxes. The most widely used taxes are income taxes, social insurance taxes, sales taxes, property taxes, and excise taxes. Governments take into account several important objectives when deciding which taxes to use: efficiency, ability to pay, horizontal equity, benefits received, and attaining social objectives. A **regressive tax** is a tax for which people with lower incomes pay a higher percentage of their incomes in tax than do people with higher incomes. A **progressive tax** is a tax for which people with lower incomes pay a lower percentage of their incomes in tax than do people with higher incomes. The **marginal tax rate** is the fraction of each additional dollar of income that must be paid in taxes. The **average tax rate** is the total tax paid divided by total income. When analyzing the impact of taxes on how much people are willing to work or save or invest, economists focus on the marginal tax rate rather than the average tax rate. The **excess burden** of a tax is the efficiency loss to the economy that results from a tax having reduced the quantity of a good produced.

 Visit **www.myeconlab.com** to complete these exercises online and get instant feedback.

## Review Questions

**2.1** Which type of tax raises the most revenue for the federal government?

**2.2** In mid-2009, it wasn't clear which of President Barack Obama's tax proposals were likely to be enacted by Congress. An article in the *Washington Post* offered the following observation:

> Since last year's campaign, President Obama has vowed repeatedly not to increase taxes for families making less than $250,000 a year. That pledge, while politically popular, has left him with just two primary sources of funding for his ambitious social agenda: about 3 million high-earning families and the nation's businesses.

If President Obama's proposals are enacted, is it likely that the U.S. tax system will become more progressive or less progressive? Be sure to provide a definition of *progressive tax* and *regressive tax* in your answer.

Source: Lori Montgomery and V. Dion Haynes, "Small Businesses Brace for Tax Battle," *Washington Post*, April 27, 2009.

**2.3** What is the difference between a marginal tax rate and an average tax rate? Which is more important in determining the impact of the tax system on economic behavior?

**2.4** Briefly discuss each of the principles governments consider when deciding which taxes to use.

## Problems and Applications

**2.5** Why does the federal government raise more tax revenue from taxes on individuals than from taxes on businesses?

**2.6** On April 1, 2009, a 62-cent increase in the federal cigarette tax went into effect. The following data is from the Gallup-Healthways Well-Being Index for 2008:

| PERCENTAGE WHO SMOKE, BY ANNUAL HOUSEHOLD INCOME | |
| --- | --- |
| **INCOME** | **PERCENTAGE WHO SMOKE** |
| Less than $12,000 | 34% |
| $12,000–$35,999 | 28% |
| $36,000–$59,999 | 22% |
| $60,000–$89,999 | 16% |
| $90,000+ | 13% |

Based on these data, would the federal cigarette tax be considered progressive or regressive? Be sure to define *progressive tax* and *regressive tax* in your answer.

Source: Lydia Saad, "Cigarette Tax Will Affect Low-Income Americans Most," *Gallup, Inc.*, April 1, 2009.

**2.7** Many state governments have begun using lotteries to raise revenue. If we think of a lottery as a type of tax, is a lottery likely to be progressive or regressive? What data would you need to determine whether the burden of a lottery is progressive or regressive?

**2.8** Use the information in Table 18-2 on page 586 to calculate the total federal income tax paid, the marginal tax rate, and the average tax rate for people with the

following incomes. (For simplicity, assume that these people have no exemptions or deductions from their incomes.)
a. $25,000
b. $125,000
c. $300,000

2.9 (Related to the *Making the Connection* on page 587) Currently, the Social Security and Medicare programs are funded by payroll taxes rather than by the federal personal income tax. In 2009, the payroll tax for Social Security was 12.4 percent on wage, salary, and self-employment income up to $106,800. Above that income level, the tax dropped to zero. The Medicare tax was 2.9 percent on all wage, salary, and self-employment income. Some economists and policymakers have proposed eliminating the payroll tax and shifting to funding Social Security and Medicare out of the federal personal income tax. Would this proposal make the federal income tax system as a whole more progressive or less progressive? Briefly explain.

2.10 Almost all states levy sales taxes on retail products, but about half of them exempt purchases of food. In addition, virtually all services are exempt from state sales taxes. Evaluate these tax rate differences, using the goals and principles of taxation on pages 589–592.

2.11 (Related to the *Making the Connection* on page 590) Suppose the government eliminates the income tax and replaces it with a consumption tax. Think about the effect of this on the market for automobiles. Can you necessarily tell what will happen to the price and quantity of automobiles? Briefly explain.

2.12 (Related to *Solved Problem 18-2* on page 592) Consider the following tax structure: Taxpayers pay nothing on the first $10,000 of income; they pay 15 percent on the next 10,000 of income; they pay 33 percent on the next $30,000; they pay 25 percent on the next $40,000; and they pay 10 percent on any income over $90,000. The Encee family earns a total household income of $125,000.
a. Is the tax progressive, regressive, or neither?
b. Calculate the total tax bill for the Encee family.
c. What is the marginal tax rate for the Encee family?
d. What is the average tax rate for the Encee family?

>> **End Learning Objective 18.2**

---

**18.3** **Tax Incidence Revisited: The Effect of Price Elasticity, pages 593–595**
LEARNING OBJECTIVE: Understand the effect of price elasticity on tax incidence.

## Summary

**Tax incidence** is the actual division of the burden of a tax. In most cases, buyers and sellers share the burden of a tax levied on a good or service. When the elasticity of demand for a product is smaller than the elasticity of supply, consumers pay the majority of the tax on the product. When the elasticity of demand for a product is larger than the elasticity of supply, sellers pay the majority of the tax on the product.

 Visit www.myeconlab.com to complete these exercises online and get instant feedback.

## Review Questions

3.1 What is meant by *tax incidence*?
3.2 Briefly discuss the effect of price elasticity of supply and demand on tax incidence.

## Problems and Applications

3.3 According to the 2004 *Economic Report of the President*, "The actual incidence of a tax may have little to do with the legal specification of its incidence." Briefly explain what this statement means and discuss whether you agree or disagree with it.

3.4 According to the 2004 *Economic Report of the President*, "Another crucial principle [of tax incidence] is that only people can pay taxes. Businesses and other artificial entities cannot pay taxes." Do you agree that businesses cannot pay taxes? Don't businesses pay the federal corporate income tax? Briefly explain.

3.5 (Related to *Solved Problem 18-3* on page 595) Use the following graph of the market for cigarettes to answer the questions.

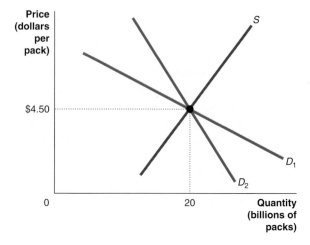

a. If the government imposes a 10-cents-per-pack tax on cigarettes, will the price consumers pay rise more if the demand curve is $D_1$ or if the demand curve is $D_2$? Briefly explain.

b. If the government imposes a 10-cents-per-pack tax on cigarettes, will the revenue to the government be greater if the demand curve is $D_1$ or if the demand curve is $D_2$? Briefly explain.

c. If the government imposes a 10-cents-per-pack tax on cigarettes, will the excess burden from the tax be greater if the demand curve is $D_1$ or if the demand curve is $D_2$? Briefly explain.

3.6 (Related to *Solved Problem 18-3* on page 595) Explain whether you agree or disagree with the following statement: "For a given demand curve, the excess burden of a tax will be greater when supply is less elastic than when it is more elastic." Illustrate your answer with a demand and supply graph.

3.7 (Related to the *Making the Connection* on page 594) Use a demand and supply model for the labor market to show the effect of the corporate income tax on workers. What factors would make the deadweight loss or excess burden from the tax larger or smaller?

3.8 Governments often have multiple objectives in imposing a tax. In each part of this question, use a demand and supply graph to illustrate your answer.

a. If the government wants to minimize the excess burden from excise taxes, should these taxes be imposed on goods that are elastic or goods that are inelastic?

b. Suppose that rather than minimizing excess burden, the government is most interested in maximizing the revenue it receives from the tax. In this situation, should the government impose excise taxes on goods that are elastic or on goods that are inelastic?

c. Suppose that the government wants to discourage smoking and drinking alcohol. Will a tax be more effective in achieving this objective if the demand for these goods is elastic or if the demand is inelastic?

3.9 (Related to the *Don't Let This Happen To You!* on page 593) According to an article in the *New York Times*, during 2009 some New Yorkers were deciding to buy existing condominiums (condos) rather than newly constructed condos. One reason given was the following: "[Some buyers] seek to avoid the 1.825 percent transfer tax that buyers must pay on a brand-new condo. (In resales, the seller pays the tax.)" Analyze this reason for buying a resale rather than a new condo.

Source: Teri Karush Rogers, "Mint Condition, Low Miles," *New York Times*, May 29, 2009.

 **End Learning Objective 18.3**

---

**18.4** **Income Distribution and Poverty,** pages 596–603

LEARNING OBJECTIVE: Discuss the distribution of income in the United States and understand the extent of income mobility.

## Summary

No dramatic changes in the distribution of income have occurred over the past 70 years, although there was some decline in inequality between 1936 and 1980, as well as some increase in inequality between 1980 and today. A **Lorenz curve** shows the distribution of income by arraying incomes from lowest to highest on the horizontal axis and indicating the cumulative fraction of income earned by each fraction of households on the vertical axis. About 12 percent of Americans are below the **poverty line**, which is defined as the annual income equal to three times the amount necessary to purchase the minimum quantity of food required for adequate nutrition. Over time, there has been significant income mobility in the United States. The United States has a more unequal distribution of income than do other high-income countries. The **poverty rate**—the percentage of the population that is poor—has been declining in most countries around the world, with the important exception of Africa. The *marginal productivity theory of income distribution* states that in equilibrium, each factor of production receives a payment equal to its marginal revenue product. The more factors of production an individual owns and the more productive those factors are, the higher the individual's income will be.

 Visit **www.myeconlab.com** to complete these exercises online and get instant feedback.

## Review Questions

4.1 Discuss the extent of income inequality in the United States. Has inequality in the distribution of income in the United States increased or decreased over time? Briefly explain.

4.2 Define *poverty line* and *poverty rate*. How has the poverty rate changed in the United States since 1960?

4.3 What is a Lorenz curve? What is a Gini coefficient? If a country had a Gini coefficient of 0.48 in 1960 and 0.44 in 2009, would income inequality in the country have increased or decreased?

4.4 Describe the main factors economists believe cause inequality of income.

**4.5** Compare the distribution of income in the United States with the distribution of income in other high-income countries.

**4.6** Describe the trend in global poverty rates.

## Problems and Applications

**4.7** (Related to the *Chapter Opener* on page 579) In his column on MSNBC.com, Robert J. Samuelson wrote, "As for what's caused greater inequality, we're also in the dark. The Reagan and Bush tax cuts are weak explanations, because gains have occurred in pretax incomes. . . . Up to a point, inequality is inevitable and desirable."

a. What are pretax incomes?

b. Evaluate Samuelson's argument that tax cuts are unlikely to have been the cause of greater income inequality in the United States.

c. Do you agree with Samuelson's argument that income inequality may be inevitable and desirable?

Source: Robert J. Samuelson, "The Rich and the Rest," MSNBC.com, April 18, 2007.

**4.8** Use the following Lorenz curve graph to answer the questions.

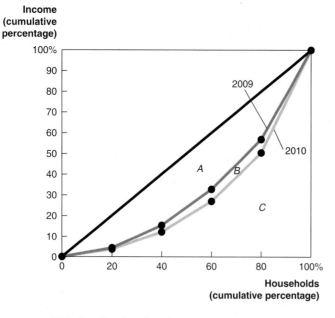

a. Did the distribution become more equal in 2010 than it was in 2009, or did it become less equal? Briefly explain.

b. If area $A = 2,150$, area $B = 250$, and area $C = 2,600$, calculate the Gini coefficient for 2009 and the Gini coefficient for 2010.

**4.9** Draw a Lorenz curve showing the distribution of income for the five people in the following table.

| NAME | ANNUAL EARNINGS |
|------|-----------------|
| Lena | $70,000 |
| David | 60,000 |
| Steve | 50,000 |
| Jerome | 40,000 |
| Lori | 30,000 |

**4.10** Why do economists often use a lower poverty threshold for poor countries than for high-income countries such as the United States? Is there a difference between *relative* poverty and *absolute* poverty?

**4.11** Suppose that Congress and the president decide on a policy of bringing about a perfectly equal distribution of income. What factors might make this policy difficult to achieve? If it were possible to achieve the goal of this policy, would doing so be desirable?

**4.12** If everyone had the same income, would everyone have the same level of well-being?

**4.13** Suppose that a country has 20 million households. Ten million are poor households that each have labor market earnings of $20,000 per year, and 10 million are rich households that each have labor market earnings of $80,000 per year. If the government enacted a marginal tax of 10 percent on all labor market earnings above $20,000 and transferred this money to households earning $20,000 or less, would the incomes of the poor rise by $6,000 per year? Explain.

**4.14** A U.S. Census Bureau report showed that 46 percent of households living below the poverty line owned their own homes, 76 percent lived in dwellings with air-conditioning, about 75 percent owned cars, and 62 percent had cable or satellite TV reception. All these levels are considerably higher than they were for households below the poverty line a generation ago, but the official poverty rate is virtually unchanged over this period, as Figure 18-5 on page 597 shows. Going back to the official definition of *poverty*, how could ownership and purchases of these goods by the poor become more common while the poverty rate stayed the same?

**4.15** In a speech, Federal Reserve Chairman Ben Bernanke made the following observation: "Although we Americans strive to provide equality of economic opportunity, we do not guarantee equality of economic outcomes, nor should we." If the federal government wanted to, how could it "guarantee equality of economic outcomes"? If the government succeeded in making the distribution of income completely equal, what would be the benefits, and what would be the costs?

Source: "Remarks by Chairman Ben S. Bernanke Before the Greater Omaha Chamber of Commerce, Omaha, Nebraska," February 6, 2007.

**4.16** In an article in the *Wall Street Journal*, Edward Lazear of Stanford University was quoted as saying: "There is some good news . . . most of the inequality reflects an increase in returns to 'investing in skills.'" Why would it be good news if it were true that most of the income inequality in the United States reflected an increase to returns in investing in skills?

Source: Greg Ip and John D. McKinnon, "Bush Reorients Rhetoric, Acknowledges Income Gap," *Wall Street Journal*, March 26, 2007, p. A2.

>> **End Learning Objective 18.4**

# Glossary

## A

**Absolute advantage** The ability of an individual, a firm, or a country to produce more of a good or service than competitors, using the same amount of resources.

**Accounting profit** A firm's net income, measured by revenue minus operating expenses and taxes paid.

**Adverse selection** The situation in which one party to a transaction takes advantage of knowing more than the other party to the transaction.

**Allocative efficiency** A state of the economy in which production is in accordance with consumer preferences; in particular, every good or service is produced up to the point where the last unit provides a marginal benefit to society equal to the marginal cost of producing it.

**Antitrust laws** Laws aimed at eliminating collusion and promoting competition among firms.

**Arrow impossibility theorem** A mathematical theorem that holds that no system of voting can be devised that will consistently represent the underlying preferences of voters.

**Asset** Anything of value owned by a person or a firm.

**Asymmetric information** A situation in which one party to an economic transaction has less information than the other party.

**Autarky** A situation in which a country does not trade with other countries.

**Average fixed cost** Fixed cost divided by the quantity of output produced.

**Average product of labor** The total output produced by a firm divided by the quantity of workers.

**Average revenue (*AR*)** Total revenue divided by the quantity of the product sold.

**Average tax rate** Total tax paid divided by total income.

**Average total cost** Total cost divided by the quantity of output produced.

**Average variable cost** Variable cost divided by the quantity of output produced.

## B

**Balance sheet** A financial statement that sums up a firm's financial position on a particular day, usually the end of a quarter or year.

**Barrier to entry** Anything that keeps new firms from entering an industry in which firms are earning economic profits.

**Behavioral economics** The study of situations in which people make choices that do not appear to be economically rational.

**Black market** A market in which buying and selling take place at prices that violate government price regulations.

**Bond** A financial security that represents a promise to repay a fixed amount of funds.

**Brand management** The actions of a firm intended to maintain the differentiation of a product over time.

**Budget constraint** The limited amount of income available to consumers to spend on goods and services.

**Business strategy** Actions taken by a firm to achieve a goal, such as maximizing profits.

## C

**Cartel** A group of firms that collude by agreeing to restrict output to increase prices and profits.

**Centrally planned economy** An economy in which the government decides how economic resources will be allocated.

***Ceteris paribus* ("all else equal") condition** The requirement that when analyzing the relationship between two variables—such as price and quantity demanded—other variables must be held constant.

**Circular-flow diagram** A model that illustrates how participants in markets are linked.

**Coase theorem** The argument of economist Ronald Coase that if transactions costs are low, private bargaining will result in an efficient solution to the problem of externalities.

**Collusion** An agreement among firms to charge the same price or otherwise not to compete.

**Command-and-control approach** An approach that involves the government imposing quantitative limits on the amount of pollution firms are allowed to emit or requiring firms to install specific pollution control devices.

**Common resource** A good that is rival but not excludable.

**Comparative advantage** The ability of an individual, a firm, or a country to produce a good or service at a lower opportunity cost than competitors.

**Compensating differentials** Higher wages that compensate workers for unpleasant aspects of a job.

**Competitive market equilibrium** A market equilibrium with many buyers and many sellers.

**Complements** Goods and services that are used together.

**Constant returns to scale** The situation when a firm's long-run average costs remain unchanged as it increases output.

**Consumer surplus** The difference between the highest price a consumer is willing to pay for a good or service and the price the consumer actually pays.

**Cooperative equilibrium** An equilibrium in a game in which players cooperate to increase their mutual payoff.

**Copyright** A government-granted exclusive right to produce and sell a creation.

**Corporate governance** The way in which a corporation is structured and the effect a corporation's structure has on the firm's behavior.

**Corporation** A legal form of business that provides owners with protection from losing more than their investment should the business fail.

**Coupon payment** An interest payment on a bond.

**Cross-price elasticity of demand** The percentage change in quantity demanded of one good divided by the percentage change in the price of another good.

## D

**Deadweight loss** The reduction in economic surplus resulting from a market not being in competitive equilibrium.

**Demand curve** A curve that shows the relationship between the price of a product and the quantity of the product demanded.

**Demand schedule** A table showing the relationship between the price of a product and the quantity of the product demanded.

**Demographics** The characteristics of a population with respect to age, race, and gender.

**Derived demand** The demand for a factor of production; it depends on the demand for the good the factor produces.

**Direct finance** A flow of funds from savers to firms through financial markets, such as the New York Stock Exchange.

**Diseconomies of scale** The situation when a firm's long-run average costs rise as the firm increases output.

**Dividends** Payments by a corporation to its shareholders.

**Dominant strategy** A strategy that is the best for a firm, no matter what strategies other firms use.

**Dumping** Selling a product for a price below its cost of production.

## E

**Economic discrimination** Paying a person a lower wage or excluding a person from an occupation on the basis of an irrelevant characteristic such as race or gender.

**Economic efficiency** A market outcome in which the marginal benefit to consumers of the last unit produced is equal to its marginal cost of production and in which the sum of consumer surplus and producer surplus is at a maximum.

**Economic growth** The ability of the economy to increase the production of goods and services.

**Economic loss** The situation in which a firm's total revenue is less than its total cost, including all implicit costs.

**Economic model** A simplified version of reality used to analyze real-world economic situations.

**Economic profit** A firm's revenues minus all its costs, implicit and explicit.

**Economic rent** (or **pure rent**) The price of a factor of production that is in fixed supply.

**Economic surplus** The sum of consumer surplus and producer surplus.

**Economic variable** Something measurable that can have different values, such as the wages of software programmers.

**Economics** The study of the choices people make to attain their goals, given their scarce resources.

**Economies of scale** The situation when a firm's long-run average costs fall as it increases output.

**Elastic demand** Demand is elastic when the percentage change in quantity demanded is *greater* than the percentage change in price, so the price elasticity is *greater* than 1 in absolute value.

**Elasticity** A measure of how much one economic variable responds to changes in another economic variable.

**Endowment effect** The tendency of people to be unwilling to sell a good they already own even if they are offered a price that is greater than the price they would be willing to pay to buy the good if they didn't already own it.

**Entrepreneur** Someone who operates a business, bringing together the factors of production—labor, capital, and natural resources—to produce goods and services.

**Equity** The fair distribution of economic benefits.

**Excess burden** A measure of the efficiency loss to the economy that results from a tax having reduced the quantity of a good produced; also known as the deadweight loss.

**Excludability** The situation in which anyone who does not pay for a good cannot consume it.

**Expansion path** A curve that shows a firm's cost-minimizing combination of inputs for every level of output.

**Explicit cost** A cost that involves spending money.

**Exports** Goods and services produced domestically and sold in other countries.

**External economies** Reductions in a firm's costs that result from an increase in the size of an industry.

**Externality** A benefit or cost that affects someone who is not directly involved in the production or consumption of a good or service.

## F

**Factor markets** Markets for the factors of production, such as labor, capital, natural resources, and entrepreneurial ability.

**Factors of production** Labor, capital, natural resources, and other inputs used to produce goods and services.

**Fixed costs** Costs that remain constant as output changes.

**Foreign direct investment** The purchase or building by a domestic firm of a facility in a foreign country.

**Foreign portfolio investment** The purchase by an individual or a firm of stocks or bonds issued in another country.

**Free market** A market with few government restrictions on how a good or service can be produced or sold or on how a factor of production can be employed.

**Free riding** Benefiting from a good without paying for it.

**Free trade** Trade between countries that is without government restrictions.

## G

**Game theory** The study of how people make decisions in situations in which attaining their goals depends on their interactions with others; in economics, the study of the decisions of firms in industries where the profits of each firm depend on its interactions with other firms.

**Globalization** The process of countries becoming more open to foreign trade and investment.

## H

**Horizontal merger** A merger between firms in the same industry.

**Human capital** The accumulated training and skills that workers possess.

## I

**Implicit cost** A nonmonetary opportunity cost.

**Imports** Goods and services bought domestically but produced in other countries.

**Income effect** The change in the quantity demanded of a good that results from the effect of a change in the good's price on consumers' purchasing power.

**Income elasticity of demand** A measure of the responsiveness of quantity demanded to changes in income, measured by the percentage change in quantity demanded divided by the percentage change in income.

**Income statement** A financial statement that sums up a firm's revenues, costs, and profit over a period of time.

**Indifference curve** A curve that shows the combinations of consumption bundles that give the consumer the same utility.

**Indirect finance** A flow of funds from savers to borrowers through financial intermediaries such as banks. Intermediaries raise funds from savers to lend to firms (and other borrowers).

**Inelastic demand** Demand is inelastic when the percentage change in quantity demanded is *less* than the percentage change in price, so the price elasticity is *less* than 1 in absolute value.

**Inferior good** A good for which the demand increases as income falls and decreases as income rises.

**Interest rate** The cost of borrowing funds, usually expressed as a percentage of the amount borrowed.

**Isocost line** All the combinations of two inputs, such as capital and labor, that have the same total cost.

**Isoquant** A curve that shows all the combinations of two inputs, such as capital and labor, that will produce the same level of output.

## L

**Labor union** An organization of employees that has the legal right to bargain with employers about wages and working conditions.

**Law of demand** The rule that, holding everything else constant, when the price of a product falls, the quantity demanded of the product will increase, and when the price of a product rises, the quantity demanded of the product will decrease.

**Law of diminishing marginal utility**  The principle that consumers experience diminishing additional satisfaction as they consume more of a good or service during a given period of time.

**Law of diminishing returns**  The principle that, at some point, adding more of a variable input, such as labor, to the same amount of a fixed input, such as capital, will cause the marginal product of the variable input to decline.

**Law of supply**  The rule that, holding everything else constant, increases in price cause increases in the quantity supplied, and decreases in price cause decreases in the quantity supplied.

**Liability**  Anything owed by a person or a firm.

**Limited liability**  The legal provision that shields owners of a corporation from losing more than they have invested in the firm.

**Long run**  The period of time in which a firm can vary all its inputs, adopt new technology, and increase or decrease the size of its physical plant.

**Long-run average cost curve**  A curve showing the lowest cost at which a firm is able to produce a given quantity of output in the long run, when no inputs are fixed.

**Long-run competitive equilibrium**  The situation in which the entry and exit of firms has resulted in the typical firm breaking even.

**Long-run supply curve**  A curve that shows the relationship in the long run between market price and the quantity supplied.

**Lorenz curve**  A curve that shows the distribution of income by arraying incomes from lowest to highest on the horizontal axis and indicating the cumulative fraction of income earned by each fraction of households on the vertical axis.

# M

**Macroeconomics**  The study of the economy as a whole, including topics such as inflation, unemployment, and economic growth.

**Marginal analysis**  Analysis that involves comparing marginal benefits and marginal costs.

**Marginal benefit**  The additional benefit to a consumer from consuming one more unit of a good or service.

**Marginal cost**  The additional cost to a firm of producing one more unit of a good or service.

**Marginal product of labor**  The additional output a firm produces as a result of hiring one more worker.

**Marginal productivity theory of income distribution**  The theory that the distribution of income is determined by the marginal productivity of the factors of production that individuals own.

**Marginal rate of substitution (MRS)**  The rate at which a consumer would be willing to trade off one good for another.

**Marginal rate of technical substitution (MRTS)**  The rate at which a firm is able to substitute one input for another while keeping the level of output constant.

**Marginal revenue (MR)**  The change in total revenue from selling one more unit of a product.

**Marginal revenue product of labor (MRP)**  The change in a firm's revenue as a result of hiring one more worker.

**Marginal tax rate**  The fraction of each additional dollar of income that must be paid in taxes.

**Marginal utility (MU)**  The change in total utility a person receives from consuming one additional unit of a good or service.

**Market**  A group of buyers and sellers of a good or service and the institution or arrangement by which they come together to trade.

**Market demand**  The demand by all the consumers of a given good or service.

**Market economy**  An economy in which the decisions of households and firms interacting in markets allocate economic resources.

**Market equilibrium**  A situation in which quantity demanded equals quantity supplied.

**Market failure**  A situation in which the market fails to produce the efficient level of output.

**Market power**  The ability of a firm to charge a price greater than marginal cost.

**Marketing**  All the activities necessary for a firm to sell a product to a consumer.

**Median voter theorem**  The proposition that the outcome of a majority vote is likely to represent the preferences of the voter who is in the political middle.

**Microeconomics**  The study of how households and firms make choices, how they interact in markets, and how the government attempts to influence their choices.

**Minimum efficient scale**  The level of output at which all economies of scale are exhausted.

**Mixed economy**  An economy in which most economic decisions result from the interaction of buyers and sellers in markets but in which the government plays a significant role in the allocation of resources.

**Monopolistic competition**  A market structure in which barriers to entry are low and many firms compete by selling similar, but not identical, products.

**Monopoly**  A firm that is the only seller of a good or service that does not have a close substitute.

**Monopsony**  The sole buyer of a factor of production.

**Moral hazard**  The actions people take after they have entered into a transaction that make the other party to the transaction worse off.

**Multinational enterprise**  A firm that conducts operations in more than one country.

# N

**Nash equilibrium**  A situation in which each firm chooses the best strategy, given the strategies chosen by other firms.

**Natural monopoly**  A situation in which economies of scale are so large that one firm can supply the entire market at a lower average total cost than can two or more firms.

**Network externalities**  A situation in which the usefulness of a product increases with the number of consumers who use it.

**Noncooperative equilibrium**  An equilibrium in a game in which players do not cooperate but pursue their own self-interest.

**Normal good**  A good for which the demand increases as income rises and decreases as income falls.

**Normative analysis**  Analysis concerned with what ought to be.

# O

**Oligopoly**  A market structure in which a small number of interdependent firms compete.

**Opportunity cost**  The highest-valued alternative that must be given up to engage in an activity.

# P

**Partnership**  A firm owned jointly by two or more persons and not organized as a corporation.

**Patent**  The exclusive right to a product for a period of 20 years from the date the product is invented.

**Payoff matrix**  A table that shows the payoffs that each firm earns from every combination of strategies by the firms.

**Perfectly competitive market**  A market that meets the conditions of (1) many buyers and sellers, (2) all firms selling identical products, and (3) no barriers to new firms entering the market.

**Perfectly elastic demand**   The case where the quantity demanded is infinitely responsive to price, and the price elasticity of demand equals infinity.

**Perfectly inelastic demand**   The case where the quantity demanded is completely unresponsive to price, and the price elasticity of demand equals zero.

**Personnel economics**   The application of economic analysis to human resources issues.

**Pigovian taxes and subsidies**   Government taxes and subsidies intended to bring about an efficient level of output in the presence of externalities.

**Positive analysis**   Analysis concerned with what is.

**Poverty line**   A level of annual income equal to three times the amount of money necessary to purchase the minimum quantity of food required for adequate nutrition.

**Poverty rate**   The percentage of the population that is poor according to the federal government's definition.

**Present value**   The value in today's dollars of funds to be paid or received in the future.

**Price ceiling**   A legally determined maximum price that sellers may charge.

**Price discrimination**   Charging different prices to different customers for the same product when the price differences are not due to differences in cost.

**Price elasticity of demand**   The responsiveness of the quantity demanded to a change in price, measured by dividing the percentage change in the quantity demanded of a product by the percentage change in the product's price.

**Price elasticity of supply**   The responsiveness of the quantity supplied to a change in price, measured by dividing the percentage change in the quantity supplied of a product by the percentage change in the product's price.

**Price floor**   A legally determined minimum price that sellers may receive.

**Price leadership**   A form of implicit collusion in which one firm in an oligopoly announces a price change and the other firms in the industry match the change.

**Price taker**   A buyer or seller that is unable to affect the market price.

**Principal–agent problem**   A problem caused by agents pursuing their own interests rather than the interests of the principals who hired them.

**Prisoner's dilemma**   A game in which pursuing dominant strategies results in noncooperation that leaves everyone worse off.

**Private benefit**   The benefit received by the consumer of a good or service.

**Private cost**   The cost borne by the producer of a good or service.

**Private good**   A good that is both rival and excludable.

**Producer surplus**   The difference between the lowest price a firm would be willing to accept for a good or service and the price it actually receives.

**Product markets**   Markets for goods—such as computers—and services—such as medical treatment.

**Production function**   The relationship between the inputs employed by a firm and the maximum output it can produce with those inputs.

**Production possibilities frontier (PPF)**   A curve showing the maximum attainable combinations of two products that may be produced with available resources and current technology.

**Productive efficiency**   A situation in which a good or service is produced at the lowest possible cost.

**Profit**   Total revenue minus total cost.

**Progressive tax**   A tax for which people with lower incomes pay a lower percentage of their income in tax than do people with higher incomes.

**Property rights**   The rights individuals or firms have to the exclusive use of their property, including the right to buy or sell it.

**Protectionism**   The use of trade barriers to shield domestic firms from foreign competition.

**Public choice model**   A model that applies economic analysis to government decision making.

**Public franchise**   A government designation that a firm is the only legal provider of a good or service.

**Public good**   A good that is both nonrivalrous and nonexcludable.

## Q

**Quantity demanded**   The amount of a good or service that a consumer is willing and able to purchase at a given price.

**Quantity supplied**   The amount of a good or service that a firm is willing and able to supply at a given price.

**Quota**   A numerical limit imposed by a government on the quantity of a good that can be imported into the country.

## R

**Regressive tax**   A tax for which people with lower incomes pay a higher percentage of their income in tax than do people with higher incomes.

**Rent seeking**   Attempts by individuals and firms to use government action to make themselves better off at the expense of others.

**Rivalry**   The situation that occurs when one person's consuming a unit of a good means no one else can consume it.

## S

**Scarcity**   A situation in which unlimited wants exceed the limited resources available to fulfill those wants.

**Separation of ownership from control**   A situation in a corporation in which the top management, rather than the shareholders, control day-to-day operations.

**Short run**   The period of time during which at least one of a firm's inputs is fixed.

**Shortage**   A situation in which the quantity demanded is greater than the quantity supplied.

**Shutdown point**   The minimum point on a firm's average variable cost curve; if the price falls below this point, the firm shuts down production in the short run.

**Social benefit**   The total benefit from consuming a good or service, including both the private benefit and any external benefit.

**Social cost**   The total cost of producing a good or service, including both the private cost and any external cost.

**Sole proprietorship**   A firm owned by a single individual and not organized as a corporation.

**Stock**   A financial security that represents partial ownership of a firm.

**Stockholders' equity**   The difference between the value of a corporation's assets and the value of its liabilities; also known as net worth.

**Substitutes**   Goods and services that can be used for the same purpose.

**Substitution effect**   The change in the quantity demanded of a good that results from a change in price, making the good more or less expensive relative to other goods that are substitutes.

**Sunk cost**   A cost that has already been paid and cannot be recovered.

**Supply curve**   A curve that shows the relationship between the price of a product and the quantity of the product supplied.

**Supply schedule**   A table that shows the relationship between the price of a product and the quantity of the product supplied.

**Surplus**  A situation in which the quantity supplied is greater than the quantity demanded.

# T

**Tariff**  A tax imposed by a government on imports.

**Tax incidence**  The actual division of the burden of a tax between buyers and sellers in a market.

**Technological change**  A change in the ability of a firm to produce a given level of output with a given quantity of inputs.

**Technology**  The processes a firm uses to turn inputs into outputs of goods and services.

**Terms of trade**  The ratio at which a country can trade its exports for imports from other countries.

**Total cost**  The cost of all the inputs a firm uses in production.

**Total revenue**  The total amount of funds received by a seller of a good or service, calculated by multiplying price per unit by the number of units sold.

**Trade**  The act of buying or selling.

**Trade-off**  The idea that because of scarcity, producing more of one good or service means producing less of another good or service.

**Tragedy of the commons**  The tendency for a common resource to be overused.

**Transactions costs**  The costs in time and other resources that parties incur in the process of agreeing to and carrying out an exchange of goods or services.

**Two-part tariff**  A situation in which consumers pay one price (or tariff) for the right to buy as much of a related good as they want at a second price.

# U

**Unit-elastic demand**  Demand is unit elastic when the percentage change in quantity demanded is *equal to* the percentage change in price, so the price elasticity is equal to 1 in absolute value.

**Utility**  The enjoyment or satisfaction people receive from consuming goods and services.

# V

**Variable costs**  Costs that change as output changes.

**Vertical merger**  A merger between firms at different stages of production of a good.

**Voluntary exchange**  A situation that occurs in markets when both the buyer and seller of a product are made better off by the transaction.

**Voluntary export restraint (VER)**  An agreement negotiated between two countries that places a numerical limit on the quantity of a good that can be imported by one country from the other country.

**Voting paradox**  The failure of majority voting to always result in consistent choices.

# W

**Winner's curse**  The idea that the winner in certain auctions may have overestimated the value of the good, thus ending up worse off than the losers.

**World Trade Organization (WTO)**  An international organization that oversees international trade agreements.

# Company Index

# Subject Index

Key terms and the page on which they are defined appear in **boldface**.

# Credits

## Photo

**Chapter 1**, *page 2*, Getty Images, Inc.; *page 14*, GraphEast RM/Photolibrary; *page 24*, © 2009 City Maps.

**Chapter 2**, *page 36*, BWM AG, HO/AP Wide World Photos; *page 39*, Herko, Robert J./ Getty Images, Inc.–Image Bank; *page 49, (top)*, Jupiter Images Picturequest–Royalty Free; *page 49, (right)*, Dan Lim/ Masterfile Corporation; *page 49, (bottom)*, Photolibrary.com; *page 49, (left)*, David Young Wolff/Getty Images Inc.–Stone Allstock; *page 51*, © Paul Sakuma/AP Wide World Photos; *page 53*, Rob Kim/Landov Media.

**Chapter 3**, *page 64*, © (Photographer)/CORBIS All Rights Reserved; *page 69*, Alex Segre/Alamy Images; *page 73*, Earl S. Cryer/AFP/Getty Images.

**Chapter 4**, *page 96*, Jeff Greenberg/The Image Works; *page 112*, Neil Guegan/ CORBIS-NY; *page 116*, Bill Aron/PhotoEdit Inc.

**Chapter 5**, *page 132*, Ron Levy/Stock Connection; *page 142*, AP Wide World Photos.

**Chapter 6**, *page 166*, Donn Thompson/Getty Images–DK Stock; *page 176*, Michelle D. Bridwell/PhotoEdit Inc.; *page 180*, photo by Krista Kennell/ZUMA Press © Copyright 2007 by Krista Kennell.

**Chapter 7**, *page 202*, Paul Sakuma/AP Wide World Photos; *page 206*, Jonathan Sprague/Redux Pictures; *page 218*, Ji Byol Lee.

**Chapter 8**, *page 236*, Charles Rex Arbogast/AP Wide World Photos; *page 247*, Ron Sherman/Ron Sherman

Photographer; *page 257*, Pallava Bagla/CORBIS-NY; *page 260*, Raul Arboleda/Getty Images, Inc. AFP; *page 274*, Michael Newman/PhotoEdit Inc.

**Chapter 9**, *page 278*, Harpo Productions Inc., George Burns/AP Wide World Photos; *page 291*, © (Photographer)/ CORBIS All Rights Reserved; *page 293*, Andrew Redington/ Getty Images, Inc.–Getty News; *page 297*, Getty Images; *page 299*, Jay Paul/The New York Times/Redux Pictures; *page 300*, Larry Kolvoord/The Images Works.

**Chapter 10**, *page 324*, Yoshikazu Tsuno/Getty Images, Inc. AFP; *page 326*, Getty Images, Inc.; *page 329*, Getty Images–Stockbyte, Royalty Free; *page 334*, (Photographer)/Agence France Presse/Getty Images; page 342, Keystone/Getty Images Inc.–Hulton Archive Photos; *page 362*, Jason DeCrow/AP Wide World Photos.

**Chapter 11**, *page 366*, Damian Dovarganes/AP Wide World Photos; *page 380*, Raymond Forbes/SuperStock, Inc.; *page 388*, Paul Sakuma/AP Wide World Photos.

**Chapter 12**, *page 400*, © Spencer Grant/Photo Edit; *page 410*, Dennis Brack/Landov Media; *page 414*, James A. Finley/AP Wide World Photos; *page 415*, Jason DeCrow/AP Wide World Photos; *page 417*, Courtesy of BIC Corporation.

**Chapter 13**, *page 430*, Chuck Pefley/Aurora Photos, Inc.; *page 439*, "These materials have been reproduced with the permission of eBay Inc." © 2009 EBAY INC. All Rights Reserved; *page 441*, matteo NATALE/fotolia; *page 448*, Damian Dovarganes/AP Wide World Photos.

**Chapter 14**, *page 460*, Marko Turk/MaXx Images; *page 463*, Koji Sasahara/AP Wide World Photos; *page 464*, Juergen Hasenkopf/Micro Photolibrary; *page 466*, Niall McDiarmid/ Alamy Images; *page 481*, AP Wide World Photos.

**Chapter 15**, *page 492*, Kim Karpeles/PhotoEdit Inc.; *page 500*, Bruce Newman/ AP Wide World Photos; *page 503*, David Young-Wolff/ PhotoEdit Inc.

**Chapter 16**, *page 520*, Getty Images; *page 534*, Theo Wargo/ Getty Images–WireImage.com; *page 536*, Getty Images; *page 543*, Safelite Group.

**Chapter 17**, *page 558*, © Bubbles Photolibrary/Alamy; *page 566*, Timothy A. Clary/Getty Images, Inc. AFP; *page 570*, www.indexopen.com; *page 571*, © 2005 Kristen Brochmann/Fundamental Photographs.

**Chapter 18**, *page 578*, REUTERS/ Kevin Lamarque/Landov Media; *page 590*, Spencer Grant/ PhotoEdit, Inc.; *page 594*, Itar-Tass/Valery Sharifulin/ Landov Media.

## Text

**Chapter 1**, *page 18*, © The Economist Newspaper Limited, London (March 5, 2009).

**Chapter 2**, *page 56*, *The Wall Street Journal*, (January 14, 2009): B1. Reprinted with permission of *The Wall Street Journal*, Copyright © 2009 Dow Jones & Company, Inc. All Rights Reserved Worldwide.

**Chapter 3**, *page 88*, Reprinted by permission of the author.

**Chapter 4**, *page 118*, Reprinted from *The Wall Street Journal* © 2008 Dow Jones & Company, Inc. All Rights Reserved.

**Chapter 5**, *page 158*, *The Wall Street Journal*, (March 28, 2009). Reprinted with permission of *The Wall Street Journal*, Copyright © 2009 Dow Jones & Company, Inc. All Rights Reserved Worldwide.

**Chapter 6**, *page 176*, Copyright © 1997, University of Chicago Press. Reprinted with permission of University of Chicago Press. All rights reserved; *page 192*, Copyright © 2008 The New York Times Company. Reprinted with permission. All rights reserved.

**Chapter 7**, *page 213*, *The Wall Street Journal*, (May 12, 2009). Reprinted with permission of *The Wall Street Journal*, Copyright © 2009 Dow Jones & Company, Inc. All Rights Reserved Worldwide; *page 220*, Copyright © 2008 *The (London) Times*. Reprinted with permission. All rights reserved.

**Chapter 8**, *page 254*, Peterson Institute for International Economics. Adapted with permission; *page 262*, Copyright © 2009 *USA Today*. Reprinted with permission. All rights reserved; *page 272*, Copyright © 2009 Time, Inc. Reprinted with permission. All rights reserved.

**Chapter 9**, *page 302*, Copyright © 2008 *The Tech Herald*. Reprinted with permission. All rights reserved.

**Chapter 10**, *page 346*, Copyright © 2008 *USA Today*. Reprinted with permission. All rights reserved.